Lecture Notes in Artificial Intelligence 4092

Edited by J. G. Carbonell and J. Siekmann

Subseries of Lecture Notes in Computer Science

T0140242

Jérôme Lang   Fangzhen Lin
Ju Wang (Eds.)

Knowledge Science, Engineering and Management

First International Conference, KSEM 2006
Guilin, China, August 5-8, 2006
Proceedings

 Springer

Series Editors

Jaime G. Carbonell, Carnegie Mellon University, Pittsburgh, PA, USA
Jörg Siekmann, University of Saarland, Saarbrücken, Germany

Volume Editors

Jérôme Lang
IRIT, Université Paul Sabatier
31062 Toulouse Cedex, France
E-mail: lang@irit.fr

Fangzhen Lin
Hong Kong University of Science and Technology
Department of Computer Science
Clear Water Bay, Kowloon, Hong Kong, China
E-mail: flin@cs.ust.hk

Ju Wang
Guangxi Normal University
Guilin, China
E-mail: jwang@mailbox.gxnu.edu.cn

Library of Congress Control Number: 2006930098

CR Subject Classification (1998): I.2.6, I.2, H.2.8, H.3-5, F.2.2, K.3

LNCS Sublibrary: SL 7 – Artificial Intelligence

ISSN   0302-9743
ISBN-10   3-540-37033-1 Springer Berlin Heidelberg New York
ISBN-13   978-3-540-37033-8 Springer Berlin Heidelberg New York

Springer is a part of Springer Science+Business Media

springer.com

© Springer-Verlag Berlin Heidelberg 2006
Printed in Germany

Typesetting: Camera-ready by author, data conversion by Scientific Publishing Services, Chennai, India
Printed on acid-free paper   SPIN: 11811220   06/3142   5 4 3 2 1 0

Preface

This volume contains the papers accepted for presentation at KSEM 2006, the First International Conference on Knowledge Science, Engineering and Management, held in Guilin, Guangxi, China, August 5-8, 2006.

The aim of this interdisciplinary conference is to provide a forum for researchers in the broad areas of knowledge science, knowledge engineering, and knowledge management to exchange ideas and to report state-of-the-art research results. While each of these three broad areas has had dedicated conferences, so far there has been no event bringing together researchers from all three areas, and KSEM aims at filling this gap.

The technical program of KSEM 2006 comprised four invited talks, given by Thomas Eiter, Ruqian Lu, Yoshiteru Nakamori, and Kwok Kee Wei, and 51 refereed contributions selected by the Program Committee out of 450 submissions. Finally, the program included two tutorials, given by Paul Buitelaar and Michael Thielscher.

This conference was initiated by Ruqian Lu, in conjunction with his project on Non-Canonical Knowledge Processing funded by the Natural Science Foundation of China (NSFC) as a Major Research Initiative. There is no doubt that without Ruqian's hard work and crucial support, this conference would not have come into being. We would also like to thank the members of this NSFC project for their support at various stages of the conference.

The success of this conference depends on the generous help of many people. We thank the Conference Chairs, Jörg Siekmann and Chengqi Zhang, for their support, particularly in helping to secure the publication of the proceedings as a volume in the Springer LNAI series. The Tutorial Chair, Cungen Cao, did a wonderful job in getting two excellent tutorials. The two Publicity Chairs, Shuigeng Zhou and Zili Zhang, did such a good job that we were literally overwhelmed by the large number of submissions.

We are grateful to the Area Chairs, the members of our Program Committee and the external referees for their thorough efforts in reviewing contributions with expertise and patience. The PC chairs would particularly like to thank Yin Chen for his help throughout the entire process. We also thank Andrei Voronkov for developing the free EasyChair system that made our difficult job manageable.

May 2006

Jérôme Lang
Fangzhen Lin
Ju Wang

Conference Organization

Conference Chairs

Jörg Siekmann (German Research Centre of Artificial Intelligence, Germany)
Chengqi Zhang (University of Technology, Sydney, Australia)

Advisory Committee

Andreas Dengel, Chair (German Research Center for AI, Germany)
David Bell (Queen's University, UK)
Didier Dubois (IRIT/UPS, Toulouse, France)
Michael Gelfond (Texas Tech University, USA)
Hector Levesque (University of Toronto, Canada)
Ruqian Lu (Chinese Academy of Sciences, China)
Yoav Shoham (Stanford University, USA)
Bo Zhang (Qinghua University, China)

Organizing Chair

Ju Wang (Guangxi Normal University, China)

Publicity Co-chairs

Shuigeng Zhou (Fudan University, China)
Zili Zhang (Deakin University, Australia)

Sponsorship Chair

Ke Liu (National Natural Science Foundation of China)

Tutorial Chair

Cungen Cao (Chinese Academy of Sciences, China)

Program Committee

Program Chairs

Jérôme Lang (IRIT / Université Paul Sabatier, Toulouse, France)
Fangzhen Lin (Hong Kong University of Science and Technology, China)

Area Chairs

Mingsheng Ying (Knowledge Science), Tsinghua University, Beijing, China
Shan Wang (Knowledge Engineering), Renmin University of China, China
Huaiqing Wang (Knowledge Management), City University of Hong Kong, China

Members

Eugene Agichtein, Microsoft Research, USA
Klaus-Dieter Althoff, University of Hildesheim, Germany
Eyal Amir, University of Illinois, Urbana-Champaign, USA
Grigoris Antoniou, FORTH, Greece
Nathalie Aussenac, IRIT-CNRS, France
Cungen Cao, Chinese Academy of Sciences, China
Xiaoping Chen, University of Science and Technology of China, Hefei, China
Yin Chen, South China Normal University, China
John Debenham, University of Technology, Sydney, Australia
Jim Delgrande, Simon Fraser University, Canada
Xiaotie Deng, City University of Hong Kong, China
Rose Dieng-Kuntz, INRIA - Sophia Antipolis, France
Chabane Djeraba, University of Science and Technology of Lille, France
Patrick Doherty, Linköping University, Sweden
Xiaoyong Du, Renmin University of China, China
Martin Dzbor, Open University, UK
Thomas Eiter, Technische Universität Wien, Austria
Hector Geffner, Universitat Pompeu Fabra, Spain
Giangiacomo Gerla, University of Salerno, Italy
Lluis Godo, Artificial Intelligence Research Institute, CSIC, Spain
Nicola Guarino, ISTC-CNR, Trento, Italy
Andreas Herzig, IRIT, CNRS / Université Paul Sabatier, France
Knut Hinkelmann, University of Applied Science, Solothurn, Switzerland
Wiebe van der Hoek, University of Liverpool, UK
Zhisheng Huang, Vrije Universiteit Amsterdam, The Netherlands
Anthony Hunter, University College London, UK
David Israel, SRI International, USA
Zhi Jin, Chinese Academy of Sciences, Beijing, China
Gabriele Kern-Isberner, Universität Dortmund, Germany
Ron Kowk, City University of Hong Kong, China
James Kwok, Hong Kong University of Science and Technology, China
Qing Li, City University of Hong Kong, China
Xuelong Li, University of London, UK
Paolo Liberatore, Università di Roma 'La Sapienza', Italy
Zuoquan Lin, Peking University, China
Chunnian Liu, Beijing University of Technology, China
Dayou Liu, Jilin University, China
Weiru Liu, Queen's University Belfast, UK
Dickson Lukose, DL Informatique Sdn Bhd, Malaysia

External Reviewers

Christian Anger
F.Y. Anthony
Colin Atkinson
Philippe Balbiani
Daniel Le Berre
Meghyn Bienvenu
Jing Chen
Liangliang Cao
Feng Chen
Hans van Ditmarsch
Helen S. Du
Ludger van Elst
Zou Feng
Giorgos Flouris
Thomas Franz
Anthony Y. Fu
Naoki Fukuta
Masabumi Furuhata
Caddie Gao
Martin Gebser
Christophe Gonzales
Olaf Grlitz
Alexandre Hanft
Michiel Hildebrand
He Hu
Ryutaro Ichise
JianMin Ji
Min Jiang
JieHui Jiang
Kathrin Konczak
Sébastien Konieczny

Markus Kroetsch
Marzena Kryszkiewicz
Guoming Lai
Rafal Latkowski
Elvis Leung
Man Li
Baoping Lin
Guohua Liu
Lin Liu
An Liu
Hai Liu
Claudio Masolo
Cdric Piette
Bertrand Mazure
Martin Memmel
Jiang Min
Yoichi Motomura
Tsuyoshi Murata
Jens Mnz
Rgis Newo
Kvin Ottens
Domenico Pisanelli
Fabian Probst
Anna Radzikowska
Axel Reymonet
Wei Sun
Sandra Sandri
Christoph Schommer
Sergej Sizov
Zhiwei Song
Patrice Perny

Olivier Spanjaard
Piotr Synak
Marcin Szczuka
Pingzhong Tang
Barbara Thönssen
Rodney Topor
Ivor Tsang
Takeaki Uno
Shankar Vembu
Emanuele Bottazzi
Holger Wache
Hongbing Wang
Liping Wang
Jian Wang
Piotr Wasilewski
Sun Wei
Robert Woitsch
Xiaofeng Xie
Xin Yan
Fangkai Yang
Haihong Yu
Bin Yu
Jilian Zhang
Deping Zhang
Kai Zhang
Qi Zhang
Yi Zhou
Fanny Feng Zou
Kai Zhang

Table of Contents

Invited Talks

Regular Papers

On Representational Issues About Combinations of Classical Theories with Nonmonotonic Rules*

Jos de Bruijn[1], Thomas Eiter[2], Axel Polleres[1,3], and Hans Tompits[2]

[1] Digital Enterprise Research Institute (DERI), Leopold-Franzens Universität Innsbruck,
Technikerstraße 21a, A-6020 Innsbruck, Austria
jos.debruijn@deri.org
[2] Institut für Informationssysteme 184/3, Technische Universität Wien,
Favoritenstrasse 9-11, A-1040 Vienna, Austria
{eiter, tompits}@kr.tuwien.ac.at
[3] Universidad Rey Juan Carlos, Campus de Mostoles,
DI-236, Calle Tulipan s/n, E-28933 Madrid, Spain
axel.polleres@urjc.es

Abstract. In the context of current efforts around Semantic-Web languages, the combination of classical theories in classical first-order logic (and in particular of ontologies in various description logics) with rule languages rooted in logic programming is receiving considerable attention. Existing approaches such as SWRL, dl-programs, and $\mathcal{DL}+log$, differ significantly in the way ontologies interact with (nonmonotonic) rules bases. In this paper, we identify fundamental representational issues which need to be addressed by such combinations and formulate a number of formal principles which help to characterize and classify existing and possible future approaches to the combination of rules and classical theories. We use the formal principles to explicate the underlying assumptions of current approaches. Finally, we propose a number of settings, based on our analysis of the representational issues and the fundamental principles underlying current approaches.

1 Introduction

The question of combining different knowledge-representation formalisms is recently gaining increasing interest in the context of the Semantic-Web initiative. While the W3C recommendation of the OWL Web ontology language [1] has been around for over two years, attention is now shifting towards defining a rule language for the Semantic Web which integrates with OWL. From a formal point of view, OWL (DL) can be seen as a syntactic variant of an expressive description logic [2], viz. $\mathcal{SHOIN}(\mathbf{D})$ [3], which is a decidable subset of classical first-order logic. In this sense, OWL follows the

---

* The first author was partially supported by the European Commission under projects Knowledge Web (IST-2004-507482), DIP (FP6-507483), and SEKT (IST-2003-506826), as well as by the Wolfgang Pauli Institute, Vienna. The second and the fourth author were partially supported by the Austrian Science Fund (FWF) under project P17212 and by the European Commission under project REWERSE (IST-2003-506779). The third author was partially supported by the CICyT project TIC-2003-9001-C02.

J. Lang, F. Lin, and J. Wang (Eds.): KSEM 2006, LNAI 4092, pp. 1–22, 2006.

tradition of earlier classical ontology languages such as KIF [4] or, more recently, the ISO Common Logic [5] effort.[1]

Declarative rule languages, on the contrary, are usually based on logic-programming methods, adopting a non-classical semantics via minimal Herbrand models. Additionally, such languages often include extensions with nonmonotonic negation [6,7]. The main differences between classical logic and rule-based languages are assumptions concerning an open vs. a closed domain and non-uniqueness vs. uniqueness of names. Combinations of ontologies, or, more generally, first-order (FO) theories, and rule bases need to take these differences into account.

There have recently been several proposals for integrating such classical ontologies (FO theories) and rule bases (e.g., [8,9,10,11,12]). Each of these approaches overcomes the differences between the paradigms in a different way, often without making the underlying assumptions of the semantics of the combination explicit.

In this paper, we study general representational issues when dealing with a combination of classical theories and rule-based languages. In particular, we specify a number of formal principles such a combination must obey, taking the fundamental differences between the classical semantics and the semantics of rule-based languages into account, as well as the different kinds of interaction between them. Furthermore, we propose a number of generic settings for such a combination, which help clarify and classify possible approaches. As formal languages underlying the classical component (ontology) and the rules component of a combined knowledge base we consider here classical first-order logic with equality and disjunctive logic programs under the stable-model semantics [7,13], respectively.

We stress that we do not consider *extensions* of a classical formalism with non-monotonic features such as default logic [14], autoepistemic logic [15], or circumscription [16,17], but start our observations based on existing approaches which *combine standard semantics* for the ontology and rules components.

2   Preliminaries

We start with a brief review of the basic elements of classical first-order logic with equality and disjunctive logic programs under the stable-model semantics. As we will see in the next section, both formalisms generalize those considered in the major approaches to combining rules and ontologies.

2.1   First-Order Logic

A first-order language $\mathcal{L}$ consists of all formulas over a signature $\Sigma = (\mathcal{F}, \mathcal{P})$, where $\mathcal{F}$ and $\mathcal{P}$ are countable sets of *function* and *predicate symbols*, respectively, and a countably infinite set $\mathcal{V}$ of *variable symbols*. Each $f \in \mathcal{F}$ and each $p \in \mathcal{P}$ has an associated *arity* $n \geq 0$; 0-ary function symbols are also called *constants. Terms* of $\mathcal{L}$ are either constants, variables, or constructed terms of form $f(t_1, .., t_n)$, where f is an n-ary function symbol and $t_1, ..., t_n$ are terms. An *atomic formula* is either a predicate $p(t_1, ..., t_n)$,

---

[1] Although Common Logic is syntactically of higher-order type, most part of it is actually first-order.

with p being an n-ary predicate symbol, or $t_1 = t_2$, where $t_1, ..., t_n$ are terms in $\mathcal{L}$. Variable-free terms (or atomic formulas) are called *ground*. A ground term is also referred to as a *name*.

Complex formulas are constructed in the usual way using the connectives $\neg$, $\wedge$, $\vee$, and $\supset$, the quantifiers $\exists$ and $\forall$ and the auxiliary symbols "(" and ")." A variable occurrence is called *free* if it does not occur in the scope of a quantifier. A formula is *open* if it has free variables, *closed* otherwise. Closed formulas are also called *sentences* of $\mathcal{L}$. By $\forall\phi$ and $\exists\phi$ we denote the universal and existential closure of a formula ϕ, respectively.

An *interpretation* of a language $\mathcal{L}$ is a tuple $\mathcal{I} = \langle U, \cdot^I \rangle$, where U is a nonempty set (called *domain*) and $\cdot^I$ is a mapping which assigns a function $f^I : U^n \to U$ to every n-ary function symbol $f \in \mathcal{F}$ and a relation $p^I \subseteq U^n$ to every n-ary predicate symbol $p \in \mathcal{P}$.

A *variable assignment* B for an interpretation $\mathcal{I}$ is a mapping which assigns an element $x^B \in U$ to every variable $x \in \mathcal{V}$. A variable assignment B' is an *x-variant* of B if $y^B = y^{B'}$ for every variable $y \in \mathcal{V}$ such that $y \neq x$. A *variable substitution* β is a set of form $\{x_1/t_1, ..., x_k/t_k\}$, where $x_1, ..., x_k \in \mathcal{V}$ are distinct variables and $t_1, ..., t_k$ are names of $\mathcal{L}$. A variable substition is *total* if it contains x/n for every variable $x \in \mathcal{V}$.[2] Given a variable assignment B and substitution β, if $\beta = \{x/t \mid x \in \mathcal{V}, t^{\mathcal{I}} = x^B$, for some name $t\}$, then β is *associated with B*.

The *application* of a variable substitution β to some term, formula, or theory is defined as follows: for a variable x, $x\beta = t$, if β contains some x/t, and $x\beta = x$ otherwise; for a formula $\phi(x_1, ..., x_n)$, where $x_1, ..., x_n$ are the free variables of ϕ, $\phi(x_1, ..., x_n)\beta = \phi(x_1\beta, ..., x_n\beta)$; for a set $\Phi = \{\phi_1, ..., \phi_n\}$ of formulas, $\Phi\beta = \{\phi_1\beta, ..., \phi_n\beta\}$.

Note that each assignment may have, depending on the interpretation, several associated variable substitutions.

Example 1. Consider a language $\mathcal{L}$ with constants $\mathcal{F} = \{a, b, c\}$, and an interpretation $\mathcal{I} = \langle U, \cdot^I \rangle$ with $U = \{k, l, m\}$ and such that $a^I = k$, $b^I = l$, and $c^I = l$. The variable assignment B is defined as follows: $x^B = k$, $y^B = l$, and $z^B = m$. B has two associated variable substitutions, $\beta_1 = \{x/a, y/b\}$ and $\beta_2 = \{x/a, y/c\}$, but no total associated variable substitution since m is an unnamed individual. □

Given an interpretation $\mathcal{I} = \langle U, \cdot^I \rangle$, a variable assignment B, and a term t of $\mathcal{L}$, $t^{I,B}$ is defined as follows: $x^{I,B} = x^B$, for a variable x, and $t^{I,B} = f^I(t_1^{I,B}, ..., t_n^{I,B})$, for $t = f(t_1, ..., t_n)$. An individual $k \in U$ which is represented by at least one name t in the language, i.e., such that $t^I = k$, is called a *named* individual, otherwise *unnamed*.

An interpretation $\mathcal{I} = \langle U, \cdot^I \rangle$ *satisfies* an atomic formula $p(t_1, ..., t_n)$ *relative* to a variable assignment B, denoted $\mathcal{I}, B \models p(t_1, ..., t_n)$, if $(t_1^{I,B}, ..., t_n^{I,B}) \in p^I$. Furthermore, $\mathcal{I}, B \models t_1 = t_2$ iff $t_1^{I,B} = t_2^{I,B}$. This is extended to arbitrary formulas as usual. In particular, we have that $\mathcal{I}, B \models \forall x\phi_1$ (resp., $\mathcal{I}, B \models \exists x\phi_1$) iff for every (resp., for some) B' which is an x-variant of B, $\mathcal{I}, B' \models \phi_1$ holds.

An interpretation $\mathcal{I}$ is a *model* of ϕ, denoted $\mathcal{I} \models \phi$, if $\mathcal{I}, B \models \phi$, for every variable assignment B. This definition is straighforwardly extended to the case of first-order

---

[2] Note that our notion of a variable substitution is slightly different from the usual one, since we only allow substitution of variables with *names* rather than with arbitrary terms.

theories. Given a theory Φ and a formula ϕ over $\mathcal{L}$, Φ *entails* ϕ, denoted $\Phi \models \phi$, iff, for all interpretations $\mathcal{I}$ in $\mathcal{L}$ such that $\mathcal{I} \models \Phi$, $\mathcal{I} \models \phi$ holds.

2.2 Logic Programs

A *disjunctive logic program* P consists of rules of form

$$h_1 \mid \ldots \mid h_l \leftarrow b_1, \ldots, b_m, \, not \, b_{m+1}, \, \ldots \, not \, b_n,$$

where $h_1, \ldots, h_l, b_1, \ldots, b_n$ are atomic formulas. $H(r) = \{h_1, ..., h_l\}$ is the set of *head atoms* of r, $B^+(r) = \{b_1, ..., b_m\}$ is the set of *positive body atoms* of r, and $B^-(r) = \{b_{m+1}, ..., b_n\}$ is the set of *negative body atoms* of r. If $l = 1$, then r is a *normal rule*. If every rule in $r \in P$ is normal, then P is normal. If $B^-(r) = \emptyset$, then r is *positive*. If every rule $r \in P$ is positive, then P is positive.

Let Σ_P denote a first-order signature which is a superset of the function, predicate, and variable symbols which occur in P and let $\mathcal{L}_P$ denote the first-order language based on Σ_P. The *Herbrand universe* U_H of $\mathcal{L}_P$ is the set of all ground terms over Σ_P. The *Herbrand base* B_H of $\mathcal{L}_P$ is the set of all atomic formulas which can be formed using the predicate symbols of Σ_P and the terms in U_H. A *Herbrand interpretation* M is a subset of B_H. With a little abuse of notation, we can view M equivalently as a first-order interpretation $\langle U_H, \cdot^I \rangle$, where $\cdot^I$ is such that $\langle t_1, ..., t_n \rangle \in p^I$ iff $p(t_1, ..., t_n) \in M$, for an n-ary predicate symbol p and ground terms $t_1, ..., t_n$. Depending on the context, we view M either as a set of atoms of $\mathcal{L}_P$ or as a first-order interpretation of $\mathcal{L}_P$.

The *grounding* of a logic program P, denoted $gr(P)$, is the union of all possible ground instantiations of P, obtained by replacing each variable in r with a term in U_H, for each rule $r \in P$.

Let P be a positive logic program. A Herbrand interpretation M of P is a *model* of P if, for every rule $r \in gr(P)$, $B^+(r) \subseteq M$ implies $H(r) \cap M \neq \emptyset$. A Herbrand model M of a logic program P is *minimal* iff for every model M' such that $M' \subseteq M$, $M' = M$. Every positive normal logic program has a single minimal Herbrand model, which is the intersection of all Herbrand models.

Following Gelfond and Lifschitz [7], the *reduct* of a logic program P with respect to an interpretation M, denoted P^M, is obtained from $gr(P)$ by deleting (i) each rule with a literal $not \, b$ in its body with $b \in M$, and (ii) all negative body literals in the remaining rules. If M is a minimal Herbrand model of the reduct P^M, then M is a *stable model* of P.

Example 2. Consider the following program P:

$$p(a); \quad p(b); \quad q(X) \mid r(X) \leftarrow p(X), not \, s(X),$$

together with the interpretation $M_1 = \{p(a), p(b), q(a), r(a)\}$. The reduct $P^{M_1} = \{p(a); p(b); q(a) \mid r(a) \leftarrow p(a), not \, s(a); q(b) \mid r(b) \leftarrow p(b), not \, s(b)\}$ has the minimal model M_1, thus M_1 is a stable model of P. The other stable models of P are $M_2 = \{p(a), p(b), q(a), r(b)\}$, $M_3 = \{p(a), p(b), q(b), r(a)\}$, and $M_4 = \{p(a), p(b), q(b), r(b)\}$. □

A disjunctive logic program P is *consistent* if it has a stable model. Furthermore, P *cautiously entails* a ground atomic formula α if $\alpha \in M$ for every stable model M of P. As well, P *bravely entails* a ground atomic formula α if $\alpha \in M$ for some stable model M of P.

The stable-model semantics [7], also referred to as the *answer-set semantics*, coincides with the minimal Herbrand-model semantics [18] for positive programs, with the perfect-model semantics [19], the well-founded semantics [6] for locally stratified programs, and with the well-founded semantics in case the well-founded model is total [7,6].

3 Current Approaches for Combining Knowledge Bases

We are concerned in this paper with knowledge bases which combine classical first-order logic and rules. A combined knowledge base $\mathcal{KB} = \langle \Phi, P \rangle$ consists of

- a first-order theory (the *classical component*) Φ, which is a set of formulas in some first-order language $\mathcal{L}_\Phi$ with signature Σ_Φ, and
- a disjunctive logic program (the *rules component*) P with signature Σ_P.

The combined signature of $\mathcal{KB}$, denoted $\Sigma_{\mathcal{KB}}$, is the union of Σ_Φ and Σ_P.

Several kinds of interactions between FO theories (or ontologies) and rules require a separation between predicates "belonging to" the FO theory component and predicates "belonging to" the rules component. We refer to predicate symbols in Σ_Φ as *classical predicates* and predicates in Σ_P as *rules predicates*. Unless mentioned otherwise, the sets of classical and rules predicates are assumed to be disjoint. *Classical atoms* are atomic formulas with a classical predicate and *rules atoms* are atomic formulas with a rules predicate. All of the approaches mentioned in this paper allow classical predicates to occur in logic programs, but do not allow rules predicates to occur in the FO theory.

In the remainder of this section we give a short survey of the most prominent approaches to combining FO theories and rules.

SWRL and Subsets. SWRL [20] is an extension of OWL DL, which corresponds to the description logic $\mathcal{SHOIN}(\mathbf{D})$, with function-free Horn-like rules.[3] SWRL allows conjunctions of atomic concepts and roles (unary and binary predicates), as well complex concept descriptions in the heads and bodies of rules. We assume here that rules in a SWRL knowledge base are positive Horn formulas. This is no real limitation, since complex concept descriptions may be replaced with new concepts which are defined equivalently to the complex descriptions in the FO theory, and rules with a conjunction of atoms in the head may be split into several rules.

A SWRL knowledge base $\mathcal{KB} = \langle \Phi, P \rangle$ can be seen as consisting of an FO theory Φ (a $\mathcal{SHOIN}(\mathbf{D})$ ontology), and a rules component P, which in turn consists of a set of positive, normal rules where atoms may be either unary, binary or (in)equality predicates. An interpretation $\mathcal{I}$ satisfies $\mathcal{KB}$ iff $\mathcal{I} \models \Phi \cup P$, where $\models$ is the classical first-order satisfaction relation. The ontology and the rules are thus interpreted as a single first-order theory.

---

[3] SWRL allows classical negation through the OWL DL axioms, but not in rules.

Notice that SWRL does not distinguish between description logic (DL) predicates and rule predicates. There is full interaction between the DL component and the rules component. As was shown in the seminal work about CARIN [21], an unlimited interaction between Horn rules and DLs leads to undecidability of key inference tasks, which also holds for the restricted form of rules allowed in SWRL. In order to recover decidability, one could either reduce the expressiveness of the DL or of the rules component (cf. [22] for a short survey on a number of restrictions which recover decidability; these restrictions reach from only allowing the expressive intersection of DLs and Horn rules [23] to leaving full syntactic freedom for the DL, but restricting Horn rules to so-called *DL-safe rules* [12] or tree-shaped rules [24]).

A drawback of SWRL from a representational point-of-view is that it does not allow the integration of nonmonotonic logic programs with ontologies. The approaches mentioned in the remainder of this section do allow the consideration of nonmonotonic rules in a combined knowledge base.

$\mathcal{DL}+log$ *and Its Predecessors.* $\mathcal{AL}$-log [25] is an approach to integrating the description logic $\mathcal{ALC}$ with positive (non-disjunctive) datalog. This approach was extended to the case of disjunctive datalog with negation under the stable-model semantics in [26] and further generalized to the case of arbitrary classical ontology languages in [8]. The latest successor in this chain is $\mathcal{DL}+log$, which allows a tighter integration of rules and ontologies than the earlier approaches. In this short survey, we will restrict ourselves to $\mathcal{DL}+log$.

The integration of rules and ontologies in a $\mathcal{DL}+log$ knowledge base $\mathcal{KB} = \langle \Phi, P \rangle$ roughly works as follows. The classical predicates are interpreted in a classical interpretation $\mathcal{I}$. The reduct of the program P with respect to $\mathcal{I}$ "evaluates" all classical atoms according to their truth value in $\mathcal{I}$. The resulting program, denoted $P_{\mathcal{I}}$, does not contain any classical predicates. This program is evaluated using the stable-model semantics as usual. For each model of the classical component, there may be zero, one, or multiple stable models M of the rules component. Models of the combined knowledge base $\mathcal{KB}$ are then of the form $\mathcal{I} \cup M$ for each model $\mathcal{I}$ of Φ and stable model M. One consequence of this definition is that if there is no stable model M for $\mathcal{I}$, then there is no combined model $\mathcal{I} \cup M$. In this way, the logic program can restrict the set of classical models, which is a form of interaction from the rules to the FO theory.

A ground atom is a consequence of the combined knowledge base iff it is true in every combined model.

In order to use the standard definitions of stable models, $\mathcal{DL}+log$ imposes the standard-names assumption, which assumes a one-to-one correspondence between names in the language and individuals in the domain of each interpretation. Another restriction is that classical predicates are not allowed to occur negatively in rule bodies. Furthermore, $\mathcal{DL}+log$ defines the weak DL-safeness restriction on variables in rules in order to retain decidability of reasoning. Each variable which occurs in the head of a rule must occur in a positive rules atom in the body. This ensures that only conclusions are drawn about individuals in the Herbrand universe. The "weak" in "weak safeness" refers to the fact that there may be variables in classical atoms in the body of a rule which do not occur in any atom in the head. This allows to express conjunctive queries over a DL knowledge base in the body of a rule, while still keeping the combined formalism decidable.

As for the various variants of safeness restrictions mentioned so far, one may argue that these restrictions are really limiting, because variables can to a large extent only range over constants which occur in the rules component. However, it is often argued that one could easily add a predicate to the rules component and add a fact $O(a)$ for each constant a which occurs in the classical component. One could then add $O(x)$ to the body of each rule for each unsafe variable x, as proposed for instance in [12].

dl-Programs. In contrast to the $\mathcal{DL}+log$ approach, the rules in a dl-program [10] do not interact with the FO theory based on single models, but rather using a clean interface which allows the exchange of ground atoms. This approach relies also on the stable-models semantics, but there is a more strict separation between the classical component and the rules component.

The interaction between the classical component and the rules component is through special query predicates in the bodies of rules, called *dl-atoms*. Allowed queries are *concept membership*, *role membership*, and *concept inclusion*. The approach allows a bidirectional flow of information: dl-atoms allow to "extend" the extensions of unary and binary rules predicates in the DL knowledge base, to be taken into account for the query to be answered.

As is the case for $\mathcal{DL}+log$, dl-programs distinguish between classical predicates and rules predicates; in dl-programs, the distinction between DL predicates and rules predicates is made implicitly—the only places where classical predicates occur in rules are the dl-atoms.

The semantics of dl-programs is defined with respect to ground logic programs. However, unlike for usual logic programs, the grounding of dl-programs is not computed with respect to the Herbrand universe of the logic program, but with respect to some arbitrary signature Σ, which might be the combined signature of the classical component and the rule component. The extended Herbrand base of a dl-program consists of all the atoms which can be constructed using the predicate and constant symbols in the signature Σ. An interpretation M is a subset of the extended Herbrand base. A ground dl-atom can be viewed as a set S^M of facts together with a ground query $Q(\mathbf{c})$, where Q is a (possibly negated) unary or binary predicate and $\mathbf{c}$ is a constant or a binary tuple of constants, respectively. A dl-atom is true in M with respect to a FO theory Φ iff

$$\Phi \cup S^M \models Q(\mathbf{c}).$$

Truth of regular atoms in the program is determined in the usual way, i.e., a ground atom α is true in M iff $\alpha \in M$. DL atoms can be removed from the ground program based on their truth value in M with respect to Φ: rules with a dl-atom in the body which is false in M with respect to Φ are removed from the program and the dl-atoms in the bodies of the remaining rules are removed. The stable-model semantics for the resulting normal program is then defined as usual.

4   Representational Issues of Combined Knowledge Bases

As we have seen in the previous section, the semantics of a combined knowledge base is defined differently for the different approaches. It is not immediately clear from the definitions what the implications are of using a particular semantics and what the expected behavior is of the combination.

When defining such a semantics of a combined knowledge base $\mathcal{KB}$, different representational issues arise which have to be dealt with. These issues stem from the different underlying assumptions in the formalisms such as open vs. closed-world assumption and unique vs. non-unique names assumption. Our main concerns are (i) the form of the domain of discourse for the quantification of the variables in the logic-program rules, (ii) implications of the unique-names assumption in the logic program, (iii) the notion of interaction from the theory to the logic program, and (iv) the notion of interaction from the rules to the theory. Each approach to combining rules and FO theory makes, either implicitly or explicitly, particular choices to deal with these issues in the definition of its semantics. In this section, we make these choices explicit by defining a number of formal principles which may underlie the semantics of a combined knowledge base.

4.1 Domain of Discourse

The semantics of logic programs is usually defined with respect to a fixed domain, viz. the Herbrand universe. An important property which holds for interpretations based on the Herbrand universe is *domain closure* [27], which means that the domain of each interpretation is limited to the Herbrand universe. In a combined knowledge base, one may want to take individuals outside of this fixed domain into account. This would require taking a larger domain of the models of P into account.

A straightforward approach is to simply use the Herbrand universe of $\mathcal{L}_P$. A drawback of this approach is that the only statements derived from Φ which are taken into account in P are the statements which involve names in the Herbrand universe. Consider the first-order theory $\Phi = \{p(a)\}$ and the logic program $P = \{r(b), q(x) \leftarrow p(x)\}$, where a is not in Σ_P. In case the variable in P quantifies only over the Herbrand universe U_H of $\mathcal{L}_P$, $q(a)$ cannot be concluded, since a is not in U_H.

An extension of this approach, which allows to consider also the names in Φ, is to consider an extended Herbrand universe, where the extended Herbrand universe consists of all names (i.e., ground terms) of the combined signature $\Sigma_{\mathcal{KB}}$. In this case, statements in Φ involving names which are not in the Herbrand universe of $\mathcal{L}_P$ are also taken into account. When considering an extended Herbrand universe as the domain of discourse, $q(a)$ could be concluded in the previous example. The potential drawback which remains with this approach is that unnamed individuals are not considered, as is demonstrated in the following example. The drawback can be overcome, however, by allowing *arbitrary domains* as the domain of discourse for P.

Example 3. Consider $P = \{q \leftarrow p(x)\}$ and $\Phi = \{\exists x p(x)\}$. If the domain of discourse of P is an extended Herbrand base, q can not be concluded, because there is no name t such that $p(t)$ can be concluded. $\quad\square$

We will now formally define a number of principles concerning the *domain of discourse* of the rules component of a combined knowledge base.

Principle 1.1 (Herbrand universe). *Given a combined knowledge base $\mathcal{KB} = \langle \Phi, P \rangle$, each interpretation M of $\mathcal{L}_P$, viewed as a pair $\langle U, \cdot^I \rangle$, has the same fixed universe*

$U = U_H$, where U_H is the Herbrand universe of $\mathcal{L}_P$. Furthermore, the interpretation function $\cdot^I$ is such that each ground term t over Σ_P is interpreted as itself, i.e., such that $t^I = t$.

Principle 1.2 (Combined signature). *Given a combined knowledge base $\mathcal{KB}=\langle \Phi, P \rangle$, each interpretation M of $\mathcal{L}_P$, viewed as a pair $\langle U, \cdot^I \rangle$, has the same fixed universe $U = U_{\mathcal{KB}}$, where $U_{\mathcal{KB}}$ is the set of ground terms of the combined signature $\Sigma_{\mathcal{KB}}$. Furthermore, the interpretation function $\cdot^I$ is such that each ground term t of $\Sigma_{\mathcal{KB}}$ is interpreted as itself, i.e., such that $t^I = t$.*

Principle 1.3 (Arbitrary domain). *Given a combined knowledge base $\mathcal{KB} = \langle \Phi, P \rangle$, each interpretation M of $\mathcal{L}_P$, viewed as a pair $\langle U, \cdot^I \rangle$, has an arbitrary first-order domain U and there are no restrictions on the interpretation function $\cdot^I$.*

Notice that Principles 1.1 and 1.2 coincide in case the names of the signatures Σ_P and $\Sigma_{\mathcal{KB}}$ coincide. The principles can be forced to coincide by extending Σ_P to include all ground terms of $\Sigma_{\mathcal{KB}}$ (see e.g. [12]); note that this may lead to an infinite logic program in case the signature is infinite.

Providing the standard-names assumption applies to the combined knowledge base, Principles 1.2 and 1.3 coincide, since then there is a one-to-one correspondence of names in the language and individuals in the domain.

4.2 Uniqueness of Names

Herbrand interpretations satisfy the unique-names assumption, i.e., for any two distinct ground terms in the Herbrand universe, their interpretations are distinct as well. There are, however, approaches which adopt a less restrictive view by axiomatizing a special equality predicate [27]. In such a case, there is a notion of default inequality: two ground terms are assumed to be unequal, unless equality between the terms can be derived.

The unique-names assumption does not hold in general for first-order interpretations. Several names in the language may be interpreted as the same individual in the domain (see, e.g., Example 1). Therefore, one may want to adopt a less restrictive view on uniqueness of names in the rules component of a combined knowledge base. We distinguish between maintaining the unique-names assumption, axiomatizing a special equality predicate, and discarding the unique-names assumption:

Principle 2.1 (Uniqueness of names). *Given a combined knowledge base $\langle \Phi, P \rangle$, for every interpretation $\langle U, \cdot^I \rangle$ of $\mathcal{L}_P$ and every pair of distinct names t_1, t_2 of $\mathcal{L}_P$, $t_1^I \neq t_2^I$ holds.*

Principle 2.2 (Special equality predicate). *Given a combined knowledge base $\langle \Phi, P \rangle$, a special binary equality predicate eq (cf. [27]) is axiomatized as part of P.*

Principle 2.3 (No uniqueness of names). *The unique-names assumption does not apply.*

Notice that Principles 1.1 and 1.2 enforce the unique-names assumption in the rules component; they cannot be combined with Principle 2.3. Notice further that in case a special equality predicate is axiomatized in P, it is generally desirable that if equality between two individuals is derived from Φ, this information is also available in P. As proposed in [28], the predicate eq may be defined in terms of equality $=$ in the classical component.

4.3 Interaction from First-Order Theories to Rules

Interaction between a first-order theory and a set of rules can take place in two directions: (a) from the FO theory to the rules and (b) from the rules to the FO theory. In this section, we consider the interaction from the FO theory to the rules; we discuss interaction from the rules to the FO theory in the next section.

We extend the notion of a logic program to distinguish between the uses of classical predicates and rules predicates. A logic program with classical atoms P consists of a set of rules of form

$$h_1 \mid ... \mid h_o \leftarrow a_1, ..., a_m, not\ b_1, ..., not\ b_n, c_1, ..., c_l, not\ d_1, ..., not\ d_k, \quad (1)$$

where a_i, b_j are rules atoms and $c_{i'}$, $d_{j'}$ are classical atoms; $c_1, \ldots, d_k$ is called the *classical component* of the body of the rule, denoted $CB(r)$, and $a_1, \ldots, not\ b_n$ is called the *rules component*, denoted $RB(r)$. We moreover define the sets $CB^+(r) = \{c_1, \ldots, c_l\}$, $CB^-(r) = \{d_1, \ldots, d_k\}$, $RB^+(r) = \{a_1, \ldots, a_m\}$, and $RB^-(r) = \{b_1, \ldots, d_n\}$.

By interaction from the FO theory to the rules we mean the conditions under which the classical atoms in the body of a rule are true or false. We distinguish two basic principles a combined knowledge base may obey with respect to the interaction from FO theories to rules: interaction based on *single models* and interaction based on *entailment*. In the former case, the truth of $CB(r)$ corresponds to satisfaction in a single model $\mathcal{I}$ of the classical component Φ; in the latter case, the truth of $CB^+(r)$ and $CB^-(r)$ is determined by entailment or non-entailment from Φ, respectively. These notions of interaction are generalizations of the notions of interaction as defined in $\mathcal{DL}+log$ [9] and dl-programs [10], respectively, as we shall see in the next section.

We now define the principles formally:

Principle 3.1 (Interaction based on single models). *Let $\mathcal{KB} = \langle \Phi, P \rangle$ be a combined knowledge base such that $\Phi \subseteq \mathcal{L}$, $\mathcal{I}$ an interpretation of $\mathcal{L}$, and B a variable assignment.*

The classical component of the body of a rule $r \in P$ is true in $\mathcal{I}$ with respect to B, denoted $\mathcal{I}, B \models CB(r)$, iff $\mathcal{I}, B \models CB^+(r)$ and $\mathcal{I}, B \not\models CB^-(r)$.

An interpretation M s-satisfies a rule r with respect to $\mathcal{I}$ and B, denoted $M, B \models_{\mathcal{I}} r$, iff $M, B \models RB(r)$ and $\mathcal{I}, B \models CB(r)$ only if $M, B \models H(r)$.

We call M an *s-model* of r with respect to $\mathcal{I}$ iff $M, B \models_{\mathcal{I}} r$, for every variable assignment B. Furthermore, M is an s-model of P with respect to $\mathcal{I}$ iff $M \models_{\mathcal{I}} r$, for every rule $r \in P$.

Principle 3.2 (Interaction based on entailment). *Let $\mathcal{KB} = \langle \Phi, P \rangle$ be a combined knowledge base such that $\Phi \subseteq \mathcal{L}$.*

The classical component of the body of a rule $r \in P$ *is* entailed by Φ *with respect to a variable substitution* β, *denoted* $\Phi \models CB(r)\beta$, *iff* $\Phi \models CB^+(r)\beta$ *and* $\Phi \not\models CB^-(r)\beta$.

An interpretation M e-satisfies *a rule* r *with respect to a variable assignment* B *and* Φ, *denoted* $M, B \models_\Phi r$, *iff, for some variable substitution* β *associated with* B, $M, B \models RB(r)$ *and* $\Phi \models CB(r)\beta$ *only if* $M, B \models H(r)$.

M is an *e-model* of r with respect to Φ iff $M, B \models_\Phi r$, for every variable assignment B. Furthermore, M is an e-model of P with respect to Φ iff $M \models_\Phi r$, for every rule $r \in P$.

Note that in case P is a ground program, the variable assignments and substitutions can be disregarded in the definitions of the principles.

Providing the combined knowledge base obeys Principle 1.1 or Principle 1.2, the variable assignment B is equivalent to its associated variable substitution β: $M, B \models \alpha$ iff $M \models \alpha\beta$, with $x/t \in \beta$ iff $x^B = t$, and the logic program P is actually equivalent to its ground instantiation with respect to U_H or the ground terms of $\Sigma_{\mathcal{KB}}$, respectively. Thus, the only case where the variable assignment is crucial in the definitions is when variables in the rule may quantify over arbitrary domains, i.e., when $\mathcal{KB}$ obeys Principle 1.3.

Stable Models for Logic Programs in Combined Knowledge Bases. In order to capture the nonmonotonic aspects of the rules components, we need to define which models are actually the intended models of P. We do this by extending the notion of stable models [7] to the case of logic programs in combined knowledge bases. For the definition of stable models, we assume the domain of discourse in an (extended) Herbrand universe (Principle 1.1 or 1.2). We first need to define the ground instantiation of P.

We augment the definition of $gr(P)$ to obtain $gr_y^{\mathcal{KB}}(P)$ as follows, where y is either H (in case of Principle 1.1) or $\mathcal{KB}$ (in case of Principle 1.2): $gr_y^{\mathcal{KB}}(P)$ is the union of all possible ground instantiations of r which are obtained by replacing each variable which occurs in a rules predicate by a term in U_y, for each rule $r \in P$.

We can now define the notion of a stable model for the logic program P in a combined knowledge base $\mathcal{KB} = \langle \Phi, P \rangle$ in view of Principle 3.1 (resp., Principle 3.2): Let M be an s-model (resp., e-model) of P with respect to $\mathcal{I}$ (resp., Φ), the *reduct* of P with respect to M, denoted $P_{\mathcal{I}}^M$ (resp., P_Φ^M) is obtained from $gr^{\mathcal{KB}}y(P)$ by removing

- every rule r such that $\mathcal{I} \not\models \exists CB(r)$ (resp., $\Phi \not\models \exists CB(r)$),
- the classical component from every remaining rule,
- every rule r such that $B^-(r) \cap M \neq \emptyset$, and
- the negative body literals from the remaining rules.

Then, M is a *stable s-model* (resp., *stable e-model*) *of P with respect to $\mathcal{I}$* (resp., Φ) iff M restricted to rules predicates is a minimal Herbrand model of $P_{\mathcal{I}}^M$ (resp., P_Φ^M).

The following example shows that there is a difference between the two principles already in simple cases.

Example 4. Consider the combined knowledge base $\mathcal{KB} = \langle \Phi, P \rangle$ with $\Phi = \{p \vee q\}$ and $P = \{r \leftarrow p, \ r \leftarrow q\}$. Note that Φ entails neither p nor q. For the case of interaction based on single models of Φ, r is included in each of the (stable) models of

P with respect to every model of Φ, since we know that for each model of Φ, either p or q (or both) is true. In case the interaction is based on entailment, r is not included in the single stable e-model of P with respect to Φ, because neither p nor q is entailed by Φ.   □

In the case of interaction based on single models, classical predicates are always interpreted classically,[4] and it is not possible to use "real" nonmonotonic negation over classical predicates or rules predicates which depend on them.

Example 5. Given the classical theory $\Phi = \{p(a)\}$ and the logic program $P = \{o(a), o(b), q(x) \leftarrow not\ p(x), o(x)\}$, where p is a classical predicate and o, q are rules predicates. Consider the interpretation $\mathcal{I}_1$ of $\mathcal{L}_\Phi$ such that $\mathcal{I}_1 \models p(a)$ and $\mathcal{I}_1 \models p(b)$. Now, $P_{\mathcal{I}_1}^M = \{o(a), o(b), q(a) \leftarrow not\ p(a), q(b) \leftarrow not\ p(b)\}$, which has one stable s-model, $M_1 = \{o(a), o(b)\}$.

Now consider the interpretation $\mathcal{I}_2$ of $\mathcal{L}_\Phi$ such that $\mathcal{I}_2 \models p(a)$ and $\mathcal{I}_2 \not\models p(b)$. Now, $P_{\mathcal{I}_2}^M = \{o(a), o(b), p(a), q(a) \leftarrow not\ p(a), q(b) \leftarrow not\ p(b)\}$, which has one stable s-model, $M_2 = \{o(a), o(b), q(b)\}$.   □

The example shows that P has at least one stable model which does not include $q(b)$ (viz. M_1), whereas one might expect $q(b)$ to be included in every stable model, because $p(b)$ is never *known* to be true.

The following example shows that there might be a discrepancy when there is interaction based on entailment and there is no unique-names assumption in Φ, but it does hold in P.

Example 6. Consider the combined knowledge base $\mathcal{KB} = \langle \Phi, P \rangle$ with $\Phi = \{\forall x, y, z\ (p(x, y) \wedge p(x, z) \supset y = z); p(a, b); p(a, c)\}$[5] and $P = \{p'(x, y) \leftarrow p(x, y)\}$, with p a classical predicate and p' a rules predicate. In every model of Φ there is at most one role filler for p (viz. $b = c$), but the single stable e-model of P contains two role fillers for p'. However, one may also argue that this is actually the expected behavior, because the unique-names assumption holds for logic programs.   □

Principles 3.1 and 3.2 can be seen as two extremes for the integration of rules and FO theories. One could imagine possibilities which lie between the two extremes. The two formulated principles are by no means the only ways of integrating rules and FO theories, but they neatly generalize current approaches in the literature.

4.4 Interaction from Rules to First-Order Theories

We now consider the interaction from the rules to the FO theory. We assume that the head $H(r)$ of a rule r may contain classical atoms.

Similar to the interaction from FO theories to rules, we distinguish between *interaction based on single models* and *interaction based on entailment*. In the case of interaction based on single models, a model M of $\mathcal{L}_P$ constrains the set of *allowed models* of

---

[4] This aspect is discussed in more detail in [28].

[5] Note that the first axiom in Φ corresponds to defining p as a functional role in description logics.

Φ; in the case of interaction based on entailment, we join the conclusions about classical predicates which can be drawn from the logic program with the FO theory. This allows to take conclusions from the logic program into account when determining entailments of the FO theory.

Principle 4.1 (Interaction based on single models). *Let* $\mathcal{KB} = \langle \Phi, P \rangle$ *be a combined knowledge base such that* $\Phi \subseteq \mathcal{L}$, $\mathcal{I} = \langle U, \cdot^I \rangle$ *an interpretation of* $\mathcal{L}_\Phi$*, and* M *an interpretation of* $\mathcal{L}_P$*, viewed as a pair* $\langle V, \cdot^J \rangle$*.*

We say that $\mathcal{I}$ *respects* M *iff, for every classical predicate* p, $p^J \subseteq p^I$*. Furthermore,* $\mathcal{I}$ *is an* s-model *of* Φ *with respect to* M *iff* $\mathcal{I} \models \Phi$ *and* $\mathcal{I}$ *respects* M*.*

For the principle of interaction based on entailment, we view the model M of a program P as a set of ground atoms that are known to be true; we do not consider the negative part of the model.

Principle 4.2 (Interaction based on entailment). *Let* $\mathcal{KB} = \langle \Phi, P \rangle$ *be a combined knowledge base such that* $\Phi \subseteq \mathcal{L}$*.*

Φ e-entails *a formula* ϕ *with respect to a model* M *of* $\mathcal{L}_P$ *iff* $\Phi \cup M \models \phi$*.*

Note that this principle views a model as a set of ground atoms and thus it can only be applied if there is a one-to-one correspondence between names in the language and elements of the domain. Thus, either Principle 1.1 or 1.2 must apply. The combination of the Principles 4.2 and 3.2 yields the following definition of the model of a program:

> An interpretation M is an *e-model* of a rule r with respect to a variable assignment B with associated variable substitution β and a FO theory Φ iff $M, B \models H(r)$ whenever $M, B \models RB(r)$ and Φ e-entails $CB(r)\beta$ with respect to M.

Stable Models for Logic Programs in Combined Knowledge Bases. We now extend the notion of a stable model introduced in the previous section. First, we need to slightly adapt the definition of a reduct of P, as before: Let x be either an s-model $\mathcal{I}$ of Φ with respect to M or Φ. Then, P_x^M is obtained from $gr_y^{\mathcal{KB}}(P)$, where y is either H (in case of Principle 1.1) or $\mathcal{KB}$ (in case of Principle 1.2), by removing

- every rule r such that $x \not\models \exists CB(r)$ if $x = \mathcal{I}$, or such that $x \not\models \exists CB(r)$ with respect to M if $x = \Phi$,
- the classical component from the body of every remaining rule,
- the classical component from the head of every rule r such that $x \not\models \forall CH(r)$ if $x = \mathcal{I}$, or such that $x \not\models \forall CH(r)$ with respect to M if $x = \Phi$,
- every rule r such that $x \models \forall CH(r)$ if $x = \mathcal{I}$, or such that $x \models \forall CH(r)$ with respect to M if $x = \Phi$, in case $CH(r) \neq \emptyset$,
- every rule r such that $B^-(r) \cap M \neq \emptyset$, and
- the negative body literals from the remaining rules.

Then, M is a *stable s-model* (resp., *stable e-model*) of P iff M restricted to the rules predicates is a minimal Herbrand model of $P_\mathcal{I}^M$ (resp., P_Φ^M).

The following example demonstrates the difference between the two kinds of interaction:

Table 1. Principles of Current Approaches

	SWRL	**dl-programs**	$\mathcal{DL}$+*log*
Domain of Discourse			
1.1 Herbrand Universe	-	-	+
1.2 Combined Signature	-	+	-
1.3 Arbitrary domains	+	-	-
Uniqueness of Names			
2.1 Names in U_H are unique	-	+	+/-[1]
2.2 Equality predicate	-	-[2]	-[2]
2.3 No uniqueness	+	-	+/-
Interaction from FO Theories to Rules			
3.1 Single models	+	-	+
3.2 Entailment	-	+	-
Interaction from Rules to FO Theories			
4.1 Single models	+	-	+
4.2 Entailment	-	+	-

[1] The combined knowledge base has the standard, and implied unique-names assumption.
[2] Both dl-programs and $\mathcal{DL}$+*log* may be extended with an equality predicate.

Example 7. Consider the combined knowledge base $\mathcal{KB} = \langle \Phi, P \rangle$ with $\Phi = \{p(a) \vee p(b)\}$ and $P = \{q \leftarrow p(a), not\ q; r \leftarrow p(b)\}$, where p is a classical predicate and q is a rules predicate. In case of interaction based on single models, r is included in every stable s-model, since for every model $\mathcal{I}$ in which $p(a)$ is true, there is no corresponding stable s-model for P.

In the case of interaction based on entailment, no such conclusion can be drawn: neither $p(a)$ nor $p(b)$ is e-entailed by Φ. In fact, the only stable e-model of P is the empty set. □

5 Representational Issues in Current Approaches

We can now compare current approaches to integrating description logics and logic programs with respect to the representational issues analyzed above. The three approaches we have selected for the comparison are SWRL [11,20], dl-programs [10], and $\mathcal{DL}$+*log* [9]. These approaches are generalizations of a number of other approaches as discussed in Section 3. The results of the classification are summarized in Table 1. In the remainder of this section, we describe the principles of the mentioned approaches in more detail. We conclude with a few remarks about stable models in these approaches.

5.1 Domain of Discourse

The domain of discourse for SWRL rules is simply the domain of the first-order interpretation of the SWRL FO theory (Principle 1.3). Thus, the variables in the SWRL rules quantify both over the named and the unnamed individuals in the DL component of the knowledge base. SWRL rules do not adhere to the unique-names assumption: several names may refer to the same individual, unless inequality between individuals is explicitly asserted. SWRL does explicitly distinguish between classical predicates and rules predicates. In fact, all predicates in a SWRL knowledge base are classical predicates.

In dl-programs, the domain of discourse corresponds one-to-one with a set of constants in some signature Σ. Typically, and most generally, this signature would be the combined signature $\Sigma_{\mathcal{KB}}$ and thus the variables in the rules may range over names in the combined signature (Principle 1.2).

$\mathcal{DL}+log$ has the standard-names assumption for the entire combined knowledge base. Additionally, it is assumed that there is always an infinite number of constant identifiers available in the signature Σ_Φ and thus in $\Sigma_{\mathcal{KB}}$. According to the definition of combined knowledge bases in $\mathcal{DL}+log$, the domain of discourse of rules in P is the set of constants in the combined signature (Principle 1.2). However, there is a restriction on the use of variables in $\mathcal{DL}+log$, the *weak DL-safeness*: every variable which occurs in an atom in the head must occur in a positive rules atom in the body. This effectively ensures that each variable which occurs in a rules predicate quantifies only over the names of $\mathcal{L}_P$. Variables which only occur in classical predicates in the body of a rule may quantify over all names in $\Sigma_{\mathcal{KB}}$. Thus, depending on where a variable occurs in a rule, the domain of discourse is either the Herbrand universe U_H^P (Principle 1.1) or the set of names in the combined signature $\Sigma_{\mathcal{KB}}$ (Principle 1.2).

5.2 Uniqueness of Names

SWRL knowledge bases do not assume the unique-names assumption (Principle 2.3), although it can be axiomatized by asserting inequality between every set of distinct constant symbols in $\Sigma_{\mathcal{KB}}$. SWRL allows the use of the equality symbol in P. One could view this as a special equality predicate, although it does not require a special axiomatization, since it is a built into the semantics. All the usual equality axioms are obviously valid in SWRL. One could thus take the point of view that there is an equality predicate in the language and this is a classical predicate and thus SWRL combines the Principles 2.2 and 2.3.

The unique-names assumption holds for the rules in a dl-program (Principle 2.1). Combined with the fact that the domain simply consists of all names of the combined signature, uniqueness of names is assumed even if two names are equal in every model of the FO theory. We illustrated this discrepancy earlier in Example 6. A possible way to overcome this discrepancy is to axiomatize an equality predicate eq in the logic program (Principle 2.2) and to define it in terms of equality statements which are derived from the FO theory:

$$eq(X, Y) \leftarrow DL[=](X, Y).$$

The unique-names assumption holds in any $\mathcal{DL}+log$ knowledge base and thus also in the rules component (Principle 2.1). One might allow arbitrary domains for Φ. As pointed out in [28], one may overcome the unique-names assumption by axiomatizing an equality predicate in P, and treating it as a classical predicate (Principle 2.2), similar to the axiomatization for dl-programs proposed above.

5.3 Interaction Between First-Order Theories and Rules

In SWRL, interaction from FO theories to rules, and from rules to FO theories, is based on single models (Principles 3.1, 4.1), since the rules and DL components in SWRL are simply part of one first-order theory. SWRL actually defines one model for both the FO theory and the rules. In terms of combined knowledge bases which we use in this paper, one could equivalently say that all predicates are classical predicates. The models for the FO theory and the rules share the same domain. Finally, an interpretation $\mathcal{I}$ is a model of $\mathcal{KB} = \langle \Phi, P \rangle$ iff $\mathcal{I}$ is an s-model of Φ with respect to every s-model M of P which shares the domain of $\mathcal{I}$.

Interaction between rules and FO theories in dl-program in both directions is based on entailment (Principles 3.2, 4.2). A (ground) dl-atom in the body of a rule in P is true if it is entailed by Φ. The interaction from rules to FO theories diverges somewhat from the description of Principle 3.2. Namely, classical predicates are not allowed to occur in the heads of rules in P. Instead, dl-atoms allow the possibility to select which part of a model M of P should be taken into account when determining truth of the dl-atom.[6] In other words, a ground dl-atom α is true in a model M with respect to FO theory Φ iff $\Phi \cup q(M) \models \alpha$, where $q(M)$ is either (a) a subset of M, (b) the negation of a subset of M, (c) the negation of a subset of the Herbrand base which is not in M, or (d) a composition of any of the above.

In $\mathcal{DL}+log$, interaction between FO theories and rules is based on single models (Principles 3.1 and 4.1), as is the case for SWRL. A model $\mathcal{I}$ is an s-model only if there is an s-model M of P which respects $\mathcal{I}$ and $\mathcal{I}$ respects M. The other direction also holds if M is additionally a stable s-model of P with respect to $\mathcal{I}$.

5.4   Stable Models in Current Approaches

SWRL does not have the notion of stable models. This is to be expected since the language does not allow default negation. A formula ϕ is entailed by a SWRL knowledge base $\mathcal{KB}$ if every model of $\mathcal{KB}$ is a model of ϕ.

In dl-programs, a model M is a stable e-model of P with respect to Φ if it is the minimal model of the reduct P_Φ^M with slightly more complicated conditions for the dl-atoms, since their form needs to be taken into account. Entailment is then defined as follows: P *bravely* entails a ground atom α if α is true in *some* stable model of P and P *skeptically* entails α if α is true in *all* stable models of P.

In $\mathcal{DL}+log$, a model M is a stable model of P if it is the minimal model of the reduct $P_\mathcal{I}^M$. A ground atom α is *entailed* by $\mathcal{KB}$ if (a) it is true in every s-model of Φ, in case α is a classical atom, or (b) it is true in every stable s-model of P, in case α is a rules atom.

6   Settings for Combining Classical Logic and Rules

Based on the analysis of the representational issues in Section 4 and as an abstraction of current approaches to combining rules and FO theories, we define three generic settings for the integration of rules and FO theories. These settings help to classify existing and future approaches to such combinations. Additionally, they help to clarify the space of possible solutions for the integration of FO theories and rules with respect to the way they resolve the representational issues we have pointed out in this paper.

---

[6] Actually, dl-atoms allow more sophisticated methods of controlling the flow of information. The negation of parts of M can be taken into account and negated information can be taken into account in the absence of information in M.

The three settings we have identified are:

1. In the *minimal interface* setting, the logic program and the FO theory are viewed as separate components and are only connected through a minimal interface which consists of the exchange of entailments. The dl-programs approach [10] falls in this setting.

2. Building an *integrated model*, where the rules and the logic program are integrated to a large extent, although there is a separation in the vocabulary between classical predicate and rules predicates. The integrated model is the union of two models, one for the FO theory and one for the rules, which share the same domain. $\mathcal{DL}+log$ [9] and SWRL [20] fall in this setting, with the caveat that SWRL does not allow negation in the rules component.

3. A final possible setting is *full integration*, where there is no separation between classical predicates and rules predicates; this makes it possible, among other things, to express nonmonotonic negation over classical predicates. We are not aware of current approaches which fall in this setting, but we can imagine approaches along this line, possibly based on first-order nonmonotonic logics [29,17,30].

The main distinction between the first and second setting is interaction based on single models (Setting 2) versus interaction based on entailment (Setting 1). In the third setting, there is not so much interaction, but rather *full integration*: one can no longer really distinguish between the FO theory and the rules. While Settings 1 and 2 are abstractions of current approaches ([9] and [10], respectively), Setting 3 is not based on current approaches, but we see this setting as a possible development towards a tighter integration of FO theories and (nonmonotonic) logic programs.

Table 2 summarizes the settings and their representational principles.

Table 2. Principles of Settings

	Minimal interface	Integrated models	Full integration
Domain of Discourse			
1.1 Herbrand Universe	-	-	-
1.2 Combined Signature	+	-	-
1.3 Arbitrary domains	-	+	+
Uniqueness of Names			
2.1 Names in U_H are unique	+	-	-
2.2 Equality predicate	-[1]	-	-
2.3 No uniqueness	-	+	+
Interaction from FO Theories to Rules			
3.1 Single models	-	+	+/-[2]
3.2 Entailment	+	-	+/-[2]
Interaction from Rules to FO Theories			
4.1 Single models	-	+	+
4.2 Entailment	+	-	-
Distinction between classical and rule predicates	+	+	-

[1] An equality predicate can be axiomatized in P

[2] Full integration requires more complex interaction than single models or entailment alone

7 Related Work

Franconi and Tessaris [22] survey three approaches to combining (the DL subset of) classical logic with rules. The three approaches are (i) (subsets of) SWRL, (ii) dl-programs, and (iii) epistemic rules [31]. The latter are a formalization of procedural rules which can be found in practical knowledge-representation systems. Franconi and Tessaris show that all three approaches coincide in case the DL component is empty and the rules component is positive, but that they diverge quickly when adding trivial axioms to the DL component. While Franconi and Tessaris look at the problem of combining classical logic and rules from the point of view of several existing approaches, we surveyed the fundamental issues which may arise when combining classical logic with rules and classified existing approaches accordingly.

Variants of logic-programming semantics without the domain-closure assumption have been studied in the logic-programming literature. In [32], the stable-model semantics is extended to open domains by extending the language with an infinite sequence of new constants. Open logic programs (see, e.g., [33]) distinguish between defined and undefined predicates. The defined predicates are given a completion semantics, similar to Clark's completion [34], and equality is axiomatized in the language. The resulting theory is then given a first-order semantics. Open logic programs were adapted to open answer-set semantics in [35].

It is worthwhile to mention some approaches which propose to use rule-based formalisms (possibly with extended domains) to reason about classical logic, and especially about description-logic theories. [12] proposes to use disjunctive datalog to reason about the description logic $\mathcal{SHIQ}$, extended with DL-safe SWRL rules. [24] uses extended conceptual logic programs to reason with expressive description logics combined with DL-safe rules. [23] proposes a subset of a description logic which can be directly interpreted as a logic program. Open logic programs have been used in [33] to reason with expressive description logics. [24] uses the open answer-set semantics [35] to reason with expressive description logics extended with DL-safe rules. [36] and [37] reduce reasoning in the description logic $\mathcal{ALCQI}$ to query answering in logic programs based on the answer-set semantics.

8 Conclusions and Future Work

There exist several different approaches to the combination of first-order theories (such as description-logic ontologies) and (nonmonotonic) rules (e.g. [8,9,10,11,12]). Each of these approaches overcomes the differences between the first-order and rules paradigms (open vs. closed domain, non-unique vs. unique names, open vs. closed world) in different ways.

We have identified a number of fundamental representational issues which arise in combinations of FO theories and rules. For each of these issues, we have defined a number of formal principles which a combination of rules and ontologies may obey. These principles help to explicate the underlying assumptions of the semantics of such a combination. They show the consequences of the choices which were taken in the design of the combination and help to characterize approaches to combining rules and FO theories according to their expressive power and their underlying assumptions.

We have used the formal principles to characterize several leading approaches to combining rules with (description-logic) ontologies. These approaches are SWRL [20], dl-programs [10], and $\mathcal{DL}+log$ [9]. It turns out that SWRL and $\mathcal{DL}+log$ are quite similar concerning their representational principles, although the approaches might seem quite different on the surface; both approaches specify the interaction between ontologies and rules based on single models, but SWRL does not allow nonmonotonic negation in the rules. The dl-programs approach has quite different underlying assumptions: the interaction between the ontology and logic program is restricted to entailment of ground facts.

Based on the formal principles, the relations between the formal principles, and generalizing existing approaches, we have defined a number of general settings for the integration of rules and ontologies. An approach may define a *minimal interface* between the FO theory and the rule base, the semantics may be based on *integrated models*, or the approach enables *full integration*, eliminating the distinction between classical and rules predicates. These settings mainly differ in the notion of interaction between FO theories and rules. In the minimal interface setting, interaction is based on entailment, whereas in the integrated models setting, the models of the FO theory and the rule base are combined to define an integrated semantics. The full integration setting requires a unified formalism which can capture both classical first-order theories and nonmonotonic logic programs.

Besides the representational principles defined in this paper, an approach to combining rules and ontologies has of course other properties which are of potential interest. To wit, computational properties such as decidability and complexity, which are concerns in several existing approaches (e.g. [21,8,9,10]), are of particular interest. Another issue in such combinations is the ease of implementation and availability of reasoning techniques. For example, the approach in [8] allows to reduce reasoning with combined knowledge bases to standard reasoning services in answer-set programming (ASP) and description-logic engines, whereas the extension to $\mathcal{DL}+log$ [9] requires non-standard reasoning services for description logics (checking containment of conjunctive queries in unions of conjunctive queries). Finally, dl-programs [10] allow a simple extension of existing algorithms for answer-set programming, using standard reasoning services of description-logic reasoners.

Our future work consists of taking the above-mentioned types of principles into account for the classification of approaches to combining FO theories and rules. Furthermore, we will continue to classify upcoming approaches and consider the combination of nonmonotonic ontology languages (e.g. [38,31,39,40]), including ontology languages with transitive closure (e.g. $\mathcal{DLR}_{reg}$ [41]), with rules.

Nonmonotonic logics seem a promising vehicle for an even tighter integration of FO theories and (nonmonotonic) logic programs than dl-programs or $\mathcal{DL}+log$, in the setting of *full integration*. One could think of an extension of a nonmonotonic description logic. For example, [42] contains a proposal for extending the MKNF-DL [39], which is based on the propositional subset of the bimodal nonmonotonic logic MBNF [43], with nonmonotonic rules. Other nonmonotonic logics which one might consider are, for example, default logic [14,29], circumscription [16,17], and autoepistemic logic [15,30].

So far we have considered rules components with the stable-model semantics [7,13]. In future work we may consider the well-founded semantics [6] for arbitrary programs. Additionally, the combination of production rules with ontologies is recently receiving some attention in the context of the W3C Rule Interchange Format (RIF) Working Group[7]. One might consider characterizing combinations of production rules with ontologies, although there are semantic challenges for such a characterization.

References

1. Dean, M., Schreiber, G., eds.: OWL Web Ontology Language Reference. (2004) W3C Recommendation 10 February 2004.
2. Baader, F., Calvanese, D., McGuinness, D.L., Nardi, D., Patel-Schneider, P.F., eds.: The Description Logic Handbook. Cambridge University Press (2003)
3. Horrocks, I., Patel-Schneider, P.F.: Reducing OWL entailment to description logic satisfiability. In: Proc. of the 2003 International Semantic Web Conference (ISWC 2003), Sanibel Island, Florida (2003)
4. Genesereth, M.R., Fikes, R.E.: Knowledge interchange format, version 3.0 reference manual. Technical Report Logic-92-1, Computer Science Department, Stanford University (1992)
5. Delugach, H., ed.: ISO Common Logic. (2006) Available at http://philebus.tamu.edu/cl/ .
6. Gelder, A.V., Ross, K., Schlipf, J.S.: The well-founded semantics for general logic programs. Journal of the ACM **38**(3) (1991) 620–650
7. Gelfond, M., Lifschitz, V.: The stable model semantics for logic programming. In Kowalski, R.A., Bowen, K., eds.: Proceedings of the Fifth International Conference on Logic Programming, Cambridge, Massachusetts, The MIT Press (1988) 1070–1080
8. Rosati, R.: On the decidability and complexity of integrating ontologies and rules. Journal of Web Semantics **3**(1) (2005) 61–73
9. Rosati, R.: $\mathcal{DL}$+log: Tight integration of description logics and disjunctive datalog. In: KR2006. (2006)
10. Eiter, T., Lukasiewicz, T., Schindlauer, R., Tompits, H.: Combining answer set programming with description logics for the semantic web. In: Proc. of the International Conference of Knowledge Representation and Reasoning (KR'04). (2004)
11. Horrocks, I., Patel-Schneider, P.F., Boley, H., Tabet, S., Grosof, B., Dean, M.: SWRL: A semantic web rule language combining OWL and RuleML. Member submission 21 May 2004, W3C (2004)
12. Motik, B., Sattler, U., Studer, R.: Query answering for OWL-DL with rules. In: Proceedings of 3rd International Semantic Web Conference (ISWC2004), Hiroshima, Japan (2004)
13. Gelfond, M., Lifschitz, V.: Classical negation in logic programs and disjunctive databases. New Generation Computing **9**(3/4) (1991) 365–386
14. Reiter, R.: A logic for default reasoning. In Ginsberg, M.L., ed.: Readings in nonmonotonic reasoning. Morgan Kaufmann Publishers Inc., San Francisco, CA, USA (1987) 68–93
15. Moore, R.C.: Semantical considerations on nonmonotonic logic. Artificial Intelligence **25**(1) (1985) 75–94
16. McCarthy, J.: Applications of circumscription to formalizing common sense knowledge. Artificial Intelligence **28** (1986) 89–116
17. Lifschitz, V.: Circumscription. In: Handbook of Logic in AI and Logic Programming, Vol. 3, Oxford University Press (1994) 298–352

---

[7] http://www.w3.org/2005/rules/wg

18. Lloyd, J.W.: Foundations of Logic Programming (2nd edition). Springer-Verlag (1987)
19. Przymusinski, T.C.: On the declarative and procedural semantics of logic programs. Journal of Automated Reasoning **5**(2) (1989) 167–205
20. Horrocks, I., Patel-Schneider, P.F.: A proposal for an OWL rules language. In: Proc. of the Thirteenth International World Wide Web Conference (WWW 2004), ACM (2004) 723–731
21. Levy, A.Y., Rousset, M.C.: Combining Horn rules and description logics in CARIN. Artificial Intelligence **104** (1998) 165 – 209
22. Franconi, E., Tessaris, S.: Rules and queries with ontologies: a unified logical framework. In: Workshop on Principles and Practice of Semantic Web Reasoning (PPSWR'04), St. Malo, France (2004)
23. Grosof, B.N., Horrocks, I., Volz, R., Decker, S.: Description logic programs: Combining logic programs with description logic. In: Proc. Intl. Conf. on the World Wide Web (WWW-2003), Budapest, Hungary (2003)
24. Heymans, S., Nieuwenborgh, D.V., Vermeir, D.: Nonmonotonic ontological and rule-based reasoning with extended conceptual logic programs. In: ESWC 2005. (2005) 392–407
25. Donini, F.M., Lenzerini, M., Nardi, D., Schaerf, A.: AL-log: integrating datalog and description logics. Journal of Intelligent Information Systems **10** (1998) 227–252
26. Rosati, R.: Towards expressive KR systems integrating datalog and description logics: A preliminary report. In: Proc. of the 1999 International Description Logics workshop (DL99). (1999) 160–164
27. Reiter, R.: Equality and domain closure in first-order databases. Journal of the ACM **27**(2) (1980) 235–249
28. Rosati, R.: Semantic and computational advantages of the safe integration of ontologies and rules. In: Proceedings of PPSWR2005, Springer-Verlag (2005) 50–64
29. Lifschitz, V.: On open defaults. In Lloyd, J., ed.: Proceedings of the symposium on computational logic, Berlin: Springer-Verlag (1990) 80–95
30. Konolige, K.: Quantification in autoepistemic logic. Fundamenta Informaticae **15**(3–4) (1991) 275–300
31. Donini, F.M., Lenzerini, M., Nardi, D., Nutt, W., Schaerf, A.: An epistemic operator for description logics. Artificial Intelligence **100**(1–2) (1998) 225–274
32. Gelfond, M., Przymusinska, H.: Reasoning on open domains. In: LPNMR 1993. (1993) 397–413
33. Van Belleghem, K., Denecker, M., De Schreye, D.: A strong correspondence between description logics and open logic programming. In: Logic Programming, Proceedings of the Fourteenth International Conference on Logic Programming, MIT Press (1997) 346–360
34. Clark, K.L.: Negation as failure. In Gallaire, H., Minker, J., eds.: Logic and Data Bases. Plenum Press, New York, USA (1978) 293–322
35. Heymans, S., Van Nieuwenborgh, D., Vermeir, D.: Guarded Open Answer Set Programming. In: 8th International Conference on Logic Programming and Non Monotonic Reasoning (LPNMR 2005). Number 3662 in LNAI, Springer (2005) 92–104
36. Baral, C.: Knowledge Representation, Reasoning and Declarative Problem Solving. Cambridge University Press (2003)
37. Swift, T.: Deduction in ontologies via ASP. In: LPNMR2004. (2004) 275–288
38. Bonatti, P., Lutz, C., Wolter, F.: Expressive non-monotonic description logics based on circumscription. In: KR2006. (2006)
39. Donini, F.M., Nardi, D., Rosati, R.: Description logics of minimal knowledge and negation as failure. ACM Transactions on Computational Logic **3**(2) (2002) 177–225
40. Baader, F., Hollunder, B.: Embedding defaults into terminological knowledge representation formalisms. Journal of Automated Reasoning **14** (1995) 149–180

41. Calvanese, D., Giancomo, G.D., Lenzerini, M.: On the decidability of query containment under constraints. In: Proc. of the 17th ACM SIGACT SIGMOD SIGART Symp. on Principles of Database Systems (PODS'98). (1998) 149–158
42. Motik, B., Rosati, R.: Closing semantic web ontologies. Technical report, University of Manchester (2006) Available at http://www.cs.man.ac.uk/ bmotik/ publications/paper.pdf.
43. Lifschitz, V.: Minimal belief and negation as failure. Artificial Intelligence **70**(1-2) (1994) 53–72

Towards a Software/Knowware Co-engineering*

Ruqian Lu

Institute of Mathematics& MADIS, AMSS
Key Lab of Intelligent Information Processing, Inst. of Computing Technology
Shanghai Key Lab of Intelligent Information Processing, Fudan University
Beijing Key Lab of Multimedia and Intelligent Software, Beijing University of Technology

Abstract. After a short introduction to the concepts of knowware, knowware engineering and knowledge middleware, this paper proposes to study the software/knowware co-engineering. Different from the traditional software engineering process, it is a mixed process involving both software engineering and knowware engineering issues. The technical subtleties of such a mixed process are discussed and guidelines of building models for it are proposed. It involves three parallel lines of developing system components of different types. The key issues of this process are how to guarantee the correctness and appropriateness of system composition and decomposition. The ladder principle, which is a modification of the waterfall model, and the tower principle, which is a modification of the fountain model, are proposed. We also studied the possibility of equipping the co-engineering process with a formal semantics. The core problem of establishing such a theory is to give a formal semantics to an open knowledge source. We have found a suitable tool for this purpose. That is the co-algebra. We also try to give a preliminary delineation of a co-algebraic semantics for a typical example of open knowledge source – the knowledge distributed on the World Wide Web.

Keywords: Knowware, knowledge middleware, software/knowware co-engineering.

1 Why Knowware?

I still keep a firm memory on the inspiring statement made by the late professor Xiwen Ma: "Software is condensed and crystallized knowledge" [1]. Every piece of software, in particular application software, contains human knowledge with respect to some domain in its condensed form. This is why software can help us to solve problems. However, usually it is the software engineers, not domain experts, who are responsible for developing software. What the domain experts have to do is only to tell the software engineers what functions they expect the software to possess. However, it is often difficult for a software engineer to acquire and master domain

* Supported by the projects 2001CCA03000, 2001AA113130, 2001CB312004 and NSF Major Program 60496324.

J. Lang, F. Lin, and J. Wang (Eds.): KSEM 2006, LNAI 4092, pp. 23–32, 2006.

knowledge within a short time. This is an important reason for many failed requirement analysis and software development. As a matter of fact, we often confuse software development with knowledge acquisition and programming, a piece of software with a package of knowledge, and particularly, the intellectual properties of software with the intellectual properties of the knowledge it used. Therefore we claim that we should separate (domain) knowledge from software, separate knowledge development from software development, and separate knowledge engineers (knowledge acquiring and programming teams) from software engineers. As pointed out by Prof. Feigenbaum, we are entering an era of "knowledge industry in which knowledge itself will be a salable commodity like food and oil. Knowledge itself is to become the new wealth of nations." [2]. We call the commercialized form of the separated knowledge as knowware. We claim further that hardware, software and knowware should be the three equally important underpinnings of IT industry [3, 4].

In this paper, we will first recall the content of [3] and [4] shortly as an introduction and preparation for the discussion in the following sections. Let us introduce the concept of knowware. Simply speaking, knowware is an independent and commercialized knowledge module that is computer operable, but free of any built-in control mechanism (in particular, not bund to any software), meeting some industrial standards and embeddable in software and/or hardware. According to the way of their production, we differentiate between three types of knowware. The first type is called naïve knowware, which has already a standard (often industrialized) form of knowledge representation. You can for example download songs and music from some web portals for your MP3 player (of course you will be charged for that). These songs are the simplest form of knowware. The second type is called transformation-based knowware. Usually, the knowledge for such type of knowware already exists in some text or multimedia form. One has to transform it to another standard form designed for knowware, which is readable and operable by some knowware managing software (called knowledge middleware, will be explained below). The process of transformation is not necessary very easy. A typical example is the knowware of tax regulations. The tax regulations of the government that should be contained in all tax calculating software form an important material of knowware production, which is used by the tax department of the government. Each time the government announces new tax rules, the knowware producer (may also be the government itself) transforms this governmental document to a knowware operable by any tax calculation software. We can even imagine that the tax rule announcing agency always publishes the new tax rules in two forms: the text form and the knowware form[1]. The third type is called search based knowware. The knowledge needed for such knowware usually is not available in a batch and ready for access way. It has to be searched or collected from various knowledge sources. The result of search is not guaranteed to be complete, even not guaranteed to be consistent. Such knowledge source can be human experts or knowledge recorded on some media, for example the digital library or the World Wide Web.

---

[1] Note that some algorithm text books carry a CD of programmed algorithms together with them.

2 Models of Knowware Engineering

Similar to the case of software engineering, where various models of software life cycle have been proposed, there should be also a corresponding concept of knowware engineering and knowware life cycle, together with their models. Besides, different types of knowware require different models of knowware life cycle. Before going into the details of knowware life cycle, we would like to mention the concept of knowledge crystal, which is common to all knowware life cycle models. A knowledge crystal can be understood as a half fabricated form of knowware, which is a well recognized and organized set of knowledge. It can be considered also as a knowledge module (compare with the micro-theory in the terminology of Lenat [5]) of a formatted and modularized knowledge base that is not necessary consistent and complete. The knowledge modules and hence the whole knowledge base are subject to a steady evolution. A knowledge crystal is usually not a commodity and does not have to take care of the commercial standard. Besides, it is more general-purpose oriented than a knowware, which is usually special purposed. It is like the half-fabricated fish and pork in the kitchen of a big restaurant, while a knowware is a well prepared dish made of these half products.

Our first model of knowware life cycle is the smelting furnace model. A smelting furnace accepts and smelts raw material inputted in a batch way, like the blast furnace smelts iron ore, or the steel furnace smelts iron blocks. This corresponds to type 2 knowware production. In the knowware practice, this smelting furnace is a massive and heterogeneous knowledge base. To give an example, we mention a project of producing ICAI systems automatically from a set of imported textbooks and technical leaflets, undertaken by our team in last decades [6]. These books and leaflets function as "knowledge ore", which will be broken in small knowledge units and smelted to knowledge magma in the knowledge base. That is, their knowledge will be extracted and reorganized in a ready to use form. Each time a new ICAI is requested by some individual, the relevant knowledge will be selected and reorganized in a knowledge crystal—the teaching course. Just as in the real smelting process, different "impurities" have to be added or removed to get quality products, the same thing will happen in this knowledge crystal production process.

Our second model of knowware life cycle is the crystallization model. Consider a vast source of knowledge like the World Wide Web. The knowledge mining process on it is just like knowledge crystallization from a knowledge solution. The crystallization core is the knowledge requirements submitted by the user. This process is not just a monotonic piling up of knowledge items. Each time a new knowledge item is acquired, an evolution of the old crystal follows. Similar knowledge items may be merged. Complimentary items may be fused. Inconsistent items may be resolved. The whole crystal may be reorganized. We need two mechanisms for maintaining the knowledge crystallization process: the knowledge pump and the knowledge kidney. A knowledge pump controls the content and granule of knowledge acquisition from the knowledge solution, while a knowledge kidney controls the metabolic process of knowledge evolution. This shows that a knowledge crystal is in a state of steady changing.

Our third model of knowware life cycle is the spiral model. Originally proposed by Nonaka and Takeuk in 1995 [7], the spiral model characterizes the formation and transformation of implicit and explicit knowledge. It circles the loop: (knowledge) externalization → combination → internalization → socialization. In the knowware practice, this knowledge spiral may very well be used to describe the spiral evolution of expert knowledge (from experience to theory). That means the knowledge spiral can serve as a model of knowledge crystal formation. Compared with the crystallization model, the knowledge spiral model puts more focus on improving the knowledge quality than on increasing the knowledge amount.

3   The Role of Knowledge Middleware

The category of software can be classified in system software and application software. For knowware there is no such classification. There is no system knowware. Every piece of knowware is application oriented. The development, application and management of knowware involve knowledge acquisition, selection, fusion, maintenance, renewing and many other functions. We need software tools, called knowledge middleware, for performing these jobs. Knowledge middleware is different from the conventional middleware concept in software engineering. Traditional middleware helps application programs to work cooperatively in a networked environment. The operation of knowware needs a network in a broader sense. This functional network connects not only knowware with knowware, but also knowware with software, knowware with knowledge source and knowware with human users. We call it the knowledge broker network, KBN for short. Thus, knowledge middleware is the underlying set of software tools based on KBN and knowledge transformation and transmission protocols, whose function is to support the effective development, application and management of knowware.

Roughly classified, we have the following kinds of knowledge middleware (KM for short): KU (Knowware-User) type KM: those helping the people to make use of knowware and helping the administrators to manage such use; CS (Crystal-Source) type KM: those functioning in the formation process of knowledge crystals; CC (Crystal-Crystal) type KM: those functioning in the evolution process of knowledge crystals; CK (Crystal-Knowware) type KM: those transforming knowledge crystals to knowware; KK (Knowware-Konwware) type KM: those combining several knowware to a more powerful knowware.

Now we come to the concept of knowware engineering. We define knowware engineering as the systematic application of knowledge middleware with the goal of knowware generation, evolution and application. Knowware engineering has life cycles, just as software engineering does. Depending on how one obtains knowledge, organizes it in knowledge crystals, maintains it, makes it evolving and transforms it to knowware, one has different kinds of life cycles for knowware engineering.

Please refer to [3] and [4] for more detailed examples of knowware and knowledge middleware.

4 A Paradigm of Software/Knowware Co-engineering

There are two different paradigms of knowware development: knowware on shelf and knowware on order. The former paradigm develops knowware independently from the development of its software environment, in which the knowware will be embedded. Such knowware is mainly for public use. For example, the knowware containing tax rules of the government will be used by any tax management system. On the other hand, the latter paradigm develops knowware together with its software environment. In this case, knowware and software are developed by a cooperative working team under a unified planning. Such knowware is mainly for private use. For example, the business policies of an enterprise will be transformed into a knowware that will form a part of the ERP of that enterprise. We also call this paradigm the paradigm of software/knowware co-engineering, which is the subject of this and next section.

This co-engineering process differs from the traditional software engineering process in many aspects. First, it is a mixed process involving both software engineering and knowware engineering issues. In addition, the knowledge middleware issues are also considered as a bridge connecting the two sides. Second, the global system requirement will be split into three partial requirements, which initiate three parallel lines (knowware, knowledge middleware, pure operational software) of system development. Third, appropriate checkpoints are established to assure the integrity and consistency of products and half products on the confluent places of the three parallel development lines. Fourth, feedbacks and loops of the process are included to meet the need of system evolution. As a result, we have the following software/knowware co-engineeing process:

Requirement specification for the whole system,

Requirement decomposition in software requirement and knowware requirement,

Software requirement decomposition in knowledge middleware requirement and pure operational software requirement,

Three parallel lines of design: pure operational software module design, knowledge middleware design and knowware design,

Composition check of three sets of designed modules: pure operational software, knowledge middleware and knowware,

Three parallel lines of implementation,

Integration and verification of the three sets of system modules,

Validation of the whole system.

Certainly this is not a brand new life cycle definition of information system engineering. One can find quite a few impacts from the software engineering concepts and techniques in the above paraphrase. However, there are special difficulties raised by this co-process definition, which do not occur in traditional software engineering process techniques. We cite a few of them:

What are the principles and techniques of decomposing a global system requirement into three partial requirements for software, knowware and knowledge middleware components?

What are the principles and techniques of generating three conforming parallel specifications from a huge combination of alternatives?

What are the principles and techniques of establishing appropriate checkpoints for assuring the integrity and consistency of the three parallel development lines?

What are the principles and techniques of performing backtrack and recurring if compatibility between the component sets is violated?

What are the principles and techniques of pursuing system evolution if both user requirements and knowledge sources are subject to change?

Some of the problems listed above will become even more serious than we might expect at a first look if the profound differences between software components and knowware components are taken into consideration.

Currently we are still far away from having a satisfying solution for all these problems. We have only got some hints from the software engineering and knowledge engineering practices. We summarize some of our thoughts in form of engineering principles in the following:

The ladder principle: this is a modification of the idea of the waterfall model of software engineering. In the waterfall model, all components of the system are implemented separately after specification and design. There is only a loose relation between the components under development. Roughly speaking, they meet each other only in the final integration test. This process looks like a diamond. Our co-engineering process model has a similarity to the waterfall model in the sense that it undergoes a stepwise refinement from the requirement analysis downwards. But it requires multiple crosschecking of the interface relations (roughly, requirement interface, design interface and implementation interface) between three kinds of system components: knowware components, knowledge middleware components and software components. The ladder principle asks for a much more frequent cross check and a much tighter relation between components. The parallel development of components looks like a ladder, rather than a diamond.

The tower principle: Because of the key role of knowledge in application software development, we suggest a knowledge centered decomposition and composition strategy. The order of decomposition is different in requirement analysis and system specification phases. During the requirement analysis phase, we first determine the pure operational software requirement, which is most close to user problem solving. Then we determine the knowledge needed by these software functions together with its sources. At last, we determine the requirement for knowledge middleware, which is a bridge between functional software and the knowledge it needs.

During the system specification phase, the workflow goes in the other way. First we specify the knowware components and their knowledge sources. Then we specify the knowledge middleware operating on them. At last, we specify the pure operational software components, which have control over the knowledge middleware.

Thus, the tower principle for decomposing a system requirement or a specification is based on the knowledge richness and knowledge processing relevance of the system components. Furthermore, among all knowledge intensive or knowledge processing relevant parts of a system, we separate the components based on the rate of stability of the knowledge content. In summary, we give always priority to those system components that are knowledge rich and subject to most frequent changes. We call it the tower principle because it simulates the idea of oil fractionating tower, where oil components with lower boiling points are first separated.

Intuitively, the tower principle is a modification of the idea of the fountain model of software engineering process. According to the tower principle, there is also a fountain, from which the objects are sprayed out. But the objects have types (software objects or knowware objects), which determine the order of objects sprayed out.

We would like also to call the system generated in this framework a synergyware, and the above co-engineering process a synergyware engineering process.

5 Towards a Formal Semantics of Co-engineering

Apart from the technical considerations discussed in last section, there are other key issues relating to the theoretical side of this co-engineering:

How to guarantee the correctness of the triple decomposition of system requirement?

How to check the correctness of the global system specification composed of the three partial specifications?

How to assure the correct composition of three sets of designed modules,

How to verify the correctness of the composed design and the integrated system?

Many of the above-mentioned issues appear also in traditional software engineering processes. Here it is not the right place for discussing all the issues in this list. What we care here is only one of them, namely how to specify a knowware formally. In particular, we want to study the formal specification of a knowledge crystal, which depends on some external knowledge source that undergoes a steady change. As example we mention the knowledge crystal of nano-technology. Assume all information about the new development of this technology is gathered from the web. As an open knowledge source, the World Wide Web is changing steadily and only a small part of it is available to a visitor by using some browser. The traditional tools of formal semantics can hardly be used to describe such a knowledge source because the programmer does not know the state space as a whole. The state space may change unexpectedly and unobserved due to other observers' interference, like a distributed database without concurrency control. In recent years, a new technique called co-algebra has been emerging to deal with these kinds of things. Different from the signature in the algebraic semantics, which generates a Σ algebra from its basic elements step by step, a co-algebra does not generate any structure from its basis, it just "observes" a currently existing state space through some "windows" and at the same time may cause some change to the state space. This mechanism can be described with the following notation:

$$X \to O(X) \times F(X)$$

where X is the state space, $X \to O(X) \times F(X)$ means an observation, $O(X)$ is the output of the observation and $F(X)$ is the modified state space after observation. It can be considered as a functor and described with categorical language.

This property is very suitable for describing knowledge sources whose internal structure is largely unknown. The process of acquiring knowledge from an open and changing knowledge source can be described with a co-algebra:

$$KnowledgeSource \times Query \rightarrow SetofAnswers \times KnowledgeSource$$

where the second occurrence of knowledge source may have been changed during the query session. Take again the World Wide Web as example, which can be considered as a state space. The browse operation can be described with co-algebra:

Browse: $Web \times Keys \rightarrow WPs \times Web$

Assume the simplest case where Keys is the query, WPs is the set of ordered sequences of observed web pages, and

No web page will be generated or deleted,
No web page changes its content
No web page changes its links to other web pages,

But we still have to take into account that the search is not always successful. Thus the browse operation can be described with the following co-algebra:

$$Browse: Web \times Keys \rightarrow \{\perp\} \cup WPs \times Web \tag{1}$$

Where $\perp$ means undefined (nothing related to the search Keys is observed with the browser). We can write it in currying form as follows:

Browse: $Web \rightarrow (\{\perp\} \cup WPs \times Web)^{Keys}$

In the practice, given any set of keywords, each browser produces a permutation of all web pages on the web. Therefore we can also rewrite the above co-algebra in the following form:

Browse: $Web \rightarrow \{\perp\} \cup WPs \times Web^{perm}$

It is trivial to prove the following proposition:

Proposition. Given a finite set WWW of web pages $\{w\}$ and a finite set $Keys$ of keywords $\{k\}$. Let $WWW' \subseteq WWW$, $Web = 2^{WWW'}$, $WPs = (WWW')^+$. Further let browse (WWW') denote the browser co-algebra with state space WWW' and assume we use the same browser for all co-algebra of such kind (in the representation of (1)). Then the final co-algebra exists. It is browse (WWW).

As we just said, this result is trivial. But it will soon become not trivial if we take the problem a bit more complicated. For example we can add some more operations on the state space:

upload: $Web \times WPs \rightarrow Web$

download: $Web \times WPs \rightarrow \{\perp\} \cup Web$

Considering the fact that many people are visiting the web at the same time. Quite a few of them may upload some new web pages at any instant. This makes the result of search non-deterministic, not yet mentioning the change of the web page content and web links. The browse co-algebra becomes:

Browse: $Web \times Keys \rightarrow \wp(\{\bot\} \cup WPs \times Web)$

Where $\wp$ means power set. As it is known in the theory of co-algebra, this time the category Coalg (Browse) does not have a final co-algebra. Its discussion becomes difficult.

As for a deep search (re-search), we'd better to consider each state as a dotted web, where each dotted web consists of a set of web pages. Each web page w is represented as a set $\{b\} \cup \{C(w)\} \cup \{v \mid$ there is a link from w to another web page v $\}$, where b is either 0 or 1, C(w) is the content of w, which we don't care for the moment. Web page w is called dotted if b = 1, otherwise called free. In this case, a browse operation will still change the current state in the way that some free (previously unobserved) web pages will become dotted (now observed by the browser) connected by reference links, where each web page is either dotted or not. Then we have:

Re-browse: $Web \times WPs \times Keys \rightarrow \wp(\{\bot\} \cup WPs \times Web)$

6 Conclusion

The co-algebraic semantics of an open knowledge source should be an interesting research topic, which must be included in the study of formal semantics of software/knowware co-engineering.

Acknowledgement. Some concepts discussed in this paper share the same name with concepts appearing somewhere else. But the meaning is different. I have listed all these literature (as far as I know it) in the reference list of this paper.

Reference

[1] Xiwen Ma, Private Communication, 1992.
[2] E.A. Feigenbaum & P. McCorduck, The fifth generation, artificial intelligence and Japan's challenge to the world, Addison-Wesley, 1983
[3] Ruqian Lu, From hardware to software to knowware: IT's third liberation? IEEE Intelligent Systems, March/April 2005, pp. 82-85
[4] Ruqian Lu & Zhi Jin, Beyond Knowledge Engineering, to appear in Journal of Computer Science and Technology. 2006.
[5] D.B. Lenat & P.V. Guha, Building Large Knowledge Based Systems: Representation and Inference in the CYC Project, Addison Wesley, 1990.
[6] Ruqian Lu, Cungen Cao, Yonghong Chen, Zhangang Han, On Automatic Generation of Intelligent Tutoring Systems, Proc. of 7th International Conference of AI in Education, 1995.

[7] I. Nonaka & H. Takeuk, The Knowledge Creating Company : How Japanese Companies Create Dynamics of Innovation, Oxford University Press, 1995

[8] N. Glance et. al., Knowledge Pump: Supporting the Flow and Use of Knowledge, in Information Technology for Knowledge Management (eds. U. Borghoff et. al.), ch3, Springer, 1998.

[9] J.F. Sowa, Representing Knowledge Soup in Language and Logic, Conference on Knowledge and Logic, Darmstadt, 2002.

[10] A. Spector, Architecting Knowledge Middleware, WWW2002, Hawaii.

Modeling and Evaluation of Technology Creation Process in Academia

Yoshiteru Nakamori

School of Knowledge Science
Japan Advanced Institute of Science and Technology
Ishikawa 923-1292, Japan

The school of knowledge science at JAIST (Japan Advanced Institute of Science and Technology) is the first school established in the world to make knowledge a target of science. At this graduate school, knowledge management research is already producing results in areas such as knowledge conversion theory, knowledge systematizing methods, and methods for the development of creativity. It is expected recently that knowledge science should help researchers produce creative theoretical results in important natural sciences. For this purpose, we have to establish a *Ba* (a Japanese term meaning: place, center, environment, space, etc.), or an environment or circumstance, that supports the development and practice of scientific knowledge creation. This paper considers the advantages and disadvantages deriving from the vagueness, depth, diversity and freedom of the definition of *Ba* given by Ikujiro Nonaka, and stresses the need to redesign *knowledge creation Ba* using systems concepts. Then, the paper proposes a systems methodology to design and evaluate *Ba* for technology creation in academia, with a report on a preliminary survey.

This research is supported by the 21st COE (Center of Excellence) Program *Technology Creation Based on Knowledge Science: Theory and Practice* of JAIST, a funds by Ministry of Education, Culture, Sports, Science and Technology, Japan.

Knowledge Management Systems (KMS) Continuance in Organizations: A Social Relational Perspective

Joy Wei He and Kwok-Kee Wei[*]

Department of Information Systems
City University of Hong Kong,
83 Tat Chee Avenue, Kowloon, Hong Kong
Tel.: +852-2788-9590; Fax: +852-2788-8192
isweikk@cityu.edu.hk

Abstract. This study explores knowledge management systems (KMS) continuance behavior in organizations. The study draws from the tenets of prior research on user acceptance and continuance of IS and the Social Capital Theory and suggest that both the technical and the situational social aspects of a KMS needs to be considered to understand KMS continuance. A conceptual model and a set of theoretical propositions are proposed as a foundation for further investigation.

Keywords: Knowledge management (KM), Knowledge management systems (KMS), Continuance, Social relationships, Organization.

1 Introduction

The phenomenon under investigation in this paper is KMS continuance in a social relational perspective. Continuance refers to post-adoption behavior[1]. We define KMS continuance as the long-term continued usage of KMS by employees in an organization.

Knowledge management (KM) is considered a strategic and value-added endeavor towards improving an organization's effectiveness in the changing the social and business environment [2]. Knowledge Management Systems (KMS) is a class of IT-based systems applied to managing organizational knowledge [3]. IS researchers have conducted a number of studies attempting to understand how KMS enables and facilitates knowledge creation, storage, sharing and application for improving organizational performance.

While these prior studies have investigated issues relating to the design, development and management of KMS, in the existing literature, very few studies provide a theoretical understanding of KMS continuance in regard to the social context of KM [4].

2 Literature Review

Given the fact that KMS are a subset of IS, we start our study with a review of IS continuance research. The literature review has three main objectives: (1) to introduce

---

[*] Corresponding author.

J. Lang, F. Lin, and J. Wang (Eds.): KSEM 2006, LNAI 4092, pp. 34–41, 2006.
© Springer-Verlag Berlin Heidelberg 2006

existing theories of IS continuance which could explain continuance behaviors in a general sense; (2) to build the KMS continuance study on prior research by identifying the key variables that determine IS continuance.

2.1 User Acceptance Models

In the last two decades, IS researchers have substantially employed intention-based models to examine the understanding of IS adoption and usage by individual users [5, 6]. In this research stream, the technology acceptance model (TAM) [5] emerges as a powerful and parsimonious model that explains IS adoption.

TAM is grounded in the theory of reasoned action [7], IS usage intention is determined by attitude towards usage as well as by the direct and indirect effects of beliefs about two factors: the perceived usefulness and the perceived ease of use of an IS. Empirical tests of TAM have showed that it can explain much of the variance in individual intention to use technology [8].

Having reviewed and empirically compared various user acceptance models, Venkatesh et al. [9] formulate a unified model, called the unified theory of acceptance and use of technology (UTAUT). UTAUT posits two main determinants of usage behavior (usage intention and facilitating conditions), and three direct determinants of intention (performance expectancy, effort expectancy, and social influence). Experience, voluntariness, gender, and age are identified as significant moderating influences. UTAUT is an integrated theory on individual acceptance of information technology and it outperforms previous user acceptance models by explaining as much as 70 percent of the variance in usage intention.

2.2 IS Continuance Models

IS continuance refers to the behaviour patterns reflecting continued use of a particular IS [1, 10]. Bhattacherjee [1] is one of the earliest researchers who explicitly elaborates the substantive differences between IS acceptance and continuance behaviors and advocates the need to understand IS continuance behavior recently [1, 10, 11].

Bhattacherjee [1] adapts Expectation-Confirmation Theory (ECT) to theorize and validate that intention to IS continuance is strongly predicted by user's satisfaction, with perceived usefulness as a second predictor. In this model, user satisfaction is in turn determined primarily by users' confirmation of expectation from prior use and secondarily by perceived usefulness. Further, confirmation of expectation also has significant influence on perceived usefulness in the post-adoption stage. The better the users' expectation are met in prior usage, the more useful the system appears to users and the more satisfied the users are.

In one of his recent work on the temporal change in continuance behavior, Bhattacherjee and his colleague [11] incorporate attitude (personal affect toward IT usage) as a second predictor of IS continuance intention. According to their two-stage model of cognition change [11], usefulness and attitude determine continuance or discontinuance. Also in this model, usefulness is depicted to determine users' attitude toward IS continuance.

It is noted that UTAUT implicitly deals with IS continuance by positing experience as a significant moderator in most of the relationships in the model. Specifically, the results of UTAUT indicate that the effect of users' effort expectancy decreases in continuance stage, while the effects of social influence on intention and the effect of facilitating conditions on continuance behavior become significant.

Another line of research argues that IS usage would transcend conscious behavior and become part of normal routine activity [10]. Prior research empirically validates that the moderating effect of habit on the relationship between IS continuance intention and continuance behavior increases over time, while the impact of IS continuance intention on continuance behavior weakens over time [10].

To summarize, IS researchers have been developing and applying richer research models to examine and explain IS continuance behavior. Based on existing IS research, perceived usefulness and users' attitude are considered to be the two key determinants of continuance intention which drives IS continuance [1, 11]. Nevertheless, the strength of intention to predict continuance may be weakened by a high level of IS habit [10]. Besides, facilitating conditions may have a direct influence on continuance behavior [9].

2.3 KMS Continuance in Organizations

Specific to the organizational context, there also exists abundant research on the organizational determinants of successful KM initiatives—for example, culture [12], leadership [13] and reward [14, 15].While the effect of reward is subject to debate [16], there is evidence that KM-specific training and personnel development programs provide incentives and rewards for knowledge sharing particularly [17]. Therefore, an organization is considered to be an active and critical player in triggering a successful KM practice, rather than simply being a background in which information systems are implemented. Organizations can thus create proper conditions to facilitate KMS use and continuance.

2.4 Social Relationships in KMS Continuance: A Social Relational Perspective

Recently, researchers have been increasingly emphasizing that knowledge transfer is a kind of social interaction among people [18]. Thomas et. al. [19] comment that all the critical issues for knowledge sharing and collaboration, such as relationships, awareness, incentives, and motivation, are all social phenomenon. As a result, researchers have proposed to examine the influence of social capital on knowledge sharing [20, 21].

Social relationship is a concept that emerged from social capital theory. It has been proved that social relationships play a significant role in determining individuals' attitude toward knowledge sharing [16]. Prior research also indicates that lack of relationship between the contributing side and the seeking side is identified as a major barrier to knowledge transfer [22]. In a study on expertise-sharing networks [23], system-mediated relationships, referring to the level of trust, respect, and tie strengths, are proved to successfully increase KMS continuance.

We propose social relationships, characterized by the level of trust, shared norms, and tie strength [20] as an important determinant of users' attitude that contributes to

KMS continuance. In this study, we examine social relationship in the context of the employee's perceptions of KMS usage by other referents in the organization with whom the employee has social interactions such as supervisors, subordinates and peers

2.4.1 Trust

People have natural tendency of hoarding knowledge [24] and it turns worse when they feel that their unique knowledge gives them authority or power in organizations [25]. Trust, defined as the extent to which users believe in the good intent, competence, and reliability of others, can reduce transactional cost and enable social relations [26]. McEvily, et. al. [27] further argue that the level of trust influences the extent of knowledge disclosure, screening, and sharing between two parties. Kankanhalli et al.[15], in their study on electronic knowledge repositories, have developed and validated the trust construct and verified trust as a significant contextual factor in knowledge contribution behavior.

2.4.2 Shared Norm

From a social viewpoint, employees are members of communities such as working groups, departments, and organizations. All of these groups have norms that reflect the commonalities among members and allow them to coordinate their actions accordingly. More specifically, shared norms within a community govern how its members behave, think, make judgments, and even how they perceive the world. Therefore, shared norms will generate propositional attitudes that tend to affect the members' behaviors in a certain way. Shared language and codes can influence the conditions for knowledge exchange [20].

2.4.3 Tie Strength

A fundamental proposition of social capital theory is that network ties provide access to resources, which means that ties can influence both access to people for knowledge exchange and anticipation of value through such exchange [20]. Tie strength characterizes the closeness and interaction frequency of a relationship between two parties [28], in this case knowledge contributors and knowledge seekers. Levin and Cross [28] find that strong, trusting ties usually help improve knowledge transfer between scientists and engineers within an organization. Furthermore, strong ties reportedly mean that people are more accessible and willing to be helpful in sharing behaviors [29].

3   The Conceptual Framework for KMS Continuance

In this section, we present a conceptual framework of KMS continuance, as depicted in Figure 1. Usefulness and attitude are two preconditions for the KMS continuance intention of employees in organizations while intention further predicts KMS continuance. The choice of usefulness and attitude as determinants of KMS continuance is grounded on IS continuance models. Since KMS is one kind of IS, it should follow the basic assumption that the usefulness of that technology – in terms of its value in performing a task, is a major driving force for usage.

We further adopt the social relational perspective to propose that social relationships act as a critical stimulus to users' attitude towards the KMS. As discussed earlier, three aspects of social relationships are particularly conducive to knowledge sharing: trust [20, 27], norms [15, 20], and tie strength [20, 28, 30]. Hence, we propose that positive social relationships of an employee with other users of KMS in the organization would stimulate positive attitude of employees in organizations and thus a critical determinant of KMS continuance. The stronger the social relationships of an employee with other users of KMS in an organization, we expect the stronger the attitude towards KMS continuance. Thus our first proposition is:

P1. *Employees who have more positive social relationships have more positive attitudes regarding KMS continuance.*

Besides continuance intention, organizational facilitating conditions are also argued to be a predictor of KMS continuance. The term facilitating factor has been defined in the model of PC utilization [31] in which it refers to some objective conditions in the environment that individuals agree make the action of usage easy to accomplish. Prior research indicates that facilitating conditions act as a direct antecedent of use behavior in IS continuance stage [9]. In our context, *organizational facilitating conditions* are operationalized as the degree to which an individual

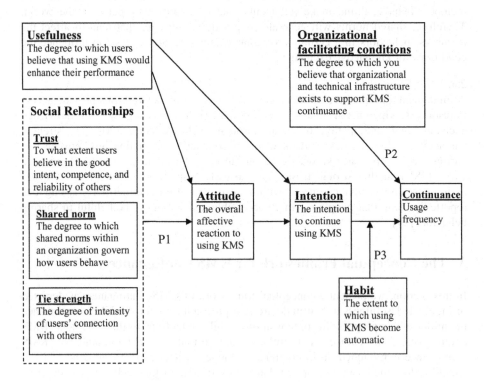

Fig. 1. Conceptual framework: Determinants of KMS continuance in organizations

believes that organizational and technical infrastructure exists to support continuance of the KMS, as in [9]. Specifically, KMS continuance might be dependent on effective organizational facilitation, such as training [32], guidance or assisting resources [31], and the availability of the technology platform [6]. Therefore, we conclude that strong organizational KM-facilitating conditions may predict actual KMS continuance. The second proposition is:

P2. *Organizational facilitating conditions would have a significant impact on employees' KMS continuance.*

In addition, recent research has noted that IS habit can moderate the relationship between continuance intention and continuance behavior [10]. Specifically, the more usage is performed out of habit, the less intentional behavior is involved. Hence, we hypothesize as follows:

P3. *Employees' intentional behavior regarding KMS continuance is dependent on their habit.*

4   Conclusions

In this research we draw from the social capital theory and develop a framework that explains how social relationships of employees have the potential to influence their KMS continuance behavior. In developing the framework, we distinguish social relationships from subjective norms because relationships focus on local patterns by which members voluntarily behave well in dealing with their colleagues, share unique knowledge connected to work life in the organization, and maintain a long-term relationship for collective expectations. We also argue that organizational KM facilitating conditions are positively associated with KMS continuance behavior. Therefore, this study contributes to the body of KMS research by providing as theoretical understanding of how an organization can establish strong, positive social relationships (with the aspects of trust, cooperative norms, and strong ties among employees) to provide a favorable context for KMS continuance. A follow-up survey with appropriate operationalisation of the social relationships constructs and its sub-constructs would help in validating the proposed framework of KMS continuance.

References

1. Bhattacherjee, A., *Understanding information systems continuance: An expectation-confirmation model.* MIS Quarterly, 2001. **25**(3): p. 351-370.
2. Liebowitz, J., *Aggressively pursuing knowledge management over 2 years: A case study at a US government organization.* Knowledge Management Research & Practice, 2003. **1**(2): p. 69-76.
3. Alavi, M. and D.E. Leidner, *Review: Knowledge management and knowledge management systems: Conceptual foundations and research issues.* MIS Quarterly, 2001. **25**(1): p. 107-136.

4. Hayes, N. and G. Walsham, *Knowledge sharing and ICTs: A relational perspective.* Social Capital and Information Technology, ed. M. Huysman and V. Wulf. 2004, London: MIT Press.
5. Davis, F.D., *Perceived usefulness, perceived ease of use, and user acceptance of information technology.* MIS Quarterly, 1989. **13**(3): p. 319-339.
6. Taylor, S. and P.A. Todd, *Understanding information technology usage: A test of competing models.* Information Systems Research, 1995. **6**(2): p. 144-176.
7. Fishbein, M. and I. Ajzen, *Belief, Attitude, Intention and Behavior: An Introduction to Theory and Research.* 1975, MA: Addison-Wesley.
8. Davis, F.D., R.P. Bagozzi, and P.R. Warshaw, *User acceptance of computer technology: A comparison of two theoretical models.* Management Science, 1989. **35**: p.982-1002.
9. Venkatesh, V., et al., *User acceptance of information technology: Toward a unified view.* MIS Quarterly, 2003. **27**(3): p. 425-478.
10. Cheung, C.M.K. and M. Limayem. *The Role of Habit in Information Systems Continuance: Examining the Evolving Relationship between Intention and Usage.* in *Proceedings of the Twenty-Sixth International Conference on Information Systems.* 2005. Las Vegas, USA.
11. Bhattacherjee, A. and G. Premkumar, *Understanding changes in belief and attitude toward information technology usage: A theoretical model and longitudinal test.* MIS Quarterly, 2004. **28**(2): p. 229-254.
12. DeLong, D. and L. Fehey, *Diagnosing cultural barriers to knowledge management.* Academy of Management Executive, 2000. **14**(4): p. 113-127.
13. Desouza, K.C., *Strategic contributions of game rooms to knowledge management: Some preliminary insights.* Information & Management, 2003. **41**(1): p. 63-74.
14. Hall, H., *Input-friendliness: Motivating knowledge sharing across intranets.* Journal of Information Science, 2001. **27**(3): p. 139-146.
15. Kankanhalli, A., B.C.Y. Tan, and K.K. Wei, *Contributing Knowledge to Electronic Knowledge Repositories: An Empirical Investigation.* MIS Quarterly, 2005. **29**(1): p. 113-143.
16. Bock, G.W., et al., *Behavioral intention formation in knowledge sharing: Examining the roles of extrinsic motivators, social-psychological forces, and organizational climate.* MIS Quarterly, 2005. **29**(1): p. 87-111.
17. Pan, S.L., M.H. Hsieh, and H. Chen, *Knowledge Sharing Through Intranet-Based Learning: A Case Study of an Online Learning Center.* Journal of Organizational Computing and Electronic Commerce, 2001. **11**(3): p. 179-195.
18. Bock, G.W. and Y.G. Kim, *Breaking the myths of rewards: An exploratory study of attitudes about knowledge sharing.* Information Resources Management Journal, 2002. **15**(2): p. 14-21.
19. Thomas, J.C., W.A. Kellogg, and T. Erickson, *The knowledge management puzzle: Human and social factors in knowledge management,* in *IBM Systems Journal.* 2001.
20. Nahapiet, J. and S. Ghoshal, *Social capital, intellectual capital, and the organizational advantage.* Academy of Management Review, 1998. **23**(2): p. 242-266.
21. Wasko, M.M. and S. Faraj, *"It is what one does": Why people participate and help others in electronic communities of practice.* Journal of Strategic Information Systems, 2000. **9**(2-3): p. 155-173.
22. Nevo, D., et al. *Exploring Meta-Knowledge for Knowledge Management Systems: A Delphi Study.* in *Proceedings of the Twenty-Fourth International Conference on Information Systems.* 2003. Seattle, USA.

23. Tiwana, A. and A.A. Bush, *Continuance in expertise-sharing networks: A social perspective.* IEEE Transactions on Engineering Management, 2005. **52**(1): p. 85-101.
24. Davenport, T.H. and L. Prusak, *Working Knowledge: How Organizations Manage What They Know.* 1998, Boston: Harvard Business School Press.
25. Orlikowski, W.J., *Learning from notes: Organizational issues in groupware implementation.* Information Society, 1993. **9**(3): p. 237-251.
26. Nooteboom, B., *The management of corporate social capital.* Social Capital of Organizations, Research in the Sociology of Organizations, ed. S.M.a.L. Gabbay, R.Th.A.J. Vol. 18. 2001, Oxford: Elsevier Science Ltd.
27. McEvily, B., V. Peronne, and A. Zaheer, *Trust as an organizing principle.* Organization Science, 2003. **14**: p. 91-103.
28. Levin, D.Z. and R. Cross, *The strength of weak ties you can trust: The mediating role of trust in effective knowledge transfer.* Management Science, 2004. **50**(11): p. 1477-1490.
29. Krackhardt, D., *The strength of strong ties.* Networks and Organizations: Structure, Form and Action, ed. N. Nohria and R.G. Eccles. 1992, Boston: Harvard Business School Press. **216-239**.
30. Reagans, R. and B. McEvily, *Network structure and knowledge transfer: The effects of cohesion and range.* Administrative Science Quarterly, 2003. **48**(2): p. 240-267.
31. Thompson, R.L., C.A. Higgins, and J.M. Howell, *Personal computing: Toward a conceptual model of utilization.* MIS Quarterly, 1991. **15**(1): p. 124-143.
32. Minbaeva, D., et al., *MNC knowledge transfer, subsidiary absorptive capacity, and HRM.* Journal of International Business Studies, 2003. **34**(6): p. 586-599.

Modelling the Interaction Between Objects: Roles as Affordances

Matteo Baldoni[1], Guido Boella[1], and Leendert van der Torre[2]

[1] Dipartimento di Informatica. Università di Torino - Italy
{baldoni, guido}@di.unito.it
[2] University of Luxembourg
leendert@vandertorre.com

Abstract. In this paper we present a new vision of objects in knowledge representation where the objects' attributes and operations depend on who is interacting with them. This vision is based on a new definition of the notion of role, which is inspired by the concept of affordance as developed in cognitive science. The current vision of objects considers attributes and operations as being objective and independent from the interaction. In contrast, in our model interaction with an object always passes through a role played by another object manipulating it. The advantage is that roles allow to define operations whose behavior changes depending on the role and the requirements it imposes, and to define session aware interaction, where the role maintains the state of the interaction with an object. Finally, we provide a description of the model in UML and we discuss how roles as affordances have been introduced in Java.

1 Introduction

Object orientation is a leading paradigm in knowledge representation, modelling and programming languages and, more recently, also in databases. The basic idea is that the attributes and operations of an object should be associated with it. The interaction with the object is made via the public attributes of the class it is an instance of and via its public operations, for example, as specified by an interface. The implementation of an operation is specific of the class and can access the private state of it. This allows to fulfill the data abstraction principle: the public attributes and operations are the only possibility to manipulate an object and their implementation is not visible from the other objects manipulating it; thus, the implementation can be changed without changing the interaction capabilities of the object.

This view can be likened with the way we interact with objects in the world: the same operation of switching a device on is implemented in different manners inside different kinds of devices, depending on their functioning.

The philosophy behind object orientation, however, views reality in a naive way. It rests on the assumption that the attributes and operations of objects are objective, in the sense that they are the same whatever is the object interacting with it.

This view has two consequences which limit the usefulness of object orientation in modelling knowledge:

J. Lang, F. Lin, and J. Wang (Eds.): KSEM 2006, LNAI 4092, pp. 42–54, 2006.

- Every object can access all the public attributes and invoke all the public operations of every other object. Hence, it is not possible to distinguish which attributes and operations are visible for which classes of interacting objects.
- The object invoking an operation (caller) of another object (callee) is not taken into account for the execution of the method associated with the operation. Hence, when an operation is invoked it has the same meaning whatever the caller's class is.
- The values of the private and public attributes of an object are the same for all other objects interacting with it. Hence, the object has always only one state.
- The interaction with an object is session-less since the invocation of an operation does not depend on the caller. Hence, the value of private and public attributes and, consequently, the meaning of operations cannot depend on the preceding interactions with the object.

The first three limitations hinder modularity, since it would be useful to keep distinct the core behavior of an object from the different interaction possibilities that it offers to different kinds of objects. Some programming languages offer ways to give multiple implementations of interfaces, but the dependance from the caller cannot be taken into account, unless the caller is explicitly passed as a parameter of each method.

The last limitation complicates the modelling of distributed scenarios where communication follows protocols.

Programming languages like Fickle [1] address the second and third problem by means of dynamic reclassification: an object can change class dynamically, and its operations change their meaning accordingly. However, Fickle does not represent the dependence of attributes and operations from the interaction.

Sessions are considered with more attention in the agent oriented paradigm, which is based on protocols ([2,3]). A protocol is the specification of the possible sequences of messages exchanged between two agents. Since not all sequences of messages are legal, the state of the interaction between two agents must be maintained in a session. Moreover, not all agents can interact with other ones using whatever protocol. Rather the interaction is allowed only by agents playing certain roles.

However, the notion of role in multi-agents systems is rarely related with the notion of session of interaction ([4]). Moreover, it is often related with the notion of organization rather than with the notion of interaction ([5]).

In this paper, we address the four above problems in object oriented knowledge representation by introducing a new notion of role. This is inspired by research in cognitive science, where the naive vision of objects is overcome by the so called ecological view of interaction in the environment. In this view, the properties (attributes and operations) of an object are not independent from whom is interacting with it. An object "affords" different ways of interaction to different kinds of objects.

The structure of this paper is as follows. In Section 2 we discuss the cognitive foundations of our view of objects. In Section 3 we define roles in terms of affordances and in Section 4 we explain how to describe roles in UML. In Section 6 we summarize how our approach to roles leads to the design of a new object oriented programming language, powerJava. Related work and conclusion end the paper.

2   Roles as Affordances

The naive view of objects sees them as having objective attributes and operations which are independent from the observer or from other objects interacting with them. Instead, recent developments in cognitive science show that attributes and operations emerge only at the moment of the interaction and change according to what kind of object is interacting with another one:

1. Objects are conceptualized on the basis of what they "afford" to the actions of the entities interacting with them. Thus, different entities conceptualize and interact with the same object in different ways.
2. The classification of entities in taxonomies of categories is not composed by uniform levels. Rather, some levels of categories have a privileged status. In the taxonomy of natural kinds this level is the level of the genus (i.e., dog, cat, pine, oak): the likely explanation is that this is the level where the characteristic ways of interacting with the entities classified by these categories are located. At the upper level (e.g., mammal, tree) no common way of interaction is possible with all the entities of the category; while at the lower level (e.g., terrier, white oak) there is less difference in the way entities of different categories are manipulated.

Interaction, thus, is the common denominator. Since we do not consider in this paper the problem of class hierarchies, we will focus on the first aspect: "affordances".

The notion of "affordance" has been made popular by Norman [6] (p. 9):

> "The term affordance refers to the perceived and actual properties of the thing, primarily those fundamental properties that determine just how the thing could possibly be used. A chair affords ('is for') support, and, therefore, affords sitting."

This is the view in which the notion of affordance has been adopted in another branch of computer science: human-computer interaction (e.g., [7]). Seeing affordances in this way, however, does not solve the problem of the subjectivity of attributes and operations, and, indeed, it is a partial reading of the original theory of affordances. We resort here to the original vision, instead.

The notion of affordance has been developed by a cognitive scientist, James Gibson, in a completely different context, the one of visual perception [8] (p. 127):

> "The affordances of the environment are what it offers the animal, what it provides or furnishes, either for good or ill. The verb to afford is found in the dictionary, but the noun affordance is not. I have made it up. I mean by it something that refers to both the environment and the animal in a way that no existing term does. It implies the complementarity of the animal and the environment...
>
> If a terrestrial surface is nearly horizontal (instead of slanted), nearly flat (instead of convex or concave), and sufficiently extended (relative to the size of the animal) and if its substance is rigid (relative to the weight of the animal), then the surface affords support...

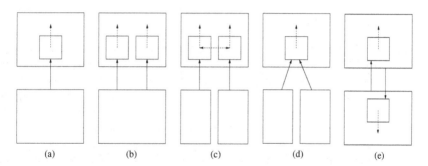

Fig. 1. The possible uses of roles as affordances

Note that the four properties listed - horizontal, flat, extended, and rigid - would be physical properties of a surface if they were measured with the scales and standard units used in physics. As an affordance of support for a species of animal, however, they have to be measured relative to the animal. They are unique for that animal. They are not just abstract physical properties. If so, to perceive them is to perceive what they afford. This is a radical hypothesis, for it implies that the 'values' and 'meanings' of things in the environment can be directly perceived.

The activity of an observer that is afforded depends on the layout, that is, on the solid geometry of the arrangement. The same layout will have different affordances for different animals, of course, insofar as each animal has a different repertory of acts. Different animals will perceive different sets of affordances therefore. ... Animals, and children until they learn geometry, pay attention to the affordances of layout rather than the mathematics of layout.

Gibson refers to an ecological perspective, where animals and the environment are complementary. But the same vision can be transferred to objects. By "environment" we intend a set of objects and by animal of a given specie we intend another object of a given class which manipulates them. Besides physical objective properties objects have affordances when they are considered relative to an object managing them.

How can we use this vision to introduce new modelling concepts in object oriented knowledge representation? The affordances of an object are not isolated, but they are associated with a given specie. So we need to consider sets of affordances. We will call a *role type* the different sets of interaction possibilities, the affordances of an object, which depend on the class of the interactant manipulating the object: the *player* of the role. To manipulate an object it is necessary to specify the role in which the interaction is made.

But an ecological perspective cannot be satisfied by considering only occasional interactions between objects. Rather it should also be possible to consider the continuity of the interaction for each object, i.e., the state of the interaction. In terms of a distributed scenario, a session. Thus a given role type can be instantiated, depending on a certain player of a role (which must have the required properties), and the *role instance* represents the state of the interaction with that role player.

3 Roles and Sessions

The idea behind affordances is that the interaction with an object does not happens directly with it by accessing its public attributes and invoking its public operations. Rather, the interaction with an object happens via a role: to invoke an operation, it is necessary first to be the player of a role offered by the object the operation belongs to. The roles which can be played depend on the properties of the player of the role (the *requirements*), since the roles represent the set of affordances offered by the object.

Thus an object can be seen as a cluster of classes gathered around a center class. The center class represents the core state and behavior of the object. The other classes, the role types, are the containers of the operations specific of the interaction with a given class, and of the attributes characterizing the state of the interaction. Not only the kind of attributes depend on the class of the interacting object, but also the values of these attributes may vary according to a specific interactant. A role instance, thus, models the session of the interaction between objects and can be used for defining protocols.

If a role represents the possibilities offered by an object to interact with it, the methods of a role must be able to affect the core state of the objects they are roles of and to access their operations; otherwise, no effect could be made by the player of the role on the object the role belongs to. So a role, even if it seems a usual object, is, instead different: it depends on the object the role belongs to and they access its state.

Many objects can play the same role as well as the same object can play different roles. In Figure 1 we depict the different possibilities. *Boxes* represent objects and role instances (included in external boxes). *Arrows* represent the relations between players and their roles, *dashed arrows* the access relation between objects.

- Drawing (a) illustrates the situation where an object interacts with another one by means of the role offered by it.
- Drawing (b) illustrates an object interacting in two different roles with another one. This situation is used when an object implements two different interfaces for interacting with it, which have methods with the same signature but with different meanings. In our model the methods of the interfaces are implemented in the roles offered by the object to interact with it. Moreover, the two role instances represent the two different states of the two interactions between the two objects.
- Drawing (c) illustrates the case of two objects which interact with each other by means of the roles of another object (which can be considered as the context of interaction). This achieves the separation of concerns between the core behavior of an object and the interaction possibilities in a given context. The meaning of this scenario for coordination has been discussed in [9].
- In drawing (d) a degenerated but still useful situation is depicted: a role does not represent the individual state of the interaction with an object, but the collective state of the interaction of two objects playing the same role instance. This scenario is useful when it is not necessary to have a session for each interaction.
- In drawing (e) two objects interact with each other, each one playing a role offered by the other. This is often the case of interaction protocols: e.g., an object can play the role of *initiator* in the Contract Net Protocol if and only if the other object plays the role of *participant* [10]. The symmetry of roles is closer to the traditional vision of roles as ends of a relation (like also in UML, see Section 7).

4   Representing Affordances in UML

Despite the conceptual difference between the traditional view of object orientation and the addition of roles as affordances, it is still possible to represent them in a object oriented modelling language like UML. So in this paper, rather than introducing new constructs in UML, we less ambitiously present how to model roles as affordances in the existing UML, to make our proposal more comprehensible.

The first problem is how to represent the roles as set of affordances of an object. Role types describe attributes and operations, so they can be modelled as classes in UML. Role instances maintain the specific values of the attributes in an interaction with the role player, so they are modelled as objects.

However, role instances are always associated with two other objects: the object of which they are roles and the object playing the role. We represent these relations by means of two composition arrows between the object and the role instance (denoted as `Class.this` in the role instance) and between the player and the role instance (denoted as `that` in the role instance). A role instance can be a role of one object only, but it can have more than one player. Instead, different role instances can have associated the same object they are role of.

Second, as discussed in Section 3, the role can access the attributes and operations of the object the role belongs to. This can be represented by saying that the namespace of the role belongs to the namespace of the class it is a role of. In UML the nested notation used in Figure 1 is not the correct way to show a class belonging to the namespace of another class. Instead, the anchor notation (a cross in a circle on the end of a line) is

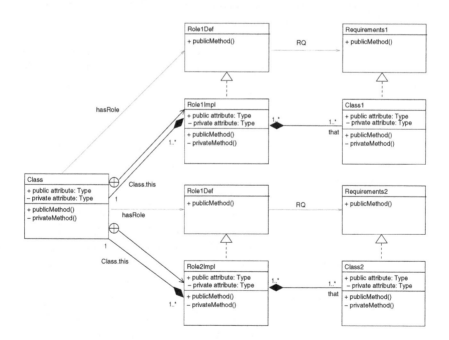

Fig. 2. Roles as affordances in UML

used between two class boxes to show that the class with the anchor icon declares the class on the other end of the line. This is the way inner classes are denoted in UML. As we discuss in Section 6 the construct of inner classes can be used to introduce roles in object oriented programming languages.

Moreover, we have to represent the dependence of a role from the properties of the player object. As discussed in Section 3, the role represents the attributes and operations which depend on a specific kind of object playing the role: a role can be played (i.e., an object can be manipulated in a certain way) only by a specific kind of players. Thus, we need to specify the requirements for playing each role class. If we specify requirements by means of a class, we restrict the set of possible players too much. We only need a partial specification to describe what is needed to play a role. Thus requirements are specified by an interface: only the objects which are instance of a class implementing the requirements can play the role.

However, there is still one unresolved issue. The class with roles cannot be given a partial specification of its interaction possibilities by means of a single interface, since the roles associated with it may share some operations but not other ones. Thus, we associate with the class a set of role definitions, one for each role class associated with it. The role definitions specify the operations which the player of the role is endowed to invoke. A role definition differs from an interface since it has associated the requirements of the role.

In Figure 2 we represent our model. We have a class class with two role definitions (hasRole relates it to Role1Def and Role2Def) representing the set affordances offered by the object to players satisfying the requirements (the interface related by the RQ association). The role definitions are implemented by classes which are connected with the class Class by a composition relation and by a namespace association (anchor link).

In Figure 2 we consider the possibility to directly interact with the class Class by directly accessing its "objective" attributes and operations. However, nothing prevents that the object does not have any public attribute or operation, so that the interaction can be only made via one of its roles.

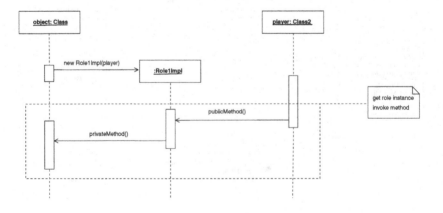

Fig. 3. The interaction with an object via a role

Finally, note that it is possible to have a single instance of a role implementation which is associated with multiple players: this can be used to represent the situation where no session is needed and it is sufficient to model multiple implementations of the same operation in a single class.

This means that we have three possibilities of interaction in our model:

- Traditional direct interaction with an object via its objective properties.
- Session-less interaction with an object via a role which presents to the object a state and operations different from the core object, but common with all the other objects playing that role (and which satisfy the role's requirements).
- Session aware interaction via a role instance representing the state of the interaction with a particular player of the role.

Thus, it is possible to select the option most suited for the situation to model, without necessarily having a role type or a role instance for each object interacting.

In summary, an object with affordances is represented by a core object associated with other objects of the classes representing the role implementations. Each role instance represents the state of the interaction with another object, and its class specifies which methods can be invoked by the players of that role if they satisfy the role's requirements.

What is still missing is how our model must be used. When another object wants to interact with it, it has to choose which role to play - assuming that it has the requirements to play it.

The sequence diagram in Figure 3 reports the interactions between the object that defines the role implementation of the role instance (`object:Class`) and a player of that role (`player:Class2`), via a role instance (`:Role1Impl`). The figure is relative to the class diagram described in Figure 2. The player and the object that defines the role exist independently from each other, while, the role instance is created in the context of the instance of the object that defines it (`object:Class`). A role instance, representing a set of affordances, depends both on the object that defines it, in the context of which it is created, and on its player, which is actually passed as a parameter during its creation. In other words, a role instance object represents an association relation with a independent state (the session of the interaction between the former two objects). The object player, in order to interact with the other object, should use an affordance of the last one, more precisely of the role instance that represents the interactions between them. First of all, it has to find the right role instance (`get role instance`) and then to invoke the method on the role instance. However, as a difference with a normal association relation, a role instance (a set of affordances) has access to the object that defines it. In this way, the role can effectively specify a way to interact with its defining object in terms of affordances, providing also a controlled access to its methods and state. In Figure 3, the role instance (`Role1Impl`) offers a way to access, in a controlled way, a private method through an affordance - i.e., a public method - used by the player. The player delegates the role instance for the access to the state of the other object, and, on the other hand, the role instance offers a power to access to the state of the other object.

5   Example

Figure 4 represents a UML object diagram of a printer which can be used in different
ways by playing different roles: SuperUser, User and AnonymousUser. Different requirements are needed to play these roles: SuperUserReq, e.g., requires the
methods getName(), getLogin() and getCertificate(). Each role provides
different operations (e.g., only a SuperUser can remove a job from a queue), or the
same operation in different manners. E.g., the print() method of a SuperUser
does not count the number of printed copies, the User's updates the copy counter
printed. The local information about the number of printed copies (printed) is
stored in the User instance, since it depends on its player. The object Printer has no
public properties. Its private operation print() is used by the print() operations
of the roles User and SuperUser, which are different from it. The private attribute
queue is accessed by the operation viewQueue() of the AnonymousUser operation. It can access the private attribute since the class AnonymousUser belongs to the
same namespace as Printer.

There are four unnamed instances of the three role types. jack, a AuthPerson,
plays two roles, so it is both part of an instance of SuperUser and of an instance of
User. As a User it has different attributes than as a SuperUser and different operations avaliable. The role AnonymousUser has only one instance since it is not necessary to keep a session for each anonymous player. The same role instance is played by
different objects implementing AnonymousReq (which requires only getName()).

The requirements can be used via the that reference, linking the role to its player.
E.g., the method print() of a SuperUser calls the private print() operation of
the Printer, passing as parameter the name of the player (that.getName()).

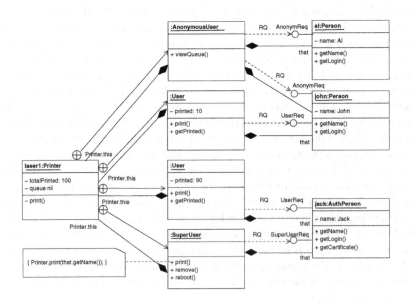

Fig. 4. Three ways of accessing a printer

6   From Modelling to Programming Languages

Baldoni *et al.* [11,10] introduce roles as affordances in powerJava, an extension of the object oriented programming language Java. Java is extended with:

1. A construct defining the role with its name, the requirements and the operations.
2. The implementation of a role, inside an object and according to its definition.
3. How an object can play a role and invoke the operations of the role.

Figure 5 shows by means of the example of Section 5 the use of roles in powerJava. First of all, a role is specified as a sort of interface (`role` - right column) by indicating who can play the role (`playedby`) and which are the operations acquired by playing the role. Second (left column), a role is implemented inside an object as a sort of inner class which realizes the role specification (`definerole`). The inner class implements all the methods required by the role specification as it were an interface.

In the bottom part of the right column of Figure 5 the use of powerJava is depicted. First, the candidate player `jack` of the role is created. It implements the requirements of the roles (`AuthPerson` implements `UserReq` and `SuperUserReq`). Before the player can play the role, however, an instance of the object hosting the role must be created first (a `Printer laser1`). Once the `Printer` is created, the player `jack` can become a `User` too. Note that the `User` is created inside the `Printer laser1` (`laser1.new User(jack)`) and that the player `jack` is an argument of the constructor of role `User` of type `UserReq`. Moreover `jack` plays the role of `SuperUser`.

The player `jack` to act as a `User` must be first classified as a `User` by means of a so-called *role casting* (`(laser1.User) jack`). Note that `jack` is not classified as a generic `User` but as a `User` of `Printer laser1`. Once `jack` is casted to its `User` role, it can exercise its powers, in this example, printing (`print()`). Such method is called a power since, in contrast with usual methods, it can access the state of other objects: its namespace shares the one of the object defining the role. In the example, the method `print()` can access the private state of the `Printer` and invoke `Printer.print()`.

```
class Printer {                          role User playedby UserReq
   private int printedTotal;                { void print();
                                               int getPrinted(); }
   definerole User {
                                          interface UserReq
      private int printed;                   { String getName();
                                               String getLogin();}
      public void print(){ ...
         printed = printed + pages;       jack = new AuthPerson();
         Printer.print(that.getName());   laser1 = new Printer();
      }                                   laser1.new User(jack);
   }                                      laser1.new SuperUser(jack);
}                                         ((laser1.User)jack).print();
```

Fig. 5. A role `User` inside a `Printer`

7 Related Work

There is a huge amount of literature concerning roles in knowledge representation, programming languages, multiagent systems and databases. Thus we can compare our approach only with a limited number of other approaches.

First of all, our approach is consistent with the definition of roles in ontologies given by Masolo *et al.* [12]. They define a role as a social entity which is definitionally dependent on another entity and which is founded and antirigid. Definitionally dependent means that a concept is used in its definition. As discussed in [13], in our approach this corresponds to the stronger property that a role is defined "inside" the object it belong to (i.e., in its namespace or as an inner class). Foundation means that the existence of a role instance requires the existence of another entity. In our model a role instance requires both the existence of a player and the existence of the object the role belongs to. Antirigidity means that the role is not a permanent feature of an entity. In our model a role can cease to exist even if both its player and the object maintain their original class.

A leading approach to roles in programming languages is the one of Kristensen and Osterbye [14]. A role of an object is "a set of properties which are important for an object to be able to behave in a certain way expected by a set of other objects". Even if at first sight this definition seems related, it is the opposite of our approach. By "a role of an object" they mean the role played by an object. They say a role is an integral part of the object and at the same time other objects need to see the object in a certain restricted way by means of roles. A person can have the role of bank employee, and thus its properties are extended with the properties of employee. In our approach, instead, by a role of an object we mean the role offered by an object to interact with it by playing the role. We focus on the fact that to interact with a bank an object must play a role defined by the bank, e.g., employee, and to play a role some requirements must be satisfied. The properties of the player of the role are extended, but only in relation with the interaction with the bank.

Roles based on inner classes have been proposed also by [15,16]. However, their aim is to model the interaction among different objects in a context, where the objects interact only via the roles they play. This was the original view of our approach [17], too. But in this paper and in [10] we extend our approach to the case of roles used to interact with a single object to express the fact that the interaction possibilities change according to the properties of the interactants.

The term of role in UML is already used and it is related to the notion of collaboration: "while a classifier is a complete description of instances, a classifier role is a description of the features required in a particular collaboration, i.e. a classifier role is a projection of, or a view of, a classifier." This notion has several problems, thus Steimann [18] proposes a revision of this concept merging it with the notion of interface. However, by role we mean something different from what is called role in UML. UML is inspired by the relation view of roles: roles come always within a relation. In this view, which is also shared by, e.g., [19,20], roles come in pairs: buyer-seller, client-server, employer-employee, *etc.*. In contrast, we show, first, that the notion of role is more basic and involves the interaction of one object with another one using one single role, rather than an association. Second, we highlight that roles have a state and add properties to their players besides requiring the conformance to an interface.

8 Conclusion

In this paper we introduce the notion of affordance developed in cognitive science to extend the notion of object in the object orientation paradigm for knowledge modelling. In our model objects have attributes and operations which depend on the interaction with other objects, according to their properties. Sets of affordances form roles which are associated with players which satisfy the requirements associated with roles. Since roles have attributes they provide the state of the interaction with an object.

The notion of affordance has been used especially in human computer interaction. In this field the difference between Gibson's interpretation of the concept and the one proposed by Norman has been clarified for example by McGrenere and Ho [21]. In particular, they notice that a feature of Gibson's interpretation is "the offerings or action possibilities in the environment in relation to the action capabilities of an actor". However, to our knowledge the fact that affordances depend on the ability of the actor has not been exploited elsewhere.

Our model allows by means of affordances a more flexible interaction with objects, composed of the non-exclusive following alternatives:

- Traditional direct interaction with an object via its objective properties.
- Session-less interaction with an object via a role which presents to the object a state and operations different from the core object.
- Session aware interaction via a role instance representing the state of the interaction with a particular player of the role.

In this paper we describe this model in UML without extending the language. In Section 6 we summarize how this model has been used to extend Java with roles.

In [17] we present a different albeit related notion of role, with a different aim: representing the organizational structure of institutions which is composed of roles. The organization represents the context where objects interact only via the roles they play by means of the powers offered by their roles (what we call here affordances). E.g., a class representing a university offers the roles of student and professor. The role student offers the power of giving exams to players enrolled in the university.

In [11] we investigate the ontological foundations of roles, while in [9] we explain how roles can be used for coordination purposes.

In this paper, instead, we use roles to articulate the possibility of interaction provided by an object.

Future work concerns the symmetry of roles as part of a relation. In particular, the last diagram of Figure 1 deserves more attention. For example, the requirements to play a role must include the fact that the player must offer the symmetric role (e.g., initiator and participant in a negotiation). Moreover, in that diagram the two roles are independent, while they should be related. Finally, the fact that the two roles are part of a same process (e.g., a negotiation) should be represented, in the same way we represent that student and professor are part of the same institution.

References

1. Drossopoulou, S., Damiani, F., Dezani-Ciancaglini, M., Giannini, P.: More dynamic object re-classification: Fickle$_{II}$. ACM Transactions On Programming Languages and Systems **24** (2002) 153–191
2. Ferber, J., Gutknecht, O., Michel, F.: From agents to organizations: an organizational view of multiagent systems. In: LNCS n. 2935: Procs. of AOSE'03, Springer Verlag (2003) 214–230
3. Juan, T., Sterling, L.: Achieving dynamic interfaces with agents concepts. In: Procs. of AAMAS'04. (2004)
4. Omicini, A., Ricci, A., Viroli, M.: An algebraic approach for modelling organisation, roles and contexts in MAS. Applicable Algebra in Engineering, Communication and Computing **16** (2005) 151–178
5. Zambonelli, F., Jennings, N., Wooldridge, M.: Developing multiagent systems: The Gaia methodology. IEEE Transactions of Software Engineering and Methodology **12(3)** (2003) 317–370
6. Norman, D.: The Design of Everyday Things. Basic Books, New York (2002)
7. Amant, R.: User interface affordances in a planning representation. Human Computer Interaction **14** (1999) 317–354
8. Gibson, J.: The Ecological Approach to Visual Perception. Lawrence Erlabum Associates, New Jersey (1979)
9. Baldoni, M., Boella, G., van der Torre, L.: Roles as a coordination construct: Introducing powerJava. Electronic Notes in Theoretical Computer Science **150** (2005)
10. Baldoni, M., Boella, G., van der Torre, L.: Bridging agent theory and object orientation: Interaction among objects. In: Procs. of PROMAS'06 workshop at AAMAS'06. (2006)
11. Baldoni, M., Boella, G., van der Torre, L.: Powerjava: ontologically founded roles in object oriented programming language. In: Procs. of OOOPS Track of SAC'06. (2006)
12. Masolo, C., Vieu, L., Bottazzi, E., Catenacci, C., Ferrario, R., Gangemi, A., Guarino, N.: Social roles and their descriptions. In: Procs. of KR'04, AAAI Press (2004) 267–277
13. Boella, G., van der Torre, L.: A foundational ontology of organizations and roles. In: Procs. of DALT'06 workshop at AAMAS'06. (2006)
14. Kristensen, B., Osterbye, K.: Roles: conceptual abstraction theory and practical language issues. Theor. Pract. Object Syst. **2** (1996) 143–160
15. Herrmann, S.: Roles in a context. In: Procs. of AAAI Fall Symposium Roles'05, AAAI Press (2005)
16. Tamai, T.: Evolvable programming based on collaboration-field and role model. In: Procs. of IWPSE'02. (2002)
17. Baldoni, M., Boella, G., van der Torre, L.: Bridging agent theory and object orientation: Importing social roles in object oriented languages. In: Procs. of PROMAS'05 workshop at AAMAS'05. (2005)
18. Steimann, F.: A radical revision of UML's role concept. In: Procs. of UML2000. (2000) 194–209
19. Masolo, C., Guizzardi, G., Vieu, L., Bottazzi, E., Ferrario, R.: Relational roles and qua-individuals. In: Procs. of AAAI Fall Symposium Roles'05, AAAI Press (2005)
20. Loebe, F.: Abstract vs. social roles - a refined top-level ontological analysis. In: Procs. of AAAI Fall Symposium Roles'05, AAAI Press (2005)
21. McGrenere, J., Ho, W.: Affordances: Clarifying and evolving a concept. In: Procs. of Graphics Interface Conference. (2000) 179–186

Knowledge Acquisition for Diagnosis in Cellular Networks Based on Bayesian Networks

Raquel Barco[1], Pedro Lázaro[1], Volker Wille[2], and Luis Díez[1]

[1] Departamento de Ingeniería de Comunicaciones, Universidad de Málaga
Campus Universitario de Teatinos, 29071 Málaga, Spain
{rbm, plazaro, diez}@ic.uma.es
[2] Nokia Networks, Performance Services, Ermine Business Park, Huntingdon,
Cambridge PE29 6YJ, UK
Volker.Wille@nokia.com

Abstract. Bayesian Networks (BNs) have been extensively used for diagnosis applications. Knowledge acquisition (KA), i.e. building a BN from the knowledge of experts in the application domain, involves two phases: knowledge gathering and model construction, i.e. defining the model based on that knowledge. The number of parameters involved in a large network is normally intractable to be specified by human experts. This leads to a trade-off between the accuracy of a detailed model and the size and complexity of such a model. In this paper, a Knowledge Acquisition Tool (KAT) to automatically perform information gathering and model construction for diagnosis of the radio access part of cellular networks is presented. KAT automatically builds a diagnosis model based on the experts' answers to a sequence of questions regarding his way of reasoning in diagnosis. This will be performed for two BN structures: Simple Bayes Model (SBM) and Independence of Causal Influence (ICI) models.

1 Introduction

The mobile telecommunication industry is undergoing extraordinary changes. In the forthcoming years, different radio access technologies (GSM, GPRS, UMTS, etc.) will have to coexist within the same network. As a consequence, operation of the radio network is becoming increasingly complex, so that the only viable option for operators to reduce operational costs is to extend the level of automation. Hence, in recent years operators have shown an increasing interest to automate troubleshooting in the radio access network (RAN) of mobile communication systems. Troubleshooting consists of detecting problems (e.g. cells with a high number of dropped calls), identifying the cause (e.g. interference) and solving the problem (e.g. improving the frequency plan). The most difficult task is the diagnosis, which is currently a manual process accomplished by experts in the RAN. These experts are personnel dedicated to daily analysing the main performance indicators and the alarms of the cells, aiming at isolating the cause of the problems. *Bayesian Networks* (BN) [17,15] is the technique that has been

J. Lang, F. Lin, and J. Wang (Eds.): KSEM 2006, LNAI 4092, pp. 55–65, 2006.
© Springer-Verlag Berlin Heidelberg 2006

adopted in this paper for the automated fault diagnosis in cellular networks [3]. BNs have been successfully applied to diagnosis in other application domains, such as diagnosis of diseases in medicine [1], fault identification in printers [12] and fault management in the core of communication networks [23]. BNs presents many advantages compared to other techniques used to model uncertainty, such as certainty factors, Dempster-Shafer theory or fuzzy logic. On the one hand, BNs have a solid base on probability theory. On the other hand, the outputs of a given BN are the probabilities of the possible causes, which are very easy to interpret.

Building a BN based on the knowledge from experts in the application domain, that is *knowledge acquisition* (KA), involves two phases. Firstly, obtaining the knowledge from experts. Secondly, model construction, that is defining the model based on the previously acquired information provided by experts. KA has been considered the bottleneck of BNs because the parameters (e.g. number of probabilities) involved in a large network are normally intractable to be specified by human experts. Hence, model construction requires a trade-off between a large and detailed model to obtain accurate results on the one hand, and, on the other hand, the cost of construction and maintenance and the complexity of probabilistic inference.

Probabilistic information can be obtained from diverse sources. The most common ones are statistical data, literature and human experts [8]. Firstly, in many application domains, such as medical diagnosis, large data collections are available [5] documenting previously solved problems. These data can be used to automatically build the BN structure and to calculate the quantitative part that best fits the available information [16,6,13]. Secondly, literature often provides probabilistic information in some application domains. However, this information is usually not directly applicable to model construction due to diverse reasons: not all probabilities are provided, probabilities are expressed in a direction reverse to the direction required by the BN, the population from which information is derived is different from the population for which the BN is being developed, etc. Finally, when there are few or no reliable data available, the knowledge and experience of experts in the domain of application is the only source of information to build the BN. In KA, several problems are often encountered. On the one hand, experts in the application domain are not normally used to the terminology used in BNs. In addition, experts feel reluctant to specify precise quantitative information. On the other hand, experts' time is scarce, whereas KA is normally a very time-consuming task. Therefore, several techniques have been proposed to simplify knowledge acquisition [20,9,7].

In mobile communication networks, currently there are not historical collections of diagnosed cases. Furthermore, diagnosis of the RAN of cellular networks is not documented in the existing literature. Thus, the experience of troubleshooting experts is, in most cases, the only source of information to build a diagnosis model.

If the diagnosis model is based on discrete BNs, quantitative information should also include the discretization of continuous variables. As this aspect is something external to the BN, literature related to construction of BNs normally does not mention this important part of the model design. Due to the fact that in mobile communication networks most symptoms are inherently continuous, discretization has been considered a crucial issue in the definition of the quantitative model.

Based on the theory presented in the following sections, a tool has been built which automatically performs knowledge acquisition, named *Knowledge Acquisition Tool* (KAT) [2]. KAT is envisaged to guide the expert through a sequence of questions regarding his way of reasoning in diagnosis. A diagnosis model is automatically constructed based on his answers. The main advantage of KAT is that it is very easy to use by troubleshooting experts and no BN knowledge is required to use the tool. As a consequence, domain experts can transfer their expertise using a language that they understand. It should be taken into account that model construction depends on the BN structure. Therefore, the user should specify which type of model he wishes to build.

The paper is structured as follows. First, section 2 gives a brief introduction to Bayesian Networks, presenting some model structures. Section 3 addresses each step of the knowledge acquisition process. Section 4 then presents model construction for different BN structures. Finally, Section 5 summarizes the most important conclusions.

2   Bayesian Networks

A Bayesian Network [17,15] is a pair (D, P) that allows efficient representation of a joint probability distribution over a set of random variables $U = \{X_1, ..., X_n\}$. D is a *directed acyclic graph* (DAG), whose vertices correspond to the random variables $X_1, ..., X_n$ and whose edges represent direct dependencies between the variables. The second component, P, is a set of conditional probability functions, one for each variable, $p(X_i|\pi_i)$, where π_i is the parent set of X_i in U.

The set P defines a unique joint probability distribution over U given by

$$P(U) = \prod_{i=1}^{n} p(X_i|\pi_i)$$ (1)

The qualitative part of the model is composed of variables (causes, symptoms and conditions) and relations among them. A *cause* or *fault* is the defective behavior of some logical or physical component which provokes malfunctioning of the cell, e.g. lack of coverage. A *symptom* is a performance indicator or an alarm whose value can be a manifestation of a fault, e.g. low received signal level. A *condition* is a factor whose value makes the probability of certain cause occurring increase or decrease, e.g. frequency hopping feature. In discrete BNs, which are the most extended ones, the quantitative part of the model is a set of probability tables. Each variable X_i has $|X_i|$ exclusive states.

The main problems encountered during model construction have relied on the definition of the BN structure, the modelling of continuous symptoms and

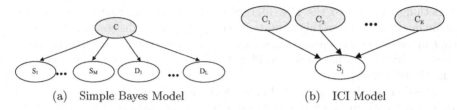

(a)   Simple Bayes Model   (b)   ICI Model

Fig. 1. BN network structures

the specification of the probabilities in the BN. Firstly, a technique often used in order to simplify model construction is to assume a given network structure. In our case, these have been the Simple Bayes Model and Independence of Causal Influence models. Secondly, continuous symptoms have been discretized into intervals, whose thresholds should be defined by diagnosis experts. Finally, probabilities should also be elicited by diagnosis experts.

2.1 Simple Bayes Model (SBM)

The SBM consists of a single parent node C and $M+L$ children nodes, $S_1, ..., S_M$, $D_1, ..., D_L$ (Fig.1(a)). The states of the parent node are the possible causes $C = \{c_1, ..., c_K\}$, whereas the children are the symptoms and the conditions, which may take any number of states.

Associated to each child, $X_i = S_i$ or D_i, there is a table of conditional probabilities $P(X_i|C)$ of size $|C| \times |X_i|$. Likewise, associated to the cause C there is a table of prior probabilities $P(C)$ of size $|C|$. Some assumptions are inherent to the SBM. First, only a fault can be present at a time. Second, children are independent given the cause.

2.2 Independence of Causal Influence (ICI)

In order to overcome the single fault assumption inherent to the SBM, in ICI models [10,22,11] each cause is represented as an independent node with two states (*no/yes*). Fig.1(b) shows part of a BN where multiple causes, $C_1, ..., C_K$, contribute to a common effect S_j. In this model, if K is large, the conditional probability table for symptom S_j may become intractable. ICI simplifies knowledge elicitation and inference by considering that the causes *independently* contribute to the effect S_j. The number of probabilities to be defined for S_j in Fig.1(b) is linear in K when assuming ICI, whereas in an unrestricted model the number of probabilities is exponential in K. BNs that we have built according to ICI structures have modelled conditions as parents of the causes. Some ICI models are the Noisy-OR [17] and Noisy-max [14].

3 Knowledge Acquisition

KA comprises the phases listed below. Table 1 summarizes the qualitative information that the expert should provide, whereas quantitative information can be found in Table 2.

Table 1. Qualitative model defined by expert

Parameters	Range	Description	Example
F_i	$i = 1, ..., W$	Fault categories W: number of fault categories	F_1 =High DCR
C_i	$i = 1, ..., K$	Causes K: number of causes	C_1 =UL interf.
S_i	$i = 1, ..., M$	Symptoms M: number of symptoms	S_{30} =% UL interf.HOs
$s_{i,j}$	$i = 1, ..., M$ $j = 1, ..., Q_i$	Symptom states Q_i: number of states of symptom S_i	$s_{30,1}$ =low
D_i	$i = 1, ..., L$	Conditions L: number of conditions	D_2 =Frequency Hopping
$d_{i,j}$	$i = 1, ..., L$ $j = 1, ..., X_i$	Condition states X_i: number of states of condition D_i	$d_{2,2}$ =on
C_r^i $= \{C_{r_1}^i, ..., C_{r_{R_i}}^i\}$	$i = 1, ..., M$	Set of causes related to symptom S_i R_i: number of causes related to S_i	$C_r^1 = \{C_3, C_4\}$
D_r^i $= \{D_{r_1}^i, ..., D_{r_{U_i}}^i\}$	$i = 1, ..., L$	Set of conditions related to cause C_i U_i: number of conditions related to C_i	$D_r^1 = \{D_2\}$

1. **Select *Fault Category*.** Fault categories are the diverse problems that the RAN may suffer, such as "High DCR" or "Congestion". A different model is built for each fault category.
2. **Define variables.** There should be a database of causes, symptoms and conditions. The expert has the chance of either selecting a variable of the database or defining a new one, which should be incorporated into the database. If the number of variables in the database is large, it may be very time-consuming to read all of them in order to find a cause similar to the one that the expert wants to define. In that case, once the user has described the variable, KAT should find and present similar variables, e.g. the terms "HW fault" and "fault in a piece of equipment" should be merged in the search [19].

   Firstly, the expert specifies the possible causes of the fault category, that is the causes of the problem in the network for which the diagnosis model is being built (e.g. "High DCR"), $\{C_1, ..., C_K\}$. It is recommended to include a cause called "Other causes", in order to cover any other possible cause of the problem not explicitly included in the defined causes. Secondly, the expert is demanded to enumerate the symptoms that may help to identify the previously defined causes, $\{S_1, ..., S_M\}$. The states, $s_{i,j}$, of each symptom, S_i, should also be specified. Lastly, the user is requested about conditions, $\{D_1, ..., D_L\}$, and their states, $d_{i,j}$, which may also help to identify the cause.
3. **Define relations.** In this phase, the user should define the causes, $C_r^i = \{C_{r_1}^i, ..., C_{r_{R_i}}^i\}$, associated to each symptom S_i. The terms "associated" or "related" are used to qualify those variables which have a strong direct interdependency. For example, the cause "Lack of coverage" is related to the symptom "Percentage of uplink samples with level < -100 dBm", whereas

the cause "uplink interference" is not related to that symptom. The explanation is that a lack of coverage reduces the received signal level in comparison to the average received signal level in a network without problems, whereas when the cause is interference, the received signal level is not normally decreased in comparison to the level in a cell without problems. The causes not related to symptom S_i will be denoted as $C_n^i = C \backslash C_r^i$.

The expert should also specify the conditions, $D_r^i = \{D_{r_1}^i, ..., D_{r_{U_i}}^i\}$, associated to each cause C_i, that is conditions whose value can modify his belief in the probability of the cause being the one causing the problem.

4. **Specify thresholds.** For each continuous symptom, S_i, interval limits (i.e. thresholds), $t_{i,j}$, between each defined interval should be requested to the user.

5. **Specify probabilities.** Verbal probability expressions are often suggested as a method of eliciting probabilistic information [18]. The number of verbal expressions should be reduced in order to avoid misinterpretations. In addition, it is advisable to use a graphical scale with numbers on one side and words on the other. In our experiments with cellular network operators, experts were asked to choose one out of five levels of probabilities: "Almost certain", "Likely", "Fifty-fifty", "Improbable" and "Unlikely". Those levels are mapped to the probabilities $0.85, 0.7, 0.5, 0.3$ and 0.1, respectively. Those mapping values have been specified by troubleshooting experts.

The procedure to define the probabilities is as follows. Firstly, the expert has to specify the prior probabilities of each of the possible causes of the problem, P_{C_i}. As causes have only two states (off/on), only the probability of the cause being present is demanded. In the case of a cause C_i related to a condition D_j, the probability of C_i should be defined for each state of D_j. If more than one condition is related to C_i, the probability of C_i should be defined for each combination of states of the associated conditions, $P_{C_i|D_i^r}$. Very often, only some combinations of states are implemented in the network. Thus, the expert should have the option of defining only those combinations that are sensible. The probabilities for impossible combinations of conditions should be set to zero. If the number of conditions is large, the number of probabilities to be defined may become intractable. However, experience with cellular network operators has shown that the number of defined conditions is normally kept low, and so is the number of demanded probabilities.

The second step is defining prior probabilities of conditions, $P_{D_{i,j}}$. The number of probabilities to be specified for each condition depends on its number of states. Hence, if the number of states is X_i, the expert should define $X_i - 1$ probabilities.

Finally, the probabilities for the symptoms are requested. For a symptom S_i, KAT should ask the probability of each state, but one of them (which is obtained from the other probabilities), given that each of the related causes, $C_k \in C_r^i$, is present and the other causes, $C_k \in C_n^i$, are absent, $P_{S_{i,j}|C_k}$. In addition, the probability of each state of the symptom, but one of them, given that none of the related causes are present should be defined, $P_{S_{i,j}|C_0}$.

Table 2. Quantitative model defined by expert

Parameters	Range	Description	N^{er} parameters
$t_{i,j}$	$i = 1, ..., M$	Threshold j for symptom S_i	
	$j = 1, ..., T_i$	T_i: number of thresholds of symptom S_i	$\sum\limits_{i=1}^{M} T_i$
$P_{C_i \mid D_r^i}$	$i = 1, ..., K$	Probability of cause $C_i = on$	
		given set of related conditions	$\sum\limits_{i=1}^{K} \prod\limits_{j=r_1}^{r_{U_i}} X_j$
$P_{D_{i,j}}$	$i = 1, ..., L$	Prior probabilities of conditions	$\sum\limits_{i=1}^{L} (X_i - 1)$
	$j = 1, ..., X_i$		
$P_{S_{i,j} \mid C_k}$	$i = 1, ..., M$	Probability of symptom $S_i = s_{i,j}$	
$\forall C_k \in C_r^i$	$j = 1, ..., Q_i$	given cause $C_k = 1$ and $C_h = 0 \ \forall h \neq k$	$\sum\limits_{i=1}^{M} R_i \cdot (Q_i - 1)$
$P_{S_{i,j} \mid C_0}$	$i = 1, ..., M$	Probability of symptom $S_i = s_{i,j}$	
	$j = 1, ..., X_i$	given cause $C_k = 0$, $\forall C_k \in C_r^i$	$\sum\limits_{i=1}^{M} (Q_i - 1)$

6. **Link symptoms and conditions to database.** The last step is linking the variables in the model to the data in the Network Management System (NMS). Thus, symptoms should be related to a parameter (performance indicator, counter, etc.) available in the NMS or a combination of parameters. For this last option, KAT should ease the construction of equations.

4   Model Construction

4.1   Model Construction for SBM

SBM was depicted in Fig.1(a). In this BN the required probabilities are the prior probabilities of causes, $P(C)$, and the probabilities of symptoms and conditions given causes, $P(S_i|C)$ and $P(D_i|C)$.

Causes are the mutually exclusive states, $c_1, ..., c_K$, of variable C. Thus, probabilities of causes should add up to 1. If the sum of the probabilities elicited by the expert is different from 1, a state c_{K+1}, named "Others", should be added to the C node, which stands for any other cause of the problem not considered by the expert. Firstly, a probability table of the cause given the conditions should be built, taking into account that $P(C_i|D_r^i, D_n^i) = P(C_i|D_r^i)$. Normally, the sum of probabilities of the states of the C node should be 1 for any column of the table (any combination of states of the conditions). However, if the probabilities introduced by the expert are different to 1 for any column, they should be normalised. The followed criterion has been to maintain constant the ratio amongst the probabilities of the same cause given different conditions. Hence, if the sum of probabilities of the states of the C node is higher than 1 for any column of the table, the sum of probabilities for that case is taken as a normalization constant B (if the sum is lower than 1 for all columns, $B = 1$). If more than a column adds 1, B is the highest sum of the columns. Then, all entries in the probability table are normalized by B. For each column, the probability of the "Others" cause is obtained as one minus the sum of the probabilities of the other causes.

Finally, the probability of each cause, $P(C = c_i)$, should be calculated according to the following equation:

$$P(C = c_i) = \frac{1}{B} \sum_{D^i_{r_1}, \dots, D^i_{r_{U_i}}} P_{C_i | D^i_{r_1}, \dots, D^i_{r_{U_i}}} \cdot P_{D^i_{r_1}} \cdot \dots \cdot P_{D^i_{r_{U_i}}} \qquad (2)$$

The expression of the probability of symptom S_i is as follows. On the one hand, the probabilities of S_i conditioned to related causes have been explicitly elicited by the expert. Their expression is:

$$P(S_i = s_{i,j} | C = C^i_{r_k}) = P_{S_{i,j} | C^i_{r_k}}, \quad j = 2 \dots Q_i, \quad k = 1 \dots R_i \qquad (3)$$

On the other hand, the expert has also defined the probability of the symptom conditioned to non-related causes, which is the same for all non-related causes:

$$P(S_i = s_{i,j} | C = C^i_{n_k}) = P_{S_{i,j} | C_0}, \quad j = 2 \dots Q_i, \quad k = 1 \dots K - R_i \qquad (4)$$

In the SBM conditions are represented as children of the parent node. Therefore, the probabilities of conditions given causes are required, whereas the available probabilities are the prior probabilities of conditions and the probabilities of causes given conditions. Assuming that conditions are independent of each other given the causes, as suggested in [21], elicited probabilities can be transformed into the required ones following the Bayes' rule:

$$P(D_j = d_{j,k} | C = c_i) = \frac{P(C = c_i | D_j = d_{j,k}) \cdot P_{D_{j,k}}}{P(C = c_i)}, \quad D_j \in D^i_r \qquad (5)$$

where $P(C = c_i)$ can be calculated following equation (2) and

$$P(C = c_i | D_j = d_{j,k}) = \frac{1}{B} \sum_{D^i_r \setminus D_j} P_{C_i | D^i_r} \cdot \prod_{(D_h \in D^i_r) \setminus D_j} P_{D_h} \qquad (6)$$

For causes which are independent of condition D_j, $D_j \in D^i_n$, instead of equation (5), the following equation should be used

$$P(D_j = d_{j,k} | C = c_i) = \frac{\left(1 - \sum_{C_h | D_j \in D^h_r} P(C = c_h | D_j = d_{j,k})\right) \cdot P_{D_{j,k}}}{1 - \sum_{C_h | D_j \in D^h_r} P(C = c_h)} \qquad (7)$$

4.2   Model Construction for ICI

In models designed following the ICI assumptions, causes are modelled as different nodes. Each cause node has two states (*false/true*) (Fig.1 (b)). Probability tables for condition variables are calculated following the expression:

$$P(D_i = d_{i,j}) = P_{D_{i,j}}, \quad j = 1...X_i \tag{8}$$

Probability tables for the cause nodes are directly built based on the information elicited by the expert according to the expression:

$$P(C_i = true|D_r^i) = P_{C_i|D_r^i} \tag{9}$$

Finally, probability tables for the symptoms are defined according to eq.(10).

$$P(S_i = s_{i,j}|C_r^i) = \sum_{\{A|g(A)=s_{i,j}\}} \prod_{k=r_1}^{r_{R_i}} P_{A_k|C_k}, \quad j = 2...Q_i, \quad A = \{A_{r_1}...A_{r_{R_i}}\} \tag{10}$$

where g is the function that defines the model, e.g. OR when it is noisy-OR model, $A = \{A_{r_1}...A_{r_{R_i}}\}$ are auxiliary variables which take on the same values as the symptom S_i and the sum varies according to all the values of the A_i.

5 Conclusions

This paper has presented how to define a knowledge acquisition tool for building diagnosis models for the RAN of cellular telecommunications networks. Although the number of existing knowledge acquisition tools is very high, normally they are focused on specific application domains. General knowledge acquisition tools are normally more complex and they are not completely suitable for this domain.

In order to increase the feasibility of the method for real usage, two BN structures which simplify KA have been selected. The information required from the expert is independent of the model structure, be it SBM or ICI. Thus, once the information has been provided by the user it is possible to build both structures from the same data and compare the results achieved by each model.

A prototype tool has been built based on this theory and it has been tested by experts in troubleshooting cellular networks. They have found the tool to be very useful to design models and to be essential in the absence of previous knowledge in BNs. Some iterative phases of refinement were carried out in order to improve the user interface, specially regarding the user-friendliness of the tool.

On the one hand, SBM and ICI models built according to the proposed methods have been compared. ICI models have shown slightly better accuracy than SBM. However, SBM is preferred to ICI due to its simplicity and similar performance [4]. On the other hand, a prototype diagnosis tool based on the SBM has been tested in a live GERAN network. The achieved diagnosis accuracy was 70%, which was similar to the accuracy obtained by a human expert [3]. Tests on UMTS networks are still on-going.

Acknowledgements. This work has been partially supported by the Spanish Ministry of Science and Technology under project TIC2003-07827 and it has been partially carried out in the framework of the EUREKA CELTIC Gandalf project.

References

1. S. Andreassen, M. Woldbye, B. Falck, and S. Andersen, "MUNIN: A causal probabilistic network for interpretation of electromyographic findings," in *Proc. International Joint Conference on Artificial Intelligence*, Milan, Italy, Aug. 1987, pp. 366–372.
2. R. Barco, "Knowledge acquisition tool specification," Nokia Networks, Málaga, Spain, Tech. Rep. AutoGERAN_KAT_2001_1H_v1_0, June 2001.
3. R. Barco, R. Guerrero, G. Hylander, L. Nielsen, M. Partanen, and S. Patel, "Automated troubleshooting of mobile networks using bayesian networks," in *Proc. IASTED Int.Conf.Communication Systems and Networks (CSN'02)*, Málaga, Spain, Sept. 2002, pp. 105–110.
4. R. Barco, V. Wille, L. Díez, and P. Lázaro, "Comparison of probabilistic models used for diagnosis in cellular networks," in *Proc. Vehicular Technology Conference (VTC)*, Melbourne, Australia, May 2006.
5. C. Blake and C. Merz. (1998) UCI repository of machine learning databases. Dept. Information and Computer Science. Irvine, CA: University of California. [Online]. Available: http://www.ics.uci.edu/~mlearn/MLRepository.html
6. W. Buntine, "A guide to the literature on learning graphical models," *IEEE Trans. Knowledge Data Eng.*, vol. 8, pp. 195–210, Apr. 1996.
7. M. J. Druzdzel and L. C. van der Gaag, "Elicitation of probabilities for belief networks: combining qualitative and quantitative information," in *Proc. Annual Conf. Uncertainty in Artificial Intelligence*, Montreal, Canada, Aug. 1995, pp. 141–148.
8. M. J. Druzdzel and L. C. van der Gaag, "Building probabilistic networks: where do the numbers come from?" *IEEE Trans. Knowledge Data Eng.*, vol. 12, no. 4, pp. 481–486, 2000.
9. L. van der Gaag, S. Renooij, C. Witteman, B. Aleman, and B. Taal, "How to elicit many probabilities," in *Proc. Annual Conf. Uncertainty in Artificial Intelligence*, Stockholm, Sweden, July 1999, pp. 647–654.
10. D. Heckerman and J. Breese, "Causal independence for probability assessment and inference using bayesian networks," Microsoft Research, Redmond, Washington, Tech. Rep. MSR-TR-94-08, Mar. 1994.
11. D. Heckerman and J. Breese, "A new look at causal independence," in *Proc. Annual Conf. Uncertainty in Artificial Intelligence*, Seattle, Washington, July 1994, pp. 286–292.
12. D. Heckerman, J. Breese, and K. Rommelse, "Decision-theoretic troubleshooting," *Communication of the ACM*, vol. 38, no. 3, pp. 49–57, Mar. 1995.
13. D. Heckerman, "A tutorial on learning bayesian networks," Microsoft Research, Redmond, Washington, Tech. Rep. MSR-TR-95-06, Mar. 1995.
14. M. Henrion, "Some practical issues in constructing belief networks," in *Uncertainty in Artificial Intelligence*, L. Kanal, T. Leuitt, and J. Lemmer, Eds. Amsterdam, The Netherlands: Elsevier Science, 1989, vol. 3, pp. 161–173.
15. F. Jensen, *Bayesian Networks and decision graphs*. New York, USA: Springer-Verlag, 2001.
16. R. Neapolitan, *Learning Bayesian Networks*. Prentice Hall, 2004.
17. J. Pearl, *Probabilistic reasoning in intelligent systems: Networks of plausible inference*. San Francisco, California: Morgan Kaufmann, 1988.
18. S. Renooij and C. Witteman, "Talking probabilities: communicating probabilistic information with words and numbers," *International Journal of Approximate Reasoning*, vol. 22, no. 3, pp. 169–194, Dec. 1999.

19. G. Salton, J. Allen, and C. Buckley, "Automatic structuring and retrieval of large text files," *Communications of the ACM*, vol. 37, no. 2, pp. 97–108, 1994.

20. C. Skaanning, F. Jensen, U. Kjærulff, and A. Madsen, "Acquisition and transformation of likelihoods to conditional probabilities for bayesian networks," in *Proc. AAAI Spring Symposium on AI in Equipment Maintenance Service and Support*, Palo Alto, California, Mar. 1999, pp. 34–40.

21. C. Skaanning, "A knowledge acquisition tool for bayesian-network troubleshooters," in *Proc. Annual Conf. Uncertainty in Artificial Intelligence*, Stanford, USA, July 2000, pp.549–557.

22. S. Srinivas, "A generalization of the noisy-or model," in *Proc. Annual Conf. Uncertainty in Artificial Intelligence*, Washington, USA, July 1993, pp. 208–215.

23. M. Steinder and A. Sethi, "Probabilistic fault localization in communication systems using belief networks," *IEEE/ACM Trans. Networking*, vol. 12, no. 5, pp. 809–822, Oct. 2004.

Building Conceptual Knowledge for Managing Learning Paths in e-Learning

Yu-Liang Chi[1] and Hsun-Ming Lee[2]

[1] Dept. of Management Information Systems, Chung Yuan Christian University,
Chung-Li, 32023, Taiwan, R.O.C.
maxchi@cycu.edu.tw
[2] Dept. of Computer Information Systems & Quantitative Methods,
Texas State University - San Marcos, TX, 78666, USA
sl20@txstate.edu

Abstract. This study develops a framework of conceptual model to manage learning paths in e-learning systems. Since learning objects are rapidly accumulated in e-learning course repositories, managing the relevant relations among learning objects are costly and error-prone. Moreover, conventional learning path management based on databases or XML metadata does not offer a sufficient conceptual model to represent semantics. This study utilizes ontology-based techniques to strengthen learning path management in a knowledgeable manner. Through establishing a conceptual model of learning paths, semantic modeling provides richer data structuring capabilities for organizing learning objects. Empirical findings are presented, which show technologies to enhance completeness of semantic representation and reduce the complexity of the path management efforts. A walkthrough example is given to present ontology building, knowledge inference and the planning of learning paths.

Keywords: Ontology, Semantic, Conceptual structure, e-Learning.

1 Introduction

E-learning systems provide fulltime education services that users can access without requiring their physical presence. The benefit of e-learning is to provide cost-effective ways of education to improve quality of learning and reduce costs of training [5]. In order to satisfy the requirements of various groups, e-learning communities endeavor to develop abundant courses and efficient learning environments. Metadata standards are recently developed for the e-learning systems to exchange a wide variety of learning materials on the Web and elsewhere [1] [16]. The Shareable Content Object Reference Model (SCORM) is an example of such standards. In addition to the effort of producing and distributing digital contents, the development of the e-learning systems is a new pedagogic opportunity. E-learning emphasizes learner-centered activities and system interactivity; therefore, remote learners can potentially outperform traditional classroom students [23]. Personalization is one of key technologies in developing such a promising e-learning environment. Personalization means customizing information for each user that is personally relevant [4] [7] [20].

J. Lang, F. Lin, and J. Wang (Eds.): KSEM 2006, LNAI 4092, pp. 66–77, 2006.

To satisfy real needs of each learner, personalized learning paths facilitate a learner-centered context for individual learning options. In a learning path, a LO is usually annotated by metadata to describe its various usages such as labs, assignments and lessons. The metadata may also describe the associations between LOs such as dependent, ancestor and sibling. Since the learning paths are composed of the LOs used in different courses, it is problematic when the paths are tangled together as a network. The worse case is that any updated or newly released LOs may cause their relation changes that increase the complexity of learning path management. Current metadata models lack direct support for data abstraction, inheritance and constraints. These limitations induce poor capabilities in deriving proper learning paths for individuals [8]. Therefore, a conceptual data model is expected to provide solutions in the semantic level.

This study proposes ontology-based techniques to design a semantic framework for addressing the learning path management problems. The framework is created from three major works. First, the general conceptual model of learning paths is gathered from experts' perception. A concept analysis approach is employed to identify hierarchical structures of concepts as an ontology prototype. Second, we use the Protégé ontology editor to build a conceptual model that includes concepts, attributes, and formal descriptions. The facts of learning objects are regarded as asserting knowledge and can be edited by the software tool. Both the conceptual model and assertion will be represented by Web Ontology Language (OWL). Third, a retrieval system employs an inference engine to support reasoning processes via rules and ontology-driven documents.

2   A Knowledge Framework for Learning Path Management

In order to develop a knowledge framework, this study utilizes ontology as a knowledge representation method. In philosophy, ontology is a resource guide for managing things systematically. In information technology, the term ontology is an explicit specification of a conceptualization [13]. It is important to note here that however the conceptualization can be accepted by the information industry only if there is a common understanding of this term. Every knowledge model is committed to some conceptualization implicitly or explicitly [15] [21]. In the ontological manner, the knowledge base can be denoted as $K=(T, A)$ [2]. The expression represents that a knowledge base (K) can be derived from intentional knowledge 'T-Box' (T) and extensional knowledge 'A-Box' (A). The T-Box contains the conceptual definitions into a terminology module (i.e., taxonomy). On the other hand, the A-Box contains the assertions about individual states into an assertional module or so called assertional knowledge.

Figure 1 shows the overall framework of the learning path management. The figure is divided by a dashed line where upper part is about the system design and lower part is the usage thereafter the learning path provided. The system design is primarily achieved through the support of ontology-based knowledge mechanisms. Three major designs are discussed as follows.

Ontology Building. The ontological architecture uses the $K=(T, A)$ knowledge model located in the right side of Figure 1. Its knowledge model, especially in the T-Box,

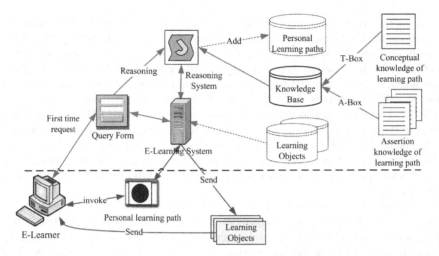

Fig. 1. A knowledge framework for learning path management. The knowledge base is based on ontologies that consist of conceptual and assertion knowledge.

can be implemented in terms of ontology building that includes the steps of capturing knowledge, designing conceptual structure and adding formal definitions. In order to represent ontologies into the information system, a well accepted knowledge representation standard is essential. Emerging XML technologies provides self describing, user definable and machine readable abilities. Since the advantages of XML are obvious, there has been strong development of ontological languages to express knowledge. The OWL (Web Ontology Language) is the newest and well-defined XML-based ontological language developed by the World Wide Web Consortium [18] [21]. This study utilizes OWL as the specification language for knowledge representation. Further details of OWL can be found at (http://www.w3c.org/2004/owl).

Reasoning System. Ontologies can be seen as a repository of the real world using knowledge perspectives. Intelligence with ontologies is created via a reasoning-driven system. Thus, a reasoning system is about to function in knowledge-based applications only if certain conceptual knowledge is defined, then assertions of real events can be followed. The reasoning consequence is derived by inferring hierarchical relations and calculating logical formalisms of concepts. Several ontology-based reasoning engines or reasoners are available such as Jena (http://jena.sourceforge.net/) and Racer (http://www.racer-systems.com/). Such reasoners are used to create additional implicitly knowledge assertions which are entailed from OWL-based repository. Thus, developers have the advantages of programming reasoning modules to manipulate ontologies.

Presentation. The end user interacts with the learning path management system through Web-based interfaces. First, after starting a learning program, the user answers a questionnaire to provide personal background and gets the response of a suggested personal learning path. He or she can make necessary modifications on the suggestion for a better learning path plan. Second, the updated personal learning path is then kept in a personal profile that will be regarded as guidance for learning path arrangement. Finally, the guidance may be updated according to the progress of each learning session.

Though various studies and experiences exist in ontological engineering literatures, no standard approach is available in this field [11] [19]. Ontology may take a variety of forms, but it usually introduces a vocabulary of terms and some specification of their meanings [12]. As mentioned earlier, a knowledge model usually consists of T-Box and A-Box. The T-Box can be considered as conceptual knowledge of domain of interest that refers to the abstract view including terms, their definitions and axioms relating them. Conceptual knowledge is definitions of things and often specialized to some domain or subject matter. It is not only the linguistic of literary but also the semantic implications that the term in the vocabulary [3].

The most challenging part of this learning path management system is the module for building ontology-based knowledge. This study adopts parts of suggestion from [22] and incorporates two tasks - capturing knowledge and building ontological knowledge. More explanations about knowledge gathering, normalization and construction are explained in the section 3 and 4.

3 Knowledge Capturing

Knowledge capturing is about how to gather human cognition of the domain of interest. Traditional information system models events only in the data level. Knowledge modeling, however, is capturing a semantic view from a set of similar objects and producing agreed characteristics of the schema that the things can be generally described. In this study, the knowledge capturing can be considered as how to acquiring the common understanding of the interested learning path semantically. Though the intuitive cognitions are all the logics of human in mind, the developers must analyze common behaviors and characteristics of the subject matters and induce them to an abstractive manner. Thus, developers have to collaborate with domain experts. Two development stages are further distinguished as expert cognitions acquiring and conceptual hierarchy normalization.

3.1 Experts Cognition Acquiring

In order to capture the key intuitive cognitions of the learning path management from experts, in-depth observations on the interested domain are essential. Knowledge developers have to reconcile intuitive cognition with abstractive cognition for describing similar things into a well accepted conceptualization. Thus, developers digest common behaviors and properties of entire things rather than dealing with individuals. For example, the learning path arrangement can be digested in terms of four possible patterns illustrated in Figure 2. The first pattern is sequence pattern and the others are extended patterns including merge, split, and accessory.

- Sequence pattern: A learning object in a sequence is enabled after the completion of another learning object in the same course.
- Merge pattern: A learning object in a sequence is enabled after the completion of multiple learning objects. It is an assumption of this pattern that each incoming background learning objects may include the same or different courses. For

examples, the Java concept, SQL and relational algebra are background courses of the JDBC.

- Split pattern: One of multiple learning objects can be chosen after the completion of a learning object. For examples, the JDBC, RMI or Beans are proper selections when a learner finishes Java basic courses.
- Accessory pattern: A learning object is accompanied with dependent accessories such as labs or practices. The accessories arrangement may be managed by using the sequence, merge or split pattern, but they are limited within the corresponding learning object.

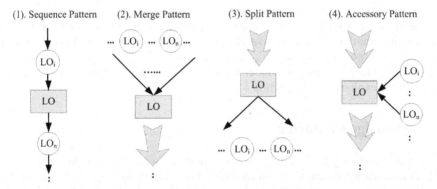

Fig. 2. Four possible learning path arrangement patterns. The symbol LO denotes a learning object, where i and n are the number to distinguish different learning objects.

Figure 2 draws abstractive cognitions that learning paths can be behaved in terms of the common understandings or "conceptualization". To further clarify the detail components of the conceptualization, a set of terms and the relevant relations are used. Referring to the patterns given in Figure 2, for example, the learning objects can be derived in various terms such as lessons and assignments for appropriately describing their corresponding atomic concepts. A set of atomic concepts is usually called universe of discourse that generally refers to the entire set of terms used in a specific discourse. Relevant relations are regarded as attributes such as "is-a" and "has-a" that are used to describe definitions of learning objects. The atomic concepts and relevant relations can be written as <*{Atomic concepts}, {Attributes}*> expression. For examples:

```
Atomic concepts: {Things, Course, Pre-Lesson, Post-
Lesson, Lesson, Learning object, Root, End, Accessory,
Lab, Assignment, Exam, ...}
```

```
Attributes: {is-learning_object, is-accessory, has-
ascendant, has-pre_lesson, has-descendant, has-
post_lesson, has-sibling, has-dependent, has-accessory,
...}
```

3.2 Conceptual Hierarchy Normalization

In previous stage, expert cognitions are formed in terms of a pair set of atomic concepts and attributes. Since ontology is like a taxonomy that is an organizational schema for

things, it needs more efforts to create a referable hierarchical structure. In order to identify a hierarchical structure of ontology, some analysis approaches such as Formal Concept Analysis (FCA) and Repertory Grid Technique (RGT) are suggested in literatures
[9] [14]. This study utilizes FCA to build the hierarchical structure since the experts
have found analysis components such as concept and attributes in the previous stage.
Within FCA approach, three processes are described as the following:

- Creating a context lattice: The initial step of FCA is to establish a context lattice
  which can be represented by a cross table. The notation 'χ' describes inside the
  table representing a binary relation that indicates an object has an attribute [10].
  The sets of objects and attributes together with their relation to each other form
  a 'formal context'.
- Finding implications of concepts: To analyze implication in the formal context,
  a computer-guided feature called attribute exploration is used. In practice, the
  exploration technique is a step-wise interactive feature that questions each implication from users. The users must then either confirm that the implication is
  always true or disagree by placed in a counterexample using existing cases.
- Building a hierarchical concept structure: The final output of concept analysis is
  usually presented by a line diagram. The line diagram comprises circles, lines
  and the tags of all objects and attributes of the given context. The line diagram
  shows dependency relationships among formal context.

Formal Concept Analysis provides a useful mean to the concept analysis of human–centered knowledge based on the mathematical theory. Knowledge engineers
exploit capabilities of FCA software tools without much development time and skill
required. Figure 3 illustrates partial results of using the FCA approach to normalize a
hierarchical structure based on definitions of concepts and attributes. The *Taxonomy*
in the left of this figure shows a conceptual hierarchy derived according to definitions
of concepts. For example, the concept "Accessory" is equivalent the following descriptions *{is-lesson} and {some has-accessory (Lab or Assignment)}*. The *Attributes*
in the right of this figure list possible attributes that are obtained from FCA attribute
exploration mechanism. The 'INV' states the inverse role of a role. For example, *haschild* and *has-parent* have the inverse relation.

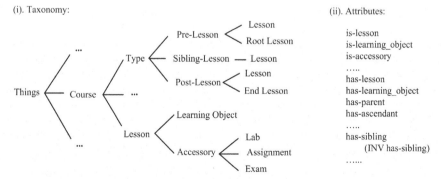

Fig. 3. (i). Learning path concepts are organized in a hierarchical classification. (ii). Attributes
used in learning path ontology are identified by using FCA attributes exploring.

4 Ontology Building

With the help of knowledge capturing, both domain expertise and conceptual hierarchy enable ontology building. Tim Berners-Lee presented the famous layer stack of semantic technologies at XML 2000 conference. Beyond knowledge representation languages of RDF, RDFS, and OWL, to fulfill his vision still needs rule and logic standardization for formal knowledge definitions. In ontology building stage, the logics are used to express formal definitions of knowledge representation. Thus, this section first introduces ontologies editing and then describes the utilization of logical formulism.

4.1 Ontology Editing

There are several graphical tools of ontology editor available, including Protégé, RICE, OWL-S, and so on. All of them offer an editing environment with a number of third party plug-ins such as the reasoner. This study utilizes Protégé as an ontology editor. The typical procedure of ontology building is editing classes (concepts), properties (relations) and constructing above components as taxonomy (T-Box). After establishing T-boxes, developers input real facts of learning materials followed the T-Box schema as assertional knowledge (A-Box). Finally, developers check the coherence of the ontology and derive inferred types of individuals to complete the ontology building. The ontology context can be stored as an OWL-based document for further utilization in reasoning systems.

4.2 Adding Description Logics

Protégé is utilized to build ontology hierarchical structure for representing conceptual knowledge. The basic relationship between concepts hierarchy is inheritance that represents *Is-a* relationship. For example, a subsumption expression *Lesson ⊑ Course* should be interpreted as the former class *Lesson* is the subclass of the later class *Course*. However, the *Is-a* hierarchy is insufficient to describe restriction criteria such as grouping, cardinality and part-whole aggregation. Thus, a logical system is expected to express a limitation on the range of types of objects.

The description logics (DLs) are derived from Horn logic and first order logic [6]. The DL has become popular and formally adopted in some knowledge representation languages such as OWL-DL and DAML+OIL [17]. To describe formal semantics, description logics are generally utilized as knowledge representation formalisms. In property descriptions, they may consist of functional characteristics such as inverse, transitive and symmetric; and apply scopes such as domains and ranges. In class definitions, the DLs notations express the semantic links which are consisted of DLs notations, properties and classes. The DLs notations are key roles to link property and concept pairs for restricting the scope of expressions. Three main DL restrictions categories can be used are:

- Quantifier restrictions: Specifying the existence of a relationship along a given property to an individual, two common quantifiers such as existential ($\exists$) or universal ($\forall$) representing some and only respectively.

- Cardinality restrictions: Describing the class of individuals that have at least (≥), at most (≤) or exactly (=) a specified number of relationships with other individuals or datatype values.
- Set operators: Set operators are used to specify unary relation such as complement (¬) and binary relation between classes such as union (∪) as well as intersection (∩).
- Expression definitions: A class that only has necessary conditions is known as a primitive class that can be use a subsumption symbol (⊑). A class that has at least one set of necessary and sufficient conditions is known as a defined class that is represent as an equivalent symbol (≡).

Protégé is capable to design DL-based ontology and typically comprises two components: T-Box and A-Box. The basic form of declaration of the T-Box is concept definition. For example, the accessory lesson can be defined as a union of several types of learning objects by writing the following declaration:

```
Accessory ≡Lab ∪ Assignment ∪ Exam
```

Logic-based knowledge presentation provides high level abstraction of the world, which can be effectively used to build intelligent applications. Modeling in DLs requires the developers to specify the concepts of the domain of discourse and characterize their relationships to other concepts and to specific individuals. The fundamental reasoning services in the T-Box are consistency and logical implication. The major reasoning services in the A-Box are instance checking and retrieval. Consequently, DL-based knowledge representation is considered the core of reasoning processes.

5 An Example

For simplicity, this study has assumed only four courses available in a learning site as our walkthrough example. Each course included several learning objects and their dependent learning materials. As illustrated in Figure 4, a learner may take a course in sequence order from top learning object to the end. However, the learning object 'Java Database Connectivity (JDBC)', for example, may have its dependent lessons such as a lab, its pre-lesson 'O-O programming' and 'Structure query language'. Of cause, each pre-lesson may have its pre-lesson. This study implements a pragmatic approach to apply ontology with available learning objects. Within this approach the following points are important.

Knowledge Capturing. In order to gather the common understanding of the domain of learning paths, eleven domain experts are invited, including three course instructors, two e-learning site developers, four experienced e-learning system users and two knowledge engineers. The major work of this stage is capturing human cognition of the learning paths. As depicted in the figure 2, the knowledge capturing task is implemented in an abstract view that only models common characteristics of this domain. Domain experts have to distinguish cognition into vocabularies (or terminologies) and attributes according to their expertise. For example, the cognition 'Pre-lesson' can be considered as a 'lesson' that is a 'learning object' and has at least one successor in terms of descendant. In this practice, a FCA context lattice involving 12 objects and 19 attributes was identified. Knowledge engineers further utilize a FCA tool to analyze relations and find implications among formal context. A prototype of conceptual hierarchy is then available for reference.

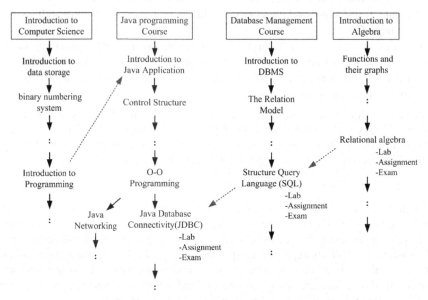

Fig. 4. A case study of learning path management

Ontology Building. Learning path ontology is built using Protégé. Within the editing tool, knowledge engineers create classes (i.e., concepts) and properties (i.e., relations); and compose classes as a hierarchical structure. Each class utilizes description logics to express formal definition of a concept. Since the inferred hierarchy derives more classification based on computation of implication discovering, this hierarchy will be useful for further utilization. In asserted conditions window, the description logic expresses formal definitions of the class 'Learning object'. The final step is entering the real facts as individuals of the ontology. Fifty-four learning objects and ninety-one dependent materials are booked in this scenario. Ontology and individuals then are kept in a repository with the OWL format.

Using Rules for Knowledge Query. The ongoing discussion of the topics related to semantic rules indicates that rule languages must be compatible and cooperate with existing logics system. This study utilizes the Semantic Web Rule Languages (SWRL) on top of the ontology layer. SWRL includes a high-level abstract syntax for Horn-like rules to be combined with an OWL knowledge base. The SWRL rules can be written by using some editor tools such as Protégé. While the abstract syntax of SWRL is representing a rule Antecedent→Consequent. Both antecedent and consequent are conjunctions of atoms using conjunction notation (∧) to connect together. As an example, consider a rule saying that the composition of ascendant and learning object properties implies the pre-lesson property would be written:

```
hasAscendant (?x, ?y)∧LearningObject(?y)➜ hasPreLesson
(?x, ?y)
```

Knowledge Retrieval. This study develops a reasoning mechanism by using Bossam that is a Java-based reasoner. The programmed mechanism provides the ability to interpret and infer OWL-based knowledge as well as SWRL queries. One the presentation side, the learning path user interface has been developed by using Java Server Page (JSP). After a user sends a questionnaire form of individual preference and background to the e-learning server, the system then replies a personal learning path suggestion to the individual user as illustrated in Figure 5. A tree-like learning path emphasizes the learner want to take a JDBC lesson. Several pre-lessons, dependent materials and follow-up lessons are recommended. If a user accepts this arrangement, then the learning path is kept in personal profile for further usage.

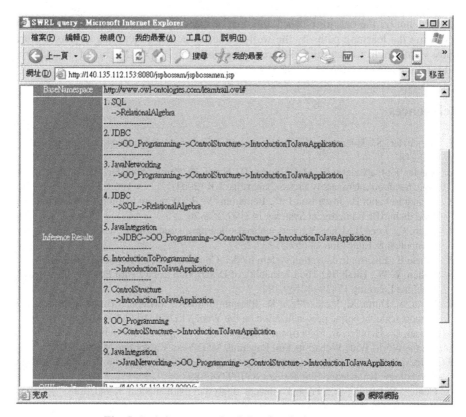

Fig. 5. An inference result of planning the learning path

6   Conclusion

This study describes a framework of knowledge building to strengthen learning path management in e-learning systems. The ontological approach is utilized to promote the management level from the data to semantic integration. This study has concisely demonstrated the details of ontological knowledge base development, including the capture of experts' cognition, conceptual structure normalization, ontologies editing and the addition of description logics for formal definition of concepts.

Our empirical findings are concluded as follows: (1). the challenge of knowledge capturing is to get the expertise in developing concepts that can be accepted in terms of a common understanding among system components. Thus, knowledge engineers must be trained to reconcile intuitive cognition with abstractive cognition for better knowledge modeling. (2). FCA can be used as an analysis approach to normalize the conceptual hierarchy among concepts and attributes. (3). Protégé is an ontology-based development environment, which provides concept building and formal logics expression for representing knowledge. (4). Bossam can be further utilized as a reasoner to facilitate knowledge inference and retrieval. The e-learning framework that takes advantages of ontological knowledge building provides efficient path management. Fundamentally, the ontology-based approach is effective to reduce the complexity of managing the learning paths by the well-defined structure of learning objects. Future study should help to determine where responsibility for SCORM should lie and provide some means to connect SCORM metadata.

References

1. Alexander, S.: E-learning developments and experiences. Education+Training 43 (2001) 240-248
2. Baader, F., Calvanese, D., McGuinness, D., Nardi, D., Parel-Schneider, P.: The description logic handbook. University Press, Cambridge UK (2003)
3. Chandrasekaran B., Josephson J. R., Benjamins V. R.: What are ontologies and why do we need them. IEEE Intelligent Systems 14 (1999) 20-26
4. Chen, C., Lee, H., Chen Y.: Personalized e-learning system using item response theory. Computers & Education 44 (2005) 237-255
5. Cloete E.: Electronic education system model. Computers & Education 36 (2001) 171-182
6. Cohen, W.W., Hirsh, H.: The Learnablity of Description Logics with Equality Constraints. Machine Learning 17 (1994) 169-199
7. Datta, A., Dutta, K., VanderMeer, D., Ramamritham, K., Navathe, S.B.: An architecture to support scalable online personalization on the Web. VLDB J. 10 (2001) 104-117
8. Fensel, D., Hendler, J., Lieberman, H., Wahlster, W.: Spinning the Semantic Web: Bringing the World Wide Web to Its Full Potential. MIT Press, Cambridge MA (2003)
9. Gaines, B.R., Shaw, M.L.G.: Knowledge Acquisition Tools based on Personal Construct Psychology. Knowledge Eng. Review 8 (1993) 49-85
10. Ganter, B., Wille, R.: Formal concept analysis: mathematical foundations. Springer-Verlag, Berlin Heidelberg New York (1997)
11. Gillam, L., Tariq, M., Ahmad, K.: Terminology and the construction of ontology. Terminology 11 (2005) 55-81
12. Gruber, T.R.: A translation approach to portable ontologies. Knowledge Acquisition 5 (1993) 199-220
13. Gruber, T.R.: Towards principles for the design of ontologies used for knowledge sharing. Int. J. of Human-Computer Studies 43 (1995) 907-928

14. Guarino, N.: Formal ontology, conceptual analysis and knowledge representation. Int. J. of Human-Computer Studies 43 (1995) 625-640
15. Guarino, N.: Understanding, building and using ontologies. Int. J. of Human-Computer Studies 46 (1997) 293-310
16. Gunasekaran, A., McNeil, R.D., Shaul, D.: E-learning: research and application. Industrial and Commercial Training 34 (2002) 44-53
17. Horrocks, I. Patel-Schneider, P.F.: Reducing OWL entailment to description logic satisfability. J. of Web Semantics 1 (2004) 345-357
18. Horrocks, I., Patel-Schneider, P.F., Harmelen, F.V.: From SHIQ and RDF to OWL: the making of a Web Ontology Language. Web Semantics: Science, Services and Agents on the World Wide Web 1 (2003) 7-26
19. Hui, B., Yu, E.: Extracting conceptual relationships from specialized documents. Data & Knowledge Eng. 54 (2005) 29-55
20. Kamba, T., Sakagami, H., Koseki, Y.: ANATAGONOMY: a personalized newspaper on the World Wide Web. Int. J. of Human-Computer Studies 46 (1997) 789-803
21. Noy, N.F., Hafner, C.D. : The State of the Art in Ontology Design. AI Magazine 18 (1997) 53-74
22. Uschold, M., Grueninger, M.: Ontologies: principles, methods and applications. Knowledge Eng. Review 11 (1996) 93-155
23. Zhang, D., Zhao, J. L., Zhou, L., Nunamaker, J. F.: Can e-learning replace classroom learning? Comm. of the ACM 47 (2004) 75-79

Measuring Similarity in the Semantic Representation of Moving Objects in Video

Miyoung Cho[1], Dan Song[1], Chang Choi[1], and Pankoo Kim[2,*]

[1] Dept. of Computer Science
Chosun University, 375 Seosuk-dong Dong-Ku Gwangju 501-759 Korea
`irune@chosun.ac.kr, songdan@stmail.chosun.ac.kr,`
`enduranceaura@gmail.com`
[2] Dept. of CSE, Chosun University, Korea
`pkkim@chosun.ac.kr`

Abstract. There are more and more researchers concentrate on the spatio-temporal relationships during the video retrieval process. However, these researches are just limited to trajectory-based or content-based retrieval, and we seldom retrieve information referring to semantics. For satisfying the naive users' requirement from the common point of view, in this paper, we propose a novel approach for motion recognition from the aspect of semantic meaning. This issue can be addressed through a hierarchical model that explains how the human language interacts with motions. And, in the experiment part, we evaluate our new approach using trajectory distance based on spatial relations to distinguish the conceptual similarity and get the satisfactory results.

1 Introduction

With the emerging technology for video retrieval, many researches are mainly emphasized on the video content. However, semantic-based video retrieval has become more and more necessary that can really reflect humans' meanings which are expressed by the natural human language during video retrieval. So, semantic-based video retrieval research has caused many researchers' attentions.

Since, the most important semantic information for video is based on video motion research which is the significant factor for video event representation. Specially, there have been a significant amount of event understanding researches in various application domains. One major goal of this research is to accomplish the automatic extraction of feature semantics from a motion and to provide support for semantic-based motion retrieval. Most of the current approaches to activity recognition are composed of defining models for specific activity types that suit the goal in a particular domain and developing procedural recognized by constructing the dynamic models of the periodic pattern of human movements and are highly dependent on the robustness of the tracking[9].

Spatio-temporal relations are the basis for many of the selections users perform when they formulate queries for the purpose of semantic-based motion retrieval. Although such query languages use natural-language-like terms, the formal definitions of these relations rarely reflect the language people would use when communicating

---

* Corresponding author.

J. Lang, F. Lin, and J. Wang (Eds.): KSEM 2006, LNAI 4092, pp. 78–87, 2006.
© Springer-Verlag Berlin Heidelberg 2006

with each other. To bridge the gap between the computational models used for spatio-temporal relations and people's use of motion verbs in their natural language, a model of these spatio-temporal relations was calibrated for motion verbs.

In the previous works, the retrieval using spatio-temporal relations is similar trajectory retrieval, it's only the content-based retrieval but not semantic-based. So, in this paper, we put forward a novel approach for mapping the similarity between different motion events(actions) to the similarity between semantic indexes based our new motion model. And, in the experiment part, we evaluate our new approach using trajectory distance based on spatio-temporal relations to distinguish the conceptual similarity and get the satisfactory results. We compare the similarity between motions with similarity between trajectories based on low-level features described by spatial relations in video.

2   Similarity Between Spatial Relations Based on Trajectory

In the video data, the trajectory of a moving object plays an important role in video indexing for content-based retrieval. The trajectory can be represented as a spatio-temporal relationship between moving objects, including both their spatial and temporal properties. User queries based on the spatio-temporal relationship are as follows: "Find all objects whose motion trajectory is similar to the trajectory shown in a user interface" or "Finds all shots with a scene that person enter the building "[5].

There have been some researches on content-based video retrieval using spatio-temporal relationships in video data. Most of the researchers retrieve information by directional relation, topological relation. John Z. Li et al.[4] represented the trajectory of a moving object as eight directions. And based on the representations for moving objects' directions, they measure similarity using distance of directional relations between the trajectory of object A and that of object B. Also, Pei-Yi Chen[8] measure velocity similarity by six possible velocity trends.

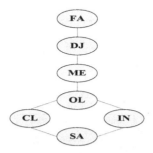

Fig. 1. The graph on topological relations

The figure 1 Shows the graph that represents distance among topological relations proposed by Shim[5]. The each node means spatial relation(SA=Same, CL=IsinCluded-by, IN=Include, OL=Overlap, ME=Meet, DJ=Disjoint, FA=Far away). Modeling topological relations is accomplished using a neighborhood graph. The

topological relation models attribute the same values at each edge of the neighborhood graphs. The table 1 describes the distance between topological relations. As it
shows, distance between same topological relations is 0, the distance between different topological relations is measured by count edge using the shortest distance.

Table 1. The distance between topological relations

	FA	DJ	ME	OL	CL	SA	IN
FA	0	1	2	3	4	5	4
DJ	1	0	1	2	3	4	3
ME	2	1	0	1	2	3	2
OL	3	2	1	0	1	2	1
CL	4	3	2	1	0	1	2
SA	5	4	3	2	1	0	1
IN	4	3	2	1	2	1	0

Considering the relations between two objects, we can measure the distance between them. In the table1, suppose we ignore the difference between FA and DJ, they
are the same.   So, the maximum distance among these relations is 4. In order to
change the motion's distance into similarity, we adopt the following method like the
formula shows:

$$sim(m_1, m_2) = S_{max} - distance[m_1, m_2]$$ (1)

Where, m_1 and m_2 mean motion to compare. S_{max} is the largest value in similarity
matrix about topological relations. For example, the figure 2 shows us similarity
measure between '*go to*' and '*enter*'.

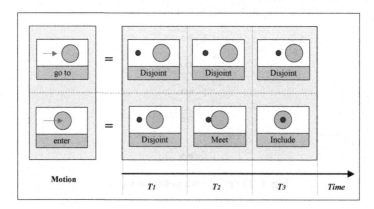

Fig. 2. Similarity between '*enter*' and '*go to*' by trajectory

'*go to*' and '*enter*' are represented as the combination of topological relations according to temporal change. The distance between two trajectories is the difference of

topological relations per each time. We can get 1.33 as distance between '*go to*' and '*enter*' by table 1. And it returns 2.67 as similarity value by equation 1.

However, most of the researches represent relation based on trajectory of moving object. They cannot describe recognition concept or meaning of motion. So, we cannot retrieve meaning or concept based information through natural language because the researches are not thorough going enough. In this paper, we represent semantic of moving objects in video using motion verbs. The basic idea of proposed method is that we build new structure on motion verbs by spatio-temporal relations. Also we reclassify motion verbs using our model.

3   Semantic Representation of Moving Objects in High-Level

Our final goal is to provide the basis for description in high-level about moving objects in video. We use motion verbs which are represented by natural language terms in video retrieval. Although there are many features to describe in high-level, we are concerned about the representation of motion verbs based on spatial relations.

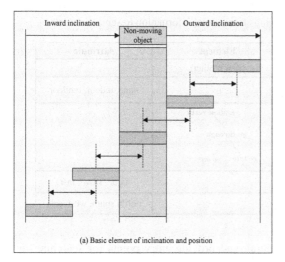
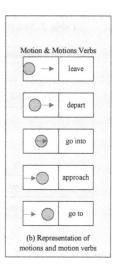

Fig. 3. Basic elements of inclination, motions and motion verbs

In the figure 3(a), it shows inclination and position of basic elements. The inclination was divided into inward and outward for representation of moving objects. We define '*leave*' and '*go to*' using inclination and position by combining FA with DJ. '*Depart*' and '*approach*' is defined using inclination and position from the definition of ME. We create 5 basic elements to represent motion of moving object based on figure 3(a)(See figure 3(b)). The distance between two adjacent elements is 1. It can apply to represent semantic motion as combination of basic terms.

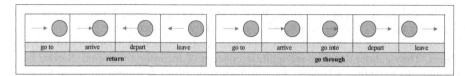

Fig. 4. Semantic Representation of Motion based on Spatio-temporal Relations

We apply our modeling which was combined the topological with directional relations to represent the semantic states based on the motion verbs. The figure 4 shows semantic representation of motions defined by the basic elements of motion verbs(*go to, arrive, depart* etc.). Specifically, semantic level observable corresponding to objects of interest are mapped directly to general concepts and become elemental terms. This is possible because the semantic meaning of each semantic level observable is clearly defined, and can be mapped directly to a word sense. The remaining semantic level information are used as contextual search constraints as described below. This formalism provides a grounded framework to contain motion information, linguistic information and their respective uncertainties and ambiguities.

Table 2. Selected mappings from visual information to semantic terms

Visual information	Element	Attribute
object	person(noun)	-
surrounding	-	none, indoor, outdoor
motion	motion verbs / go through / \ go into go out	-
motion speed	-	none, slow , fast
motion direction	-	north, south, west, east

Elemental terms are very general, and provide entry points for searching motion concept. To find more specific concepts present in the video, we need a more deterministic mapping, we have extended the concept with a small, fixed vocabulary of highly salient attributes. Concepts can be tagged with attribute values indicating that they are visible, capable of motion, and usually located indoors or outdoors. Topic attributes also indicate relevance to specific topics, by assigning topic membership to concepts.

As you can see figure 5, we represent structure using PART_OF relation. In PART_OF relation, A Concept represented by C_j is PART_OF a concept represented by C_i, if C_i has a C_j (as a part) or C_j is a part of C_i. Also, there are some antonym relations(For example, *go to* and *leave*).

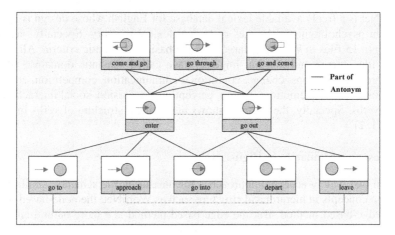

Fig. 5. Hierarchical Semantic Description for Motion Verbs

We can closely research on hierarchical structure of motion verbs. In the future works, it can be applied to semantic retrieval or indexing. Such as direction changes create the events like; person '*goes right side*' or '*goes left side*', or '*goes away*' or '*arrives*'. And velocity changes create the events person '*stops*' or '*walks*' or '*starts running*'.

4 Experiment and Evaluation

In this research, we made use of a total of 30 motion verbs and motion phrases as our experimental objects. As stated above, we omit tracking and detecting part to extract trajectory of moving object. We define a region that describes a non-moving object, while a line is used to describe the trajectory of a moving object. In order not to hurt accuracy of the experiment results, we consider the WordNet as criterion which is used to compare with our model, because WordNet describes conceptual relations among words by human knowledge.

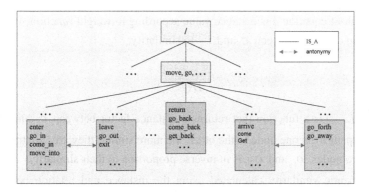

Fig. 6. Hierarchical structure about motion domain in WordNet

WordNet is a freely available lexical database for English whose design is inspired by current psycholinguistic theories of human lexical memory. Specially, verbs are divided into 15 files in WordNet, largely on the basis of semantic criteria. All but one of these files correspond to what linguists have called semantic domains: verbs of bodily care and functions, change, cognition, communication, competition, consumption, contact, creation, emotion, motion, perception, possession, social interaction, and weather verbs. Specially, the figure 6 shows hierarchical structure of verbs in motion domain [1, 2].

4.1 Measuring Similarity in High-Level

There are two widely accepted approaches for measuring the semantic similarity between two concepts in hierarchical structure such as WordNet; the node-based method and the edge-based method. But the edge-based method is a more natural and direct way of evaluating semantic similarity in hierarchical structure. So we use the former.

If the semantic distance between two adjacent nodes (one of them is a parent) is the following representation: $S_{ADJ}(c_i^l, c_j^{l-1})$. And we will expand $S_{ADJ}(c_i^l, c_j^{l-1})$ to handle the case where more than one edge is included in the shortest path between two concepts. Suppose we have the shortest path, p, from two concepts, c_i and c_j, such that $p = \{(t_0, c_0, c_1), (t_1, c_1, c_2)...(t_{n-1}, c_{n-1}, c_n)\}$. The shortest path p is the sum of the adjacent nodes. Therefore, the distance measure between c_i and c_j is as follows:

$$S_{edge}(c_i, c_j) = \sum_{k=0}^{n} W(t_k) \cdot S_{ADJ}(c_k, c_{k+1}) \qquad (2)$$

where, $W(t_k)$ indicates the weight function that decides the weight value based on the link type. The simplest form of the weight function is the step function. If the edge type is IS_A, then $W(t)$ returns 1 and otherwise returns a certain number that is more than 1 or less than 1. If the weight function is well-defined, it may return a negative value when the two concepts involved are associated by an antonym relation. However, the similarity between two concepts cannot be represented by a negative value. So we assume that the value of the antonym relation is the lowest positive value.

The result of equation 2 is distance value according to weight function. We need to change from distance between c_i and c_j to similarity.

$$Sim(c_i, c_j) = \frac{S_{edge}(c_i, c_j)}{D(L_{j \to i})} \qquad (3)$$

where, $D(L_{j \to i})$ is a function that returns a distance factor between c_i and c_j. The shorter the path from one node to the other, the more similar they are. So, the distance between two nodes, c_i and c_j, is in inverse proportion to their similarity.

The semantic similarity calculated using the distance and relation between the nodes. The similarity measure between motion verbs using equation 3 is as follows:

we try to calculate similarity between '*enter*' and '*leave*'. And we suppose the edge type between '*enter*' and '*leave*' is antonym relation. If $W(t)$ returns 0.5 by the weight function $Sim(enter, leave)$ is 0.25.

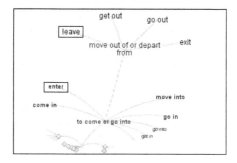

Fig. 7. Conceptual similarity calculations

4.2 Experiment

There are many features for similarity measure between trajectories. In this experiment, we measure similarity using only spatial relations that are described in section 2. We got the similarity values by the method which considers the spatial relation according to temporal change. To evaluate our model that has the good representation for the semantic information, we made a total of 30 motion verbs and motion phrases by the motion classification[3]. Appendix A lists the complete results of each similarity rating measure for each word pair, as determined by various methods, such as the WordNet-based and trajectory-based methods, as well as our proposed method.

We adopt the correlation coefficient to measure the correlation between human judgment(based on WordNet) and machine calculations(based on trajectory and our model). The correlation coefficient is a number between 0 and 1. If there is no relationship between the predicted values and the actual values the correlation coefficient is 0 or very low. A perfect fit gives a coefficient of 1. Thus the higher the correlation is coefficient the better.

Table 3. Summary of experimental results (30 verb pairs)

Similarity Method	Correlation
Trajectory-based Method	0.405
Proposed Method	0.708

The correlation values between the similarity and the human ratings in the Word-Net are listed in Table 3. It indicates that the result of our method is relatively close to the value according to human rating. Although we consider link type among concepts in this work, we cannot get the good correlation coefficient than previous work[10], because it's affected by step function of each link type. We will research on weight value by link type in the future works.

5   Conclusions and Future Works

With the development of the video retrieval technology, semantic based human language retrieval has become new trend. Among that, object motions in video based on spato-temporal relationships has been mainly concentrated. So, for catering for the users' requirement, we introduce a novel model about how to recognize the motion in video using motion verbs. We present hierarchical structure about motion (such as human action) by using spatial relations.

In the experiment, we prove our model that has the good representation for the semantic information by adopting the correlation coefficient to measure the correlation between human judgment(based on WordNet) and machine calculations(based on trajectory and our model) and get the satisfactory results. And referring to the future work, extending our novel motion verb model with more abundant motion verbs for gapping the chasm between high-level semantics and low level video feature is our further consideration.

Acknowledgement

This study was supported (in part) by research funds from Chosun University, 2004.

References

1. George A. Miller "Introduction to WordNet: An On-line Lexical Database", International Journal of Lexicography, 1990.
2. http://www.cogsci.princeton.edu/~wn/
3. Beth Levin, "English Verb Classes and Alternations", University of Chicago Press 1993.
4. John Z. Li, M. Tamer Ozsu, Duane Szafron, "Modeling of Moving Objects in a Video Database", In Proceedings of the International Conference on Multimedia Computing and Systems, pp. 336-343 , 1997.
5. Choon-Bo Shim, Jae-Woo Chang, "Spatio-temporal Representation and Retrieval Using Moving Object's Trajectories", ACM Multimedia Workshops, pp. 209-212, 2000.
6. M. Erwig and M. Schneider, "Query-By-Trace: Visual Predicate Specification in Spatio-Temporal Databases", 5th IFIP Conf. on Visual databases, 2000.
7. Z.Aghbari, K.Kaneko, A.Makinouchi, "Modeling and Querying Videos by Content Trajectories", In Proceedings of the International Conference and Multimedia Expo, pp. 463-466, 2000.
8. Pei-Yi Chen, Arbee L.P. Chen, "Video Retrieval Based on Video Motion Tracks of Moving Objects", Proceedings of SPIE Volume 5307, pp. 550-558, 2003.
9. Somboon Hongeng , Ram Nevatia , Francois Bremond, "Video-based event recognition: activity representation and probabilistic recognition methods", Computer Vision and Image Understanding, v.96 n.2, p.129-162, November 2004.
10. 10.Miyoung Cho, Dan Song, Chang Choi, Junho Choi, Jongan Park, Pankoo Kim, "Comparison between Motion Verbs using Similarity Measure for the Semantic Representation of Moving Object", CIVR 2006.

Appendix

A. Word pair semantic similarity measurement

Word pair		Similarity based on WordNet	Similarity based on trajectory	Similarity based on our model
go_to	arrive	0.25	3.5	0.6
approach	depart	0.2	3.5	0.575
go_to	go_into	0.25	2.2	0.6
approach	leave	0.25	4	0.25
go_to	cross	0.25	2.7	0.6
go_to	come_back	0.2	2.7	0.6
approach	go_back	0.25	2.7	0.6
arrive	depart	0.25	3	0.25
reach	enter	0.33	2.5	0.5
arrive	leave	0.33	3.5	0.575
reach	go_through	0.25	2.57	0.667
arrive	return	0.25	2.43	0.667
reach	come_back	0.33	2.43	0.667
arrive	go_back	0.25	2.57	0.667
depart	enter	0.25	2.25	0.5
depart	cross	0.25	2.57	0.667
go_into	leave	0.25	1	0.6
go_into	go_through	0.25	2.29	0.667
enter	return	0.25	2.64	0.5
enter	go_back	0.25	2.64	0.5
leave	go_through	0.25	2.7	0.6
leave	return	0.25	2.29	0.6
leave	come_back	0.25	2.29	0.6
return	come_back	1	4	1
return	go_back	1	2.14	1
go_to	approach	0.2	4	1
arrive	reach	0.5	4	1
go_into	enter	1	4	1
cross	go_through	0.5	4	1
come_back	go_back	1	4	1

A Case Study for CTL Model Update

Yulin Ding and Yan Zhang

School of Computing & Information Technology
University of Western Sydney
Kingswood, N.S.W. 1797, Australia
{yding, yan}@cit.uws.edu.au

Abstract. Computational Tree Logic (CTL) model update is a new system modification method for software verification. In this paper, a case study is described to show how a prototype model updater is implemented based on the authors' previous work of model update theoretical results [4]. The prototype is coded in Linux C and contains model checking, model update and parsing functions. The prototype is applied to the well known microwave oven example. This case study also illustrates some key features of our CTL model update approach such as the five primitive CTL model update operations and the associated minimal change semantics. This case study can be viewed as the first step towards the integration of model checking and model update for practical system modifications.

1 Introduction

As one of the most promising formal methods, automated verification has played an important role in computer science development. Currently, model checkers with SMV [2] or Promela [8] series as their specification languages are widely available for research, experiment, such as paper [11] and partial industry usage. Nowadays SMV, NuSMV [3], Cadence SMV [9] and SPIN [8] are well accepted as the state of the art model checkers. More recently, the MCK [5] model checker has added a knowledge operator to currently in use model checkers to verify knowledge related properties.

Buccafurri and his colleagues [1] applied AI techniques to model checking and error repairing. Harris and Ryan [6] proposed an attempt of system modification with a belief updating operator. Ding and Zhang [4] recently developed a formal approach called CTL model update for system modification, which was the first step towards a theoretical integration of CTL model checking and knowledge update. In this paper, we illustrate a case study of the microwave oven model to show how our CTL model updater can be used in practice to update the microwave oven example.

2 The Relationship Between Model Checking and Model Update

Model checking is to verify whether a model satisfies certain required properties. Model checking is performed by the model checker. The SMV model checker

J. Lang, F. Lin, and J. Wang (Eds.): KSEM 2006, LNAI 4092, pp. 88–101, 2006.
© Springer-Verlag Berlin Heidelberg 2006

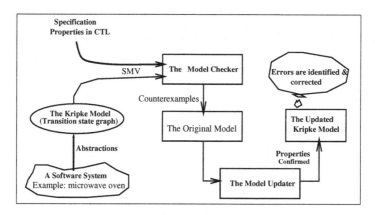

Fig. 1. The Model Checking and Model Update System

was first developed by McMillan [10] based on previous developed model checking theoretical results. This SMV model checker uses SMV as its specification language. Models and specification properties are all in the form of SMV language as the input. The SMV model checker parses the input into a structured representation for processing. Then, the system conducts model checking by SAT [2,7] algorithms. The output is counterexamples which report error messages as the result of model checking. During the model checking, there was a state explosion problem, which significantly increases the SMV model checking search space. The introduction of OBDD [2,7] in the SMV model updater solves the state explosion problem. After the first successful SMV compiler, the enhanced model checking compilers, NuSMV and Cadence SMV, were developed. NuSMV is an enhanced model checker from SMV and is more robust by the integration of a CUDD package [3]. It also supports LTL model checking. Cadence SMV was implemented for industrial use. The counterexample free concept is introduced in Cadence SMV. From SMV, NuSMV to Cadence SMV, the model checkers are developed from experimental versions to industrialized usage versions.

Model update is to repair errors in a model if the model does not satisfy certain properties. It is performed by the model updater. Our model updater updates the model after checking by the model checker if it does not satisfy the specification properties. The eventual output should be an updated model which satisfies the specification properties. In Fig. 1, the part of flow before "the original model" shows the model checking process. The part of flow after "The Original model" shows the model updater. The whole figure shows the complete process of model checking and model update.

3   The Theoretical Principles of the CTL Model Updater

Ding and Zhang [4] have developed the theoretical principle of the model updater. The prototype of the model updater described later is implemented based on these results. Before we introduce the CTL model updater, we review the CTL syntax and semantics and the theoretical results of CTL model update.

3.1 CTL Syntax and Semantics

Definition 1. *[2] Let AP be a set of atomic propositions. A Kripke model M over AP is a three tuple $M = (S, R, L)$ where 1. S is a finite set of states. 2. $R \subseteq S \times S$ is a transition relation. 3. $L : S \rightarrow 2^{AP}$ is a function that assigns each state with a set of atomic propositions (named variables in our system).*

Definition 2. *[7] Computation tree logic (CTL) has the following syntax given in Backus naur form (only listed syntax related to the case study in this paper):*

$$\phi ::= p|(\neg\phi)|(\phi \wedge \phi)|(\phi \vee \phi)|AG\phi|EG\phi|AF\phi|EF\phi$$

where p is any propositional atom.

Definition 3. *[7] Let $M = (S, R, L)$ be a Kripke model for CTL. Given any s in S, we define whether a CTL formula ϕ holds in state s. We denote this by $M, s \models \phi$. Naturally, the definition of the satisfaction relation $\models$ is done by structural induction on all CTL formulas (only listed semantics related to the case study in this paper):*

1. *$M, s \models p$ iff $p \in L(s)$.*
2. *$M, s \models \neg\phi$ iff $M, s \not\models \phi$.*
3. *$M, s \models \phi_1 \wedge \phi_2$ iff $M, s \models \phi_1$ and $M, s \models \phi_2$.*
4. *$M, s \models \phi_1 \vee \phi_2$ iff $M, s \models \phi_1$ and $M, s \models \phi_2$.*
5. *$M, s \models AG\phi$ holds iff for all paths $s_0 \rightarrow s_1 \rightarrow s_2 \rightarrow \cdots$, where s_0 equals s, and all s_i along the path, we have $M, s_i \models \phi$.*
6. *$M, s \models EG\phi$ holds iff there is a path $s_0 \rightarrow s_1 \rightarrow s_2 \rightarrow \cdots$, where s_0 equals s, and for all s_i along the path, we have $M, s_i \models \phi$.*
7. *$M, s \models AF\phi$ holds iff for all paths $s_0 \rightarrow s_1 \rightarrow s_2 \rightarrow \cdots$, where s_0 equals s, there is some s_i such that $M, s_i \models \phi$.*
8. *$M, s \models EF\phi$ holds iff there is a path $s_0 \rightarrow s_1 \rightarrow s_2 \rightarrow \cdots$, where $s_i = s$, and for some s_i along the path, we have $M, s_i \models \phi$.*

3.2 CTL Model Update with Minimal Change

Definition 4. *[4] (CTL Model Update) Given a CTL Kripke model $M = (S, R, L)$ and a CTL formula ϕ such that $\mathcal{M} = (M, s_0) \not\models \phi$, where $s_0 \in S$. An update of $\mathcal{M}$ with ϕ, is a new CTL Kripke model $M' = (S', R', L')$ such that $\mathcal{M}' = (M', s_0') \models \phi$ where $s_0' \in S'$. We use $Update(\mathcal{M}, \phi)$ to denote the result $\mathcal{M}'$.*

The operations to update the CTL model can be decomposed into 5 atomic updates called primitive operations in [4]. They are the foundation of our prototype for model update and are denoted as PU1, PU2, PU3, PU4 and PU5. PU1: adding a relation only; PU2: removing a relation only; PU3: substituting a state and its associated relation(s) only; PU4: adding a state and its associated relation(s) only; PU5: removing a state and its associated relation(s) only. Their mathematical specifications are in [4]. Model update should obey minimal change rules, which are described as follows.

Given models $M = (S, R, L)$ and $M' = (S', R', L')$, where M' is an updated model from M by only applying operation PUi on M. we define $Diff_{PUi}$ $(M, M') = (R - R') \cup (R' - R)$ $(i = 1, 2)$, $Diff_{PUi}(M, M') = (S - S') \cup (S' - S)$ $(i = 3, 4, 5)$ and $Diff(M, M') = (Diff_{PU1}(M, M'), \cdots, Diff_{PU5}(M, M'))$.

Definition 5. *[4](**Closeness Ordering***) Given three CTL Kripke models M, M_1 and M_2, where M_1 and M_2 are obtained from M by applying $PU1 - PU5$ operations. We say that M_1 is closer or as close to M as M_2. denoted as $M_1 \leq_M M_2$, iff $Diff(M, M_1) \preceq Diff(M, M_2)$. We denote $M_1 <_M M_2$ if $M_1 \leq_M M_2$ and $M_2 \not\leq_M M_1$.*

Definition 6. *[4] (**Admissible Update***) Given a CTL Kripke model $M = (S, R, L)$, $\mathcal{M} = (M, s_0)$ where $s_0 \in S$, and a CTL formula ϕ, $Update(\mathcal{M}, \phi)$ is called* admissible *if the following conditions hold: (1) $Update(\mathcal{M}, \phi) = (M', s_0')$ $\models \phi$ where $M' = (S', R', L')$ and $s_0' \in S'$; and (2) there does not exist another resulting model M'' such that $(M'', s_0'') \models \phi$ and $M'' <_M M'$.*

4   The Prototype of the CTL Model Updater

We have simulated a prototype of the CTL model updater in Linux C as the implementation of our algorithms. Unlike SMV, the input models are pre-specified in C code. Our system does not contain OBDD [7] optimization as the SMV mode updater. Thus, there is not excessive processing load for our prototype as with the SMV compiler for its parsing and checking phases. We have coded our own model checking functions to perform the model checking duty during the update process. The CTL model updater includes library functions, predefined model definition functions, a specification string parser, model checking functions and model update functions. The diagram of the code structure is shown in Fig 2. A detailed description of the system follows.

4.1   Predefined Structures and Library Functions

We have coded a set of pre-defined structures for the whole system. The most significant structures are the model definition structure, the state structure, the state data structure, and the atom and calc_pair structures for storing specification string parsing results.

The model definition structure contains the major elements of a CTL model. The definition structure contains a state pointer array and a state count, where each reachable state is defined in a state structure. The structure contains the names and number of the defined variables. The structure contains a path pointer array and a path count, where each path is defined in a path structure. The path is a structure containing a state count and array of state pointers. The

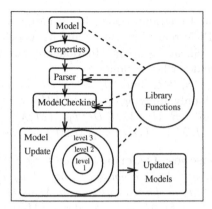

Fig. 2. The flow diagram of the Model Update System

structure in C code is as Fig 3. In this structure, "name" is the name of a model; "numvar" is the number of variables; "varname" is an array of variable names in a model; "numstates" is the number of non repeated reachable states in a model. "state[MAXSTATE]" is an array of pointers to state structures containing each non repeated reachable state; "numpaths" is the number of paths in a model; "path[MAXPATH]" is an array of pointers to the defining path structures. In our CTL model updater, the model definition structure is defined as an static instance. The change due to update on a model is eventually stored in the definition instance.

```
typedef struct {                          typedef struct {
        char name[MAXCHAR];                       int num;
        int numvar;                               boolean initial;
        char                                      boolean var[MAXVAR];
varname[MAXVAR][MAXCHAR];                         int numnext;
        int numstates;                            int next[MAXTRANS];
        state_ptr state[MAXSTATE];                int numprev;
        int numpaths;                             int prev[MAXTRANS];
        path_ptr path[MAXPATH];                   boolean result;
} state_defn;                             } state;
```

Fig. 3. The state definition structure   **Fig. 4.** The state structure in C code

The state structure is the major component defining a model. The state structure contains all information in a state in particular the values of the variables of the state, and the relations in between this state and its previous or successive states. The state structure is defined as Fig. 4. In this structure, "num" is an identifier as an integer of a state; "initial" is a boolean variable to define this state as an initial state in the model; "var[MAXVAR]" is an array of boolean variable values for this state; "numnext" is the total number of next states; "next[MAXTRANS]" is an array of the integer identifiers of next states; "numprev" is the total number of previous states; prev[MAXTRANS] is an array of the integer indentifiers of previous states. "result" is a boolean variable to store the checking result for the state.

Another major structure called "state_data" is an interface structure to actually load a state structure.

The library functions include all initializations of the model in the definition structure, simple operations for model checking and update, and printing functions for a model and its paths. For the initializations, there are functions for defining a model, its name and states, setting data in states, setting and clearing links in between states and so on. The simple operations for model checking and update include checking individual and all states in a model, checking a path or all paths in a model, adding or removing states, building or removing links in between states and calculating paths etc. The printing functions include printing states, paths and the model. The printing functions assist the user in understanding the operations performed by the model updater.

4.2 Parser

The parsing functions decompose a complex CTL formula, expressed as a string, into a number of linked structures. The components of the structures have direct equivalence to each recognizable component of the specification string as our case study illustrates below. For our system the part which needs to be parsed is the string representing the specification property, such as the property in the microwave oven model: "¬EF(Start∧ EG¬Heat)". Our parser rationalizes a CTL specification string according to the Backus Naur form [7] expressed as definition 2. There are two major structures used by our parsing library functions which store our parsing results.

An atom structure (Fig. 5) stores the results of parsing a symbol ϕ expression including ¬ and path navigation expressions. An atom structure assumes that the string contains semantics such as AG, EG and so on with a boolean atomic variable successor.

In Fig. 5, "negate1" is the negation symbol in front of "navigate" (such as AG or EG); if "negate1" is true, the negation symbol in front of "navigate" is there, otherwise, there is not a negation symbol; "negate2" is the negation symbol after "navigate". It behaves the same as "negate1"; "navigate" is the semantics about the model such as "AG" or "EG". We define numbers to represent different semantics. For example, "AF" is 4, "AG" is 5 and "EG" is 6; "varindex" is the index number of the variables in our system and represents the index position of the variable in the model definition object but includes an adder to avoid conflict with other indexes, which serves for our code only; "error" indicates whether the atom parsed correctly or not. If "error" is true, it means that the atom may not exist in our model. For example, if a string is "Start", which is a name of a variable in the model, then the structure of the parsed string should be the part of components after "operand1" and before "operand2" in Fig. 7. If a string

94   Y. Ding and Y. Zhang

```
                                         typedef struct {
                                                 boolean negate1;
                                                 boolean negate2;
                                                 int navigate;
                                                 optype operator;
typedef struct {                                 atom_ptr operand1;
        boolean negate1;                         atom_ptr operand2;
        boolean negate2;                         void * nestedpair1;
        int navigate;                            void * nestedpair2;
        int varindex;                            boolean error;
        boolean error;                   } calc_pair;
} atom;
```

Fig. 5. The atom structure in C   **Fig. 6.** The pair structure in C

is "EG¬ Heat", where "Heat" is a name of the variables in a model, then the
structure of the parsed string is the part of components after "operand2" and
before "nestedpair1" in Fig. 7.

A pair structure stores results of parsing an expression containing two ϕ expressions and a separating operator. This structure includes storage for a path
navigation expression and leading and following negate declarations. If the structure of a string is more complex than an atom, then it needs to be expressed
in a pair structure in Fig. 6. In this structure, "negate1", "negate2", "navigate"
and "error" are the same concepts as those in the atom structure; "operator" is
a logic symbol such as "∧" or "∨" and is defined as an integer in the structure;
"operand1" is the "atom" before "operator"; "operand2" is the "atom" after
"operator"; "nestedpair1" ("nestedpair2") is a casted type of "calc_pair" if the
string before (or after) "operator" is a "calc_pair", which can accommodate recursively nested "calc_pair" structures; For example, the string "AG(¬(Start∧
EG¬Heat))" can be parsed into the "calc_pair" structure as in Fig. 7. In this
figure, the elements before "nested pair1" match AG in the given string; the
elements after "nested pair1" and before "operator" are the "¬" after "AG";
"operator⋯ 22" is the "∧" in between "Start" and "EG¬ Heat"; the elements
after "operand1" and "operand2" are atoms which have been explained before
the pair structure description. During model checking and update, we select
the needed elements for any parts of the string from the corresponding parsed
structure.

The parser also contains a set of functions to rationalize negate symbols (normalize) in a specification to simplify processing. These functions use the parsing
structures as input and output.

4.3   Model Checking Functions

The model checking functions are for checking CTL semantics, such as whether
"AG", "EG", are true or not. They are continually used for the whole process
of update. Before or after each step of update, they are called to do model
checking and identify error or correct states according to different semantics or

primary pair →
    negate1 ⋯ false
    negate2 ⋯ false
    navigate ⋯ 5
    operator ⋯ 0
    operand1 ⋯ 0x00000000
    operand2 ⋯ 0x00000000
    nested pair1 →
        negate1 ⋯ true
        negate2 ⋯ false
        navigate ⋯ 0
        operator ⋯ 22
        operand1 →
            negate1 ⋯ false
            negate2 ⋯ false
            navigate ⋯ 0
            varindex ⋯ 101
            error ⋯ false
        operand2 →
            negate1 ⋯ false
            negate2 ⋯ true
            navigate ⋯ 6
            varindex ⋯ 103
            error ⋯ false
        nestedpair1 ⋯ 0x00000000
        nestedpair2 ⋯ 0x00000000
        error ⋯ false
    nestedpair2 ⋯ 0x00000000
    error ⋯ false

primary pair →
    negate1 ⋯ false
    negate2 ⋯ false
    navigate ⋯ 0
    operator ⋯ 23
    operand1 →
        negate1 ⋯ true
        negate2 ⋯ false
        navigate ⋯ 0
        varindex ⋯ 101
        error ⋯ false
    operand2 →
        negate1 ⋯ true
        negate2 ⋯ true
        navigate ⋯ 6
        varindex ⋯ 103
        error ⋯ false
    nestedpair1 ⋯ 0x00000000
    nestedpair2 ⋯ 0x00000000
    error ⋯ false

Fig. 7. The parsed structure for string "AG(¬(Start∧ EG¬Heat))"

Fig. 8. The parsed structure for string "$\neg Start \lor \neg EG \neg Heat$"

update requirements. Atomic model checking functions deal with model checking for atomic variables only. In our model checking functions, we have checking functions with "true" or "false" results to tell whether a specification property satisfies CTL semantics. To assess whether a state satisfies the required property or not, we compare the variables in a state with the variables in the required property. For particular semantics such as "EG", its model checking function is performed for each path, where each state is checked. If all states on at least one path satisfy the required property, then it means the model checking is "true" with semantic "EG". Besides, we also have functions which identify error or correct paths or states for particular CTL semantics, which will be used for model updating. For example, for semantics "EG", there are functions to identify correct or error states in a model or correct or error paths in a model. The information contained in these functions is the state or path identification numbers. If model update functions use them, they can locate the error paths or states straight away to perform model update on these states or related relations.

4.4 Model Update Functions

The model updating functions are the most important part of the system and demonstrate our previous theoretical results. They are called to update the model either on paths (eventually on states of the path) or states among all reachable states. The update functions frequently call model checking functions for each step update to see whether the updated model satisfies certain features or not. If the updated model satisfies the required feature, then the update is halted and the system returns updated models. The update obeys our minimal change rules. The resulting model could be more than one if they are not interchangeable. If the update changes the model, the definition structure containing the model is changed as well.

The update functions include atomic updates (level 1) PU1 to PU5, which update single states and their relations, and atomic update for variables in a state: adding or removing (changing) a variable. Above the atomic updates, we have 2nd level update functions for updating the semantics of a model such as AG, EG etc.. Above the 2nd level update functions, we have the outer level (level 3) update functions which are the combination of parsing, model checking and updating if the input string is not an atomic variable.

If the string representing the required property is not an atomic variable, then we parse the string before doing model checking and update. For example, if the input required property is AG(Start∧¬ Error), then all states in a model should satisfy the string after AG. The string, "Start∧¬ Error", should be parsed before further update for each state on this model. This process is performed by the functions at our 2nd and 3rd level updates which call the 1st level functions. During the process, parsing string and nested model checking and update involves certain degrees of intelligent reasoning depending on the semantics and complexity of the string. The reasoning is done by update functions on the 3rd level. If a required property is in a form such as "AG(Start)" where Start is a variable, then it can be performed by the 2nd level update functions which eventually call the 1st level update functions.

5   The Microwave Oven Model

The microwave oven model has a total of $2^4 = 16$ states, where there are 7 reachable states and one initial state, and 4 variables with boolean values. The Kripkle model of the microwave oven [2] is in Fig. 9, which shows its 7 reachable states $\{s_1, s_2, s_3, s_4, s_5, s_6, s_7\}$ and their 12 relations. The set of variables is $\{Start, Close, Heat, Error\}$ and each variable has boolean values. The specification property is "$\neg EF(Start \land EG\neg Heat)$". The result of model checking shows that the model does not satisfy the specification property. Our model updater will update the model and the updated models will satisfy the specification property.

The model is stored in an instance of the model definition structure. The specification is predefined in a char array (string). First, we should parse the specification string "$\neg EF(Start \land EG\neg Heat)$" into a parsing structure. Then, we

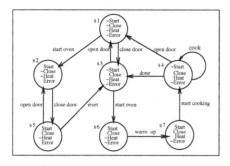

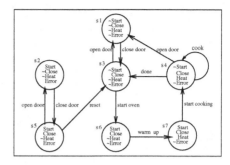

Fig. 9. The Original CTL Kripke Structure of a Microwave Oven

Fig. 10. The Updated Microwave Oven Model with Primitive Update PU2

convert the structure into a new structure corresponding to specification formula $AG(\neg(Start \wedge EG\neg Heat))$ to remove the front $\neg$. The conversion is performed by a normalize function. The parsing structure of the string "$AG(\neg(Start \wedge EG\neg Heat))$" is shown in Fig. 7.

Then, we must check each state's variables (because of AG) according to the property $\neg(Start \wedge EG\neg Heat)$ which is a nested calc_pair in our parsing structure. This is performed by a model checking process for AG which is called by level 3 update functions. We select $EG\neg Heat$ after $\wedge$" to update first, whose parsed elements are under "operand2" of "nested pair1" in Fig. 7, to apply model checking functions to identify a path (or paths) for which EG is valid. In this model, any path which has each state with variable $Heat$ false should be identified. Here, we find the paths $s_1 \rightarrow s_2 \rightarrow s_5 \rightarrow s_3 \rightarrow s_1 \cdots$ and $s_1 \rightarrow s_3 \rightarrow s_1 \cdots$ which are Strongly Connected Components (SCC) loops [2] satisfying $EG\neg Heat$. Then, we check where the states have variable $Start$ true, which is the atomic string before $\wedge$ in the specification string and maps the elements in between "operand1" and "operand2" under "nested pair1" in the parsed structure in Fig. 7. We identify states s_2, s_5,s_6 and s_7 with $Start$ true by model checking functions for AG because before $\wedge$ "$Start$" is atomic and the "AG" before "$Start$" should be mapped as the semantic symbol in front of "$Start$". Now, we must identify states which have both variables $Start$ true and $Heat$ false because of the "$\wedge$" operator between "Start" and "EG¬Heat". These states are s_2 and s_5. It means that the two states satisfy $Start \wedge EG\neg Heat$. However, the $AG(\neg$ before them in $AG(\neg(Start \wedge EG\neg Heat))$ specifies that the model should not have any state which satisfies this feature. Thus, we must update s_2 and s_5.

Now, the 2nd level update function for AG calls atomic (1st level) update functions such as PU1-PU5. The results are three equal minimal updates: for the atomic update PU2 case, relation (s_1, s_2) is deleted; for the atomic update PU5 case, state s_2 and relations (s_1, s_2), (s_2, s_5) and (s_5, s_2) are deleted; for the PU3 case, we must normalize the part of string after "AG" before PU3 is performed. $\neg(Start \wedge EG\neg Heat) = \neg Start \vee \neg EG\neg Heat$. The corresponding parsed structure for $\neg Start \vee \neg EG\neg Heat$ is as Fig. 8:

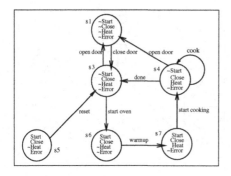

Fig. 11. The Updated Microwave Oven Model with Primitive Update PU5

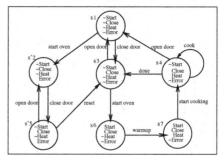

Fig. 12. The Updated Microwave Oven Model with Primitive Update PU3

Thus, eventually the faulty states s_2 and s_5 should be updated with either $\neg Start$ or $\neg EG\neg Heat$ in an update function for the $\lor$ operator. Obviously, $\neg Start$ is simpler thus is chosen. As we mentioned, the selection process involves certain intelligent reasoning.

After these updates, the resulting model $\mathcal{M}' = (M', s_1) \models \neg EF(Start \land EG\neg Heat)$. The above three resulting models are all minimally changed from the original model and are admissible. They are not interchangeable with each other due to our minimal change rules. The updated models are shown as Fig. 10, 11 and 12.

6   The Simulation Results for Updating the Microwave Oven Model

We show partial screen results by running the executable file as follows. In the beginning, the screen shows the model name, variables, states and relations in between states:

```
State Machine Model: Model name is Microwave Oven

            Variable name #1 is Start
            Variable name #2 is Close
            Variable name #3 is Heat
            Variable name #4 is Error

State Information for 7 states is ->
Id Initial        Values              Next Links       Previous Links
  1  ***  false false false false  -> 2 -> 3         <- 4 <- 3
  2       true  false false true   -> 5             <- 1 <- 5
  3       false true  false false  -> 6 -> 1         <- 1 <- 5 <- 4
  4       false true  true  false  -> 3 -> 1 -> 4   <- 7
  5       true  true  false true   -> 2 -> 3         <- 2
```

```
6        true   true   false false   -> 7                  <- 3
7        true   true   true   false   -> 4                  <- 6
```

We omit parsed structure and paths here. The states which must be updated are identified as s_2 and s_5. We only demonstrate three admissible updated results as follows.

```
Case 1: after PU2 update on the relation between state 1 & 2
```

```
State Information for 7 states is ->
Id Initial         Values             Next Links          Previous Links
 1   ***  false false false false   -> 3                  <- 4 <- 3
 2         true  false false true   -> 5                  <- 5
 3         false true  false false   -> 6 -> 1             <- 1 <- 5 <- 4
 4         false true  true  false   -> 3 -> 1 -> 4        <- 7
 5         true  true  false true    -> 2 -> 3             <- 2
 6         true  true  false false   -> 7                  <- 3
 7         true  true  true  false   -> 4                  <- 6
```

This output demonstrates the removal of the s_1 to s_2 state transition.

```
Case 2: after PU5 update on states 2 & 5
```

```
State Information for 6 states is ->
Id Initial         Values             Next Links          Previous Links
 1   ***  false false false false   -> 3                  <- 4 <- 3
 3         false true  false false   -> 6 -> 1             <- 1 <- 5 <- 4
 4         false true  true  false   -> 3 -> 1 -> 4        <- 7
 5         true  true  false true    -> 3
 6         true  true  false false   -> 7                  <- 3
 7         true  true  true  false   -> 4                  <- 6
```

This output demonstrates the removal of s_2 and its associated links.

```
Case 3: after PU3 update on states 2 & 5
```

```
State Information for 7 states is ->
Id Initial         Values             Next Links          Previous Links
 1   ***  false false false false   -> 3 -> 22            <- 4 <- 3
22         false false false true    -> 55                 <- 1 <- 55
 3         false true  false false   -> 6 -> 1             <- 1 <- 4 <- 55
 4         false true  true  false   -> 3 -> 1 -> 4        <- 7
55         false true  false true    -> 3 -> 22            <- 22
 6         true  true  false false   -> 7                  <- 3
 7         true  true  true  false   -> 4                  <- 6
```

This output demonstrates the modification of s_2 and s_5 (re-identified as 22 and 55) with updated variable values. 22 is $s'2$ and 55 is $s'5$ in Fig. 12.

7   Conclusions and Future Work

In this paper, we have demonstrated the implementation of model update theory and minimal change rules with a prototype based on the well known microwave oven example. It is an important step to advance model update from theoretical research to practice. At this stage, after we have successfully demonstrated the microwave oven example, we are coding another two well known examples: afs0 and afs1 models [11]. We intend to apply our model updater to these models as well to demonstrate hosting a more complex model with a larger number of states.

We are targeting to a formal CTL model update compiler which can accept SMV as input. Thus, our intention is that counterexamples from the existing SMV model checker will be used as part of the input of the model updater. The internal integration of our model update philosophy and the existing SMV model checker requires a comprehensive coding effort. This effort is a major future milestones for system modification and will significantly improves the usage of the SMV model checker.

Acknowledgement

The authors thank senior software engineer Neville Cockburn for his important guidance and help for this system implementation.

References

1. Buccafurri, F., Eiter, T., Gottlob, G. and Leone, N. (1999). Enhancing model checking in verification by AI techniques. *Artificial Intelligence* 112(1999) 57-104.
2. Clarke, E. Jr. et al. (1999). *Model Checking*, The MIT press, Cambridge, Massachusetts, London, England. ISBN 0-262-03270-8, Pp. 314.
3. Cimatti, A. et al. (1999). NUSMV: a new symbolic model verifier. In *Proceedings of the 11th International Conference on Computer Aided Verification*. Vol. 1633 in LNCS. Pp.495-499.
4. Ding,Y. and Zhang,Y.(2005). Model Update CTL Systems. In proceedings of The 18th Australian Joint Conference on Artificial Intelligence. Sydney, December, 2005. Pp.1-12.
5. Gammie, P. and van der Meyden, R.(2004). MCK-Model checking the logic of knowledge. In *the Proceeding of the 16th International Conference on Computer Aided Verification*. Pp. 479 - 483.
6. Harris,H. and Ryan,M. (2003). Theoretical foundations of updating systems. In *the Prodeeding of the 18th IEEE International Conference on Automated Software Engineering*. Pp.291-298.
7. Huth, M. and Ryan, M. (2000). *Logic in Computer Science: Modelling and Reasoning about Systems*. University Press, Canbridge.
8. Holzmann, Gerard. (2003). The SPIN Model Checking: Primer and Reference Manual. Addison-Wesley Professional. ISBN: 0321228626. Pp.596.

 9. McMillan,K. and Amla,N. (2002). Automatic abstraction without counterexamples. Cadence Berkeley Labs, Cadence Design Systems.
10. McMillan,K. (1992). The SMV System. `http://www.cs.cmu.edu/~modelcheck/smv.html`
11. Wing,J. and Vaziri-Farahani, M.(Oct.1995). A case study in model checking software. In proceedings of 3rd ACM SIGSOFT Symposium on the Foundations of Software Engineering.

Modeling Strategic Beliefs with Outsmarting Belief Systems

Ronald Fadel

Department of Computer Science
Stanford University

Abstract. We propose a model that formalizes the beliefs of agents in strategic environments and restricts their possible behaviors, without the typical epistemic assumptions used in game theory. We formalize the beliefs of an agent using *outsmarting belief systems* (OBS) and then propose the notion of *belief stability* to explain why some OBSs, in particular some that should occur in equilibrium, are more sensitive to perturbations than others. Also, we propose the concept of *belief complexity* as a criteria to restrict the possible OBSs. This allows us to formalize the notion of strategic communication as *belief engineering*, in which agents act in order to have other agents believe some low-complexity OBS. These concepts provide a new approach to understand why some equilibrium and non-equilibrium strategies are seen in practice, with applications to the centipede game.

1 Introduction

Explaining behavior that is not completely rational has traditionally been avoided by economists. This limitation has proven reasonable in the one agent, decision making setting, which is usually seen in microeconomics. After all, in practice, each agent is typically better off trying to approximate as much as possible the rational behavior. It is more debatable in strategic environments, which are formalized as *games* in game theory, where agents might take into account not only each other's approximation and limited rationality, but also each other's account, and so on *ad infinitum*. This might cause significant discrepancies between the "rational" expectations of the game theorist, and the empirical results (e.g. [8]).

Formally, most of game theory is built on two epistemic assumptions: common knowledge of the game and common knowledge of the rationality of the agents. These two assumptions are at the core of the concepts of rationalizable strategic behavior [1] and Nash equilibrium, where each agent plays an optimal strategy while anticipating that the other agents are doing the same. The relevance of most of the results in this field is very sensitive to these assumptions.

In this paper, we propose a new approach to characterize the behavior of agents in strategic environments, without the above common knowledge assumptions. We consider that each agent might consider other agents as not completely rational. Furthermore, each agent has a belief about which game he is playing, but he might believe the other agents to have different beliefs about this same

J. Lang, F. Lin, and J. Wang (Eds.): KSEM 2006, LNAI 4092, pp. 102–113, 2006.

game. Loosely speaking, each agent's belief and behavior can take into account that he "outsmarts" all the other agents, by thinking more steps ahead, or by knowing the game better. Note that this cannot be expressed within the logic of knowledge, as the beliefs are inconsistent. Also, it allows non-equilibrium behaviors: the agents' behaviors in the game might be inconsistent with their initial beliefs.

This approach is particularly relevant when considering cases for which the typical Nash equilibrium analysis has failed to provide a convincing explanation of experimental results. In particular, this is the case in speculative trade and the centipede game, or when bluff is involved. It is also applicable in environments where the common knowledge assumptions are disturbed by external events.

After defining our central notion of "outsmarting belief system" (OBS), we focus on characterizing the OBSs that are the most likely to occur. First of all, we define "belief stability" and we show that some OBSs that occur in Nash equilibria are not necessarily stable to perturbations in the common knowledge of the game assumption. Second, we propose a notion of "belief complexity" to reduce the set of possible OBSs by formalizing the fact that rationally bounded agents consider only the simplest (low-complexity) ones. Finally, we apply the notion of belief complexity to show that some communications and actions by an agent can be interpreted as "belief engineering", which is an attempt to change the OBSs of the other agents. To the author's knowledge, this is the first coherent use of complexity arguments to restrict the possible epistemic beliefs of agents in a game.

2   Background

2.1   The Game Theory Setting

In game theory, a strategic environment with $I = \{1, ..., I\}$ agents is modeled as a game $G : S^1 \times ... \times S^I \to \mathbb{R}^I$, with, for every single Agent i, one input $s^i \in S^i$ and one output $u^i \in \mathbb{R}$ to describe his strategy and his outcome respectively. We assume common knowledge among the agents of the game and the rationality of every agent: every agent is rational and knows the game G, and every agent knows that, every agent knows that every agent knows that etc...

In a Nash equilibrium, all agents correctly forecast each others' decisions $s_{Nash} = (s_{Nash}^1, ..., s_{Nash}^I)$, while they all individually maximize their own utilities, i.e. $s_{Nash}^i \in \arg max_{s \in S^i} G^i(s_{Nash}^1, ..., s_{Nash}^{i-1}, s, s_{Nash}^{i+1}, ..., s_{Nash}^I)$. This celebrated Nash equilibrium concept can give very accurate results about how agents behave in strategic environments. However, it has sometimes proven inaccurate, or too restrictive, to explain empirical results. In particular, a Nash equilibrium need not be unique, and need not even exist, and the concept of mixed strategy Nash equilibrium, with its controversial intuition, has only partially filled the gap.

The concept of rationalizable strategic behavior [1], close to backward induction, states that each agent plays a rationalizable strategy, which is defined circularly as a best response to the other agents' rationalizable strategies. It is less restrictive than Nash equilibrium: a Nash equilibrium strategy is necessarily a rationalizable strategy, but a rationalizable strategy need not be a Nash equilibrium strategy. However, this concept has also proven inapplicable to explain many experimental results.

2.2 Related Work

In the spirit of our work, behavioral game theory [3] has introduced psychological considerations in games. In particular, empirical studies have shown that people are not indifferent to other people's payoffs, and consider notions like fairness when choosing their strategy, which suggests that the real (utility-wise) strategic environment need not be one game, but several games, and thus contradicts the common knowledge of the game assumption. Also, other studies show that even the brightest people rarely think more than three or four steps ahead.

2.3 Main Example: The Centipede Game

Our main example in this paper is the centipede game. It is a typical example where the unique Nash equilibrium is not seen in practice.

The centipede game of depth n is a two-agent game G_n which has n steps. We assume an even number n of steps for simplicity. At each step, only one agent acts and agents alternate their turns, starting with Agent 1 who receives \$1 before his first action. At each of his turns, the agent who acts can either stop or continue the game. If he decides to stop, his outcome is whatever he has received during the game. But if he decides to continue, he has to pay \$1 while at the same time the other agent receives \$2.

The game stops at the nth step. The effective strategy of each agent is just the step at which he decides that he will stop, given that he got to this step. Hence, the strategy spaces are just $\{s_1^1, s_3^1, s_5^1, ... s_{n-1}^1, s_{never}^1\}$ for Agent 1, and $\{s_2^2, s_4^2, s_6^2, ... s_n^2, s_{never}^2\}$ for Agent 2.

We consider G_n as a function $G_n : S_n^1 \times S_n^2 \to \mathbb{R}^2$ with strategy spaces $S_n^1 = \{s_1^1, s_3^1, s_5^1, ... s_{n-1}^1, s_{never}^1\}$ and $S_n^2 = \{s_2^2, s_4^2, s_6^2, ... s_n^2, s_{never}^2\}$ and where the value of G_n gives the utility of each agent, given the strategies of the agents. A part of the game in the normal form is:

G_n	s_2^2	s_4^2	s_n^2	s_{never}^2
s_1^1	$(1,0)$	$(1,0)$	$(1,0)$	$(1,0)$
s_3^1	$(0,2)$	$(2,1)$	$(2,1)$	$(2,1)$
s_5^1	$(0,2)$	$(1,3)$	$(3,2)$	$(3,2)$
s_{n-1}^1	$(0,2)$	$(1,3)$	$(n/2, n/2-1)$	$(n/2, n/2-1)$
s_{never}^1	$(0,2)$	$(1,3)$	$(n/2\text{-}1, n/2+1)$	$(n/2+1, n/2)$

The Nash equilibrium strategies (and in fact, the only rationalizable strategies) are s_1^1 for Agent 1 and s_2^2 for Agent 2. However, empirical results show that these strategies are almost never seen in practice for a reasonably large n (say $n > 10$). Refer to [8] for more details.

3   Outsmarting Belief Systems

3.1   The Interpretation

In our approach, the actual game is not necessarily given and known by the agents. Each agent uses his own beliefs to anticipate his utility for each outcome. He also uses his beliefs about the other agents' characteristics to anticipate their beliefs about their utilities for each outcome, and so on at each step of his reasoning. In other words, the game and its contingent payoffs are not a given fact. Instead, each agent has to evaluate the environment and how the others evaluate the environment, in order to finally assess other agents' strategies and finally his own. In particular, there is an unbounded number of games to consider in each OBS: the game that the agent believes he is playing, the game that the agent believes each other agent believes he is playing and so on *ad infinitum*. Hence we reject the assumption of common knowledge of the game.

Also, we reject the common knowledge of rationality assumption: an agent may consider the other agents as irrational, or, for example, he may consider that some of the other agents consider him as irrational.

The fundamentally agent-centric view that is adopted in this paper may lead to some ambiguity. We do not make a distinction between knowing and believing, because we are not considering any "true" world. The reader should always interpret the mention of the knowledge of an agent as what he believes to be true (as what he is "confident" about, as in [5]). In particular, contrasting with the classical game theory setting, we might be in an environment where the agent does not know as much as the scientist that is trying to model his behavior.

3.2   The Formalism

For simplicity, we consider only two-agent environments. The semantics of Agent 1 having OBS $\beta = sG\beta'$ is that Agent 1 chooses strategy s, that he believes that his own outcome is determined by G, and also that he believes that Agent 2 has OBS β'. Note that G is only a *partial game*, i.e. it determines the conditional outcomes of only one agent. Formally:

Definition 1. *Let* $\xi = \{G_1, G_2, G_3...\}$ *be a set of games. Each* $G_j : S_j^1 \times S_j^2 \to \mathbb{R}^2$ *has strategy space* S_j^i *for each Agent i and* G_j *satisfies* $G_j(s_1, s_2) = (G_j^1(s_1, s_2), G_j^2(s_2, s_1))$, *where* G_j^1 *and* G_j^2 *are the partial games of* G_j. *An outsmarting belief system* β *for Agent i over* ξ *is:*

- *A single strategy:* $\beta = s^i \in \bigcup_j S_j^i$.
- *For any strategy* $s^i \in S_j^i$, *partial game* G_j^i, *and OBS* $\beta' = s^{-i}...$ *for Agent* $-i$ *such that* $s^{-i} \in S_j^{-i}$: $\beta = s^i G_j^i \beta'$.
- *For any* G_j^i *and OBS* $\beta' = s^{-i}...s^i$ *for Agent* $-i$ *such that* $s^i \in S_j^i$ *and* $s^{-i} \in S_j^{-i}$: $\beta = \beta' G_j^i \beta' G_j^i \beta' G_j^i \beta' G_j^i...$.

An OBS $s_1 G_1 s_2 G_2 s_3 G_3...$ *is valid iff, for all applicable k:*

$$s_{k-1} \in argmax_s G_{k-1}(s, s_k)$$

This formalism implies the following fact: an agent does not take into account what he believes the other agents' conditional outcomes are, only what he believes the other agents' beliefs about their conditional outcomes are.

For simplicity we might use complete games instead of partial games in our description of an OBS. For example, if the game G is common knowledge among the agents, we will describe the OBS of Agent 1 as $s_1 G s_2 G s_3 G$.... The reader should consider the first (and third, fifth etc...) mention of G in the OBS to refer to the partial game of G that gives the outcome of Agent 1, and the second (and fourth, sixth etc...) mention of G to refer to the partial game of G that gives the outcome for Agent 2.

The only restriction that we have on the OBSs is that each strategy considered in the OBS is locally optimal, in the sense that each agent maximizes his utility with respect to his belief of what is his environment, and this is, loosely speaking, commonly known. It is formalized with our notion of *validity* of an OBS. All the OBSs we consider are valid, unless stated otherwise.

We call *level* each pair consisting of a strategy followed by a game, e.g. $s_1 G$ is the first level of the OBS $\beta = s_1 G \beta'$. We call *depth* the number of levels mentioned in the OBS, e.g. $s_1 G s'$ is an OBS of depth 1. Note that if the OBS of Agent i is of depth n, it implies that Agent i considers that Agent $-i$ has an OBS of depth $n-1$. We call *decision* the strategy that the agent having a given OBS chooses (it is s_1 in $\beta = s_1 G \beta'$).

For OBSs of infinite depth, we use overlining to express infinite repetition. E.g. $s_1 G_1 \overline{s_2 G_2 s_3 G_3}$ is a contraction for $s_1 G_1 s_2 G_2 s_3 G_3 s_2 G_2 s_3 G_3...$

In case the OBS is finite, the final strategy, which we call *tail*, is the only one that is not maximizing any game. It can be considered as an initial focal point, or some initial belief. We discuss it in more details in Section 5.1.

Note that we do not take into account whether the beliefs of the agent having an OBS β correctly reflects the environment. We are only formalizing what is in one agent's mind, as incorrect as it may be.

3.3   Relation with Nash Equilibrium and Rationalizable Strategic Behavior

Proposition 1. *For any two-agent game G:*

- *The set of Nash equilibria is the set of pairs of strategies (s_1, s_2) such that the OBS $s_1 G s_2 G s_1$ is valid.*
- *The set of rationalizable strategies for any agent is the set of decisions s_1 of valid OBSs that are infinite and only mention the game G, i.e. are of the form $s_1 G s_2 G s_3 G s_4...$*

Loosely speaking, common knowledge of the game is expressed in an OBS by having only one game mentioned in the OBS, whereas common knowledge of rationality is expressed by the OBS being infinite. Proposition 1 describes how these assumptions yield the concept of rationalizable strategic behavior.

If (s_1, s_2) is a Nash equilibrium of a game G, we consider $\overline{s_1 G s_2 G}$ and $\overline{s_2 G s_1 G}$ to be OBSs associated with the equilibrium.

3.4   The Challenge

Our formalism can model in a flexible way beliefs of agents in many strategic environments that cannot be formalized in game theory, from bluff and cheating to speculative trade (see Appendix for examples). Now the challenge is to characterize the possible OBSs of the agents when they play a game. We should not expect to draw definite conclusion, as it is sometimes the case in the traditional approach, because we have fewer assumptions to start from. However, we use this formalism to investigate what can happen which leads to unexpected behaviors, and why it does happen.

4   Belief Stability

Our first application of OBSs is to study the stability of a belief, i.e. how much its decision is influenced by perturbations on the perception of the game. That is, suppose that you are an agent with an OBS β, how much will your behavior be influenced if you are suddenly less confident about what is the game played, or about what is the other agent's belief about it, or his belief about your own belief, etc...

Let G_n be the centipede game of depth n described in Section 2.3. The OBSs that correspond to the unique Nash equilibrium are $s_1^1 G_n s_2^2 G_n$ for Agent 1 and $s_2^2 G_n s_1^1 G_n$ for Agent 2. These OBSs both have in common that it would be sufficient to consider some significant change in one of the strategies or games mentioned in the first n levels to automatically need to change their decision strategies to keep the OBS valid. In other words, if I am Agent 1, it would be sufficient that I believe that you believe that I believe $[k \leq n$ times]... that I [or you] play some particular strategy $s_1' \neq s_1^1$ $[s_2' \neq s_2^2]$ for me to decide that I should not to play s_1^1.

First, we see how the games can be modified in the OBSs of the agents, and then show that the OBSs of the Nash equilibrium of the centipede game are unstable.

4.1   Game Topology

Since we are going to consider possible changes in how the game is perceived (or is believed to be perceived at some level in the OBS), we need to have a notion of distance between two games. To this end, the *game metric* quantifies by how much a game is different from another.

It is clear that small changes in the outcomes of the participants should yield a game that is close to the original one. Hence, the most straightforward game metric is defined in this simple way:

Definition 2. *The natural game metric is the function δ defined over the set of pairs $(G, G') = (G_1 \times G_2, G_1' \times G_2')$ of two-agent games such that:*

- $\delta(G, G') = \sqrt{\sum_{l=1}^{2} \sum_{(s,s') \in S} (G_l(s, s') - G_l'(s, s'))^2}$ *if G and G' have the same strategy spaces.*
- $\delta(G, G')$ *is undefined (infinite by convention) otherwise.*

Although we might construct many other game metrics, for simplicity we will use this natural game metric δ.

4.2   Stability

If we expect agents to doubt about *what* is the game, then they should doubt more about what is the game for the other agent, and even more about what is the game for them in the other agent's beliefs etc... The notion of belief stability formalizes this intuition by considering that, for an OBS to be stable, its decision should resist to small modifications in its first game and subsequent (linearly) bigger modifications in the following games. Formally

Definition 3. *The belief stability of an OBS β under the game metric δ is the largest $\sigma \in \mathbb{R}$ such that, for all OBSs β' satisfying:*

- *Let G_k and G'_k be the games in level k in β and β' respectively, then $\delta(G_k, G'_k)$ $\leq k \times \sigma$.*
- *β' is valid*

then β' has the same decision than β

Let us consider the belief stability of the OBSs associated with the Nash equilibrium of the centipede game. The higher is the belief stability of this OBS, the most robust is the Nash equilibrium prediction.

Proposition 2. *Let G_n be the centipede game with depth n. Then, as $n \to +\infty$, the stability σ_n^i of the OBS of the Nash equilibrium for every agent i goes to 0 under the natural game metric.*

Informally, with any small relaxation of the assumption of common knowledge of the game, the Nash equilibrium strategies in G_n are not entailed anymore for a sufficiently high n.

5   Belief Complexity

We define the notion of belief complexity to characterize the relevance of a given OBS given that we do not have the assumption of common knowledge of rationality. There are several reasons why agents tend to have low belief complexity OBSs:

- Having low rationality, it might be hard for them to consider far-fetched, high complexity OBSs.
- Even with high rationality, an agent might believe the other agents to have a low OBS due to their lack of full rationality, and so on, creating a focal point on low complexity beliefs.
- The fact that there are relatively fewer low-complexity than high-complexity OBSs also increases their focality.

Hence belief complexity is a criteria to choose among all possible OBSs the ones that are most likely.

5.1   Complexity Function

Using the Kolmogorov complexity [7] of the OBS $K(\alpha|I)$, where I contains all the knowledge that is given to the agents, is an intuitively appealing solution. In particular, "focal" strategies typically have low Kolmogorov complexity, and the OBSs of Nash equilibriums, although infinite, would have a finite complexity (because of the repeating patterns). However, it is well known that Kolmogorov complexity becomes relevant only with substantially high amounts of information (to offset the machine dependency of the result), and OBSs can usually be represented by a few bits.

Also, because of the semantics of OBSs, the deeper is the OBS, the more we should expect the end of the OBS to be "focal" (see [13]), because, in the considered agent's belief, this end is considered by both agents, and they both know it (and so on several times). To enforce this restriction, we consider that the tail of an OBS with low-complexity should be a "focal" strategy, but we still need to define which ones are focal, and which ones are not.

We propose the following method to decide on the complexity of an OBS, assuming common knowledge of the game. We decide on a *strategy complexity function* K over the strategy set, in the spirit of focal points and Kolmogorov complexity. In particular, K assigns a low complexity to the strategies that are in a focal Nash equilibrium, and those that are "easy" to represent. Then:

Definition 4. *Given a valid OBS β that mentions only one single game G, the belief complexity $BC(\beta)$ with strategy complexity K is defined recursively:*

- $BC(\beta) = +\infty$ *if β is not valid, or is of depth 0*
- $BC(sGs') = K(s')$
- $BC(\beta) = 1$ *if $\beta = s_1\overline{G_1s_2G_2s_3}$*
- $BC(sG\beta') = 1 + BC(\beta')$ *otherwise*

5.2   Example: Low Complexity OBSs in the Centipede Game

For each agent, it is natural to consider the most focal strategies the one that stops always (as soon as possible) and the one that never stops. They are the easiest to encode and have the particularity of being the two extremes among the set of strategies. So let's define the strategy complexity function as being $K(s_1^1) = K(s_{never}^1) = K(s_2^2) = K(s_{never}^2) = 0$ and $K(s) = +\infty$ for the other strategies. Then, the OBSs with complexity less than 1 for Agent 2 according to the belief complexity function BC are: $s_n^2Gs_{never}^1$, $s_i^2Gs_1^1$, for all i, which all have complexity 0, and $s_n^2Gs_{never}^1Gs_{never}^2$, $s_i^2Gs_1^1Gs_2^2$, for all i, and $s_i^2\overline{Gs_1^1Gs_2^2}$ for all i, which have complexity 1.

6   Belief Engineering

In the spirit of inductive reasoning, we propose the notion of belief engineering to explain, on the one hand, how the agents' behaviors are influenced by previous actions and communications, and on the other hand, how agents might use this causality to change the OBSs of each other.

6.1 Strategic Communication

Belief complexity allows us to consider some OBSs as more natural than others. Besides characterizing what are the most important OBSs, and their associated decision strategy, another application is to offer a formalization of "strategic communication" as a belief engineering process. This process describes how an agent might act in order to communicate some information, and give the other agent a particular OBS. It is based on the following assumptions:

– Agents have some inductive reasoning that makes them reject their current OBSs if it is not compatible with observation.
– Agents tend to have low complexity OBSs.
– Agents use these facts to modify each other's OBSs.

6.2 The Belief Engineering Criteria

Definition 5. *Agent i follows the belief engineering criteria of level α with respect to belief complexity function BC iff, at any point in the game, its OBS β has a complexity $BC(\beta) \leq \alpha$ and is compatible with the current history of the game, i.e. all agents' previous actions are compatible with the strategies that are assigned to them in β.*

Whereas the notion of belief stability allowed us to consider the Nash equilibrium strategies as unstable for some games, now we push the conclusion even further, still using the centipede game as an example. We get:

Proposition 3. *Suppose that Agent 2 follows the belief engineering criteria of level α with respect to the complexity function described in Section 5.2. For any α, there is a minimum depth d such that, for all $n \geq d$: Agent 2 does not choose "stop" at the second step of the centipede game G_n if Agent 1 chose "continue" at the first step.*

This proposition formalizes the following intuition: in Agent 2's beliefs, if Agent 1 does not stop at the first step, it is unlikely that he stops before a few steps from the end, because his associated OBS would have to be very complex. Furthermore, we should expect Agent 1 to use this fact: for a sufficient depth in the centipede game, and a given complexity function, if Agent 1 believes Agent 2 follows the belief engineering criteria, it is not optimal for him to have the Nash equilibrium strategy s_1^1.

7   Summary and Comments

Starting from the observation that game theory has heavily relied on strong assumptions which have sometimes yielded inappropriate results, we have proposed here an alternative way to analyze behaviors in strategic environments without the usual assumptions of common knowledge of the game and of the rationality of the agents. We formally defined outsmarting belief systems to model the beliefs of agents in a flexible and primitive way, with the goal of describing some of their beliefs that could not be described within the typical game theoretic framework. OBSs have proven to be flexible enough to yield some typical concepts of game theory, like Nash equilibrium and rationalizable strategic behavior, and also to formally represent environments like speculative trade, where agents "agree to disagree".

Then, we have shown that some OBSs that correspond to Nash equilibriums are very sensitive to perturbations on the beliefs about the game, and we have defined the concept of belief stability to formalize this intuition. To this end, we have defined a game metric to quantify how much games are different from each other.

Belief complexity aims at understanding why some beliefs, and hence their associated behaviors, are more likely to occur in an agent's mind. It relies on some other factors than the game itself, and at this point, it is not clear what the right belief complexity function should for a given game. Nevertheless, we proposed a belief complexity function that seems natural in the centipede game.

We have used the notions of OBS and belief complexity to describe the concept of belief engineering. In a bounded rationality environment, agents' are likely to act, either formally through actions in the game or, more generally, through informal communication (bargaining, commitment...), in order to make the other agents have some particular OBSs, and hence to influence the other agents' future behaviors. The concept of belief engineering aims at formalizing this strategic communication. As an example, belief engineering has been used to explain why backward induction is inapplicable in environments like the centipede game, where a first "continue" action should be seen as communicating the inapplicability of the OBSs of the Nash equilibrium, which forces the agents to have another, low-complexity OBS.

An immediate addition to the formalism is to consider probabilistic OBSs. In particular, agents may have several interpretations of the world, and hence several contradicting OBSs that they cannot rule out. Furthermore, they might believe the other agents to have several OBSs and so on. Another addition to the current formalism is to allow OBSs with more than two agents.

On the experimental side, it would be of great importance to test the concept of OBS itself by asking the agents what is their behavior, what is the rationale (game) behind it, what they believe is the strategy of the other agents, what is the rationale behind it etc... Not only would it allow us to have the OBS of the agents when they play a game, but it would also be useful to find a method to construct a good belief complexity function for any given game. This would allow us to find, in particular environments, more accurate game topologies and belief complexity functions.

We hope this approach will contribute to the understanding of strategic environments that have proven difficult to analyze within the game theoretic framework.

References

1. D. Bernheim. Rationalizable strategic behavior. *Econometrica*, 1984.
2. Gary E. Bolton and Axel Ockenfels. Erc: A theory of equity, reciprocity, and competition. *American Economic Review*, 90(1):166–193, March 2000.
3. Colin F. Camerer. *Behavioral Game Theory*. Princeton University Press, 2003.
4. Ido Erev and Alvin E Roth. Predicting how people play games: Reinforcement learning in experimental games with unique, mixed strategy equilibria. *American Economic Review*, 88(4):848–81, September 1998.
5. Yossi Feinberg. Subjective reasoning in dynamic games. In *Stanford GSB Research Paper No. 1793*, 2002.
6. Martin J.Osborn and Ariel Rubinstein. *A Course in Game Theory*. MIT Press, 1994.
7. Ming Li and Paul M. B. Vitanyi. *An Introduction to Kolmogorov Complexity and Its Applications*. Springer-Verlag, Berlin, 1993.
8. R. McKelvey and T. Palfrey. An experimental study of the centipede game. *Econometrica*, 1992.
9. P. Milgrom. *Putting Auction Theory to Work*. Cambridge University Press, 2004.
10. Ryan Porter and Yoav Shoham. On cheating in sealed-bid auctions. In *Proceedings of the 4th ACM Conference on Electronic Commerce*, pages 76–84, 2003.
11. A.E. Roth. Game theory as a part of empirical economics. *Economic Journal*, 1991.
12. Ariel Rubinstein. *Modeling Bounded Rationality*. MIT Press, 1998.
13. Thomas C. Schelling. *Strategy of Conflict*. Harvard University Press, 1960.

A   Examples of OBSs

A.1   Speculative Trade

With the usual assumptions of common knowledge of the game and the rationality of the agents, it is not possible to model speculative trade even if we allow asymmetric information. More generally, agents cannot "agree to disagree" [6].

However, there are a lot speculative behaviors happening, where the Buyer believes the security's price will go up, and the Seller believes just the opposite. Not only is this statement correct, but it is also, loosely speaking, commonly known by the two agents that they agree to have different beliefs.

The simplest one-shot speculative trade can be modeled in the following way. The (potential) Buyer has two strategies b for "buy" and nb "don't buy". Symmetrically, the Seller has s and ns for "sell" and "don't sell" respectively. However, The Buyer believes he is playing G_b whereas the Seller believes he is playing G_s, and there is, loosely speaking, common knowledge of these (contradicting) beliefs. The Buyer thinks the price of the security will go up to $p_b > p$ and the Seller believes the opposite, i.e. that it will go down to $p_s < p$. So G_b and G_s are defined as follow:

G_b	ns	s
nb	(p,p_b)	(p,p_b)
b	(p,p_b)	(p_b,p)

G_s	ns	s
nb	(p,p_s)	(p,p_s)
b	(p,p_s)	(p_s,p)

Both agents participate in the speculative trade, while anticipating the other's participation, by having the following two OBSs: $\overline{bG_bsG_s}$ for the Buyer, and

$\overline{sG_sbG_b}$ for the Seller. These two OBSs model the beliefs of the two agents, with each agent believing he outsmarts the other.

A.2   Irrationality

It can be fruitful to communicate irrationality. Consider the situation of a thief with a firearm who is surrounded by several policemen who are unarmed and who want to get him. Suppose everyone knows that there is only one bullet in the gun and that the thief cannot shoot anyone, as in this case, all the (remaining) policemen will get him and give him a worse treatment. From a rational point of view, he will be caught, but by pretending to be irrational, by successfully communicating his pretended madness, no one will dare to try to catch him first.

Formally, it can be modeled in this simple way. We consider Agent 1 as the thief and Agent 2 as one of the policemen. Agent 2 decides whether to try to catch Agent 1 or not (strategies c and nc), and Agent 1 decides whether to strike back, i.e. shoot his bullet (strategies s and ns). The game G is presented in normal form as follow (left):

G	nc	c
ns	$(0,0)$	$(-1,1)$
s	$(0,0)$	$(-10,-100)$

G'	nc	c
ns	$(0,0)$	$(-1,1)$
s	$(0,0)$	$(0,-100)$

The only (subgame perfect) equilibrium is (ns,c). However, if the policeman believes *the thief himself believes* he has plenty of bullets, i.e. they play the game G' (right above) where the thief cannot be caught, then the policeman has the OBS $\overline{ncGsG'ncG'}$ and no one will catch the thief.

Note that it is not the only way for the thief to not be caught. He can also just pretend to be irrational, and have the policemen believe he will shoot because he cannot anticipate the consequences of his actions, and is not maximizing any function. In this case, each policeman has the simple OBS $ncGs$.

This is situation where the essence of the game is not in the individual's behavior, but in successfully convincing other agents of some OBS.

We can illustrate belief engineering (see Section 6) with some modifications of the above example. Suppose the thief has 5 bullets, and there are more than five policemen. They can try to catch him each one after the other, and the more policemen he shoots, the worse they will treat him when they get him. At all equilibria or rationalizable strategy, the thief will not shoot. But by shooting the first policeman, the thief communicates that he is not fully rational, and cannot think the five steps ahead. It is likely that no one will dare to try to catch him after this action. Note that here, if the game was not dynamic (i.e. all agents had to choose their strategies from the start) and play the one-shot equivalent game, the thief would probably surrender, as he does not have the opportunity to communicate his "lack" of rationality as he did before.

Marker-Passing Inference in the Scone Knowledge-Base System*

Scott E. Fahlman

Language Technologies Institute & Computer Science Department
Carnegie Mellon University
Pittsburgh PA 12517, U.S.A.
sef@cs.cmu.edu

Abstract. The Scone knowledge-base system, currently being developed at Carnegie Mellon University, implements search and inference operations using a set of marker-passing algorithms. These were originally designed for a massively parallel hardware architecture but now are implemented completely in software. The algorithms are fast, relatively simple, and they support efficient implementation of the most heavily used KB features. This paper describes these marker-passing algorithms, their strengths and limitations, and how they are used in Scone.

1 Introduction

Scone [1] is an open-source knowledge base (KB) system being developed in the Language Technologies Institute of Carnegie Mellon University. Scone is implemented in Common Lisp. It runs stand-alone or as a server process on a 32-bit or 64-bit Linux workstation. It can also run stand-alone under Windows.

Our goal is to make Scone a practical KB system that can be used as a component in a wide range of software applications. Therefore, we place primary emphasis on Scone's expressiveness, ease of use, scalability, and on the efficiency of the most commonly used operations for search and inference.

Scone differs from other knowledge-base systems in the way it implements search and inference. Scone uses marker-passing algorithms originally designed for a hypothetical massively parallel machine, the NETL machine [2]. These marker-passing algorithms cannot, by themselves, perform every kind of search and inference that can be handled by a general theorem-prover, and the Scone operations provide no guarantee of logical completeness. However, Scone's marker-passing algorithms are fast, and they can handle the most common search and inference operations needed for common-sense reasoning in a knowledge base. These include inheritance of properties, roles, and relations in a multiple-inheritance type hierarchy; default reasoning with exceptions;

---

* Development of Scone has been supported in part by the Defense Advanced Research Projects Agency (DARPA) under contract number NBCHD030010. Thanks to Alicia Tribble and Benjamin Lambert for help in polishing this presentation.

J. Lang, F. Lin, and J. Wang (Eds.): KSEM 2006, LNAI 4092, pp. 114–126, 2006.
© Springer-Verlag Berlin Heidelberg 2006

detecting type violations; search based on set intersection; and maintaining multiple, overlapping world-views at once in the same KB.

To handle more complex reasoning tasks, we can build a general reasoner or theorem-prover on top of Scone's basic inference machinery. If we do that, Scone's marker-passing operations play a supporting role, providing a fast way to perform many of the low-level steps required by the higher-level reasoning system.

This paper describes Scone's marker-passing algorithms in greater detail, along with their application in a variety of KB tasks. It describes some of the strengths and limitations of the marker-passing approach and presents timing measurements for typical search and inference operations in a Scone knowledge base with 10^6 elements.

2 Marker-Passing Operations in Parallel Hardware

The idea for the massively parallel NETL architecture was born about 1974, while I was pondering two problems that seem to lie at the very heart of AI:

- *In any knowledge base, the amount of knowledge virtually present is very much greater than the amount of knowledge explicitly present. The extra knowledge is the result of query-time inference, which can require a lot of computation. And yet, we humans routinely perform this kind of inference quickly and in a way that seems almost effortless. We somehow do this in a knowledge base with millions of items (at least), using millisecond-speed "hardware". We're not even aware that inference is going on unless someone points this out. We don't have the same sense of mental effort that we feel when adding numbers or doing a logic puzzle.*
- *We humans also have a remarkable ability that is central to all recognition tasks: we begin with a set of observed features, a set of expectations, and a vast collection of stored descriptions; the problem is to find the stored description that best matches these features and expectations. This core operation, involving search and matching, is essentially the same whether we are talking about visual recognition, speech, or recognizing what task someone is working on after observing a few actions. Again, this is a computationally demanding task that we humans do frequently, quickly, and with no sense of mental effort.*

I came to believe that these two mysterious human abilities were related, and that they could only be explained by making effective use of the brain's massive parallelism. So if we want an AI system that can hold vast amounts of symbolic knowledge and that can do these kinds of search and inference tasks in real time, we must develop an appropriate parallel architecture and figure out how to use it.

The NETL architecture was developed to satisfy these needs. NETL was inspired in part by the work of M. Ross Quillian [3]. He proposed storing knowledge in the form of a *semantic network*, a sort of active memory with nodes representing concepts and links representing the relations between them. In his "spreading activation" model, markers flowed in parallel through all the links of the network, looking for the shortest paths between one concept node and another. NETL is similar in structure, but it uses several distinct markers, and they flow only through certain types of links under the precise control of an external, serial *control computer*. This change allows NETL to use marker propagation for more complex forms of inference.

Every node in NETL is represented by a very simple processing element that has storage for some number of *marker-bits* – typically between 16 and 32. There are a few permanently-set bits that tell the node what kind it is: an individual-node, a type-node, or some more exotic type. Each node also has a *tie-point* to which any number of links can be attached – I will say more about that below.

These nodes are all connected to the control computer by a common bus, and they can respond in parallel to simple commands like the following:

- *All nodes: turn off marker 4.*
- *All nodes with markers 1 and 2 on and marker 3 off: turn on marker 4.*
- *All nodes with marker 4 on: queue up in serial order and report your identities to the control computer.*

Every link in NETL is also a simple hardware element, and also receives its commands from the common bus. A link has several *wires*, each of which can be tied to the tie-point of any node in the knowledge base. This is a private, non-shared connection. We may think of it as physically connecting the wire to the tie-point, though in practice the connection would be established via a switching network. A generic link (in the current Scone model) has five wires: A and B (for the two concepts the link is relating), C (used in trinary relations), PARENT (what kind of link am I?), and CONTEXT (whose purpose we will describe in section 7). Some special link-types are built-in and have special meaning to the inference machinery: is-a, eq, cancel, map, and split. We will describe these below.

In addition, each link has a built-in node, complete with marker memory and a tie-point. This node, referred to as the link's *handle node*, represents the statement itself. Other links can connect to this handle node, providing meta-information about the statement: where the information came from, how certain we are, etc.

Links can sense and alter the marker-state of the nodes attached to their various wires, so they can respond, in parallel, to commands like the following:

- *All is-a links: if the node on your A-wire has marker bit 3 on and the node on your B-wire has marker 3 off, mark the B-node with marker 3.*
- *If any link took action in the previous cycle, report that on the common bus.*

The effect of the first operation is to propagate all 3-markers one level up the is-a hierarchy; the effect of the second operation is to test whether any new nodes were marked, in which case the upward-propagation step should be repeated until all superior nodes have been marked.

This massively parallel architecture can perform certain operations very fast, even as the knowledge base grows to millions of nodes and links. For example, suppose we want to mark all the gray mammals that live in Africa. We can put marker 1 on the "mammal" node and, in a few cycles, mark all the subtypes and instances of "mammal", even if there are thousands of these because of downward branching. Similarly, we can mark all the gray things with marker 2 and all the African residents with marker 3. Then, in a single cycle, we intersect these three sets by telling every node with markers 1, 2, and 3 to turn on marker 4. The 4-marked set can then be used for other operations, or its members can be reported, one by one, to the controller.

Note that only the query-time or search-time operations are fast. It may be a slow operation to add new knowledge to the KB, since this requires connecting together new nodes and links. But that seems like a good trade-off for most KB applications.

3   Pseudo-Parallel Marker-Passing Operations in Software

In the early 1980's I tried to find an economical way to build a parallel NETL machine big enough for research on "common sense" reasoning and natural language understanding. The initial goal was to create a machine that could directly implement (or efficiently simulate) 10^6 parallel NETL elements, each representing an entity or statement. I finally came to the conclusion that achieving this with the technology of that time would be impractical, especially in a university environment with limited funding. So I set this goal aside and turned my attention to other research challenges.

Daniel Hillis at MIT, and later at Thinking Machines Corporation, did make a serious attempt to implement a marker-passing machine of this type. The result was the Connection Machine [4]. But that machine took years to develop and ultimately was so expensive that few AI researchers had regular access to one. Other researchers continued to explore the parallel marker-passing approach as well. Among the most prominent were Dan Moldovan and his colleagues [5, 6, 7] and James Hendler [8, 9].

In 2000 I began to think again about the need for a practical, large-scale knowledge-base system, both for AI research and for a number of practical applications. I realized that readily available computers were now 10,000 times faster than they were in the early 1980's, and their memories were 10,000 times larger. So I began to think about implementing a NETL-like system purely in software, running on a standard workstation with enough main memory to hold the desired KB. It took some time to get this project funded and under way. Scone is the result.

I decided that Scone would retain NETL's marker-passing model, but implemented in carefully optimized software. I refer to this as the *pseudo-parallel* layer of Scone. Scone also includes a considerable body of conventional (*i.e.* less performance-critical) software built on top of this pseudo-parallel base.

It may seem like a strange decision to organize the system in this way. Even if we accept that marker passing is a good way to implement a symbolic knowledge base in parallel hardware, why would we emulate this parallel model on a serial machine? There are several reasons:

- The pseudo-parallel layer is a small, relatively simple body of code that can be carefully tuned for maximum performance.
- By basing Scone's inference on marker-passing operations, rather than on some form of resolution theorem-proving, we lock Scone into a certain part of the design space: inference is fast, following pointer chains only to relevant items in memory. There is no need for global pattern-matching in the inner loops of the program.
- Because Scone's inference algorithms are not trying to guarantee logical completeness, the damage caused if some subtle inconsistency sneaks into the KB is localized. If we say that John is a male and later assert that he is someone's mother, the "John" description may become confused, but Scone is unlikely to conclude from this that 1+1 = 3.

- Because the pseudo-parallel operations of Scone remain close to the parallel NETL model, we can easily re-implement these performance-critical parts of Scone on a data-parallel machine or on a cluster of processors. So we can develop and popularize Scone on affordable hardware and later use essentially the same model to handle much larger knowledge bases.

The software implementation of Scone's marker-passing machinery is fairly straightforward. Each knowledge-base element is implemented as a multi-word data structure in memory. One word in this structure, the *bits-word*, holds the element's marker bits, so one or two full-word Boolean operations can test the status of several markers at once: *"Does element E have all of markers 3, 4, and 7 and not marker 8?"* The link wires are implemented as pointers, and each node has back-pointers to all the links that connect to it – a separate back-pointer list for each type of wire.

For each marker M, we maintain a two-way linked list of all the elements marked with M. We call this M's *marker chain*. This chain is essential because a common operation is to scan all the elements marked with M, looking for elements that also have certain additional markers. Finally, for each marker M, we maintain a *count* of the number of nodes marked with M.

So to mark element E with marker M, we set bit M in the bits-word of E, we add element E to M's marker chain, and we increment the count of M-marked elements. To remove marker M from E, we do the opposite: clear the M bit, splice E out of M's marker chain, and decrement M's counter.

In Lisp, the frequent addition and removal of list cells from the marker chain would lead to excessive garbage collection, so we pre-allocate space for the forward and backward pointers of each marker chain in the data structure representing each element. In a system with 32 markers, this increases the size of each element by 64 pointers – 512 bytes on an implementation with 64-bit addresses. This pre-allocation is a time-space tradeoff: it makes the marking/unmarking operations much faster, at the cost of making the element data structures much larger.

As a rule, the entire active KB should be kept in main memory, since inference and search are much slower if parts of the knowledge base must be paged in from secondary storage. In a 64-bit implementation each Scone element, with its associated strings and data structures, requires about 2000 bytes of memory. So a KB with 10^6 elements, all loaded and potentially active at once, requires a machine with slightly more than 2G bytes of main memory.

4 Basic Marker Operations in Scone

Scone supports multiple inheritance through the is-a hierarchy. That is, a type or individual node may have any number of is-a links connecting it to superior (more general) types. At the top is the most general type, named "thing"; at the bottom are individual nodes. By the rules of inheritance, when we want to know some property of an individual, we must look at the individual's node and at all the type-nodes above it in the hierarchy; a property or relation could be connected to any one of these. For example, when we say that Clyde is an elephant, we connect the A-wire of an is-a link to the "Clyde" node and the B-wire to the "elephant" node. If we later ask what color Clyde is, the answer "gray" is actually inherited from the "elephant" node.

The most important pseudo-parallel operation in Scone is the *upscan*, which is used whenever we have a query about the class membership, properties, or relations of some node N. We mark N with marker M, and then propagate M to all of the type-nodes above N in the is-a hierarchy. Because we allow multiple inheritance (or upward branching) in the is-a hierarchy, an upscan might mark a large number of nodes. (Think about the number of classes of which a typical person is a member, or the number of unary predicates that may be true of that person.) The basic algorithm for an upscan is simple:

1. *Mark the starting node N with marker M.*
2. *For every element E1 newly marked with M, examine each link L that is connected to E1 by its A-wire. (A is considered to be the lower-end of the is-a link.)*
3. *If L is an active IS-A link, examine the element E2 that is attached to the B-wire of link L. (We will define "active" later, but it is a simple bit-test.)*
4. *If E2 is not already marked with M, mark E2 now.*
5. *Steps 2-4 have propagated marker M one level up the is-a hierarchy. If any new nodes have been marked with M, return to step 2 and continue iterating until we reach quiescence – that is, no new elements have been marked with M. Then stop.*

In the pseudo-parallel implementation, an upscan takes time proportional to the number of superior nodes that actually must be marked, times the average fan-out of the is-a hierarchy in the upward direction.

A *downscan* is similar to an upscan, but we cross is-a links downward, in the B-to-A direction. If we mark a type-node N with marker M and downscan, we mark all the subtypes and instances of type N. A downscan from a node high in the network, such as "physical object", might mark a large number of nodes.

In addition to is-a links, Scone has *eq-links*, which indicate that (in a given context) two nodes refer to the same entity. For example, we might have an eq-link from "George W. Bush" to "president of the U.S.". We want any marker placed on one side of an eq-link to flow to the other side, so during both upscans and downscans the markers cross active eq-links in both directions.

Upscans are used in several ways in Scone. If we want to know whether Clyde is a member of some type T, we simply upscan from Clyde and see whether the T node is marked. If we want to ask about some relation, for example to mark the set of all things that Clyde "fears" (directly or by inheritance), the algorithm is as follows:

1. *Mark the "Clyde" node with M1 and upscan to mark all its superiors.*
2. *If any active "fears" link has M1 on its A-wire, put M2 on its B-node.*
3. *Downscan all M2 markers.*

The effect of this is to put M2 on every individual or type node representing someone that Clyde fears. If there is a "fears" link from "elephant" to "mouse", we will end up with M2 on "mouse" and on "Mickey Mouse".

A similar operation can be used to detect type violations in the network. Suppose that under "person" we have two subclasses, "child" and "adult", and that these classes are disjoint. We represent this by attaching a *split-link* to these type-nodes. (A single split-link can connect to any number of nodes.) Suppose that John is known to be a child, and that someone tries to assert that John is an airline pilot, which would imply (via is-a links) that he is an adult. Before asserting this new item, we check whether doing so would violate any splits. We place marker M on both "John" and on "airline pilot", and upscan. In this case, both "child" and "adult" are marked with M. We then ask every split-link that has M on *one* of its connected nodes to check whether M is present on *more than one* of these nodes; if so, that split is violated and something is wrong. In this case, we would report that John cannot be both a child and adult, and ask the user which assertion is incorrect. (If the user really wants to assert both, the split-link can be over-ridden for John only using a cancel-link.)

The most common operation in recognition is to find the intersection of several types. We saw this in section 2, where we were looking for gray mammals in Africa. In the software version, the operation is basically the same: mark each set with a different marker, and then tell every node that has collected all of the specified markers to label itself as a winner. However, in the pseudo-parallel software version, we cannot perform the intersection in a single cycle. Instead we must scan the marker chain of one of these markers, checking each node to see whether it has the other markers. This is more efficient if we scan the marker chain with the smallest number of marked nodes; the marker counts tell us which one this is.

So in Scone the time required to intersect *n* sets is the time required to mark the members of each set, plus the time required to visit and test all the members of the smallest of the marked sets. This is slower than on the parallel machine, but it still is fast enough for most applications.

5 Default Reasoning with Exceptions

The ability of one marker to block the passage of another is used in Scone to implement a cancellation mechanism. Consider the fragment of network shown in figure 1. The dashed links in the diagram are *cancel-links*. The unlabeled arrows are is-a links. This fragment says that a bird is a flying-thing and that both canaries and penguins are birds, but a penguin is *not* a flying-thing. Tweety is a flying thing; Fred would normally be one, but he is a non-flying exception to the general rule – perhaps he is afraid of heights.

So far, we have spoken of the propagation of single markers in Scone, but in fact markers are allocated in pairs: a positive marker M and an associated *cancel-marker*, designated ~M. During an upscan, we propagate M upward from some node such as "Max", as described above. But at each step, if marker M is on the A-wire of a cancel link, we mark the B-node with ~M. During the upscan, we do not allow an M marker to cross a link that already has a ~M marker, nor do we allow an M marker to enter any node marked with ~M.

In figure 1, we also see a link L stating that birds eat worms. This statement is inherited by canaries and (as a default) by all other birds, but it is cancelled for penguins – they only eat fish. This cancellation is implemented by the cancel-link running from the "penguin" statement L (connected to L's handle-node).

Now, if we ask what Fred eats, we follow the algorithm described above for tracing relations. This marks "worm" and any subtypes or individual "worms". But if we ask what Max likes to eat, link L is cancelled (and thus rendered inactive) before any other markers can cross it. So Max only eats fish, not worms.

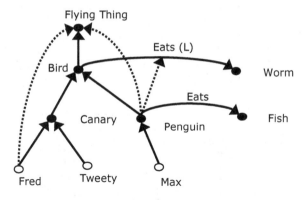

Fig. 1. Example of Cancellation

This kind of default reasoning with cancellation is a complex and controversial topic in the knowledge representation community. The examples I have presented above are straightforward and efficient, but it is possible to create networks where it is unclear whether a conclusion should be allowed or not: some paths supporting the conclusion are cancelled while others are not, and there is no clear reason to prefer one interpretation over the other. Also cancellation is incompatible with some notions of sound logical inference: it is possible to deduce a conclusion by doing a certain amount of work, and then to withdraw it when additional processing discovers that the conclusion should be cancelled.

It is beyond the scope of this paper to discuss the cancellation problem and possible solutions in greater depth. A good overview, with references to the technical literature on this subject, can be found in [10]. I will just say this: for an application-oriented system like Scone, it is impossible to live without some form of default reasoning with exceptions. The real world is full of flightless birds and white elephants. So our general approach in Scone is to try to detect all the ambiguous cases as new elements are added to the network, and to consult the user in cases where the desired meaning is not clear. Then we set up the KB network so that the runtime operations described above will yield the desired results.

The more general point is this: it is possible to use Scone-like marker passing whether or not you want to implement some form of cancellation. If you do allow cancellation, the use of cancel-markers can make this reasonably efficient at runtime.

6   Virtual Copy Semantics

In dealing with complex descriptions, Scone attempts to implement *virtual copy semantics*. Suppose we create a type-node representing a typical "family". This node serves as the container for a number of individual roles, such as "father" and "mother" and a number of type-roles, such as "child". (The type-role node stands for the typical member of a set. The set may be empty.) There are also some statements describing relations between these roles. For example, we might want to say that the mother (by default) loves the children.

The nodes and links at the top of figure 2 illustrate a somewhat simplified family for explanatory purposes: one mother, one child, and love. The dotted links signify that for every copy of "family", there will be one mother and one child.

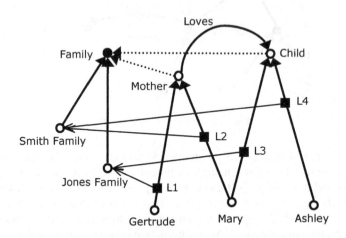

Fig. 2. Family Relations

"Smith Family" has an is-a link to family, so we want this instance to behave as if we had made a private copy of the entire "family" description. "Smith Family" has its own mother, its own child, and the mother loves the child. But we don't want to make an actual copy of all this structure; we want to create a *virtual copy* that behaves like a real copy but is implemented by inheritance and marker-passing. In general, we don't create an actual copy of an inherited node or link unless we have something to say about that specific individual; otherwise, these elements are only virtually present.

We see in figure 2 that Mary is the mother in "Smith Family". The 3-wire link L2 is a *map-link* that states this. "Smith Family" is said to be the *owner* of this map-link. The link L4 indicates that "Ashley" is the "child" in the "Smith Family". Figure 2 also shows a second instance of "family", the "Jones Family". Mary is the child in this family (link L3) and Gertrude is the mother (link L1). So Mary appears in two different copies of the "family" description, playing a different role in each.

The ability of one marker to gate the passage of another is used to good advantage in implementing virtual copies in Scone. Suppose we want to mark the nodes representing all the people that Mary loves. If we do a simple upscan, not crossing any map-links, we find nothing. But the two map-links, L2 and L3, indicate that Mary plays some role in two different descriptions; we must consider each of these descriptions separately to see if a "loves" relation is present in either of them.

Looking first at L2, we place a description marker, M_D, on its owner, "Smith Family", and upscan M_D. This *activates* the "Smith Family" description. Now we ask again whether Mary loves anyone, using the algorithm described in the previous section: upscan from Mary using M1, cross the relation link with M2, then downscan M2 on the other side. But this time, we treat any map-link as an eq-link if it is tied to an owner that is activated with M_D. So in this case, any marker arriving at one end of L2 is passed on to the other end. The same is true of L4, but L1 and L3 are inactive. So the M1 marker on Mary reaches the "mother" node, we cross the "loves" link with M2, and the resulting M2 marker on "child" propagates down into "Ashley".

Then we clear all these markers and consider the description tied to L3. We mark the owner, "Jones Family" with M_D, and repeat the procedure above. But this time L1 and L3 are active, while L2 and L4 are dormant. The M1 marker on Mary reaches the "daughter" node, but can go no further, since there is no "loves" link going in the right direction out of "daughter" – only one coming in. The final result is that, according to this piece of the network, Mary loves Ashley, but nobody else.

Note that if we had tried to look at both the "Smith Family" and "Jones Family" descriptions at the same time, it would have led to confusion. With L1, L2, L3, and L4 all active at once, we could have deduced that Gertrude loves Ashley (possible, but not supported by this network) and that Mary loves herself.

This illustrates a fundamental limitation of marker-passing: in situations where an entity plays different roles in many different virtual copies, we cannot look at all of these descriptions at once without confusion. We must look at them one by one. Or, to put it another way, each instance of a description can be viewed as a set of variable bindings: in the Smith family, "Mary" is bound to "mother" and "Britney" to "daughter". A marker-passing system cannot look at many distinct sets of variable bindings at once without confusion, though some more complex (and expensive) parallel architectures can do this. On the other hand, the marker-passing machinery makes it reasonably fast to activate and explore each of these descriptions.

7 Multiple Contexts

An important feature of Scone is its multiple-context mechanism, which allows the user to represent several different *contexts* (or states of the world) in the KB at the same time. A context is just an individual node in the KB that serves as the container for some collection of knowledge. Every link (statement) in Scone has a *context-wire* that is connected to one of these context-nodes. If that context-node is marked as active, the link is active; if not, the link is effectively turned off. Similarly, every node has a context wire that indicates the context in which its referent exists. Most of our general knowledge about the world is tied to a single large context called "general".

Contexts are connected into a hierarchy with is-a links, just like any other nodes in the Scone KB. We *activate* a context C by marking it with a special context-marker M_C and upscanning M_C to mark all the nodes above C in the hierarchy. All of the nodes and links in the M_C-marked contexts become active; all others are dormant and take no part in Scone's search and inference.

Suppose we want to create the "Harry Potter World" context, which is very similar to the real world, but in which a few people are wizards with special powers. We simply create a new individual node, "HPW" and connect an is-a link from this node to "general". At this point, "HPW" acts as an exact clone of "general": if we activate "HPW", M_C propagates upward to "general", and all the general knowledge is turned on. But now we can add some new nodes and links in the "HPW" context that are seen only when the "HPW" context is active. For example, we can assert that, in this context, a broom is a vehicle. If we return to "general", these new elements are invisible. Similarly, we can use cancel-links in the "HPW" context to turn off some specific "general" knowledge that would otherwise be active.

So in Scone, because markers can affect the behavior of other markers, we have a very powerful, lightweight, and efficient way to represent many distinct contexts in the same KB. A context can inherit all of the knowledge in some other context without the need for any actual copying – the copies are virtual. We can easily activate any context C and reason about what is true there without disturbing the contents of any other context (except for descendants of C).

Because it is inexpensive to create and populate a new context, Scone uses contexts in many ways. For example, an action or event creates two contexts, one representing the world before the event and the other representing the world after the event. If I drive from home to the airport, both I and my car are at home in the *before* context and at the airport in the *after* context. Both of these contexts inherit from "general", so all my general knowledge is present in both contexts; only a few specific things have changed as a result of the "drive" action. Contexts are also used to represent (and isolate) some person's beliefs, desires, things that are true only in certain historical periods or certain places, "what if" scenarios, and so on.

The use of multiple contexts in a KB is not a new idea. Logicians sometimes include a state term S_N in each assertion to indicate the state in which that assertion is considered to be valid. Extra formulas or rules of inference can be added to implement inheritance among these states. But reasoning with these state terms can greatly increase the amount of work that must be done by the inference system, so this mechanism is seldom used in large-scale knowledge bases.

While I am not claiming that the use of multiple contexts is a novel contribution of Scone, I will suggest that Scone's marker-passing machinery makes it efficient to use many lightweight contexts organized in a hierarchy, making this an extremely useful representational technique in Scone.

8 Performance Measurements

There are no widely accepted benchmarks for the speed of inference in a knowledge-base, and I have found very few published performance figures for the kinds of inference that are the primary focus of Scone. In order to give the reader some general idea of Scone's speed, I have run a few tests on a "synthetic" Scone knowledge base of 1,018,894 elements. We do not yet have any "real" and meaningful Scone knowledge bases of this size, so I created a synthetic KB by combining and several smaller KBs and then creating a lot of additional types and instances. I believe that the result is a fairly realistic KB in terms of its structure, though the content is not meaningful.[1] The actual KB used in these tests can be obtained from the author.

The timings given here are for the current (March 2006) version of Scone running under Steel Bank Common Lisp and Red Hat Linux. The machine is a generic workstation with a single 64-bit AMD Opteron 146 processor, rated at 2.0 GHz, and

---

[1] Of course, the complexity and structure of a "real" knowledge base will vary greatly, depending on the domain it is describing, so there probably is no such thing as a "typical" KB structure.

with 8G bytes of main memory. The machine was purchased in March 2005 for $3100. The times reported include garbage collection and (for the load tests) file I/O. For accuracy, the shorter times reported here are the result of executing the operation N times and then dividing the total time by N. In the intersection test we have set things up so that only one element is in the final intersection set.

Operation	Time	
Time to create/load 1,018,894 elements, with full type-checking	240	sec
Time per element added	236	µsec
Time to create/load 1,018,894 elements, no checking	193	sec
Time per element added	189	µsec
Downscan "thing". (Marks every node in KB, then frees marker.)	10.2	sec
Time per element marked	10	µsec
Look up an inherited property of a typical individual	.93	msec
Test whether an indv can be of a given type	.60	msec
Mark, then intersect, two sets with 10K members, one winner	49.70	msec
Mark, then intersect, three sets with 10K members, one winner	83.40	msec

9 Conclusions

Our main conclusions are these:

- *Marker passing, even on a serial machine, appears to be a good implementation technology for a knowledge-base system with goals similar to Scone's: a primary emphasis on speed, scalability, and expressiveness, with relatively less emphasis on formal guarantees of logical completeness and consistency.*
- *Marker passing algorithms in Scone support multiple inheritance with cancellation, detection of type violations, reasoning with virtual copies of complex descriptions, and multiple contexts with large amounts of shared information. Statements in Scone are first-class entities in the knowledge base, so we can make statements about statements. These features give Scone great expressive power.*
- *Programs implementing deeper, more complex forms of reasoning can be built on top of Scone's low-level pseudo-parallel machinery.*
- *The marker-passing operations in Scone can be used with or without an exception mechanism. However, if you want to use such a mechanism, marker passing provides a way to implement this facility that is efficient at query-time.*
- *For a Scone KB of 10^6 elements (nodes and/or links) running on an inexpensive workstation, speed is adequate for many applications.*
- *These marker-passing algorithms were originally designed for a massively parallel machine, and they can easily be adapted to run on most parallel machines. Some machines are better suited for KB use than others: KB operations stress memory bandwidth and communication, and make little use of floating-point arithmetic.*

In closing, I offer an informal conjecture: There are many kinds of parallelism. Parallel marker-passing, as found in NETL and as simulated in Scone, is a very simple form of parallelism that is easy to implement, and that is very fast for certain operations. But the simplicity of this model brings with it some limitations. The

processing elements are Boolean, with no arithmetic capabilities and hardly any memory. Searches and inferences that require reasoning about many simultaneous variable bindings cannot be handled in parallel by marker-passing; serial case-by-case reasoning, with a good deal of book-keeping, is required. A parallel machine with a full processor at every node could look at many such cases at once, but a marker-passing machine cannot do this.

I noted in section 2 that we humans have the ability to perform certain kinds of search and inference with almost magical ease. But when asked to solve a logical or mathematical puzzle or to prove a theorem, we experience that as hard mental work. We may require a pencil and paper. We may have to take a class to learn how to do this. Some people never learn these higher mental skills, though they usually survive anyway.

My conjecture is that the set of operations that marker-passing can handle is (more or less) co-extensive with the set of operations that are very easy for people. I am not suggesting that the human brain is implemented as a marker-passing machine; I am simply suggesting that there is a cognitively important class of computation that can be handled very well by both the human brain and by marker-passing, and another class that is difficult for both architectures. In Scone, we attempt to separate the marker-passing operations from the rest, and we give them special attention. I suspect that this separation may eventually help us to replicate some of that human magic.

References

1. Fahlman, S.E.: The Scone Knowledge Base (home page), http://www.cs.cmu.edu/~sef/ scone/
2. Fahlman, S. E.: *NETL: A System for Representing and Using Real-World Knowledge*, MIT Press, Cambridge MA (1979)
3. Quillian, M.R.: Semantic Memory. In: Minsky, M.L. (ed.): *Semantic Information Processing*, MIT Press (1968)
4. Hillis, W.D.: The Connection Machine, MIT Press, Cambridge MA, (1985)
5. Moldovan, D.I., Lee, W., Lin, C.: SNAP: A Marker-Propagation Architecture for Knowledge Processing. IEEE Trans. Parallel Distrib. Syst. 3(4): 397-410 (1992)
6. Kim, J.T., Moldovan, D. I.: Classification and Retrieval of Knowledge on Parallel Marker Passing Architecture. IEEE Trans. Knowl. Data Eng. 5(5): 753-761 (1993)
7. Harabagiu, S. M., Moldovan, D. I.: Parallel System for Text Inference Using Marker Propagations. IEEE Trans. Parallel Distrib. Syst. 9(8): 729-747 (1998)
8. Hendler, J.A.: Integrating Marker-passing and Problem Solving: A spreading activation approach to improved choice in planning, Lawrence Erlbaum, Mahwah NJ (1987)
9. Hendler, J.A.: Marker-passing over microfeatures: Towards a hybrid symbolic/ connectionist model, *Cognitive Science,* 13(1), p. 79-106 (1989)
10. Brachman, R. J., Levesque, H. J.: Knowledge Representation and Reasoning, Morgan Kaufmann, San Francisco, chapters 10 and 11 (2004).

Hyper Tableaux — The Third Version

Shasha Feng[1], Jigui Sun[1,2], and Xia Wu[1]

[1] College of Computer Science and Technology, Jilin University,
Changchun, 130012, China
[2] Key Lab of Symbolic Computation and Knowledge Engineer of Ministry of Education,
Changchun, 130012, China
`shashafeng@mail.edu.cn, jgsun@jlu.edu.cn, yexia_fw@163.com`

Abstract. The first hyper tableau suffers from blind guessing in instancing the clauses, and evolves into the unification-driven style, the second version. However, we found a counterexample of it. We modify the calculus and a new hyper tableau is represented.

1 Introduction

In [1, 2] "hyper tableaux", a sound and complete calculus for first-order clausal logic, was introduced. This calculus keeps many desirable features of analytic tableaux (such as model construction for an open branch) while having the characteristic of (positive) hyper resolution, namely to resolve away all the negative literals of a clause in a single inference step. The calculus avoids treatment of variables occurring in more than one positive literal by purifying (ground-instantiating) the selected clause before it is used for extension. Consequently the purifying operation leads to the major weakness of the calculus, which is the need to (at least partially) blindly guess ground-instantiations for certain clauses.

To eliminate the major weakness Baumgartner brought about the hyper tableaux [3] of the next generation. The blind guessing is replaced by a unification-driven technique. And another important difference is that the notion of branch closure is based on variant-ship of literals rather than syntactic identicity (modulo negation). The hyper tableaux calculus in both versions can decide the Bernays-Schoenfinkel class.

To get a competent theorem prover for first-order logic, we implemented the hyper tableaux of the next generation in Visual C++. In testing our procedure with the problems from TPTP, we encountered a counterexample. After analyzing the counterexample and the completeness proof of the calculus, especially the model construction approach for an infinite open branch, we make some modifications on the calculus and present it here as the hyper tableaux of the third version.

The new hyper tableaux calculus differs from its predecessor on the `link` rule. The new `link1` rule, adopting new criteria, can generate more instances of input clauses for the `ext` rule. The new criteria are based more on semantic interpretation than on syntactic unification.

J. Lang, F. Lin, and J. Wang (Eds.): KSEM 2006, LNAI 4092, pp. 127–138, 2006.

The rest of this paper is structured as follows: the second section gives a thorough description of the second hyper calculus, and in the third section the counterexample is presented and analyzed, in the next section our new calculus is formalized and some improvements are given. In the last section we compare our work with that of others and outline some future work.

2 The Second Version Hyper Tableaux

2.1 Preliminaries

The notions introduced here are cited from [3]. The usual notions of first-order logic are applied in a way consistent to [4]. For notions related to tableau calculi in general and the notions in clausal tableaux see [5] and [6] respectively. A clause is a multiset of literals, written as $A_1 \vee ... \vee A_m \vee \neg B_1 \vee ... \vee \neg B_n$ (where m,n ≥ 0 and the A's and B's are atoms.), or as $\mathcal{A} \leftarrow \mathcal{B}$, where $\mathcal{A} = \{A_1,..., A_m\}$ and $\mathcal{B} = \{B_1,..., B_n\}$. The literals $\mathcal{A}$ are called *head literals* and the literals $\mathcal{B}$ are called *body literals*. Clauses with $m \geq 1$ are also called *program clauses*.

A (Herbrand) interpretation I (for a given language) is represented as a (possibly infinite) set of atoms, such that atom A is true in I iff $A \in I$. As usual, $I \models X$ means that X is true in I where X is a sentence or set of sentences (interpreted conjunctively). In particular, $I \models \mathcal{A} \leftarrow \mathcal{B}$ iff $\mathcal{B}\sigma \subseteq I$ implies $\mathcal{A}\sigma \cap I \neq \emptyset$ for every ground substitution σ for $\mathcal{A} \leftarrow \mathcal{B}$.

We consider literal trees $\mathcal{T}$, i.e. finite, ordered tree, all nodes of which, except the root, are labelled with a literal. If L is a literal then $[L]$ ambiguously denotes some node N in $\mathcal{T}$ which is labelled with L. A branch of length n consisting of the nodes N_0, $N_1,..., N_n$ with root N_0 and leaf N_n is usually written as $[L_1,..., L_n]$ where L_i is the label of N_i. The letters p and q denote branches, and if $p = [L_1,..., L_{n-1}]$ then $p.[L_n]$ is the branch$[L_1,..., L_{n-1}, L_n]$ (we assume that $[L_n]$ is a new node). Any (not necessarily strict) prefix $[L_1,..., L_m]$ of a branch $p = [L_1,..., L_m, L_{m+1},..., L_n]$ is called a *partial branch (of p)*. By [ ] we denote both the root node and the partial branch from the root node to the root node.

Branches may be labelled with a "*" as *closed*; branches which are not closed are *open*. A tableau is *closed* if each of its branches is closed, otherwise it is *open*.

A literal tree is represented as the set of its branches; branch sets are denoted by the letters $\mathcal{P}$, $\mathcal{Q}$. We write $\mathcal{P}$, $\mathcal{Q}$ meaning $\mathcal{P} \cup \mathcal{Q}$. Similarly, $p,\mathcal{Q}$ means $\{p\}$, $\mathcal{Q}$. We write $X \in p$ iff X occurs in p, where X is a node or a literal label of some node in p.

The *extension of p with clause* $C = L_1 \vee ... \vee L_n$, written as $p \cdot C$, is the branch set $p.[L_1], ..., p.[L_n]$. Equivalently, in tree view this operation extends the branch p by n new nodes $N_1,..., N_n$ which are labelled with the respective literals from C. Here we say that C is the tableau clause of N_i, (for every i, $1 \leq i \leq n$). The tableau clause C of N_i is also denoted by $\mathbf{cl}(N_i)$.

For literals A and B we define $A \geq B$, A *is more general than* B, iff there is a substitution σ_A such that $A\sigma_A = B$; A and B are *variants*, written as $A \approx B$, iff $A \geq B$ and $B \geq A$; A is *strictly more general than* B, $A \succ B$, iff $A \geq B$ and not $A \approx B$. B is also said to be a *strict, or proper* instance of A then.

2.2 Informal Description

We preview the second version hyper tableau by showing the two inference rules[3]. A hyper tableau derivation for a (possibly non-ground) clause set C is the construction of a closed clausal tableau, starting with the tableau consisting of the root node only. The meanings of *branch selection* and *fair* in the calculus are the same with those in [6].

Besides an Init rule to set up the initial tableau, there are two inference rule: the Ext and the Link rule. The purpose of the Ext rule is to extend or close the selected branch. The Ext rule does not instantiate its "resources" (i.e. branch literals). The purpose of the Link rule is to generate new instances of input clauses, so that Ext will be applicable again. Link is in a sense complementary to Ext in that at least one of its resources must be properly instantiated.

Now consider the Ext rule; its application can be described as follows: let p be the selected branch; take a clause $\mathcal{A} \leftarrow \mathcal{B}$ from the "current clause set" C^{-} (which is initialized with the given input clause set C), and apply to p the β rule with $\mathcal{A} \leftarrow \mathcal{B}$, i.e. we split the clause below the leaf of p. *But* this is done only if there is a most general substitution σ such that every element $B\sigma \in \mathcal{B}\sigma$ is identical to a variant of a literal L from p. Then, all new branches with leaf $\neg B\sigma$ where $B\sigma \in \mathcal{B}\sigma$ are labeled as "closed"; the new branches (if any) with leaf from $\mathcal{A}\sigma$ are labeled as "open". If there is an open branch in the resulting tableau, select one.

Some terminology: this occurrence of the clause $\mathcal{A}\sigma \leftarrow \mathcal{B}\sigma$ is called a *tableau clause (of every branch passing through one of the literals of $\mathcal{A}\sigma \leftarrow \mathcal{B}\sigma$)*, and if the selected branch passes through a $A\sigma \in \mathcal{A}\sigma$ then we say that $A\sigma$ is selected in $\mathcal{A}\sigma \leftarrow \mathcal{B}\sigma$, which is denoted by $\mathbf{sel}(\mathcal{A}\sigma \leftarrow \mathcal{B}\sigma)$.

Obviously, the Ext rule alone is not sufficient to achieve completeness, because the clause set $\{p(x) \leftarrow, \leftarrow p(a)\}$ would admit no refutation.

The second inference rule of hyper tableau—the Link inference—can be described as follows: let p be the selected branch; take a clause $\mathcal{A} \leftarrow \mathcal{B}$ from the current clause set C^{-}, and let σ be a most general multiset unifier

$$\mathcal{B}\sigma = \{ \mathbf{sel}(C_1),\ldots, \mathbf{sel}(C_n)\}\sigma,$$

where the C_i's are new variants of some tableau clauses of p. Furthermore, in order to avoid overlapping with the Ext rule, we require that $C_i\sigma \approx C_i$ don't hold, for some i, $1 \leq i \leq n$, i.e. at least one $C_i\sigma$ must be a proper instance of C_i.

If this holds, then consecutively add $C_1\sigma,\ldots, C_n\sigma$ to the current clause set C^{-}, except those $C_i\sigma$ for which a variant is present already.

2.3 Formal Definition

In this section we give formal definitions of the inference rules of hyper tableau calculus[3].

Some preliminaries: we write $p,\mathcal{P}$ to indicate that p is selected in the branch set $p,\mathcal{P}$. Further, every open branch p is labeled with a finite set of clauses, which is denoted by $C^{-}(p)$. Intentionally, $C^{-}(p)$ provides the "current clause set" whose members can be used for extension steps (cf. the informal presentation above). Alternatively, we will also write $< p,\ C^- >$ and mean the branch p with $C^-(p) = C^-$.

The set $C^-(p)$ is complemented by the set $C^+(p)$ of tableau clauses of p, i.e. those clauses which were used in extension steps to construct p. Since p is a "path" through $C^+(p)$ (in the connection method sense) it is natural that p determines a respective selection of head literals of the clauses in $C^+(p)$. More generally, a *clause with selection* is a program clause where one of its head literals L is labeled (in some distinguished way), and L is called the *selected literal*, which is denoted by $\mathbf{sel}(C)$. A *clause set with selection* consists of clauses with selection only. In order to extract from a branch its clause set with selection we define:

$$C^+([L_1,\ldots, L_n]) = \{\ \mathbf{cl}([L_1]),\ldots, \mathbf{cl}([L_n])\}\sigma,\ \text{where}$$
$$\mathbf{sel}(\mathbf{cl}([L_1])) = L_i,\ \text{for } 1 \leqslant i \leqslant n.$$

We indicate the selected literal by underlining it.

Two clauses with selection are considered as identical iff they consist of the same literals and the same literals are selected. The qualification "disregarding selection" means to read a clause with selection as a clause without selection.

Two clauses with selection are variants iff they are variants disregarding selection; the same holds for the instance relation.

Definition 1. Hyper Tableau Inference Rules
The calculus of hyper tableau consists of the following inference rules:
The Init Inference Rule:

$$\frac{C}{<[\ ],\ C^->}$$

for given finite clause set C without selection,   where $C^- = C$.
The Ext Inference Rule:

$$\frac{<p,\ C^->,\ \mathcal{P}\ \mathcal{A}\leftarrow\mathcal{B}}{<p^*((\mathcal{A}\leftarrow\mathcal{B})\sigma),\ C^->,\ \mathcal{P}}$$

where

1. $p, \mathcal{P}$ is a branch set with selected branch p, and
2. $(\mathcal{A}\leftarrow\mathcal{B}) \in C^-(p)$, and
3. $C_1,\ldots,\ C_n$ are new and pairwise disjoint variants from clauses from C^+ (p), with the same selected literals[1], and
4. σ is a most general multiset unifier $\mathcal{B}\sigma = \{\ \mathbf{sel}(C_1),\ldots, \mathbf{sel}(C_n)\}\sigma$, and
5. $C_i \approx C_i\sigma$ for every i, $1\leq i\leq n$,   and
6. every new branch $p.[\neg B\sigma] \in p{\scriptstyle\bullet}((\mathcal{A}\leftarrow\mathcal{B})\ \sigma)$, where $B\in\mathcal{B}$, is closed, and
7. every new branch $p.[A\sigma] \in p{\scriptstyle\bullet}((\mathcal{A}\leftarrow\mathcal{B})\ \sigma)$, where $A\in\mathcal{A}$, is open and C^- $(p.[A\sigma]) = C^-(p)$.

---

[1] More precisely: the selected literal of the variant is such that when the variant is renamed back to the original clause, the selected literals will be the same.

The Link **Inference Rule:**

$$\frac{<p, \ C^->, \ \mathcal{P} \quad \mathcal{A} \leftarrow \mathcal{B}}{<p, \ C^- \cup \{\ C_1\sigma,\dots,C_n\sigma\ \}>, \ \mathcal{P}}$$

where

1. $p, \ \mathcal{P}$ is a branch set with selected branch p, and
2. $(\mathcal{A} \leftarrow \mathcal{B}) \in C^-(p)$, and
3. $C_1,\dots, C_n$ are new and pairwise disjoint variants from clauses from $C^+(p)$, with the same selected literals, and
4. σ is a most general multiset unifier $\mathcal{B}\sigma = \{\ \mathbf{sel}(C_1),\dots, \mathbf{sel}(C_n)\}\sigma$, and
5. $C_i \approx C_i\sigma$ doesn't hold for some i, $1 \le i \le n$. □

The Init inference rule is used to setup an initial tableau consisting of the root only. Notice that by the fifth Condition, the Link and Ext rule are exclusive wrt. the same $\mathcal{A} \leftarrow \mathcal{B}$, clauses $C_1,\dots, C_n$ and σ.

2.4 Model Construction

Here the calculus constructs a model for an infinite exhausted (every applicable rule has been applied) branch by the concept of "productivity", which enables redundancy based on semantics possible[3].

Definition 2. (Productive Clauses)
Let C be a program clause with selection, and let $\mathcal{C}_C{}^+$ be a possibly infinite set of clauses with selection of instances of C and let $\mathcal{C}_C{}^-$ be a set of clauses without selection of instances of C. We say that C *produces* ground atom A wrt. $< \mathcal{C}_C{}^+, \ \mathcal{C}_C{}^->$, iff there is a ground substitution γ for C such that

1. $A = \mathbf{sel}(C)\,\gamma$, and
2. there is no $D \in \mathcal{C}_C{}^+$ with $C \succ D$ and $D \ge C\gamma$,
3. there is no $D \in \mathcal{C}_C{}^-$ with $C \succ D$ and $D \ge C\gamma$.

Let $p,\mathcal{P}$ be a hyper tableau for clause set C with selected branch p. Let $C \in C$. define

$$\mathcal{C}_C{}^+(p) = \{\ D \in C^+(p)|\ C \ge D\}$$
$$\mathcal{C}_C{}^-(p) = \{\ D \in C^-(p)|\ C \ge D\}$$

We say that C *produces* ground atom A wrt. p iff C produces A wrt. $< \mathcal{C}_C{}^+(p), \mathcal{C}_C{}^-(p)>$. □

The intention of "producing clauses" is this: for given A we see if there is an instance of C in the given "positive" set $\mathcal{C}_C{}^+$ such that $\mathbf{sel}(C)$ can be instantiated to A. Condition 2 expresses that the choice of C was a most specific one. Notice that if there is a clause D as mentioned, then it can be the case that A is produced by D, namely if the selected literal in D instantiates to A. Condition 3 expresses that there is no proper instance of C in the negative set $\mathcal{C}_C{}^-$ which "cancels" C.

For example, if C = $\underline{p(x,y)}$, $r(y,z) \leftarrow q(x)$ and $C_C{}^+$ = $\{p(x,x),\ \underline{r(x,z)} \leftarrow q(x)\}$ and $C_C{}^-$ = $\emptyset$ then C produces $p(a,b)$, but C does not produce $p(a,a)$ (neither does the clause in $C_C{}^+$ produce $p(a,a)$). Now, if $C_C{}^-$ = $\{p(x,c),r(c,z) \leftarrow q(x)\}$ instead, then C still produces $p(a,b)$ but no longer produces $p(a,c)$. This is because the clause in C_C^- "cancels" any appropriate ground substitution for C.

Definition 3. (Semantics of i-paths)
Let $\mathcal{D}$ be a derivation from C and let P = q_0, ..., q_j, ... be an i-path[2] of $\mathcal{D}$. For any $C \in C$ define

$$C_C{}^+(P) = \{ D \in C^+(P) \mid C \geq D \}, \text{ where } C^+(P) = \bigcup_{j > -1} C^+(q_j)$$

$$C_C{}^-(P) = \{ D \in C^-(P) \mid C \geq D \}, \text{ where } C^-(P) = \bigcup_{j > -1} C^-(q_j)$$

We say that C *produces* ground atom A wrt. P iff C produces A wrt. $< C_C{}^+(P)$, $C_C{}^-(P)>$.

We assign an interpretation I(P) to P as follows:

$$I(P) = \{A \mid C \text{ produces } A \text{ wrt. } P \text{ for some } C \in C^+(P)\}.$$ □

In the definitions given above, we construct an interpretation for an infinite exhausted branch, which makes it possible to adopt semantic redundancy criteria (cf. [3]).

2.5 Merits of the Calculus

In our opinion the two characters make the calculus unique and sophisticated.

Firstly, as indicated in the paper, the calculus takes a unification-driven way to instantiate the clauses for extension use, avoiding the blind guessing of its predecessor, while maintaining its desirable features such as model construction for an open branch and solving all the negative literals in one reference step. With the interplay of the Ext and Link rule, the instantiated input clauses are branch local, which means much pruning of search space and less memory space needed for storing them.

Secondly, and more importantly, the calculus treats the variables in non-rigid way, different from the free variable tableau in [5] and the clausal tableau in [6]. In this way, literal P stands for any of its variants. Moreover a new notion of branch closure based on variant-ship is introduced. Consequently in constructing a model for an open branch, if P of clause C is on the branch, we make all the instances of P valid in the interpretation, except those being instances of P', a proper instance of P, from a proper instance C' of C, with the branch passing through C' also. The same idea about interpretation generation is used in FDPLL [7], the model evolution calculus [8] and the disconnection calculus [9]. We value it as the most important contribution of the hyper tableau calculus.

---

[2] i.e. an infinite and exhausted path, concise definition is referred to [3].

3 The Counterexample

Here is the counterexample[3], i.e. the problem of MSC006-1.p, an unsatisfied problem, written in our dialect[4].

$$C_2: \quad \begin{aligned} P(x,z) &\leftarrow P(x,y), P(y,z) \\ Q(x,z) &\leftarrow Q(x,y), Q(y,z) \\ Q(y,x) &\leftarrow Q(x,y) \\ P(x,y), Q(x,y) &\leftarrow \\ &\leftarrow P(a,b) \\ &\leftarrow Q(c,d) \end{aligned}$$

Below is the literal tree generated by the second version hyper tableaux.

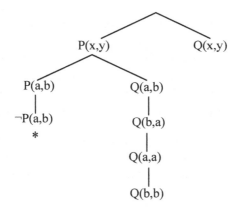

Fig. 1. The partial literal tree generated by the second calculus for the above counterexample

As is seen from above, the longest branch is left open because neither ext rule nor link rule can be applied to it. The clause set related with it is $C_2 \cup \{$ P(a,b), Q(a,b) $\leftarrow \}$. We show that no clause in the set can be used by the inference rules. Obviously there is no chance to apply ext rule or link rule with the 2nd and 3rd clauses, nor is it possible to make inference with the last three clauses in C_2, let alone the clause P(a,b), Q(a,b) $\leftarrow$. When it comes to the first clause, we try to find a unification for $B = \{P(x,y), P(y,z)\}$ and $\{P(u,u1), P(w,w1)\}$ (variants of P(x,y) on the branch). The substitution σ is $\{x \mapsto u, y \mapsto u1, z \mapsto w1, w \mapsto u1\}$. However the head literal intended to extend the branch is P(u,w1), a variant of the literal P(x,y) on the branch. The application of the Ext inference rule with this clause is redundant and this clause can't be used by the inference rules.

With an open branch in the literal tree, the clause set C_2 is decided as satisfiable according to the calculus.

---

[3] We thank Peter Baumgartner with whom we discussed the counterexample.
[4] Here u,v,w,x,y,... denote variables and a,b,...denote constants.

134   S. Feng, J. Sun, and X. Wu

According to the calculus, from the open branch we can construct an interpretation which should be a model for the clause set. The existence of the model for the clause set contradicts with the fact that it is an unsatisfied problem. Where does the problem lie? Let's begin with the *model* for the open branch. According to the above definitions, we know that in the interpretation of the branch every instance of P(x,y) except P(a,b) is valid, so are Q(a,b), Q(b,a) , Q(a,a) and Q(b,b). Obviously the interpretation falsifies the first clause representing transitivity of binary predication P. For example, the subset of the interpretation, {P(a,c), P(c,b), ¬ P(a,b)}, makes it impossible to satisfy the first clause. Thus we know that in this case the existence of an open branch doesn't entail that a model for the clause set.

To find the reasons behind, we compare the literal trees generated by the two hyper tableaux calculi. In the first hyper tableaux, we will get the subtree below P(x,y). In this calculus will the left branch still be open? Of course not. Because we can extend it with as many instances of the first clause in C_2 as we like. But in the second version calculus, when trying to extend the branch, we are confined to the clauses in the clause set related to the branch, which is increased only by the Link rule. In the counterexample, if we can add P(a,c) and P(c,b) to the branch, we may find the refutation of the problem, or conservatively at least we can eliminate the interpretation with subset of {P(a,c), P(c,b), ¬ P(a,b)} from possible models for the problem. It is hinted that the situation may be changed if we let the Link rule to generate more instances of the input clauses.

Let's have a look of the Conditions of the Link rule. The fourth Condition requires that all the body literals of $\mathcal{A} \leftarrow \mathcal{B}$ must be "solved" altogether by the proper instance of literals on the branch p (not necessarily all are proper instances, at least one is proper instance). After increasing $C^-(p)$ by the Link rule, we can apply the Ext rule to some branch p' with $\mathcal{A} \leftarrow \mathcal{B}$ (p is prefix of p') on the basis that $I(p') \models \mathcal{B}\sigma$. But can the fourth Condition entail that $I(p') \models \mathcal{B}\sigma$? The fourth Condition only considers the literals to be unified, and we can safely say that it only works on the syntactic level. However we know from the interpretation construction method, a semantic facet, that the literal L on branch p doesn't entail that all the instances of L are valid in $I(p)$. It seems that if the fourth Condition can work on the semantic level, the Link rule may generate more instances of the input clauses enough to make the calculus complete.

Below we give the third version calculus.

4 The Third Version Calculus

4.1 Formal Definition

Definition 4. Hyper Tableau Inference Rules
The calculus of hyper tableau consists of the following inference rules:
The Init Inference Rule:
The Ext Inference Rule:
The link Inference Rule:
They are all the same as their homonymies in the second version calculus.
The Link1 Inference Rule:

$$\frac{<p, \; C^- >, \; \mathcal{P} \quad \mathcal{A} \leftarrow \mathcal{B}}{<p, \; C^- \cup \{ C_1 \sigma,..., C_n \sigma \}>, \; \mathcal{P}}$$

where

1. p, $\mathcal{P}$ is a branch set with selected branch p, and
2. $(\mathcal{A} \leftarrow \mathcal{B}) \in C^-(p)$, and
3. $C_1,..., C_n$ are new and pairwise disjoint variants from clauses from C^+ (p), with the same selected literals, and
4. $\neg K \in I(p)$, and
5. σ is a most general multiset unifier $\{ \mathcal{B} \cup \{ A_j \} \} \sigma = \{ \mathbf{sel}(C_1),..., \mathbf{sel}(C_n), K \} \sigma$, for some j, $1 \leq j \leq m$, and
6. $C_i \approx C_i \sigma$ doesn't hold for some i, $1 \leq i \leq n$.
7. $I(p) \models \mathbf{sel}(C_i)\sigma$ for every i, $1 \leq i \leq n$, and $I(p) \models \neg K\sigma$.   □

We add a new Link1 rule to the calculus which can add more instances of the input clauses. The reason that we don't replace the original Link rule with the new Link1

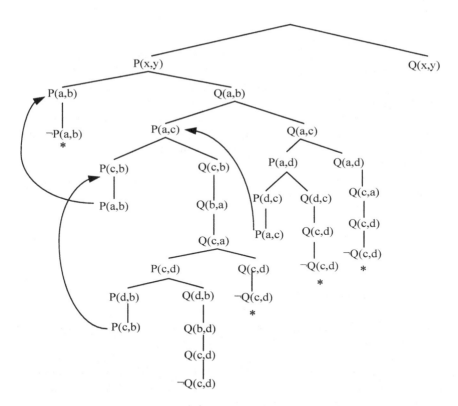

Fig. 2. The partial literal tree generated by the new calculus for the above counterexample. Node labeled with directed arc means that the pessimistic application of factorization (cf. 5.1).

rule is that we only try to apply the Link1 rule when the other two rules can't be applied to an "open" branch, just as the case in the counterexample. Since it is more complicated and time consuming to test whether a Link1 rule can be applied than to test the applicability of a Link rule, and our procedure of the second calculus showed that the second calculus was competent for some problems, we only resort to the Link1 rule when the second calculus may fail. From the definition of the new calculus and the application of the new reference rule, we know that the second calculus is a proper subset of the new calculus.

Figure 2 shows the partial literal tree generated by the new calculus for the above counterexample.

As in resolution calculi, the calculus inference rules can be applied in a don't-care nondeterministic way (the above preference is just our suggestion for faster procedure speed), as long as no possible application of an inference rule is deferred infinitely long. In other words, a concept of fairness is needed, and we can take that of the second hyper tableau calculus, with possible small modifications.

In the new calculus, the method to get $I(p)$ for a branch p is the same as before, which means that there are the same semantic redundancy criteria as those in the second calculus.

4.2 Correctness and Completeness

The new calculus is sound, because the second calculus is sound and the new Link1 rule generates only instances of input clauses in the way the Link rule does, hence logical consequences thereof.

We take the completeness proof of the second calculus as the correspondence of the new calculus, because we failed to find faults in it which render incompleteness. Since the new calculus has more instances of the input clauses for extension steps, and the concepts in the new calculus are similar to those in the second calculus, we are more justified to believe that the original completeness proof can show that the new calculus is complete.

5 Improvements

5.1 Factorization

Factorization is an important and widely used technique in tableau. Here we only discuss the optimistic application of factorization [10] and pessimistic application of factorization. In tableau community, factorization means that if node N_1 has the same labeled literal with node N_2, which is one of the nibbling of the ancestors of N_1, we can reuse the subtree below N_2 to close the branch to which N_1 belongs. The correctness of the method is guaranteed by the fact that the set of N_2's ancestors is a subset of that of N_1. The application of factorization is called optimistic if N_2 is not closed yet when factorization takes place, pessimistic otherwise.

In our calculus, the pessimistic application of factorization can be safely used without destroying the completeness, while the optimistic application of factorization is wrong because of the semantic facet of link1 rule.

5.2 Uniform for the Two Link Rules

To simplify the two Link rules into one, we borrow the idea from FDPLL by labeling the root node of the literal tree with a meta variable $\neg x$, which can be unified with any negative predication in the problem. In this way we make all the negative literals valid in the interpretation for the branch [ ], just like FDPLL and the model evolution calculus.

6 Conclusions

6.1 Related Work

Our calculus is a successor of the second version hyper tableau, with one more reference rule to generate more instances of the input clauses for extension use. So the new calculus can solve more problems than its predecessor. However the completeness of our calculus is still open.

Our calculus has small differences with its predecessor, so the comparison of our calculus with rigid hyper tableau [11], hyper resolution [12] and analytic resolution [13] can be referred to [3].

Our calculus has many similarities with the disconnection calculus. Firstly they are in tableau style, i.e. the tree branches on the clause. And secondly they have the similar model construction method. However it is shown that the disconnection calculus is not compatible with hyperlinking.

Our calculus has the similar model construction method with FDPLL and the model evolution calculus. But the latter two calculi branch on complementary literals other than literals from one clause. It is the most distinguished difference between our calculus and them.

6.2 Future Work

Complete or not
We should find whether our calculus is complete or not as soon as possible. On the one hand, we try to give a completeness proof for the calculus, and on the other hand, we try to find a counterexample of the calculus, by attempting to construct a special problem or by testing the problems in TPTP.

Implementation
We plan to make a working procedure based on the calculus. We are satisfied with the result that the future procedure would be faster in solving some classes of problems, despite that some day we may find that the calculus is incomplete.

Handle of equality
We also plan to make our calculus capable of handling equality efficiently, both in theoretical facet and working procedure.

References

1. Baumgartner P, Furbach U, Niemelä I. Hyper Tableaux (long version). from: http://www. uni-koblenz.de/fb4, Dec 1996.
2. Baumgartner P, Furbach U, Niemelä I. Hyper Tableaux. In: José Júlio Alferes, Luís Moniz Pereira, Ewa Orlowska eds. European Workshop on Logic in AI, JELIA 96. Évora, Portugal: LNCS 1126, Springer, 1996: 1−17.
3. Baumgartner P. Hyper Tableaux—The Next Generation. In: Harrie C. M. de Swart eds. TABLEAUX 98. Oisterwijk, The Netherlands: LNCS 1397, Springer, 1998: 60-76.
4. C. Chang and R. Lee. *Symbolic Logic and Mechanical Theorem Proving.* Acedemic Press, 1973.
5. M. Fitting. *First Order Logic and Automated Theorem Proving.* Texts and monographs in Computer Science. Springer, 1990.
6. R. Letz, K. Mayr, and C. Goller. Controlled integrations of the Cut Rule into Connection Tableau Calculi. *Journal of Automated Reasoning,* 13, 1994.
7. P. Baumgartner. FDPLL—A First-Order Davis-Putnam-Logeman-Loveland Procedure. In D. McAllester, editor, Proc. of CADE-17, LNAI 1831, Springer, 2000.
8. P. Baumgartner, C. Tinelli. The Model Evolution Calculus. In F. Baader eds. CADE 2003. Miami, USA: LNCS, Springer, 2003, 350-364.
9. R. Letz, G. Stenz. Proof and Model Generation with Disconnection Tableaux. In R. Nieuwenhuis and A. Voronkov (Eds), LPAR 2001, LNAI 2250, 142-156, 2001.
10. Letz R. First-Order Calculi and Proof Procedures for Automated Deduction. Darmstadt: Technische Hochschule Darmstadt, 1993.
11. Michael Kuhn. Rigid Hypertableaux. In Proc. Of KI' 97, LNAI, Springer, 1997.
12. J. A. Robinson. Automated deduction with hyper-resolution. I. J. Comput. Math., 1: 227-234, 1965.
13. D. Brand. Analytic Resolution in Theorem Proving. Artificial Intelligence, 7: 285-318, 1976.

A Service-Oriented Group Awareness Model and Its Implementation

Ji Gao-feng[1], Tang Yong[1], and Jiang Yun-cheng[1,2]

[1] Department of Computer Science, Sun Yat-sen University, Guangzhou 510275, China
isjigaofeng@163.com, issty@sysu.edu.cn
[2] College of Computer Sciences and Information Engineering, Guangxi Normal University,
Guilin 541004, China
ycjiang@mailbox.gxnu.edu.cn

Abstract. It is believed that the structure of a group is not stable which changes along with the time, the completion of goals and other random factors. After a thorough study over different kinds of group-awareness theories in recent years, and combined with the important concept Service, a new group-awareness model is proposed which is services-oriented, is called Service-Oriented Group Awareness Model (SOGAM). The awareness need of applications in heterogeneity environment and representation of the dynamic property in the group structure can be resolved by this model. The formalization to describe the awareness model, implementation of a Web-based architecture using Web Service related standards as communication model to share awareness information are given in this paper. Finally problems that need further study are pointed out.

1 Introduction

Group awareness computing focuses on the ability of a computational entity to adapt its behavior based on awareness information sensed from the physical and computational environments. In these terms, awareness is an understanding of the activities of others, which provides a context for your own activity. This context is used to ensure that individual contributions are relevant to the group's activity as a whole, and to evaluate individual actions with respect to group goals and progress. The information, then, allows groups to manage the process of collaborative working.[1] Applications depend on the availability of group awareness information in order to provide the most basic capabilities for social awareness, which includes information about the presence and activities of people in a shared environment [2].

Main issues about group-awareness research include two aspects: group-awareness model and its implementation. Group-awareness model research further dealt with its logic representation and characteristic description. Up to now, there is no standard definition for group-awareness. There is no such universal group-awareness model that could satisfy all awareness requirements in CSCW system. Reference [3] proposed a cooperative awareness model based on role, but the relation in roles' cooperation was not mentioned in this paper. Reference [4] proposed an awareness model based on spacial objects, which depict the awareness intensity between two actors by

J. Lang, F. Lin, and J. Wang (Eds.): KSEM 2006, LNAI 4092, pp. 139–150, 2006.

the intersection and union operation of the objects in users' interest space and effect space, but this model wasn't well-combined with cooperative mechanism. In reference [5], a spacial awareness model refined the awareness source in the work domain, which characterized the group-awareness through relations among its components. The hierarchy awareness model in reference [6] simply used awareness hierarchy to measure the cooperative level of different actors in collaborations. In reference [7], Tom Rodden extended the spacial objects awareness model to depict the relations among cooperative applications in non-share work domain. He measured the awareness intensity by information flow chart among application. All awareness models mentioned above have a disadvantage in common – all of them could only characterize the awareness intensity among actors in a coarse scale, none of them can measure it by precise mathematical calculations. In reference [8] and [9], the measurement of awareness intensity was more concerned in a new group-awareness model based on role and task, a measurement based on role difference was proposed. However, this model was based on a static group structure, which cannot represent the dynamic property of the group structure. Therefore, this model cannot precisely characterize the changing tasks, roles and activities in the real world.

The need for infrastructures to support building group awareness applications has also been long discussed in the literature. The main idea is to facilitate that a new application be built by reusing components that implement the desired features such as event notification [2] [10], sharing of context information [11] [12] and shared workspaces [13]. Further, those components are associated with architectural models targeted at facilitating the design as well as the evolution of applications such as Dragonfly [14] and Clover [15]. Challenges faced by developers of group awareness application include the support for several levels of heterogeneity and the distribution of responsibilities between applications and infrastructures. [16]. An alternative to deal with these two issues is to take advantage of the benefits provided by Web Service [17]. The essence of Web Services is the use of web-based standards to bridge a myriad of Internet systems independently of hardware and software heterogeneity.

This paper is organized as follows. Section 2 defines the group architecture through basic sets and relations built upon the services. Section 3 then introduces the SOGAM that can well depict group activities based on the group structure defined in Section 2. This section gives the formalization of this new model. Section 4 shows the implementation and application of SOGAM in our prototype: COP project. Section 5 talks about some further research on SOGAM.

2   The Group Structure Formalization

Group built up by different members possess certain group structure, group structure regulates all group behaviors. Therefore as a kind of group behaviors, group-awareness is restricted by group structure. It is believed that the structure of a group is not stable, and it changes along with the time, the completion of goals and other random factors. In Service-Oriented Computing the dynamic property of entity is caused by the diverse computation environment. And the dynamic property of service itself is represented in the following features: the functions provided by the service are permitted to change, the composing of service can dynamically change, and the roles service that plays in group structure also can change. All these changeable facts require that the group-awareness model could depict these changes clearly, and make new strategies according to these changes. Hence, in order to build a group-awareness model that can represent the dynamic property well based on former analysis, the concept of service is finally brought into group structure, and a Services-Oriented Group Awareness Model (SOGAM) is proposed. This section gives the formalization of this new group structure.

2.1 Basic Sets

For clearly explaining the concept model related, a service related scenario is given as follows:

There are two services: UserLogin service and JobCheck service. UserLogin service provides user registration, permission control and so on. PaperCheck service provides job submission, result notification and so on. Students login in system and submit jobs. Teachers check them and give some suggestions

Definition 1(SO): Service Object, which we can also call 'Resource', is the object manipulated in service. The state of the service can be represented by the state of SO. This is one of the core ideas in WSRF. Detail information can be found in reference [18].

For example, the SO of the JobCheck service may be papers pdf or word format. JobCheck service operates them depend on the papers' states.

Definition 2(AO): Atomic Operation is the atomic operation of system resource object which cannot be further divided. It can be denoted in two-tuples <Operation, Object>.

For example, UserLogin service provides AO like <register, user information>, <check, user permission>

Definition 3(SR): Service Role is the roles the service plays in cooperation. A service could play several different roles in different sessions in a single collaboration; many services can play the same role by possessing the same operations. Hence, it's many-many relation between roles and services.

For example, JobCheck service sometimes is a paper manager role, and sometimes is a homework inspector role.

Definition 4(S): A atomic service $S(ao_1,...,ao_n)=(Pre,Post)$ consists of

1. A finite set $Pre \in 2^{SO}$, the pre-conditions;
2. A finite set $Post \in 2^{SO}$, the post-conditions;
3. $ao_1,...,ao_n$, the operation of this service.

A composite service is a finite sequence $S_1,...,S_n$ of atomic services.

It is clear that Services are encapsulation of AOs and SOs, they offer application interfaces to users.

Definition 5(SS): Service State is the states which Service instance goes through along its execution. Let $s \in S$, then its state is represented by s(state). In SOGAM model, we have states as follows:

1. Sleeping state: a non-active state of a service.
2. Ready state: a state that all the pre-conditions of service are satisfied and the service is ready for execution.

3. Suspended state: a state that service pauses because of certain reason (such as waiting for resources).
4. Running state: a service is in execution after successful activation.
5. End state: a state denotes that the service stops (either naturally stops itself or been terminated when errors or exceptions occur).

Definition 6(TIM): Time Set: the elements in TIM could be time points or time durations. It represents the time that some role of service spends in cooperation. The time is not only system related but also people restricted.

For example, designer can restrict that JobCheck service must give a result in 24 hours from the job submission. System requires that the response time of UserLogin service is one second.

Definition 7(A): Actor: an actor is a dynamic instance generated by a role after being activated by certain service; it's a runtime agent of a service being in certain role. An Actor can be denoted in a three-tuple <s, sr, time>, in which 's' is the service that the Actor delegates, $s \in S$; 'sr' is the service role that has been activated, $sr \in SR$; 'time' is a set of Actor's life durations, time $\subseteq 2^{TIM}$.

For example: three-tuple <JobCheck, paper manager role, {8:00-10:00, 12:00}> denotes that JobCheck service worked as paper manager role during 8:00-10:00 and on 12:00 time.

Definition 8 (TASK): Task is the minimal logic unit in cooperation. It is a distinguishable behavior, can relate to multiple services. Task can be thought of a resource machine: produce new resource from old resource through services. TASK $\in 2^{SO}$.

For example, after some JobCheck service operations, paper is added new content such as comment. After UserLogin service, the information of the users is updated.

Definition 9(SD): The relations among different services are service dependence. Gutwin [19] summarize 3 kinds of activities in collaboration based on his observation and experiment: do-it-together activity, alternative activity, and producer-consumer activity. Do-it-together activity, as its name, is the kind of activity which single user cannot accomplish. It needs many users to work together at the same time. Alternative activity needs multiple users' effort, each one's job is connected to former ones'. And in producer-consumer activity, sub-activities can be divided into two different kinds, the object and information that one generates are consumed by another one. Based on the 3 collaboration activity models above, 3 service relations could be further defined according to the state of service.

1. Do-It-Together Dependence. It is defined as below:

$$DITD(s_1,s_2) \leftrightarrow post_{s_1} \cup post_{s_2} = Task \wedge pre_{s_1} \cap pre_{s_2} \neq \emptyset$$

2. Alternative Dependence. It is defined as below:

$$AD(s_1,s_2) \leftrightarrow pre_{s_1} \cap pre_{s_2} \neq \emptyset$$

Obviously, every DITD activity is the AD activity.

3. Producer-Consumer Dependence. It is defined as below:

$$PCD(s_1,s_2) \leftrightarrow post_{s_1} \supseteq pre_{s_2} \wedge pre_{s_1} \cap pre_{s_2} = \emptyset$$

Definition 10 (TAR): Target is the execution result of a series of tasks; it's the ultimate goal of cooperation. One target could be accomplished by achieving sub-tasks divided from target, the series of sub-tasks are denoted TARGET.

2.2 Basic Relations

Definition 11 (TARGET RELATION)

$$TGT =< TAR, TASK, f_{tgt} >, f_{tgt} : TAR \rightarrow 2^{TASK}$$

Target relation (TGT) is a mapping, which represents that the target of cooperation can be achieved by the decomposition of a series of tasks and then the accomplishment of each task.

Definition 12 (PARTER RELATION)

$$PAR =< A, TIM, SD, f_{par} >, f_{par} : A \times A \times TIM \rightarrow SD$$

Parter relation is a mapping, which represents the service relation among different actors at certain time in cooperation.

Definition 13 (TASK RELATION)

$$TSK =< TASK, PAR, f_{tsk} >, f_{tsk} : TASK \rightarrow 2^{PAR}$$

Task relation is a mapping, which represents that any task could be accomplished by the execution of multiple services.

Definition 14 (STATE RELATION)

$$STA =< A, TIM, SS, f_{sta} >, f_{sta} : A \times TIM \rightarrow SS$$

State relation is a mapping, which represents the state of a service in the cooperation at a certain time.

2.3 Group Structure

Definition 15 (GROUP STRUCTURE)

It has already been emphasized that the group activities is strictly restricted by group structure. By introducing the concept of 'service', a new group structure is defined as follows:

$$GS =< E, R >,$$

is a two-tuple that is composed by the relations among elements. In which:

$$E = \{TAR, TASK, A, SS, SD\},$$
$$R = \{TGT, PAR, TSK, STA\}$$

3 SOGAM

According to definition 15 it is clear that group structure characterizes the base elements and relations which constitute the group, provides the foundation for describing group-awareness. In this section, we try to characterize the group-awareness by characterizing the group members' service properties. And the group-awareness intensity can be accurately measured by the difference between services. Then a SOGAM could be set up.

Definition 16: A SOGAM is defined as a three tuple:

$$SOGAM =< E, R, ExR >$$

The definition of 'E' and 'R' can be found in DEFINITION 15, 'ExR' represents group-awareness rules, functions and relations of the extended GS, that is, task decomposition rules, single-service activity trail set and group-awareness intensity calculation function [8].

The full content of 'ExR' in DEFINITION 16 is: target decomposition rules are based on TGT, they offer groundwork for service-based awareness intensity calculation; single-service activity trail-set depicts awareness activity environment of any time; and group-awareness intensity calculation function defines the group-awareness intensity of service-to-service, actor-to-actor, and it also defines the space of service's perception ability.

3.1 Target Decomposition Rule

Any task could be regarded as a set of services related to the target. A group could dynamically generate different actors according to different targets. Hence, two target decomposition rules could be defined as follows:

Definition 17 (Existing Rule (ER)): In order to simplify the discussion, it is assumed that any target has its target decomposition. The targets that cannot be accomplished in the process of group cooperation, that means targets without target decomposition, are not in the range of our model. So they are not discussed here. Then, we have:

$$\forall tar(tar \in TAR \rightarrow \exists Tk(Tk \subseteq TASK \wedge f_{tgt}(tar) = 2^{Tk}))$$

Definition 18 (Valid Rule (VR)): After the decomposition of target, every task is assigned to an actor sequence:

$$\forall tk(tk \in TASK \rightarrow \exists Par(Par \subseteq PAR \wedge f_{tsk}(tk) = 2^{Par}))$$

According to rules above, there is an example of target decomposition tree in graph 1.

The up-most Target can be divided into two tasks: task1 and task2, which can be achieved by accomplishing a series of operations over objects Os and service Ss. Those darker objects represents that the preconditions of the services below are satisfied, one object can only offer one access to its service. Every service activates its actor according to the service status.

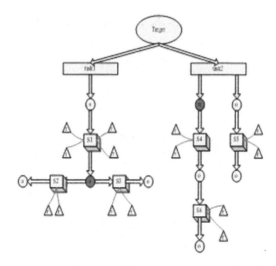

Graph 1. Target decomposition tree

3.2 Trail-Set of Single-Service Activity

In groupware, single service activity set is a sub-set of the group activity set. A three dimensional space is chosen to depict these activities. Because in the process of collaboration, the one that accomplishes the target is not services, but the actor generated dynamicly, so we use actor, service object and time as the three dimension, and corresponding activity trail-set is built up to characterize the participation and concern of a single service in the group (as in Graph 2).

The discrete point in the graph represents the role specialty and the behavior characteristic of some service at certain time. To any service object, the projection of a

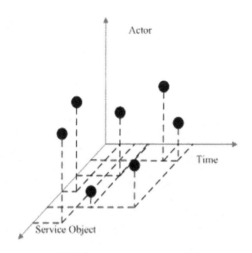

Graph 2. Single-service activity trail graph

point in the actor-time plane pictures the characteristic changing of actor's behavior over time, which is denoted by:

$$f_{so} : TIM \rightarrow A.$$

To any time point, the projection in actor-service object plane pictures the impact space and interested object space of that service, which is denoted by:

$$f_{tim} : SO \rightarrow A.$$

a_1's impact space at time tim is defined as follows:

$$IMS_{tim}(a_1) = \{a_2 / (\forall so)(so \in f_{tim}^{-1}(a_1) \wedge a_2 \in f_{tim}(so))\}$$

$$IMS(a_1) = \bigcup_{tim} IMS_{tim}(a_1)$$

a_1's interested object space at time tim is defined as follows:

$$INS_{tim}(a_1) = \{so / f_{tim}(so) = a_1\}$$

$$INS(a_1) = \bigcup_{tim} INS_{tim}(a_1)$$

Theorem 3.1
If the intersection of INS(a) and IMS(b) is not empty on sometime, then Individual a can perceive b. the proof of the 3.1 is relatively easy.

To any actor, the projection in time-service object plane pictures its activity content and quantized characteristics, which is denoted by:

$$f_{actor} : TIM \rightarrow SO.$$

And all projections of an actor picture its working domain and process track in the execution of the task.

3.3 Calculating Function of Group-Awareness Intensity

As target decomposition tree already shown in Graph 1, by extracting the actors from the graph, an actor's structure graph with awareness intensity could be set up, as in Graph 3, hence group-awareness intensity among actors and services could be defined.

When calculating group-awareness intensity, it is assumed that the awareness intensity over each other's behavior is utmost when two services, s_1 and s_2, could act the same actor; when s_1 and s_2 are unreachable in actor's structure graph, the awareness intensity between each other is 0; and when s_1 and s_2 form different actors, $actor_1$ and $actor_2$, the awareness intensity between them is in inverse ratio with the length between $actor_1$ and $actor_2$ in the actor's structure graph. With these assumptions, here come some definitions below.

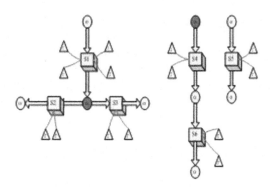

Graph 3. Actor's structure graph

Definition 19 (Awareness Intensity between Actors): in cooperation, the awareness intensity between different actors is defined as:

$$AIA(actor_1, actor_2) = \frac{K}{len(actor_1, actor_2) + 1}$$

in which K is a experience quotiety, it can be changed in different applications to achieve the best effect.

Definition 20 (Awareness Intensity between Services): Service in different cooperation could generate different actors. The awareness intensity between services is the reflection of all the multiple actors' awareness intensities.

$$AIS(s_1, s_2) = \sum_{i=1, j=1}^{i=n, j=m} Adif(actor_i, actor_j)$$

Definition 21 (Service Activity Domain): Service activity domain represents the awareness conditions of certain service over resources. It can be defined by set of SO.

$$SAD(s_1) = \{so \,/\, so \in s_2 \wedge Sdif(s_1, s_2) > 0\}$$

4 Implementation

SOGAM is based on the concept of 'service'; hence its implementation is tightly related to Web Service technologies. We developed a simple SOGAM prototype: COoperation work Platform, which we call 'COP', based on our lab's CSCW platform. COP adopts web service technologies. Its main purpose is to provide a shared work spaces and share awareness between registered applications.

First, we wrapped all modules implemented by different technique and programming languages into web services. Web services are accessed via HTTP operating on top of TCP as application by self-describing messages referencing information to understand the message. XML specifications such as WSDL (Web Service Description Language) and SOAP (Simple Object Access Protocol) are the building blocks of the Web Services architecture [17]. COP is also some Web Services that allow other applications to handle awareness information based on the classic dimensions who, where, when, what, and how discussed in the ubiquitous computing literature [20] by formalizing a set of XML-based operations associated to those dimensions. COP offers five categories of services: registry, event notification, status, storage and retrieval. The COP architecture is shown in graph 4.

COP work as follows.

1. Applications register in COP through Registry Service and obtain their identifiers and callback interfaces.
2. Designers integrate some services (the new form of applications) to achieve the target by the xml-based files which describe the target decompose tree.
3. Now we can obtain the intensity between services with the method in definition 20.
4. Services whose intensity satisfies our standard will share XML-based awareness information in SOGAM server.
5. An application can retrieve status information stored by another application by invoking Status Service and notice registered application through callback interface by invoking Notification Service.
6. Operation awareness information by means of Storage Service and Retrieval Service

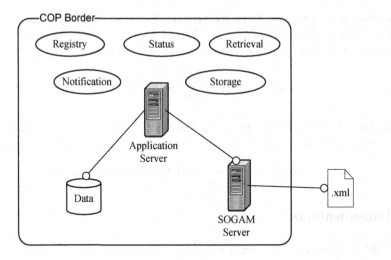

Graph 4. COP architecture

For example: follow codes describe the shared awareness information between UserLogin service and JobCheck service. The registered user Tom is A class student. He submitted his paper on 05:00 through JobCheck service

```
<!--            awareness information example -->
<awareness identifier=WS00001>
<dimensions>
<dimension="who" type="name" value="Tom"/>
<dimension="who" type="password" value="******"/>
<dimension="who" type="class" value="A"/>
<dimension="where" type="null" value="null"/>
<dimension="when" type="00:00" value="05:00"/>
<dimension="what" type="paper" value="submit"/>
<dimension="how" type="null" value="null"/>
</dimensions>
</awareness>
```

5 Conclusion and Further Study

The use of service-oriented architectures in the development of web based applications gives a new dimension to cooperative computing among different organizational units. The awareness and cooperation among them is a problem we have to confront. The main contribution of the SOGAM is relative to its proposal of a service-oriented model which resolve the need of awareness of applications in heterogeneity environment and the representation of the dynamic property in the group structure. On one hand, the cooperative efficiency can be improved. On the other hand the behavior of the service itself can be adjusted by the measured awareness information which is provided by the SOGAM model. Today, however, cooperation in group work is more common and complex that result in cooperating not only in message level but also in semantic level. There are several problems that should be done in further studies: (1) Service Description. A precondition of SOGAM is that services have rich self- description functions. Only the changing of service states are reported to SOGAM in time, can the SOGAM represent the real world's changing. So, we plan to study cooperation in groups by use of theories and methods in semantic web and AI area. (2) It is the services composition that researchers focus after SOGAM is proposed. From this paper, it is obvious that services composition is the base of the calculation of the awareness intensity. (3) The optimization strategy of actor selection. Multiple services possess similar functions (can generate same actors), therefore, some strategy for the actor selection based on the fact that every individual has an expressive self description should be set up to facilitate the cooperation.

Acknowledgement

This work is supported by the National Natural Science Foundation grant No.60373081 and the Guangdong Provincial Science and Technology Foundation grant No.05200302 and 5003348.

References

1. Dourish P, BellottiV. Awareness and coordination in shared work spaces In: Proceedings of CSCW '92 . Toronto,Canada: ACM Press, 1992, pp.107-114.
2. W.Prinz, "NESSIE: an awareness environment for cooperative settings," in Proceedings of the European Conference of CSCW, 1999, pp.391-410
3. Drury J , William s M G. A framework for role-based specification and evaluation of awareness support in synchronous collaborative applications In: Proceedings of the Eleventh IEEE International Workshops on Enabling Technologies (W ET ICE'02) . Pittsburgh: IEEE Press, 2002, pp.12-17.
4. Benford S, Fahlen L. A spatial model of interaction in large virtual environments In: Proceedings of the 3rd European Conference on CSCW (ECSCW '93). Milan, Italy: Kluwer Academic Publishers,1993, pp.13-17.
5. Gutwin C, Greenberg S. A descriptive framework of work space awareness for real-time groupware. Computer Supported Cooperative Work, 2002, (34) pp.411-446.
6. Daneshgar F, Ray P. Awareness modeling and its application in cooperative network management In: Proceedings of the 7th IEEE International Conference on Parallel and Distributed Systems. Iwate, Japan: IEEE Press, 2000, pp.357-363.
7. Rodden, T. Populating the application: a model of awareness for cooperative applications. In: Proceedings of the ACM CSCW '96 Conference on Computer-Supported Cooperative Work. Boston, MA: ACM Press, 1996, pp.87-96.
8. Ge Sheng, Ma Dianfu, Huai Jinpeng. A role-based group awareness model. Journal of Software, 2001, 12 (6), pp.864-869.
9. Linxia Yan; Jianchao Zeng. A task-based group awareness model. Computer Supported Cooperative Work in Design, 2004. Proceedings. The 8th International Conference on Volume 2, 26-28 May 2004, pp.90 - 94 Vol.2
10. G. Fitzpatrick et al., "Augmenting the workaday world with Elvin," in Proceedings of the European Conference of CSCW, 1999, pp.431-450.
11. M. Rittenbruch, "Atmosphere: towards context-selective awareness mechanisms," in Proceeding of the International Conference on Human-Computer Interaction, 1999, pp.328-332.
12. L. Fuchs, "AREA: a cross-application Notification service for groupware," in Proceedings of the European Conference of CSCW, 1999, pp.61-80.
13. T. Gross and W. Prinz, "Awareness in context: a lightweight approach," in Proceedings of the European Conference of CSCW, 2003, pp.295-314
14. G. E. Anderson, T. C. N. Graham, and T. N. Wright, "Dragonfly: linking conceptual and implementation architectures of multiuser interactive systems," in Proceedings of the ACM International Conference on Software Engineering, 2000, pp.252-261.
15. Y. Laurillau and L. Nigay, "Clover architecture for groupware," in proceedings of the ACM CSCW Conference, 2002, pp.236-245.
16. R. B. Neto et al, "A Web Service Approach for Providing Context Information to CSCW Applications," in proceedings of the WebMedia & LA-Web 2004 Joint Conference, 2004, pp.46-53
17. W3C. (2002) Web Services Activity. [Online]. Available: http://www.w3.org/2002/ws.
18. [Online].Available:http://www.oasis-open.org/committees/tc_home.php?wg_abbrev=wsrf
19. Gutwin, C. Work space awareness in real-time distributed group ware [Ph.D.Thesis]. 1997. http://w ww.cs.usask.ca/faculty/gutwin/publications.html.
20. G. Abowd, E. D. Mynatt, and T. Rodden, "The human experience," IEEE Pervasive Computing, vol. 1, no. 1, 2002, pp. 48-57

An Outline of a Formal Ontology of Genres

Pawel Garbacz

The John Paul II Catholic University of Lublin, Poland
garbacz@kul.lublin.pl

Abstract. The aim of this paper is to specify the ontological commitments of the theory of document genres proposed by J. Yates and W. Orlikowski. To this end, I construct a formal ontology of documents and genres in which to define the notions presupposed in the genre discourse. For the sake of decreasing ambiguity and confusion, I briefly describe the primitive terms in which this ontology is formulated.

1 Introduction

The idea of applying the notion of document genre in information systems is now widely recognised. There is a number of theoretical and practical studies in which documents are represented in terms of their genres. The Digital Document Track of the annual Hawaii International Conference on System Science has become an established forum for presenting these results. The specific domains of application include information and document retrieval, metadata schemas, computer-mediated communication, electronic data management, and computer-supported collaborative work.

Nonetheless, the very notion of genre is unstable and the conceptual divergences between different theories thereof are substantial. For example, it is debatable whether we should represent a genre by means of pairs <substance, form>, as suggested in [17], or triples <substance, form, functionality> ([9]) or quadruples ([13]). Some even deny that all different kinds of genres may be represented in a uniform way ([4]). There is no agreement on what kinds of genres there are and how one may organise them in a taxonomy. In particular, the theoretical status of the so called cybergenres is disputed (cf. [13], [9]).

I believe that at least some of these issues may become much more transparent if we specify the ontological commitments of the genre discourse [1]. It is usually believed in Knowledge Representation that a clear conceptualisation that stands behind a given vocabulary/database schema/taxonomy/discourse model/... may contribute both to the theoretical adequacy of the latter and to its practical applicability or efficiency. The aim of this paper is to construct a precise ontological framework in which the notion of genre may be defined in such a way that we could understand what "ontological price" we need to pay for document genres. The framework in question should clarify what entities we

---

[1] The term "genre discourse" denotes here any system of acts of communication such that they may be classified along the lines of the theory of genres.

J. Lang, F. Lin, and J. Wang (Eds.): KSEM 2006, LNAI 4092, pp. 151–163, 2006.

need to acknowledge in order for our talk about document genres not to be void. To my best knowledge, this is the first ontological inquiry into the domain of the genre discourse, thus the section 'Related work' is omitted. Let me just mention one distant cousin of this approach, namely the ontology of information objects based on the DOLCE foundational ontology (cf. [6]).

It must be emphasised that the "content" of the following ontology is strictly constrained to the theory of genres as advanced by J. Yates and W. Orlikowski. Thus, I reluctantly neglect research on discourse structure and argumentation.

2   Genres in Organisational Communication

The notion of genre I focus on in this paper originates in the theory of organisational communication. J. Yates and W. Orlikowski define it in the following way:

> A genre of organizational communication (e.g. a recommendation letter or a proposal) is a typified communicative action invoked in response to a recurrent situation. The recurrent situation or socially defined need includes the history and nature of established practises, social relations, and communication media within organizations (e.g. a request for a recommendation letter assumes the existence of employment procedures that include the evaluation and documentation of prior performance [...]). ([17], p. 301)

A genre is claimed to consist of substance and form. The former aspect encompasses the topics and needs addressed in a given act of communication and the purposes of performing of such act. The latter is claimed to be related to the physical features of the document. [17] mentions in this context the structural features, the medium in which the document is storaged, and the respective language system. Genres are dynamic entities: they are enacted, reproduced, and transformed. [17] shows how to describe such processes by means of the notion of social rule taken from the structuration theory of social institutions (cf. [7]). A genre rule associates the form and substance of a given genre with certain recurrent situations.

> For example, in the case of the bussiness letter, which is invoked in recurrent situations requiring documented communication outside the organization, the genre rules for substance specify that the letter pertain to a bussiness interaction with an external party, and the genre rules for form specify an inside address, salutation, complimentary close, and correct, relatively formal language. ([17], p. 302)

The relation between a genre and its genre rules is not very tight:

> A particular instance of a genre need not draw on all the rules constituting that genre. For example, a meeting need not include minutes or a formal agenda for it to be recognizable as a meeting. Enough distinctive

genre rules, however, must be invoked for the communicative action to be identified - within the relevant social community - as an instance of a certain genre. A chance encounter of three people at the water cooler, which is not preplanned and lacks formal structuring devices, would not usually be considered as a meeting. ([17], p. 302-303)

A coordinated sequence of genres enacted by members of a particular organisation constitutes a *genre system*. For instance, the genre system of balloting was identified as consisting of three genres: the ballot form issued by the group coordinator, the ballot replies generated by the group members, and the ballot results. ([19], p. 51)

Any (sufficiently capacious) collection of genres may be meaningfully ordered with respect to their generality. Yates and Orlikowski emphasise that any subsumption hierarchy of genres is relative to a social context.

In a series of papers: [12], [19], [18], [8], Yates and Orlikowski showed that this theoretical framework is well-suited for empirical study of electronic-supported communication in real-world organisations. The genre discourse turned out to be a fruitful methodology also in web information retrieval as attested by [4],[5], [9], and [13].

3   Ontological Commitments of the Genre Discourse

Speaking about ontological presuppositions of the genre discourse, we should distinguish between particular tokens of a certain genre and the type of this genre. The distinction between tokens and types may be characterised in terms of the relation of instantiation. Any particular token of a certain genre is said to instatiate the type of this genre. For example, a particular job application instantiates the type of the job application genre. In what follows I will call any token (i.e. instance) of a document genre a *document*. Simlarly, any type of a document genre will be called a *genre*. I assume that both documents and genres are construed along the lines of the theory of Yates and Orlikowski as sketched above.

I propose to articulate the genre discourse by means of the following primitive notions:

1. two basic general ontological categories of endurants and perdurants,
2. a specific relation of being a member of a community,
3. a general ontological category of situation-types,
4. a non-empty set *Time* of time parameters (temporal moments or regions),
5. a specific ontological category of agents and three specific relations between agents' mental attitudes and situation-types,
6. two specific relations of being a part of, one of which is atemporal and the other is temporal,

In other words, I submit that the above categories (together with their short descriptions below) are sufficient ontological commitments of the genre theory of Yates and Orlikowski. I do not claim that they are necessary; still, I conjecture that it is improbable that one can provide a less ontologically demanding framework. Although these categories are assumed here to be primitive, in order to avoid (or decrease) confusion, I will briefly characterise some of them.

All definitions and axioms below are rendered in first-order set theory.

Endurants and perdurants. The notions of endurant and perdurant are understood in the standard philosophical way. An *endurant* is an entity that is wholly present, i.e. whose all parts are present, at any time at which it exists. A *perdurant* is an entity that enfolds in time, i.e. for any time at which it exists, some of its parts are not present (see e.g. [11], [6]). How to draw a line between endurants and perdurants is a controversial isssue, however people, cars, and books are usually considered as endurants and people's lives, car races, and acts of reading are considered as perdurants. A set *End* will contain all endurants we need for a given genre discourse and a set *Perd* will contain all relevant perdurants. What is not controversial is the claim that no endurant is a perdurant.

$$End \cap Perd = \emptyset. \tag{1}$$

In our formal ontology we need both endurants and perdurants because we saw above that some documents are endurants, e.g. a memo, but other are perdurants, e.g. a meeting. Although representing a meeting as a document (of a kind) may seem counterintuitive, I follow Orlikowski and Yates' pattern to name certain perdurants as documents (in the broad sense).

Communities and their members. According to the genre theory, any document (and thereby any genre) is enacted, maintained, and transformed by and within a certain community. In this paper I will represent this aspect of the theory by introducing the relation of membership. The expression "x *in* y" is to mean that an endurant x is a member of a community y.

$$x \in Com \equiv \exists y \in End \; y \; in \; x. \tag{2}$$

Thereby I assume that communities are entities that do not change their membership trough time. If a genre x is enacted, maintained or transformed in a community y, I will say that x *comes from* y.

Situation-types, agents, and mental attitudes. The term "situation-type" is understood here as referring to such ontologically complex entities as that John is unemployed, that John's car first stopped and then burst into flames, and that Peter will steal John's book. More generally speaking, any entity to which somebody refers by means of a sentence will be called here a *situation-type*. The ontological category I have in mind here coincides with the category of situation-types as defined and used in [1]. The set of all situation-types that we need in the genre discourse will be denoted by the symbol "*Sit*". It is important to emphasise that a situation-type may obtain at one moment (temporal region) and not obtain at another. For instance, that Andrea Merkel is a chancellor obtains in January 2006 and did not obtain in March 2004.

The notion of situation-type is used here to model the conditions under which and the purposes for which a document is created. Some of such conditions refer to the objective facts. For instance, given that an annual report is created periodically, the fact that we are now in such a period is an objective situation-type. Other conditions and all purposes are related to the subjective facts such as those that somebody entertains certain belief or desire, e.g. a ballot form is issued when someone desires information about the beliefs of certain people. I isolate within the set Sit a subset Sit_0 that contains the situation-types of the former kind. Let a set $Agt \subseteq End$ contain agents, i.e. those endurants that are capable of entertaining beliefs, desires, and intentions. In order to include the subjective situations in Sit, I will use the following inductive definition:

$$Sit_{n+1} := Sit_n \cup \{< x, y >: x \in Agt \wedge y \in Sit_n\}. \tag{3}$$

$$Sit_\omega := \bigcup Sit_n. \tag{4}$$

The specific content of Sit may be established by one of the axioms of the form 5.

$$Sit := Sit_n. \tag{5}$$

Although different kinds of communities seemingly require different values of the parameter n, there seems to be two distinguished points: $n = 2$ and $n = \omega$. These points determine two different ways of modelling the notion of mutual belief, which is of crucial importance in any kind of theoretical reflection on social reality. The former point is related to the claim that we find e.g. in [15] on p. 41-51 to the effect that in most cases it is sufficient (and necessary) to define this notion in terms of second-order beliefs. Briefly speaking, all members of a community mutually believe that p iff they all believe that p and they all believe that they all believe that p. The latter point is related to the iterative notion of mutual belief (e.g. [10], p. 52-60), which requires to this end n-order beliefs, for any $n \in \omega$. Briefly speaking, all members of a community mutually believe that p iff they all believe that p, they all believe that they all believe that p, and they all believe that they all believe that they all believe that p, ... Because it is highly improbable that any member of any real-world organisation that produces and uses documents entertains such "infinite" beliefs, I adopt the former notion, which in the present framework may be defined by 7. To this end, I first fix the value of the parameter n in 5 to be equal to 2. Next, I assume that all mental attitudes to which one is committed in his genre discourse may be defined in terms of beliefs ($Bel \subseteq Agt \times Sit$), desires ($Des \subseteq Agt \times Sit$), and intentions ($Int \subseteq Agt \times Sit$). "$< x, y > \in Bel$" stands for the expression "x believes that a situation-type y obtains". Analogously, I read the abbreviations "$< x, y > \in Des$" and "$< x, y > \in Int$". Consequently, I treat beliefs, desires, and intentions as situation-types. Among different possible assumptions concerning the relationships between beliefs, desires, and intentions (see e.g. [16], p. 99-102), I adopt the modest claim to the effect that intentions entail desires.

$$Int \subseteq Des. \tag{6}$$

A community x has a mutual belief that y obtains $\equiv$ (7)

$$\equiv \forall z(z \; in \; x \rightarrow < z, y > \in Bel \land < z, < z, y >> \in Bel).$$

In what follows, I will need two auxiliary concepts defined by 8 and 9.

$$Ment\_Sit := Bel \cup Des \cup Int. \tag{8}$$

$$x \in Com \rightarrow Ment\_Sit(x) := \{< y, z > \in Ment\_Sit : y \; in \; x\}. \tag{9}$$

It should be obvious that no situation is neither an endurant nor a perdurant.

$$Sit \cap (End \cup Perd) = \emptyset. \tag{10}$$

I do not wish to take any stance on the issue whether communities are endurants or perdurants (or whether some are endurants and others are perdurants). Nevertheless, leaving this issue open, I claim that no community is a situation-type.

$$Com \cap Sit = \emptyset. \tag{11}$$

Parthood relations. Our two basic categories of endurants and perdurants need two relations of parthood. Since endurants may loose and gain (spatial) parts over time, speaking about their mereological structure, we need specify a temporal point of reference. On the other hand, since perdurants cannot loose or gain parts, we should describe their mereological structure from an atemporal point of view. This solution follows the distinction adopted in [11].

When we describe the mereological structure of a genre, we do not use the term of "part" in the sense of the standard mereological system of S. Lesniewski (see e.g. [3]). The reason for this claim is simple: such mereological theorems as the axiom of generalised sum, when applied to genres, postulate the existence of entities which are never mentioned in the genre descriptions. For instance, you do not find therein such exotic entities as the mereological sum of the second chapter of a given book and the last word in the last chapter, although you can find chapters and words. Therefore, instead of modelling such mereological structures in terms of the standard mereology, I need another, less-demanding, notion of parthood. Among different weaker theories of parthood, I opt for a theory defined in [14]. The reason for this choice is unavailability of formal theories of parthood for documents. The theory developed by P. Simons and Ch. Dement in [14] aims to capture the properties of the parthood relation in the domain of artefacts. Since we may construe documents as informational artefacts, it is reasonable to adopt the latter notion of parthood for the purposes of representing documents.

To be more precise, I will borrow Simons and Dement's theory for my temporal relation of parthood; as for its atemporal counterpart, I will simply strip this theory from its temporal indices. Let "$x \leqslant_t y$" mean that an endurant x is a part of an endurant y at t $(t, t_1, \ldots \in Time)$. Let "$exist(x, t)$" mean that an endurant x exists at t. Definitions 12 and 13 introduce two auxiliary notions.

$$x <_t y \equiv x \leqslant_t y \land \neg y \leqslant_t x. \tag{12}$$

$$x \circ_t y \equiv \exists z (z \leqslant_t x \wedge z \leqslant_t y). \tag{13}$$

$$exist(x, t) \to x \leqslant_t x. \tag{14}$$

$$x \leqslant_t y \to exist(x, t) \wedge exist(y, t). \tag{15}$$

$$x \leqslant_t y \wedge y \leqslant_t z \to x \leqslant_t z. \tag{16}$$

$$x <_t y \to \exists z (z <_t y \wedge \neg z \circ_t x). \tag{17}$$

The atemporal notion of parthood for perdurants is defined by means of definitions 18 and 19, and axioms 20, 21, and 22.

$$x < y \equiv x \leqslant y \wedge \neg y \leqslant x. \tag{18}$$

$$x \circ y \equiv \exists z (z \leqslant x \wedge z \leqslant y). \tag{19}$$

$$x \leqslant x. \tag{20}$$

$$x \leqslant y \wedge y \leqslant z \to x \leqslant z. \tag{21}$$

$$x < y \to \exists z (z < y \wedge \neg z \circ x). \tag{22}$$

Besides, I add two constraints on the ontological categories of arguments of $\leqslant_t$ and $\leqslant$.

$$x \leqslant_t y \to x, y \in End. \tag{23}$$

$$x \leqslant y \to x, y \in Perd. \tag{24}$$

At the present stage of this theory, the precise strength of the mereological principles is not crucial. For instance, instead of the weak supplementation principle (i.e. 17 and 22) we can choose the strong supplementation principle (as suggested in [2], p. 39).

4   Towards a Formal Definition of Genre

I will define a genre as a (set-theoretical) pair whose elements correspond to the informal definition from section 2 supplemented with the following extensions and modifications:

1. I carefully distinguish between a document genre and a communication genre. The former is instantiated by documents that are endurants; the latter is instantiated by documents that are perdurants. Any document of a document genre will be called a *document in the strict sense*; any document of a communication genre will be called an *act of communication* or just a *communication*.
2. Since the description of the concept of genre that we find in [17] contains heterogeneous components, I will reorganise it by splitting the aspects of substance, form, and genre rule, and joining them into two elements: use and content.

3. The *use* element of a genre is to contain the recurrent situations in which the genre is referred to and the purposes for which it is referred to. The former aspect will be represented here by a set *Trigger* of situation-types. *Trigger* is to comprise all conditions that are necessary for production of a document of a given genre. Any element of *Trigger* will be called a *trigger* both for the genre and for the documents of this genre. Because all triggers are situation-types, any document of a genre is associated with the same set of triggers. Similarly, the purpose aspect will be represented by a set *Purpose* of situation-types. Each element of *Purpose* will be called a *purpose* both of a given genre and of all documents of this genre.

4. Since any document is produced because of some mental attitude of some agent, at least one trigger for a document is a situation-type related to some mental attitude. Since any document is produced in order to evoke some mental attitude of some agent (to inform, to encourage, to request, etc.), at least one purpose of a document is a situation-type related to some mental attitude. Since any document is produced within some community, I assume that at least one trigger or purpose of a genre from a community x, belongs to $Ment\_Sit(x)$.

5. The topics addressed by a genre and its form aspect will be united together by the notion of content. The *content* of a genre consists of the medium and the language of the genre. The former is to represent the medium and structure components of the form aspect from the theory of Yates and Orlikowski. The latter is to represent their language component and, to some extent, the topics addressed by the genre. The medium component of my concept of genre contains a set of genre supports and a relation among characteristic parts of these supports. A *support* for a genre is any document of this genre. This implies that any endurant or perdurant that was, is, or will be created in a given community as an instance of some genre, is treated as a support of this genre. Since supports are particular entities, each of them has its own mereological structure. It seems all documents of a given genre should share (at least!) the same mereological pattern due to which they belong to the same genre. Consequently, I claim that for each document from a given genre, there exists a set of its parts, which will be called *characteristic* for this genre, such that a set of characteristic parts of any other document from this genre is homomorphic to the former set. Any characteristic part of a document contributes to the structural specificity of this document in so far as this specificity is determined by the genre to which this document belongs. Examples of such characteristic parts include paragraphs, titles, salutation lines, etc. In the case of documents in the strict sense, it seems obvious that only their essential parts may be characteristic. A part x of an endurant y is *essential* for y iff whenever y exists, it is a part of y.

$$x, y \in End \rightarrow [x \leqslant_{es} y \equiv \forall t \ (exist(y, t) \rightarrow x \leqslant_t y) \land \exists t \ exist(y, t)]. \quad (25)$$

6. The content of a genre will be represented as a pair $< Med, Lang >$, where a set Med characterises the medium aspect of the genre and a set $Lang$ characterises its linguistic dimension.

7. The medium of a document genre will be represented as a pair $< Supp, \leqslant_{ch}>$, where
   (a) $Supp \subseteq End$ is a non-empty set of supports of a given genre,
   (b) $\leqslant_{ch}$ is a subset of $\leqslant_{es}$ such that $\leqslant_{ch}$ is a partial order and

$$\forall x, y \in Supp < P_{\leqslant_{ch}}(x), \leqslant_{ch}> \text{ is homomorphic to } < P_{\leqslant_{ch}}(y), \leqslant_{ch}>, \tag{26}$$

   where $P_{\leqslant_{ch}}(x) := \{y \in End : y \leqslant_{ch} x\}$.

8. The medium of a communication genre will be represented as a pair $< Supp, \leqslant_{ch}>$, where
   (a) $Supp \subseteq Perd$ is a non-empty set of supports of a given genre,
   (b) $\leqslant_{ch}$ is a non-empty subset of $\leqslant$ such that $\leqslant_{ch}$ is a partial order and condition 26 is satisfied for $P_{\leqslant_{ch}}(x) := \{y \in Perd : y \leqslant_{ch} x\}^2$.

9. Notice that I do not assume that $\leqslant_{ch}$ satisfies all the axioms for $\leqslant$. The reason is that characteristic parts are defined by intentional acts performed arbitrarily by document users. On the other hand, $\leqslant_{ch}$ is assumed to be a partial order because reflexivity, symmetry, and transitivity constitute the lexical core of any mereological theory (cf. [3], p. 33-38).

10. There are no mixed genres, i.e. there is no such genre that the set of its supports contains both endurants and perdurants.

$$Supp \cap End = Supp \lor Supp \cap Perd = Supp. \tag{27}$$

11. The language element of a document genre will be modelled by a function *Lang* that maps a set of sets of equiform endurants into a set of sets of situation-types, i.e. if $X \subseteq \wp(End)$, then $Lang : X \to \wp(Sit)$. This modelling solution is based on four assumptions.
    - Some informational features of documents are equiform.
    - Any informational feature of any document is endowed with a propositional content.
    - Any such propositional content is built out of propositions.
    - Any proposition functionally corresponds to a situation-type.
    Subsequently, if $X \in Lang(Y)$, then this means that any endurant from Y conveys a piece of information represented by X.

12. The language element of a communication will be modelled by a function *Lang* that maps a set of sets of equiform perdurants into a set of sets of situation-types, i.e. if $X \subseteq \wp(Perd)$, then $Lang : X \to \wp(Sit)$. This modelling solution is based on the same assumptions as in the previous remark.

13. Although I will not provide any detailed description of *Lang*, let me just mention the need to specify the conditions under which two endurants (perdurants) are equiform. Here it suffices to claim that the relation of equiformity is an equivalence relation. This implies 28:

$$X_1, X_2 \in domain(Lang) \to X_1 \neq \emptyset \land X_2 \neq \emptyset \land X_1 \cap X_2 = \emptyset. \tag{28}$$

---

[2] Although I use the same symbol for the relation of being a characteristic part of a document in the strict sense and the relation of being a characteristic part of a communication, it must be remembered that they are actually two different relations. The same remark applies to the symbol "*Lang*" introduced later on.

Moreover, any support of any genre should contain at least one informative part:

$$\forall x \in Supp \; \exists y \; [y \leqslant x \land y \in \bigcup domain(Lang)]. \qquad (29)$$

14. The "language dimension" is tackled here rather superficially since its proper formal representation is not crucial in the genre theory. Notice that both the work of Yates and Orlikowski and the above formal framework assume that any genre is associated with exactly one language. Since this assumption seems too strong, we may treat any function $Lang$ as the "sum" of all languages associated with a given language. Obviously, this solution presupposes that we are able to deal with those word-inscriptions that in different languages convey different meanings (e.g. "was" in English and German).

Definition 1. *A genre x from a community y is a pair $< Use, Content >$ such that:*

1. *$Use =< Trigger, Purpose >$, where*
   (a) *$Trigger \subseteq Sit \land Trigger \cap Ment\_Sit \neq \emptyset$,*
   (b) *$Purpose \subseteq Sit \land Purpose \cap Ment\_Sit \neq \emptyset$,*
   (c) *$Ment\_Sit(y) \cap (Trigger \cup Purpose) \neq \emptyset$,*
2. *$Content =< Med, Lang >$, where $Med =< Supp, \leqslant_{ch} >$.*

Philosophical caveat. For a philosophically conscious reader, I should add that the above definition is to be interpreted as "A genre ... is represented as a pair ...". Strictly speaking, a genre x from a community y is an intentional entity such that

1. x generically constantly depends in its existence on the beliefs of the members of y,
2. for each trigger z for x, at least one member of y holds a belief that is equivalent to the belief that z is a trigger for x,
3. for each purpose z of x, at least one member of y holds a belief that is equivalent to the belief that z is a purpose of x,
4. for each support z of x, at least one member of y holds a belief that is equivalent to the belief that z has the characteristic parts specified by $\leqslant_{ch}$,
5. at least one member of y is a competent user of the language represented by $Lang$.

Definition 2. *A genre $x=< Use, << Supp, \leqslant_{ch} >, Lang >>$ from a community y is a document genre iff $Supp \subseteq End$. A genre $x=< Use, << Supp, \leqslant_{ch} >, Lang >>$ from a community y is a communication genre iff $Supp \subseteq Perd$.*

Definition 3. *x is a document of a genre $< Use, << Supp, \leqslant_{ch} >, Lang >>$ iff $x \in Supp$.*

Besides the constraints introduced above, I submit four axioms: 31, 32, 33, and 34, in order to exclude communicationally unreasonable cases of genres. Notice that all these axioms refer to genres enacted within a single community.

Any genre is to encompass all documents that share the same structure with respect to their characteristic parts provided that their other genre-related aspects are identical. This condition is equivalent to axiom 31 below. In order to put it in a concise way, I use the following auxiliary definition. Let X be a set of genres from a given community. Let $x_1 = <Use_1, << Y_1, \leqslant_{ch_1}>, Lang_1 >>$ and $x_2 = <Use_2, << Y_2, \leqslant_{ch_2}>, Lang_2 >>$ belong to X.

$$x_1 \approx_X x_2 \equiv [(\exists y_1 \in Y_1 \exists y_2 \in Y_2 \qquad (30)$$
$$< P_{\leqslant_{ch}}(y_1), \leqslant_{ch_1}> \text{ is homomorphic to } < P_{\leqslant_{ch}}(y_2), \leqslant_{ch_2}>) \wedge$$
$$(Use_1 = Use_2 \wedge Lang_1 = Lang_2)].$$

Notice that the relation defined by 30 is an equivalence relation in X. Let $[x]_{\approx_X}$ be a $\approx_X$-equivalence class containing $x \in X$.

$$\forall x \in X |[x]_{\approx_X}| = 1. \qquad (31)$$

The characteristic parts of a given genre are selected in order to mirror the social and informative functions of this genre. For example, the characteristic parts of business letter reflect the cultural relations within a given community and the economic interests of its members. Therefore, if two genres share their use components, then they ought to share their characteristic parts provided that the sets of their supports are identical. Enacting (within a single community) two genres such that they share their use and support components, but which differ in their characteristic parts, would be communicationally ineffective. Let $< Use_1, << Supp_1, \leqslant_{ch_1}>, Lang_1 >>$ and $< Use_2, << Supp_2, \leqslant_{ch_2}>, Lang_2 >>$ be two genres from one community.

$$Use_1 = Use_2 \wedge Supp_1 = Supp_2 \rightarrow \leqslant_{ch_1} = \leqslant_{ch_2} . \qquad (32)$$

Conversely, if two genres share their characteristic parts, then they ought to share their use elements. If two genres shared their characteristic parts, but differed in their use components, this would mean that the set of characteristic parts of one of these genres should be extended in order to discriminate the social functions of one of these genres from the social functions of the other. (Remember that by definition that $\leqslant_{ch_1} = \leqslant_{ch_2}$ implies that $Supp_1 = Supp_1$.) Let $< Use_1, << Supp_1, \leqslant_{ch_1}>, Lang_1 >>$ and $< Use_2, << Supp_2, \leqslant_{ch_2}>, Lang_2 >>$ be two genres from one community.

$$\leqslant_{ch_1} = \leqslant_{ch_2} \rightarrow Use_1 = Use_2. \qquad (33)$$

Finally, because all supports of a genre are created in order to convey information relevant for the community that enacted this genre, two genres with the same supports sets and use elements should be identical with respect to their languages. Otherwise, it would follow that the community in question may "decode" the same set of documents that it enacted in two different languages even when the community uses these documents in the same circumstances and ascribes the same purposes to them.

$$Supp_1 = Supp_2 \wedge Use_1 = Use_2 \rightarrow Lang_1 = Lang_2. \qquad (34)$$

Axioms 33 and 34 entail that two genres from one community are identical iff their characteristic parts are identical.

We are now in a position to define the relation of genre subsumption. In contradistinction to our previous definitions of the notions used by Yates and Orlikowski, we are now left with no clue as to what it exactly means that one genre subsumes another. Thus, the following definition is highly stipulative.

Definition 4. *A genre* $< Use_1, << Supp_1, \leqslant_{ch_1} >, Lang_1 >>$ *from a community* x *subsumes a genre* $< Use_2, << Supp_2, \leqslant_{ch_2} >, Lang_2 >>$ *from* x *(in a social context of* x*) iff* $\leqslant_{ch_1} \subseteq \leqslant_{ch_2}$.

The definition presupposes that the social context to which the relation of subsumption is to be relativised is given by the community parameter. This implies that only genres from the same community can be compared with respect to the subsumption relation. It is easy two observe that the relation of subsumption is a partial order on the set of all genres from a given community.

It should be obvious that our framework makes room for a number of other definitions, which are not included in this paper due to the lack of space.

5   Conclusions

Searching for the ontological commitments of the theory of genres propounded by J. Yates and W. Orlikowski, I arrived at a formal ontology of genres. Within this ontology, I showed how to represent those aspects of genres and genre documents that were mentioned by Yates and Orlikowski. It turned out that the resulting conceptual structure is complex enough to describe a broad range of communicational phenomena. Nonetheless, the set of ontological categories to which I had to resort is not sparse. The question whether we could describe the same range of phenomena on the same level of precision without such ontologically demanding categories as situation-types and mental attitudes remains open.

References

1. J. Barwise and J. Perry. *Situations and Attitudes*. A Bradford Book. The MIT Press, Cambridge (MA), 1983.
2. T. Bittner, M. Donnelly, and B. Smith. Individuals, universals, collections: On the foundational relations of ontology. In A. C. Varzi and L. Vieu, editors, *Formal Ontology in Information Systems*, pages 37–59, Amsterdam, 2004. IOS Press.
3. R. Casati and A. C. Varzi. *Parts and Places*. The MIT Press, London, 1999.
4. K. Crowston and B. H. Kwasnik. A framework for creating a facetted classification for genres: Addressing the issues of multidimensionality. In *Proceedings of the 37th Annual Hawwaii International Conference on System Sciences*, volume IV, 2004.
5. K. Crowston and M. Williams. Reproduced and emergent genres of communication on the world-wide web. In *Proceedings of the 32nd Annual Hawwaii International Conference on System Sciences*, volume VI, pages 30–39, Los Alamitos (CA), 1997. IEEE Computer Society Press.

6. A. Gangemi, S. Borgo, C. Catenacci, and J. Lehmann. Task taxonomies for knowledge content. deliverable D07, Laboratory for Applied Ontology, ISTC-CNR (Italy), 2005.
7. A. Giddens. *The consitution of society*. University of California Press, Berkeley, 1984.
8. H.-G. Im, J. Yates, and W. J. Orlikowski. Temporal coordination through communication: using genres in a virtual start-up communication. *Information, Technology and People*, 18(2):89–119, 2005.
9. A. Kennedy and M. Shepard. Cybergenre: Automatic identification of home pages on the web. *Journal of Web Engineering*, 3(3-4):236–251, 2004.
10. D. Lewis. *Convention*. Blackwell Publishing, 2002.
11. C. Masolo, S. Borgo, A. Gangemi, N. Guarino, and A. Oltramari. Wonderweb deliverable18, 2003.
12. W. J. Orlikowski and J. Yates. Genre repertoire: The structuring of communicative practices in organizations. *Administrative Science Quarterly*, 39(4):541–574, 1994.
13. T. Ryan, R. H. G. Field, and L. Olfman. Homepage genre dimensionality. In *Proceedings of the Eighth American Conference on Information Systems*, pages 1116–1128, 2002.
14. P. M. Simons and Ch. W. Dement. Aspects of the mereology of artifacts. In R. Poli and P. Simons, editors, *Formal Ontology*, pages 255–276. Kluwer Academic Publishers, Dordrecht, 1995.
15. R. Tuomela. *The Importance of Us*. Stanford Series in Philosophy. Stanford University Press, Stanford (CA), 1995.
16. M. Woolridge. *Reasoning about Rational Agents*. The MIT Press, Cambridge (MA), 2000.
17. J. Yates and W. J. Orlikowski. Genres of organizational communication. *Academy of Management Review*, 17(2):299–326, 1992.
18. J. Yates and W. J. Orlikowski. Explicit and implicit structuring in genres in electronic communication: Reinforcement and change in social interaction. *Organization Science*, 10(1):83–103, 1999.
19. J. Yates, W. J. Orlikowski, and J. Rennecker. Collaborative genres for collaboration. In *Proceedings of the Thirtieth Annual Hawwaii International Conference on System Sciences*, volume VI, pages 50–59, Los Alamitos (CA), 1997. IEEE Computer Society Press.

An OWL-Based Approach for RBAC with Negative Authorization*

Nuermaimaiti Heilili, Yang Chen, Chen Zhao, Zhenxing Luo, and Zuoquan Lin

LMAM, Department of Information Science, School of Math.,
Peking University, Beijing 100871, China
{nur, imchy, zchen, lzx0728, lz}@is.pku.edu.cn

Abstract. Access control is an important issue related to the security on the Semantic Web. Role-Based Access Control (RBAC) is commonly considered as a flexible and efficient model in practice. In this paper, we provide an OWL-based approach for RBAC in the Semantic Web context. First we present an extended model of RBAC with negative authorization, providing detailed analysis of conflicts. Then we use OWL to formalize the extended model. Additionally, we show how to use an OWL-DL reasoner to detect the potential conflicts in the extended model.

1 Introduction

The Semantic Web [1] is an evolution of the current web. It provides a common framework that allows information to be shared and reused across applications and enterprises. It is extremely important for security frameworks to capture the heterogeneous and distributed nature of the Semantic Web. Access control is an important security issue on the Semantic Web. Role-Based Access Control (RBAC) [2] has been proven to be efficient to improve security administration with flexible authorization management. Integrating RBAC with the Semantic Web helps us to reduce the complexity of web security management.

There has been lots of works about languages for security policy representation. Extensible Access Control Markup Language (XACML)[1] is a common language for expressing security policies with XML, the basic component of the Semantic Web, but XML only provides the syntax for expressing data, not the semantics. So a security framework for the Semantic Web needs a semantic language to express their security policies [3].

To meet this need, some works are presented recently. Rei [3,4], a new deontic concept-based security policy language, is currently implemented in Prolog with a semantic representation of policies in RDF-S. KAoS [5,6] uses DAML as the basis for representing and reasoning about policies within Web Services, Grid Computing, and multi-agent system platforms. And Ponder [7] is an object-oriented policy language for the management of distributed systems and networks.

---

* Supported partially by NSFC (grant numbers 60373002 and 60496322) and by a NKBRPC (2004CB318000).

[1] (http://www.oasis-open.org/committees/tc_home.php?wg_abbrev=xacml)

J. Lang, F. Lin, and J. Wang (Eds.): KSEM 2006, LNAI 4092, pp. 164–175, 2006.

From an abstract viewpoint, these works above are related to the representation of knowledge about security policies. Logic is still the foundation of knowledge representation. In fact, the logic-based approach to represent and evaluate authorization has already been studied earlier [8,9,10,11,12,13]; some of them are concerning the RBAC models [11,12,13]. We have used description logic languages to express and reason about core, hierarchical and constrained RBAC models[14].

Web Ontology Language (OWL) [15] is a standard knowledge representation language for the Semantic Web. It builds on Description Logics (DLs) [16] and includes clean and unambiguous semantics. To describe security policies by OWL helps web entities better understanding and sharing of the security policies. So we propose an OWL-based approach to represent the RBAC model.

Conventional RBAC uses the *closed world* policy [10]. This approach has a major problem that the lack of a given authorization for a given user does not prevent this user from receiving this authorization later on [17]. The concept of negative authorization is discussed in [18,17,19]. Al-Kahtani *et al.* propose the RB-RBAC-ve model, in which the concept of negative authorization to the user-role assignment is introduced [19]. In our paper, we present an extended model of RBAC with negative authorization, called RBAC($\mathcal{N}$), but our work is different from [19]. In the RBAC($\mathcal{N}$) model, negative authorization is allowed in permission-role assignment, e.g., *member* role can not access audit trails. However, the presence of positive and negative authorizations at the same time may cause conflicts.

To enforce RBAC in the Semantic Web context, we formalize the RBAC($\mathcal{N}$) model in the OWL-DL sublanguage. And then, we can use the description logic reasoner RACER [20,21] to detect potential conflicts in the RBAC($\mathcal{N}$) model. We also give a preliminary design of an authorization service based on the ideas presented in this paper.

The rest of the paper is organized into the following sections. Section 2 gives a brief introduction of OWL. We present the RBAC($\mathcal{N}$) model in Section 3. In Section 4, the formalization and reasoning on the RBAC($\mathcal{N}$) model in the OWL-DL sublanguage is developed. In Section 5, we show how to find conflicts in the RBAC($\mathcal{N}$) model using RACER. We discuss implementation considerations in Section 6 and draw conclusions in Section 7.

2   Web Ontology Language (OWL)

In the context of the Semantic Web, ontologies are used to provide structured vocabularies that describe concepts and relationships between them. Different ontology languages provide different facilities. The most recent development in ontology languages is OWL from the World Wide Web Consortium (W3C).

OWL has features from several families of representation languages such as Description Logics and frames which make it possible for concepts to be defined as well as described [22]. The logical model allows the use of a reasoner (such as RACER) which can check whether or not all of the statements and definitions in the ontology are mutually consistent and can also recognize which concepts fit under which definitions.

It is difficult to meet the full set of requirements for an ontology language: efficient reasoning support and convenience of expression for a language as powerful as a combination of RDF-S with a full logic. W3C's Web Ontology Working Group defines OWL as three different sublanguages: OWL-Lite, OWL-DL and OWL-Full. A defining feature of each sub-language is its expressiveness. OWL-DL may be considered as an extension of OWL-Lite and OWL-Full an extension of OWL-DL.

OWL-DL, the Description Logic style of using OWL, is very close to the DL language $\mathcal{SHOIN}(D)$ which is itself an extension of the the influential DL language $\mathcal{SHOQ}(D)$. OWL-DL can form descriptions of classes, datatypes, individuals and data values using constructs. In this paper, we use DL syntax(for detailed information, please refer to Fig. 1. in [22]), that is much more compact and readable than either the XML syntax or the RDF/XML syntax.

3   The RBAC Model with Negative Authorization

We introduce the concept of negative authorization (indicated by the letter $\mathcal{N}$, for "negative") into the RBAC *Reference Model* of the ANSI Standard [2]. We give a formal definition for the new model. We also provide detailed analysis of conflicts due to negative authorization.

3.1   The RBAC($\mathcal{N}$) Model

In RBAC, permissions are associated with roles, and users are made members of appropriate roles, thereby acquiring the appropriate permissions. We introduce negative authorization into permission-role assignment. Why we choose permission-role assignment rather than user-role assignment what Al-Kahtani did in [19] is that negative authorization means the denial to perform an operation on one or more RBAC protected objects and it is more reasonable to describe this with negative permission.

In the RBAC($\mathcal{N}$) model, we extend the interpretation of inheritance relations among roles as follows. We say that role r_1 "inherits" role r_2 if all privileges of r_2 are also privileges of r_1, and all prohibitions of r_1 are also prohibitions of r_2, denoted as $r_1 \geq r_2$. That is to say, the propagations of positive and negative authorization are going along two opposite directions in role hierarchy.

The RBAC reference model includes a set of sessions where each session is a mapping between a user and an activated subset of roles that are assigned to the user. For the sake of simplicity, we do not take account of sessions in the model, leaving it to implementation.

The RBAC($\mathcal{N}$) model consists of the following components:

- *Users*, *Roles*, *Perms*, (users, roles, permissions respectively),
- *RH* $\subseteq$ *Roles* $\times$ *Roles* is a partial order on *Roles* called the inheritance relation, written as $\geq$, where $r_1 \geq r_2$ only if all permissions of r_2 are also permissions of r_1, and all users of r_1 are also users of r_2,

- $UA \subseteq Users \times Roles$, a many-to-many mapping user-to-role assignment relation,
- $PA \subseteq Perms \times Roles$, a many-to-many mapping permission-to-role assignment relation describing positive authorization,
- $NPA \subseteq Perms \times Roles$, a many-to-many mapping permission-to-role assignment relation describing negative authorization,
- $permit$: $Users \rightarrow 2^{Perms}$ is a function mapping each user u to a set of permissions, user u has permissions $permit(u) = \{p| \exists r', r \geq r' \wedge (p, r') \in PA \wedge (u, r) \in UA\}$, and
- $prohibit$: $Users \rightarrow 2^{Perms}$ is a function mapping each user u to a set of permissions, user u has the permissions $prohibit(u) = \{p| \exists r', r' \geq r \wedge (p, r') \in NPA \wedge (u, r) \in UA\}$.

We use $\neg p$ to denote a negative permission, and a positive permission is just denoted as p. If $(p, r) \in NPA$, we can say that negative permission $\neg p$ is assigned to r. Negative permission here is just opposite to permission in the RBAC reference model [2], which we call positive permission.

3.2   Conflicts Due to Negative Authorization

Introducing negative authorization into RBAC may lead to conflicts because of the simultaneous presence of positive and negative authorizations . In Figure 1, permission, role and user is denoted as diamond, circle and square respectively. If a positive(negative) permission is assigned to a role, a solid(dotted) line is used to link the permission and the role. User role assignment relation is also denoted as a solid line. A solid line with an arrowhead is used to link a senior role to its junior role in the figure.

The following are four kinds of conflicts that will arise because of negative authorization and they are basic conflicts.

- Case 1: Both a positive permission p and its corresponding negative permission $\neg p$ are assigned to the same role. This case is represented by the following:
$$(p, r) \in PA \ \wedge \ (p, r) \in NPA$$

- Case 2: Role r_1 is senior to role r_2. A positive permission p is assigned to the junior role, and its corresponding negative permission $\neg p$ is assigned to the senior one. This case is represented by the following:
$$(r_1, r_2) \in RH \ \wedge \ (p, r_2) \in PA \ \wedge \ (p, r_1) \in NPA$$

- Case 3: There is no inheritance relation between role r_1 and r_2. A positive permission p and its corresponding negative permission $\neg p$ is assigned to r_1 and r_2 respectively. A user is assigned to r_1 and r_2 simultaneously. This case is represented by the following:
$$(r_1, r_2) \notin RH \ \wedge \ (p, r_1) \in PA \ \wedge \ (p, r_2) \in NPA$$
$$\wedge \ (u, r_1) \in UA \ \wedge \ (u, r_2) \in UA$$

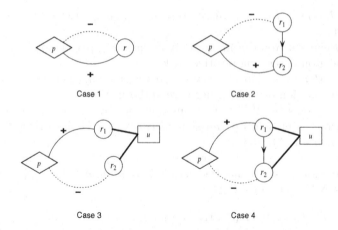

Fig. 1. Conflicts Due to Negative Authorization

- Case 4: This case is similar to Case 3. The only difference between them is that there is an inheritance relation between role r_1 and r_2 in Case 4. In the figure, role r_1 is senior to role r_2. This case is represented by the following:

$$(r_1, r_2) \in RH \ \wedge \ (p, r_1) \in PA \ \wedge \ (p, r_2) \in NPA$$
$$\wedge \ (u, r_1) \in UA \ \wedge \ (u, r_2) \in UA$$

Now we discuss them from another point of view. For a permission $p \in Perms$, We define the function $role^+(p) : Perms \rightarrow 2^{Roles}$ to denote the set of roles (including implicit assignment) that positive permission p is assigned to, and the function $role^-(p) : Perms \rightarrow 2^{Roles}$ to denote the set of roles (including implicit assignment) that negative permission $\neg p$ is assigned to. Therefore, conflicts will arise when $role^+(p) \cap role^-(p) \neq \phi$, Both Case 1 and 2 fall into this situation. Other kinds of conflicts only related to roles and permissions can be simplified to Case 1 or Case 2.

Similarly, we define the function $user^+(p) : Perms \rightarrow 2^{Users}$ to denote the set of users who have permission p, and the function $user^-(p) : Perms \rightarrow 2^{Users}$ to denote the set of users who have negative permission $\neg p$. Conflicts will also arise when $user^+(p) \cap user^-(p) \neq \phi$. Both Case 3 and 4 fall into this situation. Other kinds of conflicts related to users, roles and permissions can be simplified to all cases listed above.

To detect a conflict in the model, we just need to check whether $role^+(p) \cap role^-(p)$ and $user^+(p) \cap user^-(p)$ are empty sets for each permission $p \in Perms$.

4   Representation and Reasoning on the RBAC($\mathcal{N}$) Model in OWL-DL

OWL-DL is a natural choice as the security policy representation language for the Semantic Web. It builds on Description Logics (DLs) [16] and compared to

RDF-S, it includes formal semantics. Its one obvious advantage lies in its clean and unambiguous semantics, which helps web entities better understanding and sharing of the security policies.

In this section, we describe how to conceptualize the RBAC($\mathcal{N}$) model and construct an OWL knowledge base for it. It is feasible to assume that the role set and the permission set are finite. We choose the OWL-DL sublanguage considering its friendly syntax and decidable inference and use DL syntax instead of XML syntax for simplicity.

Given a instance of RBAC($\mathcal{N}$) model, we define an OWL knowledge base $\mathcal{K}$ as follows. The alphabet of $\mathcal{K}$ includes the following classes and properties:

- the atomic classes User, represent the users,
- the atomic classes CRole$^+$ and CRole$^-$,
- for each role $rr \in Roles$, one atomic class RR$^+$ and one atomic class RR$^-$,
- the atomic property assign, connects one user to the roles assigned to him,
- for each permission $p \in Perms$, one atomic class CRole$_p^+$ and one atomic class CRole$_p^-$,
- for each permission $p \in Perms$, one complex class User$_p^+ \equiv \exists$assign.CRole$_p^+$ and one complex class User$_p^- \equiv \exists$assign.CRole$_p^-$.

In our formalization, each role $rr \in Roles$ is an instance of concept RR$^+$, and RR$^-$, too. For each $p \in Perms$, CRole$_p^+$ and CRole$_p^-$ denotes the concept of the roles (including implicit assignment) that p and $\neg p$ is assigned to respectively. The concept $\exists$assign.CRole$_p^+$ describes the set of users assigned to some roles in CRole$_p^+$. Consequently, User$_p^+$ describes the concept of the users who get the permission p. In the same way, User$_p^-$ describes the concept of the users who get the negative permission $\neg p$.

The TBox of $\mathcal{K}$ includes two catalogs of axioms: *role inclusion axioms* and *permission assignment axioms*.

Role inclusion axioms express the role hierarchies in the RBAC($\mathcal{N}$) model. For each role hierarchy relation $rr_1 \geq rr_2$, $rr_1, rr_2 \in Roles$, role inclusion axioms have the form RR$_1^+ \sqsubseteq$ RR$_2^+$ and RR$_2^- \sqsubseteq$ RR$_1^-$. In addition, we should set up axioms RR$^+ \sqsubseteq$ CRole$^+$ and RR$^- \sqsubseteq$ CRole$^-$ for each $rr \in Roles$.

Permission assignment axioms specify positive and negative permission assignments in the RBAC($\mathcal{N}$) model. For each $(p, rr) \in PA$, permission assignment axioms have the form RR$^+ \sqsubseteq$ CRole$_p^+$. Similarly, for each $(p, rr) \in NPA$, permission assignment axioms have the form RR$^- \sqsubseteq$ CRole$_p^-$.

In the RBAC($\mathcal{N}$) model, senior roles acquire the permissions of their juniors, and junior roles acquire the negative permissions of their seniors. Permission assignment axioms capture this feature. Given two roles $rr_1, rr_2 \in Roles$, two permissions $p_1, p_2 \in Perms$, if $rr_1 \geq rr_2$, $(p_1, rr_1) \in NPA$ and $(p_2, rr_2) \in PA$, we get RR$_1^+ \sqsubseteq$ RR$_2^+$, and RR$_2^+ \sqsubseteq$ CRole$_{p_2}^+$, subsequently, RR$_1^+ \sqsubseteq$ CRole$_{p_2}^+$. Also, we can get RR$_2^- \sqsubseteq$ RR$_1^-$, and RR$_1^- \sqsubseteq$ CRole$_{p_1}^-$, then RR$_2^- \sqsubseteq$ CRole$_{p_1}^-$.

The ABox of $\mathcal{K}$ includes the following three catalogs of axioms: *Role concept assertions* declare each role to be an instance of corresponding role concept, and have the forms $\mathsf{RR}^+(rr)$ and $\mathsf{RR}^-(rr)$. *User concept assertions* specify users and have the form $\mathsf{User}(u)$. *User role assignment assertions* have the form $\mathsf{assign}(u, rr)$, indicating that user u is assigned to role rr.

After constructing an OWL knowledge base $\mathcal{K}$, we can perform some reasoning tasks on it. We can use the following query statement to check if a user u is assigned to a role rr:

$$\textsc{Ask}\{\,\exists \mathsf{assign}.\mathsf{RR}^+(u)\}$$

this refers to assert if u is an instance of $\exists \mathsf{assign}.\mathsf{RR}^+$. If we have defined $\mathsf{assign}(u, rr)$ in the ABox of $\mathcal{K}$, then $\mathcal{K} \models (\exists \mathsf{assign}.\mathsf{RR}^+)(u)$. If $\mathsf{assign}(u, rr)$ is not defined in the ABox of $\mathcal{K}$, but $\mathsf{assign}(u, rr_1)$ is defined, where role rr_1 is senior to rr, that is $rr_1 \geq rr$, then we still get $\mathcal{K} \models (\exists \mathsf{assign}.\mathsf{RR}^+)(u)$, because $\exists \mathsf{assign}.\mathsf{RR}_1^+ \sqsubseteq \exists \mathsf{assign}.\mathsf{RR}^+$. This indicates that if user u is assigned to a role rr, then u has user role assignment relation with all descendants of role rr.

We can ask $\mathcal{K}$ to query whether user u gets permission p as following:

$$\textsc{Ask}\{\mathsf{User}_p^+(u)\}$$

Similarly, we can ask $\mathcal{K}$ to query whether user u is forbidden to hold positive permission p as following:

$$\textsc{Ask}\{\mathsf{User}_p^-(u)\}$$

When we get both $\mathcal{K} \models \mathsf{User}_p^+(u)$ and $\mathcal{K} \models \mathsf{User}_p^-(u)$, there should be some conflicts in the model.

5   Conflict Detection

Security administrators prefer to detect a conflict in advance. In this section, we add some axioms into the knowledge base $\mathcal{K}$ constructed in the previous section. We use an example to describe how to find conflicts using the description logic reasoner RACER [20,21] in detail.

As we mentioned in Section 3, any kind of conflicts in the RBAC($\mathcal{N}$) will causes $role^+(p) \cap role^-(p)$ or $user^+(p) \cap user^-(p)$ not to be empty for some $p \in Perms$. Therefore, we define two axioms as follows for each permission $p \in Perms$:

$$\mathsf{Role}_p^+ \sqcap \mathsf{Role}_p^- \sqsubseteq \bot$$
$$\mathsf{User}_p^+ \sqcap \mathsf{User}_p^- \sqsubseteq \bot$$

Then once a conflict occurs, the knowledge base $\mathcal{K}$ will be inconsistent.

Assume an organization uses two roles, *manager* and *employee*. An employee has permission to *create* a purchase order, but is prohibited to *sign* a purchase order. The manager role is senior to the employee role, and has permission to sign a purchase order.

According to our formalization, there will be four classes: $\mathsf{Manager}^+$, $\mathsf{Manager}^-$, $\mathsf{Employee}^+$ and $\mathsf{Employee}^-$, and two inclusions axioms: $\mathsf{Manager}^+ \sqsubseteq \mathsf{Employee}^+$,

$\mathsf{Employee}^- \sqsubseteq \mathsf{Manager}^-$. There will also be three permission assignment axioms: $\mathsf{Employee}^+ \sqsubseteq \mathsf{CRole}^+_{create}$, $\mathsf{Employee}^- \sqsubseteq \mathsf{CRole}^-_{sign}$, and $\mathsf{Menager}^+ \sqsubseteq \mathsf{CRole}^+_{sign}$.

If we assign both the manager role and the employee to user *Bob*, the ABox will include the following assertions:

$$\mathsf{Manager}^+(manager), \mathsf{Manager}^-(manager),$$

$$\mathsf{Employee}^+(employee), \mathsf{Employee}^-(employee),$$

$$\mathsf{User}(Bob), \mathsf{assign}(Bob, employee), \mathsf{assign}(Bob, manager)$$

This should lead to a conflict (Case 4 in Figure 1).

We create an OWL ontology (Figure 2) according to the axioms and assertions above using the Protégé-OWL plugin[2]. Because OWL does not use the Unique Name Assumption (UNA), it must be explicitly stated that individuals are the same as each other, or different to each other in OWL. In order to reason over the ontologies in Protégé-OWL, a DIG[3] compliant reasoner is required. We use RacerPro 1.8 (a new version of RACER)[4], which supports OWL-DL almost completely. We send the ontology to the reasoner to check the consistency of the ontology. Then we find that the ABox is incoherent due to role *employee*.

6   Implementation Mechanism

This section outlines the basic design and implementation based on the approach presented in this paper. Figure 3 shows the components of the prototype implementation.

DIG DL reasoner interface specification [23] is a common standard to allow client tools to interact with different reasoners in a standard way. The current release of DIG standard is version 1.1. To provide maximum portability, DIG 1.1 defines a simple XML encoding to be used over an HTTP interface to a DL reasoner.

Policy Enforcement Point (PEP) is the system entity that performs access control by making decision requests and enforcing authorization decisions. Policy Decision Point (PDP) is the system entity that evaluates applicable policies and renders an authorization decision to PEP. PDP acts as a DIG client, which posts one or more actions encoded using the DIG XML schema.

RBAC policies are specified in OWL files, which can be edited via the Protégé-OWL plugin. We are currently building a graphical RBAC policy administration tool. The OWL files can be loaded into RACER by its OWL interface.

The prototype implementation operates by the following steps.

1. Security administrators write RBAC policies in OWL files, and load them into a DIG reasoner knowledge base.
2. The access requester sends a request for access to the PEP.

---

[2] Protégé-OWL plugin (http://protege.stanford.edu/plugins/owl/)

[3] DL Implementers Group (DIG) (http://dl.kr.org/dig/)

[4] RacerPro (http://www.racer-systems.com/)

```xml
<?xml version="1.0"?>
<rdf:RDF
   xmlns:rdf="http://www.w3.org/1999/02/22-rdf-syntax-ns#"
   xmlns="http://www.is.pku.edu.cn/RBAC(N).owl#"
   xmlns:xsd="http://www.w3.org/2001/XMLSchema#"
   xmlns:rdfs="http://www.w3.org/2000/01/rdf-schema#"
   xmlns:owl="http://www.w3.org/2002/07/owl#"
   xml:base="http://www.is.pku.edu.cn/RBAC(N).owl">
<owl:Ontology rdf:about=""/>
<owl:Class rdf:ID="Permission_P"/>
<owl:Class rdf:ID="sign_N">
  <rdfs:subClassOf>
   <owl:Class rdf:ID="Permission_N"/>
  </rdfs:subClassOf>
  <owl:disjointWith>
   <owl:Class rdf:ID="sign_P"/>
  </owl:disjointWith>
</owl:Class>
<owl:Class rdf:ID="User"/>
<owl:Class rdf:ID="create_P">
  <rdfs:subClassOf rdf:resource="#Permission_P"/>
  <owl:disjointWith>
   <owl:Class rdf:ID="create_N"/>
  </owl:disjointWith>
</owl:Class>
<owl:Class rdf:ID="user_sign_P">
  <owl:disjointWith>
   <owl:Class rdf:ID="user_sign_N"/>
  </owl:disjointWith>
  <owl:equivalentClass>
   <owl:Restriction>
    <owl:someValuesFrom>
     <owl:Class rdf:about="#sign_P"/>
    </owl:someValuesFrom>
    <owl:onProperty>
     <owl:ObjectProperty rdf:ID="assign"/>
    </owl:onProperty>
   </owl:Restriction>
  </owl:equivalentClass>
</owl:Class>
<owl:Class rdf:ID="Role_N">
  <rdfs:subClassOf>
   <owl:Class rdf:ID="Role"/>
  </rdfs:subClassOf>
</owl:Class>
<owl:Class rdf:ID="user_create_N">
  <owl:equivalentClass>
   <owl:Restriction>
    <owl:onProperty>
     <owl:ObjectProperty rdf:about="#assign"/>
    </owl:onProperty>
    <owl:someValuesFrom>
     <owl:Class rdf:about="#create_N"/>
    </owl:someValuesFrom>
   </owl:Restriction>
  </owl:equivalentClass>
  <owl:disjointWith>
   <owl:Class rdf:ID="user_create_P"/>
  </owl:disjointWith>
</owl:Class>
<owl:Class rdf:ID="manager_P">
  <rdfs:subClassOf>
   <owl:Class rdf:ID="employee_P"/>
  </rdfs:subClassOf>
  <rdfs:subClassOf>
   <owl:Class rdf:about="#sign_P"/>
  </rdfs:subClassOf>
</owl:Class>

<owl:Class rdf:ID="employee_N">
  <rdfs:subClassOf>
   <owl:Class rdf:ID="manager_N"/>
  </rdfs:subClassOf>
  <rdfs:subClassOf rdf:resource="#sign_N"/>
</owl:Class>
<owl:Class rdf:about="#sign_P">
  <owl:disjointWith rdf:resource="#sign_N"/>
  <rdfs:subClassOf rdf:resource="#Permission_P"/>
</owl:Class>
<owl:Class rdf:about="#employee_P">
  <rdfs:subClassOf>
   <owl:Class rdf:ID="Role_P"/>
  </rdfs:subClassOf>
  <rdfs:subClassOf rdf:resource="#create_P"/>
</owl:Class>
<owl:Class rdf:about="#Role_P">
  <rdfs:subClassOf rdf:resource="#Role"/>
</owl:Class>
<owl:Class rdf:about="#manager_N">
  <rdfs:subClassOf rdf:resource="#Role_N"/>
</owl:Class>
<owl:Class rdf:about="#user_sign_N">
  <owl:equivalentClass>
   <owl:Restriction>
    <owl:onProperty>
     <owl:ObjectProperty rdf:about="#assign"/>
    </owl:onProperty>
    <owl:someValuesFrom rdf:resource="#sign_P"/>
   </owl:Restriction>
  </owl:equivalentClass>
  <owl:disjointWith rdf:resource="#user_sign_P"/>
</owl:Class>
<owl:Class rdf:about="#user_create_P">
  <owl:equivalentClass>
   <owl:Restriction>
    <owl:someValuesFrom rdf:resource="#create_P"/>
    <owl:onProperty>
     <owl:ObjectProperty rdf:about="#assign"/>
    </owl:onProperty>
   </owl:Restriction>
  </owl:equivalentClass>
  <owl:disjointWith rdf:resource="#user_create_N"/>
</owl:Class>
<owl:Class rdf:about="#create_N">
  <rdfs:subClassOf rdf:resource="#Permission_N"/>
  <owl:disjointWith rdf:resource="#create_P"/>
</owl:Class>
<owl:ObjectProperty rdf:about="#assign">
  <rdfs:domain rdf:resource="#User"/>
  <rdfs:range rdf:resource="#Role"/>
</owl:ObjectProperty>
<employee_P rdf:ID="employee">
  <owl:differentFrom>
   <manager_N rdf:ID="manager">
    <rdf:type rdf:resource="#manager_P"/>
    <owl:differentFrom rdf:resource="#employee"/>
   </manager_N>
  </owl:differentFrom>
  <rdf:type rdf:resource="#employee_N"/>
</employee_P>
<User rdf:ID="Bob">
  <assign rdf:resource="#manager"/>
  <assign rdf:resource="#employee"/>
</User>
</rdf:RDF>
```

Fig. 2. The Example

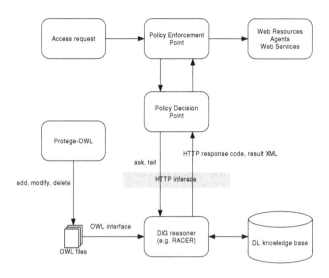

Fig. 3. The components of the prototype implementation

3. The PEP sends the request for access to the PDP.
4. The PDP constructs a DIG request to a DIG reasoner.
5. The DIG reasoner returns the response to PDP.
6. The PDP returns the authorization decision to the PEP.
7. If access is permitted, then the PEP permits access to the service; otherwise, it denies access.

To evaluate the performance impact in our prototype implementation, we measured average times taken for the PDP to get the responses from the DIG reasoner for decision requests (e.g., whether the user *Bob* has the permission of *create*). An Intel CPU 2.40 GHz machine with 1GB RAM, running Windows 2000 Server, was used to run the DIG reasoner. Our test was held in LAN. 2000 users, 100 roles and 2000 permissions were created in knowledge base $\mathcal{K}$ (we guaranteed the consistency of the $\mathcal{K}$ by the Protégé-OWL component of the system). Each user was arbitrarily assigned to 10 roles, and each role was arbitrarily assigned to 400 permissions. Test results show that the average response time is below 20 ms. In fact, the response time also depends on the structure of the $\mathcal{K}$ we built. From the test results, we can see the effectiveness of the system is quite reasonable.

In our implementation, for optimization, we described permissions and roles using OWL classes, described users using OWL individuals, and put users under role classes as role class individuals to express user-role assignment relations; We put roles under permissions as subclasses to express permission-role assignment relations.

7 Conclusion

In this paper, we first present the RBAC($\mathcal{N}$) model, which introduces the negative authorization into the RBAC of the ANSI Standard. We discuss several variations of conflicts due to negative authorization. Secondly, we give a formalization of the RBAC($\mathcal{N}$) model in the OWL-DL sublanguage. Given a RBAC($\mathcal{N}$) model, we can construct an OWL knowledge base, upon which some reasoning tasks can be performed. Then we show how to use RACER to detect the potential conflicts in the RBAC($\mathcal{N}$) model by an example. Finally, we outline the basic design and implementation based on the approach presented in this paper.

We like to note that formal semantics and reasoning support of OWL are provided through the mapping of OWL on logics, which other languages, such as OO, XML and RDF-S, lack. While OWL is sufficiently rich to be used in practice, extensions are in the making. They will provide further logical features, including rules [24]. In the future we will investigate how to use OWL extensions to represent security policies.

References

1. Berners-Lee, T., Hendler, J., Lassila., O.: The Semantic Web. Scientific American **284** (2001) 34–43
2. American National Standards Institute, I.: American national standard for information technology - role based access control (2004) ANSI INCITS 359-2004. http://csrc.nist.gov/rbac/.
3. Kagal, L., Finin, T., Joshi, A.: A policy based approach to security for the semantic web. In: Proceeding of International Semantic Web Conference (ISWC 2003). (2003)
4. Kagal, L., Finin, T., Joshi, A.: A policy language for pervasive computing environment. In: Proceedings of IEEE Fourth International Workshop on Policy (Policy 2003), Lake Como, Italy (2003) 63–76
5. Uszok, A., Bradshaw, J., Jeffers, R., Suri, N., Hayes, P., Breedy, M., Bunch, L., Johnson, M., Kulkarni, S., Lott, J.: KAoS policy and domain services: Toward a description-logic approach to policy representation, deconfliction, and enforcement. In: Proceedings of IEEE Fourth International Workshop on Policy (Policy 2003), Lake Como, Italy (2003) 93–98
6. Bradshaw, J., Uszok, A., Jeffers, R., Suri, N., Hayes, P., Burstein, M., Acquisti, A., Benyo, B., Breedy, M., Carvalho, M., Diller, D., Johnson, M., Kulkarni, S., Lott, J., Sierhuis, M., Hoof, R.V.: Representation and reasoning for daml-based policy and domain services in kaos and nomads. In: Proceedings of the Autonomous Agents and Multi-Agent Systems Conference (AAMAS 2003), Melbourne, Australia (2003) 835–842
7. Damianou, N., Dulay, N., Lupu, E., Sloman, M.: The ponder policy specification language. In: Proceedings of Workshop on Policies for Distributed Systems and Networks (POLICY 2001), Bristol, UK (2001)
8. Woo, T.Y., Lam, S.S.: Authorization in distributed systems: A new approach. Journal of Computer Security **2** (1993) 107–136

9. Massacci, F.: Reasoning about security: A logic and a decision method for role-based access control. In: Proceeding of the International Joint Conference on Qualitative and Quantitative Practical Reasoning (ECSQARU/FAPR-97). (1997) 421–435

10. Jajodia, S., Samarati, P., Sapino, M., Subrahmanian, V.S.: Flexible support for multiple access control policies. ACM Transactions on Database Systems **26** (2001) 214–260

11. Bacon, J., Moody, K., Yao, W.: A model of oasis role-based access control and its support for active security. ACM Transactions on Information and System Security (TISSEC) **5** (2002) 492–540

12. Bertino, E., Catania, B., Ferrari, E., Perlasca, P.: A logical framework for reasoning about access control models. ACM Transactions on Information and System Security (TISSEC) **6** (2003) 71–127

13. Khayat, E.J., Abdallah, A.E.: A formal model for flat role-based access control. In: Proceeding of ACS/IEEE International Conference on Computer Systems and Applications (AICCSA'03), Tunis, Tunisia (2003)

14. Zhao, C., Nuermaimaiti.Heilili, Liu, S., Lin, Z.: Representation and reasoning on RBAC: A description logic approach. In: ICTAC05 - International Colloquium on Theoretical Aspects of Computing, Hanoi, Vietnam (2005)

15. Sean Bechhofer, Frank van Harmelen, J.H.I.H.D.L.M.L.A.S.: OWL web ontology language reference (2002) `http://www.w3.org/TR/owl-ref/`.

16. Baader, F., McGuinness, D.L., Nardi, D., Patel-Schneider, P.F.: The Description Logic Handbook: Theory, Implementation and Applications. Cambridge University Press (2002)

17. Bertino, E., Samarati, P., Jajodia, S.: An extended authorization model for relational databases. IEEE Transactions on Knowledge and Data Engineering **9** (1997) 85–101

18. Bertino, E., Pierangela, Samarati, Jajodia, S.: Authorizations in relational database management systems. In: Proceedings of the 1st ACM conference on Computer and communications security, Fairfax, Virginia, United States, ACM Press New York, NY, USA (1993) 130 – 139

19. Al-Kahtani, M.A., Sandhu, R.: Rule-based RBAC with negative authorization. In: Proceedings of the 20th Annual Computer Security Applications Conference (ACSAC'04), Tucson, Arizona, USA (2004)

20. Haarslev, V., Moller, R.: Description of the RACER system and its applications. In: International Workshop on Description Logics (DL-2001), Stanford, USA (2001)

21. Haarslev, V., Moller, R.: RACER system description. In: International Joint Conference on Automated Reasoning (IJCAR'2001), Siena, Italy (2001) 18–23

22. Horrocks, I., Patel-Schneider, P.F., Harmelen, F.v.: From SHIQ and RDF to OWL: The making of a web ontology language. Jouranl of Web Semantics **1** (2003) 7–26

23. Bechhofer, S.: The DIG description logic interface: DIG/1.1 (2003) Available from: http://dl-web.man.ac.uk/dig/2003/02/interface.pdf.

24. Horrocks, I., Patel-Schneider, P.F., Boley, H., Tabet, S., Grosof, B., Dean, M.: SWRL: A semantic web rule language combining OWL and RuleML (version 0.5) (2003) `http://www.daml.org/2003/11/swrl/`.

LCS: A Linguistic Combination System for Ontology Matching

Qiu Ji, Weiru Liu, Guilin Qi, and David A. Bell

School of Electronics, Electrical Engineering and Computer Science,
Queen's University Belfast
Belfast, BT7 1NN, UK
{Q.Ji, W.Liu, G.Qi, DA.Bell}@qub.ac.uk

Abstract. Ontology matching is an essential operation in many application domains, such as the Semantic Web, ontology merging or integration. So far, quite a few ontology matching approaches or matchers have been proposed. It has been observed that combining the results of multiple matchers is a promising technique to get better results than just using one matcher at a time. Many aggregation operators, such as *Max, Min, Average* and *Weighted*, have been developed. The limitations of these operators are studied. To overcome the limitations and provide a semantic interpretation for each aggregation operator, in this paper, we propose a linguistic combination system (LCS), where a linguistic aggregation operator (LAO), based on the ordered weighted averaging (OWA) operator, is used for the aggregation. A weight here is not associated with a specific matcher but a particular ordered position. A large number of LAOs can be developed for different uses, and the existing aggregation operators *Max, Min* and *Average* are the special cases in LAOs. For each LAO, there is a corresponding semantic interpretation. The experiments show the strength of our system.

1 Introduction

The Semantic Web [1] has gained a lot progress in recent years. In this field, ontology is a key technique for the interoperability of heterogeneous systems. Currently, a large amount of ontologies have been developed in various research domains or even in the same domain. But for different ontologies, the same entity may be named differently, or defined in different ways. Even the same name may represent different entities. Ontology matching, which takes two different ontologies as input and outputs the correspondences between semantically equivalent entities (e.g., classes, properties, instances), becomes a critical solution to deal with these problems. It has been applied in many application domains, such as the Semantic Web, ontology merging or integration.

Now, quite a few ontology matching approaches or matchers [2,3,4,5,6,7] have been proposed. Good surveys of the matchers are provided in [8,9]. These matchers exploit various kinds of information in ontologies, such as entity names, entity descriptions, name paths, taxonomic structures. It has been accepted that combining the results of multiple matchers is a promising technique to get better results than just using one matcher at a time [2,3,4,10].

J. Lang, F. Lin, and J. Wang (Eds.): KSEM 2006, LNAI 4092, pp. 176–189, 2006.

Some matcher combination systems, such as LSD [3], COMA [2], CMC [10] have been developed. In general, the combination methods or aggregation operators in these systems include *Max*, *Min*, *Average* and *Weighted* (such as *Weighted Average*). It is clear that *Max* and *Min* [2] are too extreme to perform well. While *Average* [2] is inefficient to cope with the ontologies with very different structures. A *Weighted* based method [3,2,10] needs to compute the weights of different matchers. One way to get the weights is to assign them manually, and the other is by machine learning technique. Obviously, it is difficult for a person to estimate the weights by experience and rich data sets are needed to train the algorithm to obtain reliable weights for machine learning methods.

To overcome these limitations, in this paper, we propose a linguistic combination system (LCS), which combines the results of multiple matchers based on the ordered weighted average (OWA) operator and linguistic quantifiers [11]. The OWA operator generally includes three steps [12]:

- Reorder the input arguments in descending order.
- Determine the weights associated with the OWA operator.
- Utilize the OWA weights to aggregate these reordered arguments.

A weight here is associated with a particular ordered position not a specific matcher. In the OWA operator, determining weights is a key step. We adopt the way to obtain weights by a linguistic quantifier [11,13]. So we call our system the linguistic combination system (LCS). A linguistic aggregation operator (LAO) will be used for the aggregation in LCS. LAO is an OWA operator where the associated weights are obtained by the linguistic quantifiers [11]. Specifically, it is composed of the following four steps:

- Reorder the similarity values to be combined in descending order. These values are obtained by the base matchers on the current task.
- Choose or define a linguistic quantifier.
- Obtain the OWA weights by the linguistic quantifier.
- Apply the OWA weights to aggregate these similarity values.

It is interesting that existing aggregation operators like *Max*, *Min* and *Average* are special cases of LAOs. Besides, there is a semantic interpretation for each LAO to facilitate users to choose an appropriate LAO. So LAO provides a good way to supply a gap for existing aggregation operators without considering the weights to matchers.

This paper is organized as follows. Some related work is introduced in the next section. In Section 3, we give more details on the background knowledge on ontology matching and the OWA operator. The linguistic aggregation operators (LAOs) are described in Section 4. Section 5 defines the matching process which uses LAO to aggregate the results of multiple matchers. Experiment results are analyzed in Section 6. Finally, we conclude the paper and give some future work in Section 7.

2   Related Work

Ontology matchers have been developed by many researchers for all kinds of information provided in ontologies. Due to the space limitation for the paper, we only introduce some of them here. NOM [4] proposed seventeen rules by experts, which can be seen as seventeen matchers. These rules contain different aspects of an ontology, such as super concepts, sub concepts, super properties and sub properties. Cupid [5] integrates linguistic and structural matching. Importantly, it makes use of a wide range of techniques to discover mappings between schema elements. The techniques based on element names, data types, constraints and schema structures are included. In Lite [7], a universal measure for ontology matching is proposed. It separates the entities in an ontology into eight categories like classes, objects, datatypes. For an entity in a category, all the features about its definition are involved. In these papers, most of the matchers can be selected as base matchers to be combined in a combination system [10].

In existing matcher combination systems, some typical systems are mentioned as follows. LSD [3] is a data-integration system which semi-automatically finds semantic mappings by employing and extending machine-learning techniques. It aggregates multiple similarities obtained by the individual matchers by means of weighted average, where the similarities and weights are acquired by machine learning. COMA [2] exploits *Max, Min, Average* and *Weighted* strategies for combination. The *Weighted* strategy needs a relative weight for each matcher to show its relative importance. For each category in Lite [7], a set of all relationships in which the category participates is defined. And the relative weights are assigned to each relationship. Only the entities in the same category can be matched. CMC [10] combines multiple schema-matching strategies based on credibility prediction. It needs to predict the accuracy of each matcher on the current matching task first by a manual rule or a machine learning method. Accordingly, different credit for the pair is assigned. Therefore from each base matcher, two matrices including the similarity matrix and the credibility matrix are provided. It aggregates all the similarity matrices into a single one by weighted average, where the weights are determined by the credibility matrices. In NOM [4], it is mentioned that not all matchers have to be used for each aggregation, especially as some matchers have a high correlation. Both manual and automatic approaches to learn how to combine the methods are provided. The weights they use are determined manually or by a machine learning method.

To sum up, when it is not necessary or difficult to get weights for matchers, the aggregation operator which we can choose for aggregation includes *Max, Min* and *Average*. However, since each base matcher performs differently in different conditions, these operators may be not enough to show the various performance for complex situations [14].

In this paper, we propose a linguistic combination system (LCS), which includes rich linguistic aggregation operators (LAOs). And according to the semantic interpretation of LAOs we provide, it is much more convenient for users to choose an appropriate LAO.

3 Background

3.1 Ontology Matching

Typically, an ontology is to define a vocabulary in a domain of interest, and a specification of the meaning of entities used in the vocabulary. In this paper, the entities in an ontology are separated into three categories: classes, properties and instances. We only match the entities in the same category and represent ontologies in OWL[1] or RDF(S)[2].

The similarity for ontologies is defined as a similarity function: $sim(e_{1i}, e_{2j}) \in [0, 1]$, where e_{1i}, e_{2j} are two entities in the same category from a source ontology onto1 and a target ontology onto2 separately. Especially, $sim(e_{1i}, e_{2j}) = 0$ indicates e_{1i} and e_{2j} are different, and $sim(e_{1i}, e_{2j}) = 1$ shows they are the same. If the similarity $sim(e_{1i}, e_{2j})$ exceeds a threshold $th_{final} \in [0, 1]$, we call e_{2j} the matching candidate of e_{1i}. Furthermore, if there is more than one matching candidate in onto2 for e_{1i}, the one with the highest similarity is selected as its matched entity.

3.2 The Ordered Weighted Averaging (OWA) Operator

The ordered weighted averaging (OWA) operator is introduced by [11] to aggregate information. It has been used in a wide range of application areas, such as neural networks, fuzzy logic controllers, vision systems, expert systems and multi-criteria decision aids [15].

Given a set of arguments $V_1 = (a_1, a_2, ..., a_n), a_i \in [0, 1], 1 \leq i \leq n$, reorder the elements of the set in descending order and mark the ordered set as $V_2 = (b_1, b_2, ..., b_n)$, where b_j is the jth highest value in V_1. An OWA operator is a mapping F from I^n to I, $I = [0, 1]$:

$$F(a_1, a_2, ..., a_n) = \sum_{i=1}^{n} w_i b_i$$
$$= w_1 b_1 + w_2 b_2 + ... + w_n b_n,$$

where each weight $w_i \in [0, 1]$ and $\sum_{i=1}^{n} w_i = 1$.

Note that the weight w_i is not associated with a particular argument a_i, but with a particular ordered position i of the arguments. That is w_i is the weight associated with the ith largest argument whichever component it is [11].

4 The Linguistic Aggregation Operator (LAO)

From the previous section, it is obvious that a critical technique in the OWA operator is to determine the OWA weights $w_i, 1 \leq i \leq n$. So far, quite a few approaches have been proposed, for example, O'Hagan [16] introduced a procedure to generate the OWA weights by a predefined degree of orness and maximizing the entropy of the OWA weights. An interesting way to obtain the weights is developed by Yager using linguistic quantifiers [11,13].

---

[1] http://www.w3.org/TR/2004/REC-owl-guide-20040210/
[2] http://www.w3.org/TR/rdf-schema/

We adopt the linguistic quantifiers to determine the OWA weights. We use such kind of OWA operators as linguistic aggregation operators (LAOs). The following gives more details on how to aggregate the results of multiple matchers for an entity pair to be compared by LAO.

Assume there is n matchers of concern, $\{m_1, m_2, ..., m_n\}$, in an ontology matching problem. Let (x, y) be an entity pair, where x is an entity from a source ontology onto1, y from a target ontology onto2. For each matcher m_i, $m_i(x, y) \in [0, 1]$ indicates the similarity of x and y, i.e., the degree to which this matcher is satisfied by (x, y). The final similarity between x and y, $sim(x, y)$, can be computed by the results of the n matchers. That is,

$$sim(x, y) = F(m_1(x, y), m_2(x, y), ..., m_n(x, y))$$
$$= \sum_{i=1}^{n} w_i b_i$$
$$= w_1 b_1 + w_2 b_2 + ... + w_n b_n,$$

where F is the same function as that in the previous section, b_i is the ith largest value in $\{m_1(x, y), m_2(x, y), ..., m_n(x, y)\}$. According to the linguistic approach [11,13], the weight w_i is defined by

$$w_i = Q(\frac{i}{n}) - Q(\frac{i-1}{n}), \quad i = 1, 2, ..., n, \tag{1}$$

where Q is a nondecreasing proportional fuzzy linguistic quantifier and is defined as the following:

$$Q(r) = \begin{cases} 0, & \text{if } r < a; \\ (r-a)/(b-a), & \text{if } a \le r \le b, \ a, b, r \in [0, 1]; \\ 1, & \text{if } r > b, \end{cases} \tag{2}$$

where a and b are the predefined thresholds to determine a proportional or relative quantifier. $Q(r)$ indicates the degree to which r portion of objects satisfies the concept denoted by Q [17].

There are many proportional fuzzy quantifiers, such as *For all*, *There exists*, *Identity*, *Most*, *At least half(Alh)*, *As many as possible(Amap)*. Table 1 gives more details on some examples of LAOs.

From this table, it is clear that the existing aggregation operators *Max*, *Min* and *Average* are special cases of LAOs. The following simple example illustrates the use of some LAOs.

Example: Assume the similarity values to be combined are $V_1 = (0.6, 1, 0.3, 0.5)$, where each value is obtained by a base matcher on the current matching task. After re-ordering V_1 in descending order, we get $V_2=(1, 0.6, 0.5, 0.3)$.

a) For *Most*, if we let a be 0.3 and b be 0.8 (see Table 1) for Equation (2), we obtain $Q(r) = 2(r - 0.3)$, if $0.3 \le r \le 0.8$; $Q(r) = 0$, if $0 \le r < 0.3$; $Q(r)=1$, if $0.8 < r \le 1$. So, the weights for the four positions in V_2 are computed as followings by Equation (1):

$w_1 = Q(\frac{1}{4}) - Q(0) = 0$
$w_2 = Q(\frac{2}{4}) - Q(\frac{1}{4}) = 2(\frac{2}{4} - 0.3) - 0 = 0.4$

Table 1. Definitions of some LAOs

Quantifier	$Q(r)$	w_i	LAO
There exists	$Q(r) = 0$, if $r = 0$ $Q(r) = 1$, if $r > 0$	$w_i = 1$, if $i = 1$ $w_i = 0$, if $i \neq 1$	Max
For all	$Q(r) = 0$, if $r < 1$ $Q(r) = 1$, if $r = 1$	$w_i = 0$, if $i < n$ $w_i = 1$, if $i = n$	Min
Identity	$Q(r) = r$, if $0 \leq r \leq 1$	$w_i = \frac{1}{n}$, $i = 1, 2, ..., n$	Average
Most	$Q(r) = 0$, if $0 \leq r < 0.3$ $Q(r) = 1$, if $0.8 < r \leq 1$ $Q(r) = 2(r - 0.3)$, if $0.3 \leq r \leq 0.8$	$w_i = Q(\frac{i}{n}) - Q(\frac{i-1}{n})$ $i = 1, 2, ..., n$	Most
Alh	$Q(r) = 2r$, if $0 \leq r \leq 0.5$ $Q(r) = 0$, if $0.5 < r \leq 1$	$w_i = Q(\frac{i}{n}) - Q(\frac{i-1}{n})$ $i = 1, 2, ..., n$	Alh
Amap	$Q(r) = 0$, if $0 \leq r < 0.5$ $Q(r) = 2(r - 0.5)$, if $0.5 \leq r \leq 1$	$w_i = Q(\frac{i}{n}) - Q(\frac{i-1}{n})$ $i = 1, 2, ..., n$	Amap

$$w_3 = Q(\tfrac{3}{4}) - Q(\tfrac{2}{4}) = 2(\tfrac{3}{4} - 0.3) - 2(\tfrac{2}{4} - 0.3) = 0.5$$
$$w_4 = Q(1) - Q(\tfrac{3}{4}) = 1 - 2(\tfrac{3}{4} - 0.3) = 0.1$$

Hence,

$$F(0.6, 1, 0.3, 0.5) = \sum_{i=1}^{4} w_i b_i$$
$$= (0)(1) + (0.4)(0.6) + (0.5)(0.5) + (0.1)(0.3)$$
$$= 0.52$$

b) For *Alh*, we obtain $w_1 = 0.5$, $w_2 = 0.5$, $w_3 = 0$, $w_4 = 0$, by setting $a = 0$, $b = 0.5$, $n = 4$ for Equation (1) and (2). Here,

$$F(0.6, 1, 0.3, 0.5) = \sum_{i=1}^{4} w_i b_i$$
$$= (0.5)(1) + (0.5)(0.6) + (0)(0.5) + (0)(0.3)$$
$$= 0.8$$

5   An Overview of LCS

In this section, we first give an overview of ontology matching process in LCS. We then give more details on the matchers we will use for our evaluation and the semantic interpretation for LAOs.

5.1   Ontology Matching Process

Based on COMA [2], the matching process in LCS is illustrated in Figure 1, where LAO is used for the aggregation.

The entities in an ontology are classes, properties or instances. For different entity category, different matchers may be used according to the features of each category. For example, only a property has domain and range, so that the matcher of *Domain and Range* could only be used for the properties category. Similar to the matcher of *Mother Concept*, it is only suitable for instances category.

According to COMA [2] and the survey of approaches to automatic schema matching [8], matchers can be divided into three categories: individual matchers, hybrid matchers and composite matchers. We assume in this paper that individual matchers do not rely on any initial similarity matrix provided by other matchers. In contrast, a hybrid matcher needs such a matrix and directly combines several matchers, which can be executed simultaneously or in a fixed order. A composite matcher combines its independently executed constituent matchers, including individual matchers and hybrid matchers.

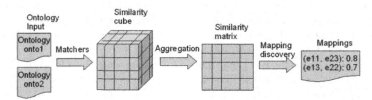

Fig. 1. Matching process in LCS

A main step of LCS is to combine the results of multiple base matchers. A base matcher is the matcher to be combined, which can be individual matcher, hybrid matcher or composite matcher. After executing each matcher, a similarity matrix is obtained. Multiple similarity matrixes form a similarity cube, which can be combined by an aggregation operator to obtain a final similarity matrix. We use LAO to combine the results of multiple base matchers. Some linguistic quantifiers for LAOs have been described in Table 1, such as *At least half*, *Most*. Others can be defined by users by adjusting the two parameters in Equation (2).

The final step of matching process is to select match candidates from the final similarity matrix. We only focus on finding the best matching candidate or matched entity from the target ontology onto2 for each entity in the source ontology onto1 if possible, which is the task of mapping discovery.

5.2   Ontology Matchers

In LCS, we choose some existing ontology matchers to evaluate our system. The details of these matchers are described as followings.

- **Name:** When comparing entity names, some preparation skills are adopted. For example, separate the name string into some tokens by the capital letters and some symbols such as '#', '_', '.'. Then delete some words like "the", "has", "an" from the token sets.
- **Name Path:** It considers the names of the path from the root to the elements being matched in the hierarchical graphs, which regards the classes or instances as nodes and relations as edges.
- **Taxonomy:** This matcher is a composite one. For classes, it consists of *super concept(Sup)*, *sub concept(Sub)*, *sibling concept(Sib)*, and *properties(Prop)*, which are the properties directly associated with the class to be matched. For properties, only *super properties(Sup)* and *sub properties(Sub)* are included here.

- **Domain and Range:** If the domain and range of two properties are equal, the properties are also similar.
- **Mother-concept:** Obviously, this matcher considers the type of an instance.

Among these matchers, *Name* is an individual matcher to provide the initial similarity matrix for other matchers. A good example for the composite matcher is *Taxonomy*. For *Name Path*, *Sup*, *Sub*, etc., they are hybrid matchers which rely on the initial matrix obtained by *Name*.

5.3   The Semantic Interpretation of LAOs

In Section 4, the definitions of some LAOs were given. We now give the semantic interpretation for them according to Yager's interpretation of the linguistic quantifiers [11,13]. The interpretation makes it convenient for users to choose an appropriate LAO for the aggregation.

Based on the definition of LAO, the explanation for some LAOs is given as followings. For an entity pair (x, y),

- **Max:** $Max(x, y) = Max\{m_1(x, y), m_2(x, y), ..., m_n(x, y)\}$. *Max* means that (x, y) satisfies at least one of the matchers, i.e., satisfies m_1 or m_2 ... or m_n.
- **Min:** $Min(x, y) = Min\{m_1(x, y), m_2(x, y), ..., m_n(x, y)\}$. *Min* means that (x, y) satisfies all the matchers, that is to say, we are essentially requiring to satisfy m_1 and m_2 ... and m_n.
- **Avg:** *Avg* (*Average*) means identity. It regards all similarity values equally.
- **Most:** Obviously, *Most* means that most of the matchers is satisfied. Usually, this operator ignores some higher and lower similarity values, that is to give small weights on them, while paying more attention to the values in the middle of the input arguments after re-ordering.
- **Alh:** *Alh* (*At least half*) satisfies at least half matchers. Actually, it only considers the first half of similarity values after re-ordering them in descending order.
- **Amap:** *Amap* (*As many as possible*) satisfies as many as possible matchers and is opposite to *Alh*. The second half of values after reordering is considered. So after an aggregation operation, the result obtained by *Alh* is always higher than that by *Amap*.

6   Experiments

The base matchers we will use in LCS for experiments include *Name*(N for short), *Taxonomy*(T for short), *Name Path*(P for short), *Domain and Range*(D for short), *Mother concept*(M for short). Moreover, for two entities from two different ontologies, if they are in the classes category, N, T and P are used to compare the two entities. If they are in the properties category, N, T and D are used. If they are in the same instances category, we use N, P and M.

The experiments are made on some ontologies provided in the context of the I^3CON conference[3]. We give more details on these ontology pairs as followings. The labels with bold font are used to represent each ontology pair.

---
[3] http://www.atl.external.lmco.com/projects/ontology/i3con.html

- **Animals:** It includes two ontologies which are defined in a similar way and around 30 entities for each ontology. They have 24 real mappings.
- **Cs:** Cs represents two computer science(cs) departments at two Universities respectively. More than 100 entities are involved in the first ontology, while about 30 entities in the second one. The number of real mappings is 16.
- **Hotel:** Hotel describes the characteristics of hotel rooms. The two ontologies in Hotel are equivalent, but defined in different ways. In each ontology, around 20 entities are defined. About 17 real mappings are identified by humans.
- **Network:** networkA.owl and networkB.owl describe the nodes and connections in a local area network. networkA.owl focuses more on the nodes themselves, while networkB.owl is more encompassing of the connections. Each ontology has more than 30 entities. In total we have 30 real mappings.
- **Pets1:** Pets1 is composed of ontology people+petsA.owl and people+petsB.owl which is a modified version of people+petsA.owl. More than 100 entities are defined in each ontology and 93 real mappings are determined manually.
- **Pets2:** Identical to Pets1 above without instance data. 74 real mappings are created.
- **Russia:** The pair of russiaA.rdf and russiaB.rdf for Russia describes the locations, objects, and cultural elements of Russia. Each of them has more than 100 entities. The total number of theoretical mappings is 117.

To evaluate LCS, the common matching quality measures are exploited in the next section. The following three sections are to show the performance of the combination methods in LCS by using some public ontologies. It is noted that, in order to discover the mapping candidates from the aggregated similarity matrix, we tune the threshold th_{final} to get the best performance by experience according to the characteristics of the combination methods and ontologies to be matched.

6.1   The Criterion of Evaluation

The standard information retrieval measures [18] are adopted by us.

- **Precision:** $precision = \frac{|I|}{|P|}$. It reflects the share of the correct mappings among all mappings returned automatically by a matcher.
- **Recall:** $recall = \frac{|I|}{|R|}$ specifies the number of correct mappings versus the real mappings determined by manually.
- **F-Measure:** $f - Measure = \frac{2*precision*recall}{precision+recall}$, which represents the harmonic mean of Precision and Recall.
- **Overall:** $overall = recall * (2 - \frac{1}{precision})$, which is introduced in [6]. It is a combined measure and takes into account the manual effort needed for both removing false and adding missed matches.

Where, $|I|$ indicates the number of the correct mappings that are found by the automatic matchers. $|P|$ is the number of all mappings that are found automatically, which includes the false and correct mappings. $|R|$ shows the number of the manually determined real mappings.

6.2   Single Matchers vs. Combination

Figure 2 shows the performance of some single matchers and combination methods on the ontology pair "network", which includes ontology networkA.owl and networkB.owl. Since there is no instance in networkA.owl, we only compare the classes and properties in two ontologies.

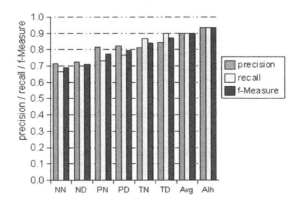

Fig. 2. Single matchers vs. combination methods

In Figure 2, each single matcher is marked as two capital letters, where the first one indicates a single matcher for classes category and the second one for properties category. For instance, "*ND*" means the matcher *Name*(*N* for short) for classes category, and the matcher *Domain and Range*(*D* for short) is used for properties category. The combination methods are *Avg* (*Average*) and *Alh* (*At least half*) based on all single matchers for each category (see Section 5.2 and the first paragraph of Section 6).

It has been shown that f-Measure increases with the increase of recall from *NN* to *Alh*. Obviously, it is much more helpful to use several matchers together at a time than just use one matcher to get better results, because more information can be obtained for multiple matchers than that for one matcher.

6.3   Comparing Different LAOs

Due to the existence of some composite matchers like *Taxonomy* for our experiments, the aggregation should be executed twice. One is for the composite matchers to combine their constituent matchers. For properties category, it needs to aggregate first the results of the constituent matchers, *Super properties* and *Sub properties*, for *Taxonomy*. The second aggregation is to combine all the base matchers, *Name*, *Domain and Range* and *Taxonomy* to get the final similarity matrix.

Since *Max*, *Min* and *Avg* are not only existing aggregation operators without weights to matchers, but the special cases in LAOs, we choose six LAOs including the three special operators to compare their performance. From Figure 3, we can

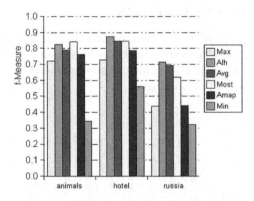

Fig. 3. The performance of several LAOs

see that: *Alh*, *Most*, *Avg* and *Amap* (*As many as possible*) outperform *Max* and *Min*. Because *Max* and *Min* are extra optimistic or too pessimistic, that is to consider one extreme similarity value at a time. While *Alh*, *Most*, *Avg* and *Amap* combine some or all the similarity values. Moreover, *Alh* could perform better than *Avg* in most cases while *Most* outperforms *Avg* in some cases because of their own characteristics.

6.4   The Comparison of *Average* and *At least half*

As *Avg* outperforms *Max* and *Min* as existing aggregation operators, we use *Alh* to compare with *Avg* on seven ontology pairs to give more details on their performances. The purpose of this experiment is to give more detail on that some operators in LAOs like *Alh* could perform better than existing aggregation operators like *Avg* in most cases. As we have said, we do not consider the weights to matchers.

Based on the matching process in LCS and the base matchers we have chosen, we compare the performance of *Avg* and *Alh* on all the ontology pairs we have

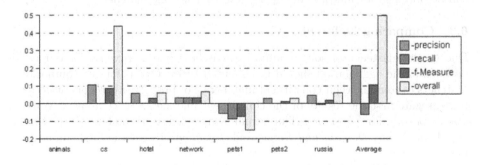

Fig. 4. Compare the performance of *Avg* and *Alh* in LCS

introduced above. See Figure 4, the data in Y axis is computed by subtracting the results of Avg from the results of Alh, where the results are expressed by precision, recall, overall and f-Measure. We use "-" in the figure to indicate the subtraction. For example, "-precision" indicates the subtraction by subtracting the precision of Avg from the precision of Alh on a specific ontology pair (O_1, O_2) (i.e., $-precision = precision_{Alh}(O_1, O_2) - precision_{Avg}(O_1, O_2)$).

From Figure 4, Alh outperforms Avg on all the ontology pairs except animals and pets by higher precision and f-Measure basing on the similar recall for each ontology pair. For animals, the performance for Avg and Alh is the same. The overall of Alh is only reduced in one out of the seven ontology pairs, while is increased in five of the seven pairs with the highest increase near 0.5, which means nearly 50% manual effort is saved.

7 Conclusion and Future Work

Ontology matching is an essential solution to deal with the interoperability of heterogeneous systems. It has been proved that, in most cases, combining the results of multiple matching approaches or matchers is a promising technique to get better results than just using one matcher at a time [2,3,4,10]. Due to the limitations of existing combination methods, we propose a new system LCS where a LAO is used for the aggregation. Through experiments, the power of LCS has been shown.

The main contribution of this paper is the introduction of OWA operator to ontology matching. The weight here is not associated with a specific matcher but a particular ordered position. We choose the linguistic quantifiers to determine the OWA weights. To our convenience, we name the OWA operator based on the linguistic quantifier to obtain weights as the linguistic aggregation operator (LAO). So a large number of LAOs can be defined according to different linguistic quantifiers. Besides, we provide a semantic interpretation of LAOs to facilitate users to select an appropriate LAO for the aggregation. Specially, some existing aggregation operators like Max, Min and $Average$ are the special cases in LAOs.

From the experiments (see Figure 3 and 4), we can see that some LAOs like Alh and $Most$, can perform better than Max, Min and Avg in most cases. So LAO provides a good way to supply a gap for existing aggregation operators without considering the weights to matchers.

In the future, we will further develop the application of OWA operators to combine multiple ontology matchers. Specifically, the following aspects are involved: First, since we intend to compare different combination methods without weights to the matchers, we provide a simple platform for such comparison. In our further work, we will compare the performance of our system with other systems. Last but not the least, we did not consider the weights of matchers, not because they are not important, but we want to propose a flexible and efficient way to aggregate the results of multiple matchers when it is not necessary to use weights. If the weights of matchers can be obtained by experts or machine learning, we can use the weighted OWA operators [19] for the aggregation.

References

1. Berners-Lee, T., Hendler, J., Lassila, O.: The semantic web. *Scientific American*, 284(5):34-43, 2001.
2. Do, H., Rahm, E.: COMA - a system for flexible combination of schema matching approaches. In *Proceedings of the 28th VLDB Conference*, pp. 610-621, 2002.
3. Doan, A., Domingos, P., Halevy, A.Y.: Reconciling schemas of disparate data sources: a machine-learning approach. *SIGMOD Record (ACM Special Interest Group on Management of Data)*, pp. 509-520, 2001.
4. Ehrig, M., Sure, Y.: Ontology mapping - an integrated approach. In *Proceedings of the First European Semantic Web Symposium, ESWS 2004, Volume 3053 of Lecture Notes in Computer Science*, pp. 76-91, Heraklion, Greece, 2004. Springer Verlag.
5. Madhavan, J., Bernstein, P.A., Rahm, E.: Generic schema matching with cupid. In *Proceedings of the Twenty-seventh International Conference on Very Large Data Bases(VLDB)*, pp. 49-58, Roma, Italy, 11-14th September 2001. Los Altos, CA, USA, Morgan Kaufmann Publishers (2001).
6. Melnik, S., Garcia-Molina, H., Rahm, E.: Similarity flooding: A versatile graph matching algorithm and its application to schema matching. In *Proceedings of Eighteenth International Conference on Data Engineering*, San Jose, California, 2002.
7. Euzenat, J. and Valtchev, P.: Similarity-based ontology alignment in OWL-Lite. In *Proceedings of the 16th European Conference on Artificial Intelligence (ECAI)*, pp. 333-337, Valencia, Spain, 2004.
8. Rahm, E., Bernstein, P.: A survey of approaches to automatic schema matching. *The International Journal on Very Large Data Bases(VLDB)*, 10(4): 334-350, 2001.
9. Shvaiko, P., Euzenat, J.: A survey of schema-based matching approaches. *Journal on Data Semantics*, No. 4, LNCS 3730, pp. 146-171, 2005.
10. Tu, K., Yu, Y.: CMC: Combining mutiple schema-matching strategies based on credibility prediction. In *Proceedings of the 10th International Conference on Database Systems for Advanced Applications (DASFAA)*, LNCS 3453, pp. 17-20, 2005, China.
11. Yager, R.R.: On ordered weighted averaging aggregation operators in multi-criteria decision making. *IEEE Trans. on Systems, Man and Cybernetics*, 18(1988): 183-190.
12. Xu, Z.: An overview of methods for determining OWA weights. *International Journal of Intelligent Systems*, 20(8): 843-865, 2005.
13. Yager, R.R.: Family of OWA operators. *Fuzzy Sets and Systems*, 59(1993): 125-148.
14. Yatskevich, M.: Preliminary evaluation of schema matching systems. *Technical Report # DIT-03-028*, Department of Information and Communication Technology, University Of Trento (Italy) (2003).
15. Yager, R. R. and Kacprzyk, J.: *The Ordered Weighted Averaging Operation: Theory, Methodology and Applications*. Kluwer Academic Publishers, pp. 167-178, Boston, 1997.
16. O'Hagan, M.: Aggregating template or rule antecedents in realtime expert systems with fuzzy set logic. In *Proceedings of the 22nd Annual IEEE Asilomar Conference on Signals, Systems, Computers*, pp. 681-689, Pacific Grove, CA, 1988.

17. Herrera, F., Herrera-Viedma, E. and Verdegay, J.L.: A sequential selection process in group decision making with a linguistic assessment approach,*Information Sciences*, 85 (1995), pp. 223-239.
18. Do, H., Rahm, E.: Comparison of schema matching evaluations. In *Proceedings of the second international workshop on Web Databases (German Informatics Society)*, 221-237, 2002.
19. V. Torra, The Weighted OWA operator, *International Journal of Intelligent Systems*, 12(1997): 153-166.

Framework for Collaborative Knowledge Sharing and Recommendation Based on Taxonomic Partial Reputations

Dong-Hwee Kim and Soon-Ja Kim

School of Electrical Engineering and Computer Science,
Kyungpook National University,
702-701, E10-822, 1370 Sankyun3-dong Buk-gu Daegu, Korea
{dewwind, snjkim}@ee.knu.ac.kr

Abstract. We propose a novel system for collaborative knowledge sharing and recommendation based on taxonomic partial reputations on web-based personal knowledge directories. And we developed a prototype of the proposed system as a web-based user interface for personal knowledge management. This system presents a personal knowledge directory to a registered user. Such a directory has a personal ontology to integrate and classify the knowledge collected by a user from the Web. And the knowledge sharing activities among registered users generate partial reputation factors of knowledge items, their domain nodes, users and groups. Then new users can obtain the knowledge items proper to their needs, by referring such reputation values of those elements. In addition, users can also take the *stem* that is a set of common knowledge items over the domains designated by them. Thus proposed system can prevent cold-start problem because our knowledge recommendation mechanisms depend on the results of the collaborative knowledge sharing activities among users.

1 Introduction

The massive accumulation of information on the Web has raised the fundamental questions over their usefulness. Though people can use search engines to obtain the information they need from a huge amount of the resources on the Web, most people may not recognize what they want actually. Moreover, only through the individual search processes, it becomes more difficult to obtain highly refined knowledge items. Therefore various investigations on knowledge acquisition and dissemination, especially on the context of e-commerce, have already conceived the useful methods which are able to bring us *knowledge* as valuable information.

Recommender Systems (RS) [1] can help people to find the information or resources they need in a certain domain of a specific knowledge, by integrating and analyzing the rated experiences or opinions of their *nearest neighbors* [7]. These systems learn about user preferences over time and find proper items or people of similar taste. *Collaborative Filtering* (CF) [2] is the most widely used technique for RS. Several collaborative filtering schemes, which have been successfully industrialized as one of

J. Lang, F. Lin, and J. Wang (Eds.): KSEM 2006, LNAI 4092, pp. 190–201, 2006.

the fundamental techniques for recommender systems, have been continuously optimized for better results of recommendation. CF techniques suggest new items or predict the usefulness of a certain item for a particular user based on the database of the ratings and opinions of other users of similar preference. Though recommender systems with collaborative filtering are achieved widespread success on the web, some potential challenges, such as *cold-start* [3] or *early-rater* [4] problems at the initial stage of RS, still remain in this context. In fact, recommender systems based on CF have failed to help in cold-start situations in many practical cases. Content-based and hybrid recommender systems perform a little better since they need just a few samples of users to find similarities among items.

Furthermore, there has been increasing efforts for developing tools for creating annotated contents over the Web and managing them. Ontologies provide an explicit specification of a conceptualization and discussed as means to support knowledge sharing. And an ontology structure provides shared vocabulary and its hierarchical relationship for expressing the knowledge on a specific domain. If some initial domain knowledge and basic user profiles are uniformly provided to a knowledge recommender system at the initial stage through the ontology corresponding to each domain of the system, then the system can prevents two known problems above. Thus, to make up for these problems of traditional recommender systems for knowledge dissemination, the items which collected in a knowledge repository should be integrated and classified by the ontology corresponding to their domains in advance.

Therefore, we propose a novel framework for collaborative knowledge sharing and recommendation through taxonomic partial reputation factors on web-based personal knowledge directories. And we implement the prototype of proposed system as a web-based user interface for knowledge management on the personal knowledge directories presented to registered users. Such a directory has a *personal ontology* as a tool for classifying and managing collected knowledge.

In our system, a new user can obtain the *stem* which represents a set of the common knowledge items over the domains designated by the user. Such a stem has the user-scalable size according to several *partial reputation factors*. Proposed system can also shorten the term of the cold-start problem of traditional recommender systems, because proposed knowledge recommendation process depends on the results of the collaborative knowledge sharing activities among users over their directories. In other words, our knowledge recommendation mechanism occurs when the initial knowledge items are accumulated enough to derive users' knowledge sharing activities over their directories.

One of the key phases in knowledge based systems construction is *knowledge acquisition* [5]. Thus knowledge acquisition problem is considered as an important subject in the context of knowledge based systems over the past year. We believe this problem can be relived by collaborative knowledge sharing activities among the users over the *personal knowledge directories* as the ontology-based sharable repositories for integrating and organizing their knowledge. Users can integrate and organize the knowledge which already restored in some other repositories on the Web through the personal knowledge directories.

Reputation is the sum of the rated trust values which given to a person by other members of the group to represents the relative level of trustworthiness, where the group is defined as the people who have the collaborative relationship to the subjects in a specific domain of their common interests. The amount of reputation of a person is a result aggregated from the subdivided reputation factors separately indicating the level of truthfulness or usefulness of the items published by the person. Therefore, we use the taxonomy-based reputation integrated in a hierarchical structure of the partial reputation values separately given to items, domains, users and groups. The gradual knowledge sharing activities among users update the reputation values for items, users and groups. And newly registered users can independently discover, capture and share the knowledge items which are proper to their needs and interests by referring such reputation values of other users or each of items in a specific domain.

In addition, recommender systems are often exposed to some attacks by malicious insider like the *copy-profile attack* [6] that a malicious user masquerades as the user who has the same profile of a target user. In this way, the attackers induce the target user to get or buy the items which have been highly rated by them in advance. The rating mechanisms included in several rating-based recommender systems without trust mechanism, always imply the weak points for those attacks. Therefore we make our reputation mechanism only depend on taxonomical structure of the collaborative network which naturally constructed by users. Thus our reputation mechanism with taxonomy-based partial reputation can absolve the attacks attempted on a small-scale.

2   Related Works

Tapestry [2], the earliest CF system, was designed to support a small community of users. A similar approach is the active collaborative filtering [3], which provides an easy way for users to direct recommendations to their friends and colleagues through a Lotus Notes database. Tapestry is also an *active collaborative filtering* system in which a user takes a direct role in the process of deciding whose evaluations are used to provide his or her recommendations. While Tapestry required explicit user action to retrieve and evaluate ratings, *automated collaborative filtering* systems such as GroupLens [8] provide predictions with less user effort. GroupLens system provides a pseudonymous collaborative filtering solution for Usenet news and movies. The original GroupLens project provides automated neighborhood for recommendations in Usenet news. When Users rate articles then GroupLens automatically recommends other articles to them. Users of GroupLens learn to prefer articles with high prediction as indicated by tie spent reading [9].

In the context of increasingly large collections of documents on the Internet, *ontologies* for information organization have become an active area of research. There is little agreement on a common definition of ontology, most works cite [10] as the common denominator of all ontology definitions. Ontologies are often used for information retrieval [11]. Using ontologies for document repositories provides for efficient retrieval of stored documents. Moreover, the structure of the ontology provides a context for the stored documents for user browsing as well as automated retrieval.

3   Personal Knowledge Directories

The framework we proposed, actually, is starting on a system for ontology-based *personal knowledge directory*. This presents a user with an web-based environment which provides registered users with the personal directory. Such directories are the repositories in which users can collect and store some knowledge items of a specific domain of their interest. These knowledge items just can simply indicate to the locations of the sources of the knowledge over the Web.

The *taxonomy*, based on the presumed *'is a kind of '* relation, can the best tool for describing a hierarchal relation among data. In this paper, the term taxonomy is thus used as both ontology and directory with inheritance hierarchy.

3.1   Ontology-Based Knowledge Directories

Knowledge sources can be any type of contents on the Web. Thus knowledge items just can include the URL addresses of some web pages, blog pages, archives, private records, etc. Users can collect and classify these items according to the *personal ontology* structured by taxonomic hierarchy of particular knowledge domains. Such items are collected from a huge number of sources over the Web. An item is located in a node as a class of a domain on one of the ontologies separately structured with heterogeneous classes and vocabularies on a specific domain of knowledge over the Web. Thus the structure and vocabularies of the personal ontologies composed by a user are different from the others.

In our system, each of registered users can make their own ontology structure by clipping out a part of the basis ontology for efficient knowledge sharing and classification. In other words, we use a unified ontology to integrate the vocabularies and structures separated among the user ontologies. And a standard ontology is structured and managed by uniformly defined taxonomy and vocabularies.

3.2   Sharable Knowledge Directories

At the early stage of the service, the system depends on the function of the users who accumulate some knowledge items in their directories independently. In this stage, users can create new knowledge items about their own know-how, experiences, opinions, etc. And they can also integrate existing knowledge items they have already got in some other places on the Web. In addition, navigating some other users' directories each of users can also take some of the items in the others' directories. Through such independent user activities to integrate and classify their accumulated knowledge, the system can indirectly and automatically accumulate the initial knowledge items over the domains on the standard ontology. Thus, strictly speaking, proposed system is not the knowledge recommender system at this stage. But, as the system accumulates items enough for a number of user groups to share those items with one another, some of users will start sharing the items with some other users. And, according to the types of sharing, users will make some relationships with other users or certain groups.

3.3 Knowledge Sharing

Available knowledge sharing activities between two users are classified into three cases: First, (1) *copying*: if a user wants to see some knowledge items or class nodes in others' directories continuously, the user can make duplicated instances of the items or whole items in a node in his or her directory. Of course, the instance can be copied from the original version of the knowledge item, or from another copied instance from one. Second, (2) *linking* is a single directional sharing function; if a user links some others' class nodes with the same nodes in his or her directory, the user can see the items in others' nodes through the corresponding nodes. And lastly, (3) *mutual linking* is a bidirectional sharing function; if a group of more than two users want to link mutually his or her nodes with another user, then they can see the items in two interconnected nodes.

3.3.1 Anonymization

Every user can refer all the information about others' activities. But, some of the users want that other users cannot know their identities connecting with their real world life. Furthermore, an anonymized user can share or takes the items or directories in some specific domains more freely or privately. So, for vigorous and natural distribution of knowledge, we added the mechanism which endows the users with anonymity by using agents. Through the anonymization process, simultaneously, each of the users takes a personal agent for finding and managing the knowledge items they need. These agents let the users can hide their identities. In other words, the agent is a unique identity that reflects their particular states on the system. In addition, they organize and update automatically the connectivity among the nodes which are dynamically connected and disconnected with others' ones. Actually, the term agents often used instead of the term users in the thesis.

3.4 Definition and Notation

In this section, we describe some definitions and notations to denote each of elements of the system, their states and relations among them.

3.4.1 Notations for Basic Elements

Agent a_u is one of agents $\mathbf{A}$; $a_u \in \mathbf{A} = \{a_1, a_2, \cdots, a_n\}$ where $|\mathbf{A}| = n$. Agent a_u has a taxonomy τ^{a_u} as a subset of the standard taxonomy τ ; $\tau^{a_u} \subset \tau$ and $\tau^{a_u} \in \mathbf{T} = \{\tau^{a_1}, \tau^{a_2}, \cdots, \tau^{a_m}\}$ where $|\mathbf{T}| = |\mathbf{A}| = m$.

A node n_j is the j-th element of the class nodes $\mathbf{N}$ on τ ; $n_j \in \mathbf{N} = \{n_1, n_2, \cdots, a_m\}$ where $|\mathbf{N}| = m$. And a node $n_k^{a_u}$ is the k-th node of the nodes $\mathbf{N}^{a_u}$ on a taxonomy τ^{a_u} which specified by an agent a_u ; $n_k^{a_u} \in \mathbf{N}^{a_u} = \{n_1^{a_u}, n_2^{a_u}, \cdots, n_\ell^{a_u}\}$ where $|\mathbf{N}^{a_u}| = \ell$.

A knowledge item i_j as a leaf node on τ is the j-th element of the items $\mathbf{I}$; $i_j \in \mathbf{I} = \{i_1, i_2, \cdots, i_n\}$ where $|\mathbf{I}| = n$. And an item i_{k,n_j} is the k-th element of a node $n_j \in \mathbf{N}$; $i_{k,n_j} \in \mathbf{I}_{n_j} = \{i_{1,n_j}, i_{2,n_j}, \cdots, i_{m,n_j}\}$ where $|\mathbf{I}_{n_j}| = m$. Then an item $i_{k,n_j}^{a_u}$ is likewise the k-th item in a node $n_j^{a_u} \in \mathbf{N}^{a_u}$ on τ^{a_u} ; $i_{k,n_j}^{a_u} \in \mathbf{I}_{n_j}^{a_u} = \{i_{1,n_j}^{a_u}, i_{2,n_j}^{a_u}, \cdots, i_{\ell,n_j}^{a_u}\}$ where $| \mathbf{I}_{n_j}^{a_u} | = \ell$. Thus the knowledge items of an agent a_u is given by $\mathbf{I}^{a_u} = \{i_1^{a_u}, i_2^{a_u}, \cdots, i_n^{a_u}\}$ where $| \mathbf{I}^{a_u} | = n$. In addition, $i_{k,n_j}^{a_u}(a_v)$ means that the original author of an item $i_{k,n_j}^{a_u}$ is the agent a_v .

We use $cA(n_j^{a_u})$ to denote the agents which copied whole items in the node $n_j \in \mathbf{N}^{a_u}$ on a taxonomy τ^{a_u} at a time. Then the agents copied an item i_k in the node $n_j \in \mathbf{N}^{a_u}$ on τ^{a_u}, is represented by $cA(i_{k,n_j}^{a_u})$ where $i_{k,n_j}^{a_u} \in \mathbf{I}_{n_j}^{a_u}$. Especially we represent the agent copied a node $n_j \in \mathbf{N}^{a_u}$ at time t by using $ca_v(n_j^{a_u})^t \in cA(n_j^{a_u})$. Similarly $ca_v(i_{k,n_j}^{a_u})^t$ denotes the agent copied an item i_k in a node $n_j \in \mathbf{N}^{a_u}$ at time t .

3.4.2 Notations for Knowledge Sharing Activities

Linking is a single directional sharing function between two agents. If an agent a_u has linked its node $n_j^{a_u}$ to corresponding node $n_j^{a_v}$ of agent a_v, then the items $\mathbf{I}_{n_j}^{a_v}$ in the linked node $n_j^{a_v}$ are shown to the agent a_u through its corresponding node $n_j^{a_u}$. We use $n_j^{a_u} \rightarrow n_j^{a_v}$ to denote this relation between two agents with their node $n_j^{a_u}$ and $n_j^{a_v}$. In addition, the node $n_j^{a_u}$ virtually includes the items in the node $n_j^{a_v}$.

Mutual linking is about that two or more agents share a node with one another equally. This relation is constituted by conjugate two single directional linking of two agents. If two agents a_u and a_v have made a relation of mutual linking to share a node n_j on each taxonomy, we use $n_j^{a_u} \leftrightarrow n_j^{a_v}$ to represent this. Then the items in the node $n_j^{a_u}$ and $n_j^{a_v}$ integrated together in their node n_j simultaneously.

3.4.3 Notations for Communities

Now, we define *communities* as the groups of the agents which collaboratively share the particular knowledge items on their common issues. In our system, *collaborative knowledge sharing* mechanism occurs in groups. In other words, the agents in a group can share multiple nodes with the others at the same time, and these shared nodes are selected and controlled explicitly by *controller agents* of the group.

We use $\mathbf{G}$ to denote a set of agent groups and g_u represents the u-th group of $\mathbf{G} = \{g_1, g_2, \cdots, g_n\}$ where $| \mathbf{G} | = n$. A group g_u is defined as the agents which have the designated taxonomy τ^{g_u} . And τ^{g_u} defined as the taxonomy includes a set of selected nodes $\mathbf{N}^{g_u}$ according to the specific domains of their common interest, where $\mathbf{N}^{g_u} = \{n_1^{g_u}, n_2^{g_u}, \cdots, n_\ell^{g_u}\}$ and $| \mathbf{N}^{g_u} | = \ell$. In addition, the agents belonged to a group g_v is denoted by using $\mathbf{A}^{g_v}$. Then we can use $a_k^{g_v}$ to represent the k-th agent in a group g_v ; $a_k^{g_v} \in \mathbf{A}^{g_v} = \{a_1^{g_v}, a_2^{g_v}, \cdots, a_m^{g_v}\}$ where $| \mathbf{A}^{g_v} | = m$.

3.5 Reputation

The partial factors of a single reputation values are involved with the knowledge sharing activities among agents. Then agents decide whether they will share an item or a node, by referring these *partial reputation factors* of the item or node over the directories in which they interest. In addition, the reputation values of some agents or groups also affect the decision of the agents who may share or take their knowledge.

3.5.1 Reputation of a Single Knowledge Item

The reputation value which given to a knowledge item is determined as follows:

(1) Knowledge Diffusion Rate

This factor represents how many agents have copied the instance of an original item into their nodes. Then *knowledge diffusion rate* $f(i_{k,n_j}^{a_u})$ of an original item $i_k \in \mathbf{I}_{n_j}^{a_u}$ is defined as

$$f(i_{k,n_j}^{a_u}) = \frac{|cA(i_{k,n_j}^{a_u})|}{t_c - t_o(i_{k,n_j}^{a_u})}$$

where t_c is current time and $t_o(i_{k,n_j}^{a_u})$ denotes the time when the item $i_{k,n_j}^{a_u}$ was created in its source node.

(2) Knowledge Propagation Distance

We denote a single *knowledge propagation* of an item $i_k \in \mathbf{I}_{n_j}^{a_u}$ by using $\mathbf{R}(i_{k,n_j}^{a_u})$ as a bundle of the knowledge propagation routes. Then a single knowledge propagation is given by $\mathbf{R}(i_{k,n_j}^{a_u}) = \{r_1(i_{k,n_j}^{a_u}), r_2(i_{k,n_j}^{a_u}), \cdots, r_\ell(i_{k,n_j}^{a_u})\}$ where $r_i(i_{k,n_j}^{a_u})$ is the *i*-th route of $\mathbf{R}(i_{k,n_j}^{a_u})$ and $|\mathbf{R}(i_{k,n_j}^{a_u})| = \ell$. And, a single *knowledge propagation route* $r_i(i_{k,n_j}^{a_u})$ is defined by the chain of the agents which copied the instance of the original item $i_k \in \mathbf{I}_{n_j}^{a_u}$ from one after another. Then, $r_i(i_{k,n_j}^{a_u})$ is obtained by $r_i(i_{k,n_j}^{a_u}) = \{a_1, a_2, \cdots, a_m\}$ where $|r_i(i_{k,n_j}^{a_u})| = m$.

The *i*-th propagation route $r_i(i_{k,n_j}^{a_u})$ of an original item $i_k \in \mathbf{I}_{n_j}^{a_u}$ has the distance value which represents a single length of the route. And the distance of the route $r_i(i_{k,n_j}^{a_u})$ is given by $d_i(i_{k,n_j}^{a_u}) = |r_i(i_{k,n_j}^{a_u})|$. And a set of the distance values is denoted by $\mathbf{D}(i_{k,n_j}^{a_u})$ where $d_i(i_{k,n_j}^{a_u}) \in \mathbf{D}(i_{k,n_j}^{a_u}) = \{d_1(i_{k,n_j}^{a_u}), d_2(i_{k,n_j}^{a_u}), \cdots, d_\ell(i_{k,n_j}^{a_u})\}$. Then the *average propagation distance* $\overline{d}(i_{k,n_j}^{a_u})$ of the original item $i_k \in \mathbf{I}_{n_j}^{a_u}$, is given by

$$\bar{d}(i^{a_u}_{k,n_j}) = \frac{\sum_{i=1}^{\ell} d_i(i^{a_u}_{k,n_j})}{|\mathbf{R}(i^{a_u}_{k,n_j})|}$$

where $d_i(i^{a_u}_{k,n_j}) \in \mathbf{D}(i^{a_u}_{k,n_j})$ and $|\mathbf{R}(i^{a_u}_{k,n_j})| = \ell$.

(3) Knowledge propagation Rate

Associating with a knowledge propagation distance $d_i(i^{a_u}_{k,n_j})$ of an original item $i_k \in \mathbf{I}^{a_u}_{n_j}$, the corresponding value of *knowledge propagation rate* $p_i(i^{a_u}_{k,n_j})$ on a knowledge propagation route $r_i(i^{a_u}_{k,n_j})$ is considered as

$$p_i(i^{a_u}_{k,n_j}) = \frac{d_i(i^{a_u}_{k,n_j})}{t_e(r_i) - t_o(i^{a_u}_{k,n_j})}$$

where $p_i(i^{a_u}_{k,n_j}) \in \mathbf{P}(i^{a_u}_{k,n_j}) = \{p_1(i^{a_u}_{k,n_j}), p_2(i^{a_u}_{k,n_j}), \cdots, p_\ell(i^{a_u}_{k,n_j})\}$ and $|\mathbf{P}(i^{a_u}_{k,n_j})| = \ell$. And $t_e(r_i)$ is the time when the instance of an original item $i^{a_u}_{k,n_j}$ lastly created by the agent on the end of the route $r_i(i^{a_u}_{k,n_j})$, and $t_o(i^{a_u}_{k,n_j})$ denotes the time when the original $i^{a_u}_{k,n_j}$ was created. Then the *average knowledge propagation rate* $\bar{p}(i^{a_u}_{k,n_j})$ of an item $i_k \in \mathbf{I}^{a_u}_{n_j}$ is defined by

$$\bar{P}(i^{a_u}_{k,n_j}) = \frac{\sum_{i=1}^{\ell} p_i(i^{a_u}_{k,n_j})}{|\mathbf{R}(i^{a_u}_{k,n_j})|}$$

where $|\mathbf{R}(i^{a_u}_{k,n_j})| = \ell$.

3.5.2 Reputation of Nodes

The reputation value given to a single domain node in the directory of an agent, is determined by following factors:

(1) Knowledge Increasing Rate

The value of the knowledge increasing rate $v(n^{a_v}_k)$ to a node $n^{a_v}_k$ is given by

$$v(n^{a_v}_k) = \frac{|\mathbf{I}^{a_v}_{n_k}|}{t_c - t_o(n^{a_v}_k)}$$

where t_c is current time and $t_o(n^{a_v}_{n_k})$ is the time when the node $n^{a_v}_k$ created.

(2) Average Knowledge Diffusion Rate

Thus we can denote the average knowledge diffusion rate $f(n_k^{a_v})$ is given by

$$f(n_k^{a_v}) = \frac{\sum_{i=1}^{m} f(i_{i,n_k}^{a_v})}{|\mathbf{I}_{n_k}^{a_v}|}$$

where $f(i_{i,n_k}^{a_v})$ is the knowledge diffusion rate of an item $i_{i,n_k}^{a_v} \in \mathbf{I}_{n_k}^{a_v}$ and $|\mathbf{I}_{n_k}^{a_v}| = m$.

(3) Neighbors

We use $h(n_k^{a_v})$ to denote the *neighbors*, which are linking to a node $n_k^{a_v}$ or mutually

sharing them. Then the value of $h(n_k^{a_v})$ is obtained by $h(n_k^{a_v}) = |\ell \mathbf{A}(n_k^{a_v})| + |s\mathbf{A}(n_k^{a_v})|$

where $|\ell \mathbf{A}(n_k^{a_v})|$ is the number of agents which are linking the node $n_k^{a_v}$ with their

node n_k and $|s\mathbf{A}(n_k^{a_v})|$ is the number of agents which are mutually sharing their node

n_k with the agent a_v.

3.5.3 Reputation of Agents

Reputation of an agent is directly connected to popularity of an agent in some specific domains. This value is determined as follows:

(1) Average Knowledge Increasing Rate

This parameter shows the average increasing velocity of the knowledge items which have being accumulated in the domain nodes of an agent. Then the value of average knowledge increasing rate $v(a_u)$ is decided by

$$v(a_u) = \frac{\sum_{k=1}^{m} v(n_k^{a_u})}{|s\mathbf{N}^{a_u}|}$$

where $m = |\mathbf{N}^{a_u}|$ and $n_k \in \mathbf{N}^{a_u}$.

(2) Average Knowledge Diffusion Rate

We define the *expanded average knowledge diffusion rate* for an agent. Thus the value of the average knowledge diffusion rate $f(a_u)$ for an agent a_u is obtained from

$$f(a_u) = \frac{\sum_{k=1}^{m} f(n_k^{a_u})}{|s\mathbf{N}^{a_u}|}$$

where $f(n_k^{a_u})$ is the value of the knowledge diffusion rate of a node n_k of an agent

a_u where $m = |\mathbf{N}^{a_u}|$ and $n_k \in \mathbf{N}^{a_u}$.

(3) Average Knowledge Sharing Rate

We define knowledge sharing rate as the ratio of the number of the neighbors $h(a_u)$ of an agent a_u to the number of shared nodes among whole existing nodes of the agent a_u. Then average knowledge sharing rate $s(a_u)$ is given by

$$s(a_u) = \frac{\sum_{k=1}^{m} h(n_k^{a_u})}{|s\mathbf{N}^{a_u}|}.$$

3.6 Knowledge Recommendation

Knowledge recommendation is a filtering process for the users who want to take a set of highly refined knowledge items from others' knowledge directories over the domains of interest. We describe these processes in detail as follows:

3.6.1 Recommendable Knowledge Directories
Now the system provides expanded function for recommendable personal knowledge directories. The recommendation processes in the system are divided as follows:

(1) Item-based Recommendation
First, this system can recommend the items to users over one or more specific domains, which have relatively high values of the partial reputation factors like the values of $f(i_{k,n_j}^{a_u})$, $\overline{d}(i_{k,n_j}^{a_u})$ and $\overline{p}(i_{k,n_j}^{a_u})$ of an item $i_{k,n_j}^{a_u}$. As we defined above, these values represent that how many agents have captured an original. And these also indicate how fast and how far the item has been propagated into other agents.

(2) Node-based Recommendation
And, our system can also recommend the nodes over one or more taxonomies of users, which have higher values of the partial reputation factors $v(n_k^{a_v})$, $f(n_k^{a_v})$ and $h(n_k^{a_v})$. These factors also indicate overall reputation of a node $n_k^{a_v}$.

(3) Agent-based Recommendation
Users may refer the knowledge collection of the agents which have got high reputation values in some specific domains of knowledge. Therefore the system can mainly recommends the users to others, which have higher values of $v(a_u)$, $f(a_u)$ and $s(a_u)$. The high values of these factors mean that the agent a_u has accumulated more valuable knowledge items and led the knowledge stream in the domain of knowledge.

(4) Stem-based Recommendation
Last, we designate a common set of the items as the term *stem*. The **stem** is denoted by $s\mathbf{I}(\mathbf{A})$ where $\mathbf{A}$ denotes a set of agents. Then, the stem means *commonly shared items in the set of common nodes* $s\mathbf{N}(\mathbf{A})$ shared by agents $\mathbf{A}$. Then agents can obtained the common items at a time over the particular agents which they designated.

For example, there are two groups g_u and g_v; $\mathbf{G}_p = \{ g_u, g_v \}$, then common items $sI(\mathbf{A}^{\mathbf{G}_p})$ are put in common nodes $sN(\mathbf{A}^{\mathbf{G}_p}) = \{ sN_1(\mathbf{A}^{\mathbf{G}_p}), sN_2(\mathbf{A}^{\mathbf{G}_p}), \cdots, sN_m(\mathbf{A}^{\mathbf{G}_p}) \}$ where $| sN(\mathbf{A}^{\mathbf{G}_p}) | = m$ and $\mathbf{A}^{\mathbf{G}_p} = \mathbf{A}^{g_u} \cup \mathbf{A}^{g_v}$. And, each set of common items $\{ sI_1(\mathbf{A}^{\mathbf{G}_p}), sI_2(\mathbf{A}^{\mathbf{G}_p}), \cdots, sI_m(\mathbf{A}^{\mathbf{G}_p}) \}$ is taken from the corresponding nodes $sN(\mathbf{A}^{\mathbf{G}_p})$. Then, if an agent want to be recommended with the stem over two groups g_u and g_v then he or she will be able to get $sI(\mathbf{A}^{\mathbf{G}_p})$.

4   Prototype of the System

As illustrated in figure 1, the prototype of the proposed system, which was implemented on MS-SQL Database Server on Windows 2000 Server, represents a web-based interface to registered users for managing taxonomically arranged knowledge items over directories. Users can browse all the knowledge items and domains under the standard taxonomy shown in the left section of the user interface in figure 1. And through the right part of the interface users can organize their knowledge items and domains on their taxonomies according to the information shown in the center section of the interface, which are about the partial reputation factors related to agents and groups in a specific domain.

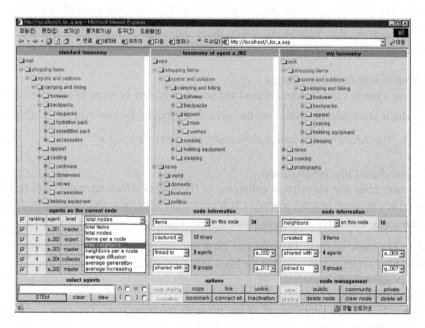

Fig. 1. Prototype of the system

5   Conclusion

In this paper, we designed and implemented a novel framework for collaborative knowledge sharing and recommendation based on taxonomic partial reputation on the personal knowledge directories. As we described above, our new knowledge sharing and recommendation schemes depend on the autonomous and collaborative relations among users. Users can promote their reputation implicitly through their knowledge sharing activities. And, as the result of recommendation process, users can take the items or nodes of which reputations have been rated relatively high. Additionally, they can be directly connected to the agents or groups as the experts on the domain in which they have got high reputation values which represent their potential ability for generating useful knowledge items. Especially, the partial reputation factors which complete a single reputation value of an agent or a group are separately calculated in the nodes on their taxonomies. Thus, not depending on overall reputation values of agents or groups, users can find some highly specified users just to a particular domain. But, the more facilitative tools for personal knowledge integration over heterogeneous their resources should be provided to users to prevent cold-start clearly.

References

1. P. Rensick and H.R. Varian, "Recommender Systems," *Communications of the ACM*, 40(3), pp. 56-58, 1997.
2. D. Goldberg, D. Nicholas, B.M. Oki and D. Terry, "Using Collaborative Filtering to Weave an Information Tapestry," *Communications of the ACM*, 35(12), pp. 61-70, 1992.
3. D. Maltz and E. Rhrlich, "Pointing the way: Active Collaborative Filtering," In *proc. of CHI'95*, pp. 202-209, 1995.
4. C. Avery and R. Zeckhauser, "Recommender Systems for Evaluating Computer Messages," *Communications of the ACM*, 40(3), pp. 88-89, 1997.
5. A. Kidd, "Knowledge Acquisition: An Introductory Framework," *Knowledge Acquisition for Expert Systems: A Practical Handbook*, pp. 1-15. 1987.
6. P. Massa and P. Avesani, "Trust-aware Collaborative Filtering for Recommender Systems," In *Proc. of Federated Int. Conference On The Move to Meaningful Internet: CoopIS, DOA and ODBASE 2004*, pp. 492-508, 2004.
7. J. S. Breese, D. Heckerman and C. Kadie, "Empirical Analysis of Predictive Algorisms for Collaborative Filtering," In *Proc. of the 14th Conference on Uncertainty in Artificial Intelligence*, pp. 43-52, 1998.
8. J. A. Konstan, B. N. Miller, D. Maltz, J. L. Herlocker, L. R. Gordon and J. Riedl, "GroupLens: Applying Collaborative Filtering to Usenet News," *Communications of the ACM*, 40(3), pp. 77-87, 1997.
9. P. Rensnick, N. Iacovou, M. Suchak, P. Bergstorm and J. Riedl, "GroupLens: An Open Architecture for Collaborative Filtering of Netnwes," In *Proc. of CSCW '94*, 1994.
10. T. R. Gruber, "Toward Principles for the Design of Ontologies used for Knowledge Sharing," Technical report, Stanford University, 1993.
11. A. Pretschner and S. Gauch, "Ontology based Personalized Search," In *Proc. 11th IEEE Intl. Conference on Tools on Artificial Intelligence*, pp. 391-398, 1999.
12. C. Welty, "Toward Semantics for the Web," In *Proc. Dagstuhl-Seminar: Semantics for the Web*, 2000.

On Text Mining Algorithms for Automated Maintenance of Hierarchical Knowledge Directory*

Han-joon Kim

Department of Electrical and Computer Engineering
University of Seoul, Korea
khj@uos.ac.kr

Abstract. This paper presents a series of text-mining algorithms for managing knowledge directory, which is one of the most crucial problems in constructing knowledge management systems today. In future systems, the constructed directory, in which knowledge objects are automatically classified, should evolve so as to provide a good indexing service, as the knowledge collection grows or its usage changes. One challenging issue is how to combine manual and automatic organization facilities that enable a user to flexibly organize obtained knowledge by the hierarchical structure over time. To this end, I propose three algorithms that utilize text mining technologies: semi-supervised classification, semi-supervised clustering, and automatic directory building. Through experiments using controlled document collections, the proposed approach is shown to significantly support hierarchical organization of large electronic knowledge base with minimal human effort.

1 Introduction

As e-business industries grow greatly today, electronic information available on networked resources including the Internet and enterprize-wide intranet becomes potentially valuable source for decision making problems; for instance, web pages, e-mail, product information, news articles, and so on. Such electronic information is rich source for building knowledge warehouse to decision-maker, which containts mostly represented in unstructured or semi-structured textual format. Recent trends in knowledge management focus on the organization of textual documents into hierarchies of concepts (or categories) due to the proliferation of topic directories for textual documents [2].

For managing knowledge data (objects) gathered from the rich information source, recent knowledge management systems have emphasized the importance of knowledge organization, i.e., building well-organized knowledge map. One of the most common and successful methods of organizing huge amounts of data is to hierarchically categorize them according to topic. The knowledge objects

---

* This research was supported by the University of Seoul, Korea, in the year of 2005.

J. Lang, F. Lin, and J. Wang (Eds.): KSEM 2006, LNAI 4092, pp. 202–214, 2006.

indexed according to a hierarchical structure (which is called knowledge directory) are kept in internal categories as well as in leaf categories, in the sense that knowledge objects at a lower category have increasing specificity. It is a shared indexing infra-structure for organizing plenty of knowledge data captured from various sources, which is also a very useful tool for delivering required knowledge to decision-makers on time, as a knowledge map. As stated in [17,18], directory have increased in importance as a tool for organizing or browsing a large volume of electronic textual information.

Currently, the directory maintained by most knowledge management systems is manually constructed and maintained by human editors. However, manually maintaining the hierarchical structure incurs several problems. First, such a task is prohibitively costly as well as time-consuming. Until now, most information systems have managed to manually maintaining their directory, but obviously they will not be able to keep up with the pace of growth and change in the networked resources through manual activities. In particular, when the subject matter is highly specialized or technical in nature, manually generated hierarchies are much more expensive to build and to maintain [1,14]. Lastly, since human experts' categorization decision is not only highly subjective but their subjectivity is also variable over time, it is difficult to maintain a reliable and consistent hierarchical structure. These limitations require knowledge systems that can provide intelligent organization capabilities with directory. In future systems, it will be necessary for users to be able to easily manipulate the hierarchical structure and the placement of a knowledge object within it. These systems should not only assist users to easily develop new organizational schemes, but they should also help them maintain extensible hierarchies of categories.

This paper describes three text mining algorithms for intelligently organizing knowledge directory. In my work, I focus on achieving evolving facilities of directory while accommodating external human knowledge, which are related to automated classification, text clustering, and directory building. As for automated classification, I propose an on-line machine learning framework for operational text classification systems. As for text clustering, a semi-supervised clustering algorithm is described that effectively incorporates human knowledge into the clustering process. Lastly, a fuzzy-relation based algorithm for directory building is proposed that uses term co-occurrence hypothesis.

2   Preliminaries

2.1   Definition of Knowledge Directory

Knowledge directory (or simply directory) is a formal system of orderly classification of knowledge obtained. In this paper, a directory is assumed to be the same as topic directory used by Yahoo search portal (http://www.yahoo.com/); that is, every child category has more than one parent category, and therefore the hierarchical structure is like a directed acyclic graph. In my work, directory structures have three elements: *knowledge object*, *category*, and *hierarchical relationship*.

- *A knowledge object* is an object data obtained with knowledge-level value, which is then classified within the knowledge directory. Since I assume the obtained knowledge is represented as unstructured or semi-structured textual format, I use a vector space model to represent the knowledge object as points in a high-dimensional topic space as in standard information retrieval systems. In the vector space model, each dimension corresponds to a unique feature (which is a term or a tag) from the knowledge collection. Thus, each knowledge object can be represented as a vector of the form $o_i = (o_{i1}, o_{i2}, \cdots, o_{in})$, where n is the total number of index features in the system and o_{ij} $(1 \leq j \leq n)$ denotes the weighted frequency that feature t_j occurs in object o_i.
- *A category* corresponds to a concept having explicit semantics to categorize obtained knowledge objects. The concept is determined by its extent and intent; the extent means all the objects belonging the category and the intent means standard terms which can characterize its category.
- *Hierarchical relationship*: Given two categories c_i, c_j, if the concept of c_i subsumes the concept of c_j in terms of generality or specificity, a hierarchical relationship $c_i \rightarrow c_j$ is produced with the category c_i as a parent and the category c_j as its child. Let C be a set of categories, then the system returns a set of hierarchical relationships $H \subset C \times C$, where H is a directory of categories with multiple inheritance.

2.2 Requirements for Automatically Maintaining Knowledge Directory

In my work, I try to achieve semi-automated directory maintenance with less human efforts. In this regard, this section presents several requirements for intelligent knowledge directory management.

- **Automated classification of knowledge objects:** It is essential to automatically assign incoming knowledge objects to an appropriate location on a predefined directory. In order to enable such an automated classification, some classification criteria need to be constructed. Recent approaches towards automated classification have used machine learning approaches to inductively build a classification model of a given set of categories from a training set of labelled (pre-classified) data. Popular learning methods include Naïve Bayes [9], k-nearest neighbor [5], and support vector machine [6]. Basically, such machine-learning based classification requires sufficiently large number of labelled training examples to build an accurate classification model. Assigning class labels to unlabelled documents should be performed by human labeller, which is a highly time-consuming and expensive task. Practically, on-line learning framework is necessary because it is impossible to distinguish training objects from unknown objects to be classified in the operational environment. In addition, classification models should be continuously updated so that its accuracy can be maintained at a high level. To resolve this problem, incremental learning method is required, in which an established model can be updated incrementally without re-building it completely.

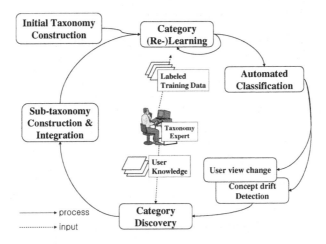

Fig. 1. Directory Maintenance Process

- **Incorporation of domain (or human) knowledge for category discovery into the system:** Basically, knowledge directory construction is a challenging problem with sufficient domain knowledge. Fully automatic construction often leads to unsatisfactory results since directory should reflect the specific requirements of an application or specific business logics than the fixed viewpoints. Furthermore, human experts' decision on directory construction is not only objective but also consistent over time. Therefore, to discover new categories for directory reorganization, I need to perform clustering under various kinds of constraints, which reflects knowledge provided by a user. However, most clustering algorithms do not allow to introduce external knowledge to clustering process.

- **Semi-automated management of evolving directory:** The directory initially constructed should change and adapt as its knowledge collection continuously grows or users' needs change. For example, when concept drift[1] happens in particular categories, or when the established criterion for classification alters with time as the content of a information collection changes, it should be possible for part of directory to be reorganized. In most cases, users desire to customize and tailor hierarchies to their own needs. Here, manual directory construction remains a time-consuming and cumbersome task. This difficulty requires the system to provide more intelligent organization capabilities with directory. When one intend to re-organize a particular part of directory, the system is expected to recommend users different feasible sub-hierarchies for that part.

---

[1] It means that the general subject matter of information within a category may no longer suit the subject that best explained those information when it was originally created.

2.3   Automated Directory Maintenance

The directory maintenance process based on text mining technologies can proceed automatically as illustrated in Figure 1. Each step of the process is described as follows.

Table 1. Procedure for hierarchically organizing knowledge objects

---

a) Initial construction of hierarchy
    i) Define an initial (seed) hierarchy
b) Category (Re-) Learning
    i) Collect a set of the controlled training data fit for the defined (or refined) hierarchy
    ii) Generate (or Update) the current classification model so as to enable a classification task for newly generated categories
    iii) Periodically, update the current classification model so as to constantly guarantee high degree of classification accuracy while refining the categories
c) Automated Classification
    i) Retrieve knowledge objects of interest from various knowledge sources
    ii) Choose significant features from the retrieved objects
    iii) Assign each of the unknown objects into the category with its maximal membership value according to the established model
d) Evolution of hierarchy (accompanied with category discovery)
    i) If concept drift or a change in the viewpoint occurs within a sub-hierarchy, reorganize the specified sub-hierarchy
    ii) If a new concept (or category) sprouts in the unclassified area, cluster the data within the unclassified area into new categories
e) Sub-hierarchy Construction and Integration
    i) Integrate the refined sub-hierarchy or new categories into the main hierarchy
f) Go to step (b)

Steps b) and c) are related to machine-learning based classification, step d) clustering for category discovery, and step e) directory building.

3   Text Mining Algorithms for Automated Directory Maintenance

This section discusses different text mining algorithms that can effectively support the directory maintenance process as discussed above. In my work, I focus particularly on optimal human intervention to the system while accommodating external human knowledge and reducing human efforts.

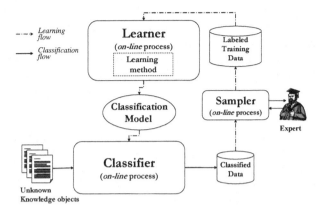

Fig. 2. Architecture of the proposed machine-learning based classification system

3.1 Semi-supervised Classification: Operational Automated Classification

Machine-learning based classification methods require a large number of good quality data for training. However, this requirement is not easily satisfied in real-world operational environments. Recently, many studies on text mining focus on the effective selection of good quality training data that accurately reflect a concept of a given category, rather than algorithm design. How to compose training examples has become a very important issue in developing operational classification systems. One good approach is a combination of 'active learning' and 'semi-supervised learning' [11]. Firstly, the active learning approach is that the learning module actively chooses the training data from a pool of unlabeled data by allowing humans to give their appropriate class label. Among different types of active learning, the selective sampling examines a pool of unlabeled data and selects only the most informative ones through a particular measure. Secondly, the semi-supervised learning is a variant of supervised learning algorithm in which classifiers can be more precisely learned by augmenting a few labeled training data with many unlabeled data [4]. For semi-supervised learning, EM (Expectation-Maximization) algorithm can be used that is an iterative method for finding maximum likelihood in problems with unlabeled data [3]. To develop operational text classifiers, the EM algorithm has been evaluated to be a practical and excellent solution to the problem of the lack of training examples in developing classification systems [12].

Figure 2 shows a classification system architecture, which supports active learning and semi-supervised learning. The system consists of three modules: *Learner*, *Classifier*, and *Sampler*; in contrast, the conventional system does not include the *Sampler* module. The *Learner* module creates a classification model (or function) by examining and analyzing the contents of training documents. The *Classifier* module uses the classification model built by the *Learner* to determine the category of each of unknown documents. In the conventional system, the *Learner* runs only once as an off-line process, but in my system, it should update the current model continuously as an 'on-line' process. To achieve the incremental learning, Naïve Bayes or support vector machine learning algorithm is preferable. This is because these algorithms can incrementally update the classification model of a given hierarchy by adding additional feature estimates to currently learned model [15]. Other than *Learner* and *Classifier* modules, the *Sampler* module that uses the selective sampling (i.e., active learning) method is required to alleviate the learning process. This module isolates a subset of candidate examples from currently classified data and returns them to a human expert for class labelling. Both selective sampling and EM algorithms assume that a stream of unlabeled objects is provided from some external sources. Practically, rather than acquiring the extra unlabeled data, it is more desirable to use the entire set of data indexed on the current populated hierarchy as a pool of unlabeled objects. As you see in Figure 2, the classified objects are fed into the *Sampler* to augment the current training examples, and they are also used by the *Learner* as a pool of the unlabeled objects for the EM process. As for the *Learner* module, not only can we easily obtain the unlabeled data used for EM process without extra effort, but also some of the mistakenly classified data are correctly classified.

3.2   Semi-supervised Clustering

To discover new categories for hierarchy reorganization, we need to perform clustering under various kinds of constraints, which reflects knowledge provided by a user. A few strategies for incorporating external human knowledge into the clustering process have already been proposed in [8,16]. My strategy is to vary the distance metrics by weighting dependencies between different components of feature vectors with the quadratic form distance for similarity scoring. That is, the distance between two object vectors o_x and o_y is given by:

$$dist_{\mathbf{W}}(o_x, o_y) = \sqrt{(o_x - o_y)^\top \cdot \mathbf{W} \cdot (o_x - o_y)} \qquad (1)$$

where each object is represented as a vector of the form $o_x = (o_{x1}, o_{x2}, \cdots, o_{xn})$, where n is the total number of index features in the system and o_{xi} $(1 \leq i \leq n)$ denotes the weighted frequency that feature t_i occurs in object o_x, $\top$ denotes the transpose of vectors, and $\mathbf{W}$ is an $n \times n$ symmetrical weight matrix whose entry w_{ij} denotes the similarity between the components i and j of the vectors. The attractive feature of quadratic form distance is its ability to represent the interrelationship of the indexing features. Each entry w_{ij} in $\mathbf{W}$ reveals how closely features t_i is associated with feature t_j. If the entry is close to 1, its corresponding two features are closely correlated. In this case, the features are used similarly across the collection of objects, and have similar functions for describing the semantics of those objects. If the clustering algorithm uses this type of distance functions, then a group of similar objects in terms of users' viewpoints will be identified more precisely.

To represent user knowledge, I introduce one or more groups of relevant (or irrelevant) examples to the clustering system, depending on the user's judgment of the selected examples from a given information collection. I refer to each of these information groups as a 'bundle'. Here, I specify two types of bundles: positive and negative ones. Examples within positive bundles (i.e., documents judged jointly relevant by users) must be placed in the same cluster while documents within negative bundles must be located in different clusters. Then, with a given set of object bundles, the clustering process induces the distance metric parameters in order to satisfy the given bundle constraints. The problem is how to find the weights that best fit the human knowledge represented as knowledge bundles. The distance metric must be adjusted by minimizing the distance between documents within positive bundles that belong to the same cluster, while maximizing the distance between documents within negative bundles. This dual optimization problem can be solved using the objective function $Q(W)$ as follows:

$$Q(\mathbf{W}) = \sum_{\langle o_x, o_y \rangle \in R_{B+} \cup R_{B-}} I(o_x, o_y) \cdot dist_{\mathbf{W}}(o_x, o_y) \qquad (2)$$

$$I(o_x, o_y) = \begin{cases} +1 & \text{if } \langle o_x, o_y \rangle \in R_{B+} \\ -1 & \text{if } \langle o_x, o_y \rangle \in R_{B-} \end{cases}$$

$$R_{B+} = \{\langle o_x, o_y \rangle | \ o_x \in B^+ \ and \ o_y \in B^+ \ for \ any \ positive \ bundle \ set \ B^+\} \qquad (3)$$

$$R_{B-} = \{\langle o_x, o_y \rangle | \ o_x \in B^- \ and \ o_y \in B^- \ for \ any \ negative \ bundle \ set \ B^-\} \qquad (4)$$

where object bundle set B^+ (or B^-) is defined to be a collection of positive (or negative) bundles, and $\langle o_x, o_y \rangle \in R_{B+}$ or $\langle o_x, o_y \rangle \in R_{B-}$ denote that a pair of objects o_x and o_y is found in positive bundles or negative bundles, respectively. Each object pair within the bundles is processed as a training example for learning the weighted distance measure. I must find a weight matrix that minimizes the objective function. To search for an optimal matrix, I adopt a gradient descent search method that is used for tuning weights among neurons in artificial neural networks [10]. As a result of searching, features involved with object bundles are assumed to be relevant in proportion to their weight while features not related to object bundles are assumed to be orthogonal.

Furthermore, given a set of bundle constraints, we can derive additional constraints that hold. The technique for deriving all constraints logically implied by a given bundle constraints is based on the following two axioms or rules.

- *Positive transitivity rule*: If $\langle o_x, o_y \rangle \in R_{B+}$ and $\langle o_y, o_z \rangle \in R_{B+}$, then $\langle d_x, d_z \rangle \in R_{B+}$
- *Negative transitivity rule*: If $\langle o_x, o_y \rangle \in R_{B-}$ and $\langle o_x, o_z \rangle \in R_{B+}$, then $\langle o_u, o_y \rangle \in R_{B-}$ holds for all $o_u \in [o_z]_{R_{B+}}$, where $[d_z]_{R_{B+}}$ is an equivalence class of o_z on R_{B+}.

As a result of the positive transitive rule, R_{B+} becomes an equivalence relation on documents occurring in R_{B+}. The rationale of the negative transitivity rule is that if d_x is irrelevant to d_y and d_x is relevant to d_z, then d_y is irrelevant to all documents relevant to d_z. Based upon these rules, each of the initial R_{B+} and R_{B-} are augmented. In particular, augmenting a relation R_{B-} according to negative transitive rule can significantly enhance the quality of the resulting clusters, since negative bundle constraints play a role in separating documents within incoherent clusters. In addition, the number of clusters that are generated can be approximately determined from the bundle constraints, although how to get the right number of resulting clusters is an open problem.

In generating object bundles, it may be necessary to allow a user to better judge the (ir-) relevance of an object to a concept. For example, the bundles can be developed by exploiting the fuzzy relevance feedback technique proposed in my previous work [7]. In this approach, object relevant to a submitted object are retrieved by using the fuzzy information retrieval method proposed in [13], and then the user can interactively develop a positive (or negative) bundle relevant to the query object while performing the relevance feedback interview.

During maintaining the directory, when a concept drift or a change in a user's viewpoint occurs within a sub-directory, the user should prepare a set of object bundles as external knowledge reflecting the concept drift or the change in viewpoint. Then, based on the prepared user constraint, the clustering process isolates categories resolving the concept drift or reflecting changes in user's viewpoint, which are incorporated into the main directory.

3.3 Automated Building of Hierarchical Relationships

To build hierarchical relationships among categories, I note that a category is represented by topical terms (or intent) reflecting its concept. This suggests that the relations between categories can be determined by considering the relations between their significant terms. That is, the generality and the specificity of categories are expressed by aggregating the relations among their terms. A hierarchical relationship between two categories is represented by membership grade in a fuzzy (binary) relation.

Therefore, I define the fuzzy relation $\mu_{CSR}(c_i, c_j)$, called 'category subsumption relation' (CSR), between two categories c_i, c_j, which represents the relational concept "c_i subsumes c_j" as follows:

$$\mu_{CSR}(c_i, c_j) = \frac{\sum_{\substack{t_i \in V_{c_i}, t_j \in V_{c_j} \\ Pr(t_i|t_j) > Pr(t_j|t_i)}} \tau_{c_i}(t_i) \times \tau_{c_j}(t_j) \times Pr(t_i|t_j)}{\sum_{t_i \in V_{c_i}, t_j \in V_{c_j}} \tau_{c_i}(t_i) \times \tau_{c_j}(t_j)} \quad (5)$$

where $\tau_c(t)$ denotes the degree to which the term t represents the concept corresponding to the category c, which can be estimated by calculating the χ^2 statistic of term t in category c since the χ^2 value represents the degree of term importance. $Pr(t_i|t_j)$ should be weighted by the degree of significance of the terms t_i and t_j in their categories, and thus the membership function μ_{CSR} for categories is calculated as the weighted average of the values of $Pr(t_i|t_j)$ for terms. The membership value μ_{CSR} indicates the strength of the relationship present between two categories.

By using the above fuzzy relation, I can build a sub-directory of isolated categories automatically according to the following procedure.

1) First, perform the proposed user-constrained clustering on a given reorganization area (see Section 3.2)
2) Calculate the CSR matrix with entries representing the degree of membership in a fuzzy relation CSR for the resulting clusters (categories) (see Equation 5)
3) Generate the α-cut matrix of the CSR matrix (denoted by CSR_α)[2] by determining an appropriate value of α
4) Create a partial sub-directory of the isolated categories from the CSR_α matrix
5) Calculate another CSR_α matrix between the sub-directory and its previous connected categories in the main directory (see Equation 5)
6) Integrate the resulting sub-directory into the main directory in accordance with the second generated CSR_α matrix.

The user determines a particular reorganization area in the main directory for reorganization, then using the clustering method proposed in Section 2, the objects within that area are decomposed into several groups under user intervention. Next, a fuzzy subsumption matrix which represents the fuzzy relation CSR among the resulting clusters is calculated, and an α-cut matrix for partial ordering is generated. As a result, the matrix is represented as a partial directory. Finally, the partial directory is integrated into the main directory. For this, the CSR matrix between the highest (or lowest) nodes in the partial directory and their mergible nodes is calculated.

4   Related Work

In terms of text mining approach for directory construction, a related system is SONIA [14] that provides the ability to organize the results of queries to networked information sources. Another related system is Athena [1] that supports management of a hierarchical arrangement of e-mail documents. In this system, a form of semi-supervised clustering algorithm was proposed that first generates incomplete clusters and then completes them by use of the classifier. Other related commercial systems include Autonomy (http://www.autonomy.com/), Inktomi Directory Engine (http://www.inktomi.com/), and Semio Directory (http://www.semio.com/), which enables a browsable web directory to be automatically built. However, these systems did not address the (semi-)automatic evolving capabilities of organizational schemes and the classification model at all. This is one of the reasons why the commercial directory-based services do not tend to be as popular as their manually constructed counterparts.

---

[2] Each entry of the matrix CSR_α represents the crisp relation that contains the elements whose membership grades in the CSR matrix are greater than the specified value of α.

5   Experimental Results

In order to evaluate the proposed text mining algorithms, I have used Reuters-21578 SGML document collection (Lewis, 1997), and documents selected from Open Directory Project (ODP) directory (http://dmoz.org) and Yahoo directory. In case of Reuters-21578, I selected 4,150 documents belonging to the 27 most frequent topics including 'Earn', 'Acq', 'Money-fx', 'Grain', 'Crude', 'Trade', 'Interest', and 'Ship' for more reliable evaluation. In this experiment, I have evaluated the proposed clustering and hierarchy building algorithms, and the proposed classification algorithm needs to be analyzed from a qualitative point of view within operational systems. In evaluating the clustering algorithm, I generated five controlled test sets (which are denoted as T1∼T5 in Figure 3) instead of using total documents because the proposed clustering algorithm is performed on a small portion of document collection for hierarchy reorganization.

Figure 3 plots the purity (or entropy) of resulting clusters while varying the supervision degree for each of the five test sets. Note that the performance of the unsupervised complete-linkage clustering algorithm corresponds to the

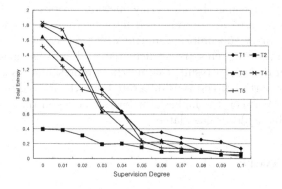

Fig. 3. The effects of supervision on clustering quality

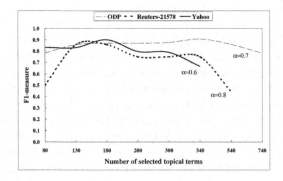

Fig. 4. Changes in the quality of discovered hierarchies from varying the number of selected topical terms

case when supervision degree is zero. This figure indicates that even a little external knowledge provides the clustering process with valuable leads to topical structures in the test sets; a small amount of supervision, covering less than approximately 5% of all of the documents, is enough to improve the performance of the clustering system.

Figure 4 shows the changes in the accuracy of automatically generated hierarchies from varying the number of selected topical terms when the threshold value α is set to 0.6~0.8: the threshold values of *Yahoo*, *ODP*, and *Reuters-21578* hierarchies are 0.6, 0.7, and 0.8, respectively. From this figure, we can see that the proposed method can recover the original hierarchical structure of manually constructed hierarchies with reasonably high quality, although it is not perfect. Note that a manually constructed hierarchy may not necessarily have higher quality than its corresponding automatically constructed one.

6   Conclusions

Towards the intelligent hierarchy management for a huge number of knowledge objects, the text-mining techniques are of great importance. In this paper, I have presented a comprehensive text-mining solution to knowledge organization problems on hierarchical directory towards intelligent directory maintenance for large textual knowledge data. My focus is on achieving evolving facilities of directory while reflecting human knowledge, through several text mining technologies. To develop operational classification systems, a combination of active learning and semi-supervised learning has been introduced together with the related system architecture that has on-line and incremental learning frameworks. In terms of category discovery, a simple representation of human knowledge has been discussed, which is used to learn the distance metric for the semi-supervised clustering. As for directory building, I have proposed a simple yet effective fuzzy-relation based algorithm without any complicated linguistic analysis. Owing to such intelligent capabilities, notwithstanding the need for user intervention, the system can significantly support hierarchical organization of large knowledge data with minimal human effort.

References

1. R. Aggrawal, R.J. Bayardo, and R. Srikant, "Athena: Mining-based Interactive Management of Text Databases," *Proc. of the 7th International Conference on Extending Database Technology (EDBT 2000)*, pp. 365–379, 2000.
2. M. Bonifacio, P. Bouquet, and P. Traverso, "Enabling distributed knowledge management managerial and technological impliations," Informatik/Informatique, Vol.3, No.1, 2002.
3. A.P. Dempster, N. Laird, and D.B. Rubin, "Maximum Likelihood from Incomplete Data via the EM Algorithm," *Journal of the Royal Statistical Society*, Vol.B39, pp. 1–38, 1977.
4. A. Demiriz, and K. Bennett, "Optimization Approaches to Semi-Supervised Learning," M. Ferris, O. Mangasarian, and J. Pang (ed.) Applications and Algorithms of Complementarity, Kluwer Academic Publishers, 2000.

5. E. Han, G. Karypis, and V. Kumar, "Text Categorization Using Weight Adjusted k-Nearest Neighbor Classification," *Proc. of the 5th Pacific-Asia Conference on Knowledge Discovery and Data Mining*, pp. 53–65, 1991.
6. T. Joachims, "Text Categorization with Support Vector Machines: Learning with Many Relevant Features," Technical Report LS8-Report, Univ. of Dortmund, 1997.
7. H.J. Kim, and S.G. Lee, "A Semi-Supervised Document Clustering Technique for Information Organization," *Proc. of the 9th Int'l Conf. on Information and Knowledge Management*, pp.30–37, 2000.
8. T. Labzour, A. Bensaid, and J. Bezdek, "Improved Semi-Supervised Point-Prototype Clustering Algorithms," *Proc. of the 7th International Conference on Fuzzy Systems*, pp. 1383–1387, 1998.
9. T.M. Mitchell, "Bayesian Learning," *Machine Learning*, McGraw-Hill, New York, pp. 154–200, 1997.
10. T. M. Mitchell. "Artificial Neural Networks," *Machine Learning*, McGraw-Hill, New York, pp.81–126, 1997.
11. I. Muslea, S. Minton, and C. Knoblock, "Active + semi-supervised learning = robust multi-view learning," *Proc. of the 19th International Conference on Machine Learning*, pp. 435–442, 2002.
12. K. Nigam, "Using Unlabeled Data to Improve Text Classification," Ph.D. thesis, Carnegie Mellon University, 2001
13. Y. Ogawa, T. Moria, and K. Kobayashi, "A Fuzzy Document Retrieval System Using the Key Word Connection Matrix and a Learning Method," *Fuzzy Sets and Systems*, 39:163-179, 1991.
14. M. Sahami, S. Yusufali, and M.Q. Baldonado, "SONIA: A Service for Organizing Networked Information Autonomously," *Proc. of the 3rd ACM International Conference on Digital Libraries*, pp. 200–209, 1998.
15. K.M. Schneider, "Techniques for Improving the Performance of Naive Bayes for Text Classification," *Proc. of the 6th International Conference on Intelligent Text Processing and Computational Linguistics (CICLing-2005)*, pp. 682–693, 2005.
16. L. Talavera, and J. Bejar, "Integrating Declarative Knowledge in Hierarchical Clustering Tasks," *Proc. of the 3rd International Conference on Intelligent Data Analysis*, pp. 211–222, 1999.
17. "Content Management, Metadata & Semantic Web: Keynote Address", Net.ObjectDAYS 2001, 2001.
18. "Innovaive Approaches for Improving Information Supply", Gartner Group Report, 2001, M-14-3517

Using Word Clusters to Detect Similar Web Documents

Jonathan Koberstein and Yiu-Kai Ng

Computer Science Department, Brigham Young University, Provo, UT 84602, USA

Abstract. It is relatively easy to detect exact matches in Web documents; however, detecting similar content in distinct Web documents with different words and sentence structures is a much more difficult task. A reliable tool for determining the degree of similarity between any two Web documents could help filter or retain Web documents with similar content. Most methods for detecting similarity between documents rely on some kind of textual fingerprinting or a process of looking for exactly matched substrings. This may not be sufficient as changing the sentence structure or replacing words with synonyms can cause sentences with similar/same content to be treated as different. In this paper, we develop a sentence-based Fuzzy Set Information Retrieval (IR) approach, using word clusters that capture the similarity between different words for discovering similar documents. Our approach has the advantages of detecting documents with similar, but not necessarily the same, sentences based on fuzzy-word sets. The three different fuzzy-word clustering techniques that we have considered include the correlation cluster, the association cluster, and the metric cluster, which generate the word-to-word correlation values. Experimental results show that by adopting the metric cluster, our similarity detection approach has high accurate rate in detecting similar documents and improves previous Fuzzy Set IR approaches based solely on the correlation cluster.

1 Introduction

Effective detection of Web documents with similar content could have many beneficial applications. For example, searching for research publication on the Internet one could find an article that discusses a subject of interest and then use the article to request a search engine to find other related articles. If the search engine could accurately detect similar Web documents, then it could retrieve other documents that discuss the same topic. The same similarity detection tool could also be used to detect plagiarism, since the ease of copying a Web document has encouraged many to make illegal use of copyright protected documents. An accurate similarity-detection tool can also assist a teacher to determine if a student uses others' work downloaded from the Internet as his/her own.

In order to discover similar documents or prevent copyright violations, the corresponding methods must be easy to use, fast, highly accurate, and not based on exact textual matches. In developing such a tool, we adopt the Fuzzy Set Information Retrieval (IR) approach as presented in [19] and significantly enhance the approach to obtain a higher degree of accuracy in discovering similar Web

J. Lang, F. Lin, and J. Wang (Eds.): KSEM 2006, LNAI 4092, pp. 215–228, 2006.
© Springer-Verlag Berlin Heidelberg 2006

documents without imposing additional overhead, or increasing the computational complexity. The Fuzzy Set IR approach detects similarity in documents by using a fuzzy set of related words. For each word w, a fuzzy set S is constructed that represents how closely related all the other words in S are to w. Since S is not the traditional bivalent set (i.e., all elements are either a member or not) and some members of the set are only partially or fuzzily included, S is known as a fuzzy set. The strength of memberships of a word w to the words in the fuzzy set of w, called *word correlation factors*, are used to determine the similarity of different documents.

In this paper, we present different approaches to compute the fuzzy sets, or word-correlation factors, of words by using the *association* and *metric clusters* [1], in addition to the *correlation cluster* adopted in [19]. The correlation cluster is the simplest clustering technique which only considers co-occurrences of words in documents to compute word similarity. The association cluster further considers the *frequency* of co-occurrences and in general is more accurate in detecting "related" words than the correlation cluster, whereas the metric cluster considers both the frequency of co-occurrences and the *distances* between the co-occurrences of different words in a document in computing the similarity of words. Word correlation factors can be used to determine the degree of similarity between two documents. We have designed and implemented our Fuzzy Set IR similarity detection approach with each of the three clustering techniques so that document similarity measures of each technique are compared to determine which technique is the most accurate in detecting similar documents. The empirical study conducted by us indicates that the metric cluster outperforms both the association and the correlation clusters. The metric cluster produces (i) half as many false positives and false negatives[1] in detecting similar documents as the correlation cluster, and (ii) only two thirds as many false positives and false negatives as the association cluster, which show that significant improvements can be obtained by using the metric cluster as opposed to the correlation and association clusters to calculate word similarities. Furthermore, our Fuzzy Set IR approach is flexible because (i) it does not use static word lists or require a specific document structure, since the correlation factors for all words are precomputed and can be used in any document regardless of the source, and (ii) it matches sentences with different structures and/or words.

This paper is organized as follows. In Section 2, we discuss work related to detecting similar documents. In Section 3, we present our similarity detection approach, which includes (i) calculating different correlation factors for words using either the correlation cluster, association cluster, or metric cluster, and (ii) computation of document similarity measures using different correlation factors. In Section 4, we verify the accuracy of each word cluster to be used for detecting similar documents by analyzing the experimental results. In Section 5, we include the computational complexity of our similarity detection approach. In Section 6, we give concluding remarks.

---

[1] *False positives (False negatives, respectively)* refer to sentences (documents) that are *different* (the *same*, respectively) but are treated as the *same* (*different*, respectively).

2   Related Work

Detecting similar documents has long been an area of research [3,9,16] Some of the previous copy-detection methods to detecting similar documents include $Diff$ (Unix/Linux man pages), $SCAM$ [16], SIF [8], $COPS$ [3], and $KOALA$ [9], which have been used to detect similar documents based on exact word matching or matching substrings. $Diff$ is a UNIX command, which analyzes two documents line by line and shows all the differences including spaces, is effective only with line-based documents with very few differences and detects exact matchings with the same sentence structure or word ordering in two documents. SCAM works reasonably well with small documents but would have more difficulty on larger documents. SIF finds similar files in a file system by using a fingerprinting scheme to characterize documents. Its drawback is that it only considers syntactic differences of documents and thus it would be unable to detect two similar documents with same ideas expressed in different words.

$COPS$ is a copy detection program specifically designed to detect plagiarism, which compares hash values between documents, but its hash function produces a large number of collisions. Also, $COPS$ can only be used on documents with at least 10 sentences and is therefore unable to be used on smaller documents. $KOALA$, like $COPS$, is also designed to detect plagiarism. $KOALA$ combines the exhaustive fingerprinting of COPS and the random fingerprinting of SIF. While KOALA is more accurate than SIF and less memory intensive, it still uses a fingerprinting technique.

Other methods for detecting similar documents [5,11,13,20] have also been proposed. [11] use the fingerprinting approach to represent a given document, which then plays the role of a query to a search engine to retrieve documents for further comparisons. As discussed earlier, the fingerprint approach is either completely syntactic or suffers from collisions. [20] introduce a statistical method to identify multiple text databases for retrieving similar documents, which along with queries are presented as vectors in the vector-space model (VSM) for comparisons. VSM is a well-known and widely used IR model [1]; however, its reliance on term frequency without considering thesaurus of index terms in documents could be a drawback in detecting similar documents. [5] characterize documents using multi-word terms, in which each term is reduced to its canonical form, i.e., stemming, and is assigned a measure (called IQ) based on term frequency for ranking, which is essentially the VSM approach. Besides using VSM, [13] also consider user's profiles [1], which describe users' preferences in retrieving documents, an approach that has not been widely used nor proven. In contrast, our similar document detection approach considers similar, in addition to exactly matched, words in computing document similarity.

3   Our Similar Document Detection Approach

In detecting document similarity, we first select the set of documents for which to compute the word-to-word similarity values, i.e., correlation factors, of various words. In the selected set of documents, we first remove all the stop words, which

are words with little meaning. Hereafter, words in the set are stemmed to reduce
all the words to their root forms, which is followed by computing the correlation
factors for all the words remaining in the set of documents. We use three different
word clusters to compute their corresponding correlation factors: the correlation
cluster, the association cluster, and the metric cluster. Using the correlation
factors, we can compute the degree of similarity of any two documents.

3.1   Document Set for Constructing Correlation Factors

The set of documents used to compute word-to-word correlation factors in our
similar document detection approach was the Oct 20, 2005 Wikipedia database
dump [17]. The database dump contains 880,388 different documents, 74,663,883
sentences, 46,861,448,677 words, and 2,389,984,085,254 characters for a total
size of 4.6 GB. Of course the most ideal set of documents to compute correlation
factors would be the set of all possible documents. However, this set is impractical
and impossible to obtain as it is not feasible to retrieve all documents on the Web
and the size of such a set would be extremely huge. The best alternative is the set
of documents that is representative of such a set. If a set of documents includes
too many documents on any given topic, then the set is not representative,
since documents on other topics are either under represented or not represented
at all. The size and nature of Wikipedia, a free on-line encyclopedia, ensures
that a variety of topics are covered. For example, Wikipedia covers topics from
"apples" to "Yahweh," and from "cooking" to "zebras." One might claim that
the set of Wikipedia documents was retrieved from one source and thus is biased.
Our counter argument is that it is not bias because the downloaded Wikipedia
documents were authored by more than 850,000 people [18]. The diversity of the
authorships of these documents leads to a representative group of documents
with different writing styles and a diversity of subject areas. No one person's style
or preferences have defined the set of documents. As a result, the set of Wikipedia
documents is an effective representative set of documents that is appropriate for
computing the general correlation factors between words.

3.2   Stop Word Removal and Stemming

Prior to using the Wikipedia documents to compute the correlation factors of
words, we first eliminate all the stop words in the documents and perform stemming on the non-stop words, a common procedure in information retrieval to
handle the quantity of distinct words. This can be accomplished in three steps.
First, stop-words, which are commonly-used words that include articles, conjunctions, prepositions, punctuation marks, numbers, non-alphabetic characters,
etc., are removed. Words, such as "and," "or," "the," and "a," carry very little
meaning and appear relatively frequently throughout all documents and thus do
not provide much information in distinguishing one document from another. Second, all the remaining words (i.e., non-stop words) are stemmed using the Porter
stemming algorithm [12]. The stemming algorithm reduces all words to their root
form, e.g., the words "attack," "attacked," and "attacks" are all stemmed to the
word "attack." Stemming dramatically reduces the number of distinct words in

a document because most words have many different variations. Third, even after performing the stop-word removal and stemming steps, there were still more than 150,000 distinct words left in the set of downloaded Wikipedia documents. With that many words left it would require more than 83 GB of memory just to store one set (i.e., one out of the three sets) of the correlation factors for each pair of words using one of the three clustering techniques. Many of the 150,000 remaining words, however, are made up of nonsensical words that only appeared in a few documents, such as "ahhh" and "yeeessss," or misspelled words, such as "teh." To further reduce the number of distinct word stems, we filtered all the remaining words using a stemmed dictionary. In order to retain as many pertinent words among the 150,000 stemmed words as possible, four different dictionaries, 12dicts-4.0 [6], Ispell [7], RandomDict [14], and Bigdict [2], were stemmed and combined, yielding a dictionary with 69,088 distinct stemmed words. Only the words among the 150,000 words that were also in the set of 69,088 stemmed dictionary words were retained in the downloaded Wikipedia documents. The final set of Wikipedia documents had 69,084 distinct stems, and only 4 of the words in the combined dictionary were not found in the set of downloaded Wikipedia documents. We use the stemmed Wikipedia documents to compute each of the three different word clusters and further determine the degrees of similarity among the stemmed documents.

3.3 Word Correlation Factors

From the reduced set of documents with only dictionary words, we compute the correlation factor between each pair of the 69,084 different words[2] by using each word-clustering approach. An entry $<i, j>$ in a word cluster is the correlation factor between word w_i and word w_j and is denoted by $C_{i,j}$, where $1 \leq i, j \leq 69,084$ and $0 \leq C_{i,j} \leq 1$. $C_{i,j} = 0$ denotes that there is no similarity between w_i and w_j, whereas $C_{i,j} = 1$ means that w_i and w_j are either the same or synonymous. A $C_{i,j}$ value between 0 and 1 indicates that w_i and w_j have only a partial degree of similarity and as such can only be treated as partially similar.

The Correlation Cluster. We first consider the correlation clustering approach to compute correlation factors of words in the Wikipedia documents. A non-normalized correlation factor is a measure of word similarity that is not in the range from 0 to 1 and often has value much larger than one. The non-normalized correlation value is denoted $P_{i,j}$, where $1 \leq i, j \leq 69,088$. In the correlation cluster, $P_{i,j}$ is simply the number of documents in which both word w_i and word w_j occur. Note that the value of $P_{i,j}$ can be from 0 to 880,388, the number of documents in the Wikipedia set, which is not our defined range for $C_{i,j}$, the correlation factor, which ranges from 0 to 1. $C_{i,j}$, the normalized correlation factor in the correlation cluster between words w_i and w_j, is defined in [1] as

$$C_{i,j} = P_{i,j}/(P_{i,i} + P_{j,j} - P_{i,j}). \tag{1}$$

---

[2] From now on, whenever we use the term *word*, we mean *non-stop, stemmed word*, unless stated otherwise.

The correlation cluster uses the *occurrence* or *absence* of two words in each document in a set as the measure of the degree of similarity for the words. For example, if the word "cat" often appears in the same document as the word "feline," but less often with the word "molecule," then the word "cat" is more similar to "feline" than to "molecule" according to the correlation cluster. Words w_i and w_j will only be highly related if they co-occur together in a significant number of documents compared to the total number of documents in which only one or the other occurs. For example, if w_i = "cat", w_j = "feline", $P_{i,i}$ = 100, $P_{j,j}$ = 150, and $P_{i,j}$ = 50, then the correlation value $C_{i,j}$ would be 50 / (100 + 150 - 50) = 0.25, a relatively large value because w_i and w_j co-occur a significant number of times, i.e., 50 out of 200 documents. However, if w_i occurred in 1,000 documents and w_j occurred in 2,000 documents and still only co-occurred in 50 documents, then $C_{i,j}$ = 50 / (1000 + 2000 - 50) = 0.017.

The Association Cluster. The second cluster that we consider is the association cluster. The association cluster is constructed by taking into account the *frequency* of co-occurrence. For example, if the words "cat" and "feline" co-occur n ($n > 1$) times in each of the m ($m \geq 1$) documents, they are more related than if they only co-occur once in each of the m documents. In the association cluster, the un-normalized correlation value $P_{i,j}$ of words w_i and w_j is given by

$$\sum_{d \in D} (F_{i,d} \times F_{j,d}) \tag{2}$$

where D is the set of all documents and $F_{i,d}$ ($F_{j,d}$, respectively) is the frequency of occurrence of word w_i (w_j, respectively) in document d. The normalized correlation value $C_{i,j}$ ($1 \leq i, j \leq 69,088$), as defined in [1], is computed by

$$C_{i,j} = P_{i,j}/(P_{i,i} + P_{j,j} - P_{i,j}). \tag{3}$$

For example, if there are only three documents with word w_i or w_j in them such that w_i = "cat", w_j = "feline", F_{i,D_0} = 2, F_{i,D_1} = 5, F_{i,D_2} = 1, F_{j,D_0} = 4, F_{j,D_1} = 2, and F_{j,D_2} = 2, then $P_{i,i}$ = (2 × 2 + 5 × 5 + 1 × 1) = 30, $P_{j,j}$ = (4 × 4 + 2 × 2 + 2 × 2) = 24, $P_{i,j}$ = (2 × 4 + 5 × 2 + 1 × 2) = 20, and $C_{i,j}$ = 20 / (30 + 24 - 20) = 0.59.

The Metric Cluster. The metric cluster uses the frequency of *occurrences* and *distances* between words in a set of documents to measure their degrees of similarity. In the metric cluster, the un-normalized correlation value $P_{i,j}$, as defined in [1], is

$$P_{i,j} = \sum_{k_i \in D} \sum_{k_j \in D} \frac{1}{r(k_i, k_j)} \tag{4}$$

where D is the set of all documents, k_i (k_j, respectively) is an occurrence of word w_i (w_j, respectively) in any document in D, and r_{k_i,k_j} is the number of words between (i.e., separating) k_i and k_j plus 1, which insures that the distance between k_i and k_j is always non-zero. $r(k_i, k_j)$ = $1/\infty$ = 0, if k_i and k_j are in different documents. Thus, in the metric cluster, words that co-occur closer together yield higher correlation values than words that co-occur farther apart, and words in separate documents will not affect the correlation values at all, since their distance values are zeros. In the metric cluster, the normalized $C_{i,j}$ is given by

$$C_{i,j} = P_{i,j}/(N_i \times N_j) \tag{5}$$

where $P_{i,j}$ is the un-normalized correlation value, and N_i (N_j, respectively) is the number of times k_i (k_j, respectively) appeared in the set of all documents.

Comparisons Between Clusters. The *correlation* clustering technique has the advantage of being simple and easy to use. However, its major drawback is that it does not take into account other factors besides the co-occurrence of two words. For example, if a book B about apples is in our set of documents and B mentions "cancer" in the dedication to a deceased loved one, "apples" and "cancer" would be treated as related to a certain degree. This allows for *false* correlations between words. If a significant number of *false* correlation factors exist, then the correlation cluster is less accurate in measuring word similarity.

The *association* cluster is a better indicator of word similarity than the correlation cluster because the former takes into account the frequency of co-occurrences. However, even using the association cluster, it is still possible that non-similar words are treated as similar. For example, if a document starts discussing how apples grow on trees and finishes with a discourse about how trucks transport apples to markets, the words "tree" and "truck" are considered related to a higher degree than supposed to be by the association cluster because the two words co-occur in the same document many times, even though intuitively "truck" and "tree" are not strongly related.

The *metric* cluster is the most difficult cluster to compute because it considers much more information, i.e., relative distances and frequency of co-occurrences of words, than the correlation and association clusters considered separately. Using the same example mentioned earlier, the measure of similarity between "tree" and "truck" would only be remotely related because they are mentioned in very distant parts of the same document, while "apple" and "tree" would be more related because they co-occur close to each other than "tree" and "truck."

3.4   Correlation Factors and Odd Ratios

With the correlation values from any of the three clusters we are able to compute the degrees of similarity of sentences in any two documents[3]. This can be accomplished by first computing how similar a word is to a sentence. Hereafter, using the word-sentence similarity values between each word in one sentence and all the words in another sentence, we can compute the degree of similarity of any pair of sentences. The similarity of sentence S_1 to sentence S_2, as well as the similarity of S_2 to S_1, decide if the two sentences are similar in content.

---

[3] Our similar document detection approach is *sentence-based*, which means that the degree of similarity between two documents is determined by the number of same/similar sentences in the documents.

The degree of similarity between a word i and a sentence S, denoted $\mu_{i,S}$, is

$$\mu_{i,S} = 1 - \prod_{j \in S}(1 - C_{i,j}) \tag{6}$$

where j is any word in S and $C_{i,j}$ is the correlation value obtained through one of the three clusters. $\mu_{i,S} \sim 1$ if $C_{i,j} \sim 1$, and $\mu_{i,S} \sim 0$ if $C_{i,j} \sim 0$, $\forall_{j \in S}$.

The similarity between sentences, denoted as $Sim(S_1, S_2)$, where S_1 and S_2 are stop-word-removed and stemmed sentences, is given by

$$Sim(S_1, S_2) = \sum_{i \in S_1} \frac{\mu_{i,S_2}}{|S_1|} \tag{7}$$

where $|S_1|$ denotes the number of distinct words in S_1. $Sim(S_1, S_2)$ measures how closely related each word in S_1 is with all the words in S_2, and $Sim(S_2, S_1)$, which does not necessary yield the same value as $Sim(S_1, S_2)$, is defined accordingly.

The equality of any two sentences S_1 and S_2 is denoted by $EQ(S_1, S_2)$, which provides an intuitive idea about the similarity of S_1 and S_2. If $EQ(S_1, S_2) = 1$, then S_1 and S_2 are the same or similar enough to be deemed equal. Conversely, if $EQ(S_1, S_2) = 0$, then S_1 and S_2 are treated as totally different. $EQ(S_1, S_2)$ is computed by

$$EQ(S_1, S_2) = \begin{cases} 1 \text{ if } MIN(Sim(S_1, S_2), SIM(S_2, S_1)) \geq pThresh \wedge \\ \quad |Sim(S_1, S_2) - SIM(S_2, S_1)| \leq vThresh \\ 0 \text{ otherwise} \end{cases} \tag{8}$$

where $pThresh$ and $vThresh$ are threshold values determined by empirical data.

The $pThresh$ value is called the *permissible threshold*, whereas the $vThresh$ value is the *variation threshold* [19]. The *permissible* threshold determines the minimum similarity value for two sentences to be considered equal, whereas the *variation* threshold insures that one sentence is not too different from the other sentence. The variation threshold further verifies the difference between two sentences when one sentence is subsumed by another such that the subsumed sentence is very related to the other, but the reverse is not necessarily true.

The $pThresh$ and $vThresh$ must be recalculated for each word cluster as the average correlation values for each cluster have very different magnitudes. In the correlation cluster, a correlation factor of 0.1 indicates that w_i and w_j are very related, whereas in the metric cluster a value of 0.0001 means that w_i and w_j are highly related. The correlation cluster has the largest average correlation factor out of the three different clusters (see Table 1). The average correlation factor in the association cluster is *smaller* than the average correlation factor in the correlation cluster by an order of 10, whereas the average correlation factor in the metric cluster is by far the *smallest*, being an order of 1,000 smaller than that of the association cluster.

The $pThresh$ and $vThresh$ values were set after running the EQ test on a set of randomly chosen sentences with 180 unique sentence combinations. Each sentence combination was evaluated beforehand to determine if they should be

Table 1. Some correlation factors in each cluster

The First Eight Correlation Factors of the Three Clusters					
Correlation	Association	Metric	Correlation	Association	Metric
2.14e-3	2.35e-4	5.56e-7	3.34e-3	6.96e-4	3.76e-8
3.84e-3	7.55e-4	6.02e-8	0	0	0
6.40e-3	1.33e-3	3.79e-8	2.49e-3	3.43e-4	1.36e-8
2.46e-2	4.35e-3	1.36e-6	8.04e-4	1.02e-4	1.96e-9

treated as equal or different. Hereafter, the threshold values that minimized the number of *false positives* and *false negatives* were used for similarity document detection. Each clustering technique is tested with the same set of sentences to insure there were no discrepancies in how the threshold values were set between the different clustering methods. Figure 1 shows the threshold values for each word-clustering technique that minimize the number of combined false positives and false negatives. The pThresh and vThresh values are 0.61 and 0.35, respectively, for the correlation cluster, 0.46 and 0.29, respectively, for the association cluster, and 0.15 and 0.11, respectively, for the metric cluster.

With the threshold values in the EQ function we can determine the degree of resemblance of a document D_1 to another document D_2. The *degree of resemblance* between two documents is defined as the number of sentences in D_1 that have an equivalent sentence over the total number of sentences in D_2, denoted by $RS(D_1, D_2)$, and is defined as

$$RS(D_1, D_2) = \frac{\sum_{i \in D_1}(1 - \prod_{j \in D_2}(1 - EQ(S_i, S_j)))}{|D_1|} \quad (9)$$

where sentence i (j, respectively) is in document D_1 (D_2, respectively).

$RS(D_1, D_2)$ represents the percentage of sentences in document D_1 that are in document D_2. The inner product in Equation 9 evaluates to *zero* if there is

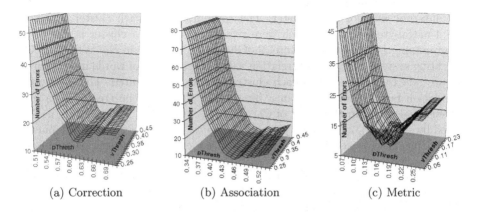

(a) Correction   (b) Association   (c) Metric

Fig. 1. pThresh and vThresh values for the correlation, association, and metric clusters

a match to sentence i in D_2, and is *one* if there is none. Thus, in effect the summation simply adds up the number of sentences in D_1 that have matching sentences in D_2. Note that $RS(D_1, D_2) = RS(D_2, D_1)$ does not necessarily hold. In order to compute a single value to evaluate the similarity of D_1 and D_2 according to the number of matched sentences, we combine $RS(D_1, D_2)$ and $RS(D_2, D_1)$, which is done by applying the *Dempster combination rule* [15] to the RS values of D_1 and D_2. According to the Dempster's combination rule, if the probability of evidence E_1 to be reliable is P_1 and the probability of evidence E_2 to be reliable is P_2, then the probability that both E_1 and E_2 are reliable is $P_1 \times P_2$. Thus, the probability that D_1 is related to D_2 is given by $RS(D_1, D_2) \times RS(D_2, D_1)$.

With the RS probability values we compute the *odds ratio* [10], or simply *odds*. Odds is the ratio of the probability (p) that an event occurs to the probability ($1 - p$) that it does not. We denote the *odds* of D_1 with respect to D_2 as $ODDS(D_1, D_2)$, when combined with the Dempster-Shafer rule, is defined as

$$ODDS(D_1, D_2) = \frac{RS(D_1, D_2) \times RS(D_2, D_1)}{1 - RS(D_1, D_2) \times RS(D_2, D_1)}. \tag{10}$$

The reasons for adopting *odds* is because it (i) is easy to compute, (ii) is a natural way to express magnitude of association, and (iii) can be linked to other statistical methods, such as Bayesian Statistical Modeling [4] and Dempster-Shafer theory of evidence [15]. In Equation 10, p and $(1 - p)$ are *odds*, and the ratio gives the *positive* (i.e., p) versus *negative* (i.e., $1 - p$) value.

4   Experimental Results

The stop-word removal and stemming of the Wikipedia documents was done in Perl on a Linux computer. This code was used to preprocess the set of downloaded Wikipedia documents and allow the clusters to be constructed. Each of the three clusters were computed only once using the Marylou4 super computer cluster at Brigham Young University. The supercomputer broke the job into 128 sub-processes for each cluster. The computation of each cluster returned 128 4-megabyte text files, which were reconstructed into a cluster in the Java programming language on an Intel 3.4Ghz dual processor in the Windows XP operating system. Since the correlation values of each pair of words in each cluster are reflexive, only half of each cluster should be computed. The computed correlation factors were saved in a binary file, which can be treated as a one dimensional array, in the order of $C_{0_1}, C_{0_2}, C_{1_2}, C_{0_3}, C_{1_3}, C_{3_2}, \ldots$ and are indexed by $j \times (j-1)/2 + i$, where $j > i$. The *Eclipse IDE* (Integrated Development Environment) was used to develop the Java code for constructing each cluster and using it to calculate $\mu_{i,S}$, Sim, EQ, RS, and $ODDS$ values.

To analyze the performance of the three different clustering methods to determine the similarity between any two documents, we used a training set of documents to set a threshold, denoted eqThresh, for the $ODDS$ value. The eqThresh value indicates which documents should be treated as equal or different. This

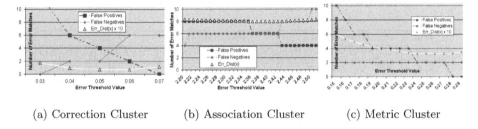

(a) Correction Cluster   (b) Association Cluster   (c) Metric Cluster

Fig. 2. Error threshold values for the correlation, association, and metric clusters

allows us to quantitatively analyze the results of different clustering methods by using false positives and false negatives as indicators of errors. A *false positive* occurs when $ODDS(D_1, D_2) > eq$Thresh and D_1 and D_2 are in fact dissimilar, whereas a *false negative* is encountered when $ODDS(D_1, D_2) < eq$Thresh and D_1 and D_2 is in fact similar. The training set used to evaluate eqThresh consists of 20 documents with 10 documents from the same Wikipedia set of documents that we used to calculate the correlation values, two groups of new, related (to a certain degree) articles, one group with five and the other one with three, and the last two articles randomly chosen, all downloaded from the Internet. Hereafter, the optimal eqThresh value was computed. We define eqThresh as the value that minimizes the function $Err\_Dist(err\_Thresh)$, where err_Thresh is a proposed threshold for the $ODDS$ values. $Err\_Dist(err\_Thresh)$ measures the distance (i.e., closeness) between err_Thresh and the values of the false positives and false negatives. $Err\_Dist(err\_Thresh)$ is given by

$$Err\_Dist(err\_Thresh) = \sum_{y=1}^{|D|} \sum_{z=1}^{|D|} |err\_Thresh - ODDS(D_y, D_z)| \times \quad (11)$$

$$Incorrect(y, z, ODDS(D_y, D_z), err\_Thresh)$$

where D is a set of documents and $Incorrect()$ is defined as:

$$Incorrect(y, z, ODDS(D_y, D_z), x) = \begin{cases} 1 \; if(ODDS(D_y, D_z) > x \wedge notamatch) \\ \quad \vee(ODDS(D_y, D_x) < x \wedge isamatch) \\ 0 \; otherwise \end{cases}$$

$$(12)$$

which returns *one* if either a false positive or false negative occurs, or *zero* if the $ODDS$ is correct for the Err_Thresh using the predetermined similarities, which is either the Boolean value in *notamatch* or its complement *isamatch*, between any two documents. The Boolean values of *notamatch* and *isamatch* of any two test documents are predefined when the 20 test documents were manually examined for similar or different. The value of the function $Err\_Dist(err\_Thresh)$ for any given $err\_$Thresh is the *distance* from all incorrect $ODDS$ values to the threshold value. Minimizing Err_Dist minimizes the distance of incorrect values (i.e., false positives and false negatives) from the threshold, which yields the

Table 2. Experimental Results on Test Sets 1, 2, 3a, and 3b

Test	Correlation					Association					Metric				
Set	Pos	FP	FN	Neg	Err	Pos	FP	FN	Neg	Err	Pos	FP	FN	Neg	Err
Set_1	10	0	25	307	7.3	16	8	20	298	8.2	22	4	13	303	5.0
Set_2	22	9	18	312	7.5	21	2	21	317	6.4	36	4	6	316	3.0
Set_{3_a}	2	0	14	376	3.1	8	2	6	376	1.5	14	0	2	376	1.0
Set_{3_b}	2	0	2	386	0.5	2	0	2	386	0.5	4	0	0	386	0
Average	9	2	15	345	5	12	3	12	344	4	19	2	5	345	2

Pos(itive); F(alse)P(ositive); F(alse)N(egative); Neg(ative); Err(or%)

eqThresh of 0.056 for the correlation cluster, 2.392 for the association cluster, and 0.258 for the metric cluster. The corresponding minimized distances or values of Err_Dist were 0.061, 7.981, and 0.322, respectively. Figure 2 shows the false positives, false negatives, and Err_Dist values as a function of err_Thresh.

With the eqThresh value for each cluster, we used three different test sets of documents to evaluate the performance of each word-clustering technique. Each test set of documents is disjoint, and the documents in each test set were composed in a similar manner as the training set, with some documents extracted from the Wikipedia set and some additional Web documents. The first two test sets, called Set_1 and Set_2, which consist of 20 documents each, were manually examined to determine which documents should be treated as similar. The third set contains 100 test documents, which yield 4,950 different combinations of pairs of distinct documents. We manually examined 20 randomly chosen document pairs twice, which yield document sets Set_{3_a} and Set_{3_b}. The false positive and false negative values, along with the number of correctly identified (dis)similar document pairs, are given in Table 2. The experimental results show that the metric cluster consistently has *lower* percentage of errors among all the three word clusters, which indicates that the *metric cluster* is able to more accurately predict similar documents than the other two.

5   Complexity Analysis of Our Word Clustering Approach

The stop-word removal and the stemming of any two Web documents can be calculated in $\mathcal{O}(n)$ time. The stop-word removal is simply a lookup in a hash table that contains all of the stop words, whereas the Porter stemming algorithm is a $\mathcal{O}(n)$ algorithm. The runtime to compute $\mu_{i,S}$, the degree of similarity between word w_i and sentence S, is $O(|S|)$, where $|S|$ is the number of words in the sentence. Since on an average the number of sentences in a document is greater than the number of words in a sentence, the time complexity for computing $\mu_{i,S}$ is $\mathcal{O}(n)$. Likewise, the time complexity for computing $Sim(S_1, S_2)$ is also $\mathcal{O}(|S|)$ or $\mathcal{O}(n)$. The time complexity for computing the EQ value is also $\mathcal{O}(n)$ as the computation of $EQ(S_1, S_2)$ consists of computing $Sim(S_1, S_2)$, $Sim(S_2, S_1)$, and a few other comparisons. In the worst case scenario, the time complexity for computing $RS(D_1, D_2)$ is $\mathcal{O}(n \times m)$, where n is the number of sentences in

D_1 and m is the number of sentences in D_2, or $\mathcal{O}(n^2)$, assuming that $n > m$, which occurs if there are no matching sentences and each sentence pair must be examined in order to determine the RS value is zero. It follows that the time complexity for computing the $ODDS(D_1, D_2)$ value is also $\mathcal{O}(n^2)$ as it requires the $RS(D_1, D_2)$ and $RS(D_2, D_1)$ values. Thus, the overall time complexity to compare two documents is $\mathcal{O}(n^2)$, since the computation of $ODDS$ values dominates over others, including the time complexity for constructing a word cluster, which comes with a $\mathcal{O}(n^2)$ time complexity, a one-time process.

6 Conclusions

We have presented a Fuzzy Set IR approach to detect similar content in Web documents. Our approach is flexible as it is not specific to any one genre or document type and is able to detect similarities in documents that do not have exact textual matches with high accuracy. Experimental results show that our detection approach, which uses the metric clustering technique, is accurate, has the least amount of false positives and false negatives, and enhances the performance of the copy-detection approach in [19] that adopts the correlation cluster.

Our similarity detection approach runs in quadratic time complexity and could be used (i) as a filter for Web search engines to locate similar documents or eliminate duplicate documents, and (ii) to help detect plagiarism by indicating how similar an unknown document is to a known (copyright protected) document.

References

1. Baeza-Yates, R., Ribeiro-Neto, B.: Modern Information Retrieval (1999)
2. http://packetstormsecurity.nl/Crackers/bigdict.gz
3. Brin, S., Davis, J., Garcia-Molina, H.: Copy Detection Mechanisms for Digital Documents. In Proc. of the ACM SIGMOD (1995) 398–409
4. Congdon, P.: Bayesian Statistical Modelling. Wiley Publishers (2001)
5. Cooper J., Coden A., Brown E.: Detecting Similar Documents Using Salient Terms. In Proc. of CIKM'02 (2002) 245–251
6. http://prdownloads.sourceforge.net/wordlist/12dicts-4.0.zip
7. http://www.luziusschneider.com/Speller/ISpEnFrGe.exe
8. Manber, U.: Finding Similar Files in Large File System. In USENIX Winter Technical Conf. (1994)
9. Nevin, H.: Scalable Document Fingerprinting. In Proc. of the 2nd USENIX Workshop on Electronic Commerce (1996) 191–200
10. Pearl, J.: Probabilistic Reasoning in Intelligent Systems: Networks of Plausible Inference. Morgan Kaufmann (1988)
11. Pereira, A.R., Ziviani, N.: Retrieving Similar Documents from the Web. Journal of Web Engineering 2(4) (2004) 247–261
12. Porter, M.: An Algorithm for Suffix Stripping. Program 14(3) (1980) 130-137
13. Rabelo, J., Silva, E., Fernandes, F., Meira S., Barros F.: ActiveSearch: An Agent for Suggesting Similar Documents Based on User's Preferences. In Proc. of the Intl. Conf. on Systems, Men & Cybernetics (2001) 549–554

14. http://www.ime.usp.br/~yoshi/mac324/projecto/dicas/entras/words
15. Ruthven, I., Lalmas, M.: Experimenting on Dempster-Shafer's Theory of Evidence in Information Retrieval. JIIS 19(3) (2002) 267–302
16. Shivakumar, N., Garcia-Molina, H.: SCAM: A Copy Detection Mechanism for Digital Documents. D-Lib Magazine (1995). http://www.dlib.org
17. http://en.wikipedia.org/wiki/Wikipedia:Database_download
18. http://en.wikipedia.org/wiki/Wikipedia:Overview_FAQ 03Feb2006
19. Yerra, R., Ng, Y.-K.: A Sentence-Based Copy Detection Approach for Web Documents. In Proc. of FSKD'05 (2005) 557–570
20. Yu, C., Liu K., Wu, W., Meng W., Rishe, N.: Finding the Most Similar Documents Across Multiple Text Databases. In Proc. of the IEEE Forum on Research and Technology Advances in Digital Libraries (1999) 150–162

Construction of Concept Lattices Based on Indiscernibility Matrices

Hongru Li[1,2], Ping Wei[1], and Xiaoxue Song[2]

[1] Department of Mathematics and Information Sciences, Yan'tai University,
Yan'tai, Shan'dong 264005, P. R. China
lihongru1126@163.com
wplhrwjy03@163.com
[2] Faculty of Science, Institute for Information and System Sciences,
Xi'an Jiaotong University, Xi'an, Shaan'xi 710049, P. R. China
songxiaoxue@stu.xjtu.edu.cn

Abstract. Formal concepts and concept lattices are two central notions of formal concept analysis. This paper investigates the problem of determining formal concepts based on the congruences on semilattices. The properties of congruences corresponding to formal contexts are discussed. The relationship between the closed sets generated by congruences and the elements of indiscernibility matrices is examined. Consequently, a new approach of determining concept lattices is derived.

Keywords: Concept lattice, Congruence, Formal context, Indiscernibility matrix, Semilattice.

1 Introduction

Formal concept analysis [3, 8] is based on mathematical order theory; in particular on the theory of complete lattices. It offers a complementary approach for rough set theory [6] in the aspect of dealing with data. As a mathematical tool for data mining and knowledge acquisition, formal concept analysis has been researched extensively and applied to many fields [1, 2, 4, 9].

The formulation of formal concept analysis depends on the binary relation provided by formal contexts. A formal context consists of an object set, an attribute set, and a relation between objects and attributes. A formal concept is a pair (objects, attributes). The object set is referred to as the extent and the attribute set as the intent of the formal concept. Determination of all the concepts in a formal context is an important problem of concept lattice theory. Ganter and Wille [3] investigate the construction of concept lattices, and present a method of generating all concepts, which is based on the properties that every extent is the intersection of attribute extents and every intent is the intersection of object intents. In this paper, we offer different approaches to obtain all the concepts of a formal context. The congruences corresponding to formal contexts are first defined. The properties of closed sets generated by the congruences are then discussed. Based on the properties and the binary relation of formal contexts, we introduce two indiscernibility matrices on objects and on attributes,

J. Lang, F. Lin, and J. Wang (Eds.): KSEM 2006, LNAI 4092, pp. 229–240, 2006.
© Springer-Verlag Berlin Heidelberg 2006

respectively. The relationships between the closed sets and the elements of indiscernibility matrices are demonstrated. Based on the relations, we can determine all concepts of a formal context by using the indiscernibility matrices. Consequently, the approaches of determining concept lattices are derived.

2 Concept Lattices and Its Properties

Let U and A be any two finite nonempty sets. Elements of U are called objects, and elements of A are called attributes. $I \subseteq U \times A$ is a correspondence from U to A, i.e., the relationships between objects and attributes are described by a binary relation I. The triple $T = (U, A, I)$ is called a *formal context*.

In a formal context (U, A, I), if $(x, a) \in U \times A$ is such that $(x, a) \in I$, then the object x is said to have the attribute a. The correspondence I can be naturally represented by an incidence table: the rows of the table are labelled by objects, columns by attributes; if $(x, a) \in I$, the intersection of the row labelled by x and column labelled by a contains 1; otherwise it contains 0.

Table 1. A formal context T

U	a	b	c	d	e
1	1	1	0	1	1
2	1	1	1	0	0
3	0	0	0	1	0
4	1	1	1	0	0

For a formal context $T = (U, A, I)$, we define two operators $i : \mathcal{P}(U) \longrightarrow \mathcal{P}(A)$; $e : \mathcal{P}(A) \longrightarrow \mathcal{P}(U)$ as follows:

$$X^i = \{a \in A : (x, a) \in I, \forall\, x \in X\},$$

$$B^e = \{x \in U : (x, a) \in I, \forall\, a \in B\},$$

where $X \subseteq U$, $B \subseteq A$, $\mathcal{P}(U)$ is the powerset of U and $\mathcal{P}(A)$ the powerset of A.

X^i is the set of attributes common to the objects in X; B^e is the set of objects which have all attributes in B.

Table 1 is an example of a formal context. In this table, for example, if we take $X = 124$ and $B = de$, then $X^i = ab$ and $B^e = 1$.

For any $X, X_1, X_2 \subseteq U$ and $B, B_1, B_2 \subseteq A$, operators "i" and "e" have the following properties [3]:

(i) $X_1 \subseteq X_2 \Rightarrow X_2^i \subseteq X_1^i$,

(ii) $X \subseteq X^{ie}$,

(iii) $X^i = X^{iei}$,

(iv) $(X_1 \cup X_2)^i = X_1^i \cap X_2^i$,

(v) $(X_1 \cap X_2)^i \supseteq X_1^i \cap X_2^i$,

(vi) $X \subseteq B^e \Leftrightarrow B \subseteq X^i \Leftrightarrow X \times B \subseteq I$.

(i)' $B_1 \subseteq B_2 \Rightarrow B_2^e \subseteq B_1^e$,

(ii)' $B \subseteq B^{ei}$,

(iii)' $B^e = B^{eie}$,

(iv)' $(B_1 \cup B_2)^e = B_1^e \cap B_2^e$,

(v)' $(B_1 \cap B_2)^e \subseteq B_1^e \cap B_2^e$,

Definition 2.1. (See [3].) Let $T = (U, A, I)$ be a context, $X \subseteq U$, $B \subseteq A$. A pair (X, B) is called a *formal concept* of the context T if it satisfies the condition: $X^i = B$ and $B^e = X$. We call X the extent and B the intent of the concept (X, B). The set of all concepts of the context T is denoted by $L(T)$ (or $L(U, A, I)$), and the sets of all extents and all intents of the context T are denoted by $EX(T)$ and $IN(T)$, respectively.

For any (X_1, B_1), $(X_2, B_2) \in L(T)$, the relation "$\leqslant$" and operations "$\wedge$" and "$\vee$" on concepts are defined as (See [3]):

$$(X_1, B_1) \leqslant (X_2, B_2) \Longleftrightarrow X_1 \subseteq X_2 \text{ (which is equivalent to } B_2 \subseteq B_1)$$

$$(X_1, B_1) \wedge (X_2, B_2) = (X_1 \cap X_2, (B_1 \cup B_2)^{ei}) \in L(T), \tag{2.1}$$

$$(X_1, B_1) \vee (X_2, B_2) = ((X_1 \cup X_2)^{ie}, B_1 \cap B_2) \in L(T). \tag{2.2}$$

In this way, the relation "$\leqslant$" is a partial ordering of the concepts. By (2.1) and (2.2), $L(T)$ is a lattice and is called the concept lattice.

From Table 1 we can see that $(124, ab)$ satisfies the conditions: $(124)^i = ab$, and $(ab)^e = 124$. Hence, $(124, ab) \in L(T)$.

Let $T = (U, A, I)$ be a formal context. Since $EX(T) \subseteq \mathcal{P}(U)$, $IN(T) \subseteq \mathcal{P}(A)$, and $EX(T)$ and $IN(T)$ are two closure systems [3], this implies that $EX(T)$ and $IN(T)$ are complete lattices. By the properties of closure system, it is easy to see that $X_1 \wedge X_2 = X_1 \cap X_2$, $B_1 \wedge B_2 = B_1 \cap B_2$, and we have the following conclusion.

Theorem 2.1. *Let* $T = (U, A, I)$ *be a formal context. For any* (X_1, B_1), (X_2, B_2) $\in L(T)$, *we define*

$$X_1 \vee X_2 = \inf\{X \in EX(T); \ X_1 \cup X_2 \subseteq X\},$$
$$B_1 \vee B_2 = \inf\{B \in IN(T); \quad B_1 \cup B_2 \subseteq B\}.$$

Then
 (i) $(X_1, B_1) \wedge (X_2, B_2) = (X_1 \cap X_2, B_1 \vee B_2) = (X_1 \wedge X_2, B_1 \vee B_2)$,
 (ii) $(X_1, B_1) \vee (X_2, B_2) = (X_1 \vee X_2, B_1 \cap B_2) = (X_1 \vee X_2, B_1 \wedge B_2)$.

Proof. (i) Since $(B_1 \vee B_2)^{ei} \in IN(T)$ and it is the smallest intent containing $B_1 \cup B_2$ (See [3]). It follows that $(B_1 \cup B_2)^{ei} = \inf\{B \in IN(T); \ B_1 \cup B_2 \subseteq B\} = B_1 \vee B_2$. From Eq. (2.1) we get that (i) is true.
 (ii) is proved analogously. $\qquad\square$

Making use of the Basic Theorem on Concept Lattices in [3], for any $(X_j, B_j) \in L(T)$, where $j \in J$ and J is an index set, we have

$$\bigwedge_{j \in J} (X_j, B_j) = (\bigcap_{j \in J} X_j, \bigvee_{j \in J} B_j) = (\bigwedge_{j \in J} X_j, \bigvee_{j \in J} B_j) \tag{2.3}$$

$$\bigvee_{j \in J} (X_j, B_j) = (\bigvee_{j \in J} X_j, \bigcap_{j \in J} B_j) = (\bigvee_{j \in J} X_j, \bigwedge_{j \in J} B_j) \tag{2.4}$$

In this way, the intersection and the union of formal concepts can be represented by the operations of complete lattices $EX(T)$ and $IN(T)$.

3   Congruences in Formal Contexts

A groupoid $(S, *)$ is called a *semilattice* if it satisfies the following conditions:

(i) If $x \in S$, then $x * x = x$;
(ii) If $x, y \in S$, then $x * y = y * x$;
(iii) If $x, y, z \in S$, then $(x * y) * z = x * (y * z)$.

Obviously, if A is a finite nonempty set, then $(\mathcal{P}(A), \cup)$ is a groupoid, and a semilattice.

Definition 3.1. (See [5].) Let $(S, *)$ be a groupoid. An equivalence relation R on S is called a *congruence* on $(S, *)$ if R satisfies the condition, for any $x, x', y, y' \in S$:

$$(x, x') \in R, \ (y, y') \in R \Longrightarrow (x * y, x' * y') \in R.$$

Theorem 3.1. *Let* $T = (U, A, I)$ *be a formal context,*

$$K_A^T = \{ (B, D) \in \mathcal{P}(A) \times \mathcal{P}(A); \ B^e = D^e \}, \tag{3.1}$$

$$K_U^T = \{ (X, Y) \in \mathcal{P}(U) \times \mathcal{P}(U); \ X^i = Y^i \}. \tag{3.2}$$

Then

(i) K_A^T *is a congruence on semilattice* $(\mathcal{P}(A), \cup)$;
(ii) K_U^T *is a congruence on semilattice* $(\mathcal{P}(U), \cup)$.

Proof. (i) It is easy to verify that K_A^T is an equivalence relation on $\mathcal{P}(A)$. Let $(B_1, D_1), (B_2, D_2) \in K_A^T$. According to the property of operator "e", $(B_1 \cup B_2)^e = B_1^e \cap B_2^e = D_1^e \cap D_2^e = (D_1 \cup D_2)^e$, i.e., $(B_1 \cup B_2, D_1 \cup D_2) \in K_A^T$. Hence, (i) is true.

Analogously as in (i), we can prove the conclusion (ii).   □

Lemma 3.2. *Let* $T = (U, A, I)$ *be a formal context,* $B \subseteq A$, $x \in U$. *Then*

$$B \subseteq x^i \Longleftrightarrow x \in B^e.$$

Proof. Since $B \subseteq x^i$ if and only if $\forall a \in B$, $(x, a) \in I$, i.e., $\forall a \in B$, $x \in a^e$. Thus, $x \in \bigcap_{a \in B} a^e = B^e$. Hence, the conclusion is true.   □

4   Relations of Congruences and Formal Concepts

Definition 4.1. (See [5]) Let $(S, *)$ be a semilattice. C is called a *closure operator* on $(S, *)$, if C satisfies the following conditions:

(i) $x \leqslant C(x)$, $\forall x \in S$;

(ii) If $x, y \in S$ and $x \leqslant y$, then $C(x) \leqslant C(y)$;

(iii) $C(C(x)) = C(x)$, $\forall x \in S$.

For an element $x \in S$, if x satisfies $C(x) = x$, then x is called C-closed.

Theorem 4.1. *Let* $T = (U, A, I)$ *be a formal context. For any* $B \in \mathcal{P}(A)$, *let*

$$C(K_A^T)(B) = \cup[B]_{K_A^T}, \qquad (4.1)$$

Then $C(K_A^T)$ *is a closure operator on semilattice* $(\mathcal{P}(A), \cup)$.

Proof. Since K_A^T is a congruence on semilattice $(\mathcal{P}(A), \cup)$, it is true by Theorem 17 in [5]. □

Let $B \in \mathcal{P}(A)$, if $C(K_A^T)(B) = B$, then B is called a $C(K_A^T)$-closed set. The set of all $C(K_A^T)$-closed sets in $\mathcal{P}(A)$ is denoted by $\mathcal{C}_{K_A^T}$.

Theorem 4.2. *Let* $T = (U, A, I)$ *be a formal context,* $X \subseteq U$, $B \subseteq A$. *Then*

$$(X, B) \in L(T) \Longleftrightarrow B \in \mathcal{C}_{K_A^T} \text{ and } B^e = X.$$

Proof. Suppose $(X, B) \in L(T)$, then $B = X^i$, $X = B^e$. If there exists $a \in A$, $a \notin B$ such that $X \subseteq a^e$, then $(B \cup a)^e = B^e \cap a^e = X \neq B^e$. Obviously, this is a contradiction. Thus, $B = \{a \in A; \ X \subseteq a^e\}$, i.e., $\forall D \subseteq A$, $D^e = B^e$ implies that $D \subseteq B$. Hence, $B = \cup[B]_{K_A^T} \in \mathcal{C}_{K_A^T}$.

Suppose $B \in \mathcal{C}_{K_A^T}$ and $B^e = X$, then $\forall D \subseteq A$, $D^e = B^e \Rightarrow D \subseteq B$. That is, $\forall a \in A$, $X \subseteq a^e \Rightarrow a \in B$. Thus, $B = \{a \in A; \ (x, a) \in I, \forall x \in X\} = X^i$. Therefore, $(X, B) \in L(T)$. □

Corollary 4.3. *Let* $T = (U, A, I)$ *be a formal context,* $B \subseteq A$. *Then*

$$B \in IN(T) \Longleftrightarrow C(K_A^T)(B) = B.$$

Proof. It can be derived directly from Theorem 4.2. □

By duality property, we have the following conclusions, it can be proved similarly.

Theorem 4.4. *Let* $T = (U, A, I)$ *be a formal context. For any* $X \in \mathcal{P}(U)$, *we let*

$$C(K_U^T)(X) = \cup[X]_{K_U^T}$$

Then $C(K_U^T)$ *is a closure operator on semilattice* $(\mathcal{P}(U), \cup)$.

Let $X \in \mathcal{P}(U)$, if $C(K_U^T)(X) = X$, then X is called a $C(K_U^T)$-closed set. The set of all $C(K_U^T)$-closed sets in $\mathcal{P}(U)$ is denoted by $\mathcal{C}_{K_U^T}$.

Theorem 4.5. *Let* $T = (U, A, I)$ *be a formal context,* $X \subseteq U$, $B \subseteq A$. *Then*

$$(X, B) \in L(T) \Longleftrightarrow X \in \mathcal{C}_{K_U^T} \text{ and } X^i = B.$$

Corollary 4.6. *Let* $T = (U, A, I)$ *be a formal context,* $X \subseteq U$. *Then*

$$X \in EX(T) \Longleftrightarrow C(K_U^T)(X) = X.$$

5   Approaches of Determining Concept Lattices

Let $T = (U, A, I)$ be a formal context, $B \subseteq A$. We let

$$r_B = \{ (x_i, x_j) \in U \times U; \quad a(x_i) = a(x_j), \ \forall a \in B \}, \tag{5.1}$$

$$\tilde{r}_B = \{ (x_i, x_j) \in U \times U; \quad a(x_i) = a(x_j) = 1, \ \forall a \in B \}. \tag{5.2}$$

It is easy to see that r_B is an equivalence relation on U; $\tilde{r}_B$ is a binary relation on U and satisfies symmetry and transitivity. The partition generated by r_B is denoted as

$$U/r_B = \{ [x_i]_{r_B}; \quad x_i \in U \},$$

where $[x_i]_{r_B} = \{x_j \in U; \ (x_i, x_j) \in r_B\}$. If $B = \{b\}$, we write $r_{\{b\}} = r_b$. Let $a, b \in A$, an operation between U/r_a and U/r_b is defined as

$$U/r_a * U/r_b = \{ [x_i]_{r_a} \cap [x_j]_{r_b}; \quad [x_i]_{r_a} \cap [x_j]_{r_b} \neq \emptyset; \ x_i, x_j \in U \}$$

when B is a finite set ($B = \{b_1, \ldots, b_k\}$), we write

$$U/r_{b_1} * \ldots * U/r_{b_k} = \prod_{i=1}^{k} U/r_{b_i}.$$

Theorem 5.1. *Let* $T = (U, A, I)$ *be a formal context,* $B \subseteq A$. *We define*

$$U/\tilde{r}_B = \begin{cases} \{ [x]_{\tilde{r}_a}; \quad x \in U \}, & B = \{a\} \\ \displaystyle\prod_{a \in B} U/\tilde{r}_a, & |B| > 1, \end{cases}$$

where, $[x]_{\tilde{r}_a} = \{y \in U; \ (x, x) \in \tilde{r}_a \Leftrightarrow (y, y) \in \tilde{r}_a\}$, $a \in A$.
Then $U/\tilde{r}_B = U/r_B$.

Proof. Let $a \in A$, $x, y \in U$. Since $(x, y) \in \tilde{r}_a \Leftrightarrow a(x) = a(y) = 1$, or $a(x) = a(y) = 0$, this implies that $(x, y) \in \tilde{r}_a \Leftrightarrow (x, y) \in r_a$. Hence, for any $a \in A$, $U/\tilde{r}_a = U/r_a$. By the definition of U/r_B, the conclusion is clear. $\qquad \square$

Theorem 5.2. *Let* $T = (U, A, I)$ *be a formal context,*

$$R_A^{\sim} = \{ (B, D) \in \mathcal{P}(A) \times \mathcal{P}(A); \quad r_B^{\sim} = r_D^{\sim} \}. \tag{5.3}$$

Then, $R_A^{\sim}$ *is a congruence on semilattice* $(\mathcal{P}(A), \cup)$.

Proof. Using the method in Theorem 3.1, it can be derived directly.   □

Theorem 5.3. *Let* $T = (U, A, I)$ *be a formal context. Then*

$$R_A^{\sim} = K_A^{'T}. \tag{5.4}$$

Proof. Let $(B, D) \in \mathcal{P}(A) \times \mathcal{P}(A)$. Since $(B, D) \in R_A^{\sim} \Leftrightarrow r_B^{\sim} = r_D^{\sim}$, and $\forall (x, y) \in U \times U$, $(x, y) \in r_B^{\sim} \Leftrightarrow (x, x) \in r_B^{\sim}$ and $(y, y) \in r_B^{\sim}$. Thus $\forall x \in U$, $(x, x) \in r_B^{\sim} \Leftrightarrow (x, x) \in r_D^{\sim}$, this implies that $b(x) = 1 \Leftrightarrow d(x) = 1$ for all $b \in B$ and all $d \in D$. Hence, $x \in B^e \Leftrightarrow x \in D^e$, i.e., $(B, D) \in K_A^{'T}$.   □

Let $T = (U, A, I)$ be a formal context, $X \subseteq U$. We let

$$r_X = \{ (a, b) \in A \times A; \quad a(x_i) = b(x_i), \; \forall x_i \in X \}, \tag{5.5}$$

$$r_X^{\sim} = \{ (a, b) \in A \times A; \quad a(x_i) = b(x_i) = 1, \; \forall x_i \in X \}. \tag{5.6}$$

Clearly, $r_X^{\sim}$ is a binary relation on A, r_X is an equivalence relation on A and

$$U/r_X = \{ [a]_{r_X}; \quad a \in A \},$$

where $[a]_{r_X} = \{ b \in A; \; (a, b) \in r_X \}$.

By duality property, it is easy to show the following theorems.

Theorem 5.4. *Let* $T = (U, A, I)$ *be a formal context. We let*

$$U/r_X^{\sim} = \begin{cases} \{ [a]_{r_{x_i}^{\sim}}; \quad a \in A \}, & X = \{x_i\} \\ \prod_{x_i \in U} A/r_{x_i}^{\sim}, & |X| > 1. \end{cases}$$

where $[a]_{r_{x_i}^{\sim}} = \{ b \in A; \; (a, a) \in r_{x_i}^{\sim} \Leftrightarrow (b, b) \in r_{x_i}^{\sim} \}$, $x_i \in U$.
Then $A/r_X^{\sim} = A/r_X$.

Theorem 5.5. *Let* $T = (U, A, I)$ *be a formal context,*

$$R_U^{\sim} = \{ (X, Y) \in \mathcal{P}(U) \times \mathcal{P}(U); \quad r_X^{\sim} = r_Y^{\sim} \}. \tag{5.7}$$

Then, $R_U^{\sim}$ *is a congruence on semilattice* $(\mathcal{P}(U), \cup)$.

Theorem 5.6. *Let* $T = (U, A, I)$ *be a formal context. Then*

$$R_U^{\sim} = K_U^{'T}. \tag{5.8}$$

For a formal context $T = (U, A, I)$, $B \subseteq A$, $X \subseteq U$. We let

$$C(R_A^\sim)(B) = \cup[B]_{R_A^\sim}, \qquad C(R_U^\sim)(X) = \cup[X]_{R_U^\sim}.$$

It is easy to see that $C(R_A^\sim)$ is a closed operator on $(\mathcal{P}(A), \cup)$, and $C(R_U^\sim)$ is a closed operator on $(\mathcal{P}(U), \cup)$. The set of all $C(R_A^\sim)$-closed sets in $\mathcal{P}(A)$ is denoted by $\mathcal{C}_{R_A^\sim}$. The set of all $C(R_U^\sim)$-closed sets in $\mathcal{P}(U)$ is denoted by $\mathcal{C}_{R_U^\sim}$. From Theorem 4.2 and Theorem 5.3 we have

$$\mathcal{C}_{R_A^\sim} = \mathcal{C}_{K_A^T} = IN(T), \qquad \mathcal{C}_{R_U^\sim} = \mathcal{C}_{K_U^T} = EX(T). \tag{5.9}$$

Eq. (5.9) presents a new way to obtain the concepts of formal contexts, i.e., we can determine the intents and extents of a formal context by means of the sets $\mathcal{C}_{R_A^\sim}$ and $\mathcal{C}_{R_U^\sim}$. The following results show the relations of set $\mathcal{C}_{R_A^\sim}$ ($\mathcal{C}_{R_U^\sim}$) and indiscernibility matrices.

Definition 5.1. Let $T = (U, A, I)$ be a formal context, $U/r_A^\sim = \{X_1, \ldots, X_k\}$, $A/r_U^\sim = \{B_1, \ldots, B_p\}$.

$$G_A^\sim = \{G_{ij}^A; \ 1 \le i, j \le k\}, \qquad G_U^\sim = \{G_{ij}^U; \ 1 \le i, j \le p\}. \tag{5.10}$$

where $G_{ij}^A = \{a \in A; \ a(X_i) = a(X_j) = 1\}$ $(1 \le i, j \le k)$, $G_{ij}^U = \{x \in U; \ b(x) = 1, \ \forall b \in B_i \cup B_j\}$ $(1 \le i, j \le p)$. $G_A^\sim$ is called an indiscernibility matrix of attributes corresponding to $r_A^\sim$ and $G_U^\sim$ an indiscernibility matrix of objects corresponding to $r_U^\sim$.

Theorem 5.7. Let $T = (U, A, I)$ be a formal context. Then
(i) $G_A^\sim \subseteq \mathcal{C}_{R_A^\sim}$;
(ii) $G_U^\sim \subseteq \mathcal{C}_{R_U^\sim}$.

Proof. (i) Suppose $B = G_{ij}^A \in G_A^\sim$. If $B = \emptyset$, then $\forall D \subseteq A$ $(D \ne \emptyset)$, $\exists a \in D$ such that $a(X_i) \ne a(X_j)$. Hence, $D \ne [\emptyset]_{R_A^\sim}$, i.e., $\emptyset = [\emptyset]_{R_A^\sim} \in \mathcal{C}_{R_A^\sim}$.

If $B = G_{ij}^A \ne \emptyset$, and $D \in [B]_{R_A^\sim}$. From $r_D^\sim = r_B^\sim$ we have $a(X_i) = a(X_j) = 1$ for all $a \in D$. This implies that $a \in B$, and so $D \subseteq B$. Since D is arbitrary, we have $\cup[B]_{R_A^\sim} \subseteq B$. $B \subseteq \cup[B]_{R_A^\sim}$ is clear. Therefore, $B \in \mathcal{C}_{R_A^\sim}$.
(ii) By the conclusion (i), it is clear.   □

Theorem 5.8. Let $T = (U, A, I)$ be a formal context. Then
(i) $A \in G_A^\sim \Leftrightarrow \exists x \in U$ such that $\forall a \in A$, $a(x) = 1$;
(ii) $U \in G_U^\sim \Leftrightarrow \exists a \in A$ such that $\forall x \in U$, $a(x) = 1$.

Proof. (i) and (ii) are obvious by Definition 5.1.   □

If a formal context $T = (U, A, I)$ satisfies the conditions: $A \notin G_A^{\sim}$, $U \notin G_U^{\sim}$, we say that T is a regular formal context.

Theorem 5.9. *Let $T = (U, A, I)$ be a regular formal context. Then*

$$G_A^{\sim} \cup A = \mathcal{C}_{R_A^{\sim}} \Longleftrightarrow \forall\, a \in A, \text{ there exists } (x_i, x_j) \in r_a^{\sim} \text{ such that}$$
$$b(x_i) \neq b(x_j) \text{ for all } b \in A - \{a\} \text{ if } r_a^{\sim} \nsubseteq r_b^{\sim}.$$

Proof. Suppose $a \in A$, and $\forall\, (x_i, x_j) \in r_a^{\sim}$, there exists $b \in A - \{a\}$ satisfying $r_a^{\sim} \nsubseteq r_b^{\sim}$, and $b(x_i) = b(x_j)$. Let $B = \cup[\{a\}]_{R_A^{\sim}}$. Clearly, $B \in \mathcal{C}_{R_A^{\sim}}$. Since $r_a^{\sim} = r_B^{\sim} = \bigcap_{b \in B} r_b^{\sim}$, $\forall\, (x_i, x_j) \in r_B^{\sim}$, $\exists\, b \in A - B$, such that $b(x_i) = b(x_j)$. If $x_i \in X_i$, $x_j \in X_j$, then $\forall\, b \in A - B$, $b(X_i) = b(X_j)$. Thus, $\forall\, 1 \leq i, j \leq k$, $G_{ij} = \{a \in A;\ a(X_i) = a(X_j)\} \neq B$. Hence, the condition is necessary.

Conversely, suppose $\forall\, a \in A$, there exists $(x_i, x_j) \in r_a^{\sim}$ such that $b(x_i) \neq b(x_j)$ for all $b \in A - \{a\}$ if $r_a^{\sim} \nsubseteq r_b^{\sim}$. From Theorem 5.7 and $A \in \mathcal{C}_{R_A^{\sim}}$ we know that $G_A^{\sim} \cup A \subseteq \mathcal{C}_{R_A^{\sim}}$ is true. Suppose $B \in \mathcal{C}_{R_A^{\sim}}$, $B \neq \emptyset$, then $\forall\, (x_i, x_j) \in r_B^{\sim} = \bigcap_{a \in B} r_a^{\sim}$ and $\forall\, b \in B$, we have $b(x_i) = b(x_j)$. Thus, $\forall\, a \in B$, $\exists\, (x_i, x_j) \in r_B^{\sim}$ such that $b(x_i) \neq b(x_j)$ for all $b \in A - \{a\}$ if $r_a^{\sim} \nsubseteq r_b^{\sim}$. By $r_B^{\sim} \subseteq r_a^{\sim}$, there exists $(x_i, x_j) \in r_B^{\sim}$ such that $b(x_i) \neq b(x_j)$ for all $b \in A - B$. That is, $B = \{a \in A;\ a(X_i) = a(X_j)\} = G_{ij}^A \in G_A^{\sim}$. Therefore, $\mathcal{C}_{R_A^{\sim}} \subseteq G_A^{\sim} \cup A$. It follows that, the sufficiency holds. $\square$

Theorem 5.10. *Let $T = (U, A, I)$ be a regular formal context. Then*

$$G_U^{\sim} \cup U = \mathcal{C}_{R_U^{\sim}} \Longleftrightarrow \forall\, x \in U, \text{ there exists } (a, b) \in r_x^{\sim} \text{ such that}$$
$$a(y) \neq b(y) \text{ for all } y \in U - \{x\} \text{ if } r_x^{\sim} \nsubseteq r_y^{\sim}.$$

Proof. By Theorem 5.9, the conclusion is clear. $\square$

To illustrate the method of determining concepts we consider two examples.

Example 5.1. Let $T_1 = (U, A, I)$ be a formal context, where $U = \{1, 2, 3, 4\}$, $A = \{a, b, c, d, e\}$, the binary relation between U and A is given by Table 1.

From Table 1 we can obtain the partitions $U/r_A^{\sim}$ and $U/r_U^{\sim}$ as

$$U/r_A^{\sim} = \{X_1,\ X_2,\ X_3\} = \{\, \{1\},\ \{2, 4\},\ \{3\} \,\},$$

$$A/r_U^{\sim} = \{B_1, \ldots, B_4\} = \{\, \{a, b\},\ \{c\},\ \{d\},\ \{e\} \,\}.$$

It is easy to verify that T satisfies the conditions of Theorem 5.9 and Theorem 5.10. Thus, we can determine the extents and the intents of T by using indiscernibility matrixes, two indiscernibility matrixes are given by Table 2 and Table 3, respectively. For the sake of brevity we write $\{i\} = i$, $\{i, j\} = ij$, $\{i, j, k\} = ijk$, $\forall\, i, j, k \in U$, and the attribute set is the same.

Table 2. Attribute indiscernibility matrix of T_1

	X_1	X_2	X_3
X_1	abde	ab	d
X_2	ab	abc	$\emptyset$
X_3	d	$\emptyset$	d

Table 3. Object indiscernibility matrix of T_1

	B_1	B_2	B_3	B_4
B_1	124	24	1	1
B_2	24	24	$\emptyset$	$\emptyset$
B_3	1	$\emptyset$	13	1
B_4	1	$\emptyset$	1	1

By Table 2 and Table 3, we have

$$G^{\sim}_A = \{\emptyset,\ d,\ ab,\ abc,\ abde\}, \qquad G^{\sim}_U = \{\emptyset,\ 1,\ 13,\ 24,\ 124\},$$

and

$$IN(T_1) = C_{R^{\sim}_A} = G^{\sim}_A \cup A = \{\emptyset,\ d,\ ab,\ abc,\ abde,\ A\},$$
$$EX(T_1) = C_{R^{\sim}_U} = G^{\sim}_U \cup U = \{\emptyset,\ 1,\ 13,\ 24,\ 124,\ U\}.$$

Hence, the concept lattice $L(T_1)$ can be derived as

$$L(T_1) = \{\ (\emptyset, A), (1, abde), (13, d), (24, abc), (124, ab), (U, \emptyset)\ \}.$$

Example 5.2. Let $T_2 = (U, A, I)$ be a formal context, where $U = \{1, 2, 3, 4, 5\}$, $A = \{a, b, c, d, e\}$, the binary relation between U and A is given by Table 4.

From Table 4 we can see that $r^{\sim}_a = r^{\sim}_b$, and a, b do not satisfy the condition in Theorem 5.9. The set $C_{R^{\sim}_A}$ here can also be determined by using the indiscernibility matrix, the method is as follows:

Since $r^{\sim}_a = r^{\sim}_b = r^{\sim}_{ab}$, and for any $B \subseteq A$, $r^{\sim}_a \neq r^{\sim}_B$ when $B \notin \{a, b, ab\}$. Therefore, $\{a, b\} = \cup[\{a\}]_{R^{\sim}_A} \in C_{R^{\sim}_A}$.

Table 4. Formal context T_2

U	a	b	c	d	e
1	1	1	0	1	1
2	1	1	1	1	0
3	0	0	0	1	0
4	1	1	1	0	1
5	1	1	0	1	1

The elements c, d and e satisfy the condition in Theorem 5.9. The indiscernibility matrix on attributes is given by Table 5.

Table 5. Attribute indiscernibility matrix of T_2

	X_1	X_2	X_3	X_3
X_1	$abde$	abd	d	abe
X_2	abd	$abcd$	d	abc
X_3	d	d	d	$\emptyset$
X_4	abe	abc	$\emptyset$	$abce$

where $U/r_A^{\sim} = \{X_1, \ldots, X_4\} = \{\{1,5\}, \{2\}, \{3\}, \{4\}\}$.
From Table 5 we get $G_A^{\sim} = \{\emptyset, d, abc, abd, abe, abcd, abce, abde\}$, and

$$IN(T_2) = G_A^{\sim} \cup A \cup \{ab\} = \{\emptyset, d, ab, abc, abd, abe, abcd, abce, abde, A\}.$$

The concept lattice $L(T_2)$ is given by Fig.1.

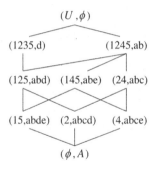

Fig. 1. Concept lattice $L(T_2)$

6   Conclusion

In this paper, we have examined the problem of determining concept lattices in formal concept analysis. The properties of congruences corresponding to formal contexts were discussed. The relationships between the closed sets induced by the congruences and indiscernibility attribute (object) sets were shown. Based on the relations, the approaches that constructs concept lattices are derived. This idea also offers some possibilities to further study data mining and knowledge acquisition.

Acknowledgements

This work is supported by the Nature Science Foundation of China (10271039) and the National 973 Program of China (2002CB312200).

References

1. Burusco, A., Fuentes-González, R., Construction of the L-fuzzy concept lattice, *Fuzzy Sets and Systems* **97** (1998) 109-114
2. Düntsch, I., Gediga, G., Algebraic aspects of attribute dependencies in information systems, *Fundamenta Informaticae*, **29** (1997) 119-133
3. Ganter, B., Wille, R., Formal Concept Analysis: Mathematical Foundations, Springer-Verlag, New York, 1999
4. Hu, K., Sui, Y., Lu, Y., Wang, J.,and Shi, C., Concept approximation in concept lattice, Knowledge Discovery and Data Mining, *Proceedings of 5th Pacific-Asia Conference*,PAKDD'01 (2001) 167-173
5. Novotný, M., Dependence Spaces of Information Systems, In: E. Orlowska(Ed.), Incomplete Informations: Rough Sets Analysis, Physica-Verlag (1998) pp, 193-246
6. Pawlak, Z., Rough sets, *International Journal of Computer and Information Sciences* **11** (1982) 341-356
7. Skowron, A., Rauszer, C.: The discernibility matrices and functions in information systems. In: Slowinski, R. (ed.), Intelligent Decision Support: Handbook of Applications and Advances of the Rough Set Theory. Kluwer Academic Publishers, Dordrecht (1992) 331-362
8. Wille, R. Restructuring lattice theory: an approach based on hierarchies of concepts, in: I. Rival (Ed.), Ordered Sets, Reidel, Dordrecht (1982) pp. 445-470
9. Yao, Y.Y., Concept lattices in rough set theory, Proceedings of 23rd International Meeting of the North American Fuzzy Information Processing Society (2004) pp. 796-801
10. Zhang, W.-X., Wei, L., Qi, J.-J., Attribute Reduction in Concept Lattice Based on Discernibility Matrix. In: Ślezak et al. (Eds.): RSFDGrC 2005, Lecture Notes in Artifical Intelligence, 3642 (2005) 157-165
11. Zhang, W.-X., Leung, Y., Wu, W.-Z., Information Systems and Knowledge Discovery, Science Press, Beijing, 2003
12. Zhang, W.-X., Qiu, G.-F., Uncertain Decision Making Based on Rough Sets, Tsinghua University Press, Beijing, 2005

Selection of Materialized Relations in Ontology Repository Management System

Man Li[1,3], Xiaoyong Du[1,2], and Shan Wang[1,2]

[1] School of Information, Renmin University of China
[2] Key Laboratory of Data Engineering and Knowledge Engineering, MOE
[3] Institute of Software, Chinese Academy of Sciences
100872 Beijing, China
{liman1, duyong, swang}@ruc.edu.cn

Abstract. With the growth of ontology scale and complexity, the query performance of Ontology Repository Management System (ORMS) becomes more and more important. The paper proposes materialized relations technique which speeds up query processing in ORMS by making the implicit derived relations of ontology explicit. Here the selection of materialized relations is a key problem, because the materialized relations technique trades off required inference time against maintenance cost and storage space. However, the problem has not been discussed formally before. So the paper proposes a QSS model to describe the queries set of ontology formally and gives the benefit evaluation model and the selection algorithm of materialized relations based on QSS model. The method in this paper not only considers the benefit in query response of the materialization technique, but also the storage and maintenance cost of it. In the end, an application case is introduced to prove the selection method of materialized relations is effective.

1 Introduction

The success of the Semantic Web strongly depends on the proliferation of ontologies. Ontology Repository Management System (ORMS) [1] is used to develop and manage ontologies in Web environment. With the growth of ontology scale and complexity, the query performance of ORMS becomes more and more important. Although existing ontology-related tools such as DLDB-OWL[2], Sesame-DB[3] etc, cannot be called ORMS because of their limited functions, the query performance for large-scale ontology is also a bottleneck of these systems, which can be seen from experimental results in reference [4]. So how to improve ontology query performance is a challenging topic.

It is well-known that RDF(S)[5] and OWL[6] define how to assert facts and specify how implicit information should be derived from stated facts. Existing ontology-related systems only store the stated facts physically while the derivation of implicit information is usually achieved at the time clients issue queries to inference engines. The process of deriving implicit information usually requires a long time, which is the main factor influencing the performance of ontology query.

J. Lang, F. Lin, and J. Wang (Eds.): KSEM 2006, LNAI 4092, pp. 241–251, 2006.
© Springer-Verlag Berlin Heidelberg 2006

Especially with the growth of ontology scale, the process of inference is complex and time consuming. Consequently query performance becomes lower.

Inspired by materialization technique in data warehouse[7], we believe that materialization is also a promising technique for fast query processing in ORMS, because read access is predominant in it. As a fine model for presenting hierarchy and semantic meaning of concepts, ontology provides semantic meaning through relations between concepts. Here two kinds of ontology relations are distinguished to discuss materialization technique conveniently. They are **base relations** that are asserted explicitly and **derived relations** that are derived from base relations. Experiences show that most of ontology queries involve derived relations, so we think it is necessary to materialize derived relations, that is to say, store them physically to avoid re-computing them for queries. In the paper the derived relations that are materialized are called **materialized relations**.

The materialized relations technique speeds up query processing by making the implicit derived relations of ontology explicit. Obviously it trades off required inference time against storage space and maintenance cost. Because ontology is not static, it is necessary to maintain materialized relations regularly to keep the consistence between materialized relations and base relations, which issues the problem of maintenance cost for materialized relations. In addition, there are large numbers of derived relations in ontology, which issues the problem of storage space cost for materialized relations. Therefore it is not practical to materialize all the derived relations, especially for the derived relations that can be acquired in short time or only used for special query requirement. To improve query performance as greatly as possible under the constraint of storage space and maintenance cost, it requires selecting some derived relations to materialize, which is called selection of materialized relations. It is a key problem for materialized relations technique; however, the problem has not been discussed formally in previous researches. Although some models and algorithms have been proposed to select materialized views in data warehouse, they are not adaptable for materialized relations, because query on ontology repository is not same as query on data warehouse. So the paper proposes a QSS model to describe ontology queries and gives the benefit evaluation model and the selection algorithm of materialized relations based on QSS model. The method in this paper considers not only the benefit in query response of the materialization technique, but also the maintenance cost and storage space of it.

The paper is organized as follows. Section 2 shows the QSS model. Section 3 proposes the benefit evaluation model and selection algorithm of materialized relations based on QSS model. Section 4 shows an application case to prove the method in this paper is effective. Section 5 introduces the related works and draws a conclusion.

2 QSS Model

Ontology is defined as an explicit formal specification of a shared conceptualization [5]. Ontology can be represented by a directed labeled graph (DLG), in which vertices represent concepts of ontology, edges represent relations between two concepts and each edge has label representing the semantics of relation. The process of ontology query can be seen as acquiring the corresponding sub-graph of ontology and query results can also be represented by a DLG. To describe ontology query formally, some definitions are given firstly.

Definition 1. For a specified ontology O and a query Q on it, the directed labeled graph QSGraph(Q, O) = <V, E, L> is called **query schema graph** of query Q on ontology O. Here V is the set of vertices, which represent ontology concepts involved in Q. V is the set of directed edges, which represent base relations between two concepts. Each edge has label, which represents the semantics of the corresponding base relation and the set of labels is denoted as L.

Example 1. Suppose that Q_1 "query all subclasses of class A" is a query on ontology O. The query schema graph of Q_1 on O is shown in Fig. 1, in which vertices represent classes involved in Q_1 and directed edges have two kinds of labels. Here R_1 represents the relation "subClassOf" and R_2 represents the relation "equivalentClass".

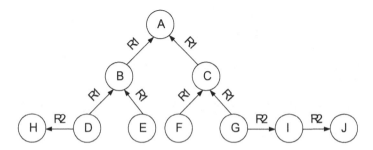

Fig. 1. A query schema graph QSGraph(Q_1, O)

It can be seen from Fig. 1, edges of query schema graph may have different labels. Here QSGraph(Q_1, O) has two kinds of labels, that is to say the set L of it has two elements R_1 and R_2. For maintenance of materialized relations, different maintenance algorithms and costs may be required according to different characteristics of relations, so it is necessary to distinguish labels in query schema graph during discussing selection of materialized relations. Therefore definition 2 is given.

Definition 2. In query schema graph QSGraph(Q, O) = <V, E, L>, if each edge has the same label, that is to say, L includes only one elements R, QSGraph(Q, O) is called **simple query schema graph on R**; otherwise, it is called **non-simple query schema graph**.

Example 2. QSGraph(Q_2, O) in Fig. 2 is a simple query schema graph on R_1.

It can be seen that QSGraph(Q_2, O) in Fig. 2 only includes one label R_1, so it is a simple query schema graph on R_1

Definition 3. For two DLGs G = <V, E, L> and G'= <V', E', L'>, if the conditions V'⊆V, E'⊆E and L'⊆L are satisfied, G' is called a **sub-graph** of G, denoted as G' ≤G.

According to the definitions about simple query schema graph and sub-graph, a query schema graph can be partitioned into some sub-graphs, each of which is a simple

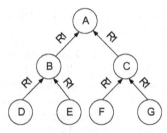

Fig. 2. A simple query schema graph QSGraph(Q_2, O)

query schema graph. Obviously, a query schema graph may have several kinds of partitions. To partition a query schema graph uniquely, definition 4 is given.

Definition 4. For query schema graph QSGraph(Q, O) = <V, E, L>, if there exists a DLG G satisfying the following conditions:

(1) G is a simple query schema graph on R;
(2) G $\leq$ QSGraph(Q, O);
(3) there does not exist a simple query schema graph G' satisfying G$\leq$G' $\leq$ QSGraph(Q, O);

G is called a ***maximum simple sub-graph on R*** of QSGraph(Q, O), denoted as G = QSGraph(Q, O)$_{[R]}$.

Based on definition 4, theorem 1 is obvious.

Theorem 1. A query schema graph QSGraph(Q, O) = <V, E, L> has |L| maximum simple sub-graphs at most, where |L| is the total number of elements in L.

Proof. To prove theorem 1 is correct, it is necessary to prove that for each R in L, QSGraph(Q, O) = <V, E, L> has one and only QSGraph(Q, O)$_{[R]}$. Suppose that QSGraph(Q, O) = <V, E, L> has more than one QSGraph(Q, O)$_{[R]}$, which are G_1 = <V_1, E_1>, G_2 = <V_2, E_2>, ..., G_i = <V_i, E_i>. Here the set of labels is omitted, because G_1, G_2, ..., and G_i only have one labels R. It is easy to construct a new graph G_n = <V_n, E_n>, which satisfies V_n = $V_1 \cup V_2$... $\cup V_i$ and E_n = $E_1 \cup E_2$... $\cup E_i$. Obviously $G_1 \leq G_n$, $G_2 \leq G_n$, ...,and $G_i \leq G_n$ are held. According to definition 4, there are $V_1 \subseteq V$, $E_1 \subseteq E$, $V_2 \subseteq V$, $E_2 \subseteq E$, ..., $V_i \subseteq V$, and $E_i \subseteq E$, so there must be $V_n \subseteq V$, $E_n \subseteq E$. And the label of G_n is R, which satisfies {R}$\subseteq$L, so there is $G_n \leq$QSGraph(Q, O) according to definition 3. It indicates that for any one G_j (G_j = QSGraph(Q, O)$_{[R]}$) there exists G_n satisfying $G_j \leq G_n \leq$QSGraph(Q, O), which is contrary to condition (3) in definition 4. The above analysis shows that the assumption that QSGraph(Q, O) = <V, E, L> has more than one QSGraph(Q, O)$_{[R]}$ does not come into existence. That is to say for each R in L, QSGraph(Q, O) = <V, E, L> has one and only QSGraph(Q, O)$_{[R]}$. So it is proven that QSGraph(Q, O) = <V, E, L> has |L| maximum simple sub-graphs at most.

Theorem 1 shows that a query schema graph could have a unique partition based on the maximum simple sub-graphs on each kind of relations in it.

Definition 5. For a specified ontology O, QSS(Q*, R*) represents a **QSS model** of ontology O, where Q* is the set of queries on O and R* is the set of base relations involved in Q*. QSS(Q*, R*) is defined as the set of QSGraph(Q, O)$_{[R]}$, where Q $\in$ Q* and R$\in$ R* are held. For any one R$\in$ R* , QSS(Q*, R*)$_{[R]}$ represents the set of QSGraph(Q, O)$_{[R]}$, where Q$\in$ Q* is held.

Definition 5 shows that QSS model consists of maximum simple sub-graphs of all query schema graphs. Different from common DLG, these graphs in QSS model have additional attributes: query frequency and computing cost.

The query frequency of a graph is equal to the "commit" frequency of query on it, which is shown in definition 6.

Definition 6. For a given graph G, suppose that G = QSGraph(Q, O)$_{[R]}$) is held, and then **query frequency** of G is denoted as F$_q$(G). The related formula is as following.

$$F_q(G) = F_c(Q); \qquad (1)$$

Here $F_c(Q)$ is the "commit" frequency of query Q.

The computing cost means the cost of computing derived relations in ontology. Because each G is a DLG, the computing cost of it is monotonic with the size of the DLG, definition 7 is given. Here the size of G is measured with the average length of paths in it.

Definition 7. For a given DLG G, suppose that G = QSGraph(Q, O)$_{[R]}$) is held, and then **computing cost** of G is denoted as C$_c$(G). The related formula is as following.

$$C_c(G) = \alpha *L_p(G) \qquad (2)$$

Here $L_p(G)$ is the average length of paths in G. α is a proportional coefficient, the value of which depends on characteristics of R, because different kinds of base relations with the same path length may require different inference times.

The query log file records all the queries descriptions of ontology in ORMS, so QSS model can be constructed by analyzing the log file. The algorithm is shown in Algorithm 1.

Algorithm 1. Construction of QSS Model
    Input: Query log file F of ontology O;
    Output: QSS Model.
    QSS (Q*, R*) is set to null;
    while (!endoffile(F))
    {
      read a query record Q from log file F;
      construct QSGraph(Q, O) = <V, E, L>;
      Q* = Q* $\cup$ Q;
      R* = R* $\cup$ L;
      for each R in L
      {
          compute QSGraph(Q, O)$_{[R]}$;
          create node N for QSGraph(Q, O)$_{[R]}$;
          if there exists node M equivalent to N
              F$_q$(M) = F$_q$(M) +1;

```
        else
        {
            insert N into QSS(Q*, R*)[R];
            Fq(N) = 1;
            compute Cc(QSGraph(Q, O)[R]);
        }
    }
}
```

In algorithm 1, the step "compute QSGraph(Q, O)[R]" is computable according to theorem 1. So algorithm 1 is feasible.

3   Selection of Materialized Relations Based on QSS Model

3.1   Benefit Evaluation Model

In QSS model, each kind of derived relations may be selected for materialization, so it is necessary to give a benefit evaluation model to compute materialization benefit of them as the criterion of materialized relations selection. In QSS(Q*, R*)[R] there may be several kinds of derived relations and the name of derived relation may be R or not. *SD(QSS(Q*, R*)[R])* is used to represent the kinds of derived relations in QSS(Q*, R*)[R]. If the derived relation R_i^d satisfies $R_i^d \in SD(QSS(Q^*, R^*)_{[R]})$, it means R_i^d can be derived from R.

Here the benefit evaluation model based on QSS model considers two factors: query benefit and maintenance cost.

Query benefit of materialized relations means the benefit on query performance by using materialized relations. It is related to query frequency and compute cost of derived relations. Obviously the query frequency is higher, and then the query benefit is greater. The compute cost is higher, which means the query performance will be improved more greatly by using materialized relations. Therefore definition 8 is given.

Definition 8. Based on QSS(Q*, R*) of ontology Q, **query benefit** for materializing derived relation R_i^d in O is denoted as $B_q(R_i^d, O)$, where $R_i^d \in SD(QSS(Q^*, R^*)_{[R]})$ ($R \in R^*$) is held. The formula is as following.

$$B_q(R_i^d, O) = \sum_{i=1}^{n} F_q(G) * (\sum_{i=1}^{n} C_c(G)) / n \qquad (3)$$

Here n is the total number of elements in QSS(Q*, R*)[R] and there is $G \in QSS(Q^*, R^*)_{[R]}$.

In definition 8, the average computing cost, i.e. $(\sum_{i=1}^{n} C_c(G)) / n$, is used to measure the saved inference time after materializing R_i^d. Here the response time of querying materialized relations is omitted, because it is very little.

In ontology the update frequency of base relations decides the frequency of re-computing materialized relations and the size of a certain kind of base relations, which is measured with average paths length of them in the DLG representing O, may affect the number of re-computing the corresponding materialized relations. Therefore the evaluation of maintenance cost is given as definition 9.

Definition 9. Based on $QSS(Q^*, R^*)$ of ontology O, **maintenance cost** for materializing derived relation R_i^d in O is denoted as $C_m(R_i^d, O)$, where $R_i^d \in SD(QSS(Q^*, R^*)_{[R]})$ ($R \in R^*$) is held. The formula is as following.

$$C_m(R_i^d, O) = F_u(R)*(\beta *L_r(O,R)) \tag{4}$$

Here $F_u(R)$ is the update frequency of base relation R, which can be acquired from the update log file of ORMS. $L_r(O,R)$ is the average length of paths with label R in the DLG representing O. β is a proportional coefficient, the value of which depends on characteristics of R, because different kinds of base relations with the same path length may require different maintenance costs for the corresponding materialized relations.

Formulas (3) and (4) are applied in the common case that for one R_i^d, there exists only one $QSS(Q^*, R^*)_{[R]}$ satisfying $R_i^d \in SD(QSS(Q^*, R^*)_{[R]})$. However, sometimes for one R_i^d there may exist several sets such as $QSS(Q^*, R^*)_{[R1]}, \ldots, QSS(Q^*, R^*)_{[Rn]}$, satisfying $R_i^d \in SD(QSS(Q^*, R^*)_{[R1]}), \ldots, R_i^d \in SD(QSS(Q^*, R^*)_{[Rn]})$. In this case, query benefit and maintenance cost of R_i^d are the average number of applying formulas (3) and (4) to every $QSS(Q^*, R^*)_{[R1]}, \ldots, QSS(Q^*, R^*)_{[Rn]}$ respectively. Due to limitation of space, the formulas will not be given here.

Obviously the benefit of materialized relation R_i^d is higher if query benefit of R_i^d is higher and maintenance cost of R_i^d is lower. So materialization benefit formula is given in definition 10.

Definition 10. Materialization benefit of R_i^d in O is denoted as Benefit(R_i^d, O). The formula based on a $QSS(Q^*, R^*)$ of ontology O is given as following.

$$Benefit(R_i^d, O) = B_q(R_i^d, O) - C_m(R_i^d, O) \tag{5}$$

In selection of materialized relations, not only materialization benefit of each relation should be considered, but also the space cost should be considered. Space cost means the required maximum storage space for materialized relations. For R_i^d ($R_i^d \in SD(QSS(Q^*, R^*)_{[R]})$), suppose that there are n concepts related to R in O and m concept-pairs having base relation R. So a directed graph G can be constructed, where vertices are the n concepts and edge are relations between two concepts. G has $n*(n-1)$ edges at most, so in O there are $n*(n-1)-m$ derived relations named R_i^d based on R at most. Therefore definition 11 is given.

Definition 11. Based on $QSS(Q^*, R^*)$ of ontology O, **space cost** for materializing R_i^d in O is denoted as $C_s(R_i^d, O)$, where $R_i^d \in SD(QSS(Q^*, R^*)_{[R]})$ ($R \in R^*$) is held. The formula is as following.

$$C_s(R_i^d, O)=(n*(n-1)-m)* \lambda \tag{6}$$

Here n is the total number of concepts related to R in O, and m is the total number of concept-pairs having base relation R. λ is the space size for storing one relation, which depends on the storage strategy of ORMS.

Formulas (6) is applied in the common case that for one R_i^d, there exists only one $QSS(Q^*, R^*)_{[R]}$ satisfying $R_i^d \in SD(QSS(Q^*, R^*)_{[R]})$. For one R_i^d, if there exist several sets such as $QSS(Q^*, R^*)_{[R1]}, \ldots, QSS(Q^*, R^*)_{[Rn]}$, satisfying $R_i^d \in SD(QSS(Q^*, R^*)_{[R1]}), \ldots, R_i^d \in SD(QSS(Q^*, R^*)_{[Rn]})$, the space cost of R_i^d is the total number of applying formulas (6) to every $QSS(Q^*, R^*)_{[R1]}, \ldots, QSS(Q^*, R^*)_{[Rn]}$.

3.2 Selection Algorithm of Materialized Relations

Based on above benefit evaluation model, the problem of selection of materialized relation can be described as: given a QSS model $QSS(Q^*, R^*)$ of ontology O and space constraint S, output the set of derived relations $\{R_1^d, R_2^d, \ldots, R_n^d\}$ required materializing, where $\sum_{i=1}^{n} C_s(R_i^d, O) \leq S$ is held and the selected relations have greater materialization benefit than others. The selection algorithm of materialized relations is shown in algorithm 2.

Algorithm 2. Selection of Materialized Relations
Input: ontology O, QSS (Q^*, R^*) of O, update log file F, space constraint S
Output: selected set of derived relations
1.   MR = { };
2.   for each R_i^d in $SD(QSS(Q^*, R^*)_{[R]}$ $(R \in R^*)$
     {
3.   if $(C_s(R_i^d, O) \leq S)$
         {
4.   compute Benefit (R_i^d, O) according to QSS (Q^*, R^*), O and F;
5.   insert R_i^d into MR by descending order of Benefit (R_i^d, O);
         }
     }
6.   Select R_i^d with the greatest Benefit (R_i^d, O) in MR;
7. $S = S - C_s(R_i^d, O)$;
8.   while $(S \geq 0)$
     {
9.   Output R_i^d;
10.   Delete R_i^d from MR;
11.   Select R_i^d with the greatest Benefit (R_i^d, O) in MR;
12. $S = S - C_s(R_i^d, O)$;
     }

In algorithm 2, derived relations are sorted by descending order of their benefit (See line 5), so that R_i^d with higher benefit can be selected priorly (see line 6 and 11) under the space constraint.

4   Case Study

To prove the validity of selection algorithm of materialized relations based on QSS model, we apply it into an economics ontology EONTO, which is developed and managed in our ORMS[1]. The browse and retrieval interface of ORMS for economic ontology is called Economics Knowledge Retrieval System, which is shown in Fig. 3.

Fig. 3. A screen snapshot of Economics Knowledge Retrieval System

Based on QSS model of EONTO and benefit evaluation model of the paper, the derived relation "subClassOf" derived from base relation "subClassOf" in EONTO has the highest materialization benefit. Despite the numerical value of its benefit, we analyze the reason that "subClassOf" has highest materialization benefit. Firstly its query benefit is high because the queries involving "subClassOf" have highest query frequency in our system and its computing cost is higher than other relations due to its transitive characteristic. Secondly because the update frequency of "subClassOf" is too slow (near to zero) and the average path length of "subClassOf" in the economics ontology is 7 (not very high), which makes its maintenance cost is very low. Consequently the materialization benefit of "subClassOf" is highest in the system. In addition, its space requirement can be satisfied easily because C_s("subClassOf", EONTO) is 120MB at most based on the storage schema[8] of our ORMS.

To prove the correctness of selection result of materialized relations, we preprocess the EONTO into five experimental ontologies with 100,000 URIs, 300,000 URIs, 500,000 URIs, 700,000 URIs and 900,000 URIs respectively. URI is used to measure the size of ontology in the paper. For each ontology, according to previous query log we perform 100 queries in two cases respectively: before materializing derived relation "subClassOf" and after materializing derived relation "subClassOf". Here the average response time of queries is used as the result of query. The experimental results are shown in Fig. 4.

Fig. 4 shows that in our system the average performance of ontology queries can be improved greatly by materializing relation "subClassOf", which also proves that the selection method of materialized relations based on QSS model is effective.

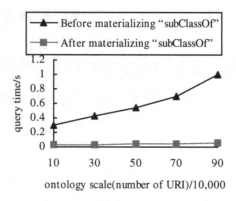

Fig. 4. The effect of materializing "subClassOf" on query time

5 Related Work and Conclusion

With the wide use of ontology, more and more researchers are interested in ontology query performance. Some of them attempt to design various ontology storage schemas to achieve high query performance [3, 8-11]. In addition, it is also assumed that materialization technique is important to achieve a scalable Semantic Web. Some researchers do research on materialized ontology views [12], however the materialized ontology views are not same as the materialized relations and we believe that the materialized relations technique will be implemented easily in ORMS. The concept of materialized ontologies proposed in reference [13] is somewhat similar with that of materialized relations, however it only discusses maintenance of materialized ontologies with changes of rules and facts in ontology. Up to now the selection problem of materialized relations has not been discussed formally in previous researches.

Although some models, such as AND-OR model [14] and Query DAG [15], have been proposed to describe queries set in data warehouse, these models are not adaptable for ontology queries. Consequently the paper proposes a novel QSS model to describe the queries set of ontology formally and gives the benefit evaluation model and the selection algorithm of materialized relations based on QSS model. The method in this paper not only considers the benefit in query response of the materialization technique, but also its maintenance cost and storage space constraint. The application case on economics ontology shows that the selection method of materialized relations in this paper is effective. However, now some values of coefficient such as α and β in our benefit evaluation model are given by experience. In the future, we will try to give more reasonable formulas for them and validate the benefit evaluation model by more experiments.

Acknowledgements

The work was supported by the National Natural Science Foundation of China (Grant No. 60496325 and No. 60573092). Thanks to group members Guo Qin, Yiyu Zhao and Yanfang Liu et al for their works to do a lot of experiments and implement the system.

References

1. Man Li, Xiaoyong Du, Shan Wang. A Study on Ontology Repository Management System for the Semantic Web. In Proc. of the 22th National Database Conference. Published by Computer Science, 2005,32(7.A):35-39.
2. Z. Pan, J.Heflin. DLDB: Extending Relational Databases to Support Semantic Web Queries. In Workshop on Practical and Scalable Semantic Systems, ISWC2003.
3. J. Broekstra, A. Kampman. Sesame: A Generic Architecture for Storing and Querying RDF and RDF Schema. In Proc. of ISWC 2002.
4. Y. Guo, Z. Pan, J. Heflin. An Evaluation of Knowledge Base Systems for Large OWL Datasets. In Proc. of International Semantic Web Conference, 2004: 274-288.
5. RDF(S). http://www.w3.org/RDF/.
6. OWL. http://www.w3.org/2004/OWL/.
7. J. Widom, editor. Special Issue on Materialized Views and Data Warehousing, IEEE Data Engineering Bulletin, 1995, 18.
8. M. Li, Y. Wang, Y. Zhao, et al. A Study on Storage Schema of Large Scale Ontology based on Relational Database. In Proc. of CNCC, 2005:216-219.
9. K. Wilkinson, C. Sayers, H. A. Kuno, D. Reynolds. Efficient RDF Storage and Retrieval in Jena2. In Proc. of SWDB, 2003: 131-150.
10. R. Agrawal, A. Somani, Y. Xu. Storage and Querying of E-Commerce Data. In Proc. of VLDB, 2001.
11. D. Beckett. The Design and Implementation of the Redland RDF Application Framework. In Proc. of WWW, 2001.
12. C. Wouters, T. Dillon, et al. Ontologies on the MOVE. In Proc.of DASFAA 2004.
13. R. Volz, S. Staab, B. Motik. Incremental Maintenance of Materialized Ontologies. In Proc. of CoopIS/DOA/ODBASE, 2003:707-724.
14. H. Gupta. Selection of Views to Materialized in Data Warehouse. In Proc. of ICDT, 1997: 98-112.
15. P. Roy, S. Seshadri, S. Sudarshan, et al. Efficient and Extensible Algorithms for Multi-query Optimization. In ACM SIGMOD Intl. Conf. on Management of Data. 2000.

Combining Topological and Directional Information: First Results*

Sanjiang Li

Department of Computer Science & Technology, Tsinghua University,
Beijing 100084, China
Institut für Informatik, Albert-Ludwigs-Universität, D-79110 Freiburg, Germany
lisanjiang@tsinghua.edu.cn

Abstract. Representing and reasoning about spatial information is important in artificial intelligence and geographical information science. Relations between spatial entities are the most important kind of spatial information. Most current formalisms of spatial relations focus on one single aspect of space. This contrasts sharply with real world applications, where several aspects are usually involved together. This paper proposes a qualitative calculus that combines a simple directional relation model with the well-known topological RCC5 model. We show by construction that the consistency of atomic networks can be decided in polynomial time.

Keywords: Qualitative Spatial Reasoning, topological relations, directional relations, consistency, realization.

1 Introduction

Spatial representation and reasoning plays an essential role in human activities. Although the mathematical theory of Euclidean space provides the most precise representation of spatial information, the qualitative approach to spatial reasoning, known as Qualitative Spatial Reasoning (QSR for short), prevails in artificial intelligence (AI) and geographical information systems (GIS) communities. This is mainly because precise numerical information is often not necessary or unavailable.

Relations between spatial entities are the most important kind of spatial information. Consequently, the development of formalisms of spatial relations forms an important research topic of QSR. Spatial relations are usually classified as topological, directional, and metric. Dozens of formalisms of spatial relations have been proposed in AI and GIS communities in the past two decades. Most research, however, has addressed only a single aspect of space. This can be contrasted with real world applications, where several aspects are usually involved

---

* This work was partly supported by the Alexander von Humboldt Foundation and the National Natural Science Foundation of China (60305005, 60321002, 60496321).

J. Lang, F. Lin, and J. Wang (Eds.): KSEM 2006, LNAI 4092, pp. 252–264, 2006.

together. Since different aspects of space are often dependent, we need to establish more elaborate formalisms that combine different types of information.

This paper concerns the integration of topological and directional information. We achieve this by combining a directional relation model with a topological one. The directional relation model, which contains 9 atomic relations, is the Boolean algebra generated by the four fundamental directional relations, viz. *north, south, west, east*. As for the topological counterpart, we choose the RCC5 algebra, which is a subalgebra of the well known RCC8 algebra introduced by Randell, Cui, and Cohn [1]. RCC5 contains five atomic topological relations, viz. *equal, proper part, discrete, partially overlap*, and the converse of *proper part*. The hybrid relation model, which contains the RCC5 atomic relations and the four fundamental directional relations mentioned earlier, has 13 atomic relations.

We call a constraint network Θ in the hybrid model *atomic* if for any two variables x, y appeared in Θ there exists a unique constraint $x\mathsf{R}y$ in Θ and R is one of the 13 atomic relations. The major contribution of this paper is to show by construction that the consistency of atomic networks can be decided in polynomial time.

The rest of this paper is organized as follows. Section 2 recalls notions and terminologies of qualitative calculus. Section 3 introduces the RCC5 algebra. The directional relation model is introduced in Section 4, where we also show that the model can be decomposed into two isomorphic components. Section 5 gives a method for deciding consistency and constructing realizations of atomic networks over the directional relation model. In Section 6 we combine topological and directional information, and give a complete method for deciding the consistency of atomic networks in the hybrid model. Section 7 concludes the paper.

2   Qualitative Spatial Calculi

We are interested in relations between bounded plane regions, where a *plane region* is a nonempty regular closed subset of the real plane. We call a plane region *simple* if it is homeomorphic to a closed disk. Note that not all regions are simple. A bounded region can have either holes or multiple components.

In what follows we write $\mathbb{U}$ for the set of bounded plane regions, and write $\mathbf{Rel}(\mathbb{U})$ for the set of binary relations on $\mathbb{U}$. With the usual relational operations of intersection, union, and complement, $\mathbf{Rel}(\mathbb{U})$ is a Boolean algebra. In QSR we are mostly interested in finite subalgebras of $\mathbf{Rel}(\mathbb{U})$. We also call such a finite subalgebra a *qualitative calculus* over $\mathbb{U}$.

Let $\mathcal{R}$ be a qualitative calculus over $\mathbb{U}$. Since $\mathcal{R}$ is finite, it is an atomic complete algebra. We call each atom in $\mathcal{R}$ an *atomic* relation, and write $\mathcal{B}$ for the set of atomic relations. Note that each relation in $\mathcal{R}$ is the union of atomic relations it contains.

For a subset $\mathcal{S}$ of $\mathcal{R}$, a constraint network Θ involving n spatial variables over $\mathcal{S}$ is a set of constraints such that all relations appeared in Θ are in $\mathcal{S}$. In other words, Θ has the form

$$\{x_i\mathsf{R}_{ij}x_j : \mathsf{R}_{ij} \in \mathcal{S}, \ 1 \leq i, j \leq n\}.$$

We call Θ *consistent* if there are n bounded plane regions $a_1, \cdots, a_n$ such that, for any two i, j, $a_i \mathsf{R}_{ij} a_j$.

The most important reasoning problem in QSR is to decide whether a constraint network is consistent. Reasoning over the whole algebra $\mathcal{R}$ is usually NP-hard. If this is the case, we are interested in finding subsets of $\mathcal{R}$ where reasoning is tractable. Of particular importance is the reasoning problem of deciding the consistency of atomic networks, i.e. constraints network over $\mathcal{B}$. Once we know that reasoning over $\mathcal{B}$ is tractable, by backtracking, the problem of deciding the consistency of arbitrary constraint networks is in NP.

For two relations $\mathsf{R}, \mathsf{S} \in \mathcal{R}$, $\mathsf{R} \circ \mathsf{S}$, the usual composition of R and S, is not necessarily a relation in $\mathcal{R}$. We write $\mathsf{R} \circ_w \mathsf{S}$ for the smallest relation in $\mathcal{R}$ which contains $\mathsf{R} \circ \mathsf{S}$, and call $\mathsf{R} \circ_w \mathsf{S}$ the *weak composition* of R and S [2, 3].

In this paper we are mainly interested in atomic networks. Given a network $\Theta = \{x_i \mathsf{R}_{ij} x_j : 1 \leq i, j \leq n\}$, we always assume that R_{ij} is $\mathsf{R}_{ji}^{\sim}$, the converse of R_{ji}.

For some qualitative calculi, the consistency of atomic networks can be decided by using the so-called path consistency algorithm. The essence of such an algorithm is to apply the following rule for any three i, j, k until the network is stable

$$\mathsf{R}_{ij} \leftarrow \mathsf{R}_{ij} \cap \mathsf{R}_{ik} \circ_w \mathsf{R}_{kj}. \tag{1}$$

We call a constraints network *path-consistent* if it is stable under the above rule.

3 RCC5 Mereological Calculus

In this section we introduce the mereological RCC5 relations. For two regions a, b, write a° and b° for the interior of a and b, respectively. Then we say

- a is *equal* to b, denoted by $a\mathbf{EQ}b$, iff $a = b$.
- a is a *part* of b, denoted by $a\mathbf{P}b$, iff $a \subseteq b$.
- a is a *proper part* of b, denoted by $a\mathbf{PP}b$, iff $a \subset b$.
- a *overlaps* b, denoted by $a\mathbf{O}b$, iff $a^\circ \cap b^\circ \neq \varnothing$.
- a is *discrete from* b, denoted by $a\mathbf{DR}b$, iff $a^\circ \cap b^\circ = \varnothing$.
- a *partially overlaps* b, denoted by $a\mathbf{PO}b$, iff $a \not\subseteq b$, $a \not\supseteq b$, and $a^\circ \cap b^\circ \neq \varnothing$.

The subalgebra of $\mathbf{Rel}(\mathbb{U})$ generated by the above relations is known as the RCC5 algebra, which contains five atomic relations, viz. $\mathbf{EQ}$, $\mathbf{PO}$, $\mathbf{DR}$, $\mathbf{PP}$, and $\mathbf{PP}^{\sim}$, the converse of $\mathbf{PP}$. RCC5 is a subalgebra of the well-known RCC8 algebra of topological relations. All relations in the RCC5 algebra can be defined by the part-of relation $\mathbf{P}$. For this reason, these relations are usually known as *mereological* relations. We write $\mathcal{B}_5$ for the set of RCC5 base relations, i.e.

$$\mathcal{B}_5 = \{\mathbf{EQ}, \mathbf{PO}, \mathbf{PP}, \mathbf{PP}^{\sim}, \mathbf{DR}\} \tag{2}$$

Renz and Nebel [4] show that reasoning over the whole RCC5 algebra is NP-hard, and reasoning over the RCC5 base relations is tractable. In fact, applying the following algorithm to any path-consistent atomic network Θ, we get a realization of Θ (also see [5, 6]).

Table 1. Weak composition table of RCC5

$\circ_w$	EQ	PP	PP$^\sim$	PO	DR
EQ	EQ	PP	PP$^\sim$	PO	DR
PP	PP	PP	$\top$	PP,PO,DR	DR
PP$^\sim$	PP$^\sim$	EQ,PP,PP$^\sim$,PO	PP$^\sim$	PP$^\sim$,PO	PP$^\sim$,PO,DR
PO	PO	PP,PO	PP$^\sim$,PO,DR	$\top$	PP$^\sim$,PO,DR
DR	DR	PP,PO,DR	DR	PP,PO,DR	$\top$

Table 2. A realization algorithm for RCC5 atomic constraints network

Given $\Theta = \{x_i R_{ij} x_j : 1 \leq i, j \leq n\}$ a path-consistent atomic network,
- take n^2 pairwise disjoint closed disks d_{ij} $(1 \leq i, j \leq n)$;
- set $a_i = d_{11}$;
- set $a_i' = a_i \cup \bigcup \{d_{ki}, d_{ik} : R_{ik} = \mathbf{PO}\}\}$;
- set $a_i'' = a_i' \cup \bigcup \{a_k' : R_{ki} = \mathbf{PP}\}$.
  Then $a_i'' R_{ij} a_j''$ for any $1 \leq i, j \leq n$, i.e. $\{a_i : 1 \leq i \leq n\}$ is a realization of Θ.

4   Cardinal Direction Calculus

Orientation is another important aspect of space, and directional relation between spatial entities have been investigated by many researchers. For example, Frank [7] proposed two methods (known as the cone-based and projection-based method) for describing the cardinal direction of a point with respect to a reference point. Later, Ligozat [8] studied computational properties of reasoning with the projection-based approach. Balbiani et al. [9] found a large tractable subclass of the rectangle algebra, which is in essence the 2-dimensional counterpart of Allen's interval algebra [10]. Another interesting approach for representing directional relations between extended spatial entities is the *direction-relation matrix* by Goyal and Egenhofer [11]. Unlike all the other approaches mentioned above, this approach does not approximate a region by a point or its minimum bounding rectangle (for definition see below). This makes the calculus more expressive. As a matter of fact, 511 (218, resp.) distinct atomic relations can be identified between bounded (connected, resp.) plane regions [12]. Recently, Skiadopoulos and Koubarakis [12] proposed an $O(n^5)$ algorithm for determining the consistency of atomic networks in this calculus.

Although the rectangle algebra and the direction-relation matrix method are very expressive, it will be difficult to combine these directional relation models into RCC5. In this section we consider a very simple model of directional relations, which contains the 8 fundamental directional relations (i.e. *east*, *northwest*, etc). The model is indeed the 2-dimensional counterpart of the interval algebra $\mathcal{A}_3$ proposed by Golumbic and Shamir [13], which is a subalgebra of Allen's interval algebra.[1]

---

[1] This fact came to us very late. Using the result obtained in [13], we can see that it is possible to extend the work reported here to larger subclasses of RCC5 and $\mathcal{R}_d$.

For a bounded region (or any bounded subset of the plane) a, define

$$\sup_x(a) = \sup\{x \in \mathbb{R} : (\exists y)(x,y) \in a\}$$

$$\inf_x(a) = \inf\{x \in \mathbb{R} : (\exists y)(x,y) \in a\}$$

$$\sup_y(a) = \sup\{y \in \mathbb{R} : (\exists x)(x,y) \in a\}$$

$$\inf_y(a) = \inf\{y \in \mathbb{R} : (\exists x)(x,y) \in a\}.$$

Note that a is bounded, $\sup_x(a), \inf_x(a), \sup_y(a)$, and $\inf_y(a)$ are well defined. Write $I_x(a)$ and $I_y(a)$, resp., for the closed intervals $[\inf_x(a), \sup_x(a)]$ and $[\inf_y(a), \sup_y(a)]$, which are called the x- and y-projection of a. It is clear that $I_x(a) \times I_y(a)$ is the minimum bounding rectangle (MBR) of a.

For two bounded regions (or bounded sets) a, b, we say

- a is *west* of b, written $a\mathbf{W}b$, if $\sup_x(a) < \inf_x(b)$;
- a is *east* of b, written $a\mathbf{E}b$, if $\sup_x(b) < \inf_x(a)$;
- a is *south* of b, written $a\mathbf{S}b$, if $\sup_y(a) < \inf_y(b)$;
- a is *north* of b, written $a\mathbf{N}b$, if $\sup_y(b) < \inf_y(a)$.

Our cardinal direction calculus, denoted by $\mathcal{R}_d$, is the subalgebra generated by $\{\mathbf{W}, \mathbf{E}, \mathbf{N}, \mathbf{S}\}$.

Note that if a is neither west nor east of b, then $I_x(a) \cap I_x(b) \neq \varnothing$. If this is the case, we say a is in *x-contact* with b, denoted by $a\mathbf{Cx}b$. Clearly, the x-contact relation $\mathbf{Cx}$ is the complement of the union of $\mathbf{W}$ and $\mathbf{E}$. Similarly, we define the *y-contact* relation $\mathbf{Cy}$ to be the complement of $\mathbf{N}$ and $\mathbf{S}$. Write $\mathcal{B}_x = \{\mathbf{W}, \mathbf{E}, \mathbf{Cx}\}$ and $\mathcal{B}_y = \{\mathbf{N}, \mathbf{S}, \mathbf{Cy}\}$. Clearly, $\mathcal{B}_x$ and $\mathcal{B}_y$ are subsets of $\mathcal{R}_d$. Denote $\mathcal{R}_x$ and $\mathcal{R}_y$, resp., for the subalgebra of $\mathcal{R}_d$ generated by $\mathcal{B}_x$ and $\mathcal{B}_y$.

Denote $\mathbf{NW} = \mathbf{N} \cap \mathbf{W}$, $\mathbf{NC} = \mathbf{N} \cap \mathbf{Cx}$, $\mathbf{NE} = \mathbf{N} \cap \mathbf{E}$, $\mathbf{CW} = \mathbf{Cy} \cap \mathbf{W}$, $\mathbf{CC} = \mathbf{Cy} \cap \mathbf{Cx}$, $\mathbf{CE} = \mathbf{Cy} \cap \mathbf{E}$, $\mathbf{SW} = \mathbf{S} \cap \mathbf{W}$, $\mathbf{SC} = \mathbf{S} \cap \mathbf{Cx}$, $\mathbf{SE} = \mathbf{S} \cap \mathbf{E}$. Then

$$\mathcal{B}_d = \{\mathbf{NW}, \mathbf{NC}, \mathbf{NE}, \mathbf{CW}, \mathbf{CC}, \mathbf{CE}, \mathbf{SW}, \mathbf{SC}, \mathbf{SE}\}$$

is the set of atomic relations in $\mathcal{R}_d$.

For a relation R in $\mathcal{R}_d$, we define the x-component (y-component) of R, written $R|_x$ ($R|_y$), to be the smallest relation in $\mathcal{R}_x$ ($\mathcal{R}_y$) containing R. The weak composition of two atomic relations R, S in $\mathcal{R}_d$ can be computed as follows:

$$R \circ_w S = \bigcup\{T \cap T' : T \in \mathcal{B}_x, T' \in \mathcal{B}_y, T \subseteq R|_x \circ_w S|_x, T' \subseteq R|_y \circ_w S|_y\}$$

This suggests that the two components of $\mathcal{R}_d$ do not interact with each other. Moreover, we have the following result on the consistency of atomic networks over $\mathcal{R}_d$. Suppose $\Theta = \{x_i R_{ij} x_j : 1 \leq i, j \leq n\}$ is an atomic network over $\mathcal{R}_d$, i.e. all R_{ij} are in $\mathcal{B}_d$. We define the *x-component* of Θ, written $\Theta|_x$, to be $\{x_i R_{ij}|_x x_j : 1 \leq i, j \leq n\}$. The *y-component* of Θ, $\Theta|_y$, is defined in the same way.

Proposition 1. *Suppose* $\Theta = \{x_i R_{ij} x_j : 1 \leq i, j \leq n\}$ *is an atomic network over* $\mathcal{R}_d$. *Then* Θ *is consistent iff both* $\Theta|_x$ *and* $\Theta|_y$ *are consistent.*

Table 3. Weak composition tables of $\mathcal{B}_x$ (left) and $\mathcal{B}_y$ (right)

$\circ_w$	**W**	**E**	**Cx**
W	W	W,E,Cx	W,Cx
E	W,E,Cx	E	E,Cx
Cx	W,Cx	E,Cx	W,E,Cx

$\circ_w$	**N**	**S**	**Cy**
N	N	N,S,Cy	N,Cy
S	N,S,Cy	S	S,Cy
Cy	N,Cy	S,Cy	N,S,Cy

Proposition 2. *Suppose* $\Theta = \{x_i R_{ij} x_j : 1 \leq i, j \leq n\}$ *is an atomic network over* $\mathcal{R}_d$. *If* $\{a_i : 1 \leq i \leq n\}$ *is a realization of* $\Theta|_x$, *and* $\{b_i : 1 \leq i \leq n\}$ *is a realization of* $\Theta|_y$, *then* $\{I_x(a_i) \times I_y(b_i) : 1 \leq i \leq n\}$ *is a realization of* Θ, *where* $I_x(a)$ *and* $I_y(b)$, *resp., are the* x- *and* y-*projection of* a.

By the above two propositions, we know that in order to decide the consistency of an atomic network over $\mathcal{R}_d$, it is enough to consider the two corresponding component problems. In the next section, we show how to find a realization of a consistent atomic network over $\mathcal{R}_d$.

5   Consistency and Realization in the Cardinal Direction Calculus

We first note that any consistent atomic network over $\mathcal{R}_x$ is also path-consistent.

Lemma 1. *Suppose* $\Theta = \{x_i R_{ij} x_j : 1 \leq i, j \leq n\}$ *is an atomic network over* $\mathcal{R}_x$. *Then* Θ *is consistent only if it is path-consistent.*

Proof. Suppose Θ is consistent. For any i, j, k, we only need to show that $\mathsf{R}_{ij} \subseteq \mathsf{R}_{ik} \circ_w \mathsf{R}_{kj}$. Since Θ is consistent, we have a realization of Θ, say $\{a_i : 1 \leq i \leq n\}$. Clearly $a_i R_{ij} a_j$, $a_i R_{ik} a_k$, and $a_k R_{kj} a_j$ hold. By the definition of relational composition, we know $\mathsf{R}_{ij} \cap \mathsf{R}_{ik} \circ \mathsf{R}_{jk} \neq \varnothing$. Since $\mathsf{R}_{ik} \circ_w \mathsf{R}_{kj}$ is the smallest relation in $\mathcal{R}_x$ which contains $\mathsf{R}_{ik} \circ \mathsf{R}_{kj}$, we know R_{ij} is contained in $\mathsf{R}_{ik} \circ_w \mathsf{R}_{kj}$.

The converse of the above lemma is, however, not true.

Example 1. Let $\Theta = \{x_i R_{ij} x_j : 1 \leq i, j \leq 4\}$ be an atomic network such that $R_{12} = R_{34} = \mathbf{W}$, $R_{21} = R_{43} = \mathbf{E}$, and all the other relations are $\mathbf{Cx}$ (see Figure 1). Note that $\mathbf{Cx} \subset \mathbf{W} \circ_w \mathbf{Cx}$, $\mathbf{Cx} \subset \mathbf{Cx} \circ_w \mathbf{Cx}$. We know Θ is path-consistent. But the following lemma shows that Θ is inconsistent.

Lemma 2. *Suppose* a, b, c, d *are four bounded regions such that* $a\mathbf{W}b$, $b\mathbf{Cx}c$, $c\mathbf{W}d$. *Then* $a\mathbf{W}d$ *holds.*

Proof. By the above assumption, we know $\sup_x a < \inf_x b \leq \sup_x c < \inf_x d$, i.e. $\sup_x a < \inf_x d$. Therefore $a\mathbf{W}d$ holds.

As a result, we know a path-consistent atomic network Θ over $\mathcal{R}_x$ is consistent only if it satisfies the following rule.

$$(\forall i, j, k, m) x_i \mathbf{W} x_j \wedge x_j \mathbf{Cx} x_k \wedge x_k \mathbf{W} x_m \rightarrow x_i \mathbf{W} x_m \qquad (3)$$

It is interesting to see that the above condition is also sufficient.

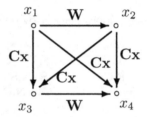

Fig. 1. A path-consistent but inconsistent atomic network over $\mathcal{R}_x$

Theorem 1. *Suppose Θ is an atomic network over $\mathcal{R}_x$. Then Θ is consistent iff it is path-consistent and satisfies (3).*

We prove this theorem by constructing a realization $\{a_i : 1 \leq i \leq n\}$ of Θ. In the rest of this section, if not otherwise stated, we assume Θ is an atomic network which is path-consistent and satisfies (3).

Set $V = \{x_i : 1 \leq i \leq n\}$ to be the set of variables in Θ. We define two relations on V as follows:

$$x_i \vartriangleleft^+ x_j \text{ iff } (\exists x_l) x_i \mathbf{W} x_l \wedge x_l \mathbf{Cx} x_j. \tag{4}$$

$$x_i \vartriangleleft^- x_j \text{ iff } (\exists x_l) x_i \mathbf{Cx} x_l \wedge x_l \mathbf{W} x_j. \tag{5}$$

Lemma 3. *Both $\vartriangleleft^+$ and $\vartriangleleft^-$ are irreflexive and transitive.*

Proof. Since $\vartriangleleft^+$ and $\vartriangleleft^-$ are similar, we take the first one as an example. The fact that $\vartriangleleft^+$ is irreflexive follows directly from the observation that $x_i \mathbf{W} x_l$ and $x_l \mathbf{Cx} x_i$ cannot hold together.

Given $x_i \vartriangleleft^+ x_j$ and $x_j \vartriangleleft^+ x_k$, we show $x_i \vartriangleleft^+ x_k$. By the definition of $\vartriangleleft^+$, we have x_l and x_m such that $x_i \mathbf{W} x_l$, $x_l \mathbf{Cx} x_j$, $x_j \mathbf{W} x_m$, and $x_m \mathbf{Cx} x_k$. Applying the rule (3), we know $x_i \mathbf{W} x_m$, hence $x_i \vartriangleleft^+ x_k$. This shows that $\vartriangleleft^+$ is transitive.

Using $\vartriangleleft^+$ and $\vartriangleleft^-$, we define two equivalence relations on V.

$$x_i \sim_{\vartriangleleft^+} x_j \text{ iff neither } x_i \vartriangleleft^+ x_j \text{ nor } x_j \vartriangleleft^+ x_i. \tag{6}$$

$$x_i \sim_{\vartriangleleft^-} x_j \text{ iff neither } x_i \vartriangleleft^- x_j \text{ nor } x_j \vartriangleleft^- x_i. \tag{7}$$

The following lemma guarantees that both $\vartriangleleft^+$ and $\vartriangleleft^-$ are equivalence relations.

Lemma 4. *Both $\sim_{\vartriangleleft^+}$ and $\sim_{\vartriangleleft^-}$ are equivalence relations on V.*

Proof. We first note that

$$x_i \sim_{\vartriangleleft^+} x_j \text{ iff } (\forall x_l) x_i \mathbf{W} x_l \leftrightarrow x_j \mathbf{W} x_l. \tag{8}$$

$$x_i \sim_{\vartriangleleft^-} x_j \text{ iff } (\forall x_l) x_l \mathbf{W} x_i \leftrightarrow x_l \mathbf{W} x_j. \tag{9}$$

Again, we take $\sim_{\vartriangleleft^+}$ as an example. Suppose $x_i \sim_{\vartriangleleft^+} x_j$ and $x_i \mathbf{W} x_l$. By $\neg(x_i \vartriangleleft^+ x_j)$, we know $\neg(x_l \mathbf{Cx} x_j)$. Moreover, $x_l \mathbf{W} x_j$ cannot hold. This is because, otherwise, we would have $x_i \mathbf{W} x_j$, which is a contradiction. Therefore we have $x_j \mathbf{W} x_l$. Similarly, $x_i \sim_{\lhd^+} x_j$ and $x_j \mathbf{W} x_l$ also imply $x_i \mathbf{W} x_l$.

On the other hand, suppose $x_i \lhd^+ x_j$. Then we have x_l such that $x_i \mathbf{W} x_l$ but $\neg(x_j \mathbf{W} x_l)$. Similarly, if $x_j \lhd^+ x_i$, then we have x_l such that $x_j \mathbf{W} x_l$ but $\neg(x_i \mathbf{W} x_l)$. Therefore (8) holds.

Lemma 5. *For $x_i \sim_{\lhd^*} x_i'$ and $x_j \sim_{\lhd^*} x_j'$, we have $x_i \lhd^* x_j$ iff $x_i' \lhd^* x_j'$, where $\lhd^* \in \{\lhd^+, \lhd^-\}$.*

Proof. Take $\lhd^+$ as an example. Suppose $x_i \lhd^+ x_j$. Then there exists x_l such that $x_i \mathbf{W} x_l \mathbf{C} x x_j$. Now since $x_i \sim_{\lhd^+} x_i'$ we have $x_i' \mathbf{W} x_l$. By $x_j \sim_{\lhd^+} x_j'$ and $x_l \mathbf{C} x x_j$, we know $x_j' \mathbf{W} x_l$ cannot hold. Therefore, $x_l \mathbf{W} x_j'$ or $x_l \mathbf{C} x x_j'$. Both cases imply $x_i' \lhd^+ x_j'$. The other direction is similar.

We now define two functions on V.

Definition 1. *For $x_i \in V$, inductively define $\delta^*(x_i)$ as follows:*

- $\delta^*(x_i) = 0$ iff $(\forall x_j) \neg (x_j \lhd^* x_i)$;
- $\delta^*(x_i) = k$ iff $(\forall x_j)[x_j \lhd^* x_i \rightarrow \delta^*(x_j) < k]$, *where $* \in \{+, -\}$.*

We have the following characterizations of $\sim_{\lhd^+}$ and $\lhd^+$ ($\sim_{\lhd^-}$ and $\lhd^-$, resp.), using δ^+ (δ^-, resp.).

Lemma 6. *For $x_i, x_j \in V$, we have*

- $\delta^*(x_i) = \delta^*(x_j)$ *iff $x_i \sim_{\lhd^*} x_j$;*
- $\delta^*(x_i) < \delta^*(x_j)$ *iff $x_i \lhd^* x_j$, where $* \in \{+, -\}$.*

Proof. This follows directly from the definitions of δ^+ and δ^-.

As a corollary, we have the following

Corollary 1. *Suppose $x \in V = \{x_i : 1 \le i \le n\}$ and $\delta^*(x) = k > 0$. Take $z_l \in V$ such that $\delta^*(z_l) = l$ for $l = 0, \cdots, k-1$. Then $z_0 \lhd^* z_1 \lhd^* \cdots \lhd^* z_{k-1} \lhd^* x$, where $* \in \{+, -\}$.*

The next two lemmas investigate the relation between atomic constraints in $\mathcal{R}_x$ and inequalities concerning the δ^* values of x_i and x_j.

Lemma 7. *For $x_i, x_j \in V$, if $x_i \mathbf{C} x x_j$, then $\delta^+(x_i) \ge \delta^-(x_j)$.*

Proof. Set $\delta^-(x_j) = k$. For convenience, we denote z_k and y_k for x_j and x_i, respectively. By Corollary 1, we have $z_l \in V$ ($l = 0, 1, \cdots, k-1$) such that $\delta^-(z_l) = l$ and $z_0 \lhd^- z_1 \lhd^- \cdots \lhd^- z_{k-1} \lhd^- x_j$ (see Fig. 2). By the definition of $\lhd^-$, we have $y_l \in V$ ($l = 0, 1, \cdots, k-1$) such that $z_l \mathbf{C} x y_l \mathbf{W} z_{l+1}$. But by $y_l \mathbf{W} z_{l+1} \mathbf{C} x y_{l+1}$ we know $y_l \lhd^+ y_{l+1}$. Therefore $\delta^+(x_i) \ge k = \delta^-(x_j)$.

Lemma 8. *For $x_i, x_j \in V$, if $x_i \mathbf{W} x_j$, then $\delta^+(x_i) < \delta^-(x_j)$.*

Proof. Set $\delta^+(x_i) = k$. For convenience, we denote z_k and y_k for x_i and x_j, respectively. By Corollary 1, we have $z_l \in V$ ($l = 0, 1, \cdots, k-1$) such that $\delta^+(z_l) = l$ and $z_0 \lhd^+ z_1 \lhd^+ \cdots \lhd^+ z_{k-1} \lhd^+ x_j$ (see Fig. 3).

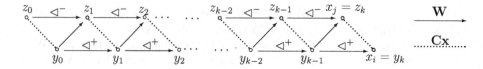

Fig. 2. Illustration of proof of Lemma 7

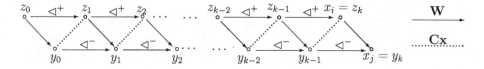

Fig. 3. Illustration of proof of Lemma 8

By the definition of $\lhd^+$, we have $y_l \in V$ $(l = 0, 1, \cdots, k - 1)$ such that $z_l \mathbf{W} y_l \mathbf{C} x z_{l+1}$. But by $y_l \mathbf{C} x z_{l+1} \mathbf{W} y_{l+1}$, we know $y_l \lhd^- y_{l+1}$. Therefore we have $z_0 \mathbf{W} y_0 \lhd^- y_1 \lhd^- \cdots \lhd^- y_k = x_j$, hence $\delta^+(x_i) = k < \delta^-(x_j)$.

In summary, we have the following

Proposition 3. *Suppose Θ is a path-consistent atomic network over $\mathcal{R}_x$ that satisfies (3). For $x_i, x_j \in V$, we have*

- *if $x_i \mathbf{C} x_j$, then $\min\{\delta^+(x_i), \delta^+(x_j)\} \geq \max\{\delta^-(x_i), \delta^-(x_j)\}$;*
- *if $x_i \mathbf{W} x_j$, then $\delta^-(x_i) \leq \delta^+(x_i) < \delta^-(x_j) \leq \delta^+(x_j)$;*
- *if $x_i \mathbf{E} x_j$, then $\delta^-(x_j) \leq \delta^+(x_j) < \delta^-(x_i) \leq \delta^+(x_i)$.*

For each i, define

$$a_i = [2\delta^-(x_i), 2\delta^+(x_i) + 1] \times \mathbb{R}. \tag{10}$$

The following proposition shows that $\{a_i : 1 \leq i \leq n\}$ is a realization of Θ.

Proposition 4. *Suppose Θ is a path-consistent atomic network over $\mathcal{R}_x$ that satisfies (3). Then $\{a_i : 1 \leq i \leq n\}$ as constructed in (10) is a realization of Θ.*

Proof. This follows directly from Proposition 3 and the definition of a_i.

Now we prove Theorem 2.

Proof (Proof of Theorem 2). The necessity part follows from Lemma 1 and Lemma 2. The sufficiency part follows from Proposition 4.

Similarly, suppose Θ is an atomic network over $\mathcal{R}_y$. Set V to be the set of variables in Θ. Write σ^+ and σ^-, resp., for the $\mathcal{R}_y$ counterparts of δ^+ and δ^-. For each i, define b_i, the counterpart of a_i, as follows:

$$b_i = \mathbb{R} \times [2\sigma^-(x_i), 2\sigma^+(x_i) + 1]. \tag{11}$$

The rule that corresponds to (3) is

$$(\forall i, j, k, m) x_i \mathbf{N} x_j \wedge x_j \mathbf{C} y x_k \wedge x_k \mathbf{N} x_m \rightarrow x_i \mathbf{N} x_m. \tag{12}$$

Then we have

Proposition 5. *Suppose Θ is a path-consistent atomic network over $\mathcal{R}_y$ that satisfies (12). Then $\{b_i : 1 \leq i \leq n\}$ as constructed in (11) is a realization of Θ.*

Theorem 2. *Suppose Θ is an atomic network over $\mathcal{R}_y$. Then Θ is consistent iff it is path-consistent and satisfies (12).*

By Proposition 1, we have the following characterization theorem.

Theorem 3. *Suppose Θ is an atomic network over $\mathcal{R}_d$. Then Θ is consistent iff it is path-consistent and satisfies (3) and (12). Moreover, $\{a_i \cap b_i : 1 \leq i \leq n\}$ is a realization of Θ, where a_i and b_i are constructed, resp., in (10) and (11).*

Remark 1. Golumbic and Sharmir [13] adopted a graph-theoretic approach to study reasoning problems in the interval algebra $\mathcal{A}_3$, which is isomorphic to our $\mathcal{R}_x$ and $\mathcal{R}_y$, and gave an $O(n^2)$ algorithm for determining whether a constraint network over $\{\{\mathbf{W}\}, \{\mathbf{E}\}, \{\mathbf{Cx}\}, \{\mathbf{W}, \mathbf{Cx}\}, \{\mathbf{E}, \mathbf{Cx}\}, \{\mathbf{W}, \mathbf{E}, \mathbf{Cx}\}\}$ is consistent. This result can be used for extending our result to larger subclasses of $\mathcal{TD}_{13}$.

6   Combining Topology with Directional Information

We now consider the smallest subalgebra of $\mathbf{Rel}(\mathbb{U})$ which contains the five atomic mereological relations and the four cardinal directional relations $\{\mathbf{N}, \mathbf{S}, \mathbf{W}, \mathbf{E}\}$. By (14) and (15), we know this algebra contains the following 13 atomic relations:

$$\mathbf{NW}, \mathbf{NC}, \mathbf{NE}, \mathbf{CW}, \mathbf{CE}, \mathbf{SW}, \mathbf{SC}, \mathbf{SE}, \mathbf{EQ}, \mathbf{PO}, \mathbf{PP}, \mathbf{PP}^{\smile}, \mathbf{CC} \cap \mathbf{DR}. \quad (13)$$

$$x\mathsf{R}y \to x\mathbf{DR}y \quad (\mathsf{R} \in \{\mathbf{N}, \mathbf{S}, \mathbf{W}, \mathbf{E}\}) \quad (14)$$
$$x\mathbf{O}y \to x\mathbf{CC}y. \quad (15)$$

We denote $\mathcal{TD}_{13}$ for this algebra and write $\mathcal{B}_{13}$ for the set of its atomic relations.

For each relation $\mathsf{R} \in \mathbf{Rel}(\mathbb{U})$, recall that we write $\mathsf{R}|_x$ ($\mathsf{R}|_y$, resp.) for the smallest relation in $\mathcal{R}_x$ ($\mathcal{R}_y$, resp.) which contains R. Similarly, we write $\mathsf{R}|_m$ for the smallest mereological relation which contains R, and write $\mathsf{R}|_d$ for the smallest relation in $\mathcal{R}_d$ which contains R. Clearly, if $\mathsf{R} \in \mathcal{TD}_{13}$, then $\mathsf{R}|_d = \mathsf{R}|_x \cap \mathsf{R}|_y$ and $\mathsf{R} = \mathsf{R}|_m \cap \mathsf{R}|_x \cap \mathsf{R}|_y$. Furthermore, if R is an atomic relation in $\mathcal{TD}_{13}$, then $\mathsf{R}|_m$, $\mathsf{R}|_d$, $\mathsf{R}|_x$, and $\mathsf{R}|_y$ are atomic relations in RCC5, $\mathcal{R}_d$, $\mathcal{R}_x$, and $\mathcal{R}_y$, respectively.

Let $\Theta = \{x_i \mathsf{R}_{ij} x_j : \mathsf{R}_{ij} \in \mathcal{B}_{13}, 1 \leq i, j \leq n\}$ be an atomic network over $\mathcal{TD}_{13}$. We now find a method for deciding the consistency of Θ. We write

$$\Theta|_m = \{x_i \mathsf{R}_{ij}|_m x_j : \mathsf{R}_{ij} \in \mathcal{B}_{13}, 1 \leq i, j \leq n\};$$
$$\Theta|_d = \{x_i \mathsf{R}_{ij}|_d x_j : \mathsf{R}_{ij} \in \mathcal{B}_{13}, 1 \leq i, j \leq n\};$$
$$\Theta|_x = \{x_i \mathsf{R}_{ij}|_x x_j : \mathsf{R}_{ij} \in \mathcal{B}_{13}, 1 \leq i, j \leq n\};$$
$$\Theta|_y = \{x_i \mathsf{R}_{ij}|_y x_j : \mathsf{R}_{ij} \in \mathcal{B}_{13}, 1 \leq i, j \leq n\}.$$

Lemma 9. *Let* $\Theta = \{x_i R_{ij} x_j : R_{ij} \in \mathcal{B}_{13}, 1 \le i, j \le n\}$ *be an atomic network over* $\mathcal{TD}_{13}$. *If* Θ *is consistent, then* $\Theta|_m$, $\Theta|_x$, $\Theta|_y$ *are also consistent.*

By (14) and (15) we know mereology and orientation are not independent. It is no surprise that the converse of the above result is not true.

Example 2. Let Θ be the atomic network over $\mathcal{TD}_{13}$ described in Fig. 4. For three regions a, b, c, if $a\mathbf{PP}b$ and $b\mathbf{N}c$, then $a\mathbf{N}c$. This shows that Θ is inconsistent. But $\Theta|_m$, $\Theta|_x$, and $\Theta|_y$ are all consistent.

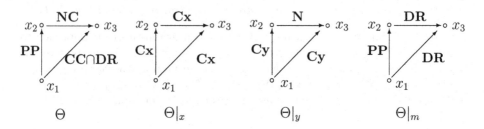

Fig. 4. An inconsistent atomic network over $\mathcal{TD}_{13}$

We now have the following result.

Proposition 6. *Let* $\Theta = \{x_i R_{ij} x_j : R_{ij} \in \mathcal{B}_{13}, 1 \le i, j \le n\}$ *be an atomic network over* $\mathcal{TD}_{13}$. *Suppose* $\Theta|_m$, $\Theta|_x$, $\Theta|_y$ *are all consistent. If* Θ *satisfies (16), then* Θ *is consistent.*

$$(\forall i, j, k) x_i \mathbf{P} x_j \wedge x_j R x_k \to x_i R x_k \quad (R \in \{\mathbf{N}, \mathbf{S}, \mathbf{W}, \mathbf{E}\}) \quad (16)$$

Proof. Without loss of generality, we assume that no R_{ij} is **EQ**. Since $\Theta|_x$ and $\Theta|_y$ are consistent, we know $\Theta|_d$ is also consistent. Let $\{a_i \cap b_i : 1 \le i \le n\}$ be the realization of $\Theta|_d$ as given in Theorem 3, where a_i and b_i are defined in (10) and (11), resp.

We note here that each $c_i \equiv a_i \cap b_i$ is a rectangle. Moreover, if $x_i \mathbf{PP} x_j$, then $c_i \subseteq c_j$. This is because, by (16), we have $\delta^-(x_j) \le \delta^-(x_i) \le \delta^+(x_i) \le \delta^+(x_j)$ and $\sigma^-(x_j) \le \sigma^-(x_i) \le \sigma^+(x_i) \le \sigma^+(x_j)$.

For $i = 1$ to n, choose four new points $p_i^1, p_i^2, p_i^3, p_i^4$ in c_i such that c_i is the MBR of $c_i' \equiv \{p_i^1, p_i^2, p_i^3, p_i^4\}$. These four points can be chosen respectively from the four edges of c_i. Note that the definition of cardinal relations can be easily extended to any bounded subsets of the plane. Since c_i is the MBR of c_i' for each i, we have $c_i' R c_j'$ iff $c_i R c_j$ for any directional relation R.

For any two i, j, if $x_i \mathbf{PO} x_j$, then choose two new points $p_{ij}, p_{ji} \in c_i \cap c_j$. For each i, define $c_i'' = c_i' \cup \{p_{ij}, p_{ji} : x_i \mathbf{PO} x_j\}$. Note that c_i is the MBR of c_i'', and $c_i'' \cap c_j'' \ne \varnothing$ iff $x_i \mathbf{PO} x_j$.

Next, for each i, we define $c_i^* = \bigcup\{c_j'' : x_j \mathbf{PP} x_i \text{ or } i = j\}$. Then c_i is the MBR of c_i^*, and hence $c_i^* R c_j^*$ iff $c_i R c_j$ for any directional relation R and any i, j.

We stress that each c_i^* contains finite points, and hence is not a region. Let $\epsilon > 0$ be the smallest distance between two different points in $P = \bigcup\{c_i^* : 1 \le i \le n\}$.

For any point p, let $B(p, \epsilon/3)$ be the closed disk centered at p with a radius $\epsilon/3$. For each i, define $r_i = \bigcup\{B(p, \epsilon/3) : p \in c_i^*\}$. Then r_i is a bounded region, and the directional relation between r_i and r_j is the same as that between c_i^* and c_j^*. Furthermore, for any two i, j, it is straightforward to check that $r_i \subseteq r_j$ iff $c_i^* \subseteq c_j^*$, and $r_i^\circ \cap r_j^\circ = \varnothing$ iff $c_i^* \cap c_j^* = \varnothing$.

Therefore $\{r_i : 1 \leq i \leq n\}$ is a realization of Θ in $\mathbb{U}$.

We now have the main result of this paper.

Theorem 4. *Let $\Theta = \{x_i R_{ij} x_j : R_{ij} \in \mathcal{B}_{13}, 1 \leq i, j \leq n\}$ be an atomic network over $\mathcal{TD}_{13}$. Then Θ is consistent iff $\Theta|_m$, $\Theta|_x$, $\Theta|_y$ are all path-consistent, and Θ satisfies (3,12,16).*

Proof. This follows directly from Proposition 6.

7   Conclusions and Further Work

In this paper we proposed a relation model that contains the five basic mereological relations and the four cardinal directional relations *north, south, west, east*. We showed that the consistency of atomic network can be decided by applying a path-consistency algorithm and three additional rules. We also gave a method for constructing realizations of consistent atomic networks.

Our results can be compared to the work of Sistla and Yu [14]. Write $*$ for the universal relation, and define $\mathcal{S}$ to be a subset of $\mathcal{TD}_{13}$ such that $\mathcal{S} = \{\mathbf{N}, \mathbf{S}, \mathbf{W}, \mathbf{E}, \mathbf{P}, \mathbf{O}, \mathbf{P}^\sim, *\}$. Sistla and Yu investigate reasoning problems over $\mathcal{S}^\cap$, which is the smallest subset of $\mathcal{TD}_{13}$ which contains $\mathcal{S}$ and is closed under intersections. Indeed, they give a complete set of rules for deciding the consistency of constraint networks over $\mathcal{S}^\cap$. Note that $\mathcal{S}^\cap$ does not contain the atomic relations $\mathbf{NC}, \mathbf{SC}, \mathbf{CW}, \mathbf{CE}, \mathbf{PO}, \mathbf{PP}, \mathbf{PP}^\sim$. Our result is 'orthogonal' to that of Sistla and Yu.

Further work will consider how to extend the approach introduced in this paper to topological RCC8 relations [1] and the cardinal directional calculus of Goyal and Egenhofer [11, 12].

References

[1] Randell, D., Cui, Z., Cohn, A.: A spatial logic based on regions and connection. In Nebel, B., Swartout, W., Rich, C., eds.: Proceedings of the 3rd International Conference on Knowledge Representation and Reasoning, Los Allos, Morgan Kaufmann (1992) 165–176

[2] Düntsch, I., Wang, H., McCloskey, S.: A relation-algebraic approach to the Region Connection Calculus. Theoretical Computer Science **255** (2001) 63–83

[3] Li, S., Ying, M.: Region Connection Calculus: Its models and composition table. Artificial Intelligence **145**(1-2) (2003) 121–146

[4] Renz, J., Nebel, B.: On the complexity of qualitative spatial reasoning: A maximal tractable fragment of the Region Connection Calculus. Artificial Intelligence **108** (1999) 69–123

264   S. Li

[5] Li, S.: On topological consistency and realization. Constraints **11**(1) (2006) 31–51
[6] Li, S., Wang, H.: RCC8 binary constraint network can be consistently extended. Artif. Intell. **170**(1) (2006) 1–18
[7] Frank, A.U.: Qualitative spatial reasoning about cardinal directions. In: Proceedings of the 7th Austrian Conference on Artificial Intelligence. (1991) 157–167
[8] Ligozat, G.: Reasoning about cardinal directions. J. Vis. Lang. Comput. **9**(1) (1998) 23–44
[9] Balbiani, P., Condotta, J.F., del Cerro, L.F.: A new tractable subclass of the rectangle algebra. In Dean, T., ed.: IJCAI, Morgan Kaufmann (1999) 442–447
[10] Allen, J.: Maintaining knowledge about temporal intervals. Communications of the ACM **26** (1983) 832–843
[11] Goyal, R., Egenhofer, M.: The direction-relation matrix: A representation for directions relations between extended spatial objects. In: The Annual Assembly and the Summer Retreat of University Consortium for Geographic Information Systems Science. (1997)
[12] Skiadopoulos, S., Koubarakis, M.: On the consistency of cardinal direction constraints. Artif. Intell. **163**(1) (2005) 91–135
[13] Golumbic, M.C., Shamir, R.: Complexity and algorithms for reasoning about time: a graph-theoretic approach. J. ACM **40**(5) (1993) 1108–1133
[14] Sistla, A.P., Yu, C.T.: Reasoning about qualitative spatial relationships. Journal of Automated Reasoning **25**(4) (2000) 291–328

Measuring Conflict Between Possibilistic Uncertain Information Through Belief Function Theory

Weiru Liu

School of Electronics, Electrical Engineering and Computer Science,
Queen's University Belfast,
Belfast, BT7 1NN, UK
w.liu@qub.ac.uk

Abstract. Dempster Shafer theory of evidence (DS theory) and possibility theory are two main formalisms in modelling and reasoning with uncertain information. These two theories are inter-related as already observed and discussed in many papers (e.g. [DP82, DP88b]). One aspect that is common to the two theories is how to quantitatively measure the degree of conflict (or inconsistency) between pieces of uncertain information. In DS theory, traditionally this is judged by the combined mass value assigned to the emptyset. Recently, two new approaches to measuring the conflict among belief functions are proposed in [JGB01, Liu06]. The former provides a distance-based method to quantify how close a pair of beliefs is while the latter deploys a pair of values to reveal the degree of conflict of two belief functions. On the other hand, in possibility theory, this is done through measuring the degree of inconsistency of merged information. However, this measure is not sufficient when pairs of uncertain information have the same degree of inconsistency. At present, there are no other alternatives that can further differentiate them, except an initiative based on coherence-intervals ([HL05a, HL05b]). In this paper, we investigate how the two new approaches developed in DS theory can be used to measure the conflict among possibilistic uncertain information. We also examine how the reliability of a source can be assessed in order to weaken a source when a conflict arises.

1 Introduction

Pieces of uncertain information that come from different sources often do not agree with each other completely. There can be many reasons for this, such as, inaccuracy in sensor data reading, nature errors occurred in experiments, reliabilities of sources, etc. When inconsistent information needs to be merged, assessing the degree of conflict among information plays a crucial role in deciding which combination mode would be best suited [DP94].

In possibility theory, the well established method is to measure the degree of inconsistency between two pieces of uncertain information. This measure is not enough when multiple pairs of uncertain information have the same degree of inconsistency. We need to further identify subsets of sources that contain information more "close" to each other. Currently, there are no approaches to fulfilling this objective, except a coherence-interval based scenario proposed in [HL05a, HL05b]. More robust methods are needed to measure the conflict among pieces of information more effectively.

J. Lang, F. Lin, and J. Wang (Eds.): KSEM 2006, LNAI 4092, pp. 265–277, 2006.

Two fundamental functions defined in possibility theory are possibility measures and necessity measures. In the context of Dempster-Shafer theory of evidence (DS theory for short), these two measures are special cases of plausibility and belief functions. Naturally, DS theory faces the same question as how conflict should be measured among belief functions. Recently, two different approaches were proposed to quantitatively judge how conflict a pair of uncertain information is [JGB01, Liu06]. One approach calculates the distance between two belief functions and another evaluates a pair of values consisting of the difference between betting commitments and a combined mass assigned to the emptyset. Both methods provide a better measure about the conflict among belief functions then the traditionally used approach in DS theory, that is, the use of the mass value assigned to the emptyset after combination.

In this paper, we take the advantage that possibility and necessity measures are special cases of plausibility and belief functions and investigate the effect of applying the two new approaches introduced above in DS theory to possibilistic uncertain information. Properties and potential applications of this investigation are explored too. In addition, we look at the issues of assessing the reliability of sources to assist resolving conflict through weakening the opinion from less reliable sources.

We will proceed as follows: in Section 2, we review the basics in possibility theory and DS theory. In Section 3, we present the relationships and properties between the two theories. In Section 4, we investigate how the approaches for inconsistent assessment in DS theory can be applied to possibilistic uncertain information. In Section 5, we examine how individual agent's judgement can be assessed, in order to discount or discarded some sources in a highly conflict situation. Finally in Section 6, we summarize the main contributions of the paper.

2   Brief Review of DS Theory and Possibility Theory

2.1   Basics of Dempster-Shafer Theory

Let Ω be a finite set containing mutually exclusive and exhaustive solutions to a question. Ω is called the *frame of discernment*.

A basic belief assignment (bba) [Sme04] is a mapping $m : 2^\Omega \to [0, 1]$ that satisfies $\sum_{A \subseteq \Omega} m(A) = 1$. In Shafer's original definition which he called *the basic probability assignment* [Sha76], condition $m(\emptyset) = 0$ is required. Recently, some of the papers on Dempster-Shafer theory, especially since the establishment of the Transferable Belief Model (TBM) [SK94], condition $m(\emptyset) = 0$ is often omitted. A bba with $m(\emptyset) = 0$ is called a normalized bba and is known as a *mass function*.

$m(A)$ defines the amount of belief to the subset A exactly, not including any subsets in A. The total belief in a subset A is the sum of all the mass assigned to all subsets of A. This function is known as *a belief function* and is defined as $Bel : 2^\Omega \to [0, 1]$.

$$Bel(A) = \Sigma_{B \subseteq A} m(B)$$

When $m(A) > 0$, A is referred to as a *focal element* of the belief function.

A *plausibility function*, denoted Pl, is defined as follows, where $Pl : 2^\Omega \to [0, 1]$.

$$Pl(A) = 1 - Bel(\bar{A}) = \Sigma_{B \cap A \neq \emptyset}\, m(B)$$

where $\bar{A}$ is the complementary set of A.

Two pieces of evidence expressed in bbas from distinct sources are usually combined using Dempster's combination rule. The rule is stated as follows.

Definition 1. *Let m_1 and m_2 be two bbas, and let $m_1 \oplus m_2$ be the combined bba.*

$$m_1 \oplus m_2(C) = \frac{\Sigma_{A \cap B = C}\, (m_1(A) \times m_2(B))}{1 - \Sigma_{A \cap B = \emptyset}\, (m_1(A) \times m_2(B))}$$

When $m_1 \oplus m_2(\emptyset) = \Sigma_{A \cap B = \emptyset}\, (m_1(A) \times m_2(B)) = 1$, the two pieces of evidence are totally contradict with each other and cannot be combined with the rule.

Definition 2. *[Sme04] Let m be a bba on Ω. Its associated pignistic probability function $BetP_m : \Omega \to [0, 1]$ is defined as*

$$BetP_m(\omega) = \sum_{A \subseteq \Omega, \omega \in A} \frac{1}{|A|} \frac{m(A)}{1 - m(\emptyset)}, \quad m(\emptyset) \neq 1 \tag{1}$$

where $|A|$ is the cardinality of subset A.

The transformation from m to $BetP_m$ is called the *pignistic transformation*. When an initial bba gives $m(\emptyset) = 0$, $\frac{m(A)}{1-m(\emptyset)}$ is reduced to $m(A)$. Value $BetP_m(A)$ is referred to as the *betting commitment to A*.

2.2 Possibility Theory

Possibility theory is another popular choice for representing uncertain information ([DP88a, BDP97], etc). At the semantic level, a basic function in possibility theory is a *possibility distribution* denoted as π which assigns each possible world in the frame of discernment Ω a value in $[0, 1]$ (or a set of graded values).

From a possibility distribution, two measures are derived, a possibility measure (demoted as Π) and a necessity measure (denoted as N). The former estimates to what extent the true event is believed to be in the subset and the latter evaluates the degree of necessity that the subset is true. The relationships between π, Π and N are as follows.

$$\Pi(A) = \max(\{\pi(\omega)|\omega \in A\}) \text{ and } N(A) = 1 - \Pi(\bar{A}) \tag{2}$$

$$\Pi(2^\Omega) = 1 \text{ and } \Pi(\emptyset) = 0 \tag{3}$$

$$\Pi(A \cup B) = \max(\Pi(A), \Pi(B)) \text{ and } N(A \cap B) = \min(N(A), N(B)) \tag{4}$$

The usual condition associated with π is that there exists $\omega_0 \in \Omega$ such that $\pi(\omega_0) = 1$, and in which case π is said to be normal. It is not always possible to obtain a possibility distribution from a piece of evidence. Most of the time, uncertain information is expressed as a set of weighted subsets (or a set of weighted formulas in possibilistic logic). A weighted subset (A, α) is interpreted as that the necessity degree of A is at least to α, that is, $N(A) \geq \alpha$.

A piece of possibilistic uncertain information usually specifies a partial necessity measure. Let $\Omega = \{\omega_1, .., \omega_n\}$, and also let $A_i = \{\omega_{i_1}, .., \omega_{i_x}\}$ in order to make the subsequent description simpler. In this way, a set of weighted subsets constructed from a piece of uncertain information is defined as $\{(A_i, \alpha_i), i = 1, .., p\}$, where α_i is the lower bound on the degree of necessity $N(A_i)$. In the following, we call a set of weighted subsets a *possibilistic information base (PIB for short)* and denote such a base as K.

There is normally a family of possibility distributions associated with a given set of weighted subsets, with each of the distributions satisfying the condition

$$1 - \max\{\pi(\omega) | \omega \in \bar{A}_i\} \geq \alpha_i$$

which guarantees that $N(A_i) \geq \alpha_i$. Let $\{\pi_j, j = 1, .., m\}$ be all the possibility distributions that are compatible with $\{(A_i, \alpha_i), i = 1, .., p\}$. A possibility distribution $\pi_l \in \{\pi_j, j = 1, .., m\}$ is said to be the least specific possibility distribution among $\{\pi_j, j = 1, .., m\}$ if $\nexists \pi_t \in \{\pi_j, j = 1, .., m\}, \pi_t \neq \pi_l$ such that $\forall \omega, \pi_t(\omega) \geq \pi_l(\omega)$.

A common method to select one of the compatible possibility distributions is to use the *minimum specificity principle* [DP87] which allocates the greatest possibility degrees in agreement with the constraints $N(A_i) \geq \alpha_i$. This possibility distribution always exists and is defined as ([DP87, BDP97])

$$\forall \omega \in \Omega, \pi(\omega) = \begin{cases} \min\{1 - \alpha_i | \omega \notin A_i\} \\ \quad = 1 - \max\{\alpha_i | \omega \notin A_i\} \quad \text{when } \exists A_i \text{ s. t. } \omega \notin A_i \\ 1 \hspace{5.5cm} \text{otherwise} \end{cases} \quad (5)$$

A possibility distribution is not normal if $\forall \omega, \pi(\omega) < 1$. The value $1 - \max_{\omega \in \Omega} \pi(\omega)$ is called *the degree of inconsistency* of the PIB and is denoted as $Inc(K)$. Given a PIB $\{(A_i, a_i), i = 1, .., p\}$, this PIB is *consistent* iff $\cap_i A_i \neq \emptyset$.

The two basic combination modes in possibility theory are the *conjunctive* and the *disjunctive* modes for merging possibility distributions ([BDP97]) when n possibility distributions are given on the same frame of discernment. For example, if we choose *min* and *max* as the conjunctive and disjunctive operators respectively, then

$$\forall \omega \in \Omega, \pi_{cm}(\omega) = \min_{i=1}^{n}(\pi_i(\omega)), \ \forall \omega \in \Omega, \pi_{dm}(\omega) = \max_{i=1}^{n}(\pi_i(\omega)) \quad (6)$$

A conjunction operator is used when it is believed that all sources are reliable and these sources agree with each other whilst a disjunctive operator is applied when it is believed that some sources are reliable but it is not known which of these sources are. A conjunction operator can lead to a new possibility distribution that is not normal when some sources are not in agreement, even though all the original possibility distributions are normal. When this happens, the merged possibility distribution expresses an inconsistency among the sources.

3   Belief Functions Verse Necessity Measures

In [Sha76], a belief function is called a *consonant function* if its focal elements are nested. That is, if $S_1, S_2, ..., S_n$ are the focal elements with S_{i+1} containing more elements than S_i, then $S_1 \subset S_2 \subset .. \subset S_n$. Let Bel be a consonant function, and Pl be its corresponding plausibility function, Bel and Pl have the following properties:

$$Bel(A \cap B) = \min(Bel(A), Bel(B)) \text{ for all } A, B \subseteq 2^{\Omega}.$$

$$Pl(A \cup B) = \max(Pl(A), Pl(B)) \text{ for all } A, B \subseteq 2^{\Omega}.$$

These two properties are exactly the requirements of necessity and possibility measures in possibility theory. Necessity and possibility measures are special cases of belief and plausibility functions.

Furthermore, a *contour function* $f : \Omega \rightarrow [0, 1]$, for a consonant function is defined through equation

$$f(\omega) = Pl(\{\omega\})$$

For a subset $A \subseteq \Omega$,

$$Pl(A) = \max_{\omega \in A} f(\omega) \tag{7}$$

Equation (7) matches the definition of possibility measure from a possibility distribution, so a contour function is a possibility distribution.

The procedure to derive a bba from a possibility distribution is stated below.

Proposition 1. *([HL06]) Let π be a possibility distribution on frame of discernment Ω and is normal. Let B_1, B_2,.., B_p and B_{p+1} be disjoint subsets of Ω such that $\pi(\omega_i) = \pi(\omega_j)$ when both $\omega_i, \omega_j \in B_i$; $\pi(\omega_i) > \pi(\omega_j)$ if $\omega_i \in B_i$ and $\omega_j \in B_{i+1}$; $\pi(\omega_i) = 0$ if $\omega_i \in B_{p+1}$ then the following properties hold:*

1. *Let $A_i = \cup\{B_j | j = 1, .., i\}$ for $i = 1, 2, .., p$, then subsets $A_1, A_2, .., A_p$ are nested;*
2. *Let $m(A_i) = \pi(\omega_i) - \pi(\omega_j)$ where $\omega_i \in B_i$ and $\omega_j \in B_{i+1}$ for $i = 1, .., p-1$. Let $m(A_p) = \pi(\omega)$ where $\omega \in B_p$. Then m is a bba on focal elements A_i;*
3. *Let Bel be the belief function corresponding to m defined above, then Bel is a consonant function.*

Subset B_1 (or focal element A_1) is called the *core* of possibility distribution π which contains the most plausible interpretations [BK01]. The nature of Proposition 1 was first observed in [DP82] where the relationship between the possibility theory and DS theory was discussed. This relationship was further referred to in several papers subsequently ([DP88b, DP98b, DNP00]).

Example 1. *Let π be a possibility distribution on $\Omega = \{\omega_1, ..., \omega_4\}$ where*

$$\pi(\omega_1) = 0.7, \pi(\omega_2) = 1.0, \pi(\omega_3) = 0.8, \pi(\omega_4) = 0.7$$

The disjoint subsets for π are

$$B_1 = \{\omega_2\}, \quad B_2 = \{\omega_3\}, \quad B_3 = \{\omega_1, \omega_4\}$$

and the corresponding focal elements as well as bba m are

$$A_1 = B_1, \quad A_2 = B_1 \cup B_2, A_3 = B_1 \cup B_2 \cup B_3$$
$$m(A_1) = 0.2, m(A_2) = 0.1, \quad m(A_3) = 0.7$$

Proposition 2. *Let π be a possibility distribution on frame of discernment Ω and be normal. Let $BetP$ be the pignistic probabilistic function of the corresponding bba m derived from π. Then $BetP(\omega_i) \geq BetP(\omega_j)$ iff $\pi(\omega_i) \geq \pi(\omega_j)$.*

Proof. Let the collection of disjoint subsets satisfying conditions in Proposition 1 be $B_1, B_2, \ldots, B_{p+1}$ and let the set of focal elements be $A_1, A_2, \ldots, A_p$. Without losing generality, we assume $\omega_i \in B_1$ and $\omega_j \in B_2$, so $\pi(\omega_i) \geq \pi(\omega_j)$. Based on Equation 1,

$$BetP(\omega_i) = \frac{m(A_1)}{|A_1|} + \frac{m(A_2)}{|A_2|} + \ldots + \frac{m(A_p)}{|A_p|}$$

and

$$BetP(\omega_j) = \frac{m(A_2)}{|A_2|} + \ldots + \frac{m(A_p)}{|A_p|}$$

It is obvious that $BetP(\omega_i) \geq BetP(\omega_j)$. $\diamond$

In fact, if the elements in Ω are ordered in the way such that $\pi(\omega_1) \geq \pi(\omega_2) \geq \ldots \geq \pi(\omega_n)$, then the inequality $BetP(\omega_1) \geq BetP(\omega_2) \geq \ldots \geq BetP(\omega_n)$ holds. Proposition 2 is valid even when a possibility distribution is not normal. In that case, $m(\emptyset) = 1 - \pi(\omega | \omega \in B_1)$. This proposition says that the more plausible a possible world is, the more betting commitment it carries.

Proposition 3. *Let π_1 and π_2 be two possibility distributions on frame of discernment Ω for two PIBs and be normal. Let K be the conjunctively merged PIB. Assume m_1 and m_2 are the bbas derived from π_1 and π_2 respectively. Then the following properties hold.*

1. *$Inc(K) = 0$ iff $m_1 \oplus m_2(\emptyset) = 0$*
2. *$Inc(K) = 1$ iff $m_1 \oplus m_2(\emptyset) = 1$*
3. *$Inc(K) > 0$ iff $m_1 \oplus m_2(\emptyset) > 0$*

Proof. We assume the conjunctive operator used in the proof is *min*. In fact, this proof is equally applicable to the other two commonly used conjunctive operators, namely, *product* and *linear product*.

Let B_{π_1} and B_{π_2} be the two cores for possibility distributions π_1 and π_2 respectively.

We first prove $Inc(K) = 0$ iff $m_1 \oplus m_2(\emptyset) = 0$. When $Inc(K) = 0$, the conjunctively merged possibility distribution of π_1 and π_2 is normal and there exists a $\omega \in \Omega$ such that $\omega \in B_{\pi_1} \cap B_{\pi_2}$. Recall that B_{π_1} and B_{π_2} are the respective smallest focal elements for m_1 and m_2, then for any A_{m_1} and A_{m_2}, two focal elements associated with m_1 and m_2 respectively, $A_{m_1} \cap A_{m_2} \neq \emptyset$. So $m_1 \oplus m_2(\emptyset) = 0$.

On the other hand, when $m_1 \oplus m_2(\emptyset) = 0$, $B_{\pi_1} \cap B_{\pi_2} \neq \emptyset$. Therefore, $\exists \omega$ such that $\omega \in B_{\pi_1} \cap B_{\pi_2}$. That is, $\pi_1(\omega) = \pi_2(\omega) = 1$ which implies $Inc(K) = 0$.

Now we prove $Inc(K) = 1$ iff $m_1 \oplus m_2(\emptyset) = 1$. When $Inc(K) = 1$, the conjunctively merged possibility distribution of π_1 and π_2 is totally inconsistent, then for any $\omega \in \Omega$ either $\pi_1(\omega) = 0$ or $\pi_2(\omega) = 0$ or both. Let $A_{m_1}^p$ and $A_{m_2}^q$ be the largest focal elements of m_1 and m_2 respectively, then $\omega \notin A_{m_1}^p \cap A_{m_2}^q$, so $A_{m_1}^p \cap A_{m_2}^q = \emptyset$. Therefore, for A_{m_1} and A_{m_2}, two focal elements associated with m_1 and m_2 respectively, $A_{m_1} \cap A_{m_2} = \emptyset$ which implies $m_1 \oplus m_2(\emptyset) = 1$.

Similar to this proof procedure, it is easy to show that when $m_1 \oplus m_2(\emptyset) = 1$, $Inc(B) = 1$.

Finally, we prove $Inc(K) > 0$ iff $m_1 \oplus m_2(\emptyset) > 0$. When $Inc(K) > 0$ there does not exist a $\omega \in \Omega$ such that $\omega \in B_{\pi_1} \cap B_{\pi_2}$ (otherwise $min(\pi_1(\omega), \pi_2(\omega)) = 1$ which violates the assumption). Since B_{π_1} and B_{π_2} are two smallest focal elements for m_1 and m_2 respectively, $B_{\pi_1} \cap B_{\pi_2} = \emptyset$ when combining these two mass functions, therefore $m(\emptyset) > 0$.

When $m(\emptyset) > 0$, we at least have $B_{\pi_1} \cap B_{\pi_2} = \emptyset$. So for any $\omega \in B_{\pi_1}$ (resp. B_{π_2}), it implies $\omega \notin B_{\pi_2}$ (resp. B_{π_1}), it follows immediately that $min(\pi_1(\omega), \pi_2(\omega)) < 1$. $\diamond$

In general conclusion $Inc(K_{12}) \geq Inc(K_{13}) \Rightarrow m_1 \oplus m_2(\emptyset) \geq m_1 \oplus m_3(\emptyset)$ does not hold.

4   Measuring Conflict Between PIBs

The conflict between uncertain information in possibility theory is measured by the degree of inconsistency induced by the information. However, this measure can only tell if two (or multiple) sources are inconsistent and to what extent, it cannot further differentiate pairs of PIBs that have the same degree of inconsistency.

Example 2. *Consider a set of four PIBs as detailed below with* $\Omega = \{\omega_1, .., \omega_4\}$.

$$K_1^1 = \{(\{\omega_1, \omega_2\}, 0.4), (\{\omega_2, \omega_3, \omega_4\}, 0.5), (\{\omega_2\}, 0.4)\}$$
$$K_2^1 = \{(\{\omega_1, \omega_2\}, 0.3), (\{\omega_1, \omega_2, \omega_3\}, 0.5), (\{\omega_1, \omega_4\}, 0.4)\}$$
$$K_3^1 = \{(\{\omega_1, \omega_3\}, 0.4), (\{\omega_2, \omega_3, \omega_4\}, 0.5), (\{\omega_3\}, 0.4)\}$$
$$K_4^1 = \{(\{\omega_2, \omega_4\}, 0.3), (\{\omega_1, \omega_3, \omega_4\}, 0.5), (\{\omega_1, \omega_4\}, 0.4)\}$$

Let $\pi_1^1, \pi_2^1, \pi_3^1$ *and* π_4^1 *be the corresponding possibility distributions of these PIBs as detailed in Table 1.*

Table 1. Four possibility distributions for the four PIBs

PIB	π	ω_1	ω_2	ω_3	ω_4
K_1^1	π_1^1	0.5	1.0	0.6	0.6
K_2^1	π_2^1	1.0	0.6	0.6	0.5
K_3^1	π_3^1	0.5	0.6	1.0	0.6
K_4^1	π_4^1	0.6	0.5	0.6	1.0

Combining any pair of the four possibility distributions conjunctively (e.g., min) produces an unnormalized possibility distribution and in all the cases, the degree of inconsistency is 0.4 (using min operator). It is, therefore, difficult to tell which two or more PIBs may be more consistent.

In this section, we deploy two approaches developed in DS theory on measuring conflict among bbas to uncertain information in possibility theory.

4.1   A Distance-Based Measure of Conflict

In [JGB01], a method for measuring the distance between bbas was proposed. This distance is defined as

$$d_{BPA}(m_1, m_2) = \sqrt{\frac{1}{2}(\tilde{m}_1 - \tilde{m}_2)^T \overset{D}{=} (\tilde{m}_1 - \tilde{m}_2)} \tag{8}$$

where $\overset{D}{=}$ is a $2^\Omega \times 2^\Omega$ dimensional matrix with $d[i,j] = |A \cap B|/|A \cup B|$ (note: it is defined that $|\emptyset \cap \emptyset|/|\emptyset \cup \emptyset| = 0$), and $A \in 2^\Omega$ and $B \in 2^\Omega$ are the names of columns and rows respectively. Given a bba m on frame Ω, $\tilde{m}$ is a 2^Ω-dimensional column vector (can also be called a $2^\Omega \times 1$ matrix) with $m_{A \in 2^\Omega}(A)$ as its 2^Ω coordinates.

$(\tilde{m}_1 - \tilde{m}_2)$ stands for vector subtraction and $(\tilde{m})^T$ is the transpose of vector (or matrix) $\tilde{m}$. When $\tilde{m}$ is a 2^Ω-dimensional column vector, $(\tilde{m})^T$ is its 2^Ω-dimensional row vector with the same coordinates. $((\tilde{m})^T \overset{D}{=} \tilde{m})$ therefore is the result of normal matrix multiplications (twice).

For example, let $\Omega = \{a, b\}$ be the frame and let $m(\{a\}) = 0.7, m(\Omega) = 0.3$ be a bba. Then $\tilde{m} = \begin{bmatrix} 0 \\ 0.7 \\ 0 \\ 0.3 \end{bmatrix}$ is a 4-dimensional column vector with row names ($\emptyset$, $\{a\}$, $\{b\}$, Ω) and $(\tilde{m})^T = [0, 0.7, 0, 0.3]$ is the corresponding row vector with column names ($\emptyset$, $\{a\}$, $\{b\}$, Ω). $\overset{D}{=}$ is a 4×4 square matrix with ($\emptyset$, $\{a\}$, $\{b\}$, Ω) as the names for both rows and columns. $((\tilde{m})^T \overset{D}{=} \tilde{m}) = 0.79$ in this example.

Example 3. (Continuing Example 2) *The four bbas recovered from the four possibility distributions in Example 2 are:*

$$m_1(\{\omega_2\}) = 0.4, m_1(\{\omega_2, \omega_3, \omega_4\}) = 0.1, m_1(\Omega) = 0.5$$
$$m_2(\{\omega_1\}) = 0.4, m_2(\{\omega_1, \omega_2, \omega_3\}) = 0.1, m_2(\Omega) = 0.5$$
$$m_3(\{\omega_3\}) = 0.4, m_3(\{\omega_2, \omega_3, \omega_4\}) = 0.1, m_3(\Omega) = 0.5$$
$$m_4(\{\omega_4\}) = 0.4, m_4(\{\omega_1, \omega_3, \omega_4\}) = 0.1, m_4(\Omega) = 0.5$$

Applying the distance-based measure defined in Equation 8 to all the pairs of PIBs, the distances between pairs of PIBs are listed below.

$$d_{BPA}(m_1, m_2) = 0.4203, d_{BPA}(m_2, m_3) = 0.4203, d_{BPA}(m_2, m_4) = 0.4203$$
$$d_{BPA}(m_1, m_4) = 0.4358, d_{BPA}(m_1, m_3) = 0.4, \quad d_{BPA}(m_3, m_4) = 0.4041$$

These results show that PIBs K_1 and K_4 are most inconsistent whilst PIBs (K_1, K_3) or (K_3, K_4) are most consistent. This detailed analysis cannot be measured by the degree of inconsistency since every pair of PIBs has the same degree of inconsistency.

A distance-based measure of a pair of bbas does not convey the same information as $m_1 \oplus m_2(\emptyset)$. More specifically, $Inc(K) = 0$ does not mean $d_{BPA} = 0$, nor does $Inc(K) = 1$ imply $d_{BPA} = 1$. For instance, a pair of possibility distributions π_1 and π_2 defined on $\Omega = \{\omega_1, \omega_2, \omega_3, \omega_4\}$ for two PIBs with

$$\pi_1(\omega_1) = 1, \pi_1(\omega_2) = 0.5, \pi_1(\omega_3) = 0.4, \pi_1(\omega_4) = 0.4$$
$$\pi_2(\omega_1) = 1, \pi_2(\omega_2) = 1, \quad \pi_2(\omega_3) = 1, \quad \pi_2(\omega_4) = 0.8$$

produces a normal possibility distribution after a conjunctive merge. The degree of inconsistency is $Inc(K_{12}) = 0$ where K_{12} is the merged PIB. However, $d_{BPA}(m_1, m_2)$

$= 0.41$ where m_1 and m_2 are the bbas for π_1 and π_2. Similarly, if we have a pair of possibility distributions π_3 and π_4 defined on the same set Ω as

$$\pi_3(\omega_1) = 1, \ \pi_3(\omega_2) = 0.6, \ \pi_3(\omega_3) = 0, \ \pi_3(\omega_4) = 0$$
$$\pi_4(\omega_1) = 0, \ \pi_4(\omega_2) = 0, \quad \pi_4(\omega_3) = 1, \ \pi_4(\omega_4) = 0.8$$

then $Inc(K_{34}) = 1$ whilst $d_{BPA}(m_3, m_4) = 0.842$ where K_{34} is the merged PIB and m_3 and m_4 are the bbas for π_3 and π_4 respectively.

This discussion shows that the distance-based measure can not replace the measure of degree of inconsistency. Both measures should be used when assessing how conflict a pair of PIBs is.

4.2 A (difBetP, $m_1 \oplus m_2(\emptyset)$) Based Measure of Conflict

The conflict between two belief functions (or bbas) in DS theory is traditionally measured using the combined mass value assigned to the emptyset before normalization, e.g., $m(\emptyset)$. In [Liu06], it is illustrated that this measure is not accurate and a new measure which is made up of two values is introduced. One of these two values is the difference between betting commitments obtained through pignistic probability functions and another is the combined value assigned to the emptyset before normalization.

Definition 3. *(adapted from [Liu06]) Let m_1 and m_2 be two bbas on Ω and $BetP_{m_1}$ and $BetP_{m_2}$ be their corresponding pignistic probability functions. Then*

$$\mathsf{difBetP}^{m_2}_{m_1} = \max_{\omega \in \Omega}(|BetP_{m_1}(\omega) - BetP_{m_2}(\omega)|)$$

is called the distance between betting commitments *of the two bbas.*

Value $(|BetP_{m_1}(\omega) - BetP_{m_2}(\omega)|)$ *is the difference between betting commitments to possible world ω from the two sources.* The distance of betting commitments, $\mathsf{difBetP}^{m_2}_{m_1}$, is therefore the maximum extent of the differences between betting commitments to all the possible worlds. This definition is a revised version in [Liu06] where in the original definition for $\mathsf{difBetP}^{m_2}_{m_1}$, ω is replaced by A (a subset). The rational for this adaptation is that we want to know how "far apart" the degrees of possibility assigned to a possible world is from the two sources.

We use the following example to show the advantage of (difBetP, $m_1 \oplus m_2(\emptyset)$) over $m_1 \oplus m_2(\emptyset)$.

Example 4. *Let m_1 and m_2 be two bbas on $\Omega = \{\omega_1, ..., \omega_5\}$ as*

$$m_1(\{\omega_1\}) = 0.8, \ m_1(\{\omega_2, \omega_3, \omega_4, \omega_5\}) = 0.2,$$

and

$$m_2(\Omega) = 1.$$

Then $m_1 \oplus m_2(\emptyset) = 0$ when m_1 and m_2 are combined with Dempster's rule, which is traditionally explained as there is no conflict between the two bbas. However, m_1 is more committed whilst m_2 is less sure about its belief as which value(s) are more plausible than others. The difference in their opinions is reflected by $\mathsf{difBetP}^{m_2}_{m_1} = 0.6$. It says that the two sources have rather different beliefs as where the true hypothesis lies.

Definition 4. *Let* (K_1, K_2) *and* (K_1, K_3) *be two pairs of PIBs and* K_{12} *and* K_{13} *be the two merged PIBs from these two pairs. Let* m_1, m_2, *and* m_3 *be the bbas for the three PIBs respectively. Assume that* $Inc(K_{12}) = Inc(K_{13})$, *then* K_1 *is more consistent with* K_2 *than with* K_3 *when the following condition holds*

$$\mathsf{difBetP}^{m_2}_{m_1} \leq \mathsf{difBetP}^{m_3}_{m_1} \text{ and } m_1 \oplus m_2(\emptyset) \leq m_1 \oplus m_3(\emptyset)$$

Example 5. *Let three PIBs on set* $\Omega = \{\omega_1, \omega_2, \omega_3, \omega_4\}$ *be*

$$K_1^2 = \{(\{\omega_1, \omega_3\}, 0.4), (\{\omega_2, \omega_3, \omega_4\}, 0.5), (\{\omega_2\}, 0.4)\}$$
$$K_2^2 = \{(\{\omega_1, \omega_2\}, 0.3), (\{\omega_1, \omega_2, \omega_3\}, 0.5), (\{\omega_1, \omega_4\}, 0.4)\}$$
$$K_3^2 = \{(\{\omega_1, \omega_2, \omega_3\}, 0.4), (\{\omega_1, \omega_2, \omega_4\}, 0.4), (\{\omega_2, \omega_3\}, 0.4)\}$$

The corresponding possibility distributions and bbas for these PIBs are

$$\pi_1^2(\omega_1) = 0.5, \; \pi_1^2(\omega_2) = 0.6, \; \pi_1^2(\omega_3) = 1.0, \; \pi_1^2(\omega_4) = 0.6,$$
$$\pi_2^2(\omega_1) = 1.0, \; \pi_2^2(\omega_2) = 0.6, \; \pi_2^2(\omega_3) = 0.6, \; \pi_2^2(\omega_4) = 0.5,$$
$$\pi_3^2(\omega_1) = 0.6, \; \pi_3^2(\omega_2) = 1.0, \; \pi_3^2(\omega_3) = 0.6, \; \pi_3^2(\omega_4) = 0.6.$$

and

$$m_1^2(\{\omega_3\}) = 0.4, \; m_1^2(\{\omega_2, \omega_3, \omega_4\}) = 0.1, \; m_1^2(\Omega) = 0.5$$
$$m_2^2(\{\omega_1\}) = 0.4, \; m_2^2(\{\omega_1, \omega_2, \omega_3\}) = 0.1, \; m_1^2(\Omega) = 0.5$$
$$m_3^2(\{\omega_2\}) = 0.4, \; m_3^2(\Omega) = 0.6,$$

$Inc(K_{12}^2) = Inc(K_{13}^2) = 0.4$. *However,* $m_1^2 \oplus m_2^2(\emptyset) = 0.20$ *and* $m_1^2 \oplus m_3^2(\emptyset) = 0.16$. *Furthermore,*

$$\mathsf{difBetP}^{m_2^2}_{m_1^2} = 0.4 + 0.1/3, \text{ and } \mathsf{difBetP}^{m_3^2}_{m_1^2} = 0.4 + 0.1/4 - 0.1/3$$

Therefore,

$$\mathsf{difBetP}^{m_3^2}_{m_1^2} < \mathsf{difBetP}^{m_2^2}_{m_1^2}$$

and

$$m_1^2 \oplus m_3^2(\emptyset) < m_1^2 \oplus m_2^2(\emptyset)$$

K_1^2 *is more consistent with* K_3^2 *than with* K_2^2.

In [Liu06], it has been shown that the $(\mathsf{difBetP}, m_1 \oplus m_2(\emptyset))$ based approach is more appropriate to measure the conflict among evidence than the distance-based approach. This can at least be seen from re-examining Example 2 using $(\mathsf{difBetP}, m_1 \oplus m_2(\emptyset))$. For example, applying this approach to the first pair of bbas derived from (π_1, π_2) in Example 2, we have $(\mathsf{difBetP}^{m_2}_{m_1}, m_1 \oplus m_2(\emptyset)) = (0.383, 0)$ which concludes that the two pieces of information are largely consistent (since $m_1 \oplus m_2(\emptyset) = 0$) but there is some disagreement among them (since $\mathsf{difBetP}^{m_2}_{m_1} \neq 0$). However, the degree of inconsistency (which is 0) as a single value cannot give us this (further) information.

5   Assessment of Agent's Judgement

When pieces of uncertain information are highly inconsistent and they have to be merged, some resolutions are needed before a meaningful merged result can be obtained. One common approach is to make use of the reliability of a source, so that the information from a source with a lower reliability can be either discarded or discounted (e.g., weakened). However, reliabilities are often required as extra knowledge and this knowledge is not always readily available. Therefore, finding ways of assessing the reliability of a source is the first step towards how to handle highly conflicting information.

In [DP94], a method for assessing the quality of information provided by a source was proposed. This method is to measure how accurate and informative the provided information is.

Let x be a (testing) variable for which all the possible values are included in set Ω and its true value (denoted as v) is known. To assess the reliability of a source (hereafter referred to as *Agent*), *Agent* is asked to provide its judgement as what is the true value for x. Assume that *Agent*'s reply is a set of weighted nested subsets in terms of possibility theory

$$K = \{(A_1, \alpha_1), ..., (A_n, \alpha_n)\} \text{ where } A_i \subset A_j, i < j$$

Then a possibility distribution π_x as well as a bba m can be constructed from this information on Ω such that

$$\pi_x(\omega) = \beta_1 = 1 \text{ when } \omega \in A_1$$
$$\pi_x(\omega) = \beta_2 \quad \text{when } \omega \in A_2 \setminus A_1 \text{ and } \beta_2 = 1 - \alpha_1$$
$$\pi_x(\omega) = \beta_3 \quad \text{when } \omega \in A_3 \setminus A_2 \text{ and } \beta_3 = 1 - \alpha_2$$
$$\vdots$$
$$\pi_x(\omega) = \beta_n \quad \text{when } \omega \in A_n \setminus A_{n-1} \text{ and } \beta_n = 1 - \alpha_{n-1}$$
$$\pi_x(\omega) = \beta_{n+1} \text{ when } \omega \notin A_n; \text{ and } \beta_{n+1} = 1 - \alpha_n$$

Then $\beta_1 \geq \beta_2 \geq \ldots \geq \beta_{n+1}$, since $\alpha_1 \leq \alpha_2 \leq \ldots \leq \alpha_n$ due to the monotonicity of N and

$$m(A_1) = \beta_1 - \beta_2, \ m(A_2) = \beta_2 - \beta_3, \ \ldots, \ m(A_n) = \beta_n - \beta_{n+1}$$

The rating of *Agent*'s judgement in relation to this variable is therefore defined as [DP94]

$$Q(K, x) = \pi_x(v) \frac{|\Omega| - ||K||}{(1 - m(A_n))|\Omega|} \tag{9}$$

where $||K|| = \Sigma_{i=1}^m (|A_i| m(A_i))$, v is the actual value of variable x, and $|\Omega|$ (resp. $|A_i|$) is the cardinality of set Ω (resp. A_i). This formula ensures that *Agent* can score high only if he is both accurate (with a high $\pi_x(v)$) and informative (with a fairly focused subset).

When $K = \{(\Omega, 1)\}$, it implies $m(\Omega) = 1$ and $\pi_x(\omega) = 1, \forall \omega \in \Omega$, then $Q(K, x) = 0$ since $||K|| = |\Omega|$. This shows that the *Agent* is totally ignorant. When $K = \{(\{v\}, 1)\}$, it implies $\pi_x(v) = 1$ and $\pi_x(\omega) = 0$ when $\omega \neq v$. Then $Q(K, x) = (|\Omega| - 1)/|\Omega|$ since $m(A_n) = 0$. This conclusion says that the *Agent*'s judgement increases along the size of the set of all values, the bigger the set, the more accurate the *Agent*'s judgement is.

When the *Agent*'s reply is not in the form of a set of weighted nested subsets, relationships between DS theory and possibility theory studies in Section 3 should be used to construct a set of nested subsets, called focal elements. Then this set of nested subsets can be used in Equation 9 for calculating the ranking of an *Agent*.

The overall rating of an *Agent* is evaluated as the average of all ratings obtained from answering a set of (testing) variables where *Agent*'s reply for each variable is judged using Equation 9. Once each *Agent*'s rating is established, suitable discounting operators ([DP01]) can be applied to weaken the opinions from less reliable *Agents* to resolve inconsistency among information.

6 Conclusion

In this paper, we have shown that additional approaches to measuring inconsistency among pieces of uncertain information are needed since the only measure used in possibility theory, e.g., the degree of inconsistency, is not adequate for situations where pairs of uncertain information have the same degree of inconsistency. We have preliminarily investigated how two recently proposed methods in DS theory on inconsistency/conflict measures can be used to measure the inconsistency among pieces of uncertain information in possibility theory. In addition, we have also looked at issues as how the reliability (or judgement) of a source can be established through assessing the quality of answers to a set of known situations.

All these studies will have an impact on which merging operator should be selected for what conflict scenario and how inconsistencies should be resolved if reliabilities of sources are known. We will investigate all these issues in depth in a future paper.

In [HL05a, HL05b], a coherence interval based method was proposed to quantitatively measure how consistent a pair of uncertain possibilistic information is. This method clearly offers a very different alternative to the two methods developed in DS theory. Comparing these three alternatives will be another objective for our future research.

References

[BDP97] S Benferhat, D Dubois, and H Prade. From semantic to syntactic approach to information combination in possibilistic logic. *Aggregation and Fusion of Imperfect Information*, 141-151, Bernadette Bouchon-Meunier (Ed.). Physica Verlag, 1997.

[BK01] S Benferhat and S Kaci. Logical representation and fusion of prioritized information based on guaranteed possibility measures: Application to the distance-based merging of classical bases. *Artificial Intelligence*, 148:291-333, 2001.

[DP82] D Dubois and H Prade. *On several representations of an uncertain body of evidence. Fuzzy Information and Decision Processes*, 167-181, Gupta and Sanchez (Eds.). North-Holland Publishing Company, 1982.

[DP87] D Dubois and H Prade. *The principle of minimum specificity as a basis for evidential reasoning. Uncertainty in Knowledge-Based Systems*, 75-84, Bouchon and Yager (Eds.). Springer-Verlag, 1987.

[DP88a] D Dubois and H Prade. *Possibility theory: An approach to the computerized processing of uncertainty.* Plenum Press, 1988.

[DP88b]   D Dubois and H Prade. Representation and combination of uncertainty with belief functions and possibility measures. *Computational Intelligence*, 4:244-264. 1988

[DP94]   D Dubois and H Prade. Possibility theory and data fusion in poorly informed environments. *Control Engineering Practice*, 2(5):811-823. 1994

[DP98a]   D Dubois and H Prade, editors. *Handbook of Defeasible Reasoning and Uncertainty Management Systems*, Volume 3. Kluwer, 1998.

[DP98b]   D Dubois and H Prade Possibility theory: Qualitative and quantitative aspects. *Handbook of Defeasible Reasoning and Uncertainty Management Systems*, Vol 1:169-226, Gabbay and Smets (eds.). Kluwer Academic Publisher, Dordrecht, 1998.

[DP01]   D Dubois and H Prade Possibility theory in information fusion. *Data Fusion and Perception*, Riccia, Lenz, and Kruse (eds.), CISM Courses and Lectures Vol 431: 53-76, Springer-Verlag, 2001.

[DNP00]   D Dubois, H Nguyen and H Prade Possibility theory, probability and fuzzy sets, Misunderstandings, bridges and gaps. *Fundamentals of Fussy Sets*, Chapter 7, 343-438, Dubois and Prade (eds.), *The Handbooks of Fuzzy Sets Series*.

[HL05a]   A Hunter and W Liu. Assessing the quality of merged information in possibilistic logic. Proceedings of ECSQARU'05:415-426, LNCS 3571, Springer, 2005.

[HL05b]   A Hunter and W Liu. A context-dependent algorithm for merging uncertain information in possibility theory (submitted), 2005.

[HL06]   A Hunter and W Liu. Fusion rules for merging uncertain information. *Information Fusion Journal* 7(1):97-134, 2006.

[JGB01]   Jousselme, A.L., Grenier, D. and Bosse, E. A new distance between two bodies of evidence. *Information Fusion*, Vol 2:91-101, 2001.

[Liu06]   W Liu. Analyzing the degree of conflict among belief functions. *Artificial Intelligence* (in press), 2006.

[SDK95]   S Sandri, D Dubois, and H Kalfsbeek. Elicitation, assessment and polling of expert judgements using possibility theory. *IEEE Transactions on Fuzzy Systems*, 3:313-335, 1995.

[Sha76]   G Shafer. *A Mathematical Theory of Evidence*. Princeton University Press, 1976.

[SK94]   Smets, Ph. and Kennes, K. The transferable belief model. *Artificial Intelligence*, 66(2):191-234, 1994.

[Sme04]   Smets, Ph. Decision making in the TBM: the necessity of the pignistic transformation. *International Journal of Approximate Reasoning* 38:133-147, 2004.

WWW Information Integration Oriented Classification Ontology Integrating Approach

Anxiang Ma, Kening Gao, Bin Zhang, Yu Wang, and Ying Yin

School of Information Science and Engineering, Northeastern University,
Shenyang 110004, China
max8025@163.com, zhangbin@mail.neu.edu.cn

Abstract. In WWW information integration, eliminating semantic hetero-geneity and implementing semantic combination is one of the key problems. This paper introduces classification ontology into WWW information integration to solve the semantic combination problem of heterogeneity classification architecture in Web information integration. However, there may be many kinds of ontology in a specific domain due to the structure of the websites, domain experts and different goals. So we have to combine all these kinds of ontology into logically unified integrated classification ontology in order to solve the problem of semantic heterogeneity commendably. This paper primarily discusses the method of building integrated classification ontology based on individual ontology, presents the definition of classification ontology, analyses the conceptual mapping and relational mapping between ontologies and solves the level conflict in the equivalent concepts.

Keywords: Information integration, Classification ontology, Semantic, Similarity.

1 Introduction

In the large space of Web data, Web information is generally organized according to the form of websites. Each website defines its own category to classify and navigate their pages in order to form the organization and structure of information. Although the structure is extractable and the auto-classification of Web pages is feasible, the criterion and classification terms of different sites are not the same when laying out. It is difficult for them to incorporate and to be compatible because of the obvious semantic difference [1]. The application of Ontology in Web directly leads to the birth of semantic web[2]. It tries to solve the semantic problems in Web information sharing, therefore, how to solve the semantic heterogeneity by means of ontology has become the point researchers focusing on.

In order to solve the semantic heterogeneity problem of Web classification architecture encountered during Web information integrating, this paper introduces classification ontology. The classification architecture integration is supported by classification ontology, forms logically unified global classification architecture under the framework and provides consistent information classification view for large Web information. The solution to classified semantic heterogeneity lies on the integrality and consistency of classification ontology. However, there may be many kinds of ontology

J. Lang, F. Lin, and J. Wang (Eds.): KSEM 2006, LNAI 4092, pp. 278–291, 2006.

in a specific domain due to the structure of the websites, domain experts and different goals. So we have to combine all these kinds of ontology into logically unified integrated classification ontology, in order to solve the problem of semantic heterogeneity.

This paper focuses on how to build integrated classification ontology based on individual classification ontology. To achieve that goal, the definition of classification ontology is given and the conceptual mapping, the relational mapping and the level conflict between equivalent concept are analyzed. Also, this paper introduces the algorithm of constructing integrated classification ontology based on the research above. At the end of this paper, the comparison of performance between the methods is given in the experiment segment.

2 Background

This paragraph presents related research, introduces the framework of WWW information integration based on the classification ontology by analyzing the feature of information source and ontology, and elaborates its theory. The key points of this paper are also stated.

2.1 Related Research

At present, it is popular home and abroad that ontology is used to solve the semantic heterogeneity, especially in the domain of information integration and information grid. Some researchers[3][4][5] presented the technology of information integration and architecture of net grid based on ontology, but they didn't further research how to solve semantic heterogeneity by means of ontology. Some researchers[6][7][8][9] presented several methods of ontology integrating, which mostly based on conceptual mapping and relational mapping. Furthermore, there are some famous integrating tools[10][11] in information integration, which integrate on the grammar level and are unable to reason the relation between concepts on the semantic level.

There are mainly two methods for conceptual mapping. One method is to extensively describe the concepts and get the relation of conceptual mapping by analyzing the extend description. For example, the 12th reference combines information reception and information integration. The author denotes the concepts by keyword vector, because the commonly used method in information reception is vector space model. In this way, the similarity of concepts converts to similarity of vectors (the cosine of the angles between vectors is commonly used). This method is objective, and reflects the similarity and difference of the words among syntax, semantic and pragmatic. It improves the accuracy of the estimation of concept similarity in a way. However, this method relies on the word library needed by training. Also its calculating is huge and the calculating method is complex. The other method is to make use of the standard semantic library (Ontology) to calculate the semantic distance between words[13]. It is effective, intuitionistic and understandable to denote the conceptual similarity by the distance the word has in the standard semantic dictionary. But this method is subjective and can't tell the truth sometimes. In the aspect of relation integration, the existing methods mostly calculate the domain and range similarity between relations respectively to estimate the similarity between relations. The accuracy will be affected in this kind of relational mapping.

In addition, most methods of integration just consider conceptual mapping and relational mapping. It's not enough for the integration of WWW classification ontology. The solution of level conflicts is crucial for effective integration of WWW classification ontology, because some equivalent concepts are in different levels in different ontologies in most of the ontology related, which is called level conflicts.

2.2 Classification-Ontology-Based WWW Information Integration

There is a remarkable feature of Web information organization that it is commonly organized in the form of websites, and the setting of the navigator, the classification of the pages to form information organization and classification architecture according to the purpose of the designer. As to Chinese portals, we have successfully extracted their classification structures, and achieved auto-classification of Web pages by the form of website. But due to the disunity of classification definition of different websites and the nonstandard terms, even the same term has different understandings in different sites because of the diversity of the consciousness and cognition. It leads to heterogeneity of classification architecture, difference of semantic and confusion of logical classification and it's hard to incorporate.

Therefore, we introduce classification ontology in WWW information integration in order to solve the semantic heterogeneity. We achieve the integration of Web classification architecture under the support of logically unified integrated classification ontology, which forms consistent global classification architecture and provides universal classification view for large Web data. The process of classification ontology based WWW information integration is shown in figure 1. Firstly, extract classification architecture and Web data from websites and classify the Web data to some category. Secondly, solve the semantic heterogeneity of the websites and achieve the classification architecture under the support of integrated classification ontology. At the same time, get the integrated data by means of redundancy-eliminating method and so on. At last, associate the classification architecture and the data to build an integrated website.

It is not difficult to figure out from the process of classification-ontology-based WWW information integration that the web data is always adhere to some classification information. The process of Web data integration is mainly about redundancy

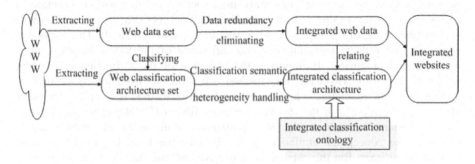

Fig. 1. Process of classification-ontology-based WWW information integration

eliminating. So the key of integrating is the integrating of classification architecture, while the heterogeneity of classification architecture is to be solved under the support of classification ontology. However, there may be many kinds of ontology in a specific domain due to the structure of the websites, domain experts and different goals. So it is crucial to build logically unified integrated ontology which is used to solve the semantic heterogeneity. This paper presents the building process of integrated classification ontology shown in figure 2 according to the features of WWW data source. Firstly, the domain experts build the local classification ontology; secondly, deal with the conceptual mapping, relational mapping and level conflict detection; at last, generate logically unified integrated classification ontology.

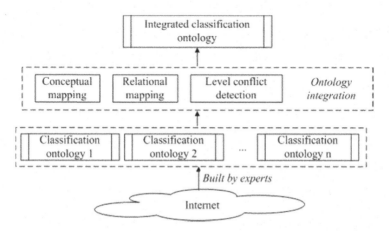

Fig. 2. Building process of integrated classification ontology

3   Mapping Relations Between Classification Ontologies

In order to build the semantic mapping relation between classification ontologies, this paragraph firstly defines the classification ontology according to features of WWW information source of classification model, and then analyses two main kinds of mapping relations between ontologies, conceptual mapping and relational mapping.

3.1   Definition of Classification Ontology

Studer and his partners presented a definition that ontology is the conceptual model which describes concepts and the relations between concepts [14]. Domain ontology is the description of concepts and relations between concepts in specific domains. We defined classification ontology(Classification ontology, CO)against classification architecture features of WWW information source.

Definition 1: Classification ontology. Classification ontology can be expressed by quintuple: CO ={C, R, H_c, I, A}, among these, C is classification concept set, R is semantic relation set, H_c is concept level, I is example set, A is ontology axiom.

Definition 2: Classification concept node set. Classification ontology could be regarded as the dendriform hiberarchy consists of the classification concepts and the relations between classification concepts. The node in the dendriform hiberarchy is called classification concept node. Classification concept node set N consists of classification concept and the level the classification concept lies in. It is defined as: N={ (c, h) | c∈ C, h= H_c}, among these, c is the concept in the classification concept set, h is the level classification concept c lies in.

Definition 3: Semantic relation set. Semantic relation set R is defined as: R={ $R_{subsumption}$, $R_{sibling}$ }, among these, $R_{subsumption}$ is subsumption relation, $R_{sibling}$ is sibling relation.

Definition 4: Direct subsumption. As to two concepts c_i and c_j, if semantic c_i contains c_j, $c_i \supset c_j$, and $Hc_j = Hc_i + 1$, then c_i and c_j has the relation of direct subsumption $R_{subsumption}$, marked as c_i $R_{subsumption}$ c_j or $R_{subsumption}$ (c_i , c_j). So c_i is one of the super-concepts of c_j and c_j is one of the subconcepts of c_i .

Definition 5: Sibling relation. As to two concepts c_i and c_j, if c_i and c_j have the same super-concept and $Hc_j = Hc_i$, then c_i and c_j has sibling relation $R_{sibling}$, marked as c_i $R_{sibling}$ c_j or $R_{sibling}$ (c_i , c_j). So c_i is one of the sibling concept of c_j .

Figure 3 shows two classification ontologies, CO_1 and CO_2, among these, the broken line indicates the equivalent mapping between ontologies.

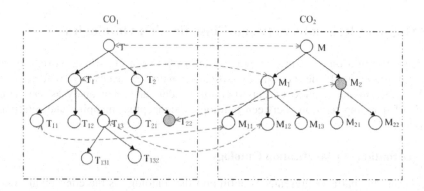

Fig. 3. Ontology and mapping between ontologies

Example 1: The expression of classification concept node set and semantic relation set of classification ontology CO_1.

The expression of classification concept node set:

N={(T, 1), (T$_1$, 2), (T$_2$, 2), (T$_{11}$, 3), (T$_{12}$, 3), (T$_{13}$, 3), (T$_{21}$, 3), (T$_{22}$, 3), (T$_{131}$, 4), (T$_{132}$, 4) , ...}

The expression of subsumption relation between concepts:

$R_{subsumption}$ (T, T$_1$), $R_{subsumption}$ (T, T$_2$), ... , $R_{subsumption}$ (T$_1$, T$_{11}$), $R_{subsumption}$ (T$_{13}$, T$_{131}$), ...

The expression of sibling relation between concepts:

$R_{sibling}$ (T$_1$, T$_2$), $R_{sibling}$ (T$_{11}$, T$_{12}$), ... , $R_{sibling}$ (T$_{21}$, T$_{22}$), $R_{sibling}$ (T$_{131}$, T$_{132}$), ...

In two related classification ontologies, there are equivalent concepts and equivalent relations, such as concept "T$_1$" in classification ontology CO$_1$ and concept "M$_1$" in classification ontology CO$_2$ are a couple of equivalent concepts, $R_{subsumption}$ (T,T$_1$) in classification ontology CO$_1$ and $R_{subsumption}$ (M,M$_1$) in classification ontology CO$_2$ are a couple of equivalent relation. Also, equivalent concepts are allowed to exist in different levels, such as concept "T$_{22}$" in classification ontology CO$_1$ and concept "M$_2$" in classification ontology CO$_2$ are a couple of equivalent concepts, but concept "T$_{22}$" in classification ontology CO$_1$ lies in level 3, and concept "M$_2$" in classification ontology CO$_2$ lies in level 2. So in order to effectively integrate classification architecture in the websites and provide logically unified integrated classification view to the users, the mapping relations between ontologies should be identified and the level conflict between equivalent concepts should be solved. By doing this, classification ontology set can be logically unified to an integrated classification ontology.

Definition 6: integrated classification ontology. Assuming that the ontologies to be integrated are: $CO_1, CO_2, \cdots, CO_n$, the integrated classification ontology ICO is defined as:

$$ICO = f_{CI \wedge AI \wedge RI}(CO_1, CO_2, \cdots, CO_n)$$
$$= f_{CI}(CO_1, CO_2, \cdots, CO_n) \wedge f_{AI}(CO_1, CO_2, \cdots, CO_n) \wedge f_{RI}(CO_1, CO_2, \cdots, CO_n)$$

Among these, f_{CI} indicates conceptual mapping, f_{AI} indicates level conflict adjusting, f_{RI} indicates relational mapping.

3.2 The Mapping Relation Between Ontologies

The mapping relation between ontologies includes conceptual mapping and relational mapping. Mapping includes equivalent mapping, containing mapping, non-intersect mapping and so on. This paper only focus on equivalent mapping.

3.2.1 Conceptual Mapping

Aimed at classification semantic heterogeneity, this paper calculates the similarity of classification concepts in two aspects. One is the semantic similarity of classification concepts itself, the other one is the similarity of subconcept set of concepts. Traditional method of concept similarity calculating is considering semantic similarity merely by concept itself, which is hard to distinguish when the same term denotes different concepts. This paper extends to consider the semantic similarity between subconcept sets while considering the semantic similarity of the concept itself. If the same term denotes different concepts, the similarity between its subconcepts is relatively low. Also, as to different terms which denote the same concept, the similarity between their subconcepts is relatively high.

The basis of calculating conceptual similarity is conceptual semantic similarity. This paper refers to the commonly used idea of conceptual semantic similarity calculating, which is that the shorter the distance of semantic, the higher the similarity. Therefore, in order to calculate conceptual semantic similarity, the concepts in classification ontology have to be mapped to standard conceptual space (WordNet or CILIN). Then calculate the similarity between concepts by means of calculating the distance between two concepts in the standard conceptual space. Assuming two related classification ontology: CO_1 and CO_2, two concepts $c_a \in CO_1$ and $c_b \in CO_2$, then the semantic similarity of c_a and c_b is :

$$sim_1(c_a, c_b) = \frac{\lambda}{\lambda + d(c_a, c_b)} \tag{1}$$

Among these, λ is an adjustable parameter which means the distance between terms when the similarity is 0.5; d is the distance of c_a and c_b.

Assuming the subconcept set of c_a、 c_b is $\{ c_{ai} | \forall_i (c_a R_{subsumption} c_{ai}), i = 1 \cdots m \}$ and $\{ c_{bj} | \forall_j (c_b R_{subsumption} c_{bj}), j = 1 \cdots n \}$ separately, then the formula of similarity calculating of concept set is:

$$sim_2(\{c_{ai}\}, \{c_{bj}\}) = \frac{1}{m} \sum_{i=1}^{m} \max_{j=1 \cdots n} (sim_1(c_{ai}, c_{bj})) \tag{2}$$

By integrating formula (1) and (2), the formula of classification concept similarity calculating is:

$$sim(c_a, c_b) = \alpha sim_1(c_a, c_b) + \beta sim_2(\{c_{ai}\}, \{c_{bj}\}) \tag{3}$$

Among these, α, β is weight, $\alpha + \beta = 1$ and $\alpha > \beta$

Definition 7: Conceptual equivalence. Assuming that the boundary is η, then if the similarity of two conception c_1 and c_2 is bigger than η, then define concept c_1 and c_2 equivalence, marked as $c_1 \equiv c_2$. It can also be described as $sim(c_1, c_2) > \eta \rightarrow c_1 \equiv c_2$.

In addition, there may be not the definition in the standard conceptual space corresponding to some specific concepts in the classification ontology. At this time, it can be reserved as standard concept, and when estimating about the equivalence with other concept, the similarity is to be decided by domain experts.

3.2.2 Relational Mapping

Relational mapping plays important role in ontology integration. For example, $R_{subsumption}$ (T, T$_1$) in classification ontology CO_1 and $R_{subsumption}$ (M, M$_1$) in classification ontology CO_2 are a couple of equivalence. Also, the two relation hasOffspring(person, person) and hasChild(person, person) come from different related ontology. Although their names are different, but it is obviously that the meaning of hasOffspring and hasChild are the same. Therefore, mapping between the equivalent relations needs to be set in order to build integrated classification ontology.

The existing methods mostly calculate the similarity of relations by means of calculating the similarity of domain and range. The method is not general. Based on this, the paper presents a method which calculates the similarity of sub-relation at the same time in order to higher the accuracy of relational mapping.

Two relations $x_1 R_1 y_1 \in CO_1$, $x_2 R_2 y_2 \in CO_2$, if relation R_1 and R_2 have the same name, then the similarity of R_1 and R_2 is:

$$sim(R_1, R_2) = sim_1(x_1, x_2)sim_1(y_1, y_2) \tag{4}$$

If relation R_1 and R_2 have different names, the similarity of sub-relations need to be considered. Assuming the sub-relations set of R_1 and R_2 are $\{ R_{1i} \mid i = 1, 2, \cdots, m \}$ and $\{ R_{2j} \mid j = 1, 2, \cdots, n \}$, then the similarity of R_1 and R_2 is:

$$sim(R_1, R_2) = \phi sim_1(x_1, x_2)sim_1(y_1, y_2) + \varphi \frac{1}{m} \sum_{i=1}^{m} \max_{j=1\cdots n} sim(R_{1i}, R_{2j}) \tag{5}$$

Among these, ϕ, φ are weight, $\phi + \varphi = 1$ and $\phi > \varphi$

Definition 8: relational equivalence. Assuming the boundary of the relational similarity is γ, then if the similarity of two relations R_1 and R_2 is above γ, then define R_1 and R_2 as equivalence, marked as $R_1 \equiv R_2$. It can also be described as $sim(R_1, R_2) > \gamma \rightarrow R_1 \equiv R_2$.

4 The Constructive Algorithm of Integrated Classification Ontology

The key of building an integrated website is to combine kinds of classification ontologies into a single logically unified integrated classification ontology. Identifying the mapping relation between ontologies is the basis of the integrating operation. However, there is level conflict in most related classification ontologies, which is the position of equivalent concepts is different in different classification ontologies. Therefore, in order to integrate classification ontologies effectively, level conflict needs to be solved. In this paragraph, the solution to level conflict is firstly given, and then constructive algorithm of integrated classification ontology based on mapping relation and solution to level conflict is given.

4.1 Solution to Level Conflict of Equivalent Concepts

In the example above, the concept T_{22} in classification ontology CO_1 and the concept M_2 in classification ontology CO_2 are a couple of equivalent concepts. However, concept T_{22} and M_2 are in different level in their own classification ontology, which is called level conflict. Therefore, in order to build integrated classification ontology, level adjustment is needed. Assuming two related ontologies: CO_1 and CO_2, and concept nodes $n_a \in CO_1$ and $n_b \in CO_2$, then the problem that equivalent concepts lie in different levels can be described as : $Q = \exists_a \exists_b (n_a.c = n_b.c \wedge n_a.h \neq n_b.h)$。

The method of equivalent concepts level adjusting is to estimate the relativity of equivalent concepts and their own sibling nodes. For example, if the relativity of concept T_{22} in classification ontology CO_1 and its sibling node T_{21} is lower than the relativity of concept M_2 in classification ontology CO_2 and its sibling node M_1, then the couple of equivalent concepts in the integrated classification ontology lie in the level of concept M_2. Assuming S_a is the sibling node set of n_a, $\forall_k (n_k \in S_a) \rightarrow R_{sibling}(n_a.c, n_k.c)$, S_b is the sibling node set of n_b, $\forall_m (n_m \in S_b) \rightarrow R_{sibling}(n_b.c, n_m.c)$, $Rel(x,y)$ represents the relativity of concept x and y, then the relativity can be measured by the possibility that two concepts appear in the same environment. corresponding integrated concept node in integrated classification ontology as n_{ICO}, then level adjusting formula is :

$$\frac{1}{|S_a|} \sum_{n_k \in S_a} Rel(n_a.c, n_k.c) > \frac{1}{|S_b|} \sum_{n_m \in S_b} Rel(n_b.c, n_m.c) \rightarrow n_{ICO}.h := n_a.h \tag{6}$$

$$Rel(c_a, c_b) = \frac{1}{|I_a| + |I_b|} \sum_{D_j \in (I_a \cup I_b)} \frac{\min(f_{aj}, f_{bj})}{f_{aj} + f_{bj}} \tag{7}$$

Among these, I_a and I_b are the instance sets of c_a and c_b, D_j represents one archive in the instance set, f_{aj} represents the frequency of c_a in archive D_j, $\min(f_{aj}, f_{bj})$ represents the minimum of f_{aj} and f_{bj}.

4.2   The Constructive Algorithm of Integrated Classification Ontology

Algorithm 1: Constructive algorithm of integrated classification ontology
Input: Classification ontologies to be integrated: $CO_1, CO_2, \cdots, CO_n$

Output: Integrated classification ontology ICO
Steps
Step 1: Add a symbol "flag" for each classification ontology to be integrated: $CO_1, CO_2, \cdots, CO_n$, initial value is "false", denotes the concept has not operated yet.

Step 2: Traversal the classification ontology $CO_i (1 \leq i \leq n)$ in the width-first order to get a concept c_i which has not been operated yet. Find out the concepts which are equivalent to it in classification ontology $CO_{i+1}, \cdots, CO_n$ using the judgment approach of concept equivalence.

1) If its equivalent concept is not found, change the flag of concept c_i into "true", and then identify the super-concept of c_i, add concept c_i to the corresponding position in ICO and build subsumption with its super-concept. Goto Step 5.

2) If the equivalent concept is found, which is marked as $\{c_j | i+1 \leq j \leq n, c_j \in CO_j\}$, then build mapping between c_i and its equivalent concept set.

$$f_{C\_equal} : \{c_j\} \rightarrow c_i \qquad (8)$$

Change the flag of concept c_i and its equivalent concepts $\{c_j\}$ into "true". Then figure out whether concept c_i and its equivalent concepts are in the same level. If yes, goto step 4; if not, goto next step.

Step 3: Calculate the relativity between every concept in equivalent concept set $\{c_j | i \leq j \leq n, c_j \in CO_j\}$ and its sibling node. Assuming concept c_a belongs to ontology CO_a, satisfying $c_a \in \{c_j | i \leq j \leq n, c_j \in CO_j\}$, and the most related to its sibling nodes. Then the level of the concept in ICO:

$$h := h_a \qquad (9)$$

Identify the super-concept of c_{top_a}, $c_{top\_a} R_{sibling} c_a$, and build subsumption with concept c_{top_a} in the ICO. Goto Step 5.

Step 4: Figure out whether the relations between every concept in equivalent concept set $\{c_j | i \leq j \leq n, c_j \in CO_j\}$ and its super-concept are equivalent.

1) If yes, map R_i to its equivalent relation set $\{R_j | i+1 \leq j \leq n, R_j \in CO_j\}$:

$$f_{R\_equal} : \{R_j\} \rightarrow R_i \qquad (10)$$

Then identify the super-concept of c_i, add c_i to the corresponding position in ICO, and build subsumption R_i with its super-concept.

2) If not, compare the relativity of each of the equivalent concept set $\{c_j | i \leq j \leq n, c_j \in CO_j\}$ with its sibling nodes, find out the concept $c_t (c_t \in CO_t)$ with the highest relativity, add c_t and the relation R_t ($R_t \in CO_t$) between c_t and its super-concept into corresponding position in ICO.

Step 5: Repeat Step 2 until all the concepts in classification ontology $CO_1, CO_2, \cdots, CO_n$ are operated.

Example 2: Integrate two classification ontology shown in figure 3 into integrated classification ontology. The integrating result based algorithm 1 is shown in figure 4.

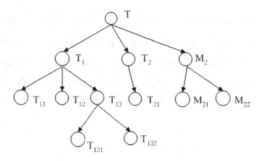

Fig. 4. Integrated classification ontology

(1) The concept T_{22} in CO_1 and the concept M_2 in CO_2 are a couple of equivalent concepts, while in different levels in their ontology, which are 3 and 2. Compare the relativity of concept T_{22} with its sibling nodes and of concept M_2 with its sibling nodes by the method of level adjusting. In this case, assuming that the relativity of concept M_2 and its sibling nodes is higher than that of concept T_{22} and its sibling nodes. So the equivalent nodes lies in level 2 in the integrated classification ontology.

(2) The concept T_1 in CO_1 and the concept M_1 in CO_2 are a couple of equivalent concepts, then build mapping between concept T_1 and M_1, and express this concept with concept T_1 in the integrated classification ontology.

5 Performance Evaluation

In the earlier study, we extracted the classification models of some portals such as SINA (http://www.sina.com.cn), SOHU (http://www.sohu.com), CHINA (http://www.china.com). In the experiment, the model system downloaded web page from the websites and recorded the structure of the sites, then extract the classification architecture with level structure, and classified Web information into corresponding category according to the auto-classifying algorithm. The results are standardized and made into corresponding classification concepts. The results are:

Table 1. Websites Classification Concepts

Classification concepts	Class of information （amount）			examples （amount of web pages）
	Level 1	Level 2	Level 3	
SINA	1	40	574	80167
SOHU	1	29	349	43532
CHINA	1	39	331	36842

Based on the experiments, this paper designed emulating experiments of conceptual mapping and relational mapping. In order to test the performance of the concept equivalence judging method (called ICCD) presented, the vector space model (VSM) in reference 12 and semantic distance of concepts calculated-only (CSD) method(see formula 1) are chosen to be compared with. The values of parameters in the experiment are: $\lambda = 18; \alpha = 0.6, \beta = 0.4;$

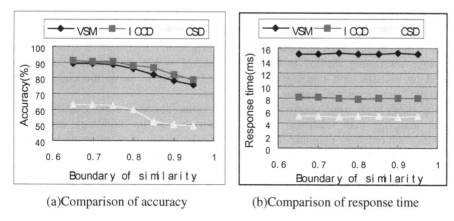

(a)Comparison of accuracy   (b)Comparison of response time

Fig. 5. Comparison of judging methods for concepts similarity

In the experiment of relational mapping, in order to compare the performance, the domain and range considered-only method in relation equivalence judgment (D_R) in reference 2 is selected as the comparing method. The method presented in this paper is called ID_R, then the values of parameters in the experiment are: $\phi = 0.6, \varphi = 0.4;$

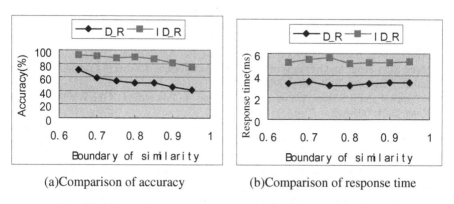

(a)Comparison of accuracy   (b)Comparison of response time

Fig. 6. Comparison of judging methods for relations similarity

It can be seen from figure 5, the accuracy of VSM and ICCD method is over 80% averagely, however, because of the complexity of VSM, its time cost is much more than ICCD. ICCD costs a little more time than CSD, but the former one considers the similarity of sub-concepts when calculating the similarity of concepts, so its accuracy is much higher than CSD. Figure 6 denotes that the relation equivalence judgment method this paper presented holds high accuracy, while the time cost is more than D_R. Compromising the accuracy and the time cost, the concept equivalence judgment method and the relation equivalence judgment method this paper presented holds high performance.

6 Conclusion

This paper applies ontology into WWW information integration, investigates the ontology integrating method in the background of WWW information integration based on classification ontology. This method is able to solve the classification semantic heterogeneity of website commendably.

This paper made some improvements aimed at the limitation of the existing conceptual mapping and relational mapping, introduced the building method of classification ontology mapping in details. The existing ontology integrating methods didn't take the level conflict of equivalent concepts into consideration. This paper presents a method that determines the level or position of equivalent concepts in the integrated ontology by means of estimating the relativity of equivalent concepts and their sibling concepts. Based on this, the integrating method of classification ontology is presented.

References

1. Aris Ouksel. Semantic interoperability in global information systems-a brief introduction to the research area and the special section. SIGMOD Record, 1999, 28(1): 5-12.
2. LI Shan-Ping. Overview of Researches on Ontology. Journal of Computer Research and Development, 2004, 41(7): 1041-1052.
3. S. Dumais. Improving the retrieval of information from external sources. Behavior Research Methods, Instruments, and Computers, 1991, 23(2):229-236.
4. Ian Foster, Carl Kesselman. The anatomy of the grid: Enabling scalable virtual organizations. International Journal of Supercomputer Applications, 2001,15(3): 200-222.
5. Meng Xiao-Peng. An Overview of Web Data Management. Journal of Computer Research and Development, 2001, 38(4): 385-395.
6. R.Agrawal and R.Srikant. On integrating catalogs. In Proceeding of the WWW-10, Hong Kong, 2001: 603-612.
7. N.F.Noy and M.A.Musen. Prompt: algorithm and tool for automated ontology merging and alignment. In Proceeeding of American Association for Artificial Intelligence (AAAI), Austin, Texas, 2000, 450-455.
8. A.Doan, J.Madhavan, and A.Halevy. Learning to map between ontologies on the semantic web. In Proceedings of WWW-2002, 11th International WWW Conference, Hawaii, 2002
9. Jie Tang, Bang-Yong Liang, Juan-Zi Li. Toward Detecting Mapping Strategies for Ontology Interoperability. The 14th International World Wide Web Conference (WWW 2005), Japan.
10. McGuinness,D.;Fikes,R..An Environment for Merging and Testing Large Ontologies. In: Proceedings of the Seventh International Conference on Principles of Knowledge Representation and Reasoning, Colorado, USA, 2000
11. F Corradini, L Mariani, E Merelli. An agent-based approach to tool integration, Journal of Software Tools Technology Transfer, 2004. 6(3):231-244

12. Xiaomeng Su, Sari Hakkarainen and Terje Brasethvik. Semantic enrichment for improving systems. interoperability. Proceedings of the 19th ACM Symposium on Applied Computing (SAC'04), ACM Press (2004) 1634-1641
13. Eneko Agirre, German Rigau. A Proposal for Word Sense Disambiguation using Conceptual Distance. Proceedings of International Conference RANLP'95, Bulgaria, 1995
14. Studer R, Benjamins V R, Fensel D. Knowledge Engineering: Principles and Methods. Data and Knowledge Engineering ,1998 ,25(122) :161 ~ 197

Configurations for Inference Between Causal Statements

Philippe Besnard[1], Marie-Odile Cordier[2], and Yves Moinard[3]

[1] CNRS, IRIT, Université Paul Sabatier
118 route de Narbonne, 31062 Toulouse cedex, France
`besnard@irit.fr`
[2] Université de Rennes I, IRISA
Campus de Beaulieu, 35042 Rennes cedex, France
`cordier@irisa.fr`
[3] INRIA, IRISA
Campus de Beaulieu, 35042 Rennes cedex, France
`moinard@irisa.fr`

Abstract. When dealing with a cause, cases involving some effect due to that cause are precious as such cases contribute to what the cause is. They must be reasoned upon if inference about causes is to take place. It thus seems like a good logic for causes would arise from a semantics based on collections of cases, to be called configurations, that gather instances of a given cause yielding some effect(s). Two crucial features of this analysis of causation are transitivity, which is endorsed here, and the event-based formulation, which is given up here in favor of a fact-based approach. A reason is that the logic proposed is ultimately meant to deal with both deduction (given a cause, what is to hold?) and abduction (given the facts, what could be the cause?) thus paving the way to the inference of explanations. The logic developed is shown to enjoy many desirable traits. These traits form a basic kernel which can be modified but which cannot be extended significantly without losing the adequacy with the nature of causation rules.

1 Motivation

Causation as entertained here concerns the usual relationship that may hold between states of affairs (thus departing from the concept favored by many people who focus on events —up to the point of insisting that causation is based on events[1]). For the relationship to hold, the cause must be what brings about the effect. Moreover, the account here is that the cause always brings about the effect (ruling out that "smoking causes cancer" may count as true). Such a strict reading makes a probabilistic interpretation of causation [16] (whether the probabilities are subjective or not) less appealing but is more sympathetic to

---

[1] The event-based approach is far from being uncontroversial: For instance, one usually says that the gravitational attraction of the moon (and of the sun) causes tides even if no event, but a principle, is indicated as the cause.

J. Lang, F. Lin, and J. Wang (Eds.): KSEM 2006, LNAI 4092, pp. 292–304, 2006.

the so-called counterfactual analysis of causation [11]. As is well-known, the idea of causal dependence is thus originally stated in terms of events (where c and e are two distinct possible events, e causally depends on c if and only if c occurs counterfactually implies e occurs and c does not occur counterfactually implies e does not occur, or if it does occur, it is due to some other rule), but facts have been reinstated [14]. Actually, statements might accommodate the technicalities pinpointed in [14] that insists on dealing with facts in a general sense (in order to capture causation involving negative existential facts for example: "she didn't get a speeding ticket because she was able to slow down early enough").

Although the counterfactual analysis of causation is meant to address the issue of truth for causation, the aim here is **not** a logic of causation: The purpose is not to give truth conditions for causal statements in terms that do not themselves appeal to causal concepts. The aim is only to provide truth-preserving conditions between causal statements. In particular, the logic will distinguish between a pair of statements essentially related as cause and effect and a pair of statements which are merely effects of a common cause (correlations being not confused with instances of causation), something conceptually troublesome for probabilistic approaches.

The logic will allow for transitivity as far as deterministic causes are concerned. No discussion on such a controversial topic is included. Instead, a single comment is as follows: Prominent authors in the defence of transitivity for causation include Lewis [13] and Hall [8] (see also Yablo [19]).

2 Introduction

When dealing with a cause (e.g., looking for something which could explain certain facts), cases involving some effect due to that cause are precious as such cases contribute to what the cause is. Accordingly, they must be reasoned upon if inference about causes is to take place. It thus seems like a good logic for causes would arise from a semantics based on collections of cases, to be called configurations that gather instances of a given cause yielding some effect(s).

The setting of configurations is what permits to discriminate correlations from instances of causes: If α and β are equivalent for example, then every situation admits both or none; when it comes to describing causation with respect to α for example, nothing requires to mention β for the reason that configurations are only supposed to take causation but not truth into account.

In the formalism to be introduced below, δ *causes* $\langle \beta \rangle$ means that δ causes the single effect β. Should α and β be equivalent, every situation is such that both α and β are true or none is; however, a configuration for δ must mention β as δ causes β but it need not be so for α (because δ does not cause α, regardless of the fact that α is true exactly when β is).

More generally, α *causes* $\langle \beta_1, \ldots, \beta_n \rangle$ means that the effects caused by α consist exactly of $\beta_1, \ldots, \beta_n$ where each β_i is *the* effect in the set $\{\beta_1, \ldots, \beta_n\}$, caused by a certain occurrence of α. Importantly, it is thus possible to express the possibility for a cause to have alternative effects like in the following example:

"Turning the wheel causes the car to go left or right". The outcome is that amongst the configurations for "turning the wheel", some include "the car goes to left" and some include "the car goes to right"[2] .

We propose a framework which is minimal in that only a few properties (all of which seemingly uncontroversial) are imposed upon it. Additional technicalities may later enrich the framework, depending on what application domain is considered. The *causes* operator is meant to be used with respect to an intended domain. A formula α *causes* $\langle \beta_1, \ldots, \beta_n \rangle$ is supposed to mean that part of our causal knowledge is that α has $\{\beta_1, \ldots, \beta_n\}$ as an exhaustive set of alternative effects. Here, "exhaustive" means that $\{\beta_1, \ldots, \beta_n\}$ accurately describes a set of alternative effects of a given kind (not precluding the existence of other kinds of effects, to be specified by means of other causal formulas).

Drastically discretizing temperatures in order to keep things simple, the example flu *causes* $\langle t_{38}, t_{39}, \ldots, t_{41} \rangle$ illustrates what is meant here: Adding t_{37}, or removing t_{38} would modify the intended meaning for the disease called flu. However, adding formulas such as flu *causes* $\langle fatigue \rangle$ is possible.

The general idea is that, from such causal formulas together with classical formulas, some consequences are to be formally derived according to the contents of the causal configurations.

According to our principled assumption requiring that causes-effects relations are captured through configurations, the following properties should not hold:

- δ *causes* $\langle \alpha \rangle \rightarrow \delta$ *causes* $\langle \alpha, \beta \rangle$ should be untrue in general – and of course so does the converse formula δ *causes* $\langle \alpha, \beta \rangle \rightarrow \delta$ *causes* $\langle \beta \rangle$.
- Neither causation nor effect should be strongly related to classical implication: $\beta \rightarrow \delta$ should entail neither δ *causes* $\langle \alpha \rangle \rightarrow \beta$ *causes* $\langle \alpha \rangle$ nor α *causes* $\langle \beta \rangle \rightarrow \alpha$ *causes* $\langle \delta \rangle$.
- Generally, δ *causes* $\langle \delta \rangle$ (reflexivity) should fail, even if it should be possible to make it hold when necessary, in special cases involving a cycling causal phenomenon.
- Chaining of nondeterministic causes is undesirable: δ *causes* $\langle \alpha, \beta \rangle$ together with β *causes* $\langle \gamma, \epsilon \rangle$ need not entail δ *causes* $\langle \alpha, \gamma, \epsilon \rangle$. The idea here is that β in full generality may cause either γ or ϵ but in the particular context where β occurs due to δ, it might well be that only γ (for instance) can happen. However, the idea of transitivity should remain, the precise formulation being postponed to the technical presentation given below in section 5. In particular, chaining of deterministic causes is desired in the form of the following property: δ *causes* $\langle \alpha, \gamma \rangle$ and α *causes* $\langle \beta \rangle$ should infer δ *causes* $\langle \beta, \gamma \rangle$.

---

[2] A question is whether a cause with alternative effects should be formalized as a cause with a single disjunctive effect. This is not the solution envisioned here because the notion of a single disjunctive effect seems somewhat shaky (it is assumed that an effect is described by means of a statement). About the well-known example that Suzy may throw a rock at a glass bottle and Billy may throw a rock at another glass bottle, some authors (Collins, Hall and Paul [5]) deny that the disjunctive item "Suzy's bottle shatters or Billy's bottle shatters" is apt to be caused: There is no such thing as a disjunctive effect.

3   Formal Definitions

The language of classical propositional logic is extended with formulas having multiple arguments: α *causes* $\langle \beta \rangle$ means that α causes the single effect β, and α *causes* $\langle \beta_1, \ldots, \beta_n \rangle$ (where n is finite) means that one of these β_i is *a* possible effect caused by a certain occurrence of α. In order to keep causal statements simple, α and $\beta_1, \ldots, \beta_n$ are atomic formulas of classical propositional logic.

Causal formulas are defined as follows, where α, β_i are propositional symbols:

1. Each propositional symbol (*propositional atom*) is a causal formula,
2. Each *causal atom* α *causes* $\langle \beta_1, \ldots, \beta_n \rangle$ is a causal formula.
3. If φ_1 and φ_2 are causal formulas, so are $\neg \varphi_1$, $\varphi_1 \wedge \varphi_2$, $\varphi_1 \vee \varphi_2$, $\varphi_1 \to \varphi_2$ and $\varphi_1 \leftrightarrow \varphi_2$.

A *propositional formula* is a causal formula without any causal atom, and "*formula*" will often be used instead of "*causal formula*". A *[causal] theory* CT is a set of formulas, the set of the propositional formulas in CT being denoted by W. As an illustration, CT may consist of $\neg(\alpha$ *causes* $\langle \beta \rangle)$ and $(\alpha$ *causes* $\langle \gamma \rangle) \to (\beta$ *causes* $\langle \gamma, \delta \rangle)$ together with $\neg(\beta \wedge \gamma \wedge \delta)$ (which makes W) where $\alpha, \beta, \gamma, \delta$ are propositional atoms.

The notion of *configuration* is to be used to specify the cases of reference between a cause and its effects. Letting $\mathcal{I}$ denote the set of interpretations in classical propositional logic, a *configuration* is a set of principal filters from $2^{\mathcal{I}}$ (hence an element of a configuration is the set of all the subsets of $\mathcal{I}$ which contain some given subset of $\mathcal{I}$). Since a set of interpretations is routinely identified with any (propositional) formula satisfied in exactly that set, a *configuration* can be assimilated with a set of conjunctions of propositional atoms.

Notice that the conjunction of 0 atoms, that is the true formula $\top$ (which corresponds to the full set $2^{\mathcal{I}}$, which is a principal filter), is an eligible element of a configuration, while the false formula $\bot$ (which corresponds to the empty set, which is not a filter), is not allowed here. Here is a simple example:

Flu causes some high temperature (either 38° or 39° or 40°) and 40° causes shiver: $\varphi_1 = flu$ *causes* $\langle t38, t39, t40 \rangle$, $\varphi_2 = t40$ *causes* $\langle shiver \rangle$.
Here are three examples of configurations:
$S_1 = \{t38, t39, t40 \wedge shiver\}, S_2 = \{shiver\}, S_3 = \{\top\}$.

Satisfaction with respect to an interpretation of classical propositional logic is denoted by means of the symbol $\models$ (e.g., $I \models \alpha$). which is also used to denote the relation of logical consequence from classical propositional logic.

A *causal interpretation* is a pair $\langle \mathcal{S}, I \rangle$ where I is an interpretation in classical propositional logic, $\mathcal{S}$ is a family (indexed by the propositional atoms) of configurations. In symbols, $I \in \mathcal{I}$ and $\mathcal{S} = \{S_\alpha, S_\beta, \ldots\}$ where each $S_\alpha \subseteq 2^{\mathcal{I}}$ is a set of principal filters and $\alpha, \beta, \ldots$ is a list of all propositional atoms.

Definition 1. *Causal satisfaction relation* and *causal inference*

A causal interpretation $\mathcal{C} = \langle \mathcal{S}, I \rangle$ satisfies a formula γ (written $\mathcal{C} \Vdash \gamma$) according to the following recursive rules:

$$\mathcal{C} \Vdash \neg \delta \quad \text{if} \quad \mathcal{C} \not\Vdash \delta \tag{1}$$

$$\mathcal{C} \Vdash \delta \vee \epsilon \quad \text{if} \quad \mathcal{C} \Vdash \delta \text{ or } \mathcal{C} \Vdash \epsilon \tag{2}$$

$$\mathcal{C} \Vdash \delta \to \epsilon \quad \text{if} \quad \mathcal{C} \not\Vdash \delta \text{ or } \mathcal{C} \Vdash \epsilon \tag{3}$$

$$\mathcal{C} \Vdash \delta \wedge \epsilon \quad \text{if} \quad \mathcal{C} \Vdash \delta \text{ and } \mathcal{C} \Vdash \epsilon \tag{4}$$

$$\mathcal{C} \Vdash \alpha \quad \text{if} \quad I \models \alpha \text{ for } \alpha \text{ propositional atom} \tag{5}$$

$$\mathcal{C} \Vdash \alpha \, causes \langle \beta_1, \ldots, \beta_n \rangle \quad \text{if} \quad \begin{cases} I \not\models \alpha \wedge \neg\beta_1 \wedge \ldots \wedge \neg\beta_n \quad \text{and} \\ \forall X \in S_\alpha \ \exists \beta_i \ \exists Y \in S_{\beta_i} \ X \models \beta_i \wedge Y, \\ \forall \beta_i \ \exists X \in S_\alpha \ \exists Y \in S_{\beta_i} \ X \models \beta_i \wedge Y. \end{cases} \tag{6}$$

We define *causal inference*, also denoted $\Vdash$, from the causal satisfaction relation as usual: $CT \Vdash \gamma$ holds iff all models of CT are models of $\{\gamma\}$.

As the configuration S_δ lists the cases describing the effects of a cause δ, the second condition $\forall X \in S_\alpha \ \exists \beta_i \cdots$ in (6) expresses that there is no case in which α causes none of $\beta_1, \ldots, \beta_n$. The third condition $\forall \beta_i \ \exists X \in S_\alpha \cdots$ expresses conversely that each of $\beta_1, \ldots, \beta_n$ does exist as an effect of α (this conditions reduces to $S_\alpha \neq \emptyset$ in case of a single effect $\langle \beta_1 \rangle$). For the reader to better grasp the intuitions underlying the above definition, let us continue our "flu" example:

Take $\mathcal{C} = \langle \mathcal{S}, I \rangle$ where $I = \emptyset$ (i.e., $I \models \neg flu$ and so on) and $\mathcal{S}$ such that $S_{flu} = \{t38, t39, t40 \wedge shiver\}$, $S_{t40} = \{shiver\}$, $S_{t38} = S_{t39} = S_{shiver} = \{\top\}$. Then, $\mathcal{C}$ is a model of $\{\varphi_1, \varphi_2\}$ (notice the mandatory occurrence of *shiver* together with $t40$ in S_{flu}). Let us verify $\mathcal{C} \Vdash t40 \, causes \langle shiver \rangle$:
– As to the first condition, $I \not\models t40 \wedge \neg shiver$ because $I \models \neg t40$.
– The second condition $\forall X \in S_{t40} \ \exists Y \in S_{shiver} \ X \models shiver \wedge Y$ is then instantiated by $X = shiver$ and $Y = \top$.
– The third condition reduces here to $S_{t40} \neq \emptyset$ (single effect).
Let us check $\mathcal{C} \not\Vdash t40 \, causes \langle t40 \rangle$: The second condition fails: X must be *shiver* here and, since $shiver \not\models t40$, we cannot get $X \models t40 \wedge Y$.

The semantics just presented bears some similarity with semantics involving a selection function for conditionals (among others, a version in [6] is: models are equipped with a family of functions indexed by $\mathcal{I}$ from the set of formulas to the powerset of $\mathcal{I}$ i.e. something fairly close to configurations). It does not come as a surprise that specifying causation-based cases shares some technical aspects with specifying counterfactual cases (would-be states of affairs). Of course, there cannot be an algebraic semantics in the usual sense that a Boolean algebra is endowed with an extra binary operation. As with logics failing substitution principles, some technical tricks would have to be used instead as in [15].

4   A Few Features of This Semantics

4.1   Two Small Typical Examples

Let us consider the following situation: $\alpha \, causes \langle \beta \rangle$, $\alpha \, causes \langle \gamma \rangle$. (S1)

We are looking for a model $\mathcal{C} = \langle \mathcal{S}, I \rangle$ of (S1). As for I, all we need is a model of the two formulas $\alpha \to \beta$ and $\alpha \to \gamma$. Let us choose $I = \{\alpha, \beta, \gamma\}$ (all propositional atoms true). As for $\mathcal{S}$, we need β and γ in each element of $S\alpha$. Here is a possibility: $S_\alpha = \{\beta \land \gamma\}$, $S_\beta = S_\gamma = \{\top\}$.

This model satisfies also the formula α *causes* $\langle \beta, \gamma \rangle$, and in fact each model of (S1) satisfies α *causes* $\langle \beta, \gamma \rangle$, meaning that we have: (S1) $\Vdash \alpha$ *causes* $\langle \beta, \gamma \rangle$.

Here is another typical situation: α *causes* $\langle \beta \rangle$, β *causes* $\langle \gamma \rangle$. (S2)

The model given above for (S1) falsifies β *causes* $\langle \gamma \rangle$. Indeed, γ must be in each element of S_β. Then, $\beta \land \gamma$ must be in each element of S_α. We can choose $I = \{\alpha, \beta, \gamma\}$ again, together with: $S_\alpha = \{\beta \land \gamma\}$, $S_\beta = \{\gamma\}$, $S_\gamma = \{\top\}$. Each model of (S2) satisfies α *causes* $\langle \gamma \rangle$, meaning that we get $(S2) \Vdash \alpha$ *causes* $\langle \gamma \rangle$. Remind that we consider transitivity as a desirable feature.

4.2   Where S_α Is the Empty Set

If $S_\alpha = \emptyset$ in a causal interpretation $\mathcal{C} = \langle \mathcal{S}, I \rangle$, then $\mathcal{C} \Vdash \neg(\alpha$ *causes* $\langle \beta_0 \cdots, \beta_n \rangle)$ and $\mathcal{C} \Vdash \neg(\beta_0$ *causes* $\langle \alpha, \beta_1, \cdots, \beta_n \rangle)$: α is neither a "cause" nor an "effect".

4.3   Irreflexivity

The condition for $\mathcal{C} \Vdash \delta$ *causes* $\langle \delta \rangle$ simplifies as $S_\delta \neq \emptyset$ and $\forall X \in S_\delta$ $X \not\models \delta$. This is why the above semantics invalidates δ *causes* $\langle \delta \rangle$.

Moreover, δ *causes* $\langle \gamma \rangle$ entails neither δ *causes* $\langle \delta \rangle$ nor γ *causes* $\langle \gamma \rangle$.

4.4   Transitivity

Chains of deterministic causes are admitted as shown by the valid inference

From δ *causes* $\langle \alpha \rangle$ and α *causes* $\langle \beta \rangle$ infer δ *causes* $\langle \beta \rangle$.

We have already stated this result with (S2) in §4.1. When it comes to chains of nondeterministic causes, the pertinent result is postponed to section 5 below. In particular, as expected (cf Introduction) the following inference is invalid:

From δ *causes* $\langle \alpha, \beta \rangle$ and β *causes* $\langle \gamma, \epsilon \rangle$ infer δ *causes* $\langle \alpha, \gamma, \epsilon \rangle$.

4.5   Sets of Effects Need Not Be Minimal in Causal Atoms

From δ *causes* $\langle \alpha_1, \cdots, \alpha_m \rangle$ and δ *causes* $\langle \beta_1, \cdots, \beta_n \rangle$,
we can infer δ *causes* $\langle \alpha_1, \cdots, \alpha_m, \beta_{i_1}, \cdots, \beta_{i_k} \rangle$
for any list $\beta_{i_1}, \cdots, \beta_{i_k}$ of elements of the set $\{\beta_1, \cdots, \beta_n\}$.

This property, which generalizes situation (S1) in §4.1, shows that cumulative effects are turned into disjunctive effects, so to speak, which is in accordance with the classical "*and* implies *or*", here applied to effects. This feature of the semantics shows that *causal atoms* are not absolutely *atomic*, but this was already clear from their definition, which involves "atoms" of different size.

Remind that having δ *causes* $\langle \alpha_1, \cdots, \alpha_m \rangle$ and δ *causes* $\langle \beta_1, \cdots, \beta_n \rangle$ is not exceptional. This is exemplified by subsection 4.4 where we get: if δ *causes* $\langle \alpha \rangle$ and α *causes* $\langle \beta \rangle$, then δ *causes* $\langle \beta \rangle$ (thus δ *causes* $\langle \alpha, \beta \rangle$).

4.6 Contradictory Effect

Our formalism does not allow causal atoms involving directly the false formula. An empty list $\langle\rangle$ can be assimilated to $\perp$ but, since we have excluded $\perp$ as an eligible element of a configuration, the second condition of (6) in Definition 1 cannot be satisfied: $\Vdash \neg(\delta \ causes \ \langle\rangle)$. Thus, we forbid empty lists $\langle\rangle$, leaving the introduction of the (single) contradictory effect for future work. This would in particular simulate some "*causal negation*", thus extending significantly the expressive power, but it is not a trivial matter.

4.7 Links with Logical Consequence

Deduction theorem: Due to the (rather traditional and classical) definition of the semantics and of the inference relation, the deduction theorem holds:

$$CT \cup \{\varphi\} \Vdash \psi \quad \text{iff} \quad CT \Vdash \varphi \rightarrow \psi.$$

Remark 1. Since condition $I \not\models \delta \wedge \neg\gamma_1 \wedge \ldots \wedge \neg\gamma_n$ is equivalent to $I \models \delta \rightarrow (\gamma_1 \vee \ldots \vee \gamma_n)$, the semantics validates the following inference:

$$\delta \ causes \ \langle\beta_1,\ldots,\beta_n\rangle \Vdash \delta \rightarrow (\beta_1 \vee \ldots \vee \beta_n)$$

which, by the deduction theorem, is equivalent to

$$\Vdash (\delta \ causes \ \langle\beta_1,\ldots,\beta_n\rangle) \rightarrow (\delta \rightarrow (\beta_1 \vee \ldots \vee \beta_n)).$$

Remark 2. Logical consequence fails in general to carry over to effects. Actually, that $\alpha \rightarrow \beta$ is a consequence of a theory CT does not entail that $\delta \ causes \ \langle\alpha\rangle \rightarrow \delta \ causes \ \langle\beta\rangle$ is a consequence of CT. Technically, the reason is that $\delta \ causes \ \langle\alpha\rangle$ imposes no condition on any configuration about β.

Remark 3. From Remark 1 we get that if δ causes α then whatever entails δ also *entails* α, but it need not *cause* α. It seems right that causation not be strongly related to logical consequence. Here is an illustration: It is certainly true that "being a compulsive gambler causes me to lose lots of money" but it seems more controversial to hold that "being a compulsive gambler and feeling sleepy causes me to lose lots of money". The above semantics fails

$$\text{if } \alpha \ causes \ \langle\gamma\rangle \text{ and } \delta \rightarrow \alpha \text{ then } \delta \ causes \ \langle\gamma\rangle,$$

which in turn invalidates

$$\text{if } \alpha \ causes \ \langle\gamma\rangle, \ \beta \ causes \ \langle\gamma\rangle, \text{ and } \delta \rightarrow \alpha \vee \beta, \text{ then } \delta \ causes \ \langle\gamma\rangle. \quad (7)$$

Remark 4. A related invalid principle is

$$\text{if } \delta \ causes \ \langle\alpha\rangle \text{ and } \alpha \leftrightarrow \beta \text{ then } \delta \ causes \ \langle\beta\rangle.$$

This principle becomes valid under the following constraint

$$\text{If} \quad W \models \alpha \leftrightarrow \beta \quad \text{then} \quad \begin{pmatrix} \forall X \in S_\delta \ \exists Y \in S_\alpha \ X \models Y \wedge \alpha \Rightarrow \\ \forall X \in S_\delta \ \exists Z \in S_\beta \ X \models Z \wedge \beta \end{pmatrix} \quad \text{(EE)}$$

Remark 5. Similarly, the above semantics invalidates

$$\text{If } \delta \text{ causes } \langle \alpha \rangle \text{ and } \delta \leftrightarrow \eta \text{ then } \eta \text{ causes } \langle \alpha \rangle$$

on the intuitive grounds that a cause is (roughly speaking) a reason for some effect(s) to happen whereas being true simultaneously with the cause is not enough for also being a reason for the effect(s).

4.8 Causes from New Premises Are Impossible

We can never infer a causal atom α *causes* $\langle \beta_1, \ldots, \beta_n \rangle$ from a theory CT which does not contain already, directly or indirectly, some causal atom α *causes* $\langle \gamma_1, \ldots, \gamma_m \rangle$. By "indirectly" here we mean allowing only "classical boolean inference", where causal atoms are dealt with as if they where new propositional atoms, e.g. inferring α *causes* $\langle \epsilon \rangle$ from δ *causes* $\langle \epsilon \rangle$ and δ *causes* $\langle \epsilon \rangle \rightarrow \alpha$ *causes* $\langle \epsilon \rangle$.

5   Proof System

The proof system $\vdash_c$ consists of any proof system for classical propositional logic extended with the following schemata

1. δ *causes* $\langle \gamma_1, \gamma_1, \gamma_2, \ldots, \gamma_n \rangle \leftrightarrow \delta$ *causes* $\langle \gamma_1, \gamma_2, \ldots, \gamma_n \rangle$.
2. δ *causes* $\langle \gamma_1, \ldots, \gamma_{i-1}, \gamma_i, \ldots, \gamma_n \rangle \rightarrow \delta$ *causes* $\langle \gamma_1, \ldots, \gamma_i, \gamma_{i-1}, \ldots, \gamma_n \rangle$.
3. δ *causes* $\langle \gamma_1, \ldots, \gamma_n \rangle \ \rightarrow \ (\delta \rightarrow \gamma_1 \vee \ldots \vee \gamma_n)$.
4. δ *causes* $\langle \gamma_1, \ldots, \gamma_n \rangle \wedge \gamma_1$ *causes* $\langle \alpha_1, \ldots, \alpha_m \rangle \rightarrow$

$$\bigvee_R \delta \text{ causes } \langle \alpha_{i_1}, \ldots, \alpha_{i_k}, \gamma_2, \ldots, \gamma_n \rangle \qquad \begin{array}{l} \text{where the range } R \text{ is} \\ \emptyset \neq \{\alpha_{i_1}, \ldots, \alpha_{i_k}\} \subseteq \{\alpha_1, \ldots, \alpha_m\}. \end{array}$$

5. δ *causes* $\langle \gamma_1, \ldots, \gamma_n \rangle \wedge \delta$ *causes* $\langle \alpha_1, \ldots, \alpha_m \rangle \rightarrow$
   δ *causes* $\langle \gamma_1, \ldots, \gamma_n, \alpha_{i_1}, \ldots, \alpha_{i_k} \rangle \qquad$ where each α_{i_j} is in $\{\alpha_1, \ldots, \alpha_m\}$.

Schemas 1 and 2 just say that the lists $\langle \gamma_1, \gamma_1, \gamma_2, \ldots, \gamma_n \rangle$ must in fact be considered as sets of formulas. Schema 3 refers to the result of *Remark 1* in § 4.7. Schema 4 describes what remains of transitivity (cf § 4.4). Schema 5 ensures that we get the result mentioned in § 4.5.

It is easy to prove that the logic presented in this text is sound, while completeness remains a conjecture:

Theorem 2. *If $CT \vdash_c \varphi$ then $CT \Vdash \varphi$.*

Two elementary typical examples of using this proof system are provided by the two situations of §4.1:

Case (S1): Point 5 gives $(\alpha \text{ causes } \langle \beta \rangle \wedge \alpha \text{ causes } \langle \gamma \rangle) \rightarrow \alpha \text{ causes } \langle \beta, \gamma \rangle$.
Case (S2): Point 4 gives $(\alpha \text{ causes } \langle \beta \rangle \wedge \beta \text{ causes } \langle \gamma \rangle) \rightarrow \alpha \text{ causes } \langle \gamma \rangle$.

6   Comments About Transitivity

6.1   A Few Valid and Invalid Principles

Here are two typical instances of schema 4:

$$\delta \; causes \; \langle \gamma_1, \ldots, \gamma_n \rangle \wedge \gamma_1 \; causes \; \langle \alpha \rangle \rightarrow \delta \; causes \; \langle \alpha, \gamma_2, \ldots, \gamma_n \rangle;$$

$$\delta \; causes \; \langle \gamma \rangle \wedge \gamma \; causes \; \langle \alpha, \beta \rangle \rightarrow \left(\begin{array}{ll} \delta \; causes \; \langle \alpha \rangle & \vee \\ \delta \; causes \; \langle \beta \rangle & \vee \\ \delta \; causes \; \langle \alpha, \beta \rangle. \end{array} \right)$$

The following are three consequences of these results, which concern what could be called "causal equivalence". We suppose that a theory contains the formula

$$(\alpha \; causes \; \langle \beta \rangle) \wedge (\beta \; causes \; \langle \alpha \rangle). \tag{8}$$

Then, we get:

$$\text{If } \delta \; causes \; \langle \alpha \rangle, \text{ then } \delta \; causes \; \langle \beta \rangle; \tag{9}$$

$$\text{If } \delta \; causes \; \langle \alpha, \alpha_1, \ldots, \alpha_n \rangle, \text{ then } \delta \; causes \; \langle \beta, \alpha_1, \ldots, \alpha_n \rangle; \tag{10}$$

$$\text{If } \alpha \; causes \; \langle \gamma \rangle, \text{ then } \beta \; causes \; \langle \gamma \rangle. \tag{11}$$

These results, which must be compared with Remark 4 in § 4.7 for cases (9) and (10), and with Remark 5 for case (11), show that "causal equivalence" is stronger than boolean equivalence, as expected. Notice however that, still supposing formula (8), the following principle remains invalid:

$$\text{If } \alpha \; causes \; \langle \gamma_1, \ldots, \gamma_n \rangle, \text{ then } \beta \; causes \; \langle \gamma_1, \ldots, \gamma_n \rangle.$$

We get no more than the disjunction obtained by point (4) in § 5:
If $\alpha \; causes \; \langle \gamma_1, \ldots, \gamma_n \rangle$, then $\bigvee_{\emptyset \neq \{\gamma_{i_1}, \ldots, \gamma_{i_k}\} \subseteq \{\gamma_1, \ldots, \gamma_n\}} (\beta \; causes \; \langle \gamma_{i_1}, \ldots, \gamma_{i_k} \rangle)$.
Here, "causal equivalence" is not stronger than the causal atom $\beta \; causes \; \langle \alpha \rangle$.

6.2   Enlarging the Semantics

Let us suppose that we have the following causal theory CT_1:

$$\alpha \; causes \; \langle \beta \rangle, \quad \beta \; causes \; \langle \gamma, \epsilon \rangle, \quad \alpha \; causes \; \langle \epsilon' \rangle; \quad \epsilon' \rightarrow \neg \epsilon.$$

Here are a few causal consequences of CT_1:
$\alpha \; causes \; \langle \beta, \epsilon' \rangle$, $\alpha \; causes \; \langle \gamma \rangle \vee \alpha \; causes \; \langle \epsilon \rangle \vee \alpha \; causes \; \langle \gamma, \epsilon \rangle$,
$\alpha \; causes \; \langle \beta, \epsilon', \gamma \rangle \vee \alpha \; causes \; \langle \beta, \epsilon', \epsilon \rangle \vee \alpha \; causes \; \langle \beta, \epsilon', \gamma, \epsilon \rangle$,
and the three implications $\alpha \rightarrow \beta$, $\beta \rightarrow (\gamma \vee \epsilon)$ and $\alpha \rightarrow \epsilon'$.

We get the expected result $\alpha \rightarrow \gamma$ (from the four implications). However the causal formula $\varphi = \alpha \; causes \; \langle \gamma \rangle$ is not a consequence of CT_1.

There are two reasons for this: The partial disconnection between causal formulas and classical formulas on one hand. The restrictions put on causal formulas which prevent negations in causal atoms on the other hand.

Here is a simple modification which will give the formula φ. Let us separate the W part of any causal theory CT into a "definitional part" WD and a remaining part. The semantics is modified by replacing the inference $\models$ in (6) of Definition 1 by $\models_{WD}$ (inference in WD), $X \models_{WD} Y$ meaning $WD \cup \{X\} \models Y$. In CT_1 here, $\epsilon' \to \neg\epsilon$ would be put in WD, and with this modified causal inference $\Vdash_D$ we get $CT_1 \quad \Vdash_D \quad \alpha$ *causes* $\langle\gamma\rangle$, in accordance with a natural expectation. The proof system in § 5 should then been modified by adding a rule generalizing to the case of not single effects the new behavior of this example, namely $CT_1 \to \alpha$ *causes* $\langle\gamma\rangle$.

Notice that this new semantics would not modify the behavior in case (7) of Remark 3 in § 4.7. One reason is that this would violate the property given in §4.8. Another way to see this is that putting $\delta \to \alpha \vee \beta$ in WD would not modify S_δ. If we wanted to get the conclusion δ *causes* $\langle\gamma\rangle$ in case (7) (which is not a desirable feature in our opinion), a more serious modification of the semantics, in the lines of condition (EE) in Remark 4 in §4.7, would be necessary.

7 Inferring Causal Explanations

There are two ways to reason from causes and effects. One is just deduction: From what is known to be true and what is known to cause what, infer what else is true. The other is abduction: From what is observed and what is known to cause what, infer what could explain the current facts. Notice that neither task is about discovering causal relationships: these are supposed to be already available and are simply used to infer deductive/abductive conclusions.

The above account of causes being rather strict, it can serve as a basis for both tasks.

As for deduction, it corresponds directly to causal inference $\Vdash$: the premises consist of facts and causal statements and the conclusions are statements expected to be true by virtue of the premises. typically, $(\alpha \vee \beta) \wedge \delta$ together with δ *causes* $\langle\gamma\rangle$ make $(\alpha \vee \beta) \wedge \gamma \wedge \delta$ to be deduced.

As for abduction, it works typically as follows: Consider the information stating that δ causes either α or β or γ. Consider further that *observation* β happens to be the case (it is a fact). Then, δ might explain that β has taken place. Hence the next definition:

Given a causal theory CT, δ *is a* causal explanation *for* β *if*
$CT \Vdash \delta$ *causes* $\langle\gamma_1, \ldots, \gamma_{i-1}, \beta, \gamma_{i+1}, \ldots, \gamma_n\rangle$.

The explanation relationship does not propagate through equivalence (Remark 5).

It must be reminded that since *possible explanations* are inferred, there is no guarantee of inferring only the "right" explanation (if any). Most of the time, the *available* causal information is anyway not enough to determine what the right explanation is and a logic is not meant to go beyond the premises it is applied to.

The relations as defined here can be considered as too strict, and in practice they should be augmented by considering some "definition formulas" WD as explained in § 6.2, which would extend the range of application of the formalism.

8   Causal Relation Versus Predictive Inference

Some logics for causal reasoning (e.g., [4,7]) satisfy apparently much more properties than the formalism presented here. However, any comparison should keep in mind that here a new specific kind of "causal formulas" has been introduced by the way of the "causal atoms". These causal atoms are not real atoms, as already remarked, since (1) they are physically made of smaller atoms, and (2) new "causal atoms" can be inferred from sets of causal atoms, as shown in § 5, and even "greater" causal atoms than those already present can be inferred, as shown in points (1) and (5) of the proof system (§ 5). However, they are "atoms" in a weak sense, which explains the relatively small number of properties allowing to derive new causal atoms.

This explains why, when making a comparison with most of the literature on the subject, the *predictive inference*, namely $\Vdash$, must be taken into account rather than the *causes* whose (presently known) properties are listed in §5.

Here are a few properties satisfied by the predictive inference $\Vdash$:

Material Implication $\{\alpha \ causes \ \langle\gamma_1,\dots\gamma_i\rangle\} \Vdash \alpha \to \gamma_1 \vee \dots \vee \gamma_i$
Strengthening $\{\alpha \ causes \ \langle\gamma\rangle, \ \delta \to \alpha, \ \delta\} \Vdash \gamma.$
Right Weakening $\{\alpha \ causes \ \langle\delta\rangle, \ \delta \to \gamma, \ \alpha\} \Vdash \gamma.$
Or (in antecedent) $\{\alpha \ causes \ \langle\gamma\rangle, \ \beta \ causes \ \langle\gamma\rangle, \ \delta \leftrightarrow \alpha \vee \beta, \ \delta\} \Vdash \gamma.$
Cut $\{\alpha \ causes \ \langle\gamma\rangle, \ \beta \ causes \ \langle\delta\rangle, \ \alpha \wedge \gamma \leftrightarrow \beta, \ \alpha\} \Vdash \delta.$

Since $\{\} \Vdash \top$ and $\{\alpha, \neg\alpha\} \Vdash \bot$ obviously hold, it looks like the predictive inference relation satisfies all the postulates of a *causal production relation* as defined in [4] and all the properties of a *disjunctive causal relation* [3]. It must be pointed out that our hypotheses are expressed here in terms of causal formulas while our conclusions pertain to classical logic.

Since the "disjunctive case" as considered e.g. in [3] does not really go "inside the disjunctive effects", formalisms such as those from [3,7] will not have the same behavior as ours when it comes to abduction. The reason is that inference in our logic strictly conforms with the causal chains which can effectively be obtained. If γ_1 happens to be inferred by means of the causal formula $\delta \ causes \ \langle\gamma_1,\gamma_2\rangle$ under the assumption δ (in symbols, $CT \Vdash \delta \ causes \ \langle\gamma_1,\gamma_2\rangle$ and $CT \cup \{\delta\} \Vdash \gamma_1$) then δ becomes an abductive conclusion but it would not be so if γ_1 were to be true for another reason (a purely deductive one). This feature seems important for a correct treatment of disjunctive effects when dealing with abduction.

9   Perspectives and Conclusion

We have provided a logical framework intended to formalize causal relations, allowing predictive and abductive reasoning. Classical propositional logic has been extended by new causal formulas describing causal relations as they are known by the user. These causal formulas follow a semantics which has been tailored in order to get the expected conclusions, and no more. Also, these formulas admit only propositional atoms as premises and only set of such atoms (intending to model disjunctive effects) as conclusions. This is to keep the definitions simple enough.

Restricting the arguments of the causal operators to propositional atomic formulas is unsatisfactory. We have evoked two ways in order to overcome this problem: (1) Considering "definitional formulas", which take a key role in the definition of the semantics, as explained in § 6.2. (2) Adopt a condition (such as (EE) in Remark 4 in §4.7), linking the causal configurations of formulas which are equivalent in W, which would extend even more the range of the predictive inference.

Yet, much remains to be done to extend the above logic to enjoy arbitrary formulas as arguments of the causal operators. Perhaps the main difficulty lies in the following incompatibility. Presumably, δ being a cause for α should not lead to the conclusion that δ is a cause for $\alpha \vee \beta$. However, δ being a cause for $\alpha \wedge \beta$ should entail that δ is a cause for α. Thus, δ being a cause for $(\alpha \vee \beta) \wedge \alpha$ should entail that δ is a cause for $\alpha \vee \beta$. As $(\alpha \vee \beta) \wedge \alpha$ is logically equivalent with α, it follows that δ being a cause for α would entail that δ is a cause for $\alpha \vee \beta$ – unless logically equivalent effects are not taken to share the same causes. Such a requirement is technically possible (as in the above logic) but is more problematic when arbitrary formulas occur as arguments of the causal operators: The statement that δ is a cause for $\alpha \leftrightarrow \neg\beta$ would fail to be equivalent to the statement that δ is a cause for $\beta \leftrightarrow \neg\alpha$ (similarly, δ causing $(\alpha \wedge \beta) \vee (\alpha \wedge \gamma)$ would not be equivalent with δ causing $\alpha \wedge (\beta \vee \gamma)$, and so on).

Another direction for generalization is to alleviate the constraint that a cause always brings about the effect. E.g., taking "Too much light causes blindness" to be true even though there would be some possibility that certain circumstances may tolerate too much light not to lead to blindness. A technical solution would be to introduce a constant $\star$ in the language to stand for a "ghost" effect. In order to encode the example just given about light and blindness, l *causes* $\langle b, \star \rangle$ would do whereas l *causes* $\langle b \rangle$ would not hold. Special rules should obviously govern $\star$, so that δ *causes* $\langle \gamma_1, \ldots, \gamma_n \rangle$ be consistent with $\neg(\delta$ *causes* $\langle \gamma_1, \ldots, \gamma_n, \star \rangle)$ and δ *causes* $\langle \gamma_1, \ldots, \gamma_n, \star \rangle$ be consistent with $\neg(\delta$ *causes* $\langle \gamma_1, \ldots, \gamma_n \rangle)$.

We have presented the basis for developing a logic taking causal relations into consideration. Once the pertinent causal relations are known, together with some background knowledge, the aim is to deduce some conclusions, or to abduce some hypotheses. Here, our goal was to define a set of basic incontestable rules. Then, real systems should be built upon this kernel, by adding some "ornament". This is the place where notions such as *strong* or *definitional knowledge* ("is-a rules" in particular), and some *weaker knowledge* should be introduced. Also, in order to facilitate tasks such as diagnosis, notions of *observable formulas* and *abducible formulas* should be considered. We consider that the basic rules cannot be extended significantly without loosing their adequacy with the nature of causation rules, and that real problems can been solved by taking care of the variety of the kinds of informations at hand. Also, some non-monotonic methods could be provided, e. g. by using the "ghost effect" evoked above.

Acknowledgments

It is a pleasure for the authors to thank the referees for their helpful and constructive comments.

References

1. Besnard Ph. and Cordier M.-O. Inferring Causal Explanations. In A. Hunter and S. Parsons (editors), *ECSQARU-99*, pp. 55–67, LNAI Vol. 1638, Springer, 1999.
2. Bell J. Causation and Causal Conditionals. In D. Dubois, C. Welty and M.-A. Williams (editors), *KR-04*, pp. 2–11, AAAI Press, 2004.
3. Bochman A. On Disjunctive Causal Inference and Indeterminism. In G. Brewka and P. Peppas (editors), *IJCAI* Workshop: *NRAC-03*, pp. 45–50, 2003.
4. Bochman A., A Causal Theory of Abduction. Common Sense 2005 pp. 33–38, 2005
5. Collins J., Hall N. and Paul L. A. (editors), *Causation and Counterfactuals*, MIT Press, 2004.
6. Chellas B. F. *Modal Logic*. Cambridge University Press, 1980.
7. Giunchiglia E., Lee J., Lifschitz V., McCain N., Turner H. Nonmonotonic Causal Theories. *Artificial Intelligence* 153(1–2):49–104, 2004.
8. Hall N. Causation and the Price of Transitivity. *Journal of Philosophy* 97:198–222, 2000.
9. Halpern J. and Pearl J. Causes and Explanations: A structural-model approach. Part I: Causes. In J. S. Breese and D. Koller (eds), *UAI-01*, pp. 194–202, Morgan Kaufmann, 2001.
10. Halpern J. and Pearl J. Causes and Explanations: A Structural-Model Approach - Part II: Explanations. In B. Nebel (ed), *IJCAI-01*, pp. 27-34, Morgan Kaufmann, 2001.
11. Lewis D. Causation. *Journal of Philosophy* 70:556–567, 1973.
12. Lewis D. *Counterfactuals*. Blackwell, 1973.
13. Lewis D. Causation as Influence. *Journal of Philosophy* 97:182–197, 2000.
14. Mellor D. H. *The Facts of Causation*. Routledge, 1995.
15. Nute D. *Topics in Conditional Logic*. Reidel, 1980.
16. Pearl J. *Causality*. Cambridge University Press, 2000.
17. Shafer G. *The Art of Causal Conjecture*. MIT Press, 1996.
18. Shafer G. Causal Logic. In H. Prade (ed), *ECAI-98*, pp. 711-720, Wiley, 1998.
19. Yablo S. Advertisement for a Sketch of an Outline of a Proto-Theory of Causation. In [5].

Taking LEVI IDENTITY Seriously: A Plea for Iterated Belief Contraction

Abhaya Nayak[1], Randy Goebel[2], Mehmet Orgun[1], and Tam Pham[3]

[1] Intelligent Systems Group, Department of Computing
Division of ICS, Macquare University, Sydney, NSW 2109, Australia
{abhaya, mehmet}@ics.mq.edu.au
[2] Department of Computing Science, University of Alberta
Edmonton, Alberta, Canada T6G 2H1
goebel@cs.ualberta.ca
[3] Thomas M. Siebel Center for Computer Science, University of Illinois
201 N. Goodwin Avenue, Urbana, IL 61801-2302
tampham2@uiuc.edu

Abstract. Most work on iterated belief change has focused on iterated belief revision, namely how to compute $(K_x^*)_y^*$. Historically however, belief revision can be defined in terms of belief expansion and belief contraction, where expansion and contraction are viewed as primary operators. Accordingly, our attention to iterated belief change should be focused on constructions like $(K_x^+)_y^+$, $(K_x^-)_y^+$, $(K_x^+)_y^-$ and $(K_x^-)_y^-$. The first two of these are relatively straightforward, but the last two are more problematic. Here we consider these latter, and formulate iterated belief change by employing the Levi identity and the Harper Identity as the guiding principles.

Keywords: Belief Change, Information State Change, Iterated Belief Contraction.

How new evidence impignes upon the knowledge of a rational agent has been the subject of vigorous discussion in the last couple of decades. Alchourrón, Gärdenfors and Makinson [1], who initiated discussion on this issue in the non-probabilistic framework provided the basic formal foundation for this discussion. Several variations and extensions of the basic framework have since been investigated by different researchers in the area including belief update, multiple belief change, iterated belief change, and belief merging. The subject of this paper is largely to do with the problem of iterated belief change.

Belief change has been viewed as any form of change in an agent's beliefs. Three forms of belief change have been investigated in the literature: expansion – simple addition of new beliefs, even if it means the agent's beliefs contradict each other; contraction – removal of a belief from one's belief corpus; and revision – addition of new beliefs while ensuring that the resulting belief corpus is consistent. The result of expanding, contracting or revising a belief corpus K by a sentence x is respectively represented as the corpora K_x^+, K_x^- and K_x^*. Properties of these operations are captured by well known rationality postulates, and constructive approaches to these operators are available in the literature [1,7,8]. K_x^+ is simply defined as $Cn(K \cup \{x\})$ where Cn is the

J. Lang, F. Lin, and J. Wang (Eds.): KSEM 2006, LNAI 4092, pp. 305–317, 2006.
© Springer-Verlag Berlin Heidelberg 2006

consequence operation of the background logic. The connection between these operators is captured by the famous Levi Identity: $K_x^* = (K_{\neg x}^-)_x^+$. So, belief revision can always be taken to be a secondary notion constructed via the primitive operations of belief expansion and belief contraction.

By *Iterated Belief Change* we refer to the problem of dealing with sequential changes in belief. On the face of it, then, iterated belief change should deal with how we can construct the corpus $(K_x^\square)_y^\diamond$ given belief corpus K, sentences x and y and belief change operations $\square$ and $\diamond$. Literature in the area have largely dealt with iterated belief revision: constructing $(K_x^*)_y^*$. Given the Levi Identity, it would appear that we could do away with revision, in favour of expansion and contraction. If so, then what we should be discussing instead are construction of corpora such as $(K_x^+)_y^+, (K_x^-)_y^+, (K_x^+)_y^-$ and $(K_x^-)_y^-$. The first two of these constructions, where the second operation is expansion, are unproblematic (given a contraction operation), since expansion is a very simple operation. It is the last two of these constructs that pose rather difficult problems. The aim of this paper is to address these two forms of iterated belief change.

Let us look at these problems in somewhat more detail. Expansion operation is not state-sensitive: K_x^+ is completely determined by K and x. But contraction operation is. The set K_x^- is not fully determined by K and x: depending on what belief state K is associated with, the value of K_x^- would be different. In particular, belief contraction inherently involves a choice among multiple candidate beliefs for removal, and the preference information that determines this choice is in the belief state but is extraneous to the belief set K. Hence what is really lacking is an appropriate account of state expansion and state contraction.

Assume that a belief set K, two sentences x and y, and an appropriate contraction operation $(-)$ are given. Since $(+)$ is not state-sensitive, $(K_x^+)_y^+$ is simply $Cn(K \cup \{x, y\})$. Similarly, $(K_x^-)_y^+$ is simply $Cn(K_x^- \cup \{y\})$, which is easily determined given that we know how the contraction operation $(-)$ behaves. But since $(-)$ is state sensitive, the construction of $(K_x^+)_y^-$ and of $(K_x^-)_y^-$ can not be subjected to such simple treatment. Assuming that K is different from K_x^+ (respectively K_x^-), they are part of different belief states, and hence the contraction operation appropriate for removing beliefs from K is not appropriate for removing beliefs from K_x^+ (respectively from K_x^-). This paper is therefore primarily about characterising the belief sets $(K_x^+)_y^-$ and of $(K_x^-)_y^-$.

In Section 1, we introduce the problem of iterated belief revision, and briefly outline the Lexicographic Revision [10], a particular approach to iterated belief revision via state revision. It is followed by a discussion of a need for accounts of state expansion and state contraction. Section 2 provides semantic accounts of state expansion and state contraction. Analogues of the Levi Identity and the Harper Identity are used to restrict the choices for state contraction operation. It is noticed that the contraction operation obtained is akin to the Lexicographic Revision in spirit. A Test Case is analysed; it is observed that Lexicographic Contraction, unlike other forms of contraction mentioned in the paper, leads to expected intuitive results for iterated contraction. In Section 3 some properties of the Lexicographic Contraction are discussed. We conclude with a short summary.

1 Background

The theory of belief change purports to model how a current theory or body of beliefs, K, can be rationally modified in order to accommodate a new observation x. A piece of observation, such as x is represented as a sentence in a propositional language $\mathcal{L}$, and a theory, such as K, is assumed to be a set of senteneces in $\mathcal{L}$, closed under a supraclassical consequence operation, Cn. Since the new piece of information x may contravene some current beliefs in K, chances are, some beliefs in K will be discarded before x is eased into it. Accordingly, three forms of belief change are recognised in the belief change framework:

1. CONTRACTION: K_x^- is the result of discarding some unwanted information x from the theory K
2. EXPANSION: K_x^+ is the result of simple-mindedly incorporating some information x into the theory K, and
3. REVISION: K_x^* is the result of incorporating some information x into the theory K in a manner so as to avoid internal contradiction in K_x^*.

The intuitive connection among these operators is captured by the following two identities named, respectively, after Isaac Levi and William Harper:

LEVI IDENTITY: $K_x^* = (K_{\neg x}^-)_x^+$, and
HARPER IDENTITY: $K_x^- = K_{\neg x}^* \cap K$.

There is another, third, identity that, though well known, has not merited special nomenclature:

THIRD IDENTITY

$$K_x^+ = \begin{cases} K_x^* \text{ if } \neg x \notin K \\ K_\perp \text{ otherwise} \end{cases}$$

The three belief change operations are traditionally introduced with three sets of *rationality postulates*. These postulates, along with motivation and interpretation for them, may be found in [7]. The expansion operation is very easily constructed: $K_x^+ = Cn(K \cup \{x\})$. Contraction and Revision operations are relatively more sophisticated operations since they deal with choice. The three identities mentioned above show that the three operations are to a large extent inter-definable. However, right from the start, the contraction and expansion operations have been taken to be more fundamental operations than the revision operation, and accordingly, the Levi Identity has typically been used to define revision via contraction and expansion.

The AGM postulates deal with "one-shot" belief change. It can deal with iterated belief revision as long as each subsequent piece of evidence does not conflict with the result of previous belief revisions, and it places no special constraints on iterated belief change when $\neg y \in K_x^*$. For instance, as pointed out by Darwiche and Pearl [6], if one initially believed (on independent grounds) that X is smart and rich, and were to accept two conflicting pieces of evidence in sequence – that X is not smart, and *then* that X is smart after all – one expects to retain the belief that X is rich in the process. However, the standard AGM account of belief revision will offer no such guarantee.

To alleviate this situation, several proposals have been advanced including Natural Revision [5], Knowledge Transmutation [13], revision by epistemic states [2] and Lexicographic Revision [9,10]. Here we briefly revisit the Lexicographic Revision, in particular its semantics, since as we will see, the problem of iterated contraction naturally leads to its counterpart, *lexicographic contraction*.

1.1 Lexicographic State Revision

Lexicographic approach to iterated belief revision is captured by a particular account of state revision [10]. The semantics of Lexicographic Revision is given in terms of an evolving belief state, where a belief state is represented as a plausibility ordering over the interpretations generated by the background language.

Definition 1. *Let Ω be the set of possible worlds (interpretations) of the background language $\mathcal{L}$, and $\sqsubseteq$ a total preorder (a connected, transitive and reflexive relation) over Ω. For any set $\Sigma \subseteq \Omega$ and world $\omega \in \Omega$ we will say ω is a $\sqsubseteq$-minimal member of Σ if and only if both $\omega \in \Sigma$ and $\omega \sqsubseteq \omega'$ for all $\omega' \in \Sigma$.*

By $\omega_1 \sqsubseteq \omega_2$ we will understand that ω_2 is not more plausible than ω_1. The expression $\omega_1 \equiv \omega_2$ will be used as a shorthand for ($\omega_1 \sqsubseteq \omega_2$ *and* $\omega_2 \sqsubseteq \omega_1$). The symbol $\sqsubset$ will denote the strict part of $\sqsubseteq$. For any set $S \subseteq \mathcal{L}$ we will denote by $[S]$ the set $\{\omega \in \Omega \mid \omega \models s \text{ for every } s \in S \}$. For readability, we will abbreviate $[\{s\}]$ to $[s]$. Intuitively, the preorder $\sqsubseteq$ will be the semantic analogue of the revision operation $*$, and will represent the belief states of an agent. We will say that $K_\sqsubseteq$ is the belief set associated with the preorder $\sqsubseteq$. It is defined as the set of sentences satisfied by the $\sqsubseteq$-minimal worlds, i.e.

$$K_\sqsubseteq = \{x \in \mathcal{L} \mid \omega \models x \text{ for all } \sqsubseteq\text{-minimal } \omega \in \Omega\}$$

An inconsistent belief state is represented by an empty relation $\sqsubseteq_\perp$: for every pair $\omega, \omega' \in \Omega, \omega \not\sqsubseteq_\perp \omega'$. Note that this violates connectedness, and hence the plausibility relation $\sqsubseteq$ is, strictly speaking, no longer a total preorder. However, this is a special case, and merits special treatment.

A modified Grove-Construction [8] is used to construct the revision operation from a given plausibility relation:

Definition 2. ($\sqsubseteq$ **to** $*$)

$$x \in K_e^{*\sqsubseteq} \text{ iff } \begin{cases} [e] \subseteq [x] & \text{if } \sqsubseteq = \sqsubseteq_\perp \\ \omega \models x \text{ for every } \omega \sqsubseteq\text{-minimal in } [e] & \text{otherwise.} \end{cases}$$

The plausibility ordering (belief state) $\sqsubseteq$, in light of new evidence e, is stipulated to evolve to the new ordering $\sqsubseteq_e^\circledast$ via the use of a state revision operator $\circledast$ as follows.

TWO SPECIAL CASES

1. If $[e] = \emptyset$ then, and only then, $\sqsubseteq_e^\circledast = \sqsubseteq_\perp$.
2. Else, if $\sqsubseteq = \sqsubseteq_\perp$, then $\omega_1 \sqsubseteq_e^\circledast \omega_2$ iff either $\omega_1 \models e$ or $\omega_2 \models \neg e$.

GENERAL CASE: Given nonempty prior ($\sqsubseteq \neq \sqsubseteq_\perp$) and satisfiable evidence($[e] \neq \emptyset$),

1. If $\omega_1 \models e$ and $\omega_2 \models e$ then $\omega_1 \sqsubseteq_e^\circledast \omega_2$ iff $\omega_1 \sqsubseteq \omega_2$
2. If $\omega_1 \models \neg e$ and $\omega_2 \models \neg e$ then $\omega_1 \sqsubseteq_e^\circledast \omega_2$ iff $\omega_1 \sqsubseteq \omega_2$
3. If $\omega_1 \models e$ and $\omega_2 \models \neg e$ then $\omega_1 \sqsubset_e^\circledast \omega_2$

1.2   State Expansion and State Contraction

Just as there is a need for iterated belief revision, there is a *prima facie* case for iterated belief expansion and iterated belief contraction. The former is trivial: $(K_x^+)_y^+ = Cn(Cn(K \cup \{x\}) \cup \{y\}) = Cn(K \cup \{x, y\})$. Iterated Belief Contraction, however, does not succumb to such an easy solution. Just like revision, contraction involves choice; hence iterated belief contraction would presuppose an account of contracting from a choice mechanism. It is little surprise that the rationality postulates of belief contraction offered by the AGM does not provide a cogent account of iterated belief contraction.

Interestingly, there is very little discussion in the literature regarding iterated belief contraction – a few exceptions being [3,4,11] and [12]. Arguably, the reason behind such reluctance is the fact that, in some sense or other, belief revision and belief expansion are "natural" operations whereas belief contraction is a "theoretical construct". Despite the persuasion of literary critics to view the *willing suspension of disbelief* as a constituting ingredient of poetic faith[1], in the belief change literature, belief contraction remains a second class citizen. However, even if belief contraction is not as natural as other forms of belief change, iterated belief contraction deserves the researchers' attention – if not for anything else, for the sake of completeness. As we argued in the introductory part of this paper, there are further compelling reasons to study iterated belief contraction – it follows from the very basic motivation behind the Levi Identity that we should be studying constructions such as $(K_x^+)_y^-$, and $(K_x^-)_y^-$. The aim of the next section is to explore this issue.

2   Approach

Given a contraction function, we can construct a revision function by first contracting everything in the belief set that would cause the addition of x to lead to inconsistency and then expanding the belief set by x. That is the intuition behind the Levi Identity. It is the Levi Identity that embodies the idea that revision is reducible to contraction and expansion – the idea that forces us to examine different combinations of contraction and expansion, different forms of *belief change*. However, the Levi Identity, as traditionally conceived, involves modification of a *belief set*, whereas iterated belief revision involves revision of a preorder over possible worlds (revision of a *belief state*): $\sqsubseteq_x^\circledast$ is taken to be the resultant preorder, when the given preorder $\sqsubseteq$ is revised in light of an accepted input sentence x. It is therefore desirable to obtain an analogue of the Levi Identity:

NEW LEVI IDENTITY $\sqsubseteq_x^\circledast = (\sqsubseteq_{\neg x}^\ominus)_x^\oplus$
where $\ominus$ is a state contraction operation, and $\oplus$ is a state expansion operator.

Therefore, our aim now is to define these two new operators $\sqsubseteq_x^\ominus$ and $\sqsubseteq_x^\oplus$ similar to $\sqsubseteq_x^\circledast$ in a way that this analogy is preserved. Once this aim is achieved, it will be sufficient to characterise any belief change by using only the contraction and expansion of preorders.

---

[1] Samuel Taylor Coleridge in *Biographia Literaria* (1817), chapter 14. Note that disbelief traditionally is taken to be a form of belief: disbelief in x is actually belief in $\neg x$; hence suspension of disbelief is a form of belief suspension.

2.1 Semantics for State Expansion

Belief expansion is the simplest form of belief change. In the AGM account, belief expansion is captured by: $K_x^+ = Cn(K \cup \{x\})$. Semantically speaking, $[K_x^+] = [K] \cap [x]$: the result of accepting information x results in a state that entertains exactly those worlds that satisfy all the old beliefs as well as the accepted piece of information. It follows that expansion does not handle inconsistency very well – if the new piece of information conflicts with the current beliefs, the agent ends up believing anything and everything.

As mentioned in Section 1, expansion can be defined in terms of belief revision (the "Third Identity"). This motivates the way we define the expansion preorder as follows:

$$\sqsubseteq_x^\oplus = \begin{cases} \sqsubseteq_x^\circledast & \text{if } \neg x \notin K \\ \sqsubseteq_\perp & \text{otherwise} \end{cases}$$

In other words, if there exists a world $\omega \in [x]$ such that ω is $\sqsubseteq$-minimal, then the resultant belief state would be the same whether we *expand* the current belief state by x or *revise* it by x. However, if the current belief does not entertain any world ω which satisfies x, then its expansion to include x will result in an inconsistent state.

With this definition of the state expansion operator, we are now in the position to construct the state contraction operator.

2.2 State Contraction and the Levi Identity

The use of a system of nested spheres of worlds to visually represent the preorder (belief state) $\sqsubseteq$ is well known [8]: a world more central in the system represents a more plausible world than one relatively less central. A sphere is a set of possible worlds and a system of spheres is a set of nested spheres which can be considered as an ordering of plausibility over the worlds; the more plausible worlds lying closer to the centre of the system of spheres. The smallest sphere at the centre of the system represents the current beliefs in the sense that it consists of exactly the worlds that satisfy the current beliefs. Two boundary cases of such representation of a belief state are:

1. FULL STATE. If $\omega \sqsubseteq \omega'$ for all worlds ω and ω', the system of sphere is conflated to a single sphere. It represents the state of complete epistemic innocence – the agent in question holds no contingent beliefs whatsoever. It is the state of null information $\sqsubseteq_\top$: the associated belief set is $Cn(\emptyset)$.
2. EMPTY STATE. If $\omega \sqsubseteq \omega'$ for *no* two worlds ω and ω', the state in question represents the "epistemic hell", a state in which the agent believes every conceivable state of affairs. This is the state of full information $\sqsubseteq_\perp$: the associated belief set is $K_\perp = Cn(\perp)$.

In order to contract from the state of null information, nothing needs to be done. So,

$$(\sqsubseteq_\top)_x^\ominus = \sqsubseteq_\top \text{ for all } x.$$

However, contracting from the state of full information is not so obvious. To contract $K_\perp$ by x, we need to allow some world which is consistent to $\neg x$ to be included in the central sphere of the resultant belief state. So it is reasonable to suggest that $(K_\bot)^-_x = Cn(\{\neg x\})$. However, in this case, the agent will end up believing $\neg x$ but this should not be allowed as there is no evidence to support either x or $\neg x$. Therefore, it is only fair that the agent will lose all the information and start his/her epistemic life again when he/she reaches this state $(K_\bot)^-_x = Cn(\emptyset)$. Accordingly we postulate that

$$(\sqsubseteq_\bot)^\ominus_x = \sqsubseteq_\top \text{ for all } x.$$

Now let us look at how state contraction should function in the principal case. Let the initial state $\sqsubseteq$ be represented by a system of spheres $[K_0] \subseteq [K_1] \subseteq [K_2] \subseteq [K_3]$ where, as illustrated in Figure 1 (top-left, state before contraction), $[K_0] = 1$, $[K_1] = [K_0] \cup 2 \cup 5$, $[K_2] = [K_1] \cup 3 \cup 6$ and $[K_3] = [K_2] \cup 4 \cup 7 = \Omega$. We are interested in contracting this state by the belief x, where $[\neg x] = 5 \cup 6 \cup 7$. In order to satisfy the original Levi Identity, it will suffice if the state resulting from this contraction centers on $[K_0] \cup 5$, since that would ensure that if K_0 was to be revised by $\neg x$, the resulting theory will hold of exactly those worlds that are minimal in $[\neg x]$, that is, 5. This effectively is the relevant *faithfulness* condition for belief contraction.

The new Levi Identity imposes one more constraint on this. It effectively says that, the resultant state after the contraction, apart from having $[K_0] \cup 5$ as the center, must ensure that the prior ordering of worlds inside $[x]$ (respectively outside $[x]$) should not be disturbed. That is, for any two worlds ω and ω' that are both inside $[x]$ (or both inside $[\neg x]$), it holds that $\omega \sqsubseteq^\ominus_x \omega'$ iff $\omega \sqsubseteq \omega'$. This condition is quite appealing,

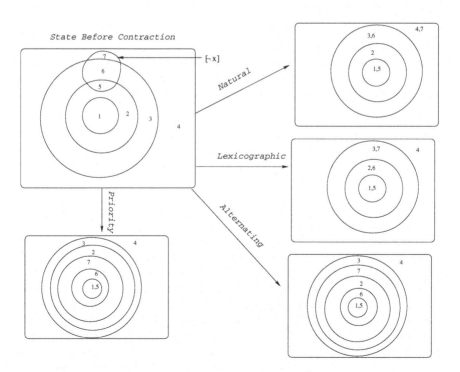

Fig. 1. States before and after the contraction

and is reminiscent of conditions well known in the context of iterated belief revision [6,10]. It turns out that in the current context, the new Levi Identity is liberal enough to allow many different constructions of the state contraction operation $\ominus$. In Figure 1, we illustrate only four of many such constructions, each of which looks reasonable, and satisfies the new Levi Identity.

1. NATURAL CONTRACTION: The only modification in the starting state effected is due to the faithfulness requirement. All other worlds are left as before.
2. LEXICOGRAPHIC CONTRACTION: Faithfulness puts $[K_0]$ and the worlds in 5 at the same footing. All other worlds are "shifted" accordingly, thus for instance, worlds in 2 and in 6 are viewed to be at par with each other.
3. ALTERNATING CONTRACTION: Faithfulness is respected. Then, repeatedly, the next best worlds in $[x]$ and $[\neg x]$ are alternated, with $[\neg x]$ being given priority.
4. PRIORITY CONTRACTION: All worlds in $[\neg x]$ are given more priority than all worlds in $[x]$, subject to the satisfaction of Faithfulness. Faithfulness is respected.

It is easily noticed that all these four constructions of a state contraction operation will satisfy the New Levi Identity. Hence, if we must identify a unique state contraction operation, and a good case can be made for it, further reasonable principles must be identified and adhered to. We find such a principle in the generalisation of the Harper Identity, as discussed below.

2.3   Harper Identity to the Rescue

In the context of classical belief change, while the Levi Identity is used to define revision in terms of contraction, the Harper Identity is used for the converse purpose: $K_x^- = K \cap K_{\neg x}^*$. Semantically the Harper Identity says that the $\sqsubseteq$-minimal worlds in Ω and the $\sqsubseteq$-minimal worlds in $[\neg x]$ are to be given equivalent status in the state resulting from the contraction of $\sqsubseteq$ by x. We generalise this Identity as follows:

NEW HARPER IDENTITY. Let B_i, $0 \leq i \leq n-1$ be the n bands ($\sqsubseteq$-equivalence classes) of worlds generated by the pre-contraction state $\sqsubseteq$, where B_0 consists of the $\sqsubseteq$-minimal worlds in Ω and $\omega \sqsubseteq \omega'$ for all $\omega \in B_i$, $\omega' \in B_j$ and $i < j$. Let C_i, $0 \leq i < k \leq n$ be the k $\sqsubseteq$-equivalent classes of worlds in $[\neg x]$, i.e., $\bigcup_{i=0}^{k-1} C_i = [\neg x]$, and $\omega \sqsubseteq \omega'$ for all $\omega \in C_i$, $\omega' \in C_j$ and $i < j$. Define $C_{i+1} = \emptyset$ for $k-1 \leq i < n-1$. The bands in $\sqsubseteq_x^\ominus$ are inductively given by $D_0 = B_0 \cup C_0$ and $D_{i+1} = (B_{i+1} \setminus [\neg x]) \cup C_{i+1}$, for $0 \leq i < n-1$.

Let's now look at Figure 2 that provides a simple illustration of lexicographic state contraction in order to gain a better appreciation of the New Harper Identity. The pre-contraction belief state is given by the bands B_0-B_8, B_0 being the set of $\sqsubseteq$-minimal worlds $[K]$. The bands C_0-C_4 (shown shaded in Figure 2) constitute $[\neg x]$, the bands with smaller index being relatively more plausible. (Note the disjointed nature of $[\neg x]$.) When we contract this state by x, the minimal worlds in the resultant state (i.e. $[K_x^-]$) is given by $[K] \cup min_{\sqsubseteq}([\neg x]) = B_0 \cup C_0$, as required by the classical Harper Identity, and is captured by D_0 as defined in the New Harper Identity. The next best worlds in the post-contraction state, namely D_1, are given by the worlds in B_1 that are *not already* accounted for, i.e. $B_1 \setminus D_0$ (denoted X_1 in Figure 2, captured by $B_1 \setminus [\neg x]$ in the New

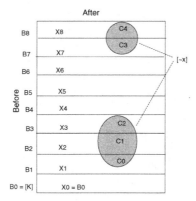

Fig. 2. State before and after a lexicographic contraction by x – a simpler view

Harper Identity), together with the next best worlds C_1 in $[\neg x]$. The other bands, D_2-D_8 are similarly constructed. Note that in this example bands C_5-C_8 are set to $\emptyset$.

In section 2.2 we noted that all that the new Levi Identity mandates is that (1) the $\sqsubseteq$-minimal worlds of Ω as well as of $[\neg x]$ be the minimal worlds in the state resulting after contraction by x, and that (2) the relative ordering of worlds inside $[x]$ as well as out side $[x]$ should not be affected by the contraction. It is easily verified that the new Harper Identity satisfies these two conditions, and thus subsumes the new Levi Identity. We invite the reader to verify that Lexicographic contraction is the only one among the four state contraction operations described earlier that satisfies the new Harper Identity.

2.4 A Test Case

We have noticed that the new Levi Identity and the new Harper Identity argue in favour of adopting Lexicographic Contraction as the correct state contraction operation. In this section we examine a test case to see how this operation fares *vis a vis* our intuitive judgment about iterated contraction. We consider a variant of a well known example due to Darwiche and Pearl [6]:

We initially believe on independent grounds that x is smart and that x is rich. That is, removing smart leaves rich undisturbed, and similarly, removing rich leaves smart undisturbed. The question is, what should we believe if we were to first remove smart followed by removal of rich. That is, what should be $(K_{smart}^{\ominus})_{rich}^{\ominus}$? Intuitively, the resultant belief set should have nothing interesting to say about smart and rich. Figure 2 below illustrates this scenario. In this figure, ij where $i, j \in \{0,1\}$ represents a world that evaluates smart to i and rich to j. In the pre-contraction state (the box on the left) $11 \sqsubset 10 \sqsubset 01 \sqsubset 00$, satisfying the requirement that both smart and rich are believed. The central column illustrates the result of the first contraction (by smart): it shows that both 01 and 11 are $\sqsubseteq_{smart}^{\ominus}$-minimal worlds according to all the four contraction strategies, thus showing that smart is removed, but rich is retained. Thus at this stage the contraction strategies behave identically at the *knowledge level*. The third column illustrates the state $(\sqsubseteq_{smart}^{\ominus})_{rich}^{\ominus}$ according to different strategies. It shows that the result of using Lexicographic Contraction concurs with our

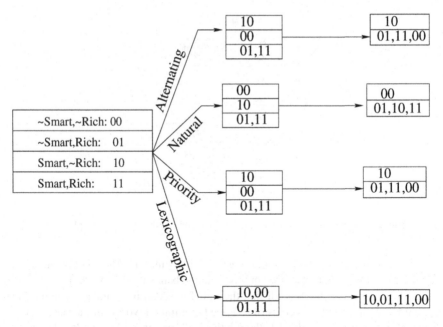

Fig. 3. A variant of Smart-Rich problem

intuitive expectation. In contrast, the other operations leave residual beliefs: the Natural Contraction allows the agent to retain the belief smart ∨ rich, while both Priority and Alternating retain smart → rich.

Thus, this test case adds further credence to Lexicographic Contraction.

3   Partial Characterisation

In this section we provide some interesting properties of the Lexicographic contraction operation. First we notice that if the second piece of information to be contracted is not believed at that point, then there is nothing to done. That is,

1. If $y \notin K_x^-$ then $(K_x^-)_y^- = K_x^-$

This directly follows from the AGM contraction postulates. Now we consider the more interesting case when the contraction is non-vacuous. We therefore assume that $y \in K_x^-$ in all the properties that are discussed below. One case of interest in this context is when y is entailed by x. In this case, one might expect that since the contraction by y from K would willy nilly remove x from K, the belief set $(K_x^-)_y^-$ would be simply K_y^-. Consider this. I believe, on independent grounds, that Tweety (the infamous bird) is both a singer and dancer, although my confidence level on Tweety's singing ability is a lot higher than on its dancing ability. However, I am first confronted with evidence that makes my doubt if Tweety has such rare joint capability (our x is sings ∧ dances); so I discard the belief that Tweety is a dancer, still retaing the belief that it can sing. The subsequent evidence I gather makes me discard the belief that Tweety can sing (our y); so in $(K_x^-)_y^-$ neither do I believe that Tweet can sing, nor do I believe that it can dance.

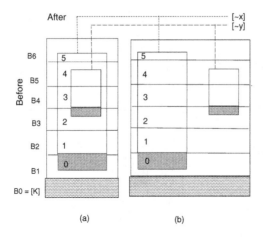

Fig. 4. Contraction when either $x \vdash y$ or $\neg x \vdash y$

On the other hand, if I were to discard the belief that Tweety sings from my initial belief corpus, I would still maintain that it can dance since I had believed them independently. that is, the belief that Tweety dances is still maintained in K_y^-. Beliefs lost in the first round of contraction remains lost in subsequent rounds. Accordingly we suggest:

2. If both $y \in K_x^-$ and $x \vdash y$, then $(K_x^-)_y^- = K_x^- \cap K_y^-$.

Note that when $x \vdash y$ we have the logical equivalence between $x \vee y$ and y. Hence this postulate can be equivalently replaced by

If both $y \in K_x^-$ and $x \vdash y$, then $(K_x^-)_y^- = K_x^- \cap K_{x \vee y}^-$.

The next case of interest is when $\neg x \vdash y$; i.e., $\vdash x \vee y$. Let's take a variant of our previous example. I believe, on independent grounds, that Tweety sings but does not dance. I am asked by a reliable party to stay prepared since Tweety might be neither a singer nor a dancer (our x is sings $\vee$ dances). After the appropriate contraction, I discard the belief that Tweety sings but retain the initial conviction that Tweety is no dancer. Subsequently I learn that Tweety might actually be a dancer, so I perform a contraction by $\neg$dances (our y). Again, it seems appropriate that the only resultant beliefs would be those that can survive both the individual contractions:

3. If both $y \in K_x^-$ and $\neg x \vdash y$, then $(K_x^-)_y^- = K_x^- \cap K_y^-$.

The following corollary to this postulate lends it further support:

If $\neg x \in K_x^-$ then $(K_x^-)_{\neg x}^- = K_{\neg x}^-$.

Note further that when $\neg x \vdash y$, we have y and $x \rightarrow y$ as logical equivalents. Hence postulate (3) can be equivalently replaced by:

If both $y \in K_x^-$ and $\neg x \vdash y$, then $(K_x^-)_y^- = K_x^- \cap K_{x \rightarrow y}^-$.

The lexicographic Contraction operation defined via the new Harper Identity satisfies both of the postulates (2) and (3). Instead of providing the formal proof, we appeal to

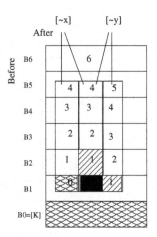

Fig. 5. A scenario depicting $(K_x^-)_y^- \neq K_x^- \cap K_y^-$: after contraction by x

the Figure 4 from which the proofs can be easily constructed. In Figure 4(a) we have $[\neg y] \subseteq [\neg x]$ representing $x \vdash y$. In Figure 4(b), since $[\neg y] \subseteq [x]$, it represents $\neg x \vdash y$. In either case, note that $min([\neg x]) \cap [\neg y] = \emptyset$ leading to the fact that $y \in K_x^-$. In each case, the result of the two sequential contractions is given by the union of the shaded portions, i.e., $B_0 \cup min([\neg x]) \cup min([\neg y])$ which is equivalent to $(B_0 \cup min([\neg x])) \cup (B_0 \cup min([\neg y]))$ which translates to $K_x^- \cap K_y^-$.

One might wonder that whenever $y \in K_x^-$, perhaps $K_x^- \cap K_y^-$ would give the result of the sequential (lexicographic) contraction $(K_x^-)_y^-$. That however is not the case. In Figure 5 we illustrate a scenario to establish this point. In this figure, a darkened out cell represents an empty intersction. Note that $min([\neg x]) \cap [\neg y] = \emptyset$ ensuring that $y \in K_x^-$. Furthermore, since neither $[\neg y] \subseteq [\neg x]$ nor $[\neg y] \subseteq [x]$, this figure represents a scenerio where $x \nvdash y$ and $\neg x \nvdash y$. In this figure, the "wavy shading" represents worlds that are $\sqsubseteq_x^\Theta$-minimal in Ω (i.e. $[K_x^-]$), and the hatched area represent worlds that are $\sqsubseteq_x^\Theta$-minimal in $\neg y$. Note that, unlike in Figure 4, here $min_\sqsubseteq([\neg y] \neq min_{\sqsubseteq^\Theta}([\neg y])$. In fact, $min_{\sqsubseteq^\Theta}([\neg y]) = min_\sqsubseteq([\neg y]) \cup min_\sqsubseteq([\neg x] \cap [\neg y])$. Consequently, $[(K_x^-)_y^-] = [K_x^-] \cup min_{\sqsubseteq^\Theta}([\neg y] = [K_x^-] \cup min_\sqsubseteq([\neg x] \cap [\neg y]) \cup min_\sqsubseteq([\neg y]) = [K_x^-] \cup ([K] \cup min_\sqsubseteq([\neg x] \cap [\neg y])) \cup ([K] \cup min_\sqsubseteq([\neg y]) = [K_x^-] \cup [K_{x \vee y}^-] \cup [K_y^-]$ whereby we get, in this particular case, $(K_x^-)_y^- = K_x^- \cap K_y^- \cap K_{x \vee y}^- \neq K_x^- \cap K_y^-$. And this is not the only exceptional scenerio.

We have not yet obtained a compact and interesting syntactic representation of these properties of lexicographic contraction. We have however obtained an interesting result that we present below:

Theorem 1. *Let x and y be any two sentences. There is some subset S of the set of belief-sets $\{K_{x \to y}^-, K_{y \to x}^-, K_{x \vee y}^-\}$ such that $(K_x^-)_y^- = \bigcap(S)$.*

The semantic intuition behind this result is that, given the new Harper Identity, no matter how $[\neg x]$ and $[\neg y]$ are configured in an initial belief state, the result $[(K_x^-)_y^-]$ will be constructed from the union of $\sqsubseteq$-minimal worlds in Ω, $[\neg x \wedge y]$, $[x \wedge \neg y]$ and $[\neg x \wedge \neg y]$.

4 Conclusion

We began with the idea of replacing the revision operator with the expansion and contraction operations in the context of iterated belief change. This was motivated by our desire to exploit the Levi Identity, which naturally led to the problem of iterated contraction. Under this formulation, we defined state expansion and state contraction operations by using an analogue of the Levi Identity appropriate for state transformations. It turned out that this analogue is not strong enough to determine a unique state contraction operation. We then argued that an analogue of the Harper Identity leads to a reasoned account of state contraction, which naturally corresponds to the idea behind lexicographic Revision. An examination of a test case provides further evidence in support of such a state contraction operation, and we have provided a partial characterisation of this operation. A complete characterisation of this operation, and its generalisation in order to complement belief merging will be pursued in our future work.

References

1. C. E. Alchourrón, P. Gärdenfors, and D. Makinson. On the logic of theory change. *Journal of Symbolic Logic*, 50:510–530, 1985.
2. S. Benferhat, S. Konieczny, O. Papini and R. Pino Pèrez. Iterated Revision by epistemic states: axioms, semantics and syntax. In W. Horn (ed.) *Proceedings of ECAI 2000: 14th European Conference on Artificial Intelligence*, pages 13-17, 2000, IOS Press.
3. A. Bochman. Contraction of epistemic states: A general theory. In M.-A. Williams and H. Rott (eds.) *Frontiers in Belief Revision*, Kluwer, pp. 195–220, 2001.
4. R. Booth, S. Chopra, A. Ghose and T. Meyer. A unifying semantics for belief change. In R. Lopez De Mantaras and L. Saitta (eds.) *Proceedings of ECAI 2004: Sixteenth European Conference on Artificial Intelligence*, pages 793-797, 2004, IOS Press.
5. C. Boutilier. Iterated revision and Minimal Revision of Conditional Beliefs. *Journal of Philosophical Logic*, **25**:262 – 304, 1996.
6. A. Darwiche and J. Pearl. On the Logic of Iterated Belief Revision. *Artifical Intelligence*, 89:1–29, 1997.
7. P. Gärdenfors. *Knowledge in Flux: Modeling the Dynamics of Epistemic States*. MIT Press, Cambridge Massachusetts, 1988.
8. A. Grove. Two modellings for theory change. *Journal of Philosophical Logic*, 17:157–170, 1988.
9. A. C. Nayak. Iterated Belief Change Based on Epistemic Entrenchment. *Erkenntnis* **41**:353 – 390, 1994.
10. A. C. Nayak, M. Pagnucco, and P. Peppas. Dynamic belief revision operators. *Artifical Intelligence*, pages 193–228, 2003.
11. H. Rott. *Change, Choice and Inference: A study of belief revision and nonmonotonic reasoning*. Oxford Science Publications, Clarendon Press, 2001.
12. H. Rott. Adjusting Priorities: Simple Representations for 27 Iterated Theory Change Operators. *Manuscrript*, October 2004.
13. M-A. Williams. Transmutations of Knowledge Systems. In J. Doyle and E. Sandewall (eds.) *Proceedings of the Fourth International Conference on Principles of Knowledge Representation and Reasoning*, pp. 619 – 629, 1994.

Description and Generation of Computational Agents

Roman Neruda[1] and Gerd Beuster[2]

[1] Institute of Computer Science, Academy of Sciences of the Czech Republic
Pod vodárenskou věží 2, 182 07 Prague 8, Czech Republic
roman@cs.cas.cz
[2] Institute of Informatics, University Koblenz-Landau
Universitätsstr. 1, 56070 Koblenz, Germany
gb@uni-koblenz.de

Abstract. A formalism for the logical description of computational agents and multi-agent systems is given. It is explained how it such a formal description can be used to configure and reason about multi-agent systems realizing computational intelligence models. A usage within a real software system *Bang 3* is demonstrated. The logical description of multi-agent systems opens *Bang 3* for interaction with ontology based distributed knowledge systems like the Semantic Web.

1 Introduction

The use of distributed Multi-Agent Systems (MAS) instead of monolithic programs has become a popular topic both in research and application development. Autonomous agents are small self-contained programs that can solve simple problems in a well-defined domain [1]. In order to solve complex problems, agents have to collaborate, forming Multi-Agent Systems (MAS). A key issue in MAS research is how to generate MAS configurations that solve a given problem [2]. In most Systems, an intelligent (human) user is required to set up the system configuration. Developing algorithms for automatic configuration of Multi-Agent Systems is a major challenge for AI research.

Bang 3 is a platform for the development of Multi-Agent Systems [3], [4]. Its main areas of application are computational intelligence methods (genetic algorithms, neural networks, fuzzy controllers) on single machines and clusters of workstations. Hybrid models, including combinations of artificial intelligence methods such as neural networks, genetic algorithms and fuzzy logic controllers, seem to be a promising and extensively studied research area [5]. *Bang 3* — as a distributed multi-agent system — provides a support for an easy creation and execution of such hybrid AI models.

Bang 3 applications require a number of cooperating agents to fulfill a given task. So far, MAS are created and configured manually. In this paper, we introduce a logical reasoning component for *Bang 3*. With this component, *Bang 3* system configurations can be created automatically and semi-automatically. The logical description of MAS opens *Bang 3* for interaction with ontology based distributed knowledge systems like the Semantic Web [6].

The description of *Bang 3* by formal logics enhances the construction, testing, and application of *Bang 3*-MAS in numerous ways:

J. Lang, F. Lin, and J. Wang (Eds.): KSEM 2006, LNAI 4092, pp. 318–329, 2006.

– System Checking
A common question in Multi-Agent System design is whether a setup has certain
properties. By the use of formal descriptions of the agents involved in a MAS and
their interactions, properties of the MAS can be (dis-)proved [7].
– System Generation
Starting with a set of requirements, the reasoning component can be used to create a MAS. The formal logical component augments evolutionary means of agent
configuration that are already present in *Bang 3* [8].
– Interactive System Generation
The reasoning component can also be used to create agents in semi-automated
ways. Here, the reasoning component acts as a helper application aiding a user
in setting up MAS by making suggestions.
– Interaction with ontology based systems
There is a growing interest in creating common logical frameworks (ontologies)
that allow the interaction of independent, distributed knowledge based system.
The most prominent one is the Semantic Web, which attempts to augment the
World Wide Web with ontological knowledge. Using formal logics and reasoning
in *Bang 3* allows to open this world to *Bang 3*.

2   Logical Description of MAS

In order to satisfy these requirements, the logical formalism must fulfill the following
requirements:

1. It must be expressive enough to describe *Bang 3* MAS.
2. There must be efficient reasoning methods.
3. It should be suitable to describe ontologies
4. It should interface with other ontology based systems.

There is a lot of research in how to use formal logics to model ontologies. The goal
of this research is to find logics that are both expressive enough to describe ontological
concepts, and weak enough to allow efficient formal reasoning about ontologies.

The most natural approach to formalize ontologies is the use of First Order Predicate
Logics (FOL). This approach is used by well known ontology description languages
like Ontolingua [9] and KIF [10].

The disadvantage of FOL-based languages is the expressive power of FOL. FOL
is undecidable [11], and there are no efficient reasoning procedures. Nowadays, the
de facto standard for ontology description language for formal reasoning is the family
of description logics. Description logics are equivalent to subsets of first order logic
restricted to predicates of arity one and two [12]. They are known to be equivalent to
modal logics [13].

For the purpose of describing multi-agent systems, description logics are sometimes
too weak. In these cases, we want to have a more expressive formalism. We decided
to use Prolog-style logic programs for this. In the following chapters, we describe how
both approaches can be combined together.

Description logics and Horn rules are orthogonal subsets of first order logic [12]. During the last years, a number of approaches to combine these two logical formalisms in one reasoning engine have been proposed. Most of these approaches use tableaux-style reasoners for description logics and combine them with Prolog-style Horn rules. In [14], Hustadt and Schmidt examined the relationship between resolution and tableaux proof systems for description logics. Baumgartner, Furbach and Thomas propose a combination of tableaux based reasoning and resolution on Horn logic [15]. Vellion [16] examines the relative complexity of SL-resolution and analytic tableau. The limits of combining description logics with horn rules are examined by Levy and Rousset [17]. Borgida [18] has shown that Description Logics and Horn rules are orthogonal subsets of first oder logic.

3   Describing *Bang 3* Agents

An *agent* is an entity that has some form of perception of its environment, can act, and can communicate with other agents. It has specific skills and tries to achieve goals. A *Multi-Agent System (MAS)* is an assemble of interacting agents in a common environment [19].

In order to use automatic reasoning on a MAS, the MAS must be described in formal logics. For the *Bang 3* system, we define a formal description for the static characteristics of the agents, and their communication channels. We do not model dynamic aspects of the system yet.

Bang 3 agents communicate via messages and triggers. Messages are XML documents send by an agent to another agent. A triggers are XML patterns with an associated function. When an agent receives a message matching the XML pattern of one of its triggers, the associated function is executed. In order to identify the receiver of a message, the sending agent needs the message itself and a link to the receiving agent. A conversation between two agents usually consists of a number of messages. For example, when a neural network agent requests training data from a data source agent, it may send the following messages:

- Open the data source located at XYZ,
- Randomize the order of the data items,
- Set the cursor to the first item,
- Send next item.

These messages belong to a common category: Messages requesting input data from a data source. In order to abstract from the actual messages, we subsume all these messages under a *message type* when describing an agent in formal logics.

Definition 1. *Message type*
A message type *identifies a category of messages that can be send to an agent in order to fulfill a specific task. We refer to message types by unique identifiers.*

The set of message types understood by an agent is called its *interface*. For outgoing messages, each link of an agent is associated with a message type. Via this link, only messages of the given type are sent. We call a link with its associated message type a *gate*.

Definition 2. *Interface*
An interface is the set of message types understood by a class of agents.

Definition 3. *Gate*
A gate is a tuple consisting of a message type and a named link.

Now it is easy to define if two agents can be connected: Agent A can be connected to agent B via gate G if the message type of G is in the list of interfaces of agent B. Note that one output gate sends messages of one type only, whereas one agent can receive different types of messages. This is a very natural concept: When an agent sends a message to some other agent via a gate, it assigns a specific role to the other agent, e.g. being a supplier of training data. On the receiving side, the receiving agent usually should understand a number of different types of messages, because it may have different roles for different agents.

Definition 4. *Connection*
A connection is described by a triple consisting of a sending agent, the sending agent's gate, and a receiving agent.

Next we define *agents* and *agent classes*. *Bang 3* is object oriented. Agents are created by generating instances of classes. An agent derives all its characteristics from its class definition. Additionally, an agent has a name to identify it. The static aspects of an agent class are described by the interface of the agent class (the messages understood by the agents of this class), the gates of the agent (the messages send by agents of this class), and the type(s) of the agent class. Types are nominal identifiers for characteristics of an agent. The types used to describe the characteristics of the agents should be ontological sound.

Definition 5. *Agent Class*
An agent class is defined by an interface, a set of message types, a set of gates, and a set of types.

Definition 6. *Agent*
An agent is an instance of an agent class. It is defined by its name and its class.

4 Describing Multi-Agent Systems

Multi-Agent Systems are assembles of agents. For now, only static aspects of agents are modeled. Therefore, a Multi-Agent System can be described by three elements: The set of agents in the MAS, the connections between these agents, and the characteristics of the MAS. The characteristics (constraints) of the MAS are the starting point of logical reasoning: In *MAS checking* the logical reasoner deduces if the MAS fulfills the constraints. In *MAS generation*, it creates a MAS that fulfills the constraints, starting with an empty MAS, or a manually constructed partial MAS.

Definition 7. *Multi-Agent System*
Multi-Agent Systems (MAS) consist of a set of agents, a set of connections between the agents, and the characteristics of the MAS.

Table 1. Concepts and roles used to describe MAS

Concepts	
mas(C)	C is a Multi-Agent System
class(C)	C is the name of an agent class
gate(C)	C is a gate
m_type(C)	C is a message type
Roles	
type(X,Y)	Class X is of type Y
has_gate(X,Y)	Class X has gate Y
gate_type(X,Y)	Gate X accepts messages of type Y
interface(X,Y)	Class X understands mess. of type Y
instance(X,Y)	Agent X is an instance of class Y
has_agent(X,Y)	Agent Y is part of MAS X

```
class(decision_tree)
type(decision_tree, computational_agent)
has_gate(decision_tree, data_in)
gate_type(data_in, training_data)
interface(decision_tree, control_messages)
```

Fig. 1. Example agent class definition

Description logics know concepts (unary predicates) and roles (binary predicates). In order to describe agents and Multi-Agent Systems in description logics, the definitions 1 to 7 are mapped onto description logic concepts and roles as shown in table 1.

An example agent class description is given in figure 1. It defines the agent class "decision_tree". This agent class accepts messages of type "control_message". It has one gate called "data_in" for data agent and emits messages of type "training_data".

In the same way, A-Box instances of agent classes are defined:

$$instance(decision\_tree, dt\_instance)$$

An agent is assigned to a MAS via role "has_agent". In the following example, we define "dt_instance" as belonging to MAS "my_mas":

$$has\_agent(my\_mas, dt\_instance)$$

Since connections are relations between three elements, a sending agent, a sending agent's gate, and a receiving agent, we can not formulate this relationship in traditional description logics. It would be possible to circumvent the problem by splitting the triple into two relationships, but this would be counter-intuitive to our goal of defining MAS in an ontological sound way. Connections between agents are relationships of arity three: Two agents are combined via a gate. Therefore, we do not use description logics, but traditional logic programs in Prolog notation to define connections:

$$connection(dt\_instance, other\_agent, gate)$$

Constraints on MAS can be described in Description Logics, in Prolog clauses, or in a combination of both. As an example, the following concept description requires the MAS "dt_MAS" to contain a decision tree agent:

$$dt\_MAS \sqsupseteq mas \sqcap has\_agent.(\exists instance.decision\_tree)$$

An essential requirement for a MAS is that agents are connected in a sane way: An agent should only connect to agents that understand its messages. According to definition 4, a connection is possible if the message type of the sending agent's output gate matches a message type of the receiving agent s interface. With the logical concepts and descriptions given in this section, this constraint can be formulated as a Prolog style horn rule. If we are only interested in checking if a connection satisfies this property, the rule is very simple:

connection(S,R,G) ←
    instance(R, RC) ∧
    instance(S, SC) ∧
    interface(RC, MT)∧
    has_gate(SC, G) ∧
    gate_type(G, MT)

The first two lines of the rule body determine the classes RC and SC of the sending agent S and the receiving agent R. The third line instantiates MT with a message type understood by RC. The fourth line instantiates G with a gate of class SC. The last line assures that gate G matches message type MT.

The following paragraphs show two examples for logical descriptions of MAS. It should be noted that these MAS types can be combined, i.e. it is possible to query for trusted, computational MAS.

Computational MAS. A computational MAS can be defined as a MAS with a task manager, a computational agent and a data source agent which are interconnected (cf. Fig. 2):

comp_MAS(MAS) ←
    type(CAC, computational_agent)∧
    instance(CA, CAC)∧
    has_agent(MAS, CA)∧
    type(DSC, data_source)∧
    instance(DS, DSC)∧
    has_agent(MAS, DS)∧
    connection(CA, DS, G)∧
    type(TMC, task_manager)∧
    instance(TMC, TM)∧
    has_agent(MAS, TM)∧
    connection(TM, CA, GC)∧
    connection(TM, DS, GD)

Trusted MAS. We define that an MAS is trusted if all of its agents are instances of a "trusted" class. This examples uses the Prolog predicate `findall`. `findall` returns a list of all instances of a variable for which a predicate is true. In the definition of predicate `all_trusted` the usual Prolog syntax for recursive definitions is used.

trusted_MAS(MAS) ←
    findall(X, has_agent(MAS,X), A))∧
    all_trusted(A)
all_trusted([]) ← true
all_trusted([F|R]) ←
    instance(F,FC)∧
    type(FC, trusted) ∧
    all_trusted([R])

5 Implementation

The above described concepts and algorithms are implemented within the *Bang 3* software system as the BOA agent. This agent works with ontological description files of the two kinds: the Description Logics description of agent hierarchies, their gates, interfaces and message types, and the Prolog clauses describing more complicated properties and concepts, such as the form of computational MAS, or the notion of trust.

5.1 Computational Multi-Agent Systems

In this section we give examples of two MAS schemes describing the computational MAS definition from section 4.

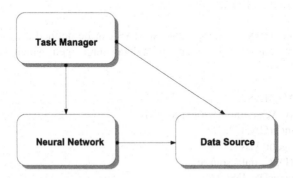

Fig. 2. Example of a small computational MAS consisting of a Task Manager agent, Data Source agent, and a computational agent (Multilayer Perceptron)

Figure 2 shows an example of the most simple computational MAS in *Bang 3* which consists only of the computational agent, data and a task manager (which can be a user interacting via GUI, or more complicated agent performing series of experiments over a cluster of workstations).

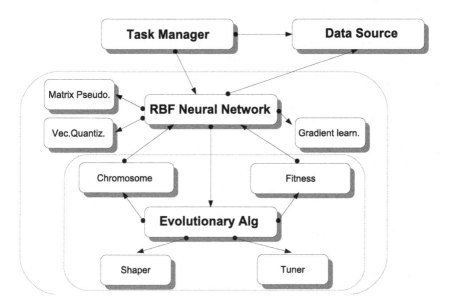

Fig. 3. Example of a more complicated computational MAS consisting of a Task Manager agent, Data Source agent, and a suite of cooperating computational agents (an RBF network agent and Evolutionary algorithm agent with necessary additional agents)

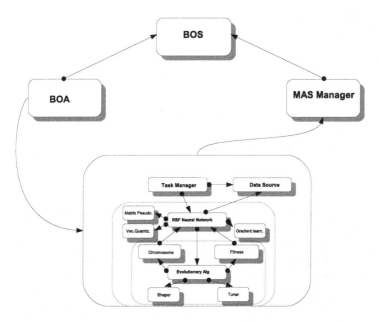

Fig. 4. The BOA agent generates a MAS configuration description and sends it to the MAS manager agent, which takes care of MAS creation and run. They both query the BOS ontology services agent.

```
(implies iAgentStdIface (and
        (some message_type agentLifeManagement)
    (all message_type agentLifeManagement)))

(implies igToYellowPages (and
        (some message_type yellowPageRequest)
    (all message_type yellowPageRequest)))

(implies Father (and (some interface iAgentStdIface)
    (all interface iAgentStdIface)
    (some gate igToYellowPages)
    (all gate igToYellowPages)))
...
;;Decision Tree
(implies aDecisionTree (and Classifier
    IterativeComputation
    Father
    classInBang))
;;Neural Networks
(implies NeuralNetwork Approximator)

;;RBF Network
(implies RBFNetworkAI (and NeuralNetwork
    IterativeComputation
    classInBang
    SimpleTaskManager
    Father
    (some gate igSolveRepresentatives)
    (some hide igCommonCompControl)
    (all hide igCommonCompControl)
    (some gate igSolveLinEqSystem)
    (all gate (or igSolveRepresentatives igSolveLinEqSystem))
    (some interface igRunNetworkDemo)
    (all interface igRunNetworkDemo)))
```

Fig. 5. Example of agent ontology description in the RACER Lisp-like formalism

A more typical computational MAS configuration is shown on figure 3. There are two more complicated computational agents, the RBF neural network (RBF) and the Evolutionary algorithm (EA) agent, that cooperate with each other within a computational MAS. Each of these two agents can itself be seen as a MAS employing several simpler agents to solve a given task. In the case of the RBF network, typically, an unsupervised learning (vector quantization), and a supervised learning (gradient, matrix inverse) agent is needed. The evolutionary algorithm agent makes use of fitness (shaper) and probabilities manager (tuner). The cooperation of RBF and EA is more intricate and takes place via the fitness and chromozome agents.

5.2 MAS Descriptions

Descriptions of the above shown — and similar — MASes are generated by the BOA agent in a formal description language. This description is then sent to the MAS manager agent, which is able to take care of physical creation of the whole system. This includes creating suitable agents (either new ones, or reusing free existing ones, or even finding suitable ones by means of ontology services), linking their gates and interfaces, sending them appropriate initialization messages, etc. This is typically followed by an (automated) trial and evaluation of the computational MAS on a particular data set.

Another way of BOA work, which is currently being developed, is an integration with GUI MAS designer, where BOA invalidates connections that are not correct, and suggests suitable partners for a connection.

Figure 5 demonstrates the above described ideas on the actual implementation of the agents hierarchy description in the RACER Lisp-like syntax. For the sake of simplicity, only the Decision Tree and RBF Neural Network are shown with several intermediate concepts missing. The complete description is included in [20].

6 Conclusion

We have shown how formal logics can be used to describe computational MAS. We presented a logical formalism for the description of MAS. In this, we combined Description Logics with traditional Prolog rules. The system we implemented allows the practical application of these technologies. We have demonstrated how this approach works in practice within the hybrid computational environment *Bang 3*.

So far, we only describe static aspects of MAS. Further research will be put in the development of formal descriptions of dynamic aspects of MAS. In particular, this means to work with ontological description of tasks and to gather knowledge about computational agents performance. Currently within *Bang 3*, there is a BDI-based mechanism that supports decisions of a computational agent based on its previous experience. This will blend smoothly with our approach, which in turn allows to provide more suitable MAS solutions. In particular, if there are more agents satisfying the constrains, we will be able to sort them according to their past performance in the required context. Thus, better partners for an agent can be supplied. Further in the future we plan to employ proactive mechanisms for an agent (again BDI-based), which will be allowed to improve its knowledge in its free time, such as trying to solve benchmark tasks and recording the results.

The hybrid character of the system, with both a logical component and soft computing agents, also makes it interesting to combine these two approaches in one reasoning component. In order to automatically come up with feasible hybrid solutions for specific problems, we plan to combine two orthogonal approaches: a soft computing evolutionary algorithm with a formal ontology-based model. So far, in [8] we have tried the isolated evolutionary approach, and the results, although satisfiable, are difficult to scale up to larger configurations. We expect synergy effects from using formal logics to aid evolutionary algorithms and vice versa.

Acknowledgments

This work has been supported by the the project 1ET100300419 of the Program Information Society (of the Thematic Program II of the National Research Program of the Czech Republic) "Intelligent Models, Algorithms, Methods and Tools for the Semantic Web Realization".

Part of this research has been been performed during R. Neruda's stay at EPCC, University of Edinburgh, under the project HPC-EUROPA (RII3-CT-2003-506079) with the support of the European Community — Research Infrastructure Action under the FP6 "Structuring the European Research Area" Programme.

References

1. Nwana, H.S.: Software agents: An overview. Knowledge Engineering Review **11**(2) (1995) 205–244
2. Doran, J.E., Franklin, S., Jennings, N.R., Norman, T.J.: On cooperation in multi-agent systems. The Knowledge Engineering Review **12**(3) (1997) 309–314
3. Krušina, P., Neruda, R., Petrova, Z.: More autonomous hybrid models in bang. In: International Conference on Computational Science (2). (2001) 935–942
4. Neruda, R., Krušina, P., Kudova, P., Beuster, G.: Bang 3: A computational multi-agent system. In: Proceedings of the 2004 WI-IAT'04 Conference, IEEE Computer Society Press (2004)
5. Bonissone, P.: Soft computing: the convergence of emerging reasoning technologies. Soft Computing **1** (1997) 6–18
6. Hendler, J.: Agents and the semantic web. IEEE Intelligent Systems **16**(2) (2001) 30–37
7. Meolic, R., Kapus, T., Brezocnik, Z.: Model checking: A formal method for safety assurance of logistic systems. In: 2nd Congress Transport – Traffic – Logistics, Portoroz, Slovenia (2000) 355–358
8. Beuster, G., Krušina, P., Neruda, R., Rydvan, P.: Towards building computational agent schemes. In: Artificial neural Nets and Genetic Algorithms — Proceedings of the ICANNGA 2003, Springer Wien (2003)
9. Farquhar, A., Fikes, R., Rice, J.: Tools for assembling modular ontologies in ontolingua. Technical report, Stanford Knowledge Systems Laboratory (1997)
10. Genesreth, M.R., Fikes, R.E.: Knowledge interchange format, version 2.2. Technical report, Computer Science Department, Stanford University (1992)
11. Davis, M., ed.: The Undecidable—Basic Papers on Undecidable Propositions, Unsolvable Problems and Computable Functions. Raven Press (1965)
12. Borgida, A.: On the relative expressiveness of description logics and predicate logics. Artificial Intelligence **82**(1–2) (1996) 353–367
13. Baader, F.: Logic-based knowledge representation. In Wooldrige, M.J., Veloso, M., eds.: Artificial Intelligence Today, Recent Trends and Developments. Springer (1999) 13–41
14. Hustadt, U., Schmidt, R.A.: On the relation of resolution and tableaux proof system for description logics. In Thomas, D., ed.: Proceedings of the 16th Internatoinal joint Conference on Artificial Intelligence IJCAI'99. Volume 1., Stockholm, Sweden, Morgan Kaufmann (1999) 110–115
15. Baumgartner, P., Furbach, U., Thomas, B.: Model-based deduction for knowledge representation. In: Proceedings of the International Workshop on the Semantic Web, Hawaii, USA (2002)

16. Vellino, A.: The relative complexity of sl-resolution and analytical tableau. Studia Logica **52**(2) (1993) 323–337 Kluewer.
17. Levy, A.Y., Rousset, M.C.: The limits of combining recursive horn rules with description logics. In: Proceedings of the Thirteenth National Conference on Artificial Intelligence, Portland, OR (1996)
18. Borgida, A.: On the relationship between description logic and predicate logic. CIKM (1994) 219–225
19. Ferber, J.: Multi-Agent Systems: An Introduction to Distributed Artificial Intelligence. Harlow: Addison Wesley Longman (1999)
20. Neruda, R., et al.: Bang web documentation (2006) http://bang.sf.org.

Knowledge Capability: A Definition and Research Model

Ye Ning, Zhi-Ping Fan, and Bo Feng

School of Business Administration, Northeastern University,
Shenyang 110004, China
ningyedbdx@163.com, zpfan@mail.neu.edu.cn, neu_fengbo@163.com

Abstract. Basing on the view of dynamic capacity and knowledge-based view, this paper explores the definition and dimensions of knowledge capability. Differing from previous literature that think knowledge capability is the sum total of the knowledge assets of organizations, this paper defines knowledge capability as including both knowledge assets and knowledge operating capacities. And it is proposed that knowledge capability is dynamic, that is to say it will reconstruct with the changing of the environment. Since there are few empirical studies on the relationship between capability and organization performance, this paper suggests a model for further empirical studies on the impact of knowledge capability on organization performance.

1 Introduction

Since 1980s, with the developing of IT and globalization of economy, the uncertainness of competitive environment has been enhanced. The theory of strategic management began to pay more attention to the internal resources and abilities rather than external industry environment. Resource-based view and core capability view threw light on the relationship between the internal resources and abilities and competitive advantage of organizations. But when we come into knowledge economy era, technology innovation has become accelerated, clustered and socialized, and resources are not key factors in competition. The developing of market and technology changes the structure of industry rapidly and the more fierce competition forces organizations to promote their core capability on and on. Teece, Pisano and Shuen proposed the theory of dynamic capability. They believe that the dynamic capability is not limited by core capability and it is on the top of the structure of capabilities. When the competitive environment changes, it can reconstruct the resources and capabilities within and without the organization and form new competitive advantage [1-3].

The definition of dynamic capability embodies the dynamic feature of capabilities and the idea that capabilities should not only be utilized but also be reconstructed with the developing of internal and external environment. The proposing of this definition adapts to the changing of the management environment resulted by the revolution of technology and so make the renewal and cultivation of capabilities a continuous and dynamic process that with no doubt contributes a lot to the establishing of competitive advantage for organizations. But we think the essence of dynamic capability should be stated more clearly. With the development of the theory of capabilities, the knowledge related features have received extensive attention. Knowledge-based view

J. Lang, F. Lin, and J. Wang (Eds.): KSEM 2006, LNAI 4092, pp. 330–340, 2006.

believes that the core capability is a knowledge system that can make the organization competitive. The knowledge system includes four dimensions: technique and knowledge, technology system, management system and value system. The four systems interact all the time. Other scholars think that the core capability is a collection of a series of techniques and knowledge that can make the key business of an organization in the top level. This view emphasizes again that the core capability is the knowledge embedded in different abilities within an organization.

Basing on the above theories, many definitions are proposed such as innovation capability, intellect capability, market knowledge capability and information technology capability etc [4-7]. Although the contents of the definitions are different, the essence of them is the specific knowledge and resources possessed by an organization, a group or an individual. It is these specific knowledge and resources that make the above capabilities hard to be imitated by competitors and so make the organization, group or individual competitive. We think this is the essence of the core capability and so define the capability with this essence as "knowledge capability". Accoring to the above literatures, knowledge capability can be divided into collective knowledge capability that is owned by an organization or a group and individual knowledge capability that is owned by an individual. In this paper, the knowledge capability we will discuss is the collective knowledge capability that is owned by an organization.

Differing from previous literatures that think the knowledge capability is the sum total of the knowledge assets of organizations, this paper defines the knowledge capability as including both knowledge resources and knowledge operating capabilities that we think can reflect the knowledge capability more fully. And it is proposed that knowledge capability is dynamic, that is to say it will reconstruct with the changing of the environment. Since there are few empirical studies on the relationship between knowledge capability and organization performance, this paper suggests a model for further empirical studies on the impact of knowledge capability on organization performance.

2 Literature Reviews on Knowledge and Capability

Historically, knowledge has been studied on different levels. In anthropological, socio-psychological, and sociological works, knowledge is seen as a social product – what members of the social system need to understand in order to function in that system. Works in cognitive psychology, emphasizing perceptual and representational knowledge and thought processes, focus on the individual decision maker's knowledge. Since the unit of analysis in developing a concept of capability is mainly the firm, its resources and social processes, a micro level concept of knowledge (individuals) needs to be merged with a macro level concept of knowledge (firms). Berger and Luckman's constructivist theories of knowledge development are in sharp contrast to the more objectivist perspective [8]. The point of disagreement is whether knowledge is dependent on the knowing subject, a person, a group or a firm, or independent of it. The theory of constructed knowledge assumes that knowledge within a group, a firm or an individual is dependent on the knowing subject transmitting knowledge through social or cognitive processes. Knowledge about "true reality" is always questionable across different firms and groups. According to Berger and

Luckman, it is not meaningful to distinguish between a constructed reality and constructed knowledge. The two are intertwined and difficult to distinguish in empirical analysis [9].

According to Tsoukas (1996), firms are distributed knowledge systems and then organizations are seen as being in constant flux, out of which the potential for the emergence of novel practices is never exhausted human action inherently creative. Management, therefore, can be seen as an open-ended process of coordinating purposeful individuals, whose actions stem from applying their unique interpretations to the local circumstances confronting them. Given the distributed character of organizational knowledge, the key to achieving coordinated action does not so much depend on those higher up collecting more and more knowledge, as on those lower down finding more and more ways of getting connected and interrelating the knowledge each one has[10].

An organization's use of unique knowledge is central to its ability to gain competitive advantage. Knowledge is critical to the firm's unique value creation schemes in several respects. Knowledge provides familiarity among various constituents within the firm. More than simply a collection of individuals, the organization is defined by its network of social interactions. As the firm proceeds through history, managers and employees develop a collective consciousness or mindset that is specific to that firm. Such familiarity provides coordinated action among employees and managers in a manner that, because of enhanced dialogue, provides rich and varied insights into the management of the firm's resources. This collective mindset fosters communication efficiency by providing a lens through which organizational members view the world [9].

The concept of capability is used in many different areas of research too, including psychology, education, management, human resources, and information systems. In management literatures, the term "capability" has been used by several authors to denote the "ability of the firm to act". Because of its strong action focus, the term capability is often used similarly to the way it is used in our daily speech; to code a broad range of our experiences related to craftsmanship, specialization, intelligence, and problem solving. As such, capability remains an experience-near concept that needs further conceptual clarification if it is to serve the purpose of theory building [9]. Webster defines capability as "The quality or state of being functionally adequate or of having sufficient knowledge, judgment, skill or strength for a particular duty" [11]. This definition of capability presupposes a particular knowledge and a particular task. Only where there exists an agreement or fit between "knowledge" (or subject) and "task" may we speak of capability. Thus, it is only meaningful to discuss capability in a specific knowledge-task context or, put another way, capability is both knowledge specific and task specific.

Bringing knowledge into the capability definition broadens the concept by making it dynamic and interactive. This acknowledges that capability is not necessarily directly linked to a specific task but relates to the ability to transfer knowledge across tasks [12]. Capability is thus non-routine, and embodies the ability to cope with complex and changing environments. Knowledge theories express this richer sense of one's capability and define knowledge as more than skills possessed by an individual. This knowledge-based approach to capability, and the idea that capability is dynamic, leads to our definition of knowledge capability of organizations.

3   Definition and Dimensions of Knowledge Capability

As for knowledge capability, many authors give their definitions from the resource-based view. For example, Allee V. defines the core knowledge capability as "the sole specialty, knowledge and technology processed by an organization" [13]. Parashar M. & Singh S. K. think that knowledge capability needs to be viewed as the sum total of the knowledge assets (both explicit and tacit) of the firm that determine its capability to absorb and create new knowledge [4]. And in IT domain, Genevieve el. defines the IT capability in business managers as "the set of IT-related explicit and tacit knowledge that a business manager possesses that enables him or her to exhibit IT leadership in his or her area of business" [7].

We agree with the above definitions on that the essence of knowledge capability is a collective learning, which is essential for organizations to obtain and sustain competitive advantage. But we do not think it is enough for the definition to include only knowledge assets possessed by an organization. Because in reality, most knowledge held and used by an organization is not owned by the organization and not in direct control of the organization so it is knowledge resource that should be concluded in knowledge capability and the core knowledge resource contribute more to knowledge capability. Besides the core knowledge resource, knowledge operating capabilities are needed to make the knowledge workable and will reconstruct the knowledge, resources and capabilities inside and outside when the competitive environment changes. This will be further discussed in section 4. So the definition of knowledge capability could be included as the "knowledge system that can synergy and reconstruct the resources, knowledge and capabilities within and without the organization to realize the harmonious development with its environment". Knowledge capability includes core knowledge resource that make the organization competitive and the knowledge operating capabilities that make the knowledge resource effective and profitable. The relationship between the two components and knowledge capability can be shown in Fig.1.

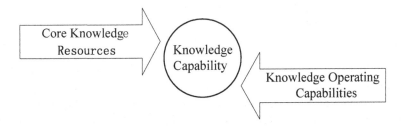

Fig. 1. Components of Organizational Knowledge Capability

An organization is a collection of different capabilities. Knowledge operating capabilities include learning capability, culture capability, communication capability and innovation capability that can be seen in Fig.2.

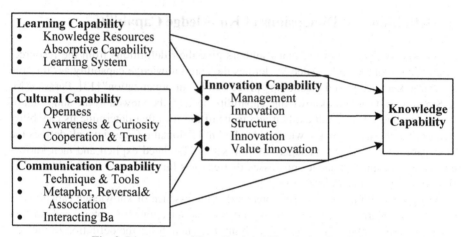

Fig. 2. Dimensions of Organizational Knowledge Capability

3.1 Learning Capability

As we have noted before, the view of dynamic capability believes that the capabilities should be reconstructed with the changing of external environment and internal resources. We think the reconstruction of the capabilities should be connected with organization learning. Senge P. proposes five disciplines to make an organization a learning organization that reflects a goal of the evolution of organizations. To some extent the competitive advantage of an organization depends on its learning capability. It is said that learning is a fundamental existing and developing manner in knowledge economy era and the more uncertain of competition the more important of learning capability. While nearly all of the organizations are learning more or less, only some of them succeed. The difference between the success and failure is the difference between their learning capabilities. The components of this capability are detailed as follows:

Knowledge Resources. Knowledge resources mainly refer to the core technique, knowledge and technology that can be used by an organization, including tacit and explicit knowledge. Explicit knowledge is the formal knowledge that can be clearly transmitted using systematic language. This type of knowledge is not sufficient to describe one's capability. One needs to be able to apply these rules to be competent. The ability to perform well is tacit knowledge, or "know-how". Practice or experience, where the individual modifies his action based on the results of previous actions, builds capability through the enrichment of know-how. Over time, individuals also develop worldviews that guide these direct experiences. These worldviews add a cognitive component to tacit knowledge that becomes embedded into an individual's action, commitment, and involvement in a specific context. An individual often knows more than he or she realizes. At the organizational level, tacit and explicit knowledge are closely linked. In their explanation of why some firms continually innovate.

Absorptive Capability. The premise of the notion of absorptive capability is that the organization needs prior knowledge to assimilate and use new knowledge. Absorptive capability refers not only to acquisition or assimilation of information by an organization but also to the organization's ability to exploit it. Absorptive capability is a dynamic capability pertaining to knowledge creation and utilization that enhances a firm's ability to gain and sustain a competitive advantage. The absorptive capability is based on the experience and knowledge acquired during long time and so it is path—dependent. So absorptive capability can make an organization absorb energy from outside and refresh the knowledge assets. To exploit and utilize these new knowledge better, the organization needs to activate original knowledge resources and combine them with the new knowledge or reconstruct them with the changing of the environment and that should be the object of knowledge capability. So we can say that absorptive capability is an important part of knowledge capability.

Learning System. Organizations learn through individuals who act as agents for them. The individuals' learning activities, in turn, are facilitated or inhibited by an ecological system of factors that is called an organizational learning system. When the learning system is only adequate enough to enable the organization to implement its existing policies and meet its stated objectives, the process at work is called single-loop—or Model I—learning. Double-loop—or Model II—learning, by contrast, performs the more difficult and comprehensive task of questioning underlying goals and assumptions [14]. An effective learning system should include the atmosphere of study, systemic thinking, acquiring, transferring and innovating of knowledge, cooperation and structure of learning. The establishment of learning system includes individual learning and organizational learning. Individual learning is a micro foundation for the accumulation and activation of organization's capabilities, while organization learning is the reflection of the accumulation and activation of organization's capabilities. An effective learning system may contribute to strengthening the motivation of learning and so increase the absorptive capability.

3.2 Cultural Capability

Organizational culture leads to a certain kind of organizational climate that can enable or destroy knowledge capability. The organizational climate should be geared to both absorb knowledge as well as connect that knowledge in new creative ways. Cultural capability acts as an enabler in creating greater knowledge assets. The components of this capability are detailed as follows:

Openness. Openness encompasses being open to new influences and ideas, willingness to step out of comfort zones and to try out new ways of doing things. Openness has been theorized to aid organizational learning. Many organizations find it difficult to practice openness because it takes them out of their comfort zone. Openness helps organizations in taking an experimental approach towards knowledge bases and towards novel combinations of these bases. Our view of getting organizations out of their comfort zone builds upon Leonard-Barton's concept of challenging core rigidities. Leonard-Barton has argued that managers need to expose their companies to a bombardment of new ideas from outside.

Awareness. The ability to spot discontinuities and abstract higher order concepts from it, to know what is going on in the vicinity and in the wider world and simultaneously stand back and see the wider perspective.

Curiosity. Which is at the very base of knowledge acquisition; these abilities help the organization see concepts in a new manner, make unconventional connections and associations between concepts, insights and facts, and turn disparate pieces of information into winning ideas [4].

Cooperation and Trust. Good cooperation can enable knowledge innovation. And cooperation is based on personal trust. According to, there are two dimensions of trust: goodwill trust and capability trust and they are closely related to the calculation of different types of perceived risk. This distinction parallels the idea that trust is the expectation of a partner fulfilling a collaborative role in a risky situation, and relies on both the partner's intention to perform and its ability to do so.

3.3 Communication Capability

Satisfactory communication can guarantee knowledge innovation, since communication can not only promote individual's ability but also can condensate the organization's capabilities and produce a strength that can far more exceed the sum of all of the capabilities. The components of this capability are detailed as follows:

Technique and Tools. The big challenge in a large organization is to facilitate the process of knowledge sharing – knowledge from within and without the organization. IT is a great enabler and many companies use it to share information across functions. Intranet sites, bulletin boards, email are common devices in organizations to link people. Communication has been shown to have a role to play in innovation in dynamic environments. Organizations should encourage both formal and informal channels of information sharing. Informal networks can be great repositories of information as well as fountainheads of innovation.

Metaphor, Reversal and Association. Ideation is usually treated like a black box, wherein the output is evaluated and the process is seen as a mystery. But if novel ideas are a result of linking insights, concepts and facts in a manner not done before, then a set of techniques can be developed to enable ideas. One of the most popular techniques is called "metaphor", where two very different concepts or themes are forced together resulting in a very different view of the world. Another more radical technique is "reversal", where opposites are brought together to create new knowledge. Reversal can be a radical technique for both product development and communication development. In a technique such as "association", one concept is associated either with a related concept or radically, with a random concept. The techniques illustrated here are only a small fraction of the established techniques like lateral thinking in use today [4].

Interacting Ba. The knowledge sharing and innovation will be limited or even hold back if there is not a shared understanding of the semantics of the language used in the communication. Too often organizations do not get this right because people attach their own semantic baggage to terms—thus communication breaks down even when they have tools, metaphors etc. We believe the concept of "ba" offered by

Nonaka can be used to answer the above question. The word means "place" or "field" or a shared space—a physical or mental space, or combination of both. No single formula defines the look or feel of originating ba, but it is a place where barriers between self and others are removed, where socialization encourages the sharing and exploration of ideas that generate new ideas. Interacting ba is the place where tacit knowledge is made explicit. Cartesian and Nishidan approaches interact as individuals discuss and analyze their ideas, developing a common understanding of terms and concepts [15].

3.4 Innovation Capability

Innovation capability is the reflection of the above capabilities that includes management innovation capability, structure innovation capability and value innovation capability.

Management Innovation. Management innovation includes managerial idea innovation, managerial style innovation, managerial tactics innovation, managerial system innovation and managerial pattern innovation etc.

Structure Innovation. Structure can influence the knowledge capability directly. Flexible structure can make knowledge capability more efficient and so the competitive advantage can be strengthened more easily. Otherwise knowledge capability would be asphyxiated and organizations' advantage would be in danger. Rapidly changing customer demands and increasingly independent professionals require entirely new structures. The extended capabilities of new technologies now enable design and management of much more highly disaggregated organizations, capable of responding to the needs of both customers and professionals. The term network organizations has been widely used to embrace a variety of these new forms, varying from flat, to horizontal matrix, to alliance, to cross-disciplinary team, to holding-company structures that merely finance a number of unrelated divisions self-coordinating on an ad-hoc basis.21 This categorization reveals little about how the various forms differ, when to use them, or how to manage them for maximum effect.

Value Innovation. Value innovation is a new idea of competition that attracts customers through creating more value for them rather than only through improving the technology competitiveness.

4 Dynamic Model of Knowledge Capability Reconstruction

As we have noted before, knowledge capability is dynamic and will reconstruct with the change of external environment and internal resources in order to realize the harmony developing with environment. Fig.3 shows the dynamic process of the reconstruction of knowledge capability.

A-B-C is the reconstruction system of knowledge capability. Ct stands for cultural capability, L stands for learning capability, C stands for communication capability, I stands for innovation capability. A-B-C is the interface between the system and the environment, t stands for the axis of time, the traverse surface of A-B-C is the static operation of knowledge capability at T_n. Learning capability and communication

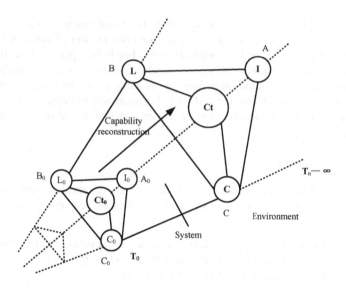

Fig. 3. Dynamic Model of Knowledge Capability Reconstruction

capability are the foundation of innovation capability and they will interact with each other so as to increase themselves constantly. Communication capability can provide technology support for learning capability and with the developing of learning capability; communication capability will be promoted too. Cultural capability is the core of the reconstruction system and it can connect the other capabilities and promote the development of the whole system. So the capability reconstruction system is dynamic.

5   The Impact of Knowledge Capability on Organization Performance

A major purpose of defining knowledge capability is to investigate whether or not it leads to positive organization performance. The research model is presented in Fig. 4. This model could be described in terms of several components or constructs. The first is knowledge capability. As we have noted before, knowledge resource and knowledge operating capabilities are connected and some particular knowledge capability is formed. This is not an end and the knowledge capability will reconstruct and develop with the changing of external and internal environment. The second part of this model is external environment, including customer demanding, competition intensity and technology change because they represent the three fundamental forces in markets: customer, competitor, and technology. The influence of these forces on the capability of organizations generally is conceived of in the literature while empirical validation is sparse. The third part of this model is internal environment and materials and technology are internal antecedent because of their significance in the research agenda. Besides that, an important area for additional research is the investigation of how features of an organization's culture influence its processes. Under the influence of the above factors, what will be the outcome of knowledge capability? Then comes the fourth part—organization performance that includes the following evaluating indexes: average income, rate of growth, finance, market share and new domain of business etc. The average income should be the average income of recent 3 or 5 years so that the persisting competitive advantage could be shown better and the haphazardness could be avoided. Rate of growth means the average of sales income and profit in recent 3 or 5 years that can show the changing situation of the performance of an organization. The above indexes can reflect the performance more totally if they are used with market share and finance indexes. New domain of business is the potential important resource of an organization's performance. Product innovation includes two indexes: the quotient of the income of new products and the total income and the quotient of the quantity of new products and total product. Customer satisfaction includes the quantity of customers and the extent of their satisfaction. Employee competence includes the employee satisfaction, employee creativity and productivity.

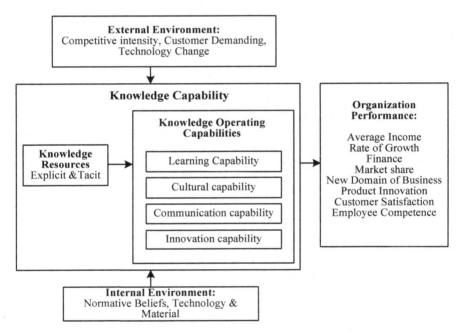

Fig. 4. A Research Model: Knowledge Capability and Organization Performance

6 Conclusions

In this paper we have proposed a definition and a dynamic model of knowledge capability. Our definition and model are based on an extensive study of the literatures, both in the theory of dynamic capability and the theory of knowledge and in the definition of knowledge and capability. From the literatures on knowledge and capability, we emphasize again that the essence of capability is a collective learning. And from the theory of dynamic capability and knowledge, we expound that knowledge capability is dynamic and will be reconstructed with the changing of the environment both inside and out-side. While we think further refinement of this theoretical definition and the development of an operational definition are needed. In conclusion, we have attempted to define a research model for further empirical study on the effects of knowledge capability on organization performance.

Acknowledgements

This work was partly supported by the National Science Fund for Distinguished Young Scholars of China (Project No. 70525002), the National Natural Science Foundation of China (NSFC, Project No. 70371050), the Teaching and Research Award Program for Outstanding Young Teachers (TRAPOYT) in Higher Education Institutions and Research Fund for the Doctoral Program of Higher Education (Project No. 20040145018), Ministry of Education, China.

References

1. Meisenhardt, K.: Dynamic Capabilities: What are They? Strategic Management Journal, Vol. 21. (2000) 1105-1122
2. Teece, D., Pisano, G., Amyshuen: Dynamic Capabilities and Strategic Management. Strategic Management Journal, Vol. 18. (1997) 509-533
3. Petroni, Alberto: The Analysis of dynamic Capabilities in a Capability-Oriented Organization. Technovation, Vol. 18. (1998) 179-190
4. Parashar, M., Singh, S. K.: Innovation Capability. IIMB Management Review, Vol. 17. (2005) 115-123
5. Quinn, J. B., Anderson, P., Finkelstein, S.: Leveraging Intellect. Academy of Management Executive, Vol. 19. (2005) 4-5
6. Li, T., Calantone, R. J.: The Impact of Market Knowledge Capability on New Product Advantage: Conceptualization and Empirical Examination. Journal of Marketing, Vol. 62. (1998) 13-29
7. Basselier, G., Reich, B. H., Benbasat, I.: Information Technology Capability of Business Managers: A Definition and Research Model. Journal of Management, Vol. 17. (2001) 159-182
8. Berger, P., Luckman, T.: The Social Construction of Reality. Penguin, New York, NY, (1967)
9. Krogh, G., Roos, J.: A Perspective on Knowledge, Capability and Strategy. Personnel Review, Vol. 24. (1995) 56-76
10. Tsoukas, H.: The Firm as a Distributed Knowledge System: a Constructionist Approach. Strategic Management Journal, Vol. 17. (1996) 11-25
11. Webster's Third New International Dictionary. Meriam-Webster, Chicago, IL,(1981)
12. Teece, D. J., Pisano, G., Shuen, A.: Firm Capabilities, Resources and the Concept of Strategy. Working Paper, University of California at Berkeley, CA. (1990)
13. Allee, V.: The Knowledge Evolution. Zhuhai Publishing House. (1998) 53
14. Argyris, C., Schon, D.: Organization Learning. Addison-Wesley, Reading, MA. (1978)
15. Cohen, D.: Toward a Knowledge Context: Report on the First Annual U.C. Berkeley Forum on Knowledge and the Firm. California Management Review, Vol. 40. (1998) 22-39

Quota-Based Merging Operators for Stratified Knowledge Bases

Guilin Qi, Weiru Liu, and David A. Bell

School of Electronics, Electrical Engineering and Computer Science
Queen's University Belfast, Belfast, BT7 1NN, UK
{G.Qi, W.Liu, DA.Bell}@qub.ac.uk

Abstract. Current merging methods for stratified knowledge bases are often based on the commensurability assumption, i.e. all knowledge bases share a common scale. However, this assumption is too strong in practice. In this paper, we propose a family of operators to merge stratified knowledge bases without commensurability assumption. Our merging operators generalize the quota operators, a family of important merging operators in classical logic. Both logical properties and computational complexity issues of the proposed operators are studied.

1 Introduction

The problem of merging multiple sources of information is important in many applications, such as database merging [14] and group decision making [15]. Priorities, either implicit or explicit, play an important role in belief merging. In classical logic, a knowledge base is a set of formulas with the same level of priority. However, an implicit ordering on the set of possible worlds can be extracted from it [11,14]. In some cases, we even assume that explicit priorities are attached to each source which takes the form of a stratified set of beliefs or goals [8,20]. That is, each source can be viewed as a stratified or prioritized knowledge base.

Merging of stratified knowledge bases is often handled in the framework of possibilistic logic [8] or ordinal conditional function [20]. Usually, the merging methods are based on the assumption that all agents use the same scale (usually ordinal scales such as [0,1]) to order their beliefs. However, in practice, the numerical information is hard to get-we may only have a knowledge base with a total pre-order relation on its formulas. In addition, different agents may use different ways to order their beliefs. Even a single agent may have different ways of modeling her preferences for different aspects of a problem [6]. In that case, the previous merging methods cannot be applied.

It is widely accepted that belief merging is closely related to social choice theory [15,7,13,9]. In social choice theory, we have a group of p voters (or agents). Each voter suggests a preference on a set of alternatives. An important problem is then to define a voting rule which is a function mapping a set of p preferences to an alternative or a set of alternatives. Many voting rules have been proposed, such as the Plurality rule [16] and the voting by quota [2].

J. Lang, F. Lin, and J. Wang (Eds.): KSEM 2006, LNAI 4092, pp. 341–353, 2006.
© Springer-Verlag Berlin Heidelberg 2006

In this paper, we propose a family of quota-based merging operators for stratified knowledge bases under integrity constraints. We assume that each stratified knowledge base is assigned to an ordering strategy. For each stratified knowledge base K and its ordering strategy X, we get a complete, transitive and asymmetric preference relation $<_{K,X}$ on subsets of the set of possible worlds. A possible world is a model of the resulting knowledge base of the quota-based merging operator if it belongs to the most preferred element of at least k preference relations. The quota-based merging operators are problematic in some cases. So we define a refined version of the quota-based merging operators.

This paper is organized as follows. Some preliminaries are given in Section 2. Section 3 introduces quota merging operators in propositional logic. In Section 4, we consider the preference representation of stratified knowledge bases. A new ordering strategy is proposed. Our merging operators are defined in Section 5. Section 6 analyzes the computational complexity of our merging operators. We then study the logical properties of our merging operators in Section 7. Section 8 discusses related work. Finally, we conclude the paper in Section 9.

2   Preliminaries

Classical logic: In this paper, we consider a propositional language $\mathcal{L}_{PS}$ from a finite set PS of propositional symbols. The classical consequence relation is denoted as $\vdash$. An interpretation (or possible world) is a total function from PS to $\{0,1\}$, denoted by a bit vector whenever a strict total order on PS is specified. Ω is the set of all possible interpretations. An interpretation w is a model of a formula ϕ iff $w(\phi) = 1$. $p, q, r,...$ represent atoms in PS. We denote formulas in $\mathcal{L}_{PS}$ by $\phi, \psi, \gamma,...$ For each formula ϕ, we use $M(\phi)$ to denote its set of models. A *classical knowledge base* K is a finite set of propositional formulas (we can also identify K with the conjunction of its elements). K is consistent iff there exists an interpretation w such that $w(\phi) = true$ for all $\phi \in K$. A knowledge *profile* E is a multi-set of knowledge bases, i.e. $E = \{K_1, ..., K_n\}$, where K_i may be identical to K_j for $i \neq j$. Let $\bigcup(E) = \cup_{i=1}^{n} K_i$. Two knowledge profiles E_1 and E_2 are equivalent, denoted $E_1 \equiv E_2$ iff there exists a bijection f between E_1 and E_2 such that for each $K \in E_1$, $f(K) \equiv K$.

Stratified knowledge base: A *stratified* knowledge base, sometimes also called ranked knowledge base [6] or prioritized knowledge base [3], is a set K of (finite) propositional formulas together with a total preorder $\leq$ on K (a preorder is a transitive and reflexive relation, and $\leq$ is a total preorder if either $\phi \leq \psi$ or $\psi \leq \phi$ holds for any $\phi, \psi \in K$)[1]. Intuitively, if $\phi \leq \psi$, then ϕ is considered to be less important than ψ. K can be equivalently defined as a sequence $K = (S_1, ..., S_n)$, where each S_i $(i = 1, ..., n)$ is a non-empty set which contains all the maximal elements of $K \setminus (\cup_{j=1}^{i-1} S_j)$ w.r.t $\leq$, i.e. $S_i = \{\phi \in K \setminus (\cup_{j=1}^{i-1} S_j) : \forall \psi \in K \setminus (\cup_{j=1}^{i-1} S_j), \psi \leq \phi\}$. Each subset S_i is called a stratum of K and i the

---

[1] For simplicity, we use K to denote a stratified knowledge base and ignore the total preorder $\leq$.

priority level of each formula of S_i. Therefore, the lower the stratum, the higher the priority level of a formula in it. A stratified knowledge profile (SKP) E is a multi-set of stratified knowledge bases. Given a stratified knowledge base $K = (S_1, ..., S_n)$, the i-cut of K is defined as $K_{\geq i} = S_1 \cup ... \cup S_i$, for $i \in \{1, ..., n\}$. A subbase A of K is also stratified, that is, $A = (A_1, ..., A_n)$ such that $A_i \subseteq S_i$, $i = 1, ..., n$. Two SKPs E_1 and E_2 are equivalent, denoted $E_1 \equiv_s E_2$ iff there exists a bijection between E_1 and E_2 such that $n = m$ and for each $K = (S_1, ..., S_l) \in E_1$, $f(K) = (S'_1, ..., S'_l)$ and $S_i \equiv S'_i$ for all $i \in \{1, ..., l\}$.

3   Quota Merging Operator

In this section, we introduce the quota operators defined in [9].

Definition 1. *[9] Let k be an integer, $E = \{K_1, ..., K_n\}$ be a multi-set of knowledge bases, and μ be a formula. The k-quota merging operator, denoted Δ^k, is defined in a model-theoretic way as:*

$$M(\Delta^k_\mu(E)) = \begin{cases} \{\omega \in M(\mu) | \forall K_i \in E \ \omega \models K_i\} & \text{if not empty,} \\ \{\omega \in M(\mu) | \sharp(\{K_i \in E | \ \omega \models K_i\}) \geq k\} & \text{otherwise.} \end{cases} \quad (1)$$

($\#L$ denotes the number of the elements in L.)

The resulting knowledge base of the k-quota merging of E under constraints μ is simply the conjunction of the bases when $\bigwedge E \wedge \mu$ is consistent. Otherwise, the models of the resulting knowledge base are the models of μ which satisfy at least k bases of E.

The choice of an appropriate k is very important to define a good quota merging operator. An interesting value of k is the maximum value such that the merged base is consistent. That is, we have the following definition.

Definition 2. *[9] Let $E = \{K_1, ..., K_n\}$ be a knowledge profile, and μ be a formula. Let $k_{max} = max(\{i \leq \sharp(E) | \Delta^i_\mu \not\models \bot\})$. $\Delta^{k_{max}}$ is defined in a model-theoretical way as:*

$$M(\Delta^{k_{max}}_\mu(E)) = \begin{cases} \{\omega \in M(\mu) | \forall K_i \in E \ \omega \models K_i\} & \text{if not empty,} \\ \{\omega \in M(\mu) | \sharp(\{K_i \in E | \ \omega \models K_i\}) = k_{max}\} & \text{otherwise.} \end{cases} \quad (2)$$

4   Preference Representation of Stratified Knowledge Bases

4.1   Ordering Strategies

Given a stratified knowledge base $K = \{S_1, ..., S_n\}$, we can define some total pre-orders on Ω.

- **best out ordering** [3]:
  Let $r_{BO}(\omega) = min\{i : \omega \not\models S_i\}$, for $\omega \in \Omega$. Then the best out ordering $\preceq_{bo}$ on Ω is defined as: $\omega \preceq_{bo} \omega'$ iff $r_{BO}(\omega) \geq r_{BO}(\omega')$

- **maxsat ordering** [6]:

  Let $r_{MO}(\omega) = min\{i : \omega \models S_i\}$, for $\omega \in \Omega$. Then the maxsat ordering $\preceq_{maxsat}$ on Ω is defined as: $\omega \preceq_{maxsat} \omega'$ iff $r_{MO}(\omega) \leq r_{MO}(\omega')$

- **leximin ordering** [3]:

  Let $K^i(\omega) = \{\phi \in S_i : \omega \models \phi\}$. Then the leximin ordering $\preceq_{leximin}$ on Ω is defined as:

  $\omega \preceq_{leximin} \omega'$ iff $|K^i(\omega)| = |K^i(\omega')|$ for all i, or there is an i such that $|K^i(\omega')| < |K^i(\omega)|$, and for all $j < i$: $|K^j(\omega)| = |K^j(\omega')|$, where $|K_i|$ denote the cardinality of the sets K_i.

Given a preorder $\preceq$ on Ω, as usual, the associated strict partial order is defined by $\omega \prec \omega'$ iff $\omega \preceq \omega'$ and not $\omega' \preceq \omega$. An ordering $\preceq_X$ is more *specific* than another $\preceq_{X'}$ iff $\omega \prec_{X'} \omega'$ implies $\omega \prec_X \omega'$. The total preorders on Ω defined above are not independent of each other.

Proposition 1. *[6] Let $\omega, \omega' \in \Omega$, K a stratified knowledge base. The following relationships hold: $\omega \prec_{bo} \omega'$ implies $\omega \prec_{leximin} \omega'$;*

4.2   A New Ordering Strategy

We now define a new ordering strategy by considering the "distance" between an interpretation and a knowledge base.

Definition 3. *[9] A pseudo-distance between interpretations is a total function d from $\Omega \times \Omega$ to N such that for every $\omega_1, \omega_2 \in \Omega$: (1) $d(\omega_1, \omega_2) = d(\omega_2, \omega_1)$; and (2) $d(\omega_1, \omega_2) = 0$ if and only if $\omega_1 = \omega_2$.*

A "distance " between an interpretation ω and a knowledge base S can then be defined as $d(\omega, S) = min_{\omega' \models S} d(\omega, \omega')$. When S is inconsistent, $d(\omega, S) = +\infty$. That is, all the possible worlds have the same distance with an inconsistent knowledge base. Two common examples of such distances are the *drastic distance* d_D and the *Dalal distance* d_H, where $d_D(\omega_1, \omega_2) = 0$ when $\omega_1 = \omega_2$ and 1 otherwise, and $d_H(\omega_1, \omega_2)$ is the Hamming distance between ω_1 and ω_2.

Definition 4. *The distance-based ordering $\preceq_d$ on Ω is defined as:*

$\omega \preceq_d \omega'$ iff $d(\omega, S_i) = d(\omega', S_i)$ for all i, or there is an i such that $d(\omega, S_i) < d(\omega', S_i)$, and for all $j < i$: $d(\omega, S_j) = d(\omega', S_j)$.

It is clear that the distance-based orderings are total preorders on Ω. Suppose $d = d_H$, the ordering $\preceq_{d_H}$ is equivalent to the total preorder $\leq_{K,Lex}$ which is defined to characterize the minimal change of a revision operator in [17].

Proposition 2. *Let $\omega, \omega' \in \Omega$, and K be a stratified knowledge base. Suppose $d = d_D$ or d_H, then we have: (1) $\omega \preceq_d \omega'$ implies $\omega \preceq_{bo} \omega'$ and $\omega \preceq_d \omega'$; (2) $\omega \prec_{bo} \omega'$ implies $\omega \prec_d \omega'$.*

5   Quota-Based Merging Operators

5.1   Voting by Quota

Let A be a finite set of objects and $N = \{1, 2, ..., n\}$ be a set of n voters (or agents), where $n \geq 2$. *Alternatives* are subsets of A. We use X, Y and Z to denote alternatives. The *ith* voter's preference relations, denoted by $\prec_i$, $\prec'_i$, etc, are complete, transitive, and asymmetric relations on 2^A (the set of subsets of A). For $X, Y \in 2^A$, $X \prec_i Y$ means X is strictly preferred to Y w.r.t voter i. Let $\mathcal{X} \subseteq 2^A$, we denote by $min(\mathcal{X}, \prec_i)$ the most preferred alternative in $\mathcal{X}$ according to $\prec_i$. Let P denote the set of all preference relations on A. A voting rule on the domain $D_1 \times ... \times D_n \subseteq P^n$ is a function $f : D_1 \times ... \times D_n \to A$, where each D_i is considered to represent the set of ith voter's preference relations.

We now introduce a voting rule, called voting by quota.

Definition 5. *[2] A vote rule $f : D_1 \times ... \times D_n \to 2^A$ is* voting by quota *if there exists k between 1 and n such that for all $(\prec_1, ..., \prec_n)$, we have $x \in f(\prec_1, ..., \prec_n)$ if and only if $\#\{i | x \in min(2^A, \prec_i)\} \geq k$.*

Voting by quota k selects the alternative consisting of objects which are in at least k most preferred alternatives of 2^A according to $\prec_i$.

5.2   Quota-Based Merging Operator

We use $\preceq_X$ to denote a total preorder on Ω, where X represents an ordering strategy. For example, if $X = bo$, then $\preceq_X$ is the best-out ordering. The idea of defining our quota-based operators can be explained as follows. First, for each stratified knowledge base K_i and the ordering strategy X_i, we obtain a complete, transitive and asymmetric preference relation on 2^Ω. We then apply voting by quota to aggregate the preferences and the obtained set of possible worlds is taken as the set of models of the resulting knowledge base.

Given a stratified knowledge base K and an ordering strategy X, Ω can be stratified with regard to the total preorder $\preceq_X$ on it as $\Omega_{K,X} = (\Omega_1, ..., \Omega_m)$ in the same way as stratifying a knowledge base. For two interpretations ω_1, ω_2, if $\omega_1 \in \Omega_i$ and $\omega_2 \in \Omega_j$, where $i < j$, then ω_1 is preferred to ω_2. A complete, transitive and asymmetric preference relation $<_{K,X}$ on 2^Ω can then be defined as follows. (1) For $W, W' \in 2^\Omega$, if $W = \Omega_i$ and $W' = \Omega_j$, where $i < j$, then $W <_{K,X} W'$; if $W = \Omega_i$ for some i, and there does not exist j such that $W' = \Omega_j$, then $W <_{K,X} W'$; (2) For elements in $2^\Omega \setminus \{\Omega_1, ..., \Omega_n\}$, we order them as $W \leq_{K,X} W'$ iff $\forall i$, $\#(W \cap \Omega_i) = \#(W' \cap \Omega_i)$ or $\exists i$ such that $\#(W \cap \Omega_i) > \#(W' \cap \Omega_i)$ and $\#(W \cap \Omega_j) = \#(W' \cap \Omega_j)$ for all $j < i$. It is possible that there exist some W_i $(i = 1, ..., k)$ such that $W_i =_{K,X} W_j$ for any pair i and j, where $W_i =_{K,X} W_j$ means $W \leq_{K,X} W'$ and $W' \leq_{K,X} W$. In that case, we arbitrary order them as $W_1, W_2, ..., W_k$ such that $W_i <_{K,X} W_j$ if $i < j$. (3) Finally, for all $W, W' \in 2^\Omega$, if $W <_{K,X} W'$, then not $W' <_{K,X} W$. It is easy to check that $<_{K,X}$ defined above is a complete, transitive and asymmetric relation on 2^Ω.

346   G. Qi, W. Liu, and D.A. Bell

Definition 6. *Let $E = \{K_1, ..., K_n\}$ be a multi-set of stratified knowledge bases, where $K_i = \{S_{i1}, ..., S_{im}\}$, μ be a formula, and let k be an integer. Let $\mathbf{X} = (X_1, ..., X_n)$ be a set of ordering strategies, where X_i ($i = 1, ..., n$) are ordering strategies attached to K_i. Suppose $<_{K_i, X_i}$ is the complete, transitive and asymmetric relation on 2^Ω obtained by K_i and X_i. The resulting knowledge base of k-quota merging operator, denoted by $\Delta_\mu^{k, \mathbf{X}}(E)$, is defined in a model-theoretic way as follows:*

$$M(\Delta_\mu^{k, \mathbf{X}}(E)) = \{\omega \in M(\mu) | \sharp(\{K_i \in E | \ \omega \in Min(2^\Omega, <_{K_i, X_i})\}) \geq k\}.$$

The models of the resulting knowledge base of the k-quota merging of E under constraints μ are the models of μ which most preferred according to at least k preference relations.

Example 1. Let $E = \{K_1, K_2, K_3\}$ be a SKP consisting of three stratified knowledge bases, where

- $K_1 = \{S_{11}, S_{12}, S_{13}\}$, where $S_{11} = \{p_1 \lor p_2, p_3\}$, $S_{12} = \{\neg p_1, \neg p_2, p_2 \lor \neg p_3, p_4\}$, $S_{13} = \{\neg p_3 \lor \neg p_4\}$
- $K_2 = \{S_{21}, S_{22}\}$, where $S_{21} = \{p_1, p_2 \lor p_3\}$ and $S_{22} = \{\neg p_2, p_4\}$
- $K_3 = \{S_{31}, S_{32}\}$, where $S_{31} = \{p_1, p_3\}$ and $S_{32} = \{p_2\}$.

The integrity constraint is $\mu = \{\neg p_1 \lor p_2\}$. The set of models of μ is $M(\mu) = \{\omega_1 = 0111, \omega_2 = 0101, \omega_3 = 0110, \omega_4 = 0100, \omega_5 = 0011, \omega_6 = 0001, \omega_7 = 0010, \omega_8 = 0000, \omega_9 = 1111, \omega_{10} = 1101, \omega_{11} = 1110, \omega_{12} = 1100\}$. We denote each model by a bit vector consisting of truth values of (p_1, p_2, p_3, p_4). For example, $\omega_1 = 0111$ means that the truth value of p_1 is 0 and the truth values of other atoms are all 1. Let $\mathbf{X} = \{X_1, X_2, X_3\}$, where $X_1 = X_2 = bo$ and $X_3 = d_H$. That is, the best out ordering strategy is chosen for both K_1 and K_2, whilst the Dalal distance-based ordering is chosen for K_3. The computations are given in Table 1 below.

Table 1

ω	K_1	K_2	K_3
0111	1	3	3
0101	2	3	5
0110	1	3	3
0100	2	3	5
0011	2	3	4
0001	2	3	6
0010	2	3	4
0000	2	3	6
1111	1	2	1
1101	2	2	3
1110	1	2	1
1100	2	2	3

In Table 1, the column corresponding to K_i gives the priority levels of strata of Ω_{K_i, X_i} where ω_i belongs to. Let us explain how to obtain the column corresponding to K_2 (other columns can be obtained similarly). Let $\omega_{13} = 1011$, $\omega_{14} = 1001$, $\omega_{15} = 1010$ and $\omega_{16} = 1000$. Since $r_{BO}(\omega_i) = 1$ for all $1 \leq i \leq 8$, $r_{BO}(\omega_i) = 2$ for $9 \leq i \leq 12$ and $14 \leq i \leq 16$, $r_{BO}(\omega_{13}) = +\infty$, we have $\Omega_{K_2, bo} = (\{\omega_{13}\}, \{\omega_9, ..., \omega_{12}, \omega_{14}, ..., \omega_{16}\}, \{\omega_1, ..., \omega_8\})$. So $l_{K_2, bo}(\omega_i) = 3$ for $1 \leq i \leq 8$ and $l_{K_2, bo}(\omega_i) = 2$ for $9 \leq i \leq 12$. Let $k=1$. Since ω_1, ω_3, ω_9 and ω_{11} are the only models of μ which belong to the level 1 of the strata of at least one of Ω_{K_i, X_i}, we have $M(\Delta_\mu^1(E)) = \{0111, 0110, 1111, 1110\}$. Let $k = 3$. Since none of models of μ is in the first level of strata of all Ω_{K_i, X_i} $(i = 1, 2, 3)$, we have $M(\Delta_\mu^3(E)) = \emptyset$.

By Example 1, the resulting knowledge base of the k-quota based merging operator may be inconsistent.

Clearly, we have the following proposition.

Proposition 3. *Let k be an integer, $E = \{K_1, ..., K_n\}$ be a multi-set of knowledge bases, and μ be a formula. Let $\mathbf{X} = (X_1, ..., X_n)$ be a set of ordering strategies, where X_i $(i = 1, ..., n)$ are ordering strategies attached to K_i. We have $\Delta_\mu^{k+1, \mathbf{X}}(E) \models \Delta_\mu^{k, \mathbf{X}}(E)$ or equivalently, $M(\Delta_\mu^{k+1, \mathbf{X}}(E)) \subseteq M(\Delta_\mu^{k, \mathbf{X}}(E))$. The converse does not generally hold.*

According to Proposition 3, the quota-based operators lead to a sequence of merged bases that is monotonic *w.r.t.* logical entailment. That is, the number of models of the merged bases may decrease when k increases. So the set of models of the merged bases may be empty for some k. We have the following definition which generalizes the k_{max}-quota operator.

Definition 7. *Let $E = \{K_1, ..., K_n\}$ be a SKP, and μ be a formula. Let $k_{max} = max(\{i \leq \sharp(E) | \Delta_\mu^{i, \mathbf{X}} \not\models \bot\})$. $\Delta^{k_{max}, \mathbf{X}}$ is defined in a model-theoretical way as:*

$$M(\Delta_\mu^{k_{max}, \mathbf{X}}(E)) = \{\omega \in M(\mu) | \sharp(\{K_i \in E | \ \omega \in Min(2^\Omega, <_{K_i, X_i})\}) = k_{max}\}.$$

Example 2. (continue Example 1) $k_{max} = 2$. So the result of merging by the $\Delta_\mu^{k_{max}, \mathbf{X}}$ operator is $M(\Delta_\mu^{k_{max}, \mathbf{X}}(E)) = \{1111, 1110\}$. That is, $\Delta_\mu^{k_{max}, \mathbf{X}}(E) = p_1 \wedge p_2 \wedge p_3$.

The following proposition states the relationship between different $\Delta^{k, \mathbf{X}}$ operators when considering different ordering strategies.

Proposition 4. *Let $E = \{K_1, ..., K_n\}$ be a SKP, μ be the integrity constraint, and let k be an integer. Let $\mathbf{X_1} = \{X_1, ..., X_n\}$ and $\mathbf{X_2} = \{X_1', ..., X_n'\}$ be two vectors of ordering strategies, where both X_i and X_i' are ordering strategies for K_i. Suppose $\preceq_{X_i}$ is more specific than $\preceq_{X_i'}$, for all i, where $X_i \in \mathbf{X_1}$ and $X_i' \in \mathbf{X_2}$, then $\Delta_\mu^{k, \mathbf{X_2}}(E) \models \Delta_\mu^{k, \mathbf{X_1}}(E)$.*

Proposition 4 shows that the operator with regard to the set of more specific ordering strategies can result in a knowledge base which has stronger inferential power.

5.3   Refined Quota-Based Merging Operator

The quota-based operators is problematic when merging knowledge bases which are jointly consistent with the formula representing the integrity constraints, i.e. $K_1 \cup ... \cup K_n \cup \phi$ is consistent.

Example 3. Let $E = \{K_1, K_2, K_3\}$ be a SKP consisting of three stratified knowledge bases, where

- $K_1 = \{S_{11}, S_{12}\}$, where $S_{11} = \{p_1 \vee p_2, p_3\}$, $S_{12} = \{\neg p_1, p_4\}$
- $K_2 = \{S_{21}, S_{22}\}$, where $S_{21} = \{p_2 \vee p_3\}$ and $S_{22} = \{p_4\}$
- $K_3 = \{S_{31}, S_{32}\}$, where $S_{31} = \{p_3\}$ and $S_{32} = \{p_2\}$.

The integrity constraint is $\mu = \{\neg p_1 \vee p_2\}$. The set of models of μ is $M(\mu) = \{\omega_1 = 0111, \omega_2 = 0101, \omega_3 = 0110, \omega_4 = 0100, \omega_5 = 0011, \omega_6 = 0001, \omega_7 = 0010, \omega_8 = 0000, \omega_9 = 1111, \omega_{10} = 1101, \omega_{11} = 1110, \omega_{12} = 1100\}$. It is clear that $\bigwedge_{S_i \in K_1 \cup K_2 \cup K_3} S_i \wedge \mu$ is consistent (the knowledge base S_i is viewed as a formula), i.e. ω_1 is its only model. Let $\mathbf{X} = \{X_1, X_2, X_3\}$, where $X_1 = X_2 = bo$ and $X_3 = d_H$. Let $k = 2$. We then have $M(\Delta_\mu^{2, \mathbf{X}}(E)) = \{\omega_1, \omega_9\}$. So $\Delta_\mu^{2, \mathbf{X}}(E) \not\equiv \bigwedge_{S_i \in K_1 \cup K_2 \cup K_3} S_i \wedge \mu$.

In Example 3, the original stratified knowledge bases are jointly consistent with μ. So intuitively, a possible world is a model of resulting knowledge base of merging if it is a model of every K_i ($i = 1, 2, 3$) and μ. However, ω_9, which is a model of $\Delta_\mu^{2, \mathbf{X}}(E)$, is not a model of K_1 because it falsifies $\neg p$. This problem will be further discussed in Section 7.

We have the following refined definition of quota-based merging operators.

Definition 8. *Let* $E = \{K_1, ..., K_n\}$ *be a SKP, μ be a formula, and let k be an integer. Let* $\mathbf{X} = (X_1, ..., X_n)$ *be a set of ordering strategies, where X_i ($i = 1, ..., n$) are ordering strategies attached to K_i. Suppose $<_{K_i, X_i}$ is the complete, transitive and asymmetric relation on 2^Ω obtained by K_i and X_i. The resulting knowledge base of refined k-quota merging operator, denoted by $\Delta_{r,\mu}^{k, \mathbf{X}}(E)$, is defined in a model-theoretic way as follows:*

$$M(\Delta_{r,\mu}^{k, \mathbf{X}}(E)) = \begin{cases} \{\omega \in M(\mu) | \forall K_i \in E \; \omega \models K_i\} & \text{if not empty,} \\ \{\omega \in M(\mu) | \sharp(\{K_i \in E| \; \omega \in Min(2^\Omega, <_{K_i, X_i})\}) \geq k\} & \text{otherwise} \end{cases}$$

Clearly, we have the following proposition.

Proposition 5. *Let* $E = \{K_1, ..., K_n\}$ *be a multi-set of stratified knowledge bases, μ be a formula, and let k be an integer. Let* $\mathbf{X} = (X_1, ..., X_n)$ *be a set of ordering strategies, where X_i ($i = 1, ..., n$) are ordering strategies attached to K_i. We have $\Delta_{r,\mu}^{k, \mathbf{X}}(E) \vdash \Delta_\mu^{k, \mathbf{X}}(E)$.*

5.4   Flat Case

In this section, we apply our merging operators to the classical knowledge bases. Since our merging operators are based on the ordering strategies, we need to consider the ordering strategies for classical knowledge bases.

Proposition 6. *Let K be a classical knowledge base. Suppose X is an ordering strategy, then*

1. *for $X = bo$ and $X = maxsat$, we have $\omega \preceq_X \omega'$ iff $\omega \models K$*
2. *for $X = leximin$, let $K(\omega) = \{\phi \in K : \omega \models \phi\}$, we have $\omega \preceq_X \omega'$ iff $|K(\omega)| \geq |K(\omega')|$*
3. *for $X = d$, we have $\omega \preceq_X \omega'$ iff $d(\omega, K) \leq d(\omega, K')$.*

By Proposition 6, the best out ordering and the maxsat ordering are reduced to the same ordering when knowledge base is flat. Furthermore, the leximin ordering can be used to order possible worlds when the knowledge base is inconsistent.

We have the following propositions.

Proposition 7. *Let $E = \{K_1, ..., K_n\}$ be a multi-set of knowledge bases, μ be a formula, and k be an integer. Suppose $X_i = bo$ or $maxsat$ for all i. Then*

$$\Delta_{r,\mu}^{k,\mathbf{X}}(E) \equiv \Delta_\mu^k(E).$$

Proposition 7 tells us that, in the flat case, the result of our refined quota-based merging operators is equivalent to that of the quota merging operators when the ordering strategies are the best out ordering or the maxsat ordering. By Proposition 1, 2, 4 and 7, we have the following result.

Proposition 8. *Let $E = \{K_1, ..., K_n\}$ be a multi-set of knowledge bases, μ be a formula, and k be an integer. Suppose $X_i = leximin$ or d, then*

$$\Delta_{r,\mu}^{k,\mathbf{X}}(E) \vdash \Delta_\mu^k(E),$$

but not vice verse.

Let us look at an example.

Example 4. Let $E = \{K_1, K_2\}$, where $K_1 = \{p_1 \vee p_2, p_3, \neg p_3\}$ and $K_2 = \{p_1, p_2, p_3\}$, $\mu = \{(p_1 \vee p_3) \wedge p_2\}$ and $k = 2$. So $Mod(\mu) = \{\omega_1 = 110, \omega_2 = 111, \omega_3 = 011\}$. Let $\mathbf{X} = (X_1, X_2)$, where $X_1 = leximin$ and $X_2 = bo$ are ordering strategies of K_1 and K_2 respectively. The computations are given in Table 2 below.

Table 2

ω	K_1	K_2
110	1	2
111	1	1
011	1	2

According to Table 2, $\omega_2 = 111$ is the only model which belong to the level 1 of the strata of both Ω_{K_1, X_1} and Ω_{K_2, X_2}. So $M(\Delta_\mu^{2,\mathbf{X}}(E)) = \{111\}$. However, if we apply the quota merging operator, since K_1 and K_2 are inconsistent, it is clear that $M(\Delta_\mu^k(E)) = \emptyset$.

6   Computational Complexity

We now discuss the complexity issue. First we need to consider the computational complexity of stratifying Ω from a stratified knowledge base. In [15], two important problems for logical preference representation languages were considered. We express them as follows.

Definition 9. *Given a stratified knowledge base K and two interpretations ω and ω', the COMPARISON problem consists of determining whether $\omega \preceq_X \omega'$, where X denotes an ordering strategy. The NON-DOMINANCE problem consists of determining whether ω is* non-dominated *for $\preceq_X$, that is, there is not ω' such that $\omega' \prec_X \omega$.*

It was shown in [15] that the NON-DOMINANCE problem is usually a hard problem, i.e **coNP**-complete. We have the following proposition on NON-DOMINANCE problem for ordering strategies in Section 3.

Proposition 9. *Let K be a stratified knowledge base. For $X = bo, maxsat$, or lexmin:*
(1) COMPARISON is in P, *where* P *denotes the class of problems decidable in deterministic polynomial time.*
(2) NON-DOMINANCE is coNP-complete.

To stratify Ω, we need to consider the problem *determining all non-dominated interpretations*, which is computational much harder than the NON-DOMINANCE problem. To simplify the computation of our merging operators, we assume that Ω is stratified from each stratified knowledge base during an off-line preprocessing stage.

Let Δ be a merging operator. The following decision problem is denoted as MERGE(Δ):

- **Input** : a 4-tuple $\langle E, \mu, \psi, \mathbf{X} \rangle$ where $E = \{K_1, ..., K_n\}$ is a SKP, μ is a formula, and ψ is a formula; $\mathbf{X} = (X_1, ..., X_n)$, where X_i is the ordering strategy attached to K_i.
- **Question** : Does $\Delta_\mu(E) \models \psi$ hold?

Proposition 10. *MERGE($\Delta^{k,\mathbf{X}}$) is CoNP-complete and MERGE($\Delta_r^{k,\mathbf{X}}$) is* BH (2)-*complete.*

The proof of Proposition 10 is similar to that of Proposition 4 in [9]. Proposition 10 shows that the complexities of both $\Delta^{k,\mathbf{X}}$ operators and $\Delta_r^{k,\mathbf{X}}$ operators are located at a low level of the boolean hierarchy. Furthermore, the computation of $\Delta^{k,\mathbf{X}}$ operators is easier than that of $\Delta_r^{k,\mathbf{X}}$ operators (under the usual assumptions of complexity theory).

7   Logical Properties

Many logical properties have been proposed to characterize a belief merging operator. We introduce the set of postulates proposed in [11], which is used to characterize Integrity Constraints (*IC*) merging operators.

Definition 10. *Let E, E_1, E_2 be knowledge profiles, K_1, K_2 be consistent knowledge bases, and μ, μ_1, μ_2 be formulas from $\mathcal{L}_{PS}$. Δ is an IC merging operator iff it satisfies the following postulates:*

(IC0) $\Delta_\mu(E) \models \mu$
(IC1) *If μ is consistent, then $\Delta_\mu(E)$ is consistent*
(IC2) *If $\bigwedge E$ is consistent with μ, then $\Delta_\mu(E) \equiv \bigwedge E \wedge \mu$, where $\bigwedge(E) = \wedge_{K_i \in E} K_i$*
(IC3) *If $E_1 \equiv E_2$ and $\mu_1 \equiv \mu_2$, then $\Delta_{\mu_1}(E_1) \equiv \Delta_{\mu_2}(E_2)$*
(IC4) *If $K_1 \models \mu$ and $K_2 \models \mu$, then $\Delta_\mu(\{K_1, K_2\}) \wedge K_1$ is consistent iff $\Delta_\mu(\{K_1, K_2\}) \wedge K_2$ is consistent*
(IC5) $\Delta_\mu(E_1) \wedge \Delta_\mu(E_2) \models \Delta_\mu(E_1 \sqcup E_2)$
(IC6) *If $\Delta_\mu(E_1) \wedge \Delta_\mu(E_2)$ is consistent, then $\Delta_\mu(E_1 \sqcup E_2) \models \Delta_\mu(E_1) \wedge \Delta_\mu(E_2)$*
(IC7) $\Delta_{\mu_1}(E) \wedge \mu_2 \models \Delta_{\mu_1 \wedge \mu_2}(E)$
(IC8) *If $\Delta_{\mu_1}(E) \wedge \mu_2$ is consistent, then $\Delta_{\mu_1 \wedge \mu_2}(E) \models \Delta_{\mu_1}(E) \wedge \mu_2$*

The postulates are used to characterize an IC merging operator in classical logic. Detailed explanation of the above postulates can be found in [11].

Some postulates in Definition 10 need to be modified if we consider merging postulates for stratified knowledge bases, i.e., $(IC2)$, $(IC3)$ should be modified as:

(IC2$'$) Let $\bigwedge E = \wedge_{K_i \in E} \wedge_{\phi_{ij} \in K_i} \phi_{ij}$. If $\bigwedge E$ is consistent with μ, then $\Delta_\mu(E) \equiv$ $\bigwedge E \wedge \mu$
(IC3$'$) If $E_1 \equiv_s E_2$ and $\mu_1 \equiv \mu_2$, then $\Delta_{\mu_1}(E_1) \equiv \Delta_{\mu_2}(E_2)$

$(IC3')$ is stronger than $(IC3)$ because the condition of equivalence between two knowledge profiles is generalized to the condition of equivalence between two SKPs. We do not generalize $(IC4)$, the fairness postulate, which is hard to be adapted in the prioritized case because a stratified knowledge base may be inconsistent and there is no unique consequence relation for a stratified knowledge base [3].

Proposition 11. $\Delta^{k,\mathbf{X}}$ *satisfies (IC0), (IC5), (IC7), (IC8). The other postulates are not satisfied in the general case. $\Delta_r^{k,\mathbf{X}}$ satisfies (IC0), (IC2), (IC5), (IC7), (IC8). The other postulates are not satisfied in the general case.*

(IC1) is not satisfied by both $\Delta^{k,\mathbf{X}}$ and $\Delta^{k,\mathbf{X}}$ because the result of merging may be inconsistent. $\Delta^{k,\mathbf{X}}$ and $\Delta_r^{k,\mathbf{X}}$ do not satisfy (IC3$'$) because some ordering strategies may be syntax sensitive. A difference between $\Delta^{k,\mathbf{X}}$ and $\Delta_r^{k,\mathbf{X}}$ is that $\Delta^{k,\mathbf{X}}$ does not satisfy the postulate (IC2$'$), whilst $\Delta_r^{k,\mathbf{X}}$ satisfies this postulate. The following proposition shows that when the ordering strategies are either best out ordering or maxsat ordering, then both operators satisfy (IC3$'$).

Proposition 12. *Suppose $X_i = bo$, maxsat, then $\Delta^{k,\mathbf{X}}$ satisfies (IC0), (IC2), (IC3$'$), (IC5), (IC7), (IC8). The other postulates are not satisfied in the general case.*

8   Related Work

Merging of stratified knowledge bases is often handled in the framework of possibilistic logic [8] or ordinal conditional function [20]. In possibilistic logic, the merging problems are often solved by aggregating *possibility distributions*, which are mappings from Ω to a common scale such as $[0,1]$, using some *combination modes*. Then the syntactic counterpart of these combination modes can be defined accordingly [4,5]. In [7], the merging is conducted by merging *epistemic states* which are (total) functions from the set of interpretations to $\mathbf{N}$, the set of natural numbers. We now discuss two main differences between our merging operators and previous merging operators for stratified knowledge bases.

First, our operators are semantically defined in a model-theoretic way and others are semantically defined by distribution functions such as possibility distributions in possibilistic logic framework. In the flat case, our merging operators belong to model-based merging operators in classical logic, so it is independent of syntactical form of the knowledge bases. In contrast, other merging operators are usually syntax-based ones in the flat case.

Second, most of previous merging operators are based on the commensurability assumption, that is, all agents use a common scale to rank their beliefs. In [4], a merging approach for stratified knowledge base is proposed which drops the commensurability assumption. However, their approach is based on the assumption that there is an ordering relation between two stratified knowledge bases K_1 and K_2, i.e. K_1 has priority over K_2. In contrast, our merging operators do not require any of above assumptions and are flexible enough to merge knowledge bases which are stratified by a total pre-ordering on their elements.

In [18], we proposed a family of lexicographic merging operators for stratified knowledge bases. Our quota-based merging operators only use the most preferred possible worlds w.r.t each ordering strategy. That is, suppose $\Omega_{K,X} = (\Omega_1, ..., \Omega_m)$, then only Ω_1 is used to define the quota-based operators. Whilst the lexicographic merging operators utilize the rest of the structure of $\Omega_{K,X}$. Therefore, the lexicographic merging operators are refinement of the quota-based operators. However, this refinement is paid by higher computational complexity.

9   Conclusions

In this paper, we have proposed a family of quota-based operators to merge stratified knowledge bases under integrity constraints. Our operators generalize the quota merging operators for classical knowledge bases. The computational complexity of our merging operators has been analyzed. Under an additional assumption, the complexities of both $\Delta^{k,\mathbf{X}}$ operators and $\Delta_r^{k,\mathbf{X}}$ operators are located at a low level of the boolean hierarchy. Furthermore, the computation of $\Delta^{k,\mathbf{X}}$ operators is easier than that of $\Delta_r^{k,\mathbf{X}}$ operators (under the usual assumptions of complexity theory). Finally, we have generalized the set of postulates defined in [11] and shown that our operators satisfy most of the generalized postulates.

References

1. Baral, C.; Kraus, S. and Minker, J. 1991. Combining multiple knowledge bases. *IEEE Transactions on Knowledge and Data Engineering*, 3(2):208-220.
2. Barberà, S.; Sonnenschein, H. and Zhou, L. 1991. Voting by committees. *Econometrica*, 59(3):595-609.
3. Benferhat, S.; Cayrol, C.; Dubois, D.; Lang, L. and Prade, H. 1993a. Inconsistency management and prioritized syntax-based entailment. In *Proc. of IJCAI'93*, 640-645.
4. Benferhat, S.; Dubois, D.; Prade, H.; and Williams, M.A. 1999. A Practical Approach to Fusing Prioritized Knowledge Bases. In *Proc. of EPIA'99*, 223-236. Springer-Verlag.
5. Benferhat, S.; Dubois, D.; Kaci, S.; and Prade, H. 2002. Possibilistic merging and distance-based fusion of propositional information. *Annals of Mathematics and Artificial Intelligence* 34:217-252.
6. Brewka, G. 2004. A rank-based description language for qualitative preferences. In *Proc. of ECAI'04*, 303-307.
7. Chopra, S.; Ghose, S. and Meyer, T. 2005. Social choice theory, belief merging, and strategy-proofness. *Journal of Information Fusion*, 7: 61-79, 2006.
8. Dubois, D.; Lang, J.; and Prade, H. 1994. Possibilistic logic. In *Handbook of logic in Aritificial Intelligence and Logic Programming*, Volume 3. Oxford University Press, 439-513.
9. Everaere, P.; Konieczny, S. and Marquis, P. 2005. Quota and Gmin merging operators. In *Proc. of IJCAI'05*, 424-429.
10. Gärdenfors P. 1988. *Knowledge in Flux-Modeling the Dynamic of Epistemic States*. Mass.: MIT Press.
11. Konieczny, S. and Pino Pérez, R. 2002. Merging information under constraints: a qualitative framework. *Journal of Logic and Computation* 12(5):773-808.
12. Konieczny, S.; Lang, J. and Pino Pérez, R. 2004. DA^2 operators. *Artificial Intelligence*, 157(1-2):49-79.
13. Konieczny, S. and Pérez, R.P. 2005. Propositional belief base merging or how to merge beliefs/goals coming from several sources and some links with social choice theory. *European Journal of Operational Research*, 160(3):785-802.
14. Liberatore, P. and Schaerf, M. 1998. Arbitration (or How to Merge Knowledge Bases). *IEEE Transaction on Knowledge and Data Engineering* 10(1):76-90.
15. Lang, J. 2004. Logical preference representation and combinatorial vote. *Annals of Mathematics and Artificial Intelligence*, 4(1-3):37-71.
16. Moulin, H. 1988. *Axioms of Cooperative Decision Making*. Cambridge University Press.
17. Qi, G.: Liu, W. and Bell, D.A. 2005. A revision-based approach to resolving conflicting information. In *Proc. of UAI'05*, 477-484.
18. Qi, G. Liu, W. and Bell, D.A. 2006. Merging stratified knowledge bases under constraints. In *Proc. of AAAI'06*, 2006.
19. Revesz, P.Z. 1997. On the semantics of arbitration. *International Journal of Algebra and Computation*, 7(2):133-160.
20. Spohn, W. 1988. Ordinal conditional functions. In William L. Harper and Brian Skyrms (eds.), *Causation in Decision, Belief Change, and Statistics*, 11, 105-134. Kluwer Academic Publisher.

Enumerating Minimal Explanations
by Minimal Hitting Set Computation

Ken Satoh and Takeaki Uno

National Institute of Informatics and Sokendai
ksatoh@nii.ac.jp, uno@nii.ac.jp

Abstract. We consider the problem of enumerating minimal explanations in propositional theory. We propose a new way of characterizing the enumeration problem in terms of not only the number of explanations, but also the number of *unexplanations*. Maximal unexplanations are a maximal set of abducible formulas which cannot explain the observation given a background theory. In this paper, we interleavingly enumerate not only minimal explanations but also maximal unexplanations. To best of our knowledge, there has been no algorithm which is characterized in terms of such maximal unexplanations. We propose two algorithms to perform this task and also analyze them in terms of query complexity, space complexity and time complexity.

1 Introduction

Abduction is a powerful logical tool to get an explanation or complement missing knowledge given observation. It has been widely used for various areas such as diagnosis, planning and natural language processing [9,2]. In abduction, one criterion for choosing better explanation among multiple explanations is *minimality*. The criterion is motivated from economy of reasoning such as Occam's razor and plausibility of the explanation (more information in explanation is used, less plausible these additional events are true).

However, to compute a minimal explanation is not so easy if the background theory is represented in a formula as pointed out in [2,3,4,5]. Only known positive result is that if a background theory is a propositional Horn theory and the observation is a positive literal, then we can enumerate all nontrivial minimal explanations for the observation in the time of the order of polynomial w.r.t. the number of clauses and number of atoms and the number of explanations. The other known results are all intractable.

In this paper, we propose another way of characterizing the enumeration problem in terms of not only the number of explanations, but also the number of *unexplanations*. Unexplanation corresponds with the phenomena that even if we add some abducible formulas, we cannot explain the observation. We give a method to enumerate interleavingly not only minimal explanations but also maximal unexplanations. To best of our knowledge, there has been no algorithm proposed which is characterized in terms of such minimal explanations and maximal unexplanations.

J. Lang, F. Lin, and J. Wang (Eds.): KSEM 2006, LNAI 4092, pp. 354–365, 2006.

In this paper, we present two versions of algorithms to enumerate minimal abducibles. One is adapted from the work by Gunopulos et. al [7,8] and the other is from our work [13,16]. Both are methods of enumerating maximal frequent itemsets in data mining.

The former algorithm has the advantages in worst time complexity in some restricted classes of abduction. The feature of the latter algorithm is that we need no memory for previously obtained solutions since the algorithm is based on depth-first search. This reduces the memory use. In order to realize the depth-first search, we use a backtracking algorithm of enumerating minimal hitting sets by one of the authors [15].

We theoretically analyze the above two algorithsm in terms of the number of explainability checks and space complexity.

2   Abductive Framework and Minimal Explanation

In this section, we define abduction.

Definition 1. *An* abductive framework *is a triple* $\langle B, H, O \rangle$ *where B be a propositional theory, H be a set of propositional formulas and O be a propositional formula.*

We call B a *background theory*, H a set of *abducibles* and O an *observation*.

Definition 2. *Let* $\langle B, H, O \rangle$ *be an abductive framework.*

- *A subset E of H is an* explanation *w.r.t.* $\langle B, H, O \rangle$ *if $B \cup E \models O$.*
- *An explanation E w.r.t.* $\langle B, H, O \rangle$ *is* consistent *if $B \cup E \not\models false$.*
- *An explanation E w.r.t.* $\langle B, H, O \rangle$ *is* minimal *if there exists no subset of H, E' s.t. $E' \subset E$ and $B \cup E' \models O$. ("$\subset$" is a strict subset relation)*

We denote all the minimal explanations w.r.t. $\langle B, H, O \rangle$ *as $MinE_{B,H}(O)$.*

If E is a minimal explanation, then if we remove any element of E, the resulting set does not explain the observation.

In this paper, we consider an enumeration algorithm of consistent minimal explanations in $MinE_{B,H}(O)$ in the condition that only explainability check is available as a query, and try to reduce the number of explainability checks.

Example 1. Consider the following abductive framework $\langle B, H, O \rangle$ where B is the conjunction of the following formulas: $P \supset T \vee U$

$Q \wedge R \wedge U \supset V$
$T \wedge S \supset false$
$U \wedge S \supset false$
$T \supset W$
$V \supset W$

and $H = \{P, Q, R, S\}$ and $O =" W"$. Then, $E_0 = \{P, Q, R, S\}$ is an explanation w.r.t. $\langle B, H, O \rangle$, but not minimal since there is an explanation $E_1 =$

$\{P, Q, R\}$ which is a subset of E_0. E_1 is a consistent minimal explanation. $E_2 = \{P, S\}$ is also a minimal explanation, but it is not consistent. In this example, $MinE_{B,H}(O) = \{E_1, E_2\}$.

For our enumeration algorithms, we use a notion of unexplainability as follows.

Definition 3. *Let $\langle B, H, O \rangle$ be an abductive framework.*

- *A subset E of H is an* unexplanation *w.r.t. $\langle B, H, O \rangle$ if $B \cup E \not\models O$.*
- *An unexplanation E w.r.t. $\langle B, H, O \rangle$ is* maximal *if there exists no subset of H, E' s.t. $E \subset E'$ and $B \cup E' \not\models O$.*

We denote all the maximal unexplanations w.r.t. $\langle B, H, O \rangle$ as $MaxUE_{B,H}(O)$.

If E is a maximal unexplanation, then if we add to E any element which is not in E, the resulting set explains the observation.

Example 2. Consider the abductive framework in Example 1. Then, $UE_0 = \{Q, R\}$ is an unexplanation w.r.t. $\langle B, H, O \rangle$, but not maximal since $UE_1 = \{Q, R, S\}$ is an unexplanation and UE_1 subsumes UE_0. In this example, $MaxUE_{B,H}(O) = \{\{P, Q\}, \{P, R\}, \{Q, R, S\}\}$.

Note that unexplainability satisfies *monotone* property meaning that if a subset of H, E does not satisfy $B \cup E \models O$ then every subset of E, E' does not satisfy $B \cup E' \models O$. Enumeration methods of maximal sets with monotone property by minimal hitting set computation have been proposed [7,8,13,16]. In this paper, we modify these algorithms in order to enumerate minimal explanations in stead of maximal unexplanations.

For our algorithms, we need the following definition of *minimal hitting set*.

Definition 4. *Let H be a finite set and $\mathcal{H}$ be a set of some subsets of H. A hitting set HS of $\mathcal{H}$ is a set s.t. for every $S \in \mathcal{H}$, $S \cap HS \neq \emptyset$. A minimal hitting set HS of $\mathcal{H}$ is a hitting set s.t. there exists no other hitting set HS' of $\mathcal{H}$ s.t. $HS' \subset HS$ (HS' is a proper subset of HS). We denote the set of all minimal hitting sets of $\mathcal{H}$ as $MHS(\mathcal{H})$.*

Example 3. Let $\mathcal{H} = \{\{R, S\}, \{Q, S\}, \{P\}\}$ Then, $\{P, R, S\}$ is a hitting set of $\mathcal{H}$ but it it not minimal since $\{P, S\}$ is a hitting set. In this example, $MHS(\mathcal{H}) = \{\{P, Q, R\}, \{P, S\}\}$.

Then, by interpreting the result in [11] to our task, we can show that there is a relationship between $MaxUE_{B,H}(O)$ and $MinE_{B,H}(O)$ through a minimal hitting set. Let $\mathcal{E}$ be a set of subsets of H. We represent $\{H \setminus E | E \in \mathcal{E}\}$ as $\overline{\mathcal{E}}$.

Proposition 5 ((adapted from [11])). *Let $\langle B, H, O \rangle$ be an abductive framework.*

$$MinE_{B,H}(O) = MHS(\overline{MaxUE_{B,H}(O)})$$

A subset E of H is included in a maximal unexplanation E' of $MaxUE_{B,H}(O)$ (in other words, E is an unexplanation) if and only if $E \cap (H \setminus E') = \emptyset$. Thus, E is an explanation if and only if E intersects $(H \setminus E')$ for every $E' \in MaxUE_{B,H}(O)$, i.e., E is a hitting set of $\overline{MaxUE_{B,H}(O)}$. Therefore, we have the above proposition.

Example 4. Consider the abductive framework in Example 1. Then, from Example 1 and Example 2, $MinE_{B,H}(O) = \{\{P, Q, R\}, \{P, S\}\}$ and $MaxUE_{B,H}(O) = \{\{P, Q\}, \{P, R\}, \{Q, R, S\}\}$. Then, $\overline{MaxUE_{B,H}(O)} = \{\{R, S\}, \{Q, S\}, \{P\}\}$. According to Example 3, $MHS(\overline{MaxUE_{B,H}(O)}) = MinE_{B,H}(O)$.

Moreover, by adapting the result in [7,8] to our task, the following holds.

Proposition 6 ((adapted from [7,8])). *Let $\langle B, H, O \rangle$ be an abductive framework, and $MaUE \subseteq MaxUE_{B,H}(O)$. Then, for every $E \in MHS(\overline{MaUE})$, either $E \in MinE_{B,H}(O)$ or E is an unexplanation.*

This proposition says that the above E is never a non-minimal explanation. Suppose the contrary. Then, E subsumed some explanation E' which are not a hitting set of $\overline{MaUE}$. Then, this means that there is a maximal unexplanation E'' in $MaUE$ such that E' does not hit $(H \setminus E'')$. This means $E' \subseteq E''$ and contradiction occurs. Therefore, the above proposition holds.

Using the following proposition in [13,8], we can enumerate maximal unexplanations without redundant explainability checks which might be done for minimal explanations which have already been found.

Proposition 7 ((adapted from [13,8])). *Let $\langle B, H, O \rangle$ be an abductive framework and $MaUE_1$ and $MaUE_2$ be subsets of $MaxUE_{B,H}(O)$. If $MaUE_1 \subseteq MaUE_2$ then*

$$MHS(\overline{MaUE_1}) \cap MinE_{B,H}(O) \subseteq MHS(\overline{MaUE_2}) \cap MinE_{B,H}(O).$$

This proposition means that if E is a minimal explanation in $MHS(\overline{MaUE_1})$, then E keeps being a minimal explanation even if we add any newly found maximal unexplanation to $MaUE_1$. A minimal hitting set E' in $MHS(\overline{MaUE_1})$ disappears by adding a new maximal unexplanation E'' to $MaUE_1$ if and only if E'' includes E'.

Suppose that we find a subset of maximal unexplanations, $MaUE$. By Proposition 5, if every set in $MHS(\overline{MaUE})$ is a minimal explanation, then we are done. Otherwise, by Proposition 6, there exists some unexplanation in $MHS(\overline{MaUE})$. Then, starting from such an unexplanation and adding each formula in H one by one to the unexplanation, we can reach a maximal unexplanation. Then, we augment $MaUE$ by the newly found maximal unexplanation and continue this process. Since the number of the maximal unexplanations is finite, we eventually enumerate $MaxUE_{B,H}(O)$. This is the algorithm adapted from the one proposed in [8] which was shown in Fig. 1. Note that this algorithm not only enumerates $MaxUE_{B,H}(O)$ but also $MinE_{B,H}(O)$.

Example 5. Consider the abductive framework in Example 1. We show the trace of Algorithm I as follows.

---

global A set of background theory B
global A set of abducible formulas H
global A set of observation O
main()
begin

1. $MaUE := \{go\_up(\emptyset)\}$ and $MiE := \emptyset$
2. $mhs = MHS(\overline{MaUE})$.
3. **for** each enumerated set $E \in mhs$, we do the following:
    if $E \in MiE$ **then continue**
    else if $B \cup E \not\models O$ **then quit loop**
    else $MiE := MiE \cup \{E\}$; output E if $B \cup E \not\models false$; **continue**
4. **if** there is no E s.t. $B \cup E \not\models O$ **then exit**
    else $MaUE := MaUE \cup \{go\_up(E)\}$ and go to 2

end

$go\_up(E)$

1. **select** an element e in $H \setminus E$
2. **if** $B \cup E \cup \{e\} \not\models O$ **then** $E := E \cup \{e\}$ and go to 1
3. **return** E

Fig. 1. Algorithm I to enumerate minimal explanations

1. Suppose $MaUE := go\_up(\emptyset) = \{\{P, Q\}\}$.
2. Since $\overline{MaUE}$ is $\{\{R, S\}\}$, we start an enumeration of $MHS(\{\{R, S\}\})$.
   (a) Suppose that $E = \{S\}$ is an enumerated set.
   Since $MiE = \emptyset$, $\{S\} \notin MiE$.
   Then, since $B \cup \{S\} \not\models O$, we quit the loop.
   Since we found that $B \cup \{S\} \not\models O$, we invoke $go\_up(\{S\})$.
   $\{Q, R, S\}$ for $go\_up(\{S\})$ is obtained.
   Then $MaUE$ becomes $\{\{P, Q\}, \{Q, R, S\}\}$.
3. Since $\overline{MaUE}$ is $\{\{R, S\}, \{P\}\}$, we start an enumeration of $MHS(\{\{R, S\}, \{P\}\})$.
   (a) Suppose that $E = \{P, S\}$ is an enumerated set.
   Since $MiE = \emptyset$, $\{P, S\} \notin MiE$.
   Then, since $B \cup \{P, S\} \models O$, MiE becomes $\{\{P, S\}\}$.
   Since $B \cup \{P, S\} \models false$, we do not output it and continue.
   (b) Suppose that $E = \{P, R\}$ is an enumerated set.
   Since $MiE = \{\{P, S\}\}$, $\{P, R\} \notin MiE$.
   Then, since $B \cup \{P, R\} \not\models O$, , we quit the loop.
   Since we found that $B \cup \{P, R\} \not\models O$, we invoke $go\_up(\{P, R\})$.
   $\{P, R\}$ for $go\_up(\{P, R\})$ is obtained.
   Then $MaUE$ becomes $\{\{P, Q\}, \{Q, R, S\}, \{P, R\}\}$.
4. Since $\overline{MaUE}$ is $\{\{R, S\}, \{P\}, \{Q, S\}\}$, we start an enumeration of $MHS(\{\{R, S\}, \{P\}, \{Q, S\}\})$.

(a) Suppose that $E = \{P, S\}$ is an enumerated set.
Since $\{P, S\} \in MiE$, we do not need to check explainability and continue.
(b) Suppose that $E = \{P, Q, R\}$ is an enumerated set.
Since $MiE = \{\{P, S\}\}$, $\{P, Q, R\} \notin MiE$.
Then, since $B \cup \{P, S\} \models O$, MiE becomes $\{\{P, S\}, \{P, Q, R\}\}$.
Since $B \cup \{P, Q, R\} \not\models false$, we output it.
Since all minimal hitting sets explain the observation, we exit.

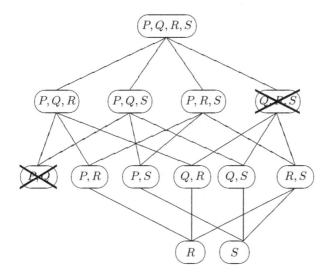

Fig. 2. $go\_up(\{S\}) = \{Q, R, S\}$

A snapshot of the trace represented in a lattice structure of H is shown in Fig. 2 at the time when we find $\{Q, R, S\}$ as the second maximal unexplanation after calling $go\_up(\{S\})$ (the first one is $\{P, Q\}$). In the figure, crossed nodes represent found maximal unexplanations. Note that since we found that $\{Q, R, S\}$ is a maximal unexplanation, we no longer have to check explainability for any subset of $\{Q, R, S\}$ thanks to monotone property of unexplainability. Therefore, any set which are not subsumed by these maximal unexplanations should be E in the next loop. This selection can be done by computing the minimal hitting sets for the complements of found maximal unexplanations. In this snap shot, the complements of maximal unexplanations, $\{P, Q\}$ and $\{Q, R, S\}$ are $\{R, S\}$ and $\{P\}$ respectively and computing the minimal hitting set of $\{\{R, S\}, \{P\}\}$ results in $\{\{P, R\}, \{P, S\}\}$ which are not subsumed by any previously found maximal unexplanations (The resulting possible sets for explanations are shown in Fig. 3).

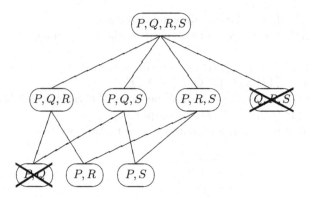

Fig. 3. After computing minimal hitting sets of $\{\{R, S\}, \{P\}\}$

Theorem 8 ((adapted from [8]))
Algorithm I in Fig. 1 enumerates $MaxUE_{B,H}(O)$ with at most

$$2 * |MinE_{B,H}(O)| + |MaxUE_{B,H}(O)| \cdot |H|$$

explainability checks. The necessary space is

$$O(|MaxUE_{B,H}(O)| + |MinE_{B,H}(O)|).$$

If explainability check can be performed in polynomial time w.r.t. the number of propositions, then the time complexity becomes the quasi-polynomial w.r.t.

$$(|MaxUE_{B,H}(O)| + |MinE_{B,H}(O)|)^1.$$

Note that in the above theorem, we assume that a check for $B \cup E \not\models false$ is done by explanation check of $false$. In the algorithm, the number of outer loops are $|MaxUE_{B,H}(O)|$ since in every iteration, one maximal unexplanation is added to $MaUE$ until $|MaxUE_{B,H}(O)|$ is obtained. To compute one maximal unexplanation by go_up, we need at most $|H|$ explainability checks. The number of inner loops for an enumerated set is at most $MinE_{B,H}(O)$ thanks to Proposition 6 but we do not need to check explainability in every iteration since we can omit previously checked explanations due to Proposition 7. This avoidance of redundant check is done by accumulating previously checked explanations in MiE in the algorithm. Then the number of checks for $MinE_{B,H}(O)$ is at most $2 * |MinE_{B,H}(O)|$ (one for explainability of O and the other for explainability of $false$). As a whole, the total number of checks becomes

$$2 * |MinE_{B,H}(O)| + |MaxUE_{B,H}(O)| \cdot |H|.$$

The necessary space is $O(|MaxUE_{B,H}(O)| + |MinE_{B,H}(O)|)$ since we have to store both of $MaxUE_{B,H}(O)$ (corresponding with $MaUE$)and $MinE_{B,H}(O)$ (corresponding with MiE). If explainability check can be performed in

---

[1] Quasi polynomial with respect to m is the polynomial of the form of $m^{\log m}$.

```
global A set of background theory B
global A set of abducible formulas H
global A set of observation O
global integer uenum; sets maxUE₀, maxUE₁,....;
main()
begin
    uenum := 0;
    construct_maxUE(0, ∅);
end

construct_maxUE(i, E)
begin
    if i == uenum then goto 1 else goto 2

    1.    if B ∪ E ⊨ O then output E if B ∪ E ⊭ false and return;
          else maxUE_uenum := go_up(E); uenum := uenum + 1;
          /* proceed to 2 */
    2.    if ‾‾maxUEᵢ‾‾ ∩ E ≠ ∅ then construct_maxUE(i + 1, E);
          else
              for every e ∈ ‾‾maxUEᵢ‾‾ s.t.
                  E ∪ {e} is a minimal hitting set of {‾maxUE₀‾, ‾maxUE₁‾, ..., ‾maxUEᵢ‾}
              do construct_maxUE(i + 1, E ∪ {e});
              return;

end
```

Fig. 4. Algorithm II to enumerate minimal explanations

polynomial time w.r.t. the number of propositions, then the complexity of the algorithm is proportional to the time of computing minimal hitting sets. Then, if we use Fredman and Khachiyan's incremental algorithm [6] for computing minimal hitting sets, we have the bound in computational time which is the quasi-polynomial of

$$(|MaxUE_{B,H}(O)| + |MinE_{B,H}(O)|).$$

The next algorithm in Fig. 4 is an adapted version of the data-mining algorithm proposed in [13,16] to our task here. This algorithm uses the irredundant minimal hitting set computation [15] in a depth-first manner. Unlike the previous Algorithm I, the algorithm cuts any redundant explainability check for a minimal explanation without storing previous check information by using a depth-first search strategy. So, this algorithm has an advantage in space complexity. Note that this algorithm not only enumerates $MaxUE_{B,H}(O)$ but also $MinE_{B,H}(O)$ as well.

Example 6. Consider the abductive framework in Example 1. We show the trace of Algorithm II as follows.

$uenum := 0;$
call $construct\_bdp(0, ∅)$

Since $i ==$ *uenum* and $B \cup \emptyset \not\models O$, we invoke $go\_up(\emptyset)$.
Suppose that $\{P,Q\}$ is obtained. $maxUE_0$ is set to $\{P,Q\}$, and *uenum* := 1.
Since $\overline{maxUE_0}$ is $\{R,S\}$ and $\emptyset \cup \{S\}(= \{S\})$ and $\emptyset \cup \{R\}(= \{R\})$ are minimal
hitting   sets   of $\{\{R,S\}\}$,   we   invoke $construct\_bdp(1, \{S\})$ and
$construct\_bdp(1, \{R\})$ in a depth-first manner.

1. $construct\_bdp(1, \{S\})$
   Since $i ==$ *uenum* and $B \cup \{S\} \not\models O$, we invoke $go\_up(\{S\})$.
   Suppose that $\{Q,R,S\}$ for $go\_up(\{S\})$ is obtained. $maxUE_1$ is set to
   $\{Q,R,S\}$, and *uenum* := 2.
   Since $\overline{maxUE_1}$ is $\{P\}$ and $\{S\} \cup \{P\}(= \{P,S\})$ is a minimal hitting set of
   $\{\{R,S\}, \{P\}\}$, we invoke $construct\_bdp(2, \{P,S\})$.
   (a) $construct\_bdp(2, \{P,S\})$
       Since $i ==$ *uenum* and $B \cup \{P,S\} \models O$ but $B \cup \{P,S\} \models false$, we
       do not output this set and return to the caller. Note that $\{P,S\} \in$
       $MinE_{B,H}(O)$.
   Since a **for**-loop is finished return to the caller.
2. $construct\_bdp(1, \{R\})$
   Since $i \neq$ *uenum*, we go directly to 2.
   Since $\overline{maxUE_1}$ is $\{P\}$ and $\{R\} \cup \{P\}(= \{P,R\})$ is a minimal hitting set of
   $\{\{R,S\}, \{P\}\}$, we invoke $construct\_bdp(2, \{P,R\})$.
   (a) $construct\_bdp(2, \{P,R\})$
       Since $i ==$ *uenum*, and $B \cup \{P,R\} \not\models O$, we compute $go\_up(\{P,R\})$.
       $\{P,R\}$ is obtained. $maxUE_2$ is set to $\{P,R\}$, and *uenum* := 3.
       Since $\overline{maxUE_2}$ is $\{Q,S\}$ and $\{P,R\} \cup \{Q\}(= \{P,Q,R\})$ is a minimal hit-
       ting set of $\{\{R,S\}, \{P\}, \{Q,S\}\}$, we invoke $construct\_bdp(3, \{P,Q,R\})$.
       Note that $\{P,R\} \cup \{S\}(= \{P,R,S\})$ is not a minimal hitting set of
       $\{\{R,S\}, \{P\}, \{Q,S\}\}$ and therefore $construct\_bdp(3, \{P,R,S\})$ is not
       invoked.
       i. $construct\_bdp(3, \{P,Q,R\})$
          Since $i ==$ *uenum* and $B \cup \{P,Q,R\} \models O$ and $B \cup \{P,Q,R\} \not\models$
          false, we output this set and return to the caller. Note that
          $\{P,Q,R\} \in MinE_{B,H}(O)$.
       Since a **for**-loop is finished return to the caller.
   Since a **for**-loop is finished return to the caller.

We can show the upper bound of the number of explainability checks for
the algorithm as follows. For every call of $go\_up(S)$, we make at most $|H|$
times of explainability checks and the number of calls of $go\_up(S)$ is at most
$|MaxUE_{B,H}(O)|$. Also, for every minimal explanation, we make exactly one
explainability check and so, the number of explainability checks for minimal ex-
planations is at most $|MinE_{B,H}(O)|$. Therefore, we have the following theorem.

Theorem 9. *Algorithm II in Fig. 4 enumerates $MaxUE_{B,H}(O)$ with at most
$2 * |MinE_{B,H}(O)| + |MaxUE_{B,H}(O)| \cdot |H|$ explainability checks. Moreover, the
space complexity of our algorithm is $O(\Sigma_{S \in MaxUE_{B,H}(O)}|S|)$.*

The space complexity is derived since we have to store only a set of maximal unexplanations to compute every minimal hitting set of these maximal unexplanations whereas Algorithm I needs to store minimal explanations to avoid redundant explainability check. Unfortunately, the above Algorithm II does not have a bound of even quasi-polynomial time complexity. since the worst time complexity of minimal hitting set computation of [15] is not bounded in polynomial. However, by the experiments in data mining setting for our original algorithm, we show that it is practically efficient [13,16].

3   Discussion and Related Work

One naive way of computing minimal explanations is that we start from the empty set of explanation and add an abducible formula one by one to check whether the set of formulas can explain the observation or not until an explanation is obtained. However, in this way, we have to check all the subsets before we encounter the minimal explanation. For example, consider the case that the propositional theory consists of n propositions and the number of minimal explanations is the constant k and the size of the minimal explanation (the number of propositions used in the explanation) is the same $\frac{n}{k}$ and every minimal explanation is disjoint each other. Then, the number of maximal unexplanation is $O(n^k)$ since a maximal unexplanation is the complement of the set each of whose element is drawn from k disjoint minimal explanations. Then, our proposed algorithms checks explainability at most in $O(n^{k+1})$ whereas the above naive algorithm needs at most $O(n^{\frac{n}{k}})$ explainability checks.

For generating all assumption-free minimal explanations (H is a set of all literals) for an observation which is a positive literal if the background theory is Horn and represented in a set of formulas, a resolution-style procedure has been presented by Eiter and Makino [3] which works in polynomial total-time. On the other hand, if an observation is a negative literal, there is no polynomial total-time algorithm exists unless $P = NP$ [4].

If we change the representation of the background Horn theory into the one based on characteristic models, Kautz et al. show that finding an minimal explanation can be done in polynomial time [10]. Eiter and Makino show that computing all minimal explanations in this model-based setting is polynomial-time equivalent to monotone dualization [5].

There are many research on consistency-based diagnosis originated by Reiter [12] using minimal hitting set computation. In these research, they compute minimal conflicts of normal behavior which contradict the observation and then compute minimal hitting set of these minimal conflicts to get a diagnosis. This can actually be regarded as a dual of our method. Let B be a background theory of the domain, and H be a set of hypotheses each of which assumes a normality of each component and O be an observation which contradicts normal behavior. Then, in our setting, the above diagnosis problem becomes an abductive framework $\langle B \cup O, H, false \rangle$ but we compute maximal unexplanations instead of computing consistent minimal explanations. In this setting, minimal explanations of *false* correspond with minimal conflicts and the complements of the maximal unexplanations corresponds with diagnoses. It is because if we remove the assumption of normality of components corresponding with the complements of the maximal unexplanations, the contradictory observation becomes consistent. Moreover, in [12] Reiter assumes that the set of minimal conflicts is computed by other machinery. However, by the observation of duality, we can compute the minimal conflicts interleavingly together with minimal diagnoses. In this direction of research, there are related works by Bailey [1] and us [14].

4   Conclusion

The contributions of this work are as follows.

- We give two algorithms to enumerate all minimal explanations and analyze the complexities of the algorithms in terms of the number of minimal explanations and maximal unexplanations.
- Algorithm I needs at most $2 * |MinE_{B,H}(O)| + |MaxUE_{B,H}(O)| \cdot |H|$ explainability checks to enumerate all consistent minimal explanations and the necessary space is $O(|MaxUE_{B,H}(O)| + |MinE_{B,H}(O)|)$. If the explainability check can be done in polynomial w.r.t. the number of propositions, then the time complexity of the algorithm is the quasi-polynomial of $(|MaxUE_{B,H}(O)| + |MinE_{B,H}(O)|)$.
- Algorithm II needs at most $2 * |MinE_{B,H}(O)| + |MaxUE_{B,H}(O)| \cdot |H|$ explainability checks to enumerate all consistent minimal explanations and the necessary space is $O(\Sigma_{S \in MaxUE_{B,H}(O)}|S|)$ thanks to the usage of backtracking-based minimal hitting computation proposed by one of the authors [15].

As future research, we need to do the following.

- We should implement an efficient explainability check.
- We should compare with other algorithm for computing abduction.
- We should search classes of problems which can be solved in a polynomial time of the number of propositions.
- We should apply this method to problems in the real domain such as diagnosis in order to show the enumeration is useful.

Acknowledgements. We would be very grateful to constructive comments of unknown reviewers.

References

1. Bailey, J., Stuckey, P. J., Discovery of Minimal Unsatisfiable Subsets of Constraints Using Hitting Set Dualization, *Proc. of PADL 2005*, pp. 174 – 186 (2005).
2. Eiter, T., Gottlob, G., The Complexity of Logic-Based Abduction, *Journal of the ACM*, 42(1), pp. 3 – 42 (1995).
3. Eiter, T., Makino, K., On Computing all Abductive Explanations, *Proc. of AAAI'02*, pp. 62 – 67 (2002).

4. Eiter, T., Makino, K., Generating all Abductive Explanations for Queries on Propositional Horn Theories, *Proceedings 12th Annual Conference of the EACSL (CSL 2003)*, LNCS 2803, pp. 197 – 211 (2003).
5. Eiter, T., Makino, K., Abduction and the Dualization Problem, *Proceedings of Discovery Science 2003*, LNCS 2843, pp. 1 – 20 (2003).
6. Fredman, M. L. and Khachiyan, L., On the Complexity of Dualization of Monotone Disjunctive Normal Forms, *Journal of Algorithms* 21(3), pp. 618 – 628 (1996).
7. Gunopulos, D., Khardon, R., Mannila, H. and Toivonen, H., Data mining, Hypergraph Transversals, and Machine Learning, *Proc. of PODS'97*, pp. 209 – 216 (1997).
8. Gunopulos, D., Khardon, R., Mannila, H., Saluja, S., Toivonen, H., Sharm, R., S., Discovering all most specific sentences, *ACM Trans. Database Syst.* 28(2), pp. 140 – 174 (2003).
9. Kakas, A. C., Kowalski, R., Toni, F., The Role of Abduction in Logic Programming , *In: Handbook of Logic in Artificial Intelligence and Logic Programming 5, pages 235-324, D.M. Gabbay, C.J. Hogger and J.A. Robinson eds., Oxford University Press* (1998).
10. Kautz, H., Kearns, M., Selman, B., Horn Approximations of Empirical Data, *Artificial Intelligence* **74** pp. 129 – 245 (1995).
11. Mannila, H. and Toivonen, T., "On an Algorithm for Finding All Interesting Sentences", *Cybernetics and Systems, Vol II, The Thirteen European Meeting on Cybernetics and Systems Research*, pp. 973 – 978 (1996).
12. Reiter, R., A Theory of Diagnosis from First Principles, *Artificial Intelligence* **32** pp. 57 – 95 (1987).
13. Satoh, K., and Uno, T., "Enumerating Maximal Frequent Sets Using Irredundant Dualization", Proc. of 6th International Conference on Discovery Science (DS2003), LNAI 2843, pp. 256 – 268 (2003)
14. Satoh, K., Uno, T., Enumerating Minimal Revised Specification using Dualization, *Proc. of the third workshop on Learning with Logics and Logics for Learning*, pp. 19 – 23 (2005).
15. Uno, T., "A Practical Fast Algorithm for Enumerating Minimal Set Coverings", *SIGAL83*, Information Processing Society of Japan, pp. 9 – 16 (in Japanese) (2002).
16. Uno, T., Satoh, K., "Detailed Description of an Algorithm for Enumeration of Maximal Frequent Sets with Irredundant Dualization", Online CEUR Workshop Proceedings of the ICDM 2003 Workshop on Frequent Itemset Mining Implementations (FIMI 2003), http://sunsite.informatik.rwth-aachen.de/Publications/CEUR-WS//Vol-90/satoh.pdf (2003)

Observation-Based Logic of Knowledge, Belief, Desire and Intention*

Kaile Su[1,2], Weiya Yue[2], Abdul Sattar[1], Mehmet A Orgun[3], and Xiangyu Luo[2]

[1] Institute for Integrated and Intelligent Systems, Griffith University
Brisbane, Qld 4111, Australia
[2] Department of Computer Science, Sun Yat-sen University
Guangzhou, 510275, China
[3] Department of Computing, Macquarie University
Sydney, NSW 2109, Australia

Abstract. We present a new model of knowledge, belief, desire and intention, called the interpreted KBDI-system model (or KBDI-model for short). The key point of the interpreted KBDI-system model is that we express an agent's knowledge, belief, desire and intention as a set of runs (computing paths), which is exactly a *system* in the interpreted system model, a well-known agent model due to Halpern and his colleagues. Our KBDI-model is *computationally grounded* in that we are able to associate a KBDI-model with a computer program, and formulas, involving agents' knowledge, belief, desire (goal) and intention, can be understood as properties of program computations. With KBDI-model, we have two different semantics to interpret our logic of knowledge, belief, desire and intention. Moreover, with respect to each semantics, we present a sound and complete proof system.

1 Introduction

The *possible worlds semantics* [1] is a fruitful approach to formalizing agent systems via modal logics, because internal mental attitudes of an agent, such as beliefs and goals, can be characterized conveniently with a model theoretic feature in terms of the belief, desire and intention accessibility relations. The well-known theory of intention [2] and the formalism of the belief-desire-intention paradigm [3], for example, are along this line. Some of those logics, say BDI_{CTL} [3], can be reduced to standard modal logics such as mu-calculus [4]. However, it is still not very clear how to obtain concrete agent models with the belief, desire and intention accessibility relations from specific agent programs. Although a number of researchers have attempted to develop executable agent languages

---

* This work was partially supported by the Australian Research Council grant DP0452628, National Basic Research 973 Program of China under grant 2005CB321902, National Natural Science Foundation of China grants 60496327, 10410638 and 60473004, and Guangdong Provincial Natural Science Foundation grant 04205407.

J. Lang, F. Lin, and J. Wang (Eds.): KSEM 2006, LNAI 4092, pp. 366–378, 2006.
© Springer-Verlag Berlin Heidelberg 2006

such as AgentSpeak(L) [5], AGENT0 [6] and 3APL [7], these agent languages are of too simple semantics to interpret formulas like $B_i(p \lor q)$ or $B_i \bigcirc p$.

The *interpreted system* model [8,9,10] offers a natural interpretation, in terms of the states of computer processes, to S5 epistemic logic. The salient point of the interpreted system model is that we are able to associate an interpreted system from a computer program, and formulas in epistemic logic that are valid with respect to the interpreted system can be understood as valid properties of program computations. In this sense, the interpreted system model is *computationally grounded* [11].

The aim of this paper is to present a computationally grounded model of knowledge, belief, desire and intention, called the interpreted KBDI-system model (or KBDI-*model* for short), by extending the interpreted system model. The key point of the KBDI-model is that an agent's beliefs, desires and intentions as well as its knowledge is characterized as a set of runs (computing paths), which is exactly a computationally grounded *system* in the interpreted system model.

Intuitively, an *interpreted KBDI-system* in KBDI-model includes a system $\mathcal{K}$ as in the interpreted system model, as well as, for each agent i, its beliefs $\mathcal{B}_i$, desires $\mathcal{D}_i$ and intentions $\mathcal{I}_i$, which are subsystems or subsets of $\mathcal{K}$. As in the the interpreted system model, agent i's knowledge is determined by the set of those runs that are consistent with its local *observations* (or local state). Similarly, agent i's beliefs are defined by the set of runs in $\mathcal{B}_i$ that are consistent with agent i's observations. Agent i's desires and intentions can also be defined in the same way. Intuitively, runs in $\mathcal{B}_i$ are possible computing paths from the viewpoint of the agent and those in $\mathcal{D}_i$ are the computing paths that the agent desires. Thus, it is reasonable to assume that $\mathcal{D}_i \subseteq \mathcal{B}_i$ because every desired computing path should be possible. Nevertheless, we need not assume that $\mathcal{I}_i \subseteq \mathcal{D}_i$ or even $\mathcal{I}_i \subseteq \mathcal{B}_i$ because an agent's intention may fail to achieve its goal and the actual computing path may be beyond the agent's belief even though the agent has chosen and completed an intentional series of actions.

The advantages of our model are that the basic element, a system, can be symbolically and compactly represented via the ordered binary decision diagram OBDD [12], which plays an essential role in symbolic model checking. Moreover, the presented model naturally characterizes the relationship between the agent's observations or local states and the dynamics of its knowledge, belief, desire and intention.

This paper is inspired by Su [13] and Su *et al* [14], which also provide agent models by extending the interpreted system model. However, Su [13] does not consider agents' belief, desire and intention. The main advantages of the present paper over Su *et al* [14] are: (1) We introduce, for each agent i, not only belief, desire and intention modalities B_i, D_i and I_i, but also a knowledge modality K_i. Moreover, the resulting axiomatic systems are more succinct and proved to be sound and complete. (2) To justify our claim that KBDI-model is computationally grounded, we show how a KBDI-model is related or generated with a program.

We present three alternative forms of KBDI-model *KBDI-Kripke structure*, *KBDI-program*, and *simplified KBDI-program*. KBDI-model is essentially a kind of an infinite model, not appropriate for model checking, while the KBDI-Kripke structure model is finite. However, the size of a KBDI-Kripke structure can be too large for a model checker to deal with. A KBDI-program is a compact and symbolic representation of a KBDI-Kripke structure; nevertheless, it is not very convenient for a programmer to code a multi-agent system as a KBDI-program. Fortunately, simplified KBDI-programs are very natural for those who are familiar with usual (distributive) programming; more importantly, they do not lose the generality of KBDI-programs.

The structure of the paper is as follows. In the next section, we briefly introduce the interpreted system model. Then, we define a new agent model of knowledge, belief, desire and intention in Section 3. In Section 4, a computationally grounded logic, called observation-based KBDI logic (or KBDI for short), is introduced and interpreted via two different semantics. Two KBDI-proof systems is presented and proven to be sound and complete with respect to two different semantics, respectively. one of them is to characterize those agents with perfect recall and a global clock. Section 5 explores how represent and generate an interpreted KBDI-system with a program, which will play an essential role in symbolic model checking KBDI logic. Finally, we discuss related work and conclude the paper with a summary.

2   Preliminaries

We start by giving some notions concerning the interpreted system model. Consider a system composed of multiple (say n) agents in an environment. We represent the system's state or the *global state* as a tuple $(s_e, s_1, \cdots, s_n)$, where s_e is the *environment's local state* and, for $1 \leq i \leq n$, s_i is *agent i's local state*.

Let L_e be a set of possible local states of the environment and L_i a set of possible local states for agent i, for $i = 1, \cdots, n$. We take $G \subseteq L_e \times L_1 \times \cdots \times L_n$ to be the set of *reachable global* states of the system. A *run* r over G is a function from the time domain–the natural numbers in our case–to G. Thus, a run over G can be identified with a sequence of global states in G. For convenience, we use g^* to denote the sequence of infinitely repeated global state g; for example, $g_0 g_1^*$ indicates a run with the initial state g_0 followed by infinitely repeated state g_1.

A *point* is a pair (r, m) consisting of a run r and time m. Given a point (r, m), we denote the first component of the tuple $r(m) = (s_e, s_1, \cdots, s_n)$ by $r_e(m)$ $(= s_e)$ and, for each i $(1 \leq i \leq n)$, the $i + 1$'th component of the tuple $r(m)$ by $r_i(m)$ $(= s_i)$. Thus, $r_i(m)$ is the local state of agent i in run r at "time" m.

The idea of the interpreted system semantics is that a run represents one possible computation of a system and a system may have a number of possible runs, so we say a *system* is a set of runs.

Assume that we have a set Φ of primitive propositions, which we can think of as describing basic facts about the system. An *interpreted system I* consists of a pair $(\mathcal{R}, \pi)$, where $\mathcal{R}$ is a set of runs over a set of global states and π is a valuation function, which gives the set of primitive propositions true at each point in $\mathcal{R}$ [8].

For every agent i, let the notation $(r, u) \sim_i (r', v)$ denote that $r_i(u) = r'_i(v)$. Intuitively, $(r, u) \sim_i (r', v)$ means that (r, u) and (r', v) are indistinguishable to agent i. We also use the notation $(r, u) \sim_i^{spr} (r', v)$ to denote the fact that $u = v$ and, for every $j \leq u$, $r_i(j) = r'_i(j)$ (here spr stands for $synchronous$ systems with $perfect\ recall$).

Let KL_n denote the language of propositional logic augmented by the future-time connectives $\bigcirc$ (next) and $\mathbf{U}$ (until) and a modal (knowledge) operator K_i for each agent i. The language KL_n can be interpreted by using an interpreted system. The related satisfaction relationship $\models_{KL_n}$ is as follows: Given $I = (\mathcal{R}, \pi)$ and a point (r, u) in $\mathcal{R}$, we define $(I, r, u) \models_{KL_n} \psi$ by induction on the structure of ψ. When ψ is of the form $K_i\varphi$, $(I, r, u) \models_{KL_n} \psi$ iff $(I, r', v) \models_{KL_n} \varphi$ for all (r', v) such that $(r, u) \sim_i (r', v)$. The semantics of atomic formulas ψ or formulas of the form $\neg\varphi$, $\varphi \wedge \varphi'$, $\bigcirc\varphi$ or $\varphi\mathbf{U}\varphi'$ can be dealt with in the usual manner.

3   The Interpreted KBDI-System Model

In this section, we present a new model of knowledge, belief, desire and intention, called the interpreted KBDI-system model (or KBDI-model for short), which extends the interpreted system model. The key point of our approach is that agents' belief, desire and intention as well as its knowledge are defined as sets of runs, that is, $systems$ in the interpreted system model.

3.1   Interpreted KBDI-Systems

Given a set G of global states and system $\mathcal{K}$ over G, an agent's $mental\ state$ over system $\mathcal{K}$ is a tuple $\langle \mathcal{B}, \mathcal{D}, \mathcal{I} \rangle$, where $\mathcal{B}$, $\mathcal{D}$ and $\mathcal{I}$ are systems (sets of runs over G) such that $\mathcal{I} \subseteq \mathcal{K}$ and $\mathcal{D} \subseteq \mathcal{B} \subseteq \mathcal{K}$. A $KBDI\text{-}system$ is a structure $\langle \mathcal{K}, \mathcal{M}_1, \cdots, \mathcal{M}_n \rangle$, where $\mathcal{K}$ is a system and for every i, $\mathcal{M}_i$ is agent i's mental state over $\mathcal{K}$.

Assume that we have a set Φ of primitive propositions which describe basic facts about agents and their environment. An $interpreted\ KBDI\text{-}system\ I$ consists of a pair $(\mathcal{S}, \pi)$, where $\mathcal{S}$ is a KBDI-system and π is a valuation function, which gives the set of primitive propositions true at each point in G.

Example 1. Let us consider the scenario of a robot cleaning a room. There are two global states: s_0 and s_1. In state s_0, the room is dirty, and in state s_1, the room is clean. Moreover, the robot believes that the room is dirty, and the goal of the robot is to clean the room.

Now we define a KBDI-system $S_0 = \langle \mathcal{K}_0, \langle \mathcal{B}_0, \mathcal{D}_0, \mathcal{I}_0 \rangle \rangle$, where

- $\mathcal{K}_0$ is the set of those runs r such that, for every natural number m, if $r(m) = s_1$ then $r(m + 1) = s_1$, which means that if the room is clean, then it will remain clean.

- $\mathcal{B}_0$ is a set of those runs $r \in \mathcal{K}_0$ with $r(0) = s_0$. This means that the robot believes the room is dirty at first. Notice that *belief* is just the information state of the robot, and there is no guarantee that robot will be able to clean the room.
- $\mathcal{D}_0$ is a subset of $\mathcal{B}_0$ such that, for every run $r \in \mathcal{D}_0$, there is a number m with $r(m) = s_1$. This means that the robot desires to clean the room.
- Finally, we may define $\mathcal{I}_0$ to be the set of runs $s_0 s_1{}^*$ and $s_1{}^*$. This indicates the robot will clean the room immediately or if the room is clean to start with, it will remain so.

We may take $\{dirty\}$ as the set Φ of primitive propositions, representing whether the room is clean or dirty. Clearly, we may naturally define $\pi_0(s_0)(dirty) = 0$ and $\pi_0(s_1)(dirty) = 1$. Thus, we obtain the interpreted KBDI-system (S_0, π_0).

3.2   KBDI-Kripke Structures

We now consider how to generate a KBDI-system.

Definition 2. *A KBDI-Kripke structure is a tuple*

$$\langle G, G_0, R_K, (R_B^1, R_D^1, R_I^1), \cdots, (R_B^n, R_D^n, R_I^n), \pi \rangle$$

where G is a set of a reachable states; $G_0 \subseteq G$ is a set of starting states; R_K and R_B^i, R_D^i, R_I^i ($0 < i \leq n$) are binary relations on G with $R_K \subseteq R_B^i \subseteq R_D^i$ and $R_K \subseteq R_I^i$; finally, π is a valuation function.

Let system $\mathcal{K}$ be the set of those runs obtained by "unwinding" the relation R_K starting from initial states in G_0. Thus, the notation $sR_K s'$ indicates that s' is a possible next state of s in system $\mathcal{K}$. Similarly, we define systems $\mathcal{B}_i$, $\mathcal{D}_i$ and $\mathcal{I}_i$ by the relations R_B^i, R_D^i and R_I^i [1], respectively. Thus, we generate a KBDI-system I by the above Kripke structure.

Suppose s is the current state of some "real" execution of the generated KBDI-system. We can determine agent i's belief, desire and intention by the relations R_B^i, R_D^i and R_I^i. Specifically, a state s' is, from agent i's views, a believable (or possible) next state iff $sR_B^i s'$; s' is one of the agent i's desired next states iff $sR_D^i s'$; finally, s' can be the next state caused by one of agent's intentional actions iff $sR_I^i s'$.

Note that the relations R_B^i, R_D^i and R_I^i capture what *next states* are, from agent i's views, believable, desired, and intentional. So, our BDI notions are future-oriented, but the "future" here is very near future, i.e. "next time". Thus, our KBDI-model significantly differers from BDI$_{\text{CTL}}$ [3,4] in that the "next time" relation and the BDI-relations in BDI$_{\text{CTL}}$ [3,4] are on different dimensions, while they are on the same dimension in our KBDI-model. This very "next time" semantics for BDI notions plays an essential role in reusing usual model checking techniques for implementing our KBDI model checker.

---

[1] Let sRa indicate that a is one of agent i's intentional actions in state s. Then, R_I^i is in turn generated by the relation R such that $sR_I^i s'$ iff there is an action a of agent i such that sRa and s' is a possible next state of s with agent i's action a.

4 KBDI Logic

This section introduces a multimodal logic of knowledge, belief, desire and intention, referred to as Observation-based KBDI logic (KBDI). As shown below, the semantics of KBDI logic is given in terms of the interpreted KBDI-system model. According to this semantics, the computation of agents' knowledge, belief, desire, and intention are based on agents' *observations*, that is, local states.

4.1 Syntax

Given a set Φ of propositional atoms, the language of KBDI logic is defined by the following BNF notations:

$$\langle wf\!f \rangle ::= \text{any element of } \Phi \mid \neg \langle wf\!f \rangle \mid \langle wf\!f \rangle \wedge \langle wf\!f \rangle \mid$$
$$\bigcirc \langle wf\!f \rangle \mid \langle wf\!f \rangle \mathbf{U} \langle wf\!f \rangle \mid$$
$$\mid K_i \langle wf\!f \rangle \mid B_i \langle wf\!f \rangle \mid D_i \langle wf\!f \rangle \mid I_i \langle wf\!f \rangle$$

Informally, $K_i \varphi$, $B_i \varphi$ and $D_i \varphi$ means that agent i knows, believes and desires φ, respectively, while $I_i \varphi$ denotes that φ holds under the assumption that agent i acts based on his intention. The formulas not containing modalities K_i, B_i, D_i and I_i $(i = 1, \cdots, n)$ are called linear-temporal logic (LTL) formulas.

4.2 Semantics

We now proceed to interpret KBDI logic formulas in terms of interpreted KBDI-systems. In the following, we inductively define the satisfaction relation $\models$ between a formula φ and a pair of interpreted KBDI-system and a point. Given an interpreted KBDI-system $I = (\mathcal{S}, \pi)$, suppose that $\mathcal{S} = \langle \mathcal{K}, \mathcal{M}_1, \cdots, \mathcal{M}_n \rangle$ and for every i, $\mathcal{M}_i = \langle \mathcal{B}_i, \mathcal{D}_i, \mathcal{I}_i \rangle$. Let r be a run in $\mathcal{K}$ and u a natural number, then we have that:

- $(I, r, u) \models K_i \varphi$ iff $(I, r', v) \models \varphi$ for those (r', v) such that $r' \in \mathcal{K}$ and $(r, u) \sim_i (r', v)$;
- $(I, r, u) \models B_i \varphi$ iff $(I, r', v) \models \varphi$ for those (r', v) such that $r' \in \mathcal{B}_i$ and $(r, u) \sim_i (r', v)$;
- $(I, r, u) \models D_i \varphi$ iff $(I, r', v) \models \varphi$ for those (r', v) such that $r' \in \mathcal{D}_i$ and $(r, u) \sim_i (r', v)$;
- $(I, r, u) \models I_i \varphi$ iff $(I, r', v) \models \varphi$ for those (r', v) such that $r' \in \mathcal{I}_i$ and $(r, u) \sim_i (r', v)$;
- $(I, r, u) \models \bigcirc \varphi$ iff $(I, r, (u + 1)) \models \varphi$;
- $(I, r, u) \models \varphi \mathbf{U} \varphi'$ iff $(I, r, u') \models \varphi'$ for some $u' \geq u$ and $(I, r, u'') \models \varphi$ for all u'' with $u \leq u'' < u'$.

Other cases involving formulas whose main connective is boolean are trivial and omitted here. We say that a formula φ is valid in an interpreted KBDI-system I, denoted by $I \models \varphi$, if $(I, r, u) \models \varphi$ holds for every point (r, u) in $\mathcal{I}$. We use $\models \varphi$ to denote that φ is valid in every interpreted KBDI-system.

According to our definition, $D_i \varphi$ is true iff φ is true along those runs that are desirable to agent i and consistent with agent i's observations. Thus, $D_i \varphi$ intuitively means that agent i's goal implies that formula φ holds.

For those agents with perfect recall and a global clock, we may use $\sim_i^{spr}$ instead of $\sim_i$ to interpret those formals with modalities B_i, D_i and I_i and get an alternative satisfaction relationship $\models^{spr}$.

Proposition 3. *The following axioms are valid with respect to both $\models$ and $\models^{spr}$:*

- $K_i\varphi \Rightarrow \varphi$
- $\Delta_i(\varphi \Rightarrow \psi) \Rightarrow (\Delta_i\varphi \Rightarrow \Delta_i\psi)$
  $\Delta_i\varphi \Rightarrow K_i\Delta_i\varphi$
  $\neg\Delta_i\varphi \Rightarrow K_i\neg\Delta_i\varphi$
  where Δ stands for K, B, D or I.
- *Relationship between knowledge, belief, desire and intention*
  $B_i\varphi \Rightarrow D_i\varphi$
  $K_i\varphi \Rightarrow B_i\varphi$
  $K_i\varphi \Rightarrow I_i\varphi$
- *Temporal operators*
  $\bigcirc(\varphi \Rightarrow \psi) \Rightarrow (\bigcirc\varphi \Rightarrow \bigcirc\psi)$
  $\bigcirc(\neg\varphi) \Rightarrow \neg\bigcirc\varphi$
  $\varphi\mathbf{U}\psi \Leftrightarrow \psi \vee (\varphi \wedge \bigcirc(\varphi\mathbf{U}\psi))$

About the relationship between belief and desire, we remark that $B_i\varphi$ means that ψ is true along those runs that are believable and indistinguishable to agent i, while $D_i\varphi$ indicates that ψ is true along those runs that are desirable and indistinguishable to agent i. However, we assume that, for agent i, desirable runs are believable ones. As a result, we have that $B_i\varphi \Rightarrow D_i\varphi$ holds.

Similarly, $D_i\varphi$ indicates that ψ is true along those runs that is intentional and indistinguishable to agent i. If we think that agent i's intentional runs are those possible runs along which agent i do his intentional serial of actions, then i's intentional runs need not to be desirable ones. Thus, $D_i\varphi \Rightarrow I_i\varphi$ is not necessarily valid. On the other hand, if we think that agent i's intentional runs are not only possibly brought about by agent i's intentional serial of actions but also desirable to agent i, then i's intentional runs are also desirable ones. In this case, $D_i\varphi \Rightarrow I_i\varphi$ is valid. In this work, we assume that agent i's intentional runs are possibly brought about by agent i's intentional serial of actions but need not to be desirable to agent i. So, we do not have that $D_i\varphi \Rightarrow I_i\varphi$ is valid.

Proposition 4. *The following axioms are valid with respect to $\models^{spr}$: $\Delta_i\bigcirc\varphi \Rightarrow \bigcirc\Delta_i\varphi$, where Δ stands for K, B, D and I.*

The formula $D_i\bigcirc\varphi \Rightarrow \bigcirc D_i\varphi$ says that if agent i's current goal implies φ holds at the next point in time, then at the next point in time her goal will imply φ, that is, agent i persists on her goal.

5   Proof Systems

In this section, we present two proof systems, called the KBDI proof system and the KBDI^{spr} proof system, respectively. The KBDI proof system is sound and complete with respect to semantics $\models$, while the KBDI^{spr} proof system is with respect to semantics $\models^{spr}$, which is for characterizing those agents with perfect recall and a global clock.

The KBDI proof system contains the axioms of propositional calculus plus those in Propositions 3. It is closed under the propositional inference rules plus for every agent i: $\frac{\vdash \varphi}{\vdash K_i \varphi}$. The KBDI^{spr} proof system is the KBDI proof system plus axioms in Proposition 4.

Theorem 5. *The KBDI proof system is sound and complete with respect to* $\models$.

The soundness part is straightforward. The completeness is a little complex, and we only present a succinct outline of its proof. With respect to the temporal dimension, our construction is similar to those previously used for completeness of dynamic logic [15] and temporal logic of knowledge [16]. We construct our model of a consistent formula out of consistent subsets of a finite set of formulas, called *the closure* of the formula. As in Halpern [16], we have a number of distinct levels of closure, forming a tree-like structure. However, when constructing a *pre-model*, we need to define those binary relations corresponding to belief, desire, and intention, which are quite different from those corresponding to knowledge as given in Halpern [16].

We first introduce some necessary notations. Given a formula ψ, let the basic closure of ψ, denoted by $cl_0(\psi)$, be the smallest set containing ψ that is closed under subformulas and contains $\neg\varphi$ if it contains φ and φ is not of the form $\neg\varphi'$. For each agent i, we define $cl_{k,i}$ ($k \geq 1$) to be the union of $cl_k(\psi)$ with the set of formulas of the form $\Delta_i(\varphi_1 \vee, \cdots, \vee \varphi_l)$ or $\neg\Delta_i(\varphi_1 \vee, \cdots, \vee \varphi_l)$, where Δ_i stands for modalities K_i, B_i, D_i and I_i, and the φ_js are distinct formulas in $cl_k(\psi)$. Finally, we take $cl_{k+1}(\psi)$ to be $\bigcup_{i=1}^{n} cl_{k,i}(\psi)$.

An index is a finite sequence $i_1 \cdots i_k$ of agents with $i_l \neq i_{l+1}$ for all $l < k$. For an index $\delta = i_1 \cdots i_k$ and agent i, let $\delta \# i$ be the index δi if $i \neq i_k$, otherwise, $\delta \# i = \delta$.

We use $ad(\varphi)$ to denote the number of alternations of modalities for distinct agents in φ. For example, $ad(p) = 0$, $ad(K_i(B_i p \vee p)) = ad(B_i p \vee p) = 1$ for a primitive p.

To construct the model of ψ, we define a *pre-model*, which is structure $\langle S, \rightarrow, R_1^K, R_1^B, R_1^D, R_1^I, \cdots, R_n^K, R_n^B, R_n^D, R_n^I \rangle$ consisting of a set of states, a binary relation $\rightarrow$ on S, and for each agent i, binary relations R_n^K, R_n^B, R_n^D and R_n^I on S.

1. The state set S consists of all the pairs (δ, X) such that δ is an index with $\mid \delta \mid \leq ad(\psi)$ ($\mid \delta \mid$ stands for the length of δ), and (a) if δ is the null sequence then X is a maximal consistent subset of $cl_d(\psi)$, and (b) if $\delta = \tau i$ then X is a maximal consistent subset of $cl_{k,i}(\psi)$, where $k = ad(\psi) - \mid \delta \mid$.
2. The relation $\rightarrow$ is defined so that $(\delta, X) \rightarrow (\tau, Y)$ iff $\delta = \tau$ and the formula $X \wedge \bigcirc Y$ is consistent [2].

---

[2] We use a finite formula set itself to denote the conjunction of all the formulas in the formula set.

3. The relation R_i^K is defined so that $(\delta, X)R_i^K(\tau, Y)$ iff (a) $\delta\#i = \tau\#i$, and
   (b) for all formulas φ of the form $K_i\alpha$, $B_i\alpha$, $D_i\alpha$ or $I_i\alpha$, $\varphi \in X$ iff $\varphi \in Y$.
   The relation R_i^B is characterized such that $(\delta, X)R_i^B(\tau, Y)$ iff (a) $\tau = \delta\#i$,
   (b) $(\delta, X)R_i^K(\tau, Y)$, and (c) $\neg B_i\neg Y$ is consistent. The relations R_i^D and R_i^I
   are defined in the same way.

The states in S of the form (δ, X) are called δ-states. For a state $s = (\delta, X)$, we
use $s \Vdash$ to denote that $\vdash X \Rightarrow \varphi$.

As shown in the following lemma, the pre-model has properties resembling
those for the truth definition for formulas in the basic closure.

Lemma 6. *For all δ-states, we have*

1. *if $\bigcirc\varphi \in clo(\psi)$, then for all states t such that $s \to t$, we have $s \Vdash \bigcirc \varphi$ iff
   $t \Vdash \varphi$.*
2. *If $\varphi_1 \mathbf{U}\varphi_2 \in clo(\psi)$ then $s \Vdash \varphi_1\mathbf{U}\varphi_2$ iff there is a sequence $s = s_0 \to s_1 \to
   \cdots \to s_l$ such that $s_l \Vdash\varphi_2$, and $s_k \Vdash\varphi_1$ for all $k < n$.*
3. *Let Δ stand for any of K, B, D and I. Assume that $| \delta\#i | \leq ad(\psi)$. Then
   $s \Vdash\neg\Delta_i\varphi$ iff there is some $\delta\#i$-state t such that $sR_i^\Delta t$ and $t \Vdash\neg\varphi$.*

We say that an infinite $\to$-sequence of states $(s_0, s_1, \cdots)$, where $s_m = (\delta, X_m)$ for
all m, is *acceptable* if for all $m \geq 0$, if $\varphi_1\mathbf{U}\varphi_2 \in X_m$ then there exists an $l \geq m$
such that $s_l \Vdash\varphi_2$ and $s_k \Vdash\varphi_1$ for all k with $m \leq k < l$.

Lemma 7. *Every finite $\to$-sequence of states can be extended to an infinite
acceptable sequence.*

For each agent i, let O_i be the function that maps the state (δ, U) to the pair
$(\delta\#i, V)$, where V is the set of those formulas in U with one of the forms $K_i\varphi$,
$\neg K_i\varphi$, $B_i\varphi$, $\neg B_i\varphi$, $D_i\varphi$, $\neg D_i\varphi$, $I_i\varphi$ and $\neg I_i\varphi$. Given an acceptable sequence
$(s_0, s_1, \cdots)$, we define a run r, called the *derived run from* $(s_0, s_1, \cdots)$, such that
for every natural number k and for every agent i, $r_e(k) = s_k$ and $r_i(k) = O_i(s_k)$.

COMPLETENESS PROOF: Assume that the given formula ψ is consistent. It
suffices to construct a KBDI-model where ψ is satisfied. For this purpose, we take
$\mathcal{K}^\psi$ to be the set of all derived runs from acceptable sequences. For each agent i,
let $\mathcal{B}_i^\psi$ be the set of all derived runs from acceptable sequences $(s_0, s_1, \cdots)$ with
$s_k R_i^B s_k$ for all $k \geq 0$. Similarly, we define $\mathcal{D}_i^\psi$ ($\mathcal{I}_i^\psi$) to be the set of all derived
runs from acceptable sequences $(s_0, s_1, \cdots)$ with $s_k R_i^D s_k$ ($s_k R_i^I s_k$) for all $k \geq 0$.
We now construct an interpreted KBDI-system $(\mathcal{S}^\psi, \pi^\psi)$, where

1. $\mathcal{S}^\psi = \langle\mathcal{K}^\psi, \langle\mathcal{B}_1^\psi, \mathcal{D}_1^\psi, \mathcal{I}_1^\psi\rangle, \cdots, \langle\mathcal{B}_n^\psi, \mathcal{D}_n^\psi, \mathcal{I}_n^\psi\rangle\rangle$
2. π^ψ is a valuation function such that for every point (r, k) and every primitive
   p, $\pi^\psi(r, k)(p) = 1$ iff $r_e(k) \Vdash p$.

To show that ψ is satisfied by the above KBDI-model, we need the following
claim:

Given $\varphi \in clo(\psi)$, $r \in \mathcal{K}^\psi$ and an index δ, assume that $r_e(m)$ is a δ-state and
$ad(K_\delta\varphi) \leq ad(\psi)$, where $K_\delta\varphi$ is an abbreviation for $K_{i_1} \cdots K_{i_k}$ if $\delta = i_1 \cdots i_k$.
Then $((\mathcal{S}^\psi, \pi^\psi), r, m) \models \varphi$ iff $r_e(m) \Vdash\varphi$.

The above claim can be proved by induction on the structure of φ. This completes the completeness proof. ∎

Theorem 8. *The KBDI^{spr} proof system is sound and complete with respect to* $\models^{spr}$.

The soundness part is easy. To show the completeness, we follow the similar line as that for the proof of Theorem 5. However, we have the following additional lemma.

Lemma 9. *Let Δ stand for any of K, B, D and I. Then for all δ-states s, t with $s \to t$, we have that for all $(\delta\#i)$-state t' with $tR_i^\Delta t'$ there exists a $(\delta\#i)$-state s' such that $sR_i^\Delta s'$ and $s' \to t'$.*

By the above lemma, we can construct an interpreted KBDI-system satisfying the consistent formula φ. Due to the limited space, we omit the details of the proof.

6   Representing and Generating a KBDI-System

6.1   Symbolic Representation of a KBDI-System

It would be satisfactory if we can derive our model from a program implemented in, say C or Java. However, to simplify the matter, we may consider some abstract programs such as *finite-state programs*, which are expressive enough from the standpoint of theoretical computer science. The Kripke structure form of a KBDI-model can be regarded as such abstract programs. Moreover, to make our model checking system practically efficient, we present those Kripke structures symbolically.

Definition 10. *A finite-state program with n agents is defined as a tuple $\mathcal{P} = \langle \mathbf{x}, \theta(\mathbf{x}), \tau(\mathbf{x}, \mathbf{x}'), O_1, \cdots, O_n \rangle$, where*

1. *$\mathbf{x}$ is a set of system variables, while $\mathbf{x}' = \{v' \mid v \in \mathbf{x}\}$ is a set of variables different from those in $\mathbf{x}$.*
2. *θ is a boolean formula over $\mathbf{x}$, called the initial condition;*
3. *τ is a boolean formula over $\mathbf{x} \cup \mathbf{x}'$, called the transition relation; and*
4. *for each i, $O_i \subseteq \mathbf{x}$, containing agent i's local variables, or observable variables.*

For convenience, we may use $\mathcal{P}(\theta, \tau)$ to denote a finite-state program with n agents $\langle \mathbf{x}, \theta(\mathbf{x}), \tau(\mathbf{x}, \mathbf{x}'), O_1, \cdots, O_n \rangle$, if $\mathbf{x}$ and $O_1, \cdots, O_n$ are clear from the context.

Definition 11. *A KBDI-program with n agents is a tuple*

$$P_A = \langle \mathcal{P}(\theta, \tau), \langle \tau_1^1, \tau_1^2, \tau_1^3 \rangle, \cdots, \langle \tau_n^1, \tau_n^2, \tau_n^3 \rangle \rangle$$

where for each agent i, and $j = 1, 2, 3$, τ_i^j is formula on $\mathbf{x} \cup \mathbf{x}'$ such that $\tau_i^j \Rightarrow \tau$ and $\tau_i^2 \Rightarrow \tau_i^1$.

From KBDI-program P_A, we can generate a KBDI-Kripke structure a tuple

$$K_{P_A} = \langle G, G_0, R_K, (R_B^1, R_D^1, R_I^1), \cdots, (R_B^n, R_D^n, R_I^n), \pi \rangle$$

where

1. G is the set of all assignments (or subsets) of $\mathbf{x}$.
2. G_0 is the set of those assignments satisfying θ.
3. For two assignments s and s' for $\mathbf{x}$, letting $N(s')$ denotes $\{v' \mid v \in s'\}$, we have that
   (a) sR_Ks' holds iff $\tau(\mathbf{x}, \mathbf{x}')$ is satisfied by the assignment $s \cup N(s')$.
   (b) For each agent i, sR_B^is', sR_D^is' and sR_I^is' hold iff the assignment $s \cup N(s')$ satisfies $\tau_i^1(\mathbf{x}, \mathbf{x}')$, $\tau_i^2(\mathbf{x}, \mathbf{x}')$ and $\tau_i^3(\mathbf{x}, \mathbf{x}')$, respectively.
4. π is a valuation function such that $\pi(s)(p) = true$ iff $p \in s$.

We use I_{P_A} to denote the interpreted KBDI-system generated by KBDI-Kripke structure K_{P_A}.

6.2 Simplified KBDI-Programs

We have developed a symbolic KBDI model checker; however, our experience with a previous version of this model checker indicated that it is inconvenient for a programmer to code a KBDI-program with n-agents because $1 + 3n$ many finite-state programs (state transition formulas) will be the result. Therefore, we simplify the definition of a KBDI-program as follows.

Definition 12. *Let* $\mathcal{P} = \langle \mathbf{x}, \theta(\mathbf{x}), \tau(\mathbf{x}, \mathbf{x}'), O_1, \cdots, O_n \rangle$ *be a finite-state program with n-agents, where, for each agent i, boolean variables WB_i, WD_i and WI_i are in $\mathbf{x}$. A simplified KBDI-program with n-agents derived from $\mathcal{P}$ is a tuple $(\mathcal{P}, P_1, \cdots, P_n)$, where for each agent i, P_i stands for $\langle \tau \wedge WB_i', \tau \wedge WB_i' \wedge WD_i', \tau \wedge WI_i' \rangle$.*

It is more convenient for a programmer to code a simplified KBDI-program with n-agents. In addition, we believe that the notion of a simplified KBDI-program not lose much generality from that of a KBDI-program.

7 Discussion

Alternating-time temporal logics: Alternating-time temporal logic (ATL) and its extensions (ATEL, for example) were proposed recently to tackle the verification of multi-agent system properties [17,18]. Using ATL one can express that a coalition of agents can achieve some properties. For example, assume that p and q are local variables of agents 1 and 2, respectively; a coalition of agents 1 and 2 can achieve $p \Leftrightarrow q$. Nevertheless, there is no practical strategy to guarantee that the formula $p \Leftrightarrow q$ holds, because agent 1 can only observe and change the value of p and so can agent 2 for variable q. It is not very convenient to use ATL to deal with incomplete information or agents' local observations, as the model checking problem of ATL with incomplete information is generally undecidable [17]. Moreover, ATL and its extensions do not deal with agents' mental states such as beliefs and desires.

Model checking BDI-agents: Model checking multi-agent systems has become an active research topic in the community of multi-agent systems. Many efforts have been devoted to model checking knowledge in multi-agent systems [19,20,13,21]. However, comparatively little work has been carried out on model checking BDI-agents. Some general approaches to model checking BDI-agents were proposed in Rao and Georgeff [22] and Benerecetti and Cimatti [23], but no method was given for generating models from actual systems, and so the techniques given there could not easily be applied to verifying real multi-agent systems. In Bordini *et al* [24], model checking techniques for AgentSpeak(L) [5] have been reported; however, AgentSpeak(L) has too simple semantics to interpret formulas like $B_i(p \vee q)$ or $B_i \bigcirc p$. The salient point of our work is that we present a general form of a BDI agent program, from which BDI agent models are generated and specifications in full BDI logics can be verified by symbolic model checking techniques.

8   Concluding Remarks

We have proposed a new KBDI-model by using interpreted systems, and developed a computationally grounded BDI logic, called KBDI logic. We interpret KBDI logic via two different semantics. One of them is based on the assumption that agents have perfect recall and there is a global clock. With respect to each of these semantics, we present a sound and complete proof system. We have explored how to represent and generate an interpreted KBDI-system with a program, which plays an essential role in symbolic model checking BDI-agents.

As for future work, we will consider applying KBDI logic in specifying and verifying security-related properties in multi-agent systems.

References

1. S. Kripke. A semantical analysis of modal logic. i: Normal modal propositional calculi. *Z. Math. Logik Grundl. Math.*, 9:67–96, 1963.
2. P.R. Cohen and H.J. Levesque. Intension is choice with commitment. *Artificial Intelligence*, 42:23–261, 1990.
3. A.S. Rao and M.P. Georgeff. Decision procedures for BDI logics. *Journal of Logic and Computation*, 8(3):293–344, 1998.
4. K. Schild. On the relationship between BDI logics and standard logics of concurrency. *Autonomous Agents and Multi-Agent Systems*, 3:259–283, 2000.
5. A.S. Rao. BDI agent speak out in a logical computable language. In *LNAI*, volume 1038, pages 42–55, 1996.
6. Y. Shoham. Agent oriented programming. *Artificial Intelligence*, 60(1):51–92, 1993.
7. K. Hindriks, F.S. de Boer, W. van der Hock, and J.-J. Ch. Meyer. Agent programming in 3APL. *Autonomous Agents and Multi-Agent Systems*, 2(4):357–402, 1999.
8. R. Fagin, J. Halpern, Y. Moses, and M. Vardi. *Reasoning about knowledge*. MIT Press, Cambridge, MA, 1995.

9. J. Halpern and L. Zuck. A little knowledge goes a long way: Simple knowledge based derivations and correctness proofs for a family of protocols. *Journal of the ACM*, 39(3):449–478, 1992.

10. J. Halpern and M. Vardi. The complexity of reasoning about knowledge and time: extended abstract. In *Proc. 18th Annual ACM Symposium on Theory of Computing*, pages 304–315, 1986.

11. M. Wooldridge. Computationally grounded theories of agency. In E. Durfee, editor, *ICMAS-00*, pages 13–22. IEEE Press, 2000.

12. R.E. Bryant. Graph-based algorithms for boolean function manipulation. *IEEE Transaction Computers*, 35(8):677–691, 1986.

13. K. Su. Model checking temporal logics of knowledge in distributed systems. In *AAAI-04*, pages 98–103. AAAI, 2004.

14. K. Su, A. Sattar, K. Wang, X. Luo, G. Governatori, and V. Padmanabhan. The observation-based model for BDI-agents. In *AAAI-05*, pages 190–195. AAAI, 2005.

15. D. Kozen and R. Parikh. An elementary proof of the completeness of PDL. *Theoretical Computer Science*, 14:113–118, 1981.

16. J. Halpern, R. van der Meyden, and M. Y. Vardi. Complete axiomatizations for reasoning about knowledge and time. *SIAM Journal of Computing*, 33(3):647–703, 2004.

17. R. Alur, T.A. Henzinger, and O. Kupferman. Alternating-time temporal logic. *Journal of the ACM*, 49:672–713, 2002.

18. W. van der Hoek and M. Wooldridge. Tractable multiagent planning for epistemic goals. In *Proc. AAMAS-02*, pages 1167–1174, 2002.

19. W. van der Hoek and M. Wooldridge. Model checking knowledge and time. In *9th Workshop on SPIN (Model Checking Software)*, Grenoble, 2002.

20. R. van der Meyden and K. Su. Symbolic model checking the knowledge of the dining cryptographers. In *Proc. of IEEE CSFW-04*, pages 280–291, 2004.

21. F. Raimondi and A. Lomuscio. Verification of multiagent system via ordered binary decision diagrams: an algorithm and its implementation. In *Proc. of AAMAS-04*, 2004.

22. A.S. Rao and M.P. Georgeff. A model theoretic approach to the verification of situated reasoning systems. In *Proc. 13th International Joint Conference on Artificial Intelligence*, pages 318–324, 1993.

23. M. Benerecetti and A. Cimatti. Symbolic model checking for multi-agent systems. In *Proc. MoChart-02*, pages 1–8, Lyon, France, 2002.

24. R.H. Bordini, C. Fisher, C. Pardavila, and M. Wooldridge. Model checking agentspeak. In *Proc. AAMAS-03*, pages 14–18, Melbourne, Australia, 2003.

Repairing Inconsistent XML Documents

Zijing Tan, Wei Wang, JianJun Xu, and Baile Shi

Department of Computing and Information Technology
University of Fudan
Shanghai, China
{zjtan, weiwang1, xujj, bshi}@fudan.edu.cn

Abstract. XML document may contain inconsistencies that violate pre-defined integrity constraints, and there are two basic concepts for this problem: *Repair* is the data consistent with the integrity constraints, and also minimally differs from the original one. *Consistent data* is the data common for every possible repair. In this paper, first we give a general constraint model for XML, which can express functional dependencies, keys and multivalued dependencies. Next we provide a repair framework for inconsistent XML document with three basic update operations: node insertion, node deletion and value modification. Following this approach, we introduce the concept of repair for inconsistent XML document, discuss the chase process to generate repairs, and prove some important properties of the chase process. Finally we give a method to obtain the greatest lower bound of all possible repairs, which is sufficient for consistent data.

1 Introduction

Generally speaking, integrity constraints are used for describing the set of all "legal" data and hence should be satisfied at all times. However, many real-life data is known to be inconsistent. We say an XML document is inconsistent if it violates some predefined integrity constraints.

Example 1. Figure 1 gives an XML document describing the information about dealers. For each dealer, we give its name(dname) and each shipment of product(plist). The shipment information is further composed of product name, product color, shipment destination and date. If not empty, values of element or attribute nodes are recorded under the node names in bold. For example, figure 1 says that a dealer named $'corp1'$ sent out $'red'$ $'desk'$ to $'dest2'$ on $'2006/1/1'$. We also list 4 integrity constraints this document should satisfy in figure 1, and we will introduce the expression of constraints further in section 2.

Note that this document violates some of the integrity constraints. For example, there are two different dealers with the same name $'corp1'$, which violate constraint 1. $'Red'$ product was shipped to $'dest2'$, which violates constraint 2. $'Desk'$ was shipped to $'dest2'$, but was not shipped to $'dest1'$, it violates constraint 3. And the date $'2006/1/1'$ for shipment violates constraint 4.

J. Lang, F. Lin, and J. Wang (Eds.): KSEM 2006, LNAI 4092, pp. 379–391, 2006.
© Springer-Verlag Berlin Heidelberg 2006

380   Z. Tan et al.

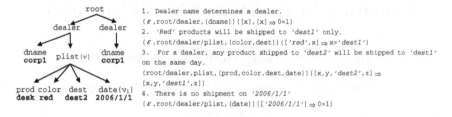

Fig. 1. An Inconsistent XML Document

Because XML is semi-structured, and the W3C standards provide limited support for constraints definition, data inconsistencies become more frequent. And because information is widely exchanged on the Web in XML format, data conflicts become more harmful. For example, today many data from different sources are integrated together to provide a single unified XML view for the users. It is difficult since it requires the resolution of many different kinds of discrepancies of the integrated data. One possible discrepancy is due to different sets of integrity constraints. Moreover, even every integrated data locally satisfies the same integrity constraints, the constraints may be globally violated. Such conflicts may fail to be resolved at all and inconsistent data can't be eliminated because of the autonomy of different data sources.

At the time inconsistencies are detected, "fixing" the document is often problematic, as there is generally not one single deterministic way of rectifying inconsistencies. What we can do is to prohibit inconsistencies from being visible by users, that is to say, to provide the *consistent data* for an *inconsistent* XML document. In this work, we extend the concept of *repairs*, originally introduced by Arenas et al.[2], to give semantics to the problem. Intuitively, a *repair* for an XML document T is a document T' satisfying the constraints, which is obtained from T by applying some "minimal change", and consistent data is the data common for every such possible repair T'. Note that the definition of consistent data talks about all possible repairs, and hence is impractical, since the number of T' can be very large or even infinite. So a remaining task is to develop effective methods to get consistent data. Given a set of integrity constraints and the original XML document T, in this paper, we provide a method to get a document T_g, which is a representation of all possible repairs for T, and thus sufficient for consistent data. T_g is an XML document which can use variables as node values, so as to accommodate the node value modification operations in repairs. Further, T_g is the greatest lower bound for all possible repairs w.r.t. a partial order $\lhd$ defined in this paper.

Related Work. There are a lot of research on inconsistent databases, including [2,5,7,8,9,12]. Because the schema, constraints, query and update operations for XML are far more complicated compared with relational ones, the discussions in relational world can not be applied to XML directly. For example, the discussions in relational field are usually bound up with first-order logic, while XML is tightly associated with path expressions. The idea of constructing a single tableau as a condensed representation of all possible repairs is introduced in [12] for relations, and we extend this method to XML.

DTD[13] and XML Schema[14] provide the basic constraints definitions for XML. Based on this, several papers have addressed the topic of how to improve the semantic expressiveness of XML. The most commonly discussed constraints are keys[6], functional dependencies[3], and multivalued dependencies[11].

[4] discusses query answers in XML data exchange, to restructure XML documents that conform to a source DTD under a target DTD, and to answer queries written over the target schema. [10] discusses the problem of repairing the inconsistency of an XML document with respect to a set of FDs in the most concise merged format. [1] presents a framework for Webhouses with incomplete information, it can represent partial information about the source document acquired by successive queries, and that it can be used to intelligently answer new queries. They differ from our goal to provide a repair and consistent data framework for inconsistent XML document.

The rest of the paper is organized as follows. Section 2 provides the basic notations. We give the repair definition in section 3. In section 4, we introduce the chase process and prove some important properties. We discuss the greatest lower bound for all repairs and consistent data in section 5, and explain the superiority of our repair definition in section 6. Section 7 draws a conclusion.

2   Preliminary Definitions

We adopt the usual view that an XML document is modelled as a node-labelled data tree, and assume that an element node is either followed by a sequence of element nodes and a set of attribute nodes, or is terminated with a text node.

Definition 1. *Assume a finite set E of element labels, a finite set A of attribute names. An XML document(tree)is defined to be $T=(V,lab,ele,att,val,v_r)$. 1)$V$ is a finite set of nodes in T, and we say T is empty iff $V=\phi$. 2)Lab is a function from V to $E \cup A$, for any $v \in V$, v is called an element node if $lab(v) \in E$, an attribute node if $lab(v) \in A$. An element node may be either followed by other nodes, or terminated with a text. 3)If v is an element node followed by other nodes, $ele(v)$ is a sequence of element nodes$[v_1, \ldots, v_n]$, and $att(v)$ is a set of attribute nodes$\{v'_1, \ldots, v'_m\}$; otherwise $ele(v)$ and $att(v)$ are undefined. 4)Function val assigns values to attribute nodes and element nodes terminated with a text, the value may be a string constant, or a string variable. For element nodes not terminated with a text, val is undefined. 5)v_r is a distinguished node in V and is called the root of T; without loss of generality, assume $lab(v_r)=r$.*

For an element node v followed by other nodes, node v' in either $ele(v)$ or $att(v)$ is called child node of v, and there is a parent-child edge from v to v'. An XML tree must have a tree structure, i.e., for each $v \in V$, there is a unique path of parent-child edges from root v_r to v. Element nodes terminated with a text and attribute nodes are called leaf nodes in T.

Our definition differs from [6] since we have extended the *val* function so that is can assign a string variable to node value. The reason for this is that we want to allow value modification as a repair primitive, and sometimes we are not concerned about the specific values used.

A symbol mapping from one symbol set A to another symbol set A' is a function h, such that for any symbol a in A, $h(a)$ is a symbol in A'. To map node values between different XML documents, we naturally extend symbol mapping to nodes and XML documents. Let the symbol set for XML document T be composed of all the constants and variables from node values. Given a symbol mapping h, for a node v in T, $lab(h(v)) = lab(v)$, and $val(h(v)) = h(val(v))$. Let the root of T be v_r, $h(T)$ is an XML document rooted at $h(v_r)$, and for any node v in T, if v is the kth child node of v', then $h(v)$ is the kth child node of $h(v')$ in $h(T)$. To summarize, the symbol mapping affects only the node values, while leave the node label and tree structure unchanged. In the rest of paper, we consider h that preserves constants. That is, if a is a constant, $h(a)$=a.

Let v and v' be two nodes in V. v and v' are value equal, denoted as $v \equiv v'$ iff $(1)lab(v) = lab(v')$, and $(2)val(v) = val(v')$.

A simple path in DTD D is a sequence of node names, with the form $P ::= \epsilon \mid e/P$. Here ϵ represents the empty path, $e \in E \cup A$, and "/" denotes concatenation of two paths. If the first element of P is r, we call P root path.

In XML document T, we say that a node v_2 is reachable from node v_1 by following the path P, iff $(1)v_1 = v_2$, and $P = \epsilon$, or $(2)P = P'/e$, there is a node v' such that v' is reachable from node v_1 by following P', and v_2 is a child of v' with label e. We write $\lfloor v\{P\}\rfloor$ for the set of nodes in T that can be reached by following P from v. In particular, when there is only one node in $\lfloor v\{P\}\rfloor$, we use $v\{P\}$to denote this node. If v is the *root* node, we write $\lfloor P\rfloor$ for $\lfloor v\{P\}\rfloor$. For example in figure 1, we have $\lfloor root/dealer/plist\rfloor=\{v\}$, $v\{date\}=v_1$.

Definition 2. *A Generalized Integrity Constraint Model.*

The constraint is either of the form $(R_1, R_2, (Q_1, \ldots, Q_n))(X_1, \ldots, X_m \Rightarrow X_{m+1})$, *or of the form* $(R_1, R_2, (Q_1, \ldots, Q_n))(X_1, \ldots, X_m \Rightarrow u = w)$. *Here R_1 is a root path, or $R_1 = \epsilon$. $R_1/R_2/Q_1, \ldots$, $R_1/R_2/Q_n$ are all root paths. $X_j(j \in [1, m + 1])$ is a sequence of values $[x_{j1}, \ldots, x_{jn}]$ that may contain variables. $u(and \ w)$ is either a variable or a constant. We require all the variables in constraints are bound, that is, all the variables in X_{m+1}, u, or w should also occur in $X_1, \ldots, X_m$. Let the symbol set for constraint be composed of all the variables and constants in $X_1, \ldots, X_m, X_{m+1}$, u and w.*

A constraint σ is satisfied by an XML tree T, denoted as $T \models \sigma$ iff: For any symbol mapping h from σ to T, $\forall v \in \lfloor R_1 \rfloor$, if $(1)\exists v_j \in \lfloor v\{R_2\}\rfloor$, and (2)there is only one leaf node in $\lfloor v_j\{Q_i\}\rfloor$, and $(3)val(v_j\{Q_i\}) = h(x_{ji})$, $(i \in [1, n]$, $j \in [1, m])$, and

    a. If $\sigma=(R_1, R_2, (Q_1, \ldots, Q_n))(X_1, \ldots, X_m \Rightarrow X_{m+1})$, then $\exists v_{m+1} \in \lfloor v\{R_2\}\rfloor$, there is only one leaf node in $\lfloor v_{m+1}\{Q_i\}\rfloor$, and $val(v_{m+1}\{Q_i\}) = h(x_{(m+1)i})$ $(i \in [1, n])$;

    b. If $\sigma=(R_1, R_2, (Q_1, \ldots, Q_n))(X_1, \ldots, X_m \Rightarrow u = w)$, $h(u)=h(w)$.

For a set of constraints Σ, if $T \models \sigma$ for any $\sigma \in \Sigma$, we write $T \models \Sigma$. Below we use τ to denote the constraint of the form $(R_1, R_2, (Q_1, \ldots, Q_n))(X_1, \ldots, X_m \Rightarrow$

X_{m+1}), and use γ for $(R_1, R_2, (Q_1, \ldots, Q_n))(X_1, \ldots, X_m \Rightarrow u = w)$. The constraint model proposed is defined based on paths, such that it can accommodate the tree structure of XML document, and express both absolute constraints and relative constraints. The absolute constraints hold inside the whole document, while relative constraints hold in only part of the document. The introduction of variables, constants and symbol mapping in the definition improves the semantic expressiveness, and makes the definition more generalized. For example, it can express keys, functional dependencies and multivalued dependencies.

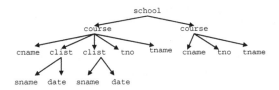

Fig. 2. Integrity Constraint

Example 2. Figure 2 describes the situation in a school. The courses are listed with the course name as identifiers, and also catalog the teacher no and teacher name. Further, *clist* gives the detailed teaching info, regarding each student and each class date. We give the constraints in this document as follows:

1. course name is the key for a course.
   $(\epsilon, school/course, (cname))([x], [x] \Rightarrow 0 = 1)$
2. The teacher no determines teacher name.
   $(\epsilon, school/course, (tno, tname))([x, y_1], [x, y_2] \Rightarrow y_1 = y_2)$
3. Assume every student attends every class, then for a given course, student name multidetermines class date.
   $(school/course, clist, (sname, date))([x_1, y_1], [x_2, y_2] \Rightarrow [x_1, y_2])$
4. If student 'Tom' attends a given course, so does student 'Jerry'.
   $(school/course, clist, (sname, date))(['Tom', x] \Rightarrow ['Jerry', x])$
5. There is no course on '2005/11/1'.
   $(\epsilon, school/course/clist, (date))(['2005/11/1'] \Rightarrow 0 = 1)$

Constraints 3 and 4 are relative, which hold for a given course, not for the whole document. Similarly, we can give the constraints in figure 1.

3   From Mend to Repair

A repair R for an XML document T w.r.t a set of constraints Σ is an XML document consistent with Σ, and is also as close as possible to T. In this paper, we consider three update operations for fixing an XML document, the operations are node insertion, node deletion and node value modification. To describe the semantics of "as close as possible", we assume the repairing is done according to some partial order. The order $\subseteq$ below can describe node insertion and node deletion only, the order $\preceq$ is further defined based on symbol mapping, and it can describe all the three update operations.

Definition 3. *Let S, T be two XML documents, if T is empty, $T \subseteq S$. Otherwise let the root node for T be r_T, the root node for S be r_S, the child nodes of r_T be $\{v_1, \ldots, v_n\}$, and the child nodes of r_S be $\{u_1, \ldots, u_m\}$. We use T_{v_i} to denote the subtree rooted at v_i in T, and S_{u_j} to denote the subtree rooted at u_j in S. $T \subseteq S$ iff*

1. *$r_T \equiv r_S$;*
2. *$\forall T_{v_i}$, $\exists S_{u_j}$, such that $T_{v_i} \subseteq S_{u_j}$; ($i \in [1,n]$, $j \in [1,m]$)*
3. *For T_{v_i} and T_{v_k}, there exists subtree S_{u_j} and S_{u_f}, such that $T_{v_i} \subseteq S_{u_j}$ and $T_{v_k} \subseteq S_{u_f}$. And if $i \neq k$, $j \neq f$. ($i,k \in [1,n]$, $j,f \in [1,m]$)*

Definition 4. *Let S, T be two XML documents, we write $T \preceq S$ iff there exists a symbol mapping h from T to S, such that $h(T) \subseteq S$. If $T \preceq S$, and $S \preceq T$, we write $T \sim S$. If $T \preceq S$, and $T \not\sim S$, we write $T \prec S$.*

It is clear that if $S \subseteq T$, $S \preceq T$. Note that $\subseteq$ ignores the order of sibling nodes, and $\preceq$ allows different symbol sets for node values. We have the following conclusions for $\preceq$ and $\subseteq$, and the proofs are trivial.

Theorem 1. *Let T, S be two XML documents:*

1. *$\subseteq$ and $\preceq$ satisfy reflexivity and transitivity.*
2. *$\sim$ satisfies reflexivity, symmetry and transitivity.(equivalence relation)*

For the three basic update operations, we can summarize the relationship between T and S w.r.t $\preceq$ as follows, which can be verified by the definition easily.

1) If S is obtained from T by node deletion, $S \preceq T$; 2) If S is obtained from T by node insertion, $T \preceq S$; 3)If S is obtained from T by node value modification, to replace a constant by a variable, $S \preceq T$; 4)If S is obtained from T by node value modification, to replace a variable by a constant or a variable, $T \preceq S$.

We get repairs in the following way: Starting from the original XML document T, we find document M first, and M subsatisfy Σ. Here 'subsatisfy' means that we can further find a document R based on M, and $R \models \Sigma$. To be specific, when getting M from T, we "remove" those data from T, which conflicts with Σ. This is done by nodes value modifications, to replace a constant by a variable, or by nodes deletions. The insertion of nodes will not help to "solve" the conflict, so it will not be used in this step. Please note that $M \preceq T$. When obtaining R from M, we "add" some information from Σ to M. It is done by nodes value modifications, to replace a variable in M by a constant, or to replace a variable in M by another variable in M. It can also be done by some nodes insertions. In this step, deletion of nodes will not be used, and $M \preceq R$. Further, to accommodate the "as close as possible" requirement, M should be the document meeting the requirements, and be the closest to T w.r.t $\preceq$. And R should be the document meeting the requirements, and be the closest to M w.r.t $\preceq$.

Definition 5. *Let T be an XML document and Σ a set of constraints, an XML document S is said to subsatisfy Σ iff there exists an XML document J, such that S ⪯ J, and J⊨ Σ.*

A mend for T and Σ is an XML document M⪯T, M subsatisfy Σ; and there does not exist M', such that M⪯M'⪯T, and M' subsatisfy Σ.

A repair for T and Σ is an XML document R, R⊨Σ; and there exists a mend M for T and Σ, such that M⪯R, and for any R', M⪯R'⪯R, R' ⊭ Σ.

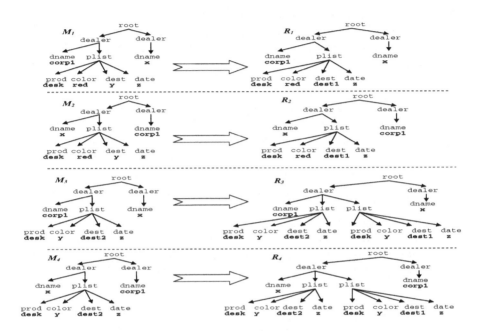

Fig. 3. Mend and Repair

Example 3. We can give all the mends and the corresponding repairs in figure 3, other mends are ∼ to them. In the 4 possible mends, we replace either 'corp1' as variable x, replace '2006/1/1' as variable z, and replace either 'dest2' or 'red' as variable y. Intuitively, the mends replace untrustworthy node values by variables. Node deletion is not used in M_1 to M_4, although it is allowed. For example, if we delete the leftmost *dname*, replace '2006/1/1' as variable z, and replace 'dest2' as variable y, we can get a document M', which subsatisfies Σ. But $M' \preceq M_2$, M' is not a mend. Our definition of ⪯ implies that, if possible, we prefer node value modification to node deletion. Repairs will add information from Σ to mends. For example, in R_1, we will replace y as 'dest1', which is implied by constraint 2. And in R_3, we will insert new nodes describing the shipment to 'dest1', which is suggested by constraint 3. In fact, they are the chase results introduced in the next section. After getting all the repairs, we are sure that there is a shipment to 'dest1', as it is the common part for all possible repairs, although the original document has no information about the shipment to 'dest1' at all.

4   Chasing Repairs

From original document T, we use node deletion, or replace a constant by a variable to get the candidates of mend. So the number of possible candidates are limited w.r.t. $\sim$. By definition 5, a mend candidate is a mend if we can further find a repair based on it. In this section, we introduce the chase process for this purpose, and it can also justify whether a mend candidate is a mend indeed.

Definition 6. *The chase process may fail to find a repair for some mend candidates, so we introduce a special XML document, denoted $\square$, for such situations. Let S and T be XML documents, and Σ a set of constraints. We write $T \vdash_{\Sigma} S$ if S can be obtained from T by a single application of one of the following rules:*

1. $\square \vdash_{\Sigma} \square$;
2. *if $T \models \Sigma$, $T \vdash_{\Sigma} T$; otherwise $\exists \sigma \in \Sigma$, $T \not\models \sigma$. By definition, there is a mapping h from σ to T, $\exists v \in \lfloor R_1 \rfloor$, $\exists v_j \in \lfloor v\{R_2\} \rfloor$, with only one leaf node in $\lfloor v_j\{Q_i\} \rfloor$, and $val(v_j\{Q_i\}) = h(x_{ji})$, which violate σ:*
   (a) *$\sigma = \tau = (R_1, R_2, (Q_1, \ldots, Q_n))(X_1, \ldots, X_m \Rightarrow X_{m+1})$. S is obtained from T by nodes insertions: Insert child node v_{m+1} for node v matching path R_2, insert child nodes for v_{m+1} matching paths $Q_1, \ldots, Q_n$, and set $val(v_{m+1}\{Q_i\}) = h(x_{(m+1)i})$;*
   (b) *$\sigma = \gamma = (R_1, R_2, (Q_1, \ldots, Q_n))(X_1, \ldots, X_m \Rightarrow u = w)$. If $h(u)$ and $h(w)$ are two distinct constants, $S = \square$. Otherwise assume without loss of generality that $h(u)$ is a variable, S is obtained from T by a symbol mapping g: $g(h(u)) = h(w)$, and g preserves other variables.*

A chase of T by Σ is a maximal sequence $T = T_1, T_2, \ldots, T_n$ of XML documents such that for every $i \in \{1, \ldots, n\}, T_i \vdash_{\Sigma} T_{i+1}$, and $T_i \neq T_{i+1}$.

In figure 3, it can be verified that R_i is the chase result of M_i respectively($i \in [1, 4]$). Next we prove some properties of the chase. The chase can terminate in finite steps according to theorem 2. By theorem 2 and 4, We can 'chase' repair from T iff T subsatisfies Σ. Theorem 3 shows that the chase result is a repair indeed. Theorem 5 proves that for any two possible chase results S_1 and S_2, $S_1 \sim S_2$. For two mends which $\sim$, theorem 7 proves that the corresponding chase results also $\sim$.

Theorem 2. *Let $T \neq \square$ be an XML document and Σ a set of constraints:*

1. *If S is an XML document in a chase of T by Σ and $S \neq \square$, $T \preceq S$;*
2. *If $S \neq \square$ is the last element of a chase of T by Σ, $S \models \Sigma$;*
3. *Each chase of T by Σ is finite.*

Proof. 1. Let the chase be $T = T_1, \ldots, T_n$, and $S = T_i$. We prove by induction on i. $T \preceq S = T_1$ is trivial. Assume $T \preceq T_k$, next we prove $T \preceq S = T_{k+1}$. Since $S \neq \square$, if S is obtained from T_k by nodes insertion, $T_k \preceq S$. Otherwise S is obtained from T_k by a symbol mapping, $T_k \preceq S$. By transitivity, $T \preceq T_k \preceq S$.

2. Let the chase be $T=T_1,\ldots,T_i$, we prove by induction on the length i. If $i=1$, by definition 6, $S = T \models \Sigma$. Assume when $i = k$, $T_k \models \Sigma$. Next we prove when $i = k + 1$, $T_{k+1} \models \Sigma$. The chase of T_2 is $T_2,\ldots,T_{k+1}$, and the length is k. By induction hypothesis, $T_{k+1} \models \Sigma$.
3. By definition, all the variables in constraints are bound, so the chase will not introduce new variables and constants other than the ones in T and Σ. The application of τ may insert new subtrees to extend T_{i-1}. Note that the same subtree will not be inserted by the application of τ repeatedly, otherwise T_{i-1} will satisfy τ itself. Because the path expressions in Σ, the variables and constants in T and Σ are limited, the subtrees that can be inserted are also limited. To summarize, the chase is finite.

Theorem 3. *Let T and F be XML documents, both distinct from $\Box$, and Σ a set of constraints. Let $S \neq \Box$ be a document in a chase of T by Σ, if $T \preceq F$, and $F \models \Sigma$, $S \preceq F$.*

Proof. Let the chase be $T=T_1,T_2,\ldots,T_n$, and $S = T_i$, we prove by induction on i. If $i=1$, $S=T \preceq F$ is given. With the induction hypothesis $T_k \preceq F$, there exists mapping f from T_k to F, and $f(T_k) \subseteq F$. Next we prove $T_{k+1} \preceq F$, T_{k+1} is obtained from T_k:

1. T_{k+1} is obtained by application of τ. For a given mapping h from τ to T_k, we insert nodes to T_k and set the node values. Since $F \models \tau$, F contains all the inserted nodes(maybe with different node variable values). Otherwise it can be verified that F violates τ with the mapping $f \circ h$. Since the application of τ will not introduce new variables, $f(T_{k+1}) \subseteq F$, $T_{k+1} \preceq F$;
2. T_{k+1} is obtained by application of γ. Without loss of generality, we assume $T_{k+1}=g(T_k)$, $g(h(u)) = h(w)$. Since $h(u)$ and $h(w)$ are symbols in T_k, and $F \models \gamma$, $f(h(u)) = f(h(w))$. The mapping g preserves all the other variables, $f(T_{k+1})= f(g(T_k))=f(T_k) \subseteq F$, $T_{k+1} \preceq F$.

Theorem 4. *Let T and F be XML documents, both distinct from $\Box$, and Σ a set of constraints. If $\Box$ is the last element of a chase of T by Σ and $T \preceq F$, $F \not\models \Sigma$.*

Proof. Let S be the last but one element in the chase of T that ends with $\Box$, that is, $S \vdash_\Sigma \Box$. If $S \not\preceq F$, $F \not\models \Sigma$ by theorem 3. Next assume $S \preceq F$, and a mapping f such that $f(S) \subseteq F$.

$S \vdash_\Sigma \Box$ because of the application of γ, so there is a mapping h from γ to S, such that $\exists v \in \lfloor R_1 \rfloor$, $\exists v_j \in \lfloor v\{R_2\} \rfloor$, with only one leaf node in $\lfloor v_j\{Q_i\} \rfloor$, $val(v_j\{Q_i\}) = h(x_{ji})$, and $h(u)$ and $h(w)$ are two distinct constants. In document F, for the mapping $f \circ h$, $\exists f(v) \in \lfloor R_1 \rfloor$, $\exists f(v_j) \in \lfloor f(v)\{R_2\} \rfloor$, with only one leaf node in $\lfloor f(v_j)\{Q_i\} \rfloor$, $val(f(v_j)\{Q_i\}) = f(val(v_j\{Q_i\})) =f(h(x_{ji}))$. f does not change the value of constants, and $h(u)$ and $h(w)$ are two distinct constants, so $f(h(u))$ and $f(h(w))$ are two distinct constants, F violates γ.

To conclude, $S \not\preceq F$, then $F \not\models \Sigma$.

Theorem 5. *Let $T \neq \Box$ be an XML document, and Σ a set of constraints. If two chases of T end with $S_1 \neq \Box$ and $S_2 \neq \Box$ respectively, $S_1 \sim S_2$.*

Proof. By theorem 2, $T \preceq S_2$, and $S_2 \models \Sigma$. S_1 is a document in a chase, by theorem 3, $S_1 \preceq S_2$. Similarly, $S_2 \preceq S_1$. It follows $S_1 \sim S_2$.

By theorem 5, the different results of chase T by Σ are $\sim$-equivalence. Without loss of generality, we choose an arbitrary result as a representative, and denote it as $chase(T, \Sigma)$.

Theorem 6. *Let $T \neq \Box$ be an XML document, and Σ a set of constraints. T subsatisfies Σ iff $chase(T,\Sigma) \neq \Box$.*

Proof. This is the immediate corollary of theorem 2 and theorem 4.

Theorem 7. *Let T and S be XML documents, both distinct from $\Box$, and Σ a set of constraints. If $S \preceq T$, $chase(S,\Sigma) \neq \Box$, and $chase(T,\Sigma) \neq \Box$, then $chase(S,\Sigma) \preceq chase(T,\Sigma)$. If $S \sim T$, $chase(S,\Sigma) \sim chase(T,\Sigma)$.*

Proof. If $S \preceq T$, by theorem 2, $S \preceq T \preceq chase(T, \Sigma)$, and $chase(T, \Sigma) \models \Sigma$. So $chase(S, \Sigma) \preceq chase(T, \Sigma)$ by theorem 3. Similarly, $chase(T, \Sigma) \preceq chase(S, \Sigma)$ if $T \preceq S$. Thus if $S \sim T$, $chase(S, \Sigma) \sim chase(T, \Sigma)$.

5 Greatest Lower Bound and Consistent Data

To get the consistent data from the original XML document, all the repairs need to be merged together. We use function η for this purpose, and it is defined for variables, nodes and trees in sequence.

(1) $\eta(x,y)$: if $x=y$ is the same constant a, $\eta(x,y)=$a; otherwise $\eta(x,y)$ is a variable, and $\eta(x_1, y_1)=\eta(x_2, y_2)$ iff $x_1=x_2$, $y_1=y_2$. (2)$\eta(v_1, v_2)$: if v_1 and v_2 are of the same node type(e.g. element node), and $lab(v_1) = lab(v_2)$: $\eta(v_1, v_2)$ is a node v having the same node type and label as v_1, and $val(v) = \eta(val(v_1), val(v_2))$. Otherwise $\eta(v_1, v_2)$ is undefined. (3)Assume two XML trees T_1 and T_2, the root of T_1 is r_1, the root of T_2 is r_2, the child nodes of r_1 is $\{v_{11}, \ldots, v_{1n}\}$, and the child nodes of r_2 is $\{v_{21}, \ldots, v_{2m}\}$. $\eta(T_1, T_2)$ is defined as a tree T iff $\eta(r_1, r_2)$ is defined. Let the root of T be r, $r \equiv \eta(r_1, r_2)$; for any subtree T_{1i} rooted at v_{1i} in T_1 and any subtree T_{2j} rooted at v_{2j} in $T_2(i \in [1, n], j \in [1, m])$, if $\eta(v_{1i}, v_{2j})$ is defined, $\eta(v_{1i}, v_{2j})$ is a child node of r in T, and $\eta(T_{1i}, T_{2j})$ is a subtree rooted at $\eta(v_{1i}, v_{2j})$ in T.

Without loss of generality, we consider two documents in the definition of η, and it can be extended to n documents as well. Practically, in η every subtree in T_1 is combined with every subtree in T_2 at the same level. For example, we give the η for repairs R_2 and R_3 in figure 4(a). Note that figure 4(a) $\npreceq R_2$. $\preceq$ is too strict for η, as it requires comparison of the number of child nodes. We introduce $\lhd$ below to show the relationship between $\eta(T_1, T_2)$ and T_1.

Definition 7. *Let S, T be two XML documents, we denote $T \lhd S$ iff:*

1. *T is empty, or;*
2. *Let the root node for T be r_T, the root node for S be r_S, the child nodes of r_T be $\{v_1, \ldots, v_n\}$, and the child nodes of r_S be $\{u_1, \ldots, u_m\}$. There exists mapping h from T to S, such that:*

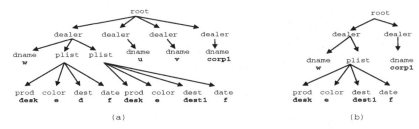

Fig. 4. η of repairs R_2 and R_3

(a) $h(r_T) \equiv r_S$;

(b) for any subtree T_{v_i} rooted at $h(v_i)$ in $h(T)$, there exists subtree S_{u_j} rooted at u_j in S, such that $T_{v_i} \lhd S_{u_j}$; $(i \in [1,n], j \in [1,m])$

If $T \preceq S$, $T \lhd S$. We write $T \sim \lhd S$ iff $T \lhd S$, and $S \lhd T$. $\lhd$ neglects node ranks(the number of child nodes) in the XML tree, for different T_{v_i} and T_{v_k}, we may use a single S_{u_j} to $\lhd$ them. For example, figure 4(a)$\sim \lhd$ figure 4(b). It is trivial that figure 4(b)$\lhd$ figure 4(a). And we can find a mapping h, h={u/corp1,v/corp1,d/dest1}, which makes figure 4(a)$\lhd$ figure 4(b).

Next we prove that η will generate the greatest lower bound(glb) for a set of repairs $\{R_1, \ldots, R_n\}$ w.r.t. $\lhd$. That is, $\eta(R_1, \ldots, R_n) \lhd R_i$ for $i \in [1,n]$, and if $T' \lhd R_i$ for $i \in [1,n]$, $T' \lhd \eta(R_1, \ldots, R_n)$.

Theorem 8. T_1, T_2 are two XML documents, $\eta(T_1, T_2)$ is a glb of T_1 and T_2.

Proof. Let the root of T_1 be r_1, the root of T_2 be r_2, the child nodes of r_1 be $\{v_1, \ldots, v_n\}$, the child nodes of r_2 be $\{u_1, \ldots, u_m\}$. Let $\eta(T_1, T_2)=T$, the root of T be r, and the child nodes of r be $\{w_1, \ldots, w_k\}$.

We define a mapping h from T to T_1, $h(\eta(x,y)) = x$. h preserves the constants, since $h(\eta(x,y))$=a iff $x = y$=a; h is valid because $\eta(x_1,y_1)=\eta(x_2,y_2)$ iff $x_1 = x_2$, $y_1 = y_2$. It can be easily verified that h makes $T \lhd T_1$; similarly $T \lhd T_2$, so T is the lower bound of T_1 and T_2.

Assume $T' \lhd T_1$, and $T' \lhd T_2$, next we prove $T' \lhd T$. Let the root of T' be r', and the child nodes of r' be $\{z_1, \ldots, z_l\}$. By definition, there exists mapping h, which makes $T' \lhd T_1$, and exists mapping g, which makes $T' \lhd T_2$. Next we construct a mapping f from T' to T, $f(x) = \eta(h(x), g(x))$. f preserves the constants, so it is valid. It is clear that $f(r') \equiv r$. Let T_i' be a subtree rooted at z_i in T', it can be verified that $f(T_i') \lhd \eta(h(T_i'), g(T_i'))$. Since $T' \lhd T_1$, by definition T_1 has subtree T_{1j} rooted at v_j, which makes $h(T_i') \lhd T_{1j}$; similarly T_2 has subtree T_{2e} rooted at u_e, which makes $g(T_i') \lhd T_{2e}$. By the construction of η, there exists subtree T_d rooted at w_d in T, $T_d = \eta(T_{1j}, T_{2e})$, thus $f(T_i') \lhd T_d$. Since T_i' is arbitrary, $T' \lhd T$. $(i \in [1,l], j \in [1,n], e \in [1,m], d \in [1,k])$

If S and T are all glbs of $\{R_1, \ldots, R_n\}$, by definition $T \sim \lhd S$. We assume there is an arbitrary selection rule that picks a representative of this $\sim \lhd$-equivalence class and denote it as $glb(R_1, \ldots, R_n)$. Note that if $T \sim \lhd S$, T bears the same information as S with regard to the constant-valued nodes, including node labels, node values, and paths from root node to arbitrary nodes.

Definition 8. *Given a constraint set Σ, an XML document T, assume the repair set for T w.r.t Σ be $\{R_1, \ldots, R_n\}$, the consistent data from T is defined to be the node labels, node values and the paths from root node to arbitrary nodes for constant-valued nodes in $glb(R_1, \ldots, R_n)$.*

Example 4. It can be verified that figure 4(b) is a *glb* for $\{R_1, R_2, R_3, R_4\}$. The constant-valued nodes requirement excludes the information about *color* and *date*. The consistent data from the original inconsistent XML document is that: there is a dealer named *'corp1'*, and there exists a shipment of *'desk'* to *'dest1'*. But it is uncertain whether this shipment is carried out by dealer *'corp1'*.

6   More About Repairs

Finally we make a further explanation about the superiority of our *repair* definition. In this paper, we define *repair* based on the introduction of *mend* first. A more direct definition can be given as follows, to avoid confusion, we call it *Fix*.

Definition 9. *Given XML document T and a constraint set Σ, we say F is a fix for T w.r.t Σ iff $F \preceq T$, $F \models \Sigma$, and for any $F \preceq F' \preceq T$, $F' \not\models \Sigma$.*

Example 5. Figure 5 gives a fix F_1. Here we replace the right *'corp1'*, *'red'*, *'dest2'* and *'2006/1/1'* as variable x, y, z and w respectively. It can be verified that F_1 is a fix.

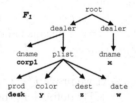

Fig. 5. Fix F_1

If we define *consistent data* based on *fix*, the information about the shipment to *'dest1'* will be lost, as it does not appear in F_1. Note that we have $F_1 \preceq R_1$. In fact, it can be proved that for every fix F, we have a repair R such that $F \preceq R$, so that our definition of *repair* can always preserve more information from the original document than *fix*.

Theorem 9. *Assume F is a fix for T w.r.t Σ, 1)there always exists a mend M for T w.r.t Σ, such that $F \preceq M \preceq T$; and 2)there always exists a repair R based on M, such that $F \preceq R$.*

Proof. 1) This is trivial. Because if there exists no mend M, such that $F \prec M \preceq T$, since $F \models \Sigma$, by definition 5, F itself is a mend.

2) Because $F \models \Sigma$, $F=chase(F, \Sigma)$. Since $F \preceq M$, by theorem 7, $F=chase(F, \Sigma) \preceq chase(M, \Sigma)$. By theorem 5, $chase(M, \Sigma) \sim R$, so $F \preceq R$.

7   Conclusion

We study the inconsistency problem in the field of XML. We introduce a repair and consistent data framework for XML document, give the chase process to generate repairs, and provide a method to get the *glb* of all repairs.

References

1. S. Abiteboul, L. Segoufin, V. Vianu. Representing and Querying XML with Incomplete Information. In PODS, 2001. 35-47.
2. M. Arenas, L. E. Bertossi, J. Chomick. Consistent Query Answers in Inconsistent Databases. In PODS, 1999. 68-79.
3. M. Arenas, L. Libkin. A Normal Form for XML Documents. TODS, 2004, 29(1):195-232.
4. M. Arenas, L. Libkin. XML Data Exchange: Consistency and Query Answering. In PODS, 2005. 13-24.
5. P. Bohannon, W. F. Fan, M. Flaster, R. Rastogi. A Cost-Based Model and Effective Heuristic for Repairing Constraints by Value Modification. In SIGMOD, 2005. 143-154.
6. P. Buneman, S. Davidson, W. Fan, C. Hara, W. Tan. Reasoning about Keys for XML. In Database Programming Languages, 2002. 133-148.
7. L. Bravo, L. Bertossi. Logic programs for consistently querying data integration systems. In IJCAI, 2003. 10-15.
8. J. Chomicki, J. Marcinkowski. Minimal-Change Integrity Maintenance Using Tuple Deletions. Information and Computation, 2005, 197(1-2): 90-121.
9. G. Greco, S. Greco, E. Zumpano. A logical framework for querying and repairing inconsistent databases. IEEE Transaction on Knowledge and Data Engineering, 2003, 15(6):1389-1408.
10. W. Ng. Repairing Inconsistent Merged XML Data. In DEXA, 2003. 244-255.
11. M. W. Vincent, J. Liu. Multivalued Dependencies and a 4NF for XML. In CAISE, 2003. 14-29.
12. J.Wijsen. Database Repairing Using Updates. TODS, 2005, 30(3):722-768.
13. Extensible Markup Language (XML) 1.0 (Second Edition). W3C Recommendation, October 2000. http://www.w3.org/TR/REC-xml
14. XML Schema Part 1: Structures. W3C Recommendation, May 2001. http://www.w3.org/TR/xmlschema-1/

A Framework for Automated Test Generation in Intelligent Tutoring Systems

Tang Suqin[1] and Cao Cungen[2]

[1] College of Computer Science and Information Technology,
Guangxi Normal University, Guilin 541004, China
[2] Key Laboratory of Intelligent Information Processing,
Institute of Computing Technology,
Chinese Academy of Sciences, Beijing 100080, China
suqint@sina.com

Abstract. Intelligent tutoring systems have being extensively researched, and are viewed as cost-effective alternatives to traditional education. However, it has been long recognized that development of such systems is labor-intensive and time-consuming, and that a certain degree of automation in the development process is necessary. This paper proposes a framework for automating test generation – one of the key components in an intelligent tutoring system. The core of the framework is a domain conceptual model, a collection of testing goals, and a collection of test-generation rules, and the latter two are formulated from an analysis of various modes of error and on the basis of the domain conceptual model.

Keywords: Intelligent tutoring system, test generation, domain conceptual model, testing goal, test-generation rules, individualized testing.

1 Introduction

As a cost-effective alternative to traditional school education, automated intelligent tutoring has being extensively researched (Katz, Lesgold, Gary, *et al.*, 1992; Cao, 2000; Lu, Cao and Chen,*et al.*, 1996; Wiemer-Hastings, Graesser and Harter, 1998; Ning and Cios, 1989; Futtersack and J.-M.Labat, 1992; Beck, Stern and Haugsjaa, 1996). However, it has been long recognized that developing such systems is labor-intensive and time-consuming, and that a certain degree of automation in the development process is necessary (Beck, Stern and Haugsjaa, 1996; Lu, Cao, Chen, *et al.*, 1996).

One of the labor-intensive tasks in developing an intelligent tutoring system (ITS) is to manually design tests to determine, posterior to a single lesson, whether a student has properly mastered the taught concepts. For example, after teaching diabetes, insulin-dependent diabetes, non-insulin-dependent diabetes, and gestational diabetes in a lesson, it is sensible for an ITS to test whether the student has really mastered the taxonomic structure of all these concepts.

However, it is extremely both labor-intensive and tedious to design such post-lesson tests, and thus should be automated somehow. This paper introduces a framework for

J. Lang, F. Lin, and J. Wang (Eds.): KSEM 2006, LNAI 4092, pp. 392–404, 2006.

this automation. The core of our framework consists of three components: A conceptual model for a domain to be taught to students, A collection of testing goals to indicate what are needed to be tested, and A collection of test-generation rules for achieving those goals.

Testing goals are founded both on the domain conceptual model[1] that an ITS system expects a student to build up in the course of study, *and* on an analysis of errors that are possibly made by students in building up their conceptual model of a domain. While human error has been extensively and intensively studied for more than two decades (e.g. Reason 1990; Senders and Moray, 1991; Cao, 1998), this paper focuses on three modes of error – *error of omission, error of insertion* and *error of substitution*, because we are mainly interested to test the conceptual structure of concepts learned by a student, and other errors (e.g. slips) are more associated with student behavior, which are out of the scope of this paper.

A test-generation rule is an executive agent for generating tests to achieve a certain testing goal; provides a number of conditions of when to test; and generates a number of *separate* tests for testing a student's conceptual model from different perspectives. Note that a test-generation rule does not specify which of the generated tests is used to test a student. This specification requires knowledge of a student's characteristics. Put in another way, each test should be individualized – this is of course complementary to individualized instruction.

The paper is organized as follows. The next section outlines the framework. In section 3, we present and discuss a list of testing goals on the basis of different modes of error. In section 4, we present and explain some of the test-generation rules formulated on the basis of testing goals and the domain conceptual model. Section 5 discusses individualized testing, where relationships between test generation and an individual student's modes of error are analyzed. Section 6 concludes the work, and raises two related issues on our future research agenda.

2 Framework Overview

The core of our framework is constituted of three basic components: a domain conceptual model, a collection of testing goals, and a collection of test-generation rules. The following sections will explain each component in turn.

2.1 Domain Conceptual Modeling

Generally, a *domain conceptual model* consists of a set of domain concepts, each of which has a number of attributes, and a collection of relations among the concepts. Formally, we use $\sum=(\copyright, \circledR)$ to represent a domain conceptual model, where $\copyright$ is the set of domain concepts, and $\circledR$ the set of conceptual relations among the concepts in $\copyright$.

As illustration, in the domain of diabetes diagnosis, the conceptual model $\sum$ may contain the following concepts: $\copyright=\{$diabetes, insulin-dependent diabetes,

---

[1] We will abbreviate 'domain conceptual model' as 'conceptual model' throughout the paper, whenever no confusion is caused.

non-insulin-dependent diabetes, gestational diabetes, pancreas, Beta cells, pancreas malfunction, insulin, insufficient insulin secretion}, and the relations ®={is-a, part-of, caused-by}.

In this work, the ontology of a domain conceptual model is generalized to contain a lot of most common relationships[2]:

1. is-a(C_1, C_2): concept C_1 is a superconcept of C_2, e.g. is-a(diabetes, insulin-dependent diabetes).
2. directly-caused-by(C_1, C_2): concept C_1 is *directly* caused by C_2, e.g. directly-caused-by(diabetes, insufficient insulin secretion).
3. caused-by(C_1, C_2): concept C_1 is *directly* or *indirectly* caused by C_2, e.g. caused-by(diabetes, pancreas malfunction). By the definition, it is obvious that directly-caused-by(C_1, C_2) implies caused-by(C_1, C_2).
4. temporally-before(C_1, C_2): concept C_1 is *temporally before* C_2, e.g. temporally-before(insufficient insulin secretion, diabetes).
5. temporally-coexist(C_1, C_2): concept C_1 is *temporally coexist with* C_2, e.g. temporally-coexist(pancreas malfunction, insufficient insulin secretion).
6. part-of(C_1, C_2): concept C_1 is a part of C_2, e.g. part-of(Beta cells, pancreas).
7. substance-of(C_1, C_2): concept C_1 is an integral substance of C_2, e.g. substance-of(H, H_2O).
8. own-attribute(C, A): concept C has an attribute A, e.g. own- attribute (insulin-dependent diabetes, onset).
9. own-essential-attribute(C, A): concept C has an essential[3] attribute A, e.g. own-essential-attribute(insulin-dependent diabetes, onset).
10. attribute-value-is(C, A, V): concept C has an attribute A whose value is V, e.g. attribute-value-is(insulin-dependent diabetes, onset, juvenile).

It should be noted that there are many other temporal relationships between concepts, but here we only present two of them for illustration. For more discussion on temporal relationships, see (Allen, 1983; Allen, 1984).

2.2 Testing Goals, Test-Generation Rules

A testing goal highlights or identifies a possible error made by a student in developing his or her knowledge structure, whereas a test-generation rule is an executive agent for generating tests to achieve the goal.

To formulate testing goals, we focus on possible errors made by a student in learning a course of a domain. Reason classifies human errors into three basic categories at three different levels of abstraction (Reason, 1990). However, since we are more interested to test the knowledge structure of a student, we classify a student's errors into three observable modes, namely omission, insertion and substitution:

---

[2] It should be stressed that these are the most common relationships in every domain. In WordNet, for example, semantic concepts essentially have 4 relationships, which are of course covered by our domain conceptual model below.

[3] An essential attribute of a concept is an attribute that plays a characterizing or identifying role for the concept. In the example of diabetes diagnosis, the onset is essential, because it can be used to differentiate the diagnosis of insulin-dependent diabetes and non-insulin-dependent diabetes – the onset of the former is teenage, and the latter adult.

1. *Error of omission*: an error of omission in a knowledge structure means that some concept is missing or left out in the conceptual model of a student.
2. *Error of insertion*: an error of insertion in a conceptual model is characterized by the fact that some irrelevant concepts are inserted in the wrong place of the conceptual model.
3. *Error of substitution*: an error of substitution in a conceptual model is defined as an appropriate concept being replaced with an inappropriate one. Note that this error is *not* primitive. In fact, it can be reduced to an error of omission plus an error of insertion. Nevertheless, we still incorporate it here for easy presentation.

Test-generation rules are executive agents for achieving testing goals. As illustration, assume that a concept C has $C_1,...,C_n$ as all its subconcepts. To identify an error of omission in a student's conceptual model, a test-generation rule may generate a test, asking if $C_i, ..., C_j$ are *all* the subconcepts of C, where $\{C_i,...,C_j\} \subset \{C_1, ...,C_n\}$. If a student answers yes, then we can claim that the student makes an error of omission – he or she neglects other subconcepts.

To end this section, we would stress that a testing goal plays a double role in our framework: It is *both* a guideline of how test-generation rules are formalized, *and* a justification of the formalized rules. In this very sense, we say that our proposed test-generation framework is rational.

3 Testing Goals

3.1 Overview

From different perspectives, we have identified seven testing goals for both guiding and justifying test generation. (We do not claim that the list of goals, though most common and important, is exhaustive. As will be described shortly, more specific goals could be added in at any time, because of the generality and scalability of the proposed framework.)

Goals 1 to 5 are fundamental in the sense that they test whether a student has established a *static big picture* of learned domain concepts – a systematic, high-level understanding of the static conceptual structure, whereas goals 6 and 7 are towards the other end of the knowledge 'spectrum' – testing whether a student has properly built up a *dynamic big picture* of learned domain concepts.

3.2 Goal 1: To Test Student's Taxonomic Structure of Concepts

For each domain, the taxonomic structure of domain concepts is its fundamental backbone, and developing such a proper structure is a basic yet crucial requirement in student learning. However, a common problem in student learning is that students may not build up the taxonomic structure appropriately: the structure may be incomplete (an error of omission), mixed up with irrelevant concepts (an error of insertion), or both (an error of substitution).

The test for goal 1 can be either a *single-level* or a *multiple-level* test. A single-level test checks whether a student has mastered a concept and its subconcepts completely, whereas a multiple-level test determines whether the student has properly organized the learned concepts into multiple levels of abstraction (for more details, see figure 11 in Section 4.2.2).

3.3 Goal 2: To Test Student's Meronymic Structure of Concepts

Quite similar to the taxonomic structure, a student may encounter problems in learning a meronymic (or part-whole) structure of a domain concept. The learned whole-part structure may be incomplete, mixed up with irrelevant concepts, or both.

3.4 Goal 3: To Test Student's Substantial Structure of Concepts

It is very important for a student to master the substantial structure of a concept. However, it is sometimes difficult for a student to fully master all integral substance of a complicated concept.

For instance, after the concept *dioxyline phosphate* is taught to a medicine student, the student is expected to know all the substances of dioxyline phosphate. But he or she may fail to do so.

3.5 Goal 4: To Test Student's Differential Structure of Concepts

In each domain, many concepts are quite similar, and differentiating them is both a challenging instructional goal on the side of the instructor and a challenging learning task on the side of a student.

For example, differentiating insulin-dependent diabetes from non-insulin-dependent diabetes is not an easy task for some students, because both share similar symptoms.

3.6 Goal 5: To Test Student's Attributive Structure of Concepts

An attribute of a concept is usually viewed as a descriptor of the concept. The concept may have numerous attributes that may sometimes be out of a student's memory (thus errors of omission). Further, some attributes of the concept are so important that students should be expected to understand and memorize.

3.7 Goal 6: To Test Student's Temporal Structure of Concepts

Temporality and causality are closely related facets of concepts. Causality generally implies temporality, but the converse generally does not apply.

Whenever both temporality and causality prevails in a domain conceptual structure, students tend to make mistakes in appreciating the real relationships among the involved concepts.

3.8 Goal 7: To Test Student's Causal Structure of Concepts

Like the taxonomy and meronymy of concepts, causal knowledge prevails in a domain (e.g. medicine). It represents a deep understanding of the domain that should be achieved by students.

Unlike the taxonomy and meronymy of concepts, however, the causal structure of concepts is more complex.

For example, a student may mistake concept C' as a direct cause of concept C. The reason might be that the student has not understood the intermediating causes of concept C (see Section 4.2 for more discussion).

4 Test-Generation Rules

Given testing goals, we now define corresponding test-generation rules for achieving them. In the following, we assume that the domain conceptual model is $\Sigma=(\copyright,\circledR)$. We use C, C1,..., Cn, D1,..., Dm, E1,..., Ek to stand for concepts in $\copyright$, and A, A1,..., An to denote attributes of some concepts in $\copyright$.

4.1 Some Useful Predicates

To specify test-generation rules concisely[4]., we need a few predicates with variable arity:

1. taught-concepts($C_1,...,C_n$) $\equiv_{def.}$ $C_1,...,C_n$ have already be taught (to a student).
2. taught-attributes($A_1,..., A_n$) $\equiv_{def.}$ $A_1,...,A_n$ have already be taught.
3. taught-concept-attributes($C,A_1,...,A_n$) $\equiv_{def}$ taught-concepts(C) $\bigwedge$ taught-attributes ($A_1, ...,A_n$).
4. classified-into($C; C_1,...,C_n$)[5].$\equiv_{def.}$ $\forall$ $1\leq i\leq n$: is-a(C_i,C)$\bigwedge$ $C'\in\copyright$:is-a(C', C)$\to C'$ $\in\{C_1, ...,C_n\}$ meaning that C is conceptually partitioned into and only into $C_1,...,C_{n-1}$, and C_n.
5. structurally-partitioned-into($C; C_1,...,C_n$)$\equiv_{def.}$$\forall$ $1\leq i\leq n$:part-of(C_i, C) $\bigwedge$ $\forall C'$ $\in\copyright$: part-of(C', C)$\to C'\in\{C_1, ...,C_n\}$ meaning that C is structurally partitioned into and only into $C_1,...,C_{n-1}$,and C_n.
6. substantially-partitioned-into($C; C_1, ..., C_n$) $\equiv_{def.}$ $\forall$ $1\leq i\leq n$: substance-of(C_i, C) $\bigwedge$ $\forall$ $C'\in\copyright$: substance-of(C', C)$\to C'\in\{C_1, ...,C_n\}$ meaning that C is substantially partitioned into and only into $C_1,...,C_{n-1}$, and C_n
7. directly-caused-by($C; C_1, ..., C_n$) $\equiv_{def.}$ $\forall$ $1\leq i\leq n$: directly-caused-by(C,C_i) $\bigwedge$ $\forall$ $C' \in\copyright$: directly-caused-by(C,C')$\to C'\in\{C_1,...,C_n\}$ meaning that C is directly caused by and only by $C_1, ... C_{n-1}$, or C_n. (Also see definition 8.)
8. caused-by($C; C_1, ..., C_n$) $\equiv_{def.}$ $\forall$ $1\leq i\leq n$: caused-by(C, C_i) $\bigwedge$ $\forall C'\in\copyright$: caused-by(C, C')$\to C'\in\{C_1,...,C_n\}$ meaning that C is caused by and only by $C_1, ... C_{n-1}$, or C_n. By definition, it is easy to verify that directly-caused-by(C, $C_1, ..., C_n$) implies caused-by(C, $C_1, ..., C_n$).
9. own-attributes($C; A_1, ...,A_n$) $\equiv_{def.}$ $\forall$ $1\leq i\leq n$: own-attribute($C; A_i$) $\bigwedge$ $\forall A$: own-attribute($C; A$)$\to A\in\{A_1, ..., A_n\}$ meaning that $A_1, ...,A_n$ are *all* the attributes of C. (Also see definition 10.)

---

[4] Otherwise, we would incorporate all the specifications into the premise part of a rule, which may complicate the semantics of the rule.

[5] Here, the semicolon plays the same role as a comma. We use a semicolon to indicate that C is a special argument in the predicate. This also applies to the predicates partitioned-into(), directly-caused-by(), and caused-by().

10.   own-essential-attributes$(C; A_1,...,A_n) \equiv_{def.}$

$\forall 1{\le}i{\le}n$:own-essential-attribute$(C; A_i) \bigwedge$

$\forall A$: own-essential-attribute$(C; A){\rightarrow}A \in \{A_1, ..., A_n\}$ meaning that $A_1, ..., A_n$ are *all* the essential attributes of C.

11.   essential-attribute-difference$(C_1, C_2; A) \equiv_{def.} \forall 1{\le}i{\le}2$: own- essential- attribute

$(C_i; A) \bigwedge \forall 1{\le}i{\le}2$: own-essential-attribute$(C_i; A, V_i) \bigwedge V_1 {\ne} V_2$ meaning that A is a common essential attribute of C_1 and C_2, and their respective values (i.e. V_1 and V_2) differ. (Also see definition 12)

12.   essential-attributes-difference$(C_1, C_2; A_1 ,..., A_n) \equiv_{def.} \forall 1{\le}j{\le}n$:

own-essential-differences$(C_1, C_2; A_j) \bigwedge$

$\forall A$: essential-attribute-difference$(C_1, C_2; A) \rightarrow A \in \{A_1, ..., A_n\}$ meaning that $A_1 ,..., A_n$ are *all* the common essential attribute of C_1 and C_2, where their respective values differ.

4.2 Test-Generation Rules

4.2.1 Format of Test-Generation Rule

In our framework, each test-generation rule consists of 5 components:

Rule-ID. Rule identifier.

Testing goal. The goal for which this rule generates tests to achieve.

Premises. Premises specify the circumstances where the rule is used. Typically, the circumstances are the concepts taught to a student so far; and knowledge structure of the taught concepts in the domain conceptual model. We will discuss student-specific information in Section 5, "Individualized Testing".

Variable declaration. This component defines variables in generated tests.

Test generation. This component lists the generated test(s). A test is in the form of 'ask if <predicate>'. Here, <predicate> is viewed as an *inquiring predicate*. In actual practice, it is straightforward to translate an inquiring predicate, e.g. with translation templates, into a domain-specific textual question to be presented to a student. For instance, the test "ask if classified-into$(C; C1, ..., Cn)$" can be translated into "Is C classified into $C1,..., Cn$?" or "What are the taxonomic relationships among the concepts $C,C1,...,Cn$?"

4.2.2 Some Test-Generation Rules.

We begin with goal 7 – to test the causal knowledge structure of a student. Table 1 presents a test-generation rule which generates three separate tests. (Notice that this rule has two free variables X and Y. At this moment, we do not attempt to determine the values of X and Y, because their choices depend on information of individual students in their student models. We will turn to this issue in the next section.)

$Test_1$ asks a student whether $C_1, ...,C_n$ are the direct causes of C. This kind of test conveys more information than $test_2$, because, at least, all the subconcepts are given in

---

[6] To save space, we will only present a few test-generation rules spanning all the formulated testing goals, and explain their meanings, respectively.

Table 1. A test-generation rule which generates three separate tests

---

Rule-ID: #1
Testing Goal: Goal 7
Premises:
      taught-concepts(C, C_1, ...,C_n), and   directly-caused-by (C; C_1, ...,C_n)
Variable declaration:
      $\varnothing \neq X \subset \{C_1, ...,C_n\}$;$\{C_1, ...,C_n\} \subset Y \subseteq ©$
Test generation:
      $Test_1$: Ask if directly-caused-by (C; C_1, ..., C_n)
      $Test_2$: Ask what are the direct causes of C
      $Test_3$: Ask if directly-caused-by(C; X)
      $Test_4$: Ask if directly-caused-by(C; Y)

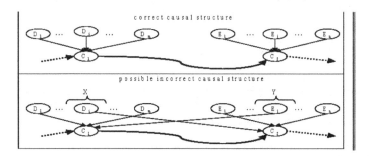

Fig. 1. A complicated causal structure

the test. Selecting a *proper* subset of $\{C_1, ...,C_n\}$, i.e. X, test$_3$ asks the student whether C is directly caused *only* by a concept in X. If the student answers yes, he or she makes an error of omission, since X is only a proper subset of all the possible causes $\{C_1, ..., C_n\}$. In this sense, we call A similar explanation applies to test$_4$.

Table 2. Another test-generation rule for goal 7

Rule-ID: #2
Testing Goal: Goal 7
Premises:
      taught-concepts(C_1, C_2), and taught-concepts(D_1, ..., D_m), and
      taught-concepts(E_1, ..., E_n), and caused-by(C_2; C_1), and
      directly-caused-by(C_1; D_1, ...D_m), and directly-caused-by(C_1; E_1, ...E_n), and caused-by(C'_2, C_3)
Variable declaration:
$U \subset \{D_1, ...,D_m\}$, and $V \subset \{E_1, ...,E_n\}$;$X = V \cup \{D_1, ...,D_m\}\backslash U$;$Y = U \cup \{E_1, ...,E_m\}\backslash V$
Test generation:
      $Test_1$: ask if directly-caused-by(C_1; X)
      $Test_2$: ask if directly-caused-by(C_2; Y)

Table 2 presents another test-generation rule for goal 7. This rule is more complicated because it generates tests to check whether a student has mastered a complicated causal structure of concepts as illustrated in fig.1. When two causally related concepts have separate direct causes (see the upper part of fig.1), a student may tend to have difficulty in placing the concepts in a right causal order, thus leading to errors of insertion and substitution. A similar argument applies to rule 3 in table 3.

Table 3. A similar argument applies to rule 3

Rule-ID: #3
Testing Goal: Goal 6
Premises:
    taught-concepts(C, D, C_1, ...,C_n, D_1,...,D_n), and   temporally-before(C; C_1, ...,C_m), and temporally-coexist(D; D_1, ...,D_n)
Variable declaration:
    $\varnothing \neq X \subset \{C_1, ...,C_n\}$, and $\{C_1, ...,C_n\} \subset Y \subseteq ©$
Test generation:
    $Test_1$: Ask if temporally-before(C; C_1, ...,C_n)
    $Test_2$: Ask if temporally-coexist(D; D_1, ...,D_n)
    $Test_3$: Ask if temporally-before(C; X)
    $Test_4$: Ask if temporally-coexist(C; Y)

Table 4. Depicts a test-generation rule for goal 5

Rule-ID: #4
Testing Goal: Goal 5
Premises:
taught-concept-attributes(C, A_1, ..., A_n), and attribute-value-is(C, A_i, V_i)
Variable declaration:
$\varnothing \neq X \subset \{A_1, ..., A_n\}$, and $\{A_1, ..., A_n\} \subset Y \subseteq ©$ $1 \leq i \leq n i \neq j$
Test generation:
    $Test_1$: Ask if own-attributes(C; A_1, ..., A_n)
    $Test_2$: Ask if own-attributes(C; X)
    $Test_3$: Ask if own-attributes(C; Y)
    $Test_4$: Ask if own-essential-attributes(C_i; X)
    $Test_5$: Ask if own-essential-attributes(C_i; Y)
    $Test_6$: Ask what is the value of A_i

Table 4 depicts a test-generation rule for goal 5. Although the generated tests are simple, they are not trivial at all. For example, asking a student which attribute is an essential one for a concept is not trivial: The student has to do a lot of reasoning in order to single out essential properties of the concept from other non-essential properties.

To better understand a domain conceptual model, it is important for a student to grasp the differences among different concepts. Rule #5 in table 5 aims to test, through some essential attribute, whether a student has really learned differences between two concepts.

Table 5. Test whether a student has really learned differences between two concepts

Rule-ID: #5
Testing Goal: Goal 4
Premises:
 taught-concepts(C_1, C_2); taught-attribute(A_1, ..., A_n)
 essential-attributes-difference(C_1, C_2; A_1, ..., A_n)
Variable declaration:
 $j \in \{1,...,n\}$
Test generation:
 Test$_1$: Ask if essential-attribute-difference(C_1,C_2; A_j)

It is sometimes difficult for a student to master all integral substance of a complicated concept. For example, after the concept *dioxyline phosphate* is taught to a medicine student, the student is expected to know all the substance of dioxyline phosphate. A similar argument applies to rule #6 in table 6.

Table 6. A similar argument applies to rule #6

Rule-ID: #6
Testing Goal: Goal 2
Premises:
taught-concepts($C,C_1,...,C_n$), and structurally-partitioned-into($C, C_1,...,C_n$)
Variable declaration:
 $\varnothing \neq X \subset \{C_1, ...,C_n\}$, and $\{C_1, ...,C_n\} \subset Y \subseteq ©$
Test generation:
 Test$_1$: Ask if structurally-partitioned-into(C; C_1, ...,C_n)
 Test$_2$: Ask if structurally-partitioned-into(C; X)
 Test$_3$: Ask if structurally-partitioned-into(C; Y)

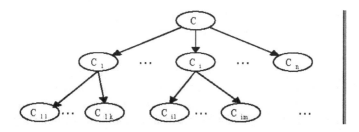

Fig. 2. A multi-level conceptual taxonomy

The test-generation rule in table 7 generates three separate tests to check whether a student has mastered a single-level conceptual taxonomy for a *root concept* C (see fig. 2), whereas table 8 gives a test-generation rule for testing whether a student masters a multi-level taxonomy of numerous learned concepts.

Table 7. Check whether a student has mastered a single-level conceptual taxonomy

---

Rule-ID: #7
Testing Goal: Goal 1
Premises:
> taught-concepts(C, C_1, ...,C_n), and   classified-into(C; C_1, ...,C_n)

Variable declaration:
> $\varnothing \neq X \subset \{C_1, ...,C_n\}$, and $\{C_1, ...,C_n\} \subset Y \subseteq ©$

Test generation:
> $Test_1$: Ask if classified-into(C; C_1, ...,C_n)
> $Test_2$: Ask if classified-into(C; X)
> $Test_3$: Ask if classified-into(C; Y)

Table 8. Test whether a student masters a multi-level taxonomy of numerous learned concepts

---

Rule-ID: #8
Testing Goal: Goal 1
Premises:
> taught-concepts(C, C_i, C_{ij}), and classified-into(C_i; C_{i1}, ...,C_{ik})

Variable declaration:
> $\varnothing \neq X \subset \{C_1, ...,C_n\}$, and $\{C_1, ...,C_n\} \subset Y \subseteq ©$

Test generation:
> $Test_1$: ask if classified-into(C_i; C_{i1}, ...,C_{ik})
> $Test_2$: ask what the complete taxonomy of C.

A multi-level taxonomy of domain concepts is illustrated in fig.2. It is usually a big challenge for both average and good students to understand and memorize such a complex structure. This is especially true when sibling subconcepts are similar or causally related. Therefore, it is worth to test whether a student makes errors of insertion and substitution, as done by rule #8.

5 Individualized Testing

As one may have noticed that, a test-generation rule is 'under-specified': We have not constrained scopes of variables X, Y, Z, etc., nor the applicability conditions of generated tests (e.g. which test is best for which type of student?). All this is relevant to characteristics of a student that is modeled in a so-called *student model* .[7].

In this paper, we assume that a student model has three important statistics, corresponding to the three modes of error – omission, insertion and substitution. Notice that some classes of student models, e.g. *overlay model*, may not have such statistics, but fortunately using our framework to encode these statistics into a student model is

---

[7] A full discussion of student modeling is out of the scope of this paper. See [King, 1998] for an overview of student modeling issues and methods.

not difficult. In fact, the tests generated by the test-generation rules play an important role in analyzing and updating a student's model, as will be seen below.

For illustration, let's individualize rule #1 in table 1. The same analysis applies to all other test-generation rules as well.

First, for a *good* student who makes little errors, test$_2$ appears more reasonable. This type of test is actually both a challenge to and a reinforcement of the student's memory. Moreover, we believe that test$_1$ is not appropriate for the (good) student, just because it conveys more *reminding* information.

Second, for a student who tends to make errors of omission and substitution[8], it is sensible to apply test$_1$ and test$_4$ to the student, because this *type* of test has more information, and thus reminds the student of the correct conceptual structure of concepts.

Finally, for a student who tends to make errors of insertion and substitution, both test$_1$ and test$_3$ are appropriate. The reason for using test$_3$ is that this type of test would lead the student to constrain the scope of direct causes of a concept.

In summary, when we consider a student's characteristics in test generation and selection, the testing outcome is much sensible and thus the whole process of automated intelligent tutoring is more individualized.

6 Conclusion

In this paper, we presented a generic framework for automating one of the key components in an ITS, i.e. post-lesson test generation. The core of the framework is a domain conceptual model, and a collection of testing goals, and a collection of test-generation rules. We believe that this effort can reduce the labor in ITS development considerably.

The testing goals are formulated on the basis of a thorough understanding of a domain conceptual structure, and therefore they are objective. Test-generation rules are well justified by the testing goals, and thus the generated tests should be objective as well.

The proposed framework aims to generate tests to detect possible errors in a student's conceptual model. In other words, the framework acts as an 'error-detector'. Two related issues are remaining on our future research agenda. First, we will consider the problem of abducing possible cognitive causes for the detected errors, and use these causes to adjust the instruction process. Second, we will extend our framework to generate tests to check a student's overall domain conceptual model in a synthetic manner.

Acknowledgements

This work is supported by the Natural Science Foundation (grant nos. 60573010, 60273019, 60496326, 60573063, and 60573064), and the National 973 Programme (grants no. 2003CB317008 and G1999032701).

---

[8] Recall that an error of substitution is not primitive.

References

1. Allen, J. Toward a General Theory of Action and Time. Artificial Intelligence, vol. 23(2): 123-154. 1984.
2. Cao, C.: Student Belief System and Its Application in Intelligent Tutoring. Proceedings of the 6th National Joint Conference on Artificial Intelligence, 2000.
3. Cao,C.: Expert-oriented Knowledge Acquisition. China Science Press, Beijing. 1998.
4. Beck, J., M.Stern and E.Haugsjaa: Applications of AI in Education. ACM Crossroads Article. 1996.
5. Katz, S., A.Lesgold, E.Gary, M.Gordin and L.Greenberg: Self-adjusting Curriculum Planning in Sherlock-II. Lecture Notes in Computer Science, vol. 602, 343-355. 1992.
6. King, R.: Classification of Student Modeling Approaches for Intelligent Tutoring. Tech Report MSSU-COE-ERC-98-4, Mississipi State University. 1998.
7. Lu,R., C.Cao, Y.Chen, et al.: A PNLU Approach to ICAI System Generation. Science in China (Series A), vol.38, 1-10. 1996.
8. Tang S. and Cao C.: A Rule-Based Approach to Modeling Student's Cognitive State In Intelligent Tutoring Systems. Computer Science and Technology in New Century, ICYCS,1228-1230, 2001
9. Senders, J. and N.Moray, Human Error: Cause, Prediction and Reduction. Lawrence Erlbaum Associates, Hillsdale, NJ. 1991.
10. Wiemer-Hastings, P., A.Graesser and D.Harter: The Tutoring Research Group: The Foundation and Architecture of Autotutor. Lecture Notes in Computer Science, vol.1452, 334-343. 1998.
11. Tang S.: Researches of Teaching Strategy based on domain-specific ontology. Computer Engineering and Applications, vol. 40(2),194-197,2004
12. Julika Siemer. and Marios C.: A comprehensive method for the evaluation of complete intelligent tutoring system. Decision Support Systems,22(1998)85-102
13. Evaluating and Improving Educational Material and Tutoring Aspects of Distance Learning Systems. Christos Pierrakeas, and Michalis Xenos and Panayiotis Pintelas, Studies in Educational Evaluation 29 (2003) 335-349.
14. Miguel Nussbaum, Ricardo Rosas, Isabel Peirano, and Francisco CaÂ rdenas, Development of intelligent tutoring systems using knowledge structures. Computers & Education 36 (2001) 15-32

A Study on Knowledge Creation Support in a Japanese Research Institute*

Jing Tian[1], Andrzej P. Wierzbicki[1,2], Hongtao Ren[1], and Yoshiteru Nakamori[1]

[1] School of Knowledge Science,
Japan Advanced Institute of Science and Technology (JAIST)
Asahidai 1-1, Nomi, Ishikawa 923-1292, Japan
{jtian, andrzej, hongtao, nakamori}@jaist.ac.jp
[2] National Institute of Telecommunications,
Szachowa 11, 04-894 Warsaw, Poland

Abstract. With the knowledge civilization development, the creation of knowledge and technology attracts an increasing interest in scientific research and practice. Universities and research institutes play a vital role in creating and transmitting scientific knowledge. Thus, enhancing the scientific knowledge creation in academia is a significant issue. In the paper, we investigate what aspects of knowledge creation processes in academic research we should support in particular. A questionnaire-based survey was conducted in a Japanese research institute (JAIST). By using a multiple criteria formulation and reference point method, we extract useful information and knowledge from the data base of survey results. Most critical and important problems are discovered by the negative and positive evaluations with respect to the conditions of scientific creativity. The results of the investigation give also valuable information for research and development management in universities and research organizations.

Keywords: Scientific knowledge creation, questionnaire-based survey, creativity support.

1 Introduction

Knowledge discovering, possession, handling and enhancement seem to become an issue of increasing importance and actuality in contemporary society. In order to sustain competitive competencies, new knowledge and technologies are faster required by individual, organizations, even nations. Thus, the creation of knowledge and technology requires increasing attention in scientific research and practice.

Universities and research institutes play a vital role in creating and transmitting scientific knowledge, which is the fundamental source and driver for society progress and development. Thus, enhancing the scientific knowledge creation in academia is a quite significant issue.

---

* The research is supported by 21st COE (Center of Excellence) Program "Technology Creation Based on Knowledge Science" of JAIST, funded by Ministry of Education, Culture, Sports, Science and Technology (MEXT, Japan).

J. Lang, F. Lin, and J. Wang (Eds.): KSEM 2006, LNAI 4092, pp. 405–417, 2006.
© Springer-Verlag Berlin Heidelberg 2006

Creation, at a certain point, means a new combination of different data, information, knowledge or wisdom [1]. Usually, new knowledge is created through interactions between tacit and explicit knowledge [2]. The capability of the interaction depends on the individual scientists as well as the context. If the appropriate methods or techniques are used to support the process of scientific research, it is possible to raise the performance of the creativity. At the School of Knowledge Science of JAIST (Japan Advanced Institute of Science and Technology), we are conducting research related to systems and environment for supporting knowledge management and creation in academic. Some special and diverse requirements as well as hidden obstructions have been discovered [3], while a systems-thinking framework for knowledge management in scientific laboratories was proposed [4]. However, as discussed in the concept of *Creative Space* [5], knowledge creation processes are extremely diversified and rich. How should we choose what creativity support should be considered in particular?

The way we chose as a possible answer is to concentrate first on the variety of knowledge creation theories, then analyze possible creativity processes, then select creative transitions that are judged most important for these processes and finally develop creativity support. As mentioned in Nakamori [6], "it is vital to begin to continuously and systematically develop the theory of technology creation, verifying the theory in scientific laboratories, and improving the theory by feedback from practice".

In the work described here, we focus on supporting the creative process of academic research in its *normal* character [7]. In order to investigate what aspects of knowledge creation processes we should support in particular, we conduct a survey in a Japanese scientific research institute (JAIST) based on characterizing creativity processes [8]. By using *a family of achievement functions* in the *reference point approach*, we extract useful information and knowledge from the data base of survey results. Most critical and important problems are discovered by the negative and positive evaluations with respect to the conditions of scientific creativity. Although the particular results are limited naturally to the context of JAIST, we believe that the methods proposed and questions asked have a more general validity.

The rest of this paper is organized as follows. Section 2 shortly recalls a *Triple Helix* theory and other spirals of knowledge creation processes. Section 3 is an overview of the survey, its goals, scope, study assumption and instrument. A detailed analysis method and survey findings are presented in Section 4. Section 5 contains brief concluding remarks.

2 Knowledge Creation Processes

Until the last decade of the 20th century we could distinguish two main streams, two schools of thinking how knowledge is created [9]. The first stream maintained that knowledge creation is essentially different activity than knowledge validation and verification – thus distinguishing *the context of discovery* from *the context of verification*. The second stream kept to the old interpretations of science as a result of induction and refused to see creative acts as irrational.

However, precisely these subconscious or unconscious aspects, the concepts of tacit knowledge, of intuition and of group collaboration resulted since the last decade of 20th century in quite new approaches to knowledge creation. The first of such approaches is *Shinayakana Systems Approach* [10]. Influenced by the soft and critical systems tradition, it specifies a set of principles for knowledge and technology creation. Parallel, in management science, another approach, SECI spiral, was developed by Nonaka and Takeuchi [2]. It is renowned with a process-like, algorithmic principle of organizational knowledge creation (*Socialization-Externalization-Combination-Internalization*). Furthermore, a systemic and process-like method to knowledge creation called *I-System* [11] was developed based on *Shinayakana Systems Approach.* Five ontological elements of this system are *Intervention* (problem and requirement perspective), *Intelligence* (public knowledge and scientific dimension), *Involvement* (social motivation), *Imagination* (creative dimension), and *Integration* (synthesized knowledge). All transitions between diverse dimensions of creative space are free according to individual needs.

Many other theories of creating knowledge for the needs of today and tomorrow were developed. We might call them *micro-theories of knowledge creation* [5], as distinct from the philosophical theories of knowledge creation on the long term, historical macro-scale that usually, however, do not help in current knowledge creation. All such micro-theories take into account the tacit, intuitive, emotional, even mythical aspects of knowledge. Many of them can be represented in the form of spirals of knowledge creation processes, describing the interplay between tacit and explicit or intuitive and rational knowledge, such as in *SECI spiral.*

In Wierzbicki and Nakamori [5], an integration and synthesis of such micro-theories of knowledge creation takes the form of so-called *Creative Space* – a network-like model of diverse creative processes with many nodes and transitions between them, starting from a generalization of the *SECI Spiral.* Many spirals of knowledge creation can be represented as processes in *Creative Space;* one of interesting observations is that we should distinguish between group-based, industrial *organizational knowledge creation processes* – such as the *SECI Spiral,* or its Occidental counterpart called *OPEC Spiral* [12], or an older and well known organizational process called *brainstorming* that can be also represented as a *DCCV Spiral* [13] –as opposed to *academic knowledge creation processes,* describing how knowledge is normally created in academia and research institutions.

For the latter type, three processes of normal knowledge creation in academia are described in Wierzbicki and Nakamori [5]: *hermeneutics* (gathering scientific information and knowledge from literature, web and other sources and reflecting on these materials), represented as the *EAIR (Enlightenment-Analysis-Immersion-Reflection) Spiral; debate* (discussing in a group research under way), represented as the *EDIS (Enlightenment-Debate-Immersion-Selection) Spiral; experiment* (testing ideas and hypotheses by experimental research), represented as the *EEIS (Enlightenment-Experiment-Interpretation-Selection) Spiral.* Since all of these spirals begin with having an idea, called the *Enlightenment* (*illumination, aha, eureka*) effect, they can be combined into a *Triple Helix of normal knowledge creation,* typical for academic work, see Fig. 1.

The triangles in Fig. 1 indicate the phenomenon *Enlightenment* – generating an idea, a transition from individual intuition to individual rationality, analyzed in

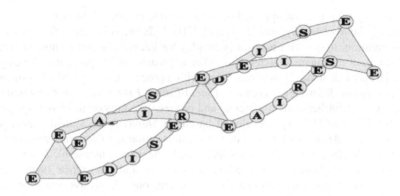

Fig. 1. The *Triple Helix* of normal academic knowledge creation

Wierzbicki and Nakamori [5] in detail. Since this is a joint transition to all three spirals, it can be used for switching between these spirals or for performing them in parallel.

The humanistic concept of *hermeneutics* (interpreting texts) is used here to describe the most basic activity for any research – that of gathering from outside sources relevant information and knowledge, called here *research materials,* interpreting them and reflecting on them. A full cycle of the *EAIR Spiral* consists of: *Enlightenment,* having a research idea, then following it with ideas where and how to find research materials; *Analysis,* which is a rational analysis of the research materials; *hermeneutic Immersion,* which means some time necessary to absorb the results of analysis into individual intuitive perception of the object of study; *Reflection,* which denotes intuitive preparation of the resulting new ideas. *Hermeneutic EAIR* is the most individual research spiral, but its importance should be well understood even in fully organizational, industrial group-based research. No knowledge is lost during all these transitions and each transition can add new perspectives, ideas, or insights, contributing to a deeper enlightenment on the next process repetition. Thus, this process guarantees knowledge creation, in smaller or bigger steps, depending on the situation.

Another, *intersubjective EDIS Spiral* describes also one of the most fundamental and well known processes of normal knowledge creation in academia: after having an idea due to the *Enlightenment* phenomenon, an individual researcher might want to check it intersubjectively through *Debate*. Scientific debate actually has two layers: one is verbal and rational, but after some time for reflection we also derive intuitive conclusions from this debate. This is the extremely important and in fact difficult transition called *Immersion* (of the results of debate in group intuition); it occurs as a transition from *group rationality* to *group intuition*. An individual researcher does not necessarily accept all the results of *group intuition;* she or he makes his own *Selection* in the transition from *group intuition* to *individual intuition*. This process can again proceed repetitively, and thus can be described as a spiral; again, knowledge can be only increased during each transition.

However, academic knowledge creation is not only hermeneutic and intersubjective; in many disciplines it requires also experimental research. This is described by a corresponding *experimental EEIS Spiral* that also starts with the transition *Enlightenment,* this time indicating the idea of an experiment, but is followed by *Experiment* performing the actual experimental work, then by *Interpretation* of the experimental results reaching into intuitive experimental experience of the researcher, finally *Selection* of ideas to stimulate a new *Enlightenment.* This cycle can be repeated as many times as needed, but usually requires support in experiment planning, reporting, etc.

These three spirals contained in the *Triple Helix* are separate, not a part of one larger spiral, because we can perform them not only parallel, but also separately. For example, research in humanities (history, literature, etc.) concentrates on *Hermeneutics;* but also other sciences, even technology creation, need hermeneutic reflection and interpretation of written scientific literature. These three spirals do not exhaustively describe all what happens in academic knowledge creation, but we might ask several questions.

Can we *falsify* the *Triple Helix* theory, see [14]? Yes, if we found an example of a university where knowledge creation proceeds without reading and interpreting scientific literature, experimenting or debating, or proceeds using only rational, not intuitive and emotional aspects of knowledge creation – which, we believe, is barely possible. But we can ask also a question that can be researched: *do these spirals describe the most essential elements of academic research?* On the one hand, gathering and interpreting information and knowledge, debating and experimenting are no doubt essential; on the other hand, it is always good to test such conclusions by a survey of opinions. Since these spirals are individually oriented (e.g., the motivation for and the actual research on preparing a doctoral thesis is mostly individual), even if a university and a laboratory does support them, we can test their importance by asking about individual opinions of researchers.

3   A Survey of Scientific Creativity Support

To answer the questions proposed above, we performed a questionnaire-based survey in JAIST in order to measure what aspects of knowledge creation processes are evaluated as either most critical or most important by responders.

With respect to the analyses of the *Triple Helix* theory of normal academic knowledge creation, the questionnaire should concentrate on selected four main topics, i.e. *Enlightenment* (generating an idea), *Hermeneutics* (gathering scientific information and knowledge from diverse sources and reflecting on the materials; represented as *Analysis* and *Reflection*), *Debate* (discussing the idea in a group research under way), *Experiment* (testing idea by experimental research); but the theory of *I-System* suggests also fifth topic, *Research Planning.*

A long questionnaire was prepared corresponding to above five topics; it consisted of total of 48 questions, organized in five parts. The questions were of three types. The first type was *assessment questions,* assessing the situation between students and at the university; the *most critical* questions of this type might be selected as those that correspond *worst* to a given reference profile. The second type was *importance questions,* assessing importance of a given subject; the *most important* questions might be considered as those that correspond *best* to a reference profile. For those two types of questions, responders were required to tick appropriate responses showing a preference ranking. The third type was *controlling questions,* testing the answers to the first two types by indirect questioning revealing responder attitudes or asking for a detailed explanation. The multiple choice questions were given and phrased usually with a single option or a single option with an "others- please specify" possibility. The entire questionnaire consisted of:

- Part one: Conditions for gathering scientific materials and ideas, including 6 assessment questions and 2 controlling questions;
- Part two: Conditions for experimental work, including 3 assessment questions, 5 importance questions and 2 controlling questions;
- Part three: Conditions for discussing ideas and research results, including 17 assessment questions;
- Part four: Conditions for creating ideas; including 3 assessment questions and 4 controlling questions;
- Part five: Conditions for planning research, including 3 assessment questions and 3 controlling questions.

The respondents of this survey included all graduate students (preparing for a master or doctoral degree), post doctors and research associates/assistants. The survey base included demographic information about the responders' affiliation (three schools), status, and nationality (Japanese and foreign), which will help us subdivide the responders.

The initial questionnaire was in English. Because most of responders are Japanese, we also prepared a Japanese version. Both of them were published on the intranet. The responders were motivated to take the questionnaire seriously by a competitive award (a trip to an international conference for most critical and detailed response). A total of 143 responses were received, which constituted about 14% response rate, not bad for such a detailed questionnaire.

4 Analysis of Survey Results

The initial analysis of the survey answers resulted in several ideas on the method of evaluating questionnaires results. These results could be considered as a data base from which a user (a dean, manager, decision maker, etc., - a person using this result) could get support in his/her work. For this, we must come up with a way of extracting knowledge from such a data base and finding most important options between all these questions and types of responders. A natural continuation of this idea is that *the extracted knowledge must respond to the preferences of the user*, as in any decision support system. We express these preferences in the form of *reference distribution* of outcomes of the survey that the user would consider satisfactory. We aggregate the results – any *actual distribution* of outcomes of the survey concerning a given question and a given type (nationality, school, status) of responders – by using a family of *achievement functions* in the *reference point approach*, proposed by Wierzbicki [15], since then developed by many researchers and summarized in the book [16]. We slightly extend the family of achievement functions for the purpose of evaluating the results of the survey and extracting knowledge from them. The particular process of extracting knowledge from the survey results could be described as follows:

1) The user specifies what he would consider as good results, satisfactory for him, by specifying *a reference distribution of results* that he considers good enough, in a sense *aspiration distribution.* He might also specify, if he wishes, some *parameters of the achievement function.* In our research, several *synthetic users* were specified and some standard values of these parameters were used.

2) Then, a special software system was developed for computing the *achievement degrees* – the values of the achievement function – for all questions, all total or partial (for all types of responders) distributions.

3) Then the system orders the questions (first for total distributions of answers, then also for various types of distributions) according to the achievement degrees (starting with the worst), thus preparing *a ranking list of questions* starting with the most critical ones. At the top of the list the user thus obtains the worst assessed by responders (either by all or by a given type or responders); he should turn his attention mostly to them. At the bottom of the list the user obtains the questions where the answers of responders were the best from the perspective of his requirements. *The ranking list of questions represents the knowledge extracted from the data base,* relative to user preferences expressed in the form of reference distribution.

4) Finally, we analyze all such results qualitatively and derive the conclusions.

4.1 Reference Profiles and Achievement Functions

In our questionnaire, all questions of first two types – assessment questions and importance questions – allowed five options of answers, variously called but signifying similar opinions: "very good – good – average – bad – very bad" or "very important – important – indifferent – not important – negatively important". Thus, answers to all questions of first two types can be evaluated on a common scale, as a percentage distribution of answers VG – G – A – B – VB, while a different wording of the answers would be appropriately interpreted. Let us denote by y_i, $i \epsilon I = \{vg, g, a, b, vb\}$, the values of quality indicators. Then we denote by y_{ijk} the percentage of responses i ($i \epsilon I = \{vg, g, a, b, vb\}$) to the question number $j \epsilon J$ (J is the set of all questions of first two types which can be evaluated in the way as assumed here), for the type of responders $k \epsilon K$ (K is the set of all types of responders; by $k = t$ we shall denote the totality of responders). Thus, the sum $\Sigma_{i \epsilon I} y_{ijk} = 100\%$ for all $j \epsilon J$ and $k \epsilon K$. The sequence $\{y_{ijk}\}_{i \epsilon I} = \mathbf{y}_{jk}$ is called *the distribution* of answers to the question j for the type k of responders.

In this application, answers *VG* and *G* were considered as positive outcomes (quality indicators that should be maximized), while *VB* and *B*, but also *A*, were all considered as negative outcomes (quality indicators to be minimized; in the case of "average" answer *A*, it means that too many responders in this category indicate some problem related to the corresponding question). Thus we considered $i \epsilon G$ ($G = \{vg, g\}$) as positive outcomes and $i \epsilon B$ ($B = \{a, b, vb\}$) as negative outcomes.

We denote by $\mathbf{r} = \{r_i\}_{i \epsilon I}$ the *reference distribution* – a distribution of outcomes that user considers satisfactorily good. We do not assume here that user should define the

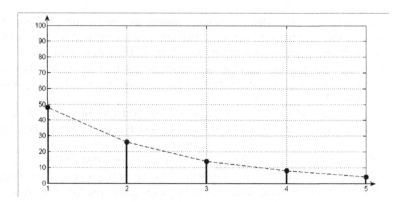

Fig. 2. An example of a reference distribution

reference distribution separately for different questions j and types of responders k, he can adapt the reference distribution to his needs by changing it in an interactive analysis of results. An example of a reference distribution is given below in Fig. 2.

With the vector of quality indicators y_{jk} and the reference profile or distribution r, the scalar evaluation or *achievement index* is $s_j = \sigma(y_j, r, \alpha)$, where σ is the achievement function and α denotes additional parameters of this function.

For example, the most basic achievement function [16], after adapting it to our case, has the form:

$$\sigma_1(y_j, r, \varepsilon) = min_{i=1,...k}\,(y_{ijk} - r_i)\,sign_i + \varepsilon \sum_{i=1,...k}(y_{ijk} - r_i)\,sign_i. \tag{1}$$

where $sign_i = +1$ if $i \epsilon G$ and $sign_i = -1$ if $i \epsilon B$ (means simply change the sign for bad outcomes) and ε is a small parameter, always smaller than 1 (we test $\varepsilon = 0.1; 0.2; 0.5$ in our research). The function (1) is increasing with the improvement of quality indicators, has value zero if all quality indicators equals their reference values, is positive if the quality indicators are better than their reference values (larger in maximized indicators, $i \epsilon G$, smaller in minimized indicators, $i \epsilon B$), and is negative if the quality indicators are worse than their reference values (smaller in maximized indicators, $i \epsilon G$, larger in minimized indicators, $i \epsilon B$). The achievement degree – the value of the achievement function – can be also measured in % and can be interpreted as the value of the smallest improvement of quality indicators over their reference values, slightly corrected by the sum of all improvements. This principle – improving the worst case first – might be interpreted as an application of the *theory of justice* of Rawls [17] to multiple criteria decision making.

The function (1) is only one member of a broad family of achievement functions [16]; all such functions preserve and approximately represent the partial order in multiple criteria space. This means that they are *strictly monotone* with respect to this order (strictly increase when a quality indicator vector is replaced by another, better in all components and strictly better with respect to the order – at least in one component). Moreover, their *level sets* (sets of points where the function values are greater than or equal to a given value) approximate *the positive cone* representing the partial order. Beside these theoretical properties, however, achievement functions can be diverse.

We introduce in this paper another achievement function, resulting from an adaptation of the *theory of regret* of Kahneman und Tversky [18]. This theory says that decision makers feel stronger regret for not achieving their aspirations than satisfaction from overachieving their aspirations. The function $\sigma_1(y_j,\ r,\ \varepsilon)$ described above has, in fact, such property, but it is expressed indirectly and must be shown by analyzing level sets of this function. But we can specify a similar achievement function by directly using the property suggested by the *theory of regret*:

$$\sigma_2(y_j, r, \delta) = (2/(k(1+\delta)))(\sum_{i=1,...k}((y_{ijk}-r_i)\,sign_i)_+ + \delta\sum_{i=1,...k}((y_{ijk}-r_i)\,sign_i).)\,. \quad (2)$$

where $(x)_+ = max(0,\ x)$ and $(x). = min(0,\ x)$ denote the positive and negative parts of a number x, respectively (if the number x is, e.g., negative, then its positive part is zero and the number is equal to its negative part, and vice versa), and the parameter δ is another example of parameters α: $\delta \geq 1$ is the *coefficient of regret*, in the case when $\delta = 1$ we have the simplest linear aggregation. The scaling coefficient $2/(k(1+\delta))$ is applied in order to obtain a similar to the function (1) scale of values of achievement indicators – in the simplest case when $\delta = 1$, this scaling coefficient is $1/k$, and the values of $\sigma_2(y_j,\ r,\ \delta)$ represent the average improvement of quality indicators over their reference values.

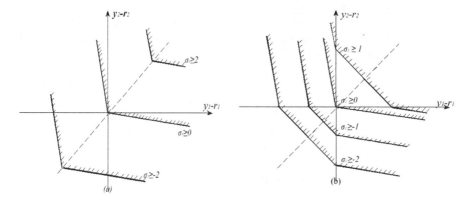

Fig. 3. Comparison of level sets of $\sigma_1(y_j,\ r,\ \varepsilon)$ (a) and $\sigma_2(y_j,\ r,\ \delta)$ (b)

The function $\sigma_2(y_j,\ r,\ \delta)$ belongs in fact to the same family of *piece-wise linear functions* as the function $\sigma_1(y_j,\ r,\ \varepsilon)$, but has slightly different level sets and is differently parameterized (the parameter δ has analogous effects as $1 + 1/\varepsilon$). In Fig. 3, the level sets of these two functions are compared for the simple case when $k = 2$, both quality indicators are maximized, $\delta = 6$ and $\varepsilon = 0.2$. In further sections, we shall compare the effects of using these functions for ranking units and data sets in a practical application.

4.2 Survey Result Analysis and Findings

A special software system was developed for computing the distributions of answers, defining and changing reference profile distributions, computing ranking lists of questions (with special exposure to a given number of the worst and the best ranked questions), repeating these computations for all or part of responders – e.g., for foreign students, or doctoral students, or students of a given School of JAIST, etc. For research reasons, beside the two achievement functions (1) and (2), four different types of reference profile distributions were compared by computing of the software system, specified in the Table 1. A special attention should be paid to:

1) The worst evaluated assessment questions of the first type, indicating some critical conditions for scientific creativity;
2) The best evaluated importance questions of the second type, indicating issues that are most important in the opinion of responders.

Table 1. Four different types of reference profile distributions

Name	Symbol	VG	G	A	B	VB
Regular	r_A	36%	28%	20%	12%	4%
Demanding	r_B	48%	26%	14%	8%	4%
Stepwise	r_C	42%	42%	7%	5%	4%
Average	r_D	21%	38%	22%	14%	5%

The reference distribution called *Average* (r_D) represents the actual average of percentages of answers for all questions (of the first and second type) and all responders. This distribution might be taken as the basic one, because it results from the experimental data and might be considered as independent from the preferences of the decision maker - although, theoretically, average aspirations result only in average, not necessarily interesting answers (actually, this theoretical conclusion was confirmed in practice, see later comments). Truly interesting results might correspond to more demanding aspirations, hence beside the average distribution we postulated *synthetic users* and considered three more demanding ones, which were characterized by the types of neutral reference distributions. The one called *Regular* (r_A) was almost linearly decreasing; the one called *Stepwise* (r_C) was almost uniform for positive and for negative outcomes; while the one called *Demanding* above (r_B) was almost hyperbolically decreasing and actually the most demanding.

It was found that changing the achievement function or the type of reference distribution does not essentially, qualitatively change the questions evaluated as worst, most critical; it influences, although slightly only, the best, most important or best provided for. In seven worst evaluated questions, almost all were consistently repeated independently of these changes; thus, we can count them as the most critical questions of the first type. These are questions related to not good enough situations concerning:

1) Because of language reasons, difficulty in discussing research questions with colleagues from other countries;
2) Easiness of sharing tacit knowledge;
3) Critical feedback, questions and suggestions in group discussions;
4) Organizing and planning research activities;
5) Preparing presentations for seminars and conferences;

6) Designing and planning experiments;
7) Generating new ideas and research concepts.

Most of these results actually corresponds to some elements of the three spirals of normal academic knowledge creation: *Intersubjective EDIS Spiral* – items 2), 3) and 5); *Experimental EEIS Spiral* – item 6); *Hermeneutic EAIR Spiral* (as well as the earlier mentioned spirals) – item 7). However, they also stress the importance of another spiral: *Roadmapping (I-System) Spiral* [19] of planning knowledge creation processes – item 4).

The importance of these spirals is also stressed by the positive evaluation of the importance of other elements of these spirals in response to questions of the second type. Among the seven best evaluated questions, the following questions of the second type were consistently (independently of the changes of achievement function form or reference profile) listed as most important:

1) Learning and training how to do experiments;
2) Help and guidance from the supervisor and colleagues;
3) Frequent communication of the group.

Besides the qualitative analysis of the assessment and importance questions, we also summarized the results of the third type questions, i.e. *controlling questions*. The indirect questioning revealed responders' attitudes and detailed explanation corresponding to the answers of the first two types' questions. For instance, concerning the seventh one of the most critical questions – "Generating new ideas and research concepts", when we asked if responders felt there were not good enough conditions for creating and finding new idea, what could be improved? The large numbers of the answers focused on "better discussions and idea exchange in the group", "rich research reference and scientific literature" and "better access to the research program". When we asked why you felt you are not efficient (also belong to an aggregation *B*) in generating new ideas and research concepts, the responses showed they did not know how to evaluate their works and then improve it, and they thought they did not catch the efficient method of research. Moreover, we asked what was perceived as the most important factor to promote finding and creating new ideas. We found the responders thought "communication and discussion with other researchers" and "catch the research trends in time" were most important factors.

We gathered all suggestions and comments concerning the support of the creativity environment as well as complains about not enough support, they concentrated on:

1) Plentiful information and knowledge source;
2) Training and guiding on research method and experiment skill;
3) Communication and discussion with other researchers either from a same lab or from the different labs, different subjects, or other institutes.

The analysis results of controlling questions emphasized the findings from assessment and importance questions, and also confirmed some elements of the three spiral of normal academic knowledge creation: items 1) and 3) correspond to *EDIS Spiral*; item 2) corresponds to *EAIR* and *EEIS Spiral*. In addition, item 2) also reflected on *Roadmapping (I-System) Spiral* in a certain extent, since researchers should know how they can reach their research targets [19]. However, according to Popper [14], no amount of empirical evidence can finally confirm any theory, hence such confirmation is always partial. Moreover, we used a novel type of questionnaire and a novel method of evaluation of obtained results when testing the significance of a novel theory; naturally, it is necessary to repeat and investigate in more detail such tests in future.

Beside a partial empirical confirmation of the essential character of the three spirals of the *Triple Helix* of normal academic knowledge creation and the conclusion about the importance of the fourth *I-System Roadmapping Spiral*, the results of the investigation give also valuable information for university management: what aspects of knowledge creation processes should be improved.

One subject is the language barrier: English-speaking seminars should be much more frequently used in JAIST, Japanese students should be encouraged to use English language more frequently. Another subject relates to encouraging and teaching methods of critical debate at seminars, or to teaching how to plan generally research activities and in particular how to plan experiments. The help in preparation of presentations at seminars and conferences already functions quite well in JAIST, but perhaps it should be intensified even further.

6 Conclusion

This study focused on the process of academic knowledge creation and explored which aspects of this process should be addressed when developing creativity support to enhance knowledge creation and research management. A questionnaire-based survey was conducted to investigate the conditions for scientific creativity in a Japanese scientific research institute (JAIST). We used a multiple criteria formulation and reference profiles for result analysis and knowledge acquisition from complex data sets and got the promising results. The seven most critical questions and three most important questions were evaluated by responders with respect to academic knowledge creation process. The suggestions and comments summarized from controlling questions also helped us in considering what elements should be included in creativity support. We hope our experience can be widely used for reference in research and development management in universities, research organizations and companies.

Other conclusion from this study is a partial empirical confirmation of the essential importance of the three spirals of normal academic knowledge creation contained in the *Triple Helix*: the *Intersubjective EDIS Spiral*, the *Experimental EEIS Spiral*, and the *Hermeneutic EAIR Spiral*. The research stresses also the importance of the *Roadmapping (I-System) Spiral* of planning knowledge creation processes. Although the results are limited naturally to the context of the research institute investigated (JAIST), we believe that the methods proposed and questions asked have a more general validity.

References

1. Nakamori, Y.: Introduction to a COE Program at JAIST. Proceedings of International Forum 'Technology Creation Based on Knowledge Science: Theory and Practice', Nov. 10-12, JAIST, Japan, pp. 1-4, 2004.

2. Nonaka, I., and Takeuchi, H.: The Knowledge-Creating Company: How Japanese Companies Create the Dynamics of Innovation. Oxford University Press, New York, 1995.
3. Tian, J., Nakamori, Y., Xiang, J. and Futatsugi, K.: Knowledge Management in Academia: Survey, Analysis and Perspective. International Journal of Management and Decision Making, to appear on Vol. 7, No. 2/3, 2006, pp.275–294.
4. Tian, J. and Nakamori, Y.: Knowledge Management in Scientific Laboratories: a Survey-based Study of a Research Institute. Proceeding of the Second International Symposium on Knowledge Management for Strategic Creation of Technology, Nov. 14-17, Kobe, Japan, pp. 19-26, 2005.
5. Wierzbicki, A.P. and Nakamori Y.: Creative Space: Models of Creative Processes for the Knowledge Civilization Age. Springer Verlag, Berlin-Heidelberg 2006.
6. Nakamori, Y.: Technology Creation Based on Knowledge Science. Proceedings of the First International Symposium on Knowledge Management for Strategic Creation of Technology, JAIST, Japan, pp.1-10, 2004.
7. Kuhn T.S.: The structure of scientific revolutions. Chicago University Press, Chicago 1962
8. Wierzbicki, A.P., Tian, J. and Ren, H.: The Use of Reference Profiles and Multiple Criteria Evaluation in Knowledge Acquisition from Large Database. Submit to 4th US-European Workshop on Logistics and Supply Chain Management, June 8&9, 2006, University of Hamburg, Germany.
9. Wierzbicki, A.P. and Nakamori, Y.: Knowledge Creation and Integration: Creative Space and Creative Environments. Proceeding of the 38th Annual Hawaii International Conference of System Science (CD/ROW), Computer Society Press, 2005, 10 pages.
10. Nakamori Y. and Sawaragi Y.: Shinayakana Systems Approach in Environmental Management. Proceedings of 11th World Congress of International Federation of Automatic Control, Tallin. Pergamon Press, vol 5 pp 511-516, 1990.
11. Nakamori, Y.: Systems Methodology and Mathematical Models for Knowledge Management. Journal of Systems Science and Systems Engineering, Vol.12, No.1, pp49-72, 2003.
12. Gasson S.: The Management of Distributed Organizational Knowledge. In Sprague RJ (ed) Proceedings of the 37th Hawaii International Conference on Systems Sciences (CD/ROW). IEEE Computer Society Press, 2004.
13. Kunifuji S.: Creativity Support Systems in JAIST. Proceedings of JAIST Forum 2004: Technology Creation Based on Knowledge Science, pp 56-58, 2004.
14. Popper K.R.: Objective knowledge. Oxford University Press, Oxford 1972
15. Wierzbicki, A.P.: The Use of Reference Objectives in Multiobjective Optimization. in G. Fandel and T. Gal (eds), Multiple Criteria Decision Making: Theory and Applications, Vol. 177 of Lecture Notes in Economic and Mathematical Systems, Springer-Verlag, Berlin, Germany, 1988.
16. Wierzbicki, A.P., Makowski M. and Wessels J.: Model-Based Decision Support Methodology with Environmental Applications. Kluwer, Dordrecht 2000.
17. Rawls J.: A Theory of Justice. Belknap Press, Cambridge, Mass 1971.
18. Kahneman D. und Tversky A.: The Psychology of Preferences. Scientific American 246:150-173, 1982.
19. Ma, T., and Nakamori, Y.: Roadmapping and i-System for Supporting Scientific Research. Proceedings of the 5th International Symposium on Knowledge and Systems Sciences, JAIST, Japan, Nov. 10-12, 2004.

Identity Conditions for Ontological Analysis

Nwe Ni Tun and Satoshi Tojo

Japan Advanced Institute of Science and Technology
1-1 Asahidai, Nomi, Ishikawa 923-1292
{nitun, tojo}@jaist.ac.jp

Abstract. The role of ontologies is to provide a well-defined structure of domain knowledge that acts as the heart of any system of knowledge representation on that domain for the purposes of reasoning, knowledge sharing, and integration. Thus, it is essential to clarify the structure of knowledge in ontologies. In this paper, we discuss how ontology developers can define the identity conditions of classes explicitly, and can utilize them to develop structured taxonomies with adequate consistency. The background of this paper is OntoClean which is a domain independent methodology for ontology modeling using some philosophical notions. We exemplify the classification of sorts with necessary conceptual constraints. Then, we provide an explicit, simplified, and practical ontological analysis system regarding our subsumption constraints.

1 Introduction

Today, a number of domain ontologies are available in the ontology libraries of the Web, including OWL ontology library[1], DAML ontology library[2], SchemaWeb ontology library[3], and so on. They are very useful for learning ontologies and for developing ontology-based applications.

However, we observe that there are two difficulties for the purpose of ontology reuse and management concerning the ontologies available on the Web. First, the classes are conceptualized in poorly structured taxonomies with inadequate semantics. An example of this is a DAML ontology on the wine domain given at http://ontolingua.stanford.edu/doc/chimaera/ontologies/wines.daml. The second difficulty concerns mapping and merging where heterogeneities occurr between similar domain classes. Those heterogeneities can be categorized into three groups: subsumption heterogeneity (different levels of subsumption), schema heterogeneity (different sets of properties), and terminological heterogeneity (different names or labels between classes, between properties, and between individuals).

Since the Web is a distributed environment that allows independent conceptualization and modeling, heterogeneities can appear between ontologies. It

---

[1] http://protege.stanford.edu/plugins/owl/owl-library/
[2] http://www.daml.org/ontologies/
[3] http://www.schemaweb.info/

J. Lang, F. Lin, and J. Wang (Eds.): KSEM 2006, LNAI 4092, pp. 418–430, 2006.

is difficult to avoid such heterogeneities in practical cases. However, if classes were well structured in subsumption relationships with adequate semantics, it would be much easier to resolve the heterogeneities by analyzing the inherited properties between classes. For that purpose, we need a systematic method of ontological analysis.

One available solution is OntoClean [2], a domain independent methodology of ontology modeling that supports well-formed ontologies. In OntoClean, a number of subsumption constraints are provided based on philosophical notions of *identity, rigidity* (essence), *unity*, and *dependency* (called meta-properties). In our experience, the methodology is theoretically sound and very useful in rendering relevant meta-level notions for ontological analysis. However, the approach of defining those meta-properties for each class is idealistic and vague. It makes ontology developers a bit confused and it is hard to apply. Therefore, we considered a more expressive and practical approach, that would guide ontology developers regarding how to do a structured conceptualization and analysis of their ontologies effectively.

There are two major purposes of this paper. First, we would like to adopt some notions of OntoClean (mainly identity) by giving the semantics of classes in an expressive way. Second, we wish to provide a practical framework for ontological analysis using identity conditions and taxonomic constraints.

The paper is organized as follows. In the next section, we give a formal definition of identity conditions (ICs) and present the relations between ICs and subsumption. Moreover, we distinguish global ICs from local ICs in terms of rigidity. A classification of sorts—classes with identity—and a typical taxonomic structure are also provided. In Section 3, a practical method of ontological analysis is defined, and demonstrated step-by-step. Then, in the next section, a representation of sortal ontologies in terms of OWL and an implementation framework using Protégé OWL editor are introduced. We summarize our contribution by comparing it with related works and discuss future directions in Section 5.

2   Identity Conditions and Subsumption of Sorts

First of all, we give a brief description of the ontological terminology which we use in this paper. Ontology is a collection of classes with subsumption (or subset) relationships. Each class is defined by a set of properties. Each property is a function on a specific domain and range. Also, a class is interpreted as a set of individuals—entities which are countable and identifiable. Some conceptual and taxonomic constraints are also defined for classes and properties.

2.1   Identity, ICs, and Sorts

We mainly focus on identity and identity conditions for ontological analysis. **Identity** is related to the problem of distinguishing a specific individual of a certain class from other individuals by means of an identity condition. Identity Condition (IC) of a class is a characteristic function that provides a unique IC value for each individual of the class. As examples, we can use *hasFingerprint*, *hasStudentID*, *hasISBN*, *hasURI*, *hasWineAppellation*[4], *hasLatitudeLongitude*, and *hasCurrency* as the ICs of *Person*, *Student*, *Book*, *WebResource*, *Wine*, *Location*, and *Money* respectively. IC is one of the properties that belong to a class. However, IC is differentiated from other properties by its characteristic of one-to-one relationship between domain and range. We traced the literature of identity [3,4,5,7,9,11] and observed the following important notions what encourage us to pay attention on identity conditions of a class.

"No entity without identity" (Quine, 1969)[14]
"No individual can instantiate both of two sorts if they have different criteria of identity associated with them." (Lowe, 1989) [6]
"If something can be identified and is a whole, then we say it is individual. A class is called a sort if it introduces or carries an IC." (Welty & Guarino, 2000) [4]

Following the above statements, it seems that ICs are strongly related to classes and individuals. Here, we need to explain the term 'sort'. In the ontology literature related to philosophy, ontological classes can be classified into sortals (or sorts) and non-sortals concerning identity. If a class has an IC, then it is a sort; otherwise it is not. An example of non-sortal is '*Red*' which is a kind of attribution for individuals. For example, *Wine* is a primitive class under ⊤ (topmost class). Then, *RedWine* is a sub-class of *Wine*. For *RedWine*, there is a property *Color* which is restricted by *Red*. Thus, we consider sorts as classes and non-sortals as the properties of sorts. Now, we will discuss the identity conditions (ICs) of sorts. The original formalization of IC given in Definition 4 of OntoClean[2], is as follows.

$$\Box(\ (E(x,t) \land \phi(x,t) \land E(y,t') \land \phi(y,t') \land x = y \rightarrow \Sigma(x,y,t,t'))\ ) \tag{1}$$

$$\Box(\ (E(x,t) \land \phi(x,t) \land E(y,t') \land \phi(y,t') \land \Sigma(x,y,t,t') \rightarrow x = y)\ ) \tag{2}$$

"An identity condition is a *sameness formula* Σ that satisfies either (1) or (2) assuming the predicate E for actual existance. An IC is *necessary* if it satisfies (1) and *sufficient* if it satisfies (2), and need not be both."

Suppose that *hasISBN* is the IC of sort *Book*. Then we say it is necessary to have the same ISBN for the same book or two individual books with the same ISBN are sufficient to identify as the same book. We assume that all copies of the same ISBN as the same book. If a modeler considers his/her conceptualization level to such copies, a further IC should be defined. As examples, a librarian may use a catalog number or a book shopper may use a bar-code to distinguish a copy of the same ISBN from others. We revise the formalization of IC preserving identity characteristic, however we omit temporal aspect because we interpret a possible world as a state of a specific situation and do not like to restrict it only by time. In the next section, we will discuss local and global IC which are interpreted in terms of Kripke's possible world semantics[1].

---

[4] WineAppellation means a designation of a certain wine, that consists of appellation and vintage.

Definition 1 (Revised IC). *IC of a sort, generally denoted by ι, is a functional property that provides a unique IC value for each individual of the sort. Formally,*

$$\iota(c_1 : s) = \iota(c_2 : s) \text{ iff } c_1 = c_2 \tag{3}$$

where $c : s$ represents individual c of sort s.

If an IC is explicitly defined for a sort, every individual of the sort must have a specific IC value that can distinguish it from other individuals. That is known as identity. Moreover, ICs are useful to examine a membership relation between an individual and a class. For example, suppose that *hasFingerprint* is the IC of *human_being* (or Person), thus each individual person has a unique fingerprint, also that a certain individual having a fingerprint guarantees that individual is a person. It is also similar that if we define *hasStudentID* as the IC of *Student*, then for a specific individual who has a studentID is definitely a student. We examine membership relations with using other common characteristics among individuals. Here, we consider ICs as an alternative but a more reliable property for membership relation. In summary, ICs are differentiated from other properties by facilitating not only for identity—are two individuals the same?—but also for membership relation—what is an individual?

2.2 ICs and Subsumption

For a sort s, there is a set of properties $P(s)$. For example,

$$P(Book) = \{hasTitle, hasAuthor, hasPublishedYear, \text{hasISBN}\}.$$

For every $p \in P(s)$, there is a specific domain and range such that $p : \mathcal{D}_s \to \mathcal{R}_p$. $\iota \in P(s)$ if sort s owns IC ι. Sorts are mainly organized with subsumption relationship $\sqsubseteq$ that allows inheritance: if $s_1 \sqsubseteq s_2$ then $P(s_2) \subseteq P(s_1)$. Similarly, a sort inherits the ICs of its super-sorts. We call a set of ICs that all belong to a specific sort s IC set denoted by $I(s)$. For example, $I(Student) = \{hasDNA, \text{hasFingerprint}, \text{hasStudentID}\}$ through $Student \sqsubseteq Person \sqsubseteq Living\_being$ where $\iota_{Student}$ is *hasStudentID*, ι_{Person} is *hasFingerprint*, and ι_{Living_being} is *hasDNA*.

According to inheritance, we define subsumption between sorts using their IC sets and call that **subsumption by IC sets**, i.e., for two sorts s_1 and s_2,

$$\text{if } s_1 \sqsubseteq s_2 \text{ then } I(s_2) \subseteq I(s_1). \tag{4}$$

Moreover, we consider **sub-property relationship** $\ll$ between ICs, which configures the structure of domains and ranges related to ICs with set-theoretical inclusion relation, that is, for $\iota_1 \colon \mathcal{D}_1 \to \mathcal{R}_1$, and $\iota_2 \colon \mathcal{D}_2 \to \mathcal{R}_2$,

$$\iota_1 \ll \iota_2 \text{ iff } \mathcal{D}_1 \subseteq \mathcal{D}_2 \text{ and } \mathcal{R}_1 \subseteq \mathcal{R}_2. \tag{5}$$

Suppose that ι_{Wine} is *hasWineAppellation*, $\iota_{FrenchWine}$ is *hasFrenchWineAppellation*, and $\iota_{BurgundyWine}$ is *hasBurgundyAppellation*. If we define *Burgundy*

$Wine \sqsubseteq FrenchWine \sqsubseteq Wine$ with $hasBurgundyAppellation \ll hasFrench$
$WineAppellation \ll hasWineAppellation$, then the subsumption is consistent.
Thus, for two sorts s_1 and s_2 with ICs ι_{s_1} and ι_{s_2}, there is a **subsumption
with sub-property relationship**:

$$\text{if } \iota_{s_1} \ll \iota_{s_2} \quad \text{then} \quad s_1 \sqsubseteq s_2. \tag{6}$$

Multiple inheritance is allowed in ontologies, so that we can construct a subsumption with multiple super-sorts such that $DryWhiteWine \sqsubseteq (DryWine \sqcap$
$WhiteWine)$—a $DryWhiteWine$ is both a $DryWine$ and a $WhiteWine$. However, we prohibit multiple inheritance with incompatible ICs as Lowe stated
in above. For example, $Apple \sqsubseteq (Fruit \sqcap Tree)$ defined in a single taxonomy is inconsistent because the ICs of apple fruit and apple tree are different
as well as incompatible. No individual is instantiated by such an $Apple$. However, $AppleFruit \sqsubseteq Fruit$ and $AppleTree \sqsubseteq Tree$ are consistent under different
taxonomies even in a single ontology.

2.3   IC vs Global ICs

We divided ICs into global IC and local IC according to the rigidity of sort.
Rigidity is strictly related to the philosophical notion of $essence$[2]. According
to the First-order Kripke model provided in [10], where every sort s is represented
as a unary predicate p_s, sort s is **rigid** iff:

$$\Vdash \Box\forall x[p_s(x) \to \Box(E(x) \to p_s(x))]. \tag{7}$$

A sort s is **anti-rigid** iff:

$$\Vdash \Box\forall x[p_s(x) \land \Diamond(E(x) \to \neg p_s(x))]. \tag{8}$$

The unary predicate $E(x)$ expresses the actual existence of an individual in an accessible world. In a precise translation, if any individual of a rigid sort in world w
exists in an accessible world w' such that wRw', then it must be an individual of
the same sort. Every person is a person in every possible world while he/she has
different roles in different worlds, such as $Student, Part-timeResearcher$. Thus,
person is a rigid sort and student is an anti-rigid sort. Here, we re-interpret the
original ontological modality by Guarino[3] to the accessibility of knowledge,
regarding each possible world as a partial knowledge-base with an ontology.

Definition 2 (Global IC). *If an IC returns the same IC value for the same
individual in any accessible world of a Kripke model such that wRw', then the
IC is called a global IC, denoted by ι^+. Formally, ι_s^+ is the global IC of sort s if
it satisfied $\iota_s^+(c\colon s)^w = \iota_s^+(c\colon s)^{w'}$.*

A rigid sort originates a global IC, but an anti-rigid sort can not. If an IC does
not qualify as a global IC, then we call it *local IC*. Generally, anti-rigid sorts
create local IC depending on possible worlds.

Example 1. *Suppose that studentID gives a unique identification number to each student in both University 1 (or U_1) and University 2 (or U_2).*

$$\begin{cases} hasStudentID(c_1\colon Student) = \text{`320025'} \text{ at } U_1 \\ hasStudentID(c_1\colon Student) = \text{`210'} \quad \text{at } U_2 \end{cases}$$

However, the *studentID* value of student c_1 is different from U1 to U2. By $Student \sqsubseteq Person$ with $\iota^+_{Person} = hasFingerprint$,

$$\text{hasFingerprint}(c_1\colon Student)^{U_1} = \text{hasFingerprint}(c_1\colon Student)^{U_2}.$$

It is a proof that *Student* is anti-rigid and its IC is local, while the global IC *hasFingerprint* carried from the rigid sort *Person* can provide the same IC value.

Anti-rigid sorts have a dependency on other disjoint sorts. **Dependency** is a notion that expresses the relation of a certain sort to another sort, in which both sorts are semantically disjoint. Precisely speaking, if a sort has a dependency then the semantics of the sort is described in close relation to its dependent sort. Consider *'Student is a person who studies in a school'*. *Student* sort has dependency on another sort *School* with *'study'* relationship. It means that we do not define a person who does not study at a school as a student. Similarly, *'DessertWine is a Wine which is served as a Dessert'* and *'CookingWine is a Wine which is used in cooking of certain dishes'*. In general, rigid sorts do not have dependency.

Though *Wine* is a rigid sort, *DessertWine* is an anti-rigid sort because any individual of *DessertWine* in a world may stop being *DessertWine* in any accessible world.

Example 2. *Suppose that 'Santa Margherita 2004' is defined as DessertWine in restaurant w but it may be changed to a CookingWine at restaurant w' and to an AppetizerWine in restaurant w''. However, it is still a wine in all restaurants and the IC value 'Santa Margherita 2004' carried from Wine does not change.*

Figure 1 is an illustration of rigid sorts and anti-rigid sorts.

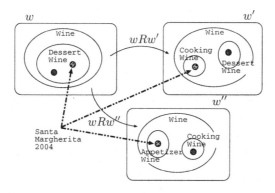

Fig. 1. Rigid sorts and anti-rigid sorts

There are two issues concerning ICs. The first issue is whether ICs are always *intrinsic* or not. In our approach, both intrinsic and extrinsic properties can be used as ICs if they satisfy Definition 1. As examples, fingerprint is intrinsic to a person but studentID is rather extrinsic. The next issue is related to temporal aspects. While a global IC can identify an individual through all possible worlds, a local IC changes world by world. As a person can be a student and a part-time employee even at the same time, we interpret a possible world as a state of a specific situation, and do not like to restrict it only by time.

2.4   A Classification of Sorts

We categorize sorts into four groups based on the classification provided in Figure 2 of OntoClean[2]. However, we redefine each group in terms of our interpretations of rigidity, global IC, and dependency.

1. **Type**: A sort is called a type if it is rigid and it originates a new global IC. Some examples of type are *Person, Book, Wine, WebResource*, and *Organization*, with global ICs *hasFingerprint, hasISBN, hasWineAppellation, hasURI, hasOrgID* respectively.
2. **Quasi-type**: A sort is called a quasi-type if it is rigid but does not originate a new global IC. It is a subdivision of a type by a structural property p—a property which distinguishes the sort from its siblings with a common attributive value v for all of its individuals such that $\forall x \, p(x : s, v : Value)$. For example, *Vertebrate, EducationalInstitution*, and *RedWine*, are the quasi-types of *Animal, Organization*, and *Wine*, with structural properties *hasBackbone.Yes, purposeFor.Education*, and *hasColor.Red* respectively.
3. **Role**: A sort is called a role if it is anti-rigid and has dependency. Thus, if a sort is a role, then a structural property between the sort and its dependent sort should be described explicitly, such as *belongTo*(c_1 : *Professor*, c_2 : *University*), *servedAs*(c_3 : *DessertWine*, c_4 : *Dessert*). A role may or may not create a local IC. As examples, *Professor, Student*, and *DessertWine* are roles. *Professor* and *Student* are re-identified with local ICs *hasProfessorID* and *hasStudentID* respectively. In the case of *DessertWine*, there may not a definite local IC.
4. **Sub-role**: A sort is called a sub-role if it is a sub-division of a role. Sub-roles never create an additional local IC, and just carry the IC from its role if the IC is available. Similarly to quasi-type, there must be a structural property p which distinguishes it from other siblings. For example, *ResearchStudent, Supervisor*, and *Non-sweetDessertWine*, are 'sub-roles' with the following structural properties: '*ResearchStudent is a Student who does research work*', '*Supervisor is a Professor who advises a ResearchStudent*', and '*Non-sweetDessertWine is a DessertWine which is not sweet*'.

According to the above classification of sorts, we summarize **conceptual constraints** of each group as follows. If sort s is a

- *type*, then there is a global IC $\iota_s^+ \in P(s)$;
- *quasi-type*, then there is a structural property $p \in P(s)$ with a common attributive value;
- *role*, then there is a structural property $p \in P(s)$ which describes a relation to dependent sort s' such that $p(c_1 : s, c_2 : s')$; and
- *sub-role*, then there is a structural property $p \in P(s)$ with a common attributive value.

Preserving "anti-rigid sorts never subsume rigid sorts" in a structured taxonomy [2], we define three **subsumption constraints**:

1. the sort after the topmost sort $\top$ must be a type,
2. a number of quasi-types can exist under a type, and then additional types can be defined under a type or quasi-type, and
3. a role can never subsume a type.

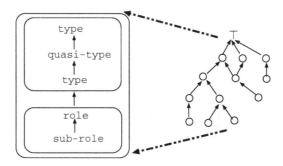

Fig. 2. A typical model of a structured taxonomy

A typical model of a structured taxonomy is presented in Figure 2. Consider the following two taxonomies to realize the importance of our constraints for a structured ontology.

$$ChablisWine \sqsubseteq DryWhiteWine \sqsubseteq Wine \sqsubseteq \top \tag{a}$$

$$VolnayWine \sqsubseteq NonsweetDessertWine \sqsubseteq DessertWine \sqsubseteq Wine \sqsubseteq \top \tag{b}$$

According to our subsumption constraints, (a) is a structured taxonomy but (b) is not, because *DessertWine* is a role and *NonsweetDessertWine* is a sub-role while *VolnayWine*, *ChablisWine*, and *Wine* are types, and *DryWhiteWine* is a quasi-type. Our objective in relying on those subsumption constraints together with conceptual constraints is to provide a structured hierarchy of sorts.

3   A Practical Method for Ontological Analysis

We provide a practical method to develop structured ontologies as follows.

1. Define a set of sorts, S, together with $P(s)$ for each sort $s \in S$ including ICs.
2. Classify the sorts of S into the groups of type, quasi-type, role and sub-role.
   (a) First, divide S into rigid sorts and anti-rigid sorts concerning equation numbers (7) and (8) given in Section 2.3.
   (b) Second, divide rigid sorts into types and quasi-types, and also anti-rigid sorts into roles and sub-roles by the classification given in Section 2.4.
3. By our conceptual constraints, check whether the description of each sort satisfies them or not.
4. According to the subsumption constraints, construct sort hierarchies for S.
5. Then, check whether each subsumption relationship satisfies equation number (4) or (6) given in Section2.2, or not.
6. If 'No', then go to Step 1 and repeat the steps to restructure the sorts.

Now, we demonstrate our method with some sorts from the French wine domain in Example 3.

Example 3 (Wine Ontology). *According to step (1), suppose that*
$S = \{Wine, FrenchWine, LoireWine, RedWine, WhiteWine, DessertWine, DryWine, BurgundyWine, ChablisWine, SparklingWine, Chardonnay Wine, Pinot\_NoirWine\}$.
Then, the description of each sort is given as follows:
$FrenchWine \equiv Wine \sqcap producedFrom.French$
$LoireWine \equiv Wine \sqcap producedFrom.Loire$
$BurgundyWine \equiv Wine \sqcap producedFrom.Burgundy$
$RedWine \equiv Wine \sqcap hasColor.Red$
$WhiteWine \equiv Wine \sqcap hasColor.White$
$DessertWine \equiv Wine \sqcap servedAs.Dessert$
$DryWine \equiv Wine \sqcap hasSugar.Dry$
$ChablisWine \equiv DryWine \sqcap WhiteWine \sqcap producedFrom.Chablis \sqcap$
$\qquad\qquad madeFromGrape.Chardonnay$
$SparklingWine \equiv Wine \sqcap hasTaste.Sparkling$
$ChardonnayWine \equiv Wine \sqcap madeFromGrape.Chardonnay \sqcap hasColor.White$
$Pinot\_NoirWine \equiv Wine \sqcap madeFromGrape.Pinot\_Noir \sqcap hasColor.Red$
$Loire \sqsubseteq French, Chablis \sqsubseteq Burgundy \sqsubseteq French$
$\iota^+_{Wine} = \text{hasWineAppellation}, \iota^+_{FrenchWine} = \text{hasFrenchAppellation}$
$\iota^+_{LoireWine} = \text{hasLoireAppellation}, \iota^+_{ChablisWine} = \text{hasChablisAppellation}$
$\iota^+_{BurgundyWine} = \text{hasBurgundyAppellation}$
$hasLoireAppellation \ll hasFrenchAppellation \ll hasWineAppellation$
$hasChablisAppellation \ll hasBurgundyAppellation \ll hasFrenchAppellation$

Note that symbol '$\equiv$' is for equivalence and '.' is for having a specific value or sort. In the above descriptions, each kind of wine is interpreted unambiguously. As an example, every *ChablisWine* is a dry and white wine that is made from a white grape, Chardonnay, and is produced from Chablis which is located in Burgundy. And the set of properties that belong to *ChablisWine* is:

$$P(ChablisWine) = \{producedFrom, hasColor, hasSugar, hasChablisAppella$$
$$tion\}.$$

In Step 2.(a), only *DessertWine* is an anti-rigid sort and others are rigid sorts. In Step 2.(b), we divide the sorts into four groups as shown below.

type = {*Wine, FrenchWine, LoireWine, BurgundyWine, ChablisWine*}
quasi-type = {*RedWine, DryWine, WhiteWine, SparklingWine, Chardonnay Wine, Pinot_NoirWine*}
role = {*DessertWine*}
sub-role = { }

The main characteristic in the above categorization is global IC. In Step 3, we check whether the sorts in each category satisfy the conceptual constraints or not. In Step 4, according to the specification of each sort given in the previous steps, the sorts are structured as shown in Figure 3. In Step 5, we checked the consistency of each subsumption relationship by Definition 1, and equation number (6) given in Section2.2.   ■

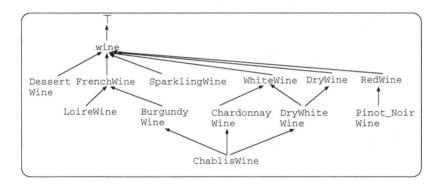

Fig. 3. A taxonomy of wine sorts

Our method is also flexible in adding new sorts into ontologies, and in repeating ontological analysis. Suppose that we would like to extend this wine ontology with the additional sorts given below.

$BourgogneWine \equiv Wine \sqcap producedFrom.Bourgogne$
$BourgogneWhiteWine \equiv BourgogneWine \sqcap ChardonnayWine$
$BourgogneRedWine \equiv BourgogneWine \sqcap Pinot\_NoirWine$
$NonsweetDessertWine \equiv DessertWine \sqcap hasSugar.Dry$
$Bourgogne \sqsubseteq Burgundy, \iota_{BourgogneWine} = hasBourgogneAppellation$
$hasBourgogneAppellation \ll hasBurgundyAppellation$

Then, by following the given analysis steps, the additional sorts are added into the previous wine ontology as shown in Figure 4. Note that *nonsweetDessertWine* is a *sub-role* of *DessertWine*.

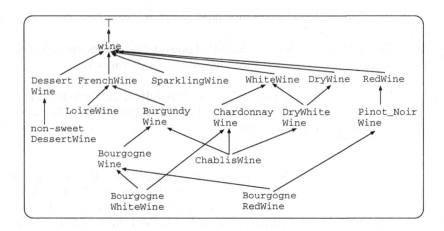

Fig. 4. The wine taxonomy with additional sorts

4   Representation and Implementation of Sortal Ontologies

Sortal ontologies are ontologies that organize sorts in subsumption relationships together with ICs.

Definition 3 (Sortal Ontologies). *A sortal ontology is a quadruple $O = \langle S, \sqsubseteq, P, A \rangle$ where S is a collection of sorts, $\langle S, \sqsubseteq \rangle$ is a lattice-based taxonomy for S such that $\sqsubseteq = \bigcup \{s_1 \sqsubseteq s_2 | s_1, s_2 \in S\}$, P is a set of properties belonging to S such as $P = \bigcup \{P(s) | s \in S\}$, and A is a set of conceptual and subsumption constraints.*

4.1   Representation of Sortal Ontologies Using OWL

For a sortal ontology $O = \langle S, \sqsubseteq, P, A \rangle$, every sort $s \in S$ is defined as an instance of *owl:class* together with a specific IC by a restriction of 'cardinality is exactly 1'. IC is represented using *owl:DatatypeProperty* with the restriction 'FunctionalProperty'. Figure 5 is a sample representation of Wine sort and its IC 'WineAppellation' in terms of OWL source code [5].

4.2   Implementation of Sortal Ontologies Using Protégé

In this section, we provide some instructional guidelines for users to develop sortal ontologies using Protégé OWL 3.2 beta [6]. The reasons we selected Protégé OWL as an editor for sortal ontologies are its use of frame-based representation, and its generation of OWL source code.

---

[5] http://www.w3.org/TR/owl-ref/
[6] http://protege.stanford.edu/download/prerelease/full/

```
<owl:Class rdf:ID="Wine">
  <rdfs:subClassOf>
    <owl:Restriction>
      <owl:onProperty>
        <owl:DatatypeProperty rdf:ID="WineAppellation"/>
      </owl:onProperty>
      <owl:cardinality
            rdf:datatype="http://www.w3.org/2001/XMLSchema#int">1
      </owl:cardinality>
    </owl:restriction>
  </rdfs:subClassOf>
  <rdfs:subClassOf rdf:resource="http://www.w3.org/2002/07/owl#Thing"/>
</owl:Class>
<owl:DatatypeProperty rdf:about="WineAppellation">
  <rdf:type rdf:resource="http://www.w3.org/2002/07/owl#FunctionalProperty"/>
    <rdfs:domain rdf:resource="#Wine"/>
    <rdfs:range rdf:resource="http://www.w3.org/2001/XMLSchema#String/>
</owl:DatatypeProperty>
```

Fig. 5. The representation of sort and IC in terms of OWL

We can develop sortal ontologies by following the Protégé OWL tutorial [7]. For a sortal ontology $O = \langle S, \sqsubseteq, P, A \rangle$, every sort $s \in S$ is defined as a class under the topmost class *owl:Thing*. As we mentioned above, the IC of a class is implemented as an instance of *owl:DatatypeProperty*, and the IC to be *functional* as well as *= cardinality is 1*. The individuals of each sort can be given via an 'instance' tab, and the IC value of each individual is automatically restricted not to be empty and also to be unique by the above specification of IC. In Protégé, sub-property relationship is provided and thus the sub-property relationships between our ICs can be represented.

After developing a sortal ontology, OWL code can be generated by the option of 'show RDF/XML source code' under 'code' menu. In Protégé, there is a plugin 'OWLviz' to view the visual graphs of ontologies. Our example 'SortalWines.owl' is published at http://protege.cim3.net/cgi-bin/wiki.pl?Protege OntologiesLibrary. The important step in transforming Web ontologies into sortal ontologies is explicitly defining the IC for each sort.

5   Conclusions

In this paper, we discussed how to represent the ICs of sorts explicitly and how to utilize them for ontological analysis. Our typical model of structured ontologies with necessary conceptual constraints can also be used as an ontology modeling framework.

There are not many closely related works. Methontology [8] is a complementary methodology that provides the guidelines for building and re-engineering ontologies, while OntoClean provides a methodology to clean the taxonomic structure of ontologies. In the work of Tamma and Capon [12,13], meta-level attributes such as mutability over time, modality, prototypes and exceptions, etc.,

---

[7] http://www.co-ode.org/resources/tutorials/ProtegeOWLTutorial. pdf

are discussed based on the meta-properties of OntoClean. Their objective is for ontology merging between heterogeneous ontologies. However, a formal representation and demonstration were not clearly presented for that purpose. Among the meta-properties of OntoClean, only identity allows inheritance through subsumption. Thus, we mainly focused on ICs and classified sorts. Compared with OntoClean, we provided an explicit, simplified, and practical framework for ontological analysis regarding our classification of sorts. That is our advantage over OntoClean. However, the scope of our method limits ontologies to be sortal.

In [10], we have also presented a new ontology mapping technique, in which sort mappings are found using the sameness relationship between the ICs of sorts. In future work, we will discuss ICs for further ontology management processes such as merging, alignment, and versioning.

References

1. A. Chagrov and M. Zakharyaschev. Modal Logic. *Oxford Science Publications*. 1997.
2. C. Welty and N. Guarino. Supporting ontological analysis of taxonomic relationships. *Data & Knowledge Engineering*, vol.39, pages 51-74, Elsevier 2001.
3. C. Welty and N. Guarino. Identity and Subsumption. *LADSEB-CNR Internal Report*. 2001.
4. C. Welty and N. Guarino. Identity, Unity and Individuality: Towards a Formal Toolkit for Ontological Analysis. *Proceedings of ECAI-2000*. 2000.
5. C. Welty and N. Guarino. A Formal Ontology of Properties. *Proceedings of the EKAW-2000: The Conference on Conceptual Modeling. Springer-Verlag LNCS.*. 2000.
6. E. J. Lowe. *What is a Criterion of Identity*. The Philosophical Quarterly, Vol.39, pp: 1-21, 1989.
7. M. Carrara and P. Giaretta. Identity Criteria and Sortal Concepts. *In Proceedings of the International Conference on Formal Ontology in Information Systems, 234-243. ACM Press.* 2001.
8. M. Fernández-López, A. Gómez-Pérez, A. Pazos-Sierra, and J. Pazos-Sierra. Building a Chemical Ontology using METHONTOLOGY and the Ontology Design Environment. *IEEE Intelligent Systems and their Applications*, 37-46, 1999.
9. N. Guarino., M. Carrara, and P. Giaretta. An Ontology of Meta-level Categories. *In Proceedings of the 4th International Conference on Principles of Knowledge Representation and Reasoning, 270-280. Morgan Kaufmann.* 2001.
10. N. N. Tun and S. Tojo. IC-based Ontology Expansion in Devouring Accessibility. *Australian Ontology Workshop (AOW 2005)*, Vol. 58, pp: 99-106, 2005.
11. T. Gruber. Towards Principles for the Design of Ontologies used for Knowledge Sharing . *In Journal of Human-Computers Studies, 43(5,6):907-928.* 1995.
12. V. Tamaa and T. J.M.B. Capon. An Enriched Knowledge Model for Formal Ontological Analysis. *In Proceedings of the international conference on formal ontology and information systems (FOIS01), ACM Press*, New York, 2001.
13. V. Tamaa and T. J.M.B. Capon. Attribute Meta-properties for Knowledge Sharing. *In Proceedings of KR2003*, 2003.
14. W. V. O. Quine. *Ontological Relativity and Other Essays*. Columbia University Press, 1969.

Knowledge Update in a Knowledge-Based Dynamic Scheduling Decision System

Chao Wang, Zhen-Qiang Bao, Chang-Yi Li, and Fang Yang

Department of Computer Science and Engineering, Yangzhou University,
Yangzhou, 225009, China
wangchaoeric@sohu.com

Abstract. Through the interrelated concept of the job shop production, this paper constructs a dynamic scheduling decision system based on knowledge, and gives five attributes of resource agent and corresponding task, time, cost, quality, load and priority. Using the fuzzy set and rough set, the classified knowledge of the attribute is generated, and is used as the states criteria in the Q-learning. To initialize Q value of the decision attribute, we collect the knowledge from experts. The Q-learning algorithm and initial parameter values are presented in knowledge based scheduling decision model. By the algorithmic analysis, we demonstrate its convergence and credibility. Applying this algorithm, the system will update the knowledge itself continuously, and it will be more intelligent in the changeful environment, also it will avoid the subjectivity and invariance of the expert knowledge.

1 Introduction

A new paradigm called agent technology has been widely recognized as a promising paradigm for developing software applications able to support complex tasks. An agent can be viewed as a computational module that is able to act autonomously to achieve its goal. In fact, agents can be used to represent physical shop-floor components such as parts, machines, tools, and even human beings. Each agent is in charge of information collection, data storage, and decision-making for the corresponding shop floor component. A popular scheme to achieve cooperation among autonomous agents is through the negotiation-based contract-net protocol [1]. The contract-net protocol provides the advantage of real-time information exchange, making it suitable for shop floor scheduling and control. The idea of the agent-based approaches has also offered a promising solution for controlling future manufacturing systems requiring flexibility, reliability, adaptability, and reconfigurability[2][3].

In the former paper [1], we present a dynamic scheduling system based on knowledge. The material objects in shop floor are abstracted as Task Agent, Resource Agent, Scheduling Agent, and so on. Through the method of rough, fuzzy set and with the expert knowledge, the attributes of the task and the resource can be used to design the knowledge model of scheduling decision. Then the system can be used to make the scheduling decision. But this system has some disadvantages as follows: (1) The knowledge of the scheduling decision is given by the experts, so it is unilateral

J. Lang, F. Lin, and J. Wang (Eds.): KSEM 2006, LNAI 4092, pp. 431–441, 2006.

and subjective. (2) The knowledge of scheduling decision in this system is unchangeable, but in fact the scheduling decision may be dynamic in different circumstance. Directing to the two points, the reinforcement learning method is introduced in this paper, the knowledge of scheduling decision system will learn by itself all the time, and then the system will be more practical and flexible.

2 Reinforcement Learning

Reinforcement learning is a kind of machine learning method [2]-[7], which can permit an single agent to learn its optimal action policy through a series of trial-and-error interactions with dynamic environment. The main idea behind it is to strengthen the good behaviors of agent while weaken the bad behaviors of it through delay rewards given by the environment. During the course, the agent will get positive rewards if its behaviors are seemed as good, otherwise negative rewards[9].

There are many RL algorithms. Among them, Q-learning is a popular one[2][3]. It's a model-free method and the learned decision policy is determined by the state-action value function, Q (state, action), which estimates long-term discounted reward for each (state, action) two-tuple. It needn't training simples to find the solution but using the trial-and-error. It is very competent for solving problem in dynamic environment. And now Q-learning is widely applied, such as industry control, robotic soccer, agent system, and so on.

Exploration and exploitation is another important issue in RL problems[4]. Exploration entails the agent trying something that has not been done before in order to get more reward, while in exploitation the agent favors actions that were previously taken and rewarded. Exploitation may take advantage of guaranteeing a good expected reward in one play, but exploration provides more opportunities to find the maximum total reward in the long run. One popular approach to deal with this trade-off issue is the ε–greedy method. The ε–greedy method involves selecting, with probability $(1 - \varepsilon)$, the action with the best value (exploitation), otherwise, with small probability ε, an action is selected randomly (encouraging exploration)[2].

3 Knowledge-Based Dynamic Scheduling Decision System

3.1 Related Concepts in Shop Floor

Knowledge-based dynamic scheduling decision system is constructed using CNP as the bid mechanism of task allocation and resource scheduling. Scheduling Agent plays the global control role of system decision-making floor which is in charge of generating schemes according to task requirements and the actuality of resources. When a task is sent down to the scheduling system, the tasks should be decomposed into many processes or sub tasks, which can be accomplished by one resource agent solely[8].

$E(T_i)$: Type of resource agent required by Task T_i .

$\rho(T_i)$: Priority of Task T_i , and $\rho(T_i) = \dfrac{T_e(T_i) - T_e}{T_l(T_i)}$. In this function, we re-

gard $T_e(T_i)$ as due time of Task T_i , T_l as the time in advance of leftover scheme and

T_e as current time. If $\rho \leq 1$, T_i is crucial task; otherwise, it is also not.

$C(A_p, T_i)$: Cost standard of Task T_i .

$Q(A_p, T_i)$: Basic quality requirement of Task T_i .

$T_s(A_p, T_i)$: Start time in scheme of Task T_i , and $T_s(A_p, T_i) > T_e$.

$T_e(A_p, T_i)$: End time in scheme of Task T_i .

If TS is a set of tasks which should be accomplished during a period (or in scheme), it is regarded as Task Set of scheduling system. Consequently, scheduling agent will invite bids to resource agent for each task in Task Set in order to generate a scheme.

Suppose SR_p is the set of resource agents which are dominated by scheduling agent A_p. So, the invitation of bid, which contains management information of Task T_i , is sent to corresponding resource agents that match with $E(T_i)$ in SR_p . Then, A_p will wait for replies.

After receiving invitation of bid, resource agent evaluates its capacity. And then, it replies A_p to bid. Bids sent to A_p by Resource Agents contain their own information as bellow:

$E(A_i)$: Task Resource Agent A_i bid for.

$C(A_i, T_j)$: Cost for A_i to accomplish T_j .

$T(A_i, T_j)$: Time for A_i to accomplish T_j .

$Q(A_i, T_j)$: Highest quality level A_i reaches to accomplish T_j .

$T_e(A_i, T_j)$: End time for A_i to accomplish T_j .

L_i : Current load of A_i , which means the time for A_i to finish all tasks committed from now on.

As a result, the bidders, which bid for Task T_i , constitute the bid-set BD_i of T_i . Through using the knowledge of scheduling rules to reason, A_p should evaluate all the bids and give the winner, at the end, form a scheduling.

3.2 Attribute Knowledge

According to the management information of tasks and the capacity of resources, condition attributes may be classified into these kinds[1]: (a) Time, (b) Cost, (c) Quality, (d) Load, (e) Priority. They are defined as below:

1) Time:

   1- $T_e(A_i,T_j) \leq T_e(A_p,T_j) - k_1 T(A_i,T_j)$, it means A_i can accomplish T_j ahead of schedule.

   2- $T_e(A_p,T_j) - k_1 T(A_i,T_j) \prec T_e(A_i,T_j) \leq T_e(A_p,T_j)$, it means A_i can accomplish T_j on schedule.

   k_1 is a constant, and $0 < k_1 < 1$.

2) Cost:

   1- $C(A_i,T_j) \leq C(A_p,T_j)$, it means A_i can accomplish T_j under the standard of cost.

   2- $C(A_i,T_j) \succ C(A_p,T_j)$, it means A_i can accomplish T_j beyond the standard of cost.

3) Quality:

   1- $\dfrac{Q(A_i,T_j)}{Q(A_p,T_j)} \leq 1 - k_3$, it means A_i can accomplish T_j on a high quality level.

   2- $\dfrac{Q(A_i,T_j)}{Q(A_p,T_j)} \leq 1 - k_2$, it means A_i can accomplish T_j on an equal quality level to requirement.

   3- $\dfrac{Q(A_i,T_j)}{Q(A_p,T_j)} = 1$, it means A_i can accomplish T_j on a low quality level.

   k_2, k_3 are constants, and $0 < k_2 < k_3 < 1$.

4) Load: 1- $T_c + L_i \leq T_s(A_p,T_j) + k_4(T_e(A_p,T_j) - T_s(A_p,T_j))$,   it means A_i is insufficiently loaded.

   2- $T_c + L_i \succ T_s(A_p,T_j) + k_4(T_e(A_p,T_j) - T_s(A_p,T_j))$, it means A_i is fully loaded.

   k_4 is a constant, and $0 < k_4 < 1$.

5) Priority:

   1- $\rho(T_j) \leq 1$, it means T_j is a crucial task.

   2- $\rho(T_j) \succ 1$, it means T_j is not crucial task.

The information of resource agent capacity, which is shown in bid, is transformed into knowledge of standardized condition attributes according to above definitions. They are used for antecedent of scheduling rules.

   Moreover, the evaluation to resource agent's bid is regarded as decision attribute. It is used for consequent of rule and also assorted into three levels:

1-Precedence, means it is perfect.

2-Feasible, means it is feasible.

3-Defective, means there is some defection in somewhere.

3.3 Scheduling Decision Knowledge Rules

Through observing the scheduling in the shop floor by the experts, noting the scheduling data every time, then standardization them and delete the repeated rules, we can get the scheduling decision knowledge rules as table 1.

Table 1. Scheduling Decision knowledge rules

U	a	b	c	d	e	f	U	a	b	c	d	e	f
1	1	1	1	1	1	1	25	1	1	1	1	2	1
2	2	1	3	1	1	2	26	1	1	1	2	2	1
3	1	1	2	1	1	1	27	1	1	2	1	2	1
4	1	1	2	2	1	1	28	1	1	2	2	2	1
5	1	1	3	1	1	2	29	1	1	3	1	2	2
6	1	1	3	2	1	2	30	1	1	3	2	2	2
7	1	2	1	1	1	1	31	1	2	1	1	2	2
8	1	2	1	2	1	1	32	1	2	1	2	2	2
9	1	2	2	1	1	1	33	1	2	2	1	2	2
10	1	2	2	2	1	1	34	1	2	2	2	2	2
11	1	2	3	1	1	2	35	1	2	3	1	2	3
12	1	2	3	2	1	2	36	1	2	3	2	2	3
13	2	1	1	1	1	1	37	2	1	1	1	2	1
14	2	1	1	2	1	1	38	2	1	1	2	2	1
15	2	1	2	1	1	1	39	2	1	2	1	2	1
16	2	1	2	2	1	1	40	2	1	2	2	2	1
17	1	1	1	2	1	1	41	2	1	3	1	2	2
18	2	1	3	2	1	3	42	2	1	3	2	2	2
19	2	2	1	1	1	2	43	2	2	1	1	2	2
20	2	2	1	2	1	2	44	2	2	1	2	2	2
21	2	2	2	1	1	2	45	2	2	2	1	2	2
22	2	2	2	2	1	2	46	2	2	2	2	2	2
23	2	2	3	1	1	2	47	2	2	3	1	2	3
24	2	2	3	2	1	3	48	2	2	3	2	2	3

4 Q-Learning in the Scheduling Decision System

In table 1, according to the given value of condition attributes, there is a value of decision attribute, and it is unchangeable. As we know in the dynamic environment, the scheduling decision will be changed sometimes, i.e. the same condition value of attributes, the scheduling decision may be changeable. So we use the Q-learning algorithm in the system. Through exploitation and exploration, the good scheduling decision is strengthened and the better scheduling decision will be found. The knowledge of the system can be updated continually.

4.1 Q-Learning Algorithm

Table 2 is the table of state policy. All combinations of the five attributes are the states of the Q-learning.

Table 2. State policy

state	State criteria					*f1*	*f2*	*f3*
	a	b	c	d	e	Q(f1)	Q(f2)	Q(f3)
1	1	1	1	1	1	Q(1,1)	Q(1,2)	Q(1,3)
2	2	1	3	1	1	Q(2,1)	Q(2,2)	Q(2,3)
3	1	1	2	1	1	Q(3,1)	Q(3,2)	Q(3,3)
$\vdots$	$\vdots$	$\vdots$	$\vdots$	$\vdots$	$\vdots$	$\vdots$	$\vdots$	$\vdots$
46	2	2	2	2	2	Q(46,1)	Q(46,2)	Q(46,3)
47	2	2	3	1	2	Q(47,1)	Q(47,2)	Q(47,3)
48	2	2	3	2	2	Q(48,1)	Q(48,2)	Q(48,3)

Processing algorithm:

1) From the knowledge-based scheduling decision system and the knowledge of experts, initialize the Q value.
2) Perception the current state, s_0.
3) Follow a certain policy (ε-greedy), select an appropriate action (a) for the given state (s_0).
4) Execute the selected action (a), receive immediate reward (r), and perceive the next state s_1.
5) Update the value function as follows:

$$Q(s_0,a) = Q(s_0,a) + \alpha[r + \gamma \max_b Q(s_1,b) - Q(s_0,a)] \qquad (1)$$

6) Let $s_0 = s_1$.
7) Go to step 3 until state s_0 represents a terminal state.
8) Repeat steps 2-7 for a number of episodes.

4.2 Parameter Initialization

1) Q value:

$$f = \begin{cases} 1, Q(s_1,1) = 10; Q(s_1,2) = Q(s_1,3) = 0 \\ 2, Q(s_2,2) = 10; Q(s_2,1) = Q(s_2,3) = 0 \\ 3, Q(s_3,3) = 10; Q(s_3,1) = Q(s_3,2) = 0 \end{cases} \qquad (2)$$

In formula (2), s_1, s_2 and s_3 are the aggregates in table 1 when f is 1, 2 and 3 respectively. $s_1 \cup s_2 \cup s_3 = U$. The Q value is prepared for table 2. For example, when U=1 in table 1, Q(1,1)=10, and Q(1,2)=Q(1,3)=0 in table 2. Similarly, all the Q values will be obtained.

2) r: It is the reward function. In this paper, r is gained from the condition attributes by comparison. Before the scheduling, there is a group of condition attributes values forecasted. After it, there is a group of real condition attributes values. Then we compared the two groups of values. The formula of reward criteria is as follows.

$$r = \begin{cases} 10, & \text{if } x = 5 \\ 6, & \text{if } x = 4 \\ 2, & \text{if } x = 3 \\ -2, & \text{if } x = 2 \\ -6, & \text{if } x = 1 \\ -10, & \text{if } x = 0 \end{cases} \qquad (3)$$

Where x is the number of the pairs of attributes which have the same value in the two groups. For example, when there are five pairs of attributes have the same value, then its r (reward) is 10 in this scheduling.

$\gamma, \alpha, \varepsilon$: γ, is the discount-rate parameter. As it approaches zero, the agent is more myopic because it takes immediate reward into account more strongly. On the other hand, as it approaches 1, the agent will be more farsighted reducing the impact that recent results have on the learned policy. α, is a small positive fraction that influences the learning rate. ε is a Parameter in ε–greedy method. In this paper, we set the ε =0.1. It means that 90 percent of the probability will use the action which has the biggest value, and the 10 percent of probability will use the other action to find the better scheduling decision. Several example systems, such as those illustrated in [2][3] apply the Q-learning algorithm with the setting of γ=0.9, α =0.1, ε =0.1. This paper uses the same common parameter setting.

5 Algorithmic Analysis

The application background of the system is a Precision Machinery company in Yangzhou. Its tasks are simplex, but the tasks' processes are more complicated. For the purpose of finding better scheduling, CNP and QL are used in this company.

Given a task, and it has many processes. The states are generated corresponding to each process. We suppose a state whose value is 2 is processing. In our experiment, we schedule for 300 times in 15 groups, so each group has 20 times of scheduling. But in the course of the experiment, the environment was changed (The company was attach importance to the time and Quality in the first 140 times of scheduling, but they had much time and the quality is not so important after it), then the scheduling decision was changed consequently during the experiment. The data of the experiment are shown in table 3.

Table 3. Data of the experiment

G	f	r	Q	t	G	f	r	Q	t
0	f1	null	0	null	8	f1	6	9.13	2
	f2	null	10	null	(141-	f2	6	15.11	17
	f3	null	0	null	160)	f3	-6	2.89	1
1	f1	-2	0.7	1	9	f1	10	11.00	2
(1-20)	f2	6	14.25	18	(161-	f2	2	11.69	17
	f3	-6	0.3	1	180)	f3	-6	2.90	1
2	f1	-2	1.33	1	10	f1	6	14.33	17
(21-	f2	6	14.89	18	(181-	f2	-2	10.80	2
40)	f3	-6	0.57	1	200)	f3	-2	3.31	1
3	f1	2	2.30	1	11	f1	10	18.30	18
(41-	f2	10	18.38	18	(201-	f2	-6	10.16	1
60)	f3	-2	1.21	1	220)	f3	-6	3.28	1
4	f1	2	3.95	2	12	f1	10	18.88	17
(61-	f2	10	18.90	17	(221-	f2	-6	8.68	2
80)	f3	-2	1.79	1	240)	f3	-2	3.65	1
5	f1	6	5.06	1	13	f1	10	18.98	17
(81-	f2	10	19.00	18	(241-	f2	-10	7.72	1
100)	f3	-6	1.91	1	260)	f3	-2	4.29	2
6	f1	6	6.95	2	14	f1	10	19.00	18
(101-	f2	10	19.00	18	(261-	f2	-6	7.24	1
120)	f3	-2	1.91	0	280)	f3	-2	4.56	1
7	f1	6	7.75	1	15	f1	10	19.00	18
(121-	f2	6	15.67	17	(281-	f2	-6	6.819	1
140)	f3	-2	2.88	2	300)	f3	-6	4.40	1

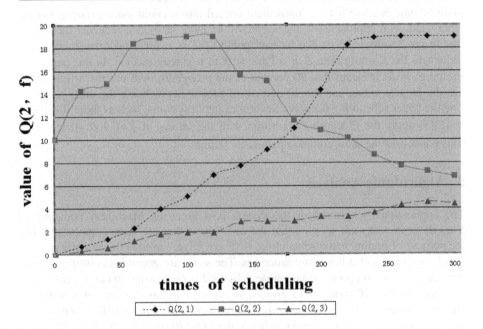

times of scheduling

---♦--- Q(2,1)   —■— Q(2,2)   —▲— Q(2,3)

Fig. 1. Change of the Q values

In table 3, G represents the group of scheduling; f means scheduling decision; r means reward function; Q means Q value corresponding to decision; t means scheduling times of the corresponding decision. For example, in group 2, we can know that f1 is taken once, and the reward is -2; f2 is taken for 18 times with the reward of 6; f3 is taken once with the reward of -6. So are the others. After we scheduled for 300 times, the change of Q values is shown as figure 1.

In figure 1, we can find that the Q value will change corresponding to the dynamic environment. When $Q(2,2) < Q(2,1)$, the scheduling decision also had changed from f2 to f1. After the change of the environment for a long time, the Q value will be convergence. In our system, the convergence value is 19.

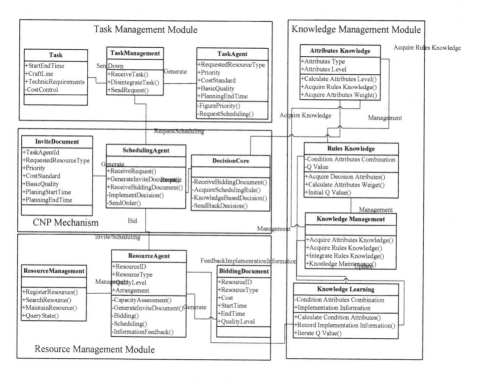

Fig. 2. Class diagram

6 System Structure

We design the structure of the scheduling decision system. It is divided into four modules: the task management module is in charge of acceptance of the tasks sent from superiors, generating of task agents and conveying the scheduling requests of task agents; the duty of the resource management module are maintaining and controlling the available resources, generating resource agents which participate in bidding; the mechanism of inviting and deciding bids is made up of two parts: one takes charge of the activity of inviting bids and sending scheduling orders, another makes decision for resource scheduling; the knowledge management module manages the knowledge of attributes, the knowledge of scheduling rules and the records of resources scheduled to support system to make decision.

7 Conclusions

The paper presents a Q-learning algorithm for the dynamic Scheduling System based on knowledge. Through this method, the scheduling decision knowledge will update with dynamic environment continually, and the scheduling decision system becomes more intelligent, practical and flexible. But it just updates the knowledge of the scheduling agent. How can we update all the agents' knowledge in multi-agent system is a complex problem. At the same time, the algorithm cost too much time to convergent, and the response of the environment has a little delay. So in our later study, we will pay more attention to the above problems.

Acknowledgements

This paper is supported by the National Natural Science Foundation of China under Grant No. 70471073; Natural Science Foundation of Jiangsu Education Department of China under Grant No. 04KJB520169; Natural Science Foundation of High Education of Jiangsu Province of China under Grant No. 05KJB120156; The project of demonstrating and popularizing science and technology achievements of Yangzhou under Grant No. YZ2004042-8.

References

1. Zhen-qiang Bao, Ning-sheng Wang, Zong-tan Cai: Research on the model of scheduling agent based on bid using Rough-Fuzzy sets. Machine Engineering of China, Vol. 14, No. 22, (2003) 1943-1946.
2. Yi-Chi Wang, John M. Usher: Learning policies for single machine job dispatching, Robotics and Computer-Integrated Manufacturing, Vol. 20, (2004) 553-562.
3. M.Emin Aydin, Ercan Öztemel: Dynamic job-shop scheduling using reinforcement learning agents, Robotics and Autonomous System, Vol. 33, (2000)169-178.
4. Yang Gao, Shi-fu Chen: Research on Reinforcement Learning Technology: A Review, ACTA AUTOMATICE SINICA, Vol. 30, NO.1, (2004)89-100.
5. Lian-Fang Kong, Jie Wu: Dynamic single machine scheduling using Q-learning Agent, Proceedings of Fourth International Conference on Machine Learning and Cybernetics, (2005)3237-3241.
6. Jing Huang, Bo Yang, Da-you Liu: A distributed Q-learning algorithm for multi-agent team coordination, Proceedings of Fourth International Conference on Machine Learning and Cybernetics, (2005) 108-113.
7. Luis C. Rabelo, Albert Jones, Yuewern Yih: Development of a real-time learning scheduling using reinforcement learning concepts, 1994 IEEE International Symposium on Intelligent Control, Columbus Ohio USA, (1994)291-296.

8. Zhen-qiang Bao, Chang-yi Li, Xin Zhou, wen-yu, Bian: A Knowledge-based Dynamic Scheduling Decision System, Proceedings of 2005 international conference on management science & engineering(12th), Incheon, R.Korea, (2005) 1554-1559.
9. Sutton R S, Precup D, Singh S: Between MDPs and semi-MDPs: a framework for temporal abstraction in reinforcement learning, Artificial Intelligence, Vol. 112, No.1 (1999)181-211.

Knowledge Contribution in the Online Virtual Community: Capability and Motivation

Chih-Chien Wang and Cheng-Yu Lai

Grad. Inst. of Information Management, National Taipei University, P.O. Box 179 - 45,
Taipei City, 11699, Taiwan
wangson@mail.ntpu.edu.tw, s79385002@tpnet.ntpu.edu.tw

Abstract. With the popularization of the Internet, virtual communities offer a new way for knowledge exchange. Previous research focused on the individuals' motivation to knowledge contribution. However, the exchange of knowledge is facilitated not only when individuals are motivated but also when individuals have the ability to engage in it. This study examines the influence of capability to the knowledge contribution in the virtual community as compared to individual motivation. An online questionnaire survey and partial least squares (PLS) were used to analyze and verify the proposed hypotheses. The results indicated that perceived self-efficacy and professional experience positively influence knowledge contribution in the online virtual community. However, individual motivations, which often are regarded as important influential factors in the real world, did not significantly influence knowledge contribution in the online virtual community.

1 Introduction

Due to a growing understanding of the importance of knowledge, people participate in knowledge exchange through various ways. Traditionally, knowledge exchange took place during physical interaction. People shared knowledge with colleagues in exchange with others' contribution of knowledge. These knowledge exchange participants had prior and subsequent relationships and might know each other physically. In this situation, factors about personal relationship may influence individual motivations toward knowledge contribution. In recent years, online virtual communities, such as the online groups, listserv service, and bulletin board systems, have served as a new way for people who have the same interests or expertise to share experience or knowledge with each other. Since that virtual community is anonymous and based in cyberspace, most virtual community participants have no physical personal relationship with each other and do not physically know each other. Some virtual community participants may play the role of free-riders and choose to get knowledge from these virtual communities but do not, in turn, contribute any of their knowledge. Hence, it is an interesting instance of individuals' willingness to share their knowledge in the virtual community, even if they recognize the existence of free-riders.

Individuals' motivation is a common reason influencing the individuals' willingness to contribute their knowledge. In the last few years, much research was concerned with the influence of individual motivation towards knowledge contribution.

J. Lang, F. Lin, and J. Wang (Eds.): KSEM 2006, LNAI 4092, pp. 442–453, 2006.

Burgess [1] used both qualitative and quantitative methods to measure what motivates individuals to transfer their knowledge. Bock et al. [2] proposed a framework with motivators and the theory of reasoned action (TRA) to assess behavior intention in knowledge-sharing. Both of them suppose that knowledge-sharing probably is occurring when individuals have adequate motivation. A number of studies had also found motivation to be very important for knowledge contribution [3-5].

However, the exchange of knowledge is not only facilitated when individuals are motivated but also when individuals have the capability to engage in it. Even if individuals are motivated to participate in knowledge exchange, having knowledge is still a basic requirement when they hope to contribute knowledge [6]. Constant et al. [3] argued that expertise is as important as motivation when individuals contribute their knowledge. The study of Kankanhalli et al. [7] also showed that both motivation and self-efficacy will influence individuals' willingness to share their knowledge in the organization.

Within the extensive literature on knowledge management, most of the research focused on knowledge exchange within the organization or cross-organization. Only a few studies had paid attention to the knowledge exchange in the virtual community. Most of these studies of virtual community knowledge exchange mainly focused on the knowledge contribution motivations of the individuals. The influence of individual capability on the knowledge contribution in the virtual community seldom has been discussed.

The purpose of this study is to examine the influence of capability on the knowledge contribution as compared to individual motivations in the virtual community. In view of the prior research purposes, the following questions were proposed: Is capability a prerequisite condition for members in the virtual community to contribute their knowledge? Are individuals definitely contributing their knowledge when they have the motivation that is mentioned in the real-world knowledge contribution?

The remaining parts of this paper are structured as follows: The second section deals with the theoretical foundations for proposing the hypotheses and the research model. Then, the research design and methodology are presented. The results of the statistical analysis are detailed in the following section four and five. Finally, conclusions and the need for future research are discussed in the last section.

2 Literature Review and Hypotheses Development

In a virtual community, knowledge contribution occurs when individuals are motivated to review the posted questions and take their time and effort to reply a response [6]. Over the past few years, many researchers used motivation as an indicator to measure the knowledge-sharing by the individual in an organization [2,3,7]. Davenport and Prusak [8] proposed that individuals participate in knowledge exchange when they expect to acquire some rewards that can be summarized as reputation, reciprocity or altruism.

Gary [9] indicated that an individual may lose the ownership of the knowledge that they have and the benefits based on this knowledge when contribute knowledge in the organization. As a result, sufficient incentive is necessary for individuals to engage in sharing knowledge [8]. An aspect of social exchange theory also suggests that the expectation of getting advantage, such as the promotion of status or the increase of reputation, is essential for an individual to participate in social interaction [10]. Since reputation is important for an individual to engage in the community and can be gained through knowledge contribution by showing others their expertise [3,11]. An individual who perceives that participation in knowledge exchange will enhance their reputation will contribute more responses to the community [6]. Thus, the expectation that contributing knowledge will enhance one's reputation and status may motivate an individual to contribute knowledge. This leads to the first hypothesis.

Hypothesis 1. **Reputation has a positive influence on knowledge contribution in the virtual community.**

Reciprocity means the intensive to be reciprocal to others [12]. Prior research showed that high-reciprocity perception individuals seem to have positive attitudes toward knowledge contribution [2]. The research of Wasko and Faraj [13] also indicated that knowledge contribution in an online community is facilitated by reciprocity. High-reciprocity perception individuals are people who believe that their contributed knowledge helps solve others' problems in the community will also be reciprocated by the people whom they helped. These high-reciprocity perception individuals will participate in knowledge exchange more frequently. Rheingold [14] indicated that an individual is likely to acquire the knowledge they need more quickly if they helped others frequently in the virtual community.

However, a free-rider may be a serious problem in a public virtual community. When a virtual community is open to the general public, all individuals could join it. If most people play the role of "free-rider" in the virtual community, members of virtual community can not expect others to respond to their question, even if they have answered others' questions. When an individual is in high-reciprocity, they may find that the virtual community is not a good place to contribute their knowledge, due to some free-riders never will provide feedback. Since free-riders are common phenomena in the virtual community, the influence of reciprocity to knowledge contribution might be negative.

From the side of the free-rider perspective, reciprocity has a negative influence on knowledge contribution. From the research conducted by previous studies, reciprocity may positively influence knowledge contribution. Since two different direction inferences exist, this study proposed that reciprocity has no significant influence on knowledge. This leads to the second hypothesis, which follows.

Hypothesis 2. **Reciprocity has no significant influence on knowledge contribution in the virtual community.**

Previous research shows that an individual may gain satisfaction by revealing their altruistic behavior, such as contributing their knowledge [13]. Altruism occurs when the individual helps others without expecting any return [15]. Kankanhalli et al. [7] pointed out that enjoying helping others is positively related to knowledge contributors in the organization. Wasko and Faraj [6] also provided evidence that individuals are motivated to contribute more helpful knowledge to others because they enjoy helping others in community/society. Therefore, individuals who gain enjoyment by solving others' problems in the virtual community will possess higher motivation to contribute their knowledge. This leads to the following hypothesis.

Hypothesis 3. **Altruism has a positive influence on knowledge contribution in the virtual community.**

The concept of self-efficacy refers to confidence in one's capability to fulfill a specific performance [16]. The extent of self-efficacy will influence people to choose the behavior that they are capable of and the sustainability of the behavior that they choose [16,17]. Kankanhalli et al. [7] indicated that knowledge self-efficacy is positively related to the knowledge contribution in an organization. Therefore, individuals with higher levels of self-efficacy seem to participate in knowledge contribution more frequently [18]. Although the majority of past research on self-efficacy focuses on the organization, this study suggests that self-efficacy is also a relevant capability indicator for evaluating why individuals contribute their knowledge in the online virtual community. This leads to the following hypothesis.

Hypothesis 4. **Self-efficacy has a positive influence on knowledge contribution in the virtual community.**

In addition to self-efficacy, prior research shows that the extent of one's expertise is positively related to the value of knowledge contribution [3]. Besides, individuals who participate in a virtual community or have been learning about the topic for a long time will tend to have more expertise or experience that can be contributed [6]. Therefore, the individual's professional experience can be seen as another capability indicator to assess the knowledge contribution in the virtual community. This leads to the following hypothesis.

Hypothesis 5. **Professional experience has a positive influence on knowledge contribution in the virtual community.**

As discussed above, this study proposes the research model as depicted in figure 1.

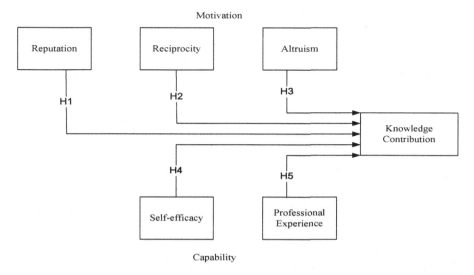

Fig. 1. Research model

3 Methodology

3.1 Instrument Development

This study adapted an online questionnaire survey to examine the influence of individuals' motivation and capability on knowledge contribution. This study discusses three individual motivations for knowledge contribution: reputation, reciprocity and altruism. Reciprocity and altruism were assessed using a scale modified from Kankanhalli et al. [7]; reputation was measured using a scale modified from Wasko and Faraj [6]. All individual motivation items were measured along a five-point Likert-type scale.

Besides these three motivation factors, the study undertook two individual capability factors: self-efficacy and professional experience. The scale measuring self-efficacy was adapted from a five-point Likert-type scale developed originally by Kankanhalli et al. [7]. Elsewhere, two items were used to assess the community members' professional experience. The questionnaire also collected demographic data.

To measure knowledge contribution, this study adapted the method practiced by Wasko and Faraj [6], which assesses knowledge contribution through helpfulness and volume of the contribution. At first, content analysis was performed to determine whether the messages posted by community members were questions, responses to questions, or others. The category "others" was used to omit the messages which were neither questions nor responses to questions, usually announcements or spamming and unrelated to knowledge contribution. The messages in the category "others" are not included for analysis. Messages belonging to the "response to question" category then were reviewed to evaluate their value, based on the extent of the knowledge contribution, and rated as very valuable, valuable, somewhat valuable and valueless to the question asked. The response directly answering the question with the explanation of the answer and/or the knowledge source for future study was rated as very valuable and received a score of 4, whereas the response directly answering the question with neither the reason for the answer nor the source of knowledge was rated as valuable and received a score of 3. The response rated as "somewhat valuable" answered the question indirectly, providing a hint, a partial answer, or a link only, and gets a score of 2. If the response answers the question but provides little value to the knowledge seeker—such as an answer to the question with a simple word like "Yes" or "No"—was rated as valueless and only scores 1. This study counted the number of responses posted by a community member as the volume of contribution and calculated the scores of knowledge value each individual got as the helpfulness of contribution.

3.2 Data Collection

Data were collected in the period of four months, July to October 2005, from an online virtual community that discusses JAVA-relevant topics on a bulletin board system. Of the 1,881 messages collected in this study, 602 were questions and 891 were responses to the questions. These questions and responses were contributed by 552 members of the virtual community. E-mail questionnaires were sent to these members, and 114 (20.7%) fully completed questionnaires were received for data analysis. Of them, 91 (79.8%) were male and 23 (20.2%) were female. The subjects were 23.07 years old, on average. Only 14 (12.3%) stated that they had the JAVA certificate authorized by Sun Microsystems.

4 Data Analysis

This study adopted partial least squares (PLS) to measure the model proposed in this study. PLS is a component-based analysis that has been used as an alternative to co-variance-based analysis such as LISREL, EQS, and AMOS [19]. PLS can be used to analyze measurement and structure models with minimal demands on measurement scales, sample size, and residual distributions, and is widely used in IS research [2,6,20]. In general, the sample size in PLS can be equal to the larger of the following strong rule of thumb: (a.) 10 times the scale with the largest number of formative indicators, or (b.) 10 times the largest number of structural paths directed at a particular construct in the structural model. In this study, the largest number of formative indicators is four and the largest number of structural paths directed at a particular construct is five. As a result, 114 completed questionnaires are enough for PLS analysis.

A PLS model usually is analyzed and interpreted in two steps: (a.) the reliability and validity of the measurement model is assessed firstly, and then (b.) the structural relationships are examined subsequently.

4.1 Reliabilities and Validation

The reliability of the five scales used in this study was assessed using the Cronbach alpha. The Cronbach alpha of reputation, altruism, reciprocity, professional experience and self-efficacy are 0.694, 0.823, 0.831, 0.855 and 0.522, respectively. Since the Cronbach alpha value of self-efficacy is not well above the commonly-acceptable level, this study therefore performed confirmatory factor analysis to assess the scale items for self-efficacy. As the result of confirmatory factor analysis, two insignificant items were deleted. The recalculated Cronbach alpha of self-efficacy, after deleting two items, is 0.718, and thus well within acceptable range. The resulting data are shown in Table 1.

Table 1. Scale Dimensions Reliability Analysis

Scale dimensions	Cronbach's α
Reputation	0.694
Altruism	0.823
Reciprocity	0.831
Professional experience	0.855
Self-efficacy	0.718

Table 2. Correlations and Square Root of AVE values. **: Correlations significant at p<0.05. Values in the catercorner are square root of AVE and others are correlations.

		1	2	3	4	5	6
1	Reputation	**0.73**					
2	Altruism	0.16**	**0.79**				
3	Reciprocity	0.31**	0.30**	**0.81**			
4	Self-efficacy	0.04	0.18**	-0.01	**0.90**		
5	Professional Experience	-0.02	-0.04	-0.22**	0.31**	**0.94**	
6	Knowledge Contribution	0.10	0.14	-0.15**	0.34**	0.39**	**0.99**

Convergent validity was accessed by examining the average variance extracted (AVE) of each construct. As shown in Table 2, all AVE values in this study were well above the value of 0.5 suggested by Fornell and Larcker [21]. We therefore can verify the convergent validity.

Discriminant validity refers to the extent to which evaluations of different constructs are unique from each other [22]. The model is achieved when the AVE of each construct exceeds the squared correction among other constructs [21]. All AVE values in this study are the highest squared correlation in the corresponding rows and columns as Table 2 listed, indicating that discriminant validity has been accepted.

5 Hypothesis and Model Testing

Since PLS has no prior claim on distribution assumptions, it requires a re-sampling procedure as a significant test; the proposed model and hypotheses were estimated using 100 iterations of the bootstrap technique in PLS-Graph version 3.0. The explanatory power of a structural model is measured through the R^2 value. The results of the hypothesis and model test are shown in Figure 2 and summarized in Table 3.

As shown in figure 2, hypothesis 1 is not supported. Reputation is not a significantly influential factor for knowledge contribution in the anonymous virtual community, although it is an important factor in real-world knowledge contribution. One explanation for this difference is that the reputation gained in anonymous cyberspace is not equal to physically-gained reputation. For an anonymous virtual community, such as the bulletin board systems where this study collected data, users must use an account/identification to participate in knowledge exchange. The reputation gained in virtual community is linked to the account/identification in the virtual community rather than their physical role position in the real world. The reputation in the cyberspace could not be used in the real world. Hence, reputation may not motivate an individual to contribute their knowledge in the virtual community.

Besides, the coefficients of reciprocity are not significant, as hypothesis 2 forecasted. This result consists with the research conducted by Ye et al. [23], reciprocity

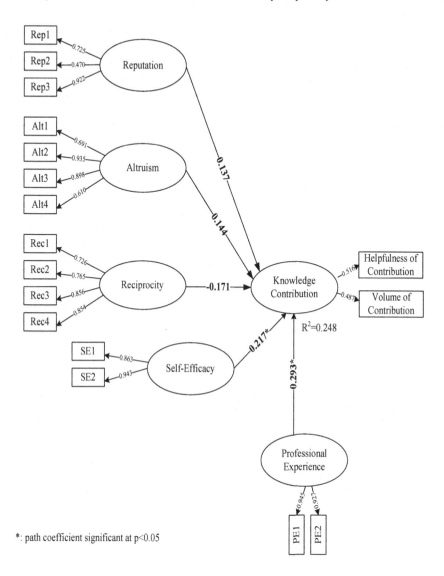

Fig. 2. Results of PLS Analysis

has no influence to the knowledge contribution in the virtual community. More efforts are need to discuss why reciprocity has influence to the knowledge contribution in the real world as previous studies indicated and has no influence in the virtual communities as this study and Ye et al. [23]'s study found. One explanation this study proposed is that the free-rider problem is a common phenomenon in the virtual community and causes individuals who possess knowledge to have less willingness to share. As a result, hypothesis 2 is supported.

In addition, although previous research shows that altruism will influence the willingness of individuals to contribute their knowledge, the influence of altruism to knowledge contribution is not significant in this study. One possible explanation for the insignificant relationship between altruism and knowledge contribution is that there exists a bystander effect for the influence of altruism on helping behavior [24]. The "bystander effect" explains the phenomenon that an individual would not provide favors to others when they find the existence of bystanders. They "think" that other bystanders will help the guy who needs help. There are a lot of bystanders in the virtual community, at least 552 members in the bulletin board system where this study collected data. As a result, individuals may think that others will help the guy who needs help in the virtual community. This bystander effect reduces individuals' willingness to share knowledge. Therefore, hypothesis 3 is not supported.

The empirical results of this study showed that self-efficacy has a significant influence on knowledge contribution, as hypothesis 4 predicted. When individuals are confident that they have capability to contribute knowledge in the virtual community, they tend to share knowledge more frequently and helpfully. This result is consistent with previous knowledge exchange research [7,18]. In addition, professional experience is also a significant influence to the knowledge contribution in this study. An individual who participates in the community or has been learning/studying a particular topic for a long time tends to have more professional experience and thus appears to have more willingness to contribute knowledge. As a result, hypothesis 5 is also supported.

Table 3. Results of Hypothesis Testing

	Hypothesis	Result	Statistic Analytical Details
H1	Reputation has no significant influence on the knowledge contribution in the virtual community.	Not Supported	There is no significant evidence (coefficient=0.137; t=1.02) that reputation will influence individuals to contribute their knowledge in the virtual community.
H2	Reciprocity has no significant influence on the knowledge contribution in the virtual community.	Supported	Reciprocity has no effect (coefficient=-0.171; t=1.49) on knowledge contribution in the virtual community.
H3	Altruism has no significant influence to the knowledge contribution in the virtual community.	Not Supported	Altruism has no significant influence (coefficient=0.144; t=1.07) on the knowledge contribution in the virtual community.
H4	Self-efficacy has positive influence on the knowledge contribution in the virtual community.	Supported	Self-efficacy has positive influence (coefficient= 0.217; t=2.27) on the knowledge contribution in the virtual community.
H5	Professional experience has positive influence on the knowledge contribution in the virtual community.	Supported	Professional experience has positive influence (coefficient= 0.293; t=3.80) on the knowledge contribution in the virtual community.

6 Discussion

This study examines the influence of individual motivation and capability to the knowledge contribution. An online questionnaire survey was adapted to confirm five research hypotheses formulated in this research. PLS was used to assess the veracity of the proposed model. Several results can be obtained from this research.

1. Three individual motivations in this study do not significantly influence knowledge contribution in the virtual community.
2. Both self-efficacy and professional experience influence the willingness of individuals to contribute their knowledge in the virtual community.

Compared to other studies of knowledge contribution, the results of this study are somewhat different. Wasko and Faraj [6] used the aspect of social capital to examine knowledge contribution in the virtual community and found that reputation and reciprocity have significant influence on knowledge contribution. However, the results of this study show that reputation and reciprocity have no influence on knowledge contribution. Explanation for the different results of reputation is that users can not use their real names but must use an account/identification to participate in the anonymous virtual community we examined. Moreover, the virtual community Wasko and Faraj [6] examined is hosted by a legal professional association. Participation in that virtual community is not anonymous, and the first and last names of the participants are visible as part of the message header. Therefore, reputation is important to the participants of that virtual community. However, this study collected data from a public community. This public community allows users to participate in knowledge exchange anonymously, and therefore the free-rider problem is a common phenomenon and diminishes individuals' willingness to contribute the knowledge they possess in the community.

Furthermore, Ye et al. [23] used individual, knowledge and environment factors to investigate individuals' inclination toward knowledge contribution in the virtual communities. The results indicated that three individual factors (enjoyment in helping others, self-image and knowledge self-efficacy) are significant influences upon individuals' knowledge contribution intention in the virtual community. However, the results of this study show that the influence of altruism to knowledge contribution is not significant. One possible explanation for the different results is that there exists discrepancy between the subjects of the two studies. There are more then fifty thousand participants in the virtual community this study examined, the bystander effect may happen frequently and therefore diminish individuals' willingness to contribute their knowledge altruism. When the population of virtual community reduces, the bystander effect might also drop down.

Several implications can be drawn from this study. First of all, capability is a prerequisite for an individual to contribute knowledge, even though they have motivation to contribute knowledge in the virtual community. The extent of self-efficacy will influence an individual's willingness to contribute their knowledge in the virtual community. People who have higher self-efficacy will tend to have more confidence to contribute their knowledge in the virtual community. Moreover, the extent of professional experience also influences knowledge contribution directly. Individuals who have more professional experience are likely to share their knowledge in the virtual community more frequently.

To practice, although prior research suggested that it is important to stimulate individuals' motivation for knowledge-sharing, the results of this study indicated that promoting individuals' capability seems more important. Encouraging individuals to promote their expertise not only increases their confidence about their knowledge but also facilitates the knowledge contribution in the virtual community. Furthermore, keeping individuals for long-term participation in a virtual community is also important for knowledge-sharing.

However, there are several limitations in this research. One limitation is that the investigation was conducted in a virtual community only and may restrict the applicability of the findings. Further research may examine this topic across different virtual/physical communities, countries and cultures to see whether there exists variation. Another limitation of this study is that the virtual community we examined was only one kind of the virtual community. However, Hangel III and Armstrong [25] indicated that a virtual community could be classified as interest, relationship-building, fantasy, and traction four categories. Individuals in different kinds of virtual communities may have different behaviors in knowledge-sharing. This needs to be studied further. A comparison of knowledge-sharing between physical and virtual community might also be conducted in the future.

References

1. Burgess, D.: What Motivates Employees to Transfer Knowledge Outside their Work Unit? Journal of Business Communication, 42 (2005) 324-348
2. Bock, G.W., Zmud, R.W., Kim, Y.G., Lee, G.N.: Behavioral Intention Formation in Knowledge Sharing: Examining the Roles of Extrinsic Motivators, Social-Psychological Forces, and Organizational Climate. MIS Quarterly, 29 (2005) 87-111
3. Constant, D., Sproull, L., Kiesler, S.: The Kindness of Strangers: The Usefulness of Electronic Weak Ties for Technical Advice. Organization Science: A Journal of the Institute of Management Sciences, 7 (1996) 119-135
4. Osterloh, M., Frey, B.S.: Motivation, Knowledge Transfer, and Organizational Forms. Organization Science: A Journal of the Institute of Management Sciences, 11 (2000) 538
5. Szulanski, G.: The Process of Knowledge Transfer: A Diachronic Analysis of Stickiness. Organizational Behavior & Human Decision Processes, 82 (2000) 9-27
6. Wasko, M.M. and Faraj, S.: Why should I Share? Examining Social Capital and Knowledge Contribution in Electronic Networks of Practice. MIS Quarterly, 29 (2005) 35-57
7. Kankanhalli, A., Tan, B., Wei, K.K.: Contributing Knowledge to Electronic Knowledge Repositories: An Empirical Investigation. MIS Quarterly, 29 (2005) 113-143
8. Davenport, T.H., Prusak, L.: Work Knowledge: How Organizations Manage What They Know. Harvard Business School Press, Boston MA (1998)
9. Gray, P.H.: The Impact of Knowledge Repositories on Power and Control in the Workplace. Information Technology and People, 14 (2001) 368-384
10. Blau, P. M.: Exchange and Power in Social Life. Wiley, New York (1964)
11. Ba, S., Stallaert, J., Whinston, A. B.: Research Commentary: Introducing a Third Dimension in Information Systems Design--the Case for Incentive Alignment. Information Systems Research, 12 (2001) 225

12. Fehr, E., Gächter, S.: Reciprocity and Economics: The Economic Implications of Homo Reciprocans. European Economic Review, 42 (1998) 845-859
13. Wasko, M.M. and Faraj, S.: It is What One Does: Why People Participate and Help Others in Electronic Communities of Practice. Journal of Strategic Information Systems, 9 (2000) 155-173
14. Rheingold, H.: The Virtual Community: Homesteading on the Electronic Frontier. MIT Press, Cambridge MA (2000)
15. Wilson, E.O.: Sociobiology: The New Synthesis. Cambridge, Mass: Harvard University Press (1975)
16. Bandura, A.: Social Foundations of Thought and Action. Prentice-Hall, Englewood-Cliffs NJ (1986)
17. Gist, M.E., Mitchell, T.R.: Self-Efficacy: A Theoretical Analysis of its Determinants and Malleability. Academy of Management Review, 17 (1992) 183-211
18. Cabrera, Á, Collins, W.C., Salgado, J.F.: Determinants of Individual Engagement in Knowledge Sharing. International Journal of Human Resource Management, 17 (2006) 245-264
19. Chin, Wynne, W.: Issues and Opinion on Structural Equation Modeling. MIS Quarterly, 22 (1998) 1
20. Chin, W.W., Todd, P.A.: On the use, Usefulness and Ease of use of Structural Equation Modeling in MIS Research: A Note of.. MIS Quarterly, 19 (1995) 237-246
21. Fornell, C., Larcker, D.F.: Evaluating Structural Equation Models with Unobservable Variables and Measurement Error. Journal of Marketing Research (JMR), 18 (1981) 39-50
22. Bagozzi, R.P.:An Examination of the Validity of Two Models of Attitude. Multivariate Behavioral Research, 16 (1981) 323-359
23. Ye, S., Chen, C.P., Jin X.L.: An Empirical Study of What Drives Users to Share Knowledge in Virtual Communities. First International Conference on Knowledge Science, Engineering and Management, Guilin City, China (2006)
24. Darley, J.M., Latan□, B.: Bystander Intervention in Emergencies: Diffusion of Responsibility. Journal of Personality and Social Psychology, 8 (1968) 377-383
25. Hangel III, J., Armstrong, A.G.: Net Gain: Expanding Markets Through Virtual Communities. Mckinesy and Company (1996)

Effective Large Scale Ontology Mapping

Zongjiang Wang, Yinglin Wang, Shensheng Zhang, Ge Shen, and Tao Du

Dept. of Computer Science
Shanghai Jiaotong University, 200030, China
microw@sjtu.edu.cn

Abstract. Ontology mapping is the key point to reach interoperability over ontologies. It can identify the elements corresponding to each other. With the rapid development of ontology applications, domain ontologies became very large in scale. Dealing with the large scale ontology mapping problems is beyond the reach of the existing algorithms. To improve this situation a modularization-oriented approach (called MOM) was proposed in this paper. This approach tries to decompose a large mapping problem into several smaller ones and use a method to reduce the complexity dramatically. Several large and complex ontologies have been chosen and tested to verify this approach. Experimental results indicate that the MOM method can significantly reduce the time cost while keeping the high mapping accuracy.

1 Introduction

Mapping is a critical operation in many well-known application domains such as schema/ontology integration, semantic web, data warehouse, e-commerce, etc. The increasing awareness of the benefits of ontologies for information processing has lead to the creation of a number of such ontologies for real world domains. Many different solutions have been proposed to the matching problem. Examples include Cupid, COMA, Glue, Rondo, and S-Match, etc[1-5]. However, in complex domains such as medicine these ontologies can contain thousands of concepts. The previous approaches were typically applied to small ontologies in which most correspondences could be automatically determined without much difficulty in a reasonable time. However, as surveyed in, most small ontologies are structurally rather simple and of the size of ontology are less than 100 components (classes, properties). Unfortunately, the effectiveness of automatic match techniques studied so far may significantly decrease for larger scale ontologies[2] because larger ontologies increase the likelihood of false matches. To improve this situation a modularization-oriented approach (called MOM) was proposed in this paper. This approach tries to decompose a large mapping problem into several smaller ones and use a method to reduce the complexity dramatically.

The rest of the paper is organized as follows. Section 2 provides the related definitions. In section 3, we firstly give a brief introduction of our system architecture, and then describe the components of system in detail. The experiments and evaluation are given in section 4. Finally, before conclude our work with a discussion, we gives the survey of the related work.

J. Lang, F. Lin, and J. Wang (Eds.): KSEM 2006, LNAI 4092, pp. 454–465, 2006.

2 Definitions

This section introduces two basic definitions used throughout the paper: one is the ontology, and the other is the ontology mapping.

2.1 Ontology

Information systems process the information in a domain. Any information is based on a concept framework that is called ontology. An ontology specifies a conceptualization of a domain in terms of concepts, properties, and relations[6]. We use the OWL-Lite to represent ontologies. Ontology can be defined by a seven tuple[7]. $O := (C, Hc, Rc, Hr, I, Ri, A)$

An ontology O is a tuple consisting the following. The concepts C (instances of "owl:Class") of the ontology are arranged in a hierarchy $Hc \in C \times C$ (instances of "rdfs:subClassOf"). Relations Rc (instances of "rdf:Property") can also be arranged in a hierarchy Hr ("rdfs:subPropertyOf"). Instances I of a specific concept are interconnected by property instances Ri. Axioms A, expressed in a logical language, can be used to infer knowledge from existing one.

For a concept $c \in C$, we define $I_c \subset I$ as the set of its instances. Let i_c be an instance of c, i.e $i_c \in I_c$. Let j denote a value of c's data property $r_d \in R_C$ or its object property $r_o \in R_I$. We call the triple (i_c, r_d, j) a data property instance and triple (i_c, r_o, j) an object property instance, respectively.

2.2 Ontology Mapping

Ontology mapping takes two ontologies as input and creates a semantic correspondence between the entities in the two input ontologies[8]. We adopt the following definition for the term "mapping": Given two ontologies O_1 and O_2, mapping from ontology O_1 to another O_2 means for each entity in ontology O_1, we try to find a corresponding entity, which has the same intended meaning, in ontology O_2 [9]. Ontology O_1 is called source ontology and O_2 is called target ontology.

An ontology mapping function can be defined by the following way:

$$f = \mathrm{Map}(\{e_{i_1}\}, \{e_{i_2}\}, O_1, O_2) \qquad (1)$$

where $e_{i_1} \in o_1, e_{i_2} \in o_2 : \{e_{i_1}\} \xrightarrow{f} \{e_{i_2}\}$. $\{e_{i_1}\}$ denotes a collection of entities, $e_{i_1} \in C \cup R_C \cup R_I$. f can be one of the mapping types (e.g. equivalentClass, subclass, sameIndividualAs, unionOf, disjointWith, etc.) or null. When equivalent mapping is the only concern, we usually leave out O_1 and O_2 and write as $\mathrm{Map}(\{e_{i_1}\}, \{e_{i_2}\})$. We use the notation $\mathrm{Map}(O_1, O_2)$ to indicate all entity mappings from O_1 to O_2. Once a mapping $\mathrm{Map}(\{e_{i_1}\}, \{e_{i_2}\})$, between two ontologies O_1 to O_2 is established, we also say that "entities $\{e_{i_1}\}$ is mapped onto entities $\{e_{i_2}\}$". For each pair of entity set$(\{e_{i_1}\}, \{e_{i_2}\})$, we call it candidate mapping.

In this paper, we only consider the 1:1 mappings between single entities.

3 A Modularization-Oriented Ontology Mapping Approach

For large ontologies matching, it is likely that large portions of one or both input ontologies have no matching counterparts[10]. The standard approach trying to match the input ontologies completely, however, will often lead not only to performance problems (long execution times), but also to poor match quality with many false matches.

We thus propose a Modularization-based Ontology Mapping approach (we call it MOM later). This is a divide-and-conquer strategy which decomposes a large match problem into smaller sub-problems by matching at the level of ontology modules. As illustrated in Fig.1, the strategy encompasses four steps: (1) partition the large ontologies into suitable modules, (2) identify the most similar modules in two sets of modules, (3) use the OPM algorithm to match two similar modules, and (4) combine the module match results. By reducing the size of the mapping problem we not only can obtain better performance but also can improved match quality compared to previous ontology mapping methods.

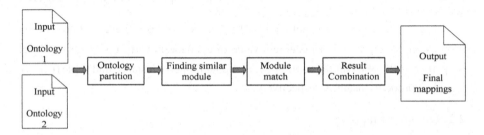

Fig. 1. Mapping process in MOM

3.1 Ontology Partition

In this section, we show how to partition the large ontologies into small modules, (see Fig.2). We take the approach of[11].

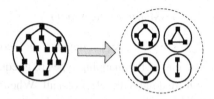

Fig. 2. Ontology Partition

This method takes the E-connection as the theoretical foundation[12]. In a Semantic web context, E-connection contains a set of "E-connected" ontologies. Each of the E-connection is modeling a different application domain, while the

E-connection is modeling the union of all domains. For brevity, an E-connection is an extended OWL-DL, which adds the functions to define and use the link property.

After introducing a series of definitions, such as semantic encapsulation, strongly encapsulating and module, the authors then try to find the relevant axioms for each entity in the original ontology. The main idea of this approach is to transform the input ontology into an E-connection with the largest possible number of connected knowledge bases and keep the semantics of the original ontology in a specific way. The algorithm uses the obtained E-Connected ontologies to generate, for each entity, its E-module, which is the minimal strongly encapsulating component that can be obtained from the E-Connection.

The main advantage of using E-Connections is that the soundness of the partitioning process can be guaranteed, because the E-module for each entity is strongly encapsulating. This algorithm is worst-case quadratic in the size of the input ontology.

3.2 Finding Similar Modules

In the last step, through the modularization, we partition the large ontology and get two sets of modules. The goal of this step is to identify modules of the two ontologies that are sufficiently similar to be worth matching in more detail. This aims at reducing match overhead by not trying to find correspondences between irrelevant modules of the two ontologies. Assume the first ontology has M modules, and the second one has N modules, and the approach should execute $M \times N$ mappings. With the help of modules matcher, we remove the irrelevant module-pairs and obtain the L similar module-pairs. Generally, L is much smaller than $M \times N$, and this will avoid unnecessary calculation if compared with other methods.

The problem of finding the most similar L module-pairs may be transformed to the problem of finding the maximum bipartite match[13]

Definition: a bipartite graph $G=(X,Y,E)$ is a simple graph defined as follows:

- X is the set of vertices which denotes a modules of first ontology
- Y is the set of vertices which denotes a modules of second ontology
- E is the set of edges which all go between the X and Y. The weight of the edge is the similarity of the vertices.

The question is to find a match $M \subseteq E$ such that $w(M)=\sum_{e \in M} w(e)$ is the maximum.

To solve the maximum bipartite match problem, we use the Hungary arithmetic which can find out the match of bipartite graph and the Kuhn arithmetic which can find out the maximum one based on Hungary arithmetic[13].

Now we introduce how to get the similarity of the two modules.

In order to compare two modules (they are parts of the ontologies) and measure the similarity between them, we use the similarity measure $Sim(O_1,O_2)$ between two ontologies, O_1 and O_2, which is based on two values: (1) lexical similarity and (2) conceptual similarity[14].

3.2.1 Lexical Similarity

We use edit distance method to compare two lexical terms.

$$\text{Sim}(L_i,L_j) = \max(0, \frac{\min(|L_i|,|L_j|)-ed(L_i,L_j)}{\min(|L_i|,|L_j|)}) \in [0,1] \qquad (2)$$

where $\bar{L}_1$ is a lexicon of ontology O_1 which includes a set of terms for ontology concepts L_1^C, and a set of terms for ontology relations L_1^R. L_i is a term of $\bar{L}_1$, and L_j is a term of $\bar{L}_2$. $\text{Sim}(L_i,L_j)$ returns a number between 0 and 1, where 1 stands for perfect match and zero for no match. Then we can get the lexical similarity between the two ontologies:

$$\text{Sim}(\bar{L}_1,\bar{L}_2) = \frac{1}{|\bar{L}_1|} \sum_{L_i \in \bar{L}_1}^{n} \max_{L_j \in \bar{L}_2} \text{Sim}(L_i,L_j) \qquad (3)$$

We notice that $\text{Sim}(\bar{L}_1,\bar{L}_2)$ is an asymmetric measure that determines the level to which the lexical level of a sign system $\bar{L}_1$ (the target) is covered by the one of a second sign system $\bar{L}_2$ (the source). Obviously, $\text{Sim}(\bar{L}_1,\bar{L}_2)$ may be quite different from $\text{Sim}(\bar{L}_2,\bar{L}_1)$. For instance, if $\bar{L}_2$ contains not only all the strings of $\bar{L}_1$, but also plenty of strings outside $\bar{L}_1$, then $\text{Sim}(\bar{L}_1,\bar{L}_2)=1$, but $\text{Sim}(\bar{L}_2,\bar{L}_1)$ may be close zero. Let us definite the relative number of hits:

$$\text{SetHit}(\bar{L}_1,\bar{L}_2) = \frac{|\bar{L}_1 \cap \bar{L}_2|}{|\bar{L}_1|} \qquad (4)$$

To make the $\text{Sim}(\bar{L}_1,\bar{L}_2)$ correct in all conditions, we must assure the value of $\text{SetHit}(\bar{L}_1,\bar{L}_2)$ is less than 1.

3.2.2 Conceptual Similarity

Conceptually, we may compare semantic structures of ontologies O_1, O_2 that vary for concepts A_1, A_2. In our model the conceptual structures consist of two parts: one is the similarity between the two taxonomies of the ontologies, another is the similarity between the two sets of the relations of the ontologies[14].

3.2.3 Total Similarity

The total similarity between two ontologies is the combination of lexical similarity and conceptual similarity

Here, a fixed weighting scheme is applied for the combination. The weights can be chosen by the expert experience.

$$\text{Sim}(O_1,O_2) = W_{lexical} * Sim_{lexical} + W_{conceptual} * Sim_{conceptual} \qquad (5)$$

where $W_{lexical} + W_{conceptual} = 1$

3.3 Module Match

Here we used a mapping method OPM (Ontology Parsing graph-based Mapping method). The algorithm has 5 steps: ontology parsing, ontology parsing graph generation, lexical similarity calculation, similarity iteration, and graph match.

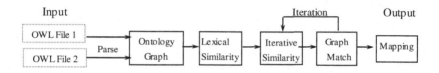

Fig. 3. Architecture of OPM

3.3.1 Ontology Parsing
Here, we used the OWL API, developed by Manchester University, to parse the ontology [15]. With it, we can easily get a clear data structure which reflects all kinds of relationships between the entities in ontologies, such as class, property, restriction, cardinality, etc. These relationships are very important to ontology mapping, and they provide valuable clues for further processing.

3.3.2 Ontology Parsing Graph
The similarity between vertices of the ontology parse graph (we call it OP-graph) follows two principles: (1) it depends on the category X of vertex considered and (2) it takes into account all the features of this category (e.g., superclasses, properties)[16]. We build OP-graph by extending the general concept of graph and encode the type information into vertices and edges. The OP-graph can be built through the following steps:

(1)   Parse the ontology and obtain all the elements of ontology;
(2)   Represent the concept of ontology entity as the vertices of graph. OP-graph has the following categories of vertices: class, object, relation, property, property instance, datatype, etc.
(3)   Represent the relations between vertices as the edges of graph. These edges, like the vertices, have each own types.

OP-graph structure makes the relations between ontology language elements more explicit (Fig 4). After constructing OP-graph, the problem of searching the optimal mapping between two heterogenous ontologies, is translated into a problem of finding the optimal match between two OP-graphs.

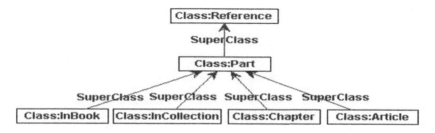

Fig. 4. A parsing graph of ontology "Reference"

3.3.3 Lexical Similarity

The similarity of the vertices is a real number in [0, 1], in which 0 (1) stands for completely different (similar) entities. The similarity of the vertices is the foundation in the process of finding the graph matching. The similarity of the vertices calculated by the lexical information is as the initial value of the lexical similarity. Here we use two methods to compute the lexical similarity: WordNet-based approach and StringDistance-based approach.

3.3.4 Iterative Similarity

According to the ontology semantics, we get the OP-graph and lexical similarity between the vertices. Now the iterative similarity between vertices of the OP-graph is defined based on the following four principles:

(1) There is no meaning to compute the similarity between different categories vertices.

(2) Since vertices of different categories reflect different ontology logic relation, so the similarity definitions of these vertices are not the same.

(3) The definitions of the vertices should take into account all the adjacent relations among vertices

(4) The similarity is normalized as the value between 0 and 1

The formula of iterative similarity stems from the third principle. Assume we calculate the iterative similarity between N_a and N_b, where N_a is a vertex of G_a and N_b is a vertex of G_b. S_a is the set of adjacent vertices of N_a in G_a, and S_b is the set of adjacent vertices of N_b in G_b. We assume all vertices belong to Class category, and all edges belong to SuperClass category. Hence, S_a and S_b are the sets of vertices linked by the "SuperClass" edge. The iterative similarity is a weighted average of two parts, the previous iterative similarity and SSim between S_a and S_b (explained later):

$$Sim(i)(N_a,N_b) = W_1 * Sim(i-1)(N_a,N_b) + W_2 * SSim_{(i-1)}(S_a,S_b) \quad W_1+W_2=1 \quad (6)$$

For example, let us compute the iterative similarity between the "Class:Part" in Fig.4 and the "Class:Employee" in Fig.5.

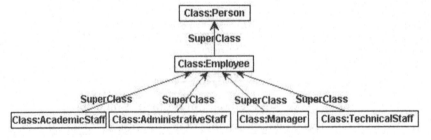

Fig. 5. A parsing graph of ontology "University Faculty"

Na=Class:Part,   Sa={Class:InBook,   Class:InCollection,   Class:Chapter, Class:Article, Class:Reference }

Nb=Class:Employee, Sb={Class:Person, Class:Manager, Class:AcademicStaff, Class:AdministrativeStaff , Class: TechinalStaff }

Assume W_1 = 0.4, W_2= 0.6, Sim (i-1) (Class:Part, Class:Employee) = 0.2, Ssim (i-1)(Sa, Sb) = 0.3.

So, Sim(i)(Class:Part, Class:Employee) = 0.4 * 0.2 + 0.6 * 0.3 = 0.26

The similarity of the set SSim is the total of the similarity of the vertices pairs which is the optimal match between two sets. i stands for the iteration times.

$$SSim_{(i)}(Sa,Sb)=\frac{Max(\sum_{k,j}(S_{ak},S_{bj}))}{Max(|S_a,S_b|)} \quad (7)$$

where (S_{ak},S_{bj}) is a mapping pair.

In OP-graph, different types of vertices connect to other vertices by different types of edges. Therefore we can integrate these adjacent vertices' SSim into the IteSim with weights

$$Sim(i)(N_a,N_b) = W_1 * Sim(i-1)(N_a,N_b) + W_2 * SSim_{(i-1)}(S_a,S_b) \quad W_1+W_2=1$$

$$Sim_{(i)}(N_a,N_b)=W_1*Sim_{(i-1)}(N_a,N_b)+\sum_e (W_e*\frac{Max(\sum_{i=1}^n Sim(S_{aei},S_{bei}))}{Max(|S_{ael}|,|S_{bel}|)}) \quad (8)$$

where W_e is the weigh of the similarity of the sets comprised of the edges type of e.

3.3.5 Graph Match

Now we compute the overall similarity between two OP-graphs. We build a bipartite graph based on two OP-graphs. Vertices of the bipartite graph are the union of the vertices of two OP-graphs. The edges are created between vertices pairs which have valid similarity values, and weights of edge are assigned to be the similarity values. Then the overall similarity between two OP-Graphs is equivalent to the maximum match of bipartite graph. To solve the bipartite maximum match problem, we adopt the Hungary arithmetic which can find the match of bipartite graph and the Kuhn arithmetic which can find the maximum one based on Hungary arithmetic. The $O(|V||E|^2)$ complexity of arithmetic is effective to find the mapping between mid-scale ontologies.

After updating the similarity of the all element pairs through the iterations, we can get the graph similarity between the two OP-graphs with the graph match algorithm. Then we compare it with the previous result. If the difference between the present one and the previous one falls into the predefined admissible range, the iteration stops; otherwise, the iteration goes on until it reaches maximum allowed number of iterations.

Finally according to the correspondent relationships between the vertices of the OP-graph and the elements of the ontology, we obtain the optimal (final) mapping between the two ontologies.

The complexity of OPM is $O(|N|^{5.5})$, where N is the number of the entities of the OP-graph.

3.4 Result Combination

Because our task is to determine the match result for two complete ontologies, so the match correspondences for two modules mapping need to be combined with the match result into a complete one.

3.5 Analysis of Run-Time Complexity

Now we discuss the complexity of the MOM. We consider two situations:

(1) For the ontologies that cannot be modularized, the complexity of the partition module is $O(|V|^5)$. Since the complexity of the exact mapping module is $O(|V|^{5.5}) \sim O(|N|^{5.5})$ (N stand for the number of entities of the OP-graph), therefore, the complexity of the whole algorithm is $O(|N|^{5.5})$, which is same as the complexity without modularizing. (2) For the ontologies that can be modularized, the complexity of the partition module is $MO(|U|^5)$, where $N=MU$, and M is the modules number. From the above, we know the complexity of the module match is $O(|V|^{5.5}) \sim O(|U|^{5.5})$. So the complexity of the MOM algorithm is $MO(|U|)^5 + MO(|U|^{5.5}) \sim MO(|U|^{5.5})$. The complexity of the algorithm without modularization is $O(|N|^{5.5}) = O(|MU|^{5.5}) = O(|M|^{5.5})\ O(|U|^{5.5})$. Comparing the two results, we know the complexity of the whole algorithm decreases by $O(|M|^{4.5})$ after modularizing the large ontologies.

4 Experimental Evaluation

In order to evaluate our approach, we have conducted some experiments. We wanted to investigate and get an intuition about whether our MOM approach is effective for large scale ontology mapping. In the experiment, we evaluated MOM on some practical large data sets: web services ontologies, medical ontologies and tourism ontologies. These ontologies are from different places and have 172-646 concepts. (see Table 1) The ontologies of each pair are similar to each other.

Table 1. Ontologies in experiments

ontologies		concepts	Properties		Instances number	manual mapping
			Data properties	object properties		
Web services	1	209	8	228	16	171
	2	172	13	122	246	158
Medical	1	398	9	166	163	236
	2	443	13	206	247	251
Tourism	1	549	8	312	262	398
	2	646	21	241	354	407

We use standard information retrieval metrics to evaluate our method and compare with other methods[17].

$$\Pr ec = \frac{|m_a \cap m_m|}{|m_a|}, \operatorname{Re} c = \frac{|m_m \cap m_a|}{|m_m|} \qquad (9)$$

where m_a are mappings discovered by MOM(or OPM) and m_m are mapping assigned by experts.

We took the OPM as the baseline method to test the effect of MOM.

OPM - It uses the two ontologies as the input, and does not consider the size of the ontologies.

MOM - It focus on the large scale ontology mapping problems.

Table 2. Experimental comparison between OPM and MOM

Data set	mapping	OPM		MOM	
		Prec	Rec	Prec	Rec
Web services	1 to 2	76.1	73.2	76.0	73.1
	2 to 1	75.2	71.4	75.8	71.6
Medical	1 to 2	71.1	69.2	70.8	69.0
	2 to 1	76.7	74.2	76.8	74.1
Tourism	1 to 2	80.3	73.6	79.1	75.6
	2 to 1	78.5	73.3	79.2	74.6

Table 2 shows the comparison between OPM and MOM. From Table 2, we can found some results of MOM are not as good as the results of OPM. But, from Fig.6,

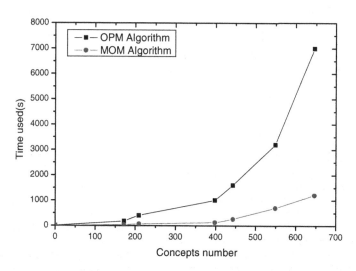

Fig. 6. Testing result comparison between the MOM and OPM

we know the time cost of MOM is much less than the cost of OPM. After analyzing the whole process of MOM, we find the reason which affects mapping accuracy. For some well designed large ontologies, the E-connection based partition approach is effective. But it is not suitable for some poor organized ontologies. A few of uncertain nodes can not be assigned to the correct module. So, in the future, we will develop new partition method to fit all kinds of ontologies.

In short, compared to OPM, for large scale ontologies, our algorithm MOM can significantly reduce the time complexity while keeping the high mapping accuracy. The experiments results show that MOM is very promising for large scale ontologies mapping.

5   Conclusion and Future Work

Large and complex ontologies are still not well supported by current ontology matching prototypes, thereby limiting the practical applicability of such systems. We propose a modularization-orient approach to decompose a large match problem into smaller ones and use a method to significantly reduce the mapping time. Our technique includes sub-steps for large ontology partitioning, finding similar modules, module matching and result combination. The experiments show that our approach is more effective in mapping the large scale ontologies than the traditional approach which directly matches the two large ontologies.

In the future, we would like to continue the work in several directions: (1) in OPM, using machine learning techniques to get all kinds of weight to make our method more effective. (2) Discovery of complex mapping.

Acknowledgments

The authors would like to thank the Natural Science Funds of China (Grant No. 60374071) and the National High Technology Research and Development Program of China (863 Program, Grant No.2002AA411420) for the financial support of this research.

References

1. M. Jayant, A. B. Philip, and R. Erhard. Generic Schema Matching with Cupid, in *Proceedings of the 27th International Conference on Very Large Data Bases*: Morgan Kaufmann Publishers Inc., 2001.
2. H.H.Do and E. Rahm. COMA - a system for flexible combination of schema matching approaches, in *Proceedings of VLDB* 2001, pp. 610-621.
3. D. AnHai, M. Jayant, D. Robin, D. Pedro, and H. Alon. Learning to match ontologies on the Semantic Web. The VLDB Journal, 12(4): 303-319, 2003.
4. M. Sergey, R. Erhard, and A. B. Philip. Rondo: a programming platform for generic model management, in *Proceedings of the 2003 ACM SIGMOD international conference on Management of data*. San Diego, California: ACM Press, 2003.
5. F. Giunchiglia, P. Shvaiko, and M. Yatskevich. S-Match: an algorithm and an implementation of semantic matching, in *Proceedings of ESWS*, 2004, pp. 61-75.

6. R. G. Thomas. Toward principles for the design of ontologies used for knowledge sharing. Int. J. Hum.-Comput. Stud., 43(5-6): 907-928, 1995.
7. M. Ehrig and S.Staab. QOM: Quick ontology mapping, in *Proceedings of ISWC*, 2004.
8. R. Erhard and A. B. Philip. A survey of approaches to automatic schema matching. The VLDB Journal, 10(4): 334-350, 2001.
9. S. Xiaomeng. A text categorization perspective for ontology mapping. Technical report, 2002.
10. R. Erhard, D. Hong-Hai, M. Sabine, and mann. Matching large XML schemas. SIGMOD Rec., 33(4): 26-31, 2004.
11. B. C. Grau, B. Parsia, E. Sirin, and A. Kalyanpur. Modularizing OWL Ontologies, in *the 4th International Semantic Web Conference (ISWC-2005)*, 2005.
12. K. Oliver, L. Carsten, W. Frank, and Z. Michael. E-connections of abstract description systems. Artif. Intell., 156(1): 1-73, 2004.
13. J. Hopcroft and R. Karp. An $n^{5/2}$ algorithm for maximum matchings in bipartite graphs. SIAM Journal on Computing 2(4)225–231, 1973.
14. A. Maedche and S. Staab. Measuring similarity between ontologies, in *Proceedings of EKAW*, 2002.
15. http://owl.man.ac.uk/api.shtml.
16. J.Euzenat and P.Valtchev. Similarity-based ontology alignment in OWL-lite, in *Proceedings of ECAI*, 2004.
17. H.H.Do, S.Melnik, and E.Rahm. Comparison of schema matching evaluations, in *Proceedings of workshop on Web and Databases*, 2002.

A Comparative Study on Representing Units in Chinese Text Clustering

Wang Hongjun[1,2], Yu Shiwen[1], Lv Xueqiang[2], Shi Shuicai[2], and Xiao Shibin[2]

[1] Institute Of Computing Linguistics Peking University, Beijing 100080;
[2] Chinese Information Processing Center Beijing Information Technology Institute,
Beijing 100101
wang.hongjun@trs.com.cn

Abstract. Words and n-grams are commonly used Chinese text representing units and are proved to be good features for Chinese Text Categorization and Information Retrieval. But the effectiveness of applying these representing units for Chinese Text Clustering is still uncovered. This paper is a comparative study of representing units in Chinese Text Clustering. With K-means algorithm, several representing units were evaluated including Chinese character N-gram features, word features and their combinations. We found Chinese word features, Chinese character unigram features and bi-gram features most effective in our experiments. The combination of features didn't improve the results. Detailed experimental results on several public Chinese Text Categorization datasets are provided in the paper.

Keywords: Chinese text Clustering; N-gram feature; Bi-gram feature; Word feature.

1 Introduction

Text clustering has been investigated for use in a number of different areas of text mining and information retrieval. It plays an important role for efficient document organization, summarization, navigation and retrieval [1][2][3][4][5].

In text clustering, a text or document is always represented as a bag of words. There is no boundary between Chinese words, so segmentation is the basis for Chinese Text Processing. Many effective segmentation methods have been proposed in the previous studies. However, when a large number of new words such as names, location names and company names appear in the text, the result of segmentation is usually dissatisfactory [6]. Some researchers tried to use Chinese character N-gram features in Chinese text categorization and information retrieval and proposed their experiment results [7][8][9]. But how to choose appropriate representing units for Chinese text clustering is still a problem.

This paper uses Chinese words, N-grams and their combinations as representing units and compares their performance in document clustering.

The experiment used several public Chinese Text categorization datasets, so the results can be comparable with others.

J. Lang, F. Lin, and J. Wang (Eds.): KSEM 2006, LNAI 4092, pp. 466–476, 2006.

2 Overview of Document Clustering

The task of document clustering is to group a set of documents into clusters, make that the documents in same cluster are similar and the documents in different clusters are dissimilar.

Document clustering includes three steps: represent each document by a vector; computing the similarity between vectors; group vectors into clusters.

(1) Represent each document by a vector

We use the vector space model (VSM) [10] to represent documents as points in a high dimensional space, where each dimension corresponds to a unique word or n-gram from the corpus. The mapping process extracts a list of unique units from each document, assigns each unit a weight, and represents the document with a vector using these units. The vector is defined as:

$$d_i = (w_{i1}, w_{i2}, \ldots , w_{in})$$

In this paper, tf*Idf was used to calculate the weight of each unit w_{in}.

(2) Compute the similarity between vectors

There are a number of possible measures for computing the similarity between documents, but the most common one is the cosine measure, which is defined as:

$$cosine(\ d_1, d_2\ ) = (d_1 \cdot d_2) / \|d_1\| \|d_2\|$$

(3) Group vectors into clusters

Agglomerative hierarchical clustering and K-means are two clustering techniques that are commonly used for text clustering. This paper choose K-means algorithm for document clustering [11].

K-means have a time complexity, which is linear in the number of documents: $O(n*k*t)$. (n: Number of documents; k: Number of clusters; t: Number of iterations) For this reason, it's suitable for large-scale document clustering.

K-means Algorithm for finding *K* clusters.

1. Randomly select K seed documents as the centroids of initial clusters.
2. Assign each document to the cluster with the nearest centroid.
3. Re-compute the centroids of the clusters.
4. Repeat step 2 and 3 for 't' times.

In the experiment, we set Number of iterations 't' = 10.

Since K-means clustering algorithm is easily influenced by selection of initial centroids[12], we random produced 20 sets of seed documents as initial centroids for each dataset and averaged 20 times performances as the final clustering performance.

3 Text Representing Units Selection

Word and n-gram are commonly used text representing units.

In Chinese natural language processing, words are the most frequently used units. There is no boundary between Chinese words, so word segmentation is an essential step. Because there are some difficulties in Chinese word segmentation which haven't been overcame, some researchers tried to use Chinese character N-gram features in Chinese NLP.

N-gram features are fixed length characters that continuously occur in text. Compare to words, Chinese character N-gram features contain some non-words features, which have good statistical qualities on some occasions. But n-grams also have more garbage features than words.

The experiments in Chinese text categorization by Libaoli[7], De-jun Xue[8] show that: Chinese character bi-gram features are good features for Chinese Text Categorization and get comparable performance as word features.

Nie[9] proposed a Chinese text indexing method for information retrieval, combined N-gram and word as index units. The experiment in Chinese retrieval datasets showed that, this method improved the performance of Chinese information retrieval.

These experiments show that: N-gram features have superiority of statistical, and play an important role in Chinese natural language processing.

To compare the relative effectiveness of Chinese representing units to text clustering, we used several different features and compare their performance in text clustering:

1. Chinese word features.
2. Chinese character unigram features.
3. Chinese character bi-gram features.
4. Chinese character trigram features.
5. Chinese character 4-gram features.
6. Chinese character 5-gram features.
7. Combinations of Chinese character unigram features and bi-gram features.
8. Combinations of Chinese character bi-gram features and trigram features.

For example, to a Chinese sentence "文本聚类技术得到了广泛的应用", the features are:

1."文本", "聚类", "技术", "得到", "了", "广泛", "的", "应用"
2."文", "本", "聚", "类", "技", "术", "得", "到", "了", "广", "泛", "的", "应", "用"
3."文本", "本聚", "聚类", "类技", "技术", "术得", "得到", "到了", "了广", "广泛", "泛的", "的应", "应用"
4."文本聚", "本聚类", "聚类技", "类技术", "术得到", "得到了", "了广泛", "广泛的", "泛的应", "的应用"
5."文本聚类", "本聚类技", "聚类技术", "类技术得", "技术得到", "术得到了", "得到了广", "到了广泛", "了广泛的", "泛的应用"
6."文本聚类技", "本聚类技术", "聚类技术得", "类技术得到", "技术得到了", "术得到了广", "得到了广泛", "到了广泛的", "了广泛的应", "广泛的应用"
7."文", "本", "聚", "类", "技", "术", "得", "到", "了", "广", "泛", "的", "应", "用", "文本", "本聚", "聚类", "类技", "技术", "术得", "得到", "到了", "了广", "广泛", "泛的", "的应", "应用"

8."文本", "本聚", "聚类", "类技", "技术", "术得", "得到", "到了", "了广",
"广泛","泛的", "的应", "应用",

"文本聚", "本聚类", "聚类技", "类技术", "术得到", "得到了", "了广泛",
"广泛的","泛的应", "的应用"

High dimensionality of feature space is a crucial obstacle for N-gram Text
Clustering. Noisy features can lead to misleading clusters, so feature selection is
needed. We adopt a simple method based on Document Frequency (DF) and DF
method is used in text categorization [13]. Document frequency is the number of
documents in which a feature occurs in a dataset. An N-gram or a word is not useful if
it appears in every document or it appears only in one or few documents. So we
remove N-grams or words with a very small DF (DF=2). Feature selection can also
reduce running time.

4 Experimental Procedures and Evaluation

4.1 Evaluation Metrics

To measure the quality of clusters, several measures have been proposed such as
entropy, precision (also called purity), F-measure, overall similarity and so on.

F-measure is more suitable for measuring the effectiveness of the hierarchical
clustering[2][3][14][15]. K-means method used in our experiment is not a hierarchical
clustering method. Overall similarity should be used in the absence of any external
information, such as class labels[3]. As we shall see in the next section, all test
documents used in our experiment are tagged with class labels.

For these reasons, F-measure and overall similarity aren't appropriate measures for
our experiment and we use entropy and precision to evaluate cluster quality. The two
measures are widely used to evaluate the performance of unsupervised clustering
algorithms.[2][3] [13][14][15]

If one representing unit performs better than other representing units on both two
measures, we can have some confidence that it is truly the best representing units for
the situation being evaluated.

(a) Entropy
Entropy measures the uniformity or purity of a cluster.

Let C and C' denote the number of obtained clusters and the number of original
classes respectively. Let A denote the set of documents in an obtained cluster, and the
class label of each document is denoted as label(d_i) . The entropy for all clusters is
defined by the weighted sum of the entropy for all clusters, as shown in the equation
(1):

$$\text{Entropy} = -\sum_{k=1}^{C'} \frac{|A_k|}{N} \sum_{j=1}^{C} P_{jk} * \log(p_{jk}) \qquad (1)$$

$$P_{jk} = \frac{1}{|A_k|} |\{d_i \mid label \ (d_i = c_j)\}| \qquad (2)$$

(b) Precision
The precision measure evaluates the degree to which each cluster contains documents from a single category.

For each cluster, it commonly consists of documents from several different classes. So we choose the class label that shares with most documents in this cluster as the final class label. Then, the precision for each cluster is defined as:

$$\text{Precision}(A) = \frac{1}{|A|}\max(|\{d_i \mid label \ (d_i = c_j)\}|) \tag{3}$$

To avoid the possible bias from small clusters with high precision, the final precision is defined by the weighted sum of the precision for all clusters, as shown in the equation (4):

$$\text{Precision} = \sum_{k=1}^{G'} \frac{A_k}{N} \Pr ecision \ (A_k) \tag{4}$$

Lower entropy means better results while higher precision means better results.

4.2 Document Collections

There are several Chinese text datasets for Chinese Text categorization: PKU Tianwang TC corpus (html), 863 TC corpus, People Daily Corpus (1997), Fudan University TC corpus. Every document in these datasets is tagged with class labels. These datasets can also be used for testing Chinese text clustering.

Since document clustering performance may varies greatly on different dataset, we use several different text datasets to evaluate its performance, which include 863 TC corpus, People Daily Corpus (1997), Fudan University TC corpus and Internet News TC corpus (colleted by us) as our datasets. Table 1 shows their detail info.

Table 1. Summary description of datasets

Datasets	Classes Num	Document Num	Size
863 TC corpus	36	3600	20.3M
People Daily corpus (1997)	5	1252	1.36M
Internet news TC corpus	10	2620	3.48M
Fudan University TC corpus	20	9833	137M

Since we used standard public datasets to evaluate document clustering, the experiments could be comparable with others.

5 Experimental Results and Discussions

5.1 Experimental Results

In the experiment, we used four datasets. In each dataset, we random produced 10 group documents as the seed documents of K-Means.

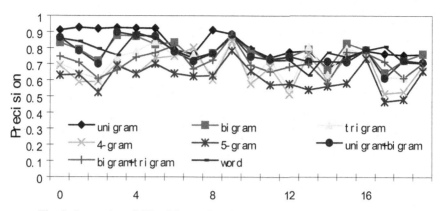

Fig. 1. Comparison Of Precision on People Daily (20 group seed documents)

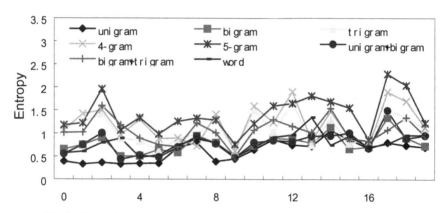

Fig. 2. Comparison of Entropy on People Daily (20 group seed documents)

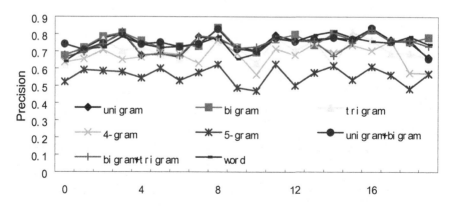

Fig. 3. Comparison of Precision on Internet News (20 group seed documents)

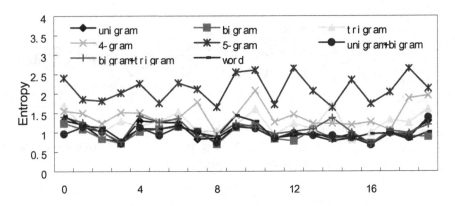

Fig. 4. Comparison of Entropy on Internet News (20 group seed documents)

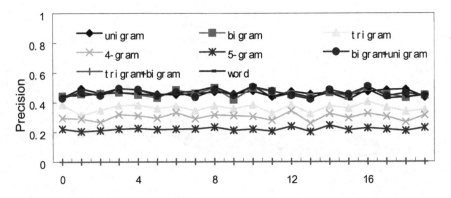

Fig. 5. Comparison of Precision on 863 Corpus (20 group seed documents)

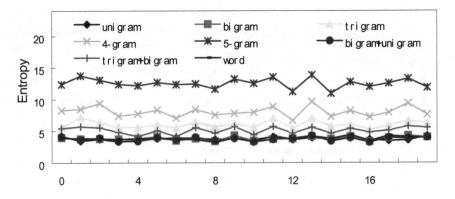

Fig. 6. Comparison of Entropy on 863 Corpus (20 group seed documents)

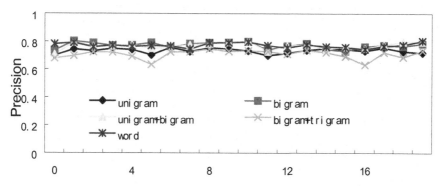

Fig. 7. Comparison of Precision on Fudan Corpus (20 group seed documents)

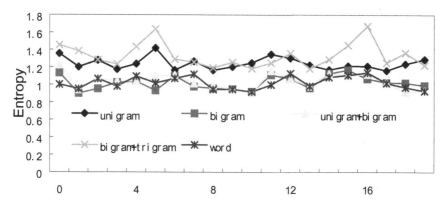

Fig. 8. Comparison of Precision on Fudan Corpus (20 group seed documents)

Table 2. Comparison of Precision on 4 datasets (* means the result was omitted)

Representing Units	People Daily	Internet News	863 Corpus	Fudan Corpus
1-gram	**0.8225**	0.7431	**0.4650**	0.7337
2-gram	0.7795	0.7592	0.4586	**0.7724**
3-gram	0.7067	0.7093	0.3625	*
4-gram	0.6674	0.6761	0.3027	*
5-gram	0.6172	0.5597	0.2207	*
2-gram+1-gram	0.7678	**0.7541**	0.4630	0.7694
3-gram+2-gram	0.7120	0.7382	0.3967	0.7089
Word	0.7792	0.7445	0.4573	0.7732

Figure 1,3,5,7 show the precision results of each datasets using different features. X-axis represents the 20 group different seed documents used by K-Means; Y-axis represents the precision of each group seed group.

Figure 2,4,6,8 show the entropy results of each datasets using different features. X-axis represents the 20 group different seed documents used by K-Means; Y-axis represents the entropy of each group seed group.

Table 2 shows the precision comparison on 4 datasets.

Table 3. Comparison of Entropy on 4 datasets (* means the result was omitted)

Representing Units	People Daily	Internet News	863 Corpus	Fudan Corpus
1-gram	**0.6147**	1.0223	3.7568	1.2453
2-gram	0.7792	**0.9567**	3.8339	**1.0230**
3-gram	1.0895	1.2505	6.0478	*
4-gram	1.2117	1.4421	8.0789	*
5-gram	1.4170	2.1174	12.5426	*
2-gram+1-gram	0.8023	0.9751	**3.7327**	1.0437
3-gram+2-gram	1.0551	1.1030	5.1236	1.3334
Word	0.7923	1.0334	3.8395	1.0257

5.2 Experimental Discussions

According the above figures and tables, Chinese word features, Chinese character unigram features and bi-gram features got the best results, 3-gram、4-gram、5-gram got worse result. N-gram's combinations didn't improve the result effectively.

Compare to Chinese character n-gram features, Chinese word features have intuitively better semantic qualities and contains fewer garbage words than n-gram features. In the experiment word features got good result and the feature number is stable.

Chinese character bi-gram features got a good result and their features numbers are slightly larger than the numbers of word features after feature selection using DF.

In Chinese, most words consist of two Chinese characters. Word features and bi-gram features share a large quantity same features. Bi-gram features also contain some non-words features, which have good statistical qualities on some occasions. So bi-gram features got good results in the experiment.

Chinese character unigram features also got good results and its feature number is the smallest. Commonly, Chinese character unigram features couldn't express complete meanings themselves. So they are rarely be used in text clustering, text categorization and other applications. But this experiment got a different result and it proved that unigrams are good features for text clustering.

In the experiments, we found that both word features and N-gram features contain a lot of garbage features that do no help to text clustering. How to remove these garbage features is an important research issue. Compare to N-gram features, word features have a good advantage: many linguistic features can be utilized to remove garbage words, such as POS [16], semantic relations and so on. We expect these domain knowledge will improve Chinese text clustering in our future experiments.

6 Conclusions

This paper presents the results of an experimental study on representing units in Chinese text clustering. Several representing units were evaluated including Chinese character N-gram features, word features and their combinations. We found that Chinese word features, Chinese character unigram features and bi-gram features got the best results. But their combinations didn't improve the results.

We only used K-Means method in this experiment, other method will be tested and more public datasets will be used. Our future work also includes utilizing linguistic features to improve Chinese text clustering.

Acknowledgement

This work is supported by the National Grand Fundamental Research 973 Program of China (No. 2004CB318102); the National Natural Science Foundation of China (No.60272084); Beijing Natural Science Foundation Program and Scientific Research Key Program of Beijing Municipal Commission of Education (KZ200310772013); the Scientific Research Common Program of Beijing Municipal Commission of Education (M200510772008, KM200610772008).

References

[1] Cutting, D., Karger, D., Pedersen, J. and Tukey, J. W., Scatter/Gather: A Cluster-based Approach to Browsing Large Document Collections, SIGIR 92, 318– 329 (1992).(5)

[2] B. Larsen and C. Aone. Fast and effective text mining using linear-time document clustering. In Proc. 5th ACM SIGKDD Int. Conf. on Knowledge Discovery and Data Mining, 1999.

[3] M. Steinbach, G. Karypis, and V. Kumar. A comparison of document clustering techniques. In KDD Workshop on Text Mining, 2000

[4] Tao Liu, Shengping Liu, Zheng Chen, Wei-Ying Ma. An Evaluation on Feature Selection for Text Clustering. ICML2003

[5] Krishna Kummamuru, Rohit Lotlikar, Shourya Roy. A Hierarchical Monothetic Document Clustering Algorithm for Summarization and Browsing Search Results. WWW2004, May 17–22, 2004, New York,USA.

[6] Huaping Zhang, Qun Liu, Hao Zhang, Xueqi Cheng, Automatic Recognition of Chinese Unknown Words Based on Role, Tagging 19th International Conference on Computational Linguistics, SigHan Workshop, 2002.8.

[7] Li Baoli, Chen Yuzhong, Bai Xiaojing, Shiwen Yu. Experimental Study on Representing Units in Chinese Text Categorization. CICLing 2003: 602-614

[8] De-jun Xue. A Study on Key Issues of Automated Text Categorization for Chinese Documents. PHD theses, Tsinghua University. 2004

[9] Jian-Yun Nie, and Fuji Ren. Chinese information retrieval: using characters or words? Information Processing and Management. 1999, 35:443-462

[10] Salton,G. Automatic Text Processing: The Transformation, Analysis, and Retrieval of Information by Computer, Addison-Wesley, Reading, MA. 1989.

[11] Faber, V. Clustering and the Continuous k-Means Algorithm, Los Alamos Science, November 22, 1994.
[12] Paul Bradley and Usama Fayyad, *Refining Initial Points for K-Means Clustering*, Proc of ICML1998(pp. 91-99).
[13] Yang, Y., & Pedersen, J. O. A comparative study on feature selection in text categorization. Proc. Of ICML1997 (pp. 412-420).
[14] Y. Zhao and G. Karypis. Evaluation of hierarchical clustering algorithms for document datasets. In Proceedings of the International Conference on Information and Knowledge Management, 2002.
[15] Y. Zhao and G. Karypis. Empirical and theoretical comparisons of selected criterion functions for document clustering. Machine Learning, 55(3), 2004.
[16] Mihai Surdeanu, Jordi Turmo, Alicia Ageno, A hybrid unsupervised approach for document clustering, Proceeding of the eleventh ACM SIGKDD international conference on Knowledge discovery in data mining, August 21-24, 2005
[17] Jinying Chen, Martha Stone Palmer: Chinese Verb Sense Discrimination Using an EM Clustering Model with Rich Linguistic Features. ACL 2004: 295-302

A Description Method of Ontology Change Management Using Pi-Calculus*

Meiling Wang, Longfei Jin, and Lei Liu**

Key Laboratory of Symbolic Computation and Knowledge
Engineering of Ministry of Education of P.R. China,
College of Computer Science and Technology, Jilin University,
Changchun, 130012, P.R. China
liulei@jlu.edu.cn

Abstract. In an open and dynamic environment, due to the changes in the application's domain or the user's requirements, the domain knowledge changes over time and ontology evolves continually. Pi-calculus is a kind of mobile process algebra which can be used for modeling concurrent and dynamic systems. Based on the pi-calculus, this paper proposes a kind of ontology process model used for solving the change implementation and propagation problems in ontology evolution process. This solution is discussed at three levels: the change implementation of single ontology evolution, the push-based synchronization realization for the change propagation in the evolution of multiple dependent ontologies within a single node, and the pull-based synchronization realization for the change propagation of the distributed ontologies evolution.

1 Introduction

In the Semantic Web, ontology is a shared and machine-executable conceptual model in a specific domain of interest [1], and is seen as the key aspect of Semantic Web [2].

Currently, in a more open and dynamic environment, due to the changes in the application's domain or the user's requirements, the domain knowledge changes over time and ontology evolves continually [3]. A modification in one part of an ontology may generate some subtle inconsistencies in the other parts of the same ontology, in the ontology-based instances as well as in the dependent ontologies and applications [4]. After applying a change to a consistent ontology, the ontology itself, its instances, its dependent ontologies and applications must remain in (another) consistent state. Thus a consistent evolution is needed to guarantee the consistency of ontology when changes.

* This paper is sponsored by European Commission under grant No.TH/Asia Link/010 (111084) and Jilin province science development plain project of China under grant No. 20050527.
** Corresponding author.

J. Lang, F. Lin, and J. Wang (Eds.): KSEM 2006, LNAI 4092, pp. 477–489, 2006.
© Springer-Verlag Berlin Heidelberg 2006

Ontology evolution is the timely adaptation of an ontology to the arisen changes and the consistent propagation of these changes to dependent artefacts [5], and it facilitates the modification of an ontology by preserving its consistency. The complexity of ontology evolution increases as ontology grows in size, so a structured ontology evolution process is required. A six-phase evolution process [6] is proposed: (1) change capturing; (2) change representation; (3) semantics of change; (4) change implementation; (5) change propagation; and (6) change validation.

In a distributed setting like the World Wide Web, to enable the information reuse and interoperability, multiple and distributed ontologies must be supported, and ontology evolution becomes more difficult. Pi-calculus is a kind of mobile process algebra used for modeling concurrent and dynamic systems [7], thus a kind of ontology process model for ontology change management is proposed in this paper. Based on the process model, the change implementation and propagation problems of ontology evolution process are discussed at three levels: the change implementation of single ontology evolution, the synchronization realization for the change propagation in the evolution of multiple dependent ontologies within a single node and the distributed ontologies.

Section 2 gives a brief introduction to pi-calculus. Section 3 describes a process model for ontology using pi-calculus as a basis for ontology change management. Section 4 elaborates respectively on managing changes at three levels. Section 5 is an overview of related work. Section 6 concludes the paper and discusses some further work.

2   An Overview of Pi-Calculus

Pi-calculus proposed by Robin Milner is an extension of process algebra CCS (Calculus of Communication System) [8], and is considered as a concurrent theory with the research emphasis on mobile communication between processes. The basic computing entities of pi-calculus are names and processes, and the communication between two processes is realized by transferring objects along their link (port). Link names belong to the same category as the transferred objects, thus the link name between two processes can be transferred so as to change interconnections as they interact. For this reason, pi-calculus has been called a calculus of "mobile" processes and is used to model concurrent and dynamic systems [9].

A simple communication between P and Q is shown in Fig.1. P and Q are processes, x, y and z are link (port) names; P sends a message along $\overline{y}$, and Q receives the message from y. The syntax of pi-calculus [10] is:

$$P ::= 0|\overline{y}x.P|y(x).P|\tau.P|P + Q|P|Q|(x)P|[x = y]P|A(x_1, x_2, \cdots, x_n).$$

1). 0 is the empty process, which cannot perform any actions.
2). $\overline{y}x.P$ is an output prefix, where $\overline{y}$ is an output port and x is a datum sent out along that port. The intuition is that x is sent along $\overline{y}$ and thereafter the process continues as P.

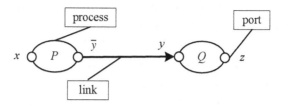

Fig. 1. Communication between P and Q

3). $y(x).P$ is an input prefix, where y is an input port and x is a variable which will get its value from y. The intuition is that x is received along the y and thereafter x is the placeholder for the received name. After the input, the process will continue as P but with the newly received name replacing x.

4). $\tau.P$ is a silent prefix which represents a process that can evolve to P without any interaction with the environment.

5). $P + Q$ is a sum representing a process that can enact either P or Q.

6). $P|Q$ is a parallel composition which represents the combined behavior of P and Q executing in parallel. P and Q can act independently, and may also communicate if one performs an output and the other one performs an input along the same port.

7). $(x)P$ is a restriction. The process behaves as P but the name x is local, meaning that it cannot immediately be used as a port for the communication between P and its environment. However, x can be used for the communication between the components within P.

8). $[x = y]P$ is a match, which will behave as P if x and y are the same name, else will do nothing.

9). $A(x_1, x_2, \cdots, x_n)$ is an identifier, where n is the arity of A. Every identifier has a definition $A(x_1, x_2, \cdots, x_n) \overset{def}{=} P$, where the x_i must be pairwise distinct, and the intuition is that $A(y_1, y_2, \cdots, y_n)$ behaves as P with y_i replacing x_i for each i. So a definition can be thought as a process declaration, $x_1, x_2, \cdots, x_n$ as formal parameters, and the identifier $A(y_1, y_2, \cdots, y_n)$ as an invocation with actual parameters $y_1, y_2, \cdots, y_n$.

Structural congruence and *operational semantics* are omitted for the length limitation.

3   Ontology Process Model

Based on the pi-calculus in section 2, this paper proposes a kind of ontology process model for ontology change management. Entities of a concrete ontology including concepts, properties and instances are presented as processes; associations between entities are denoted as the links between processes (entities), and an entity can interoperate with another one associated with it by the link between them. Fig.2 is a simple ontology example, and if d is a link name between concept *Person* and *Student*, thus *Person* can send a message to *Student* along the port $\bar{d}$, and *Student* can receive the message from *Person* by the port d, vice versa. The process model of the ontology in Fig.2 is shown in Fig.3.

All the entities of an ontology including concepts, properties and instances are denoted as processes, thus the ontology itself can be denoted as a complex process equal to the parallel composition of all the entity processes contained. The ontology process of Fig.3 is described as:

$$Root|Person|Project|Works\_at|Prof|Student|PhD|MSc|WiHi$$

$$|ResearchProject|Ontologging.$$

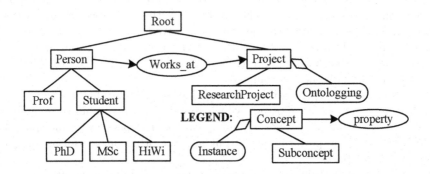

Fig. 2. A simple ontology

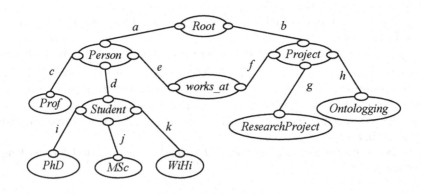

Fig. 3. An ontology process model

4   Managing Changes in Ontology Evolution Using Pi-Calculus

Based on the ontology process model described in the section 3, this section will solve the implementation and propagation problems of the changes in ontology evolution process using pi-calculus, especially three aspects are discussed: section

4.1 is about the change implementation of single ontology evolution; section 4.2 discusses the change propagation realization in the evolution of multiple dependent ontologies within a single node, and section 4.3 discusses the change management of the distributed ontologies evolution.

4.1 Single Ontology Process Model Evolution

Three elementary change operations: *CreateEntity*, *DeleteEntity* and *ModifyEntity* are defined as the processes as follows:

Fig. 4. *CreateEntity*

$$CreateEntity(E_1, E_2, x) \stackrel{def}{=} \overline{x}(CREATE).x(msg_1).[msg_1 = CREATE$$

$$-ACK]\overline{x}(END).E_2|x(msg_2).[msg_2 = CREATE]\overline{x}(CREATEACK).E_1$$

Fig. 5. *DeleteEntity*

$$DeleteEntity(E_1, E_2, x) \stackrel{def}{=} \overline{x}(DELETE).x(msg_1).[msg_1 = DELETE$$

$$-ACK]0|x(msg_2).[msg_2 = DELETE]\overline{x}(DELETEACK).E_1$$

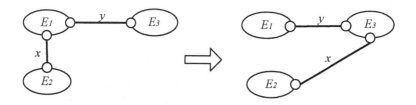

Fig. 6. *ModifyEntity*

$$ModifyEntity(E_1, E_2, E_3, x, y) \stackrel{def}{=} \overline{x}(MODIFY).x(msg_1).[msg_1 = MO$$

$$-DIFYACK]\overline{x}(END).E_2|x(msg_2).[msg_2 = MODIFY]\overline{y}(MODIFY).$$

$$y(msg_3).[msg_3 = MODIFYACK]\overline{x}(MODIFYACK).\overline{y}(x).E_1|y(msg_4).$$

$$[msg_4 = MODIFY]\overline{y}(MODIFYACK).y(z).E_3$$

$$MsgName = \{CREATE, CREATEACK, DELETE, DELETEACK,$$

$$MODIFY, MODIFYACK, BEGIN, END\}$$

Message names in the set *MsgName* are used for the synchronization of change operations: *CREATE* and *CREATEACK* are for *CreateEntity*, *DELETE* and *DELETEACK* are for *DeleteEntity*, and *MODIFY* and *MODIFYACK* are for *ModifyEntity*. Complex change operation is defined as the composition of elementary operations, and *BEGIN* and *END* are for the composition. *CreateEntity* takes precedence over *ModifyEntity*, and *ModifyEntity* takes precedence over *DeleteEntity*.

For single ontology evolution process [11], the essential phase is the *semantics of change*, whose task is to maintain ontology consistency. A single ontology is consistent if it satisfies a set of conditions or invariants and all used entities are defined [12]. Applying a change to an ontology will not always leave it in a consistent state, so some additional changes those guarantee the transition into a consistent state are needed; however, for some change, different sets of additional changes may be generated to lead it to the different final consistent states. An *evolution strategy* unambiguously defines the way how an ontology change will be resolved resulting not in an arbitrary consistent state but in a consistent state fulfilling the user's preferences [6].

A particular evolution strategy is typically chosen by the user at the start of the evolution process. Assume that the chosen evolution strategy determines that for the concept removal to reconnect subconcepts to the parent concepts. By selecting this strategy, the removal of a concept *Student* from the process model of Fig.3 will be implemented as

$$\overline{d}(BEGIN).(i(msg_1)|j(msg_2)|k(msg_3)).[msg_1 = END][msg_2 = END]$$

$$[msg_3 = END]DeleteEntity(Person, Student, d)|d(msg).[msg = BEGIN]$$

$$(ModifyEntity(Student, PhD, Person, i, d)|ModifyEntity(Student, MSc,$$

$$Person, j, d)|ModifyEntity(Student, WiHi, Person, k, d))$$

The reconnection from *PhD*, *MSc* and *WiHi* to *Person* must take precedence over the deletion of *Student*, otherwise the deletion of *Student* would cause the deletion of all its subconcepts and induce wrong result.

4.2 Evolution of Multiple Dependent Ontology Process Models

According to the open-closed reuse principle [13], each ontology should be a closed, consistent, and self-contained entity, but be open to the extensions in the other ontologies, thus reuse can be supported by allowing an ontology process model to include some other ontology process models to obtain the union of the definitions of all the included models.

Consider the inclusion relationships among the ontologies within one node, except for cyclical inclusions and subsets inclusions. Fig.7 presents four ontology process models: Sports Ontology (SO), Bicycle Ontology (BO), Climbing Ontology (CO), and Integrated Catalog Ontology (ICO). BO and CO each include SO, and ICO includes BO and CO. In SO and CO, Sports Utility does not have any subconcepts or superconcepts, but in BO it has one subconcept Bicycle and in ICO it has one superconcept Catalog Item. On the right-hand side, the direct acyclic inclusion graph is shown. SO is indirectly included in ICO twice, once through BO and once through CO, but ICO will contain all the elements of SO only once.

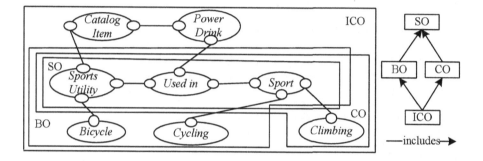

Fig. 7. Four Dependent Ontologies

An ontology that includes some other ontologies is called a *dependent ontology*. A dependent ontology is consistent if the ontology itself and all its included ontologies, observed alone and independently of the ontologies in which they are reused, are single ontology consistent [12]. As an included ontology is changed, the consistency of the dependent ontologies may be invalidated, thus maintaining the consistency of not only single ontologies but also dependent ontologies should be taken into account. For example of Fig.7, if *Sports Utility* of SO is deleted, BO and ICO will become inconsistent since *Bicycle* and *Catalog Item* will have a superconcept and a subconcept undefined respectively.

The consistency maintenance of multiple dependent ontologies within one node may be achieved by the *push-based* synchronization approach[1]: changes of the changed ontology are propagated to dependent ontologies as they happen [14]. To avoid temporal inconsistency, changes should be pushed immediately as they occur [15].

According to the inclusion relationship, all the ontologies within a single node are ordered: for each ontology O_1 and O_2, if O_1 includes O_2 directly or indirectly, then O_2 occurs before O_1 in the order; if O_1 and O_2 do not include each other

---

[1] The other approach is pull-based synchronization approach.

and both include the same ontologies or are included by the same ontologies, then they are parallel in the order. The order is so-called *ontology propagation order*. When changes are propagated to the dependent ontologies, only those ones that include the changed ontology and follow it in the ontology propagation order must be visited. In order to propagate changes to an ontology, firstly they must be processed by all the ontologies included in the target ontology, and only the induced changes but not the original ones should be propagated further up the ontology inclusion order, otherwise an invalid evolution process would be caused since a change cannot be processed twice. The processing order of the changes propagated from other ontologies is important: ontology O should process the changes generated by the ontologies that O directly includes before process the ones generated by the ontologies that O indirectly includes, otherwise the indirectly included ontologies would generate some additional changes in O that would be received later from the directly included ones, finally resulting in the same change processed twice.

With respect to the example of Fig.7, the propagation order is $SO \rightarrow BO|CO \rightarrow ICO$; suppose that the links between BO and SO, CO and SO, BO and ICO, CO and ICO are x, y, z and t respectively; if SO is changed and the operation is *action*, then the *push-based* synchronization based on the ontology process model will be realized as follows:

$$action.action_1.(\overline{x}(BEGIN)|\overline{y}(BEGIN)).SO$$

$$|x(msg_1).[msg_1 = BEGIN]action_2.\overline{z}(BEGIN).BO$$

$$|y(msg_2).[msg_2 = BEGIN]action_3.\overline{t}(BEGIN).CO$$

$$|(z(msg_3).[msg_3 = BEGIN]action_4$$

$$|t(msg_4).[msg_4 = BEGIN]action_5).action_6.\overline{t}(END).ICO$$

In which $action_1$, $action_2$, $action_3$ and $action_6$ denote the additional change operations generated by *action* on SO, BO, CO and ICO respectively; $action_4$ denotes the additional change operation generated by $action_2$ on ICO; and $action_5$ denotes the additional change operation generated by $action_3$ on ICO.

4.3   Evolution of Distributed Ontology Process Models

In Semantic Web, ontologies spread across many different nodes and reuse is achieved by replicating the distributed ontologies locally and including them in other ontologies.

A *distributed dependent ontology* is an ontology that depends on the ontologies residing at the different nodes in the distributed environment. Fig.8 shows a distributed ontology system. SO and CO are defined at service provider A, because CO is defined at the same node as SO, no replication is necessary. BO is defined at service provider B, so to reuse SO it must be replicated to B. ICO is defined at service provider C, so SO, BO and CO must be replicated to C. In order to

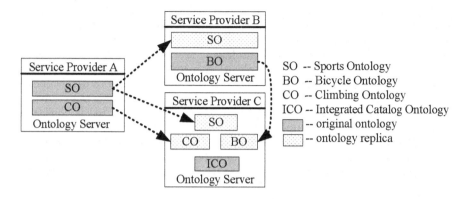

Fig. 8. Distributed ontologies

replicate an ontology model, it must be physically accessed, thus each ontology model is associated with a physical URI: unambiguously identifies the location of the model and contains all the information necessary to access the model.

Replication introduces a kind of significant inconsistency. An example is that *SO* at *B* is inconsistent if it has not been updated according to the changes of its original at *A*; since *BO* at *B* includes *SO* which is inconsistent, then *BO* is inconsistent; so is *ICO* at *C*.

An ontology is *replication consistent* if it is equivalent to its original and all its included ontologies (directly and indirectly) are replication consistent [12]. To solve the replication inconsistency between distributed ontologies, restrict that modification should always be directly performed at the original but not replicas and be propagated to the replicas, and adopt pull synchronization approach between originals and replicas. According to the pull synchronization approach, information of the included ontologies is stored in the dependent ontology, the original ontologies are checked periodically to detect changes and collect deltas[2], and loose consistency which permits temporary inconsistency is allowed to increase performance. Each ontology must contain an associated version number, create an instance of special evolution log and keep its physical URI. Each replica must contain a physical URI of its original and its original's evolution log. Evolution log tracks the history of the original changes from which deltas are identified. The deltas extracted from evolution logs are merged into a list of changes. Replication and dependency inconsistency must be resolved together in one step. An ontology can be included in many other ontologies, and its changes will be included into the logs of all these ontologies, thus the changes from different deltas caused by the same change of a common included ontology should be grouped and the duplication must be eliminated. After determining the directly included replicas of the ontologies to be updated, the logs of these ontologies are accessed.

---

[2] Changes that have been applied to the original since the last synchronization of replica.

486   M. Wang, L. Jin, and L. Liu

The version number of ontology increases each time when it is changed. Replication consistency is performed by determining the equivalence of ontology with its original by version number comparison and by recursively determining the replication consistency of included ontologies [12]. For example of Fig.8, service provider C wants to resolve the replication inconsistency of ICO. ICO is an original and directly includes the replicas of BO and CO, thus to determine the replication consistency of BO and CO recursively. If BO or CO is not equivalent with its original by version number comparison and the original is consistent, then the replica should be updated and SO should be considered recursively; else if the original is not consistent, then the determination of replicas is aborted because the originals of BO and CO should be consistent to obtain the changes from SO through them. The pull synchronization process is realized as follows:

$$(\overline{z}(BEGIN)|\overline{t}(BEGIN)).(z(msg_1)|t(msg_2)).[msg_1 = END][msg_2 = END$$

$$]action_1.ICO|z(msg_3).[msg_3 = BEGIN]\overline{c}(IFCONSISTENT).c(msg_4).$$

$$([msg_4 = CONSISTENT]\overline{x}(BEGIN).x(msg_5).([msg_5 = END]\overline{z}(END).$$

$$action_2 + [msg_5 = NOTREADY]\overline{z}(NOTREADY)) + [msg_4 = INCON$$

$$-SISTENT]\overline{z}(NOTREADY)).BO|t(msg_6).[msg_6 = BEGIN]\overline{b}(IFCON$$

$$-SISTENT).b(msg_7).([msg_7 = CONSISTENT]\overline{y}(BEGIN).y(msg_8).([$$

$$msg_8 = END]\overline{t}(END).action_3 + [msg_8 = NOTREADY]\overline{t}(NOTREADY))$$

$$+[msg_7 = INCONSISTENT]\overline{t}(NOTREADY)).CO|(x(msg_9)|y(msg_{10})).$$

$$[msg_9 = BEGIN][msg_{10} = BEGIN]\overline{s}(IFCONSISTENT).s(msg_{11})$$

$$([msg_{11} = CONSISTENT](\overline{x}(END)|\overline{y}(END)).action_4 + [msg_{11} = IN$$

$$-CONSISTENT](\overline{x}(NOTREADY)|\overline{y}(NOTREADY))).SO$$

Suppose that the links between BO and SO, CO and SO, BO and ICO, CO and ICO are x, y, z and t respectively. b, c and s respectively denote the links of physical URI between the replicas of BO, CO and SO at C and their originals. $IFCONSISTENT$, $CONSISTENT$ and $INCONSISTENT$ are the messages used for the synchronization between originals and replicas. $NOTREADY$ is returned by the included replica when its original is inconsistent and the process will be suspended. $action_1$ is the change operation on ICO which may be caused by the replication inconsistencies of BO, CO and SO; $action_2$ and $action_3$ are respectively the change operations on BO and CO which may be caused by the replication inconsistencies of itself and SO; $action_4$ is the change operation on SO which may be caused by its replication inconsistency.

5   Related Work

Ontologies are increasing in popularity, and are applied in more and more application areas. Ontology evolution is a very complex problem of ontology engineering and is very significant for the Semantic Web. Much related work has been done on the ontology evolution investigation.

[6] identifies a six-phase evolution process introduced in section 1. [5] defines three types of change discovery and proposes an evolution log based on an evolution ontology for the KAON ontology model. An implementation of data-driven change discovery is included in the KAON tool suite [16]. [17] describes a set of changes for the OWL ontology language based on an OWL meta-model. [18] presents the *PromptDiff* ontology-versioning environment, which compares and presents *structural* changes rather than changes in text representation of ontologies. [19] proposes an approach for analyzing and classifying the operations on ontology according to their impact on metadata. [20] discusses OntoView, a web-based change management system for ontologies. [12] presents an approach for evolution in the context of dependent and distributed ontologies. [21] presents an approach to model ontology evolution as the reconfiguration-design problem solving. In [22] a model transformation based conceptual framework for ontology evolution is presented.

Pi-calculus is an expertise for describing mobile process [23] and enables dynamic system modeling and synchronization detection. As a powerful and mature formal method, a large number of tools are provided for correctness detection and related application, such as JACK tool set, pi-calculus based language PICT, executable pi-calculus EPI and value-passing process algebra tool VPAM [24]. For the aptness for pi-calculus to model concurrent and dynamic systems, this paper proposes to manage the changes in ontology evolution using pi-calculus.

6   Conclusions and Further Work

Based on the pi-calculus, this paper proposes a kind of ontology process model for ontology change management: entities including the concepts, properties and instances are described as processes; associations between the entities are denoted as the links between processes (entities) and one entity can interoperate with another one associated with it by the link between them; an ontology as a set of entities is described as a complex process equal to the parallel composition of all the entity processes.

Based on the process model, the change implementation and propagation problems of ontology evolution process are discussed at three levels: change implementation and precedence order of single ontology evolution, realization of the push-based synchronization for the change propagation in the evolution of multiple dependent ontologies within a single node, and the realization of the pull synchronization for the change propagation of distributed ontologies evolution.

A lot of work is needed to do, just explain a few. To refine the ontology process model and the elementary change operations, to define the complex change operations, to consider the change validation based on the model and develop the tools supporting the evolution process for single ontology, multiple dependent ontologies within a single node and distributed ontologies.

References

1. Bussler, C., Fensel, D., and Maedche, A. A Conceptual Architecture for Semantic Web Enabled Web Services. SIGMOD Record, 31(4): 24-29, 2002.
2. T. Berners-Lee, J. Hendler, and O. Lassila. The semantic web. Scientific American, 2001(5), 2001. available at http://www.sciam.com/2001/0501issue/0501berners-lee.html.
3. D. Fensel. Ontologies: dynamics networks of meaning. In Proceedings of the 1st Semantic web working symposium, Stanford, CA, USA, 2001.
4. M. Klein, and D. Fensel. Ontology versioning for the Semantic Web. In Proceedings of International Semantic Web Working Symposium, USA, 2001.
5. Ljlijana Stojanovic. Methods and Tools for Ontology Evolution. PhD thesis, University of Karlsruhe, 2004.
6. Ljiljana Stojanovic, Alexander Mädche, Boris Motik, and Nenad Stojanovic. User-driven ontology evolution management. In Proceedings of the 13th European Conference on Knowledge Engineering and Management (EKAW 2002), number 2473 in Lecture Notes in Computer Science, pages 285-300, Siguenza, Spain, October 2002. Springer-Verlag.
7. Jun Liao, Hao Tan, and Jinde Liu. Describing and Verifying Web Service Using Pi-Calculus. CHINESE JOURNAL OF COMPUTER, 28(4): 635-643, 2005.
8. R. Milner. A Calculus of Communicating Systems. number 92 in Lecture Notes in Computer Science, 1980. Springer-Verlag.
9. U. Nestmann, and B. Victor. Calculi for mobile processes: Bibliography and web pages. Bulletin of the EATCS, 64: 139-144, 1998.
10. J. A. Bergstra, A. Ponse, and S. A. Smolka, editors. Handbook of Process Algebra. Elsevier, 2001.
11. Peter Haase, and Ljiljana Stojanovic. Consistent Evolution of OWL Ontologies. In Proceedings of the 2nd European Semantic Web Conference (ESWC 2005), number 3532 in Lecture Notes in Computer Science, pages 182-197, Heraklion, Greece, May 29-June 1, 2005. Springer-Verlag.
12. Alexander M., Boris M., and Ljiljana S. Managing multiple and distributed ontologies in the semantic web. VLDB Journal, 12(4): 286-302, 2003.
13. B. Meyer. Object-Oriented Software Construction, Second Edition. Prentice Hall, 1997.
14. Bhide M., Deoasee P., Katkar A., Panchbudhe A., and Ramamritham K. Adaptive push-pull: disseminating dynamic Web data. IEEE Trans Comput, 51(6): 652-668, 2002.
15. Pierre G., and van Steen M. Dynamically selecting optimal distributing strategies on Web documents. IEEE Trans Comput, 51(6): 637-651, 2002.
16. FZI Karlsruhe, and AIFB Karlsruhe. KAON The Karlsruhe Ontology and Semantic Web Framework. Developer's Guide for KAON 1.2.7, 2004.
17. Michel K. Change Management for Distributed Ontologies. PhD thesis, Vrije Universiteit Amsterdam, 2004.

18. Natalya F. Noy, Sandhya Kunnatur, Michel Klein, and Mark A. Musen. Tracking Changes During Ontology Evolution. In Proceedings of 3rd International Semantic Web Conference (ISWC 2004), number 3298 in Lecture Notes in Computer Science, pages 259-273, Hi-roshima, Japan, November, 2004. Springer-Verlag.

19. Paolo Ceravolo, Angelo Corallo, Gianluca Elia, and Antonio Zilli. Managing Ontology Evolution Via Relational Constraints. In Proceedings of the 8th International Conference on Knowledge-Based Intelligent Information and Engineering Systems (KES 2004), number 3215 in Lecture Notes in Artificial Intelligence, pages 335-341,Wellington, New Zealand,September 2004. Springer-Verlag.

20. Michel K., Atanas K., Damyan O., and Dieter F. Finding and characterizing changes in ontologies. In Proceedings of the 21st International Conference on Conceptual Modeling(ER2002), number 2503 in Lecture Notes in Computer Science, pages 79-89, Tampere, Finland, October 2002. Springer-Verlag.

21. Ljiljana Stojanovic, Alexander Maedche, Nenad Stojanovic, and Rudi Studer. Ontology evolution as reconfiguration-design problem solving. In Proceedings of the 2nd International Conference on Knowledge Capture (KCAP 2003), pages 162-171, Sanibel, Florida, October 2003. ACM, OCT.

22. Longfei Jin, Lei Liu, and Dong Yang. A Model Transformation Based Conceptual Framework for Ontology Evolution. In Proceedings of the 9th International Conference on Knowledge-Based, Intelligent, Information, and Engineering Systems (KES 2005), number 3681 in Lecture Notes in Artificial Intelligence, pages325-331, Melbourne, Australia, September 2005. Springer.

23. Milner R. Communicating and Mobile Systems: The Pi-Calculus. Cambridge University Press, 1999.

24. Huimin Lin. A verification tool for value-passing process algebras. IFIP Transactions C-16: Protocol Specification, Testing and Verification, North-Holland, 1993, 79-92.

On Constructing Environment Ontology for Semantic Web Services

Puwei Wang[1,2], Zhi Jin[1,3], and Lin Liu[4]

[1] Institute of Computing Technology, Chinese Academy of Sciences
[2] Graduate University of Chinese Academy of Sciences
[3] Academy of Mathematics and System Sciences, Chinese Academy of Sciences
[4] School of Software, Tsinghua University
Beijing 100080, China
wangpw@ict.ac.cn

Abstract. This paper proposes constructing an environment ontology to represent domain knowledge about Web services. The capability of a Web service is considered in terms of the effects it imposes on the environment during execution. Thus, more fundamental and precise semantic specification for service capability than conventional interface-based description language can be obtained. Basic concepts of the ontology include resources residing in the environment. For each environment resource, there is a corresponding hierarchical state machine specifying its dynamic characteristics. Thus, the influence of a machine on its environments can be modelled with the state machines of the environment resources. Rules and algorithms to construct an environment ontology on the basis of generic domain ontology are introduced. And then guidelines for specifying Web service capability semantically based on the constructed environment ontology are given.

1 Introduction

To implement reliable, large-scale interoperation of Web services, the fundamental need is to make such services computer interpretable–to create a Semantic Web of services which are encoded in an unambiguous, machine understandable description [1]. And the Semantic Web relies heavily on formal ontologies for the comprehensive and transportable machine understanding. Therefore, the realization of the Semantic Web of services is underway with the development of ontology markup languages, such as OWL-S [2] and WSMO [3], etc. OWL-S (formerly DAML-S) took the initiative to provide an ontology markup language expressive enough to describe Web services semantically. And WSMO also proposes its own ontology markup languages. The goals of these efforts are to provide a world-wide standard for semantic description of Web services. They have made many successful steps towards the semantic specification of Web services.

Researches on the semantic capability specification of Web services usually regard it as a functional procedure, i.e. a Web service is considered as a one-step process. It has its own limitation for advertising Web services. Currently,

J. Lang, F. Lin, and J. Wang (Eds.): KSEM 2006, LNAI 4092, pp. 490–503, 2006.

an interesting idea is that behavior is expected to be the capability specification of Web services. Research results reflecting this idea are coming forth. A.Wombacher presents an approach for service matchmaking by using a business process description, i.e. a behavior description, rather than a one-step process description [4][5][6]. On the other hand, the behavior descriptions are globally predefined to assure their consistency in service discovery. It may not be suitable for specifying the capability of Web services which are published by different teams in different terms without negotiation in advance.

Furthermore, most current behavior-based capability specifications may be tied too closely with implementation to express exactly what Web services can do, i.e. the behavior descriptions are usually mingled with personal preferences of each developer of Web services. These personal preferences may have influence on service matchmaking in Web service discovery. Moreover, their behavior description, which may contain some critical information of Web services, may be unwilling to be advertised in public by its provider. This paper proposes environment ontology to be fundamental for specifying the capability of Web services semantically attempting to stride over above limitations. The capability of a Web service is considered in terms of the effects it imposes on the environment during its execution. Therefore, an environment ontology is designed to be shared knowledge which describes domain environment of different Web services. It assures that the behavior-based capability specification of a Web service, which is generated from the effects that the Web service imposes on its environment, can be understood by other Web services without negotiation in advance.

The rest of this paper is structured as follows: Section 2 gives the definition of the environment ontology. Section 3 describes the procedure for constructing the environment ontology, and an example of environment ontology is described to illustrate its definition in section 4. Section 5 outlines an approach for specifying the capability of Web services semantically. Finally, section 6 analyzes current related works and draws a conclusion. Moreover, we also have a discussion about future works.

2   Formation of the Environment Ontology

Environment in dictionary is generally defined as follows: "the circumstance of conditions that surround one; the totality of circumstances surrounding an organism or group of organisms, especially". By analogy with the organism, it is harmless to say that the circumstances of a Web service are those controllable resources that the Web service can interact with or can bring effects to. In this sense, the environment of a Web service then can be viewed as a finite set of various controllable resources surrounding the Web service. A controllable resource is a stateful entity, and its state transitions are triggered by outside inputs. For example, *ticket* is a controllable resource. It has two states: *onsale* and *soldout*. And we can change its state from *onsale*, i.e. *ticket* is on sale, to *soldout*, i.e. *ticket* is sold out. Moreover, controllable resources are domain-relevant and independent to any Web services. Therefore, the conceptualization of controllable resources, i.e. the environment ontology, can constitute the shared domain knowledge for different Web services. We call the concept on the controllable resource the *resource concept* in the environment ontology.

Most of the general ontology structures, such as the one defined in [7], only contain the declarations of the concepts and the relations between them. They don't characterize the states of the concepts and the relations between the states. Then, we extend the general ontology structure by attaching each resource concept a hierarchical state machine for specifying its dynamic characteristics. On the basis of above analysis, the definition of the environment ontology is given in follows:

Definition 1. *An Environment Ontology is depicted as a 6-tuple.*
$\mathcal{E}nv\mathcal{O} \overset{\text{def}}{=} \{Rsc, \mathcal{G}^c, \mathcal{H}^c, \mathcal{HSM}, inter, res\}$, *in which:*

- *Rsc is a finite set of resource concepts,*
- $\mathcal{G}^c \subseteq Rsc \times Rsc$ *is an ingredient relation between the resource concepts,* $\forall c_{r1}, c_{r2} \in Rsc$, $< c_{r1}, c_{r2} > \in \mathcal{G}^c$ *means that* c_{r1} *is an ingredient of* c_{r2},
- $\mathcal{H}^c \subseteq Rsc \times Rsc$ *is a taxonomic relation between the resource concepts, which forms the resource concept's hierarchy.* $\forall c_{r1}, c_{r2} \in Rsc$, $< c_{r1}, c_{r2} > \in \mathcal{H}^c$ *means that* c_{r1} *is a subconcept of* c_{r2},
- $\mathcal{HSM}$ *is a finite set of hierarchical state machines (called "HSM"),*
- *inter* $\subseteq \mathcal{HSM} \times \mathcal{HSM}$ *is a message exchange relation between HSMs.* $hsm_1, hsm_2 \in \mathcal{HSM}$, $<hsm_1, hsm_2> \in inter$ *means that* hsm_1 *and* hsm_2 *interact with each other,*
- *res* : $Rsc \leftrightarrow \mathcal{HSM}$ *is a bijective relation.* $\forall c_r \in Rsc$, *there is one and only one hsm* $\in \mathcal{HSM}$, $hsm = res(c_r)$. *It's called that hsm is the HSM of* c_r.

Before detailing HSM of resource concept, we first introduce a basic state machine of resource concept. There is a primitive definition before defining the basic state machine. Let $c_r \in Rsc$ be a resource concept.

Definition 2. *The Set of States of Resource Concept*
Let $c_r.Attrs = \{\alpha_1, \alpha_2, ..., \alpha_n\}(n \geqslant 1)$ *be the set of attributes of* c_r, *and* $\alpha_i.value$ $(n \geqslant i \geqslant 1)$ *be the countable value range of* $\alpha_i \in c_r.Attrs$. *Then, the set of states of* c_r *is:*

$$c_r.State \overset{\text{def}}{=} \{< \alpha_i, v > \mid \alpha_i \in c_r.Attrs, v \in \alpha_i.value\}$$

This definition makes it clear that state of a resource concept is defined as the pair of an attribute of the resource concept and a certain value within its countable value range. For example, the resource concept *ticket* has an attribute *salecond*, and onsale is a value of *salecond*. Therefore, *onsale* that is a state of *ticket* can be defined as $<salecond$, onsale$>$.

Then we can figure out a basic state machine ("BSM") of resource concept. Let $c_r \in Rsc$ be a resource concept and $\alpha \in c_r.Attrs$ is an attribute of c_r.

Definition 3. *A Basic State Machine of* c_r *is defined as a 5-tuple:*
$\mathcal{N} \overset{\text{def}}{=} \{\mathcal{S}, \Sigma, \mathcal{T}, f, \lambda_0\}$, *in which:*

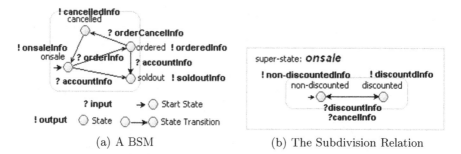

(a) A BSM   (b) The Subdivision Relation

Fig. 1. Example of BSM and the Subdivision Relation

- $\mathcal{S} = \{< \alpha, v > \mid v \in \alpha.value\}$ *is a finite set of states of* c_r ($\mathcal{S} \subseteq c_r.State$),
- Σ *is a finite set that is partitioned into the two subsets:* Σ^{in} *and* Σ^{out} *for input and output messages (called "inputs" and "outputs") respectively,*
- $\mathcal{T} \subseteq \mathcal{S} \times \Sigma^{in} \times \mathcal{S}$ *is a set of state transitions,*
- $f : \mathcal{S} \rightarrow \Sigma^{out}$ *is an output function. A state sends out an output message,*
- $\lambda_0 \in \mathcal{S}$ *is the start state.*

Fig.1(a) depicts a basic state machine of resource concept *ticket* in terms of its attribute *salecond* and its value range {onsale, ordered, cancelled, soldout}. Among the set of states, *onsale* is the start state.

And then, we can add new features to the BSM, namely the hierarchy. Concretely, states (called "super-states") of a BSM could be further subdivided into other BSMs (called "sub-BSMs"). Informally, such hierarchy is obtained by recursively subdividing each super-state into a set of BSMs. The relation between super-states and BSMs is called *subdivision relation*. Let c_r be a resource concept, $c_r.\mathcal{BSM} = \{\mathcal{N}_1, ..., \mathcal{N}_n\}$ ($n \geqslant 1$) be the set of BSMs of c_r and $\mathcal{S}(\mathcal{N})$ mean the set of states $\mathcal{S}$ in a BSM $\mathcal{N}$.

Definition 4. $\mathcal{D} \subseteq c_r.State \times c_r.\mathcal{BSM}$ *is a subdivision relation.* $s \in c_r.State, \mathcal{N} \in c_r.\mathcal{BSM}$ *and* $s \notin \mathcal{S}(\mathcal{N})$, $< s, \mathcal{N} >\in \mathcal{D}$ *means that* s *can be subdivided into* $\mathcal{N}$ *and* s *is called super-state of* $\mathcal{N}$ *(Accordingly,* $\mathcal{N}$ *is called sub-BSM of* s).

For example, Fig.1(b) gives another basic state machine $\mathcal{N}_{sub}$ of *ticket*, which is constructed on the basis of the attribute *discountcond* and its value range {non-discounted, discounted}. State *onsale* of *ticket* (shown in Fig.1(a)) is a super-state that can be subdivided into $\mathcal{N}_{sub}$ (i.e. $< onsale, \mathcal{N}_{sub} >\in \mathcal{D}$). Moreover, the subdivision relation has the property: A BSM cannot have more than one super-states. Formally, if $< s, \mathcal{N} >\in \mathcal{D}$, then $\forall s' \in c_r.State, s' \neq s$, we have $< s', \mathcal{N} >\notin \mathcal{D}$. Each state in $\mathcal{N}$ is called sub-state of s.

Then, the definition of hierarchical state machine of resource concept, which is like the recursive definition of tree, is presented as follows. Let $c_r \in Rsc$ be a resource concept and $c_r.\mathcal{BSM} = \{\mathcal{N}_1, ..., \mathcal{N}_n\}$ (n $\geqslant 1$) be the set of BSMs of c_r.

Definition 5. *A Hierarchical State Machine of* c_r *is depicted as a 2-tuple:*
$hsm(c_r) \stackrel{def}{=} \{c_r.\mathcal{BSM}, \mathcal{D}\}$:

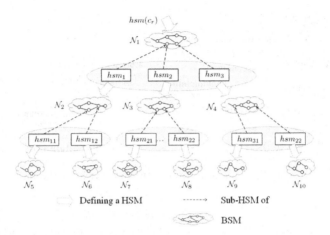

Fig. 2. Example of a Hierarchical State Machine

- *There is a special BSM in $c_r.\mathcal{BSM}$ that called the root (denoted by $\mathcal{N}_{root} \in c_r.\mathcal{BSM}$) of the HSM.*
- *The remaining BSMs are partitioned into $n>0$ disjoint sets $\mathcal{B}_1, ..., \mathcal{B}_n$, where each of them can also constitute a HSM hsm_i (i.e. $hsm_i = \{\mathcal{B}_i, \mathcal{D}_i\}, \mathcal{D}_i \subseteq \mathcal{D}$). If $\mathcal{N}_{root}^{\mathcal{B}_i} \in \mathcal{B}_i$ is the root of hsm_i, then $\exists s \in \mathcal{S}(\mathcal{N}_{root})$, such that $< s, \mathcal{N}_{root}^{\mathcal{B}_i} > \in \mathcal{D}$ (hsm_i can be called sub-HSM of s).*

Finally, we define the message exchange relation between HSMs. Let hsm_1 and hsm_2 be two HSMs, $\mathcal{S}(hsm_i)$ be the set of states in hsm_i, and $\mathcal{T}(hsm_i)$ be the set of state transitions in hsm_i ($1 \leqslant i \leqslant 2$).

Definition 6. *Message Exchange Relation inter*
The message exchange relation between HSMs is:

$$inter \overset{def}{=} \{<hsm_1, hsm_2>|\exists s \in \mathcal{S}(hsm_i), t \in \mathcal{T}(hsm_j), 1 \leqslant i \neq j \leqslant 2, s \uparrow t\}$$

Table 1. Message Exchanges

State↑Transition	Meaning
$valid\uparrow(ordered \rightarrow soldout)$	The output from *creditcard*'s state *valid* is the input which can trigger the state transition of *ticket* from *ordered* to *soldout*.
$valid\uparrow(onsale \rightarrow soldout)$	The output from *creditcard*'s state *valid* the input which can trigger the state transition of *ticket* from *onsale* to *soldout*.
$soldout\uparrow(non\text{-}charged \rightarrow charged)$	The output from *ticket*'s state *soldout* the input which can trigger the state transition of *creditcard* from *non-charged* to *charged*.

where $s \uparrow t$ means that output from state s is the input which can trigger transition t. For example, there are a message exchange relation between $hsm(creditcard)$ and $hsm(ticket)$ because of Table 1.

3 Construction of the Environment Ontology

Different from the ontology learning which focuses on extracting and refining knowledge from a mass of rough-and-tumble information, such as the works in [7], the environment ontology can be constructed from the existing general ontology with the help of the domain experts. Concretely, a majority of resource concepts have been specified in the existing general ontology, as well as the hierarchy and the ingredient relations between these resource concepts. Therefore, the first step for constructing the environment ontology is to refine resource concepts and the hierarchy and the ingredient relations between resource concepts from the existing general ontology. And then, the second step is to construct HSMs of these resource concepts. The HSM of a resource concept is defined in terms of attributes of the resource concept. These attributes could be acquired mostly from the relations between concepts in the existing general ontology. To acquire the attributes, the relations in the existing general ontology are classified into the three categories:

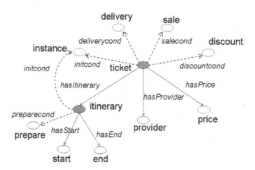

Fig. 3. A Segment of the Existing General Ontology *Ticket*

1. The first one contains those relations which represent characteristics of concepts (called "characteristic relation" for short). For example, in the ontology *Ticket* (shown in Fig.3. The dark gray ellipse denotes resource concepts, and the dash-line with arrowhead denotes characteristic relations), the relations *deliverycond, salecond* and *discountcond* of the concept *ticket* are characteristic relations. Actually, the characteristic relations can be corresponding to attributes, which are fundamental to construct HSM.
2. The second one contains those relations which are the composition or inheritance relations between concepts, i.e. the ingredient or hierarchy relations. For example, the relation *hasItinerary* is an ingredient relation in the ontology *Ticket* (Fig.3). The relations are realized concretely as subsumption or

inheritance between resource concept's attributes. Hence, they play important roles in the procedure for constructing HSM.

3. The rest relations compose the third one. It's beyond the scope of the paper.

Based on the existing general ontology and the classification, the procedure for constructing HSM can be presented. The first step of the procedure is to construct BSMs which are basic elements of a HSM. Let $c_r \in Rsc$ be a resource concept in an environment ontology. The algorithm for constructing BSMs of c_r with the help of the domain experts is given in follows:

Algorithm 1. ConstructingBSMs

Require: $\mathcal{O}$ is an existing general ontology, and c is the concept in $\mathcal{O}$ corresponding to c_r.

Ensure: generated BSMs of resource concept c_r

   Acquiring $\mathcal{R}_c$ that is a set of relations associated with c in $\mathcal{O}$

   for all $r_c \in \mathcal{R}_c$ **do**

   if r_c is a characteristic relation **then**

   1) Acquiring the attribute α from r_c,

   2) Extracting the value range $\alpha.value$,

   3) Creating $\mathcal{S}=\{s|s=<\alpha, v>, v \in \alpha.value\}$,

   4) Creating the set of state transitions $\mathcal{T} \subseteq \mathcal{S} \times \Sigma^{in} \times \mathcal{S}$,

   5) Creating output function f, for each state $s \in \mathcal{S}$, $f(s) = m^{out}$, m^{out} is an output.

   6) Ensuring a start state λ_0.

   end if

   end for

After constructing these BSMs of c_r, the ingredient $\mathcal{G}^c$ and the hierarchy $\mathcal{H}^c$ relation between resource concepts would play important roles in the next step. If c_r has no the ingredient or the hierarchy relations with other resource concepts, this step only is to construct the subdivision relations on these BSMs. Otherwise, $\mathcal{G}^c$ and $\mathcal{H}^c$ should be taken account of.

The *Algorithm.2.* constructs the HSM of c_r in terms of the hierarchy relation $\mathcal{H}^c$. Let $c_{r1}, c_{r2}, ..., c_{rn} \in Rsc$ be n resource concepts, and HSMs of $c_{r2}, ..., c_{rn}$ have been constructed, and c_r has the hierarchy relation $\mathcal{H}^c$ to $c_{r1}, c_{r2}, ..., c_{rn}$. The underlying idea of the algorithm is that c_r inherits attributes of $c_{r1}, c_{r2}, ..., c_{rn}$, for c_r inherits $c_{r1}, c_{r2}, ..., c_{rn}$. Therefore, the BSMs and the subdivision relations of these HSMs ($hsm(c_{r1}), ..., hsm(c_{rn})$) could be reused during the construction of $hsm(c_r)$. The operation semantics of overloading and ambiguous derivation during the reuse procedure are to create the *inheritance threads* from BSMs of c_r to those reusable constructed BSMs of $c_{r1}, c_{r2}, ..., c_{rn}$.

The *Algorithm.3.*, which constructs the HSM of c_r in terms of the ingredient relation $\mathcal{G}^c$, is similar to the *Algorithm.2.*. In this algorithm, the BSMs and the subdivision relations of $hsm(c_{r1}), ...,$ and $hsm(c_{rn})$ can be reused. Its difference from *Algorithm.2.* is that the algorithm need not to deal with the problem of overloading and ambiguous derivation. During the algorithm, the BSMs constructed in terms of the attribute *inticond* should be combined.

Algorithm 2. Constructing HSM in terms of Hierarchy Relation

Require: $\mathcal{O}$ is an existing general ontology, c is the concept in $\mathcal{O}$ corresponding to c_r.
Ensure: HSM of resource concept c_r: $hsm(c_r)$
  $hsm(c_r) = \{\mathcal{BSM}_{cr}, \mathcal{D}_{cr}\}$, $\mathcal{BSM}_{cr} = \phi$, $\mathcal{D}_{cr} = \phi$,
  $\mathcal{BSM}_{new} = ConstructingBSMs(c_r, \mathcal{O})$,
  $\mathcal{BSM}_{cr} = \mathcal{BSM}_{new}$,
  for all $c'_r \in \{c_{r1}, ..., c_{rn}\}$ **do**
    /* Reusing HSMs of $\{c_{r1}, ..., c_{rn}\}$ */
    $hsm(c'_r) = \{\mathcal{BSM}'_{cr}, \mathcal{D}'_{cr}\}$,
    $\mathcal{BSM}_{cr} = \mathcal{BSM}_{cr} \cup \mathcal{BSM}'_{cr}$, $\mathcal{D}_{cr} = \mathcal{D}_{cr} \cup \mathcal{D}'_{cr}$.
  end for
  for all $\mathcal{N}_i \in \mathcal{BSM}_{new}$ **do**
    while $\exists \mathcal{N} \in \mathcal{BSM}_{cr}, attribute(\mathcal{N}) == attribute(\mathcal{N}_i)$ **do**
      Overloading $(\mathcal{N}, \mathcal{N}_i)$.
    end while
    if $\exists s \in \mathcal{N} \in \mathcal{BSM}_{cr}, \mathcal{D}(s, \mathcal{N}_i)$ **then**
      /* Creating the subdivision relation */
      $\mathcal{D}_{cr} = \mathcal{D}_{cr} \cup \{< s, \mathcal{N}_i >\}$.
    end if
  end for

Algorithm 3. Constructing HSM in terms of Ingredient Relation

Require: $\mathcal{O}$ is an existing general ontology, c is the concept in $\mathcal{O}$ corresponding to c_r.
Ensure: HSM of resource concept c_r: $hsm(c_r)$
  $hsm(c_r) = \{\mathcal{BSM}_{cr}, \mathcal{D}_{cr}\}$, $\mathcal{BSM}_{cr} = \phi$, $\mathcal{D}_{cr} = \phi$,
  $\mathcal{BSM}_{new} = ConstructingBSMs(c_r, \mathcal{O})$,
  $\mathcal{BSM}_{cr} = \mathcal{BSM}_{new}$,
  for all $c'_r \in \{c_{r1}, ..., c_{rn}\}$ **do**
    $hsm(c'_r) = \{\mathcal{BSM}'_{cr}, \mathcal{D}'_{cr}\}$, $\mathcal{BSM}_{cr} = \mathcal{BSM}_{cr} \cup \mathcal{BSM}'_{cr}$, $\mathcal{D}_{cr} = \mathcal{D}_{cr} \cup \mathcal{D}'_{cr}$.
  end for
  for all $\mathcal{N}_i \in \mathcal{BSM}_{new}$ **do**
    while $\exists \mathcal{N} \in \mathcal{BSM}_{cr}, attribute(\mathcal{N}) == attribute(\mathcal{N}_i) == initcond$ **do**
      Combining $(\mathcal{N}, \mathcal{N}_i)$.
    end while
    if $\exists s \in \mathcal{N} \in \mathcal{BSM}_{cr}, \mathcal{D}(s, \mathcal{N}_i)$ **then**
      $\mathcal{D}_{cr} = \mathcal{D}_{cr} \cup \{< s, \mathcal{N}_i >\}$.
    end if
  end for

4 Example of an Environment Ontology

A segment of the Budget Travelling Environment Ontology (called "*BTO*") is given to illustrate above definitions. In this segment, five resource concepts are focused. They are *hotelroom*, *creditcard*, *merchandise*, *ticket* and *itinerary* respectively. Table 2 summarizes the associations among them and their HSMs. And then, the next is to introduce how to construct their HSMs.

Table 2. Associations in BTO

Association	
$\mathcal{H}^c$	
ticket→merchandise	hotelroom→merchandise
$\mathcal{G}^c$	
itinerary→ticket	
res	
ticket↔hsm(ticket)	itinerary↔hsm(itinerary)
hotelroom↔hsm(hotelroom)	creditcard↔hsm(creditcard)
merchandise↔hsm(merchandise)	
$inter$	
hsm(ticket)‖hsm(creditcard)	hsm(hotelroom)‖hsm(creditcard)

The section summarizes the procedure for constructing the HSM of resource concept *ticket*, i.e. *hsm(ticket)* in BTO. Other HSMs in BTO could be constructed in the same way. Fig.4 and Fig.5 depict *hsm(itinerary)*, *hsm(ticket)*, *hsm(hotelroom)* and *hsm(creditcard)*. According to the *Algorithm*.3. that constructs HSM in terms of ingredient relation, the precondition for constructing *hsm(ticket)* is that *hsm(itinerary)* has been constructed. For *itinerary*, the construction of its HSM with the help of domain expert is presented:

1) Construction of *hsm(itinerary)*:
Step 1: Four relations associated with the concept *itinerary* obtained from the general ontology $Ticket$ (Fig.3). Among them, *initcond* and *preparecond* are characteristic relations.
Step 2: (Constructing BSMs of *itinerary*)

BSM	attribute, value range
$\mathcal{N}_1$	*initcond*, {non-instantiated, instantiated}
$\mathcal{N}_2$	*pareprecond*, {planned, designed, formulated}

Step 3: (Constructing the subdivision relation)
The BSM $\mathcal{N}_2$ is sub-BSM of the state *instantiated* in $\mathcal{N}_1$, i.e. $< instantiated, \mathcal{N}_2 > \in \mathcal{D}$. Consequently, *hsm(itinerary)* is constructed.

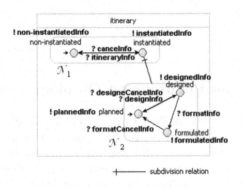

Fig. 4. The HSM of *itinerary*

(2) Construction of $hsm(ticket)$**:**

Step 1: Seven relations associated with $ticket$ obtained from the general ontology $Ticket$ (Fig.3). Among them, $initcond, salecond, discountcond, deliverycond$ are characteristic relations. Moreover, $hasItinerary$ is an ingredient relation from $itinerary$ to $ticket$.

Step 2: (Constructing BSMs of $ticket$)

BSM	attribute, value range
$\mathcal{N}_3$	$initcond$, {non-instantiated, instantiated}
$\mathcal{N}_4$	$salecond$, {onsale, ordered, cancelled, soldout}
$\mathcal{N}_5$	$discountcond$, {non-discounted, discounted}
$\mathcal{N}_6$	$deliverycond$, {non-delivered, delivered}

Step 3: Reusing $\mathcal{N}_1, \mathcal{N}_2$ and subdivision relation of $hsm(itinerary)$, and $\mathcal{N}_1$ is combined into $\mathcal{N}_3$.

Step 4: (Constructing the subdivision relation) $hsm(ticket)$ is constructed.

- $\mathcal{N}_4$ is sub-BSM of state $formulated$ of $\mathcal{N}_2$, i.e. $< formulated, \mathcal{N}_4 > \in \mathcal{D}$,
- $\mathcal{N}_5$ is sub-BSM of state $onsale$ of $\mathcal{N}_4$, i.e. $< onsale, \mathcal{N}_5 > \in \mathcal{D}$,
- $\mathcal{N}_6$ is sub-BSM of state $soldout$ of $\mathcal{N}_4$, i.e. $< soldout, \mathcal{N}_6 > \in \mathcal{D}$.

A message exchange relation has been introduced between $hsm(creditcard)$ and $hsm(ticket)$. In the same way, $hsm(creditcard)$ also has a message exchange relation with $hsm(hotelroom)$. They are denoted by the thick light-gray line with double arrowheads in Fig.5.

5   The Semantic Capability Specification of Web Services

Then, an approach for semantic capability specification of Web services is presented in the section. It acquires the capability specification from the effects that Web services imposes on resource concepts in the environment ontology. An effect on a resource concept is described as a triplet which contains an initial state, a target state and a set of middle states (i.e. they are concluded in the trace from the initial state to the target state) of this resource concept. Let c_r be a resource concept.

Definition 7. $effect(c_r) \overset{\text{def}}{=} < s_i, \mathcal{S}_m, s_t >, s_i, s_t \in c_r.State, \mathcal{S}_m \subseteq c_r.State$, in which s_i is an initial state, s_t is a target state and $\mathcal{S}_m$ is a set of middle states.

The traces from s_i to s_t via $\mathcal{S}_m$ consist of: (1) state transitions in the basic state machines or (2) transitions from a state to its sub-state. For example, an effect that a simple ticket-selling service imposes on resource $ticket$ can be described as $< onsale, \{ordered\}, soldout >$. Based on the effect, we can acquire the trace from $hsm(ticket)$: $onsale \rightarrow ordered \rightarrow soldout$.

Environment ontology is a knowledge base for both the registers and the providers of Web services. The capability profile of a Web service, which is for advertising itself, can be described based on the effects that Web services impose on resource concepts in their environments. And then, the registers can

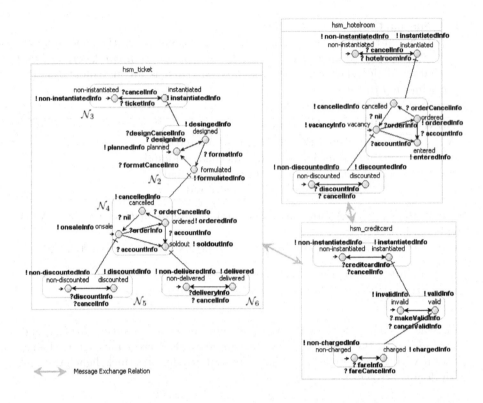

Fig. 5. HSMs of *ticket*, *hotelroom*, and *creditcard*

reason on environment ontology in terms of the capability profile to acquire specific behavior-based capability specification of Web services. Concretely, by traversing a HSM of resource concept in an environment ontology, the traces from initial state to target state via the set of middle states can be created. The traces constitute a reduced HSM. The HSM actually can be a behavior-based specification of Web services. Due to the space limitation, we don't give the algorithm. The capability profile is defined as follows:

Definition 8. $capProfile \stackrel{\text{def}}{=} \{Rsc_{sub}, \mathcal{M}s, effs\}$, *in which Rsc_{sub} is a set of resource concepts in an environment ontology that the Web service is situated in, $\mathcal{M}s$ is a set of inputs that the Web service needs and outputs that the Web service produces, and $effs$ is a set of the effects that the Web service imposes on these resource concepts in Rsc_{sub}.*

For an instance, there is a Web service "Budget Travelling Agency" (called "BTA"). It has the basic capability for customers: purchasing tickets and booking hotel rooms. Its environment has been specified as BTO (depicted in Table 2, Fig.4 and Fig.5). BTA imposes effects on the two resource concepts *ticket* and *hotelroom* in BTO, and the HSMs $hsm(ticket)$ and $hsm(hotelroom)$ have been given in Fig.5. Then, the XML-based capability profile of *BTA* can be presented as follows:

```
<capability Id="BudgetTravelling">
  <resources>BTO:ticket,BTO:hotelroom</resources>
  <inputs>
    <input res="ticket">orderInfo,orderCancelInfo,deliveryInfo</input>
    <input res="hotelroom">orderInfo,orderCancelInfo</input>
  </inputs>
  <outputs>
    <output res="ticket">deliveredInfo</output>
    <output res="hotelroom">orderedInfo</output>
  </outputs>
  <effects>
    <effect res="ticket">
      <initialState>onsale</initialState>
      <middleSet>ordered,cancelled<middleSet>
      <targetState>soldout</targetSstate>
    </effect>
    <effect res="hotelroom">
      <initialState>vacancy</initialState>
      <middleSet>cancelled<middleSet>
      <targetState>ordered</targetState>
    </effect>
  </effects>
</capability>
```

Fig.6 is the screenshot for showing the HSMs which are generated in terms of the capability profile **BudgetTravelling**. The *ws_ticket* in Fig.6 depicts a reduced HSM, which is generated in terms of the effect that *BTA* imposes on *ticket*. In the same way, *ws_hotelroom* is generated in terms of the effect that *BTA* imposes on *hotelroom*. These HSMs can be semantics of capability specification of *BTA*. Then, service matchmaking can be regarded as model matching for HSMs.

Fig. 6. Screenshot of HSMs generated from **BudgetTravelling**

6 Related Work and Conclusion

Semantic web service is an active research area attracting growing interests. The semantic capability specification is a fundamental for automatic Web service discovery, which is a goal of semantic Web services. In OWL-S [2] and WSMO [3], the capability specification of Web services is based on a functional procedure. OWL-S defined an ontology of Web services to provide three essential types of knowledge about Web services. The capability specification is presented as ServiceProfile [2] which describes what Web services do. The method has shown its limitations for specifying exactly capability of Web services. For an instance, a limitation of the OWL-S ServiceProfile argued in [8] arises due to the lack of logical relationships underlying the inputs and outputs of the functional procedure. Hence, the OWL-S ProcessModel, which is primarily designed for specifying how a Web service works, is expected to be the capability specification of a Web service in these researches [8][9]. Currently, semantic behavior-based capability description of Web services as an improvement from the conventional functional procedure description has a promising prospect. Moreover, [10] has proposed hierarchical state machine to specify software requirement and has shown its efficiency.

This paper proposes the environment ontology to be a domain ontology which describes environment of Web services. It's able to be fundamental for specifying Web service capability semantically. It enables that hierarchical state machine can be generated automatically from the effects that Web services impose on resources in their environments. Consequently, the hierarchical state machines, which is derived from the environment ontology, can be a semantic capability specification of Web services. The approach has the several qualities: (1) Our behavior-based capability specification is derived from the environment ontology. Hence, it assures that the behavior-based capability specification can be understood by other Web services without pre-negotiation in service discovery. (2) For derived from shared environment ontology, the capability specification isn't be too relevant with implementation to be unwilling to be published. (3) More importantly, this approach will support more intelligent discovery and matchmaking of Web services.

In our future work, the state machine-based capability specification will be related to current popular semantic description language of Web services. Rules and algorithm for intelligent service discovery and matchmaking based on our capability specification also will be specified.

Acknowledgment

This work is partly supported by the National Natural Science Key Foundation of China under Grant No.60233010, and Grant No.60496324, the National Key Research and Development Program under Grant No.2002CB312004.

References

1. Sheila A.McIlraith, Tran Cao Son, and Honglei Zeng, "Semantic Web Services", IEEE Intelligent Systems, vol. 16, no. 2, Mar./Apr. 2001, pp. 46-53.
2. The OWL Services Coalition, OWL-S: Semantic Markup for Web Services, 2004 http://www.daml.org/services/owl-s/1.1/overview/
3. WSMO project site (Web Service Modeling Ontology), http://www.wsmo.org
4. Andreas Wombacher, Peter Fankhuaser, Bendick Mahleko et al, "Matchmakeing for Business Processes based on Choreographies," EEE 2004
5. Andreas Wombacher, Peter Fankhuaser, Erich Neuhold, "Transforming BPEL into annotated Deterministic Finite State Automata for Service Discovery," ICWS 2004
6. B. Mahleko, and A.Wombacher, "A grammar-based index for matching business processes," ICWS 2005
7. Alexander Maedche and Steffen Staab, "Ontology Learning for the Semantic Web," IEEE intelligent systems, Mar./Apr. 2001, pp.72-79
8. Sharad Bansal and Jose M.Vidal. "Matchmaking of Web Services Based on the DAML-S Service Model," AAMAS 2003, July 14-18, 2003, ACM.
9. Antonio Brogi et al. "Flexible Matchmaking of Web Services Using DAML-S Ontologies," ICSOC 2004 November 15-18.
10. Mats P.E. Heimdahl and Nancy G. Leveson, "Completeness and Consistency in Hierarchical State-Based Requirments", IEEE Transaction on software engineering, vol 22, no.6, June 1996

Knowledge Reduction in Incomplete Systems Based on $\gamma-$Tolerance Relation

Da-kuan Wei

[1] School of Information Engineering, Hunan University of
Science and Engineering, Yongzhou, Hunan, 425006, P.R. China
[2] School of Automation, Nanjing University of Science
and Technology, Nanjing, Jiangsu, 210094, P.R. China
weidakuan@126.com

Abstract. The traditional rough set theory is a powerful tool to deal with complete information system, and its performance to process incomplete information system is weak, M.Kryszkiewcz has put forward the tolerance relation to handle the problem. however,the method may not be perfect on account of excessively many intersectional elements between classifications. This paper improves the tolerance relation proposed by M.Kryszkiewcz to obtain the $\gamma - tolerance$ relation and $\gamma - tolerance$ classes, presents rough set model for incomplete information system based on the $\gamma - tolerance$ relation. The method of $\gamma - tolerance$ relation is proved to be more superior to that of M.Kryszkiewcz's tolerance relation. Finally, the conception of $\gamma - attributes$ reduction is defined, and the algorithm of $\gamma - attribute$ reduction is provided.

Keywords: Rough set, Tolerance relation, $\gamma - tolerance$ relation, incomplete information system, $\gamma - attribute$ reduction.

1 Introduction

Rough set theory, proposed by Polish mathematician Pawlak in 1982, is a new mathematical tool to handle imprecision, uncertainty, and vagueness. After more than 20 years' research and development, It has made great progress in both theories and applications.Especially it has also been applied in many fields, such as pattern recognition, data mining, decision analyzing, machine learning, knowledge acquiring, approximation reasoning, etc., successfully.

The investigative object for the classical Pawlak rough set theory is complete information table, its domain of conditional attribute values is complete and traditional Contor set, that is, each element has certain attribute value under conditional attributes [1-3]. And in practical applications, there exist many such information tables, called incomplete information systems,that their partial conditional attribute values are unknown for a certain piece of information vacating or missing; the classical rough set theory can not cope with the kinds of incomplete information systems. Although there are many scholars (for instances, Kryzkiewicz; Wu & Zhang; Lingras & Yao; Hong et al.)to have been studied

J. Lang, F. Lin, and J. Wang (Eds.): KSEM 2006, LNAI 4092, pp. 504–513, 2006.

them [4-12] , the methods to handle the incomplete information systems are too coarse (that is, there exist many intersectional elements between tolerance classes) to be effectually used in all experimental studies.

In the former paper [12], the improved-tolerance relation was suggested, although the classifications produced by it are not coarser than classification produced by M.Kryszkiewcz's tolerance relation, the approach to classification is wished to be further perfect. In order to more efficiently solve the problem—classification is quite coarse , $\gamma - tolerance$ relation is proposed, which is tolerance relation as $\gamma = 1$. The rough set model of the incomplete information system under $\gamma - tolerance$ relation is defined, and it is the generalization of the rough set model in complete information system. Finally, we give its knowledge reduction and its algorithm in incomplete information system.

2   Basic Theories

In this section, we mainly narrate the basic concepts and correlative contents about incomplete information system .

2.1   Approximation Set

Let $S = (U, A, V, f)$ be an information system,where U is a nonempty finite set of objects called universe of discourse, A is a nonempty finite set of conditional attributes; and for every $a \in A$, such that $f : U \rightarrow V_a$, $V = \cup_{a \in A} V_a$, where V_a is called the value set of attribute a.

Definition 1. Let $S = (U, A, V, f)$ be a information system. Then $R = \{(x, y) \in U \times U : \forall a \in A, a(x) = a(y)\}$ is called an equivalence relation on U, $[x]_R = \{y \in U : (x, y) \in R\}$ is called the equivalence class of the object $x \in U$ with respect to the set A of conditional attributes.

Evidently, if $[x]_R \neq [y]_R$, then $[x]_R \cap [y]_R = \phi$ and $\cup_{x \in U} [x]_R = U$. Therefore, $\{[x]_R : x \in U\}$ forms a partition of U with respect to the equivalence relation R.

Definition 2. Let $S = (U, A, V, f)$ be an information system. R be an equivalence relation on U, $X \subseteq U$. the upper-approximation set and lower-approximation set of X with regard to set A of conditional attributes under the equivalence relation R can be defined as:

$$\overline{R}(X) = \{x \in U : [x]_R \cap X \neq \phi\} = \cup\{[x]_R : x \in X\},$$

$$\underline{R}(X) = \{x \in U : [x]_R \subseteq X\} = \{x \in X : [x]_R \subseteq X\}$$

respectively .

Lemma 1. Let $S = (U, A, V, f)$ be an information system, and $X \subseteq U$; $B \subseteq A$. Then:(1) $\underline{R}(X) \subseteq X \subseteq \overline{R}(X)$; (2) $\overline{R_A}(X) \subseteq \overline{R_B}(X)$ and $\underline{R_A}(X) \supseteq \underline{R_B}(X)$,where R_A and R_B represent the equivalence relation on U with regard to sets A and B of conditional attributes separately.

2.2 Incomplete Information System [1]

Definition 3. If some of the precise attribute values in an information system are unknown, i.e., missing or known partially, then such a system is called an incomplete information system and which is still denoted with convenience by the original notation $S = (U, A, V, f)$. That is, if there exist at least a attribute $a \in B \subseteq A$, such that V_a includes null values, then the system is called an incomplete information system, the sign * usually denotes null value. Otherwise the system is called a complete information system.

Many scholars have been deeply researching on rough set methods of the system and have got many good results in recent years.

Definition 4. Let $S = (U, A, V, f)$ be an incomplete information system, and $T(B) = \{(x,y) \in U \times U : \forall b \in B, b(x) = b(y) \vee b(x) = * \vee b(y) = *\}$, where $B \subseteq A$, then $T(B)$ is called a M.Kryszkiewcz's tolerance relation or called a tolerance relation in short [4-5].

Evidently, $T(B) = \cap_{b \in B} T(\{b\})$ holds, T is reflexive and symmetric , but not transitive.

Let $T_B(x) = \{y \in U : (x,y) \in T(B)\}$, and then $T_B(x)$ is called the tolerance class of the object $x \in U$ with respect to the set $B \subseteq A$ of conditional attributes. $T_B(x)$ is constituted by all objects in universe U which is possibly indiscernible with x.

Suppose that $U/T(B) = \{T_B(x) : x \in U\}$ represents classifications, then the elements in $U/T(B)$ are tolerance classes. Generally, the tolerance class in $U/T(B)$ don't form the partition of U, they may be subsets of each other or may overlap, but consist a cover, i.e., $\cup U/T(B) = U$.

Definition 5. Let $S = (U, A, V, f)$ be an incomplete information system, and $X \subseteq U, B \subseteq A$, the upper-approximation set and lower-approximation set of the set X with regard to set B of conditional attributes under the tolerance relation T can be defined as:

$$\overline{T}_B(X) = \{x \in U : T_B(x) \cap X \neq \phi\} = \cup\{T_B(x) : x \in X\},$$

$$\underline{T}_B(X) = \{x \in U : T_B(x) \subseteq X\} = \{x \in X : T_B(x) \subseteq X\}$$

respectively.

Lemma 2. Let $S = (U, A, V, f)$ be an incomplete information system, and $X \subseteq U, C \subseteq B \subseteq A$. Then: (1) $\underline{T}_B(X) \subseteq X \subseteq \overline{T}_B(X)$; (2) $\overline{T}_B(X) \subseteq \overline{T}_C(X)$ and $\underline{T}_B(X) \supseteq \underline{T}_C(X)$.

3 $\gamma - Tolerance$ Relation

From the definition of tolerance relation, we can see that if the attribute values of two objects, with respect to every attribute in attribute set, are equivalent or the set of attribute values of at least an object includes null values, then the two objects must belong to the same tolerance class; in other words, the null may take arbitrary values. Therefore such a tolerance class is not totally suit for the reality. In this section, we are going to improve the tolerance relation.

Let $S = (U, A, V, f)$ be an incomplete information system, $b \in B \subseteq A, V_b = \{b(x) : b(x) \neq *, x \in U\}$, and it be possible that V_b contains the same elements, $|V_b|$ represents the number of all the elements in V_b, and the same elements is calculated by the number of these same elements, $|b(x)|$ expresses the number of $b(x)$ which is the non-null attribute value .

Definition 6. Let $S = (U, A, V, f)$ be an incomplete information system, $x, y \in U$, $b \in B \subseteq A$, and there exist at least a $b(z) \neq *$ in V_b, then the probability that $b(x)$ equals $b(y)$, denoted by $p_b(x, y)$, is defined as follows:

$$
p_b(x, y) = \begin{cases}
1, & b(x) \neq * \wedge b(y) \neq * \wedge b(x) = b(y) \\
\frac{|b(y)|}{|V_b|}, & b(x) = * \wedge b(y) \neq * \\
\frac{|b(x)|}{|V_b|}, & b(y) = * \wedge b(x) \neq * \\
1, & b(x) = * \wedge b(y) = * \\
0, & b(x) \neq * \wedge b(y) \neq * \wedge b(x) \neq b(y)
\end{cases}
$$

Definition 7. Let $S = (U, A, V, F)$ be an incomplete information system, $x, y \in U, B \subseteq A$, the probability that x and y have the same attribute values on B, denoted by $p_B(x, y)$, is defined as : $p_B(x, y) = \Pi_{b \in B} p_b(x, y)$. $p_B(x, y)$ is also called the probability that x equals y on B.

Evidently, if $C \subseteq B$, then $p_B(x, y) \leq p_C(x, y)$.

Similarity to the paper [10], a section-value γ $(0 \leq \gamma \leq 1)$ can be used to ascertain a tolerance relation in the incomplete information system. As the probability that x is equal to y on B is not less than γ, we believe that x and y belong to the same class.

Definition 8. Let $S = (U, A, V, f)$ be an incomplete information system, $x, y \in U, B \subseteq A$. Then: $T^\gamma(B) = \{(x, y) : x \in U \wedge y \in U \wedge p_B(x, y) \geq \gamma\}$ is called $\gamma - tolerance$ relation, and $T_B^\gamma(x) = \{y : y \in U \wedge (x, y) \in T^\gamma(B)\}$ is named $\gamma - tolerance$ class of x.

From definition 7 and 8, we can know that $\gamma-tolerance$ relation and $\gamma-tolerance$ class of x change into M.Kryszkiewcz's tolerance relation and tolerance class as $\gamma = 1$ separately, furthermore they are equivalence relation and equivalence class when the system S is a complete information system and $\gamma = 1$ respectively.

Suppose that $U/T^\gamma(B) = \{T_B^\gamma(x) : x \in U\}$ stands for classifications, then the elements in $U/T^\gamma(B)$ are $\gamma-tolerance$ classes. Generally, $\gamma-tolerance$ classes in $U/T^\gamma(B)$ don't consist the partition of U, but form a cover, i.e., $\cup U/T^\gamma(B) = U$.

Under $\gamma - tolerance$ relation, $T_B^\gamma(x) = \{y : y \in U \wedge (x, y) \in T^\gamma(B)\}$ implies the maximal set of objects that are possibly indiscernible by B with x.

From definition 8, we also easily obtain the following two simple conclusions.

Theorem 1. $\gamma - tolerance$ relation has reflexivity and symmetry properties, but may not have transitivity property.

Theorem 2. Let $S = (U, A, V, f)$ be an incomplete information system, $C \subseteq B \subseteq A$, $\gamma \in [0,1]$. The following properties hold: (1) $T^\gamma(B) \subseteq T^\gamma(C)$; (2) $T^\gamma(B) \subseteq \cap_{b \in B} T^\gamma(\{b\})$; (3) $T^\gamma(B) \subseteq T(B)$.

Proof. (1) $\forall(x,y) \in T^\gamma(B) \Rightarrow p_B(x,y) \geq \gamma$, and $C \subseteq B \subseteq A$, then $p_C(x,y) \geq p_B(x,y) \geq \gamma \Rightarrow (x,y) \in T^\gamma(C) \Rightarrow T^\gamma(B) \subseteq T^\gamma(C)$; (2) $\forall(x,y) \in T^\gamma(B) \Rightarrow p_B(x,y) \geq \gamma \Rightarrow \Pi_{b \in B} p_b(x,y) \geq \gamma \Rightarrow p_b(x,y) \geq \gamma$ for every $b \in B \Rightarrow p_{\{b\}}(x,y) \geq \gamma \Rightarrow (x,y) \in T^\gamma(\{b\}) \Rightarrow (x,y) \in \cap_{b \in B} T^\gamma(\{b\}) \Rightarrow T^\gamma(B) \subseteq \cap_{b \in B} T^\gamma(\{b\})$; (3) If $(x,y) \notin T(B)$, then for every $b \in B$ such that $b(x) \neq b(y) \Rightarrow p_b(x,y) = 0 \Rightarrow (x,y) \notin T^\gamma(B)$.

From above definition 8, theorem 1 and 2, there are the following theorems for $\gamma - tolerance$ relation.

Theorem 3. Let $S = (U, A, V, f)$ be an incomplete information system, $B \subseteq A$, $0 \leq \gamma_1 < \gamma_2 \leq 1$. Then: (1) $T^{\gamma_1}(B) \supseteq T^{\gamma_2}(B)$; (2) $T_B^{\gamma_1}(x) \supseteq T_B^{\gamma_2}(x)$, for each $x \in U$.

Proof. (1) $\forall(x,y) \in T^{\gamma_2}(B) \Rightarrow p_B(x,y) \geq \gamma_2 > \gamma_1 \Rightarrow (x,y) \in T^{\gamma_1}(B) \Rightarrow T^{\gamma_1}(B) \supseteq T^{\gamma_2}(B)$; (2) Let $x_0 \in T_B^{\gamma_2}(x)$, Suppose that $x_0 \notin T_B^{\gamma_1}(x)$, then $p_B(x, x_0) \geq \gamma_2$ and $p_B(x, x_0) < \gamma_1$, Further, there would be $\gamma_2 < \gamma_1$ which contradicts the condition $\gamma_1 < \gamma_2$, therefore, $x_0 \in T_B^{\gamma_1}(x)$, the conclusion(2) in theorem 3 holds.

Theorem 4. Let $S = (U, A, V, f)$ be an incomplete information system, $C \subseteq B \subseteq A$, $\gamma \in [0,1]$. Then $T_B^\gamma(x) \subseteq T_C^\gamma(x)$.

Proof. Assume that $x_0 \in T_B^\gamma(x)$, we then have $P_B(x_0, x) \geq \gamma$. Since $C \subseteq B \subseteq A$. hence $p_B(x_0, x) \leq p_C(x_0, x)$, or equivalently, $p_C(x_0, x) \geq \gamma$, namely $x_0 \in T_C^\gamma(x)$. Consequently, $T_B^\gamma(x) \subseteq T_C^\gamma(x)$ which completes the proof.

Theorem 5. Let $S = (U, A, V, f)$ be an incomplete information system, $B \subseteq A$. Then $T_B^\gamma(x) \subseteq T_B(x)$ for every $\gamma \in [0,1]$.

Proof. Form theorem 2(3), we can directly gain the consequence.

By theorem 5, we immediately gain the following conclusion.

Corollary. Let $S = (U, A, V, f)$ be an incomplete information system, $B \subseteq A$, $x, y \in U$, Then: $T_B^\gamma(x) \cap T_B^\gamma(y) \subseteq T_B(x) \cap T_B(y)$.

The corollary states that the number of the intersectional elements between $\gamma - tolerance$ classes is not greater than that between tolerance classes.

Example 1. Table 1 gives an incomplete information system(IIS in short) $S = (U, A, V, f)$, where $U = \{x_1, x_2, ..., x_9\}$ is the set of objects, $A = \{a_1, a_2, a_3, a_4\}$ is the set of conditional attributes, $*$ represents null values.

If $\gamma = 0.2$, 0.3, 0.4 respectively, then all the $\gamma - tolerance$ classes of objects in U are given as follows (Table 2):

From table 2, we can see the number of elements in $\gamma - tolerance$ classes is decreasing as γ is gradually increasing, this is consistent with theorem 3(2).

Table 1. IIS

	x_1	x_2	x_3	x_4	x_5	x_6	x_7	x_8	x_9
a_1	1	1	3	1	*	3	3	3	2
a_2	2	*	2	2	2	1	2	1	3
a_3	1	3	3	*	1	*	*	2	*
a_4	1	1	*	1	1	3	*	3	2

Table 2. $\gamma - Tolerance$ Classes w.r.t. $A(\gamma = 0.2, 0.3, 0.4)$

	$T_A^\gamma(x_1)$	$T_A^\gamma(x_2)$	$T_A^\gamma(x_3)$	$T_A^\gamma(x_4)$	$T_A^\gamma(x_5)$	$T_A^\gamma(x_6)$	$T_A^\gamma(x_7)$	$T_A^\gamma(x_8)$	$T_A^\gamma(x_9)$
0.2	$\{x_1, x_4, x_5\}$	$\{x_2, x_4\}$	$\{x_3, x_7\}$	$\{x_1, x_2, x_4\}$	$\{x_1, x_5\}$	$\{x_6, x_8\}$	$\{x_3, x_7\}$	$\{x_6, x_8\}$	$\{x_9\}$
0.3	$\{x_1, x_4, x_5\}$	$\{x_2\}$	$\{x_3, x_7\}$	$\{x_1, x_4\}$	$\{x_1, x_5\}$	$\{x_6\}$	$\{x_3, x_7\}$	$\{x_8\}$	$\{x_9\}$
0.4	$\{x_1, x_4\}$	$\{x_2\}$	$\{x_3, x_7\}$	$\{x_1, x_4\}$	$\{x_5\}$	$\{x_6\}$	$\{x_3, x_7\}$	$\{x_8\}$	$\{x_9\}$

4   Rough Set Model

The rough set model considered below is based on $\gamma - tolerance$ relation in an incomplete information system.

Definition 9. Let $S = (U, A, V, f)$ be an incomplete information system, $B \subseteq A$, $T^\gamma(B)$ is a $\gamma-tolerance$ relation with regard to B, $T_B^\gamma(x) = \{y \in U : (x, y) \in T^\gamma(B)\}$ is $\gamma - tolerance$ class contained x. For every set $X \subseteq U$, let:

$$\overline{T_B^\gamma}(X) = \{x \in U : T_B^\gamma(x) \cap X \neq \phi\} = \cup\{T_B^\gamma(x) : x \in X\},$$

$$\underline{T_B^\gamma}(X) = \{x \in U : T_B^\gamma(x) \subseteq X\} = \{x \in X : T_B^\gamma(x) \subseteq X\}.$$

Then $\overline{T_B^\gamma}(X)$ and $\underline{T_B^\gamma}(X)$ are said to be upper-approximation set and lower-approximation set of X based on $\gamma-tolerance$ relation, or shortly said to be $\gamma - upper - approximation$ set and $\gamma - lower - approximation$ set of X respectively.

$$\overline{T_B^\gamma} : P(U) \to P(U) \quad and \quad \underline{T_B^\gamma} : P(U) \to P(U)$$

are called a pair of upper-approximation operator and lower-approximation operator separately, where $P(U)$ is the power set of U.

From definition 9 known, as (U, A, V, f) is complete information system, $B \subseteq A$, and $T^\gamma(B)$ becomes equivalence relation $R_B(just\ now\ \gamma = 1)$, $\overline{T_B^\gamma}(X)$ and $\underline{T_B^\gamma}(X)$ are:

$$\overline{T_B^\gamma}(X) = \{x \in U : [x]_{R_B} \cap X \neq \phi\} = \overline{R_B}(X),$$

$$\underline{T_B^\gamma}(X) = \{x \in U : [x]_{R_B} \subset X\} = \underline{R_B}(X).$$

Namely, $\overline{T_B^\gamma}(X)$ and $\underline{T_B^\gamma}(X)$ become into the classical Pawlak supper-approximation set and lower-approximation set of X respectively.

Example 2. (continued example 1) Table 1 gives a data-table of incomplete information system, and table 2 provides the relevant $\gamma - tolerance$ classes

($\gamma = 0.2, 0.3, 0.4$ separately). Now we let $X = \{x_1, x_3, x_6, x_7, x_8\}$. According to definition 9 we obtain :

$$\overline{T_A^{0.2}}(X) = \overline{T_A^{0.3}}(X) = \{x_1, x_3, x_4, x_5, x_6, x_7, x_8, x_9\},$$

$$\overline{T_A^{0.4}}(X) = \{x_1, x_3, x_4, x_6, x_7, x_8\},$$

$$\underline{T_A^{0.2}}(X) = \underline{T_A^{0.3}}(X) = \underline{T_A^{0.4}}(X) = \{x_3, x_6, x_7, x_8\}.$$

Theorem 6. Let $S = (U, A, V, f)$ be an incomplete information system, $X \subseteq U$, $B \subseteq A$, $\gamma \in [0, 1]$. Then upper-approximation operator $\overline{T_B^\gamma}$ and lower-approximation operator $\underline{T_B^\gamma}$ have the following properties:

(1) $\underline{T_B}(X) \subseteq \underline{T_B^\gamma}(X) \subseteq X \subseteq \overline{T_B^\gamma}(X) \subseteq \overline{T_B}(X)$;

(2) If $X_1 \subset X_2$, Then : $\overline{T_B^\gamma}(X_1) \subseteq \overline{T_B^\gamma}(X_2)$, $\underline{T_B^\gamma}(X_1) \subseteq \underline{T_B^\gamma}(X_2)$;

(3) $\overline{T_B^\gamma}(\overline{T_B^\gamma}(X)) \supseteq \overline{T_B^\gamma}(X) \supseteq \underline{T_B^\gamma}(\overline{T_B^\gamma}(X)), \underline{T_B^\gamma}(\underline{T_B^\gamma}(X)) \subseteq \underline{T_B^\gamma}(X) \subseteq \overline{T_B^\gamma}(\underline{T_B^\gamma}(X));$

(4) $\overline{T_B^\gamma}(X) = (\underline{T_B^\gamma}(X)^C)^C$, $\underline{T_B^\gamma}(X) = (\overline{T_B^\gamma}(X)^C)^C$.

Where T_B represents M.Kryszkiewcz's tolerance relation with respect to B, X^C indicates the complementary set of X.

Proof. (1) From definition 9, we have: $\underline{T_B^\gamma}(X) \subseteq X \subseteq \overline{T_B^\gamma}(X)$. Due to theorem 5, $T_B^\gamma(x) \subseteq T_B(x)$, we also have: $\underline{T_B}(X) = \{x \in U : T_B(x) \subseteq X\} \subseteq \{x \in U : T_B^\gamma(x) \subseteq X\} = \underline{T_B^\gamma}(X)$ for every $\gamma \in [0, 1]$, namely, $\underline{T_B}(X) \subseteq \underline{T_B^\gamma}(X)$. Analogically, $\overline{T_B^\gamma}(X) \subseteq \overline{T_B}(X)$. Therefore, $\underline{T_B}(X) \subseteq \underline{T_B^\gamma}(X) \subseteq X \subseteq \overline{T_B^\gamma}(X) \subseteq \overline{T_B}(X)$.

(2) The proof is very simple.

(3) From the results of (1) and (2), we can immediately gain the proof.

(4) $x \in (\underline{T_B^\gamma}(X^C))^C \Leftrightarrow x \notin \underline{T_B^\gamma}(X^C) \Leftrightarrow x \notin \{y \in U : T_B^\gamma(y) \subset X^C\} \Leftrightarrow x \notin \{y \in U : T_B^\gamma(y) \cap X = \phi\} \Leftrightarrow x \in \{y \in U : T_B^\gamma(y) \cap X \neq \phi\} \Leftrightarrow x \in \overline{T_B^\gamma}(X)$. Consequently $\overline{T_B^\gamma}(X) = (\underline{T_B^\gamma}(X^C))^C$.

Analogically, the second formula in (4) can be proved.

5 $\gamma - Attribute$ Reductions

5.1   The Concept of $\gamma - Attribute$ Reduction

First of all, the definition of attribute reduction is introduced.

Definition 10. $S = (U, A, V, f)$ be an incomplete information system, $B \subseteq A$, $\gamma \in [0, 1]$. If for every $x \in U$, such that $T_A^\gamma(x) = T_B^\gamma(x)$ and $T_B^\gamma(x) \neq T_{B-\{b\}}^\gamma(x)$ for each $b \in B$, then B is called a $\gamma - attribute$ reduct or a $\gamma - knowledge$ reduct of the system $S = (U, A, V, f)$.

Theorem 7. Let $S = (U, A, V, f)$ be an incomplete information system, Then there must exist a $\gamma - attribute$ reduct of S for every $\gamma \in [0, 1]$.

Proof. If $T_A^\gamma(x) \neq T_{A-\{a\}}^\gamma(x)$ for every $x \in U$ and each $a \in A$, then A itself must be a $\gamma - attribute$ reduct of S.

If there is $a \in A$ such that $T_A^\gamma(x) = T_{A-\{a\}}^\gamma(x)$ for every $x \in U$, then we consider the attribute subset $B_1 = A - \{a\}$ of A. If $T_{B_1}^\gamma(x) \neq T_{B_1-\{b_1\}}^\gamma(x)$ for every $b_1 \in B_1$, then B_1 is a $\gamma-attribute$ reduct of S. If there is $b_1 \in B_1$ such that $T_{B_1}^\gamma(x) = T_{B_1-\{b_1\}}^\gamma(x)$, we consider $B_2 = B_1 - \{b_1\}$. Since A is finite, continuing the process obtains $B \subseteq A$ such that $T_A^\gamma(x) = T_B^\gamma(x)$ and $T_A^\gamma(x) \neq T_{B-\{b\}}^\gamma(x)$ for every $b \in B$. Consequently B is a $\gamma - attribute$ reduct of S.

Generally, $\gamma - attribute$ reduct may not be unique.

5.2 $\gamma-$ Attribute Reduction Algorithm

In fact, the proof of theorem 7 provides the main parts of $\gamma-$ attribute reduction algorithm.

$\gamma-$ Attribute Reduction Algorithm

• **Input:** $S = (U, A, V, f)$, and the valid values of γ ($0 \leq \gamma \leq 1$), where $U = \{x_1, x_2, ..., x_n\}$, $A = \{a_1, a_2, ..., a_n\}$.

• **Output:** $\gamma-$ attribute reduct B ($B \subseteq A$) of the system S.

Step 1. Find all the $\gamma-$ tolerance classes with respect to A : $T_A^\gamma(x_1), T_A^\gamma(x_2)$, ..., $T_A^\gamma(x_n)$.

Step 2. Let $B_k^1 = A - \{a_k\}$, $k = 1, 2, ..., m$, and calculate $T_{B_k^1}^\gamma(x_1), T_{B_k^1}^\gamma(x_2), ..., T_{B_k^1}^\gamma(x_n)$.

Step 3. If $\{T_A^\gamma(x_1), T_A^\gamma(x_2), ..., T_A^\gamma(x_n)\} \neq \{T_{B_k^1}^\gamma(x_1), T_{B_k^1}^\gamma(x_2), ..., T_{B_k^1}^\gamma(x_n)\}$ for every $k \in \{1, 2, ..., m\}$, then A is a $\gamma-$ attribute reduct of system S, and stop. Otherwise, if there is a $k_1 \in \{1, 2, ..., m\}$, such that $\{T_A^\gamma(x_1), T_A^\gamma(x_2), ..., T_A^\gamma(x_n)\} = \{T_{B_{k_1}^1}^\gamma(x_1), T_{B_{k_1}^1}^\gamma(x_2), ..., T_{B_{k_1}^1}^\gamma(x_n)\}$, then let $A_1 = B_{k_1}^1 = A - \{a_{k_1}\}$ and return 2.

Step 4. Continuing step 2 and step 3 until finding a $B \subseteq B_{k_h}^h \subseteq A (h \leq m - 1$ is a positive integer number) satisfies that $T_A^\gamma(x) = T_B^\gamma(x)$ and $T_A^\gamma(x) \neq T_{B-\{b\}}^\gamma(x)$ for every $b \in B$

Example 3 (continued example 1). Table 1 gives a data-table of an incomplete information system and table 2 presents various $\gamma-$ tolerance classes ($\gamma = 0.2, 0.3, 0.4$) with respect to A. Now let $B = \{a_1, a_2, a_3\}$, then the $\gamma-$tolerance classes are as follows(Table 3).

From table 2 and 3, we certainly know that:

$$\{T_A^{0.2}(x_1), ..., T_A^{0.2}(x_9)\} \neq \{T_B^{0.2}(x_1), ..., T_B^{0.2}(x_9)\},$$

Table 3. $\gamma - Tolerance$ Classes w.r.t. $B(\gamma = 0.2, 0.3, 0.4)$

	$T_B^\gamma(x_1)$	$T_B^\gamma(x_2)$	$T_B^\gamma(x_3)$	$T_B^\gamma(x_4)$	$T_B^\gamma(x_5)$	$T_B^\gamma(x_6)$	$T_B^\gamma(x_7)$	$T_B^\gamma(x_8)$	$T_B^\gamma(x_9)$
0.2	$\{x_1, x_4, x_5\}$	$\{x_2, x_4\}$	$\{x_3, x_7\}$	$\{x_1, x_2, x_4\}$	$\{x_1, x_5, x_7\}$	$\{x_6, x_8\}$	$\{x_3, x_5, x_7\}$	$\{x_6, x_8\}$	$\{x_9\}$
0.3	$\{x_1, x_4, x_5\}$	$\{x_2\}$	$\{x_3, x_7\}$	$\{x_1, x_4\}$	$\{x_1, x_5\}$	$\{x_6\}$	$\{x_3, x_7\}$	$\{x_8\}$	$\{x_9\}$
0.4	$\{x_1, x_4\}$	$\{x_2\}$	$\{x_3, x_7\}$	$\{x_1, x_4\}$	$\{x_5\}$	$\{x_6\}$	$\{x_3, x_7\}$	$\{x_8\}$	$\{x_9\}$

$$\{T_A^{0.3}(x_1), ..., T_A^{0.3}(x_9)\} = \{T_B^{0.3}(x_1), ..., T_B^{0.3}(x_9)\},$$

$$\{T_A^{0.4}(x_1), ..., T_A^{0.4}(x_9)\} = \{T_B^{0.4}(x_1), ..., T_B^{0.4}(x_9)\}.$$

By calculating, we also have:

$$\{T_B^{0.3}(x_1), ..., T_B^{0.3}(x_9)\} \neq \{T_C^{0.3}(x_1), ..., T_C^{0.3}(x_9)\} \text{ and}$$

$$\{T_B^{0.4}(x_1), ..., T_B^{0.4}(x_9)\} \neq \{T_C^{0.4}(x_1), ..., T_C^{0.4}(x_9)\} \text{ for every subset } C \text{ of } B.$$

For these reasons, B are both a $0.3-$attribute reduct and a $0.4-$attribute reduct of S.

6   Conclusion

The $\gamma - tolerance$ relation and $\gamma - tolerance$ class based on the probability that objects equal on the set of conditional attributes have been proposed in this paper, with variation of γ value, intersectional elements between $\gamma - tolerance$ classes are variable, for this reason, the $\gamma - tolerance$ relation is superior to M.Kryszkiewcz's tolerance relation in some way. At the meantime, the paper still has presented rough set model under $\gamma - tolerance$ relation, the model is the generalization of the Pawlak rough set model in complete information system. Finally, the paper introduced the definition of $\gamma-$attribute reduction and its reduction algorithm in incomplete information system based on $\gamma-$tolerance relation and $\gamma-$tolerance classes. The research for knowledge reduction of the system with γ changing is our next work.

Acknowledgements

The paper is supported by National Science Foundation of China (No.70571032).

References

1. Wang G.-Y.: *Rough Set Theory and Knowledge Discovery.* Xi'an JiaoTong University Press, Xi'an(2001)
2. Liu Q.: *Rough Set and Rough Reasoning.* Science Press, Beijing(2001)
3. Zhang W.-X., Leung Y., Wu W.-Z.: *Information System and Knowledge Discovery.* Science Press, Beijing(2003)
4. Kryszkiewicz M.: Rough set approach to incomplete information system. *Information Sciences*, 112(1998) 39-49

5. Marzena Kryszkiewicz: Rules in incomplete information systems. *Information Sciences*, 113(1999) 271-292
6. Wu W.-Z., Mi J.-S., Zhang W.-X.: A New Rough Set Approach to Knowledge Discovery in Incomplete Information System. *Proceedings of the Second International Conference on Machine Learning and Cybernetics*, Xi'an, 2-5 November 2003 (1713-1718)
7. Roman Slowinski, Danel Vanderpooten: A Generalized Definition of Rough Approximation Based on Similarity. *IEEE Transactions on Knowledge and Data Engineering*, Vol.12(2),2000, 331-336
8. Zhang H.-Y., Liang J.-Y.: Variable Precision Rough Set Model and a Knowledge Reduction Algorithm for Incomplete Information System. *Computer science*, Vol.30(4),2003, 153-155
9. Wang G.-Y.:Extension of Rough Set under Incomplete Information System. *Journal of Computer Reseach and Development*, Vol.39(10),2002,1238-1243
10. He W., Liu C.-Y., Zhao J., Li H.: An Algorithm of Attributes Reduction in Incomplete Information System. *Computer science*, Vol.31(2),2004, 153-155
11. Huang B., Zhou X.-Z.: Extension of Rough Set Model Based on Connection Degree under Incomplete Information System. *Systems Engineering –Theory and Practice.* 1 (2004) 88-92
12. Wei D.-K., Zhou X.-Z., Zhu Y.-G.: Knowledge Reduction in Incomplete Information Systems Based on Improved-tolerance Relation. *Computer Science*,Vol.32(8A),2005, 53-56

An Extension Rule Based First-Order Theorem Prover

Xia Wu[1,2], Jigui Sun[1,2], and Kun Hou[1,2,3]

[1] College of Computer Science and Technology, Jilin University,
130012 Changchun, China
[2] Key Laboratory of Symbolic Computation and Knowledge Engineer of Ministry of Education,
130012 Changchun, China
[3] College of Computer Science and Technology, Northeast Normal University,
130017 Changchun, China
yexia_fw@163.com, jgsun@jlu.edu.cn, bluebloodhk@163.com

Abstract. Methods based on resolution have been widely used for theorem proving since it was proposed. The extension rule (ER) method is a new method for theorem proving, which is potentially a complementary method to resolution-based methods. But the first-order ER approach is incomplete and not realized. This paper gives a complete first-order ER algorithm and describes the implementation of a theorem prover based on it and its application to solving some planning problems. We also report the preliminary computational results on first-order formulation of planning problems.

1 Introduction

Automated theorem proving (ATP) has matured into one of the most advanced areas of computer science. The usually used deduction methods in ATP include resolution based method, tableau based method, sequent calculus and nature deduction method etc. The traditional idea used in TP is to try to deduce the empty clause to check the unsatisfiability. Resolution based TP is a paradigm of this idea. But the ER based TP[1] proceeds inversely to resolution. Namely, the ER approach checks the unsatisfiability by deducing the set of clauses consisting of all the maximum terms. Therefore, it is a new theorem proving method.

As a new reasoning method, whether or not the ER method can be applied well in ATP relies on the efficiency. Since first-order ER method is reduced to a series of ground-level satisfiability problems, the behavior of propositional ER will affect the behavior of first-order ER directly. Thus, it seems the speed of the propositional ER method is so important. To accelerating the ER methods in proposition logic, we improved them and obtained more speedup[2][3].

Unfortunately, Lin's first-order ER method[1] is incomplete. We have described the improvements of the incomplete first-order ER approach in [4] by (a) revise the definition of the potential blockage, give a complete first-order ER algorithm, (b) increasing the case M-satisfiability by giving a bound M, so as to make the ER method more useful for theorem proving and logic programming, and (c) accelerating it through invoking the more efficient proposition ER approach. The correctness of the improved ER

J. Lang, F. Lin, and J. Wang (Eds.): KSEM 2006, LNAI 4092, pp. 514–524, 2006.

method described in this paper for first-order logic with functions as well as termination on unsatisfiable formulas are shown in [4].

Our purpose of this paper is to develop a basic practical inference algorithm for non-Horn first-order logic with functions and report some preliminary computational results.

2   The Extension Rule Methods in Proposition Logic

Propositional ER algorithm is very important in first-order theorem proving because in every iteration we need to solve a propositional satisfiability problem obtained by treating variants of first-order predicates as the same atom.

2.1   The Basic ER Method in Proposition Logic

We run back over the central idea of the ER method at first. The details can be found in [1]. The extension rule is defined as follows.

Definition 2.1. Given a clause C and an atom set M: $C'=\{C\vee a, C\vee\neg a \mid$ "a" is an atom, $a\in M$, $''\neg a''$ and $''a''$ does not appear in C$\}$. The operation proceeding from C to C' is the extension rule on C. C' is the result of the extension rule.

Definition 2.2. A clause is a maximum term on an atom set M if and only if it contains all atoms in M in either positive form or negative form.

The ER method uses the inverse of resolution together with the inclusion-exclusion principle to solve TP problems. So if we want to decide whether a set of clauses is satisfiable, we can proceed by finding an equivalent set of clauses such that all the clauses in it are maximum terms by using the extension rule. Evidently, all of the maximum term set consist of n atoms must include 2^n elements. The number of maximum term extended by a clause set can be calculated by using the inclusion-exclusion principle. Once a set of clauses deduces that the set of all the maximum terms is unsatisfiable, we can decide the clause set is unsatisfiable.

Example 2.3. Check the satisfiability of the clause set $\Phi=\{\neg A\vee B\vee\neg C, A\vee C, \neg A\}$. The maximum term number extended by Φ: $S=2^0+2^1+2^2-0-2^0-0+0=6$. Because $6<2^3$, clause set $\Phi=\{\neg A\vee B\vee\neg C, A\vee C, \neg A\}$ is satisfiable.

2.2   The IER and RIER Methods in Proposition Logic

The idea of algorithm IER[1] is to use a more efficient but incomplete algorithm followed by a complete algorithm and to hope that the problem can be solved by using the more efficient algorithm. When the ER Algorithm runs, it is actually searching through the entire space of all maximum terms and checking if any maximum term cannot be extended, while in fact it is possible to search through a subspace and check if any maximum term cannot be generated in this smaller space. If so, we can draw the conclusion that Φ is satisfiable. Otherwise, it cannot tell whether Φ is satisfiable since it is possible that a maximum term out of the subspace cannot be extended. In this case, fall back to the original Algorithm ER.

In order to obtain more efficiency, we improved ER methods by speeding up the algorithm ER and IER with several rules in DP method[2][3]. There are some clauses in the set of clauses having nothing to do with the satisfiability, such as the clause containing pure literal, the clause including tautology and the clause implied by other clause, etc. Hence, we can use some rules to delete these clauses, and then check the satisfiability of the reduced clause set by ER or IER.

Four rules, tautology rule, pure literal rule, inclusion rule, and single literal rule, are used to reduce the primary clause set. Denote tautology rule by RT, pure literal rule by RP, inclusion rule by RI, and single literal rule by RS. Let RL={RT, RP, RI, RS}, the RIER algorithm in proposition logic invoked by our first-order ER method is given below.

```
Algorithm RIER (Reduced Improved Extension Rule)
1. Let Φ={C₁, C₂, …,Cₙ}.
   While Φ satisfies any rule in RL
   Loop
   Φ₁:= using RL to deal with Φ
   If Φ₁ is empty then stop: return satisfiable
   Else If Φ₁ includes empty clause set
        then stop: return unsatisfiable
   Φ:=Φ₁
   End loop
2. Let Φ={C₁, C₂, …,Cₚ}(p≤n), M(|M|=m)be its set of at-
   oms, and let C be an arbitrary clause whose atoms ap-
   pear in M.
3. Φ':= Φ
4. For all the clauses D in Φ'
   (a) If D and C have complementary literal(s)
        then Eliminate D from Φ'
   (b) Call ER to check the satisfiability of Φ'
5. If Φ' is satisfiable then Stop: return satisfiable
   Else call Algorithm ER with Φ
```

Theorem 2.4.[3] Algorithm RIER is sound and complete for proposition logic theorem proving.

The efficiency of RIER is much better than IER[3], and this causes a big speed-up in the first-order ER algorithm.

3 Algorithm RFOER (Revised First-Order Extension Rule)

We assume that a first-order formula is given in prenex clausal form, $F= \overset{m}{\underset{i=1}{\wedge}} \forall x_i C_i$, where x_i is a vector of all the variables appearing in clause C_i. The clauses are standardized apart, meaning that no two contain a common variable. The basic concepts and symbols in this paper can refer to [1] and [4].

Definition 3.1. Two formulas are said to be variants of each other when they can be unified by renaming substitutions.

Definition 3.2. Given a quantifier-free formula F, a pair of atoms $P(t)$, $P(t')$ is potentially blocked if:

(1) $P(t)$ appears positively in F;
(2) $P(t')$ appears negatively in F;
(3) $P(t)$ and $P(t')$ have a most general unifier (mgu), such that $P(t)\sigma = P(t')\tau$; and
(4) There are clauses C and C′ in F of which $P(t)$ and $P(t')$ are respectively their atoms, and for which either (a) $C\sigma$ is not a variant of any clause in F or (b) $C'\tau$ is not a variant of any clause in F.

An atom is potentially blocked if it is a member of a potentially blocked pair, and F is potentially blocked if some atom is potentially blocked.

To ensure termination of the first-order ER algorithm, we include only potential blockages between terms whose unification results in nesting depth at most M. We will say that a pair of atom is "M-potentially blocked" when at least one potential blockage is of this sort.

Definition 3.3. Given a quantifier-free formula F, a pair of atoms $P(t)$, $P(t')$ is M-potentially blocked if they are potentially blocked and their mgu (σ, τ) is such that $P(t)\sigma$ and $P(t')\tau$ contains no terms of nesting depth strictly greater than M.

Definition 3.4. Say F is M-satisfiable if there is some Herbrand interpretation I such that every ground instance of F is true in I or contains a term with nesting depth greater than M.

Now we present the revised first-order ER method. For M=0, 1,... the algorithm tries to find a potential blockage for the given formula F that is not M-potentially blocked. If it finds a pair atoms that is M-potentially blocked, it partially instantiates two clauses that cause the potential blockage and conjoins them with F, so that a stronger formula is checked for satisfiability in the next iteration. The procedure terminates when (a) if F_k is unsatisfiable, in which case F is unsatisfiable; or (b) a pair of atoms which is not potentially blocked is found, in which case F is satisfiable.

It will be shown later that if F is unsatisfiable, the algorithm terminates with a proof of unsatisfiability. Because first-order logic is semi-decidable, there is no assurance of termination if F is satisfiable.

Algorithm RFOER (Revised First-Order Extension Rule):
Let $F = \forall x_1 C_1 \land ... \land \forall x_m C_m$ be a first-order formula.
1. Set $F_0 := C_1 \land ... \land C_m$, k:=0, and M:=0.
2. Check the satisfiability of F_k by algorithm RIER, where treats variants of the same clause as the same clause.
3. **If** F_k is unsatisfiable, **then** stop: return *unsatisfiable*.
    Otherwise, if F_k is not potentially blocked, **then** Stop: return *satisfiable*.
    Otherwise, if F_k is not M-potentially blocked, **then** return *M-satisfiable*. Let M:=M+1, go to step 3.

4. (F_k is M-potentially blocked) Let C_h and C_i be two clauses in F_k whose atoms are M-potentially blocked, $P(t)$ and $P(t')$ are the M-potentially blocked atoms in C_h and C_i respectively. Let (σ,τ) be a mgu of $P(t)$ and $P(t')$. Set $F_{k+1}:=F_k \land C_h\sigma \land C_i\tau$, k:=k+1, go to step 2.

There are many potentially blocked atom pairs, yet if the particular atom pair in Step 2 is not M-potentially blocked, we can claim that F is M-satisfiable. Although a different atom pair could be M-potentially blocked, that M-potentially blocked would be resolved and ultimately F would be found to be M-satisfiable.

The following three theorems have been proved in [4].

Theorem 3.5. If a fixed upper bound M^* is placed on M, the algorithm RFOER terminates after a finite number of steps.

Theorem 3.6. (soundness) The algorithm RFOER indicates (a) unsatisfiability only if F is unsatisfiable, (b) satisfiability only if F is satisfiable, and (c) M-satisfiability only if F is M-satisfiable.

Theorem 3.7. (completeness) If F is unsatisfiable then RFOER terminates with an indication of unsatisfiability.

4 A Description of the Algorithm

There are two schools of practice in instantiation based methods, differing in the techniques used to control instance generation. Uncontrolled instance generation as used in early attempts was not very successful because of combinatorial explosion of the numbers clauses. One way of controlling instance generation is the use of semantics to guide the search of theorem provers[5][6]. The other school of thought is the Jeroslow school[7] that uses blockage testing as a way of control over generation of instances. Our potential blockage is such a version.

4.1 A Description of the Algorithm

The set of clauses that form a first-order formula in skolem normal form is a terse representation of a (usually infinite) set of ground clauses that are equivalent to a (usually infinite) formula in propositional logic. The compactness theorem[8] says that for an unsatisfiable first-order formula, there is a finite set of ground clauses which is unsatisfiable as a propositional formula. This finite set is constructed by substituting variables with all constants whose depth is less than a particular finite value (initially unknown).

This leads us to the instantiation procedure for testing satisfiability wherein we construct a set of ground clauses by substituting variables with constants upto depth 0, test for satisfiability, construct another set by substituting variables with constants upto depth 1, test, ..., construct another set by substituting variables with constants upto depth n and test again. If the formula is unsatisfiable, we are guaranteed to find that the set is unsatisfiable when we construct it by substituting variables with constants of some finite depth.

We can see that atoms with universally quantified variables represent a (usually infinite) set of ground atoms. At each stage the RFOER algorithm solves a propositional satisfiability problem consisting of the universally qualitified formula without its quantifiers (but with skolem functions generated by existential quantifiers in the original formula). Some of the atoms are only partially instantiated, but all atoms are treated equally as atomic propositions. Atoms that are variants of each other, however, are regarded as identical (two atoms are variants if they are the same but for renaming of variables). If the proposition algorithm returns the satisfiability, RFOER finds the potential blockage atom pairs among the clauses. If C_1, C_2 are the clauses containing potential blockage, then instantiate them by the mgu of the potentially blocked atom pair to generate clauses C_1', C_2', which are added to the formula. When the propositional satisfiability is re-solved, the conflict is resolved.

To ensure finite termination of the RFOER algorithm for unsatisfiable formulas, we need to modify the procedure by resolving, among the several potential blockages that may exits at the same point of time, any one of those having the least nesting depth of the mgu. By doing this, we ensure that we fully explore the set of ground clauses obtained using constants only upto a certain depth, before proceeding to the next level.

When complementary factor is high, namely there are more complementary literals in the clause set, propositional ER algorithm RIER has a relatively good performance[3]. This result in RFOER is more effective when there are more complementary literals in the clause set.

4.2 Incremental Potentially Blockage Testing

Potential blockage testing is done by checking whether the atoms of any pair of clauses are unifiable, and if so, whether the substituted clauses are variants of any clause in the formula. Let $\Phi=\{C_1, C_2, \ldots\ldots, C_n\}$ be the clause set gotten from formula F and m be the average length of the clauses in Φ. Consider the unification and variant tests between two clauses firstly. In the first unification and variant tests, the optimal complexity is $O(n^2)$ and the worst and average complexity are both $O(n^2m^2)$. When attempt to unify and be variant in after each loop test, the optimal complexity is $O(n)$ (it is just the most ideal situation in theory and not happed in practice actually) and the worst and average complexity are both $O(nm^2)$. In fact, the RFOER is more effective for those clause sets which clause length is different widely. The number of potential blockage and the most nesting depth also affect the speed of RFOER. It is the worst case to solve all of the potential blockages to get decidable result, so it needs not solve all of the potential blockages in general.

We note the potentially blocked atom pairs which are not instantiated this time are still the potentially blocked atom pairs in the next iteration. This led to the idea of testing potential blockages incrementally by re-using the results of the potential blockage tests (mgus and variants) that were obtained in the previous iteration.

As shown in figure 1, to implement incremental potential blockage testing, we associate with each clause, a list of results with a node for each subsequent clause. Each result node stores a pointer to the clauses when the tests were last carried out, and the results of the tests (i.e. whether the mgu was found, if so, what was the mug, and whether the variant test succeeded or not). The very first time, all these nodes are empty, but as we perform potential blockage tests, we store the results in this list. When a clause is added, we add an empty result node to each of the clauses in the formula. If the new clause is an instantiation of some clause C_i then its mugs are the subset of C_i's mugs. So it needs not to test the mgus between the new clause and those clauses having no mug with C_i.

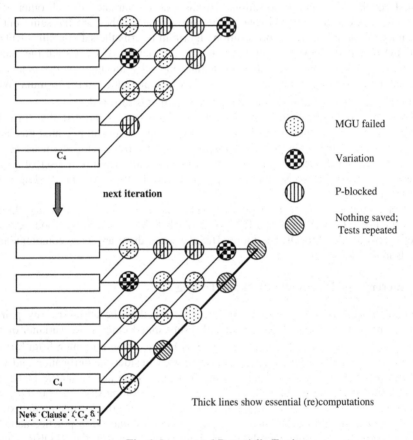

Fig. 1. Incremental Potentially Testing

5   Experimental Results

This section shows the solutions of two kinds of standard and representative planning problem commonly used to study methods of solution of planning problems. These solutions were obtained by using RFOER to implement the first-order theorem proving technique for planning. The experiments were performed on a Pentium 2.80GHz.

To ensure termination in a finite number of steps, the RFOER explores the Herbrand Universe level by level (breadth-first). This feature causes it to generate the shortest plans when it is used to solve planning problems.

We use Kautz's formal method[9] to encoding these planning problems into SAT format problem in first-order logic. In the planning as satisfiability approach, a planning problem is not a theorem to be proved; rather, it is simply a set of axioms with the property than any model of the axioms corresponds to a valid plan. Some of these axioms describe the initial and goal states. The other axioms describe the actions in general. To find the sequential plans, we state that only one action occurs at a time, and assert that some action occurs at every time.

5.1 The Shortest Plan Problem (SPP)

One can move though initial position to goal position in single steps or jumps of two. How does one go from initial position to goal position in the fewest number of steps?

Take the problem 1 as an example, which is a directed graph with cycle given in Figure 2. The number of the node set and the arc set are 11 and 15 respectively. When nesting depth M is 8, the algorithm returns unsatisfiable. It means the problem 1 has solution, namely it has the shortest path. Moreover, the test time is 2.313 seconds and the generated clause number is 267.

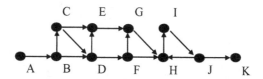

Fig. 2. SPP with 11 notes and 15 arcs

By Kautz's formal method, it can be written,
$P(A, s) \wedge (\neg P(A, s) \vee P(B, step(s))) \wedge (\neg P(B, s) \vee P(C, step(s))) \wedge$
$(\neg P(C, s) \vee P(D, step(s))) \wedge (\neg P(D, s) \vee P(E, step(s))) \wedge (\neg P(E, s) \vee P(F, step(s))) \wedge$
$(\neg P(F, s) \vee P(G, step(s))) \wedge (\neg P(G, s) \vee P(H, step(s))) \wedge (\neg P(H, s) \vee P(I, step(s))) \wedge$
$(\neg P(I, s) \vee P(J, step(s))) \wedge (\neg P(J, s) \vee P(K, step(s))) \wedge (\neg P(A, s) \vee P(C, jump(s))) \wedge$
$(\neg P(B, s) \vee P(D, jump(s))) \wedge (\neg P(C, s) \vee P(E, jump(s))) \wedge (\neg P(D, s) \vee P(F, jump(s))) \wedge$
$(\neg P(E, s) \vee P(G, jump(s))) \wedge (\neg P(F, s) \vee P(H, jump(s))) \wedge (\neg P(G, s) \vee P(I, jump(s))) \wedge$
$(\neg P(H, s) \vee P(J, jump(s))) \wedge (\neg P(I, s) \vee P(K, jump(s))) \wedge (\neg P(J, s) \vee P(H, jump(s))) \wedge$
$\neg P(K, s)$.
P(A, s) means that the initially position is A, $(\neg P(A, s) \vee P(B, step(s)))$ means that one can step from A to B, $(\neg P(A, s) \vee P(C, jump(s)))$ means that one can jump from A to C, P(K, s) means that one can not move from A to K.

Table 1 shows the computational results on SPPs. The Problem 1 and 2 in table 1 are the directed graph with cycle and without cycle respectively. Both of them have solutions. So RFOER terminates and returns unsatisfiability. The Problem 3 and 4 are the directed graph with cycle and Problem 5 and 6 are acyclic directed graph. All of them have no solutions. RFOER terminates and returns satisfiability for Problem 3 and 4. RFOER stops and returns M-satisfiability for any given M for Problem 5 and 6. Namely they are those satisfiable without termination problems.

Table 1. Shortest Plan Problems

SPP		Prob.1 (11, 15) Cycle	Prob.2 (11, 14) Non-cycle	Prob.3 (8, 12) Non-cycle	Prob.4 (11, 13) Non-cycle	Prob.5 (6, 9) Cycle	Prob.6 (8, 13) Cycle
M=3	Result	3-SAT	3-SAT	3-SAT	3-SAT	3-SAT	3-SAT
	Time	0.078	0.062	0.063	0.031	0.047	0.093
	Clauses	63	59	58	44	42	69
M=4	Result	4-SAT	4-SAT	4-SAT	4-SAT	4-SAT	4-SAT
	Time	0.234	0.187	0.187	0.078	0.140	0.406
	Clauses	94	84	83	57	68	122
M=5	Result	5-SAT	5-SAT	5-SAT	5-SAT	5-SAT	5-SAT
	Time	0.484	0.359	0.328	0.141	0.375	1.297
	Clauses	130	109	101	68	105	208
M=6	Result	6-SAT	6-SAT	6-SAT	6-SAT	6-SAT	6-SAT
	Time	0.875	0.546	0.406	0.188	0.859	6.141
	Clauses	171	132	108	77	155	355
M=7	Result	7-SAT	7-SAT	SAT	7-SAT	7-SAT	7-SAT
	Time	1.484	0.750	1.219	0.234	1.875	18.485
	Clauses	218	152	108	84	226	598
M=8	Result	UNSAT	UNSAT	——	8-SAT	8-SAT	8-SAT
	Time	2.313	0.921	——	0.265	5.906	51.844
	Clauses	267	166	——	88	325	979
M=9	Result	——	——	——	SAT	9-SAT	9-SAT
	Time	——	——	——	1.078	12.422	141.047
	Clauses	——	——	——	88	462	1575
M=10	Result	——	——	——	——	10-SAT	10-SAT
	Time	——	——	——	——	25.468	640.625
	Clauses	——	——	——	——	651	2539

5.2 The Blocks World Problem (BWP)

In the blocks world, the robot can pick up or put down a block in each single step, the goal is to make a predetermined stack.

Table 2 shows the computational results on BWPs. In table 2, the blocks of Problem 1 to 5 are 4, 6, 8, 10 and 12 respectively. Take the problem 1 as an example. There are 4 blocks in the initial state, when nesting depth M is 3, the algorithm returns unsatisfiable. It means the problem 1 has solution, namely the 4 blocks have changed into the required shape in three movements sequence. The test time is 0.297 seconds and the generated clause number is 77.

Table 2. Blocks World Problems

BWP		Prob.1 (4)	Prob.2 (6)	Prob.3 (8)	Prob.4 (10)	Prob.5 (12)
M=3	Result	UNSAT	3-SAT	3-SAT	3-SAT	3-SAT
	Time	0.297	<0.001	<0.001	0.015	0.031
	Clauses	77	47	67	92	120
M=6	Result	——	UNSAT	6-SAT	6-SAT	6-SAT
	Time	——	0.953	<0.001	0.015	0.031
	Clauses	——	137	67	92	120
M=9	Result	——	——	UNSAT	9-SAT	9-SAT
	Time	——	——	2.390	0.015	0.031
	Clauses	——	——	217	92	120
M=13	Result	——	——	——	UNSAT	13-SAT
	Time	——	——	——	5.265	0.031
	Clauses	——	——	——	318	120
M=16	Result	——	——	——	——	UNSAT
	Time	——	——	——	——	10.343
	Clauses	——	——	——	——	438

6 Conclusions

Testing for potential blockage remained a bottleneck. It involves checking whether the atom pairs of any pair of clause are unifiable, and if so, whether the partially instantiated clauses so obtained are variants of any clause in the current formula F. Therefore, it is difficult to solve complex problems.

Another problem is that the number of potential blockages resolved before reaching unsatisfiability depends upon the order in which they are removed. There is reason to search for heuristics that help choose such potential blockage to be resolved, that unsatisfiability is reached with a near minimum number of blockage resolved.

Reasoning about knowledge has found applications in such diverse fields as economics, linguistics, artificial intelligence, and computer science. Within computer science, reasoning about knowledge plays an extremely important role in contemporary theories of intelligent agents. Although there exists a number of theories of reasoning about knowledge, which are formulated in the framework of modal logics, the work on practical proof methods for the expressive logics involved in these theories has been sparse.

We have extended ER method to modal logics by destructive approach[10] and functional translation method[11]. We are going to extend first-order ER method to modal logics by relational translation in the future. Based on these works, we will give some modal theorem prover in the future and take the suitable one as the deduction methods for knowledge and belief.

Acknowledgments

This paper was supported by National Natural Science Foundation of China (Grant No.60273080, 60473003), the Science and Technology Development Program of Jilin Province of China (Grant No.20040526), the Outstanding Youth Foundation of Jilin Province of china (Grant No.20030107), the Basic Theory and Core Techniques of Non Canonical Knowledge Specialized Research Fund for the Doctoral Program of Higher Education Grant No. 20050183065, the NSFC Major Research Program 60496321 and also by Science Foundation for Yong Teachers of Northeast Normal University Grant No. 20051001.

References

1. Lin, H., Sun, J.G., Zhang, Y. M., Theorem proving based on extension rule, Journal of Automated Reasoning, Springer, (2003)31:11-21.
2. Wu, X., Sun, J.G., Lu, S., Yin, M.H., Propositional extension rule with reduction, International Journal of Computer Science and Network Security, (2006) 6: 190-195.
3. Wu, X., Sun, J.G., Lu, S., Li, Y. and Meng, W., Improved propositional extension rule, In Proceeding of 1st International Conference on Rough Sets and Knowledge Technology (RSKT2006), Chongqing, China, 2006, to appear.
4. Wu, X., Sun, J.G., Hou, K., Extension rule in first order logic, In Proceeding of 5th International Conference on Cognitive Informatics (ICCI 2006), Beijing, China, 2006, to appear.
5. Chu, H., and Plaisted, D.A., Semantically Guided First-Order Theorem Proving Using Hyper-Linking, In Proceeding of 12th Conference on Automated Deduction, Nancy, France, (1994): 192-206.
6. Paramasivam, M., Plaisted, A. D., A replacement rule theorem prover, Journal of Automated Reasoning, (1997) 18:221-226.
7. Jeroslow, R. G., Computation-oriented reductions of predicate to propositional logic, Decision Support Systems, (1988) 4:183-197.
8. Chang, C., Lee, R. C., Symbolic logic and mechanical theorem proving, Academic Press, 1973.
9. Kautz, H., Selman, B, Planning as satisfiability, In Proceeding of the 10th European Conference on Artificial Intelligence, Vienna, Austria, (1992): 359-363.
10. Wu, X., Sun, J.G., Feng, S. S., Destructive extension rule in modal logic K, Proceeding of International Conference of Computational Methods, Singapore, 2004.
11. Wu, X., Sun, J.G., Lin, H., Feng, S. S., Modal extension rule, Process In Natural Science, China, (2005) 6: 550-558.

An Extended Meta-model for Workflow Resource Model

Zhijiao Xiao[1], Huiyou Chang[1], Sijia Wen[1], Yang Yi[1], and Atsushi Inoue[2]

[1] School of Information Science and Technology, Sun Yat-sen University,
510275 Guangzhou, China
mmousecindy@yahoo.com.cn
[2] Computer Science Department, Eastern Washington University,
99004 WA, USA

Abstract. Workflow resource model describes all kinds of resources that support the execution of workflows. The meta-model for workflow resource model presents the constituents of workflow resource model. It is one of the three correlative sub-meta-models for workflow model. Based on the analysis of existed studies and real cases, an extended meta-model for workflow resource model was introduced by extending and modifying the meta-model for organizational model proposed by WfMC. The detail of entities and their relationships were described. The relationships between workflow resource model and process model were discussed. XML was used to describe the meta-model. In the end, a conclusion and proposals for future research directions were presented.

1 Introduction

Workflow is the automation of a business process, in whole or part, during which documents, information or tasks are passed from one participant to another for action, according to a set of procedural rules[1]. WfMS (Workflow Management System) is a system that defines, creates and manages the execution of workflows through the use of software, running on one or more workflow engines, which is able to interpret the process definition, interact with workflow participants and, where required, invoke the use of IT tools and applications[1]. Nowadays, workflow technology has received much attention by its capability to support today's complex business processes.

A workflow needs to access resources during its execution. The importance of resources involved in workflow management system has been pointed out by many researchers[2-4]. Resource management is an important issue in workflow management system, and the effective modeling of resources is the basis of the effective managing of resources. There are two kinds of resource models: one is integrated into workflow process model, and the other is separated from the process model. The latter is widely used since the life-cycle of the resources within an enterprise typically varies from the life cycles of the enterprise's processes. In addition, the separation enables workflow designers to create workflow models that are independent of changes of workflow resources, adding to their robustness[4].

WfMC (Workflow Management Coalition) proposed a organizational meta-model which identifies several types of workflow participants and their relationships[3]. But

J. Lang, F. Lin, and J. Wang (Eds.): KSEM 2006, LNAI 4092, pp. 525–534, 2006.

it is not enough to describe complicated structures of resource models. Many further researches have been done and several different complicated meta-models have been proposed[4-6].

Based on the deep analysis of existed studies and real cases, an extended meta-model for workflow resource model was introduced in this paper by extending and modifying the meta-model for organizational model proposed by WfMC. The rest of this paper is organized as follows. In section 2, the meta-model for workflow resource model is proposed. The detail of all the entities and their relationships are described. In section 3, the relationships between workflow resource model and process model are discussed. In section 4, XML is used to describe the meta-model. Finally, a conclusion and proposals for future research directions are presented in section 5.

2 Meta-model for Workflow Resource Model

Meta-models are used to define the semantic and syntactic structures and rules of models. They are models that describe models. Workflow meta-models are used to describe the constituents of workflow models. There are three correlative sub-meta-models for workflow model: meta-model for process, meta-model for information and meta-model for resource. They describe different attributes of workflow from different views.

Workflow resource models describe all kinds of resources that support the execution of workflows, including human and nonhuman resources. The design of the meta-model should guarantee that all kinds of workflow resource models can be constructed using the elements from the meta-model. And the resource models constructed based on the meta-model should have good flexibility and robustness.

There are two forms of resource classification[8]. One is based upon functional properties and the other is based upon position within the organization. Based on these two classifications, the design of the resource model should follow two different directions. The meta-model for resource model should support the modeling of resources in these two directions.

In order to satisfy all the requirements mentioned above, an extended meta-model for workflow resource model, as shown in figure 1, is proposed by extending and modifying the meta-model for organizational model proposed by WfMC.

Resource is the core of the resource meta-model. Based on the two kinds of classification, the model is divided into two parts: functional view and organizational view.

A functionally-based resource class is known as a *role*[8]. From a process perspective, a role represents the capabilities and authorities required for the proper execution of an activity. For a resource perspective, a role represents the combined capabilities and authorities of a process participant[4]. The introduction of role improves the flexibility and robustness of workflow model through separating workflow process model and resource model.

Resources can also be classified according to their place in the organization. The place of a resource in the organization is called a *station*. A station is the role of a resource within the organization. A station belongs to an *organizational unit*. The introduction of station separates organizational structure from concrete resources.

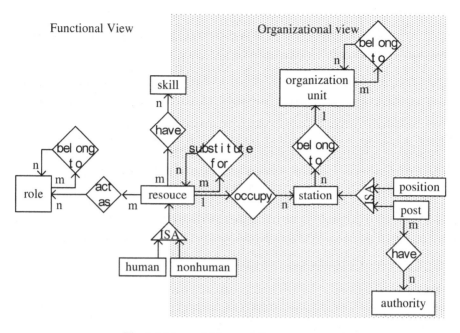

Fig. 1. Meta-model for workflow resource model

2.1 Entities

Resource: A resource is any entity required by a workflow for its execution. Depending on the application domains, resources can be human resources or nonhuman resources, such as machines, money, software etc. Here, we use RES to denote the resource set, $resource_i \in$ RES denotes a resource whose identifier is i; HUM denotes the human resource set, $human_j \in$ HUM denotes a human resource whose identifier is j; NHUM denotes the nonhuman resource set, $nonhuman_k \in$ NHUM denotes a nonhuman resource whose identifier is k. The basic attributes of a resource include identifier, name, description, skills, substitute requirements, etc. There are some dynamic attributes of a resource, such as state, workload, history, etc.

Skill: A skill is an ability of being able to fulfill certain functions. It is the proficiency, facility, or dexterity that is acquired or developed through training or experience. Skill is a direct property of a resource and remains associated with the resource, even if the position of the resource in the enterprise changes[4]. For example, Mike can type. "Typing" is one of the skills Mike has. The skills of a resource determine to some extent that if it can act as certain roles, or occupy certain stations, or substitute for certain resources. We use SKI to denote the skill set, $skill_i \in$ SKI denotes a skill whose identifier is i. Different resources have different level in different skills. For example, Mike can type 100 words in one minute. "100 words in one minute" is the level of Mike in the "typing" skill. We use $level(resource_i, skill_j)$ to denote the level of $resource_i$ in skill $skill_j$.

Role: A role is a set of common characteristics such as structures, properties, behaviors, rights and obligations. In workflow context, a role is a logical group of resources that can conduct certain tasks. According to different characteristics of roles, a hierarchy structure of roles can be built to describe that a certain role supervises another. We use ROLE to denote the role set, $role_i \in$ ROLE denotes a role whose identifier is i. The basic attributes of a role include identifier, name, description, father, requirements, etc.

Station: A stations is an organization position. It is the building block of the formal organizational structure of an enterprise. We use STA to denote the station set, $station_i \in$ STA denotes a station whose identifier is i. For human resources, stations are called posts and their holders are granted the necessary authorities to perform the activities associated with these posts. $post_j \in$ POST denotes a post whose identifier is j, and POST is the post set. As far as nonhuman resources are concerned, stations are called positions. $position_k \in$ POSI denotes a position whose identifier is k, and POSI is the position set. The basic attributes of a station include identifier, name, description, organization unit, duties, requirements, etc.

Authority: An authority is a right to access objects, or a permission to conduct certain operations. Authority is a property of a post. For example, financial manager can sign an expense account under \$100,000. "Sign an expense account under \$100,000" is an authority of the post "financial manager". We use AUT to denote the authority set, $authority_i \in$ AUT denotes an authority whose identifier is i.

Organization Unit: An organization unit, such as a department or a work team, is a group of stations. We use ORU to denote the organization unit set, $organization\ unit_i \in$ ORU denotes an organization unit whose identifier is i. An organization unit belongs to one or more superior organization units. The basic attributes of an organization unit include identifier, name, description, superior, etc.

Table 1. Entities and their attributes. This table summarizes several main entities and their attributes.

Entity	Attributes
Resource	Id, Name, Description, Skill List, Substitute Requirements, State, Workload, History, Extended Attributes
Skill	Id, Name, Description, Extended Attributes
Role	Id, Name, Description, Requirements, Father, Extended Attributes
Organization Unit	Id, Name, Description, Superior, Extended Attributes
Station	Id, Name, Description, Duties, Requirements, Organization Unit, Extended Attributes
Post	Id, Name, Description, Duties, Requirements, Organization Unit, Authorities, Extended Attributes
Authority	Id, Name, Description, Extended Attributes

2.2 Relationships

ISA: X→Y. X is a sub-class or an instance of Y. X inherits Y's attributes.
BELONGTO: X→Y. X belongs to Y. X is part of Y. For instance, *post$_i$* that belongs to *organization unit$_j$* can be expressed as

    <post$_i$> BELONGTO *<organization unit$_j$>*.

HAVE: X→Y. X is an attribute of Y.
SUBSTITUTEFOR: X→Y. X satisfies the substitute requirements of Y, so X can substitute for Y if Y is absent. For instance, *resource$_i$* that can substitute for *resource$_j$* can be expressed as

    <resource$_i$> SUBSTITUTEFOR *<resource$_j$>*.

OCCUPY: X→Y. X satisfies the requirements of Y, so X can occupy Y, and take Y's responsibilities, where $X \in$ RES, $Y \in$ STA. If $Y \in$ POST, $X \in$ HUM, else $Y \in$ POSI, $X \in$ NHUM. For instance, if a human resource *human$_i$* satisfies the requirements of *post$_j$*, then *human$_i$* can occupy *post$_j$*.

    <human$_i$> OCCUPY *<post$_j$>*.

The human resource occupied a post will be entitled with the authority associated with that post.

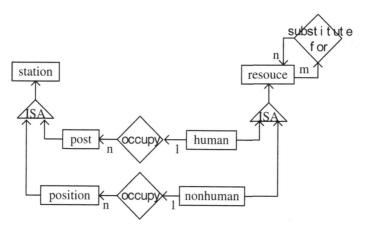

Fig. 2. The "occupy" relationship between resource and station. This figure shows some details of the "occupy" relationship between resource and station.

ACTAS: X→Y. X satisfies the requirements of Y, so X can act as Y, where $X \in$ RES, $Y \in$ ROLE. A resource can act as more than one role, and a role can be acted by one or more resources.

The "actas" relationship has two special attributes: competence and preference[10-11]. The competence indicates the ability of a resource to carry out tasks effectively or well. It can be evaluated in terms of many factors, such as resource's skill level, resource's current workload, processing cost, and the like. Some strategies can be used to combine these factors into a scalar value called *competence*. We use *competence(resource$_i$, role$_j$)*, whose value is between 0 and 1, to denote the competence of *resource$_i$* act as role *role$_j$*. The preference means the property that a resource likes to carry out some tasks more than others. It is subjective, but can be measured based on the workload of the resource, biding rate to the same type of tasks, etc. We use *preference(resource_i, role_j)*, whose value is between 0 and 1, to denote the preference of *resource_i* act as role *role_j*.

For instance, resource *human_i* that can act as role *role_j* having competence and preference with certain values can be expressed as

<*human_i*> ACTAS <*role_j*> COMPETENCE (0.8) PREFERENCE (0.4).

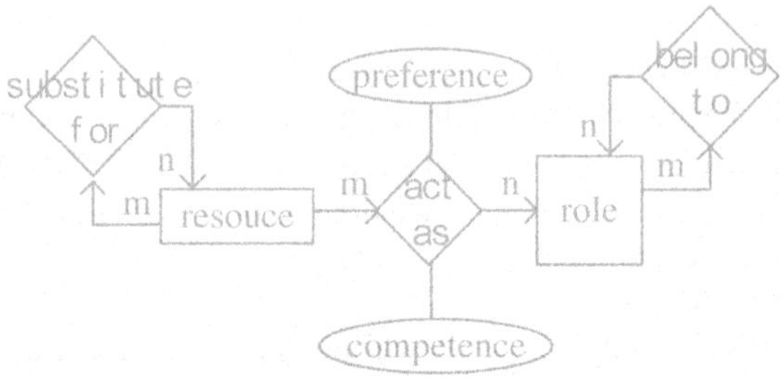

Fig. 3. The "actas" relationship between resource and role. This figure shows some details of the "actas" relationship between resource and role.

3   Relationships Between Resource Model and Process Model

The resource model built using the meat-model proposed in this paper is separated from the process model. All the resources in the resource model can act as a participant to become the performer of workflow processes or activities, which connect the process

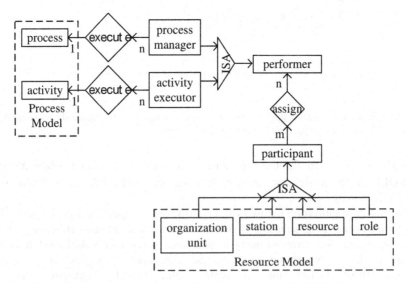

Fig. 4. Relationships between process model and resource model. This figure shows some details of the relationships between process model and resource model.

model and the resource model as a whole. The interfaces, as shown in figure 4, support the interaction between the process model and the resource model.

Participant assignment links the process model and the resource model. The particular resources, which can be assigned to perform a specific activity or a process, are specified as a performer which is an attribute of the activity or the process. There are four types of workflow participant which can be assigned to a performer to be involved into the execution of workflows: organization unit, station, resource, and role.

In general, there are two ways of resource assignments: direct or indirect. The direct way is through biding concrete resources for processes or activities. This kind of assignment is static and usually be done during workflow build-time. In this way, process model and resource model are tightly coupled. The utilization of resources is inefficient. Exception or waiting would happen frequently when the required resources are not available. But in this way, there is no time spent on searching for suitable resources for the execution during the run-time.

The indirect assignment of resources is done by assigning roles, stations, and organization units as performers. In this way, assignment is separated into two parts. First, roles, stations, or organization units are assigned as performers during the process build-time, and the mapping between roles, stations, or organization units and resources is done in the resource model build-time. Then, during the run-time, resources are evaluated and a concrete resource is selected to participate in the execution.

4 XML Based Description of the Meta-model

4.1 XML Resource Definition Language (XRDL)

In order to keep the resource model clearly separated from the process model and to provide a interchange basis for different resource models from different workflow management systems in distributed and heterogeneous environments, a workflow resource definition language XRDL (XML Resource Definition Language) is proposed based on XML. It provides an XML file format to interchange resource models between tools. All the elements and their relationships in the meta-model for workflow resource model are defined by XML schemas. Due to the limited space, we only give the "actas" relationship that is defined by an XML schema as an example:

```
<xsd:element name="ActAs">

    <xsd:complexType>

        <xsd:attribute name="Id" type="xsd:NMTOKEN"
use="required"/>

        <xsd:attribute name="ActorId" type="xsd:NMTOKEN"
use="required"/>

        <xsd:attribute name="RoleId" type="xsd:NMTOKEN"
use="required"/>

        <xsd:sequence>

            <xsd:element ref="XRDL:Competence"
minOccurs="0"/>
```

```
          <xsd:element ref="XRDL:Preference"
minOccurs="0"/>

       </xsd:sequence>

    </xsd:complexType>

 </xsd:element>
```

4.2 Extensions to XPDL

XPDL (XML Process Definition Language) is proposed by WfMC to provide a common interchange standard that enables products to continue to support arbitrary internal representations of process definitions with an import/export function to map to/from the standard at the product boundary[12]. XPDL has been widely accepted and implemented in many commercial and open-source products.

XPDL is a process definition language. It provides a participant declaration which may define some simple types of resource. Through making some small extensions and modifications to XPDL definition of "ParticipantType", the process model described by XPDL can refers to the resource model built based on the meta-model proposed in this paper and described by XRDL well and effectively.

The participant in XPDL is one of the following types: resource set, resource, organizational unit, role, human, or system. We confine it to the following types: resource, organizational unit, role, or station. Since we can assign more than one resource to perform an activity or a process, resource set and role set are not consider as one of the participant type. The extensions and modifications to the XPDL description of "ParticipantType" are shown as follow:

```
<xsd:element name="ParticipantType">

  <xsd:complexType>

    <xsd:sequence>

       <xsd:any namespace="##other"
processContents="lax" minOccurs="0"
maxOccurs="unbounded"/>

    </xsd:sequence>

    <xsd:attribute name="Type" use="required">

      <xsd:simpleType>

        <xsd:restriction base="xsd:NMTOKEN">

           <xsd:enumeration value="RESOURCE"/>

           <xsd:enumeration
value="ORGANIZATIONAL_UNIT"/>

           <xsd:enumeration value="STATION"/>

           <xsd:enumeration value="ROLE"/>

        </xsd:restriction>

      </xsd:simpleType>
```

```
    </xsd:attribute>

    <xsd:anyAttribute namespace="##other"
processContents="lax"/>

    </xsd:complexType>

</xsd:element>
```

5 Conclusions

An extended meta-model for workflow resource model is proposed in this paper based on the organizational meta-model proposed by WfMC. It enriches the building elements for resource modeling and is able to model complex resource models. It can be used to model human and nonhuman resources. It improves the flexibility and robustness of the workflow model by separating process model and resource model, organizational structure and concrete resources. It supports direct and indirect resource assignment. It describes the competence and preference of resources which can facilitate the optimization of resource assignment.

An XML based resource definition language XRDL is proposed to describe the meta-model, which provide the facility for the interchange of different resource models in distributed and heterogeneous environments.

Limited to the space, the details of resource modeling and management based on the meta-model is not mentioned. In our project, we developed a tool for resource modeling based on the meta-model proposed in this paper which can be used to build resource models conveniently. We also developed a resource manager to process the interaction between resource model and process model at build-time and run-time.

In our project, database technologies are used to realize the storage and management of resource models. But there are some requirements that can not be satisfied using database technologies. For a future work, policies of resource management and resource query language can be proposed. Some researches have been done on those areas[13-14].

Acknowledgement

The work reported in this paper is supported in part by the National Natural Science Foundation of China under grant No. 60573159, as well as the Natural Science Foundation of Guangdong Province of China under grant No. 05100302.

References

1. Workflow Management Coalition: Terminology & Glossary. WfMC-TC-1011, Workflow Management Coalition (1999)
2. Li, W., Zeng, G. Z., Wang, X. L.: A Workflow Model Based on Timed Petri Net. Journal of Software 13, 8 (2002) 1666-1671. (in Chinese)
3. Workflow Management Coalition: Interface 1: Process Definition Interchange Organisational Model. WfMC-TC-1016-O, Workflow Management Coalition (1998)

4. Michael Zur Muehlen: Organizational Management in Workflow Applications – Issues and Perspectives. Information Technology and Management 5 (2004) 271-291
5. Li, H. C., Shi, M. L.: Workflow Models and Their Formal Descriptions. Chinese Journal of Computers 26, 11 (2003) 1456-1463.(in Chinese)
6. Hu, C. C.: Organization Model and Solution in Workflow System. http://www.javafox.org (2004). (in Chinese)
7. Zhao, W., Hu, W. H., Zhang, S. K., Wang, L. F.: Study and Application of a Workflow Meta-Model. Journal of Software 14, 6 (2003) 1052-1059. (in Chinese)
8. Aalst, W. M. P., Hee, K.V.: Workflow Management: Models, Methods, and Systems. The MIT Press, Cambridge, MA (2002)
9. Hee, K. van, Serebrenik, A., Sidorova, N., Voorhoeve, M.: Soundness of resource-constrained workflow nets. In: G. Ciardo and P. Darondeau (Eds.): ICATPN 2005, LNCS 3536 (2005) 250-267
10. Senkul, P., Toroslu, I. H.: An architecture for workflow scheduling under resource allocation constraints. Information Systems 30 (2005) 399-422
11. Lee, K. M.: Adaptive resource scheduling for workflows considering competence and preference. In: M. Gh. Negoita er al. (Eds.): KES 2004, LNAI 3214 (2004) 723-730
12. Workflow Management Coalition. Process Definition Interface -- XML Process Definition Language. WfMC-TC-1025, Workflow Management Coalition (2005)
13. Huang, Y., Shan, M.: Policies in a resource manager of workflow system: modeling, enforcement and management. In: International Conference on Data Engineering (1999)
14. Du, W., Davis, J., Huang, Y., Shan, M.: Enterprise workflow resource management. In: International Workshop on Research Issues in Data Engineering, Sydney, Australia (1999) 108-115

Knowledge Reduction Based on Evidence Reasoning Theory in Ordered Information Systems*

Wei-Hua Xu[1], Ming-Wen Shao[2], and Wen-Xiu Zhang[3]

[1] Faculty of Science, Institute for Information and System Sciences,
Xi'an Jiaotong University, Xi'an, Shaan'xi 710049, P.R. China
datongxuweihua@126.com
[2] School of Information Technology, Jiangxi University of Finance & Economics,
Nanchang, Jiangxi 330013, P.R. China
shaomingwen1837@163.com
[3] Faculty of Science, Institute for Information and System Sciences,
Xi'an Jiaotong University, Xi'an, Shaan'xi 710049, P.R. China
wxzhang@mail.xjtu.edu.cn

Abstract. Rough set theory has been considered as a useful tool to model the vagueness, imprecision, and uncertainty, and has been applied successfully in many fields. Knowledge reduction is one of the most important problems in rough set theory. However, in real-world most of information systems are based on dominance relations in stead of the classical rough set because of various factors. To acquire brief decision rules from systems based on dominance relations, knowledge reductions are needed. The main aim of this paper is to study the problem. The basic concepts and properties of knowledge reduction based on evidence reasoning theory are discussed. Furthermore, the characterization and knowledge reduction approaches based on evidence reasoning theory are obtained with examples in several kinds of ordered information system, which is every useful in future research works of the ordered information systems.

1 Introduction

The rough set theory, proposed by Pawlak in the early 1980s[1], is an extension of set theory for the study of intelligent systems characterized by inexact, uncertain or vague information and can serve as a new mathematica tool to soft computing. This theory has been applied successfully in machine learning, patten recognition, decision support systems, expert systems, data analysis, data mining, and so on. Since its introduction, the theory has generated a great deal of interest among more and more researchers.

Knowledge reduction is one of the hot research topics of rough set theory. Much study on this area had been reported and many useful results were

---

* This work is supported by the National 973 Program of China(2002CB31200).

J. Lang, F. Lin, and J. Wang (Eds.): KSEM 2006, LNAI 4092, pp. 535–547, 2006.

obtained until now[2-8]. However, most work was based on consistent information systems, and the main methodology has been developed under equivalence
relations which are often called indiscernibility relations. In practise, most of
information systems are not only inconsistent, but also based on dominance relations because of various factors. In order to obtain the succinct decision rules
from them by using rough set method, knowledge reductions are needed. In recent years, more and more attention has been paid to research of rough set.
Many types of knowledge reductions have been proposed in the area of rough
sets[9-15].

However, the original rough sets theory approach does not consider attributes
with preference-ordered domains, that is, criteria. In many real situations, we are
often face with the problems in which the ordering of properties of the considered
attributes plays a crucial role. One such type of problem is the ordering of objects. For this reason, Greco, Matarazzo, and Slowinski[16-20]proposed an extension rough sets theory, called the dominance-based rough sets approach(DRSA)
to take into account the ordering properties of criteria. This innovation is mainly
based on substitution of the indiscernibility relation by a dominance relation.
In DRSA, where condition attributes are criteria and classes are preference ordered, and many studies have been made in DRSA[21-25]. But useful results
of knowledge reductions are very poor in ordered information systems until
now.

In this paper the main objective is to study the problem. The basic concepts and properties of knowledge reduction based on evidence reasoning theory
are discussed. Furthermore, the characterization and knowledge reduction approaches based on evidence reasoning theory are obtained with examples in several kinds of ordered information system, which is every useful in future research
works of the ordered information systems.

2   Rough Sets and Ordered Information Systems

This section recalls necessary concepts of rough sets and ordered information
systems. Detailed description of the theory can be found in [12, 24].

In rough set theory, an information system(IS) is an quadruple $\mathcal{I} = (U, AT,
V, f)$, where U is a finite nonempty set of objects and AT is a finite nonempty set
of attributes, $V = \bigcup_{a \in AT} V_a$ and V_a is a domain of attribute a, $f : U \times AT \to V$ is
a total function such that $f(x, a) \in V_a$ for every $a \in AT, x \in U$ called information
function.

A decision table is a special case of an information system in which, among the
attributes, we distinguish one called a decision attribute. The other attributes
are called condition attributes. Therefore, $\mathcal{I} = (U, AT \cup \{d\}, V, f)$ and $AT \cap
\{d\} = \phi$,where set AT contains so-called condition attributes and d, the decision
attribute.

For an information system (U, AT, V, f), $A \subseteq AT$,

$$R_A = \{(x_i, x_j) | f(x_i, a) = f(x_j, a), a \in A\}$$

is an equivalence relation(indiscernibility relation,Pawlak). So U can be classified in terms of R_A. The set which includes x can be expressed as $[x]_A$ and has the following properties:

$$[x]_{AT} \subseteq [x]_A, \quad R_{AT} \subseteq R_A.$$

The total of the classifications of U in terms of R_A can be represented as following:

$$U/R_A = \{[x]_A | x \in U\}.$$

It describes the meta-knowledge that can be represented by attribute A. In addition, the object set involved with the meta-knowledge of U/R_A can be represented by attribute A. It is denoted as $\sigma(U/R_A)$.

For any $X \subseteq U$, the upper and lower approximations can be represented as

$$\overline{R_A}(X) = \{x | [x]_A \cap X \neq \phi\}$$

$$\underline{R_A}(X) = \{x | [x]_A \subseteq X\}.$$

If $\overline{R_A}(X) = \underline{R_A}(X) = X$, X is the knowledge which can be represented by A and X is called a definable set. Otherwise, X is the knowledge which cannot be represented by A, and is called a rough set.

In an information systems, if the domain(scale) of a condition attributes is ordered according to a decreasing or increasing preference, then the attributes is a criterion.

Definition 2.1. An information system is called an ordered information system(OIS) if all condition attributes are criterions.

It is assumed that the domain of a criterion $a \in AT$ is complete pre-ordered by an outranking relation $\succeq_a$, and $x \succeq_a y$ means that x is at least as good as y with respect to criterion a. In the following, without any loss of generality, we consider a condition criterion having a numerical domain, that is, $V_a \subseteq \mathcal{R}(\mathcal{R}$ denotes the set of real numbers) and being of type gain , that is, $x \succeq y \Leftrightarrow f(x,a) \geq f(y,a)$(according to increasing preference) of $x \succeq y \Leftrightarrow f(x,a) \leq f(y,a)$(according to decreasing preference), where $a \in AT, x, y \in U$. For a subset of attributes $A \subseteq AT$, we define $x \succeq_A y \Leftrightarrow x \succeq_a y, \forall a \in A$. That is to say x is at least as good as y with respect to all attributes in A. In general, the domain of the condition criterion may be also discrete, but the preference order between its values has to be provided.

The dominance relation that identifies granules of knowledge is defined as follows.

For a given OIS, we say that x dominates y with respect to $A \subseteq AT$, if $x \succeq_A y$, and denoted by $xR_A^{\geq}y$. Namely,

$$R_A^{\geq} = \{(y, x) \in U \times U | y \succeq_A x\}.$$

If $(y, x) \in R_A^{\geq}$, then y dominates x with respect to A.

Given $A \subseteq AT$ and $A = A_1 \cup A_2$,where attributes set A_1 according to increasing preference, A_2 according to decreasing preference. The granules of knowledge induced by the dominance relation $R_A^{\geq}$ are the set of objects dominating x,

$$[x]_A^{\geq} = \{y \in U | f(y, a_1) \geq f(x, a_1) \ (\forall a_1 \in A_1)$$
$$and \ f(y, a_2) \leq f(x, a_2) \ (\forall a_2 \in A_2)\}$$
$$= \{y \in U | (y, x) \in R_A^{\geq}\}$$

and the set of objects dominated by x,

$$[x]_A^{\leq} = \{y \in U | f(y, a_1) \leq f(x, a_1) \ (\forall a_1 \in A_1)$$
$$and \ f(y, a_2) \geq f(x, a_2) \ (\forall a_2 \in A_2)\}$$
$$= \{y \in U | (x, y) \in R_A^{\geq}\}$$

Which are called the $A-dominating$ set and $A-dominated$ set with respect to $x \in U$, respectively.

Let $U/R_A^{\geq}$ denote classification, which is the family set $\{[x]_A^{\geq} | x \in U\}$. Any element from $U/R_A^{\geq}$ will be called a dominance class. Dominance classes in $U/R_A^{\geq}$ do not constitute a partition of U in general. They may be overlap.

In the following, for simplicity, without any loss of generality, we only consider condition attributes with increasing preference.

Proposition 2.1. Let $R_A^{\geq}$ be a dominance relation. The following hold.

(1) $R_A^{\geq}$ is reflexive,transitive, but not symmetric, so it is not a equivalence relation.

(2) If $B \subseteq A \subseteq AT$, then $R_{AT}^{\geq} \subseteq R_A^{\geq} \subseteq R_B^{\geq}$.

(3) If $B \subseteq A \subseteq AT$, then $[x_i]_{AT}^{\geq} \subseteq [x_i]_A^{\geq} \subseteq [x_i]_B^{\geq}$.

(4) If $x_j \in [x_i]_A^{\geq}$, then $[x_j]_A^{\geq} \subseteq [x_i]_A^{\geq}$ and $[x_i]_A^{\geq} = \cup\{[x_j]_A^{\geq} | x_j \in [x_i]_A^{\geq}\}$.

(5) $[x_j]_A^{\geq} = [x_i]_A^{\geq}$ iff $f(x_i, a) = f(x_j, a) \ (\forall a \in A)$.

(6) $\mathcal{J} = \cup\{[x]_A^{\geq} | x \in U\}$ constitute a covering of U.

For any subset X of U, and A of AT define

$$\underline{R_A^{\geq}}(X) = \{x \in U | [x]_A^{\geq} \subseteq X\},$$

$$\overline{R_A^{\geq}}(X) = \{x \in U | [x]_A^{\geq} \cap X \neq \phi\},$$

$\underline{R_A^{\geq}}(X)$ and $\overline{R_A^{\geq}}(x)$ are said to be the lower and upper approximation of X with respect to a dominance relation $R_A^{\geq}$. And the approximations have also some properties which are similar to those of Pawlak approximation spaces.

Proposition 2.2. Let (U, AT, V, f) be an OIS and $X, Y \subseteq U$, then its lower and upper approximations satisfy the following properties.

(1) $\underline{R_A^{\geq}}(X) \subseteq X \subseteq \overline{R_A^{\geq}}(X)$.

(2) $\overline{R_A^{\geq}}(X \cup Y) = \overline{R_A^{\geq}}(X) \cup \overline{R_A^{\geq}}(Y)$;
$\underline{R_A^{\geq}}(X \cap Y) = \underline{R_A^{\geq}}(X) \cap \underline{R_A^{\geq}}(Y)$.

(3) $\underline{R_A^{\geq}}(X) \cup \underline{R^{\geq}}(Y) \subseteq \underline{R_A^{\geq}}(X \cup Y)$;
$\overline{R_A^{\geq}}(X \cap Y) \subseteq \overline{R_A^{\geq}}(X) \cap \overline{R^{\geq}}(Y)$.

(4) $R_A^\geq(\sim X) = \sim \overline{R_A^\geq}(X); \overline{R_A^\geq}(\sim X) = \sim \underline{R_A^\geq}(X).$

(5) $\underline{R_A^\geq}(U) = U; \overline{R_A^\geq}(\phi) = \phi.$

(6) $\underline{R_A^\geq}(X) \subseteq \underline{R_A^\geq}(\underline{R^{\geq A}}(X)); \overline{R_A^\geq}(\overline{R_A^\geq}(X)) \subseteq \overline{R_A^\geq}(X).$

(7) If $X \subseteq Y$, then $\underline{R_A^\geq}(X) \subseteq \underline{R_A^\geq}(Y)$ and $\overline{R_A^\geq}(X) \subseteq \overline{R_A^\geq}(Y).$

where $\sim X$ is the complement of X.

Example 2.1. Given an OIS in Table 1.

Table 1

$U \times AT$	a_1	a_2	a_3
x_1	1	2	1
x_2	3	2	2
x_3	1	1	2
x_4	2	1	3
x_5	3	3	2
x_6	3	2	3

From Table 1, we can see that the dominance classes determined by AT are

$$[x_1]_{AT}^\geq = \{x_1, x_2, x_5, x_6\}; [x_2]_{AT}^\geq = \{x_2, x_5, x_6\};$$

$$[x_3]_{AT}^\geq = \{x_2, x_3, x_4, x_5, x_6\}; [x_4]_{AT}^\geq = \{x_4, x_6\};$$

$$[x_5]_{AT}^\geq = \{x_5\}; [x_6]_{AT}^\geq = \{x_6\};$$

If $X = \{x_2, x_3, x_5\}$, then

$$\underline{R_{AT}^\geq}(X) = \{x_5\} \subseteq X; \overline{R_{AT}^\geq}(X) = \{x_1, x_2, x_3, x_5\} \supseteq X$$

Definition 2.2. An ordered decision table(ODT) is an ordered information system $\mathcal{I} = (U, AT \cup \{d\}, V, f)$, where $d(d \notin AT)$ is an overall preference called the decision, and all the elements of AT are criterions.

Definition 2.3. For an ODT $\mathcal{I} = (U, AT \cup \{d\}, V, f)$, if $R_{AT}^\geq \subseteq R_d^\geq$, then this ODT is consistent, denoted by CODT, otherwise, this ODT is inconsistent(IODT).

Example 2.2. Given an CODT based on Table 1 in Table 2.
From the table, we have

$$[x_1]_d^\geq = [x_3]_d^\geq = \{x_1, x_2, x_3, x_4, x_5, x_6\};$$

$$[x_2]_d^\geq = [x_5]_d^\geq = [x_6]_d^\geq = \{x_2, x_5, x_6\};$$

$$[x_4]_d^\geq = \{x_2, x_4, x_5, x_6\}$$

Table 2

$U \times (AT \cup d)$	a_1	a_2	a_3	d
x_1	1	2	1	1
x_2	3	2	2	3
x_3	1	1	2	1
x_4	2	1	3	2
x_5	3	3	2	3
x_6	3	2	3	3

Obviously, by the above and Example 2.1, we have $R_{AT}^{\geq} \subseteq R_d^{\geq}$, so the DOT in Table 2 is CODT.

Example 2.3. We can obtain a IODT(Table 3) in stead of the value domain of d by $\{3,2,1,2,3,1\}$, respectively in Example 2.2.

Table 3

$U \times (AT \cup d)$	a_1	a_2	a_3	d
x_1	1	2	1	3
x_2	3	2	2	2
x_3	1	1	2	1
x_4	2	1	3	2
x_5	3	3	2	3
x_6	3	2	3	1

From the table, we have

$$[x_1]_d^{\geq} = [x_5]_d^{\geq} = \{x_1, x_5\}; \quad [x_2]_d^{\geq} = [x_4]_d^{\geq} = \{x_1, x_2, x_4, x_5\};$$

$$[x_3]_d^{\geq} = [x_6]_d^{\geq} = \{x_1, x_2, x_3, x_4, x_5, x_6\}.$$

Obviously, by the above and Example 2.1, we have $R_{AT}^{\geq} \not\subseteq R_d^{\geq}$, so the ODT in Table 3 is IODT.

3   Knowledge Reduction Approach Based on Evidence Reasoning in OIS and ODT

For an information system (U, AT, V, f) in Pawlak rough set theory, if $R_A = R_{AT}$ when $A \subset AT$, for any $a \in A$, $R_{A-\{a\}} \neq R_{AT}$, then A is a reduction of the information system. Moreover, reduction exists and is not unique[11]. The set of attributes that is included in all reductions is called the core. Similarly, the following can be found in [16].

Definition 3.1. For an ordered information system OIS (U, AT, V, f), if $R_A^{\geq} = R_{AT}^{\geq}$ when $A \subset AT$, for any $a \in A$, $R_{A-\{a\}}^{\geq} \neq R_{AT}^{\geq}$, then A is a reduction of the information system. The set of attributes that is included in all reductions is called the core.

Definition 3.2. For an consistent ordered decision table CODT $\mathcal{I} = (U, AT \cup \{d\}, V, f)$, if $R_A^{\geq} \subseteq R_d^{\geq}$ when $A \subset AT$, for any $a \in A$, $R_{A-\{a\}}^{\geq} \not\subseteq R_d^{\geq}$, then A is a reduction of the CODT.

Let $\mathcal{I} = (U, AT \cup \{d\}, V, f)$ be an IODT , and for any set $A \subseteq AT$, $R_A^{\geq}, R_d^{\geq}$ be dominance relations derived from condition attributes set AT and decision attributes set $\{d\}$ respectively,denote

$$U/R_A^{\geq} = \{[x_i]_A^{\geq} | x_i \in U\},$$

$$U/R_d^{\geq} = \{d_1, d_2, \cdots, d_r\},$$

$$\sigma_A^{\geq}(x) = \{d_j | d_j \cap [x]_A^{\geq} \neq \phi, x \in U\},$$

where $[x]_A^{\geq} = \{y \in U | (y, x) \in R_A^{\geq}\}$.

From the above, we can have the following propositions immediately.

Proposition 3.1. The following always hold.
(1) $\overline{R_A^{\geq}}(d_j) = \cup\{[x]_A^{\geq} : d_j \in \sigma_A^{\geq}(x)\}$.
(2) If $B \subseteq A$, then $\sigma_A^{\geq}(x) \subseteq \sigma_B^{\geq}(x), \forall x \in U$.
(3) If $[x]_A^{\geq} \supseteq [y]_A^{\geq}$, then $\sigma_A^{\geq}(x) \supseteq \sigma_A^{\geq}(y), \forall x, y \in U$.

Definition 3.3. Let $\mathcal{I} = (U, AT \cup \{d\}, V, f)$ be an IODT. If $\sigma_A^{\geq}(x) = \sigma_{AT}^{\geq}(x)$, for all $x \in U$, we say that A is an assignment consistent set of $\mathcal{I}$. If A is an assignment consistent set, and no proper subset of A is assignment consistent set, then A is called an assignment consistent reduction of IODT.

An assignment consistent set is a subset of attributes set that preserves the possible decisions of every object.

Obviously, the reductions of OIS and ODT also exist and is not unique.

In evidence reasoning, for a universe U a mass function can be defined by a map $m : 2^U \to [0, 1]$, which is called a basic probability assignment and satisfies two axioms:

$$(1) \quad m(\phi) = 0$$

$$(2) \quad \sum_{X \subseteq U} m(X) = 1.$$

A subset $X \subseteq U$ with $m(X) > 0$ is called a focal element. Using the basic probability assignment, belief and plausibility of X are expressed as

$$Bel(X) = \sum_{Y \subseteq X} m(Y),$$

$$Pl(X) = \sum_{Y \cap X \phi} m(Y).$$

In [26], the authors discussed the interpretations of belief functions in the theory of Pawlak rough sets. For an information system (U, AT, V, f), $X \subseteq U, A \subseteq AT$, it is represented as follows:

$$Bel(X) = \frac{|\underline{R_A}(X)|}{|U|} = \sum_{Y \subseteq X} m(Y)$$

$$Pl(X) = \frac{|\overline{R_A}(X)|}{|U|} = \sum_{Y \cap X = \phi} m(Y)$$

Then $Bel(X)$ is the belief function and $Pl(X)$ is the plausibility function of U.

For an OIS and for any set $A \subseteq AT$, the classification of $U = \{x_1, x_2, \cdots, x_k\}$ by the dominance relation $R_{AT}^{\geq}$ is denoted as

$$U/R_{AT}^{\geq} = \{[x_1]_{AT}^{\geq}, [x_2]_{AT}^{\geq}, \cdots, [x_k]_{AT}^{\geq}\}.$$

Let

$$D = \{(x_i, x_j)|i, j \in \{1, 2, , \cdots, k\}\}$$

then the element number of D is k^2.

And we note that

$$W(x_i, x_j) = \{a|f(x_i, a) < f(x_j, a)\}$$

Specially, when $W(x_i, x_j) = \phi$, we denoted as

$$D' = \{(x_i, x_j)|W(x_i, x_j) = \phi\}$$

$$H(A) = \{(x_i, x_j)|W(x_i, x_j) = A\}.$$

Then

$$m(A) = \frac{|H(A)|}{|D - D'|} \qquad (A \subseteq AT)$$

is the mass function on AT. As a result, we have belief function $Bel(A)$ and plausibility function $Pl(A)$.

Proposition 3.2. For an OIS $\mathcal{I} = (U, AT, V, f)$, if $A \subset AT, Pl(A) = 1$ and if $B \subseteq A$ and $B \neq A$, we have $Pl(B) < 1$, then A is a reduction of the OIS $\mathcal{I}$.

Proof. Since $Pl(A) = 1$ if and only if

$$\sum_{B \cap A \neq \phi} m(B) = 1.$$

This means that, for any $m(B) \neq 0$, B must have the form of $B \cap A \neq \phi$, i.e. for any $H(B) \neq \phi$, we have $B \cap A \neq \phi$. Then $U/R_{AT}^{\geq}$ can be identified by A. For the dame reason, $Pl(B) < 1$ if there exist B' such that $H(B') \neq \phi$ but $B' \cap B = \phi$. Therefore $U/R_{AT}^{\geq}$ cannot be identified by B' completely.

Example 3.1. Let we consider the OIS $\mathcal{I} = (U, AT, V, f)$ in Example 2.1 here. Note that

$$A_1 = \{a_1, a_3\} \quad A_2 = \{a_3\} \quad A_3 = \{a_2\} \quad A_4 = \{a_1, a_2\}$$
$$A_5 = AT = \{a_1, a_2, a_3\}$$

The classification of $U/R_{AT}^{\geq}$ is as follows:

$$[x_1]_{AT}^{\geq} = \{x_1, x_2, x_5, x_6\}; [x_2]_{AT}^{\geq} = \{x_2, x_5, x_6\};$$
$$[x_3]_{AT}^{\geq} = \{x_2, x_3, x_4, x_5, x_6\}; [x_4]_{AT}^{\geq} = \{x_4, x_6\};$$
$$[x_5]_{AT}^{\geq} = \{x_5\}; [x_6]_{AT}^{\geq} = \{x_6\};$$

Then the matrix of $W(x_i, x_j)$ is as in Table 4.

Table 4

	x_1	x_2	x_3	x_4	x_5	x_6
x_1	ϕ	A_1	A_2	A_1	A_5	A_1
x_2	ϕ	ϕ	ϕ	A_2	A_3	A_2
x_3	A_3	A_4	ϕ	A_1	A_4	A_5
x_4	A_3	A_4	ϕ	ϕ	A_4	A_4
x_5	ϕ	ϕ	ϕ	A_2	ϕ	A_2
x_6	ϕ	ϕ	ϕ	ϕ	A_3	ϕ

From the above, we have $|D - D'| = 20$, and $m(A_1) = 4/20$, $m(A_2) = 5/20$, $m(A_3) = 4/20$, $m(A_4) = 5/20$, $m(A_5) = 2/20$.

Therefore, for $A = \{a_2, a_3\}$, we can find $A \cap A_i \neq \phi (i = 1, 2, \cdots, 5)$, and $Pl(A) = 1$. Since $Pl(\{a_2\}) = Pl(A_3) = 4/20$ and $Pl(\{a_3\}) = Pl(A_2) = 5/20$. Hence, $A = \{a_2, a_3\}$ is a reduction of the OIS.

Next, we will mainly consider the method of the reduction in ODT.

Firstly, the CODT is considered.

For the consistent information system $\mathcal{I} = (U, AT \cup \{d\}, V, f)$ with target d, i.e. CODT.

For any set $A \subseteq AT$ we note that

$$W(x_i, x_j) = \begin{cases} \{a|f(x_i, a) < f(x_j, a)\}, & f(x_i, d) < f(x_j, d). \\ \phi, & f(x_i, d) \geq f(x_j, d). \end{cases}$$

And

$$H(A) = \{(x_i, x_j)|W(x_i, x_j) = A\}.$$
$$D = \{(x_i, x_j)|i, j \in \{1, 2, \cdots, k\}\}.$$

Another, when $W(x_i, x_j) = \phi$, we denoted as

$$D' = \{(x_i, x_j)|W(x_i, x_j) = \phi\}$$

Then

$$m(A) = \frac{|H(A)|}{|D - D'|} \qquad (A \subseteq AT)$$

is the mass function on AT. As a result, we can calculate the belief function $Bel(A)$ and plausibility function$Pl(A)$.

Proposition 3.3. For an CODT $\mathcal{I} = (U, AT \cup \{d\}, V, f)$, if $A \subset AT, Pl(A) = 1$ and if $B \subseteq A$ and $B \neq A$, we have $Pl(B) < 1$, then A is a reduction of the CODT $\mathcal{I}$.

Example 3.2. Here the CODT $\mathcal{I} = (U, AT \cup \{d\}, V, f)$ in Example 2.2 be considered. Note that

$$A_1 = \{a_1, a_3\} \quad A_2 = \{a_1, a_2\} \qquad A_3 = AT = \{a_1, a_2, a_3\}$$

Then the matrix of $W(x_i, x_j), i, j \in \{1, 2, \cdots, 6\}$ is as in Table 5.

Table 5

	x_1	x_2	x_3	x_4	x_5	x_6
x_1	ϕ	A_1	ϕ	A_1	A_3	A_1
x_2	ϕ	ϕ	ϕ	ϕ	ϕ	ϕ
x_3	ϕ	A_2	ϕ	A_1	A_2	A_3
x_4	ϕ	A_2	ϕ	ϕ	A_2	A_2
x_5	ϕ	ϕ	ϕ	ϕ	ϕ	ϕ
x_6	ϕ	ϕ	ϕ	ϕ	ϕ	ϕ

We have $|D - D'| = 11$, and $m(A_1) = 4/11, m(A_2) = 5/11, m(A_3) = 2/11$.
Therefore, for $A = \{a_2, a_3\}$ and $A' = \{a_1\}$, we can find $A \cap A_i \neq \phi$, and$A' \cap A_i \neq \phi(i = 1, 2, 3)$, moreover $Pl(A) = Pl(A') = 1$. Since $Pl(\{a_2\}) = 7/11$ and $Pl(\{a_3\}) = 6/11$. Hence, $A = \{a_2, a_3\}$ and $\{a_1\}$is a reduction of the CODT.
Finally, we will give the approach to reduction of IODT.
For any set $A \subseteq AT$ we note that

$$W(x_i, x_j) = \begin{cases} \{a|f(x_i, a) < f(x_j, a)\}, \sigma^{\geq}_{AT}(x_i) \subset \sigma^{\geq}_{AT}(x_j). \\ \phi, \qquad\qquad\qquad \sigma^{\geq}_{AT}(x_i) \not\subset \sigma^{\geq}_{AT}(x_j). \end{cases}$$

And

$$H(A) = \{(x_i, x_j)|W(x_i, x_j) = A\}.$$
$$D = \{(x_i, x_j)|i, j \in \{1, 2, \cdots, k\}\}.$$

Another, when $W(x_i, x_j) = \phi$, we denoted as

$$D' = \{(x_i, x_j) | W(x_i, x_j) = \phi\}$$

Then

$$m(A) = \frac{|H(A)|}{|D - D'|} \qquad (A \subseteq AT)$$

is the mass function on AT.

Hence, we can obtain the following.

Proposition 3.4. For an IODT $\mathcal{I} = (U, AT \cup \{d\}, V, f)$, if $A \subset AT, Pl(A) = 1$ and if $B \subseteq A$ and $B \neq A$, we have $Pl(B) < 1$, then A is an assignment consistent reduction of the IODT $\mathcal{I}$.

Example 3.3. IODT $\mathcal{I} = (U, AT \cup \{d\}, V, f)$ in Example 2.3 be considered. Note that

$$A_1 = \{a_1, a_3\} \quad A_2 = \{a_1, a_2\} \quad A_3 = \{a_3\} \quad A_4 = AT = \{a_1, a_2, a_3\}$$

Then the matrix of $W(x_i, x_j), i, j \in \{1, 2, \cdots, 6\}$ is as in Table 6.

Table 6

	x_1	x_2	x_3	x_4	x_5	x_6
x_1	ϕ	ϕ	ϕ	A_1	ϕ	A_1
x_2	ϕ	ϕ	ϕ	A_3	ϕ	A_3
x_3	ϕ	ϕ	ϕ	A_1	ϕ	A_4
x_4	ϕ	ϕ	ϕ	ϕ	ϕ	A_2
x_5	ϕ	ϕ	ϕ	A_3	ϕ	A_3
x_6	ϕ	ϕ	ϕ	ϕ	ϕ	ϕ

We have $|D - D'| = 9$, and $m(A_1) = 3/9, m(A_2) = 1/9, m(A_3) = 4/9, m(A_4) = 1/9$.

Therefore, for $A = \{a_2, a_3\}$ and $A' = \{a_1, a_3\}$, we can find $A \cap A_i \neq \phi$, and $A' \cap A_i \neq \phi (i = 1, 2, 3, 4)$, moreover $Pl(A) = Pl(A') = 1$. Since $Pl(\{a_1\}) = 5/9$, $Pl(\{a_2\}) = 2/9$ and $Pl(\{a_3\}) = 8/9$. Hence, $A = \{a_2, a_3\}$ and $\{a_1, a_3\}$ is an assignment consistent reduction of the IODT.

4   Conclusion

It is well-known that rough set theory has been regarded as a generalization of the classical set theory in one way. Furthermore, this is an important mathematical tool to deal with vagueness. We proposed a new technique of knowledge reduction using rough sets with evidence reasoning theory. The basic concepts and properties of knowledge reduction based on evidence reasoning theory are discussed. Furthermore, the characterization and knowledge reduction approaches based on evidence reasoning theory are obtained with examples in several kinds of ordered information system, which is every useful in future research works of the ordered information systems. The successful applications of rough set theory in a variety of intelligent systems will amply demonstrate heir usefulness and versatility.

Acknowledgements. The authors would like to thank the anonymous referees for their very constructive comments.

References

1. Z. Pawlak, Rough sets, International Journal of Computer and Information Science, 11(5)(1982) 341-356.
2. Q. Liu, S.H. Liu, F. Zheng, Rough Logic and its Applications in Data Reduction (in Chinese), Journal of Software, 12(2001) 415-419.
3. M. Kryszkiewicz, Comprative Studies of Alternative Type of Knowledge Reduction in Inconsistent Systems, International Journal of Intelligent Systems, 16(2001) 105-120.
4. W.X. Zhang, J.S. Mi, W.Z. Wu, Approaches to Knowledge Reductions in Inconsistent Systems(in Chinese), Chinese Journal of Computers, 26(2003) 12-18.
5. R. Slowinski (Ed.), Intelligent Decision Support: Handbook of Applications and Advances of the Rough sets Theory, Kluwer academic Publishers, Boston(1992).
6. M. Kryszkiewicz, Rough Set Approach to Incomplete Information System, Information Sciences, 112(1998) 39-49.
7. D. Slezak, Searching for Dynamic Reducts in Inconsisten Decision Tables, In: Proceedings of IPMU'98, Paris, France, Vol.2 (1998) 1362-1369.
8. D. Slezak, Approximate Reducts in Decision Tables, In: Procedings of IMPU'96, Vol.3, Granada, Spain(1996) 1159-1164.
9. M. Beynon, Reducts with in the Variable Precision Rough Set Model: a further investigation. European Jourmal of Operational reasearch, 134(2001) 592-605.
10. H.S. Nguyen, D. Slezak, Approximations Reducts and Assoisiation Rules Correspondence and Complexity Results, in: N.Zhong, A.skowron, S.Oshuga(Eds.), Proceedings of RSFDGrC'99, Yanaguchi, Japan, LNAI 1711, 1999, 137-145.
11. Z. Pawlak, Rough Sets:Theoretical Aspects of Reasonging About Data, Kluwer Academic Publishers, Boston ,1991.
12. W.X. Zhang, W.Z.Wu, J.Y. Liang, D.Y.Li, Theory and Method of Rough sets, Science Press, Beijing, 2001.
13. M. Quafatou, α−RST: a generalization of rough set theory, Information Science, 124(2000) 301-316.
14. R. Slowinski, C. Zopounidis, A.I. Dimititras, Prediction of Company Acquisition in Greece by Means of the Rough set Approach, European Journal of Operational reasearch,100(1997) 1-15.
15. M. Zhang, L.D. Xu, W.X Zhang, H.Z. Li, A Rough Set Approach to Knowledge Reduction Based on Inclusion Degree and Evidence Reasoning Theory, Expert Systems, Vol.20(2003), 5:298-304.

16. S. Greco, B. Matarazzo, R. Slowingski, Rough Approximation of a Preference Relatioin by Dominance Relatioin. ICS Research Report 16 / 96, Warsaw University of Technology; 1996 and in Eru H Oper Res 1999, 117:63-83.

17. S. Greco, B. Matarazzo, R. Slowingski, A New Rough Set Approach to Multicriteria and Multiattribute Classificatioin. In: Polkowsik L, Skowron A, editors. Rough sets and current trends in computing (RSCTC'98), Lecture Notes in Artificial Intelligence, Vol 1424. Berlin:Springer-Verlag; 1998.60-67.

18. S. Greco, B. Matarazzo, R. Slowingski, A New Rough Sets Approach to Evaluation of Bankruptcy Risk. In: Zopounidis X,editor. Operational tools in the management of financial risks. Dordrecht: Kluwer. 1999, 121-136.

19. S. Greco, B. Matarazzo, R. Slowingski, Rough Sets Theory for Multicriteria Decision Analysis. Eur J Oper Res, 2001, 129: 11-47.

20. S. Greco, B. Matarazzo, R. Slowingski. Rough Sets Methodology for Sorting Problems in Presence of Multiple Attributes and criteria. Eur J Oper Res 2002, 138:247-259.

21. K. Dembczynski, R. Pindur, R. Susmaga, Generation of Exhaustive Set of Rules within Dominance-based Rough Set Approach. Electron. Notes Theor Comput Sci 2003, 82(4).

22. K. Dembczynski, R. Pindur, R. Susmaga, Dominance-based Rough Set Classifier without Induction of Decision Rules. Electron. Notes Theor Comput Sci 2003, 82(4).

23. Y. Sai, Y.Y. Yao, N. Zhong. Data Analysis and Mining in Ordered Information Tables. Proc 2001 IEEE Int Conf on Data Mining. IEEE Computer Society Press, 2001, 497-504.

24. M.W. Shao, W.X. Zhang, Dominance Relation and Relus in an Incomplete Ordered Information System, Inter J of Intelligent Sytems, Vol.20(2005), 13-27.

25. W.H. Xu, W.X. Zhang, Knowledge Reductions in Inconsistent Information Systems Based on Dominance Relation, 11th International Fuzzy Systems Association World Congress, Beijin, China,2005, 1493-1496.

26. Y.Y. Yao, P. Lingras, Interpretations of Belief Functions in The Theory of Rough Sets, Information Sciences, Vol.104(1998), 81-106.

A Novel Maximum Distribution Reduction Algorithm for Inconsistent Decision Tables

Dongyi Ye, Zhaojiong Chen, and Chunyan Yu

College of Math. and Computer, Fuzhou University, Fuzhou 350002, China
yiedy@fzu.edu.cn

Abstract. A maximum distribution reduction is meant to preserve not only all deterministic information with respect to decision attributes but also the largest possible decision class for each object of an inconsistent decision table. Hence, it is useful to compute this type of reduction when mining decision tables with data inconsistency. This paper presents a novel algorithm for finding a maximum distribution reduct of an inconsistent decision table. Two functions of attribute sets are introduced to characterize a maximum distribution reduct in a new and simple way and then used as a heuristic in the algorithm to search for a reduction. Complexity analysis of the algorithm is also presented. As an application example, the presented algorithm was applied to mine a real surgery database and some interesting results were obtained.

1 Introduction

Many types of attribute reduction of a decision table have been proposed in the context of rough sets[1][2][3]. Each type of reduction has its own scope of adaptability when applied to real-world problems. The classic attribute reduction based on indiscernibility relations was proposed by Professor Z. Pawlak [1]. This type of attribute reduction is meant to preserve the deterministic(or certain) information with respect to decision attributes of a decision table and is therefore often used and shown appropriate for extracting deterministic decision rules from the table. However, there is no guarantee for such attribute reduction to preserve non-deterministic decision information of an inconsistent decision table.

The distribution reduction is a more complete knowledge reduction that is characterized by preserving the class membership distribution for all objects of a decision table [3]. In other words, such reduction preserves not only all deterministic but also non-deterministic information of an inconsistent decision table. The distribution attribute reduction, though keeping more information than the classic attribute reduction, must satisfy a larger number of more stringent conditions. Hence, there are fewer distribution reducts than classic reducts for a given inconsistent decision table. Moreover, the decision rules derived from distribution reduction are generally less compact and more complicated than those derived from classic attribute reduction. The concept of maximum distribution reduction proposed in [4] may be a good trade-off between the capability of preserving information with respect to decisions and the compactness of derived rules.

J. Lang, F. Lin, and J. Wang (Eds.): KSEM 2006, LNAI 4092, pp. 548–555, 2006.
© Springer-Verlag Berlin Heidelberg 2006

Different from the distribution reduction, the maximum distribution reduction is characterized by preserving only the largest class membership distribution of objects and thus eliminates the strict requirements of the distribution reduction.Though missing some non-deterministic information, the maximum distribution reduction preserves all deterministic information as well as the largest possible decision class for each object. Hence, it is a good choice to compute maximum distribution reduction when mining inconsistent data.

Like the case of classic reduct computation, computing all maximum distribution reducts of an inconsistent decision table is a NP-hard problem. Therefore, it is more practical and often sufficient in practice to design an algorithm that computes just one maximum distribution reduct instead of all reducts. However, no such algorithms have been given in the literature. This paper presents a novel algorithm for finding a maximum distribution reduct. Two useful functions of attribute sets are introduced and some of their properties are presented. It turns out that they can be used together to characterize a maximum distribution reduct in a new way. Hence, the two functions serve as a heuristic in the algorithm to search for a maximum distribution reduct.

This paper is organized as follows. Section 2 presents some basic concepts and notations of rough sets. Section 3 introduces two summation functions of attribute sets and discusses their properties. In Section 4, a new greedy algorithm for computing a maximum distribution reduct based on the two functions is described. Section 5 contains the complexity analysis of the algorithm and some experimental results tested on several data sets from the UCI machine learning repository. Section 6 presents the application of the algorithm to a real world mining problem. Section 7 concludes the paper.

2   Some Basic Concepts and Notations

For convenience of presentation, we introduce in this section some basic concepts and definitions. For more details, readers can refer to [1][3] and [4].

Formally, a decision table can be represented as a quadruple $L = \{U, A, V, F\}$ [1], where $U = \{x_1, \cdots, x_n\}$ is a non-empty finite set of objects called universe of discourse, A is a union of condition attributes set C and decision attributes set D , V is the domains of attributes belonging to A, and $F : U \times A \longmapsto V$ is an information function assigning attribute values to objects belonging to U. We assume that C contains m condition attributes and without loss of generality that D contains only one decision attribute which takes $k(> 1)$ distinct values. For a subset $P \subseteq A$, $IND(P)$ represents the indiscernible relation induced by the attributes belonging to P and there should be no confusion if we use U to represent either a set of attributes or the relation $IND(P)$. A subset $X \subseteq U$ represents a concept and the partition induced by $IND(P)$ is called a knowledge base and denoted by $U/IND(P)$. In particular, $U/IND(D) = \{Y_1, \cdots, Y_k\}$ is the knowledge base of decision classes.

Let $X \subseteq U$ and $R \subseteq C$. The R–lower approximation of X is defined as $\underline{R}X = \{x \in U : [x]_R \subseteq X\}$, where $[x]_R$ refers to an equivalence class of $IND(R)$

determined by element x . The R–approximation quality with respect to decisions is given by

$$\gamma_R = \sum_{i=1}^{k} \frac{|\underline{R}Y_i|}{|U|},$$

where $|\cdot|$ denotes the cardinality of a set. The membership function of object x to concept X with respect to the equivalence class $IND(R)$ is given by

$$\alpha_R^X(x) = \frac{|[x]_R \bigcap X|}{|[x]_R|}.$$

In other words, the value of $\alpha_R^X(x)$ gives the accuracy of a decision rule induced from object x concerning concept X under $IND(R)$. It may be of interest not only the membership of an object in a particular class but also the membership in all classes determined by the decision attribute D. Such membership, also called class membership distribution, is defined as a mapping $\mu_R : U \to [0,1]^k$, where $\mu_R(x) = (\alpha_R^{Y_1}(x), \cdots, \alpha_R^{Y_k}(x))$.

Definition 1. *Let $R \subseteq C$. If R is a minimal set satisfying $\gamma_R = \gamma_C$, then R is said to be a relative reduct of C or simply a reduct. The intersection of all reducts is called the attribute core of C and denoted as $Core_A(C)$.*

Definition 2. *Let $R \subseteq C$. If R is a minimal set satisfying $\mu_R(x) = \mu_C(x), \forall x \in U$, then R is said to be a distribution reduct of C .The intersection of all distribution reducts is called the distribution core of C and denoted as $Core_T(C)$*

Let

$$\lambda_R(x) = \max\{\alpha_R^{Y_1}(x), \cdots, \alpha_R^{Y_k}(x)\}.$$

Definition 3. *Let $R \subseteq C$. If R is a minimal set satisfying $\lambda_R(x) = \lambda_C(x), \forall x \in U$, then R is said to be a maximum distribution reduct of C .The intersection of all maximum distribution reducts is called the maximum distribution core of C and denoted as $Core_M(C)$.*

It can be observed that a distribution reduction needs to satisfy more conditions than a maximum distribution reduction. The above three types of attribute reductions are identical to each other when the decision table under consideration is consistent. If the decision table is inconsistent, we know that a distribution reduction is itself a maximum distribution reduction and a maximum distribution reduction is also a classic attribute reduction[4]. But the reverse is not true. As for the relationship between different types of cores, we have the following inclusions: $Core_A(C) \subseteq Core_M(C) \subseteq Core_T(C)$.

Let $R \subseteq C$ and $Z_i \in IND(R)$. It is easy to see that

$$\alpha_R^X(x) = \alpha_R^X(y), \lambda_R(x) = \lambda_R(y), \forall X \subseteq U, \forall x, y \in Z_i.$$

Thus, as a convention, we shall use in the remainder of this paper $\alpha_R^X(Z_i)$ and $\lambda_R(Z_i)$ to represent respectively $\alpha_R^X(x)$ and $\lambda_R(x)$ for any $x \in Z_i$.

3 Two Functions of Attribute Sets and Their Properties

In this section, we introduce two summation functions of attribute sets that will be useful for characterizing a maximum distribution reduction in a new way. For $R \subseteq C$, let

$$\xi_R = \sum_{x \in U} \lambda_R(x). \tag{1}$$

and

$$\delta_R = - \sum_{x \in U} \ln \lambda_R(x) \tag{2}$$

Lemma 1. *Let $R \subseteq P \subseteq C$ and $Z_i \in IND(R)$.*
(1)$\sum_{x \in Z_i} \lambda_R(x) \leq \sum_{x \in Z_i} \lambda_P(x)$
(2)If $\sum_{x \in Z_i} \lambda_R(x) = \sum_{x \in Z_i} \lambda_P(x)$, then $- \sum_{x \in Z_i} \ln \lambda_R(x) \leq - \sum_{x \in Z_i} \ln \lambda_P(x)$

Proof. Since $R \subseteq P \subseteq C$, we have $IND(P) \subseteq IND(R)$. Suppose that

$$Z_i = \bigcup_{l=1}^{t_i} X_{il}, X_{il} \in IND(P), l = 1, \cdots, t_i$$

Then by our convention,

$$\sum_{x \in Z_i} \lambda_R(x) = |Z_i| \lambda_R(Z_i) \tag{3}$$

and

$$\sum_{x \in Z_i} \lambda_P(x) = \sum_{l=1}^{t_i} |X_{il}| \lambda_P(X_{il}) \tag{4}$$

Suppose that

$$\lambda_R(Z_i) = \alpha_R^{Y_j}(Z_i)$$

for some $Y_j \in IND(D)$ and

$$|X_{il}| = N_{il}, |X_{il} \bigcap Y_j| = a_{jl}, l = 1, \cdots, t_i,$$

then

$$\alpha_P^{Y_j}(X_{il}) = \frac{|X_{il} \bigcap Y_j|}{|X_{il}|} = \frac{a_{jl}}{N_{il}} \tag{5}$$

Thus,

$$|Z_i| \alpha_R^{Y_j}(Z_i) = |Z_i| \frac{|Z_i \bigcap Y_j|}{|Z_i|} = \sum_{l=1}^{t_i} a_{jl} = \sum_{l=1}^{t_i} N_{il} \frac{a_{jl}}{N_{il}} \tag{6}$$

yielding by (5)

$$|Z_i| \lambda_R(Z_i) = \sum_{l=1}^{t_i} |X_{il}| \alpha_P^{Y_j}(X_{il}) \leq \sum_{l=1}^{t_i} |X_{il}| \lambda_P(X_{il}) \tag{7}$$

In view of (3) and (4), the proof of the first part of Lemma 1 is thus done. We now proceed to prove the second part. By (3),(4)and the hypothesis , we see that $|Z_i|\lambda_R(Z_i) = \sum_{l=1}^{t_i} |X_{il}|\lambda_P(X_{il})$, or equivalently

$$\lambda_R(Z_i) = \sum_{l=1}^{t_i} \frac{|X_{il}|}{|Z_i|}\lambda_P(X_{il}) \tag{8}$$

Since $\sum_{l=1}^{t_i} \frac{|X_{il}|}{|Z_i|} = 1$, the convexity of function $f : x \to -\ln x$ gives

$$-\ln \sum_{l=1}^{t_i} \frac{|X_{il}|}{|Z_i|}\lambda_P(X_{il}) \le -\sum_{l=1}^{t_i} \frac{|X_{il}|}{|Z_i|} \ln \lambda_P(X_{il}) \tag{9}$$

We then get by (8)

$$-|Z_i| \ln \lambda_R(Z_i) \le -\sum_{l=1}^{t_i} |X_{il}| \ln \lambda_P(X_{il}) \tag{10}$$

Hence, $-\sum_{x \in Z_i} \ln \lambda_R(x) \le -\sum_{x \in Z_i} \ln \lambda_P(x)$.
The proof is thus completed.

The following corollary is straightforward.

Corollary 1. Let $R \subseteq P \subseteq C$.
(1) $\xi_R \le \xi_P$;
(2)If $\xi_R = \xi_P$, then $\delta_R \le \delta_P$.

Theorem 1. Let $R \subseteq C$. Then $\lambda_R(x) = \lambda_C(x), \forall x \in U$ if and only if $\xi_R = \xi_C$ and $\delta_R = \delta_C$

Proof. Let $IND(R) = \{Z_1, \cdots, Z_M\}$. The only-if part is straightforward by definition.

Now suppose that $\xi_R = \xi_C$ and $\delta_R = \delta_C$. Then for any $Z_i \in IND(R)$, by Lemma 1(1), we have $\sum_{x \in Z_i} \lambda_R(x) = \sum_{x \in Z_i} \lambda_C(x)$. By Lemma 1(2), we see that

$$-\sum_{x \in Z_i} \ln \lambda_R(x) \le -\sum_{x \in Z_i} \ln \lambda_C(x) \tag{11}$$

Since $\delta_R = \delta_C$, it holds that

$$\sum_{x \in Z_i} \ln \lambda_R(x) = \sum_{x \in Z_i} \ln \lambda_C(x) \tag{12}$$

Following the idea in proving the second part of Lemma 1, we can similarly conclude using the strict convexity of function $f : x \to -\ln x$ that $\lambda_R(x) = \lambda_C(x), \forall x \in Z_i$. The proof is done.

By Theorem 1, the verification of a maximum distribution reduct becomes simpler. Thus, *it suffices to check only two conditions instead of formally as many conditions as the number of elements of the universe.*

4   Algorithm for Finding a Maximum Distribution Reduct

Theorem 1 gives another way to characterize a maximum distribution reduction and suggests, in combination with the monotone property of ξ_R, an intuitive heuristic for guiding a reduction search process. More precisely, given a subset $R \subseteq C$ and attribute $a \in C \backslash R$, the values of $\xi_{R \cup a}$ and $\delta_{R \cup \{a\}}$ can be used to determine whether adding a to subset R is helpful or not for finding a maximum distribution reduction. This idea leads to our algorithm for computing a maximum distribution reduction.

The basic steps of the algorithm can be described as follows:

Step 1. Compute the classic attribute core $Core_A$ using the method presented in [5]. Let $R = Core_A(C)$;

Step 2. If $\xi_R = \xi_C$ and $\delta_R = \delta_C$, then goto step 4; If $\xi_R < \xi_C$, then choose an attribute $a*$ which maximizes $\xi_{R \cup \{a\}}, a \in C \backslash R$. If there are many such attributes, choose the one that has the least number of attribute values. Goto step 3; If $\xi_R = \xi_C$ and $\delta_R < \delta_C$, then choose an attribute $a*$ which maximizes $\delta_{R \cup \{a\}}, a \in C \backslash R$ and goto step 3.

Step 3. Set $R = R \cup \{a*\}$ and go back to step 2;

Step 4. If R is minimal, then output R and exit; Otherwise, eliminate redundant attributes in R to assure its minimality and exit.

By Theorem 1, the outcome of the algorithm is a maximum distribution reduct. To extract decision rules from the computed reduced table, a value reduction would be needed to remove duplicated records in the reduced decision table. This is similar to classic attribute value reductions. Readers can refer to [6] for a detailed discussion.

5   Complexity Analysis and Experiment

Let us analyze the computational complexity of the algorithm step by step. $Core_A(C)$ can be obtained within $O(mn^2)$ comparisons [5]. For any $R \subseteq C$, the computational cost for $IND(R)$ is also bounded by $O(mn^2)$. Hence, we can get ξ_R and δ_R at the cost of $O(mn^2)$ computations. At each iteration, a new attribute is added to the current candidate set R. Thus, the job on the first three steps of the algorithm will be done after at most m repetitions. The redundancy elimination in Step 4 can be accomplished within less than m trials. Therefore, the algorithm terminates within at most $O(m)$ iterations and has a total complexity of $O(m^2 n^2)$.

To verify its performance, the algorithm was implemented on a 2.8GHz machine running Windows XP with 256 MB of main memory and then tested on several real data sets obtained from the UCI machine learning repository. These data sets were picked due to their inclusion of data inconsistency. Table 1 shows the results of this experiment. In the table, nbrMDR represents the number of attributes in a maximum distribution reduct computed by the algorithm and the name of each data set is followed by a numeral bracketed indicating the number of all condition attributes belonging to the data set. Moreover, the approximation quality γ_C is included in the table to show the inconsistency degree of each data set.

Table 1. Experiment Results

name of data set	nbrMDR	running time	γ_C
Flare(10)	8	10s	0.558
Solar(12)	10	2s	0.718
Primary-tumo(17)	16	10s	0.844
Breast-cancer(9)	7	4s	0.960
Solar-flare(10)	6	0.5s	0.798

It can be observed that the algorithm could terminate in a reasonable amount of time for all test problems.

6   An Application Example

In this section, we shall describe the application of the proposed algorithm to a real world rule mining problem. The data set we dealt with is a surgery database with more than 50000 records that describe the results of surgical operations performed in a provincial hospital during the past ten years. After discretizing some of its continuous-valued attributes, the database was transformed into a decision table with 9 condition attributes and one decision attribute. The condition attributes are respectively age of a patient, gender of a patient, duration of operation, season of operation, environment of operation, anesthesia, category of operation, date of hospitalization and date of check-out. Incision is taken as the only decision attribute. The characteristics of some typical attributes are as follows:

Incision(3 values):
1. Non-infect(healing up); 2.Inflammation; 3 Purulency .
Category of operation(12 values):
1.Neurosurgery; 2.Gland; 3.The five sense organs; 4.Thorax; 5.Blood vessel; 6.Lymph; 7.Digestive system; 8.Colic; 9.Retina; 10.Urogenital system; 11. Orthopaedics; 12. Non-operating
Anesthesia(5 values):
1.Epidural block; 2.General anesthesia; 3.Local anesthesia; 4.Acupuncture anesthesia; 5.Other anesthesia
Environment of operation(3 values):
1.Clean; 2.Carrying bacteria; 3.Dirty

This decision table is inconsistent since $\gamma_C = 0.61$. We applied the proposed algorithm to compute a maximum distribution reduct of it. The algorithm was run on a 2.8GHz machine with 256 MB of main memory and ended within 2 minutes. The reduct found is composed of 3 condition attributes, namely,

environment of operation, anesthesia, and category of operation. 27 deterministic and 108 non-deterministic decision rules were extracted from the reduced decision table by further eliminating some redundant attribute values. 11 percent of the rules turned out to be interesting. Some of these rules are listed as follows:
(1) If *Category of operation* is on *urogenital system* and *Environment of Operation = clean,* and *Anesthesia = local anesthesia,* then *Incision = healing up(* accuracy =0.91);
(2)If *Category of operation* is on *thorax* and *Environment of Operation = carrying bacteria,* and *Anesthesia = Epidural block,* then *Incision = inflammation(* accuracy =0.83);

7   Conclusion

We address in this paper the problem of computing a maximum distribution reduct which has not been well explored so far. We present a simpler way to characterize maximum distribution reductions by introducing two summation-based functions of attribute sets. A new greedy algorithm for computing a maximum distribution reduction is developed based on the functions. The computational complexity of the algorithm is analyzed. Some experimental results are presented to show the feasibility of the proposed algorithm.

Acknowledgement. This work was funded by Key Projects of Science and Technology of Fujian province of China(No.K04005 and No.2005H028).

References

1. Pawlak Z., Slowinski R., Rough set approach to multi-attribute decision analysis. European Journal of Operational Research, **72** (1994)443–459
2. Bazan, J., A Comparison of Dynamic and non-Dynamic Rough Set Methods for Extracting Laws from Decision Tables, In: L. Polkowski, A. Skowron(eds.), Rough Sets in Knowledge Discovery, Heideberg, Physica-Verlag,(1998)321–365
3. Kryszkiewicz M. Comparative studies of alternative type of knowledge reduction in inconsistent systems. International Journal of Intelligent Systems, **16** (2001)105–120
4. Zhang Wenxiu, Mi Jusheng,Wu Weizhi, Knowledge reductions in inconsistent information systems, Chinese Journal of Computers, 26(2003) 12–18
5. Ye Dongyi, Chen Zhaojiong, A New discernibility matrix and the computation of a core, Acta Eletronica Sinica, 30(2002)1086–1088
6. Wang Guoyin, Rough set and knowledge aquisition, Xian Jiaotong Unversity Press, 2001

An ICA-Based Multivariate Discretization Algorithm*

Ye Kang[1,2], Shanshan Wang [1,2], Xiaoyan Liu[1], Hokyin Lai[1],
Huaiqing Wang[1], and Baiqi Miao[2]

[1] Department of Information Systems, City University of Hong Kong
[2] Management School, University of Science and Technology of China,
HeFei, AnHui Province
kye@mail.ustc.edu.cn, sswang@ustc.edu

Abstract. Discretization is an important preprocessing technique in data mining tasks. Univariate Discretization is the most commonly used method. It discretizes only one single attribute of a dataset at a time, without considering the interaction information with other attributes. Since it is multi-attribute rather than one single attribute determines the targeted class attribute, the result of Univariate Discretization is not optimal. In this paper, a new Multivariate Discretization algorithm is proposed. It uses ICA (Independent Component Analysis) to transform the original attributes into an independent attribute space, and then apply Univariate Discretization to each attribute in the new space. Data mining tasks can be conducted in the new discretized dataset with independent attributes. The numerical experiment results show that our method improves the discretization performance, especially for the nongaussian datasets, and it is competent compared to PCA-based multivariate method.

Keywords: Data mining, Multivariate Discretization, Independent Component Analysis, Nongaussian.

1 Introduction

Discretization is one of preprocessing technique used frequently in many data warehousing and data mining applications. It is a process of converting the continuous attributes of a data set into discrete ones. In most of databases, data is usually stored in mixed format: the attribute can be nominal, discrete or continuous. In practice, continuous attribute needs to be transformed discrete one so that some machine learning methods can operate on it. Furthermore, discrete values are more concise to represent and specify and easier to process and comprehend, because they are closer to knowledge-level representation. Therefore, discretization can highlight classification tasks and improve predictive accuracy in most cases[1].

Univariate Discretization is one of commonly used discretization strategy. It aims to find a partition of a single continuous explanatory attribute of a dataset at one time. But attributes in multivariate datasets are usually correlated with each other, discretizing them without considering the interaction between them can not get a global optimal result. Thus, Multivariate Discretization, which means discretizing attributes

---

* Supported by a SRG Grant (7001805) from the City University of Hong Kong.

J. Lang, F. Lin, and J. Wang (Eds.): KSEM 2006, LNAI 4092, pp. 556–562, 2006.

simultaneously or considering multiple attributes at the same time, draws more and more attention in recent years. However, few effective algorithms of Multivariate Discretization have been provided until now.

As the dataset usually comes with correlated attributes, to make them independent but the attribute information is not lost is a possible way for Multivariate Discretization. In this paper, a new Multivariate Discretization Algorithm using ICA (Independent Components Analysis) is presented. In this algorithm, we transform the original attributes into a new attributes space with ICA, and then conduct Univariate Discretization on the attributes of new space one by one as they are independent of each other after transform. Finally, a global optimal discretization results can be obtained. ICA is a statistical method, which can extract independent features from database, and then the database can be newly reformed approximately by the independent features as attributes. The accuracy of classification on this discretization results with the Multivariate Discretization algorithm proposed in this paper shows that this algorithm is competent to the published Multivariate Discretization approaches such as PCA-based Multivariate Discretization [2], especailly for nongaussian data.

The remainder of the paper is organized as follows: Section 2 gives an overview of related work, in Section 3 we discuss our transformation algorithm, and in Section 4 we report our experimental results. Finally we give our conclusion in Section 5.

2   Related Work

A large number of discretization algorithms have been proposed in past decades. Most of them are the Univariate Discretization methods. Univariate Discretization can be categorized in several dimensions: supervised or unsupervised, global or local, dynamic or static, merging(bottom-up) or splitting(top-bottom)[3]. For example, Chimerge[4] is a supervised, bottom-up algorithm, Zeta[5]is a supervised splitting algorithm, and Binning is a unsupervised splitting one. In discretization algorithms, stop criteria is an important factor. Most commonly used discretization criteria are Entropy measure, Binning, Dependency, Accuracy and so on [1]. Except that, recently Liu [6] provided Heterogeneity as another new criteria to evaluate a discretization scheme.

In the Univariate Discretization algorithms, each attribute is viewed as independently determining the class attribute. Therefore, it can not generate global optimal intervals by discretizing all the involved attributes in a multivariate dataset one by one. A solution to this problem is to discretize attributes simultaneously, that is to consider multiple attribute at a time, which is known as Multivariate Discretization. Several approaches about this have been presented.

Ferrandiz′ [7] discussed the multivariate notion of neighborhood, which is extending the univariate notion of interval. They proposed Bipartitions based on the Minimum Description Length (MDL) principle, and apply it recursively. This method is thus able to exploit correlations between continuous attributes. However it reduces predictive accuracy as it makes only local optimization.

Bay [8] provided an approach to the Multivariate Discretization problem considering interaction among attributes. His approach is to finely partition each continuous attribute into n basic regions and iteratively merge adjacent intervals with similar multivariate distribution. However, this approach is not very effective because of its high computational complexity.

Sameep [2] proposed a PCA-based Multivariate Discretization method. His method first computes a positive semi-defined correlation matrix from the dataset. Suppose its eigenvalues are $\lambda_1 \geq \lambda_2 \geq \cdots \geq \lambda_d$ of which the corresponding eigenvectors are e_1, e_2, ..., e_d. Only the first k ($k<d$) eigenvectors with greater variance from the data are retained. Then all the data in original space are projected to the eigenspace which is spanned by the retained eigenvectors. Since each dimension in eigenspace is not correlated, the new attributes can be discretized separately by simple Distance-based Clustering or the Frequent Item Sets method. Once cut points are obtained, they are projected to the original data set which correlated most closely with this corresponding eigenspace dimension. This approach considers the correlation information among attributes through PCA transform. But PCA which relies on second-order statistics of the data often fails where the data are nongaussian [9].

In this paper, a new ICA-based multivariate discretization algorithm is proposed. The original attributes are transformed into a new attributes space with ICA, and then conduct Univariate Discretization on the attributes of new space one by one. The numerical experiment results show that this method impoves discretization performance, especially for the nongaussian datasets, and it is competent to other Multivariate Discretization method, such as PCA-based method.

3   ICA-Based Multivariate Discretization Algorithm

This section gives a detailed description of our algorithm and the background of it will also be introduced.

3.1   ICA (Independent Component Analysis)

ICA is on the base of Central Limit Theorem which tells that a sum of independent variables tends to follow a Gaussian distribution. Assuming there are n features, we denote x_j as the j-th feature and X as the random vector composed of x_1, ..., x_n. The objective of ICA is to find n independent components s_i of X:

$$x_j = a_{j1}s_1 + a_{j2}s_2 + \ldots + a_{jn}s_n, \text{ for all } j \tag{1}$$

Let A be the matrix with element a_{ij} and S be the vector (s_1, ..., s_n), then the above equation can be rewritten as follows:

$$X=AS \tag{2}$$

$$S=A^{-1}X=WX \tag{3}$$

where W denotes the weighed matrix of X which is the inverse of A. All we observe is the random vector X, but we must estimate both A and S from it. The final aim of this estimation process is to obtain the values of W that can make S maximally nongaussianity, and they are just the independent components of X.

Since there are many ICA algorithms provided by researchers such as Kernel [10], Hyvärinen and Oja [11], and Comon [12], in this paper we adopted FastICA algorithm which was introduced by Hyvärinen and Oja[11] due to low linear computational complexity.

From Central Limit Theorem it is known that the sum of two independent variables is more Gaussian than themselves. So X is more Gaussian than S. In other words, S is more nongaussian than X. As the linear sum of Gaussian distribution components still follows Gaussian distribution, ICA is only fit for nongaussian datasets (i.e., the more nongaussian the attribute variable of a data set is, the better). One of the classical measures of nongaussianity is kurtosis. The kurtosis of a variable y is defined by the following equation:

$$kurt(y) = E\{y^4\} - 3(E\{y^2\})^2 \qquad (4)$$

where y is zero-mean and of unit variance. Kurt will be zero for Gaussian variable. So the absolute value of kurtosis $|kurt(y)|$ is usually used as measure of non-gaussianity. And ICA is more suited to the variable with larger value of $|kurt(y)|$.

3.2 ICA-Based Discretization Algorithm

Our method is composed of the following four steps:

(1) Centering and whitening
Given a multivariate dataset, let x_i denotes (i=1, ..., n) it's the i-th attribute which consists of m records, then the most basic and necessary step is to center x_i before the application of the ICA algorithm. Centering x_i is to subtract its mean value so as to make x_i zero-mean. This preprocessing can simplify ICA algorithm.

After centering, whitening as another important preprocessing should be taken, which transform the observed random vector X into white vector (i.e., the components are uncorrelated and their variances equal unity) denoted by Y. One popular whitening method is adopted here, which is using the eigenvalue decomposition (EVD) of the covariance matrix $E\{XX^T\} = EDE^T$, where E is the orthogonal matrix of eigenvectors of $E\{XX^T\}$ and D is the diagonal matrix of its eigenvalue, $D = \mathrm{Diag}(d_1, d_2, ..., d_m)$. Thus,

$$Y = ED^{-1/2}E^T X \qquad (5)$$

Where the matrix $D^{-1/2}$ is computed by a simple component-wise operation as $D^{-1/2} = \mathrm{Diag}(d_1^{-1/2}, ..., d_n^{-1/2})$. It is easy to check that now $E\{YY^T\} = I$.

(2) Transforming attributes space by FastICA into new attributes space
After centering and whitening, FastICA is used to transform the original multi-attribute space into new independent multi-attribute space. Let z_i (i=1,..., n) denotes a new attribute which contains m data points, and each of them is independent of others. Finally, the class attribute is appended to the new space accordingly, and each instance

in the new dataset has the same class label as before. During transform, attribute information contained in the original dataset is preserved maximally in the new dataset.

(3) Using Univariated Discretization

After the new attributes z_i, ($i=1, \ldots, n$) are obtained, we apply Unviariated Discretization method to each of them, and finally get the discretized intervals of the new attributes.

So far, many Univarivated Discretization have been proposed, in our experiment, we use the MDL method of Fayyad and Zrani [13] which is the only supervised discretization method provided in Weka and is also known for its good performance.

4   Experiments

In this section, we validate the Multivariate Discretization method proposed in our paper in terms of the quality of the discretization results. Here we use the results of Classification tasks on our discretization data to test the performance of our algorithm.

4.1   Experiment Setting

All the datasets used in this experiment are from UCI repository[1]. In order to simplify our experiment, those datasets with only continuous attributes were chosen. Table 1 gives a description of the chosen datasets. We used WEKA[2], software which contains Classification and Discretization tool packages to evaluate our discretization results.

Table 1. Data Sets Used in Evaluation

Dataset	Records	Attributes	Num of Class labels
Iris	150	4	3
Waveform	300	21	3
Glass	214	9	7
Cancer	683	8	2

Having chosen the datasets, we first took away the class attribute of each dataset, then centered and whitened the remaining continuous attributes, and transformed the original datasets by FastICA algorithm into new attributes space. A Matlab imple-mentation of the FastICA algorithm is available on the World Wide Web free of charge[3]. At last we obtained a new dataset with independent attributes carrying the

---

[1] http://www.ics.uci.edu/~mlearn/MLRepository.html
[2] http://www.cs.waikato.ac.nz/~ml/
[3] http://www.cis.hut.fi/projects/ica/fastica/

information of the original dataset attributes. After transformat, the class attribute taken away before it was appended, then a new dataset was completed.

Discretization tool package of WEKA includes both supervised and unsupervised Univariate Discretization methods. The supervised discretization method is based on MDL [13]. As the attributes in the new transformed space are independent, they can be discretized separately. The discretized datasets was then processed by four classification algorithms of WEKA, respectively, C4.5, IBK, PART, NaiveBayes, and the error rates of classification using 10-fold cross-validation are reported in Table 2.

Table 2. Classification Error Comparison

Dataset	Mean kurtosis		C4.5	IBK	PART	NB	PCA+C4.5
Waveform	2.9237	Original	24.56	25.34	23.6	18.24	N
		ICA	17.32	16.86	16.72	18.12	
Iris	2.8941	Original	6	6	4.67	6	4.9
		ICA	1.3	1.3	1.3	1.3	
Glass	2.2055	Original	26.19	21.50	24.30	25.23	29
		ICA	27.57	28.04	29.91	29.91	
Cancer	1.6425	Original	4.25	3.07	4.25	2.49	4.1
		ICA	6.59	6.88	6.30	5.41	

Two groups of datasets were used in this experiment, one was composed of the original datasets that was downloaded from UCI Repository, and the other was composed of the new independent attribute data sets that were transformed from the original data sets using ICA. The supervised Univariate Discretization based on MDL was conducted on both the group's data sets. And their classification errors are reported in Table 2. From Table 2, for the datasets Waveform and Iris, ICA-based discretization method improved the classification accuracy significantly. However, it did not work very well on the datasets Glass and Cancer. This is because ICA has its roots for datasets with nongaussian distribution. We have mentioned before that kurtosis is one classic measure of nongaussianity, so the kurtosis of each dataset is given in the second column of the table. As there are more than one attributes for each dataset, the given value is the mean kurtosis of all the attributes. It can be seen that Waveform and Iris are much more nongaussian than Glass and Cancer as they have larger mean kurtosis. This can explain why our method works better for the former two datasets. The last column lists the results of the PCA-based Multivariate Discretization method from[2]. And we can see that our method is competent.

5 Conclusions

In this paper, we proposed ICA-based Multivariate Discretization method. It uses ICA to transform original dataset to a new dataset in which the attributes are independent of each other, and then conducts the Univariate Discretization on the new dataset. The numerical experiment results show that the discretization results of this method could improve the classification accuracy, especially for the nongaussian datasets, and it is competent compared to other multivariate method, such as PCA-based method and so on.

References

1. LIU, H., *Discretization: An Enabling Technique*. Data Mining and Knowledge Discovery, 2002. **6**: p. 393-423.
2. Sameep Mehta, *Toward Unsupervised Correlation Preserving Discretization*. IEEE TRANSACTIONS ON KNOWLEDGE AND DATA ENGINEERING, 2005. **17**(9): p. 1174-1185.
3. Dougherty, J., Kohavi, R., & Sahami, M. *Supervised and unsupervised discretization of continuous features*. in *Proceedings of the Twelfth International Conference on Machine Learning*. 1995.
4. Kerber, R. *Chimerge discretization of numeric attributes*. in *Proceedings of the 10. th. International. Conference on Artificial Intelligence*. 1991.
5. K.M.HO. *Zeta: A Global Method for Discretization of Continuous Variables*. in *The Third International Conference on Knowledge Discovery and Data Mining*. 1997.
6. Liu, X. and H. Wang, *A Discretization Algorithm Based on a Heterogeneity Criterion*. IEEE Transactions on Knowledge and Data Engineering, September 2005. **17**(9): p. 1166-1173.
7. Ferrandiz, S. *Multivariate Discretization by Recursive Supervised Bipartition of Graph*. in *4th International Conference, MLDM 2005,Leipzig, Germany,July 9-11. Proceedings*. 2005.
8. Bay, S.D., *Multivariate Discretization of Continuous Variables for Set Ming*. Knowledge and Information Systems, 2001. **3**(4): p. 491-512.
9. Yaping HUANG and S. LUO. *Genetic Algorithm Applied to ICA Feature Selection*. in *Proceedings of the International Joint Conference on Neural Networks*. 2003.
10. Bach, F.R. and M.I. Jordan, *Kernel Independent Component Analysis*. Journal of Machine Learning Research, 2002. **3**.
11. Hyvärinen, A., *Independent Component Analysis:Algorithms and Applications*. Neural Networks, 2000. **13**: p. 411-430.
12. Comon, P., *Independent component analysis, A new concept?* Signal Processing, 1994. **36**: p. 287-314.
13. Fayyad, U. and K.B. Irani. *Multi-Interval Discretization of Continuous-Valued Attributes for Classification Learning*. in *Proceeding of 13th International Joint Conference on Artificial Intelligence*. 1993.

An Empirical Study of What Drives Users to Share Knowledge in Virtual Communities

Shun Ye[1], Huaping Chen[1], and Xiaoling Jin[2]

[1] School of Management, University of Science and Technology of China,
Hefei 230026, Anhui, China
yeshun@mail.ustc.edu.cn, hpchen@ustc.edu.cn
[2] Department of Information Systems, USTC-CityU Joint Advanced Study Institute,
Dushu Lake, Industrial Park Suzhou, China
xljin@mail.ustc.edu.cn

Abstract. This paper proposes and tests a new model that helps explain knowledge contribution in virtual communities. Grounded on a communication-based view, we examined key drivers of user intention to share knowledge in virtual communities from three aspects: the knowledge to be shared, the individual self and the environment. In particular, a self-concept-based motivation model was employed to investigate individuals' motivational factors. An empirical study of 363 virtual community users demonstrated the salient and dominant influences of enhanced knowledge self-efficacy and self-image on knowledge contribution intention. Enjoyment in helping others, trust and system usability were also found to be important motivations for knowledge sharing. Implications for both researchers and practitioners are discussed.

1 Introduction

Virtual communities (VCs) are groups of people with common interests and practices that communicate regularly and for some duration in an organized way over a common communication medium, such as a bulletin board or a news group [1]. The emergence of VCs brings together geographically dispersed, like-minded people to form a network for knowledge exchange [2]. Since participation in VCs is open and voluntary and participants are typically strange to each other [3], researchers are interested in what motivates VC users to spend their valuable time and effort on sharing their valuable knowledge. A small but growing body of studies have investigated factors that influence knowledge contribution (intention) in VCs [3,4,5,6,7]. However, most of these studies focused on individual motivations (e.g., anticipated reciprocity) and/or environmental factors (e.g., generalized trust), neglecting factors involved with knowledge. According to existing psychology literature, people are unwilling to share an item they consider pretty valuable [8,9]. Many studies have also implied the potential influence of knowledge factors on sharing behavior by terms as "loss of knowledge power" [10,11]. This study, therefore, proposes a new model with knowledge factors included to help explain user intention to contribute knowledge in VCs.

J. Lang, F. Lin, and J. Wang (Eds.): KSEM 2006, LNAI 4092, pp. 563–575, 2006.
© Springer-Verlag Berlin Heidelberg 2006

Other studies have also inspected additional factors that facilitate knowledge contribution in VCs. For instance, Wang and Lai [12] studied knowledge sharing in VCs based on a motivation-capability framework. They focused on the significance of capability as compared to that of motivations. Nevertheless, they considered too few motivations and overlooked factors related with the knowledge and environment. Our study aims at (1) building a more comprehensive model of motivations for knowledge contribution and (2) investigating the dominant role of self-concepts. We examined motivating factors from a communication-based perspective. To stress the importance of self-concepts in predicting knowledge contribution as indicated by self-based theories like social identity theory [13] and self-efficacy theory [14], a self-concept-based motivation model [15] which incorporates and emphasizes self-concepts is adopted.

The rest of this paper begins with the theoretical background and hypotheses. Then it describes the methodology and research design, followed by a discussion of the main findings. Finally, it highlights implications for research and practice as well as suggestions for future research.

2   Research Model and Background

In studying knowledge transfer in virtual teams and distributed environments, a communication-based perspective [16] is often used [17,18], from which five basic elements potentially influencing knowledge transfer are identified: channel, message, context, source and recipient characteristics [18,19]. The first four characteristics are related with knowledge contribution in VCs, an important aspect of knowledge transfer. Channel characteristics refer to the properties of VCs and context characteristics refer to the contextual factors such as sharing norms in VCs. They are all environmental factors. Message characteristics refer to the traits of shared knowledge and source characteristics refer to knowledge contributors' factors. Thus, we will examine influential factors of knowledge contribution intention in VCs from three perspectives: the knowledge to be shared, the contributor self and the environment. Fig.1 describes our research model.

2.1   Knowledge Factors

Prior literature suggests that knowledge contributors may feel that their knowledge sharing behavior will result in a loss of unique value and power related with the shared knowledge [20,21]. Such a perception is acting as an obstacle to knowledge sharing [10,20]. Within the psychology field, it has been found that the more valued an item is, the less likely an individual is to share it [8,9,22]. In the organizational context, Ford and Staples [23] found that perceived value of knowledge (PVK), namely the value of knowledge perceived by its holder, had an impact on employees' intention to share knowledge. Based on these findings, we propose that in VCs PVK is negatively associated with users' knowledge contribution intention.

H1: Perceived value of knowledge has a negative effect on an individual's knowledge contribution intention in VCs.

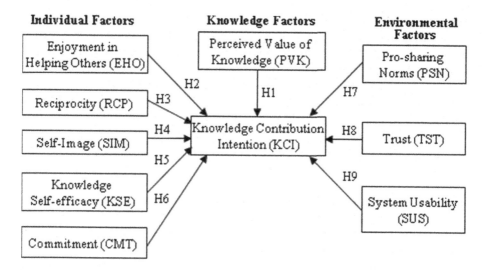

Fig. 1. The Research Model of Knowledge Contribution Intention

2.2   Individual Factors

Different from previous studies, we employed a self-concept-based motivation model which emphasized the importance of self-concepts [15], instead of traditional motivation model [24], to identify individual motivations. We adopted the self-concept-based motivation model for two reasons. First, self-concepts have been found to be important in predicting human behavior [13,14]. Human beings have a fundamental need to maintain or enhance their self-concepts and they are motivated to behave in ways that are consistent with existing self-perceptions [25]. These findings imply that knowledge contributors' sharing intention may be greatly influenced by their self-concepts. Second, several studies have indicated that self-concepts could influence individuals' decisions of whether or not to contribute knowledge to a great extent [4,5,11]. According to the self-concept-based motivation model, there are five basic sources of motivation: intrinsic process motivation, instrumental motivation, external self-concept-based motivation, internal self-concept-based motivation and goal internalization.

Intrinsic Process Motivation. Individuals who are primarily motivated by intrinsic process motivation perform a task because they consider it a fun and challenge. They enjoy the task and feel rewarded simply by performing the task [15,24]. Researchers have found that individuals may contribute their knowledge to others in VCs just because they think it is interesting to help others solve challenging problems and because they enjoy helping others [4,5]. This leads to the following hypothesis:

H2: Enjoyment in helping others has a positive effect on an individual's knowledge contribution intention in VCs.

Instrumental Motivation. Individuals are motivated by instrumental motivation when they believe that their behavior will result in certain outcomes they are focusing on [15,26]. In other words, individuals are looking for some extrinsic rewards when participating in a chosen activity. In VCs, knowledge sharing is facilitated when there is a strong sense of reciprocity which means what is given is expected to be paid back in the future [3,5]. It has been pointed out that in VCs people seemed to get more quick answers for their questions if they had regularly helped others before [27]. Thus, we hypothesize:

H3: Reciprocity has a positive effect on an individual's knowledge contribution intention in VCs.

External Self-Concept-Based Motivation. Individuals motivated by external self-concept-based motivation attempt to meet the expectations of others by behaving in ways that satisfy reference group members to gain acceptance and status [15,28]. Sharing knowledge with others earns contributors respect and a better image [29,30]. People contributing knowledge to others can benefit from improved self-concepts [5]. When individuals feel that the behavior of contributing knowledge to others will enhance their status and others' recognition of them, they will be attracted to contribute their valuable knowledge to others [4]. Therefore perceived improvement of self-image can serve as a motivator for users to share their knowledge in VCs [5,29]. This leads to the following hypothesis:

H4: Self-image has a positive effect on an individual's knowledge contribution intention in VCs.

Internal Self-Concept-Based Motivation. Individuals pursuing improved perceptions of competency are motivated by internal self-concept-based motivation. For these individuals, the need for a higher level of traits, competency and values in their important identities spurs them to perform a task [15,28]. Knowledge self-efficacy refers to the confidence in one's ability to provide knowledge that is valuable to others [11]. Through sharing useful knowledge to the organization, people feel more confident in what they can do [30]. And this perception of enhanced self-efficacy can motivate employees to contribute their knowledge to others [31]. Similarly, contributing knowledge to others helps enhance VC users' learning and self-efficacy [4]. This elicits the following hypothesis:

H5: Knowledge self-efficacy has a positive effect on an individual's knowledge contribution intention in VCs.

Goal Internalization. Individuals motivated by goal internalization behave congruently with their value systems. Achieving internalized values and goals of the team or organization is the driving force behind this source of motivation [15]. Commitment represents a strong belief in and acceptance of the organization's goals and values, a willingness to exert considerable effort on behalf of the organization, and a strong desire to maintain membership in the organization [32]. Prior findings suggest that commitment to the organization make employees more willing to share knowledge with others [29]. Individuals who are committed to VCs feel a strong sense of responsibility to help others in the network on the basis of shared membership [3,4]. Therefore, we postulate that commitment to VCs positively influences knowledge contribution intention.

H6: Commitment has a positive effect on an individual's knowledge contribution intention in VCs.

2.3 Environmental Factors

Jarvenpaa and Staples [33] implied a positive relationship between perceived ease of use of VCs and knowledge contribution. A large number of poor-organized information and lack of efficient searching techniques would impede knowledge sharing in VCs [34]. In this sense, a VC's system usability may be an important predictor of individuals' knowledge contribution intention [7].

In a network of human relationships, there is an important nonmonetary resource called social capital which refers to the sum of resources that embedded within the network [35]. Trust and pro-sharing norms are two key aspects of social capital that also exist in VCs [3,27]. They provide necessary contextual conditions for the occurrence of knowledge exchange [35]. Trust, more accurately referring to generalized trust in this study, is a belief in other members' benevolence, competence and reliability. It resides not for a specific individual but rather the whole community [11,36]. Trust has been proved to be an important facilitator in cooperation and knowledge exchange [37]. Several studies implied that distrust caused by fear of losing face and possible "personal attacks" could hamper knowledge sharing in VCs [4,6].

Pro-sharing norms stand for consensuses on knowledge sharing among users in VCs. Previous literature suggests that pro-sharing norms could enhance the climate for knowledge sharing and thus encourage individuals to contribute their knowledge to a group or team [10,33]. In VCs where pro-sharing norms are strong, members who voluntarily conform to the norms will be more willing to join in knowledge contribution activities. Hence, we postulate:

H7: System usability has a positive effect on an individual's knowledge contribution intention in VCs.

H8: Trust has a positive effect on an individual's knowledge contribution intention in VCs.

H9: Pro-sharing norms has a positive effect on an individual's knowledge contribution intention in VCs.

3 Research Design

3.1 Data Collection

A self-administered questionnaire was designed to gather data needed to test the model. We delivered 500 questionnaires and received 363 usable ones, with a high response rate of 72.6%. Among the respondents, 63% were male and 37% were female. Over 50% of the respondents aged between 21 and 25. A majority of the respondents were university students, although our sample included a diversity of education levels that ranged from less than high school to doctorates. More than 50% of the respondents visited their chosen VCs at least every 2 days. On average, the respondents had used their respective VCs for 2.2 years and spent over an hour at each visit.

3.2   Measures

All the items used in this study were adapted from previous studies, with minor modifications to ensure contextual consistency. PVK was adapted from Ford and Staple [23]; enjoyment in helping others, reciprocity, knowledge self-efficacy, trust and pro-sharing norms were adapted from Kankanhalli et al. [11]; self-image was adapted from Wasko and Faraj [3]; commitment was adapted from Mowday et al. [32]; system usability was adapted from McKinney et al. [38]; knowledge contribution intention was adapted from Bock et al. [39]. All the question items were measured on a 7 point Likert type scale from strongly disagree(1) to strongly agree(7). Before formal data collection, 35 VC members are invited to participate in the pilot test of the survey. Questions that did not demonstrate construct validity, content validity or reliability were eliminated.

3.3   Data Analysis

We used the partial least squares (PLS) structural equation modeling approach for to validate the construct measures and test the hypotheses in the research model. PLS [40] is a structural technique that can specify both the relationships among the conceptual factors of interest and the measures underlying each construct. Furthermore, the non-normality and medium size of the data make PLS a better choice over covariance-based approaches like LISREL. Thus, PLS-Graph version 3.00 was chosen for data analysis.

4   Results and Discussion

4.1   The Measurement Model

Convergent validity indicates the extent to which items of a scale that are theoretically related should be related in reality. In PLS, rather than using Cronbach's alpha, which represents a lower bound estimate of internal consistency due to its assumption of equal weights of items, a better estimate can be gained by using the internal consistency reliability (ICR) [41]. An ICR of 0.70 or above and an average variance extracted (AVE) of more than 0.50 are considered to be acceptable [42]. In this study, All ICR and AVE values meet the recommended threshold, suggesting adequate convergent validity. Table 1 summarizes the measurement model results.

Discriminant validity indicates the extent to which a given construct is different from other constructs. One criterion for adequate discriminant validity

Table 1. Correlation Matrix and Psychometric Properties of Key Constructs[1]

	ICR	AVE	1	2	3	4	5	6	7	8	9	10
PVK	0.89	0.57	**0.76**									
EHO	0.92	0.74	0.33	**0.86**								
RCP	0.88	0.65	0.20	0.72	**0.81**							
SIM	0.93	0.88	0.18	0.44	0.44	**0.94**						
KSE	0.87	0.77	0.32	0.41	0.44	0.54	**0.88**					
CMT	0.87	0.57	0.46	0.42	0.40	0.32	0.42	**0.75**				
SUS	0.88	0.65	0.28	0.40	0.38	0.31	0.37	0.43	**0.81**			
TST	0.87	0.63	0.26	0.34	0.37	0.28	0.37	0.41	0.38	**0.79**		
PSN	0.83	0.71	0.23	0.42	0.44	0.33	0.42	0.41	0.37	0.39	**0.84**	
KCI	0.93	0.81	0.31	0.57	0.43	0.51	0.60	0.42	0.45	0.44	0.43	**0.90**

is that the square root of the AVE represented as the diagonal elements in the constructs correlation matrix should be greater than the off-diagonal elements in corresponding rows and columns [41]. As shown in Table 1, our measurement model demonstrates adequate discriminant validity.

Another way to evaluate convergent and discriminant validity is to examine the factor loadings of each indicator. Each indicator should have higher loadings on the construct of interest than on any other construct [41]. Table 2 shows factors loadings and cross-loadings for the multi-item measures. An inspection of this table demonstrates that the measurement model provides adequate discriminant and convergent validity.

4.2 The Structural Model

Fig. 2 presents the results of the PLS structural model assessment with overall explanatory power and estimated path coefficients (all significant paths are indicated with an asterisk). Tests of significance of all paths were performed using the bootstrap resampling procedure.

As shown in Fig. 2, knowledge self-efficacy and enjoyment in helping others were found to be the two most influential factors of knowledge contribution intention, with path coefficients of 0.275 and 0.216 respectively. Neither PVK nor reciprocity was significantly linked to knowledge contribution intention. The path from self-image to knowledge contribution intention was positive and significant ($\beta = 0.125, p < 0.05$). The relationship between commitment to VCs and knowledge contribution intention was in the expected direction but only approached significance ($\beta = 0.096, p < 0.10$). System usability had a positive and significant effect on knowledge contribution intention ($\beta = 0.095, p < 0.05$). Trust in VCs was also positively and significantly linked to knowledge contribution intention ($\beta = 0.11, p < 0.05$). The association between pro-sharing norms and knowledge contribution intention was positive but not significant. Overall,

---

[1] Bold diagonal elements are the square root of AVE values for each construct; off-diagonal elements are the correlations between constructs.

Table 2. Factor Loadings and Cross-Loadings

	PVK	EHO	RCP	SIM	KSE	CMT	SUS	TST	PSN	KCI
PVK1	**0.65**	0.17	0.07	0.10	0.19	0.31	0.15	0.09	0.16	0.13
PVK2	**0.70**	0.32	0.18	0.20	0.26	0.42	0.31	0.17	0.25	0.29
PVK3	**0.77**	0.25	0.18	0.15	0.26	0.32	0.37	0.18	0.15	0.22
PVK4	**0.79**	0.25	0.18	0.14	0.25	0.39	0.21	0.25	0.17	0.23
PVK5	**0.81**	0.25	0.14	0.08	0.23	0.30	0.20	0.24	0.18	0.24
PVK6	**0.80**	0.21	0.13	0.12	0.24	0.34	0.18	0.23	0.14	0.23
EHO1	0.27	**0.86**	0.55	0.38	0.31	0.31	0.34	0.24	0.31	0.48
EHO2	0.30	**0.88**	0.59	0.39	0.36	0.37	0.37	0.32	0.32	0.50
EHO3	0.29	**0.86**	0.65	0.39	0.36	0.34	0.30	0.30	0.36	0.50
EHO4	0.28	**0.86**	0.68	0.38	0.38	0.32	0.38	0.32	0.46	0.48
RCP1	0.17	0.63	**0.79**	0.33	0.34	0.31	0.30	0.36	0.38	0.43
RCP2	0.13	0.55	**0.80**	0.36	0.37	0.30	0.32	0.24	0.35	0.46
RCP3	0.16	0.57	**0.84**	0.34	0.32	0.32	0.28	0.26	0.34	0.43
RCP4	0.19	0.57	**0.78**	0.39	0.37	0.38	0.33	0.32	0.33	0.42
SIM1	0.15	0.40	0.40	**0.93**	0.49	0.30	0.27	0.22	0.31	0.45
SIM2	0.18	0.42	0.43	**0.94**	0.53	0.34	0.31	0.30	0.30	0.50
KSE1	0.25	0.38	0.41	0.56	**0.91**	0.34	0.33	0.35	0.38	0.59
KSE2	0.32	0.33	0.34	0.37	**0.84**	0.40	0.33	0.30	0.35	0.44
CMT1	0.35	0.30	0.29	0.21	0.32	**0.80**	0.29	0.34	0.32	0.40
CMT2	0.42	0.44	0.44	0.26	0.29	**0.70**	0.34	0.27	0.30	0.36
CMT3	0.27	0.22	0.21	0.22	0.30	**0.69**	0.24	0.30	0.34	0.28
CMT4	0.33	0.30	0.30	0.27	0.35	**0.76**	0.31	0.29	0.30	0.33
CMT5	0.36	0.31	0.29	0.33	0.33	**0.81**	0.41	0.34	0.30	0.41
SUS1	0.15	0.36	0.33	0.24	0.29	0.31	**0.69**	0.18	0.36	0.29
SUS2	0.26	0.32	0.26	0.24	0.23	0.38	**0.83**	0.31	0.27	0.29
SUS3	0.25	0.31	0.30	0.29	0.36	0.35	**0.86**	0.35	0.24	0.40
SUS4	0.22	0.32	0.34	0.24	0.32	0.34	**0.83**	0.34	0.35	0.43
TST1	0.18	0.31	0.33	0.25	0.31	0.29	0.38	**0.76**	0.28	0.40
TST2	0.22	0.22	0.21	0.24	0.27	0.35	0.26	**0.80**	0.18	0.31
TST3	0.22	0.27	0.28	0.20	0.36	0.30	0.27	**0.83**	0.35	0.32
TST4	0.22	0.26	0.31	0.20	0.25	0.34	0.25	**0.78**	0.41	0.35
PSN1	0.18	0.37	0.37	0.27	0.31	0.33	0.28	0.32	**0.83**	0.36
PSN2	0.22	0.34	0.37	0.28	0.39	0.36	0.35	0.34	**0.85**	0.38
KCI1	0.28	0.53	0.52	0.44	0.51	0.38	0.42	0.37	0.42	**0.89**
KCI2	0.26	0.54	0.51	0.44	0.52	0.43	0.36	0.40	0.38	**0.91**
KCI3	0.29	0.48	0.44	0.49	0.58	0.48	0.44	0.41	0.37	**0.90**

the explained variance R^2 was 0.548, indicating that the antecedents of knowledge contribution intention explained 54.8 percent of the variance.

4.3   Discussion of Results

Our results provide support for the theoretical model and qualified support for most of our hypotheses. The results indicate that important predictors of knowledge contribution intention include knowledge self-efficacy, perception of

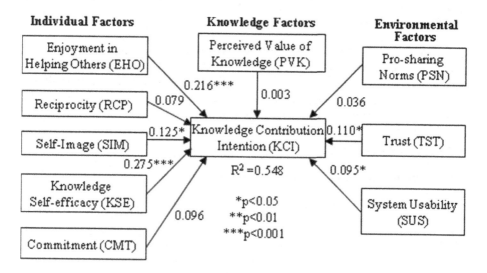

Fig. 2. Results of the PLS Analysis

enhanced self-image, enjoyment in helping others, trust in VCs and system usability. These findings are consistent with previous studies.

It is clearly seen from the PLS results that knowledge self-efficacy and self-image had a strong influence on knowledge contribution intention, weighing the first and the third respectively. This result not only emphasizes the importance of self-concepts in predicting human behavior but also provides strong support for the adoption of the self-concept-based motivation model.

The negative relationship between PVK and knowledge contribution intention was not confirmed. This may be due to the nature of knowledge. An individual can share knowledge with others without losing access to or use of that knowledge, and consequently without losing its value. While in psychology research, the act of sharing results in a loss of value since what was shared was often a physical object [23].

The path between reciprocity and knowledge contribution intention was nonsignificant. One possible explanation is that reciprocity in VCs may be generalized [43]. Generalized reciprocity occurs when one's giving is not reciprocated by the recipient, but by a third party [3]. The nonexistence of direct reciprocity weakens the influence of reciprocity on knowledge contribution intention.

The supposed link between commitment and knowledge contribution intention was marginally nonsignificant. One potential explanation for this is that it is often people who are receiving knowledge rather than contributing knowledge that are committed to VCs [3].

The association between pro-sharing norms and knowledge contribution intention was not supported. It is probably because VC members are rational ones who want to maximize their benefits such as enhanced self-image and knowledge self-efficacy rather than altruistic individuals who voluntarily conform to pro-sharing norms without gains.

5   Conclusion

The aim of this study is to better understand the underlying drivers of user intention to share their knowledge in VCs. We examined potential factors influencing knowledge contribution intention from three perspectives and developed a more comprehensive model compared with previous studies. The empirical test provides support for the employment of a self-concept-based motivation model and the whole research model. The findings have important implications for both researchers and practitioners.

5.1   Implications for Theory and Research

Our study broadens the scope of antecedents of knowledge contribution intention. Precisely, knowledge factors, individual factors and environmental factors need to be inspected when examining predictors of knowledge contribution intention. Other elements of the three aspects may need further investigation. For instance, with respect to environmental factors, a VC's personalization ability, namely the ability to match users' idiosyncratic preferences, may have an impact on users' usage intention [44] and subsequent contribution intention.

Another implication for researchers is that they should realize the importance of self-concepts in predicting and determining human behavior. In our case, knowledge self-efficacy and self-image influence knowledge contribution intention to a great extent. Researchers studying human behavior in knowledge management, especially knowledge contribution, should therefore include self-concepts into their research. Other self-concepts like self-esteem is worthy of further research.

5.2   Implications for Practice

One obvious implication for practitioners is that they should focus attention on encouraging knowledge contribution by the allure of enhanced self-concepts. A recognition mechanism or a rating system for improved self-image may be useful for fostering activities of knowledge sharing among VC users. VC managers can also notify contributors of how they have contributed to the whole community to improve their perceptions of enhanced knowledge self-efficacy.

In addition, VC managers should try to better system usability, especially when the community becomes larger and larger. They should always ensure a clear design and good organization of contents. Ways of making the system friendlier and easier to use should be a concern for VC designers and managers.

5.3   Limitations and Future Research

At least two limitations of this study should be noted. First, though the response rate was high, the sample size was relatively small. A larger sample would bring more statistical power. Second, a majority of the respondents were university students. They usually join in VCs that exist outside organizations. The replication of this study targeting members of VCs inside organizations is necessary before the results can be generalized to other types of VCs.

An outcome of the current study is the identification of several areas for future research. First, the study should be extended to investigate actual knowledge contribution behavior, which may provide additional insights into the understanding of knowledge contribution. Second, knowledge sharing is only one aspect of knowledge transfer. Future research can focus on knowledge receivers and the potential factors influencing receiving behavior. This might help build a better understanding of knowledge transfer.

Acknowledgements

The work was supported by Provincial Natural Science Foundation of Anhui under Grant No. 050460404. We would like to thank the PC chairs and anonymous reviewers for their valuable advices. Special thanks to Kwok-Kee Wei for his insightful comments on earlier drafts of this work.

References

1. Ridings, C.M., Gefen, D., Arinze, B.: Some Antecedents and Effects of Trust in Virtual Communities. Journal of Strategic Information Systems 11 (2002) 271-295
2. Wellman, B., Gulia, M.: Net-Surfers Don't Ride Alone: Virtual Communities as Communities. In: Wellman, B. (ed.): Networks in The Global Village. Boulder, CO: Westview Press (1999) 331-366
3. Wasko, M.M., Faraj, S.: Why Should I Share? Examining Social Capital and Knowledge Contribution in Electronic Networks of Practice. MIS Quarterly 29(1) (2005) 35-57
4. Wasko, M.M., Faraj, S.: "It Is What One Does": Why People Participate And Help Others in Electronic Communities of Practice. Journal of Strategic Information Systems 9(2/3) (2000) 155-173
5. Kollock, P.: The Economics of Online Cooperation: Gifts, and Public Goods in Cyberspace. In: Smith, M., Kollock, P. (eds.): Communications in Cyberspace. Routledge New York (1999)
6. Ardichvili, A., Page, V., Wentling, T.: Motivations and Barriers to Participating in Virtual Knowledge Sharing Communities of Practice. Journal of Knowledge Management 7(1) (2003) 64-77
7. Tedjamulia, S.J.J., Olsen, D.R., Dean, D.L., Albrecht, C.C.: Motivating Content Contributions to Online Communities: Toward a More Comprehensive Theory. Proceedings of the 38th Hawaii International Conference on System Sciences (2005)
8. Cialdini, R.B.: Influence: Science and Practice. MA: Allyn and Bacon, Boston (2001)
9. Kalman M.E., Monge, P., Fulk, J., Heino, R.: Motivations to Resolve Communication Dilemmas in Database-mediated Collaborations. Communication Research 29(2) (2002) 125-154
10. Orlikowski, W.J.: Learning From Notes: Organizational Issues in Groupware Implementation. Information Society 9(3) (1993) 237-251
11. Kankanhalli, A., Tan, B., Wei, K.K.: Contribution Knowledge to Electronic Knowledge Repositories: An Empirical Investigation. MIS Quarterly 29(1) (2005) 113-143

12. Wang, C.C., Lai, C.Y.: Knowledge Contribution in the Online Virtual Community: Capability and Motivation. Proceedings of the 1st International Conference on Knowledge Science, Engineering and Management (2006)

13. Tajfel, H., Turner, J.C.: The Social Identity Theory of Group Behavior. In: Worchel, S., Austin, L.W. (eds.): Psychology of Intergroup Relations. Nelson-Hall Chigago (1986)

14. Bandura, A.: A Self-efficacy Mechanism in Human Agency. American Psychologist 37 (1982) 122-147

15. Leonard, N.H., Beauvais, L.L., Scholl, R.W.: Work Motivation: The Incorporation of Self-Concept-Based Processes. Human Relations 52(8) (1999) 969-998

16. Jablin, F.M., Putnam, L.L.: The New Handbook of Organizational Communication: Advances in Theory, Research, and Methods. Thousand Oaks CA: Sage (2001)

17. Tan, B., Wei, K.K., Huang, W.W., Ng, G.: A dialogue Technique to Enhance Electronic Communication in Virtual Teams. IEEE Trans. Profess. Commun. 43(2) (2000) 153-165

18. Sarker, S., Sarker, S., Nicholson, D.B., Joshi, K.D.: Knowledge Transfer in Virtual Systems Development Teams: An Exploratory Study of Four Key Enablers. IEEE Trans. Profess. Commun. 48(2) (2005) 201-218

19. Szulanski, G.: The Process of Knowledge Transfer: A Diachronic Analysis of Stickiness. Organizational Behavior and Human Decision Process 82(1) (2000) 9-27

20. Davenport, T.H., Prusak, L.: Working Knowledge: How Organizations Manage What They Know. Harvard Business School Press, Boston (1998)

21. Gray, P.H.: The Impact of Knowledge Repositories on Power and Control in the Workplace. Information Technology and People 14(4) (2001) 368-384

22. Bregman, N.J., Lipscomb, T.J., McAllister, H.A., Mims, M.: Sharing Bahavior: Effect of Denomination Value and Number. Journal of Genetic Psychology 144 (1984) 131-135

23. Ford, D.P, Staples, D.S.: Perceived Value of Knowledge: Shall I Give You My Gem, My Coal? Proceedings of the 38th Hawaii International Conference on System Sciences (2005)

24. deCharms, R.: Personal Causation: The Internal Affective Determinants of Behavior. Academic Press, New York (1968)

25. Snyder, R.A., Williams, R.R.: Self Theory: An Integrative Theory of Work Motivation. Journal of Occupational Psychology 55 (1982) 257-267

26. Shamir, B.: Calculations, Values and Identities: The Sources of Collective Work Motivation. Human Relations 43 (1990) 313-332

27. Rheingold, H.: The Virtual Community: Homesteading on the Electronic Frontier. Cambridge, MA: MIT Press (2000)

28. Wynn, D.E.: Leadership and Motivation in Open Source Projects. Proceedings of the 7th Annual Conference of the Southern Association for Information Systems (2004) 324-329

29. Constant, D., Sproull, L., Kiesler, S.: The Kindness of Strangers: The Usefulness of Electronic Weak Ties for Technical Advice. Organization Science 7(2) (1996) 119-135

30. Constant, D., Kiesler, S., and Sproull, L.: What's Mine Is Ours, or Is It? A Study of Attitudes about Information Sharing. Information Systems Research 5(4) (1994) 400-421

31. Bock, G.W., Kim, Y.G.: Breaking the Myths of Rewards: An Exploratory Study of Attitudes about Knowledge Sharing. Information Resource Management Journal 15(2) (2002) 14-21

32. Mowday, R.T., Steers, R.M., Porter, L.: The Measurement of Organizational Commitment. Journal of Vocational Behavior 14 (1979) 224-247
33. Jarvenpaa, S.L., Staples, D.S.: The Use of Collaborative Electronic Media for Information Sharing: An Exploratory Study of Determinants. Journal of Strategic Information Systems 9(2/3) (2000) 129-154
34. Preece, J.: Online communities: Designing Usability, Supporting Sociability. John Wiley and Sons, New York (2000)
35. Nahapiet, J., Ghoshal, S.: Social Capital, Intellectual Capital, and Organizational Advantage. Academy of Management Review 23(2) (1998) 242-266
36. Putnam, R.D.: The Prosperous Community: Social Capital and Public Life. The American Prospect 4 (1993)
37. Adler, P.S.: Market, Hierarchy, and Trust: The Knowledge Economy and the Future of Capitalism. Organization Science 12 (2001) 215-234
38. McKinney, V., Yoon, K., Zahedi, F.M.: The Measurement of Web-Customer Satisfaction: An Expectation and Disconfirmation Approach. Information Systems Research 13(3) (2002) 296-315
39. Bock, G.W., Zmud, R.W., Kim, Y.G., Lee, J.N.: Behavioral Intention Formation in Knowledge Sharing: Examining the Roles of Extrinsic Motivators, Social-Psychological Force, and Organizational Climate. MIS Quarterly 29(1) (2005) 87-111
40. Wold, H.: Introduction to the Second Generation of Multivariate Analysis. In: Wold, H. (ed.): Theoretical Empiricism. New York, USA: Paragon House (1989)
41. Chin, W.W.: The Partial Least Squares Approach to Structural Equation Modeling. In: Marcoulides, G. (ed.): Modern Methods for Business Research. Mahwah, NJ: Lawrence Erlbaum Associates (1998) 295-336
42. Fornell, C., Larcker, D.: A Second Generation of Multivariate Analysis: Classification of Methods and Implications for Marketing Research. In: Houston, M.J. (ed.): Review of Marketing. American Marketing Association, Chicago (1987) 407-450
43. Wasko, M.M., Teigland, R.: The Provision of Online Public Goods: Examining Social Structure in a Network of Practice. Proceedings of the 23rd Annual International Conference on Information Systems (2002) 163-171
44. Tiwana, A., Bush, A.A.: Continuance in Expertise-Sharing Networks: A Social Perspective. IEEE Transactions on Engineering Management 52(1) (2005) 85-101

A Method for Evaluating the Knowledge Transfer Ability in Organization

Tian-hui You, Fei-fei Li, and Zhu-chao Yu

School of Business Administration, Northeastern University,
Postfach 110004, Shenyang, P.R. China
thyou@mail.neu.edu.cn

Abstract. Knowledge transfer as an important aspect of knowledge management has been considered as an effective way to promote the knowledge ability and the core competence of an organization. In this paper, a method to evaluate knowledge transfer ability in organization is proposed. Firstly, the main factors which affect the knowledge transfer ability to be found out through the analysis of the relevant research of domestic and international knowledge transfer, then, an index system is set up to evaluate knowledge transfer ability using the method of questionnaire investigation and statistical analysis as knowledge transmission ability, knowledge receptive ability, interactive ability and organizational supporting ability, etc.. According to the index system and the characteristics of linguistic assessment information provided by experts, a multi-index linguistic decision-making method based on linguistic assessment information is proposed using LWD operator and LOWA operator developed in recent years. Finally, an example is given to explain the method.

1 Introduction

Accompany with the arriving of knowledge economy times, the organization traditional management models is being under serious impact, knowledge management as a new business management model to appear the formidable superiority, becomes an important supporting platform to strengthen the core competitive ability in organization. Knowledge transfer takes the knowledge management an important aspect, can enhance organization's performance level, avoid the repetition development of knowledge and the full use already the knowledge resources which has. At present, the researches on knowledge transfer have already aroused the attention of scholars, and the content of these researches focus on such aspects as knowledge transfer model [1-3], factors which affect successful knowledge transfer [4-8] and mechanism [9-11] which are based on Nonaka's SECI model and Szulanski's intercourse model. Among the models Nonaka's SECI model is a most famous one in which the concept of explicit knowledge and tacit knowledge is proposed and clarified the implementation of knowledge production and innovation through a spiral process between explicit knowledge and tacit knowledge [1]. Szulanski compartmentalized knowledge transfer process into four stages: stating, implement, regulate and conformity [3]. Many academic literatures have developed factors affecting knowledge transfer such as characteristics of the source of knowledge,

J. Lang, F. Lin, and J. Wang (Eds.): KSEM 2006, LNAI 4092, pp. 576–585, 2006.

the recipient, the context and the knowledge itself [5], the nature of the social network and tie [6], network structure [7] and so on. Cummings and Teng through case study found that knowledge transfer success was associated with several key variables and proposed nine factors influencing knowledge transfer success, they are embeddedness and articulability of knowledge context, organizational, physical, knowledge and norm distance of relational context, project priority and learning culture of recipient context and activity context [8]. Knowledge transfer mechanism involve personnel move, training, technology transfer, patent, consuetude repeat, communication, relations of alliance and other organizations and so on[11]. For the research method, there is not only theoretical study, but also abundant empirical study which especially concerning the cooperative R&D [12], strategic alliance [13] and parent-subsidiary corporation [14]. While effective knowledge transfer depends greatly on knowledge transfer ability in organization, the researches on knowledge transfer ability are still rare [15-17]. Cohen and Levinthal state that knowledge transfer ability consists of conveying and absorbing capability [15]; Hamel attributes successful knowledge transfer to three factors: intent, transparency and receptivity, and further expatiates the determinants of the factors [16]; Schlegelmilch and Chini distinguish knowledge transfer capabilities between transmission channels, knowledge management infrastructure and knowledge processes capability[17]. These researches are all qualitative analysis about knowledge transfer ability; quantitative analysis has not been involved. So our research addresses this gap by analyzing and evaluating the knowledge transfer ability in organization.

2 Index System of Knowledge Transfer Ability

The efficiency and velocity is different when knowledge is transferred between different actors and units. The ability to control velocity, extent, quality and quantity, direction of knowledge flow is called knowledge transfer ability. In order to enhance the efficiency and velocity of knowledge transfer and reduce knowledge innovation cost, an organization must possess considerable knowledge transfer ability. Knowledge transfer in an organization is a series of processes that valuable knowledge is diffused, replicated and shared, and can take place in different layers (individual, group, department and organization). There are four variables involves in this process, namely, knowledge to be transferred, knowledge source, knowledge recipient and the "bridge" which connects the both ends of knowledge transfer. Therefore, assessing an organization's knowledge transfer ability not only need considering knowledge transmission ability and receptive ability, but also taking into account interactive ability and organization supporting ability.

The main factors which affect the knowledge transfer ability to be found out through the analysis of the relevant research of domestic and international knowledge transfer, then an index system is set up to assess this ability using the method of questionnaire investigation and statistical analysis, which including four dimensions and sixteen basic indexes (shown in figure 1), because space restricts, only the main analysis result are provided here, these abilities are mainly as follows:

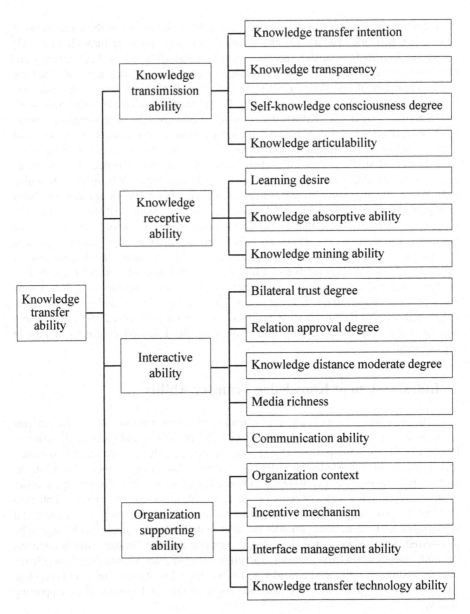

Fig. 1. Index system of knowledge transfer ability

(1) Knowledge transmission ability. The knowledge transmission ability refers to the ability that guarantees the knowledge resource to be transmitted effectively to the knowledge recipient through suitable way in organization. This kind of ability is mainly embodied by the knowledge transfer intention, the knowledge transparency, the self-knowledge consciousness degree as well as the knowledge articulability. (a) Knowledge transfer intention is a kind of driving factor, which reflects the initiative

and goal of knowledge transfer, and can adjust the process of knowledge transfer. Generally, the stronger the transfer intention is the easier the knowledge transfer will be carried out. (b) Knowledge transparency refers to the degree of openness and accessibility of the knowledge which the knowledge resource willing to transfer, and it can affect the quantity and quality of the transferred knowledge. A higher level of transparency allows a more effective knowledge transfer. (c) Self-knowledge consciousness degree presents the degree to which knowledge resource understands what aspect knowledge and how much knowledge it holds. It largely decides the ability of an organization's engaging in knowledge transfer. The fuller knowledge resource realizes self-knowledge, the more it will be advantageous to knowledge transfer. (d) Knowledge articulability refers to the ability that the knowledge resource presents its knowledge which needs to be understood by the knowledge recipient. The stronger the knowledge articulability is, and the better the transfer result will be.

(2) Knowledge receptive ability. The knowledge receptive ability refers to the ability that knowledge recipient understands and accepts knowledge and then transforms to their own knowledge storage. This kind of ability is mainly embodied by the learning desire, the knowledge absorptive ability and the knowledge mining ability. (a) Learning desire is the tendency that the recipient takes knowledge transfer as an opportunity to learn new skills but not to obtain the properties of the other part. Lacking of learning desire can lead difficulty to knowledge transfer. But, if the recipient has high learning desire, they can frequently behave enormous endurance and overcome difficulties in the course of knowledge transfer. (b) Knowledge absorptive ability refers to the ability that the recipient cognizes the value of the new knowledge, and assimilates it and makes it for further application. This kind of ability depends greatly on the previous knowledge accumulation, the learning ability and the diligently degree. Knowledge absorptive ability is strong and the knowledge transfer ability will be strong too. (c) Knowledge mining ability manifests the recipient's initiative to participate in knowledge transfer and ability for deep acquiring knowledge from the knowledge resource. This kind of ability may impel the knowledge resource to be more willing and in a more appropriate way to transfer knowledge.

(3) Interactive ability. The interactive ability mainly embodies the ability that both sides of knowledge transfer together affect knowledge transfer's result, including the bilateral trust degree, the relational approval degree, the knowledge distance moderate degree, the media richness as well as communication ability. (a) Trust can promote exchange information, experience and knowledge between staff. When existing trusts between both sides of knowledge transfer, staff will be more willing to give the opposite party useful knowledge, simultaneously also will be willing to accept and absorb the knowledge which other staff provide. The higher the bilateral trust degree is, the more they are willing to participate in knowledge transfer activities. (b) Relation approval degree mainly includes intimacy, durability and mutually identity between the two sides, it is mainly manifested in the aspect of values, organization culture, social position, management method and so on. It will be much easier to produce admire and learning intention if there is higher relation approval degree between two sides, and thereupon will accelerate knowledge transfer. (c) Knowledge distance is the gap between the

knowledge source and recipient on knowledge accumulation level, or the degree to which the source and recipient possess similar knowledge. When transferring knowledge between departments or communities on different knowledge accumulation level, the bilateral knowledge distance or "the gap" is too big or too small will both hindrance knowledge transfer activities, just the moderate knowledge distance then can promote knowledge to be transferred effectively. (d) Media richness refers to the ability that the media has to change people's comprehension by explaining ambiguous questions, it can affect the depth of knowledge transfer, and it portrays the media's ability to raise organization's learning ability in a certain time. The higher the degree of media richness, the stronger knowledge transfer ability is. (e) Perfect communication ability can promote both sides to participate in knowledge transfer, as well as effective exchange and communication in organization, and then increase the effectiveness of knowledge transfer.

(4) Organization supporting ability. Organization supporting ability is mainly embodied in such aspects as organization context, incentive mechanism, interface management ability and knowledge transfer technology ability. (a) Organization context refers to the entire organization's environment, including organization structure, organization culture, and organization's recognition and supporting degree on the knowledge transfer and so on. Organization structure influences organization's absorptive ability and deferent ability, thus enhances or reduces the effectiveness of cognizing relevant knowledge transfer. Concretely speaking, the network organization structure is much advantaged to promote exchange and share information and experience and more effective to facilitate knowledge transfer than the functional organization structure. Organization culture has huge influence on the flows, transformation and innovation of tacit knowledge. If it can form one kind of favorable environment and atmosphere which can promote the knowledge to flow, transformed and innovation, and one kind of more perfect learning organization culture in organization, then the knowledge transfer will be promoted enormously. (b) Incentive mechanism plays a vital role in encouraging members to participate positively in organization's knowledge management activities especially the knowledge transfer activities. Knowledge transfer can not occur automatically. Only by establishing perfect incentive mechanism and placing importance on rewarding the active staff, can they naturally be willing to participate in knowledge transfer. (c) Interface management ability reflects the ability that an organization manages knowledge flow, which on the one hand can enable to fully use of knowledge being learned, on the other hand can guarantee the essential knowledge not to be divulged. Better interface management ability is helpful to transfer knowledge in organization and develop organization's own ability. (d) Knowledge transfer technology mainly comprise the knowledge discover technology, knowledge repository technology, intelligent agent technology, group technology, knowledge network technology and the knowledge management system which integrates these technologies above. These technologies affect the velocity of knowledge transfer, so it will enormously advance successful realization of knowledge transfer by developing and innovating knowledge transfer technology in an organization timely.

3 A Method to Evaluate the Knowledge Transfer Ability

In order to evaluate knowledge transfer ability in an organization, usually experts present their linguistic assessment information, and then aggregate the linguistic assessment information to obtain group assessment information. Taking into account that those assess indexes are qualitative and fuzzy, a multi-index linguistic decision-making method is given based on LWD (Linguistic Weighted Disjunction) operator [18] and LOWA (Linguistic Ordered Weighted Averaging) operator [19, 20] to assess knowledge transfer ability in organization. The principle is as follows.

In the course of assessing knowledge transfer ability in an organization, let $P = \{P_1, P_2, ..., P_q\}$ ($q \geq 2$) be a non-empty and finite set of decision indexes, where P_j is the jth ability index. Let $E = \{E_1, E_2, ..., E_m\}$ ($m \geq 2$) be a non-empty and finite set of experts, where E_k is the kth expert. Let $R^k = (r_1^k, r_2^k, ..., r_q^k)^T$ be the weight vector of indexes given by E_k, where r_j^k is chosen from a nature linguistic assessment terms set S. Finally, let $A = (a_j^k)_{m \times q}$ be an assessment matrix, where a_j^k is the kth group member's assessment value of the jth index from a nature linguistic assessment terms set S. S is a pre-established ordinal nature linguistic assessment terms set consisting of odd linguistic terms, which describes the importance of P_j. In this paper, a set of five terms S could be given such as $S = (S_i) = \{S_0 = $ VL(Very Low), $S_1 = $ L(Low), $S_2 = $ M(Moderate), $S_3 = $ H(High), $S_4 = $ VH(Very High) $\}$.

Usually, in these cases, it is required that in the linguistic terms set there exists:

(1) The set is ordered: $S_i \geq S_j$ if $i \geq j$.

(2) There is a negation operator: $\text{Neg}(S_i) = S_j$ such that $j = T - i$ (T+1 is the cardinality).

(3) Maximization operator and minimization operator: $\text{Max}(S_i, S_j) = S_i$ if $S_i \geq S_j$; $\text{Min}(S_i, S_j) = S_j$ if $S_i \geq S_j$.

In order to manage and calculate the linguist terms conveniently, the calculation steps of the multi-index linguistic decision-making method in virtue of the LWD operator and LOWA operator are given as follows:

Step 1. Aggregate the ability indexes of linguist assessment information given by each expert. First, the linguist assessment information of a_j^k and r_j^k given by each expert are aggregated into integrated values by virtue of LWD operator and LOWA operator using the following formula:

$$(a^k, r^k) = \phi[(a_1^k, r_1^k), (a_2^k, r_2^k), \cdots, (a_q^k, r_q^k)] . \tag{1}$$

Where $k = 1, 2, \cdots, m$; a^k is the integrated value of knowledge transfer ability given by the expert E_k; r^k is the importance of the expert E_k and ϕ is LWD operator. a^k and r^k can be calculated as follows:

$$a^k = \max_{j=1,\cdots,q} \min(a_j^k, r_j^k), \quad k = 1, 2, \cdots, m \ . \tag{2}$$

$$r^k = \phi_Q(r_1^k, r_2^k, \cdots, r_q^k), \quad k = 1, 2, \cdots, m \ . \tag{3}$$

where ϕ_Q is LOWA operator. ϕ_Q is defined as:

$$
\begin{aligned}
\phi_Q(r_1^k, r_2^k, \cdots, r_q^k) &= W^{\mathrm{T}} B \\
&= \xi^q \{w_t, r_{\sigma(t)}^k, t = 1, 2, \cdots, q\} \\
&= w_1 \otimes r_{\sigma(1)}^k \oplus \xi^{q-1} \{\beta_h, r_{\sigma(h)}^k, h = 2, 3, \cdots, q\} \ .
\end{aligned}
\tag{4}
$$

where $W = (w_1, w_2, \cdots, w_q)^{\mathrm{T}}$ is a weighted vector, such that: $w_t \in [0,1]$, $\sum_{t=1}^{q} w_t = 1$, $\beta_h = w_h / \sum_{t=2}^{q} w_t$, $h = 2,3,\cdots q$ and $B = \{b_1, b_2, \cdots b_m\}$ is a vector associated to R^k, such that, $B = \sigma(A) = (r_{s(1)}^k, r_{s(2)}^k, \cdots, r_{s(q)}^k)^{\mathrm{T}}$, where $r_{s(j)}^k \le r_{s(i)}^k, \forall i \le j$, with σ being a permutation over the set of labels R^k. ξ^q is the convex combination operator of q terms. $\otimes$ is the general product of a term by a positive real number and $\oplus$ is the general addition of terms. If $q = 2$, then ξ^q is defined as:

$$\xi^2 \{w_t, r_{\sigma(t)}^k, t = 1, 2\} = w_1 \otimes S_j \oplus (1 - w_1) \otimes S_i = S_l, \quad S_j, S_i \in S(j \ge i) \ . \tag{5}$$

where $l = \min(\mathrm{T}, i + \mathrm{round}(w_1 \cdot (j - i)))$, "round($\cdot$)" is the usual round operation, and $r_{\sigma(1)}^k = S_j$, $r_{\sigma(2)}^k = S_i$.

In the case of a non-decreasing proportional quantifier, w_t is given by this expression:

$$w_t = Q(t/q) - Q((t-1)/q), \quad t = 1, 2, \cdots, q \ . \tag{6}$$

where $Q(u)$ is fuzzy quantifier operator, which can be represented as:

$$
Q(u) =
\begin{cases}
0 & \text{if } u < d, \\
\dfrac{u - d}{f - d} & \text{if } d \le u \le f, \\
1 & \text{if } u > f.
\end{cases}
\tag{7}
$$

where $d, f, u \in [0,1]$. The corresponding parameter (d, f) is $(0, 0.5)$, $(0.3, 0.8)$ and $(0.5, 1)$, respectively representing "half at least", "majority", "as much as possible".

Step 2. Aggregate the integrated assessment values of each expert into the integrated assessment value of the group. a^k and r^k are aggregated into the integrated assessment value of the group by virtue of LWD operator and LOWA operator, namely,

$$(a,r) = \phi[(a^1, r^1), (a^2, r^2), \cdots, (a^m, r^m)] \; . \tag{8}$$

where a is the assessment value of the group, $a \in S$; r is the credibility degree of the information given by the expert group, $r \in S$. a and r are calculated separately as follows:

$$a = \max_{k=1,2,\cdots m} \min(a^k, r^k) \; . \tag{9}$$

$$r = \phi_Q(r^1, r^2, \cdots r^m) \; . \tag{10}$$

where the method to calculate r is as same as the method given before to calculate r^k and no longer go into details here.

Step 3. Judge the current situation of knowledge transfer ability in an organization. The current situation of knowledge transfer ability in an organization can be known by virtue of the value of a calculated before, and meanwhile, the credibility degree of the information given by the expert group can be known by virtue of the value of r.

The process to assess knowledge transfer ability is also a process to understand organization's condition of knowledge transfer. This process can help organization find out its insufficiency for implementing knowledge transfer, and then contributes to the organization's taking corresponding measures to promote the transfer of knowledge in organization.

4   Illustrative Example

There is a software development company containing multi software development teams. Each team implements one or more projects at the same time, and a mass of knowledge and experience in these teams can be shared. Therefore, for promoting knowledge transfer among teams and avoiding the repetition development of knowledge and the full use of company's knowledge resources, the company is going to assess its interior knowledge transfer ability. The organization invites three experts (i.e., E_1, E_2, E_3) to participate in assessing. The weight vectors and assessment matrix provided by experts for the four dimensions such as the knowledge transmission ability, the knowledge receptive ability, the interactive ability and the organization supporting ability are respectively as follows:

$R_1^1 = (VH, H, L, VH)^T$, $R_1^2 = (H, VH, VL, M)^T$, $R_1^3 = (VH, H, M, H)^T$,

$R_2^1 = (H, VH, M)^T$, $R_2^2 = (VH, M, VL)^T$, $R_2^3 = (VH, H, L)^T$,

$R_3^1 = (VH, H, M, L, VH)^T$, $R_3^2 = (VH, VH, M, VL, VL)^T$, $R_3^3 = (VH, L, M, M, VH)^T$,

$R_4^1 = (VH, L, M, M)^T$, $R_4^2 = (VH, VH, M, VL)^T$, $R_4^3 = (L, M, M, H)^T$.

$$A_1 = \begin{bmatrix} L & VL & M & L \\ VL & L & L & M \\ L & M & M & H \end{bmatrix}, \quad A_2 = \begin{bmatrix} M & H & L \\ H & L & M \\ VH & M & L \end{bmatrix},$$

$$A_3 = \begin{bmatrix} VH & M & M & H & H \\ M & H & VL & VL & VH \\ M & VH & VL & VL & L \end{bmatrix}, \quad A_4 = \begin{bmatrix} H & VH & VL & M \\ M & M & L & VL \\ VH & M & L & H \end{bmatrix}.$$

First, according to the formulas (1) and (2), aggregate the nature linguistic assessment information given by experts to linguistic assessment value a_j^k of jth dimension, we can obtain $a_1^k = (L, M, H)^T$; $a_2^k = (H, H, VH)^T$; $a_3^k = (VH, H, M)^T$; $a_4^k = (H, M, H)^T$. When adopting the principle of "as much as possible", the parameter (d, f) is (0.5, 1) corresponding to $Q(u)$. According to the formulas of (3)~(7), we can obtain $r_1^k = (M, M, M)^T$; $r_2^k = (M, L, M)^T$; $r_3^k = (L, M, M)^T$; $r_4^k = (M, L, M)^T$. Then according to the formulas of (8)~(10), we get the assessment value of each dimension, namely $a_1 = M$; $a_2 = M$; $a_3 = M$; $a_4 = M$, and the credibility $r_1 = M$; $r_2 = L$; $r_3 = L$; $r_4 = L$. Finally, according to the formulas of (8)~(10) again, we obtain the assessment value of the group, namely, $a = M$. Meanwhile, the credibility degree of the information given by the expert group is obtained, $r = L$. Through calculation, we come to the conclusion that the ability assessment result of knowledge transfer in organization is "Moderate".

5 Conclusions

This paper analysis the knowledge transfer ability in organization and proposes a multi-index linguistic decision-making method to evaluate it. The method is based on the linguistic assessment information and use LWD operator and LOWA operator. And the credibility degree of the information given by the expert group is obtained. The method helps to judge the ability situation of knowledge transfer in an organization, and then help the organization to take corresponding strategies to enhance knowledge transfer ability.

References

1. Nonaka, I., Takeuchi, H.: The Knowledge-Creating Company, Oxford University Press, New York(1995)
2. Gilbert, M., Cordey-Hayes, M.: Understanding the Process of Knowledge Rransfer to Achieve Successful Technological Innovation. Technovation. vol. 16, 6(1996) 301-312
3. Szulanski, G.: Exploring Internal Stickiness: Impediments to the Transfer of Best Practice within the Firm. Strategic Management Journal. 17(Summer special issue) (1996) 27-43
4. Chang, L., Zou, S.G., Li, S.C.: Research of Influential Elements on Knowledge Diffusion Based on Knowledge Chain. Science Research Management. vol. 22, 5(2001) 122-127

5. Szulanski, G.: The Process of Knowledge Transfer: A Diachronic Analysis of Stickiness. Organizational Behavior and Human Decision Processes. vol. 82, 1(2000) 9-27

6. McEvily, B., Zaheer, A.: Bridging ties: A source of firm heterogeneity in competitive capabilities. Strategic Management Journal. vol. 20 (1999) 1133-1156

7. Reagans, R., McEvily, B.: Network structure and knowledge transfer: The effects of cohesion and range. Administrative Science Quarterly. vol. 48 (2003) 240-267

8. Cummings, J.L., Teng, B.S.: Transferring R&D knowledge: the key factors affecting knowledge transfer success. J. Eng. Technol. Manage. vol. 20(2003) 39-68

9. Galbraith, C.S.: Transferring core manufacturing technologies in high technology firms. California Management Review. vol. 32, 4 (1990) 56-70

10. Mowery, D.C., Oxley, J.E., Silverman, B.S.: Strategic Alliances and Inter-firm Knowledge Transfer. Strategic Management Journal. 17(winter special issue)(1996) 77-91

11. Luo, P.L., Zhou, Y., Guo, H.: A Literature Review on the Mechanism of Knowledge Transferring among Virtual R&D Organizations. R&D management. vol. 16, 5(2004): 18-25, 81 in Chinese

12. Schweizer, L.: Knowledge transfer and R&D in pharmaceutical companies: A case study. J. Eng. Technol. Manage. vol. 22(2005) 315-331

13. Gomes-Casseres, B., Hagedoorn, J., Jaffe, A.B.: Do alliances promote knowledge flows? Journal of Financia Economics. vol, 80(2006) 5-33

14. Wang, P., Tong, T.W., Koh, C.P.: An integrated model of knowledge transfer from MNC parent to China subsidiary. Journal of World Business. vol. 39(2004)168-182

15. Cohen, W.M., Levinthal, D.A.: Absorptive Capacity: A New Perspective on Learning and Innovation. Administrative Science Quarterly. vol. 35, 1(1990)128-152

16. Hamel G.. Competition for competence and inter-partner learning within international strategic alliances. Strategic Management Journal. vol. 12. (1991) 83-103

17. Schlegelmilch, B.B., Chini, T.C.: Knowledge transfer between marking functions in multinational companies: a conceptual model. International Business Review. vol. 12 (2003) 215-232

18. Herrera, F., Herrera-Viedma, E., Verdegay, J.L.: Choice Process for Non-homogeneous Group Decision Making in Linguistic Setting . Fuz. Set. Sys. vol. 94, 3(1998) 287-308

19. Herrera, F., Herrera-Viedma, E., Verdegay, J.L.: Direct Approach Processes in Group Decision Making Using Linguistic OWA Operators . Fuz. Set. Sys. vol. 79, 1(1996) 175-190

20. Herrera, F., Herrera-Viedma, E.: Linguistic Decision Analysis: Steps for Solving Decision Problems under Linguistic Information. Fuz. Set. Sys. vol. 115, 1(2000) 67-82

Information Extraction
from Semi-structured Web Documents*

Bo-Hyun Yun[1] and Chang-Ho Seo[2]

[1] Dept. of Computer Education, Mokwon University
800, Doan-dong, Seo-ku, Taejon, 302-729, Korea
ybh@mokwon.ac.kr
[2] Dept. of Applied Mathematics, Kongju University
182, Shinkwan-dong, Kongju-City, 305-350, Korea
chseo@kongju.ac.kr

Abstract. This paper proposes the web information extraction system that extracts the pre-defined information automatically from web documents (i.e. HTML documents) and integrates the extracted information. The system recognizes entities without labels by the probabilistic based entity recognition method and extends the existing domain knowledge semiautomatically by using the extracted data. Moreover, the system extracts the sub-linked information linked to the basic page and integrates the similar results extracted from heterogeneous sources. The experimental result shows that the global precision of seven domain sites is 93.5%. The system using the sub-linked information and the probabilistic based entity recognition enhances the precision significantly against the system using only the domain knowledge. Moreover, the presented system can extract the more various information precisely due to applying the system with flexibility according to domains. Thus, the system can increase the degree of user satisfaction at its maximum and contribute the revitalization of e-business.

1 Introduction

The Web has presented users with huge amounts of information, and some may feel they will miss something if they do not review all available data before making a decision. These needs results in HTML text mining. The goal of mining HTML documents is to transform HTML texts into a structural format and thereby reducing the information in texts to slot-token patterns.

The objective of information extraction is to extract only the user interests in a lots of web documents and to convert them into the formal form. A user provides the information extraction system with web sites, as the input, that are on a topic or event of interest. Based on this input from the user, the system extracts the most interesting part from web sites that are on the desired topic or event. The information extraction system can enhance the degree of the user

* This work was supported by grant No. R01-2005-000-10200-0 from Korea Science and Engineering Foundation.

satisfaction in web surfing, because the system extracts the specific part from various web sites and suggests the integrated results.

Conventional approaches[9,10] dealing with the data extraction in the web are to induce the wrapper which encapsulates the heterogeneity within various data sources. The wrapper is the extraction rule representing the interesting data location and the structure about the specific information source. These wrapper system regards the web page as the set including the useful information.

For example, the only specific data has the importance in the semi-structured web pages as the result of goods information retrieval. Thus, it is important to produce the wrapper which can extract the useful information within them. These wrapper application systems can provide users with the information service satisfying the intellectual curiosity of users. In order to enhance the performance of the wrapper, we must consider the following elements :

- Entity without labels
  Inducing the wrapper in the information source, we recognize the web page including the label by the domain knowledge. However, we can't recognize the entity in the web page without the label, because there aren't clues of the entity. Therefore, we need the method recognizing the entity without the label.
- Expansion of domain knowledge
  Generally, the first domain knowledge is constructed by the domain expert and is also expanded manually by them. The manual expansion of domain knowledge is needed to apply the wrapper to a lots of domains. However, the manual expansion can't often reflect the dynamic properties and the fast update of the web. These domain knowledge results in extracting the deficient information in the web pages. Thus, it is necessary to expand automatically the first domain knowledge.
- Sub-linked web page
  Most web sites provide only the brief information in the first web page and show the detailed information in the sub-linked pages. These can reduce the system overhead and provide the information concisely and fast. Thus, the wrapper induction has to consider the sub-linked web pages.

In order to satisfy the three kinds of considerations, this paper proposes the web information extraction system that extracts the pre-defined information automatically from web documents (i.e. HTML documents) and integrates the extracted information. The system recognizes entities without labels by the probabilistic based entity recognition method and extends the existing domain knowledge semiautomatically by using the extracted data. Moreover, the system extracts the sub-linked information linked to the basic page and integrates the similar results extracted from heterogeneous sources.

2   Related Works

Conventional approaches of the wrapper induction can be divided into three types of systems such as the manual method, the semi-automatic method, and the automatic method. The manual method[10] produces the extraction rules manually in the specific domains. However, the method takes the long time to make the rules by the manual and can't expand the rules flexibly.

The semi-automatic wrapper induction method[18] receives the user input at the least to learn the XWRAP wrapper and alleviates the problem of the manual method. XWRAP constructs the HTML documents as the hierarchical structure and receives the user input about the only meaning part. However, this method also has to receive the user input. Even if the convenient interface is provided to users, the precise input is not guaranteed. Moreover, the method can't learn the wrapper on the HTML documents which are not constructed as the hierarchical tree.

The automatic wrapper induction method can be divided into the machine learning method[3-9,12-17,19,20], the data mining method[1,2], and the concept modelling method[11]. The machine learning method regards a lots of information in the web as the correlating data and induces the wrapper based on the machine learning. The data mining method analyzes the set of example objects from users and extracts new objects of new web pages by the bottom-up extraction. Finally, the concept modelling method parses the ontology(i.e. the instances of concept model) and produces the schema of the database automatically. And then, the method recognizes the data in the semi-structured web pages and stores the data in the schema of the database.

The above automatic wrapper induction methods have the following problems. First, the methods can recognize the entities corresponding to the domain knowledge but not extract the entities without the exactly corresponding labels. Second, the methods can not expand the new domain knowledge automatically by the existing domain knowledge. Third, the methods do not consider the sub-linked web pages and extract the data in only the first pages.

3   Automatically Extracting Web Information

The system configuration of our method is shown in Figure 1. In the preprocessing module, the query form analyzer analyzes the query expression of web sites and stores the analyzed results. The analyzed results are used in the time of extracting the information by the information extracting module. The query form analyzer is needed because each site has the query form respectively. Then, we parse the HTML web pages by the structure analyzer.

The wrapper learner learns the wrapper based on the learning data and the wrapper producer produces the wrapper by using the results of analyzing the wrapper configuration and the domain knowledge in the wrapper induction engine. In the phase of wrapper induction, we improves the precision of the extraction by using both the domain knowledge and the probabilities estimating the entities without labels. The information extractor extracts the information automatically in the web sites based on the results of analyzing queries in the preprocessor and the wrapper constructed in the wrapper induction engine. The result integrator integrates the information extracted from the heterogeneous web sites because several web sites often have the redundant data.

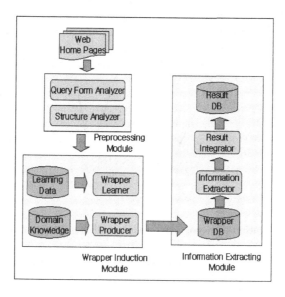

Fig. 1. System Configuration of Information Extraction System

3.1 Recognizing Entities Without Labels

When inducing the wrapper in the information source, web pages having the labels are recognized automatically by the domain knowledge. However, without labels the system can not recognize the entities even if the domain knowledge is used. The reason is that there are no clues to be identified in the web pages. Therefore, this paper presents the probabilistic model to recognize the entities without labels.

At first, we define the related term before explaining the model. *entity* is the basic unit that can be used in the each domain. For example, in the movie web sites, the entities are the title, the director, or the protagonist. *label* is the clue that can be provided to recognize the entities in the information source. Labels of the title can be *title*, *movietitle*, or *titleofthemovie*. *item* is the basic unit of the information providing in the information source. Most web pages show several items by the list type or the table type. In other words, items are defined as the tuples of the database. *token* is the part which can be the value of the entity in the text. For example, the token of the title is $Titanic$ and the token of the director is $JamesCameron$. *tokenset* is the collection of the tokens about each entity. *tokensetsequence* is several token sets.

Accordingly, we define the above situation mathematically.

1. Let $\{t_1, t_2, ..., t_n\}$ be n tokens recognized for one item.
2. Let $\{e_1, e_2, ..., e_n\}$ be n entities assigned.
3. Let $\{t'_1, t'_2, ..., t'_m\}$ be m tokens not recognized for one item.
4. Let $\{e'_1, e'_2, ..., e'_q\}$ be q entities not assigned. Here, e'_k is the entity set E defined in the domain knowledge subtracted by the entity observed in the

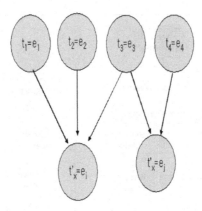

Fig. 2. Relation of Recognized Tokens and Non-recognized Tokens

current information source. Since the entities of tokens are given exclusively, the already observed entities have to be removed in the entity set.

5. Let v be items for one information source.
6. Let $\{T_1, T_2, ..., T_n\}$ be n token set for one information source. And then, let $T_i = \{t_{i1}, t_{i2}, ..., t_{iv}\}$ be v tokens for one token set.
7. Let $\{T'_1, T'_2, ..., T'_m\}$ be m token set not recognized for one information source. And then, let $T_i = \{t'_{j1}, t'_{j2}, ..., t'_{jv}\}$ be v tokens for one token set.
8. Let $(n + m)$ be the number of entities in the domain knowledge.

By definition, we propose the probability based model which gives the token set the name of entities exclusively. This method is to use the context information within one item and to consider the labels within the same item as the token. The reason is that the usage of the text part already recognized can estimate the labels of tokens not recognized. Thus, we can solve the problem of the current site by the extracted information of the other information source.

For example, suppose that $Titanic$ of the movie title is not recognized because of the omission of the labels. The director of $Titanic$ is $JamesCameron$ and the protagonist is $LeonardoDiCaprio$. If $JamesCameron$ is already recognized as the director entity, the token of $Titanic$ can be estimated as the title entity. The reason is that $\{(title = Titanic), (director = JamesCameron), (protagonist = LeonardoDiCaprio)\}$ from other information source can be appended to the learning data. In addition, if $LeonardoDiCaprio$ is recognized as the protagonist, the token of $Titanic$ can be probably regarded as the title entity. If $\{(director = JamesCameron), (production = Titanic)\}$ exists in the learning data, the system can not see if $Titanic$ is the title entity or the production entity. In this case, $(protagonist = LeonardoDiCaprio)$ plays the important role in estimating $Titanic$ as the title entity.

The context information is used in order to identify the entity of the token not recognized. The value of these probabilities can be calculated by the extracted data. Moreover, the system do not use only the context information of one item but consider the context information of several items. The reason is that the context information of several items can obtain the distinguishable probability more than that of one item.

As shown in Figure 2, we present the model to identify the entities of the token by using the context information. This model uses the token information $\{(t_1 = e_1), (t_2 = e_2), (t_3 = e_3), (t_4 = e_4)\}$ to know if the token t'_x is recognized as the entity e'_i or as the entity e'_j. If the number of the case which t_1 is e_1 and t'_x is e'_i, t_2 is e_2 and t'_x is e'_i, and t_3 is e_3 and t'_x is e'_i is larger than that of the case which t_3 is e_3 and t'_x is e'_j and t_4 is e_4 and t'_x is e'_j, t'_x will be e'_i more than e'_j. Therefore, in Figure 2, the meaning of the arrow is the probability of the case existing in the two below nodes. The more the probability of the arrow is large and the number of the arrow is numerous, the more the probability of the unassigned entity of the node is great.

Using the above concept, we define the equation to represent the degree which the known node information supports the new node information to be recognized. By the following steps, we can obtain the probability of the model.

1. Construct the learning data from several information sources.
2. Collect the data suggesting in the premise to extract the information within the information source.
3. Compute the probability which the token belongs to the entity. When $\{(t_1 = e_1), (t_2 = e_2), (t_3 = e_3),$ and $(t_4 = e_4)\}$ is recognized, the probability which a token t'_j is an entity e'_i can be defined by the following equation.

$$P(t'_j = e'_i | t_1 = e_1, t_2 = e_2, ..., t_n = e_n) \tag{1}$$

Here, n is the number of tokens and entities. By the total probability, the equation (1) is converted to the equation (2).

$$\sum_{k=1}^{n} P(t'_j = e'_i | t_1 = e_1, t_2 = e_2, ..., t_n = e_n) = \sum_{k=1}^{n} P(t'_j = e'_i, t_k = e_k) \tag{2}$$

By the equation (2), when $\{t_1 = e_1, t_2 = e_2, t_3 = e_3, t_4 = e_4\}$ is recognized, the probability which the token set $T'_j, j = 1, ..., n$, is the entity e'_i is the equation (3).

$$P(T'_j = e'_i | T_1 = e_1, T_2 = e_2, T_3 = e_3, T_4 = e_4)$$
$$\cong \frac{1}{v} \sum_{h=1}^{u} \sum_{k=1}^{n} P(T'_j = e'_i | T_1 = e_1, T_2 = e_2, T_3 = e_3, T_4 = e_4) \tag{3}$$

Because several items exist in the information source, to compute the probability which the token set belongs to the entity is reliable more than to compute the probability which the token belongs to the entity. Thus, the $P(t'_{jk} = e'_i | t_{hk} = e_h)$ is the value which the entity e'_i is the token t'_{jk} and the number of tuples that the entity e_h is the token t_{hk} is divided by the total number of tuples in the learning data. $P(t_{hk} = e_h)$ is the value which the number of tuples that the entity e_h is the token t_{hk} is divided by the total number of tuples in the learning data.

4. Choose the entity e'_i of the highest probability and assign it as the entity of the token set T'_j. However, if the probability is smaller than the threshold, we don't assign the probability.

5. Remove the token set T'_j from the sequence of the first token set and create the sequence of the new token set $T'_1, T'_2, ..., T'_m$. For the sequence of the new token set, the step (3) and (4) is applied repeatedly.

By the above model, the method of computing the probability is as follows:

1. Construct the learning data. Let us assume that the u number of the tuples exists.

2. Compute the probability. The probability which the token t'_1 not recognized belongs to the entity e'_2 is computed by the equation (4). Let us suppose that the token t_4 is recognized as the entity e_4, the token t_5 is as the entity e_5, and the token t_6 is as the entity e_6. Here, u is the number of the tuples in the learning data, and $\sharp of item$ is the number of items satisfying $t'_1 = e'_2$ and $t_i = e_i$ at the same time for any i.

$$
\begin{aligned}
P(t'_1 = e'_2 | t_4 &= e_4, t_5 = e_5, t_6 = e_6) \\
&= P(t'_1 = e'_2, t_4 = e_4) + P(t'_1 = e'_2, t_5 = e_5) + P(t'_1 = e'_2, t_6 = e_6) \\
&= \frac{\sharp of item(t'_1 = e'_2 \& t_4 = e_4)}{u} \times \frac{\sharp of item(t_4 = e_4)}{u} \\
&+ \frac{\sharp of item(t'_1 = e'_2 \& t_5 = e_5)}{u} \times \frac{\sharp of item(t_5 = e_5)}{u} \\
&+ \frac{\sharp of item(t'_1 = e'_2 \& t_6 = e_6)}{u} \times \frac{\sharp of item(t_6 = e_6)}{u}
\end{aligned} \tag{4}
$$

3.2   Semi-automatic Domain Knowledge Expansion

Semi-automatic domain knowledge expansion is to extract the expandable candidates automatically from the first manual domain knowledge and to select the domain knowledge to be expanded manually. Most wrappers are induced based on the domain knowledge constructed by the first domain expert. However, when the entry of domain knowledge does not exist, the system can not induce the wrapper of the sites. These occur because labels of sites are not found in the entries of domain knowledge and because the kinds of the format or the delimiter are different. Therefore, it is necessary to expand the first domain knowledge in order to deal with the structure and content changes. In case of failing the wrapper induction, we try to expand the domain knowledge to induce the wrapper which can recognize the structure of the current sites by using the extracted data. Labels and delimiters extracted previously will be the value in the domain knowledge. However, it is impossible to extract new labels and new delimiters by the extracted result. Since the value can recognize several formats, we can induce labels and delimiters by expanding the domain knowledge semi-automatically.

Let us suppose the following for the learning of the domain knowledge.

- The slot is composed of the label, the delimiter, and the value. The template is the set of slots.
- The element information of slots is composed of the value type representing of the format of the value and the property representing the relation information among the elements.
- Delimiters consist of symbols and, by using them, we can separate the text into several formats.
- The value of slots is used to determine the most appropriate entities by using the learning data. If entities are determined, labels are enrolled as labels of entities and delimiters are enrolled as delimiters of the entities.

For sites of failing the induction of the wrapper, we analyze the structure of the sites and produce the tree of the object. If the object is identified, the candidates of the value are selected to expand the domain knowledge. And then, we determine values, labels, and delimiters and compute the probabilities by using them. The entities, the labels and the properties are decided by the computed probabilities. The determined elements are added to the appropriate part of the domain knowledge. Finally, the wrapper is reproduced. Because the domain knowledge is expanded by using the learning data, the new induced wrapper can extract the more precise information. The following steps are repeated in all slots of the templates.

- The recognition of the value
  We compare the data of the object site to the data of the existing sites. At first, we compare the types and, in case of the same value types, compute the probabilities on the same slots. The more many word sets of the existing site and the object site are overlapped, the more the probabilities of the slots are high. We calculate the vector similarity between the word vector of the extracted data and the word vector of the candidate object. We determine the slots of the high similarity.
- The recognition of the labels
  If the slots and the values are decided, we choose the labels in the candidate objects. Labels are the different values with the existing domain knowledge and can be the combined value between the enrolled symbols and values.
- The recognition of the delimiters
  If the value and the labels are chosen, we can determine the delimiters. The most appropriate entities, labels, and delimiters are expanded in each item of the domain knowledge.

3.3   Information Integration of Sub-linked Pages

Information integration of sub-linked pages is to integrate the extracted result of the current pages and sub-linked pages by searching the sub-linked pages of the current pages. Many sites show only the brief information in the first page. When users want to see the detailed information of the items, the sites show the detailed information linked by the hyperlinked pages. This construction of the sites can make users recognize the brief information at a glance. However, if the first page of the sites provides too much information to users, they may take a long time to examine the first page. Moreover, in order to show much information to users, the sites have to take much data at a time from the database. This may cause the operation time of the web program to be long. Thus, it is inconvenient for users to obtain the necessary information because of the slow access time. Therefore, in order to acquire the sufficient information about the items, we must consider the sub-linked pages properly. Our system extracts the detailed information of items by using the hyperlink as follows:

- When inducing the wrapper
    1. The system identifies the boundary of each item by analyzing the pattern of the information in the first page.
    2. The system confirms the useful information by tracking the hyperlink within the identified boundary. The useful information is the pages which many entities are identified by referencing the domain knowledge.
    3. If the sub-linked information is useful, the system stores the identified entities and the location of the link in the wrapper.
- When extracting the information
    1. The system reads the wrapper and decides if the information of the sub-linked page is extracted.
    2. The system extracts the information in the first page and, if there is the extraction mark of the hyperlink, extracts the information in the sub-linked page.
    3. The system integrates the information between the first page and the sub-linked page.

4   Experimental Results

In this paper, after the wrapper is induced, the system constructs the learning data by the induced wrapper. Our system constructs the learning data by the batch process automatically, not manually, according to the domain. When the learning data are constructed at first, the system can induce the improper wrapper. The reason is that the first learning data is insufficient. By expanding the learning data, the more the wrapper is induced, the more the wrapper is precise. The evaluation data of the wrapper induction are seven movie sites such as Core Cinema, Joy Cinema, and so on. Because movie sites have the characteristics to be updated periodically, wrapper induction is performed about recent data to detect slot-token patterns. Since our knowledge for wrapper induction is composed of Korean language, we test our method about Korean movie sites. We determine 12 of entities such as title, genre, director, actor, grade, music, production, running time, and so on. Table 1 shows seven web sites used in the experiments.

Table 1. Seven web sites used in the experiments

Domain	Name	Site URL
Movie	Site	http://www.corecine.co.kr/movie/list_cinecore.htm
Movie	Site	http://www.joycine.com/omni/time.asp
Movie	Site	http://www.maxmovie.com/join/cineplex/default.as
Movie	Site	http://www.maxmovie.com/movieinfo/reserve/movieinfo_reserve.asp
Movie	Site	http://www.nkino.com/moviedom/coming_movie.as
Movie	Site	http://www.ticketpark.com/Main/MovieSearch.asp
Movie	Site	http://www.yesticket.co.kr/ticketmall/resv/movie_main.as

The first evaluation measure is the extraction precision of sites in the equation (5).

$$Precision = \frac{the\ number\ of\ the\ extracted\ entities}{the\ number\ of\ the\ entities\ to\ be\ extracted} \times 100 \qquad (5)$$

Here, the number of the extracted entities is the number of entities recognized in learning the wrapper and the number of the entities to be extracted is the number of the entities defined in the movie domain. In addition, the average precision of all sites is computed by the equation (6).

$$Average\ precision = \frac{the\ total\ precision\ of\ each\ site}{the\ number\ of\ sites} \qquad (6)$$

We evaluate three kinds of extraction methods such as 'Knowledge Only', 'Link Extraction', and 'Label Detection'. 'Knowledge Only' is the method of extracting movie information by using only knowledge without considering hyperlinking and token probability based recognition. This method is to extract the information according to XML based knowledge. 'Link Extraction' means the method of using hyperlinking in addition to the baseline method. 'Label Detection' is the method of considering both hyperlinking and token probability based recognition in addition to the baseline method. Table 2 shows the precision of three kinds of methods.

The average precision of each method is shown in Figure 3. The performance of 'Link Extraction' and 'Label Detection' is better than that of 'Knowledge Only'

Table 2. Results of three kinds of methods

Sites	Knowledge Only	Link Extraction	Label Detection
Site A	0.73	0.84	0.93
Site B	0.76	0.83	0.94
Site C	0.78	0.87	0.96
Site D	0.64	0.84	0.94
Site E	0.72	0.85	0.93
Site F	0.73	0.87	0.94
Site G	0.72	0.82	0.91

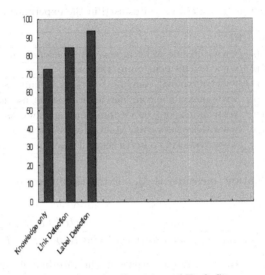

Fig. 3. Average Precision of Each Site

significantly. In other words, experimental results show that it is important to consider hyperlinking and token probability based recognition in inducing the wrapper and our system can extract the information appropriately.

The comparison between our system and other systems is shown in Table 3. The eight information extraction systems based on structured web sites don't extract the information in the free text. 'Mutislot' is the factor to compare if the system can extract the information of multisolts. That is, it represent the integration of several related information. 'WIEN', 'STALKER' and our system can process the multislots. Moreover, our system can extract information by the probabilistic based method for entities without labels. We can extract the detailed information by using hyperlink. Finally, through the expansion of the domain knowledge, we can extract the data of new formats by considering the dynamic properties.

Table 3. Comparison with other systems

	Structured Document	Multislot	No Label	Hyperlink	Knowledge Expansion
ShopBot	O	X	X	X	manual
WIEN	O	O	X	X	manual
SoftMealy	O	X	X	X	manual
STALKER	O	O	X	X	manual
RAPIER	O	X	X	X	manual
SRV	O	X	X	X	manual
WHISK	O	O	X	X	manual
Proposed Method	O	O	O	O	semiautomatic

5   Conclusion

In this paper, we propose the probabilistic wrapper induction system which can extract the information in the web pages efficiently. Our system tries to expand the domain knowledge semiautomatically, to use the hyperlink for the detailed information, and to utilize the probabilistic based method for the unlabeled entity. The experimental results show that our system can extract the web information precisely without the user intervention. Our system can perform the real-time extraction. That is, if the wrapper is induced, the system can extract the web information periodically and rapidly. Moreover, through the expansion of the domain knowledge, we can extract the data of new formats by considering the dynamic properties. Finally, our system provides the convenient graphic user interface for the wrapper induction and the information extraction.

However, our method can't extract the text information from the imaged data and the dynamic data(i.e flash). Many web pages have the imaged button, the imaged character, and the flash. In order to extract the text information from these data, we will try to work the pattern recognition technique and the flash analyzed technique in the future.

References

1. B. Adelberg, NoDoSE- A tool for Semi-Automatically Extracting Structured and Semistructured Data from Text Documents, ACM SIGMOD, 1998.
2. A. Arasu, H. Garcia-Molina, Extracting structured data from web pages, ACM SIGMOD, 2003.
3. R. Baumgartner, S. Flesca, G. Gottlob, Declarative Information Extraction, Web Crawling, and Recursive Wrapping with Lixto, Lecture Notes in Computer Science, 2001.
4. A. Blum, T. Mitchell, Combining Labeled and Unlabeled Data with Co-Training, Proceedings of the 1998 Conference on Computational Learning Theory, 1998.
5. D. Buttler, L. Liu, and C. Pu, A Fully Automated Object Extraction System for the World Wide Web, Proceedings of the 2001 International Conference on Distrubuted Computing Systems, May 2001.
6. M. E. Califf. Relational Learning Techniques for Natural Language Information Extraction, PhD thesis, University of Texas at Austin, August 1998.
7. F. Ciravegna. Learning to Tag for Information Extraction from Text, Workshop Machine Learning for Information Extraction, European Conference on Artifical Intelligence ECCAI, August 2000. Berlin, Germany, 2000.
8. W. Cohen, M. Hurst, and L. S. Jensen. A flexible learning system for wrapping tables and lists in html documents, The Eleventh International World Wide Web Conference WWW-2002, 2002.
9. V. Crescenzi, G. Mecca, P. Merialdo, RoadRunner: Towards Automatic Data Extraction from Large Web Sites, Proceedings of 27th International Conference on Very Large Data Bases, 2001.
10. L. Eikvil,Information Extraction from World Wide Web: A Survey, Report No. 945, ISBN 82-539-0429-0, July, 1999.

11. D.W. Embley, D.M. Campbell, Y.S. Jiang, Y.-K. Ng, R.D. Smith, S.W. Liddle, D.W. Quass, A Conceptual-Modeling Approach to Extracting Data from the Web, International Conference on Conceptual Modeling / the Entity Relationship Approach, 1998.
12. D.Freitag,Machine Learning for Information Extraction in Informal Domains, PhD thesis, Computer Science Department, Carnegie Mellon University, Pittsburgh, PA, November 1998.
13. D. Freitag, N. Kushmerick. Boosted Wrapper Induction, Proceedings of the Seventh National Conference on Artificial, pages 577-583, 2000.
14. J. R. Gruser, L. Raschid, M. E. Vidal, and L. Bright, Wrapper Generation for Web Accessible Data Sources, Proceedings of the 3rd IFCIS International Conference on Cooperative Information Systems, NewYork, August, 1998.
15. C. N. Hsu, C. C. Chang, Finite-State Transducers for Semi-Structured Text Mining, Workshop on Text Mining IJCAI 99, 1999.
16. M. Junker, M. Sintek, M. Rinck. Learning for Text Categorization and Information Extraction with ILP, Proc. Workshop on Learning Language in Logic, June 1999.
17. N. Kushmerick, Gleaning the Web, IEEE Intelligent Systems, vol.14, no.2, pp. 20-22, 1999.
18. N. Kushmerick, B. Thomas. Intelligent Information Agents R&D in Europe: An AgentLink perspective, chapter Adaptive Information Extraction: A Core Technology for Information Agents. Springer, 2002.
19. L. Liu, C. Pu, and W. Han, XWRAP: An XML-enabled Wrapper Construction System for Web Information Sources, Proceedings of the 16th International Conference on Data Engineering, 2000.
20. P. Merialdo, P. Atzeni, G. Mecca, Design and development of data-intensive web sites: The araneus approach, ACM Transaction on Internet Technology TOIT 3(1): 49-92, 2003.

Si-SEEKER: Ontology-Based Semantic Search over Databases

Jun Zhang[1,2,3], Zhaohui Peng[1,2], Shan Wang[1,2], and Huijing Nie[1,2]

[1] School of Information, Renmin University of China, Beijing 100872, P.R. China
{zhangjun11, pengch, swang, hjnie}@ruc.edu.cn
[2] Key Laboratory of Data Engineering and Knowledge Engineering
(Renmin University of China), MOE, Beijing 100872, P.R. China
[3] Computer Science and Technology College, Dalian Maritime University,
Dalian 116026, P.R. China

Abstract. Keyword Search Over Relational Databases(KSORD) has been widely studied. While keyword search is helpful to access databases, it has inherent limitations. Keyword search doesn't exploit the semantic relationships between keywords such as hyponymy, meronymy and antonymy, so the recall rate and precision rate are often dissatisfactory. In this paper, we have designed an ontology-based semantic search engine over databases called Si-SEEKER based on our i-SEEKER system which is a KSORD system with our candidate network selection techniques. Si-SEEKER extends i-SEEKER with semantic search by exploiting hierarchical structure of domain ontology and a generalized vector space model to compute semantic similarity between a user query and annotated data. We combine semantic search with keyword search over databases to improve the recall rate and precision rate of the KSORD system. We experimentally evaluate our Si-SEEKER system on the DBLP data set and show that Si-SEEKER is more effective than i-SEEKER in terms of the recall rate and precision rate of retrieval results.

1 Introduction

Keyword Search Over Relational Databases(KSORD) has been widely studied [1], and many prototypes have been developed, such as SEEKER[2], IR-Style[4], BANKS[6], and DBXplorer[5],etc. While keyword search is helpful to access databases, it has inherent limitations. Keyword search is only based on keyword matching and doesn't exploit the semantic relationships between keywords such as hyponymy, meronymy, or antonymy, so the recall rate and precision rate are often dissatisfactory.

With the increasing research interest on ontology and semantic web, ontology-based semantic search has attracted more and more attention in Information Retrieval(IR) community [16,17] and database community[7,8,9].

An ontology consists of a set of concepts linked by directed edges which form a graph. The edges in the ontology specify the relationships between the concepts(e.g. "subClassOf" or "partOf"). The ontology could be formal with respect to the implementation of a transitive "subClassOf" hierarchy, which connects all

J. Lang, F. Lin, and J. Wang (Eds.): KSEM 2006, LNAI 4092, pp. 599–611, 2006.
© Springer-Verlag Berlin Heidelberg 2006

concepts. Although other hierarchies can be defined , the "subClassOf" hierarchy is the most important relationship between the concepts and mainly used for query processing[18]. Ontology can be used to provide semantic annotations for text data in the database to create semantic indexes which support semantic search, just like the full-text indexes to support keyword search.

Ontology-based semantic search is to utilize domain-specific knowledge to obtain more accurate answers on a semantical basis by comparing concepts rather than keywords. Not only the syntactical keywords between a user query and text objects are matched, but also the meaning of them[10].

Database community has been studying how to exploit ontology to support semantic matching in RDBMS[7]. However, to the best of our knowledge, none of the existing KSORD systems currently exploits domain-specific ontology to provide semantic search over databases.

We design a novel ontology-based semantic search engine over databases called Si-SEEKER based on our i-SEEKER system. i-SEEKER is a KSORD system extending SEEKER[2] with our candidate network selection techniques, while Si-SEEKER extends i-SEEKER with semantic search. The overview of an Ontology-based Semantic Search Over Relational Database(OSSORD) system comparing with that of a KSORD system is shown in Fig. 1. A KSORD system employs the full-text index and database schema to search databases by keyword matching, while an OSSORD system utilizes more metadata including ontology and semantic indexes to search databases by semantic matching.

Our Si-SEEKER exploits hierarchical structure of domain-specific ontology to compute semantic similarity between a user keyword query and annotated data, and returns more semantic results in a higher recall rate and precision rate than the KSORD system. In Si-SEEKER, the data in databases are annotated with the concepts in the ontology. Thus semantic indexes are created before

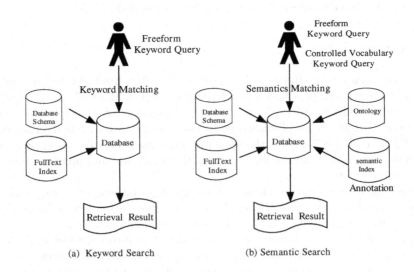

(a) Keyword Search   (b) Semantic Search

Fig. 1. Comparing keyword search with semantic Search over databases

query processing. When a user keyword query comes, it is transformed into a concept query in the same concept space of the ontology, and a generalized vector space model(GVSM)[11] is employed to compute semantic similarity between the concept query and annotated data. As a result, semantic results will be returned. We also combine semantic search with keyword search to tolerance to the incompleteness of ontology and annotations of data for the sake of robustness. Our experiments show that the framework is effective.

The rest of this paper is organized as follows. Section 2 reviews existing work and analyzes their limitations and drawbacks. Section 3 describes our novel framework in detail. Our experiments are presented in Section 4, and we conclude with summary and future work in section 5.

2   Related Work

Currently, many KSORD systems, such as SEEKER[2],IR-Style[4],BANKS[6], and DBXplorer[5], rely on the IR engine of Relational Database Management System(RDBMS) to index and retrieve text attributes, and to rank the retrieval results. One of their drawbacks is that they lack semantic search capability. Thus, even though they answer user keyword queries with 100% precision, the recall of these systems is relatively low. ObjectRank[3] system applies authority-based ranking to keyword search in databases modeled as labeled graphs. It has semantic search capability to some extent, for it could retrieve the results which have no occurrences of user query keywords. While ObjectRank has limited semantic search capability, our work exploits domain ontology to provide more powerful semantic search over databases.

Souripriya Das et al. presented a method to support ontology-based semantic matching in RDBMS[7], and built a prototype implementation on Oracle RDBMS. However, their approach makes ontology-based semantic matching available as part of SQL. Piero Bonatti et al. proposed an ontology extended relation(OER) model which contained an ordinary relation as well as an associated ontology that conveyed semantic meaning about the terms being used, and extended the relational algebra to query OERs[9]. However, our Si-SEEKER is fundamentally different from the above works, for it extends a KSORD system to implement ontology-based semantic search over databases in a simpler manner to access databases.

In IR community, David Vallet et al. proposed an ontology-based information retrieval model to improve search over large document repositories[16]. [17] presented an ontology-based information retrieval method. Both of them employed TF-IDF algorithm[19,20] to compute the weight of annotations, while TF-IDF algorithm is useful in long documents, but not in short documents like the text attributes in databases[14]. The former made use of classic Vector Space Model(VSM)[19] to compute the semantic similarity, while the latter computed the intersection of query concepts and document concepts in an ontology.

In semantic search, a key issue is how to compute semantic similarity. Several distance-based methods for computing semantic similarity were introduced in [11,10], while information content based method was proposed in [15]. Troels Andreasen et al[10]. studied ontology-based querying. [13] discussed using knowledge hierarchies to overcome keyword search limitations. We employ a Generalized Vector Space Model(GVSM) to compute the semantic similarity between a user query and annotated data by exploiting the hierarchical domain structure[11].

3 Our Framework

3.1 System Architecture

After analyzing i-SEEKER system, we find out it is Tuple Set(TS) creator in the KSORD system that does simple keyword search based on the IR engine of RDBMS and lacks semantic search capability. TS creator exploits full-text indexes to search databases and creates a tuple set for each relation with text attributes in the database(see Fig.2(a)).

We propose a novel ontology-based semantic search engine architecture called Si-SEEKER which extends the TS creator of i-SEEKER with other three semantic related components: COncept(CO) extractor, SEmantic(SE) searcher and Tuple Sets(TS) merger(see Fig.2(b)).

In Si-SEEKER system, when a freeform or controlled keyword query comes, on the one hand, TS creator performs its original keyword search based on the

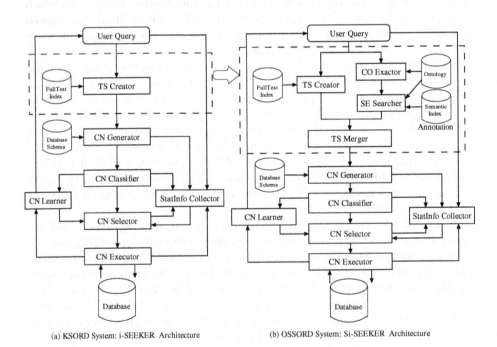

(a) KSORD System: i-SEEKER Architecture   (b) OSSORD System: Si-SEEKER Architecture

Fig. 2. Comparing i-SEEKER with Si-SEEKER

IR engine of RDBMS and creates a keyword-based tuple set(KTS) for each relation with text attributes(R) in the database. On the other hand, CO extractor extracts concepts from the user query keywords and transforms the user query into a concept query, and SE searcher executes semantic search to generate a semantic tuple set(STS) for each R by exploiting preconstructed semantic indexes and GVSM to compute semantic similarity between the concept query and annotated data in the database. TS merger integrates KTS and STS into a combined tuple set(CTS) for each R. So, candidate networks(CNs) will be generated by CN generator based on those combined tuple sets. Intuitively, a CTS with semantic tuples holds more tuples than the relevant KTS, thus more semantic results will be generated, so the recall rate and precision rate of Si-SEEKER ought to increase. However, the quality of semantic search depends heavily on the completeness of the domain-specific ontology and the quality of the annotations of data in the database. For the sake of robustness, we combine semantic search with keyword search through the component of TS merger.

3.2 Ontology, Annotation, Semantic Index and Concept Extractor

We use ACM Computing Classification System(1998)(ACM CCS1998)[1] as a simple ontology on computer science domain to support semantic search on DBLP[2] data set. There are 1475 concepts and 2 relationships(subClassOf, relatedTo) in this ontology. We mainly exploit the hierarchical domain structure(subClassOf hierarchy) to compute the semantic similarity between a user keyword query and annotated data in the database(see Fig.3).

The annotations come from the category information of SIGMOD XML data set[3], and semantic indexes are created based on the annotations. There are 477 annotated papers and 1369 semantic index entries.

ACM digital library[4] adopts ACM CCS1998 to classify all of their collected papers, and can provide an extended keyword query language like CCS:'Data models' to do simple classification search which doesn't exploit the hierarchical domain structure or compute semantic similarity between a user query and classified papers. DBLP bibliography server provides keywords querying and subjects browsing. However, we exploit the ACM CCS1998 hierarchical domain structure to provide semantic search over DBLP data set.

Concept Extractor has been widely studied in natural language processing [12]. We implemented a simple concept extractor based on Stanford Parser[5].

3.3 Semantic Similarity

A key issue of semantic search is how to compute semantic similarity between a user query and the query data. Our framework mainly exploits the hierarchical

---

[1] http://www.acm.org/class/1998/ccs98.html

[2] http://dblp.uni-trier.de/

[3] http://www.sigmod.org/record/xml/XMLSigmodRecordMar1999.zip

[4] http://portal.acm.org/dl.cfm

[5] http://nlp.stanford.edu/software/lex-parser.shtml

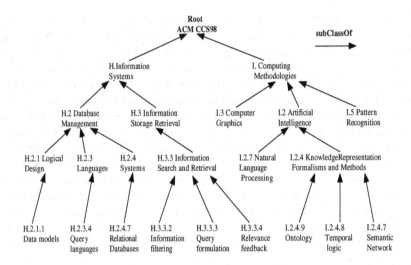

Fig. 3. A portion of Computer Science domain ontology from ACM CCS1998

domain structure(e.g. subClassof) of domain-specific ontology and GVSM[11] to compute the semantic similarity between a user query and annotated data in the database.

An ontology can be formally represented as a hierarchy of a concept space, user queries and data are all mapped to the same concept space. Then, the semantic similarity between a user query and annotated data can be computed on the concept space. First, we give some definitions(definition 1, 3 and 4 come from [8,11]).

Definition 1. Hierarchy $H(S, \leq)$: *Suppose $(S, \leq)$ is a partially ordered set. A hierarchy $H(S, \leq)$ for $(S, \leq)$ is the Hasse diagram for $(S, \leq)$, which is a directed acyclic graph whose set of nodes is S and has a minimal set of edges such that there is a path from u to v in the Hasse diagram iff $u \leq v$.*

Definition 2. Ontology $O(C, R, H)$: *A ontology is represented as $O(C, R, H)$, where C is a set of concepts $\{c_1, c_2, ..., c_i\}$, R is a set of relationships $\{r_1, r_2, ..., r_j\}$, and H is a set of hierarchies $H(C,r)$. There is a root in $H(C,r)$ which is the most abstract concept in C.*

For example, in the ontology of ACM CCS1998, r is the relationship of 'subClassOf'. A portion of H(C,subClassOf) is shown in Fig.3. Although other hierarchies can be defined , the 'subClassOf' hierarchy is the most important relationship between concepts and is mainly used for query processing.

Definition 3. Concept Depth $depth(c)$: *Define the depth of a concept c node(denoted as depth(c)) in a hierarchy $H(C,r)$ of ontology $O(C, R, H)$ is the number of edges on the path from the root of O to that concept node.*

Definition 4. Lowest Common Ancestor $LCA(c_1, c_2)$: *Given two concepts c_1 and c_2 in O, define the Lowest Common Ancestor $LCA(c_1, c_2)$ to be the node of greatest depth that is an ancestor of both c_1 and c_2. This LCA is always well defined since the two concepts have at least one common ancestor, the root node, and no two common ancestors can have the same depth.*

So, for any two concepts c_1 and c_2, their dot product is defined as[11]:

$$\overrightarrow{c_1} \cdot \overrightarrow{c_2} = \frac{2 * depth(LCA_O(c_1, c_2))}{depth(c_1) + depth(c_2)} \quad (1)$$

where in the GVSM $\overrightarrow{c_1}$ and $\overrightarrow{c_2}$ are asserted to be not really perpendicular to each other since they are somewhat similar to the LCA. This is different from the classic vector space model in which any two different vectors are supposed to be perpendicular to each other and the dot product of them is zero.

Example 1. *Take the ontology of ACM CCS1998 as an example(see Fig.3). Let c_1 is H.2.3.4, c_2 is H.2.4, then $LCA(c_1, c_2) = LCA(H.2.3.4, H.2.4) = H.2$, $depth(c_1) = depth(H.2.3.4) = 4$, $depth(c_2) = depth(H.2.4) = 3$, $depth(LCA(c_1, c_2)) = depth(H.2) = 2$. So, $\overrightarrow{c_1} \cdot \overrightarrow{c_2} = (2 * 2)/(4 + 3) = 0.5714$.*

Suppose a relation R has m textual attributes and n tuples, $a_i(1 \le i \le m)$ stands for a textual attribute in R, and $r(r \in R)$ stands for a tuple in R.

In keyword search, keyword queries and data are viewed as keyword vectors. So, we can define a keyword query Q_k and the similarity between Q_k and tuple r in relation R as follows:

Definition 5. Keyword Query Q_k: *A keyword query Q_k is a set of keywords, denoted as $Q_k(k_1, k_2, ..., k_l)$, $k_j(1 \le j \le l)$ is a keyword, and each keyword k_j has a weight W_{qj}. Suppose Q_k is OR semantics among the query keywords.*

The similarity $Sim_k(a_i, Q_k)$ between a_i and Q_k comes from the IR engine of RDBMS, while the similarity $Sim_k(r, Q_k)$ between r and Q_k can be defined as:

$$Sim_k(r, Q_k) = \frac{\sum_{i=1}^{m} Sim_k(a_i, Q_k)}{m} \quad (2)$$

But in semantic search, keyword queries and data are viewed as concept vectors. We define a concept query Q_c and a_i as:

Definition 6. Concept Query Q_c: *A concept query Q_c is a set of Concepts which are extracted from a user keyword query by concept extractor, denoted as $Q_c(c_1, c_2, ..., c_{l_1})$, $c_j(1 \le j \le l_1)$ is a concept in an ontology O, and each concept c_j has a weight W_{qj}. We suppose Q_c is OR semantics among the query concepts, and define the vector of Q_c as:*

$$\overrightarrow{Q_c} = \sum_{j=1}^{l_1} W_{qj} \overrightarrow{c_j} \quad (3)$$

Definition 7. Concept Text Attribute a_i: *Define each textual attribute a_i as a vector of concepts which are manually semantically annotated based ontology O, denoted as $a_i(c_1, c_2, ..., c_{l_2})$, $c_k(1 \leq k \leq l_2)$ is a concept in the ontology O, and each concept c_k has a weight W_{a_ik}. We define the vector of a_i as:*

$$\vec{a_i} = \sum_{k=1}^{l_2} W_{a_ik}\vec{c_k} \tag{4}$$

The concept weight W_{qj} in the concept vector of Q_c captures the relative concept importance($W_o(c)$) in the domain ontology, which can be assigned manually by ontology designers. In addition to $W_o(c)$, the concept weight W_{a_ik} in text attribute a_i also captures the relative concept importance in itself, which can be assigned manually by data annotators.

So, we can define the semantic similarity $Sim_s(a_i, Q_c)$ between concept text attribute a_i and concept query Q_c by the generalized cosine-similarity measure (GCSM)[11] as:

$$Sim_s(a_i, Q_c) = \frac{\vec{a_i} \cdot \vec{Q_c}}{\sqrt{\vec{a_i} \cdot \vec{a_i}}\sqrt{\vec{Q_c} \cdot \vec{Q_c}}}$$
$$= \frac{\sum_{k=1}^{l_2} \sum_{j=1}^{l_1} W_{a_ik}W_{qj}\vec{c_k} \cdot \vec{c_j}}{\sqrt{\sum_{k=1}^{l_2} \sum_{j=1}^{l_2} W_{a_ik}W_{a_ij}\vec{c_k} \cdot \vec{c_j}}\sqrt{\sum_{k=1}^{l_1} \sum_{j=1}^{l_1} W_{qk}W_{qj}\vec{c_k} \cdot \vec{c_j}}} \tag{5}$$

where the dot product of $\vec{c_k}$ and $\vec{c_j}$ can be computed as equation 1.

The semantic similarity $Sim_s(r, Q_c)$ between tuple r in R and concept query Q_c can be defined as:

$$Sim_s(r, Q_c) = \frac{\sum_{i=1}^{m} Sim_s(a_i, Q_c)}{m} \tag{6}$$

3.4   Semantic Search

In Si-SEEKER, semantic searcher creates a semantic tuple set(ST) for each relation R(denoted as STS(R)). $Sim_s(r, Q_c)$ will be computed for each tuple r in R, and the tuple r will be picked out if its $Sim_s(r, Q_c)$ is greater than a semantic similarity threshold(denoted as ε_{ssim}). ε_{ssim} is an experience parameter which we determine empirically as 0.5(see Sect. 4.3). Our semantic search algorithm is shown in Algorithm 1..

In order to perform efficient semantic search, we have done some pre-computing work, including the depth of every concept c of ontology O, the LCA of any two concepts, and the dot product of any two concepts. However, we find that our semantic searcher is not so efficient as the IR engine of RDBMS. In this paper, we mainly evaluate the effectiveness of our framework and confine ourselves to the improvement of the recall rate and precision rate of the KSORD system. We leave the improvement of efficiency of our framework to future work.

Algorithm 1.   Semantic Search Algorithm (SSA)

Input: $Q_k(K_1, K_2, ..., K_t)$,Database Schema(DS),ε_{ssim}
Output: a set of STS(R)
Begin

  1: convert Q_k to Q_c by CO extractor
  2: **for** each relation R in DS with m text attributes and n tuples **do**
  3:   **for** j = 1 to n **do**
  4:     $Sim_s(r, Q_c) = 0$;
  5:     **for** i = 1 to m **do**
  6:       $Sim_s(r, Q_c)+ = sim_s(a_i, Q_c)$ computed as equation 5;
  7:     **end for**
  8:     $Sim_s(r, Q_c)/ = m$
  9:     **if** $(Sim_s(r, Q_c) > \varepsilon_{ssim})$ **then**
10:       add r to STS(R);
11:     **end if**
12:   **end for**
13: **end for**
14: return a set of STS(R);

End.

3.5 Combining Semantic Search and Keyword Search

The quality of semantic search depends heavily on the completeness of the domain-specific ontology and the quality of the annotations of data. If domain-specific ontology and its semantic annotations are incomplete, semantic searcher in Si-SEEKER performs poorly. For incomplete ontology, none of concepts could be extracted from some keyword queries, and for incomplete annotations of data, semantic searcher may return no results. So, it is necessary to combine semantic search with keyword search through the component of TS merger for the sake of system robustness.

However, merging KTS and STS is not so simple. Firstly, our semantic similarity score(Sim_s) always ranges between 0 and 1, while the keyword similarity score(Sim_k) from the IR engine of different RDBMS may range differently. For example, the IR-style score from Oracle 9i RDBMS ranges between 0 and 100, and that from PostgreSQL RDBMS ranges between 0 and 1. So, we need to normalize Sim_k to the range [0,1] when we use Oracle RDBMS. We employ min-max normalization performing a linear transformation on the Sim_k to the range [0,1] in the following formula:

$$Sim_k = \frac{Sim_k - min(Sim_k)}{max(Sim_k) - min(Sim_k)} \qquad (7)$$

where $min(Sim_k)$ and $max(Sim_k)$ are the minimum and maximum values of Sim_k. Take Oracle 9i RDBMS as an example, $min(Sim_k)$ is 0 and $max(Sim_k)$ is 100.

Secondly, even though Sim_s and Sim_k are in the same range or have the same value, it is difficult to determine how to combine the two kinds of similarity measures.

Our TS merger combines Sim_s with Sim_k for a relation R to generate a combined tuple set as the following formula[16]:

$$Sim_c(r, Q) = t \times Sim_s(r, Q_c) + (1 - t) \times Sim_k(r, Q_k) \qquad (8)$$

where t is an experience parameter and may differ for different data set. We adopt the following adjustment to the equation 8 in our experiments:

$$t = \begin{cases} 0.6 & \text{if } Sim_s(r, Q_c) \neq 0 \text{ and } Sim_k(r, Q_k) \neq 0 \\ 1 & \text{else if } Sim_k(r, Q_k) = 0 \\ 0.3 & \text{else } Sim_s(r, Q_c) = 0 \end{cases} \qquad (9)$$

4   Experimental Evaluation

4.1   Experimental Environment

We ran our experiments using the Oracle 9i RDBMS on the platform of Windows XP SP2 and IBM NoteBook computer with Intel Pentium 1.86GHZ CPU and 1.0GB of RAM memory. Based on i-SEEKER system, we implemented our Si-SEEKER in Java and connected to the RDBMS through JDBC. The IR engine was the Oracle9i Text extension.

We used the DBLP data set for our experiments, which we decomposed into relations according to the schema shown in Fig. 4. We used ACM CCS1998 as our test ontology which has 1475 concepts and 2 relationships(subClassOf, relatedTo). We mainly exploited the subClassOf domain hierarchy to compute semantic similarity(see Fig.3). The annotations came from the category information of SIGMOD XML data set, and semantic indexes were created based on these annotations. There were 477 annotated papers and 1369 semantic index entries.

4.2   Evaluation Methodology

We extracted all the concepts which had annotations from our ontology O as a query concept list, and constructed all our benchmark concept queries(BCQs). For a BCQ $Q_c(c_1, c_2, ..., c_l)$, we extracted all annotation instances of the query's concepts and their sub-concepts in the ontology O as the benchmark results of Q_c. So, we could evaluate the effectiveness of our semantic search and keyword search in terms of the recall rate and precision rate. We explain our evaluation methodology through the following example(recall that user queries are OR semantic). As for top-k results, we got only the top k results to evaluate the effectiveness of our framework.

Example 2. *As for the relation Papers(see Fig.4), suppose the concept query $Q_c(H.2)$(see Fig.3), and the concept H.2 is 'Database Management', the query concept H.2 and its all sub-concepts(e.g. H.2.1,H.2.2,H.2.3,H.2.1.1,etc) have a set of annotation instances T={pid1, pid2, pid3, pid4, pid5}, which are viewed as the benchmark results for $Q_c(H.2)$. pid1,pid2 and so on denote the paper ids which identify tuples in the relation Papers.*

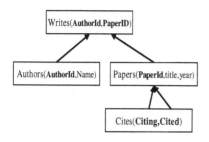

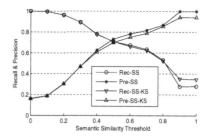

Fig. 4. The DBLP schema graph

Fig. 5. recall and precision of different semantic similarity threshold

When the keyword query Q('Database Management') comes, suppose the set K={pid1,pid10,pid11,pid30} is created by keyword search for keyword query $Q_k('DatabaseManagement')$, and the set S={pid1,pid2,pid3,pid4,pid6,pid7} is created by semantic search for concept query $Q_c(H.2)$ with ε_{ssim}. Then, the recall rate of Q_c is $|T \cap S|/|T| = 4/5 = 0.8$, while the precision of Q_c is $|T \cap S|/|S| = 4/6 = 0.667$. Similarly, the recall rate of Q_k is $|T \cap K|/|T| = 1/5 = 0.2$, while the precision of Q_k is $|T \cap K|/|K| = 1/4 = 0.25$.

4.3   Semantic Similarity Threshold

Semantic similarity threshold(ε_{ssim}) is a key parameter for semantic search which may vary with different data sets. ε_{ssim} is a tradeoff between the recall rate and the precision rate. Generally,the smaller ε_{ssim} is, the greater the recall rate is and the smaller the precision rate is, for more results are returned. If ε_{ssim} is set to zero, the recall rate may approach 100% while the precision may approach 0%. On the contrary, if ε_{ssim} is set to 1, the recall rate may approach 0% while the precision may approach 100%.

In Si-SEEKER, ε_{ssim} is determined empirically as 0.5, then a relatively good recall rate(70.8%) and precision rate(73.2%) on average may be achieved(see Fig.5 where let Rec_SS be the recall rate of semantic search(SS), Prec_SS be the precision rate of SS, Rec_SS_KK be the recall rate of semantic search combined with keyword search(SS_KS) and Prec_SS_KK be the precision rate of SS_KS). In fact, ε_{ssim} is not only related to a specific data set, but also related to the number of query concepts transformed from a user keyword query. Thus ε_{ssim} may be adjusted dynamically in runtime. ε_{ssim} may be set to different values by different end-users, who may prefer a high recall(precision) rate of retrieval results to a high precision(recall) rate.

4.4   Effectiveness Evaluation of Our Framework

The recall rate and precision rate of Si-SEEKER were averaged over 80 user keyword queries, where each keyword was selected randomly from the set of extracted concept list. We compared three search methods: keyword search(KS), semantic search(SS), semantic search combined with keyword search(SS_KS). In the following figures, let topk be the value of top-k.

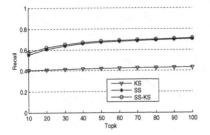
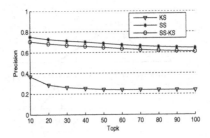

Fig. 6. Recall: Fix $\varepsilon_{ssim} = 0.5$, and var; topk

Fig. 7. Precision: Fix $\varepsilon_{ssim} = 0.5$, and vary topk

Figure 6 shows the effect of topk on the recall rate of three different search methods, while figure 7 shows the effect of topk on the precision rate of those methods. With the growing number of topk, the recall rate increases while the precision rate decreases. The two figures also state that SS outperforms KS by 56.8% more in the recall rate and 165% more in the precision rate on average, and that SS_KS outperforms KS by 59.4% more in the recall rate and 149.8% more in the precision rate. We also can see SS_KS has slightly greater recall rate than SS, but slightly smaller precision rate than SS.

5   Conclusion and Future Work

We have presented a novel ontology-based semantic search engine called Si-SEEKER to perform semantic search over databases which exploits hierarchical structure of domain ontology and GVSM to compute semantic similarity between a user query and annotated data. The effectiveness of our framework was evaluated in terms of the recall rate and precision rate of retrieval results. Our experiments show that Si-SEEKER outperforms i-SEEKER in the quality of retrieval results. In the future work, we will annotate more data in the DBLP data set to adjust the semantic similarity computing model for higher recall rate and precision rate, and also improve the efficiency of our semantic searcher.

Acknowledgement

This work is supported by the National Natural Science Foundation of China under Grant No.60473069 and 60496325.

References

1. S. Wang, K. Zhang. Searching Databases with Keywords. Journal of Computer Science and Technology, 20(1). 2005:55-62
2. J. Wen, S. Wang. SEEKER: Keyword-based Information Retrieval Over Relational Databases. Journal of Software,16(7). 2005:1270-1281

3. A. Balmin, V. Hristidis, Y. Papakonstantinou. ObjectRank: Authority-Based Keyword Search in Databases.VLDB,2004:564-575
4. V. Hristidis, L. Gravano, Y. Papakonstantinou. Efficient IR-Style Keyword Search over Relational Databases. VLDB, 2003:850-861.
5. S. Agrawal, S. Chaudhuri, and G. Das. DBXplorer:A System for keyword Search over Relational Databases.ICDE, 2002:5-16.
6. V. Kacholia, S. Pandit, S. Chakrabarti, et al. Sudarshan, Rushi Desai, Hrishikesh Karambelkar: Bidirectional Expansion For Keyword Search on Graph Databases. VLDB 2005:505-516.
7. S. Das, E.I. Chong, G. Eadon, J. Srinivasan. Supporting Ontology-Based Semantic matching in RDBMS. VLDB,2004:1054-1065
8. E. Hung, Y. Deng, V.S. Subrahmanian. TOSS: An Extension of TAX with Ontologies and Similarity Queries.SIGMOD,2004:719-730
9. P.A. Bonatti, Y. Deng, V. Subrahmanian. An Ontology-Extended Relational Algebra. In Proceedings of the IEEE International Conference on Information Reuse and Integration (IEEE IRI). 2003:192-199
10. T. Andreasen, H. Bulskov, and R. Knappe. On Ontology-based Querying. 18th International Joint Conference on Artificial Intelligence, Ontologies and Distributed Systems(IJCAI). 2003. 53-59
11. P. Ganesan, H. Garcia-Molina, and J. Widom. Exploiting Hierarchical Domain Structure to Compute Similarity. ACM Trans. Inf. Syst. 21(1). 2003:64-93
12. N. Bennett, Q. He, C. Chang, and B.R. Schatz. Concept extraction in the interspace prototype. Technical report, Dept. of Computer Science, University of Illinois at Urbana-Champaign, 1999.
13. R. LaBrie,R.S. Louis. Information Retrieval from Knowledge Management Systems: Using Knowledge Hierarchies to Overcome Keyword Limitations. Proceedings of the Ninth Americas Conference on Information Systems (AMCIS), 2003:2552-2562
14. B. Kang. A novel approach to semantic indexing based on concept.Proceedings of the 41st Annual Meeting on Association for Computational Linguistics,2003:44-49
15. P. Resnik. Using Information Content to Evaluate Semantic Similarity in a Taxonomy.Proceedings of IJCAI,1995:448-453
16. D. Vallet, M. Fernndez, P. Castells. An Ontology-Based Information Retrieval Model. ESWC 2005: 455-470
17. P. Varga, T. Mszros, C. Dezsnyi, et al. An Ontology-Based Information Retrieval System. IEA/AIE 2003: 359-368
18. J. Kohler, S. Philippi, M. Lange. SEMEDA: ontology based semantic integration of biological databases. BIONINFORMATICS,19(18),2003:2420-2427.
19. R. Baeza-Yates, B. Ribeiro-Neto, et al. Modern Information Retrieval. ACM Press,1999.
20. G. Salton, C. Buckley. Term-Weighting Approaches in Automatic Retrieval. Information Processing and Management, 24(5).1998: 513-523.

Efficient Computation of Multi-feature Data Cubes*

Shichao Zhang[1,2], Rifeng Wang[1], and Yanping Guo[1]

[1] Department of Computer Science, Guangxi Normal University, Guilin, China
[2] Faculty of Information Technology, University of Technology, Sydney, Australia
zhangsc@it.uts.edu.au, wrfgm@163.com, yp-go@163.com

Abstract. A Multi-Feature Cube (MF-Cube) query is a complex-data-mining query based on data cubes, which computes the dependent complex aggregates at multiple granularities. Existing computations designed for simple data cube queries can be used to compute distributive and algebraic MF-Cubes queries. In this paper we propose an efficient computation of holistic MF-Cubes queries. This method computes holistic MF-Cubes with *PDAP* (Part Distributive Aggregate Property). The efficiency is gained by using dynamic subset data selection strategy (Iceberg query technique) to reduce the size of materialized data cube. Also for efficiency, this approach adopts the chunk-based caching technique to reuse the output of previous queries. We experimentally evaluate our algorithm using synthetic and real-world datasets, and demonstrate that our approach delivers up to about twice the performance of traditional computations.

1 Introduction

Data cube queries compute aggregates over large datasets at different granularities and are an important part of Decision Support System (DSS) and On-line Analytical Processing (OLAP) applications. The main difference between the data cube query and traditional SQL query is that data cube not only models and views the multi-dimensional data, but also allows the computation of aggregate data at multiple levels of granularity. The core part of multidimensional data analysis is the efficient computation of aggregations across many sets of dimension that are also called granularities generally. There are many algorithms designed for optimizing the aggregation of multiple granularities [2-5]. Most of these algorithms aiming to minimize the aggregation of varied granularities base on simply data cube queries that always aggregate with single distributive or algebraic function in existing query systems. And there are only few attentions to a complex query based on data cube. However, with the development of data mining techniques and the demand of business competition, complex queries, which can provide more information and stronger support to decision-maker than simple queries, are seriously challenging to

* This work is partially supported by Australian large ARC grants (DP0449535, DP0559536 and DP0667060), a China NSFC major research Program (60496327), a China NSFC grant (60463003) and a grant from Overseas Outstanding Talent Research Program of Chinese Academy of Sciences (06S3011S01).

J. Lang, F. Lin, and J. Wang (Eds.): KSEM 2006, LNAI 4092, pp. 612–624, 2006.

existing simple data cube query computing techniques. It is in exigent demand to develop data cube technology nowadays. In fact, existing decision support systems aim to provide answers to complex queries over very large databases. Unfortunately, there is only little research into complex decision support queries that compute multiple dependent aggregates at different granularities. Two typical examples of complex query are as follows:

Q1. Grouping by all subsets of {customer, item, month} to find the maximum price among all tuples in 2005, and the total sales among all tuples of such maximum price.

Q2. Grouping by all subsets of {customer, item, month} to find the minimum price among all tuples in 2005, and the fraction of the total sales due to tuples whose price is within 25%, within 50%, and within 75% of the minimum price.

From the above examples, we can conclude two characteristics of a complex query as follows.

- A complex query computes complicated aggregation over the relation R at 2^k different granularities. For a complex query, the computation of aggregate is much more difficult than a simple one when the complex query consists of many sub-queries.

Considering *Q1*, two sub-queries are involved in this complex query; both of them are distributive aggregate functions and compute at 2^3 granularities : {month}, {customer}, {item}, {month, customer }, {month, item}, {customer, item}, {month, customer, item} and {ALL}.

- A complex query involves multiple simple sub queries that aggregate with multiple dependences at multi-granularities. This dependent relationship between the sub-queries is the main feature of complex queries (always proposed by single user based on the logic of query task), in comparison to query flows (usually proposed by multi-users based on the sequence of time), and it not only exists in the aggregate conditions of former-later sub-queries but also may be in the output of former-later sub-queries.

Considering example *Q2*, the first sub-query computes MIN(Price), then it computes SUM(Sale) in those tuples whose price is within 1.25*MIN(Price) in the second sub-query, and so on. Moreover, we can also see that the result of the third sub-query contains the result of the second sub-query. These two relationships of dependence are usually existed in complex queries, especially the former one.

From above characteristics of complex queries, we can conclude that the cost of aggregation in a complex query is always much higher than that in a simple query, its response time is much longer than that of the simple one. Therefore, we must develop efficient techniques to deal with the complex query problem.

1.1 Motivation

In [1], a Multi-Feature Cube (MF-Cube) was named to compute a complex-data-mining query and it can efficiently answer many complex data mining queries. The authors classified the MF-Cubes into three categories based on the extent to which finer granularity results can be used to compute coarser granularity results. The three types of aggregate function, including distributive, algebraic and holistic functions, determine the categories of MF-Cubes. We call them the distributive, algebraic and holistic MF-Cube in a simple way accordingly. From above, a multi-feature cube is an extension of simple data cube. This encourages us to explore optimizing computations of MF-Cube from the methods of computing simple data cube query. Like a simple data cube query, the type of MF-Cube determines the approaches used in its computation. For distributive MF-Cubes aggregated on distributive aggregate functions, it can use the coarser-finer granularities optimizing techniques (i.e., the results of coarser granularities can compute directly with the output of finer granularities). And the algebraic MF-Cubes can transform into distributive MF-Cubes through extending distributive aggregate functions and thus it can also use coarser-finer granularities optimizing technique. The methods of computing these two types of MF-Cubes are mainly discussed in [1] and they can use many simple data cube optimizing algorithms, e.g., [3-5]. However, for holistic MF-Cube, it pointed out that there is not an efficient technique and only presented a straightforward method [1]: first partition the data cubes, and then compute all the 2^n granularities separately. A major problem related to this method, however, is that the required storage space can be exponential if all the granularities are pre-computed, especially when the cube has many *CUBE BY* attributes, and the computation of aggregates will become much more complex when the size of data is very large.

On the other hand, most existing algorithms are designed for distributive or algebraic aggregate functions and there is rarely work concerning holistic and user-defined aggregate functions. And distributive and algebraic functions can also be used in new Decision Support Systems (DSS) as standard functions. However, they could not satisfy the request of decision-makers nowadays, especially when the task of data analysis becomes more complex and fast response is desired. It is challenging for decision support systems to aggregate at holistic and user-defined functions on multi-dimensional data analysis. Furthermore, aggregate functions for holistic MF-Cube may be a combination of distributive, algebraic, holistic and user-defined types according to the definition in [6]. Consequently, the time-space cost of computing holistic MF-Cubes is far more than the other queries. This encourages us to seek new and efficient techniques for computing holistic MF-Cubes.

1.2 Our Approach

In this paper we propose an efficient computation of holistic MF-Cube queries. Specifically, we

- Identify the distributive and algebraic functions contained in each sub-query of complex queries for which Part Distributive Aggregate Property defined in this paper can be used.
- Use a new dynamic subset selection strategy——Iceberg query technique to minimize the materialization of the data cube.
- Use the chunk-based caching technique that allows later sub-queries to partially reuse the results of previous sub-queries.

Our goal is to simplify the process of aggregation over multiple granularities, minimize the computing cost on multiple sub queries, reduce the response time of complex query and answer the user as soon as possible. With these three strategies, we experimentally evaluate our method with synthetic and real-world data sets, and the results show that our approach delivers up to about twice the performance of traditional computations.

The rest of this paper is organized as follows: In Section 2, we mainly illustrate the two properties of MF-Cube and give two definitions corresponding to the properties. In Section 3 we describe our optimizing strategies and our algorithm in detail. Then we experiment our method and show the significant results in Section 4. In the last section, a laconic conclusion is presented to summarize our works.

2 Properties of Multi-feature Cubes

In [1], a multi-feature cube was defined as: for n given *CBUE BY* attributes $\{B_1,...,B_m\}$, a multi-feature cube is a complex data cube which computes dependent aggregation of complex query at 2^n granularities. We call it MF-Cube for short. We present a brief definition of three categories of MF-Cubes according to [1] .

Definition 2.1. *(Distributive, Algebraic and Holistic MF-Cubes)*

Consider a MF cube query Q. let $\tilde{B}_1$ and $\tilde{B}_2$ denote arbitrary subsets of the CUBE BY attributes $\{B_1, B_2, ... , B_k\}$, such that $\tilde{B}_1$ is a subset of $\tilde{B}_2$. Let Q1 and Q2 denote the same subquery at granularity $\tilde{B}_1$ and $\tilde{B}_2$ separately. Query Q is said to be a distributive MF-Cube query if there is computable function F such that for relation R and all Q1 and Q2 as above Output(Q1,R) can be computed via F as F(Output(Q2,R)); Q said to be an Algebraic MF-Cube query if there exists a Q' obtained by adding aggregates to the syntax of query Q, such that Q' is Distributive MF-Cube; Otherwise, Q is said to be a Holistic MF-Cube query. For simplification, we present examples of MF-Cubes when we describe the properties below.

For the paper size restriction, we only present the properties of distributive and holistic MF-Cube and omit algebraic MF-Cube's below to aid intuition.

Property 2.1. *A distributive MF-Cube only uses distributive aggregate functions in all its sub-queries.*

We can conclude this property directly from the definition of distributive MF-Cube [1]. It is obviously that if a data cube is distributive; all of aggregate functions in its each sub query are distributive.

Example 2.1. Consider *Q1*, *Q1* is a typical distributive MF-Cube for it only contains two distributive aggregate functions: MAX() and SUM() in its two sub queries. So it can use the optimizing techniques between its coarser and finer granularities.

For simplification, we define this coarse-fine optimizing property as Distributive Aggregate Property (DAP) to describe the dependent relationship of coarser-finer granularities.

Definition 2.2. *(Distributive Aggregate Property, DAP)*

Given two granularities $\tilde{B}_i$ and $\tilde{B}_j$ ($\tilde{B}_i \subset \tilde{B}_j$), if the output of coarse granularity ($\tilde{B}_i$) only uses the output of the finer granularity ($\tilde{B}_j$) aggregation, we name this property as Distributive Aggregate Property.

DAP is the typical characteristic of distributive aggregate functions of data cube query and the distributive MF-Cube is named after it.

Example 2.2. We show that *Q1* is a distributive MF-Cube and conforms to this property. Consider two coarser-finer granularities {Customer, Item} and {Customer, Item, Month}. Suppose that we have computed the aggregates of the granularity {Customer, Item, Month} and have kept both MAX (Price) and SUM (Sales) for each group. We now wish to compute the aggregates for the granularity {Customer, Item}. We can combine the twelve pairs of values (one per month) into an annual pair of values, as follows: (a) Compute the maximum of the monthly MIN (Price) values. This is the annual MIN (Price) value. (b)Add up the Monthly SUM (Sales) for those months whose monthly MIN (Price) value is equal to the annual MIN (Price) value. This is the annual SUM (Sales) value.

Property 2.2. *A holistic MF-Cube includes holistic or user-defined aggregate functions, or the combination of distributive, algebraic, holistic and user-defined aggregate functions.*

In [1], a holistic MF-Cube is simply defined as follow: If a multi-feature cube is not distributive or algebraic, it is holistic. According to this definition, we can judge that Q2 is a holistic MF-Cube, for it could not conform to DAP.

In particular, due to the dependent relationship of complex query, besides the standard aggregate functions already defined in query systems, there may be another kind of aggregate condition function in complex query for constraining the range of aggregation. For example, in Q2, the function 1.25* MIN(Price) is used to constrain the aggregation SUM(Sales) in the second sub query, the same as 1.5*MIN(Price) and 1.75*MIN(Price). These aggregate condition functions also take important role in the complex query, so we cover them into the category of aggregate function as a new kind, user-defined aggregate functions, when they are not exactly standard query functions, even if they may partly contain existing standard functions, i.e., 1.25* MIN (Price). This is a new extension for aggregate function of holistic MF-Cube.

So, we can conclude that holistic MF-Cube has most complex aggregate functions in comparison to distributive and algebraic MF-Cube, which may include: distributive, algebraic, holistic and user-defined functions at the same time.

Example 2.3. In *Q2*, there are not only distributive but also user-defined aggregate functions: MIN(Price),SUM(Sales) and 1.25*MIN(Price), 1.5*MIN(Price), 1.75*MIN(Price). In Example 2.4, a different feature among coarser-finer granularities aggregation shows to us (Example 2.4).

Example 2.4. Suppose that we've computed these aggregates for the granularity {Customer, Item, Month} and have kept all of MIN(Price), SUM(R1.Sales), SUM(R2.Sales) and SUM(R3.Sales) for each group. We now wish to compute the aggregates for the granularity {Customer, Item}. Unfortunately, we cannot simply combine the twelve tuples of values (one per month) into a global tuple of values for the MIN(Price) in each month group may be different from the annual's. Suppose that (for some group) the minimum price over the whole year is $110, but that the minimum price for January is $120. Then we do not know how to combine January's SUM(R2.Sales) of $1000 came from tuples with price at most $165; the figure $1000 includes contributions from tuples with price up to $180. This indicates that the computing process of holistic MF-Cube is different from other MF-Cubes.

The most important optimizing technique in distributive and algebraic MF-Cube is DAP, so, if a holistic MF-Cube contains distributive or algebraic aggregate functions and if we can use DAP in these sub queries, it can simplify the process of aggregation greatly. Moreover, there may partly contain distributive or algebraic aggregate functions in user-defined functions, whether we can partly use DAP in this case is worth of thinking. We are glad to have approved our assumption in our experiments. So we definite these two optimizing computation processes as Part Distributive Aggregate Property as follows.

Definition 2.3. *(Part Distributive Aggregate Property, PDAP). A PDAP of a holistic MF-Cube is one of the following two instances:*

Case 1: *some aggregate functions in sub-query are distributive or algebraic and others are holistic or user-defined;*

Case 2: *the user-defined functions in some sub-queries partly consist of distributive or algebraic functions.*

We can use *PDAP* in these sub queries in the two cases above. We name these optimizing processes as part-*DAP*, for we only partly use *DAP* in holistic MF-Cube, in comparison with all-*DAP* used in all of the sub queries of distributive ones. Furthermore, when user-defined functions consist of distributive or algebraic aggregate functions, they also conform to *DAP* partly.

Example 2.5. Considering Query *Q2*, there are four sub-queries that include one distributive aggregate function and three user-defined aggregate functions. Besides, all the user-defined aggregate functions contain the distributive aggregate functions. So we can use *PDAP* in these sub-queries on multiple granularities: when computing the first sub-query, MIN(Price), we can use *DAP* directly on the coarser-finer granularities. And for the rest sub-queries, because their aggregate functions contain distributive aggregate functions, we can test whether we can use the optimizing property. For example, suppose the annual min(price) is $110, and if there are 5 months' the same as the annual's, then we can combine the output of these 5 months' into annual's and need to compute another 7 months' only. As a consequence, we can save the cost of computing aggregation greatly with *PDAP*.

3 Optimizing Strategies for Holistic MF-Cubes

In Sections 1 and 2, we have presented the characteristics and properties of MF-Cube, especially for holistic MF-Cube in detail. In this section, we propose three strategies for holistic MF-Cubes.

3.1 Optimizing Strategies

The three optimizing strategies are as follows.

● Strategy 1. *Using PDAP to aggregate dependently.*

If a holistic MF-Cube uses distributive or algebraic aggregate function, we can use this property to maximize optimizing aggregations. In this case, the granularities can be computed dependently rather than independently which induce more time cost, as we have described in Section 2.

- Strategy 2. *Using a dynamic subset selection strategy——iceberg query technique to partly materialize data cube.*

The iceberg query technique first proposed in [7] is a popular method to reduce the size of data cube and improve the performance efficiently. Instead of computing a complete cube, an iceberg query performs an aggregate function over an attribute (or a set of attributes) and then eliminates aggregate values that are below some user-specified aggregate threshold, thus the iceberg cube can be computed partly. It is so-called iceberg query because the results of the above threshold are often very small (the tip of an iceberg), relative to the large amount of input data (the iceberg). There are many methods researched based on iceberg-cube, such as [4, 8, 10]. Since we know each aggregate function of sub-query before computing data cubes, we can set a condition according to the query to choose efficient data for part-materialization of the data cubes. In [10], several complex constraints have been proposed to compute iceberg-cube more efficiently, which include a significant constraint that we use in our paper, as shown in our algorithm in Section 3.2. In our algorithm, the iceberg condition using to select efficient tuples is varying with the input data, so it is a dynamic selection.

- Strategy 3. *Using the chunk-based caching technique to reuse the results of previous sub queries.*

The chunk-based caching scheme is proposed in [9] mainly to resolve the problem of overlap results between the previous query and the later query for multidimensional query flows by dividing the multidimensional query space uniformly into smaller chunks and caching these chunks. Since chunks are smaller than query level caching units, so they can be reused to compute the partial result of an incoming query. One of the main features of MF-Cube is the dependent relationship among sub-queries, so we can partition cube into smaller chunks and reuse the caching results as possible as we can. It is easy to test this case in example *Q2*.

We combine these three strategies into our algorithm and experiment with the above examples. We name our algorithm *PDIC* (Part Distributive_Iceberg_Chunk) and illustrate it in Section 3.2.

3.2 PDIC Algorithm

3.2.1 Process of PDIC Algorithm
We describe our algorithm PDIC in four steps:

(i) *Partition data cube into small memory-cubes using the method in [2].*

The Partitioned-Cube algorithm described in [2] uses a divide-and-conquer strategy to divide the data cube into several simpler sub datacubes with one of CUBE BY attributes each time. In comparison to another method of dividing data cube mentioned in [3, 6], the former is better suited to compute holistic MF-Cube in that it maintains all tuples from a group of the data cube simultaneously in memory and allows for the computation of the holistic MF-Cube aggregate over this group. The later one which partitions the data cube by all CUBE BY attributes simultaneously maintains partially computed aggregates. The process of partitioning is: first choose one of the CUBE BY attributes and partition data cube by it, if the sub cube is also larger than memory size, partition the sub-cube by another CUBE BY attribute, and so on.

(ii)   *Order the paths of the 2^n granularities and pre-sort sub-cubes according to these orders.*

Before computing the aggregates, we should order the paths of granularities for sorting and aggregating with these sequences. An algorithm computing paths is shown in [2], and we also use it in our algorithm. When sorting the sub-cubes, we use the existing algorithm Pipe-Sort to share the sorting work, as described in [5]. For understanding easily we simply point out the sequences of aggregate of granularities: first aggregate all the granularities involving the partitioned attributes in each sub cube. Before aggregating the others, partition the data cube again with another CUBE BY attribute where the data cube contains attributes less one than last time. The following operations repeat as above.

(iii)   *Compute iceberg-cube with iceberg-query techniques.*

For each sorted-sub datacube, we use iceberg-query techniques with iceberg conditions which come from the complex query, i.e., <1.75*MIN(Price) in example Q2. We use this constraint to select efficient data while we aggregate the MIN(Price) of each group. When the MIN(price) changes, so as the value of 1.75*MIN(Price). Whatever the change of the MIN(Price), the data larger than 1.75*MIN(Price) are excluding in the tip of iceberg.

(iv) *Compute the complex aggregates with PDAP and use chunk-based caching techniques when answering the multi-sub queries on the tip of iceberg of the iceberg-cube.*

As has been described in Sections 2 and 3.1, both of these two strategies can be used to optimize the aggregates of holistic MF-Cube when there are distributive or algebraic aggregate functions in a holistic MF-Cube and the results of former-later sub queries are overlap.

3.2.2 Algorithm *PDIC*

Algorithm *PDIC* (R , {B_1 , … , B_k} , A , GFs)

INPUT : R: the relation to aggregate;   {B_1 , …, B_k}: *CUBE BY* attributes ;

        A: aggregate of test attributes ;   GFs: aggregate functions ;

OUTPUT: aggregates of MF-Cubes Query

METHOD:

1 . Dim=$B_i \in$\{B_1,…,B_k\}; n=Cardinality(B_i);

2 . R_1,…,R_n =*Partitioned-cube*(R, Dim, n, Countdata[Dim],{B_1,…,B_k});

        //partitioned data cube , Countdata[Dim]=the number of tuples

3 . For(i=0;i<n; i++)

4 . {

5 .   *Initialize* accumulators at granularities which include B_i;

6 .   *SortR=Sort*(R_i, $\widetilde{B}_i$)   // $\widetilde{B}_i$ =subset of {B_1 , … , B_k}

7 .   For (j=0;j< Countdata[i];j++)

8 .   {T= tuple in SortR;   x=GF(T.A);   Iceb_Cond=F(x)

9 .   if (value(T.A)<Iceb_Cond)   //Iceberg-query

10 .   Select tuple T; Else Prone T;

11 .   }

12 .   For queries which contain distributive and algebraic functions

13 .   {*PartDistribAggre* (SortR , GF(T.A));   //PDAP

14 .   *Chunked_Cube*(Iceberg-cube,n_query, cond_subquery[n_query])

15 .   }   //Chunk-based caching

16 .   For rest sub-queries

17 .   {*GranulAggre* (SortR,GF(T.A))

18 .   *Chunked_Cube*(Iceberg-cube, n_query, cond_subquery[n_query])

19 .} }

20 . Dim=$B_j\in\{B_1,...,B_k\}$ and $B_j \neq B_i$; n=Cardinality(B_j);

21 . $R_1,...,R_n$= *Partitioned-cube*(R,Dim,n,Countdata[Dim],$\{B_1,...,B_{i-1},B_{i+1}, ... ,B_k\}$);

22 . Repeat 3 to 19;

4 Experiments and Performance

4.1 Experimental Data

There are three classes of dataset used in our experiments. The first two are synthetic datasets with dense and skew data generated by a synthetic dataset generator designed as [8]. The other is the real-world dataset containing weather conditions at various weather stations in September 1991 [11]. We select 7 dimensions in each dataset with six base dimension attributes and one measure attribute consisted in them. We generate 10 groups of Zipf distributive skew datasets in which α varies from 0 to 3 only on measure attribute with 10^6 tuples, as described with the parameters in Table 1, and 5 groups of dense datasets with the parameters showing in Table 2. And the parameters of the weather datasets are shown in Table 3.

4.2 Experimental Evaluations

To check the efficiency of the proposed algorithm in answering the holistic MF-Cube, a comprehensive performance study is conducted by testing *PDIC* algorithm against the traditional algorithm *ModiPC*, which is modified from Partitioned-Cube to suit for holistic MF-Cube. Both of the algorithms are coded using

Table 1. Parameters of Skew Datasets

	CUBE BY attributes			Base Attributes		Measure Attribute	Data Sets
Items	A	B	C	D	E	F	
Cardinality	10	100	100	100	100	[500,1500]	10 datasets of 10^6 tuples
α	0, 0.2, 0.4, 0.5, 0.6, 0.8, 1, 1.5, 2, 3						

Table 2. Parameters of Dense Datasets

	CUBE BY Attributes			Base Attributes		Measure Attribute	Data Sets
Items	A	B	C	D	E	F	5 datasets of 10^6-5*10^6 tuples
Cardinality	10	10	10	10	100	[500,1500]	

Table 3. Parameters of Weather Datasets

	CUBE BY Attributes			Base Attributes		Measure Attribute	Data Sets
Items	Change Code	Low-cloud type	Date	Station number	Total-cloud cover	longitude	One datasets of 10^6 tuples
Cardinality	10	12	30	100000	9	[0,36000]	

VC++6.0 on a DELLWorkstation PWS650 with 2G main memory and 2.6G CPU. The operating system is Windows 2000. As the evaluations are mainly to compare the performance of the two algorithms, we only test the CPU time of computing aggregations on a holistic MF-Cube, for both of the times of partitioning and sorting are the same in these two algorithms and to be excluded in our results. We run one holistic MF-Cube query *Q2* in our experiment, and the different parameters in our experiments are changed similarly according to this query. The symbols in the result figures denote as follows: |CB| =number of *CUBE BY*-attributes, |T|= number of tuples, |SQ|=number of sub-queries. TD=type of datasets, SK=skew datasets, DS=dense datasets, WD= weather data sets of real-world.

a. Experiment with Skew Datasets

The first set of experiments studies the effectiveness of skew datasets. With the parameters described as Table 1, we test the two algorithms with skew datasets and show the results in Table 4, Figures 1 and 2.

From Figure 1, we can see that there is a little effect on the performance of *PDIC* algorithm when the Zipf factor varies from 0 to 3. when the factor α is 0 meaning uniform distribution of the datasets, the iceberg tip coming from iceberg queries is 37.8% of the base data cube, as is shown in Table 4, which make the best performance of iceberg queries. As the factor increases gradually, the iceberg queries performances drop on the other way round and become invalid when αequals to 3. Meanwhile, the result cube of queries in *PDIC* is obviously predominant, varying

Table 4. Different I/O data size between two algorithms

Skew factor	PDIC Alg		ModiPC Alg
α	Iceberg Tip	Resultcube1 of Query	ResultCube2 of Query
0	37.8% of DB	99.2% of Iceberg Tip	243% of ResultCube1
0.2	45.9% of DB	99.4% of Iceberg Tip	274% of ResultCube1
0.4	55.5% of DB	99.9% of Iceberg Tip	298% of ResultCube1
0.5	60.6% of DB	99.9% of Iceberg Tip	304% of ResultCube1
0.6	65.9% of DB	99.9% of Iceberg Tip	320% of ResultCube1
0.8	77.2% of DB	100% of Iceberg Tip	342% of ResultCube1
1	86.9% of DB	100% of Iceberg Tip	358% of ResultCube1
1.5	98.5% of DB	100% of Iceberg Tip	389% of ResultCube1
2	99.8% of DB	100% of Iceberg Tip	393% of ResultCube1
3	99.9% of DB	100% of Iceberg Tip	393% of ResultCube1

243% to 393% in *ModiPC* more than *PDIC*. As a result, despite of little effect of the skew data, our algorithm is about 200% superior than *ModiPC* algorithm, varying from 214% to 171% while skew factor is from 0 to 3, as is shown in Figures 1 and 2. Besides of the effective iceberg queries and chunk-based caching techniques, the PDAP takes most important role in improving the performance of holistic MF-Cubes.

    b.   Experiment with Dense Datasets of Different Number of CUBE BY-Attributes

    The more the number of *CUBE BY*-Attributes is, the more the response time in answering the complex queries will be. For testing the effect of our algorithm in different attributes of CUBE BY, we experiment with 2-4 attributes and glad to see that the similar superiority to the straightforward method, advancing 226% in average (as shown in Figures 3-6). The main contribution of our algorithm is using three optimizing strategies to improve the performance of holistic MF-Cube through minimizing the aggregation of multi-granularities and reducing the cost of computation over multiple sub queries. We don't take the different data structure into account and use the same in both of the two algorithms. As a result, whatever the type of dataset is, dense or sparse, dose not affect the performance of the algorithms. We use dense datasets in our experiments.

    c.   Experiment with Dense Datasets of Different Number of Sub-queries

    Based on complex query *Q2*, we test the holistic MF-Cube respectively with one distributive function in the first sub-query and vary the distributive function number of rest sub-queries from 1 to 4.As results showing in Figure 7, we conclude that there are also similar improvements of performances in different number of sub-queries, averagely excelled 224% than *ModiPC* algorithm.

    d.   Experiment with Weather Dataset of Real-World

    We also choose 6 items of the weather dataset from file sep91L.dat in [11], as described in table3, which consists of 0.98 million tuples and over 27M data. We choose longitude as measure attribute and its value varies from 0 to 36000. In our

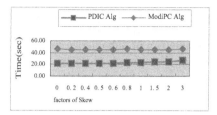

Fig. 1. |CB|=3,T=10^6,|SQ|=3,DT=SK

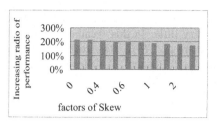

Fig. 2. |CB|=3,T=10^6,|SQ|=3,DT=SK

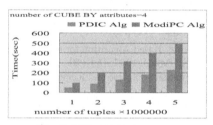

Fig. 3. |CB|=2,|SQ|=3,DT=DS

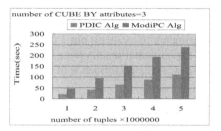

Fig. 4. |CB|=3, |SQ|=3,DT=DS

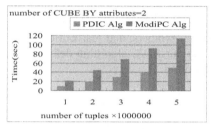

Fig. 5. |CB|=4,|SQ|=3,DT=DS

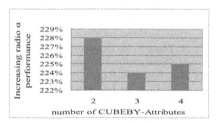

Fig. 6. |SQ|=3,DT=DS

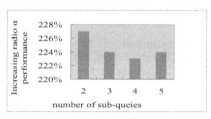

Fig. 7. |CB|=3,T=10^6,DT=DS

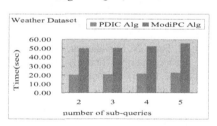

Fig. 8. |CB|=3,T=0.98×10^6,DT=WD

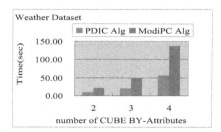

Fig. 9. | SQ|=3,T=0.98×10^6,DT=WD

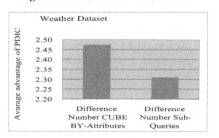

Fig. 10. T=0.98×10^6,DT=WD

experiments, we accordingly change the conditions in *Q2*, for the MIN longitude may be very little. In this weather dataset, we also test the two algorithms on different numbers of *CUBE BY*-Attributes and different numbers of sub-queries to compare their performances. As shown in Figures 8 to 10, the average advantage of *PDIC* algorithm is more than 200%.

5 Conclusion

In this paper, we have proposed a new computation of holistic MF-Cube that takes into account the different types of aggregate function. We have conducted extensive experiments to evaluate our *PDIC* algorithm with synthetic and real-world datasets. The experimental results have demonstrated that our *PDIC* algorithm delivers up to about twice the performance of the *ModiPC* algorithm.

References

[1] K.A. Ross, D. Srivastava and D. Chatziantoniou. Complex Aggregation at Multiple Granularities. In: Proc. of EDBT'98, 1998: 263-277.
[2] K. Ross and D. Srivastava. Fast computation of sparse datacubes. Athens, Greece, Aug. 1997. In: Proc. Int. Conf. Very Large Data Bases, 1997: 116–125.
[3] Y. Zhao, P. M. Deshpande, J. F. Naughton. An Array-Based Algorithm for Simultaneous Multidimensional Aggregates. In: Proc. of ACM SIGMOD, 1997: 159-170
[4] K.S. Beyer, R. Ramakrishnan. Bottom-Up Computation of Sparse and Iceberg Cubes. In: Proc. Of ACM SIGMOD, 1999: 359-370.
[5] S. Agarwal, R. Agrawal, P.M. Deshpande, A. Gupta, J. F. Naughton, R. Ramakrishnan, and S. Sarawagi. On the Computation of Multidimensional Aggregates. In: Proc. Int' Conf. Very Large Data Bases, 1996: 506-521.
[6] Gray, A. Bosworth, A. Layman, and H. Pirahesh. Datacube: A relational aggregation operator generalizing group-by, cross-tab, and sub-totals. In: Proc. of the IEEE ICDE, 1996: 152-159.
[7] M. Fang, N. Shivakumar, H. Garcia-Molina, R. Motwani and J. D. Ullman. Computing iceberg queries efficiently. In: Proc. of 24th VLDB Conf., New York, 1998: 299-310.
[8] Han, J. Pei, G. Dong, and K. Wang. Efficient Computation of Iceberg Cubes with Complex Measures. In: Proc. ACM-SIGMOD Int'l Conf. Management of Data, 2001: 1-12.
[9] P. M. Deshpande, K. Ramasamy, A. Shukla. Caching Multidimensional Queries Using Chunks. In: Proc. ACM SIGMOD, 1998: 259-270.
[10] Guozhu Dong, Jiawei Han, Joyce, M. W. Lam. Mining Constrained Gradients in Large Databases. In: IEEE TKDE, 2003.
[11] Hahn C, Warren S, London J. Edited synoptic cloud reports from ships and land stations over the globe. (1996) Available on http://cdiac.esd.ornl.gov/cdiac/ndps/ndp026b.html

NKIMathE – A Multi-purpose Knowledge Management Environment for Mathematical Concepts

Qingtian Zeng[1,2], Cungen Cao[1], Hua Duan[2], and Yongquan Liang[2]

[1] Key Laboratory of Intelligent Information Processing,
Institute of Computing Technology, Chinese Academy of Sciences,
Beijing 100080, China
[2] College of Information Science and Technology,
Shandong University of Science and Technology,
Qingdao 266510, China
{zqtian, cgcao}@ict.ac.cn

Abstract. In 2001, *NKIMath*, as the mathematics knowledge component of National Knowledge Infrastructure, was initiated to elaborate in China. In order to help knowledge engineers acquire and manage the mathematical knowledge especially the conceptual knowledge, a knowledge management environment, *NKIMathE* has been designed and developed. *NKIMathE* integrates three main components: (1) a platform for knowledge acquisition, syntax checking and organization for mathematical concepts; (2) a module for multi-lingual knowledge translation and transform for mathematical concepts; and (3) a Web-based and a mobile knowledge Q-A platforms for mathematical concepts.

1 Introduction

Knowledge presentation and acquisition are two of the main topics within knowledge engineering. Mathematical knowledge representation and acquisition are important and useful for many mathematical applications, including knowledge-based automatic theorem proving, integration of different mathematical software systems, mathematical semantic Web, and high-level mathematical instruction [1]. Wiedijk [2] compared 15 mathematical provers on MKM2003 including Otter/Ivy [3], HOL [4], PVS [5], Theorema [6], etc., among which there are eight provers needing a large mathematical library to support. So, knowledge-based automatic theorem proving promotes knowledge representation and acquisition for mathematics. Traditionally, there are no communications between different mathematical software systems, and it is difficult to share codes or resources between these systems. In 1995, Homann [7] pointed out the integration of all kinds of mathematical software systems is one of the main technologies for mathematics automation. In the integration process, there is one problem necessary to be solved, which is the knowledge representation satisfying different systems, since the knowledge representation is the foundation for integration.

J. Lang, F. Lin, and J. Wang (Eds.): KSEM 2006, LNAI 4092, pp. 625–636, 2006.

626   Q. Zeng et al.

Recently, with the development and application of Web technology, mathematical mark language for the content and the context of mathematics toward Web, such as MathML [8], OpenMath [9] and OMDoc [10], have been received more attention. And, a lot of projects about mathematical domain knowledge base have been started including MBase [11], HELM [12], MOWGLI [13], and NKI-Math [1,14] etc.

In 1999, a long-term research project (called the National Knowledge Infrastructure, or NKI) was initiated in China to develop shareable knowledge bases of different domains and relevant underlying systems. Currently, the NKI contains knowledge from more than 20 domains, e.g. medicine, biology, history, geography, mathematics, music, ethnology, and archaeology [1,15,16,17,18,19]. The knowledge of NKI is acquired from encyclopedia, dictionaries, handbooks, textbooks, and so on, by semi-automatic and automated knowledge acquisition. NKI has two main purposes, one of which is to provide society-oriented knowledge services by Web, telephone, Email, etc., and another of which is to provide KAPI (knowledge application programming interface) for computer systems including language system, digital library, machine translation and so on.

NKIMath [1,14] is the mathematical knowledge component of NKI, which is important for building the whole NKI project, not only because mathematics is a useful subject about science and engineering, but also is mathematics the foundation of lots of subjects, such as physics, mechanics, and so on.

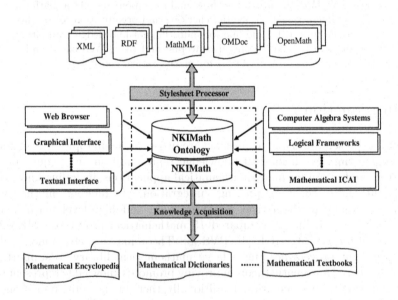

Fig. 1. The Framework of *NKIMath* Knowledge Base System

The framework of the *NKIMath* knowledge base system is shown in Fig. 1. The knowledge source of *NKIMath* includes mathematical encyclopedia, mathematical dictionaries, mathematical textbooks, and so on. Knowledge engineers acquire knowledge from these sources and store them into the knowledge base. The knowledge acquired is expected to serve for lots of knowledge-enable applications, including:

- **Mathematical Knowledge Query.** Users can query the knowledge within *NKIMath* through a Web browser, textual interface or graphical interface. Similarly, users can send the questions to the knowledge server by their PDA or mobile phone, and then the answers for questions can be returned to the users. A web-based knowledge question and answering system has been developed for users, which will be presented in the Section 4.
- **Mathematical Knowledge Instruction.** While building the knowledge base of mathematical concepts, the relations between concepts can also be built. With the associational relations between concepts, a set of instruction strategies can be generated automatically, which decides the instruction sequences between mathematical knowledge.
- **Mathematical Knowledge Reasoning.** The conceptual knowledge within *NKIMath* can be used for knowledge reasoning. A set of mathematical theorems can be proved through an automatic theorem prover based on *NKI-Math*.
- **Mathematical Knowledge Designing.** The requirements for the same mathematics knowledge of different users, for example students, teachers, and engineers and so on, are usually different. The user-adapted knowledge texts are expected to be produced from *NKIMath* based on the information models of different users.

With the elaborating of *NKIMath*, a computer-assistant knowledge management environment, *NKIMathE* has been designed and developed to help knowledge engineers acquire, organize and manage the knowledge base. *NKIMathE* integrates three main components: (1) a platform for knowledge acquisition and organization for mathematical concepts; (2) a module for knowledge translation and transform for mathematical concepts; and (3) a knowledge Q-A (Question and Answering) system for mathematical concepts.

In this paper, we will introduce the knowledge management environment for mathematical concepts within *NKIMath*. Section 2 presents the platform for knowledge acquisition and organization for mathematical concepts. Section 3 introduces the module for knowledge translation and transform for mathematical concepts. Section 4 presents the Q-A system for mathematical concepts. Conclusions are given in Section 5.

2   Knowledge Acquisition and Organization for Mathematical Concepts

The user interface of the platform for knowledge acquisition and organization for mathematical concepts is shown in Fig.2. The main performances of this platform include knowledge acquisition, knowledge error and abnormity checking, knowledge editor, and knowledge organization.

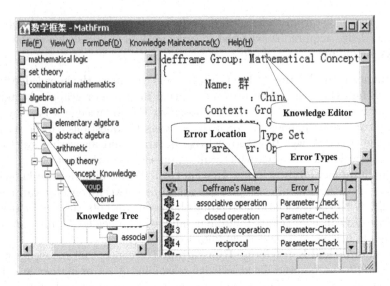

Fig. 2. Knowledge Acquisition and Organization for Mathematical Concepts

The platform can help knowledge engineers with knowledge edit, query, compilation, knowledge error and abnormity checking. The main functions of the platform include,

- **Knowledge Acquisition.** Knowledge can be acquired within the knowledge editor, and the attributes and relations of the knowledge frame can be added automatically. When completed, knowledge frame is added into the knowledge base automatically. The log file is created to record the name of the knowledge engineer, the time of knowledge acquisition or modification.
- **Knowledge Checking.** According to the knowledge representation language, the representation errors in the knowledge frame can be checked and corrected automatically, which includes the definitions and types of attributes and relations, the number and type of the parameters within predicate and function and so on.
- **Knowledge Organization.** The conceptual knowledge frames within *NKI-Math* are classified and organized as a tree based on the CONTEXT attribute of the knowledge frame. While a new knowledge frame is added into the knowledge base, the platform can add a correct position in the knowledge tree for the new concept.

2.1   Knowledge Abnormity Checking

All the knowledge in the frame of an mathematical concept should be correct; otherwise the correctness of the whole knowledge base will be affected. For each concept, an attribute FD (Formal Definition) presents a machine-oriented formal definition with a formal formula in first-order logic, which are mainly used for knowledge reasoning and theorem proving, and also the foundations for building

Table 1. Abnormities and Errors about the Formal Definition of Mathematical Concept

Error Type	Examples	Error Reasons

Undefined Parameters	$def frame\ Group: Mathematical\ Concept$
	 {
	 $Parameter: G$
	 $: Type\ Set$
	 $Parameter: op$
	 $: Type\ Operation$
	 $FD: Monoid(G, op) \land Have\_Inverse(S, op)$
	 }
		The parameter S in $Have\_Inverse$ (S, op) is not defined in the frame.

Number of Parameters Mismatching	$def frame\ Group: Mathematical\ Concept$
	 {
	 $Parameter: G$
	 $: Type\ Set$
	 $Parameter: op_1$
	 $: Type\ Operation$
	 $Parameter: op_2$
	 $: Type\ Operation$
	 $FD: Monoid(G, op_1, op_2) \land Have\_Inverse(G, op_1)$
	 }
		With the knowledge frame of $Monoid$, $Monoid(G, op_1, op_2)$ should be a binary predicate.

Parameters Unused	$def frame\ Group: Mathematical\ Concept$
	 {
	 $Parameter: G$
	 $: Type\ Set$
	 $Parameter: op_1$
	 $: Type\ Operation$
	 $Parameter: op_2$
	 $: Type\ Operation$
	 $FD: Monoid(G, op_1) \land Have\_Inverse(G, op_1)$
	 }
		The parameter op_2 is not used.

Syntax Error	$def frame\ Group: Mathematical\ Concept$
	 {
	 $Parameter: G$
	 $: Type\ Set$
	 $Parameter: op$
	 $: Type\ Operation$
	 $FD: Monoid(G, op) \land Have\_Inverse(G, op))$
	 }
		The number of brackets is not matching.

Semantic Error	$def frame\ Group: Mathematical\ Concept$
	 {
	 $Parameter: G$
	 $: Type\ Set$
	 $Parameter: op$
	 $: Type\ Operation$
	 $FD: Monoid(G, op) \rightarrow Have\_Inverse(G, op)$
	 }
		The $\rightarrow$ operation should be $\land$.

the relations between concepts to realize knowledge inheritance. Unfortunately, the FD is obtained manually by the knowledge engineers, so a lot of abnormities and errors can be occurred in FD during knowledge acquisition.

Table 1 lists several kinds of abnormities and errors frequently occurred in the formal definitions and points out the error reasons, where we take knowledge frame of *Group* as all examples. Generally, the errors can be divided into two kinds:

- **syntax errors**, including undefined parameters, unused parameters, unknown keywords, and mismatching brackets and so on, the main reasons of which are the careless of knowledge engineers;
- **semantic errors**, the main reasons of which are the misapprehensions of knowledge.

The syntax errors or abnormities are usually obvious and easy to be checked, while the semantics errors are inconspicuous and must be verified by right methods. We have presented the formal definitions for several kinds of knowledge abnormities and errors about mathematical concepts, and given the checking rules and algorithms. By now, the knowledge checking module within *NKIMathE* has been realized to check all kinds of syntax errors about mathematical concepts. In this paper, we will not have more discussions about the knowledge analysis and checking on the mathematical concepts. More discussions can be seen in [20].

2.2   Organization for Knowledge Frames

The conceptual knowledge frames within *NKIMath* are classified based on the CONTEXT attribute of the knowledge frame, and all the concepts belonging to a same branch are organized as a tree. If concept C_2 is used to define concept C_1, C_2 is a child node of C_1 in the tree. There are three kinds of leaf nodes in the tree respectively labeled with "*new*", "*old*" and "*meta*". The leaf nodes labeled with "*new*" are the "*unknown*" concepts, which must be acquired in order to keep knowledge completeness. The leaf nodes labeled with "*old*" mean that it is no necessary to continue constructing the sub tree of these nodes in order to reduce the dimensions of the knowledge tree, because they have been constructed in other places. The leaf nodes labeled with "*meta*" are primary concepts, which mean the definitions of these concepts don't depend on any other concepts. Part of the knowledge tree constructed is shown in Fig.3.

The knowledge tree is convenient for knowledge browse, search and edit according to the subject branches of mathematics, and the outline of the concept relations of each branch is clear. From the knowledge tree, it is easy to discover the backbone about the mathematical concepts, for example, there is a relation chain "*Group* $\rightarrow$ *Monoid* $\rightarrow$ *Semi* $-$ *group*" in the tree ($C_1 \rightarrow C_2$ representing C_1 is defined based on C_2). An $IS - A$ relation chain "*Semi* $-$ *group* $\rightarrow$ *Monoid* $\rightarrow$ *Group*", where $C_1 \rightarrow C_2$ represents that $IS - A(C_1, C_2)$, can be obtained by reversing the chain of "*Group* $\rightarrow$ *Monoid* $\rightarrow$ *Semi* $-$ *group*".

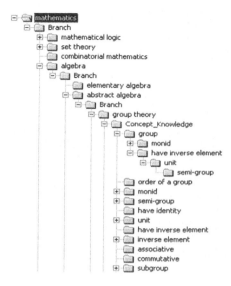

Fig. 3. Part of *NKIMath* Knowledge Tree

3   Knowledge Translation and Transform for Mathematical Concepts

NKIMath is language-independent, since it is easy to translate *NKIMath* into multi-lingual bases with knowledge translation patterns. At the same time, it is also easy to transform between NKIMath and OMDoc [10]. These can ensure *NKIMath* can serve for many mathematical systems or be used by different users with different native language.

3.1   Auto-generation of Multi-lingual Mathematical Knowledge Base

At present, the statement and formal knowledge representation for mathematical concepts within *NKIMath* is represented in Chinese, but the knowledge base is language-independent. Given the knowledge base with FD (formal definition) in any language version, multi-lingual bases can be auto-generated with the different language translation PATTERNs.

In the knowledge representation frame of *NKIMath*, a knowledge translation PATTERN attribute is added to exhibit a standard pattern for different languages, which serves for multi-lingual translation for mathematical knowledge . With the different language PATTERNs for each concept, a shareable knowledge in multi-lingual versions can be auto-generated to meet for users with different native languages.

For example, Fig.4 gives three patterns designed for concept *Group* in Chinese, English and German. The formal syntax of PATTERN is not discussed with more details in this paper. In Fig.4, $<?G>$ indicates that G is a variable, which can

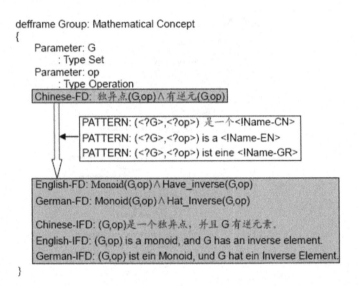

Fig. 4. Result about the Auto-generation of Multi-Lingual Mathematical Knowledge Base

be replaced by any variable symbol of predicate *Group*. $<!NAME>$ indicates that $NAME$ is a constant, which can be replaced by the true value of $NAME$ in different language in the *Group* knowledge frame during the translation process.

Based on these patterns designed, the knowledge can be translated into multi-lingual versions easily. By now, the translator of *NKIMathE* can translate the FD (Formal Definition) of mathematical concept from Chinese into English and German, and the FD from Chinese to IFD (Informal Definition) in Chinese, English and German based on the translation PATTERNs of concepts. With the PATTERNs of the concept *Group* given in Fig.4, the results of translating Chinese FD of *Group* into English and German FDs as well as into Chinese, English and German IFDs are shown in Fig.4.

3.2   Transform Between *NKIMath* and OMDoc

OMDoc is used for knowledge representation in many mathematical knowledge systems [10], and it will be accepted as the international standard for mathematical document marked language. The knowledge representation of *NKIMath* follows lots of similarities with OMDoc, for example, the FD and IFD attributes in *NKIMath* correspond to the FMP and CMP elements in OMDoc respectively. Fig.5 shows the corresponding relationships between OMDoc and *NKIMath*.

A transform toolkit has been developed to realize the transformation between *NKIMath* and OMDoc with each other. The advantages of this toolkit are obvious:

- Transforming knowledge in *NKIMath* into OMDoc can ensure NKIMath can be shared by other mathematical knowledge system.

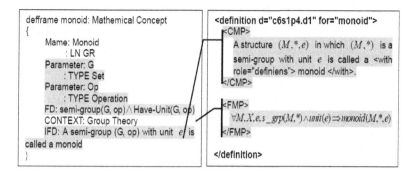

Fig. 5. The Corresponding Relationships between OMDoc and *NKIMath*

- Transforming OMDoc into *NKIMath* provides an auto-acquisition method for the knowledge in *NKIMath* from the mathematical documents in OMDoc format.

4 Knowledge Q-A System for Mathematical Concepts

To satisfy knowledge requirements of users, two human-machine knowledge interfaces have been developed. One is Web-based for users to query knowledge through internet, and another is a mobile knowledge Q-A system, with which users can send message using their mobile phone or PDA to obtain the knowledge they need.

4.1 Web-Based Knowledge Q-A System for Mathematical Concepts

A Web-based knowledge Q-A system for mathematical concepts has been realized with which users can query knowledge within *NKIMath* in natural language through internet.The user interface for knowledge Q-A for mathematical concepts is shown in Fig.6, including the question-input window and the answer-output window. Users can input questions in flexible natural language, for example, users can query the definition for concept *Monoid* as followings,

- *What is Monoid?*
- *I want to know what the definition of Monoid is.*
- *Please tell me how to define a Monoid.*

After submitting the questions by users, the knowledge query system sends the questions to the knowledge sever. The server finds the answers and feeds back to the query system, thus users can obtain the answers within the answer-output window.

4.2 Mobile Knowledge Q-A System for Mathematical Concepts

Besides a Web-based knowledge Q-A system for mathematical concepts, another mobile knowledge interface for mathematical concepts within *NKIMath* has been

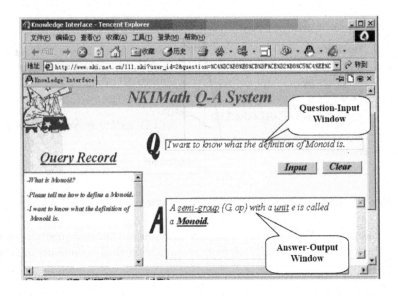

Fig. 6. Web-based Knowledge Q-A System for Mathematical Concepts

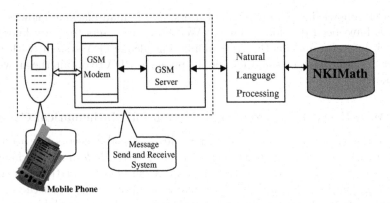

Fig. 7. Mobile Knowledge Q-A System for Mathematical Concepts

developed, the framework of which is shown as in Fig.7. Users can send a message in natural language to the GSM server to acquire the knowledge he requires. After GSM server receives the message, the message is processed by NLP (Natural Language Processing) so as to the questions understood by system. After finding the knowledge in *NKIMath* corresponding to the questions, the answer will be returned to the user's mobile phone by GSM server.

5   Conclusion

Knowledge processing for mathematical concepts is a large project, which includes knowledge representation and acquisition, knowledge analysis and verification, knowledge organization and management. With the enlargement of the scale of knowledge base, the necessary for a knowledge management environment for mathematics like *NKIMathE* will be obvious. *NKIMathE* is only a primary knowledge management platform for mathematics, especially for mathematical concepts. *NKIMathE* integrates three main components: (1) a platform for knowledge acquisition, syntax checking and organization for mathematical concepts; (2) a module for knowledge translation and transform for mathematical concepts; and (3) a knowledge Q-A system for mathematical concepts.

As a knowledge management environment for mathematical concepts, there are lots of works to be continued with *NKIMathE* , which include,

- auto-construction for knowledge inheritance hiberarchy of mathematical concepts based on the knowledge frames,
- knowledge semantics checking, including knowledge redundancy, knowledge consistency, etc.,
- different-lingual knowledge generation for other languages besides Chinese, English and German, and
- knowledge application platforms about mathematical concepts, for example, mathematical instruction.

In this paper, we only have a discuss on the knowledge management of mathematical concepts. In the future, the knowledge processing and management about mathematical theorems should also be considered. As one of the best and most important applications of mathematical knowledge, *NKIMath* will be considered to combine one of theorem provers so as to have theorem proving in the future.

Acknowledgement

This Work is supported by the National Natural Science Foundation of China under Grant (No.60273019, 60496326, 60573036, and 60573064), the National 973 Programme (No. 2003CB317008 and G1999032701), the Taishan Scholar Program of Shandong Province, and Science Development Foundation of SDUST (No. 05g001).

References

1. Zeng, Q., Cao, C., Tian, G., Sui, Y., Liu, H.: Methods for mathematical concept knowledge representation, acquisition and management within NKIMath. In: Second International Conference on Knowledge Economy and Development of Science and Technology. (2004) 27–35
2. Wiedijk, F.: Comparing mathematical provers. In: Proceedings of MKM 2003. (2003) 188–202
3. Otter/Ivy. (Website) http://www.mcs.anl.gov/AR/otter/ and http://www-.unix.mcs.anl.gov/mccune/acl2/ivy/
4. HOL. (Website) http://www.cl.cam.ac.uk/Research/HVG/HOL.

5. PVS. (Website) `http://pvs.csl.sri.com/`.
6. Theorema. (Website) `http://www.theorem.org/`.
7. Homann, K., Calmet, J.: Combining theorem proving and symbolic mathematical computing. In: AISMC. (1994) 18–29
8. Carlisle, D., Ion, P., Miner, R., Poppelier, N.: Mathematical Markup Language (MathML) version 2.0. W3c recommendation, World Wide Web Consortium (2001) Available at http://www.w3.org/TR/MathML2.
9. Caprotti, O., Cohen, A.M.: Draft of the Open Math standard. The Open Math Society, `http://www.nag.co.uk/projects/OpenMath/omstd/` (1998)
10. Kohlhase, M.: OMDoc: An open markup format for mathematical documents (version 1.1) (2001) `http://www.mathweb.org/omdoc/omdoc.ps`.
11. Franke, A., Kohlhase, M.: System description: MBASE, an open mathematical knowledge base. In: Conference on Automated Deduction. (2000) 455–459
12. Asperti, A., Padovani, L., Coen, C.S., Schena, I.: HELM and the semantic Math-Web. Lecture Notes in Computer Science **2152** (2001) 59–74
13. MOWGLI. (Website) `http://www.mowgli.cs.unibo.it/`.
14. Zeng, Q., Cao, C., Sui, Y., Si, J., Tian, G.: Ontology-based knoweldge acquistion and knowledge inheritance mechanism for mathematics. Microelectronics and Computer **20**(9) (2003) 19–27
15. Cao, C.: Medical knowledge acquisition from the electronic encyclopedia of China. In: Artificial Intelligence Medicine, 8th Conference on AI in Medicine in Europe, AIME 2001, Cascais, Portugal, July 1-4, 2001, Proceedings. Volume 2101 of Lecture Notes in Computer Science., Springer (2001) 268–271
16. Cao, C., Feng, Q., Gao, Y., Gu, F., Si, J., Sui, Y., Tian, W., Wang, H., Wang, L., Zeng, Q., Zhang, C., Zheng, Y., Zhou, X.: Progress in the development of national knowledge infrastructure. Journal of Computer of Science and Technology **17**(5) (2002) 523–534
17. Cao, C., Wang, H., Sui, Y.: Knowledge modeling and acquisition of traditional Chinese herbal drugs and formulae from text. Artificial Intelligence in Medicine **32**(1) (2004) 3–13
18. Gu, F., Cao, C., Sui, Y.F., Tian, W.: Domain-specific ontology of botany. Journal of Computer of Science and Technology **19**(2) (2004) 238–248
19. Zhang, C., Cao, C., Gu, F., Si, J.: Domain-specific formal ontology of archaeology and its application in knowledge acquisition and analysis. Journal of Computer of Science and Technology **19**(3) (2004) 290–301
20. Zeng, Q.: Research on knowledge acquisition and analysis of mathematical concepts. PhD thesis, Institute of Computing Technology, Chinese Academy of Sciences (2005)

Linguistic Knowledge Representation and Automatic Acquisition Based on a Combination of Ontology with Statistical Method

Dequan Zheng, Tiejun Zhao, Sheng Li, and Hao Yu

MOE-MS Key Laboratory of Natural Language Processing and Speech
Harbin Institute of Technology, Harbin, 150001
{dqzheng, tjzhao, lisheng, yu}@mtlab.hit.edu.cn

Abstract. Due to the complexity and flexibility of natural language, linguistic knowledge representation, automatic acquisition and its application research becomes difficult. In this paper, a combination of ontology with statistical method is presented for linguistic knowledge representation and acquisition from training data. In this study, linguistic knowledge representaiton is firstly defined using ontology theory, and then, linguistical knowledge is automatically acquired by statistical method. In document processing, the semantic evaluation value of the document can be get by linguistic knowledge. The experimention in Chinese information retrieval and text classification shows the proposed method improves the precision of nature language processing.

1 Introduction

Linguistic knowledge representation and automatic acquisition is one of the cores of natural language processing and is applied to information retrieval, data mining, machine translation, etc. However, the poor linguistic knowledge and polysemy restrict the natural language processing.

The knowledge acquisition bottleneck has become the major impediment to the development and application of effective information processing. To remove this bottleneck, new document processing techniques must be introduced for knowledge representation and acquisition from various types of documents. Landauer et al use the latent semantic analysis theory for knowledge representation and acquisition[1], Stevens et al suggest the class method[2]. Tang et al propose to use document structure for knowledge acquisition[3], Boeg et al use fuzzy set theory[4]. Peters and Shrobe make use of semantic networks for knowledge representation[5]. Ontology-based method is recently proposed for acquire various knowledge[6~8].

Ideally, computer should firstly "understand" the nature language, and then process the document. If computer could learn and accumulate linguistic knowledge continuously, its intellection and precision will be enhanced. However, previous researches have failed to consider the semantic information of natural language and have ignored the environment of changeful topics. In order to overcome above shortcomings, in this paper, a combination of ontology with statistical method is presented for linguistic knowledge representation and acquisition.

J. Lang, F. Lin, and J. Wang (Eds.): KSEM 2006, LNAI 4092, pp. 637–649, 2006.

In this study, we determined the structure of such a combination of Ontology with statistical method. This structure is firstly comprised of an ontology description framework for Chinese words and a representation of Chinese linguistic knowledge. Subsequently, a Chinese linguistic knowledge will be automatically acquired by determining, for each word, its co-occurrence with semantics, pragmatics, and syntactic information from the training corpus. For document processing, the usage of Chinese keywords will be gotten from linguistic knowledge to act as a semantic evaluation value of document. Finally we make use of evaluation value for effective information processing.

The rest of this paper is organized as follows. In section 2, we describe the knowledge representation method. In section 3, we propose our strategy for linguistic knowledge acquisition. In section 4, we give the application method of linguistic knowledge. In section 5, we present two groups of experiment and evaluate the performance of the proposed method. In section 6, we give the conclusion and future works.

2 Linguistic Knowledge Representation

Ontology was recognized as a conceptual modeling tool, which can descript an information system in the semantics and knowledge[9]. After ontology was introduced in the field of Artificial Intelligence[6], it was combined with natural language processing and applied in many field, such as knowledge engineering[10], information retrieval, and semantic Web[11]. Its succeed provides with theory to construct the word sense ontology and acquire linguistic knowledge.

The goal of statistical language modeling (SLM) is to estimate the likelihood (or probability) of a word string[12]. Some statistical information like word frequency, documents frequency is becoming a component of SLM and successfully applied to many fields such as automatic speech recognition[13], statistical machine translation[14], information retrieval[15], etc.

2.1 Word Sense Description Framework

In practical application, ontology can be described in natural languages, framework structure, semantic web, logical language, etc[16]. At present, some popular methods, such as Ontolingua[17], CycL[10], Loom[18], are all based on logical language.

Despite the strong logical expression, it is not easy for logical language to deduce the process. In this study, we provided a framework structure of such a Chinese keyword. This structure is a readable format by computer and comprises of domain, definition, part of speech (POS), semantic information, relationship, synonym, sub-domain information. Figure 1 shows the word sense description framework for Chinese words.

In this study, we automatically construct the Chinese word sense description based on a combination of HowNet[19], Chinese thesaurus, Chinese-English bilingual dictionary and other information.

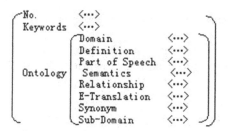

Fig. 1. Word sense description framework

2.1.1 Semantic

The Semantic information is mainly from the semantic definition of Chinese word in HowNet. There is only a number to denote the semantic definition in "HowNet-Definitions"[18] and the number will replace the semantic information in this paper.

For example, '爱好' is 'DEF={fact|事情:{FondOf|喜欢:target={~}}}' and its number is 10086, then its semantic information is replaced by number 10086.

We developed a semantic tagging system based on HowNet and the precision is over 85%.

2.1.2 POS

The POS information is from the Chinese POS tagging set developed by our laboratory. It has 52 labels including 10个punctuations and the label is from 0 to 51 and we define the POS of keyword as label 52.

We used a Chinese dictionary that contains about 85,000 items to develop a Chinese word segmentation system and developed a POS tagging system, the precision is over 98% and 95% respectively.

2.1.3 English Translation

The English translation is from a Chinese-English bilingual dictionary developed by our laboratory and the dictionary contains basic Chinese-English word 102,615 pairs and auxiliary Chinese-English word 23,067 pairs.

2.1.4 Synonym

We referred to the Chinese thesaurus (expanded) developed by information retrieval laboratory of Harbin Institute of Technology. The thesaurus got rid of some useless words and is expanded to 77,343 words. We listed part of the synonym in common use in word sense Ontology description.

2.1.5 Relationship

There are 16 relationships representation between Chinese words defined in the HowNet, we referred to part of relationship such as infliction, receiving, modifier, collocation, etc.

2.2 Linguistic Knowledge Representation Method

Linguistic knowledge plays an important role in information processing. In this paper, we will consider multi-elements of the keyword and its co-occurrence such as POS, semantic, location and co-occurrence probability and construct the linguistic knowledge.

We define an expression to describe the word sense of a keyword including its definition, POS, semantic information and English translation.

$$Keyword_{Onto\log y} \overset{def}{=} Keyword(Def, POS, Sem, Tran) \tag{1}$$

Where, *Def* denotes the definition of keyword, *POS* is part of speech, *Sem* denotes the semantic information of Keyword defined in Hownet, Tran is English translation.

We define an expression to describe the linguistic knowledge representation of a keyword, which considers the multi-elements of keyword in context.

$$Keyword_{Onto\log y} \overset{def}{=} \left(\overset{m}{\underset{l=1}{Y}} \left(Sem_l, POS_l, L, \overline{C_l}\right) / \overset{n}{\underset{r=1}{Y}} \left(Sem_r, POS_r, L, \overline{C_r}\right) \right) \tag{2}$$

Where, $Keyword_{Ontology}$ denotes the keyword description. The right represents linguistic knowledge of the keyword that acquired from training data. $\left(Sem_l, POS_l, L, \overline{C_l}\right)$ denotes the left *l-th* co-occurrence of the *keyword*, which comprises of semantic, *POS*, the position and the weighed average co-occurrence distance, $\left(Sem_r, POS_r, L, \overline{C_r}\right)$ denotes the right *r-th* co-occurrence. The symbol "/" separates the left and right of the keyword. The symbol " ∪ " denotes the aggregate of co-occurrence of the *Keyword*.

We define the *Keyword* and (*Sem_i*, *POS_i*, L) as a semantic pair to mark with <*Keyword*, (*Sem_i*, *POS_i*, L)> and only denote the *Keyword* and its co-occurrence. $\overline{C_l}$ denotes the weighed average co-occurrence distance of the semantic pair <*Keyword*, (*Sem_l*, *POS_l*, L)> in all training data.

$$\overline{C_l} = (1 + w_l) \frac{1}{all} \sum_{i=1}^{all} C_i \quad w_l = (0 \sim 1) \tag{3}$$

Where, C_i denotes the *i-th* co-occurrence distance of the semantic pair <*keyword*, (*Sem_i*, *POS_i*, L)>; all is the times in all training data; w_l denotes the weighing of the semantic pair and the more much times the semantic pair appears, the more the weighing is big.

Formula 2 is the representation of the linguistic knowledge of a *keyword*, total keywords and their linguistic knowledge construct the knowledge bank in a specific field. Formula 4 is the representation of linguistic knowledge bank.

$$LingOnto_{Field} \overset{def}{=} \sum_{all} Keyword_{Onto\log y} \tag{4}$$

3 Linguistic Knowledge Acquisition

To acquire linguistic knowledge of keywords, we first need to know their *POS* and semantic information in a sentence, and then, get the **Characteristic String** to replace

Table 1. Characteristic string representation

Items	Results ("游客" acts as keyword)
Chinese sentence	外国游客来北京游玩。
Segmentation	外国 游客 来 北京 游玩 。
POS tagging	外国 nd/ 游客Keyword/来 vg/ 北京nd/ 游玩vg/ 。 wj/
Semantic tagging	外国 nd/021243 游客 Keyword/070366来 vg/017545 北京 nd/021243 游玩 vg/092317 。 wj/-1
Characteristic String	nd/021243 游客Keyword/070366 vg/017545 nd/021243 vg/092317

this sentence, subsequently, acquire linguistic knowledge. An example is shown in table 1.

Figure 2 is the sketch map of the co-occurrence and location of the *Keyword*, where, W_1, W_2, ..., *Keyword*, ..., W_i constructs the **Characteristic String**, *l* and *r* denote the location of the *Keyword* and its co-occurrence and will be regarded as a processing unit.

Fig. 2. The co-occurrence and location of Keyword

In this study, we will acquire the linguistic knowledge by learning the usage of the keywords and their co-occurrence in semantics, pragmatics and syntactic information in all training data. Algorithm 1 is the processing of knowledge bank acquisition.

Algorithm 1

Step1: corpus pre-processing.

For every document D_i, we will use the Ontology description of the keywords to make all synonyms into the same one. Subsequently, extract the sentence that includes the Keywords to construct a temporary file and regard a sentence as processing units. And then, do word segmentation, *POS* tagging, semantic tagging and get rid of the auxiliary word likes "的、地、得、了、吧、呀" etc to get a **Characteristic String**.

Step2: Calculate the co-occurrence distance.

We take the Keyword as center word, and define the left and right distance factor B_l and B_r by formula 5. Where, *m* and *n* denote the number of the left side and right side words.

$$B_l = \frac{1-\frac{1}{\alpha}}{1-\left(\frac{1}{\alpha}\right)^m} \qquad B_r = \frac{1-\frac{1}{\alpha}}{1-\left(\frac{1}{\alpha}\right)^n} \qquad (5)$$

Subsequently, we respectively get the co-occurrence distant between a semantic pair of the keywords by formula 6 (here, we definite α equal to 2).

$$C_{li}=\left(\frac{1}{\alpha}\right)^{i-1}B_l \qquad C_{rj}=\left(\frac{1}{\alpha}\right)^{j-1}B_r \qquad (6)$$

Step3: Calculate the weighed average co-occurrence distance between a semantic pair of every word.

Documents learned, keywords and their co-occurrence information $\left(Sem_i, POS_i, L, \overline{C_i}\right)$ construct the linguistic knowledge.

4 Linguistic Knowledge Application

In this paper, we define two symbols, *Sem_Word$_i$* and *Sem_Pair$_i$*. *Sem_Word$_i$* denotes the relation information appeared in document, including semantic label, POS, location, and *Sem_Pair$_i$* denotes the semantic pair constructed by the *Keyword* and its co-occurrence.

$$Sem\_Word_i \overset{Def}{=} (Sem_i, POS_i, i)$$

$$Sem\_Pair_i \overset{Def}{=} <Keyword, Sem\_Word_i>$$

In actual document processing, we will first acquire the **Characteristic String** of every sentence, and then, regard the *keyword* as the center to define the left semantic evaluation value of keyword *Evaluation_Left*.

$$Evaluation\_Left = \prod_{i=1}^{m} P(Sem\_Word_{li} \mid Sem\_Pair_{li-1})$$

Where, $P(Sem\_Word_{li} \mid Sem\_Pair_{li-1})$ is the conditional probability, *Sem_Word$_0$* and *Sem_Pair$_0$* denotes the *Keyword*, and then,

$$\log Evaluation\_Left = \sum_{i=1}^{m} \log P(Sem\_Word_{li} \mid Sem\_Pair_{li-1})$$

According to the presentation of linguistic knowledge and the monotony of logarithm, this paper replaces the conditional probability with the weighed average co-occurrence distance of the semantic pair, so, the define is as follows,

$$Evaluation\_Left = \sum_{i=1}^{m} \overline{C_{li}} \qquad (7)$$

In a similar way, the right evaluation value is defined.

And then, the semantic evaluation value of the keyword in a sentence is the sum of left evaluation value and right evaluation value.

$$Evaluation\_Keyword_s = Evaluation\_Left + Evaluation\_Right \qquad (8)$$

The semantic evaluation value of the keyword in a document is defined as follows (t is the number of sentence in a document),

$$Evaluation\_Keyword = \sum_{S=1}^{t} Evaluation\_Keyword_s \qquad (9)$$

So, the semantic evaluation value of the document is defined as follows (k is the number of the *Keyword* in a document),

$$Evaluation\_Docment = \sum_{D=1}^{k} Evaluation\_Keyword_D \qquad (10)$$

To avoid data sparseness, the weighed average co-occurrence distance is defined with 0.01 if the linguistic knowledge of a semantic pair does not appeared in knowledge bank.

5 Experiment and Discussion

To evaluate the performance of the proposed method, we do two groups of experiment, i.e. Chinese information retrieval and text classification.

5.1 Chinese Information Retrieval

5.1.1 Chinese Information Retrieval Strategy
In this study, we use Chinese words as indexing units, we firstly do an initial retrieval according to user query, and we expand user query based on Ontology description of keywords. Subsequently, we respectively acquire the linguistic knowledge of keywords from user query, and then, compare the similarity between user query and retrieval documents according to the linguistic knowledge to reorder the initial retrieval document set.

5.1.2 Linguistic Knowledge of Topic
In this study, we use NTCIR-3 workshop [20] formal Chinese test collection. For every topic, we will extract its Keywords and acquire the linguistic knowledge from its description type by agorithm1. For example,

Title: 复制小牛之诞生
(The birth of a cloned calf)
Description: 与使用被称为体细胞核移植的技术创造复制牛相关的文章
(Articles relating to the birth of cloned calves using the technique called somatic cell nuclear transfer)

After Chinese words are segmented, we select "体细胞, 移植, 技术, 创造, 复制, 牛" to act as the keyword of this topic and acquire the linguistic knowledge of every topic from its description type run (D-Run) by algorithm 1. Figure 3 is the presentation of linguistic knowledge.

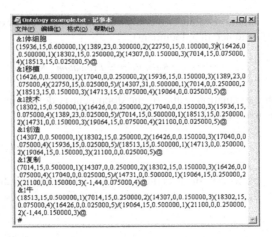

Fig. 3. Presentation of linguistic Ontology knowledge

5.1.3 Initial Document Set Acquisition

For Chinese information retrieval, single Chinese character, bi-gram and words (characters) are the most used as indexing units. In this paper, we consider Chinese words as indexing units.

We select the description field (D-run) as indexing type to evaluation the proposed method. We consider Chinese words (i.e. keywords of every topic) as initial indexing units to get their ontology representation as the query expansion and get the initial retrieval document set.

5.1.4 Documents Ranking

For the initial retrieval documents, we will acquire the linguistic knowledge of every document by algorithm 1, and then, compare the similarity by calculating the semantic evaluation value of the retrieval documents and user query respectively, final, reorder the initial retrieval documents.

Algorithm 2

   Step1: Get the Chinese word segmentation and selection keywords.
   Step2: Acquire the linguistic knowledge of the topic by algorithm 1.
   Step3: Calculate the evaluation value of every topic.
   We make the accumulative total for the average co-occurrence distance $\overline{C}$ of a semantic pair *<Keyword, (Sem, POS, L)>* in the description type run (D-Run), and mark with *Evaluation-Topic*.
   Step4: Get the initial retrieval document set
   We regard the description information as retrieval type and regard Keywords and their expansion as retrieval unit to get an initial retrieval document set;
   Step5: Acquire the linguistic Ontology knowledge of the document.
   Acquire the linguistic Ontology knowledge from every document of the topic by algorithm 1.

Step6: Calculate the evaluation value of every document.

We make the accumulative total for the average co-occurrence distance $\overline{C}$ according to the same as semantic pair $<Keyword, (Sem, POS, L)>$ that appears in the topic, and mark with $Evaluation\text{-}Doc_i$;

Step7: Judge the similarity between user queries and retrieval documents.

We define a formula to calculate the similarity between user queries and documents, and re-ranking the initial retrieval documents by the similarity.

$$Similarity_{ratio-Doc_i} = \frac{Evaluation - Doc_i}{Evaluation - Topic} \qquad (11)$$

5.1.5 Experimental Results

We use NTCIR-3 Formal Chinese Test Collection, which contains 381,681 Chinese documents and 42 topics, and select 42 D-runs type query to evaluate our method. We use the two kinds of relevant measures, i.e. relax-relevant and rigid-relevant[21] and compare the results with other group submission.

Table 2. The average precision of C-C runs (Relaxed)

Topic Fields	# of Runs	Average	Maximum	Minimum
C	4	0.2605	0.2929	0.2403
D	14	0.2557	0.3617	0.0443
DC	1	0.2413	0.2413	0.2413
T	1	0.2467	0.2467	0.2467
TC	4	0.3109	0.3780	0.2389
TDC	1	0.3086	0.3086	0.3086
TDN	1	0.3499	0.3499	0.3499
TDNC	8	0.3161	0.4165	0.0862
Total	34	0.2806	0.4165	0.0443
HLM-D	*1*	*0.4481*	*0.4481*	*0.4481*

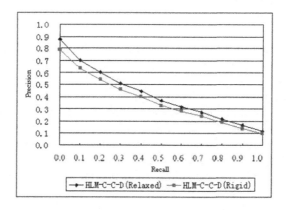

Fig. 4. C-C Run 11-Point Precision (HLM-D-Runs)

In NTCIR-3 workshop, in total, 8 different combinations of topic fields and 34 runs are used in Chinese-Chinese (C-C) single language information retrieval (SLIR) track. Table 2 shows the distribution and the corresponding average, maximum, minimum of average precision[22], and HLM-D is the result of the D-runs that is proposed method.

HLM-D-runs improve the performance than other runs. Figure 4 show the relaxed relevance C-C run and rigid relevance C-C run according to the proposed method. In total, there are about an average 9.34% increase in precision can be achieved than the submission in NTCIR-3 workshop.

5.2 Text Classification

5.2.1 Text Classifiers Construction
For actual document, first, we will acquire the different kind of linguistic knowledge respectively by learning different training data to determine different text classifiers. Subsequently, respectively get the semantic evaluation value of the document by different kind of linguistic knowledge. And then, the text categorization will be judged by the highest semantic evaluation value. Algorithm 3 describes the process of text category by the proposed method.

Algorithm 3

Step1, extract the keywords of documents
We firstly get Chinese word segmentation for total training data, and then, extract i keywords by $tf*idf$ strategy for every document in a text category.

Step2, respectively acquire the linguistic knowledge of every text category by algorithm 1.

Step3, regard the linguistic knowledge for every text category as its text classifier.

Step4, calculate the semantic evaluation value of every testing document
We respectively calculate the semantic evaluation value of every testing document using formula 10 according to the linguistic knowledge of every text category, and mark with $Evaluation\text{-}Document_{ij}$. $Evaluation\text{-}Document_{ij}$ denotes the semantic evaluation value of the $i\text{-}th$ document that acquires from the $i\text{-}th$ text classifier.

Step4, judge text category
We will judge the text category by the maximum of the semantic evaluation value $Evaluation\text{-}Document_{ij}$.

5.2.2 Data Collections and Evaluation
We collect and clean up 10 kinds of 8,450 Chinese documents from Internet including computer, current affairs, sports, education, environment, economy, medicine, military affairs, art, traffic and select 4,450 documents as training data for acquiring linguistic knowledge to determine text classifiers, the others act as testing data to evaluate performance of text classifiers. Table 3 is the data distribution on total text categories.

Table 3. Data distribution on different text categories

Items	Comp	Current affairs	Sports	Edu	Env	Eco	Medi	Military affairs	Art	Traf
Training data	500	550	500	500	400	400	400	400	400	400
Testing data	420	470	460	470	390	370	370	330	340	380

To measure the performance of a classifier that produces a ranked list of categories for each test document, with a confidence score for each candidate. We adopt an approach called interpolated 11-point average precision[23] and the recall and the precision for one specific document are defined to be:

$$recall(r) = \frac{Number\ of\ categories\ found\ that\ are\ correct}{Total\ mumber\ of\ true\ categories} \quad (12)$$

$$precision(p) = \frac{Number\ of\ categories\ found\ that\ are\ correct}{Total\ mumber\ of\ categories\ found} \quad (13)$$

Another evaluation criterion that combines recall and precision is the F_1-measure:

$$F_1 = \frac{2 * p * r}{p + r} \quad (14)$$

5.2.3 Experimental Results

In the proposed method, we firstly extract 5 keywords from every training document by $tf*idf$ strategy to form a keyword set for different text category, and acquire the linguistic knowledge of this text category by algorithm 1 to determine the text classifiers. Subsequently, we extract 10 keywords from every testing document and judge its text category by algorithm 3.

To evaluating the proposed hybrid language modeling, we use total testing data in table 3 and compare the text categorization results with Bayes, kNN, SVM. Multinomial model is used in Bayes method[24]. In kNN method, k equals to 50. Multinomial kernel function is selected in SVM method and its dimension is 3 and the One-vs-Rest method is used for multi-class text categorization[25]. Table 4 is a comparison of average precision among Bayes, kNN, SVM and the proposed method in this paper.

Table 4. Comparison of average precision on different text categorization methods (%)

Number of Documents	Bayes	KNN	SVM	Method in this paper
200	84.46	91.65	93.38	96.54
500	84.12	91.11	92.66	96.32
1000	83.33	90.76	91.79	95.41
2000	82.79	90.23	90.87	94.23
3000	82.24	89.88	90.21	93.77
4000	81.69	89.53	89.62	93.08

In table 4, it is shown that compared with Bayes, kNN and SVM, the proposed method respectively increases about 12.41%、 4.41% and 3.61% in the same number of testing documents.

6 Conclusion

In this paper, we gave a combination of Ontology with statistical method for linguistic knowledge representation and acquisition. In this study, first, we construct ontology description and acquire linguistic knowledge, in documents processing, the semantic evaluation value of every document will be calculated. The experiment in Chinese information retrieval and text classification shows a good performance than previous works.

On the other hand, in the current method, we only use a part of Ontology description and combined with some co-occurrence information, such as semantics, POS, position, distance, etc. We are faced with some problems and further work include: (1) use more semantic relation, (2) combine with some NLP technologies, (3) improve the model to increase the performance of information retrieval, (4) apply this method to other fields.

Acknowledgement

This paper is supported by the National Natural Science Foundation of China (No.60435020, 60302021).

References

1. Landauer, T. K. & Dumais, S. T. A solution to Plato's problem: The Latent Semantic Analysis Theory of the Acquisition, Induction, and Representation of Knowledge. Psychological Review, 1997,104: 211-140
2. Steven, W. Knowledge Acquisition and Knowledge Representation with Class: the Object-oriented Paradigm. Expert Systems with Applications, 1998, 15(2): 235-244
3. Tang, Y. Y., Yan, C. D., Suen, C. Y. Document Processing for Automatic Knowledge Acquisition. IEEE Transactions on Knowledge and Data Engineering, 1994, 6(1): 3-21
4. Boeg, K., Adlassnig K. P., Hayashi, Y., Rothenfluh T. E., Leitich H. Knowledge Acquisition in the Fuzzy Knowledge Representation Framework of a Medical Consultation System. Artificial Intelligence in Medicine, 2004, 30(1): 1-26
5. Peters, S., Shrobe, H. E. Using Semantic Networks for Knowledge Representation in an Intelligent Environment. Proceedings of the PerCom 2003, 2003: 323-329
6. Gruber, T. R. Toward principles for the design of ontologies used for knowledge sharing. International Workshop on Formal Ontology, 1993
7. Guarino, N. Formal Ontology, Conceptual Analysis and Knowledge Representation, International Journal of Human-Computer Studies, 1995, 43(2/3): 625-640
8. Stevens, R., Goble, C. A. and Bechhofer, S. Ontology-based knowledge representation for bioinformatics. Brief. Bioinform, 2000, 398–414

9. Neches, R., Fikes, R., Finin, T., Gruber, T., Patil, R., Senator, T., and Swartout, W. R. Enabling Technology for Knowledge Sharing. AI Magazine, 1991, 12(3): 16~36

10. CycL. http://www.cyc.com

11. W3C Semantic Web. http://www.w3.org/2001/sw

12. Gao, J. F., Lin, Ch. Y. Introduction to the Special Issue on Statistical Language Modeling, ACM Transactions on Asian Language Information Processing, 2004, 3(2)

13. Jelinek, F. Self-organized language modeling for speech recognition. In Readings in Speech Recognition, 1990: 450-506.

14. Brown, P., Pietra, S. D., Pietra, V. D., and Mercer, R. The mathematics of statistical machine translation: Parameter estimation. Computational Linguistics, 1993, 19(2): 269-311

15. Croft, W. B. and Lafferty, J. Language Modeling for Information Retrieval. Kluwer Academic, 2003

16. Uschold M. Building Ontologies-Towards A Unified Methodology. In expert systems 96, 1996

17. Ontolingua. http://www.ksl.stanford.edu/software/

18. Loom. http://www.isi.Edu/isd/LOOM/

19. Dong, Zh. D. http://www.keenage.com/

20. NTCIR-3. http://research.nii.ac.jp/ntcir-ws3/

21. Yang L. P, Ji, D. H, T, L. Document Re-ranking Based on Automatically Acquired Key Terms in Chinese Information Retrieval. In Proceedings of the COLING'2004, 2004: 480-486

22. Chen, K. H., Chen, H. H., Kando, N., Kuriyama, K., lee, s., Myaeng, S. H., Kishida, K., Eguchi, K. and Kim, H. Overview of CLIR Task at the Third NTCIR Workshop. In proceedings of the NTCIR-3, 2002, 1~37

23. Yang Y. M. An evaluation of statistical approaches to text categorization. Information Retrieval, 1999, 1(1): 76~88.

24. Eyheramendy S., Lewis D. D., Madigan D. On the naive bayes model for text categorization. Proceedings of the Ninth International Workshop on Artificial Intelligence and Statistics, Key West, Florida, 2003, 1~8

25. Hsu C. W., Lin C. J. A comparison on methods for multi-class support vector machines. IEEE Transactions on Neural Networks, 2002, 13(2): 415~425

Toward Formalizing Usefulness
in Propositional Language

Yi Zhou and Xiaoping Chen

Multi-agent System Lab, Computer Science Department,
University of Science and Technology of China (USTC). HeFei, AnHui, China
zyz@mail.ustc.edu.cn, xpchen@ustc.edu.cn

Abstract. In this paper, we attempt to capture the notion of *usefulness* in propositional language. We believe that classical implication captures a certain kind of usefulness, and name it *strict usefulness*. We say that a formula P is strictly useful to a formula Q under a formula set Γ if and only if P implies Q under Γ in classical propositional logic. We also believe that classical implication is too strict to capture the whole notion of usefulness. Therefore, we extend it in two ways. The first one is *partial usefulness*, which means that if P is true, then Q will be partially true under the background of Γ. The second one is *probabilistic usefulness*, which means that the probability of Q is true will increase by given P is true under Γ. This paper provides semantic definitions of them respectively in propositional language, and discusses the fundamental properties of them.

Keywords: Knowledge representation, usefulness, partial implication, probabilistic relevance.

1 Introduction

The concept of usefulness has long existed in AI community. In [12], Newell gave his views on the principle of rationality as follows: "If an agent has knowledge that one of its actions will lead to one of its goals, then the agent will select that action". Doyle concluded this kind of rationality as "if it seems useful, do it" [4], and he also pointed out the lack of formalization in the concept of usefulness. According to Newell and Doyle, the fundamental issue is that, given an agent's belief and its goals, which formulas and actions are useful to the agent's goals under its current belief? These formulas and actions play essential roles on rational decision making of agents. They are alternatives in the current decision step, and if chosen, they provide guidance and restrictions for later decisions.

This paper attempts to provide an exploration on the formalization of usefulness. Suppose that the agent's belief is a formula set and the agent's goal is a formula, and given a set of actions and formulas, which ones are useful? We mainly focus on the case of formulas here and leave the case of actions into future directions. And we restrict our discussions in propositional language. Thus, the problem turns into: given a proposition set Γ and two propositions P and Q, is P useful to Q under Γ ?

J. Lang, F. Lin, and J. Wang (Eds.): KSEM 2006, LNAI 4092, pp. 650–661, 2006.

We must argue that there are several different kinds of usefulness. Classical logic captures a certain kind of it, that is, if Q is not true under Γ and P implies Q under Γ, then we can say that P is useful to Q under Γ. In other words, with the help of P, Q holds under Γ. However, this doesn't capture the whole notion of usefulness. Therefore, we extend it in two ways.

The first one is partial usefulness, which means that if P is true, then Q will be partially true under the background of Γ. We adopt the partial implication semantics [13] to address this issue. The second one is probabilistic usefulness, which means that the probability of Q *is true* will increase by given P *is true*. Technically, we introduce the notion of probabilistic relevance into propositional language to formalize this kind of usefulness.

The rest of this paper is organized as follows. In the following section, we give an example and analyze three different kinds of usefulness informally. In section 3, partial implication and probabilistic relevance are formalized in propositional language semantically. And Section 4 investigates their main properties. In section 5, we define three kinds of usefulness based on classical implication, partial implication and probabilistic relevance respectively. Then, related works are discussed in section 6. Finally, we draw our conclusions.

2 Informal Analysis

Let's consider the following example. Here, x, y and z are atoms:

Example 1. *Assuming that Γ is empty, and given the proposition $Q = x \wedge y$, are the following propositions useful to Q?*
P_1: $x \wedge y$; P_2: $x \wedge y \wedge z$; P_3: $x \wedge \neg y$; P_4: x; P_5: $x \vee y$; P_6: $x \wedge z$; P_7: $x \vee z$.

P implies Q under Γ means that in the background Γ if the agent achieves P then Q will also be achieved; hence we treat classical implication as a certain kind of usefulness. In the example above, P_1 and P_2 are useful to Q. However, there is no doubt that P_4 should be useful to Q. But in classical propositional logic, P_4 doesn't imply Q. We can see that classical implication is sometimes too strict to capture the whole notion of usefulness. Therefore, other criterions of usefulness are needed.

We can broaden the restrictions of Q *is true* from two aspects. Firstly, although Q is not true, part of Q is true; and we can continue to achieve Q based on the contribution of P. We call it partial usefulness. Secondly, although Q is not true, the probability of Q *is true* increases by given P *is true*. We call this probabilistic usefulness.

In [13], Zhou and Chen introduced partial implication semantics. P partially implies Q can be understood as that P is "useful and harmless" to Q in any situation. Here, "useful" means that if P is true, then part of Q is true. And "harmless" means that under the contribution of P we can achieve Q. P_4 is a typical example of partial implication. x partially implies $x \wedge y$, since x achieves part of $x \wedge y$ (x); and under the contribution of x, we can achieve $x \wedge y$ (if we achieve y). However, P_3 doesn't partially imply Q, because although P_3 achieves part of Q (x), P_3 makes Q unachievable ($\neg y$ holds). And P_7 doesn't partially imply Q either, because P_7 can't ensure the "in any situation" condition (if only z holds). We'll employ partial implication semantics to formalize partial usefulness.

Correspondingly, we'll use probabilistic relevance to formalize probabilistic usefulness. Probabilistic relevance is usually defined as $\Pr(Q \mid \Gamma \cup \{P\}) > \Pr(Q \mid \Gamma)$ [3]. Probabilistic relevance, also known as confirmation or evidence, has been studied by a lot of philosophers and Bayesians. Though some researchers criticized this criterion of probabilistic relevance [1], we still advocate this point of view and introduce it into propositional logic. That P is probabilistically relevant to Q under Γ is defined as: for each possible probabilistic distribution of propositions, $\Pr(Q \mid \Gamma \cup \{P\}) > \Pr(Q \mid \Gamma)$. In example 1, whatever the probabilistic distribution is, we can get $\Pr(x \wedge y \mid \{x\}) > \Pr(x \wedge y)$.

3   Formalization

We will restrict our discussion within a propositional language, denoted by L. The formulas of L are formed as usual from a finite set of atoms, $Atom= \{x_1, x_2 \ldots\}$, and the standard connectives $\neg, \vee, \wedge, \rightarrow$ and $\leftrightarrow$. Let Γ, Γ', etc. denote sets of consistent propositional formulas in L, x, y atoms, l literals, and P, Q, R formulas in L.

Definition 1 (Prime Implicant). *A consistent literal set π is a prime implicant of formula P under Γ, if:*
(1) $\Gamma \cup \pi$ is consistent;
(2) $\Gamma \cup \pi \models P$;
(3) There is no other consistent literal set π' satisfying (1), (2), and $\pi' \subset \pi$.

We write $\Gamma(P)$ to denote the set of all prime implicants of P under Γ.

Definition 2 (Partial Implication). *We say that P partially implies Q under Γ, denoted by $\Gamma \models P \succ Q$, if:*
(1) $\Gamma(P)$ is not empty.
(2) For each $\pi \in \Gamma(P)$, there exists $\pi' \in \Gamma(Q)$, such that $\pi \cap \pi'$ is not empty and $\pi \cap -\pi'$ is empty.
Here, $-\pi'$ denotes the literal set of all negations in π'.

Next, we'll introduce probabilistic relevance into propositional logic. A truth assignment is a literal set, and for each atom $x \in Atom$, exactly one of x or $\neg x$ is in it. A truth assignment can also be considered as a formula in L. The value of a truth assignment T in a probabilistic assignment is the multiple of all literals in it.

Definition 3 (Probabilistic Assignment). *A probabilistic assignment M is a mapping from formulas to $[0, 1]$ $M: L \rightarrow [0, 1]$, such that:*
For each literal l, $M(l)=1-M(\neg l)$;
For each truth assignment T, $M(T)= \Pi (M(l) \mid l \in T)$;
For each formula P, $M(P)= \Sigma (M(T) \mid T \models P)$.

Based on the definition of probabilistic assignment, we can introduce the notion of probabilistic relevance into propositional language as follows.

Definition 4 (Probabilistic Relevance). *We say that P is probabilistic relevant to Q under* Γ, *denoted by* $\Gamma \models P \mapsto Q$, *if:*

(1) For every M,
$$\frac{\sum\limits_{T\models\Gamma\cup\{P,Q\}} M(T)}{\sum\limits_{T\models\Gamma\cup\{P\}} M(T)} \geq \frac{\sum\limits_{T\models\Gamma\cup\{Q\}} M(T)}{\sum\limits_{T\models\Gamma} M(T)} \; ;$$

(2) There exists M, such that
$$\frac{\sum\limits_{T\models\Gamma\cup\{P,Q\}} M(T)}{\sum\limits_{T\models\Gamma\cup\{P\}} M(T)} > \frac{\sum\limits_{T\models\Gamma\cup\{Q\}} M(T)}{\sum\limits_{T\models\Gamma} M(T)} .$$

This definition captures the intuitive sense of probabilistic relevance of $\Pr(Q \mid \Gamma \cup \{P\}) > \Pr(Q \mid \Gamma)$ to some extent, though there are other possible definitions of the probabilistic relevance in propositional language.

As a matter of convenience, we omit Γ when it is empty. The following section will discuss the fundamental properties of partial implication and probabilistic relevance.

4 Main Properties

First of all, we enumerate some instances of the partial implication and probabilistic relevance to illustrate their characteristics over atoms. Some of them can be found in [13]. In order to compare partial implication with probabilistic relevance, we reuse them for convenience here. In partial implication semantics and probabilistic relevance, these propositions do not necessarily hold for formulas. As an example, we can get $\models x \succ x \land y$ when Γ is empty, but $\not\models P \succ P \land Q$ for all formulas P and Q (e.g. let $P = x \lor y$ and $Q = \neg y$).

Example 2 (Partial Implication and Probabilistic Relevance Relationships over Atoms)

(p-1-1) $\models x \succ x \land y;$ *(p-1-2)* $\models x \mapsto x \land y;$

(p-2-1) $\models x \land y \succ y;$ *(p-2-2)* $\models x \land y \mapsto y;$

(p-3-1) $\models x \succ x \lor y;$ *(p-3-2)* $\models x \mapsto x \lor y;$

(p-4-1) $\not\models x \lor y \succ x;$ *(p-4-2)* $\models x \lor y \mapsto x;$

(p-5-1) $\not\models x \succ y;$ *(p-5-2)* $\not\models x \mapsto y;$

(p-6-1) $\not\models x \land \neg y \succ x \land y;$ *(p-6-2)* $\not\models x \land \neg y \mapsto x \land y;$

(p-7-1) $\models x \land z \succ x \land y;$ *(p-7-2)* $\models x \land z \mapsto x \land y;$

(p-8-1) $\models x \succ x \wedge (\neg x \vee y)$; (p-8-2) $\models x \mapsto x \wedge (\neg x \vee y)$;

(p-9-1) $\not\models \neg x \succ x \wedge (\neg x \vee y)$; (p-9-2) $\not\models \neg x \mapsto x \wedge (\neg x \vee y)$;

(p-10-1) $\not\models (x \wedge y) \vee (r \wedge s) \succ (x \wedge \neg y) \vee (r \wedge s)$;

(p-10-2) $\not\models (x \wedge y) \vee (r \wedge s) \mapsto (x \wedge \neg y) \vee (r \wedge s)$;

(p-11-1) $\not\models (x \wedge y) \vee (\neg x \wedge z) \succ (x \wedge r) \vee (\neg x \wedge s)$;

(p-11-2) $\not\models (x \wedge y) \vee (\neg x \wedge z) \mapsto (x \wedge r) \vee (\neg x \wedge s)$;

(p-12-1) $\models x \succ (x \wedge y) \vee (\neg x \wedge \neg y)$;

(p-12-2) $\not\models x \mapsto (x \wedge y) \vee (\neg x \wedge \neg y)$;

(p-13-1) $\models \neg x \succ (x \wedge y) \vee (\neg x \wedge \neg y)$;

(p-13-2) $\not\models \neg x \mapsto (x \wedge y) \vee (\neg x \wedge \neg y)$;

(p-14-1) $\not\models x \wedge \neg y \succ (x \wedge y) \vee (\neg x \wedge \neg y)$;

(p-14-2) $\not\models x \wedge \neg y \mapsto (x \wedge y) \vee (\neg x \wedge \neg y)$;

(p-15-1) $\{\neg y\} \not\models x \succ (x \wedge y) \vee (\neg x \wedge \neg y)$;

(p-15-2) $\{\neg y\} \not\models x \mapsto (x \wedge y) \vee (\neg x \wedge \neg y)$;

In the following, we explore some basic properties about partial implication and positive relevance. Most of the properties about partial implication are already stated in [13].

We say that a proposition P is trivial under Γ iff $\Gamma \models P$ or $\Gamma \models \neg P$, otherwise, we say that P is non-trivial under Γ.

Theorem 1 (Partial Implication and Classical Implication). *If* $\Gamma \models P \rightarrow Q$ *and both P and Q are non-trivial under* Γ, *then* $\Gamma \models P \succ Q$.

Theorem 2 (Probabilistic Relevance and Classical Implication). *If* $\Gamma \models P \rightarrow Q$ *and both P and Q are non-trivial under* Γ, *then* $\Gamma \models P \mapsto Q$.

Theorem 1 and theorem 2 show that both partial implication and probabilistic relevance are extensions of classical implication to some extent.

Proposition 1 (Partial Implication and Probabilistic Relevance). $\Gamma \models P \succ Q$ *doesn't imply* $\Gamma \models P \mapsto Q$; $\Gamma \models P \mapsto Q$ *doesn't imply* $\Gamma \models P \succ Q$.

For instance, from Example 2, we have $\models x \succ (x \wedge y) \vee (\neg x \wedge \neg y)$ (p-12-1), $\not\models x \mapsto (x \wedge y) \vee (\neg x \wedge \neg y)$ (p-12-2). Therefore, $\Gamma \models P \succ Q$ doesn't imply $\Gamma \models P \mapsto Q$. Similarly, the comparison between (p-4-1) and (p-4-2) shows that, $\Gamma \models P \mapsto Q$ doesn't imply $\Gamma \models P \succ Q$. Partial implication and probabilistic relevance are not subsystems of each other. This shows that partial implication and probabilistic relevance are two different directions of extending classical implication.

Proposition 2 (Non-triviality of Partial Implication and Probabilistic Relevance). *If P or Q is trivial under* Γ, *then* $\Gamma \models P \succ Q$ *doesn't hold and* $\Gamma \models P \mapsto Q$ *doesn't hold.*

Theorem 3 (Independence of syntax). *If* $\Gamma \models P \leftrightarrow Q$, *then* $\Gamma \models P \succ R$ *implies* $\Gamma \models Q \succ R$; $\Gamma \models R \succ P$ *implies* $\Gamma \models R \succ Q$; $\Gamma \models P \mapsto R$ *implies* $\Gamma \models Q \mapsto R$; $\Gamma \models R \mapsto P$ *implies* $\Gamma \models R \mapsto Q$.

Proposition 3 (Non-transitivity of Partial Implication and Probabilistic Relevance). $\Gamma \models P \succ Q$ *and* $\Gamma \models Q \succ R$ *doesn't imply* $\Gamma \models P \succ R$. $\Gamma \models P \mapsto Q$ *and* $\Gamma \models Q \mapsto R$ *doesn't imply* $\Gamma \models P \mapsto R$.

For example, $\models x \succ x \wedge y$ (p-1-1), $\models x \wedge y \succ y$ (p-2-1), but $\not\models x \succ y$ (p-5-1). So, transitivity of partial implication does not hold. Similarly, $\models x \mapsto x \wedge y$ (p-1-2), $\models x \wedge y \mapsto y$ (p-2-2), but $\not\models x \mapsto y$ (p-5-2). General transitivity of probabilistic relevance doesn't hold either.

Proposition 4 (Non-monotonicity of Partial Implication and Probabilistic Relevance). $\Gamma \models P \succ Q$ *doesn't imply that for any R,* $\Gamma \cup \{R\} \models P \succ Q$. $\Gamma \models P \mapsto Q$ *doesn't imply that for any R,* $\Gamma \cup \{R\} \models P \mapsto Q$.

Counterexample of monotonicity of partial implication: let Γ be empty, $P=x$, $Q=(x \wedge y) \vee (\neg x \wedge \neg y)$, $R=\neg y$. Counterexample of monotonicity of probabilistic relevance: let Γ be empty, $P=\neg x \vee y$, $Q=\neg x \vee z$, $R=x \wedge z$.

Theorem 4. *If* $\Gamma \models P \mapsto Q$, *then* $\Gamma \models Q \mapsto P$.

Theorem 4 doesn't hold for partial implication. For instance, $\models x \succ x \vee y$ (p-3-1), but $\not\models x \vee y \succ x$ (p-4-1).

Theorem 5. *If* $\Gamma \models P \mapsto Q$, *then* $\Gamma \models \neg P \mapsto \neg Q$.

Theorem 5 doesn't hold for partial implication. For instance, $\models x \wedge y \succ x$, but $\not\models \neg x \vee \neg y \succ \neg x$.

Theorem 6. *There doesn't exist* Γ, *P and Q, such that* $\Gamma \models P \mapsto Q$ *and* $\Gamma \models \neg P \mapsto Q$.

However, partial implication allows that P and $\neg P$ partially imply Q simultaneously. For example, $\models x \succ (x \wedge y) \vee (\neg x \wedge \neg y)$ (p-12-1) and $\models \neg x \succ (x \wedge y) \vee (\neg x \wedge \neg y)$ (p-13-1) hold at the same time.

Next, we examine some basic schemas in partial implication and probabilistic relevance. Here, > denote both $\succ$ and $\mapsto$ in a basic schema.

Proposition 5 (Some Basic Schemas)

Basic schemas	Counterexample of partial implication	Counterexample of probabilistic relevance
If $\models P \rightarrow Q$ and $\models R{>}P$, then $\models R{>}Q$	$P=x \wedge y$ $Q=y$ $R=x$	$P=x \wedge y$ $Q=y$ $R=x$
If $\models P{>}Q$ and $\models P{>}R$, then $\models P{>}Q \wedge R$	$P=x$ $Q=(x \wedge y) \vee z$ $R=(x \wedge \neg y) \vee z$	$P=x$ $Q=(x \wedge y) \vee z$ $R=(x \wedge \neg y) \vee z$
If $\models P{>}Q$ and $\models P{>}R$, then $\models P{>}Q \vee R$	$P=x$ $Q=(x \vee y) \wedge z$ $R=(x \vee \neg y) \wedge z$	$P=x$ $Q=(x \vee y) \wedge z$ $R=(x \vee \neg y) \wedge z$
If $\models P{>}Q$ and $\models R{>}Q$, then $\models P \wedge R{>}Q$	$P=x$ $Q=(x \wedge y) \vee (\neg x \wedge \neg y)$ $R=\neg y$	$P=(x \wedge y) \vee z$ $Q=x$ $R=(x \wedge \neg y) \vee z$
If $\models P{>}Q$ and $\models R{>}Q$, then $\models P \vee R{>}Q$	$P=x \wedge y$ $Q=(x \wedge r) \vee (\neg x \wedge s)$ $R=\neg x \wedge z$	$P=(x \vee y) \wedge z$ $Q=x$ $R=(x \vee \neg y) \wedge z$
If $\models P \wedge Q{>}R$, then $\models P{>}R$ or $\models Q{>}R$	$P=x \vee \neg y$ $Q=x \vee y$ $R=x$	$P=x \wedge (\neg r \vee s)$ $Q=(\neg x \vee y) \wedge r$ $R=x \wedge r$
If $\models P \vee Q{>}R$, then $\models P{>}R$ or $\models Q{>}R$	$P=(x \wedge y) \vee (r \wedge s)$ $Q=(x \wedge \neg y) \vee (r \wedge \neg s)$ $R=(x \wedge \neg y) \vee (r \wedge s)$	$P=x \vee (\neg r \wedge s)$ $Q=(\neg x \wedge y) \vee r$ $R=x \vee r$
If $\models P{>}Q \wedge R$, then $\models P{>}Q$ or $\models P{>}R$	$P=x \vee y$ $Q=x$ $R=y$	$P=x \wedge r$ $Q=x \wedge (\neg r \vee s)$ $R=(\neg x \vee y) \wedge r$
If $\models P{>}Q \vee R$, then $\models P{>}Q$ or $\models P{>}R$	$P=x \vee y$ $Q=x$ $R=y$	$P=x \vee r$ $Q=x \vee (\neg r \wedge s)$ $R=(\neg x \wedge y) \vee r$

Here, x, y, r, s are atoms. As listed above, none of these basic schemas holds in partial implication and probabilistic relevance. Accordingly, further studies are required on other possible properties of partial implication and probabilistic relevance.

To sum up, partial implication and probabilistic relevance are both extensions of classical implication (theorem 1 and theorem 2), and are not subsystems of each other (proposition 1). They have many similar properties (proposition 2, 3, 4, 5, theorem 3), but there also exists fundamental differences (theorem 4, 5 and 6) between them.

One may argue that these two formalizations are both too weak, since that transitivity and many of the schemas don't hold. We believe that an intuitive formalization is more important. From the counter-examples listed above, one can see that transitivity and some schemas is not appropriate for the concept of usefulness. And it is also the reason of nonuse of modal logic as the basis.

5 Usefulness

This section will define three kinds of usefulness, namely, strict usefulness, partial usefulness and probabilistic usefulness.

Definition 5 (Strict Usefulness). *We say that proposition P is strictly useful to proposition Q under* Γ *iff P and Q are non-trivial and* $\Gamma \models P \to Q$.

Strict usefulness is a trivial definition based on classical logic. As we pointed out in section 1, it can't capture the whole notion of usefulness. So, we give the definition of partial usefulness and probabilistic usefulness based on the semantics of partial implication and probabilistic relevance.

Definition 6 (Partial Usefulness). *We say that proposition P is partially useful to proposition Q under* Γ *iff* $\Gamma \models P \succ Q$.

Definition 7 (Probabilistic Usefulness). *We say that proposition P is probabilistically useful to proposition Q under* Γ *iff* $\Gamma \models P \mapsto Q$.

In Example 1 we mentioned in section 2, the answer is that P_1 and P_2 are strict usefulness to Q while the others are not. P_1, P_2, P_4, P_5, P_6 are partial usefulness to Q, while the others are not. P_1, P_2, P_4, P_5, P_6, P_7 are probabilistic usefulness to Q, while the others are not.

Now, we defined two more kinds of usefulness between two propositions under a background theory. And the useful relationships between actions (sequence of actions) with respect to a proposition under a background theory are also important. Here, we simply employ the effect of an action under a background to represent it.

The formalization of usefulness provides guidance for decision making of rational agents. The propositions and actions useful to the goal will be the alternatives in the current decision step. And those propositions and actions which are not useful to the goal will be neglected. Once an agent chooses a certain useful proposition or action, it will become the intention of the agent. Let's examine the decision processes in following examples.

Example 3 (Beer and Beef)
Joey wants to have beer and beef $(x \wedge y)$. *And there are three stores that offer the followisng services respectively:*

Store1 offers beer, but Joey is not sure if there is beef or not (x);
Store2 offers beer, but there is no beef (x ∧ ¬y);
Store3 offers a service, you can buy a certain pack, and there will be either beer or milk in it. And there is no more information about beef (x ∨ z).

None of these choices are strict useful to the agent's goal. Accordingly, there is no explicit way to achieve the agent's goal under the current beliefs. However, going to store1 is partially useful to the agent's goal (as well as probabilistically useful), and going to store3 is probabilistically useful to the agent's goal. Therefore, they can both be alternatives for Joey. Note that going to store3 is not partially useful to the goal. We can choose different understandings of usefulness on requirements.

Example 4 (Which Way to Go)
Alice and Bob are in a square and they can't contact each other. There are two directions to go, north and south. At the end of the roads, there are park and supermarket respectively. Their goal is to meet in either of the places $((n_1 \wedge n_2) \vee (s_1 \wedge s_2))$. Should Alice go north or south?

The agent's belief is $\Gamma = \{\neg(n_1 \wedge s_1), \neg(n_2 \wedge s_2)\}$. According to our definitions, going north (n_1) and going south (s_1) are both partially useful but not probabilistically useful to the goal. They can both be rational alternatives. It's rational since alternatives are not choices. We can't make a difference between n_1 and s_1 without additional information. However, if Alice knows that Bob would go to the park, then going north (n_1) is the only alternative in the current situation ($\Gamma = \{\neg(n_1 \wedge s_1), \neg(n_2 \wedge s_2), n_2\}$). She will definitely go to the park too.

Due to the incomplete knowledge and the dynamic environments, the agent may not be able to find an action sequence to achieve its goal. Obviously, it's better for the agent to do something rather than nothing. And the problem coming up is which action (action sequence) should be chosen now? From the viewpoint of usefulness, if there is no action sequence to completely achieve the goal, the agent can find a useful one instead. As we can see that the concept of usefulness plays a very important role in rational decision making. This formalism of usefulness provides a method to generate alternatives of agent.

We believe that these three sorts of usefulness don't capture the whole notion of usefulness either. For example, a conditional desire rule (if *P*, desire *Q*) [2, 10] can not be represented in our criteria.

6   Related Works

There are several works closed to the formalization of usefulness in AI community. From the viewpoint of the classical logic and AI planning, the concept of usefulness is treated as follows: an action (action sequence) that enables the agent to achieve its goal is useful. However, this so-called "all-or-nothing" criterion of usefulness is not adequate for autonomous agents in uncertain and dynamic environments [5]. On the one hand, since the knowledge is incomplete, the agent can't always find an action sequence to achieve its goal even when the way actually exists. Moreover, because of the dynamic environment, there may exist no action sequence achieving the goal in the beginning, and after some actions taken, there might emerge a possible way to achieve the goal. In many situations, if no actions were taken in the earlier stages, the agent may lose the chance to finally achieve the goal. Therefore, we need new criterions for usefulness.

In decision theory, explicit values are assigned to alternative actions to represent the degree of usefulness. The actions with higher values are more useful to the agent. However, decision theory cares more about preference relationships among alternatives rather than what the alternatives are. And these values are experimental and numerical, which are not readily available to the agents [2].

Haddawy and Hanks have pointed out a way to combine the AI planning and decision theory [5]. They studied partial satisfaction relationship between propositions and the agent's goal. A mapping from these propositions to [0, 1] is given to represent the degree of satisfaction, and an action (action sequence) which achieves a proposition with non-trivial value (e.g. 0.8) is treated as partial satisfaction of goals. Different from decision theory, they gave direct values to propositions but not to actions. However, their proposal of "partial satisfaction" is not formalized.

Also, there are some similar notions from the logic perspectives. Relevance logic mainly discusses relevant implication instead of material implication. Although partial implication and probabilistic relevance both have the characteristic of relevancy, the basic motivation and results are different. Partial implication and probabilistic relevance are both a generalization of material implication, while relevant implication is a restriction of it. For instance, both $\models x \succ x \wedge y$ and $\models x \mapsto x \wedge y$ hold, which doesn't hold in relevance logic apparently.

Perhaps the most related notions of usefulness are the series of meta-level relevance in propositional logic, including formula variable independence [9,10], relevance to a subjective matter [6,7], novelty [11,9] etc. These notions study informational relationships between formulas or between atom sets and formulas. To some extent, the notion of usefulness can be viewed as satisfaction relationships between formulas.

In [10], Lang et. al. defined a notion of formula variable independence. A formula P is said to be semantically variable independent on an atom x if and only if there is a formula Q such that $P \leftrightarrow Q$ holds and x doesn't occur in Q. A formula P is said to be semantically variable independent on an atom set π if and only if P is semantically variable independent on every atom of π.

Theorem 7. *A formula P is semantically variable independent on an atom x if and only if $\not\models x \succ P$ and $\not\models \neg x \succ P$.*

However, this doesn't hold for probabilistic relevance. We have $\not\models x \mapsto (x \wedge y) \vee (\neg x \wedge \neg y)$ and $\not\models \neg x \mapsto (x \wedge y) \vee (\neg x \wedge \neg y)$, while $\succ (x \wedge y) \vee (\neg x \wedge \neg y)$ isn't semantically variable independent on x.

Theorem 8. *If a formula P is semantically variable independent on an atom x, then $\not\models x \mapsto P$ and $\not\models \neg x \mapsto P$.*

From Theorem 7 and Theorem 8, we can easily get the following two corollaries.

Corollary 1. *A formula P is semantically variable independent on an atom set* π *if and only if for all x in* π, $\not\models x \succ P$ *and* $\not\models \neg x \succ P$.

Corollary 2. *If a formula P is semantically variable independent on an atom set* π, *then for all x in* π, $\not\models x \mapsto P$ *and* $\not\models \neg x \mapsto P$.

These two corollaries can be extended into more general theorems.

Theorem 9. *A formula P is semantically variable independent on an atom set* π *if and only if for all formula Q only mentioning atoms in* π, $\not\models Q \succ P$.

Theorem 10. *If a formula P is semantically variable independent on an atom set* π, *then for all formula Q only mentioning atoms in* π, $\not\models Q \mapsto P$.

Lakemeyer introduces several notions of relevance [6,7]. We show that the relationships between these notions and partial.

Definition 8 (relevance to a subjective matter [6]). *A formula P is relevant to an atom set* π *if and only if there is a prime implicate of P mentioning an atom in* π.

Theorem 11 ([10]). *A formula P is relevant to an atom set* π *if and only if P is not semantically variable independent on* π.

As a consequence, A formula P is relevant to an atom set if and only if there exists an atom x in π, such that $\models x \succ P$ or $\models \neg x \succ P$.

Lakemeyer also introduces several notions of strict relevance to a subjective matter.

Definition 9 (strict relevance to a subjective matter [7]). *A formula P is relevant to an atom set* π *if and only if there is a prime implicate of P mentioning an atom in* π *and every prime implicate of P mentions only atoms in* π.

Theorem 11 ([10]). *A formula P is strict relevant to an atom set* π *if and only if P is not semantically variable independent on* π *and P is semantically independent on* $Atom \backslash \pi$.

As a consequence, A formula P is strictly relevant to an atom set if and only if there exists an atom x in π, such that $\models x \succ P$ or $\models \neg x \succ P$ and there doesn't exist an atom y in π, such that $\not\models y \succ P$ and $\not\models \neg y \succ P$.

Another related notion is positive novelty [9,11]. P is positive new to Q under a background theory Γ if and only if there is a minimal abductive explanation for Q under $\Gamma \cup \{P\}$ but not under Γ. This criterion is quite different from both partial implication and positive relevance.

7 Conclusion

This work provides an exploration on the formalization of the concept usefulness. We distinguished three kinds of usefulness: strict usefulness, partial usefulness and probabilistic usefulness. Partial implication semantics is employed to formalize partial usefulness and probabilistic relevance is introduced to formalize probabilistic usefulness respectively. Also, we examined the fundamental properties. We believe that this work captures some of the essential notions of usefulness and we also pointed out that our work may not cover the whole notion of usefulness.

There are a lot of works that can be done in the future. Firstly, these three sorts of usefulness didn't capture the whole notion of usefulness, and a further understanding of usefulness is worth pursuing. Secondly, more properties on partial implication and probabilistic relevance are required, and extension to the formalizations into first order language is needed. Thirdly, in this paper we only discussed the useful relationships between propositions, and it is also important to study the useful relationships between actions and propositions. Fourthly, usefulness in multi and conflict goals situations should also be investigated.

Acknowledgments. The authors would like to thank the anonymous reviewers very much for their tremendous valuable comments. Clearly, their comments are carefully considered by the authors. But some of them are not explicitly involved in this final version. This work is supported by NNSF(60275024) and 973 programme(2003CB317000).

References

[1] P. Achinstein. *The book of evidence.* Oxford University Press, 2001.

[2] C. Boutlier. Toward a logic for qualitative decision theory. *In Proceedings of KR'94*, pages 75-86, 1994. Morgan Kaufmann.

[3] R. Carnap. *Logic foundations of probability.* 2nd edition. Chicago: University of Chicago Press, 1962.

[4] J. Doyle. Rationality and its roles in reasoning. *Computational Intelligence.* 8(2): 376-409. 1992.

[5] P. Haddawy and S. Hanks. Utility models for goal-directed decision-theoretic planners. *Computational Intelligence*, 14(3): 392-429, 1998.

[6] G. Lakemeyer. A logic account of relevance. In proceedings of IJCAI'95, pp. 853-859, 1995.

[7] G. Lakemeyer. Relevance from an Epistemic Perspective. Artif. Intell. 97(1-2): 137-167 (1997).

[8] J. Lang, P. Liberatore and P. Marquis. Conditional independence in propositional logic. *Artificial Intelligence*, 141(1-2): 79-121, 2002.

[9] J. Lang, P. Liberatore and P. Marquis. Propositional Independence - Formula-Variable Independence and Forgetting. Journal of Artificial Intelligence Research 18:391-443, 2003.

[10] J. Lang, L. van der Torre, E. Weydert. Hidden uncertainty in the logical representation of desires. *In Proceedings of IJCAI'03.* 685-690, 2003.

[11] P. Marquis. Novelty revised. In proceedings of ICMIS'91. LNAI Vol. 542. 550-559. Springer, New York, 1991.

[12] The knowledge level. *Artificial Intelligence*, 18(1): 87-127. 1982.

[13] Y. Zhou and XP Chen. Partial implication semantics for desirable propositions. In Proceedings of the Ninth International Conference on Principles of Knowledge Representation and Reasoning, pages 606-611, 2004.

Author Index

Lecture Notes in Artificial Intelligence (LNAI)

Vol. 3890: S.G. Thompson, R. Ghanea-Hercock (Eds.), Defence Applications of Multi-Agent Systems. XII, 141 pages. 2006.

Vol. 3885: V. Torra, Y. Narukawa, A. Valls, J. Domingo-Ferrer (Eds.), Modeling Decisions for Artificial Intelligence. XII, 374 pages. 2006.

Vol. 3881: S. Gibet, N. Courty, J.-F. Kamp (Eds.), Gesture in Human-Computer Interaction and Simulation. XIII, 344 pages. 2006.

Vol. 3874: R. Missaoui, J. Schmidt (Eds.), Formal Concept Analysis. X, 309 pages. 2006.

Vol. 3873: L. Maicher, J. Park (Eds.), Charting the Topic Maps Research and Applications Landscape. VIII, 281 pages. 2006.

Vol. 3863: M. Kohlhase (Ed.), Mathematical Knowledge Management. XI, 405 pages. 2006.

Vol. 3862: R.H. Bordini, M. Dastani, J. Dix, A.E.F. Seghrouchni (Eds.), Programming Multi-Agent Systems. XIV, 267 pages. 2006.

Vol. 3849: I. Bloch, A. Petrosino, A.G.B. Tettamanzi (Eds.), Fuzzy Logic and Applications. XIV, 438 pages. 2006.

Vol. 3848: J.-F. Boulicaut, L. De Raedt, H. Mannila (Eds.), Constraint-Based Mining and Inductive Databases. X, 401 pages. 2006.

Vol. 3847: K.P. Jantke, A. Lunzer, N. Spyratos, Y. Tanaka (Eds.), Federation over the Web. X, 215 pages. 2006.

Vol. 3835: G. Sutcliffe, A. Voronkov (Eds.), Logic for Programming, Artificial Intelligence, and Reasoning. XIV, 744 pages. 2005.

Vol. 3830: D. Weyns, H. V.D. Parunak, F. Michel (Eds.), Environments for Multi-Agent Systems II. VIII, 291 pages. 2006.

Vol. 3817: M. Faundez-Zanuy, L. Janer, A. Esposito, A. Satue-Villar, J. Roure, V. Espinosa-Duro (Eds.), Nonlinear Analyses and Algorithms for Speech Processing. XII, 380 pages. 2006.

Vol. 3814: M. Maybury, O. Stock, W. Wahlster (Eds.), Intelligent Technologies for Interactive Entertainment. XV, 342 pages. 2005.

Vol. 3809: S. Zhang, R. Jarvis (Eds.), AI 2005: Advances in Artificial Intelligence. XXVII, 1344 pages. 2005.

Vol. 3808: C. Bento, A. Cardoso, G. Dias (Eds.), Progress in Artificial Intelligence. XVIII, 704 pages. 2005.

Vol. 3802: Y. Hao, J. Liu, Y.-P. Wang, Y.-m. Cheung, H. Yin, L. Jiao, J. Ma, Y.-C. Jiao (Eds.), Computational Intelligence and Security, Part II. XLII, 1166 pages. 2005.

Vol. 3801: Y. Hao, J. Liu, Y.-P. Wang, Y.-m. Cheung, H. Yin, L. Jiao, J. Ma, Y.-C. Jiao (Eds.), Computational Intelligence and Security, Part I. XLI, 1122 pages. 2005.

Vol. 3789: A. Gelbukh, Á. de Albornoz, H. Terashima-Marín (Eds.), MICAI 2005: Advances in Artificial Intelligence. XXVI, 1198 pages. 2005.

Vol. 3782: K.-D. Althoff, A. Dengel, R. Bergmann, M. T.R. Roth-Berghofer (Eds.), Professional Knowledge Management. XXIII, 739 pages. 2005.

Vol. 3763: H. Hong, D. Wang (Eds.), Automated Deduction in Geometry. X, 213 pages. 2006.

Vol. 3755: G.J. Williams, S.J. Simoff (Eds.), Data Mining. XI, 331 pages. 2006.

Vol. 3735: A. Hoffmann, H. Motoda, T. Scheffer (Eds.), Discovery Science. XVI, 400 pages. 2005.

Vol. 3734: S. Jain, H.U. Simon, E. Tomita (Eds.), Algorithmic Learning Theory. XII, 490 pages. 2005.

Vol. 3721: A.M. Jorge, L. Torgo, P.B. Brazdil, R. Camacho, J. Gama (Eds.), Knowledge Discovery in Databases: PKDD 2005. XXIII, 719 pages. 2005.

Vol. 3720: J. Gama, R. Camacho, P.B. Brazdil, A.M. Jorge, L. Torgo (Eds.), Machine Learning: ECML 2005. XXIII, 769 pages. 2005.

Vol. 3717: B. Gramlich (Ed.), Frontiers of Combining Systems. X, 321 pages. 2005.

Vol. 3702: B. Beckert (Ed.), Automated Reasoning with Analytic Tableaux and Related Methods. XIII, 343 pages. 2005.

Vol. 3698: U. Furbach (Ed.), KI 2005: Advances in Artificial Intelligence. XIII, 409 pages. 2005.

Vol. 3690: M. Pěchouček, P. Petta, L.Z. Varga (Eds.), Multi-Agent Systems and Applications IV. XVII, 667 pages. 2005.

Vol. 3684: R. Khosla, R.J. Howlett, L.C. Jain (Eds.), Knowledge-Based Intelligent Information and Engineering Systems, Part IV. LXXIX, 933 pages. 2005.

Vol. 3683: R. Khosla, R.J. Howlett, L.C. Jain (Eds.), Knowledge-Based Intelligent Information and Engineering Systems, Part III. LXXX, 1397 pages. 2005.

Vol. 3682: R. Khosla, R.J. Howlett, L.C. Jain (Eds.), Knowledge-Based Intelligent Information and Engineering Systems, Part II. LXXIX, 1371 pages. 2005.

Vol. 3681: R. Khosla, R.J. Howlett, L.C. Jain (Eds.), Knowledge-Based Intelligent Information and Engineering Systems, Part I. LXXX, 1319 pages. 2005.

Vol. 3673: S. Bandini, S. Manzoni (Eds.), AI*IA 2005: Advances in Artificial Intelligence. XIV, 614 pages. 2005.

Vol. 3662: C. Baral, G. Greco, N. Leone, G. Terracina (Eds.), Logic Programming and Nonmonotonic Reasoning. XIII, 454 pages. 2005.

Vol. 3661: T. Panayiotopoulos, J. Gratch, R. Aylett, D. Ballin, P. Olivier, T. Rist (Eds.), Intelligent Virtual Agents. XIII, 506 pages. 2005.

Vol. 3658: V. Matoušek, P. Mautner, T. Pavelka (Eds.), Text, Speech and Dialogue. XV, 460 pages. 2005.

Vol. 3651: R. Dale, K.-F. Wong, J. Su, O.Y. Kwong (Eds.), Natural Language Processing – IJCNLP 2005. XXI, 1031 pages. 2005.

Vol. 3642: D. Ślęzak, J. Yao, J.F. Peters, W. Ziarko, X. Hu (Eds.), Rough Sets, Fuzzy Sets, Data Mining, and Granular Computing, Part II. XXIII, 738 pages. 2005.

Vol. 3641: D. Ślęzak, G. Wang, M. Szczuka, I. Düntsch, Y. Yao (Eds.), Rough Sets, Fuzzy Sets, Data Mining, and Granular Computing, Part I. XXIV, 742 pages. 2005.

Vol. 3635: J.R. Winkler, M. Niranjan, N.D. Lawrence (Eds.), Deterministic and Statistical Methods in Machine Learning. VIII, 341 pages. 2005.